Graham A. Reid

LONDON, 18th April

HISTORICAL RECORDS

•••••

OF THE FIVE DYNASTIES

Ouyang Xiu's letter to Su Shi in Original calligraphy.
Courtesy of the National Palace Museum, Taipei.

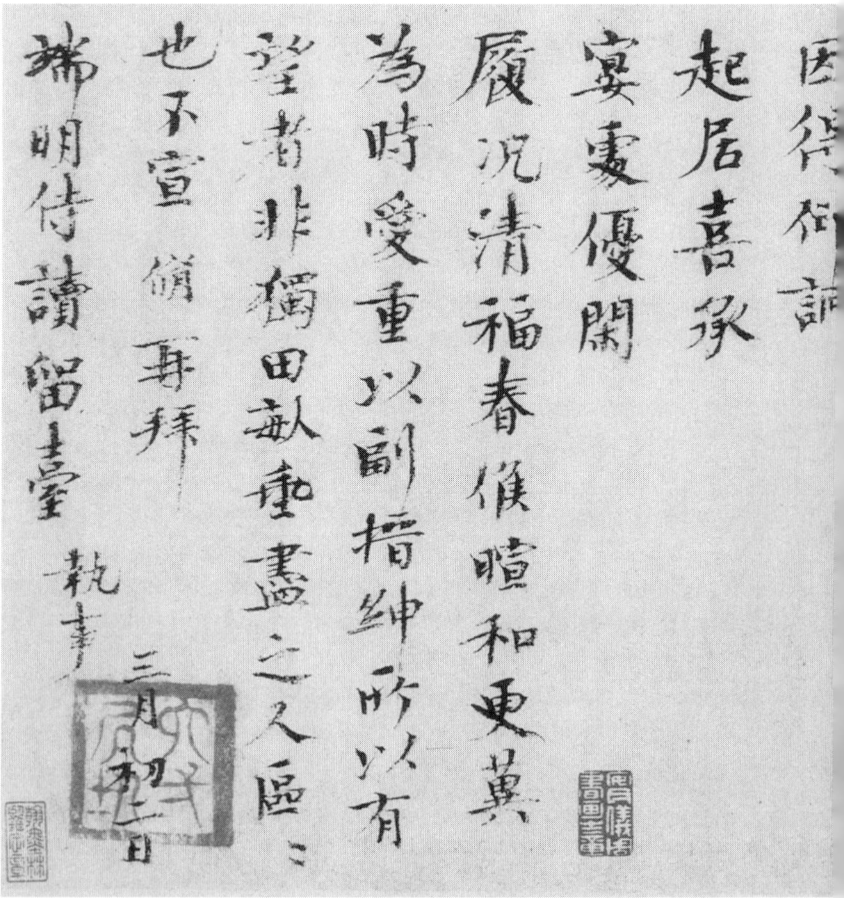

起居喜承
宴處優閑
履況清福春候暄和更冀
為時愛重以副搢紳所以有
望者非獨田畝垂盡之人區區
也不宣 脩再拜
端明侍讀留臺執事 三月初七日

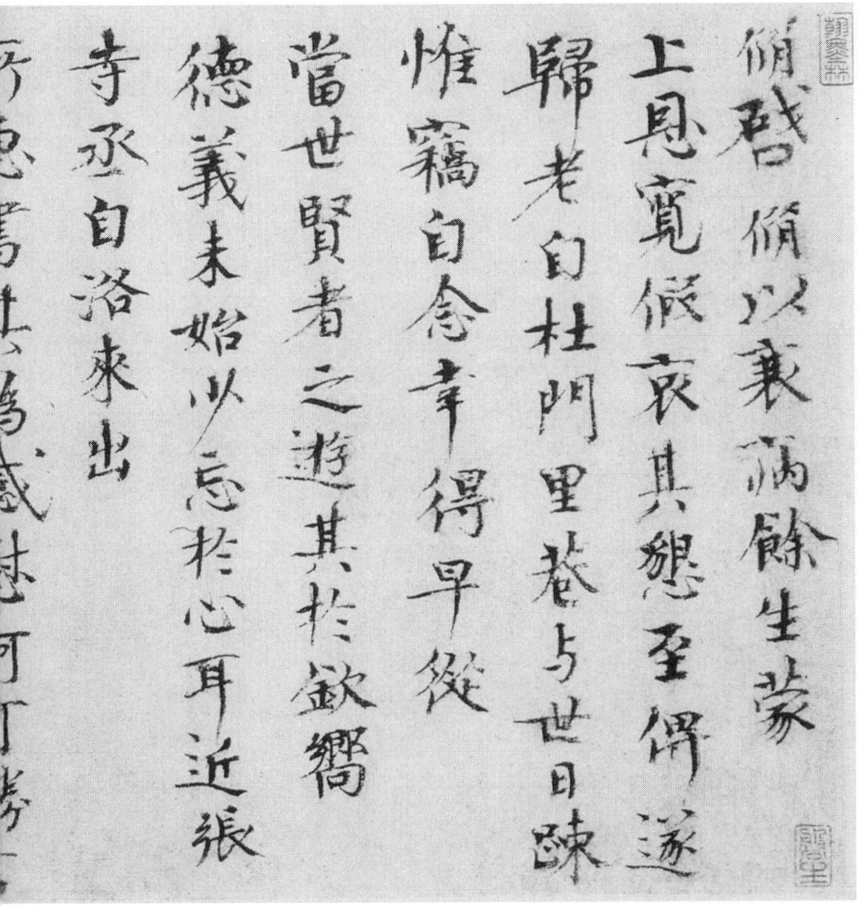
僩啓 僩以衰病餘生蒙
上恩寬假哀其懇至俾遂
歸老自杜門里巷与世日踈
惟竊自念幸得早從
當世賢者之遊其於欽嚮
德義未始少忘於心耳近張
寺丞自洛來出

HISTORICAL RECORDS
OF THE FIVE DYNASTIES

Ouyang Xiu

Translated, with an Introduction by
RICHARD L. DAVIS

COLUMBIA UNIVERSITY PRESS
NEW YORK

Columbia University Press wishes to express its appreciation for assistance given by Brown University and the Chiang Ching-kuo Foundation for International Scholarly Exchange in the publication of this book

Columbia University Press
Publishers Since 1893
New York Chichester, West Sussex

Library of Congress Cataloging-in-Publication Data
Ouyang, Xiu, 1007–1072.
[Wu dai shi ji. English]
Historical records of the five dynasties / Ouyang Xiu, translated with an introduction by Richard L. Davis.
p. cm.
Includes bibliographical references and index.
ISBN 978–0–231–12826–1 (cloth : alk. paper) —
ISBN 978–0–231–12827–8 (pbk. : alk. paper)
1. China—History—Five dynasties and the Ten kingdoms, 907–979.
I. Davis, Richard L. II. Title. III. Series
DS749.5.O9313 2004
951'.018—dc21 2003055286
∞

Columbia University Press books are printed on permanent and durable acid-free paper
Printed in the United States of America

c 10 9 8 7 6 5 4 3 2 1
p 10 9 8 7 6 5 4 3 2 1

IN MEMORY OF A NOBLE
SISTER AND FRIEND
GAYLE RUTHERFORD, M.D.

CONTENTS

....

* An asterisk (*) indicates translation of only select biographies for the cluster of chapters, although each biography is translated in full. Omitted altogether were the following: "Consistent Conduct" (Yixing, chapter 34), "Treatise on Astronomy" (Sitian kao, chapters 58–59), "Treatise on Administrative Geography" (Zhifang kao, chapter 60), "Timeline for the Hereditary Houses of the Ten Kingdoms" (Shiguo shijia nianpu, chapter 71), and "Appendixes on the Four Barbarians" (Siyi fulu, chapters 72–74).

ACKNOWLEDGMENTS

The *Historical Records of the Five Dynasties* has fascinated me for nearly two decades as both historical craft and social commentary, although producing a translation of the current scope was far from my initial intent. In 1988 I drafted part of a monograph on eleventh-century historiography that focused on three works: the two dynastic histories associated with Ouyang Xiu, the *New History of the Tang* and *Historical Records of the Five Dynasties*, and Sima Guang's *Comprehensive Mirror for the Advancement of Governance*. After some drafting, however, I found the three works and the two authors difficult to compare, and many of my initial assumptions about them were difficult to justify as well. I also became convinced of the need for a corpus of Ouyang Xiu's historical writings in English translation. The more immersed in the text I became, the more convinced I was that this particular work, like few histories from the period, truly deserved to be brought to a wider audience. No historical text from China's middle period has ever been translated, except in fragments. Moreover, author Ouyang Xiu's standing as a towering intellect, his classical and literary works even more celebrated than his histories, makes for an appeal across modern disciplines. As a historian of Song-dynasty political culture and historical method, my preeminent interest in the text is historical; the tools and sensitivities that I bring to the translation are historical as well. Readers more philologically or literarily inclined will doubtless find a disciplinary bias in my interpretations of events and terms, but the breadth of coverage should compensate for deficiencies in expression.

Roughly two-thirds of the Chinese original has been rendered in English. Sections critical to understanding the politics and personality of the time appear in full: "Basic Annals" (chapters 1–12) and "Royal Families" for the north (chapters 13–20), plus "Hereditary Houses" for the south (chapters 61–70), mostly. Biographical clusters based on moral categories (chapters 31–33, 35–38) also appear in their entirety, indispensable as they are to appreciating the Confucian moral agenda that permeates the work and inspires its rich commentary. A major pruning occurs with the other biographical clusters. My selections were informed by the need for the most important figures to be represented; otherwise, biographies of greater length and detail were given priority over less developed stories, biographies with important commentary over those without. I wanted temporal and topical balance as well, so there are disproportionately more biographies for poorly represented dynasties such as Jin, Han, and Zhou, and fewer for the Later Tang, the best-documented period in the *Historical Records.* Biographies chosen for inclusion are translated in full without abbreviation or deletion, thereby better representing the narrative strengths of the original, although fuller coverage made it necessary to limit the number of biographies. Left untranslated altogether are two treatises on astronomy and administrative geography and the concluding chapters on the "Four Barbarians," which do not lend themselves to translation. Ouyang Xiu's strongest chapters are the biographies, where he weaves literary sources into historical documents and provides the depth of personality and perspective wholly absent in the original official history for the period. The biographies allowed the author to play a role particularly suited to him, that of the storyteller, with every story conveying some higher truth or fitting some broader agenda.

My appreciation of the Chinese text as a masterpiece of the classical style, at once direct and nuanced, was greatly assisted by the privilege of organizing classes around it during a teaching stint in Taiwan from 1996 to 1998. I am grateful to undergraduates at Tung-wu (Soochow) University in Taipei and graduate students at Chung-cheng University in Chia-yi for indulging my interests in the text and providing a modern perspective on it. Administrators at the two universities also deserve credit for their faith in this foreigner's potential to teach Chinese history to their students. I am at once grateful and humbled. Conference organizers and university lectureships in Taiwan, mainland China, and the United States provided invaluable venues for discussing the work with fellow historians. My friend Liu Xiao, a Yuan-dynasty historian at the Academy of Social Sciences in Beijing, deserves special mention for a methodical reading of the entire translation, his scrupulous eye sparing me numerous errors. The text further benefited from readings from colleagues at Brown such as David Lattimore, plus undergraduate and graduate students on whom I tested the manuscript, especially Luc Nguyen. A colleague in the Korean language, Angela Jong-eun Lee-Smith, assisted with the transliteration of Korean names in the Basic Annals. Maps were produced in Taiwan with assistance from a friend of long standing, Chiang Jung-yuan. Another debt is owed three readers for Columbia University Press, whose critical yet measured input proved invaluable and whose suggestions for change have been largely adopted. I thank the executive editor there, Jennifer Crewe, for readily recognizing the importance of the text and the need to make it accessible to scholars and students alike. Manuscript editor Gregory McNamee labored hard and well on the final product, as did Cheng-hua Fang with final corrections.

My understanding of the late Tang and the Five Dynasties, several centuries before my earlier specialty, has benefited immensely from the expertise of Huang Ch'ing-lien, at the Academia Sinica's Institute of History and Philology, an old Princeton friend always generous with his time. As early as 1977, the Academia Sinica was my research base in Asia, when director Chü Wan-li took me under his wing. Its doors opened once again during my sabbatical in 2000–2001 amid further drafting and revision. I thank the current director, fellow Song-dynasty historian Huang K'uan-ch'ung, for the continuing hospitality and cherished friendship. A yearlong sabbatical was made possible with a research fellowship from the Chiang Ching-kuo Foundation for International Scholarly Exchange. Imperial China tends to receive low priority among grant programs at universities and private endowments, so CCK must be commended for so liberal a casting of its funding net.

My mentor at Princeton University, the late James T. C. Liu (1919–1993), wrote the first and still the leading multidisciplinary biography of Ouyang Xiu in 1967, a book that remains the point of departure for my work and all else on this remarkable figure. The book inspired me as a college student to pursue studies in the Song dynasty, and many readings later, I still leave with fresh insights. The book has stood the test of time. My investment in this translation project emanates not from simple devotion to a teacher's memory, however. James was never given to producing students in his own image, and my assessment of Ouyang Xiu as historian differs considerably from his. The appeal of the project came instead from the opportunity to immerse myself in a single text, thereby reinvigorating my skills as a sinologist while expanding forays into Chinese historiography. Such rather selfish motivation should not diminish, I trust, the broader value of this book.

I owe a final acknowledgment to the many friends in Taiwan, beyond the academic circuit, who continue to draw me back: they have given more than I ever expected, more than I can ever repay. Above all, to You Tzung-chun, whose meaning defies description and leaves this man of words utterly wordless.

LIST OF MAPS

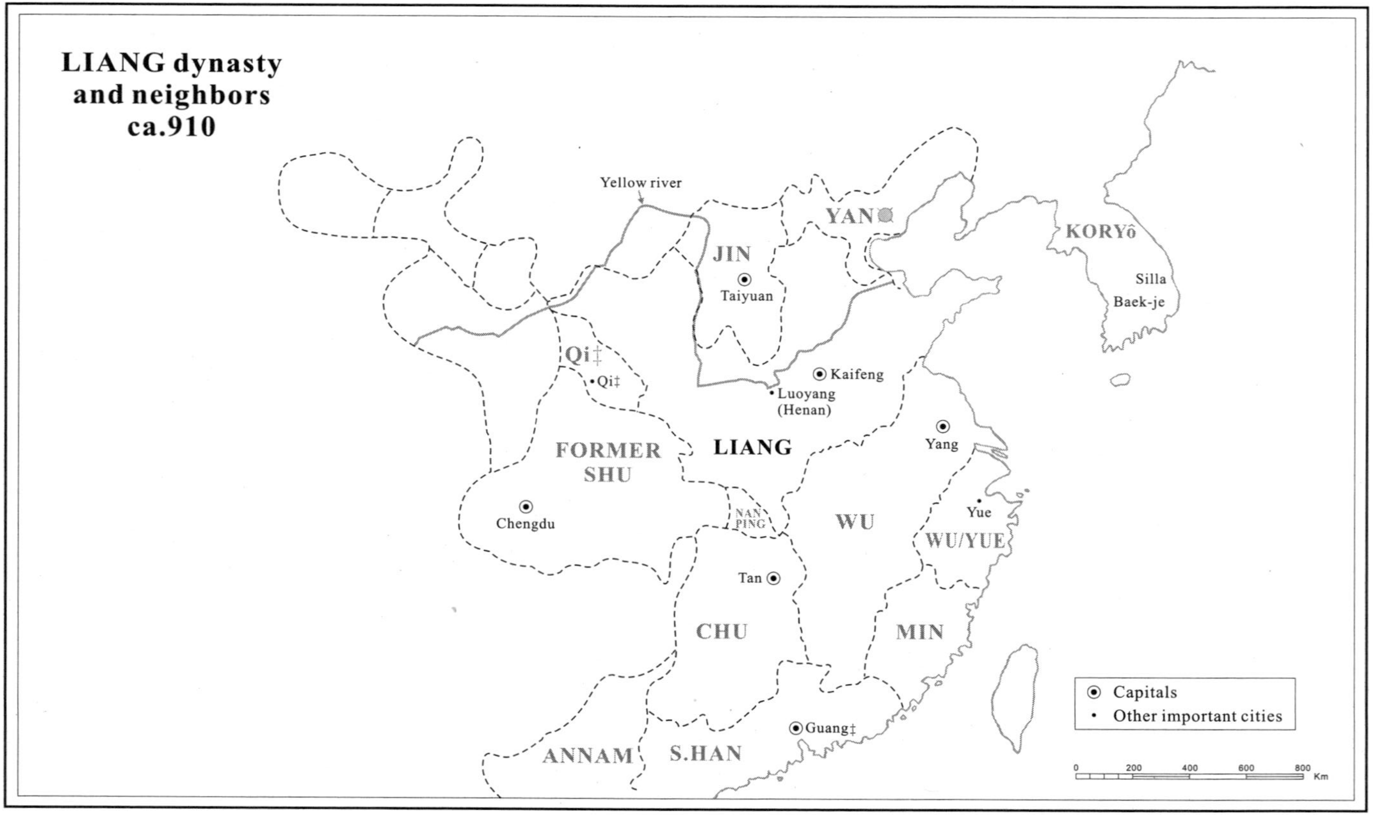
LIANG dynasty
and neighbors
ca.910
Yellow river
YAN
KORYŏ
Silla
Baek-je
JIN
Taiyuan
Qi‡
•Qi‡
Kaifeng
Luoyang
(Henan)
Yang
LIANG
FORMER
SHU
Chengdu
NAN
PING
WU
Yue
WU/YUE
Tan
CHU
MIN
Guang‡
ANNAM
S.HAN
Capitals
Other important cities
0
200
400
600
800
Km

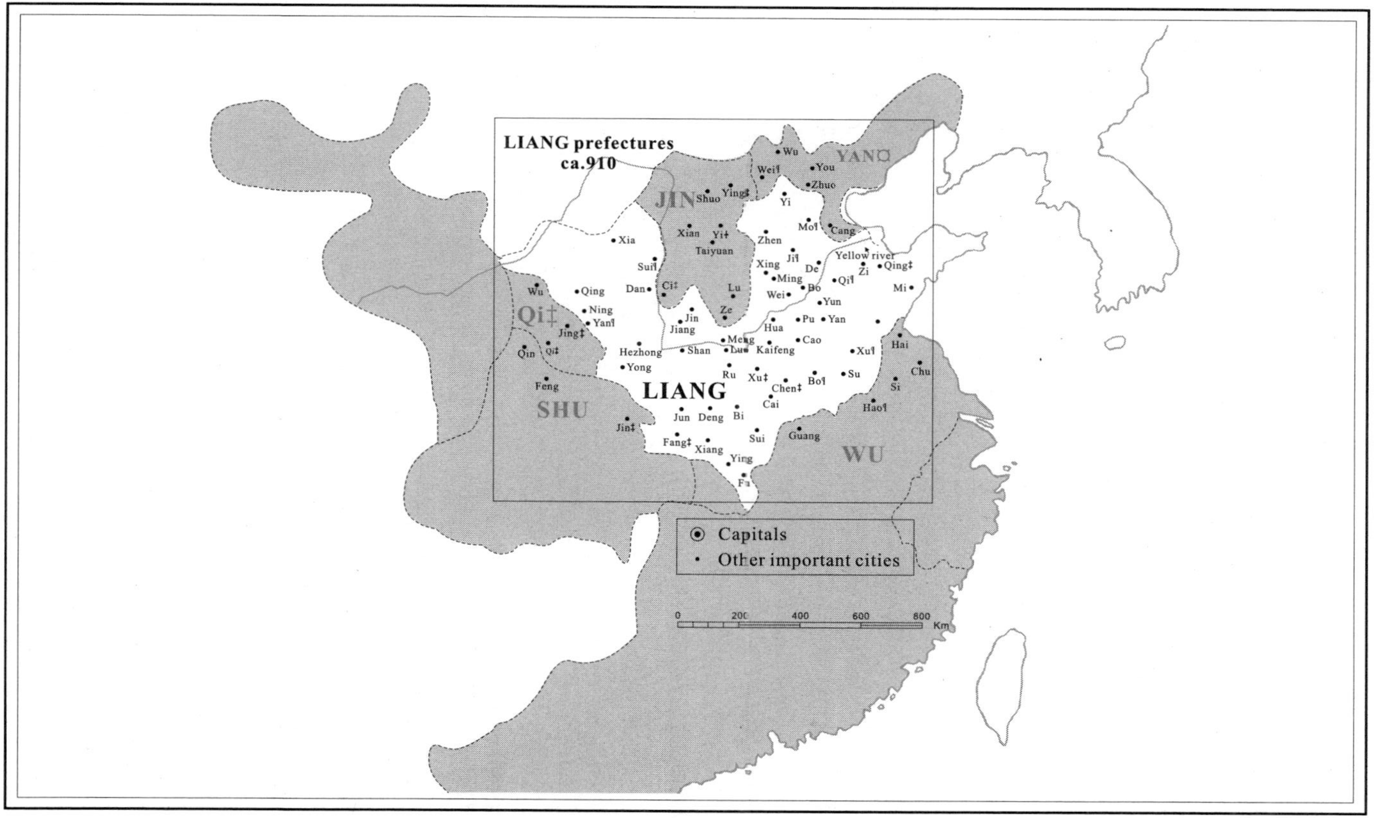

LIANG prefectures
ca.910
YAN
JIN
Qi‡
SHU
LIANG
WU
Wu
Wei¶
You
Zhuo
Shuo
Ying‡
Yi
Mo¶
Cang
Xian
Yi‡
Taiyuan
Zhen
Xia
Sui¶
Ci‡
Dan
Lu
Ze
Xing
Ji¶
De
Ming
Bo
Wei
Yellow river
Qing‡
Zi
Qi¶
Mi
Wu
Qing
Ning
Yan¶
Jing‡
Qin
Qi‡
Feng
Jin
Jiang
Hezhong
Shan
Yong
Meng
Lu
Kaifeng
Hua
Yun
Pu
Yan
Cao
Xu¶
Hai
Chu
Ru
Xu‡
Chen‡
Bo¶
Su
Si
Cai
Hao¶
Jun
Deng
Bi
Jin‡
Fang‡
Xiang
Sui
Guang
Ying
Fa
Capitals
Other important cities
0
200
400
600
800
Km

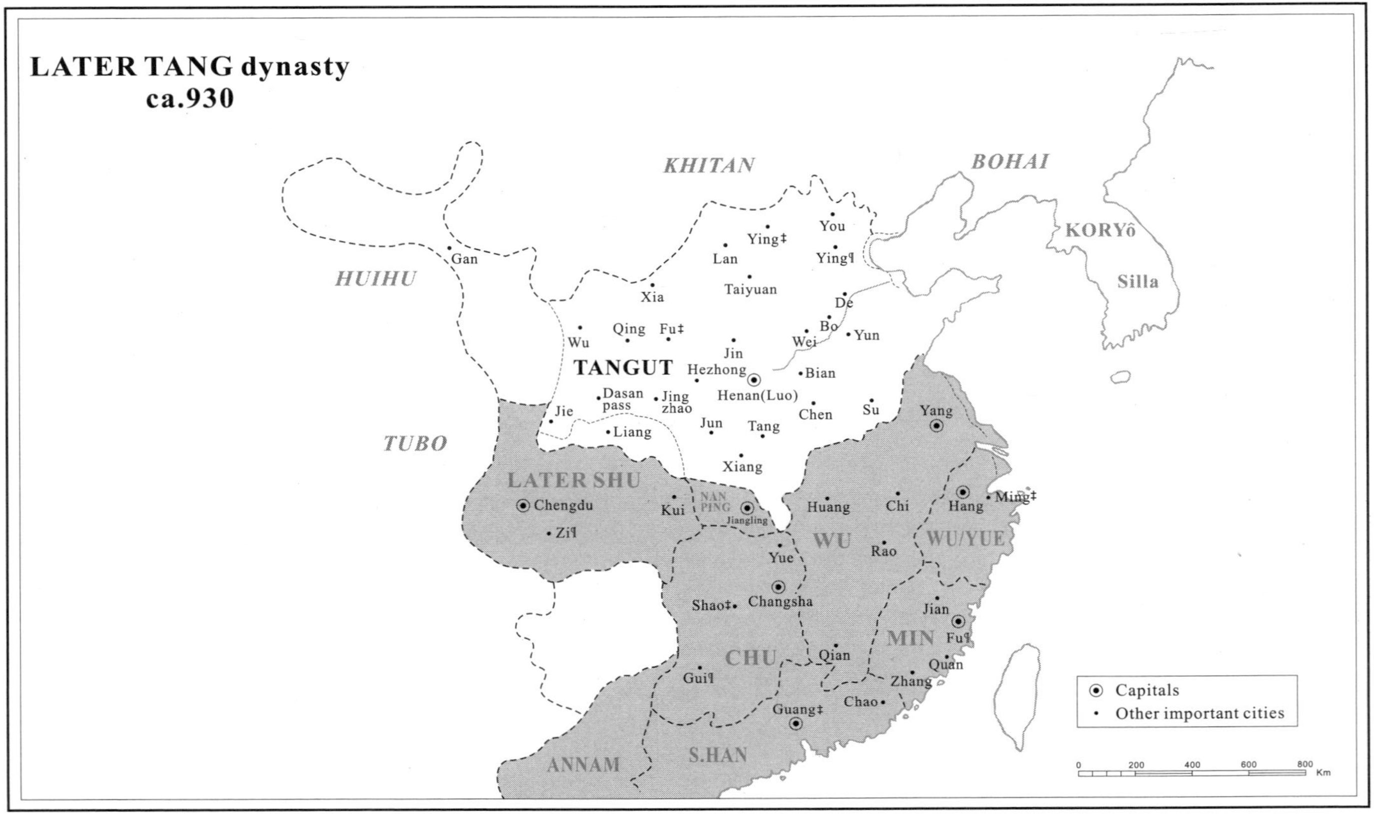
LATER TANG dynasty
ca.930
KHITAN
BOHAI
KORYŎ
Silla
HUIHU
TUBO
TANGUT
Gan
You
Ying‡
Ying¶
Lan
Taiyuan
Xia
De
Bo
Yun
Wei
Qing
Fu‡
Wu
Jin
Hezhong
Henan(Luo)
Bian
Dasan pass
Jing zhao
Jie
Liang
Jun
Tang
Chen
Su
Xiang
Yang
LATER SHU
Chengdu
Zi¶
Kui
NAN PING
Jiangling
Huang
Chi
Hang
Ming‡
WU
Rao
WU/YUE
Yue
Changsha
Shao‡
Jian
Fu¶
MIN
CHU
Qian
Quan
Gui¶
Zhang
Chao
Guang‡
ANNAM
S.HAN
Capitals
Other important cities
0
200
400
600
800
Km

LATER JIN-HAN dynasties ca.940-950

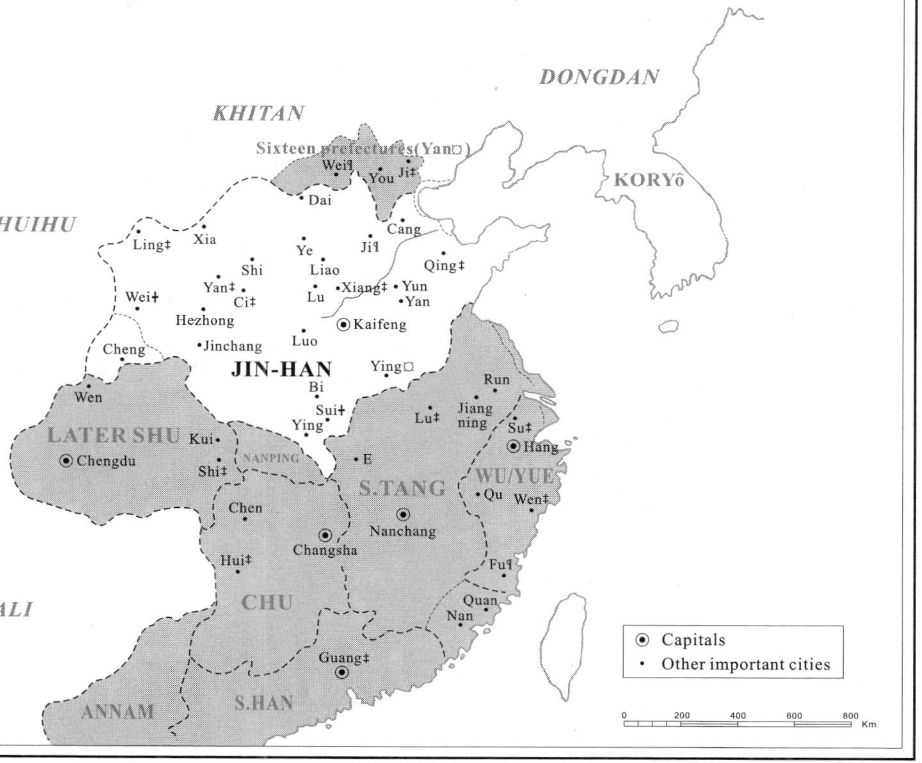

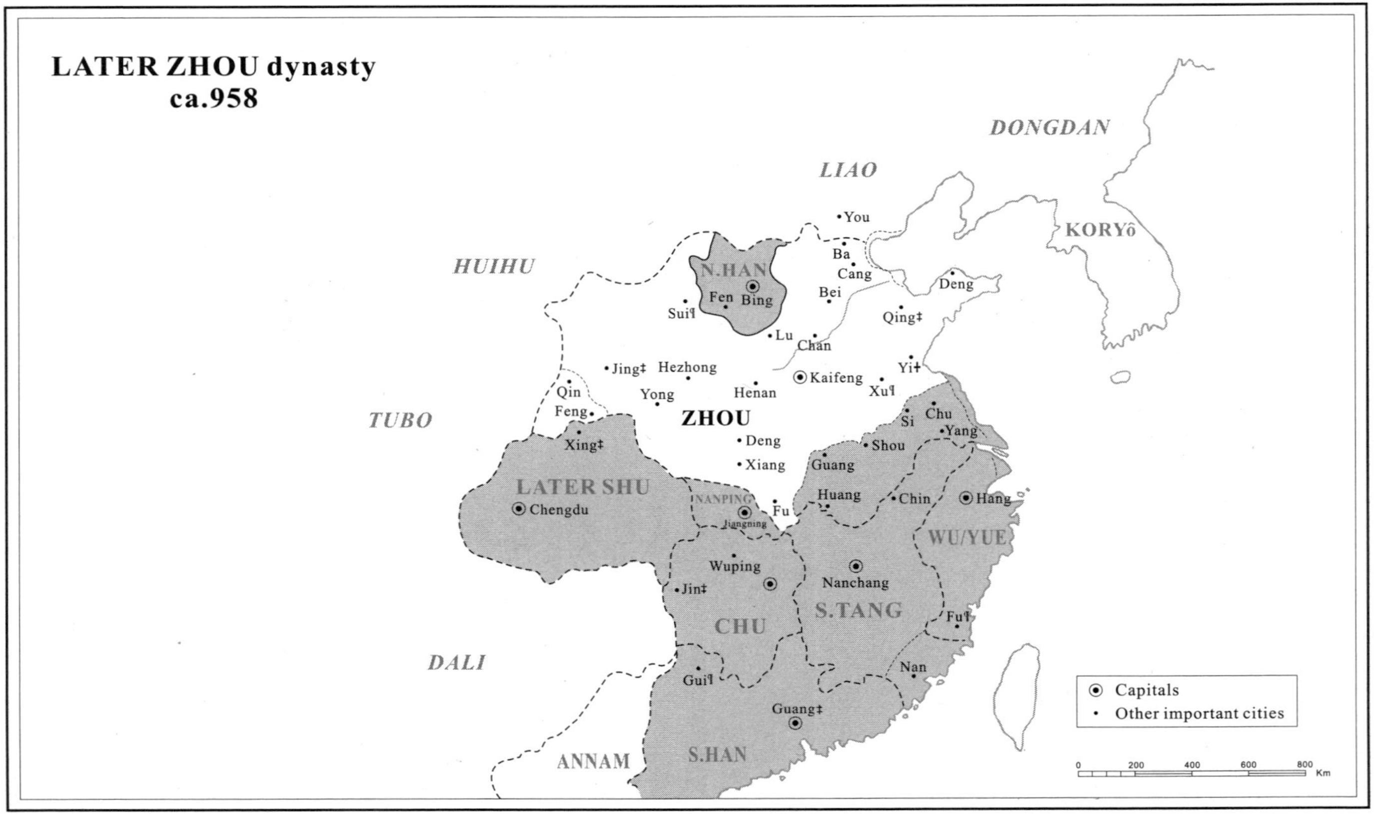
LATER ZHOU dynasty
ca.958
DONGDAN
LIAO
KORYŏ
HUIHU
TUBO
DALI
ANNAM
N.HAN
ZHOU
LATER SHU
NANPING
CHU
S.TANG
WU/YUE
S.HAN
You
Ba
Cang
Bei
Deng
Qing‡
Fen
Bing
Sui¶
Lu
Chan
Yi‡
Kaifeng
Xu¶
Jing‡
Hezhong
Henan
Qin
Yong
Feng
Xing‡
Deng
Xiang
Si
Chu
Yang
Shou
Guang
Huang
Chin
Hang
Chengdu
Jiangning
Fu
Wuping
Nanchang
Jin‡
Fu¶
Gui¶
Nan
Guang‡
Capitals
Other important cities
0
200
400
600
800
Km

RULERS OF THE FIVE DYNASTIES AND TEN KINGDOMS

THE FIVE DYNASTIES

LIANG

Zhu Wen (Quanzhong, 852–912), Taizu, r. 907–912
Zhu Yougui, Prince of Ying, r. 912–913
Zhu Youzhen (888–923), Emperor Mo, r. 913–923

LATER TANG

Li Keyong (856–908), Emperor Wu, Taizu
Li Cunxu (885–926), Zhuangzong, r. 923–926
Li Siyuan (867–933), Mingzong, r. 926–933
Li Conghou (887–937), Emperor Min, r. 933–934
Li Congke (887–937), Emperor Fei, r. 934–937

JIN

Shi Jingtang (892–942), Gaozu, r. 937–942
Shi Chonggui (b. 914), Emperor Chu, r. 942–947

HAN

Liu Zhiyuan (895–948), Gaozu, r. 947–948
Liu Chengyou (932–951), Emperor Yin, r. 948–951
Liu Yun (d. 951), Duke of Xiangyin, r. 951

ZHOU

Guo Wei (904–954), Taizu, r. 951–954
Chai Rong (921–959), Shizong, r. 954–959
Guo Zongxun (953–973), Emperor Gong, r. 959–960

THE TEN KINGDOMS

WU

Yang Xingmi (842–905)
Yang Wo (886–908)
Yang Longyan (897–922)
Yang Pu (901–938), r. 921–937

SOUTHERN TANG

Li Bian (888–943), r. 937–943
Li Jing (898–961), r. 943–961
Li Yu (937–978), r. 961–975

FORMER SHU

Wang Jian (847–918), r. 908–918
Wang Yan (d. 926), r. 918–926

LATER SHU

Meng Zhixiang (d. 934), r. 925–934
Meng Chang (919–965), r. 934–965

SOUTHERN HAN

Liu Yin (874–911), r. 917–942
Liu Yan (889–942), r. 942
Liu Pin (920–943), r. 942–943
Liu Cheng (920–958), r. 943–958
Liu Chang, r. 958–971

CHU

Ma Yin (852–930)
Ma Xisheng (d. 932)
Ma Xifan (899–947), r. 932–947
Ma Xiguang (d. 950), r. 947–950
Ma Xi'e, r. 950–951

WU/YUE

Qian Liu (852–932), r. 923–932
Qian Yuanguan (890–944), r. 932–941
Qian Zuo (928–947), r. 941–947
Qian Chu (929–988), r. 947–978

MIN

Wang Shenzhi (862–925)
Wang Yanhan, r. 925–926
Wang Lin (Yanjun), r. 927–936
Wang Jipeng, r. 936–939
Wang Xi, r. 939–944
Wang Yanzheng, r. 944–946

NANPING

Gao Jixing (858–928)
Gao Conghui (891–948)
Gao Baorong (920–960), r. 948–962
Gao Baoxu (924–962)
Gao Jichong, r. 962–963

EASTERN HAN

Liu Min (896–955), r. 951–955
Liu Chengjun, r. 954–968
Liu Ji'en, r. 968–974
Liu Jiyuan, r. 974–979

CHRONOLOGY OF EVENTS IN THE FIVE DYNASTIES[i]

873 (*XIANTONG*[ii] 14)

Emperor Xizong accedes to Tang throne, 7th mo.
Tang takes military action against Shatuo
Rebellion of Wang Xianzhi begins

875 (*QIANFU* 2)

Huang Chao joins rebellion

878

Wang Xianzhi killed by Tang armies
Datong governor Duan Wenchu killed as Li Keyong becomes interim regent
Huang Chao captures Guangzhou‡

879

Gao Pian named Huainan governor

880 (*GUANGMING* 1)

Huang Chao occupies Tang capital, 12th mo.
Tang campaigns against Shatuo

....

i. Chronology based on Xiao, *Lidai diwang nianbiao*, with substantial modification based on the *Historical Records*, both narrative chapters and chronological chart (chapter 71). The information on natural disasters derives from *Wudai huiyao*, chaps. 10–11, pp. 172–186.
ii. From 907 to 959, reign names appear for the Five Dynasties of North China only, not the coterminous Ten Kingdoms, which are too numerous to cite. Tang reign names appear before and Song reign names after this period.

881 (*ZHONGHE* 1)

Tang capital recaptured, 4th mo.

882

Dong Chang becomes Hangzhou prefect

883

Qin Zongquan surrenders to Huang Chao
Zhu Quanzhong (Wen) becomes Bian prefect and Xuanwu governor
Li Keyong succeeds father Guochang at Hedong
Huainan governor Gao Pian murdered by rebel Bi Shiduo as Yang Xingmi occupies Yangzhou

884

Huang Chao is killed
Zhu Quanzhong fails to capture Li Keyong at Shangyuan Post

885 (*GUANGQI* 1)

The Tang Emperor returns to Changan, 3d mo.; flees to Fengxiang, 12th mo.

886

Zhu Quanzhong becomes Prince of Wuxing

888 (*WENDE* 1)

Tang Emperor returns to Changan, 2d mo.
Emperor Xizong dies and Zhaozong succeeds, 3d mo.

889 (*LONGJI* 1)

Qin Zongquan executed after abortive raid on Bianzhou

890 (*DASHUN* 1)

Pang Shigu routed in campaign against Huainan

891

Yangzhou mutineer Sun Ru killed by Yang Xingmi

892 (*JINGFU* 1)

Shi Pu and Sun Ru thwarted at Huainan

893

Shi Pu commits suicide
Wang Jian executes Tian Lingzi

895 (*QIANNING* 2)

Dong Chang rebels at Yuezhou‡, becoming Luoping Emperor
Li Keyong becomes Prince of Jin; Yang Xingmi named Huainan governor

896

Qian Liu occupies Yuezhou‡ and eliminates Dong Chang
Liu Yin occupies Guangzhou‡

898 (*GUANGHUA* 1)

Zhu Quanzhong routs Li Keyong

901 (*TIANFU* 1)

Emperor abducted by eunuchs to Fengxiang, 10th mo.
Ma Yin occupies five prefectures in Chu
Zhu Quanzhong elevated to Prince of Liang

902

Yang Xingmi becomes Prince of Wu
Qian Liu becomes Prince of Yue and later Wu/Yue

903

Li Maozhen executes eunuchs as Tang Emperor returns to capital, 1st mo.
Zhu Quanzhong becomes Prince of Liang; son Youning killed in Huainan
Wang Jian becomes Prince of Shu, 8th mo.

904 (*TIANYOU* 1)

Tang Emperor forcibly relocated to Luoyang, 4th mo.
Zhu Quanzhong murders Emperor Zhaozong and installs Emperor Ai (Prince of Jiyin), 6th mo.

Governors Li Maozhen, Wang Jian, and Li Jihui launch joint campaign against Zhu Quanzhong

905

Sons of Zhaozong murdered by Zhu Quanzhong, 2d mo.
Massacre of Tang literati occurs at Baima Post, 6th mo.
Yang Xingmi dies and Yang Wo succeeds as Prince of Wu, 11th mo.
Empress dowager and Liu Can murdered by Quanzhong, 12th mo.
Li Keyong joins fraternal alliance with Khitan

907 (*KAIPING* 1)

Zhu Quanzhong purges Tang and assumes Liang throne, 4th mo.
Locusts despoil Cai, Chen†, Ru, Xu‡, and Ying¤ prefectures, 6th mo.
Bianzhou renamed Kaifeng and designated eastern capital; Luoyang redesignated as western capital
Wang Jian becomes emperor of Former Shu, 9th mo.
Governor Liu Rengong jailed by son Shouguang

908

Zhu Quanzhong murders the former Tang emperor, 1st mo.
Li Keyong dies and son Cunxu succeeds as Prince of Jin, 1st mo.
Xu Wen of Huainan murders Yang Wo and installs Longyan, 5th mo.

909

Liang capital relocated to Luoyang
Xu Wen consolidates control of Huainan
Wang Shenzhi becomes Prince of Min; Liu Shouguang named Prince of Yan

910

Yang Longyan installed as King of Wu
Flooding in Hao, Ji¶, Song, and Ying¤ prefectures, 7th mo.

911 (*QIANHUA* 1)

Prince of Jin routs Liang armies at Baixiang [Zhaozhou]
Liu Shouguang becomes Emperor of Yan, 8th mo.
Liu Yin succeeded by brother Liu Yan at Southern Han

912

Liang founder killed by son Zhu Yougui, 6th mo.
Prince of Jin defeats Liang armies at Youzhou

913

Zhu Yougui murdered by Zhu Youzhen, Emperor Mo, 2d mo.
Prince of Jin captures Liu Rengong and Shouguang

914

Liu Shouguang murdered at Taiyuan

915 (*ZHENMING* 1)

Weizhou surrenders to Prince of Jin; routs Liang armies at Zhending, 6th mo.
Liu Yan of Lingnan [Han] severs ties with Liang
Shu acquires four prefectures

916

Khitan ruler Abaoji becomes emperor

917

Liu Yan becomes emperor of Southern Han
Khitan blockade Youzhou, routed by Prince of Jin

918

Prince of Jin campaigns against Liang; standoff at Yangliu

919

Wang Jian dies and son Zongyan succeeds as King of Shu, 6th mo.

920

Yang Longyan is purged by brother Pu as King of Wu, 5th mo.

921 (*LONGDE* 1)

Zhang Wenli rebels at Zhao, killing Wang Rong; he dies months later
Zhu Youneng rebels

922

Prince of Jin routs Khitan at Zhenzhou

923 (*TONGGUANG* 1)

The Prince of Jin becomes Tang Emperor, 4th mo.
The Liang Emperor dies in a purge, 10th mo.
Tang shifts capital from Weizhou to Luoyang, naming Guo Chongtao as minister
Chu and Nanping submit tribute to Tang

924

Nanping offers tribute to Tang and receives its investiture
Li Maozhen dies as King of Qin

925

Tang invasion of Shu led by Prince of Wei and Guo Chongtao, purging Wang Zongyan, 11th mo.
Locusts despoil Zhenzhou, 9th mo.
Flooding ruptures dikes along the Yellow River, 9th mo.
Major earthquake at Si, Wei, and Xu¶ prefectures, 11th mo.
Wang Yanhan succeeds father Shenzhi as king of Min

926 (*TIANCHENG* 1)

Prince of Wei (Jiji) kills Guo Chongtao in Shu, 1st mo.; he is killed, 4th mo.
Deposed Shu emperor Zongyan is killed, 3rd mo.
Actor Guo Congqian kills Tang Emperor Zhuangzong, as Li Siyuan occupies Luoyang and succeeds as Emperor Mingzong, 4th mo.
Khitan invade Bohai (Parhae), changing name to Dongdan
Khitan ruler Abaoji dies and second son Yelü Deguang succeeds
Wang Lin succeeds brother Yanhan as king of Min, 12th mo.

927

Tang campaigns against Nanping, 2d mo.
Major earthquake at Zhengzhou, 7th mo.
Meng Zhixiang murders Li Yan in Shu
Tang court invests King of Chu

928

Wang Yanqiu routs Khitan
Gao Conghui succeeds Jixing as Nanping governor, winter
Tang invests Min ruler as king
Chu armies rout Nanping

930 (*CHANGXING* 1)

Shu magnates Dong Zhang and Meng Zhixiang rebel, 9th mo.
Ma Xisheng succeeds Yin at Chu
Tang commander Shi Jingtang fails to subdue Shu, 12th mo.

931

Tang court executes An Chonghui and cohort, 5th mo.
Earthquake at Taiyuan, 6th mo.
Gao Xifan inherits power at Nanping

932

Flooding in region of Hao, Song, and Ying¤ prefectures, 7th mo.
Ma Xifan succeeds Xisheng as Chu potentate
Qian Yuanguan succeeds father Qian Liu as king of Wu/Yue
Meng Zhixiang claims eastern Chuan region
Min kings claim title of emperor

933

Li Congrong dies in rebellion; Li Conghou succeeds Mingzong as Emperor Min, 11th mo.
Meng Zhixiang becomes King of Shu; Min king declares himself emperor

934 (*YINGSHUN* 1)

Meng Zhixiang becomes emperor of Later Shu, int. 1st mo.
Li Congke murders Tang Emperor Min, succeeding as Emperor Fei, 4th mo.

935

Meng Zhixiang dies and son Chang succeeds as Shu emperor, 6th mo.
Wang Chang (Jipeng) of Min murders father Lin and succeeds him
The Khitan invade Tang
Koryô (Gaoli) supplants the Silla (Xinluo) regime in southeastern Korea

936 (*TIANFU* 1)

Shi Jingtang rebels to establish Jin dynasty as Gaozu, 1st mo., ceding sixteen prefectures centering on Youzhou to Khitan
Tang Emperor Fei commits suicide at Luoyang, intercalary (int.) 10th mo.

937

Jin dynasty capital moves to Bianzhou (Kaifeng)
Fan Yanguang rebels at Tianxiong command, 6th mo.; he dies in 940
Yang Pu relinquishes Wu throne to Li Bian, who establishes Southern Tang with capital at Jinling, 10th mo.
Khitan adopt Liao as dynastic name
Koryô supplants Baek-je (Later Baiji) to unify the Korean Peninsula

938

Fires kill more than a thousand residents of Xiangzhou

939

Major flood near Luoyang, 7th mo.
Wang Xi murders nephew Chang and succeeds as Emperor of Min

941

Dikes rupture along Yellow River at Hua and Xing prefectures, 9th mo.
An Chongrong rebels against Jin dynasty
Wu/Yue king dies, succeeded by son Qian Zuo
Min ruler Wang Xi becomes emperor

942

Locusts despoil Shandong, Henan, and Guanxi regions for a year, starting 4th mo.
Imperial nephew Shi Chonggui succeeds Gaozu of Jin
An Chongrong rebellion suppressed
Liu Pin succeeds as Southern Han ruler

943

Yang Guangyuan rebels against Jin, inviting Khitan intervention, 12th mo.
Li Jing succeeds Bian as Southern Tang ruler
Southern Han ruler murdered by successor Liu Cheng

944 (*KAIYUN* 1)

Khitan intervene against Jin dynasty, but fail, 1st mo.
Wang Xi murdered at Min and succeeded by Yanzheng, 3d mo.
Yellow and Luo rivers flood, affecting Zhengzhou, 6th mo.
Yang Guangyuan murdered by son, who surrenders to Jin, 12th mo.

945

Jin dynasty rallies against Khitan, dismissing minister Sang Weihan

946

Wang Yanzheng of Min (Yin) purged by Zhu Wenjin, prompting Southern Tang intervention, 2d mo.
Khitan begin invasion of Jin, 6th mo., capturing the emperor and murdering Sang Weihan in 12th mo.
Southern Tang invades Min and wins its surrender

947

Liu Zhiyuan mutinies at Taiyuan, assuming Han throne as Gaozu, 3d mo.
Khitan withdraw from Bianzhou, 3rd mo.; Yelü Ruan (Wuyu, Shizong) succeeds as their ruler, 4th mo.
Khitan invaders expelled from Zhenzhou, 8th mo.
Ma Xiguang inherits power at Chu
Qian Chu inherits power at Wu/Yue

948 (*QIANYOU* 1)

Han emperor dies and son Chengyou succeeds as Emperor Yin, 2d mo.
Li Shouzhen of Hezhong rebels, 3d mo.; killed by Guo Wei in 949
Locusts despoil Cao, Mi, Qi¶, Qing‡, Xing, Yan, Yi†, Yun prefectures, 7th mo.
Gao Baorong succeeds father Conghui as potentate of Nanping

949

Khitan invade Zhao and Wei prefectures, early winter

950

Guo Wei reassigned to Ye capital, as Han emperor attempts assassination, 4th mo.

Guo Wei murders coterie of officials, Emperor Yin dies, 11th mo.; the heir-designate for Han, Liu Yun, is killed, 12th mo.
Ma Xi'e inherits power in Chu

951 (*GUANGSHUN* 1)

Guo Wei accedes throne as Taizu of Zhou, with Kaifeng capital, 1st mo.
Liu Yun's father, Liu Chong, establishes rival Northern (Eastern) Han at Taiyuan, 1st mo.
Khitan ruler Yelü Ruan falls to assassin; succeeded by cousin Yelü Jing (Muzong)
Southern Tang invades Chu, relocates magnates to Jinling to end the dynasty

952

Flooding near Kaifeng, 7th mo.
Murong Yanchao rebels
Northern Han ruler receives Khitan investiture

953

Khitan invasion repulsed at Dingzhou

954 (*XIANDE* 1)

Chai Rong succeeds to Zhou throne as Shizong, 1st mo.; routs Northern Han and Khitan armies at Gaoping, 3d mo.

955

Zhou campaigns against Later Shu, 5th mo., and Southern Tang, 11th mo.
Northern Han ruler is succeeded by son Liu Chengjun, 11th mo.

956

Zhou emperor personally joins Southern Tang offensive; Zhao Kuangyin becomes chief director of the Imperial Guard
Southern Tang liquidates scions of former Wu ruling family
Wu/Yue raids Southern Tang

957

Emperor Shizong personally conquers Shouzhou, 3d mo.
Northern Han armies repulsed at Luzhou, the Zhou reclaiming the Three Passes, 4th mo.

958

Zhou troops withdraw after Southern Tang cedes all lands north of Yangzi River and relinquishes imperial trappings, 3d mo.
Liu Chang succeeds Cheng to Southern Han throne, autumn

959

Shizong personally leads campaign against Khitan, 4th mo., dying of illness and succeeded by Emperor Gong, 6th mo.

960 (*JIANLONG* 1)

Zhao Kuangyin purges Zhou to rule over Song dynasty, 1st mo.
Huainan governor Li Chongjin vanquished by Song armies
Gao Baoxu succeeds brother as Nanping potentate

961

Li Yu succeeds Jing as Southern Tang ruler at Jinling, 6th mo.

962

Gao Jichong succeeds uncle as Nanping potentate, 11th mo.

963 (*QIANDE* 1)

Nanping surrenders to Song, 9th mo.

965

Later Shu ruler Meng Chang surrenders to Song, 1st mo.

967

Liu Ji'en succeeds his stepbrother to the Northern Han throne

968

Song campaign against Northern Han fails after Khitan intervention

970

Song campaign against Southern Han led by Pan Mei

971

Southern Han ruler Liu Chang surrenders to Song, 2d mo.
Southern Tang relinquishes kingdom status, 2d mo.

974

Song launches campaign against Southern Tang led by Cao Bin
Liu Jiyuan inherits power at Northern Han during Song campaign

975

Southern Tang surrenders to Song

976 (*TAIPING-XINGGUO* 1)

Song armies rout Northern Han at Taiyuan as Khitan intervene
Taizong succeeds to the Song throne

978

Qian potentates of Wu/Yue relinquish empire and relocate to Song capital

979

Song succeeds in conquering Northern Han

MAJOR DISTRICT COMMANDS OF THE FIVE DYNASTIES[i]

NORTH CHINA

Anguo	Xing, Ming, Ci prefectures (Later Tang–Zhou dynasties)
Anyi	Luzhou (Tang–Zhou)
Anyuan	An (Tang, Jin)
Baoxin	Luzhou‡ (Zhou)
Baoyi	Shanzhou (Tang–Song)
Chengde	Zhenzhou (Tang, Han)
Datong	Yingzhou‡ (Liang)
Ganhua	Huazhou‡ (Tang–Zhou)
Guide	Songzhou (Tang–Zhou)
Hedong	Bing (Tang)
Henghai	see Yichang
Huaide	Jin‡ (Jin)
Huguo	Jin (Liang)
Jianxiong	Jin (Tang)
Kuangguo	Xuzhou‡ (Liang), Tongzhou (Tang-Zhou)
Kuangyi	Luzhou (Liang)
Luoyang	western capital (Liang, Jin, Han, Zhou); Luojing (Tang)
Rongzhao	Jin‡ (Jin)
Shannan east	Xiang (Tang–Zhou)

....

i. Based on Ouyang Xiu, *Wudai shiji*, chap. 60, pp. 737–740. The list here provides the administrative seat for each command but does not include other prefectures and counties subordinate to it. For greater detail and full chronology of assignments to the district commands, see Zhu, *Wudai shiguo fangzhen*; Wang, *Wudai huiyao*, chap. 24, pp. 382–385.

Shunde	Zhen (Jin)
Shunyi	Yao (Tang–Zhou)
Tianxiong	Wei, also called Chanzhou (Liang, Tang); Daming (Liang, Han, Zhou), Guangjin (Jin), Xingtang (Tang), including Xiang‡ (Liang, Tang)
Weisai	Xin (Tang–Zhou)
Weisheng	Deng (Tang)
Weixin	Cao (Jin, Zhou) [also Zhangxin]
Wusheng	Deng (Zhou)
Wushun	Zhen (Liang)
Xihai	Yan (Liang) [also Taining] Tang-Zhou
Xuanwei	An (Liang)
Xuanwu	Bian or Kaifeng, eastern capital (Liang–Zhou), including Cao (Liang, Tang), Song (Liang)
Xuanyi	Hua (Liang)
Yichang	Cang, You
Yicheng	Hua (Tang–Zhou)
Yisheng	Yao (Liang) [Jingsheng]
Yongan	Fu† (Jin, Zhou)
Zhangde	Xiang‡ (Jin)
Zhangguo	Ying‡ (Tang–Zhou)
Zhangwu	Yan‡ (Tang–Zhou)
Zhaoyi	Ze, Xing, Ming, Ci (Liang), Lu (Liang, Jin)
Zhen'an	Chen‡ (Jin, Zhou)
Zhenguo	Shan (Liang), Hua‡ (Tang–Zhou)
Zhenning	Chan (Jin–Zhou)
Zhongwu	Chen‡ (Liang, Tang); Tong (Liang), Xu‡ (Tang-Zhou)
Zhongyi	Xiang (Liang), including Yan‡ (Liang)
Zhongzheng	Shou (Zhou)

SOUTH CHINA

Huainan	Yang (Wu, S. Tang)
Jiannan east	Yi¤, Zi‡ (Shu) [Xichuan]
Jianwu	Yong‡ (S. Han)
Jingjiang	Gui† (Chu)
Jingnan	Jiangling (S. Tang)
Ningguo	Xuan (Wu, S. Tang)
Ningyuan	Rong‡ (S. Han)
Qiannan	Qian‡ (Shu)

Qinghai	Guang‡ (S. Han)
Shannan west	Xingyuan (Shu)
Wu'an	Tan (Chu)
Wuchang	E (Wu, S. Tang)
Wuding	Yang‡ (Shu)
Wuwei	Fu¶ (Min, Wu/Yue)
Wuxin	Suizhou (Shu)
Zhendong	Yue (Wu/Yue)
Zhenhai	Hang (Wu/Yue)
Zhennan	Hong (Wu, S. Tang)

INTRODUCTION

Few early civilizations can match imperial China in the precociousness of its historical writings. For nearly three thousand years, the Chinese have produced works astonishingly advanced in method and monumental in volume, thereby making it difficult to speak of a single epochal Golden Age for the historical genre. Conceivably, though, the Eastern Zhou (ca. 770–256 B.C.E.) was such a time: in this classical period, history first asserted its independence from literary and cosmological writings to assume an autonomy of its own. Every major epoch contributed distinctively to the philosophy and technique of historical scholarship, yet the Song dynasty (C.E. 960–1279) can rival the very best.[1] Historical innovators of the time drew inspiration from classical traditions, yet they adjusted traditional forms to meet the current needs of politics and the expectations of scholarship. The *Historical Records of the Five Dynasties*, or *Wudai Shiji*, so uniquely succeeded in combining tradition with innovation, empirical rigor with didactic message, that the government promptly sanctioned it as official history. It was the last of the dynastic histories by an individual author and the last written in a wholly private capacity.

The Five Dynasties era (C.E. 907–979), with its pandemic tumult and personal tragedy, differed from the times of author Ouyang Xiu (Ou-yang Hsiu, 1007–1072) like night and day. In the earlier period, a mighty military machine commonly subverted civilian controls, lackluster favorites wreaked havoc on a succession of royal palaces, and emperors typically acted on whim and their officials on greed while northern China succumbed to a string of alien occupiers. Ouyang Xiu writes in indignation and disbelief, his history laden with emotionally evocative commentary that indicts the immoral many with the same stridency with which it celebrates the ethical few. His colorful characterizations add humanistic depth to ethical abstractions, highlighting the high drama and moral malaise of the day. Focused on the tenth century, the *Historical Records* nonetheless contains insights and agendas that are distinctly eleventh-century in origins: the great debates on dynastic legitimation and factional politics, religious conflict and border affairs permeate the work. Indeed, the not-so-subtle historical presentism was one among many reasons for its lasting appeal.

The *Historical Records*, published posthumously in 1077, is radical in method. By drastically streamlining the text to make the work more narrative-focused than document-driven, the editing yields a story that is uniquely compelling as both literature and history. Clustering biographies around moral themes such as political ethics reveals a distinctly philosophical thrust to the history. Annotation for terms and techniques suggests a philological precociousness centuries ahead of its time, as does the author's empiricist rigor as reflected in strict standards for representing people and events. On the other hand, the *Historical Records* is a quintessentially and conservatively Confucian work. Both narrative and commentary are manipulated to maximize moral lessons. A conservative message is further reflected in the celebration of Chinese heroes, denigration of the "barbarian" other, and rhetoric against assertive women, bankrupt politics, and eroding family values. Such a mix of novel methods and traditional message forced the author to walk a difficult tightrope in attempts to prove history's capacity to be at once moral and empirical.

Ouyang Xiu was not only a giant among giants on the eleventh-century intellectual landscape, but also a godfather of the cultural renaissance underway at the time. He could boast a string of professional attainments from assistant minister to political reformer to chief examiner of the civil service.[2] These provided merely a launching pad, however, for an awesome array of cultural breakthroughs. Almost single-handedly, he led a literary revolution to replace the awkward "contemporary" prose current in his day with the "classical" style of the Spring and Autumn period, making it the dominant style by mid-century.[3] For too long, the effective expression of ideas was held hostage to a rigid literary regimen. Ouyang Xiu had "a genius for the natural," according to official biographers, "his words simple and clear, credible and broad."[4] The *Historical Records* serves as vivid testament to the power of ordinary words in the hands of a true artist. In addition, Ouyang Xiu produced exquisite *shi* poetry in the stylized traditional forms as well as the free-flowing lyrical *ci* style that he personally helped to popularize.[5] His advocacy of ancient traditions went beyond writing forms to include textual content. In interpreting such classics as the *Rites of Zhou*, the *Odes*, or the *Spring and Autumn An-*

nals, he stressed the original texts over a millennium of later commentary, deploying internal evidence and modern reasoning to access the original intent of the sages.[6] Coinciding with these other pursuits was the study of history, an enterprise enriched by the rare intellectual diversity of the author. His history thus emerges as no simple narration of people and events, but as a work that transcends barriers of specialty and discipline. Literary scholars are often baffled that China developed fiction rather late relative to history and poetry. The sheer richness of its historical experience is much to blame, as the *Historical Records* will attest.

His son Ouyang Fa (1040–1085), reflecting back on the times when the book in manuscript form circulated only among friends, asserted with pride, "literati of the time who managed to acquire a few dozen words of the text tended to hide it away like a jewel."[7] Intense interest continued for centuries. Perhaps the most discriminating historical critic for traditional China, Zhao Yi (1727–1814), lavished praise on Ouyang Xiu's rare feat: "With a straightforward presentation and careful assessment of events, the *Historical Records* deserves to be deemed an exemplary history. . . . Not only does Ouyang's literary style approach the original *Historical Records* in lucidity, but a methodology grounded in the *Spring and Autumn Annals* with praise and blame embedded in the Annals and Biographies is a feat that eluded even Sima Qian."[8] Writing seven centuries after the death of Ouyang Xiu and nearly two millennia after Sima Qian, Zhao Yi clearly placed the *Historical Records* among the epic works in China's long historiographic tradition.

The Text

In the simple selection of a title, Ouyang Xiu affirmed unequivocally the inspiration behind his work: the *Historical Records of the Five Dynasties* was named after the *Historical Records*, or *Shiji*, often rendered as the *Records of the Grand Historian*, by Sima Qian (b. 145 B.C.E.). Although he was writing a universal history for all times, Sima Qian created a format for the dynastic history in later times: the "composite annal/biographical" form *(ji zhuan ti)* provided a political chronology at the outset, with a full complement of biographies for individuals and treatises on institutions in later chapters.[9] Containing both a concise chronology to illustrate cause and effect and detailed stories to humanize the record, the original *Historical Records* contained in a single work the virtues of the premier histories to precede it: the *Spring and Autumn Annals (Chun Qiu)*, attributed to Confucius, and the *Narratives of Zuo (Zuo Zhuan)* that supplemented the chronology with stories.[10] Ouyang Xiu's debt to Sima Qian went beyond mere format, however.

He found still greater inspiration in Sima Qian's critical spirit: a healthy skepticism toward the sources, a reasoned explanation of events, and objectivity in presentation.[11] The ideal of objectivity is reflected in the separation of text from commentary, fact from opinion. It also emerges in an eclectic selection and critical use of source materials, balancing private writings against official documents. No word exists in classical Chinese for "objectivity," but the principle was practiced all the same. Sima Qian is famed for stressing human agency in the forging of history, eschewing explanations based on heavenly intervention or supernatural events: monarchs and courtiers who "feared ghosts" or "indulged spirits" did not fare well at his hand.[12] Sima Qian was not altogether consistent in his rationalist impulses, but he established a foundation for later historians to build upon.[13] Apart from skepticism, the historical realism of Sima Qian appealed to Ouyang Xiu as well. The tyrannical and short-lived Qin dynasty (221–206 B.C.E.), for example, had been widely repudiated as illegitimate in Sima's own time, yet his history insisted on respecting its legality, if not legitimacy, by writing "Basic Annals" *(Benji)* for Qin, alongside the legitimate rulers of China's past. Sima acknowledged, in effect, the regime's practical achievement at unifying the empire, however despicable its two self-destructive rulers.[14] Even the controversial Empress Lü, who reigned as veritable ruler mere decades before his birth, received an Annal in his history, an honor otherwise reserved for males.[15] Sima Qian thus set a high empirical standard for the earliest dynastic history.

No such rigor and forethought existed in the original history of the Five Dynasties, later dubbed the *Old History* (*Jiu wudai shi*). Under the nominal direction of chief minister Xue Juzheng (912–981) and the stewardship of his assistant Lu Duoxun (934–985), the work was completed in 974 under the auspices of a newly enthroned Song court, even as much of southern China and parts of the north still eluded its rule.[16] The *Old History* in 150 chapters seemed unjustifiably long for a period of only six decades; by comparison, the original dynastic history for the Tang (618–907) contained only 240 chapters.[17] An exasperating citation of documents, an uncritical reliance on official sources, and too little balance between the Five Dynasties of the north and the coexisting Ten Kingdoms mostly in the south—the *Old History* seemed little more than a sourcebook devoid of selectivity or purpose. Finally, even as a reference work, the *Old History* was difficult to access, having been organized into five "books" *(shu)*, one for each of the Five Dynasties, each with self-contained Annals and Biographies.

In overhauling the *Old History*, Ouyang Xiu created a distinct format: the Annals for each of the Five Dynasties were clustered together in twelve short chapters, then a biographical cluster for each era placing imperial consorts alongside imperial clansmen in eight chapters, then clusters of individual biographies in thirty-seven chapters, treatises limited to astronomy and administrative districts in three chapters, chronicles for the Ten Kingdoms in ten chapters, and appendixes on the "four barbarians" in three chapters.[18] A more integrated work, it proved more compact as well: the *Historical Records of the Five Dynasties* in seventy-four chapters was half the length of the *Old History*. Much of the streamlining came through massive reduction in the citation of documents, especially in the Annals. Treatises on calendars and commodities, civil service and military institutions, and laws and punishments were deleted as well.[19] Biographical chapters were trimmed down in the spirit of "more facts and fewer words" *(shi zeng wen sheng)*, that is, including more people but being selective about details. Thus, every passage serves a purpose. An area of major expansion occurred with coverage for the Ten Kingdoms: five chapters in the *Old History* were expanded to ten chapters by Ouyang Xiu and dubbed "Hereditary Houses" *(Shijia)*, a term coined by Sima Qian. These chapters included information on potentates whose surrender in the mid- to late 970s came after completion of the official history. In effect, Ouyang Xiu went beyond revising the older work to set new paradigms for understanding the times.

Relative to other dynastic histories attributed to a single author, the *Historical Records of the Five Dynasties* comes perhaps closest to actually representing a single author's industry and intellect. The original *Historical Records* may be widely attributed to Sima Qian, yet father Sima Tan initiated the project and authored some parts.[20] The other history of comparable fame to emerge from the eleventh century, the *Comprehensive Mirror for the Advancement of Governance (Zizhi tongjian)* edited by Sima Guang (1019–1086), contains even less of his own original writing.[21] Some writers posit that Ouyang Xiu's *Historical Records* benefited from the initial input of a friend, Yin Shu (1001–1047), but the supposition has not gone unchallenged, and any influence was probably confined to the Annals, Yin having died early.[22] Later on, annotation on terms, methods, and symbolic meaning was added; attributed to his student Xu Wudang although likely guided by the author, they appear as footnotes in the translation that follows. (My own notes appear as endnotes.) Still, without dispute, the overwhelming bulk of the initial drafting and later revision was assumed by a singular Ouyang Xiu, the entire narrative in his inimitable pen and rich commentary wedded to a lifetime of philosophical positions.

Ouyang Xiu originally drafted the text during exile in Yiling and Qiande counties in south-central China from the tenth month of 1036 until the sixth month of 1039.[23] Nonetheless, it remained with him until his death in 1072, when the Song court ordered retrieval for publication in 1077. Modern scholars can find no compelling cause for the author's adamancy against publication, despite permitting extensive circulation of the draft among friends.[24] As late as 1060, Ouyang Xiu declined a court invitation to publish the work, citing the need to "further refine and emend it" *(fu jingjia kaoding)*, a process allegedly impeded by official posting away from the capital, with its rich repositories of documents.[25] Yet as early as 1053, a letter to a long-time friend refers to the history in seventy-four chapters, precisely its current form, implying that later alterations were modest, at least in scope.[26] The same letter contains a highly curious statement. "I have simply reconstituted the *History of the Five Dynasties* in seventy-four chapters, which I dare not distribute widely," Ouyang Xiu says with part humility, part subtle symbolism. He adds, "The work should not be seen by ordinary men, yet neither should good men be denied access."[27] What sort of "ordinary" or "vulgar" men *(suren)* were of concern to him?[28] What issues of content, either in the history's narrative or commentary, might have provoked such "vulgar" critics? How did such perceived criticisms inform later revisions? There are no definitive answers, although analysis of the text suggests substantive revisions, not just cosmetic rewrites, well into the author's later years, particularly in the lengthy and magisterially executed commentaries, where the author's historical vision and political views are best articulated and where contemporary import is most in evidence.

Ouyang Xiu's substantive revision of the *Historical Records* through the 1050s is irrefutably evidenced in comments on "legitimate succession." His original essay of 1040, *Zhengtong lun*, had evoked a vociferous debate over its recognition of dynasties widely assailed as morally bankrupt, such as the ancient Qin or the more recent Later Liang. To many, he seemed an apologist for the hegemon. In his concluding commentary to the "Annals of Liang" in the *Historical Records*, Ouyang Xiu personally alludes to a controversy now some years old: "Ever since Later Tang times, a world long despising the Liang had largely deemed the dynasty illegitimate. In my own assessment of the Five Dynasties, however, I singularly refused to dismiss the Liang, causing some critics to reprove me for a grave disservice to the maxims of the *Spring and Autumn Annals*." He then proceeds with a brief presentation of the negative criticisms in order to dispute them, one after another. Without question, this commentary in chapter 2 was written many years after his controversial essay of 1040, which had coincided with the initial drafting of the *Historical Records*. Moreover, the content and even wording of commentary in chapter 2 are nearly identical to another, noticeably different writing on legitimacy from Ouyang Xiu's later years, *Exposition on the Wei and Liang (Wei/Liang jie)*.[29]

The original 1040 essay, despite allusion to interregna (*wutong* or *juetong*) for other periods, does not cast the Five Dynasties in that mold.[30] Precisely the early presumption of legitimacy for the Five Dynasties, in fact, explains the organization of the *Historical Records* around those regimes. Many years, perhaps decades, later, Ouyang Xiu's essay on legitimation theory in "three parts," *Zhengtong san lun*, shifts significantly to reject the entire period as an interregnum. "Some regimes lack rectitude from beginning to end, while failing to unite the world. How can they be deemed legitimate? The Wei and the Five Dynasties are precisely such cases. . . . The men who seized power in the Five Dynasties were all renegades. Dismissing the Liang as singularly illegitimate reflects the prejudice of the dynasty's detractors. If the Liang must be deemed illegitimate, how do we sanction the Later Tang, Jin, Han, and Zhou? I now reject them all."[31] In the tension between Confucian moralism and historical realism, an aging Ouyang Xiu seemed to shift toward the former. The change of heart came too late to inform the overall structure of the *Historical Records*, but it is subtly reflected in the author's careful evasion of the broader issue of legitimate rule for the period: the commentary for chapter 2 never specifically asserts the legitimacy of the Five Dynasties, but merely justifies the author's "unbiased" approach to the Liang, a theme common to early and later writings.

Ouyang Xiu's commentary on "factions," appearing as the concluding commentary to "Six Courtiers of Tang," also suggests considerable evolution since 1044, when his memorial and the subsequent "Discourse on Factions" *(Pengdang lun)* were written. The "Discourse," less than two thousand characters long, proved perhaps even more explosive than his legitimation writings, for he wrote not about some historiographic abstraction but in defense of fellow political reformers at court. In the face of a millennium of Confucian rhetoric equating factional alliances with political subterfuge, Ouyang Xiu argued that the factional activities of moral men can actually benefit the state and should be condoned. "It is only natural that moral men tend to enter partisan alliance with other moral men based on shared principles, while petty men ally with other petty men for mutual profit. Your Servant, in fact, contends that petty men actually have no factions; only moral men can form them."[32] He then proceeds to attribute the "supreme governance" of ancient kings Yao and Shun to their elevation of "factions of morally superior men" *(junzi zhi peng)*, attributing the "pervasive tumult" of the late Han and Tang dynasties to the purge of moral men, as petty sorts take control. Biographer James T. C. Liu argues that Ouyang Xiu contradicts himself in another memorial only a year later, where he characterizes as patently "false" the charge of factionalism against fellow reformers.[33] Whether this was a genuine change of heart or merely a strategic retreat we can never know. Commentary in the *Historical Records* begins by denouncing those who "raise the factionalist banner," as if to reflect his later approach to the problem. Yet the last three paragraphs of the same commentary affirm that, "it is naturally inherent for moral men to relish in associating with others of common character" (chapter 35). This might suggest a merging of earlier and later views, with Ouyang Xiu warning against false labels even as he defends the right of moral men to associate. The new synthesis, representing the writer's more mature views, implies continuing work on the commentaries well into his later life.

The time Ouyang Xiu invested in historical comments clearly demonstrates the centrality of commentary to text. Thus, the *Historical Records* is by far the most intensely polemical of the twenty-four dynastic histories. In subsequent centuries, official histories came to be compiled by committees of erudite men often competent with sources but short on conviction, men who obsess over facts but slight commentary. It was perhaps the richness of commentary in the *Historical Records*, in contrast, that explains its appeal even beyond the borders of Song China. After all, it was under Jurchen Jin-dynasty rule over North China, in 1207, that the *Historical Records* first received sanction as the "official version," supplanting the *Old History* in curricula at the Imperial University.[34] It remained the standard version in successive dynasties for the next half millennium, commonly dubbed the *New History of the Five Dynasties (Xin Wudai Shi)*, and for a while, the *New Historical Records of the Five Dynasties (Xin Wudai Shiji)*.[35] The original history faced such pervasive neglect, on the other hand, that efforts at full reproduction in the eighteenth century proved impossible: the extant version today, reconstructed from other sources, is not complete.[36]

The wide and enduring appeal of the *Historical Records* at the expense of the *Old History* also relates to presentation: not only is the editing flawless, but the structure is also remarkably spontaneous. The *Old History* had conformed to the traditional format of confining commentary to a few lines at the end of chapters, preceded by the words "comments of the court historians" *(shichen yue)*, in formal and formulaic manner. Ouyang Xiu does not confine his comments to the predictable places: they appear wherever they are rhetorically most effective, including the opening of a chapter as a prolonged preface. Never are comments merely pro forma or obligatory. Some chapters have none and others have comments many paragraphs long. Still more unprecedented, commentary is invariably preceded with the words *wuhu*, the sound of a long and anguished cry. All comments were essentially mournful outbursts against the tumult of the times. The word "lament" in English originally related to the sound of weeping as well, so *wuhu* is rendered, "We Lament," rather than the standard, "Alas!"

Ouyang Xiu's history is a model of the "classical prose" *(guwen)* that he personally celebrated and popularized. Literary and classical sensibilities also inspired the precise use of words, as evidenced in the glossing of terminology that appears as footnotes in the translation that follows, annotation attributed to student Xu Wudang in consultation with the author.[37] Chapters 2 and 3 are especially replete with such notes, rich in philological as well as historiographic insights. At one point the author explains his reasoning in selecting different verbs to describe assorted military actions, stating, "Four terms are used with reference to the deployment of armies: when two equals attack each other, the term employed is 'attack'; when the mighty attacks the weak, it is 'campaign'; when action is taken as punishment for a crime, it is 'punitive drive'; when the Son of Heaven personally accompanies his men, it is an 'expedition' " (chapter 2). Often moral implications or judgments are reflected in the annotation, as when the reader is informed, later in the same chapter, "The 'defector' turns against one regime and joins another, becoming a subject of the other power. The 'rebel' is an inferior who conspires against his superior, committing a higher level of treachery." Such distinctions are made in the interests of "language consistency," literally, "patterns" or "rules" of language *(wenli)*, the specificity of language serving to augment his history's moral thrust. *Historical Records of the Five Dynasties* is the earliest dynastic history with such meticulous glosses appended to the original text, a tool previously more common with philosophical texts.

The organization of biographical chapters is also unique. The *Old History* did not contain a special cluster for the "Loyal and Righteous" *(Zhongyi)*, despite the fact that these had become a staple of the dynastic history in recent centuries.[38] The rationale of official historians was never articulated, but an indignant Ouyang Xiu overhauled the biographical section from chapters 32–57 to enumerate a rigorous set of Confucian duties. A two-chapter cluster for "Martyrs to Virtue" *(Sijie)* and "Martyrs in Service" *(Sishi)* celebrated the lives of the loyal few as it created a hierarchy of loyalty determined by whether death was voluntary or involuntary. Ouyang Xiu also clusters together civil and military men who served a single dynasty as "subjects" *(chen)*; the ethically compromised who served multiple dynasties appear later under "Miscellaneous Biographies" *(Zazhuan)*. The word for "miscellaneous," *za*, has the dual meaning of something mixed and impure, akin to "motley assemblage." Even placement in the history reflects a ranking grounded in moral principles: sequences for exemplary personages appear before the ethically ambiguous.

Moral indoctrination notwithstanding, the *Historical Records* stands out for another equally emphatic message: the historian's need for realism *(shi)* and reason *(li)*. Realism involved respecting historical fact and avoiding deception by biased or misleading sources. As stated in the commentary to chapter 18, "We can afford nothing less than caution where omissions in the historical literature are involved: recording dubious points in the inherited record permits credible portions to receive a credible reception, after all." He was alluding specifically to inadequate information about an historical event, yet traditional sources based on government records often contained blatant fabrications, particularly pertaining to prodigies and omens. Since the earliest times, irregularities of nature—anomalies on earth or in the heavens—were taken as ominous signs of heaven's pleasure or displeasure. The *Old History of the Five Dynasties*, like earlier dynastic histories, contained detailed chapters on astronomical portents.[39] It also cited birth-related prodigies that portended the rise of future emperors: red vapors above the Liang founder's home, white vapors hovering over the Jin founder, red lights and thunderous roars heralding in the Zhou founder, and the marathon thirteenth-month pregnancy yielding the Tang founder.[40] And when virtuous dynasties or rulers were purged by the less virtuous, the *Old History* often attributes such events to an inscrutable Heaven.[41] Such citations were likely gleaned uncritically from contemporary documents and presented as simple fact.

Each of the aforementioned prodigies in the *Old History* was deleted from the *Historical Records* or cited with the clear intent of censure. For example, when the waters of the usually murky Yellow River reportedly turned clear after the Liang ascent to power, the citation came with a caveat, "I cite such omens to expose the inauspiciousness of it all."[42] A far more emphatic case appears in chapter 63, where chronicles for the Former Shu contain numerous citations of prodigies such as the dragon or phoenix, presented in tongue-and-cheek fashion. A long commentary at the end of the chapter proceeds to lambaste the regime for such incredible reports: "In reading the *History of Shu*, I found it perplexing that auspicious omens ostensibly associated with kingly rule such as the tortoise, dragon, unicorn, phoenix, and white *zouyu* tiger would ultimately surface in this domain, of all places!" Without denying the existence of such legendary beasts in ancient times, Ouyang Xiu casts doubt on their appearance in an inauspicious age like the Five Dynasties and a setting like Shu, remote and mismanaged. The conclusion is based upon "common sense" or "ordinary reasoning" *(chang li)*,[43] as he affirms in a note to chapter 5. "Things that cause injury such as floods, droughts, storms, and locusts are natural disasters and thus cited. But events that contravene common experience and occur inexplicably are prodigies; these lie beyond our ability to comprehend and are not cited."[44] In a later chapter not translated here, Ouyang Xiu dismisses accounts of fire ablaze on water or beans raining from heaven, insisting that such things "have never met the eyes nor ears of the Middle Kingdom."[45] In effect, historical reasoning grounded in human experience and tangible evidence should exclude the unreasonable. "All things have understandable reasons," he affirms in private writings, and these require only exhaustive analysis to be revealed.[46] Thus, natural and supernatural phenomena must be handled skeptically.

Undue attention to omens and prodigies ran against Ouyang Xiu's rule of "common sense" but entailed political dangers as well, pretenders of the Five Dynasties having patently exploited them to legitimize illicit power.[47] He cites the example of a youthful Qian Liu, founder of the regime of Wu/Yue: anointed a prodigy by some prognosticator, the tale later provided a pretext to usurp power (chapter 67). Concluding that chapter is the comment, "The links between Heaven and humanity can defy explanation. Since antiquity, not only have occultists won favor through the novel, but also ultimately valorous men turning to insurrection often anointed themselves through prodigies and omens. . . . The predictions of occultists often miss the mark and are rarely on target. Why do men so relish in citing the few accurate hits?" The historian's highest duty thus rests with exposing political fraud of the sort, reasserting the centrality of personal merit to political development. Thus, the *Historical Records* contains few references to heavenly intervention in human affairs, far fewer than even the *New History of the Tang*, published in 1060 under the general editorship and partial authorship of Ouyang Xiu.[48] When speaking as an individual author in a private capacity, he is unequivocal: "The principle behind dynastic splendor or ruin is the Mandate of Heaven, some say. Yet how can we possibly deny human actions?"[49] One writer portrays a once skeptical Ouyang Xiu as turning more superstitious with age.[50] There is scant evidence of such change in the *Historical Records*, still in his hands at the time of death.

Such skepticism among historians toward the supernatural probably had its roots in the middle Tang, particularly the writings of Liu Zhiji (661–721) and Du You (735–812). They had decried the old fascination with destiny and religion, omens and auguries as an unhealthy distraction from analysis of the "human condition," whose impact on history is far greater.[51] Intellectual hostility toward omens and auguries was likely reinforced, in the early decades of the Song, through the policies of founding emperors Taizu (r. 960–976) and Taizong (r. 976–997), who imposed strict bans on books of astrology and fortune-telling for fear of destabilizing the new dynasty.[52] But the suppression of such information by the historian presents another set of problems. Legends can figure prominently in the unfolding of history, swaying the hearts of prospective subjects. By stripping the narrative of fortune-telling and the like, the events themselves become difficult to understand in full measure. In other words, strict adherence to historiographic principle can have a deleterious impact on historical meaning.

Ouyang's personal skepticism ultimately extended beyond mere attitudes toward omens and auguries to include religious beliefs in general. In a path-breaking essay "On Fundamentals," for example, he once likened Buddhism to a "disease" gnawing at the moral fabric of the country, a parasitic institution draining the empire of its human and material resources.[53] He also warned, elsewhere, of Buddhism's grip on human emotions and its consequent capacity to mobilize or "stir up the people," as he puts it, with the potential for wreaking every sort of disruption.[54] Ouyang Xiu was proud of relating the story of uncles who had targeted the Buddhist establishment, coercing monasteries to contribute to famine relief or indicting crazed monks for abuses against commoners.[55] His anti-Buddhist predisposition would powerfully inform characterizations of Emperor Shizong of Zhou, the Five Dynasties ruler who commanded Ouyang Xiu's greatest respect.[56] In commentary on the reign (chapter 12) he writes: "Only a year after his accession, Shizong eliminated 3,336 Buddhist temples across the empire. The Middle Kingdom faced a shortage of copper cash at the time, so the confiscation of all Buddhist statuary of bronze was mandated for recasting as coin. He once commented, 'Tradition has it that the Buddha viewed human existence as unreal, yet out of an urge to profit mankind [through his teachings], he chose to retain his true body. Having once chosen to forgo personal salvation to profit the world, how could he possibly begrudge us a bunch of bronze statues?' " Shizong's trivialization of Buddhist rituals seemed tailored to the personal sentiments of Ouyang Xiu, who saw hypocrisy in the religion's denigration of the material while its institutions amassed vast wealth. Such strong sentiments against religion and for reason were probably not characteristic of eleventh-century intellectuals, yet they reflect an important agenda for some, one that Ouyang Xiu persuasively articulated.

Overall, the unique methodology and message of Ouyang Xiu's history suggest some important changes, none as critical as historical audience. Dynastic histories, many centuries before the Song period, were mostly written under state sponsorship and usually in the early reigns of a new regime. Their immediate audience was discernibly the throne and its advisors, who then set a course for the new dynasty informed by the recent past. Ouyang Xiu's history, written generations later and sanctioned as the official version only after his death, is unique in not being constrained by such short-term court agendas. This permitted an unprecedented broadening of readership—a conscious objective of the author, I believe. The pervasive concern for Confucian loyalty only makes sense for a work directed at scholars and officials in the broadest sense, not simply or even chiefly court insiders. A meticulous methodology stressing precision of speech, scrupulous skepticism toward the inherited record, and an exhaustive exploration of human agency to elevate historical reasoning suggests another audience: practicing or aspiring historians. A history shorn of the usual charts and treatises on institutions, where the bulk of information is buried in biographies, appeals to another cluster of more leisured readers drawn preeminently to the personality of history over the institutional nuts and bolts, readers placing literary or moral edification before simple information. This further underscores the self-consciousness of the author in composing the *Historical Records*, writing for posterity but keeping a keen eye on contemporary needs.

The Times

Most historians are drawn to topics out of nostalgia or pride, yet Ouyang Xiu studied the Five Dynasties for its largely negative lessons, particularly pertaining to the military leaders who dominated and were the source of turmoil, to his mind. And indeed, in comments on a cluster of military men, he minces no words in linking political bankruptcy to the martial identity of leaders—views more characteristic of the eleventh century, when civil power was restored, than the tenth century that he writes about. "Rulers of the Five Dynasties all emerged from the ranks of military men, the fearless officers and ferocious warriors beneath them appropriating land and noble titles for themselves. How is this different from having wolves shepherd men?"[57] "Fearless and ferocious," desirable traits in warriors, were precisely those that made them the worst of rulers, for they resorted to the heavy-handed tactics of pressure and extortion, with no sense of higher duty. Rule backed by professional armies with negligible popular support gave rise to an escalating dependence on arms. A sense of higher duty also eluded the military generally, the "purge of rulers and overthrow of dynasties" largely perpetrated by the military elite: in the Five Dynasties, the military *coup d'état* replaced the peasant rebellion as the primary route to imperial power. The divorce of political power from popular bases, compounded by the indifference of military men to civil traditions, led to moral and political malaise, or, in the idiom of the *Historical Records*, "turmoil" *(luan)* and "destruction" *(huai)*.[58]

The reign of warriors was rooted in the eighth century, as was the expanding autonomy of military governors *(jiedushi)*, simplified in my translation as "governors." These men began as agents of the court responsible for logistics and troop support in the border provinces, but in the wake of mutinies in mid-century, they proved a persistent threat to civil power.[59] A century of struggle between center and periphery ensued, the government's cause largely lost by the mid-880s, as the rebel Huang Chao (d. 884) ravaged the empire and governors across the realm asserted autonomy. The authority of governors, once scrupulously sanctioned by the court, turned hereditary in the last decades of the dynasty, to pass from father to son or from patron to protégé. The court employed rival armies in or near the capital to oversee governors in the provinces, the "palace armies" led by commissioners of the "northern" and "southern" bureaus *(xuanhui shi)*, mostly eunuchs in the late Tang. Unwittingly, the action created a cause for governors in the provinces to rally against.[60] Governor jockeyed against governor and against the palace while amassing stupendous fortunes. The recently unearthed tomb of Wang Chuzhi, whose biography appears in chapter 39, offers stunning evidence of the resources and stature enjoyed by them. Some twelve meters in circumference, the tomb in Quyang County (modern Hebei Province) rivals those of royal princes in size and sumptuous decor.[61]

The founder of the first of the Five Dynasties, Zhu Wen, usually referred to in the text rather wryly as Quanzhong (Wholeheartedly Loyal), the name conferred by rulers of Tang, began humbly as a lieutenant to the rebel Huang Chao. Reverting to the Tang cause in 882, he quickly rose to governor of the Xuanwu command at Bianliang (Kaifeng), in the heart of north-central China along the Grand Canal.[62] He succeeded in defending his charge against predators such as the ruthless Qin Zongquan to his south, while expanding from that base to the north and west. In the capital, Zhu allied with courtiers such as Cui Yin against the powerful eunuch faction. Engineering the liquidation of more than seven hundred eunuchs in 903, he thereby effected the forcible relocation of the Tang emperor, Zhaozong, from the western capital at Chang'an (hereafter Changan) to the eastern capital at Luoyang, closer to his own base. Only a year later, the emperor fell to Zhu's assassin, an affair elaborated upon in the biography of Li Yanwei. Zhu Quanzhong ruled briefly through a puppet before declaring the Liang dynasty in 907, his primary capital at Bianzhou, east of the two historic capitals.

In commentary, Ouyang Xiu characterizes the Liang dynasty as "evil," "depraved," and "despised by the world." Its founder committed despicable acts of treason to the Tang by heartlessly liquidating his ruler and leading courtiers. The disciplining of his own armies was unthinkably brutal as well. When a commander or his lieutenant perished in battle, Zhu insisted on liquidating all subordinate officers who survived, ostensibly for their cowardice.[63] Even the royal family was consumed by assassination, the founder himself succumbing to the intrigues of a son. Boundless lechery also menaced the regime.[64] Zhu acquired several hundred women in time, according to "Royal Family" chapters of the *Historical Records*. The biography of Zhang Quanyi reveals that the emperor, visiting a trusted commander, raped both his wife and daughter, barely escaping retribution from the son. The emperor's affair with the wife of another commander, Yang Chongben, caused Chongben to defect to rival Li Maozhen. Such personal depravity and ruthless governance has few parallels among the fifty-five other rulers or potentates of the period, save for one or two hereditary houses in the south.

Moral bankruptcy of this sort explains Ouyang Xiu's reticence to acknowledge the political feats of the Liang, which were surprisingly numerous for a rule of sixteen years. Most notably was the elimination of more than a century of eunuch power by a sweeping liquidation in and away from the capital in 903. The military powers once vested in eunuchs now shifted to an independent military commission, initially the Bureau for Venerable Governance (*Chongzhengyuan*) and later the Bureau of Military Affairs (*Shumiyuan*). Eunuch power never recovered from the setback, not in the Five Dynasties nor even the subsequent Song period. Moreover, the dynasty's second ruler, Emperor Mo, ambitiously endeavored to break the back of the preeminently powerful Tianxiong command, centered on Weizhou, by splitting it in two. The ploy backfired, permitting the dynasty's premier rival to win a major ally in its very backyard and precipitating the Liang's unraveling. Emperor Mo would have changed the course of history had he prevailed.

The progenitors of the Later Tang, Li Guochang[65] and his son Keyong, commonly called the Princes of Jin, hailed from Shatuo tribes, or "federations," of Turkish ancestry with three separate bases extending from Central Asia to the northern border of China, the Taiyuan area of modern Shanxi.[66] The Shatuo initially aligned with the Tibetans (Qiang) and the Uighurs (Huihu or Huihe), reverting to the Tang by the early ninth century. The distinguished service of its men in various high-level border posts caused the Tang court to confer upon them the imperial surname Li, a common ploy to win the loyalties of border mercenaries.[67] Guochang and Keyong operated from a base considerably north of Zhu Quanzhong, yet by the early 890s Keyong presented a sufficient threat that Quanzhong often targeted him for raids and incessantly intrigued to incite rifts between him and the court. Still, it was Keyong who rescued Emperor Zhaozong from the cabal of governors intent on overturning him, initially in 895 and again in 898.[68] And his son proved a persistent and ultimately fatal foe for Liang armies along the Yellow River, overturning the dynasty in 923.

The Shatuo hereafter adopted the Tang namesake in honor of the dynasty's beneficence. Known to history as the Later Tang, the dynasty lasted more than twelve years and, relative to its predecessor, ruled over a domain extending farther to the north, the west, and the southwest. It was the only northern dynasty to reign, however briefly, over a sizable part of Shu, modern Sichuan, whose conquest appears in the biographies of Guo Chongtao, Kang Yanxiao, and the Prince of Wei, Jiji. Such feats were partly attributable to more ethnically inclusive armies. The "multiracial armies of Inner Asians and

Chinese" *(Fan/Han jun)*, which second emperor Mingzong commanded, clearly evolved into an elite force with a stunning record. Other cross-cultural accommodations are in evidence, the Later Tang laying an institutional foundation destined to last for centuries: it organized an Imperial Guard and Imperial Bodyguard *(Shiwei qinjun)* to enhance palace control over the military and a finance commission *(sansi)* to assert court prerogatives to collect and allocate revenues.[69] The collection of taxes in cash, rather than grain, began under Tang rule.[70] Its rulers governed from a plethora of capitals, starting with Taiyuan, Weizhou, and Zhenzhou, and later adding Changan, Luoyang, and Kaifeng. The geographic mobility inherent in such an arrangement provided a rare political and military visibility. Ouyang Xiu concedes in commentary that Later Tang dynast Mingzong, a ruler both disciplined and humane, reigned over "a time when wars had abated and harvests were bountiful." Despite seizing power by military coup against his brother by adoption, Zhuangzong, he ruled from the heart. In a conversation with his military commissioner on the appropriateness of military expenditures, Mingzong laments, "To fatten war horses, I have to emaciate my people—this would shame me!" (see Fan Yanguang). Forces of nature seemed to conspire against the circumspect ruler all the same, his reign beset with a constant stream of natural disasters and anomalies. Earthquakes are reported in 927 and 931, major floods in 932, and five solar eclipses from 926 to 931, plus a succession of lunar eclipses, falling stars, and assorted celestial anomalies from 928 to 931.[71] The symbolism of such events, never lost on the Chinese, surely undermined an otherwise credible regime.

More important, Shatuo leaders could never, or perhaps preferred not to, disabuse themselves of alien customs and religions.[72] The ritual impropriety of burning paper money on "Cold foods festival" offers one of many examples.[73] Ouyang Xiu's many references to royal excursions, hunts, and cockfights in the Basic Annals of Tang and Jin clearly serve as censure, not simple points of information. Military practices such as conveying orders attached to arrows *(chuanjian)*, rather than employing written orders in Chinese fashion, proved confounding as well (see Huo Yanwei). Emperor Zhuangzong's unthinkable decision in 925 to level his own altar of accession, merely to make way for a polo field, presents another case of clashing customs (see Zhang Xian). The cavalier adoption of hundreds of sons, a practice lambasted by Ouyang Xiu in chapter 36 as politically destabilizing, may similarly have its origins in nomadic ways.

Rulers of the Later Tang were not without fatal flaws of personality either. Founder Zhuangzong, a legendary romantic, possessed an imposing facility in classical Chinese and liked nothing more than composing songs and performing alongside actors and musicians. He kept an entourage of a thousand actors and twice that number in female consorts and paramours, or so the histories say.[74] The flamboyant ruler also spent lavishly on gambling and palace décor, impulses initially harnessed by Guo Chongtao and Zhang Chengye, his seasoned minister and senior eunuch, as well as the powerful Dowager Cao, his mother. At the same time, Zhuangzong tried to resuscitate eunuch power at court, summoning back to the capital hundreds who had eluded execution under the previous dynasty by hiding in the locales. This proved an enormous blunder, according to Ouyang Xiu's commentary to chapter 38. Still greater misjudgment appears in the chapter on "Court Musicians and Actors." Perhaps the most tragic chapter in this or any history, it exposes Zhuangzong as being as deficient in political savvy as he was gifted in the martial and literary arts, precisely why he succumbed to a coup after only three years. Successor Mingzong began with the symbolic act of purging and liquidating most eunuchs, ushering in a nearly eight-year reign of prosperity and stability, according to the biography of Feng Dao. His successors proved poor substitutes, however, and the house fell to nomadic cousins.

Later Tang royals retreated to their Taiyuan base once Shi Jingtang, a descendant of Zhuye tribes ethnically related to the Shatuo Turks, founded the Jin dynasty (distinct from the Jin "princely domain" of Li Keyong). The translation here generally employs "the Jin dynasty" or "Shi-Jin" with reference to this second Shatuo regime.[75] A leading figure in the Imperial Guard and brother-in-law of Emperor Mingzong, Jingtang mutinied in 936, buttressed by fellow governors and the Khitan, one-time allies of the Later Tang now expanding in North China.[76] The Khitan monarch, Yelü Deguang (r. 927–947), intervened as well to purge the Tang from its base at Taiyuan.[77] Jingtang's success could not have occurred without Khitan intervention, and Khitan intervention would not have come if the last Tang emperor had adopted the appeasement policies then under consideration at court, as outlined in the biography of Lü Qi.

Modern historians credit Shi Jingtang, or Emperor Gaozu of Jin, with strengthening the center against local military power by broadening the powers of trusted palace officials; he also reorganized the bodyguard to enhance its responsiveness to the throne.[78] The Basic Annals for his reign further allude to the abolition of abusive forms of taxation, such as collecting taxes two to four years in advance or prodding officials to pay for imperial banquets as an informal assessment. He aspired to some virtue, yet the regime never stabilized and remained perennially strapped for cash. The court was reduced to plying the governors to cover burial costs for the dynasty's founder, as the Annals for Emperor Chu reveal. Natural disasters struck so frequently, especially in 943, that the court felt compelled to declare a succession of amnesties for lawbreakers, triggering a lively debate on the historical purpose and limits of amnesties (chapter 57, Zhang Yun‡). The northern strongholds of the Jin dynasty, at Mingzhou and later Taiyuan, proved vulnerable to pressures from the Khitan. And setting capitals in the Chinese heartland, initially Luoyang and then Kaifeng, only modestly diminished the threat, so Jingtang swore allegiance to Khitan ruler Yelü Deguang. In diplomatic protocol, Jingtang served him as "son" and consulted him about major policy decisions, including the simple selection of an heir. Such loss of face was compounded by the cession of strategically vital lands, the "sixteen prefectures" clustered near modern Beijing—the "defense line" for all of northeast China, in the words of one author.[79] This effectively denied the Jin a needed buffer.[80] The alliance proved highly unpopular with the governors, with some, such as An Chongrong, invoking it as cause to rebel.

An adopted son of little promise inherited the Jin throne in 942. From the outset, Emperor Chu seemed reckless and immoral. In the very midst of his father's funeral wake, he broke the most sacred of mourning rules by taking an empress, Lady Feng, the widow of his own uncle (chapter 17). His political judgment seemed scarcely better, as power devolved on the arrogant and arrantly stupid Jing Yanguang. Trade with the Khitan was abruptly curtailed and their envoys spurned, needlessly ruining relations and triggering wars that consumed the Jin in its last three tumultuous years.[81] These years also witnessed an unusual share of natural disasters. The dual costs of war and disaster led to reviving the old policy of collecting taxes years in advance, a desperate government threatening execution for the hoarding of grain.[82] Emperor Chu, deposed by the Khitan, ended up deep in Manchurian wastelands to live out his days in destitution. The details of his journey northward and the hardships endured as an exile are passionately presented in the biographies of Empress Li and Zhang Yanze and eerily resemble the travails of Song royals themselves in 1126, a mere five decades after Ouyang Xiu's death. The story thus reverberates for later readers in ways unknown and inconceivable to the author.

The Khitan overran the Jin capital at Kaifeng with aid from key courtiers such as Du Chongwei, men alienated by the throne's ineptitude. They proceeded to exercise direct control over the residual Chinese empire in the early months of 947. Many refused to acquiesce in Khitan rule, however.[83] The common people stood in open defiance through rebellion and other forms of roguery, reacting to excessive taxes and needless plunder. The military establishment defied the Khitan as well, with the next dynasty, Han, established by one such defiant governor, Liu Zhiyuan of Taiyuan, the former satrapy of Jin rulers. Descended of the Shatuo, he was chief inspector of the Imperial Guard upon seizing Luoyang and Kaifeng in early 947. But the unstable regime was overturned by 951, making it the shortest of the Five Dynasties. It had come to power largely through the vacuum attending a succession crisis among the Khitan and the withdrawal of their best armies. The Han summarily severed diplomatic ties with the Khitan. It even sought to contain their cultural influence by banning Khitan-style costumes and paraphernalia.[84] Domestically, the dynasty initially adopted severe laws to curtail abusive extractions and bribes by the ruling class. It was undermined, however, by the defiance of leading military figures such as the wily Du Chongwei, whose resistance lasted nearly a year. Furthermore, the dynasty's founder, posthumously called Gaozu, died within a year of enthronement. His successor, Emperor Yin, shy of sixteen years old upon assuming power, allegedly "frolicked within the palace with petty men."[85] Moreover, the young emperor made major decisions on the advice of such "petty men" as Murong Yanchao without consulting a broader officialdom. His greatest insanity, in late 950, involved murdering an entire cohort of influential officers, including Yang Bin and Shi Hongzhao, and plotting against chief commander Guo Wei, a ploy inciting Guo to mutiny and purge the Han house. The only virtuous personality in the palace was his stepmother, Dowager Li, but even her strident rebuke could not reform the monarch. She could only stand by as the military purged and murdered Yin, placing a puppet on the throne for over a month as prelude to outright usurpation.[86] Historically in China, short-lived dynasties have not been ruined so much by megalomaniac-founders as by mediocre second emperors—a rule borne out repeatedly by the Five Dynasties' experience.

The Zhou dynasty, founded in 951, represents the return of Chinese rule after nearly three decades of Shatuo or Khitan dominance, a factor clearly behind Ouyang Xiu's enthusiasm for the regime. Founder Guo Wei had enjoyed the special favor of Shi Jingtang, who as governor found him indispensable and brought him along from one assignment to the next. In his youth, there were reports of "drinking, gambling, and heroic escapades without regard for nuanced behavior."[87] As an adult, however, Guo Wei acquired a sense of compassion, camaraderie, and humility to match the martial daring for which he was also famed. Such exceptional traits partly explain the rare trust of Dowager Li, wife of the Han founder, who ultimately relinquished to him the throne of child monarch Liu Yun in a remarkably peaceful transfer of power.[88] Guo Wei reigned for only three years, half of which saw him in declining health.[89] But at the outset, with amazing gall, he intentionally incited the powerful Khitan by launching a campaign against the Eastern or Northern Han, a Khitan protectorate, triggering their invasion to the south.[90] It must have seemed an act of foolish ambition for a new and vulnerable regime, or perhaps a stroke of genius. Might Guo Wei have anticipated that the newly enthroned Khitan ruler was vulnerable to the assassination that did indeed claim his life, abruptly ending their campaign?

Upon the founder's untimely death, the regime found a second hero in Chai Rong, posthumously called Shizong.[91] Serving under Guo Wei in the 940s, Chai Rong assisted him on campaigns and continued campaigning after taking the throne, his own martial prowess complemented by a talented cohort of subordinate commanders, including the future founder of the Song dynasty, Zhao Kuangyin (927–976). In only six years Shizong expanded the Zhou domain to surpass all other empires of the Five Dynasties save for the Later Tang. In contrast with the Later Tang's focus on expansion in the southwestern Shu region, he adopted the brilliant strategy of Wang Pu, cited at length in chapter 31, where the target of expansion shifted to the southeast. Shizong surely saw this vast region ruled by the Southern Tang as politically vulnerable, based on the declarations of war against it (chapter 62). His was a bold move yielding a stunning string of military gains for the short-term, while a generation later providing the Song dynasty a blueprint to conquer the world. Ouyang Xiu heralds Shizong as "heroic" in some contexts and "wise" in others, a man with the requisite martial gifts to prevail over awesome enemies, along with an intuitive eye for talent and a drive for positive change. His relations with Confucian ritualists and civilian counselors are celebrated as uniquely cordial, a sign of reemerging civilian power after nearly a century of eclipse.[92] Many policies commonly associated with the Song have their origins in the Zhou: in a word, the Song revolution began in 951, not 960.

Shizong's heroic stature relates partly to his embrace of new military strategies and technologies. After prioritizing conquest of the lower Huai and Yangzi regions, he amassed a fleet of warships and legions of sailors with such stunning speed that one visiting ambassador shrieked, "They must have fallen from heaven!"[93] He tended to set seemingly impossible goals and then proceed to fulfill them, as in 957, when he shocked departing envoys in vouching that the safer land route would be available upon their return, inasmuch as he needed only a few months to conquer the southern Huai, in its entirety![94] Shizong had the unique capacity to court civilian advisors, even as he maintained independence of action, his military instincts driving policy above all else. Most civilian courtiers opposed aggression against the rival kingdoms, according to the biography of Wang Pu. Leading the charge was senior courtier Feng Dao (882–954), whose admonition against the Northern Han campaign appears in his biography. Feng doubtless feared that the thirty-three-year-old Shizong was no match for the seasoned ruler of Han, more than twenty years his senior and closely allied to the still more powerful Khitan. "I have heard that Taizong of Tang, in pacifying the world, personally campaigned against all foes, great and small alike," Shizong asserted. "Your Majesty has not reached the point to invite comparisons with Tang Taizong," Feng replied in arrogant condescension.[95] The withering retort was not altogether off the mark, for heavy losses eventually forced Zhou armies to retreat. Military capacities aside, Feng seemed to find preposterous Shizong's propensity for presenting himself as a modern-day Taizong, whose wide-ranging feats several centuries earlier were now legendary. Ouyang Xiu clearly objects to Feng Dao's underestimation of his ruler, the passage censuring him as much as celebrating Shizong.

The Zhou dynasty presented historian Ouyang Xiu with a minefield of problems. First, the accession of Guo Wei to the throne in 951 closely parallels that of Zhao Kuangyin to the Song throne in 960. Both men purged child monarchs to seize power from leadership positions in the Imperial or Palace Guard. Both men also deferred their imperial ambitions for weeks or even months in order to mobilize support among civilian and military leaders. When characterizing Guo Wei as deferring his accession out of "shame," Ouyang Xiu might be seen as censuring the founder of his own dynasty (chapter 20). To avoid this, he buried the comment in an inconspicuous place at the end of biographical clusters for the Zhou royal family, leaving the Annal of Taizu without comment at all. One finds similar angst in his narrative on the purge of the Zhou house by the Song. "The [Zhou] Emperor relinquished the throne," he states, the annotation by student-collaborator Xu Wudang adding, " 'relinquishing' implies 'obeying'—that is, the capacity to obey the Mandate of Heaven" (chapter 12). Conspicuously absent are allusions to the Zhou dynasty's being "overturned" or "brought to ruin" *(wang)*, the common idiom for earlier dynasties, the author preferring to be vague. In a note, Xu Wudang accuses Guo Wei of "deceiving the world" by installing a child emperor only to purge him months later. Such strong words are absent from the text itself, again suggesting special sensitivity to characterizations of Guo Wei for fear of inferences pertaining to the Song dynasty. Indeed, to avoid intruding into contemporary history, Ouyang Xiu shuns any elaborate discussion of the Song founder, save for a few celebrated exchanges with rulers of the Ten Kingdoms.

Another sensitive area pertains to the "Biographies of Zhou Subjects." The chapter, translated below in full, contains only three biographies, in contrast to similar chapters for earlier dynasties that are much longer. There were certainly other candidates available for inclusion, but by Chinese historiographic tradition, persons living into the subsequent Song dynasty, especially persons entering service under the Song, rightfully belong to the history for the later dynasty. Ouyang Xiu was partly conforming to that tradition, but at the same time conveniently avoiding a more sensitive problem of judging the virtue of Zhou-dynasty officials to serve under his own dynasty. Is virtue compromised when old subjects serve a new dynasty, even when that dynasty has a superior claim to the Mandate of Heaven? Three hundred years later, when the dynastic history for the Song, *Song shi*, was compiled, official historians drafted biographies of "Three Subjects of Zhou." The three biographies, at the very end of *Song shi*, contain a preface specifically critical of Ouyang Xiu for failing to include the three men as Zhou Subjects, although their careers were concentrated in the dynasty.[96] Yet official historians of the fourteenth century were too insensitive. For example, the first of the three men quietly omitted from the *Historical Records*, Han Tong, actually died before the Song dynasty's formal founding. He was killed by a minor military officer immediately after the mutiny at Chenqiao that catapulted Taizu to the Song throne. Official historians absolve Taizu of any culpability in the affair, but Ouyang Xiu could hardly write on Han Tong without broaching the complicated and controversial mutiny at Chenqiao, a potential minefield of problems still shrouded in taboo and disinformation. Evasion was his only recourse.

The authors of the *Old History*, presuming legitimacy for the Five Dynasties of the north, organized the history around them. The coterminous Ten Kingdoms were emphatically presented as illegitimate and their chronicles, at the end of the history, subsumed under either "Hereditary Regimes" *(Shixi)* or "Illicit Usurpers" *(Jianwei)*, the former nominal vassals of the north and the latter unabashed pretenders to imperial power.[97] Ouyang Xiu may have hailed from the south,[98] but in the convention of northern historiography he presumes the preeminent sovereignty of northern regimes and categorically rejects claims of the south, home to nine of the Ten Kingdoms. Thus, when the phrase "Middle Kingdom" is used in the *Historical Records*, the north is implied.[99] Chapters on "Hereditary Houses," in fact, denounce the Ten Kingdoms as self-absorbed and indulgent, obsessed merely with perpetuating themselves. The perspective is that of a Han-Chinese chauvinist who champions a unity imposed from the north, the cradle of early civilization and the historical unifier of the country. "There is a saying, 'When a fresh wind arises, perpetrators of darkness will submit; when the sun and moon come out, torches will be extinguished,'" he states in celebration of the Zhou and later Song dynastic ascents (chapter 61). The Ten Kingdoms emerge as obstacles to be overcome by a disciplined and focused leader of the Chinese heartland. For most southern kingdoms, the greatest enemy was internal: potentates given to frivolous conduct and sufficiently secure, unlike rulers of the north, to perpetuate such practices indefinitely.

The *Historical Records* highlights the political and military inadequacies of the southern kingdoms while slighting their multifaceted attainments. Modern historians of economy, for example, trace the invention of paper currency, in the early eleventh century, to the Shu region of the mid-tenth century: with fragmentation of the Chinese realm causing shortages in precious metals, promissory notes emerged to sustain commerce.[100] Students of scientific innovation attribute the spread and perfection of printing technology to the southern kingdoms, cities such as Chengdu in the west and Hangzhou in the east emerging as centers for publishing to rival the north.[101] Cultural historians celebrate the lavish sums of local wealth committed to art and architecture, libraries and temples across the south. Wealth was available for cultural purposes because of lower levels of military spending relative to the north, but also because of less siphoning northward of southern wealth in the absence of a central government.[102] Coastal regimes exploited both trade and piracy to fill their coffers, creating a new orientation to ocean trade and enhancing China's presence on the high seas. The wealth thereby won permitted advances in technology, especially shipbuilding. The naval superiority of the south is evidenced in the Zhou dynasty's early campaigns against the Southern Tang, in the 950s, when the north had to commandeer southern ships to build a navy capable of conquering the south, the Zhou having begun with no navy at all.[103] The Southern Tang long held the advantage in shipbuilding as well as trained seamen, advantages that reflect sustained investment. The southern kingdoms survived nearly forty years on average—several times the longevity of northern regimes—due precisely to ingenuity and investment of this sort. They further benefited from a vast buffer between them and the many nomadic groups to menace North China throughout the Five Dynasties era.

Defense and Security

Of all the realignments of the Five Dynasties period, none was as momentous as strategic alignments to the north and west. The premier border presence in Tang times was the Tujue, Turkish tribes originating in the Altai Mountains region who built a loose confederation extending from the Aral Sea through much of Mongolia and parts of Manchuria in the far east.[104] The Eastern khanate governing Inner Asia prospered, in the sixth and seventh centuries, through control over the Silk Road. Its decline by the eighth century paved the way for new groups to emerge, many of them former subjects or allies of the Turks. The Uighurs offer one example of vassal-turned-lord, becoming a critical link in the transition from the Tang to the Five Dynasties.

As residents of the Mongolian steppe, the Altai Mountains to their north and the Gobi Desert to their south, the Uighurs (Huihe or Huihu) asserted their autonomy from the Tujue in the mid-eighth century, then supported the Chinese government in suppressing domestic rebels during the late 750s to early 760s.[105] They managed to wrest a sizable part of the lucrative silk trade away from the Tujue Turks, further undermining that empire while creating a stable source of income for themselves. Soon to turn on their Chinese hosts, the Uighurs conducted raids on such cities as Luoyang, deep in the interior of China. Their empire lasted only a century or so, ruined by the combination of natural disasters in their homeland and raids by the Kirghiz to the north and the Tibetans (Qiang) to the south. The Uighurs, more sedentary in lifestyle than the Turks, subscribed to Manichaeism and brought "civilization" to the steppe, according to one author, as they ruled from permanent capitals and governed by the written rule of law.[106] Upon losing their empire in the mid-ninth century, residual Uighur tribes retreated to the oases of Turkestan to create petty kingdoms at Ganzhou and Khocho under the Five Dynasties.

The Uighurs and earlier the Tuoba, also known as Toba and Tagbach, had both influenced and at different times ruled over a new confederacy destined to eclipse both groups in the tenth century. Ancestors to the Mongol and Manchu alike, the Khitan (Qidan) hailed from western Manchuria and the eastern stretches of Mongolia, centering on the modern provinces of Liaoning and Jilin.[107] Under nominal Uighur control until 842, the decline of Tang power there gave the Khitan an opportunity to expand. By the turn of the tenth century, a new leadership under Abaoji (d. 926) of the Yila clan, later renamed Yelü, managed to subdue three rivals in Manchuria: the Shiwei to the north, the Jurchen to the northeast, and the Xi to the south. Abaoji also broke an alliance, in 917, with a far more powerful adversary to his south, the Shatuo, although permanent gains were few. The Wugu (Onggirad) of eastern Mongolia similarly succumbed to Khitan dominance during these years, as did the Tuyuhun (often simplified as "Tuhun" in the *Historical Records*).[108] Residents of the Gobi Desert and a mixture of Tibetan and Xianbei, the Tuyuhun maintained diplomatic relations with North China through the dynastic twists and turns of the tenth century, as evidenced in the Basic Annals that follow.

Perhaps the most spectacular conquest, in the last year of Abaoji's life, involved Bohai (Parhae), a vast empire centering on eastern Manchuria and extending southward to the Korean Peninsula.[109] Bohai had been a tributary of the Liang, the first of the Five Dynasties, so the Khitan conquest symbolized a diminished Chinese presence in the northeast. The Khitan, on the other hand, consolidated their control over a contiguous domain extending from Central Asia to the Pacific Ocean. They produced a highly successful second monarch as well, Yelü Deguang (Taizong, r. 926–947). Chapter 17 of the *Historical Records* characterizes him as a formidable foe. The Khitan and the Shatuo were the two leading nomadic federations to dominate the Five Dynasties. The Shatuo, in successfully ruling the Chinese heartland, accomplished a feat never achieved by the Khitan, whose attempt at direct rule in 947 lasted scarcely a few months. Khitan power proved more enduring, however. Confined mostly to regions north of China proper, their empire survived into the eleventh and early twelfth centuries.

The Khitan began as less sophisticated than the Uighurs, subscribing largely to folk religions and lacking a written language before the 920s. After a stunning string of conquests, however, Abaoji chose to abandon the title of Khaghan common for nomadic rulers and proclaim himself "Emperor," Chinese-style, in 916. He inaugurated a tributary system for conducting foreign affairs and a succession from father to son, both distinctly Chinese modes of governing.[110] He also helped the Shatuo consolidate their dominance of northern China, a "fraternal alliance" established as early as 905; that alliance would falter once Shatuo princes became emperors of the Later Tang. His son and successor, Yelü Deguang, entrenched the regime further by adopting the dynastic name of Liao in 937. Deguang proved a formidable rival to North China's rulers, his own stability contrasted with their instability. Khitan numbers must have grown considerably by then. During an intervention in China in 935, their armies of a reputed 100,000 filled columns a hundred *li* long and fifty *li* wide, according to the biography of Zhang Jingda. Thus, even before the founding of a Song empire in 960, the Liao had a permanent presence south of the Great Wall, particularly over the "sixteen prefectures" clustered near Beijing (the Yan¤ command centered on Youzhou). The Middle Kingdom's sovereignty over that strategic beltway would take centuries to recover. Moreover, the precedent of North China providing tribute to the Khitan and accepting protocol as peers, established under the Jin dynasty, set expectations that informed relations with the Song dynasty.

Another powerful confederation to emerge in the tenth century was Tangut (Dangxiang or Dangxiang Qiang).[111] Descended chiefly of the Qiang tribesmen from northeastern Tibet, the Tangut originated in the region of Xiazhou and Yichuan (modern Ningxia), before extending into southern Mongolia and Gansu Province. To their west were the Tuyuhun and the Uighur, the Khitan to the northeast. Assorted Tibetan groups bordered their south, including a Tibetan group called Tubo (Tufan), whose regular missions to North China are cited in the Basic Annals. The Tangut had allied with a succession of Inner Asian powers, from the Tuoba to the Tuyuhun to the Tujue, accepting Chinese sovereignty in the early Tang. The alliance with China continued into the early years of the Five Dynasties, the Tangut allying with the Liang dynasty against its rival, the Shatuo, only to realign with the Shatuo upon their conquest of China proper, the Later Tang serving as a wedge against the Khitan. The Tangut continued to identify with the Chinese court in the wake of Later Tang rule: mending relations with the Khitan during their indirect rule under the Jin dynasty, allying with the Han dynasty once it supplanted the Jin, and identifying with the Zhou after its ascent. The Five

Dynasties of the north provided invaluable trade and protection for the Tangut, regimes that in turn appreciated the value of neutralizing a people whose proximity had afforded familiarity with Chinese culture in potentially threatening ways.

Included in the *Historical Records* are three concluding chapters on assorted "barbarian" groups of the tenth century, not translated here. Most modern scholars of Inner Asia consider it highly flawed, while a profusion of names and terms makes for difficult reading. The chapters gave Ouyang Xiu a venue for casting alien peoples and their ways in a uniquely Song perspective, prejudices and all. Enough characterizations appear elsewhere of "barbarian customs" and the "barbarian nature" to understand that perspective without reading an entire treatise. The rhetoric, it seems, relates more to present politics than history: by maligning the trustworthiness of aliens, he could impugn the appeasement policies current in his own day. "For those who collude with barbarians in conducting affairs without knowing the entire course of events, calamity is the common outcome, but never good fortune," he comments under Subjects of Jin. The historical presentism is palpable.

The military challenge for the Five Dynasties, apart from harnessing alien menaces to the north and west, involved taming the domestic infidel and military institutions evolved to contain an ever-changing threat.[112] The purge of the Tang dynasty in 907 by the arrogant governor Zhu Quanzhong represents the victory of governors over the throne, periphery over the center, military men over civilian monitors. At the same time, the Liang dynasty that he established also accelerated a process of recentralizing military power by building new structures in the capital to offset the preponderant power of local magnates.[113] In the final years of Tang rule, an enfeebled central government at Luoyang could probably command a mere 30,000 troops, in contrast to the estimated 240,000 men under the banner of assorted governors.[114] The single Xuanwu command of Zhu Quanzhong had garnered an armed force of 60,000 in the waning years of Tang rule, a force further ballooning several times on the eve of the Tang dynasty's purge. Such an imbalance was hardly acceptable once Liang upstarts were in power, so the capital was moved eastward to the old satrapy at Kaifeng and local military resources were deployed to the task of centralizing imperial power.

The district governors had a personal guard (*yabing* or *yaya*), commanded by attachés *(yajiang)*, to advance their own agendas of expansion and intrigue. This force was originally responsible for securing city walls, only to assume an autonomy that empowered it to buttress the governor or to subvert him, as with the powerful Wei/Bo command.[115] The governors had military retainers in the form of assisting commanders *(pijiang)*, detachment commanders *(biejiang, pianjiang)*, commanders' attendants *(kejiang)*, and quasi-military administrative aides *(li, shuli)*.[116] (See Appendix for standard translation of offices.) This array of local resources provided the foundation, by Later Tang times, for the elite Imperial Bodyguard in the capital, literally the "personal" guard *(qinjun)*.[117] Controlled by the emperor, it was commanded by a cohort of longstanding associates, each army with ten directors *(zhihuishi)* and one chief director *(du zhihuishi)*. The Imperial Bodyguard should be distinguished from the Imperial Guard (*shiwei* or *jinjun*), or "Six Armies" *(liujun)*, each headed by professional commanders *(tongjun)*; lacking comparable personal ties to the emperor, imperial guardsmen were often seen as less responsive relative to the bodyguard.[118] The Later Tang further introduced a "supreme marshal" *(yuanshuai)* to coordinate and scrutinize activities of the Six Armies, originally naming an imperial clansman to enhance the guard's responsiveness to the throne.[119] Thus, under the initial two of the Five Dynasties of North China, an expansion of armed forces in the capital coincided with the elevation of the bodyguard. Indeed, the Six Armies disappeared as a formal structure after the Later Tang owing to such marginalization.

A second momentous reform of the early Liang was to introduce military secretaries at court, dubbed Commissioners of Venerable Governance *(chongzhengshi)*, abolishing the eunuch-run Secretariat of Palace Armies *(nei shumishi)*.[120] In the late ninth century, the Secretariat for Palace Armies had enabled eunuchs to lead armies against unruly governors, conduct inspections and collect taxes locally, and even serve as liaisons between the palace and the periphery. They incurred the wrath of governors in the process. With the mass liquidation of eunuchs in 903, perpetrated by the chief minister at the prodding of Zhu Quanzhong, the eunuch secretariat was abolished. Moreover, the new commissioners of venerable governance were to be "literati"—that is, men with some literacy, although not exclusively civilian sorts. Zhu Quanzhong also selected close confidantes such as Jing Xiang as commissioners, thereby creating military advisors at court and a command structure in the capital that enjoyed the emperor's full trust. The Bureau of Venerable Governance became the Bureau of Military Affairs *(Shumiyuan)* in later dynasties, which continued to be staffed by imperial confidantes as part of the outer court.

The Liang dynasty presided over another shift in power: the commissioners of the northern or southern courts of palace armies *(bei/nan xuanhuishi)* were replaced by "officers of palace services" *(gongfengguan)*, eunuchs supplanted by trusted aides to the emperor.[121] As personal representatives of the palace, often serving at important state ceremonies or negotiating with rival neighbors on its behalf, they served an important quasi-military role in and away from the capital. Palace services officers existed in Tang times and earlier, but are more visible in the Five Dynasties owing to the relative absence of eunuchs and the more restricted role of the military-affairs commissioners compared to palace secretaries of old. Eunuchs were once overseers for palace access, but under the Liang and Later Tang, additional auxiliaries to the emperor's bodyguard emerge to secure his safety at home or serve as his emissary abroad. These included commissioners of palace security *(huangchengshi)*, masters of diplomatic accommodations *(keshengshi)*, and masters of auxiliary palace gates *(gemenshi)*.[122]

Imperial interests were protected at-large by assorted military overseers *(jianjun)* and adjutants *(xingjun sima)*, defense commissioners *(fangyushi)* and surveillance officers *(guanchashi)*. Such offices had roots in earlier times but were used with greater effectiveness as agents of the central government deployed to harness regional powers or fill military vacuums locally.[123] The policy of redeploying the resources of governors to serve the interests of the court is reflected in the new rules toward appointing prefects *(cishi)*. As chief administrators for the prefectures responsible to the governors, prefects were largely military men selected directly or indirectly by the governor as reward for merit in battle.[124] The Liang dynasty began imposing restrictions by invoking the right to approve the governor's nominees, often assigning confidantes of the court. The posting of "acting prefects" *(quanzhi zhoushi)*, often civilians chosen to monitor the military prefect, also acquired appeal during this period. These provisional appointments might occur in the absence of a permanent prefect, but service concurrent with the local military prefect also occurred, creating overlapping authority. The Later Tang even restricted the term of prefects to twenty-five months and imposed examinations to weed out incompetents, policies continued under successor dynasties.[125]

Shatuo rulers of the Later Tang chose to embrace many of the military reforms of the Liang. They continued to institutionalize military decisions in the outer court and to select commissioners of military affairs from a cohort of trusted and experienced aides, the most eminent perhaps Guo Chongtao. They carried centralization to a new level by formalizing the Imperial Bodyguard *(qinjun)* as the premier force in the capital.[126] Its second emperor, Mingzong, having come to power through mutiny, added a bodyguard of loyalists destined for a permanent place in the military infrastructure. The earliest references to the Imperial Bodyguard appear under the year 927, in his Basic Annals, emerging in the immediate wake of Mingzong's usurpation of the throne and coexisting alongside the Six Armies and the Imperial Guard. The process culminated under the Zhou, when another upstart, Shizong, reorganized a cluster of favored armies into the elite Palace Guard *(dianqianjun)*.[127] By then the Six Armies no longer existed, the Palace Guard now joining the Imperial Bodyguard in commanding center stage. From the Palace Guard, the founder of Song, Zhao Kuangyin (Taizu), eventually usurped power to end the Five Dynasties. Modern historians see great symbolism in the fact that the coups d'état toward the end of the Five Dynasties, catapulting Guo Wei to the Zhou throne in 951 and Zhao Kuangyin to the Song throne in 960, both emanated from military professionals in the capital, as military commissioners or Palace Guard chiefs.[128] This contrasts with the foundings of the Liang, Later Tang, Jin, and Han, where the upstarts were governors in the provinces who owed their powers to hereditary privilege as much as battle experience, men whose lives personified the fragmentation of dynastic power. The emerging preeminence of the Palace Guard in the politics of the late Five Dynasties marks a radical shift in power whose stunning speed is matched by its enduring impact. The military institutions of the next three centuries were born of the tumult of the Five Dynasties, the centralization of military power under the Song at once a reaction to tenth-century excesses and an elaboration on emerging structures to contain those excesses.

A final note on institutions: many posts were supernumerary and involved few powers. "Commander for reserve cavalry" *(fuma duwei)*, for example, was simply an honorary post given to imperial in-laws. Governorships usually involved real powers, but many received honorary assignment as governor with no powers, which is often specified in the text. There were ideally three chief ministers representing "directors" *(shilang)* from each of the three ministries: Chancellery, Palace Secretariat, and Secretariat. Such posts in ordinary times would be held by highly literate men, but often went to marginally educated military men during the Five Dynasties, so-called commander-ministers *(jiangxiang)*. In other cases, individuals received honorary ministerial standing with no ministerial powers. The same holds for appointees as prefect. Thus, the plethora of titles should not obscure the fact that the civil and military services were actually quite modest in size.

Confucian Ethics

Across the spectrum from military affairs to social relations, no theme is reiterated more in the *Historical Records* than chaotic discontinuity. And no figure seems to typify the prevailing moral malaise more than Feng Dao, Ouyang Xiu's caustic critique of him perhaps the most familiar passage to modern readers (chapter 54). Feng Dao clearly emerges as a lightning rod for Confucian theorists of the eleventh-century. "Having served four royal houses and ten sovereigns, he increasingly presumed upon bygone merits to glorify himself," Ouyang Xiu writes. A minister to Mingzong of Tang for nearly seven years, Feng Dao proceeded to embrace Mingzong's adopted son, the future Emperor Fei, and facilitated Fei's purge of Emperor Min. He was also implicated in the decision to sidestep the younger son of Shi Jingtang, against the emperor's dying wishes, in favor of an older son by adoption.[129] Thus, early on he emerges as a brazen manipulator of imperial powers by imposing his own will on vulnerable monarchs—a serious crime irrespective of motivation.

Feng Dao's association with a series of alien rulers seemed particularly offensive. He had deserted the Liang dynasty to serve the Prince of Jin as early as 911, over a decade before Jin pretenders unified the north.[130] To abandon Chinese rulers and ally with alien upstarts, long before any change in Heaven's Mandate is in evidence, seemed the deed of a traitor to his people. Feng later evinced such an affinity for another alien ruler, Yelü Deguang, that he exclaimed in Yelü's presence, "Times like ours would be hard to salvage even for the Buddha, should he appear. Only a man like Your Majesty will do." His words seemed a virtual endorsement of Khitan rule, and indeed, Feng served as Khitan surrogate in the brief interval between the Jin and Han dynasties. Contrasting with his esteem for the Khitan ruler is Feng's inexplicably cavalier treatment of a Chinese, Shizong of Zhou, whom he disparages over and again. Several hostile exchanges between the two men are recorded in the *Historical Records*, where Feng Dao consistently diminishes the emperor's martial abilities and questions his ambitions. Almost forty years the emperor's senior, Feng was extended extraordinary latitude, yet the political acuity of youth is less in evidence in his last year or so of life.

In his preface to the biography, Ouyang Xiu decries the lack of "shame" in men like Feng Dao, who indiscriminately sell their services to any ruler, much like a prostitute. Invoking the story of Woman Li is highly symbolic: her adamant adherence to principles of chaste devotion to a dead husband, to the point of maiming herself after the slightest violation by a man, reflects precisely the sense of integrity absent among most Confucian men. In effect, the Five Dynasties was a topsy-turvy world where women were more moral than men, warriors more dedicated than civilian statesmen—defying the social hierarchy of Confucian tradition.[131]

Ouyang Xiu's critique of Feng Dao is less about him personally as civil responsibility in the abstract. The chapters on "Martyrs to Virtue" *(Sijie)* and "Martyrs in Service" *(Sishi)* are unique to the *Historical Records*. Dynastic histories since the late sixth century, beginning with the court-sponsored *History of the Wei*, contained chapters on the "Loyal and Righteous" *(Zhongyi)*, a fairly broad cluster of persons offering exceptionally candid criticism or other forms of dedicated service, but usually not at the cost of their lives.[132] Ouyang Xiu creates a more exclusive cluster: martyrs only. He further sets standards so high for "Martyrs to Virtue," the supreme martyrs, that he can identify only three candidates.[133] The premier criterion for inclusion in the first cluster is service to a single dynasty. Within the second cluster of fifteen "Martyrs in Service" are individuals who died serving a second house, men who began as ethically compromised only to redeem themselves later on, "by ultimately dying in the service of humanity." A second criterion for both martyr clusters appears to be voluntary death, not necessarily in an act of suicide like Xia Luqi, but in the spirit of accepting death as civic duty, subordinating self to state. As reiterated in the concluding commentary to chapter 32, "Men subsisting on the salaries of mankind must accept possible death in its service." Withdrawing from office is the responsible recourse for the disaffected, not surrender or flight. Other chapters further elaborate on navigating such difficult ethical waters.

In the biographical cluster for "Subjects of Tang," Ouyang Xiu affirms the higher duty demanded of persons at the top of the political hierarchy, ministers such as Feng Dao but also local leaders. Zhang Xian was metropolitan custodian of Taiyuan in 926, when mutineers seized his family to compel his surrender. He responded by executing the messenger in an affirmation of resolve, an act deemed noble by Ouyang Xiu, who celebrates the placing of principle before personal concerns. Zhang Xian's political standing was critical to determining expectations of civic duty: the region's defenses depended on him as chief presiding officer at Taiyuan. Elsewhere, officials of lesser importance are expected to place family before civic duty, Ouyang Xiu stressing that family duty is an equally important Confucian imperative (see chapter 24, Wu Zhen).

Perhaps the most delicate maneuvering of civic and family duties occurs with the judicious Emperor Shizong. As revealed under "Royal Family of Zhou" (chapter 20), his layman father, Chai Shouli, once murdered an innocent man, and Shizong, as emperor, opted to suppress the incident over punishing his father. "He could countenance the indiscretion of bending laws to invigorate the moral way of father and son, his actions in accord with righteous principle and reflecting his appreciation of relative worth," Ouyang Xiu argues. "Punishing a single person will not necessarily create a world where no one kills. Yet the murder of one's father involves negation of one's natural constitution and disavowal of human mores." The story and its nuanced commentary reveal that Ouyang Xiu did not judge people in a vacuum: family values remain the foundation for higher ethical aspirations, the unfilial son a poor candidate for ethical leadership.

A corollary to his demand for male fidelity to political authority is Ouyang Xiu's call for women to submit to the authority of men. Commentary from the *Historical Records* suggests that a critical component in the turbulence of the times was women favored by the throne but lacking in circumspection, creating rifts within the royal houses and tensions at court that ultimately unraveled the dynasties. The preface to chapter 13, "Royal Family of the Liang," declares, "Without peer in the world, the Liang had the might of tigers or wolves, so to speak. Yet eventual downfall occurred through fancy for a few women, culminating in men hacking at the chests or the bowels of fellow men to butcher one another like swine. In the calamity erupting between father and son, we can know the potential for the sensuous woman to ruin mankind." The reader will doubtless be surprised to read the subsequent six short biographies for empresses and concubines of the Liang, who exuded personal and political virtues far exceeding their husbands. Ouyang's invective is not directed at them, but at women described later in the same chapter, starting with those involved in the death of Taizu and the usurpation of Zhu Yougui.

The Liang founder had an eldest son by adoption, Zhu Youwen, who proved highly capable. He enjoyed the emperor's favor as well, prompting an ailing Taizu in his last hours to anoint Youwen as successor. Yet the founder also had an illegitimate son, Zhu Yougui, the product of some "amorous affair with a married woman." Yougui later became an important figure in the capital and the corridors of the palace, along with his wife, née Zhang. Yougui's wife happened to be caring for the ill emperor when she learned of the impending installation of rival Youwen and reputedly goaded her husband to seize power by force. Under cover of night, he and a coterie of sympathetic guardsmen entered the palace to murder the emperor in a brutal act of disembowelment, then killed his designated heir. Yougui reigned for only a half year, falling in a conspiracy by the third son of Taizu, the future Emperor Mo. Ouyang Xiu clearly blames women for the tumultuous succession—the married woman whose affair yielded the bastard pretender and Woman Zhang for spying on the emperor and precipitating the assassination plot. Wholly ignored are the notorious lechery and raging temper of the father, not to mention the unbridled ambitions of the son—far more critical factors in the violence and instability to plague the regime. A parallel case occurs in the Later Tang, where imperial uncle Li Kening's abortive attempt to overthrow Zhuangzong is presented in the *Historical Records* as the handiwork of a scheming wife.

The Liang dynasty was further destabilized by another woman of the Taizu era, née Liu, whose scandalous sexual conduct appears in the biography of Jing Xiang, the prominent minister (chapters 21–23). Consort and later wife of two prominent Liang courtiers, Shi Pu and Jing Xiang, she continued an amorous affair with Emperor Taizu concurrent with her marriage to Jing Xiang, "her movements in and out of his bedroom" unaffected by the emperor's accession and her own marriage. She subsequently brokered her influence in the palace, "employing a reception's officer to conduct business with governors, while fraternizing with the rich and powerful." Here is another case where Taizu's lechery triggers a problem for which a woman bears principal blame. Yet the reader is also shocked by the nonchalance of this woman toward marital fidelity, signs of a broader moral slump.

Under the first emperor of Later Tang, Zhuangzong, the "profusion of women" suddenly recruited for his palace provided grist for court scandal. The great passion of his life, Lady Liu, the beauty to bear his favorite son, Jiji, turned out an enormous political liability (chapter 14). Zhuangzong displaced his legal wife to install her as empress, making for a turbulent start. A strong faith in Buddhism caused her to lavish wealth on clerics and religious institutions, even to cultivate the emperor's own "delusion" by the faith. At the same time, she had infamous propensities for hoarding material possessions, carried to such extremes that taxes were siphoned off to her own palace as soldiers went unpaid. When they lost their families to starvation, the soldiers deserted and Zhuangzong died for lack of security, his death seemingly a direct consequence of her gross insensitivity. Empress Liu is even accused of fornicating with an in-law in the immediate wake of her husband's death, adding moral turpitude to her other vices.

The rare power of women in the Five Dynasties is further reflected in their control over men as mothers. Without doubt, the most intimidating yet respected woman was the mother of Zhuangzong, Dowager Cao. She commanded such filial devotion from him that he would hasten home three or four times a year, even under the pressure of protracted campaigns (chapter 14). The biography of eunuch Zhang Chengye, in chapter 38, contains a remarkable story where a self-indulgent Zhuangzong, sometime before accession, had needlessly threatened the highly circumspect Zhang, an offense conveyed to the empress dowager. When she summoned the son to her quarters, a "petrified" Zhuangzong immediately tried to mend relations with the eunuch before meeting her. A day later, Dowager Cao accompanied her son to the eunuch's residence to make formal apologies, having already affirmed by letter that "the youth has been flogged with light rod for his rudeness." Zhuangzong must have been in his early thirties at the time! The *Historical Records* reports another flogging of a Later Tang royal man, probably in his late teens, by his mother: a practical joker, Jiji was chastised with light rod for participating in an elaborate hoax on his mother, Empress Liu (chapter 37). The heavy-handedness of Later Tang empresses might be attributed to the greater freedom afforded women in nomadic culture, as mirrored in the Khitan royal family at the same time.[134] By all indications, however, both Dowager Cao and Empress Liu, Zhuangzong's mother and his wife, were of Chinese ancestry.

The powers of palace women after 930 do not diminish so much as shift, their influence greatest during succession disputes or transitions of dynastic power as mediators between the palace and the military. In 934, when Emperor Min fled his capital and rival Fei seized the throne, it was another Dowager Cao who legalized the coup through her mandates, according to the Annals of Fei. More than a decade later, as Khitan armies invaded the Jin capital to purge the emperor and take the royal family hostage, it was Empress Dowager Li (d. 950) who directed talks with Yelü Deguang (chapter 17). Long opposed to her adopted son's severing of relations with the Khitan—the act that triggered their invasion—her deft negotiations in 947 probably spared his life. Her letter to Deguang on Emperor Chu's behalf is cited in full in her biography. Under the next dynasty, another empress dowager, also surnamed Li (d. 960), similarly facilitated the transfer of dynastic powers (chapter 18). She was the mother of Emperor Yin of Han, a sixteen-year-old upon succession who quickly proved inept. Refusing to consult courtiers about major decisions, his reckless ploy to purge the Palace Guard leadership brought on the rebellion of Guo Wei, the influential chief guardsman. A child initially reigned as nominal successor to Han rule, the empress dowager serving initially as regent. Some forty days later, the empress dowager relinquished her own powers to Guo Wei, who now established the Zhou dynasty. The *Historical Records* similarly cites her edict of abdication, which is unthinkably amicable and perhaps a poor reflection of the real maneuvering behind the scenes through so many weeks. The final female regent to relinquish imperial powers, at the end of Zhou, was a consort of Shizong. Empress Fu's regency over the six year-old Guo Zongxun, in 959, lasted a half-year, after which she transferred power to another Palace Guard chief, Zhao Kuangyin, founder of the Song. The matter is mentioned only in passing in the Basic Annals (chapter 12), owing to lingering sensitivity in Song times. For the Jin, Han, and Zhou dynasties, the heightened political visibility of palace women relates to the inexplicably short lives of a succession of dynastic founders, whose powers passed to incompetent youth. In each case, the women acted with circumspection, although ultimately they were active participants in the subterfuge of relinquishing dynastic powers.

The *Historical Records of the Five Dynasties* contains no chapter on "notable" or "chaste" women *(lienü)*. For earlier histories, such women hailed mostly from upper-class families and personified some sort of moral lesson; they were not typically women of the palace, and their biographies derived from a range of sources, many unofficial. Presumably, such sources were fewer owing to the turmoil of the Five Dynasties, which makes all the more valuable the detailed account of the Woman Li, as preface to the biography of Feng Dao (chapter 54). The wife of a minor official who died on assignment near the western capital, Woman Li had gathered his remains and headed for the northeast when an innkeeper declined accommodations. There ensued an appalling confrontation where the widow refused to leave the premises and the innkeeper grabbed her by the arm, forcibly evicting her. The Woman saw the simple touch as tantamount to sexual violation and lopped off the violated arm with an axe, purportedly declaring, "How have I, the wife of another man, failed to protect my chastity by allowing this arm to be touched by another?" "Literati lacking similar regard for their physical person, men suffering shame for the simple sake of survival, should be considerably ashamed to learn of this woman's integrity," Ouyang Xiu adds. Such moral conviction seems less common for society's most privileged, men and women alike, which is precisely why the word "shame" carries such sting.

The story of Woman Li, with her strong reaction to physical violation by an anonymous man, must be read within the context of the Five Dynasties, where the absence of local order, particularly in North China, had permitted the violation of women at unthinkably high levels. Biographical clusters on the "Royal Families" are replete with stories of young girls and married women being abducted by marauding troops, sometimes ending up as imperial consorts, as with Empress Li of the Later Han or empresses Liu and Wei of the Later Tang. More commonly they ended up as a concubine of some decorated soldier or friend of the court, as with the Woman Liu, the eventual wife of Liang minister Jing Xiang, given to him only after Zhu Quanzhong personally had his way with her (chapter 21). Many such girls were abducted quite young and likely abused well before the socially acceptable marriage age of fourteen *sui*.[135] Forcible sex for married abductees was perhaps the norm, for their sensual appeal is specifically cited in the narrative as the cause for their abduction. The moral dilemmas for such women, particularly those already married, can well be imagined. Certainly from the Song-dynasty perspective of Ouyang Xiu, such women should have maimed or even killed themselves rather than accept violation.[136] In any case, the times left women with some unsavory choices. Contrary to common assumption, abducted women did not always come from the lower classes. The story of the Virtuous Consort Dong in chapter 19 reveals that upper-class women were abducted as well, although her ordeal doubtless had a happier ending than most.

A Note on the Translation

Translated in full are the "Annals" for the Five Dynasties (chapters 1–12), which provide key names, dates, and basic facts. Such chapters in the *Old History* were once replete with details on events, but Ouyang Xiu relegated details to biographical chapters, his Annals serving as simply a point of reference. A single event can be mentioned in several biographies, often with different inference or new information. The translation contains less repetition than the original, inasmuch as I intentionally avoided repetition in the selection of biographies, especially from the "Miscellaneous" sections (chapters 39–57).

To enhance the fluency of the text, I have avoided bracketed insertions, except when adding information not implied by the author. Classical Chinese often deletes subject and object, sometimes even the verb. When the inference is clear, no further notation is given; only in cases of ambiguity does the information appear in brackets. Information in parentheses represents background provided by the author, not the translator.

By tradition, Chinese emperors were referred to by a posthumous temple name, such as Taizu or Gaozu, "Exalted Ancestor," in the case of dynastic founders, with taboos imposed on the use of their personal names for the duration of that dynasty. Historians writing under successor regimes were no longer bound by old taboos, but they tended to respect them all the same. Thus, Ouyang Xiu prefers to cite an emperor's secondary name (Zhu Quanzhong, not Zhu Wen), switching to his posthumous title after accession; this reflects respect for the institution of dynasty, not necessarily the person in power. The translation generally follows the nomenclature original to the *Historical Records*, the names of rulers inserted in brackets when ambiguities emerge. A full list of rulers with personal and temple names precedes this introduction. In the case of individuals, Ouyang Xiu preferred the use of personal name over courtesy or other names; any departure from this norm will be noted.

In Western scholarship, historical figures are referred to either by full name or simply surname for purposes of brevity: "Feng," for example, is the short form of "Feng Dao." When Chinese historians wish to abbreviate a name, they instead employ the individual's personal or courtesy name: "Quanzhong," for example, is the short form of "Zhu Quanzhong." Surnames do not appear without the suffix of "Gentleman" *(gong)* or "Mister/Miss" *(shi)*. In the translation, Chinese conventions are followed, so "Dao" is the abbreviated form for "Feng Dao." Educated Chinese men usually have a "courtesy name" *(zi)* and some have a "style name" or "sobriquet" *(hao)*. Military men often had nicknames such as "Brocade General," but usually no courtesy names, an important class distinction reflected in the biographies. A convention of nomenclature peculiar to the *Historical Records* is to delete the word "governor" when command is indicated: "Zhu Quanzhong of the Xuanwu command" infers the governor of Xuanwu (centered on Kaifeng). If a place name such as Kaifeng precedes the name, the reference is to an individual from that place, not the governor. In cases of confusion, I have added the needed wording.

To avoid confusion in place names, symbols are added to prefectures otherwise indistinguishable in romanized form, a full glossary of Chinese characters appearing as Appendix. The most commonly cited prefectures appear without suffix, while lesser-used homonyms are followed by a symbol [‡ ¶ † ¤ •]. The designation for metropolitan area or prefecture, *zhou*, appears variously as *zhou* or prefecture, but sometimes is deleted to save space. Thus, Jinzhou can appear as Jin Prefecture or as simply Jin when prefecture is implied; prefixed by "the," it indicates a princely domain of Jin or the Shi-Jin dynasty. Strategically important cities or towns were sometimes called "commanderies" *(jun)* or "garrisons" *(zhen)*, rather than simply prefectures. The word "command" refers to the district of a governor, often dubbed *jiedu* or *fanzhen* in the text, and generally spans multiple prefectures.

The reader should note that Chinese are considered one year old at birth, the consequence of China's historically having had no concept of zero; on the first lunar New Year after birth they are considered to be two years old. Chinese age counted in *sui* thus tends to be a year or year and a half older than the same age in the West. The age dates of individuals that appear in brackets in the translation have already been adjusted by one year.

Finally, a simple rule for weights and measures is[137]:

AREA	WEIGHT	LENGTH
	bushel (*dan*, 30 kg)	foot (*chi*, 22 cm)
mou (342 meters)	catty (*jin*, 250 grams)	pace (*bu*, 185 cm)
qing (100 *mou*)	ounce (*liang*, 15.6 grams)	*she* (league, 30 *li*)
	peck (*dou*, 2000 cc)	*li* (1/3 mile or 415 meters)

For readers wishing further information on Chinese military technology and strategy, see *Science and Civilisation in China*.[138] My translation of most technical terms pertaining to weapons and military affairs is based on this source.

HISTORICAL RECORDS

•••••

OF THE FIVE DYNASTIES

CHAPTER 1

ANNALS I: BASIC ANNALS OF LIANG[i]

Taizu [Zhu Wen, Quanzhong, C.E. 852–912], the Divinely Martial, the Originally Sagacious, and the Filial Emperor, surnamed Zhu, was native to Wugou hamlet, Dangshan County, Songzhou. His father, Zhu Cheng, an instructor in

....

i. *Annotation by [student] Xu Wudang.* As for the names of the various kingdoms, the "Basic Annals of Liang" refers to the dynasty as Liang beginning with its ruler's investiture as Prince of Liang; the "Basic Annals of Tang" refers to the dynasty as Jin beginning with its ruler's investiture as Prince of Jin and shifts to Tang only after the formal adoption of Tang as dynastic designation—each in accord with actual conditions. But beginning with biographical chapters, official historians had revised dynastic names retroactively, such that an empire was cited as Liang, or Jin, or Tang even before its rulers were invested and its empire established. The Later Tang once called itself Jin, as did Shi Jingtang's dynasty; and Li Bian assumed the Tang name. Liu Yan adopted Han for his dynasty, as did Liu Min. Wang Jian adopted the designation Shu, as did Meng Zhixiang. The Jin of Shi royals ruled as a single dynasty and can be identified without further modifiers. But words like "East" and "South," "Former" and "Later" are added to the Tang, Han, and Shu to distinguish hereditary houses. The Liang founder initially held investitures as lord of Pei as well as Dongping, the Southern Tang initially calling itself Qi, but the three designations were rarely cited even by contemporaries and can be omitted here. The Five Dynasties being an age of tumult, names and titles were convoluted and inconsistent. For historians composing a narrative of events, it matters most that events are arranged in a comprehensible fashion, permitting the reader to access the particulars.

The term "Basic Annals" [*Benji*] conforms to longstanding practice: *ben* implies tracing the origins of a dynasty's ascent, while *ji* infers a sequential arrangement of events chronologically. Before an imperial accession, the narrative is overly detailed to explore the origins of a ruler's rise and expose the ripple or rush of dynastic ascent. After an imperial accession, the narrative is brief: the exalted station and weighty responsibility of monarchs lends great import to their deeds, so a concise narrative allows normative rules [*fa*] to be established.

the Five Classics, sired three sons: Quanyu, Cun, and Wen.[ii] Cheng died, leaving the three boys in poverty with no means to support themselves, so they joined their mother in laboring for board in the household of Liu Chong of Xiao County [Xuzhou¶]. Quanyu had few other talents, although he was modestly more mature in character. Cun and Wen proved brave and burly, and the latter particularly savage.

In the fourth year of Qianfu, under the Tang ruler Xizong [C.E. 877], as Huang Chao rose in rebellion at Cao and Pu prefectures, Cun and Wen cast their lot with the rebels. It was during Chao's assault against Lingnan that Cun died in battle. Chao later overran the capital [Changan] and appointed Wen vanguard for at-large armies on the southeastern front. Wen raided and felled Tongzhou, becoming defense commissioner of the prefecture. At the time, the Son of Heaven was sheltered at Shu [Sichuan], as assorted governors combined forces to suppress the bandits.[iii] After successive defeats by Wang Chongrong of Hezhong, Wen pleaded with Chao for reinforcements, requests suppressed by deputy commandant Meng Kai and never communicated to Chao. His own attendant, Xie Tong, now addressed Wen, stating,

> The house of Huang Chao arose from grass and marsh lands when the Tang happened to be vulnerable and chaotic—his feat one of simply exploiting internal rifts to seize Tang lands. He has no promise as an accomplished and rising King. How does such a man merit our collaboration? With the Son of Heaven now in Shu, the various governors daily converge in colluding to revive dynasty—a sign that humanity has not yet spurned the Tang legacy. Moreover, commanders like you fight vigorously beyond the capital, but lackeys control matters within. This was why Zhang Han once repudiated Qin to revert to Chu [in B.C.E. 207].

Wen concurred, so he assassinated military overseer Yan Shi and returned personally to Hezhong, where he surrendered to Wang Chongrong. General commander Wang Duo conveyed the imperial writ confirming Wen as commandant of the Imperial Insignia Left Guard and deputy commissioner of bandit suppression for at-large forces at Hezhong. The Son of Heaven further conferred the personal name of Quanzhong.

ii. On altering taboo names and citing personal names, see the note below on "nomenclature for kings."

iii. Contemporary nomenclature is employed for "assorted governors." By Tang practice, the commanderies and prefectures administered by regional governors were called "frontier commands" [*fanzhen*], so texts speak of "assuming a command" or "changing commands."

In the third month of the third year of Zhonghe [C.E. 883], Quanzhong was named prefect of Bianzhou [Kaifeng] and governor of its Xuanwu command. The governors' combined armies crushed Chao and restored the capital, in the fourth month, forcing Chao to flee to nearby Lantian. Quanzhong returned to Xuanwu on the third day of the seventh month. The following events occurred this year: via Lantian Pass, Huang Chao overpowered Caizhou, where governor Qin Zongquan defected to Chao before besieging Chenzhou‡. Shi Pu of Xuzhou,¶[iv] as general commander of infantry and cavalry at large on the southeastern front, allied with the eastern governors to rescue Chenzhou‡. The prefect of Chen‡, Zhao Chou, further sought relief from Quanzhong. Shi Pu refused to direct armies in person, despite his duties as general commander.

In the fourth year [C.E. 884], Zhu Quanzhong personally commanded the relief of Zhao Chou, leading the combined armies of the governors in a successful raid on Huang Ye, Shang Rang, and other lieutenants of Huang Chao. In this way, Zhao Chou felt obliged to Quanzhong and began submitting to him. At the time Li Keyong of Hedong had led troops down the Taihang Mountains, crossed the Yellow River, and from Luoyang assisted armies of the east in pummeling Huang Chao. A beleaguered Chao was already in retreat when pursuers, Quanzhong and Keyong, defeated him at Yancheng. Chao fled to Zhongmou, only to be defeated once more at Wangman. He fled to Fengqiu to face a decisive defeat. Then, barely managing to break away, he proceeded eastward as far as Langhu gorge, at Mount Tai, where troops of Shi Pu in hot pursuit killed him.

In the ninth month, the Son of Heaven bestowed titles on Zhu Quanzhong as honorary dignitary for education with ministerial standing, his noble status advanced to Marquis of Pei. In the third month of the second year of Guangqi [C.E. 886], his noble status was advanced to "Prince." Mutineers at the Yicheng command had purged governor An Shiru and elevated governor's guard commander Zhang Xiao to interim regent. Shiru sought sanctuary with Quanzhong, who killed him before sending Zhu Zhen and Li Tangbin to subdue Huazhou; he named Hu Zhen interim regent there. A new investiture as Prince of Wuxing occurred in the twelfth month.

With Huang Chao dead, Qin Zongquan proclaimed himself emperor and overran the prefectures of Shan, Luo, Huai‡, Meng, Tang, Xu‡, Ru, and Zheng. He further dispatched commanders Qin Xian, Lu Tang, and Zhang Zhi to attack Bianzhou. Xian forted his men at Banqiao, Zhi at its northern suburbs, and Tang at Wansheng, as thirty-six palisades encircled Bianzhou.

....

iv. Citations like "a certain person of a certain prefecture" all allude to the governor there.

The Prince[v] appraised his armies as inadequate and dared not leave, sending Zhu Zhen to enlist soldiers to the east while soliciting relief from Yan and Yun prefectures. In the spring of the third year [C.E. 887], Zhen returned with ten thousand fresh troops and several hundred horses. An assault on Qin Xian of Banqiao ensued, his four fortifications decimated. Another assault occurred, this time on Lu Tang of Wansheng, as a vanquished Tang leaped into the water to drown.

Learning of the defeat of Lu Tang and cohort, Qin Zongquan personally led several thousand elite warriors in placing fortifications in the northern suburbs of Kaifeng. In the fifth month, Zhu Jin of Yan Prefecture and Zhu Xuan[vi] of Yun came to lend assistance to the Prince. Halfway through a banquet for them in his barracks, the Prince stood as if to use the toilet, then exited through the northern gate with light infantry to raid Zhang Zhi, the sound of music continuing inside with no interruption. Zhi remained unaware of the Prince's arrival when contingents from Yan and Yun joined the Prince in an attack that devastated Zhi and yielded more than twenty thousand enemy heads. Zongquan and Zhi now fled by night: passing through Zhengzhou, they massacred its people before absconding.

Upon reaching Cai Prefecture, Qin Zongquan again dispatched Zhang Zhi to attack Bian. When the Prince learned of Zhi's return, he climbed a mound behind Fengchan Monastery to survey the passing of his troops. The Prince instructed Zhu Zhen to trail him, but with a stipulation: "Zhi will surely stop after sighting our men. Once he stops, return promptly without engaging him." Zhi did, indeed, halt upon detecting Zhen to his rear, Zhen returning immediately. The Prince now had Zhen lead soldiers to a vast forest to hide; he personally headed eastward with crack cavalry, using large grave mounds as cover. Zhi stopped to eat. After finishing, he clutched his banners for a sally against Zhen, whose men offered only modest resistance. The Prince now led a coordinated rally of troops in ambush, splitting the army of Zhi into three. Joined in battle, Zhi was defeated resoundingly and fled for his life, only for a furious Zongquan to behead him.

Meanwhile, the forces loyal to Qin Zongquan at Heyang, Shan, and Luoyang prefectures scattered randomly upon learning that crack troops from Cai had been exterminated at Bian. This permitted Li Hanzhi to seize Heyang, as Zhang Quanyi, a commander under Zhuge Shuang, seized Luoyang in surrender to the Prince. In the tenth month, the Son of Heaven's emissaries pre-

....

v. Citations occur in increments: initially acknowledging Quanzhong by personal name, then by noble rank, and eventually by imperial title. Citing noble rank only after investiture serves to expose the haste of Quanzhong [in pursuit of power].

vi. The rumor that Zhu Xuan had earlier followed the Prince is erroneous.

sented the Prince with a stone tablet called "Commemorative Record of Achievements."

The armies of Zhu Xuan and Zhu Jin, having assisted in reclaiming Bianzhou, returned eastward after crushing Qin Zongquan. The Prince had a notice delivered to Yan and Yun prefectures: maligning its leadership for luring eastward the fugitive soldiers from Bian, he sent a contingent to punish them, thereby claiming Cao and Pu prefectures. He now orchestrated a raid on Yunzhou by Zhu Zhen, who returned after a rout. In the twelfth month, the Son of Heaven's emissaries arrived to present the Prince with an iron writ of immunity and a stone tablet for virtuous governance.

The death of Gao Pian, governor of Huainan circuit, had enabled Yang Xingmi to occupy Yangzhou. The Son of Heaven thus conferred on the Prince concurrent powers as governor of Huainan. The Prince proposed Xingmi's accommodation as deputy governor while naming manager-adjutant Li Fan as interim regent to Yangzhou. Xingmi rejected Fan upon his arrival.

In the inaugural month of the first year of Wende [C.E. 888], the Prince departed for Huainan, returning after reaching Songzhou. Qin Zongquan, at the time, had recently seized Xiang Prefecture and installed Zhao Deyin as governor. Deyin rebelled against him and reverted to the Prince, however. The Son of Heaven hence confirmed the Prince as general commander of at-large forces for the four fronts at Caizhou with Deyin as his deputy.

On the third day of the third month [April 17[1]], Emperor Xizong expired. A mutiny erupting at the Tianxiong command [Weizhou] had reduced governor Le Yanzhen to a captive. His son Congxun, prefect of Xiang‡ Prefecture, attacked the Wei insurgents and requested military assistance of the Prince, who sent Zhu Zhen for a raid on Wei. Wei upstarts assassinated Yanzhen, while Congxun perished in battle. They now installed Luo Hongxin as successor to Yanzhen, as Zhen returned to home base. Zhang Quanyi soon swept Heyang and ran off Li Hanzhi, who fled westward to Hedong circuit. Li Keyong had already dispatched troops to besiege Heyang when pleas for assistance arrived from Quanyi. The Prince charged Ding Hui and Niu Cunjie with the relief. They defeated the Hedong armies at Yanhe.

In the fifth month, at-large armies campaigning at Cai Prefecture, despite a blockade of more than a hundred days, could not prevail. Shi Pu was already general commander of the southeastern front when the Prince also received command of at-large armies, with Shi Pu still acknowledged as general commander. So, the Prince submitted a memorial censuring Pu for lack of distinction in the Caizhou suppression, while rebuking the court for failure to remove him as general commander. He thereby instigated Pu's taking up arms.

Some time earlier, the death of Gao Pian having wreaked havoc on the southern Huai, Chuzhou prefect Liu Zan fled westward, where the Prince extended sanctuary to him. Once the armies of the Prince failed to take Cai Prefecture by force and returned, he wanted to attack Xu¶, and he ordered Zhu Zhen to lead several thousand men eastward, purportedly to escort Zan back to Chuzhou. Shi Pu, already angered by the Prince's criticisms and further incensed by news of the impending arrival of Zhen's men, ultimately unleashed his own men to intercept them. But Zhen battled them at Wukang to deliver a devastating blow, claiming the two counties of Feng and Xiao. Zhen hence attacked Suzhou to the south, which also fell. Garrisoned at Xiao County, he commissioned Pang Shigu to advance against another target: Xuzhou¶. In the inaugural month of the inaugural year of Longji [C.E. 889], Pang Shigu crushed Shi Pu at Lüliang.

Shen Cong, military attaché of the western Huai governor, managed to capture Qin Zongquan, lop off his feet, and convey him by cage to the capital. But Cong was assassinated by Guo Fan, a detachment commander who abducted Zongquan in order to deliver the prisoner in person. The Prince decided to entrust the prisoner's delivery to Li Fan, his own manager-adjutant, asking the court to confirm Guo Fan as interim regent for the western Huai as well. The Son of Heaven elevated the Prince's noble status to Prince of Dongping in the third month. Zhu Zhen assassinated Li Tangbin, in the seventh month. The Prince reacted by proceeding to Xiao County to seize and murder Zhen before launching a raid on Xuzhou¶. Heavy rains and flooding that winter impeded the further deployment of troops, so he returned.

Some time earlier, the rebel Qin Zongquan had unleashed his younger brother Zongheng to plunder the southern Huai region. Zongheng was murdered this year by one of his own commanders, Sun Ru, who now attacked Yang Xingmi at Yangzhou. With the lower Huai in utter tumult, Xingmi fled southward to Xuan Prefecture, permitting Ru to take Yangzhou.

In the spring of the first year of Dashun [C.E. 890], the Prince directed Pang Shigu's strike against Sun Ru in Huainan. He returned after a rout. A local commander, Zhang Yun, recaptured Suzhou for Shi Pu, in the fourth month. The Prince assumed personal command of an offensive against Suzhou in retaliation, without prevailing.

Previously, in the wake of Huang Chao's defeat and flight, Li Keyong had pursued him as far as Yuanqu, but regrouped after failing to catch up.[2] Passing through Bianzhou, he rested troops at the northern suburbs when the Prince invited him to a banquet at Shangyuan Post, only to raid him by night. Keyong eluded his would-be assailants by leaping over a wall, then lodged a complaint in the capital over the incident. The Son of Heaven fully appraised the Prince at Bian as culpable but mediated the matter. By this time, chief minister Zhang Jun was secretly conspiring with Bian authorities, the Prince bribing him lavishly. Jun thus proposed a campaign against Hedong at the behest of Bianzhou. The high officials of Tang uniformly opposed the opening of hostilities, but Jun grew ever adamant under pressure from Bian, the Son of Heaven only able to concede.

During the fifth month, the court appointed Zhang Jun general commander of at-large forces along the four fronts at Taiyuan, with the Prince named commissioner of bandit suppression for the southeastern theater. The Prince refused to preside personally over the relevant armies, assigning only two thousand men to Jun, then garrisoned at Yindi. A mutinous commander of Hedong, Feng Ba, assassinated the defending commander of Luzhou, Li Kegong, to surrender to the Prince. Ge Congzhou subsequently received orders to occupy Luzhou. Li Keyong thereby deployed Kang Junli to attack Congzhou and precipitate his flight to Heyang.

The Prince departed for Heyang in the ninth month, the Son of Heaven conferring concurrent powers over the Xuanyi command in the next month. He later left for Huazhou, where he sought passage through Wei [to the north] in advance of a strike against Hedong [to the west] and even demanded provisions for his men. Again, he wanted to anger the Wei military and incite war. Wei leaders did, indeed, reject both requests, noting the inappropriateness of issuing troops from their direction and declining provisions due to scarcity. Thus began the invasion of Wei. During the eleventh month, the forces of Zhang Jun met resounding defeat at Yindi. In the inaugural month of the second year [C.E. 891], the Prince engaged Wei troops at Neihuang, routing them and conducting a massacre at the old Yuancheng. Gestures of goodwill arrived from local magnate Luo Hongxin. Suzhou was conquered in the tenth month. A commander at Caozhou, Guo Shaobin, assassinated prefect Guo Rao to surrender the prefecture during the eleventh month. Ding Hui vanquished Zhu Jin at Jinxiang in the twelfth.

A drive against Yunzhou began in the inaugural year of Jingfu, the second month [C.E. 892], the forward divisions of Zhu Youyu suffering defeat at Doumen. Troops of the Prince, arriving late, retreated after a similar defeat. Youyu seized neighboring Puzhou sometime that winter, his assault on Xu¶ Prefecture ensuing. During the fourth month of the second year [C.E. 893], Pang Shigu overran Xu¶ and killed Shi Pu. As the Prince departed for Xu¶, Shigu became interim regent and proceeded to conduct operations against Yan and Yun prefectures.

In the inaugural year of Qianning, the second month [C.E. 894], the Prince engaged Zhu Xuan at Yushan and routed him. In the second year, the eighth month [C.E. 895], he again defeated Xuan at Liangshan, and once more at Juye during the eleventh month. The prefectures of Yan and Yun turned to Hedong for relief. Li Keyong dispatched relief troops to assist them, troops that later trespassed upon Wei territory and were harassed by Wei patrols. An angry Keyong thus unleashed a mass of men against Wei. Luo Hongxin begged the Prince for aid, and he committed Ge Congzhou to the effort. Li Keyong was invested Prince of Jin during this year.

In the third year, the fifth month [C.E. 896], the son of Li Keyong, Luoluo, was captured amid combat at Huanshui [Xiangzhou‡] and sent to Weizhou, where authorities killed him. In the seventh month, Li Maozhen of Fengxiang raided the capital, and the Son of Heaven took sanctuary at Huazhou‡. The Prince offered military assistance to the beleaguered monarch, but the Son of Heaven politely enjoined him to stay away. The Prince proposed relocation of the capital to Luoyang as well, an idea spurned by the throne.

With Pang Shigu triumphant at Yun Prefecture, in the inaugural month of the fourth year [C.E. 897], the Prince departed for Yun and designated Zhu Youyu interim regent. The Prince then attacked Yan Prefecture. Zhu Jin had absconded for Huainan by now, so Ge Congzhou became interim regent for Yan. The drive on Huainan began during the ninth month: Pang Shigu set forth from Qingkou and Ge Congzhou from Anfeng, while the Prince's men quartered at Suzhou. Yang Xingmi had unleashed Zhu Jin for a preemptive strike against Qingkou, however, defeating and killing Shigu. Returning in haste with his men, Congzhou was again defeated along the Pi River, by Zhu Jin. The Prince, alarmed, abruptly withdrew.

In the inaugural year of Guanghua, the third month [C.E. 898], the Son of Heaven gave the Prince concurrent powers as the Tianping governor [of Yunzhou]. In the fourth month, the Prince dispatched Ge Congzhou to raid Jin positions [of Li Keyong] to the east of the mountain. He eventually won the three prefectures of Xing, Ming, and Ci. Meanwhile, Zhao Kuangning of Xiangzhou, ever since his father Deyin had submitted to the Prince, had simultaneously entered secret talks with Yang Xingmi and Li Keyong, so news of the offensive slipped out. In the seventh month, the Prince ordered Shi Shucong and Kang Huaiying to attack Kuangning; they claimed the three prefectures of Bi, Sui, and Deng.[3] Hostilities ceased only after Kuangning sued for peace. Li Hanzhi surrendered Luzhou during the twelfth month.

In the second year [C.E. 899], Liu Rengong of Youzhou attacked Wei, compelling Luo Shaowei to solicit relief. The Prince came to the Wei's defense by defeating Rengong at Neihuang. He ordered Shi Shucong to storm the Jin at Taiyuan, in the fourth month, with no success. Li Keyong captured Ze and Lu prefectures in the seventh month. During the eleventh month, mutineers at the Baoyi command assassinated Governor Wang Gong and elevated his military attaché Li Fan to interim regent. But one of Fan's underlings, Zhu Jian, in turn assassinated him to surrender the region. The Baoyi governorship reverted to Jian as reward.

In the fourth month of the third year [C.E. 900], the Prince sent Ge Congzhou to raid Cang Prefecture, the domain of Liu Rengong. Congzhou engaged Rengong at Laoyati; after Rengong's loss of De Prefecture, Congzhou inflicted decided defeat. The Jin captured Mingzhou in the eighth month, but the Prince of Liang personally led men to reclaim the prefecture. Zhen and Ding prefectures were allied to Jin at the time, so an attack on Zhen ensued. Lincheng soon fell and Wang Rong, its presiding officer, made overtures of peace to the Prince. The Prince proceeded with a drive against Dingzhou, where presiding officer Wang Gao fled to the Jin as subordinate Wang Chuzhi surrendered the prefecture.

The Tang eunuch Liu Jishu, having induced tumult, had confined the Son of Heaven to the eastern palaces. In the inaugural year of Tianfu [C.E. 901], the inaugural month, imperial security chief Sun Dezhao intervened to execute Jishu and restore the Son of Heaven to power. The Prince was now invested Prince of Liang. He soon sent Zhang Cunjing to attack Wang Ke at Hezhong circuit: with troops issuing by way of Hanshan, Cunjing overran Jin and Jiang prefectures. Wang Ke had initially sought relief from the Jin, but its inability to assist forced Ke to surrender to the Prince.

A major offensive against the Prince of Jin was launched in the third month. Approaching via the Taihang Mountains, Shi Shucong first laid claim to Ze and Lu prefectures. The troops of Ge Congzhou, Zhang Cunjing, Hou Yan, and Zhang Guihou rendezvoused with armies from Zhen and Ding prefectures in converging on Taiyuan; a siege ensued without effecting a surrender, so they withdrew under heavy rains. In the fifth month, the Son of Heaven affirmed the Prince of Liang's concurrent powers as metropolitan custodian of Hezhong and governor of the Huguo command. The Jin took the prefectures of Ci‡ and Xi in the sixth month.

With Liu Jishu and his close associates now executed, chief minister Cui Yin allied externally with the Liang, expecting to prevail upon its armies to liquidate all eunuchs. But Li Maozhen of Fengxiang, Wang Xingyu of Bin/Ning, and others sent their own close kinsmen to form an elite force within the Son of Heaven's bodyguard, a force of which eunuchs such as Han Quanhui expected to avail themselves. As the Son of Heaven began laying plans with minister Yin, eunuchs with alert ears overheard, and they planted female beauties within the palace precincts to ferret out the facts discreetly. In time, they heard a story of Yin's scheme to liquidate eunuchs in a petition to the throne. The news utterly terrified Quanhui and cohort, who tearfully wrung their hands from day to night, contemplating a cabal against Yin to save themselves. Intuiting his scheme exposed and matters urgent, Yin forged an imperial rescript summoning the armies of Liang to enter the capital to murder the eunuchs.

In the tenth month, the Prince mobilized armies against Hezhong from the Xuanwu, Xuanyi, Tianping, and Huguo commands—a combined force of seventy thousand. They acquired Tong Prefecture, then assaulted Hua‡, securing the surrender of Han Jian. As the armies of Liang approached the capital, eunuch Quanhui and others promptly deployed contingents from Qi‡ and Bin prefectures, currently on assignment with the Imperial Guard, to abduct the Son of Heaven for flight to Fengxiang. The Prince now wrote a letter exposing Cui Yin's intent to summon him to the capital, inciting the Son of Heaven to remove Yin as chief minister and demote him to minister of public works. The armies of Liang were mandated to return to home base. The Prince of Liang withdrew troops, but opened hostilities against Binzhou, his men quartered at Sanyuan. Soon, the governor of Bin, Yang Chongben, surrendered the four prefectures of Bin, Ning, Qing, and Yan¶. Cui Yin hence absconded for Huazhou‡.

In spring of the second year [C.E. 902], the Prince withdrew his men to Hezhong. Armies of the Prince of Jin [Li Keyong] raided the prefectures of Jin and Jiang. The Prince retaliated by deploying Zhu Youning against them. Youning stormed Pu County and captured Fen, Ci‡, and Xi prefectures in the wake of a Jin defeat. Advancing to blockade Taiyuan, Youning did not triumph and withdrew, causing Fen, Ci‡, and Xi to revert to Jin control. During the fourth month, Youning led his men westward to Xingping, where they battled Li Maozhen at Wugong and defeated him handily. When armies of the Prince raided Fengxiang, Maozhen repeatedly emerged from the city to engage them; he was swiftly vanquished, and an encirclement ensued. Li Zhouyi of Fu/Fang led his men in the relief effort for Fengxiang, during the eleventh month. The Prince responded with a surprise storm against Fuzhou‡ led by Kong Jing, who captured the relatives of Zhouyi for relocation to Hezhong, the surrender of Zhouyi occurring soon thereafter. At the time, the forces of Qizhou‡ had sustained frequent losses after a long siege: the city's provisions exhausted, everyone from the Son of Heaven to women of his inner palace suffered from exposure and hunger.

During the inaugural month of the third year [C.E. 903], Li Maozhen assassinated Han Quanhui and others, some twenty eunuchs in all, stringing up their heads to show the Liang military, while predicating release of the Son of Heaven upon a lifting of the Liang siege. On the twenty-second day [February 22], the Son of Heaven emerged to meet with Liang troops.[4] The Prince sent an express courier summoning chief minister Cui Yin, but Yin declined on the pretext of illness. The Prince's messenger tried to inveigle him, saying, "I have never met the Son of Heaven and fear an imposter, so you should come to ascertain things." The Son of Heaven's entourage had reached Xingping when Cui Yin led the official rank and file in greeting him. Personally holding the Emperor's horse reins was the Prince, who rode and wept at once, the tears subsiding only after the passage of ten *li*. Onlookers all presumed his genuine loyalty.

On the twenty-seventh day [February 27], the Son of Heaven arrived from Fengxiang: changing into mourning apparel, he wept before the Imperial Ancestors' Temple. Now entering his palace, he ordered the liquidation of over seven hundred eunuchs. On the third day of the second month [March 4], the Son of Heaven cited the Prince as "Subject of Merit Who Rejuvenates Celestial Powers, the Supremely Loyal and Upright." The Prince of Hui, Li Zuo, was named supreme marshal empirewide and the Prince of Liang named deputy supreme marshal. As the Prince prepared to return eastward with his men, son Zhu Youlun stayed behind as director of imperial security and bodyguard to the Son of Heaven. The Son of Heaven received the Prince in banquet at Yanxi mansion, presenting five songs on the "willow branch" theme.

Liang armies had previously returned westward when Wang Shifan of Qing‡ Prefecture unleashed commander Liu Xun to storm Yan, Liang territory, successfully occupying it. The Prince was personally at his Liang satrapy, but departed for Yun Prefecture during the fourth month, dispatching [his nephew] Zhu Youning to raid Qing‡ in retaliation. Shifan defeated him at Shilou, however, and Youning died. In the ninth month, Yang Shihou vanquished Qing‡ forces at Linqu to capture Di Prefecture. Wang Shifan then relinquished Qing‡, the surrender of Liu Xun ensuing. Zhu Youlun died after he was thrown from a horse in a polo match. An infuriated Prince, convinced that minister Cui Yin had murdered his son, sent Zhu Youqian to the capital to assassinate Yin and all others involved in that fateful match.[5]

Ever since the Son of Heaven's flight from Huazhou‡, the Prince had petitioned for the capital's relocation to Luoyang [Henan Prefecture]. The Emperor declined, but the Prince directed Zhang Quanyi of Henan to proceed with renovation of the Luoyang palaces in anticipation of the relocation. In the inaugural year of Tianyou [C.E. 904], the Prince departed for Hezhong Prefecture. He sent his military attaché Kou Yanqing to the western capital to petition, once again, for imperial relocation to Luoyang, including the forced resettlement eastward of residents of Changan. The Son of Heaven, reaching Shanzhou, held an audience in this provisional capital, then departed for the eastern capital in advance of the Prince. The men in the Six Armies had largely scattered by now, so the Emperor was accompanied eastward by only a dozen or so young eunuchs, along with two hundred kickball players and palace boys. As the imperial entourage approached Gushui [Shanzhou], the

Prince prodded imperial doctor Xu Zhaoyuan to allege treacherous schemes on the part of these men, causing their liquidation and even replacement prior to informing the throne. By now, the aides to the Son of Heaven were all cronies of the Liang. The Son of Heaven arrived from the western capital on the tenth day of the [intercalary] fourth month [May 27].[6] News of the Son of Heaven's coerced relocation to Luoyang prompted consideration of punitive action against the Liang by Li Keyong (Prince of Jin), Li Maozhen (Prince of Qi‡), Zhao Kuangning (Prince of Chu), Wang Jian (Prince of Shu), and Yang Xingmi (Prince of Wu). It was a terribly frightening prospect for the Prince.

In the sixth month, Yang Chongben once again reverted to Qizhou‡. The Prince led his men toward Hezhong with the expressed intent of retaliating against Chongben, while discharging Zhu Yougong, Shi Shucong, Jiang Xuanhui, and others to commit regicide against Zhaozong, who expired. In the tenth month, the Prince held court in the capital, murdering Zhu Yougong and Shi Shucong [to silence them]. He directed a drive against the southern Huai and captured Guangzhou in the eleventh month. Another drive against Shouzhou, unsuccessful, ended in retreat.

In the second month of the second year [C.E. 905], the Prince dispatched Jiang Xuanhui to Jiuquchi to assassinate the nine royal princes of Tang, including the Prince of De, Li Yu. Massacre of the dignitary for public works Pei Zhi, along with a hundred others, occurred during the sixth month. Messengers of the Son of Heaven arrived in the seventh month with a stone tablet for the Prince, "Commemorating Merit in the Imperial Reception." The Prince, wishing to supplant the Tang dynasty, notified the governors through messengers. Zhao Kuangning of Xiangzhou voiced opposition, so the Prince unleashed Yang Shihou against the seven prefectures of Tang, Deng, Fu, Ying, Sui, Jun, and Fang‡, capturing them. The Prince now departed for Xiangzhou, forting his men north of the Han River. During the ninth month, Shihou breached Xiangzhou as Kuangning absconded for Huainan. Jingnan was also captured, as interim regent Zhao Kuangming absconded for Shu. Shihou raided Shou Prefecture from bases at Guang, failing to prevail.

At the altars of the southern suburbs, the Son of Heaven conducted divination and prayers to heaven. The action incited the Prince, who believed that Jiang Xuanhui and cohort were praying to Heaven to prolong the life of Tang. A nervous Son of Heaven thus restricted ceremonies to divination only. On the twenty-seventh day of the eleventh month [December 25], invested Prince of Wei, the Prince received honors as chancellor of state and supreme statesman. The Son of Heaven confirmed, as Wei territory, the twenty-one commands of Xuanwu, Xuanyi, Tianping, Huguo, Tianxiong, Wushun, Youguo, Heyang, Yiwu, Zhaoyi, Wuning, Baoyi, Zhongyi, Wuzhao, Wuding, Taining, Pinglu, Kuangguo, Zhenguo, Jingnan, and Zhongwu. He also conferred the "nine official privileges with vestments," which the Prince refused to accept in indignation [for his parsimony].[7]

In the twelfth month, the Son of Heaven confirmed the Prince as supreme marshal for armed forces worldwide. The Prince, bitter still, sent a messenger accusing palace military secretary Jiang Xuanhui and Empress Dowager He of improper intimacies. Consequently, Xuanhui was murdered and his body set afire, as the Empress succumbed to regicide in the Jishan palace. Also murdered was chief minister Liu Can; chamberlain of ceremonials Zhang Yanfan was dismembered by horse-drawn carts. The Son of Heaven ordered the suspension of divination ceremonies owing to the Dowager's death.

During the third year, spring [C.E. 906], Luo Shaowei of Weizhou, planning to liquidate his personal guard, requested reinforcements in anticipation of a backlash. The Prince had led his men northward to attack Liu Rengong at Cangzhou and their passage through Wei coincided with Shaowei's liquidation of his guard; those guardsmen in the suburbs rebelled and occupied the prefectures of Bei, Wei‡, Chan,[8] and Bo. The entire lot was liquidated by the Prince before he proceeded with the campaign against Cangzhou, forting his men at Changlu. In the interim, Liu Rengong turned to the Jin for assistance and together they captured Luzhou. The Prince withdrew his men.

CHAPTER 2

ANNALS II: BASIC ANNALS OF LIANG

In the spring,[1] the inaugural month of the inaugural year of Kaiping, the twenty-fifth day [C.E. March 11, 907], the Son of Heaven delegated Xue Yiju, the censor-in-chief, to visit the Prince and render honors to troops.[2] Chief minister Zhang Wenwei joined leading courtiers in imploring the Prince to advance himself further. On the sixteenth day of the fourth month, the Prince adopted the personal name of Huang and assumed the throne as Emperor on the eighteenth day [June 1].[i] On the twenty-second he announced a general amnesty,[ii] changed the calendar, adopted Liang as dynastic name, and invested the deposed ruler of Tang as Prince of Jiyin.[iii] Bianzhou was elevated to the Kaifeng metropolitan area and designated the eastern capital. The eastern capital of Tang times [Luoyang] now became the western capital, the metropolitan district of Jingzhao [Changan] renamed Yongzhou.[iv] A day of drink and merriment was an-

i. Once a ruler is in power, only the following sorts of events are noted: events of historic dimensions, changes in traditional practices, events out of the ordinary, events of symbolic import, and events that cause a later reaction. Apart from these five, all else is excluded.
ii. Extant texts for imperial pardons all read, "a general amnesty for the entire world was declared." Here, the word "general" is recorded in order to convey the aim of the amnesty to extend far and wide, but not "the entire world," for the domain never actually extended that far.
iii. Here, reference to the Son of Heaven as "ruler of Tang" reflects the idiom of the original documents.
iv. On the formation and elimination of prefectures and counties, see the "Treatise on Administrative Geography." Here, only changes pertaining to the capital will be noted.

nounced for the new eastern capital. The recipient of gown and staff, Meilau, reached the capital as envoy of Khitan ruler Abaoji.[v]

On the first day of the fifth month [June 14], the court appointed former ministers of Tang, Zhang Wenwei and Yang She, as deputy directors of the Chancellery, censor-in-chief Xue Yiju becoming deputy director of the Palace Secretariat, each with concurrent powers as chief ministers. Envoys sent by the Bohai [Parhae] kingdom and the Khitan arrived on the second day.[vi] On the ninth, elder brother Quanyu was invested as Prince of Guang, imperial sons Youwen as Prince of Bo,[vii] Yougui as Prince of Ying, Youzhang as Prince of Fu, Youzhen as Prince of Jun, and Youhui as Prince of Jian, and imperial nephews Youliang invested as Prince of Heng, Youneng as Prince of Hui, and Youhui‡ as Prince of Shao. On the eighteenth day, the Military Affairs Bureau was renamed the Venerable Governance Bureau,[3] with the former chamberlain for palace revenues, Jing Xiang, designated commissioner. During this month, the chief director of at-large forces at Luzhou, Li Si'an, engaged Jin troops in battle and met defeat.[viii]

On the ninth day of the sixth month [July 21], the governor of the Pinglu command, Han Jian, was appointed dignitary for education with concurrent powers as chief minister. In autumn, the seventh month, the twenty-fourth day [September 4], posthumous honors as "Emperor" were extended to paternal ancestors and "Empress" given their wives: the imperial great-great-grandfather, An, renamed Xuanyuan, received the temple designation of Suzu; the sobriquet Xuanxi went to his wife, née Fan. Great grandfather Maolin, renamed Guangxian, received the temple designation of Jingzu; the sobriquet Guangxiao went to his wife, née Yang. Grandfather Xin, renamed Zhaowu, received the temple designation of Xianzu; the sobriquet Zhaoyi went to his wife, née Liu. Imperial father Cheng, renamed Wenmu, received the temple designation of Liezu; the sobriquet Wenhui went to his wife, née Wang.

....

v. When barbarians arrive, there is no reference to "attending audience" because they are not expected to know ritual protocol, nor is there reference to tributary items because their gifts are not valued; thus, they are simply said to "arrive." In a chaotic age like the Five Dynasties, the fact of their coming to court in no way reflects on the quality of governance here, one way or the other. For an age of chaos, in fact, the frequency of their visits is nothing of which to be proud.

vi. The name and rank of some barbarian rulers and their officials are sometimes given, sometimes not. Citation is not necessary partly because such information is given in detail in the *Old History*; embassies are noted here only to indicate symbolic import.

vii. Zhu Youwen is referred to as son when, in fact, he was not; for explanation, see "Biographies of the Liang Royal Family" [chapter 13].

viii. In the interests of consistency of language [*wenli*]: when the government suffers defeat, the term *baiji* is employed; when the opponent is defeated, the term *baizhi* is used. The location of battle is not cited in the case of at-large detachments.

On the twenty-second day of the eighth month [October 2], hordes of green caterpillars struck Tongzhou. And at Xizhou, the waters of the Yellow River appeared to be clear.[ix] Horses were appropriated in the ninth month. Military exercises took place at the Fan terrace in the winter, fifteenth day of the tenth month [November 23]. On the twenty-ninth day of the eleventh month [C.E. January 5, 908], the palace announced an amnesty for military deserters at large and criminals sentenced to tonsure or tattoo.[x]

In the second year, spring, twenty-fifth day of the inaugural month [February 29], envoys from Bohai reached the capital. On the twenty-seventh day [March 2], the Emperor conducted divination ceremonies at the western capital. Regicide against the Prince of Jiyin occurred.[xi] Envoys of Khitan ruler Abaoji arrived on the thirtieth day of the second month [April 3]. On the first day of the third month, the Monarch departed for the western capital,[xii] then for Huai‡ Prefecture on the fifth day,[xiii] and finally Ze on the sixth. On the seventh day, the master of court ceremonials, Li Song, invested Duke of Laiguo, was confirmed as ritual heir to the two deceased princes of Tang.[xiv] On the eleventh day, the Kuangguo governor, Liu Zhijun, became bandit-suppressing commissioner of at-large armies at Luzhou. The court postponed divination ceremonies on the twenty-second. Chief minister Zhang Wenwei passed away.[4]

In summer, the third day of the fourth month [May 5], the court dismissed Yang She as chief minister and named vice-minister of personnel Yu Jing as deputy director of the Palace Secretariat and Zhang Ce, the Hanlin current recipient of edicts and vice-minister of rites, as vice-minister of punishments, both with ministerial standing. The monarch reached Zezhou on

....

ix. These omens are cited to expose the inauspiciousness of it all.

x. In an age when men tend to murder with relish, minor amnesties should be cited to reveal the continued potential for compassion toward men.

xi. For a subject, the act of regicide [*shi*] is a grave crime. The title "Prince of Jiyin" is cited to reflect the reality [of the Former Monarch's current standing as mere "prince"]; the word *shi* defines properly the nature of the Liang crime.

xii. [For an imperial progress,] the term *xing* implies completion of the act of "going to," while *ru* implies "departing for" without necessarily reaching the destination. The word *ru* implies that the Emperor is en route and indicates an official purpose for the trip.

xiii. The Five Dynasties being an age of turmoil, its armies had scarcely a day of rest, so every military action cannot possibly be mentioned. Therefore, when armies deployed are neither victorious nor vanquished, when cities under assault are neither won nor lost, then no citation is made. But it is a manifestly important matter for senior commanders to be mandated to join the Son of Heaven in a royal movement, as occurs here; departure for Huaizhou and Zezhou reflects the ongoing siege of Luzhou.

xiv. [In conformity with current taboo practices], the Liang once changed the character *wu* to *wu*‡ [for the *wuyin* (seventh) day]; the *Old History* reverted all such renderings back to *wu* [a convention adopted here].

the twelfth day. On the nineteenth day of the fifth month [June 20], the chief inspector of at-large forces at Luzhou, Kang Huaiying, engaged Jin forces along city walls and met defeat.[xv] On the twenty-eighth day, three ritual temples to Tang were erected. Envoys of the Khitan arrived. On the third day of the sixth month [July 3], in preparation for a campaign against Qi‡, the court named the Zhongwu governor, Liu Zhijun, commissioner of bandit-suppressing forces at large in the western circuits.[xvi] The assassination of Wang Shifan, generalissimo for the Imperial Insignia Right Guard, occurred on the tenth day, his clansmen liquidated as well.[xvii] The troops of Liu Zhijun battled Qi‡ warriors at Mogu on the seventeenth, defeating them.

In autumn, the ninth day of the ninth month [October 6], the Monarch departed for Shanzhou,[xviii] naming Zhu Youwen, the Prince of Bo, interim custodian of the eastern capital. He arrived from Shanzhou in the autumn, ninth day of the tenth month. Zhang Ce was dismissed on the twenty-fifth day of the eleventh month [December 21]. Yang She, left associate at the Imperial Secretariat, now held concurrent powers as chief minister. On the second day of the twelfth month, the Duke of Jie [ritual heir to Tang] was designated "revered heir to the three princes," the Dukes of Xi and Lai named heirs to the "two princes."

In spring of the third year, seventh day of the inaugural month [C.E. January 31, 909], the Monarch departed for the western capital. He again burned lanterns in prayers for prosperity.[xix] On the twenty-third, he offered ancestral sacrifices at the Imperial Ancestors' Temple, performing offerings at the southern altars on the twenty-fourth.[xx] A general amnesty ensued. On the twenty-ninth, the multitude of courtiers further venerated their monarch as the "Profoundly Civil, Sagaciously Martial, Expansive and Filial Emperor."

....

xv. Barricades had been erected around the entire periphery of Luzhou; location is indicated because battle occurred within the walls of the city.

xvi. Four terms are used with reference to the deployment of armies: when two equals attack each other, the term employed is "attack" [*gong*]; when the mighty attacks the weak, it is "campaign" [*fa*]; when action is taken as punishment for a crime, it is "punitive drive" [*tao*]; when the Son of Heaven personally accompanies his men, it is an "expedition" [*zheng*]. Distinctions are absolutely necessary in the narration of events; there is no inference of "praise and blame" in the terminology.

xvii. When death is justified, the term "execution" [*fuzhu*] is used; when death is not justified, then the word "murder" [*sha*] is employed as among peers.

xviii. He did so because Jinzhou and Jiangzhou had come under attack by the Prince of Jin.

xix. The "burning of lanterns," by historic custom, involved the celebration of a common bounty and goodwill by everyone in the realm, from the monarch to the masses. But at a time of serious corruption of those customs, I note the Emperor's declaration to expose the failings of his rule.

xx. As for "sacrifices to heaven at the southern altars," the phrase "performance of offerings" [*youshi*] is employed to conform to the idiom of the day.

Military exercises took place at the Xixin gardens on the twenty-sixth day of the second month. On the twenty-eighth day, Gao Wanxing of Yanzhou‡ defected from the Qi‡ satrapy to surrender to Liang.[xxi]

Envoys of the king of Bohai, Dayin Zhuan, arrived on the sixth day of the third month [March 29]. On the ninth day, the Monarch departed for Hezhong[xxii] and appointed the governor of Shannan east circuit, Yang Shihou, commissioner of bandit-suppressing forces at large along the four fronts at Luzhou. Liu Zhijun captured Danzhou. By summer, the eleventh day of the fourth month, he had further conquered the three prefectures of Yan‡, Fu‡, and Fang.[xxiii] The Monarch arrived from Hezhong on the fifteenth day of the fifth month [June 5], murdering the Youguo governor, Wang Chongshi. On the sixteenth day of the sixth month [July 6], Liu Zhijun orchestrated the defection of Liu Han, the Youguo governor, who surrendered to Qi‡.[xxiv] The Monarch left for Shanzhou on the seventeenth day.[xxv] The Prince of Ji, Zhu Youqian, became commissioner of bandit suppression for at-large regiments in eastern Tongzhou, on the twenty-first day. Liu Zhijun fled to Qi‡. A mutiny within the Danzhou military caused prefect Song Zhihui to be purged.

During autumn, the seventh month, the armed forces of Shangzhou mutinied and overthrew prefect Li Chou, who fled to Qi‡. On the second day [July 21], Danzhou was retaken and Wang Xingsi, chief culprit in the mutiny, apprehended.[xxvi] The Monarch returned from Shanzhou on the twelfth day. On the twenty-first, mutineers within the Xiangzhou military murdered their interim regent, Wang Ban.[xxvii] Prefect Yang Qian of Fangzhou‡ surrendered

....

xxi. In the turmoil of the late Tang—when the strong and the weak were in constant contest and when men freely reverted to this or that domain with no sense of permanence—it is difficult to decide where blame rightly rests. Employment here of the term "treason" [*pan*] represents a first step toward properly fixing the duty of subjects.

xxii. He did so because, in the aftermath of Gao Wanxing's surrender, the troops of Liu Zhijun had attacked Fu‡ and Yan‡ prefectures.

xxiii. In the simple interest of language consistency, territory acquired relatively easily is "captured" [*qu*], acquired with difficulty is "seized" or "conquered" [*ke*].

xxiv. Also in the simple interest of language consistency: to surrender one's person is called *xiang*, to surrender land is called *fu*. As governor for the Zhongwu command, Zhijun relinquished to Qi‡ the land of Tongzhou. Here, the defection of Zhijun is noted without specifying the territory surrendered, for the Zhongwu command has been cited earlier.

xxv. He did so due to the defection of Liu Zhijun.

xxvi. The chief culprit was originally unknown, so I say simply that "the army mutinied"; only after reclaiming the prefecture was his identity learned. The name of the principal commander behind the Danzhou conquest, the noble titles for Xingsi, and the date of his execution are all missing—these were never recorded in the *Old History*.

xxvii. Wang Ban died because he lacked the intelligence to protect his own life and lacked the cunning to manage his underlings, so no reference occurs to "dying honorably in battle" [*sizhi*] to expose the circumstances under which he died. A volitional death represents a badge of integrity for a subject—a matter not to be treated trivially.

to Shu [Sichuan]. The court ordered, on the eighteenth day of the eighth month [September 5], a reduction in punishment for prisoners facing death sentences. On the twenty-eighth, the prefect of Junzhou, Zhang Jingfang, wrested Fang‡ away from Yang Qian and apprehended him. Envoys of the Khitan arrived in the capital on the eleventh day of the intercalary eighth month [September 27]. A royal inspection of farming occurred at Xiyuan on the seventeenth.

It was the tenth day of the ninth month [October 26] that Chen Hui, the commissioner of bandit-suppressing forces at large and generalissimo of the Left Bodyguard, seized Xiangzhou and apprehended the chief renegade Li Hong.[xxviii] On the fifteenth day, the court named the Baoyi governor, Wang Quan, commissioner of bandit-suppressing forces at large in eastern Luzhou. The court dismissed ministers Han Jian and Yang She on the nineteenth. Chamberlain for ceremonials Zhao Guangfeng became deputy director of the Palace Secretariat and Du Shao, recipient of edicts at the Hanlin academy and vice-minister of works, became vice-minister of revenues—both with concurrent ministerial powers. Li Hong and Yang Qian were executed on the twenty-ninth day. The summer solstice occurred in winter, the second day of the eleventh month [December 17]. Prayers of gratitude were conducted in the southern suburbs.[xxix] The court inaugurated a search for the wise and noble, on the seventeenth. The Zhenguo governor, Kang Huaiying, directed a punitive campaign against Qi‡. In the twelfth month, Huaiying seized the three prefectures of Ning, Qing, and Yan¶, only to be defeated in a contest with Liu Zhijun at Shengping.

In spring of the fourth year, first day of the inaugural month [C.E. February 13, 910], the performance of music was revived at court.[xxx] Military exercises took place at Yulin on the sixteenth day. On the twenty-ninth day of the second month, a royal inspection of farming occurred at Gushui. On the ninth day of the eighth month [September 15], the Monarch departed for

…………

xxviii. The commissioning of Chen Hui to suppress the rebels is overlooked in the *Old History* and appears for the first time here. The identity of the chief culprit was learned only after reclamation of the area, which is why the earlier citation simply mentions a "mutiny in the armed forces."

xxix. The summer solstice usually does not merit mention; I do so here only because the solstice prompted prayers of gratitude: citation is merited because the ruler's prayers of gratitude are in response to the solstice. Like the wording in original sources, no citation here occurs for the "performance of offerings" [*youshi*] at the southern altars—after all, "prayers of gratitude" are more ritualistically informal than the "performance of rites" at the southern altars.

xxx. Since the turmoil of the late Tang, rites and music had vanished. The revival of music having begun at this point, it deserves mention.

Shanzhou,[xxxi] naming the metropolitan custodian of Henan Prefecture, Zhang Zongshi, interim custodian of the western capital. On the fourteenth, the campaign against Qi‡ was entrusted to Yang Shihou, the Huguo governor now empowered as commissioner of bandit suppression for at-large forces in the western circuits. The Monarch reached the capital from Shanzhou on the third day of the ninth month. He pronounced a search for the wise and good on the twenty-fifth. On the third day of the eleventh month [December 7], the Ningguo governor, Wang Jingren, was charged with the campaign against Zhao as commissioner of bandit suppression for at-large forces in the northern circuits. Defections to the Jin occurred by the Prince of Zhao, Wang Rong, and the Prince of Beiping, Wang Chuzhi. Jin forces now came to the rescue of Zhao. Drafts of laws and statutes were promulgated on the seventeenth day of the twelfth month.

In the spring of the inaugural year of Qianhua, second day of the inaugural month [C.E. February 3, 911], Wang Jingren fought Jin forces at Baixiang [Zhaozhou], a defeat ensuing. On the fifth, the court issued an amnesty for criminal sentences of banishment and below, soliciting critical dialogue and constructive remonstrance. It designated, on the eighth, Tianxiong governor Yang Shihou as commissioner of bandit suppression for at-large forces to the north. In summer, eighteenth day of the fourth month [May 19], envoys of the Khitan ruler Abaoji reached the capital. A general amnesty was announced on the first day of the fifth month, the current calendar changed to Qianhua. The Monarch visited Zhang Zongshi at home, on the tenth.

In autumn, seventeenth day of the eighth month [September 12], a royal inspection of farming occurred at Yulin. Envoys of Bohai reached the capital. A grand tour of polo grounds at Xing'an took place on the twenty-seventh. In his procession to the Wenming palace, on the first day of the ninth month, the Monarch entered by the auxiliary side door.[xxxii] He departed for Wei Prefecture on the twentieth,[xxxiii] designating Zhang Zongshi as interim custodian of the western capital. A grand tour of the eastern suburbs of Wei occurred in winter, twenty-sixth day of the tenth month[5] [November 19]. Gao Wanxing acquired Yanzhou† during the eleventh month. The Monarch arrived from Wei

....

xxxi. This is because men of Qi‡ and Jin had attacked Xiazhou.

xxxii. To refer to "an imperial progress to the palace" [*yudian*] by noting a "procession through the auxiliary door" [*ruge*] represents the original phraseology: it serves to illustrate the breaches of protocol common to the time; see the biography of Li Qi for details. The protocol, repeated in later times, is not cited again; one citation is sufficient to expose the ritual shortcomings of the era.

xxxiii. He did so because Jin forces had attacked Wei.

on the twelfth day.[xxxiv] Envoys of the Huihu Uighurs and Tubo Tibetans reached the capital on the fifteenth.

In the spring of the second year, eighth day of the second month [C.E. February 28, 912], the court named its chamberlain for imperial recreations, Lu Bi, emissary to Shu. The Monarch departed for Wei on the fifteenth, leaving Zhang Zongshi as interim custodian of the western capital. At the next destination, Baima, he murdered the left cavalier of palace remonstrance Sun Zhi, right master of admonition Zhang Yan, and Ministry of War associate Zhang Jun. He departed for Beizhou on the twenty-ninth, and on the seventh day of the third month [March 28] perpetrated a slaughter at Zaoqiang [Jizhou].[xxxv] The Monarch again departed for Wei Prefecture on the eighth day. He arrived from Wei in the summer, twenty-first day of the fourth month [May 10],[xxxvi] departing for the western capital on the thirteenth.

On the ninth day of the fifth month [May 28], the palace announced an "imperial grace,"[xxxvii] reducing all criminal sentences of capital punishment and below. Sentences of penal servitude were rescinded and proscriptions imposed on the slaughter of animals. Envoys from Bohai reached the capital. Chief minister Xue Yiju passed away sometime this month. The Monarch's health deteriorated during the sixth month. The Prince of Ying, Yougui, rebelled.[xxxviii] The Emperor expired on the second day [July 18].[xxxix]

We lament. Ever since Later Tang times, a world long despising the Liang had largely deemed the dynasty illegitimate. In my own assessment of the Five Dynasties, however, I singularly refused to dismiss the Liang, causing some critics to reprove me for a grave disservice to the maxims of the *Spring*

....

xxxiv. He did so because Jin forces had allied with Zhen and Ding prefectures in a drive against Xiang‡ and Wei.
xxxv. The word "slaughter" is used to stress the severity of his savagery.
xxxvi. "He departed for the western capital," mentioned in the following line, infers having previously reached the eastern capital.
xxxvii. An "imperial grace" [*deyin*] represents a small-scale amnesty. The original phraseology is kept in tact to demonstrate its actual scope.
xxxviii. The "defector" [*panzhe*] turns against one regime and joins another, becoming a subject of the other power. The "rebel" [*fan*] is an inferior who conspires against his superior, and commits a higher level of treachery. No fixed principle is adopted for citing or not citing dates, and admittedly, some events simply cannot be assigned a date: rebellion, for example, is never confined to a single day or night and thus cannot be fixed to a single date, so the precise dates of rebellions are not cited below.
xxxix. He lived to be sixty-one *sui*. The place of expiration is not given, thereby stressing the unnatural conditions surrounding his death. In the eleventh month of the second year of Qianhua, he was buried by Yougui at Yinque County, Henan, and given the tomb name Xuanling. Burial data is withheld in the text, for he died an unnatural death.

and Autumn Annals.[6] They say, "The Liang represents an horrific evil that deserves eradication from history. To elevate the regime, instead, is tantamount to condoning usurpers, a position contrary to the thrust of the *Annals*!" This is precisely the thrust of the *Annals*, I would contend. When Duke Huan of Lu assassinated Duke Yin to enthrone himself, when Duke Xuan assassinated Zichi to enthrone himself, when Duke Li of Zheng expelled his heir Hu to install himself, and Gongsun Piao of Wei expelled ruler Kan to enthrone himself—in no case did the Sage Confucius, in his *Annals*, deny their sovereignty. Likewise, I am embracing the rules of the *Spring and Autumn Annals* by not casting the Liang as bogus. "But did the *Annals* also condone usurpation?" I would simply say that the intent of the *Annals* is amply evident in its refusal to disavow the rule of these four figures.

In the *Spring and Autumn Annals*, the Sage was profound in expressing intent and thereby persuaded or dissuaded incisively; he was credible with words and thereby clarified virtue and vice. He aspired to expose misdeeds to later generations by stressing "adherence to reality." If reality entailed reign as ruler, "ruler" was written; if reality involved usurpation, "usurpation" was written. He recorded real conditions to earn posterity's trust, and in the process, made the misdeeds of these four rulers impossible to conceal. When rulers cannot conceal their vice, men will recognize that ill repute is unshakeable and the inclination to commit evil will thereby virtually cease. This is the meaning of "profound expression of intent whereby persuasion is incisive" or "the credible use of words to clarify virtue and vice." For ancient tyrants Jie and Zhou, the stripping of kingly titles was unnecessary for thousands of generations to despise them. The *Spring and Autumn Annals*, in refusing to eradicate from history these rulers of great infamy, did not undermine the celebration of goodness and censure of vice. In fact, it was only by scrupulously depicting misdeeds without cost to realism that later generations deemed the work credible. And by acknowledging sovereignty without concealing vice, it stymied the misdeeds of others. Only after comprehending such purport in the *Spring and Autumn Annals* can one appreciate my own principle in not disallowing the Liang.

CHAPTER 3

ANNALS III: BASIC ANNALS OF LIANG

Emperor Mo [Zhu Youzhen, C.E. 888–923] was the third son of Taizu, named Youzhen.[i] He possessed a handsome exterior, a staid demeanor, sparing use of words, plus an enduring affection for Confucian literati. Invested as Prince of Jun upon the accession of Taizu, he became left commandant of the Heavenly Ascent Guard and chief director of infantry and cavalry in the eastern capital.

During the sixth month of the second year of Qianhua [C.E. 912], Emperor Taizu succumbed to an act of regicide and Zhu Yougui enthroned himself. He also murdered Youwen, the Prince of Bo, intending to blame him for the regicide. He further named the Prince of Jun as interim custodian of the eastern capital and metropolitan custodian of Kaifeng, Jing Xiang as deputy director at the Palace Secretariat with concurrent powers as chief minister, and minister of revenue Li Zhen commissioner of the Bureau of Venerable Governance. The calendar year was changed to Fengli, effective as of next year [C.E. 913].

During the second month, after arriving at the eastern capital, the Prince of Jun began plotting secretly with Zhao Yan, the honorary commandant for reserve cavalry,[1] and sent Mao Shenjiao to Weizhou to lay plans with Yang Shihou. Shihou dispatched junior lieutenant Wang Shunxian to Luoyang to enlist Yuan Xiangxian, general commander of the Dragon and Tiger Left Guard, as chief bandit suppressor [against Yougui]. At the time, a mutiny had

i. Mo, "The Last Emperor," is not an official posthumous title, but I follow the idiom of original documents.

erupted in the Dragon-Prancing regiments quartered at Huaizhou‡. Amid apprehensions among the culprits, the Prince of Jun forged an imperial edict in the name of Yougui, "the entirety of Dragon-Prancing forces, both left and right divisions now assigned to the eastern capital, are recalled to Luoyang." And to incite their fury, he added, "The Son of Heaven pursues you, in the wake of the Huaizhou‡ mutiny, intending to bury you all alive." Such words left the entire command in tears and baffled over how to respond. The Prince continued, "The Former Emperor committed thirty years to constructing a kingly enterprise, only to lie dead today at Yougui's hands. How can you possibly escape death yourselves?" Displaying a portrait of Taizu to the various commanders, he said between sobs, "By hastening to Luoyang to arrest the renegades, you might still turn calamity into good fortune." The soldiers all cheered "Ten thousand years" as they beseeched the Prince to become ruler. The Prince, meanwhile, sent a messenger to rally Yuan Xiangxian and cohort.

On the seventeenth day [March 27], Xiangxian led palace guardsmen in punishing the thugs, as Yougui perished and Du Xiao was murdered. He also dispatched Zhao Yan to the eastern capital to take possession of the imperial seal for dynastic succession. He entreated the Prince to enter Luoyang, but he reported back, "Yimen [Kaifeng County] is where Taizu launched his imperial enterprise. To the north is Bing and Fen prefectures, to the east Huaiyang and Donghai, while numerous governors' commands are located to the east as well. In coordinating commanders and mobilizing men, the advantage lies in proximity."

During the same month, Emperor Mo acceded to the throne at the eastern capital.[ii] He reverted to the Qianhua reign, year three, and restored the official and titular rank of Youwen, the deceased Prince of Bo.[2] On the fourth day of the third month [April 13], his personal name was changed to Huang.

In summer, the fifth month, Yang Shihou captured Cangzhou. In autumn, the fifth day of the ninth month [October 7], censor-in-chief Yao Ji rose to deputy director at the Palace Secretariat with ministerial powers. Jin forces [of Li Cunxu] acquired Youzhou in winter, the twelfth month. In the summer of the fourth year, eleventh day of the fourth month [C.E. May 8, 914], the court demoted Yu Jing to manager-adjutant to the governor of Laizhou. Once the Wuning governor Jiang Yin rebelled, the Tianping governor Niu Cunjie led the suppression.

....

ii. Succession to the throne is an important event, but reflecting the severe turmoil of the day, in place of the exact date only "sometime this month" appears in extant documents. The phrase "at the eastern capital" connects to earlier comments above.

In the spring, the inaugural year of Zhenming, the inaugural month [C.E. 915], Cunjie vanquished Xuzhou¶.[iii] On the seventh day of the third month [April 23], Zhao Guangfeng was dismissed as minister. Pinglu governor He Delun was reassigned as Tianxiong governor.[iv] The three prefectures of Xiang‡, Chan, and Wei‡, formerly administered by the Tianxiong command, were partitioned to form the new Zhaode command, with palace-armies commissioner Zhang Yun as governor. A mutiny at the Tianxiong command, on the twenty-ninth day, culminated in He Delun's defection and surrender to Jin.[v] Meanwhile, Li Baoheng of Bin Prefecture defected from the Qi‡ satrapy to submit to Liang rule.

In summer, first day of the sixth month [July 15], the Prince of Jin, Li Cunxu, occupied Weizhou and soon thereafter Dezhou. The Prince of Kang, Zhu Youzi, rebelled and was executed in winter, the twenty-fourth day of the tenth month [December 3].[vi] On the ninth day of the eleventh month, the reign year was changed retroactively to Zhenming. Wen Zhaotu at Yaozhou betrayed Qi‡ and reverted to dynasty. The Monarch changed his personal name to Zhen sometime this year.[vii]

The court dismissed Yang She as chief minister in the spring of the second year, eleventh day of the second month [C.E. March 17, 916]. Zhennan governor Liu Xun engaged armies of Jin at the old Yuancheng, during the third month and fled in defeat to Huazhou. Jin forces seized Wei‡ and Hui prefectures. Li Ba, the chief commander for alien suppression, rebelled and was executed. Another chief commander for alien suppression, Zhang Wen, defected to the Jin and surrendered his charge during the sixth month, summertime. Jin armies captured Xiangzhou‡ in the seventh month, autumn, and governor Zhang Yun fled for the capital, as the defecting Anguo governor, Yan Bao, surrendered to the Prince of Jin.

On the fifteenth day of the eighth month [September 14], the former grand tutor to the heir-apparent, Zhao Guangfeng, became dignitary for pub-

....

iii. Because Jiang Yin died by setting himself afire, no mention is made of "execution."
iv. The appointment of officials is generally not cited unless the act is beyond the ordinary and impacts on some other event. Here, the citation serves as background to the Tianxiong mutiny.
v. With reference to military mutinies, only the chief culprit is usually cited, but here, Delun is identified as defector due to his greater culpability as a man of senior stature. Delun should not rightfully be credited with leading the mutiny, yet he deserves censure for failing to die nobly in the face of a mutiny. The ringleader was actually Zhang Yan, but he was a man of no great consequence whom Delun could have executed and did not, so his name has been dropped and blame placed solely on Delun.
vi. Dates are not given for rebellions, but are given for the execution of rebels.
vii. The exact month and day is missing from the *Old History*.

lic works and concurrently deputy director at the Chancellery with ministerial powers. Jin armies captured Cangzhou during the ninth month, causing Henghai governor Dai Siyuan to seek sanctuary in the capital. Jin forces also overwhelmed Beizhou, where defending commander Zhang Yuande perished honorably in battle.[viii] In winter, fifteenth day of the tenth month [November 13], the court conferred ministerial powers on Zheng Jue, deputy director of the Palace Secretariat.

In the summer of the third year, thirteenth day of the fourth month [C.E. May 6, 917], the court designated Liu Qu, commandant for the Thousand-Bull Right Guard, as emissary to the Khitan. In winter, the twelfth month, Xuanyi governor He Gui was reassigned commissioner of bandit-suppressing forces at large on the northern front. On the twenty-fourth day [C.E. February 8, 918], the Monarch departed for the western capital to conduct divination ceremonies. Jin troops captured Yangliu district [Jizhou].

In the inaugural month of the fourth year, the Monarch, unable to perform the divination rituals, arrived from the western capital on the fifth day [February 18]. In the summer, the seventh day of the fourth month [May 19], vice minister of personnel Xiao Qing became deputy director of the Palace Secretariat with ministerial powers, Zhao Guangfeng dismissed as minister on the twenty-seventh [June 8]. On the first day of the twelfth month, commissioner He Gui murdered subordinate commanders Xie Yanzhang, Meng Shencheng, and Hou Wenyu. Engaging Jin armies at Huliu on the twenty-fourth, he was defeated. Taining governor Zhang Shoujin defected to the Jin and surrendered his charge sometime this year.[ix] The suppression was entrusted to Liu Xun, the former military training commissioner for Haozhou now designated commissioner of pacification and regional order for Yanzhou.

In the spring, the inaugural month of the fifth year [C.E. 919], the Jin quartered troops at Desheng Commandery [Puzhou].[x] On the first day of the eighth month [August 28], the court reassigned the metropolitan custodian of Kaifeng, Wang Zan, to commissioner of bandit-suppressing regiments at large along the northern front. Liu Xun overwhelmed defectors at Yanzhou and executed Zhang Shoujin in winter, the tenth month. Jin armies captured Puyang County in the twelfth month. The newly named commissioner of bandit-suppressing forces at large for the north was Huo Yanwei, the former Tianping governor.

....

viii. "To perish in battle" [*sizhi*] means an honorable death.

ix. Owing to an oversight in the *Old History*, the month and day are unknown, so these events are cited at the year's end as backdrop to next year's conquest of Yanzhou.

x. In the absence of victory or defeat, the deployment of armies is generally not noted [as indicated earlier], except here, where the event affects the balance of power between Liang and Jin.

In the summer of the sixth year, seventh day of the fourth month [C.E. April 28, 920], the court announced a reduction for all criminal sentences of capital punishment and below. On the thirteenth, the left secretary at the Imperial Secretariat, Li Qi, became deputy director at the Palace Secretariat with concurrent powers as chief minister. Tongzhou fell to Zhu Youqian, the Hezhong governor, who killed standing governor Cheng Quanhui before surrendering to the Prince of Jin. Charged with the suppression was the Taining governor, Liu Xun. In autumn, the seventh month, the diabolical renegade Wu Yi, of nearby Chenzhou‡, proclaimed himself "Son of Heaven." On the second day of the ninth month [October 16], palace services officer Lang Gongyuan received commission as goodwill ambassador to the Khitan. Rebel Wu Yi was executed in the tenth month, winter.

In spring, the inaugural year of Longde [C.E. 921], the Zhao commander Zhang Wenli, after killing his ruler Wang Rong, requested reinforcements of Liang, a request denied.[xi] On the first day of the third month, the court proscribed the intermingling of monks and nuns. Zhu Youneng, the Prince of Hui and prefect of Chenzhou‡, rebelled. In summer, the first day of the fifth month [June 9], the court announced a minor amnesty, the retroactive inauguration of a new reign name [Longde], and reduction in sentences below banishment. It issued a pardon for Youneng, sometime that autumn, his noble status reduced to Marquis of Fangling. It also named the Tianping governor, Dai Siyuan, commissioner of bandit suppression for forces at large on the northern front. Siyuan faced Jin armies in battle at Qicheng, during the tenth month, ending in defeat.

In the spring, the inaugural month of the second year [C.E. 922], Dai Siyuan stormed Weizhou and claimed Cheng'an County. In autumn, the eighth month, the interim regent for infantry and cavalry at Huazhou, Duan Ning, attacked Weizhou‡ and apprehended its prefect, Li Cunru. Dai Siyuan seized Qimen, Gongcheng, and Xinxiang.

In the spring, the third month of the third year [C.E. 923], Li Jitao defected from the Jin to surrender Luzhou. In summer, the fourth intercalary month, Tang armies[3] captured Yunzhou.[xii] On the seventeenth day of the fifth month [July 3], the Xuanyi governor Wang Yanzhang became commissioner of bandit suppression for forces at large on the northern front; he captured the

....

xi. Wenli, formerly adopted by Rong, is also known by the name "Wang Deming." Referring to him here as "Zhang Wenli" merely follows convention in the *Old History*.

xii. The Prince of Jin, even before becoming emperor, considered himself a peer with Liang as rival to power. His adoption of the dynastic name of Tang had neither positive nor negative effect on the Liang and, therefore, is not cited here. Reference to "men of Tang" [no longer Jin], in the wake of formally declaring dynasty, appears because events dictate.

southern city of Desheng Commandery. Replacing him as commissioner of bandit-suppressing at-large forces, in the eighth month of autumn, was Duan Ning. Vanguard commander Kang Yanxiao defected and surrendered to the Tang.

In winter, the fourth day of the tenth month [November 14], the Xuanyi governor Wang Yanzhang engaged Tang armies in battle at Zhongdu County [Yanzhou].[xiii] Defeated, he perished in battle. The men of Tang captured Caozhou. Some thugs pilfered the imperial seals and fled to Tang.[4] On the eighth day, the Emperor expired.[xiv] The Liang collapsed.[xv]

....

xiii. Official appointments tend not to be cited, except as in this case: Yanzhang went into battle against the Tang after dismissal as bandit-suppressing commander—that is, he assumed command of armies without a court commission.

xiv. He was thirty-six *sui*.

xv. Writing that "the Liang collapsed" stresses the haste with which Zhuangzong of Tang came to power: Zhuangzong was enthroned as sovereign of Tang in the fourth month, whereas Liang rule did not expire until the tenth—proof that the Tang refused to defer its own dynastic ambitions until completely annihilating its rival.

CHAPTER 4

ANNALS IV: BASIC ANNALS OF TANG

Zhuangzong[1] [Li Cunxu, C.E. 885–926], the Radiantly Sagacious, Divinely Earnest, and Filial Emperor, descended from a people initially known as Zhuye who originated among the western Tujue Turks. In later times, they identified themselves as Shatuo and adopted Zhuye as surname.

In the reign of Tang Emperor Dezong [C.E. 780–804], a certain Zhuye Jinzhong resided at Jinman Prefecture of the Beiting region [Jimusaier, Xinjiang]. When a chieftain of Tubo Tibetans conquered Beiting, in the Zhenyuan era [C.E. 785–804], he relocated Jinzhong eastward to Ganzhou to serve as frontier guard. But the succeeding chieftain was defeated by the Huihu Uighurs, permitting Jinzhong to flee eastward with his son, Zhiyi. An angry chieftain, in response, pursued them to Shimen Pass, where Jinzhong died in battle. Thus, Zhiyi personally made the flight farther east on his own, submitting to Tang rule and accepting sanctuary at Yanzhou†. There, he entered the ranks of Fan Xizhao, the governor of Hexi. The reassignment of Xizhao as governor of Taiyuan caused Zhiyi to join him and assume residence at the new city of Shenwuchuan, Dingxiang County. His legions ten thousand strong—all brave and brash and adept as archers and horsemen—hence formed the so-called Shatuo Army.

Zhuye Zhiyi left a son, Chixin [d. C.E. 883], at the time of his death. During the tenth year of Xiantong, in the reign of Emperor Yizong [C.E. 869], the commandant of the Divine Strategy Guard, Kang Chengxun, led eighteen assisting commanders in a punitive strike against the rebel Pang Xun at Xuzhou¶. Zhuye Chixin assisted by directing a third platoon of Shatuo tribesmen as suppression brigades at large for Taiyuan. His merit in the crushing of Xun led to assignments as grand protector of the nomads and governor of the Zhenwu command, as well as conferral of the name Li Guochang and registry as a subject of Tang. As the Shatuo tend to be aggressive, Guochang grew progressively arbitrary as he persevered for recognition by the court, behavior that Emperor Yizong found troubling. In the thirteenth year [C.E. 872], Guochang was reassigned as prefect of Yunzhou‡ and defense commissioner of Datong command, but he declined the post on the pretext of illness.

The son of Guochang, *Li Keyong* [C.E. 856–908], grew into a man so adept at mounted archery that he could hit twin flying ducks from a reclining position. He became a defense coordinator for Yunzhou‡. Once Guochang rejected the court's reassignment, Keyong moved to murder the current defense commissioner at Datong, Duan Wenchu, and seize control of Yun‡, where he installed himself as interim regent. The Tang court responded by reassigning its equerry for the imperial stud, Lu Jianfang, as the Zhenwu governor charged with the suppression, assisted by forces from You and Bing prefectures. Jianfang's men made it as far as Lanzhou when they were routed. Thereafter, the Shatuo could pillage the region north of Dai and create a permanent border menace.

Emperor Xizong acceded to power a year later [C.E. 873]. Believing the former Taiyuan governor, Li Ye, to have once enjoyed Shatuo goodwill, he hoped to win them over by arranging, upon Ye's death, for his son Jun to become the Lingwu governor and commander of reconciliation for the three tribes of Shatuo across six prefectures.[i] Li Keyong was appointed defense commissioner of the Datong command. Guochang had lived in Taiyuan for some time before leaving to launch an assault against the Tangut, in response to which Helian Duo, a man of Tuhun extraction, overpowered Zhenwu with a surprise hit. When word reached Keyong, he attempted a rescue mission for his father from the direction of Yunzhou‡, but authorities there had similarly sealed off the surrounding passes to resist him. Father and son, now with nowhere to go, plundered the region of Wei¶ and Shuo, where they eventually acquired some three thousand soldiers. Guochang thereby secured Weizhou¶ as Keyong reoccupied the new city. Emperor Xizong consequently launched a punitive campaign against the Shatuo, with Helian Duo as governor of Datong and Li Jun as bandit-suppressing commissioner for the northern Dai area.

....

i. I lack evidence on the location of the "six prefectures" and the identity of the "three tribes," although the *History of Tang* contains references to the assignment of commissioners over them.

In the fifth year of Qianfu [C.E. 878], the Shatuo overpowered Zhelu Commandery, then Kelan, as Tang armies faced successive defeats. The greatly emboldened Shatuo proceeded to occupy Wei¶ and Shuo to the north, while to the south intruding as far as the prefectures of Xin‡, Dai, Lan, and Shi, even up to Taigu County [Taiyuan]. A drive against the Shatuo began during the inaugural year of Guangming [C.E. 880]: commissioner of bandit suppression Li Zhuo rendezvoused with Li Keju of Youzhou and Helian Duo of Yunzhou‡. A standoff between Keyong and Keju occurred at the Xiongwu command, but the uncle of Keyong, Youjin, relinquished to Li Zhuo the prefectures of Wei¶ and Shuo, the news forcing a speedy retreat for Keyong and his men. But chased by Keju, he was routed at the Yao'ershan. At Weizhou¶, Li Zhuo assisted others in a pincer action against Keyong, dashing him once more. In the face of such devastating defeats for the Shatuo, father and son absconded for Tartar domains.

Brave and brash in youth, Li Keyong was dubbed by troops as "Li the Crow" [Ya'er]. After rising in stature, he also came to be called the "One-Eyed Dragon," having lost one eye. Throughout the northern Dai region his reputation swelled. Yet the longer he lingered in Tartar lands, the more he agonized over ambitions unrealized, even suspecting his hosts of scheming against him. Thus, he often went hunting with men of similar prowess. While driving a spike into wood or brandishing a horsewhip, he could simultaneously hit targets with an arrow from a hundred feet away, causing even this courageous cohort to defer to him as divinely gifted.

The rebel Huang Chao had already overrun the capital when a militia recruiter for the northern Dai region, Chen Jingsi, dispatched the earliest wave of Shatuo mercenaries, in the inaugural year of Zhonghe [C.E. 881]. Some ten thousand Tuhun mercenaries under Anqing had departed for the capital when a mutiny erupted within Shatuo ranks at Jiangzhou. A massive pillage ensued and they withdrew. Jingsi now deduced that Keyong alone could command the Shatuo, so he was summoned by imperial orders to serve in Tartar lands as prefect for Daizhou and governor of at-large armies north of Yanmen. He led a contingent some ten thousand strong, a combination of Chinese and aliens, in departing from the Shiling Pass, only to demand campaign subsidies for his army upon reaching Taiyuan. When governor Zheng Congdang delivered only a thousand strings of cash and a thousand piculs of rice, Keyong deemed him parsimonious and unleashed marauders to plunder widely before returning north.

In the eleventh month of the second year [C.E. 882], Chen Jingsi and Li Keyong prepared once more to deliver seventeen thousand men to the capital, a combination of infantry and cavalry. They departed Hezhong in the inaugural month of the next year [C.E. 883]. Upon pitching camp at Qiankeng [southern Tongzhou], the cronies of Huang Chao shrieked in alarm, "The Crow's army is here!" He prevailed over a Chao lieutenant, Huang Ye, at Shidi Gorge in the second month, then over Zhao Zhang and Shang Rang at Liangtian Slope in the third month, leaving a trail of corpses some thirty *li* long.

At the time, the armies of assorted governors had converged on Changan in a massive battle at Wei bridge. Defeated, the bandits retreated into the city, but Keyong exploited the momentum of victory to pursue them through the Guangtai gates, doing battle at the Wangchun mansion's Shengyang palace. A vanquished Chao fled to Lantian Pass, and peace returned to the capital, Keyong's military merits premier among the governors. The Son of Heaven honored Keyong as interim dignitary for public works with ministerial standing, assigned governor of Hedong. Guochang became governor of at-large regiments north of Yanmen, dying in the tenth month.[2]

During the eleventh month, Li Keyong directed younger brother Kexiu to raid Meng Fangli, the Zhaoyi governor. Kexiu captured the two prefectures of Ze and Lu, while Fangli fled to the eastern mountain region [Shandong]. The three prefectures of Xing, Ming, and Ci were subsequently reorganized under a new Zhaoyi command.[ii] As Huang Chao retreated to the south, he won the surrender of Qin Zongquan at Caizhou, then raided Chen‡ Prefecture. Keyong directed a force of fifty thousand in the relief of Chen‡, during the fourth year [C.E. 884]. His troops issuing from Tianjing Pass, he requested passage through Heyang, an accommodation refused by Zhuge Shuang, so he had to cross the Yellow River from Hezhong Prefecture. In the fourth month, he routed Shang Rang at Taikang and Huang Ye at Xihua. The rebel Chao continued to fight as he retreated, but Keyong chased him to Zhongmou and caught up before he could cross the river. The rebels were rendered a stunning setback. They lost again at Fengqiu as Huang Chao fled for his life. Keyong trailed in hot pursuit, covering some two hundred *li* over a full day and night, but could not overtake Chao's men, so he turned around at Yuanqu.

During passage through Bianzhou [Kaifeng], as Li Keyong rested his armies at Fengchan Monastery, Zhu Quanzhong invited him to a banquet at Shangyuan Post. As the night progressed and the wine abated, Keyong lay in a drunken stupor when Quanzhong's hidden men emerged to set random fires. An attendant to Keyong, Guo Jingzhu, then extinguished nearby candles and hid him beneath a bed, splashing water on his face to alert him to the crisis. A

....

ii. The Zhaoyi command, under the Tang, originally consisted of five prefectures in the circuits both east and west of the mountains; but Ze and Lu now belonged to Jin, while Xing, Ming and Ci were occupied by Meng Fangli. Thus, there existed two separate Zhaoyi commands at the time.

heavy rain happened to pour from the heavens to extinguish the fires. And by the mere light of lightning, Keyong and attendants "Stone Mountain Xue" and "He the Uighur" managed to locate the Weishi gate and scuttle down, finding safe passage to their own barracks. Upon returning to Taiyuan in the seventh month, Keyong lodged a complaint over the matter with the Tang court, seeking the augmenting of forces against Kaifeng. He even arranged for younger brother Kexiu to quarter some ten thousand men at Hezhong in anticipation of action. Emperor Xizong preferred to mediate the matter, while citing Keyong's merit in the Huang Chao suppression to invest him as Prince of Longxi.

In the inaugural year of Guangqi [C.E. 885], tensions emerged between Wang Chongrong of Hezhong and eunuch Tian Lingzi, causing Chongrong's reassignment to Yanzhou. His replacement as governor of Hezhong was Wang Chucun of Dingzhou, the court ordering Keyong[iii] to provide a military escort for Chucun to his district. Chongrong prompted someone to inveigle Keyong, saying, "The Son of Heaven has ordered Chongrong to await your arrival, then join Chucun in executing you." The agent even feigned to have an imperial edict, showing it to [an illiterate] Keyong and attributing the affair to the "schemes of Zhu Quanzhong." Keyong believed him and petitioned the court, eight times in all, for a punitive strike against Quanzhong. Emperor Xizong's repeated refusals utterly riled Keyong.

Chongrong was now in defiance of reassignment orders, so Emperor Xizong resorted to punitive action, commissioning Zhu Mei of Binzhou and Li Changfu of Fengxiang. Keyong rebelled, however, and extended military aid to Chongrong. Defeating Mei at Shayuan [Tongzhou], he proceeded to raid the capital, setting random fires and plundering widely. The Son of Heaven fled the capital for sanctuary at Xingyuan, as Keyong withdrew to quarter troops at Hezhong. Zhu Mei also rebelled, sending his men to stalk the Son of Heaven, but not succeeding. They apprehended instead the Prince of Xiang, Li Wen, pressing him to proclaim himself emperor as they pitched camps at Fengxiang. Emperor Xizong deemed Keyong the only man capable of crushing Mei, even though deployment proved unfeasible. Keyong had close ties to the chief director of local forces, Yang Fugong, dating back to the Huang Chao suppression in the capital. The Emperor thus had master of admonition Liu Chongwang present an imperial summons to Keyong to lead the campaign against Mei, conveying this as the personal wish of Fugong. Keyong feigned consent yet refused to act.

....

iii. Having yet to claim illicit titles, Keyong is not cited as "Prince."

Meng Fangli died during the next year [C.E. 886] and younger brother Meng Qian succeeded him as governor. Li Keyong stormed and overran Qian in the inaugural year of Dashun [C.E. 890], claiming the three prefectures of Xing, Ming, and Ci. He further delegated An Jinjun to direct the drive against Helian Duo at Yunzhou‡. Li Kuangwei of Youzhou came to Duo's assistance, however, and in a contest at Weizhou¶ prevailed decidedly over Jinjun. Losses of the sort by Keyong led Kuangwei, Duo, and Zhu Quanzhong to petition the court for a campaign against him. Emperor Zhaozong opposed military action, noting Keyong's exceptional distinction in the Huang Chao suppression. The matter was referred to executives above rank four at the three departments, where majority opinion also opposed military action. Chief minister Zhang Jun singularly favored a campaign. Shatuo aggression against Emperor Xizong that once forced him to flee to Xingyuan, he argued, demanded a lethal retaliation. Military furnishings officer Yang Fugong, on cordial terms with Keyong, remonstrated aggressively against the action, convincing Emperor Zhaozong, who formally notified Quanzhong and cohort of his decision. Zhang Jun nonetheless grew ever rigid in his position, having been secretly bribed by Quanzhong. Emperor Zhaozong had no alternative. Jun was assigned general commander of at-large infantry and cavalry for the four fronts at Taiyuan, with Han Jian as deputy commander.

At the time, a mutinous commander at Luzhou, Feng Ba, had defected from Li Keyong and surrendered to the Liang, which authorized Ge Congzhou to occupy the city. The Tang court responded by assigning the current metropolitan custodian of Jingzhao, Sun Kui, as the Zhaoyi governor [of Luzhou]. Keyong dispatched Li Cunxiao to detain Kui at Zhangzi and instead had Kang Junli claim Luzhou. In the eleventh month, the armies of Zhang Jun and Li Keyong battled at Yindi Pass: for all three contests, Jun lost each time, forcing him and Han Jian to flee for cover. Keyong's men could now conduct a massive plunder of Jin and Jiang prefectures, scavenging an area of a thousand *li* all the way to Hezhong. Keyong memorialized the court in self-reproach, his words crudely insulting. The Son of Heaven responded with magnanimity, taking personal fault for the problem.

In the second month of the second year [C.E. 891], the court reinstated Keyong as the Hedong governor and Prince of Longxi, bestowing titular rank as honorary grand preceptor and palace secretary. In the fourth month, Keyong attacked Helian Duo at Yunzhou‡ and imposed a blockade to last over a hundred days, forcing Duo to flee to the Tuhun. In the wake of a great gathering at Taiyuan, in the eighth month, Keyong confederates departed Jin and Jiang prefectures to plunder Huai‡ and Meng, extending eastward to Xing. A drive against Wang Rong now ensued at Zhenzhou. Keyong constructed palisades to the west of Changshan, permitting ten or so horsemen to cross the Hutuo River and spy on the enemy. He encountered heavy rains, however, as flatlands developed puddles several feet deep. In this way, Zhen defenders rushed Keyong and forced him to take cover in a forest. There, trying to calm his horse, he said, "For generations at Taiyuan, our horses have never neighed." And, indeed, the horse happened not to whine, sparing him exposure. Meanwhile, the advance armies of Li Cunxiao captured Lincheng and proceeded northward to attack Yuanshi [Zhaozhou]. But when Li Kuangwei intervened on behalf of Wang Rong, Keyong's men returned to Xingzhou.

In the inaugural year of Jingfu [C.E. 892], Wang Rong raided Xing Prefecture, Li Cunxin and Li Sixun vanquishing him at Yaoshan. Li Keyong assisted Wang Chucun in an offensive against Rong at the new city [Zhenzhou] during the second month, Rong prevailing this time. In the eighth month, Li Kuangwei raided Yun‡ Prefecture with the intent of drawing out the troops of Keyong, but Keyong penetrated the Yun‡ theater undetected and hit Kuangwei from the rear, forcing his retreat. Li Cunxiao defected at Xingzhou in the tenth month.

In the second year [C.E. 893], Li Cunxiao had turned to Wang Rong for assistance, causing Keyong to deploy regiments at Jingxing in a preemptive strike against Rong. Keyong also struck hard against the holdings of Rong at Pingshan, even as a letter was sent to sway him. Hard-pressed, Rong struck a truce with Keyong, presenting some five hundred thousand bolts of silk and committing regiments to join the Xingzhou offensive. During the third month of the inaugural year of Qianning [C.E. 894], Keyong apprehended and killed Li Cunxiao. A drive against Youzhou began sometime that winter, Li Kuangchou forced to abandon the city and flee to Jingcheng [Cangzhou], where stalkers murdered him. Liu Rengong replaced him as interim regent.

In the second year [C.E. 895], the death of Wang Chongying of Hezhong triggered a succession feud between two of his sons, Ke and Gong. Li Keyong petitioned for the installation of Ke, while Gong's selection enjoyed the support of Li Maozhen of Fengxiang, Wang Xingyu of Binning, and Han Jian of Huazhou‡. Initially uncomfortable selecting either man, Emperor Zhaozong reassigned chief minister Cui Yin to the Hezhong governorship, later accepting Keyong's counsel to install Ke. The decision infuriated Li Maozhen and sympathizers, who combined the armies of three districts to assault the capital, only to disband upon news of Keyong's similar deployment of armies. In the sixth month, Keyong attacked Jiangzhou and beheaded prefect Wang Yao: the younger brother of Gong, Yao had sided with him in the succession feud. As Keyong reached Hezhong in the seventh month, Wang Xingyue of Tongzhou fled to the capital. Professing that "a hundred thousand Shatuo had arrived," he had conspired to escort the Son of Heaven to Binzhou. A similar scheme to forcibly relocate the Emperor, this time to Fengxiang, had been concocted by

Yan Gui, the purported son of Li Maozhen. Chaos pervaded the capital, Emperor Zhaozong taking refuge at Shimen Pass [Yuanzhou].

For over a month, the armies of Li Keyong remained stationary without advancing when clansmen Li Jiepi (Prince of Yan) and Li Yun (Prince of Dan) were sent to Keyong at the Emperor's behest: employing brotherly courtesies, they apprised him of the emergency. Keyong responded by advancing his men to Wei bridge, during the eighth month, the court now naming him general commander of at-large forces on the Bin/Ning command's four fronts. Emperor Zhaozong hence returned to the capital. In the eleventh month, Keyong stormed Bin Prefecture, whose fall forced Wang Xingyu to flee to Qing where he was killed. Keyong then withdrew to quarter troops at Yunyang and request authorization for a strike against Maozhen. Emperor Zhaozong reasoned that by commending Keyong, he could deflate his rivalry with Maozhen and ameliorate current tensions, so Keyong was honored as "Subject of Merit, Devout and Proper, Who Tames the Menacing" and invested Prince of Jin.

At the time, armies of the Prince of Jin had been garrisoned north of the Wei River, where rains had fallen for sixty days. Some encouraged Keyong to proceed to the capital, but he proved indecisive. Ge Yu, the governor's chief military attaché, advised him to the contrary, "The Son of Heaven, since returning from Shimen Pass, has enjoyed not a moment's rest. The hearts of mankind will take no solace in the Prince's crossing of the Wei River with his armies! Delivering your ruler from harm should suffice. Why bother to appear at court?" A humored Keyong exclaimed, "If Ge Yu has no faith in me, what can I expect of the world?" He thus regrouped his men and withdrew.

In the inaugural month of the third year [C.E. 896], Emperor Zhaozong prepared to restore Zhang Jun as chief minister. Li Keyong characterized this as the "handiwork of Zhu Quanzhong" and petitioned the court: "On the morning that Your Majesty names Jun minister, I swear before sunset to reach the royal palaces." Such threats horrified the capital and caused Jun's nomination to be abruptly aborted. During the campaign of Zhu Quanzhong against Yan and Yun prefectures, Keyong dispatched Li Cunxin to negotiate passage through Weizhou in order to assist Zhu Xuan. But as Cunxin personally quartered troops at Shen County, his men trespassed upon and plundered the outskirts of Wei. They were ambushed by Luo Hongxin, Cunxin fleeing westward to Mingzhou in defeat. Keyong now personally commanded a rush on Wei, engaging the enemy at Huanshui County and losing his son, Luoluo. In the sixth month, he captured over ten districts belonging to Wei, including Cheng'an, Huanshui, and Linzhang. He further overwhelmed Wei defenders at Bailong Lake, in the tenth month, before advancing against Guanyin Gate. Only the arrival of relief from Quanzhong caused Keyong to desist.

In the fourth year [C.E. 897], Liu Rengong rebelled against Jin, causing Li Keyong to deploy a force of fifty thousand in a retaliatory strike against him, but Keyong was roundly defeated at Ansai. During the inaugural year of Guanghua [C.E. 898], Zhu Quanzhong charged Ge Congzhou with offensives against the three prefectures of Xing, Ming, and Ci, which succumbed. In retaliation, Keyong unleashed Zhou Dewei, who departed from Qingshankou and engaged Congzhou at Zhanggongqiao. Dewei was badly beaten. The defending commander of Lu Prefecture, Xue Zhiqin, died sometime that winter and his prefecture came under the occupation of Li Hanzhi, who defected to surrender Luzhou to Quanzhong.

During the second year [C.E. 899], Zhu Quanzhong deployed Shi Shucong in the successful raid on Chengtian Commandery. Shucong followed through with the conquest of Liaozhou, expanding as far as Yuci County when routed by Zhou Dewei at Dongwo Post. Ze and Lu prefectures were reclaimed sometime that autumn by Li Sizhao. In the third year [C.E. 900], Sizhao thwarted the Bianzhou armies [of Zhu Quanzhong] at Shahe, reclaiming Mingzhou. Quanzhong responded by personally organizing a blockade of the city, as Sizhao fled. Encountering an ambush by Bian forces at Qingshankou, Sizhao was severely beaten. Huaizhou‡ was claimed by Sizhao sometime that autumn. In this year, the armies of Bian struck Zhen and Ding prefectures, which hereafter broke with the Jin and submitted to Quanzhong.

Zhu Quanzhong, invested Prince of Liang in the inaugural year of Tianfu [C.E. 901], proceeded to conquer the prefectures of Jin, Jiang, and Hezhong, apprehending Wang Ke. In the wake of losing three dependent states, the Jin sued for peace with Liang, conveying by envoy the requisite documents and gratuities. The Prince of Liang perceived the Jin as vulnerable to conquest, declaring, "The Jin speaks of alliance, but its letters are composed in arrogance." He hence launched a massive campaign against the Jin. In the fourth month, Shi Shucong approached from Tianjing Pass, Zhang Wenjing from Xinkou Pass, Ge Congzhou from Tumen Pass, Wang Chuzhi from Feihu, and Hou Yan from Yindi. Shucong succeeded in taking Ze and Lu prefectures, his lieutenant Bai Fengguo seizing Chengtian Commandery. Capitulation to Liang forces also occurred at Liao Prefecture, by defending commander Zhang E, and at Fen by defending commander Li Tang. Such turns struck terror in Jin leaders. Then, heavy rains happened to fall from the heavens, unleashing contagious diseases within the Liang army that caused its men to scatter. The Jin recaptured Fen and executed defector Li Tang, during the fifth month. Zhou Dewei and Li Sizhao acquired Ci‡ and Xi prefectures in the sixth month.

An offensive against Jin and Jiang prefectures, begun in the second year [C.E. 902], ended in a rout at Pu County [Xizhou]. The armies of Liang now exploited this new momentum to crush the three prefectures of Fen, Ci‡, and Xi. A blockade of Taiyuan ensued. Such developments terrified Keyong, who contemplated absconding either to Yunzhou‡ or to Xiongnu lands. In the midst of his indecision, a sweeping epidemic broke out within the Liang military, forcing it to disband. Zhou Dewei could thereby retake Fen, Ci‡, and Xi prefectures.

In the fourth year [C.E. 904], the Tang capital was moved to Luoyang by Liang leaders, the reign changed to Tianyou. Keyong believed that the Liang had coerced the Son of Heaven into relocating the court and regarded Tianyou as a bogus reign, so spurning it, he continued to acknowledge the former Tianfu reign. A meeting with Khitan ruler Abaoji occurred at Yunzhong, during the fifth year [C.E. 905], where they entered a "fraternal" alliance.

During the sixth year [of Tianfu, C.E. 906], the Liang raided Cangzhou, part of the Yan¤ domain. The Prince of Yan, Liu Rengong, thus sought reinforcements from Keyong. Resenting the previous duplicity of Rengong, Keyong was inclined to refuse when son Cunxu admonished:

> This is our moment to surge ahead! Today, some seven or eight out of ten parts of the world come under Liang control. Even such mighty foes as Zhao, Wei, and Zhongshan dare not disobey its directives. In effect, no serious challenge to the Liang can be found north of the Yellow River—Rengong and ourselves the only remaining threats. Should Yan¤ and Jin consolidate powers, it would not bode well for the Liang, to be sure. For men who aspire to rule the world, rushing to a rival's assistance after successive ordeals—to wit, refusing to cling to petty grievances—represents a generosity certain to win its goodwill. This is, as the saying goes, "obtaining multiple fruits through a single good deed," an opportunity we can ill afford to squander.

Keyong concurred, and on behalf of Yan¤, launched a successful raid on Lu Prefecture and forced Liang besiegers to withdraw. He named Li Sizhao interim regent for Lu. In the seventh year [C.E. 907], a Liang force of a hundred thousand campaigned against Lu and employed dual ramparts around the entire city wall. In response, Zhou Dewei was sent to relieve Lu, his men forting at Luanliu. Keyong fell ill that winter. Sometime this year, the Liang overthrew the Tang, but Keyong acknowledged the Tang calendar: fourth year of Tianyou.

In the inaugural month of the fifth year [of Tianyou], nineteenth day [C.E. February 23, 908], Li Keyong died at the age of fifty-three *sui*. Son Cunxu succeeded him, burying Keyong at Yanmen Pass [Daizhou].

WE LAMENT. Frequent is the loss of information as generations pass, losses scarcely attributable to official historians alone. Presumably, the ancestors of the Li house originated among the western Tujue Turks and were initially dubbed Zhuye. They personally assumed the designation "Shatuo" in later generations and Zhuye as their surname, while honoring Bayegu as progenitor. The preface [to the *Old History*] states,[3] "The Shatuo belonged to the barren lands of Beiting. During the Tang-dynasty reign of Taizong, the various tribes of western Tujue were broken and the Tongluo and Pugu peoples resettled across that wilderness. Forming the special prefecture of Shatuo, their ancestor Bayegu became protector-general and bequeathed the post in hereditary fashion to sons and grandsons. After serving for generations as protector-generals at Shatuo, his descendants came to call themselves 'Shatuo.'" Having scrutinized extant records, however, I find such representations all erroneous.

Northern barbarians have no surnames, after all, so Zhuye simply designates a tribe. Moreover, Bayegu was contemporary with the Zhuye, not some progenitor. No prefecture of Shatuo existed in the Tang reign of Taizong either. After conquering the western Tujue, Taizong dispersed their tribes and established the thirteen prefectures, Tongluo entrusted with the Guilin protectorate, Pugu with the Jinwei protectorate, and Bayegu with the Youling protectorate. There was no Shatuo intendancy. Among the Tie'le tribes of the western Tujue, at the time, the Yantuo and Ashina were the largest subgroups. Other tribes included the Tongluo, Pugu, and Bayegu, more than ten in all and rather small. Smaller still were the tribes of Chuyue and Chumi. Zhuye merely signifies an ancillary tribe of the Chuyue. The Tang had forced the Bayegu into submission by the twenty-second year of Emperor Taizong [C.E. 648], and only a year later, Ashina Helu rebelled. In the second year of Yonghui during Gaozong's reign [C.E. 651], Zhuye Guzhu followed Helu in battle at Laoshan, where defeat came at the hands of Heli of the Qibi. He hereafter vanished. Another hundred and fifty or sixty years later, in the reign of Emperor Xianzong, Zhuye Jinzhong and son Zhiyi surfaced in the Middle Kingdom, assuming the designation Shatuo and the surname Zhuye.

"Shatuo" refers to a vast wasteland south of the Jinsha Mountains and east of the Pulei Sea. And since the time of the Chuyue, occupiers of such lands have been dubbed the Shatuo-Tujue. But the northern barbarians lack a written language to preserve their past, and the Zhuye were too small to be noted elsewhere, their posterity losing touch with their own legacy. Once the imperial surname, Li, was conferred on the grandson of Jinzhong, the house assumed such prominence that barbarian peoples came to speak of the Shatuo as noble stock.

CHAPTER 5

ANNALS V: BASIC ANNALS OF TANG

Li Cunxu was the eldest son of Keyong. Previously, when Keyong vanquished Meng Fangli at Xingzhou [C.E. 890] and withdrew his men to Shangdang, they banqueted at Sanchui Ridge as musicians performed the "Song to Longevity." Already wasted by age, his voice assumed a cavernous melancholy as listeners sat in solemnity. By his side was Cunxu, five *sui* at the time.[1] A pensive Keyong stroked his beard as he pointed to the boy, saying with a smile, "I am rich in experience and see a true prodigy in this boy. Who is to say, twenty years hence, that he will not replace me on a battlefield like this?" At eleven *sui*, Cunxu accompanied Keyong in the rout of Wang Xingyu, later appearing in the capital for the formal pronouncement of victory. Emperor Zhaozong, astonished by his robust exterior, conferred gifts of water-foul goblet and kingfisher platter. Patting him on the back, he remarked, "This boy, endowed with fabulous features, will certainly enjoy fame and fortune someday. You should not forget your royal family." As an adult, Cunxu proved gifted as horseman and archer and exuded a bravado exceeding that of ordinary men. He was also modestly familiar with the *Spring and Autumn Annals* and could appreciate its principal thrust. He especially reveled in singing, dancing, and theatrical performances.

In the inaugural month of the fifth year of Tianyou [C.E. 908], he inherited powers as Prince at Taiyuan. His uncle Kening subsequently assassinated Li Cunzhi, the military inspector-in-chief, such that charges of sedition were leveled against Kening by palace favorite Shi Jingrong. In the second month, after apprehending and slaying him, Cunxu informed Zhou Dewei of the mourning underway for the deceased Prince and troubles triggered by his uncle. Dewei thereby returned with his men from Luanliu to Taiyuan.

Upon learning of a state funeral underway at Jin and Dewei's withdrawal of his men, Liang besiegers slightly slackened their alert along the dual ramparts. The Prince [Cunxu] proposed to commanders, "Liang leaders know that I happen to be in formal mourning, they also regard my youth and inexperience as precluding constructive action. We should rightfully exploit their inattentiveness to strike fast." Thus, he and his men rushed Shangdang [Luzhou]. En route, he sighed after reaching Sanchui Ridge, "At precisely this site, the Former Prince once banqueted his men." A vast fog happened to fill the sky and absorb the daylight. His troops advanced through the fog to attack the dual ramparts of Liang besiegers and pierce them, dealing a shattering blow to the enemy. He returned triumphantly to announce the feat before the ancestral temple. In the ninth month, Wang Jian, the Prince of Shu and Li Maozhen, the Prince of Qi attended Yang Chongben in an assault on Da'an Commandery, Liang territory. The Prince of Jin similarly had Zhou Dewei attack Liang contingents at Jinzhou, vanquishing them at Shenshan.

In the sixth year [C.E. 909], the Liang defector Liu Zhijun approached the Prince of Jin for military assistance. The Prince personally commanded a force to Yindi Pass while also directing Zhou Dewei to raid Jinzhou. Liang troops were defeated at Mengkeng. During the winter of the seventh year [C.E. 910], as the Liang deployed Wang Jingren in a drive against Zhao, the Prince of Zhao, Wang Rong, approached the Prince for relief. The various commanders, apprehensive that Wang Rong might be duplicitous, opposed the issuing of troops; the Prince did not concur and chose to assist Zhao. In the inaugural month of the eighth year [C.E. 911], Liang men were defeated at Baixiang County [Zhaozhou]: twenty thousand men lost their heads, three hundred commanders and their lieutenants were captured, and three thousand horses procured. A drive against Xingzhou ensued. In the absence of victory, a contingent was left behind to encircle the prefecture, the Prince personally scurrying for a raid against Weizhou. Zhou Dewei was sent separately to storm Xiajin and Gaotang counties, Liang territory, as part of a drive against Bozhou. Dewei prevailed at Dongwu and Chaocheng counties, suddenly to descend on Liyang, Linhe, and Qimen counties, as Xinxiang and Gongcheng were plundered.

Liu Shouguang, the Prince of Yan, began augmenting his military owing to the penetration of Jin armies so deep into the Liang domain. Despite professing support for the Jin cause, the Prince of Jin felt sufficiently threatened to pull back his men. A meeting with Wang Rong, the Prince of Zhao, took place at Chengtian Commandery during the seventh month, as Liu Shouguang declared himself emperor at Yan¤. In the inaugural month of the ninth year [C.E. 912], the court sent Zhou Dewei to rendezvous with troops from Zhen and Ding in the campaign against Yan¤. Shouguang turned to the Liang for relief. It responded with a raid against Zhao and a massacre at Zaoqiang, as Li Cunshen fled in defeat. Zhu Youqian defected from the Liang during the eighth month, surrendering the Hezhong command to the Prince. After the Liang had dispatched Kang Huaiying for a punitive strike against Youqian, he reversed allegiances back to Liang while keeping covert ties to Jin. In the tenth month of the tenth year [C.E. 913], Liu Shouguang offered his fealty. Once the Prince left for Youzhou, however, he betrayed his promise and refused to surrender, so he was crushed militarily. The Prince of Yan, Liu Shouguang, was murdered at Taiyuan during the eleventh year [C.E. 914], his father Rengong "sacrificed" at Yanmen.[i] Wang Rong (Prince of Zhao) and Wang Chuzhi (Prince of Beiping) now formally petitioned for the Prince's promotion to imperial secretary, as local branches of the Imperial Secretariat were introduced [for administration]. A raid on the Liang prefecture of Xing occurred in the seventh month, with Jin armies badly beaten at Zhanggongqiao.

During the twelfth year [C.E. 915], a mutiny within the Weizhou military permitted He Delun, defecting from the Liang, to cede to the Prince the two prefectures of Wei and Bo. Entering Wei territory, the Prince executed the mastermind behind the mutiny, Zhang Yan, upon reaching Yongji, then organized five hundred of Yan's men into a bodyguard dubbed the "Silver-Lance Advance Corps." The Prince assumed powers as governor of the Wei/Bo command, in the sixth month, concurrent with other duties. He proceeded to capture De Prefecture, then Chan in the seventh month. The armies of Liu Xun were garrisoned at Huanshui when the Prince led a hundred horsemen to spy on their camp. He was ambushed by Xun in a ring of men several layers thick, but managed to break the ring and escape, losing seven or eight horsemen. In the eighth month, the Liang recaptured Chan Prefecture, so Jin armies erected ramparts opposite Xun's men at Shen County and repeatedly attempted to lure the enemy into action, but Xun sealed up the city and refused to leave.

The Prince arranged for Li Cunshen to remain at Shen County in the inaugural month of the thirteenth year [C.E. 916], personally professing to return westward. News that the Prince of Jin had already departed prompted Xun to lead men in storming the eastern wall of Weizhou. The Prince had reached Beizhou only to turn around to surprise Xun and inflict a stunning defeat. He pursued Xun to the former Yuancheng and prevailed once more as

....

i. This refers to cutting out the heart in sacrifice at the grave [of Li Keyong].

Xun fled to Liyang. He led the attack on the Liang prefecture of Wei‡ in the third month, its prefect Mi Zhao surrendering. He conquered Cizhou as well and murdered prefect Jin Zhao. Ming Prefecture was conquered in the fourth month, while a blockade of Xing induced the surrender of governor Yan Bao during the eighth month. Another governor of Liang, Zhang Yun, abandoned Xiangzhou‡, as did Dai Siyuan at Cangzhou, permitting acquisition of these two prefectures. And the Beizhou military murdered the defending commander of Liang, Zhang Yuande, to surrender the prefecture.

The Khitan invaded Weizhou¶ and apprehended the Zhenwu governor, Li Siben. In the fourteenth year [C.E. 917], they invaded Xin and then You prefectures. Li Siyuan [the future Mingzong] retaliated to expel them. That winter, Liang governor Xie Yanzhang was garrisoned at Yangliu [Jizhou], which the Prince attacked during the twelfth month. Personally carrying bales of hay to clog the city's moats, the Prince succeeded in breaking its defenses. During the inaugural month of the fifteenth year [C.E. 918], as the armies of Liang and Jin faced off at Yangliu, Xie Yanzhang pierced dikes along the Yellow River to permit its waters to split Jin armies. The Prince crossed the river for a sortie against Yanzhang, in the sixth month, razing four of his fortresses. A grand inspection of Weizhou occurred in the eighth month: a total of a hundred thousand infantry and ten thousand horsemen converged on Majia crossing, representing the combined forces from the Lulong, Henghai, Zhaoyi, and Anguo commands, plus the prefectures of Zhen and Ding. Xie Yanzhang forted at Xingtai. Jin troops advanced to Linpu in the twelfth month, whereupon Liang pursuers engaged them at Huliu. The Jin army suffered a major setback, Zhou Dewei perishing with honor. At dusk, Liang forces were resting on a mound when the Jin struck again and routed them. Jin armies hence deployed at Desheng would erect dual ramparts.

In the inaugural month of the sixteenth year [C.E. 919], the Prince became the Lulong governor, current with other commissions. A Liang offensive led by Wang Zan against the southern city of Desheng Commandery [Puzhou] proved fruitless, the Jin expanding the northern city in the tenth month. In the twelfth month, Liang armies were defeated south of the Yellow River. During the seventeenth year [C.E. 920], the Zhu Youqian raid on Tong Prefecture caused the Liang to retaliate, commissioning Liu Xun. Liang troops at Tong were vanquished by Li Cunshen.

In the inaugural month of the eighteenth year [C.E. 921], a Buddhist monk from Weizhou, Chuanzhen, presented a "seal confirming Heaven's mandate to the Tang." A commander at Zhao, Zhang Wenli committed regicide against his ruler, Wang Rong, petitioning the Jin for confirmation of office. Wenli was named interim military regent for Zhenzhou, in the second month. During the third month, petitions for the Prince to become emperor came from Hezhong governor Zhu Youqian, Zhaoyi governor Li Sizhao, Henghai governor Li Cunshen, Yiwu governor Wang Chuzhi, Anguo governor Li Siyuan, Zhenzhou interim regent Zhang Wenli, Tianping provisional governor Yan Bao, Datong governor Li Cunzhang, Zhenwu governor Li Cunjin, and Kuangguo governor Zhu Lingde. Occasioning each of the Prince's three declensions were three petitions from Youqian and the others. "I will consider it," the Prince now pronounced.

In the eighth month, the Prince directed Fu Xi, a one-time Zhao commander under Wang Rong, to assist Yan Bao and Shi Jiantang in a drive against Zhang Wenli at Zhenzhou. Wenli died when Jiantang captured Zhaozhou, but his son Chujin sealed off Zhenzhou in defense. Jiantang died in battle there during the ninth month. In the tenth month, the Liang lieutenant Dai Siyuan raided Desheng Commandery's northern city, only to be defeated by Li Siyuan at Qicheng. Defector Wang Chuzhi surrendered his charge to the Khitan, causing son Wang Du to incarcerate him and change loyalties to the Jin. In the twelfth month, the Khitan invaded Zhuo Prefecture, then Ding Prefecture.

In the inaugural month of the nineteenth year [C.E. 922], the Khitan were vanquished at Xincheng and Wangdu, the pursuit of them extending as far as Youzhou. The defeat of Yan Bao at Zhenzhou, in the third month, led to his replacement by Li Sizhao. Sizhao died in battle during the fourth month, replaced by Li Cunjin. The Liang captured Weizhou‡ in the eighth month. Cunjin prevailed over Zhenzhou forces at Dongyuan in the ninth month, but later died in battle. Li Cunshen overpowered Zhenzhou in the tenth month, the Prince assuming concurrent powers as the Chengde governor.

In the inaugural year of Tongguang, spring, the third month [C.E. 923], Li Jitao surrendered Luzhou to the Liang upon defecting from Jin. Summer, the twenty-fifth day of the fourth month [May 13], the Emperor formally acceded to the throne, announced a general amnesty, inaugurated a new reign name, and adopted the dynastic designation of Tang. He appointed left provisional minister Doulu Ge as deputy director of the Chancellery and right provisional minister Lu Cheng as deputy director of the Palace Secretariat, both empowered as chief ministers. Named commissioners of military affairs were Guo Chongtao, senior military advisor, and Zhang Juhan, military overseer for the Zhaoyi command.[ii] Weizhou was renamed the "eastern capital," Taiyuan the "western capital," and Zhenzhou the "northern capital."

············

ii. The Tang had formerly appointed eunuchs to be commissioners of military affairs [*shumishi*], so it was a lesser post. Hereafter, literati came to be consulted and its powers paralleled ministers of state, so appointments are cited here alongside those of ministers.

In the intercalary month, posthumous honors as "Emperor" were extended to paternal ancestors and "Empress" given to their wives: the imperial great-grandfather, Zhiyi, and great grandmother, née Cui, both received the posthumous sobriquet of Zhaolie and the temple designation of Yizu; imperial grandfather Guochang and grandmother, née Qin, both received the posthumous sobriquet of Wenjing and the temple designation of Xianzu; the imperial father [Keyong] received the posthumous sobriquet of "Martial" and the temple designation of Taizu. Temples were erected at Taiyuan for emperors of former Tang times from Gaozu and Taizong to Yizong and Zhaozong, known as the "seven temples."[iii]

On the twenty-eighth day [June 15], Li Siyuan acquired Yunzhou.[iv] On the eighteenth day of the fifth month [July 4], Liang forces claimed the southern town of Desheng Commandery. A confrontation with Wang Yanzhang at his new ramparts ended in his defeat. Lu Cheng was relieved of ministerial duties sometime this month. In autumn, the eighth month, Liang forces seized Zezhou[v] and defending commander Pei Yue perished with honor. On the twenty-seventh day of the ninth month [November 8], the armies of Li Siyuan and Wang Yanzhang engaged at Difang, Siyuan prevailing.

In winter, the second day of the tenth month [November 12], the Emperor departed for Yunzhou in a sortie against the Liang,[vi] capturing Zhongdu on the fourth day and Caozhou on the seventh. The Liang dynasty collapsed on the ninth day as Jing Xiang committed suicide.[vii] Zheng Jue was demoted to fiscal manager for Lai Prefecture, Xiao Qing to fiscal manager for Deng‡

....

iii. Implicit in the posthumous honoring of imperial ancestors is the erection of temples for them, so there is no need to cite "temple" each time. For this specific citation, however, a precedent is set by devoting four temples to Gaozu, etc. [rulers of the preceding Tang dynasty]. So important an event, yet the *Old History* gave no date.

iv. The "Army of Righteous Sons" established by Taizu of the Later Tang contained many men like Li Sizhao. From the outset, each received from Taizu a personal name and surname, but were not treated entirely as sons. In this citation pertaining to Li Siyuan, therefore, I refer to his adopted name without acknowledging him as royal son, in contrast with Youwen and Congke [sons formally adopted].

v. Ze and Lu both belonged to Jin during the late Tang. The Liang once acquired Zezhou in its early years, but it reverted briefly to Jin, only now to be reclaimed by Liang through conquest. The intervening date for the Jin reclamation of Zezhou does not appear, as the *Old History* failed to mention it. For a period of turmoil with endemic wars and conquests such as the Five Dynasties, there are often no consistent rules for citations about the outcome of conflicts, as here.

vi. Having taken the enemy by surprise with a sudden offensive, the word "sortie" [*xi*] is used in the interest of consistency [*wenli*], with no inference of praise or blame.

vii. Xiang, a subject of Liang, was behind many of its schemes to subvert the original Tang dynasty. Despite dying when the Liang collapsed, no reference occurs to "dying honorably" [*sizhi*], but rather "committing suicide." This shows that an honorable death is a great ethical feat and that its acknowledgement is not made casually.

on the sixteenth day. Li Zhen, Zhao Yan, Zhang Hanjie, and Zhu Gui were slain and their families liquidated. An imperial grace, announced on the nineteenth day, reduced punishment for capital offenses and released convicts sentenced to banishment and less.

On the fifth day of the eleventh month [December 15], the "northern capital" was renamed Zhenzhou, Taiyuan becoming the new "northern capital." On the sixteenth, Bianzhou was redesignated Xuanwu command. On the seventeenth, the left minister at the Imperial Secretariat, Zhao Guangyin, became deputy director at the Palace Secretariat with concurrent powers as chief minister, as did Wei Yue, the current vice minister of rites. Envoys of Kim Bak-yeong [Jin Puying], the King of Silla [Xinluo], arrived on the eighteenth. The Yongping command became the new "western capital" on the twenty-first. The Emperor departed for the "Luo capital" on the twenty-fourth [C.E. January 3, 924].[viii] On the inaugural day of the twelfth month, the Emperor arrived from Bian Prefecture. Li Jitao was executed on the twelfth. The younger brother of Jitao, Jida, murdered elder brother Jichou at Lu.[ix] A royal hunt took place at Yique on the twenty-third.

In spring, the inaugural month of the second year, the metropolitan prefect for Henan, Zhang Quanyi, led assorted governors in presenting housewarming gifts for the palace. On the tenth day [February 17], a search was ordered for eunuchs of the Tang.[x] On the eleventh, emissaries arrived from the King of Silla, Kim Bak-yeong, as well as the governor of Quanzhou, Wang Fenggui. On the sixteenth, Dayumo reached the capital as official envoy of the king of Bohai, Dayin Quan. The Emperor departed for Heyang on the twenty-first, returning on the twenty-second.[xi] On the twenty-eighth, the idol known as "Spiritual Master of the Seven Ancestral Temples" arrived from Taiyuan, worship to which occurred at the Imperial Ancestors' Temple. Sunrise rituals took place at the Supreme Mysteries Temple. On the twenty-ninth day, rites for the ancestors were undertaken at the Imperial Ancestors' Temple.

On the inaugural day of the second month [March 8], attending ritual offerings at the southern suburbs, a general amnesty declared. On the fifth, the

....

viii. The word "Luo capital" [for Luoyang] is used in conformity with contemporary usage.

ix. In employing the words "Jichou was murdered" [*beisha*], the intent is not to deny him an "honorable death" [*sizhi*], but to hold him culpable for Jida's murder of their brother. Jida's act was not unlike "regicide against a sovereign."

x. In citing such insidious deeds, no additional censure is needed: a simple citing of the facts is sufficient to expose the severity of the deed.

xi. The Emperor did so to greet the Empress Dowager, née Cao, his own mother. Upon acceding to power, Zhuangzong had commissioned Lu Cheng to present her with the formal vestments of empress dowager. Neither the *Old History* nor the *Veritable Records* indicate the date of investiture, so it is not given here.

multitude of courtiers honored the Monarch as the "Luminously Literate, Intelligently Martial, Illustrious and Filial Emperor." A royal visit to the home of Li Siyuan occurred on the tenth. The Lady Liu was installed as empress on the fifteenth [March 22].[xii] Tangut envoys arrived on the eleventh day of the third month. On the twelfth, the cohort of loyal officers distinguished for either pacifying Bianzhou or occupying Luoyang's southern suburbs received honors from the palace. Director of public works Li Tu was named dignitary for inspecting the royal tombs, on the twenty-second day.[xiii] Yang Li, a commander at Luzhou, rebelled.

In summer, the fifth day of the fifth month [June 9], director of music Chen Jun and the steward for palace gardens Chu Deyuan were named prefects for Jingzhou and Xianzhou, respectively.[xiv] The king of Bohai, Dayin Quan, sent an envoy who arrived on the nineteenth. Li Siyuan conquered Luzhou on the twenty-ninth.[xv] On the ninth day of the sixth month, [Luzhou rebel] Yang Li was executed. The king of the Huihe Uighurs, Renmei, was invested Khan of Yingyi, on the twenty-second. In the autumn, the twelfth day of the seventh month [August 15], the Emperor departed for Mount Lei [Mongolia] to raise up effigies to the heavenly spirits.[xvi] Heavy rains persisted during the eighth month, causing the Yellow River to expand. On the sixteenth day of the ninth month [October 17], water was placed at the gates of the capital in prayers[xvii] to Mars.[2] A royal visit to the residence of Guo Chongtao occurred on the eighteenth. On the twentieth, envoys arrived from the Black River region. In winter, the sixth day of the tenth month [November 5], the wife of Zhao Hui, a commander in the Brave-as-Bears Left Guard, gave birth[3]

....

xii. Of the thirteen rulers of the Five Dynasties, only seven would formally install empresses and the phrasing of edicts varies from case to case. When the formal wife is installed, the phrasing goes, "the Concubine known as X or the Wife surnamed Y became empress." When a woman is not formal wife, the phrase simply says that "a woman surnamed X was installed as empress." The objective here is to avoid the indiscriminate conflating of such formal and informal wives, with no other inference of praise or blame.

xiii. This refers to the tombs of the Tang emperors.

xiv. Civilian appointments are generally not cited, except as in this case, owing to its excessiveness [see chapter 37].

xv. No mention is made of this commander's assignment, as the *Old History* fails to indicate.

xvi. This is a barbarian ritual.

xvii. The Basic Annals generally cite natural disasters, but not prodigies. Yet inasmuch as the placing of water in prayers to Mars does not appear in ritual texts, the action is indicative of the prevailing anxieties about disaster as well as the prevailing ignorance about how to express humility before heaven by simply rectifying one's virtue. Things that cause injury such as floods, droughts, storms, and locusts are natural disasters and thus cited. But events that contravene common reasoning [*changli*] and occur inexplicably are prodigies; these lie beyond our ability to comprehend and are not cited.

to male triplets.[xviii] On the ninth day of the eleventh month, a royal hunt took place at Yique, the Emperor returning on the twelfth.[xix] A chieftain of the Huihu Uighurs, Anqianxiang, arrived as their envoy on the twenty-third. In the twelfth month, the sixth day, the Emperor and Empress visited Zhang Quanyi at his residence.

In spring of the third year, seventh day of the inaugural month [C.E. February 2, 925], the Emperor departed for the "eastern capital," the altar where he had acceded the throne leveled for a polo field.[4] Men gathered for polo on the new field, on the sixth day of the second month, hunting wild geese at Wang Mang River [Weizhou] on the twelfth. On the eighteenth, envoys arrived representing the Turkish leader Hunjielou and the king of Bohai, Dayin Quan. A hunt for wild geese in the northern suburbs took place. Ducks were hunted at Guopo on the twenty-second, wild geese in the northern suburbs on the twenty-seventh.

The third day of the third month [March 29], on the winter solstice, the "mountain sacrifice" occurred at the western suburbs.[xx] The Emperor returned from the "eastern capital" on the twenty-eighth. On the twenty-ninth, the "eastern capital" was renamed the "Ye metropolis" and the Luo capital renamed "eastern metropolis." In summer, thirteenth day of the fourth month [May 8], the Emperor and Empress visited the residences of Guo Chongtao and Zhu Hanbin. There was drought. Zhao Guangyin died on the twenty-eighth. Consort Dowager Liu died on the sixth day of the fifth month [May 30], the Emperor suspending audience for five days.[xxi] Envoys from the Black River as well as Jurchen regions arrived on the eighteenth. On the fourth day of the sixth month, the chamberlain for the imperial clan, Li Shu, received the commission to conduct new divinations for the tomb sites of Tang Emperors Zhaozong and Shaodi.[xxii] Horses were appropriated. In autumn, the eleventh day of the seventh month [August 3], Empress Dowager Cao ex-

....

xviii. The citing of a prodigy such as this reflects my focus on human affairs: such events have been regarded by later generations as auspicious omens, but by noting their occurrence in an age of such turmoil, the belief is exposed as wrong.

xix. The time of his return from Yique [less than fifty kilometers south of Luoyang] is indicated to expose his severe sloth: he stayed for four full days.

xx. Being a vulgar rite outside the prescribed rituals, it merits mention.

xxi. For the legal wife of Taizu and formal mother of Zhuangzong, calling her "Consort Dowager" and merely "suspending court" [upon her death] reveals the ritual bankruptcy and meager recognition common to this age of chaos.

xxii. "Shaodi" refers to the Prince of Jiyin. The Liang once posthumously named him "Emperor Ai," the Bereaved, but the Later Tang preferred "Shaodi," the Young, a convention adopted here.

pired.[xxiii] The metropolitan prefect for Henan, Luo Guan, was murdered on the twenty-third day of the eighth month.

On the tenth day of the ninth month [September 30], a punitive campaign was launched against Shu, with the Prince of Wei, Jiji, as general commander of at-large forces on the four fronts of western Chuan and Guo Chongtao as commissioner of bandit suppression. Rains had persisted since the sixth month. A hunt for wild geese occurred at Jian Mountain on the twenty-third. In winter, the twenty-third day of the tenth month [November 11], envoys arrived from tribes of the Xi [southern Manchuria], the Tuhun, and the Tujue Turks. The "Chaste and Austere" Empress Dowager was interred at the Kunling mausoleum on the twenty-ninth. Envoys of Koryô [Gaoli] arrived on the eighteenth day of the eleventh month [December 6]. On the twentieth, Wang Yan surrendered.[xxiv] Guo Chongtao murdered Wang Zongbi and his younger brothers, Zongwo and Zongxun, annihilating their clan. On the twentieth day of the twelfth month, a royal hunt took place at Baisha, the Emperor returning on the twenty-fourth. In the intercalary month, the twenty-third day, the Emperor invested his younger brothers: Cunmei as Prince of Yong¶, Cunba as Prince of Yong, Cunli as Prince of Xue, Cunwo as Prince of Shen, Cunyi as Prince of Mu, Cunque as Prince of Tong, and Cunji as Prince of Ya.

In spring of the fourth year, fifth day of the inaugural month [C.E. February 19, 926], a reduction for sentences of capital punishment and below was mandated. The Prince of Wei, Jiji, killed Guo Chongtao and his two sons in Shu, on the seventh day.[xxv] Khitan envoy Meilao Xieli arrived on the eleventh. On the twenty-first [March 7], the Emperor assassinated younger brother Cunyi, Prince of Mu, along with the Huguo governor at Hezhong, Li Jilin, liquidating the families of both men. On the twenty-eighth, envoys arrived from the northwest potentate of Shazhou, Cao Yijin, envoys of Aduoyu, the Huihu Uighur, arriving a day later. On the thirtieth, the court murdered former commanders of Li Jilin, including Shi Wu, Xue Jingrong, Zhou Tangyin, Yang Shitai, Wang Jing, Lai Ren, and Bai Fengguo, their families liquidated as well.

....

xxiii. As for why no mention is made of her "investiture as empress dowager," see earlier notes.

xxiv. When the armies of Tang entered Shu, they won the surrender of ruler and subjects alike without a single battle. Thus, the simple facts of the incident are given. For more on the ruler's death and his territory's surrender, see "the murder of Yan" below.

xxv. In fact, Empress Liu had authorized Jiji to murder Chongtao. In stating, "Jiji killed him," I refer to Jiji's personal direction of troops in the provinces. A directive from the Empress is not synonymous with a mandate from the Son of Heaven, and Jiji had the option of refusing.

On the second day of the second month [March 18], the commissioner of the southern court of palace armies, Li Shaohong, was promoted to commissioner of military affairs. On the sixth, a commander at the Ye command, Zhao Zaili, rebelled at Beizhou.[xxvi] A royal hunt at Lengquan occurred a day later. Zhao Zaili overran the Ye capital, as Wuning governor Li Shaorong retaliated. A mutiny erupted at Xingzhou by commander Zhao Tai. Entrusted with the punitive campaign against him was Li Shaozhen, the commissioner of bandit suppression for the northeast. The suppression of Zhao Zaili was entrusted to the Chengde governor, Li Siyuan, on the sixteenth day.

Sometime during the third month Zhao Tai was executed, Li Siyuan rebelled, and defending commander Zhai Jian of Bozhou installed himself as prefect. Wang Yan and his entire family was murdered on the eighth day [April 22].[xxvii] The Emperor departed for Bianzhou on the ninth, then Xingze [Zhengzhou] on the sixteenth. Yao Yanwen, director of the Dragon-Prancing Guard, surrendered his vanguard to Li Siyuan, who then occupied Bian. The Emperor reached the capital from Wansheng on the seventeenth.[xxviii] The director of cavalry rotations, Guo Congqian, rebelled. In summer, the first day of the fourth month [May 15], the Emperor expired.[xxix]

....

xxvi. No dates are generally cited for rebellions, an exception being made for Zaili to illustrate the progression of his disillusionment, the details of which appear in his biography. Zaili had no inclination to rebel at the outset, but was provoked to rebel on this day. While wishing to pass judgment on his grave transgression, it is also necessary to distinguish this particular defection from the defection of others, by exploring his original intent. For precisely this reason, arbitrary judgments should be avoided in treating the moral decency or indecency of men.

xxvii. To reprieve Wang Yan, then murder him along with his entire family in the wake of surrender, is worse than killing the innocent; yet no distinctions are made in the narrative here, the symbolism of which is clear from previous comments on the "surrender of Yan."

xxviii. The Emperor had reached Wansheng Garrison [the western suburbs of Kaifeng] only to return upon learning of Siyuan's occupation of Bianzhou.

xxix. He lived to be forty-three. The Emperor's body was set afire by court actors and musicians [chapter 37]. When Mingzong occupied Luoyang, he retrieved the remains and buried them in Xin'an County, Henan, during the seventh month of the inaugural year of Tiancheng [C.E. 926], naming the mausoleum Yongling—a name changed to Yiling during the Jin dynasty owing to taboo restrictions. The text here makes no mention of burial for reasons already cited under Emperor Taizu of Liang.

CHAPTER 6

ANNALS VI: BASIC ANNALS OF TANG

Mingzong [Li Siyuan, C.E. 867–933] the Sagacious and Moral, Harmonious and Martial, Scrupulous and Filial Emperor, hailed from generations of barbarians without surnames. His father, Ni, a chieftain among Yanmen tribes [northern Hedong], sired Miaojilie, who employed his skills as horseman and archer to serve Taizu [Li Keyong]. A man direct, genuine, and sparing in words, he conducted affairs with fervid dedication. Taizu thus adopted him as son, conferring the name Siyuan.

Amid the Liang assault on Yan and Yun prefectures, Zhu Xuan and Zhu Jin requested reinforcements, and Taizu assisted by dispatching Li Cunxin with thirty thousand men. But Cunxin stayed behind at Shen County and sent Siyuan instead with three thousand soldiers in a separate raid, whereupon the Liang armies dispersed. Having lingered at Shen County, Cunxin came under attack from Luo Hongxin and fled in defeat. Siyuan alone dared to pursue him prior to returning, inspiring Taizu to rename the five hundred crack horsemen under Siyuan's command as the "Squad of the Furious Stampede."

During the raid on Xing and Ming prefectures, Liang territory, in the third year of Guanghua [C.E. 900], Li Sizhao's approach from the Qing Mountains caused an encounter with Ge Congzhou's men. Vastly overwhelmed, Sizhao fled in defeat with Liang warriors on his heels. Siyuan arrived soon thereafter via a bypass route, proposing to Sizhao, "Sir, allow me to fight for you!" Dismounting his horse to sharpen a javelin, Siyuan proceeded to an elevated position and drew column lines along the left and right—lines that the Liang pursuers failed to notice as they approached. "I have taken a lesson from Gentleman Ge Congzhou," he shouted impetuously. "Your men must not move!" His cavalry struck fast with intermittent broadsides as Sizhao personally followed up, forcing the Liang men to withdraw. Arrows had punctured his body in four places, inspiring Taizu to honor him by removing his own clothing for the wound while offering medicines. Hereafter, the reputation of "Li, the furious stampede man" reverberated throughout the four corners.

In its standoff with the Jin at Baixiang [Zhaozhou], the Liang organized its Dragon-Prancing Guard by the color of their horses, red or white, with colors to match the horses emblazoned on the banners and armor of the two groups. The mere sight of them terrified most Jin fighters. The future Zhuangzong once raised a goblet in a toast to Siyuan, asking, "Does the sight of the red and white horses of the Liang frighten you? Well, they scare even me!" Siyuan replied with jocular ease, "They are merely a mirage. By tomorrow, their horses will revert to our own corrals." "Your fury alone is enough to swallow the enemy alive," Zhuangzong commented with relish in drinking from a goblet. Then, seizing a cudgel, Siyuan charged forth by chariot to raid the white horse regiments and apprehend two attending commanders of the enemy before returning. The Liang rout resulted in the promotion of a meritorious Siyuan to prefect of Daizhou.

During the campaign of Zhuangzong against Liu Shouguang, Li Siyuan and Li Sizhao led a force of thirty thousand from Feihu County, pacifying Shanhou to claim the prefectures of Wu, Gui¶, and Ru [Hebei north circuit]. Zhuangzong had pacified Wei Prefecture when Ci and Xiang‡ also succumbed, causing Siyuan to be named prefect of Xiangzhou‡ and governor of the Zhaode command, and even, in time, Anguo governor. After the Khitan assault on Youzhou, Zhuangzong commissioned Siyuan to repulse them, combining forces with Yan Bao.

Li Siyuan's reassignment as Henghai governor came in the inaugural year of Tongguang [C.E. 923]. The Liang and Tang were in the midst of a standoff along the Yellow River when Li Jitao defected and relinquished Luzhou to the Liang. The event left Zhuangzong perceptibly anxious, so he summoned Siyuan to his tent, asking, "Jitao has already surrendered Shangdang to the Liang, while Liang troops are in the middle of a broadside against Zezhou. What do you think of a surprise storm on Yunzhou to sever the Liang's right arm?" Siyuan responded, "The military standoff along the river has lasted far too long. Unless some extraordinary step is taken, no break can occur on our larger agenda. Allow me to handle the matter on my own." With five thousand men, a combination of infantry and cavalry, he crossed the Yellow River at Jizhou and proceeded southward to Yunzhou. Troops at the prefecture were unprepared, and they succumbed. In this way, Siyuan became Tianping governor and deputy supervisor of multiracial infantry and cavalry.

Palisades to the south of Desheng Commandery having been overrun by Liang regulars, Zhuangzong had to retreat to Yangliu. Wang Yanzhang exploited the moment to pummel Yunzhou, but Zhuangzong invested his entire army in the relief of Yunzhou, with Siyuan as vanguard for assailing Liang belligerents. Pursuing them as far as Zhongdu, Siyuan eventually apprehended Yanzhang and Zhang Hanjie, a military inspector for the Liang.

The defeat of Yanzhang notwithstanding, residual Liang armies all fell under Duan Ning's command and were quartered on the northern side of the Yellow River. Zhuangzong could not decide the best approach, although his commanders largely preferred exploiting the current momentum to claim Qing‡ and Qi¶ prefectures. Li Siyuan countered, "Ning has yet to learn of Yanzhang's defeat. Once he learns, another three days of indecision will ensue before a recourse emerges. If he succeeds at anticipating our approach and promptly unleashes relief forces, he must cross the Yellow River at Liyang County, and the ships needed to move tens of thousands of warriors can scarcely be assembled in a single day. Yet we are merely several hundred *li* from Bianzhou [the Liang capital], with no natural obstacles in the way. We can arrive within two nights, if we proceed in square formation. With the conquest of Bian, Duan Ning can hardly cause concern!" Guo Chongtao similarly urged the occupation of Bian. Having been persuaded, Zhuangzong dispatched Siyuan with an advance of a thousand horsemen. The raid on the city's Fengqiu gate induced Wang Zan to open the gates in surrender. Zhuangzong arrived later and, at the very sight of Siyuan, grabbed him by the clothes to butt heads, cheering, "The world is ours!" Siyuan was named palace secretary.

During the second year [C.E. 924], Zhuangzong worshipped Heaven at the southern suburbs and bestowed an iron writ of immunity upon Siyuan. Yang Li at Luzhou was vanquished by Siyuan in the fifth month. Reassigned as Xuanwu governor, Siyuan concurrently served as supervisor for multiracial infantry and cavalry empirewide in the sixth month. He defeated the Khitan at Zhuozhou, after incursions against Yuyang [Jizhou‡] that winter.

In the third year [C.E. 925], the court reassigned Siyuan as Chengde governor [Zhenzhou]. During Zhuangzong's tour of the Ye capital, Siyuan requested an audience in the provisional capital but was refused. When the Chaste and Austere Dowager took ill, Siyuan sought to enter the palace to pay respects, a request again denied. He further petitioned after the Dowager's death to visit her hillside mausoleum, receiving permission only to cancel because of border raids by the Khitan. He did appear in audience at Luoyang during the twelfth month.

In the inaugural year of Tiancheng [C.E. 926],[i] slanders had caused Guo Chongtao and Zhu Youqian to die, and Siyuan was now a target of suspicion because of his high visibility. Once Zhao Zaili rebelled at Weizhou, senior advisors all begged for Siyuan's deployment to suppress the renegades. Zhuangzong initially demurred, although relentless petitions from courtiers forced him to concede. On the sixth day of the third month [April 20], Siyuan reached Wei and quartered his men to the south of Yuhe. Zaili apologized for misdeeds from a tower atop the walled city. A mutiny erupted in the armed forces on the eighth day, and Siyuan now entered Weizhou to mend relations with Zaili. He departed that night, stopping at Wei County. On the eleventh, he led his own troops southward and had Shi Jingtang direct three hundred horsemen as an advance force. Passing through the village of Julu, Siyuan plundered two thousand horses from small wards to augment his cavalry. He entered Bianzhou on the twenty-sixth.

On the first day of the fourth month [May 15], Emperor Zhuangzong expired. Siyuan occupied Luoyang on the third day. Assuming direction of state affairs, Siyuan met with ranked officiary at the Ascending Sage Palace on the eighth. A day later, senior military advisor An Chonghui became commissioner of military affairs. Yuan Xingqin was murdered, along with revenues commissioner Kong Qian. The commandant of the Valorous Left Guard, Kong Xun, became commissioner of military affairs on the sixteenth day. On the twentieth, funeral offerings were initiated at the western palace.[ii] The Emperor assumed the throne before the coffin of Zhuangzong,[iii] changing from the coarse clothing of mourning to ordinary imperial garb.[iv] The Prince of Wei, Jiji, died on the twenty-sixth.[v] On the twenty-eighth [June 11], the court

....

i. This was, in fact, the fourth year of Tongguang. "The inaugural year of Tiancheng" is cited in association with the general amnesty and reign changes noted below. The Basic Annals of Zhuangzong above gives "fourth year of Tongguang," whereas another reign name is acknowledged here: no need to shun the use of overlapping reign names.

ii. The citation "funeral offerings were initiated" serves to expose the tardiness of Siyuan [in conducting rites]: some twenty days had passed since Luoyang's occupation, on the third day.

iii. To accede to the throne before the coffin [of the deceased monarch] is a rite of transition for the new ruler. For the treasonous subject who employs the rituals of orthodox succession in the wake of illicitly installing himself, the facts are cited without altering words from the original text. With the earlier mention of "a rebellion," the character of the crime has already been clarified. By citing the facts, here, Siyuan's personal sense of shame and desire to evade historical responsibility for his awful crime becomes readily apparent.

iv. Having employed the rituals of orthodox succession, Siyuan hastily casts off mourning clothes and dons ordinary imperial garb—an event described here to expose his deceit.

v. The deaths of royal princes are usually not cited, but the citation here exposes Mingzong's deployment of armies as an actual act of rebellion. A treasonous Congqian had committed regicide at the time, giving Mingzong the pretext of "responding to distress." The eldest son of Zhuangzong, still alive at the time of accession, relinquished his inheritance to Mingzong.

announced a general amnesty and change of reign name. Dachen Lin, envoy of the king of Bohai, Dayin Quan, reached the capital. Zhang Juhan was dismissed sometime this month.

On the first day of the fifth month [June 13], advisor to the heir-apparent Zheng Jue and minister of public works Ren Huan both became deputy directors at the Palace Secretariat with ministerial powers. Zhao Zaili was named Yicheng governor on the thirteenth day.[vi] In the sixth month, the twelfth day [July 24], a mutiny erupted within the Crane-Commanding Guard at Bianzhou, director Zhang Jian having killed provisional prefect Gao Ti; the execution of Jian occurred on the fourteenth. In autumn, the sixth day of the seventh month [August 16], An Chonghui murdered Ma Yan, deputy for the palace, at the gate of the Censorate.[vii] Arrivals were announced for the Khitan envoy Meilao Shugu and the Bohai envoy Dazhao Zuo. On the twenty-fifth, the court demoted Doulu Ge to prefect for Chen Prefecture and Wei Yue to prefect of Xu, then ordered exiles for Ge and Yue, respectively, to Ling and He prefectures, on the thirtieth.

On the first day of the eighth month [September 10], a resident of Xiashi County, Shanzhou, Gao Cun, reported the delivery of male triplets by his wife. On the thirteenth, thirty-two ivory handstaffs were distributed to courtiers without them.[viii] A royal inspection of farming occurred at the Lengquan palace and game reserve. The Khitan violated the border on the fifteenth. On the twenty-third, Pinglu governor Huo Yanwei assassinated Wang Gongyan, the prefect of Dengzhou‡, in his district. On the thirtieth, imperial doctor Zhang Zhizhong became deputy metropolitan custodian of Taiyuan. On the fifth day of the ninth month [October 14], the Emperor visited the Zhide palace [his old residence as Prince] and the home of Yuan Jianfeng. In winter, the fourth day of the tenth month [November 11], arrival was announced for the grand oracle, Funeng Hehua, as envoy of Li Beiwan, the supreme oracle for assorted southern-barbarian spirits in Yunnan's Lianglin district and commandant of the Martial Right Guard. On the eighteenth, Khitan envoy Mogunei arrived to announce mourning for ruler Abaoji; court was suspended for three days in his honor. After a long drought, it rained on the twenty-eighth.

In spring of the second year, first day of the inaugural month [C.E. February 5, 927], the Emperor changed his personal name to Dan. On the eleventh,

....

vi. Zaili deserved death for having started the succession turmoil, but Mingzong used him to justify his own rebellion, then rewarded his merit with an appointment as governor—cause for this citation.

vii. The Censorate exists to investigate the improper deeds of officials; to murder someone at the gates of the Censorate is an abomination.

viii. This is written to reveal the prevailing level of degeneracy at court.

Duanming academician and vice minister of war Feng Dao and chamberlain for imperial ceremonials Cui Xie were named deputy directors of the Palace Secretariat with ministerial powers. In the second month, the first day, envoy Jang Boon [Zhang Fen] of Silla reached the capital. Meng Zhixiang, the governor of western Chuan, murdered his military director-in-chief, Li Yan. An amnesty was announced for prisoners within the capital on the fifteenth day. Guo Congqian was named prefect of Jingzhou and soon murdered.[ix] On the seventeenth, the governor of Shannan east circuit, Liu Xun, became bandit-suppressing commissioner for the southern front charged with the campaign against Jingnan [Nanping].[x] On the first day of the third month [April 5], the Emperor toured the Huijie gardens, where courtiers entertained him.[xi] A mutiny at the Lutai command resulted in the death of its commander, Wu Zhen. The envoy for Silla, Lim Eon [Lin Yan], reached the capital.

In summer, the tenth day of the fourth month [May 13], the treasonous commanders at Lutai, Long Zhi and cohort, were executed. On the seventh day of the sixth month, Ren Huan was dismissed. On the occasion of a royal visit to Baisima Slope on the twenty-first, the Emperor sacrificed to spirits of the Tujue Turks.[xii] In autumn, the fifteenth day of the seventh month [August 15], the prefect of Suizhou, Xifang Ye, claimed the prefectures of Kui, Zhong, and Wan [of Shu]. Doulu Ge and Wei Yue were murdered on the twenty-fourth. On the seventh day of the eighth month, emissaries [from the southwest] reached the capital: Song Chaohua representing Zangke tribes and others for Kunming. On the twenty-second day of the ninth month, an envoy of the Tangut known as Rulianshan arrived, as on the twenty-fourth did Meilao, an envoy for the Khitan.

In the winter, the seventh day of the tenth month [November 4], the Emperor departed for Bianzhou. Xuanwu governor Zhu Shouyin defected.

....

ix. This is cited because Congqian, after committing regicide, received an official appointment instead of punishment. His crime the same as Zaili, he deserved to be "executed," but the citation calls it "murder." Mingzong having shared in the commission of that crime, he could not preside over a lawful execution, so the word "murder" is employed as among peers.

x. At the time, Jingnan had seceded from the Middle Kingdom and submitted to the sovereignty of Wu, so the word "campaign" [*fa*] is preferable to "punitive expedition" [*tao*], for no measure of punishment was involved. This affirms the rule that, in the absence of bonds as ruler-subject, Jingnan cannot be held accountable as defector.

xi. Informal travels are minor events that do not merit mention, except as signs of excess. Here, they are noted only for the reigns of Zhuangzong [of Tang] and Chu of Jin to expose their intemperance. Mingzong, however, was diligent and frugal by the standards of rulers of the Five Dynasties, and not excessive in his travels. The citation here is intended, rather, to expose the failings of ruler-subject protocol as reflected in the practice of courtiers "paying to banquet" the Emperor.

xii. [Rites to the Tujue spirits] is a practice of the barbarians.

Dying honorably in battle was Ma Yanzhao, the chief director cavalry and infantry. Shouyin committed suicide on the eleventh day.[xiii] On the seventeenth, the retired junior guardian to the heir-apparent, Ren Huan, was murdered.[xiv] The release of criminals attended a minor amnesty on the twenty-third. Sometime this winter, the palace conveyed an arrow [with military orders] to Huo Yanwei.[xv] On the twenty-eighth day of the eleventh month [December 24], Khitan envoy Meilao reached the capital.

On the twelfth day of the twelfth month, envoys from Tubo, western neighbors of the Huihu Uighurs, came to the capital. On the twenty-seventh, a royal hunt occurred in the eastern suburbs. On the twenty-ninth, posthumous honors as "Emperor" were extended to paternal ancestors and "Empress" given to their wives: great-great grandfather Yu, renamed Xiaogong, received the temple designation of Huizu; the sobriquet Xiaogongzhao went to his wife, née Liu. Great grandfather Ao, renamed Xiaozhi, received the temple designation of Yizu; the sobriquet Xiaozhishun went to his wife, née Zhang. Grandfather Yan, renamed Xiaojing, received the temple designation of Liezu; the sobriquet Xiaojingmu went to his wife, née He. The imperial father, renamed Xiaocheng, received the temple designation of Dezu; the sobriquet Xiaochengyi went to his wife, née Liu. Temples were erected at Yingzhou‡.

In spring of the third year, the tenth day of the inaugural month [C.E. February 4, 928], the Khitan overran Pingzhou. The protector-general for the Tuhun, Li Shaolu, came to court. On the nineteenth, Kong Xun was dismissed. Envoy Li Ashan, representing the Huihu Uighurs, arrived on the twenty-second. On the first day of the third month, the palace issued a request for candid criticism. Zheng Jue was dismissed on the thirteenth. The Chengde governor, Wang Jianli, became associate director of the Secretariat with chief ministerial powers, on the seventeenth. Xifang Ye seized Guizhou. Commissioner of the southern court of palace armies Fan Yanguang became military affairs commissioner.

In the summer, third day of the fourth month [April 25], Yanguang was dismissed. Envoys of the Tartars arrived on the tenth. Yiwu governor Wang

....

xiii. No citation appears for the "conquest" of Bianzhou, for the Son of Heaven who personally led his men in this campaign occupied the city without a single battle. Earlier, the "fall of the prefecture" was mentioned in lieu of noting the "committing of suicide"; here, the "committing of suicide" is mentioned in lieu of the "fall of the prefecture."

xiv. In fact, An Chonghui had forged the edict ordering the murder, but it is not written that Chonghui killed him: Mingzong knew of the deed without censuring him, and even issued an edict of reprimand for Ren Huan. Thus, it is said here that Mingzong personally killed him.

xv. This is a practice among the barbarians. [Chapter 46, Huo Yanwei.]

Du defected. On the twenty-seventh day, the court designated Guide governor Wang Yanqiu as bandit-suppressing commissioner for northern forces at large. In the fifth month, the Khitan commander Tunei occupied Dingzhou. On the nineteenth day [June 9], generalissimo of the Right Guard Zhao Jingyi became commissioner of military affairs. The khan of the Huihu Uighurs, Renyu, was invested "Shunhua Khan."

In the autumn, sixteenth day of the seventh month [August 4], the defense commissioner for Qizhou¶, Cao Tingyin, was murdered. During the eighth month, Lulong governor Zhao Dejun apprehended Hemiao, a leading Khitan and administrator for royal affairs. The defense commissioner for Qingzhou, Dou Tingwan, rebelled. Jingnan governor Li Jingzhou received orders to suppress Tingwan during the tenth month, winter. On the sixteenth day [November 30], Zhang Mujin reached the capital as envoy of the Tujue Turks. On the eleventh day of the eleventh month, an envoy of the Tuhun, Nianjiu, arrived. Wang Jianli was dismissed on the twenty-third day. In the twelfth month, Li Jingzhou conquered Qingzhou, executing Dou Tingwan. The Emperor visited Kang Yicheng's residence on the tenth.

In spring, the twenty-first day of the inaugural month [C.E. March 5, 929], envoy of the Huihu Uighurs, protector-general Chebo, reached the capital. Wang Yanqiu captured Dingzhou on the second day of the second month.[xvi] Yanqiu presented, on the twenty-first, prisoners of war and the left ears of the dead. Zhao Jingyi passed away. Cui Xie died on the twenty-seventh. The Monarch arrived from Bianzhou on the thirtieth. Royal nephew Congcan died by assassination on the sixteenth day of the third month.

In the summer, the fourth month, the Khitan invaded Yunzhou‡. On the fourteenth day [May 25], Khitan envoy Liaokuo Meili came to demand the return of Tunei; the envoy was killed. On the fifteenth, the Duanming academician and vice minister of war Zhao Feng won appointment as deputy director at the Chancellery, concurrent minister of public works, and chief minister. On the first day of the fifth month, the Emperor met with ranked officiary to celebrate the new moon.[xvii] On the seventeenth, [the last] Emperor of Tang, Shaodi, received posthumous recognition as the "Luminously Manifest, Radiantly Devout, and Filial Emperor." The Khitan invaded Yunzhou‡.

xvi. Wang Du died after setting himself afire, so no citation for execution appears.

xvii. Rather than he "held formal audience," he is said to "celebrate the new moon" to expose the lack of ritual propriety. The holding of audience, being a commonplace event, is not usually cited. But "celebration of the new moon on the fifth month" derives from Daoist thought and began to be practiced in Tang times. It is cited here to illustrate that such breaches of ritual principles, in a time of turmoil, were not taken seriously. This rite was repeated in later times, but no further citation occurs, the reasoning similar to that provided under "procession to the auxiliary palace."

In autumn, the fifth day of the seventh month [August 12], the generalissimo of the Imperial Insignia Right Guard, Mao Zhang, was murdered. Envoy Guzhi reached the capital from the Black River region, on the ninth day of the eighth month [September 10], as did the leader of the Tuhun, Nian'gongshan, on the eleventh, the Tangut Sheyuming on the nineteenth, and the ambassador Jang Bin [Zhang Bin] on the twenty-third, for the King of Koryô, Wang Geon [Wang Jian]. The officer of palace services, Wu Zhaoyu, was murdered on the twenty-seventh day of the ninth month, then the county magistrate of Xiping, Li Shang, on the sixth day of the twelfth month, in winter.

In the spring of the inaugural year of Changxing, second day of the inaugural month [C.E. February 3, 930], horses were inspected at their pastures. Zhu Hongzhao, commissioner of the southern court of palace armies, was promoted to interim custodian of the imperial precincts on the twenty-sixth. Envoy for the Black River tribes, Wuer, arrived on the fourth day of the second month. The Tianxiong governor, Shi Jingtang, became commissioner of the imperial encampment on the eleventh day. Dedication ceremonies occurred at the Taiwei Temple on the nineteenth. Offerings to the ancestors occurred at the Imperial Ancestors' Temple, on the twentieth, and at the southern suburbs on the twenty-first day. The palace announced a general amnesty and a new reign name. It installed the Pure Consort, née Cao, as empress on the twenty-sixth day of the third month [April 27].

In the summer, the fifth day of the fourth month [May 5], at the instigation of An Chonghui, the director of the governor's special forces at Hezhong, Yang Yanwen, purged governor Li Congke from office. Suppression efforts began on the ninth day, led by the interim custodian of the western capital, Suo Zitong, and the director of infantry in the Imperial Guard, Yao Yanchou. Zitong apprehended Yanwen on the eighteenth and murdered him.[xviii] On the twenty-fifth, leading courtiers elevated the Monarch to the "Sagaciously Enlightened, Divinely Martial, Literarily Virtuous, Reverent and Filial Emperor." The chieftain of Tubo, Yuboge, reached the capital on the twenty-eighth. During the fifth month, envoys arrived for the Huihu Uighurs: Nielizu on the fourteenth day and Anheilian on the seventeenth.

In autumn, twenty-first day of the seventh month [August 17], a search was ordered for the burial places of the sons and grandsons of Emperor Zhuangzong.[xix] On the fourth day of the eighth month [August 30], Zhongwu

....

xviii. Yanwen was guilty of a crime, but Zitong had orders to capture him alive and therefore acted improperly by killing him, so the word "murder" is employed instead of "execute."

xix. The uncertain burial spots for Zhuangzong's sons and grandsons reveals that Mingzong's raising of troops did not go unchallenged. The harm to victims was lamentable, yet initiating searches for them only now reveals the tardiness of his actions. It was no act of grace.

governor Zhang Yanlang became commissioner of the Three Fiscal Agencies.[xx] The murders of Li Xingde, chief director of the Sage-Sustaining Guard, and squad leader Zhang Jian occurred on the eleventh day; their extended families were liquidated as well. The Tuhun arrived to offer fealty. Imperial son Congrong received investiture as Prince of Qin. On the seventeenth, Haizhou commander Wang Chuanji murdered prefect Chen Xuan to repudiate Wu sovereignty and surrender to the Tang. The Tuhun, Kanghebi, reached the capital on the twenty-fourth. Imperial son Conghou was invested Prince of Song on the twenty-fifth. On the second day of the ninth month [September 25], Tubo Tibetan envoy Wang Manru arrived. The governor of eastern Chuan, Dong Zhang, rebelled. The court designated Chengde governor Fan Yanguang as military affairs commissioner, on the twenty-fourth, and Shi Jingtang as chief commissioner of the bandit-suppressing at-large forces in eastern Chuan, on the twenty-seventh.

In winter, seventh day of the tenth month [October 31], the court began storing ice. On the fourteenth day, the retired generalissimo of the Valorous Guard, Zhang Yun, donated supplemental rations for the troops. Dong Zhang overran Langzhou‡ on the fifteenth, killing governor Li Renju, as military director Yao Hong died with honor. Meng Zhixiang rebelled [in Shu]. On the first day of the eleventh month, Congrong the Prince of Rong received investiture. The Emperor toured the Imperial Ancestors' Temple.[xxi] The [deposed] Khitan Prince of Dongdan, Tuyu,[1] fled to offer fealty on the twenty-seventh day.[xxii] On the eighteenth day of the twelfth month, the court suspended audiences for a day after the death of Yang Renju, the former heir to the two princes of Tang, deputy director of the Palace Library, and Duke of Xi. On the twenty-eighth, Huihu envoy Zhaimosi reached the capital, representing the khan of Xunhua, Renyu. An Chonghui led the suppression against Dong Zhang.[xxiii] Envoys of Cao Yijin of Shazhou arrived.

In spring of the second year, ninth day of the inaugural month [C.E. January 20, 931], the Tangut envoy Sheqiyi reached the capital. Tartar emissary Lieliuxueniangju arrived on the twenty-first. The Emperor visited the residence of An Yuanxin on the ninth day of the second month. Envoys arrived on the tenth day for the Tujue Turks and the Tuhun: Du Ashu and Kang

....

xx. The appointment of commissioners for the Three Fiscal Agencies began at this time, a practice retained to this very day.

xxi. The rites of investiture were largely suspended in this age of chaos, such that this isolated instance of implementation is noteworthy.

xxii. Barbarians cannot be judged by the rules of propriety, so, it is not said that Tuyu "defected from the Khitan."

xxiii. Orders did not include commanders' names, as Chonghui left on his own authority as commissioner of military affairs.

Wanlin, respectively. The court dismissed An Chonghui on the thirteenth day and Zhao Feng sometime during the third month, designating chamberlain for imperial ceremonials, Li Yu‡, deputy director at the Imperial Secretariat with ministerial powers on the twenty-ninth day [April 19].

In the summer, sixteenth day of the fourth month [May 5], Zhao Yanshou, commissioner of the northern court of palace armies, became commissioner of military affairs. Dong Zhang conquered Suizhou‡ on the twenty-sixth, Wuxin governor Xia Luqi dying with honor. A day later, in the wake of persistent drought, amnesties went out for those sentenced to lifetime banishment and less. Murdered in the intercalary fifth month, the fifth day were An Chonghui, the retired grand preceptor to the heir-apparent, his wife née Zhang, and sons Chongzan and Chongxu.

In the autumn, the sixth day of the eighth month [September 20], Khitan envoy Yeguer reached the capital. On the third day of the ninth month, falcons and hawks on the five reservations were released. In the winter, fifteenth day of the eleventh month [December 26], envoys for the Tubo Tibetans arrived. The court authorized banner and post for the home-door of Xing Zhao, a subject at Dizhou on the eighteenth.[xxiv] In the twelfth month, the first day, the ban on iron production was suspended; hereafter, taxes were imposed on farm implements.[xxv] On the sixth day, an emissary from Xiliang Prefecture reached the capital, as did Huihu envoy Anqiusi on the sixteenth, and Wen Chengjiao of Bohai on the eighteenth. The Tangut attacked Fangqu.

In spring of the third year, eighteenth day of the inaugural month [C.E. February 26, 932], Khitan envoy Yegu reached the capital, envoys from Bohai and the Huihu Uighurs arriving on the twenty-seventh. On the twenty-seventh day of the second month, Jingnan governor Yao Yanchou engaged Tangut armies at Niu'ergu and defeated them. Khitan envoys arrived on the second day of the third month. In the summer, eighth day of the fourth month [May 16], an emissary from Silla reached the capital. On the eighth day of the fifth month, the heir to the two princes of Tang and inspector over the heir-apparent's household, Yang Yanshao, inherited the title of Duke of Xi. On the twenty-second day, Meng Zhixiang attacked Dong Zhang to topple the prefecture of Mian [in Shu]. Wang Geon was invested King of Koryô, on the third day of the sixth month, his superintendence over the Dae-eui [Dayi] command confirmed. Meng Zhixiang murdered Dong Zhang to over-

....

xxiv. For times of war, with the kingly way extinct and ritual propriety lost, it is indeed worth noting such dual acts of goodness: commoners still conscious of filial and fraternal ways and their ruler authorizing banner and post, intent on promoting such conduct among the people.

xxv. The practice continues to this day, thus the citation here.

run eastern Chuan. Tartar chieftain Xiege joined tribesmen in coming to submit to dynasty. In the autumn, thirtieth day of the eighth month [October 2], an envoy from Tubo reached the capital. In the winter, twelfth day of the tenth month, the monarch visited Shi Jingtang's residence.

In spring of the fourth year, thirteenth day of the inaugural month [C.E. February 10, 933], the Duanming academician and vice minister of war, Liu Xu, became deputy director of the Imperial Secretariat with ministerial powers. Zhu Huang, an envoy of Meng Zhixiang, reached the capital on the twelfth day of the second month.[xxvi] On the twenty-eighth day of the third month, the Lady of Jin, née Xia, was posthumously invested as empress. In the summer, third day of the fifth month [May 29], imperial sons Congke[xxvii] and Congyi were invested as Princes of Lu and Xu, respectively. Imperial nephews were also invested: Congwen as Prince of Yan, Congzhang as Prince of Yang, and Congmin as Prince of Jing. Khitan envoy Shuguqing reached the capital.

On twenty-first day of the seventh month [August 14], the autumn, the protector-general for the Huihu Uighurs, Limo, came to the capital with offerings of white falcons, the court ordering their release.[2] A general amnesty was declared on the fourth day of the eighth month. On the twenty-fifth day of the ninth month, the court dismissed Zhao Yanshou and replaced him as military commissioner by the governor of Shannan east, Zhu Hongzhao. In the winter, seventeenth day of the tenth month [November 7], Fan Yanguang was dismissed as military commissioner, replaced by Feng Yun, the current commissioner of the Three Fiscal Agencies. The Monarch took ill while visiting Shihe pavilion on the twenty-ninth day.[xxviii] In the eleventh month, the twentieth day [December 9], the Prince of Qin, Congrong, infiltrated the Xingsheng palace with a contingent of soldiers; unable to prevail, execution ensued.[xxix] On the twenty-third, fiscal commissioner Sun Yue was murdered by

....

xxvi. The Ten Kingdoms are extraneous and generally not mentioned [in the Annals for the north]. In this case, Zhixiang was a former Tang subject who once rebelled against it and here reverses himself to declare fealty. He had severed ties because the court would not accept his autonomy and later converted because he still hoped to revert to good. Yet his messenger came without conforming to the proper protocol for a subject, so the form of citation here follows that for barbarian tributaries [who send envoys].

xxvii. Congke was not imperial son, but the word "son" is employed; the rationale here is the same as above, under Youwen, the Prince of Bo in Liang times. [See chapter 2, footnote vii.]

xxviii. I write that he "took ill"; details appear under narrative for Congrong.

xxix. For a son, after his ruler takes ill, to enter the palace accompanied by troops to demand his own installation, rather than seeking to care for the sick, is a crime worthy of death, thus the word "execution" is employed. He believed that the Emperor had already died, and fearing a possible disinheritance, simply deployed troops to secure his enthronement; this was not sedition, so the word "rebellion" is not employed.

Kang Yicheng, chief director of the Imperial Guard and Imperial Bodyguard. The Emperor expired in the Yonghe palace on the twenty-sixth day [December 15].[xxx]

WE LAMENT. Since antiquity, times of good governance are the aberration and tumult the norm. Kings of the Three Dynasties ruled the world for hundreds of years, yet a mere handful of its rulers merit much mention. More can hardly be expected of later times, let alone the Five Dynasties!

Elders have said to me that, "Mingzong, despite his barbarian stock, could be genuinely honorable in character and magnanimous in benevolent love for the people." He rightfully deserves recognition by the standards of Five Dynasties' rulers. Once burning ritual incense by night, he peered to the heavens in prayer, saying, "This servant of yours, barbarian in origin, is scarcely fit to order the world. Tumult has persisted for far too long and I beseech Heaven to sire a Sage-king soon." From the outset of his reign, he curtailed or even discharged staffs of palace ladies and actor-musicians, while eliminating the palace privy such that revenues from locales across the world were all reverted to official repositories. When fires damaged the Guangshou palace and specialists charged with the restoration requested an extra application of red lacquer [to protect the wood], he glumly lamented, "Heaven deploys fire to admonish me. How can further waste possibly be fitting?" One year in the wake of a drought, some snow fell. Sitting in his courtyard exposed to the snow, Mingzong directed workers not to shovel palace precincts, insisting, "This is Heaven's gift to me." He often queried Chief minister Feng Dao and cohort about afflictions upon the common people. They noted that grain and silk were affordable and the people free of pestilence, as Mingzong commented gleefully, "I can hardly accept credit, and indeed, should join You Gentlemen in doing noble deeds to repay Heaven." Whenever aides were found guilty of graft, he imposed summary death, calling them "bloodsuckers of the people." He issued an edict, at the same time, citing honest aides like Sun Yue as an example for the world. In his compassion for the people and concern for things, he certainly aspired to good governance.

Although advanced in years upon his accession, Mingzong never indulged in the sensual, never delighted in the distant hunt. He ruled for seven years, the longest for Five Dynasties' monarchs, when warfare had somewhat abated and material bounty repeatedly surfaced. He nourished the people, quite simply, by giving them rest. But barbarians are by nature intemperate

....

xxx. He was sixty-seven *sui*. In the inaugural year of Qingtai [C.E. 934], he was buried in Luoyang County, Henan. He may have died of natural causes, but was buried by a renegade, so no details pertaining to the burial appear [in the text].

and their benevolence lacks clarity such that courtiers were often executed without good reason. They cannot anticipate and avert, therefore, the ruinous rifts between father and son symbolized by Congrong. Rather, apostasy erupted suddenly with the parties eventually succumbing to horrific evil, the Emperor himself consumed by bitterness upon death.

The vice minister of justice at the time, Kang Cheng, once counseled in a petition on current affairs, "There are five phenomena that need not worry the ruler of men and six phenomena that should rightfully alarm him. He need not worry if the sun, moon, and stars are off orbit, nor worry if change is visible in the heavens, nor worry over the beguiling words of petty men, nor worry if mountains shatter and rivers turn dry, nor worry about the calamities of flood, drought, locusts, and other insects. However, he should rightfully be alarmed if literati of wisdom insist on seclusion, alarmed if the four classes of people change professions, alarmed if superiors commingle with inferiors, alarmed if the sense of honesty and shame wanes, alarmed if truth is corrupted by slander and flattery, and utterly terrified if candid counsel is not heard." Men of knowledge all recognized his words to contain many biting criticisms of prevailing misdeeds. Incidents like the mutiny of Congrong or the deaths of Ren Huan and An Chonghūi may indeed emanate from superiors commingling with inferiors or truth corrupted by slander and flattery. Cheng's words bear relevance to maladies well beyond his own times, so persons aspiring to govern cannot but take heed!

CHAPTER 7

ANNALS VII: BASIC ANNALS OF TANG

Emperor Min [Li Conghou, C.E. 914–934], fifth son of Mingzong, had the personal name Conghou. Physically stout and sturdy, he had a propensity to be sparing in words and steeped in propriety, winning the special love of Mingzong, whom he closely resembled. In the second year of Tiancheng [C.E. 927], with the rank of honorary dignitary of education, Conghou became metropolitan custodian of Henan and overseer of the Six Armies, and later, honorary grand guardian with ministerial standing. Conghou's consort was the daughter of Kong Xun, and Xun's feat of marrying his daughter to Conghou had infuriated An Chonghui, who arranged Xun's dismissal as commissioner of military affairs and Conghou's assignment away from the capital as Xuanwu governor, in the third year [C.E. 928]. Reassignment as Hedong governor occurred a year later. In the inaugural year of Changxing [C.E. 930], invested Prince of Song, Conghou became Chengde governor, then Tianxiong governor in the second year, with concurrent standing as palace secretary conferred later.

In the fourth year [C.E. 933], the eleventh month, the Prince of Qin, Congrong, was executed. Mingzong, gravely ill at the time, had dispatched the eunuch Meng Hanqiong to summon the Prince of Song from Ye. The Emperor expired in the interim, but for six days secrecy was imposed on public mourning. On the first day of the twelfth month [December 20], mourning rites commenced in the western palace, the new Emperor assuming power before the royal coffin. He convened with officialdom on the eastern steps of the palace, then resumed position at the royal bier, donning mourning attire at the western palace, on the fourth.[i] He climbed the stairs to the Guangzheng gate, on the eighth, to inquire of the well-being of civil and military subjects. The wardrobe stewardess, Miss Wang, was slain on the ninth. Court business resumed as usual on the eleventh. Ceremonials stewardess Miss Kang was murdered on the thirteenth. On the fifteenth [C.E. January 3, 934], the court designated Feng Dao as special dignitary for the grand procession to the imperial mausoleum, minister of revenues Han Yanyun as associate dignitary, Palace Secretariat drafter Wang Yan as assisting emissary, minister of rites Wang Quan as deputy for funeral ceremonies, minister of war Li Lin as escort for the royal carriage, deputy-censor Long Min as master of funeral regalia, and left associate at the Imperial Secretariat and provisional administrator for Henan, Lu Zhi, as master for accommodations and transportation. Final mourning observances were held on the twenty-fifth.

In the inaugural year of Yingshun, spring, first day of the inaugural month [January 18], formal audience occurred at the Guangshou palace.[ii] The protector-general for the Khitan, Mo Layu, reached the capital as envoy on the fourth day. On the seventh, a general amnesty, change in reign name, and restoration of musical performances were pronounced. Arrivals in the capital were acknowledged for envoys of Renmei [Renyu], khan of the Huihu Uighurs, and emissaries from Sha and Gua prefectures. On the twenty-fourth, Zhu Hongzhao and Feng Yun donated monies to assist in erecting the royal mausoleum. Investiture of the Empress Dowager occurred on the fifth day of the intercalary month [February 21],[iii] and of the Consort Dowager Wang on the thirteenth. The interim custodian of the northern capital, Shi Jingtang, donated silver and silk to defer construction costs for the hillside mausoleum.

On the twentieth day of the second month [April 6], the Emperor inspected the imperial mausoleum under construction. The Prince of Lu and governor of Fengxiang, Congke, rebelled. On the twenty-first, the interim custodian of the western capital, Wang Sitong, was named chief officer of at-large forces on the western front; deputy officer for the same front was Yao Yanchou, the Jingnan governor. The armies of Sitong met defeat on the six-

....

i. After two dynasties and five rulers, finally we witness revival of the practice whereby a sovereign acceding to power immediately assumes mourning for a predecessor. For the deceased monarch to meet a natural end and the new monarch to enjoy a legitimate beginning, thereby avoiding calamity among courtiers and subjects, is a rare occurrence for such an age of usurpation and turmoil. Thus, more than the usual detail is given.

ii. A lack of ritual propriety is reflected here.

iii. The Empress Dowager's surname is not cited, that is, I refuse to say that "so-and-so was invested as empress"; honors for royal mothers cannot be slighted [as occurred here]. For more on the affair, see biographical chapters.

teenth day of the third month [May 2]: the directors of the Awesome Duty Guard, Yin Hui, and the Forest of Feathers Guard, Yang Siquan, defected in submission to Congke. Murdered on the twenty-first was the chief director of the Imperial Guard and Imperial Bodyguard, Zhu Hongshi. On the twenty-third, the court named Kang Yicheng, governor for the three cities of Heyang, as chief commissioner of bandit suppression for at-large forces at Fengxiang, with Wang Sitong serving as his deputy. The deputy custodian of the western capital, Liu Suiyong, defected in surrender to Congke. Sitong rushed back to the capital [Luoyang], but did not succeed and died with honor. On the twenty-seventh, a mutiny by the inspector of military police in the capital, An Congjin, caused the assassination of Feng Yun and the suicide of Zhu Hongzhao. Congjin conveyed their two heads to Congke. On the twenty-eighth, the Emperor departed for Weizhou‡.[iv]

Emperor Fei [Li Congke, C.E. 887–937] was native to Pingshan, Zhenzhou. Originally surnamed Wang, his family had been obscure and humble for generations, his mother, née Wei, widowed young. She was later abducted by the future Mingzong, when he commanded cavalry through Pingshan. The Woman Wei's son, Asan, then over ten years in age, would be raised by Mingzong as son and given the name Congke. As the youth matured, he acquired a daring and imposing demeanor, a scrupulous integrity and cautious tongue, plus a dauntless valor and combat prowess that caused Mingzong to love him dearly. Ever since the Prince of Jin's armies battled the Liang along the Yellow River, Congke's string of victories caused Zhuangzong, employing his nickname, to exclaim, "Asan is not only the same age as me, but his daring in battle resembles me also!"

In the second year of Tongguang [C.E. 924], he became director of light cavalry for the Weizhou‡ prefect, his armies garrisoned at Shimen. Mingzong's armies, involved in the suppression of rebel Zhao Zaili, abruptly returned southward [in mutiny] from Weizhou. [A sympathetic] Congke deployed garrison men from Quyang and Yu counties, departing from Changshan, to try to catch up with Mingzong. With few troops so far south, Mingzong and his armies rallied passionately upon learning of Congke's men to their rear. After taking the throne, he thus named Congke governor for Hezhong and Prince of Lu. Once Mingzong grew advanced in years, the Prince emerged as eldest among the royal sons. Military commissioner An Chonghui deemed him sufficiently threatening to forge an edict ordering his

....

iv. No citation appears for the Emperor's expiration, for regicide against the Prince of E should rightfully be included in the Annals of Emperor Fei.

elimination by Yang Yanwen, the assistant commander of Hezhong. The Prince was inspecting horses at Huanglong hamlet when Yanwen closed the city gates in defiance. The Prince remained at Yuxiang to report to Mingzong. Summoned back to the capital, he was confined to a residence on Qinghua lane. Chonghui repeatedly demanded the application of martial law in this case, Mingzong refusing to listen. Chonghui was himself later assassinated and the Prince resuscitated as commandant of the Left Guard and interim custodian of the western capital.

In the third year of Changxing [C.E. 932], the Prince became governor of Fengxiang. The Prince's son, Li Chongji, had managed palace armies since Mingzong's oversight over the Crane-Commanding Guard. Chongji was stripped of all military posts after the accession of Emperor Min due to the court dominance of Zhu Hongzhao and Feng Yun, banished to military training commissioner at Bozhou¶. Further reassigned custodian of the northern capital, the private notice had not arrived when the public announcement revealed Li Congzhang as his replacement. Earlier, An Chonghui had fallen from favor and was banished to Hezhong, Congzhang replacing him. Chonghui's subsequent murder left the Prince ever unsettled, his rebellion and occupation of the city ensuing. Emperor Min dispatched Wang Sitong to join a suppression effort with the other governors, but Sitong fled in the wake of defeat, the governors' armies all vanquished.

In the inaugural year of Qingtai, seventeenth day of the third month [C.E. May 3, 934], the Prince led soldiers eastward. He reached Changan on the twentieth and deputy custodian of the western capital, Liu Suiyong, turned against the Tang court to embrace the Prince. Proceeding to Huazhou‡ on the twenty-fourth, the Prince apprehended Yao Yanchou. He then advanced to Lingbao and Tang defectors reverted to him, on the twenty-sixth, led by An Yanwei of Hezhong and Kang Sili of Shan Prefecture. He proceeded to Shanzhou on the twenty-ninth, as Kang Yicheng embraced the Prince and repudiated the Tang court. He murdered the commissioner of palace armies, Meng Hanqiong. Emperor Min assumed exile at Weizhou‡.

On the third day of the fourth month [May 18], summer, the Prince entered the capital as Feng Dao led the official rank and file in greeting him at Jiangqiao. The Prince spurned the gathering, entering the western palace to weep before meeting with officialdom. Feng Dao offered a bow and the Prince reciprocated. He hereafter assumed residence in the Zhide palace. On the fourth, the Son of Heaven was demoted to Prince of E and the Prince of Lu instructed to preside over the empire, by order of the Empress Dowager. The Prince acceded to the throne as emperor on the seventh day. The personal property of Henan residents was diverted to reward troops, on the eighth. A day later, urban property taxes were collected five months in advance as subsidy for troops. The Prince of E fell to regicide on the tenth,[v] the prefect of Ci [Ci‡], Song Lingxun, dying honorably in his service. A general amnesty and change of reign name were announced on the seventeenth. Kang Yicheng and Yao Yanchou were murdered on the twentieth.[vi]

On the seventh day of the fifth month [June 21], Duanming academician and left master of admonition Han Zhaoyin became commissioner of military affairs, with the commissioner of royal estates Liu Yanlang serving as deputy commissioner. Feng Dao was dismissed as minister on the eleventh. Tianxiong governor Fan Yanguang became military commissioner. On the fifteenth, offices were conferred on candidates and imperial clansmen who formerly endorsed Fei's accession. Imperial visits to the residences of Fan Yanguang and Suo Zitong occurred in the sixth month, the eleventh day.

In the autumn, the thirteenth day of the seventh month [August 25], the court named chamberlain for imperial ceremonies Lu Wenji deputy director of the Imperial Secretariat with ministerial powers. It invested as empress the Lady of Pei, née Liu, on the nineteenth. In the eighth month, the third day, it named Yao Yi, left director of the Imperial Secretariat, deputy director of the Palace Secretariat with ministerial powers. Officials preselected by the palace were approved.[vii] The Khitan violated the border during the ninth month. In winter, the eleventh day of the tenth month [November 20], Li Yu‡ and Liu Xu were dismissed. On the ninth day of the twelfth month, Xiongwu governor Zhang Yanlang rose to deputy director of the Palace Secretariat with ministerial standing. The Khitan raided Yunzhou‡. On the twenty-fourth, the Monarch visited Longmen [Loyang]. There was drought.

In spring of the second year, ninth day of the second month [C.E. March 16, 935], Fan Yanguang was dismissed. On the twenty-fourth, the Grand Lady of Lu, née Wei, received posthumous honors as Empress Dowager.[viii] On the seventh day of the third month, the court designated Zhongwu governor Zhao Yanshou as commissioner of military affairs. In the summer, twenty-seventh day of the fifth month, it designated commissioner of the southern

....

v. The import of wording here is the same as above, under "regicide against the Prince of Jiyin."

vi. Having defected from Emperor Min, Yicheng committed a crime deserving of "execution." However, Emperor Fei himself committed a similarly heinous act of murder, so the word "murder" is employed.

vii. The phrase "officials preselected by the palace" doubtless refers to men given office due to association with Emperor Fei when first raising troops in rebellion. Inasmuch as they were not formally chosen by the Ministry of Personnel, their selection required an imperial edict. No lessons, positive or negative, can be inferred by the practice, which would otherwise not be cited; but the *Old History* lacked details, so this point of ignorance is acknowledged to alert the reader to ambiguities.

viii. This investiture is noted because the Lady Wei was not formal mother.

court of palace armies, Liu Yanhao, as commissioner of military affairs. The Khitan pillaged the border. The official multitudes donated horses to military companies, on the twentieth day of the sixth month.[ix] Arriving in the autumn, fifth day of the seventh month [August 6], was Chen Fuhai, protector-general under the khan of the Huihu Uighurs, Renmei [Renyu]. Military commissioner Liu Yanhao was dismissed, as minister of punishments Fang Gao replaced him at the military bureau on the seventeenth day of the ninth month. Envoys from Bohai arrived on the twenty-third.

In spring of the third year, fifth day of the inaugural month [January 31, 936], envoys arrived from Baek-je [Baiji]: imperial son Joong Mee [Chong Mei] received investiture as the Prince of Ong [Yong], on the seventeenth. On the seventeenth day of the third month [April 11], Hanlin academician and vice minister of rites Ma Yinsun was nominated deputy director at the Palace Secretariat with ministerial powers. Hedong governor Shi Jingtang rebelled [at Taiyuan].

In the summer, eighteenth day of the fifth month [June 17], Jianxiong governor Zhang Jingda was named chief commissioner of bandit suppression for the four fronts at Taiyuan, Yiwu governor Yang Guangyuan named deputy. On the twentieth, vanguard director An Shenxin mutinied to surrender to Shi Jingtang, as did An Chongrong, a commander of garrison forces at the Zhenwu command, a day later. On the twenty-fourth day, Tianxiong governor Liu Yanhao was purged by Zhang Lingzhao, inspector-in-chief for the Sage-Sustaining Guard, on assignment there. On the sixth day of the sixth month [June 27], the court employed Ling Zhao as commander of the Thousand-Bull Right Guard and acting prefect of Tianxiong.[x] On the seventeenth, it named Xuanwu governor Fan Yanguang as commissioner of bandit suppression for the four fronts at Tianxiong.

In the autumn, twenty-second day of the seventh month [August 11], Weizhou was conquered and Zhang Lingzhao executed on the twenty-sixth. A day later, the director of the Sage-Extolling Guard, Zhang Wandi, rebelled in surrender to Shi Jingtang. Khitan nobles arrived as ambassadors on the second day of the eighth month. In the ninth month, the eighteenth day, Zhang Jingda was defeated in battle with the Khitan at Taiyuan, then encircled by them at Jin'an. The Emperor departed for Heyang on the twenty-second. In the winter, ninth day of the tenth month [October 26], horses were appropriated and commoners inducted into the military. On the third day of the eleventh month, Lulong governor Zhao Dejun was named general com-

....

ix. The term "company" refers to a unit of troops.
x. The word "employ" [*yi*] is usually not used for the appointment of officials. Use of the word in this context underscores Ling Zhao's willingness to be "employed."

mander of at-large forces. The Khitan established the Jin dynasty on the twelfth day [November 28]. In the intercalary month, the ninth day, the mutinous Yang Guangyuan murdered Zhang Jingda and submitted to the Khitan.[xi] Armies of the Khitan and the Jin dynasty reached Luzhou on the nineteenth day. Emperor Fei departed for Heyang on the twenty-second day, expiring on the twenty-sixth [C.E. January 11, 937].[xii]

WE LAMENT. Between ruler and subject there is much that confounds. The enlightened can anticipate an incident before it erupts, while the muddled apprised of imminent danger remains indifferent. Those who speak up before an incident, however loyal, will not be believed. Those who allow an incident to erupt, only to express regrets after the fact, are anything but timely! Only An Chonghui consistently portended the peril of the Prince of Lu but did not counter him effectively, at the ultimate cost of losing the lives of himself and his extended family. His undoing derived from this. The deceased Emperor Min was buried at Huiling, the sight of his tumulus anguishing passersby. If Mingzong had known, his chagrin over Chonghui would have been palpable. A true pity!

....

xi. Rather than "die with honor," Jingda is said to have been "murdered." As a leading general, he was obliged to execute Guangyuan for his transgressions. If he had failed and ended up murdered by Guangyuan, he could still have died "honorably." However, Jingda induced Guangyuan to murder him to facilitate Guangyuan's defection—the citation here reflecting Jingda's own wishes. [Chapter 33.]

xii. He was fifty-one *sui*. The Emperor died by setting himself afire. Emperor Gaozu of the Jin dynasty ordered the burial of his remains at the Huiling frontier.

CHAPTER 8

....

ANNALS VIII: BASIC ANNALS OF JIN

Gaozu [Shi Jingtang, C.E. 892–942], the Sagaciously Literate, Martially Enlightened, Virtuous and Filial Emperor was sired by Nieliji, originally a western barbarian who joined Zhuye tribes in relocating to the Yin Mountain region upon conversion to the Tang dynasty. Subsequently, the Prince of Jin, Li Keyong, rose in rebellion in the vicinity of Yun‡ and Shuo prefectures. And Nieliji, skilled as horseman and archer, often attended the Prince of Jin on campaigns, proving accomplished. Appointments culminated in prefect of Mingzhou. Nieliji fathered Jingtang and assumed the surname Shi, although the origins of the surname are unknown. By character, Jingtang was solemnly sincere and sparing in words. The future Mingzong of Tang so favored him as to offer a daughter in marriage: the Princess Yongning. For this reason, Jingtang often served under Mingzong's command, his unit known as the Left Brigade of Archers.

After the acquisition of Weizhou by the future Zhuangzong, Liang commander Liu Xun stormed Qingping. Zhuangzong rushed to its rescue, but even before his men could fight, he was surrounded by Xun. Shi Jingtang and a dozen or so cavalrymen now charged forth with lances to retrieve Zhuangzong for a safe return. Zhuangzong acknowledged his heroism with a hearty clap on the back, picking up morsels of the cheese and chewy cakes that barbarians treasure to feed him by hand. Hereafter, Jingtang's reputation reverberated throughout the military. In the fifteenth year [C.E. 918], as Zhuangzong fought at Huliu, his vanguard Zhou Dewei died in battle. Jingtang's Left Brigade of Archers thereafter assisted Mingzong in another victory over Liang armies. Liang commanders such as Hu Lutao and Yang Cun did defeat Mingzong, yet he was often delivered from danger by Shi Jingtang.

Mingzong was leading the suppression of turncoat Zhao Zaili when his men mutinied at Weizhou [to enthrone him]. He originally considered going personally to the Son of Heaven to distinguish himself from the rebels, yet Jingtang reckoned to him, "Scarcely can a military mutiny erupt on the frontier without the leading generals goading the rebels. Moreover, hesitancy is the bane of military men, speedy action the better alternative. Provide several hundred horsemen and I will lead an advance raid on Bianzhou. Owing to the strategic import of Yimen to the empire, if you can acquire it, your higher mission is achievable." Mingzong agreed and provided Jingtang with three hundred crack horsemen as vanguard, crossing the Yellow River at Liyang, as he proceeded to occupy Bianzhou. Zhuangzong arrived later from Luoyang and could not enter the city, so his troops scattered in defeat as he returned westward. Mingzong had placed the vanguard against him under Jingtang's direction, in the interim, and it rushed Sishui to capture the remnant troops of Zhuangzong, who fell in an act of regicide as Mingzong assumed power. Jingtang was rewarded with the Baoyi governorship and conferred the appellation, "Subject of Merit, Exhaustive in Loyalty and Accomplished as Strategist and Dynastic Resuscitator." He served currently as deputy commissioner of the Six Armies.

At Shanzhou, Jingtang is said to have governed with honesty. At the time, local overlords often refused to abide by the laws, such that Tao Qi of Deng Prefecture and Li Ye of Bozhou¶ both proposed sentences of death for graft and other official improprieties. Mingzong responded by issuing an edict praising honest officials such as An Chongruan of Pu‡ Prefecture, Zhang Wanjin of Ming, and Sun Yue of Yao, using them as examples to the world. Jingtang topped the list.

In the second year of Tiancheng, the tenth month [C.E. 927], Shi Jingtang accompanied the Emperor to Bianzhou as commissioner of the imperial encampment. Advanced to the Xuanwu governor and chief director of cavalry and infantry in the Imperial Guard and Imperial Bodyguard, Jingtang retained his old post as deputy commissioner of the Six Armies. His title of honor now became "Subject of Merit, Luminously Loyal, Unstintingly Steadfast, and Enduringly Ethical." In the fourth month of the third year [C.E. 928], reassigned to the Tianxiong governorship as metropolitan custodian of Xingtang, the court conferred ministerial standing. Honors as chief commander of reserve cavalry came in the fifth month. During the rebellion of Dong Zhang in eastern Chuan, Jingtang served as commander of bandit-suppressing forces at large. He returned after failing to prevail over Dong Zhang, reassuming concurrent powers as deputy commissioner for the Six Armies.

Jingtang was in the midst of reassignment as governor of the three cities of Heyang when the Khitan, Tuhun, and Tujue Turks all launched invasions. Congrong, the Prince of Qin, was then serving as general commander of the Six Armies, and Jingtang was apprehensive about continuing to serve as his deputy, convinced that Congrong would someday bring peril. He thus offered to assume the commissionership itself. When orders arrived retaining him as deputy, Jingtang promptly declined the assignment altogether. Mingzong repeatedly quizzed senior courtiers about prospective appointees, Fan Yanguang and Zhao Yanshou all concurring about Jingtang. In this way, the court named him governor of Hedong, chief coordinator for the multiracial force of cavalry and infantry for the Datong, Zhangguo, Zhenwu, and Weisai commands. He now acted on orders, inasmuch as deputy oversight over the Six Armies had been dropped.

In the subsequent year [C.E. 933], Mingzong expired and Emperor Min acceded to power, elevating Shi Jingtang to palace secretary before reassignment as Chengde governor, in the third month. During the fifth month of the inaugural year of Qingtai [C.E. 934], upon reappointment as governor of Taiyuan, he came to the capital for an audience. The rebellion at Fengxiang of Congke, the Prince of Lu, had just erupted, and Emperor Min, fleeing the capital, encountered Jingtang on the highway. Jingtang murdered more than a hundred in the Emperor's entourage, then incarcerated him at Weizhou‡ before departing. Once Emperor Fei assumed power, he felt certain of Jingtang's rebel designs.

In the fifth month of the inaugural year of Tianfu [C.E. 936], Shi Jingtang was named Tianping governor, an appointment he ultimately declined. "The Former Monarch long ago conferred the Taiyuan command, so reassignment today without cause can only infer suspicion of possible rebel intent," he confided to a subordinate. "Moreover, Taiyuan has difficult terrain and plenty of food. Is it not feasible to issue a call to arms to the various governors at home while soliciting assistance from the Khitan abroad?" Sang Weihan, Liu Zhiyuan, and others uniformly concurred with the plan. Jingtang now petitioned the court, denouncing the installation of Emperor Fei and requesting enthronement instead of Congyi, the Prince of Xu, as heir to Mingzong. Emperor Fei promptly stripped Jingtang of all offices and titles, ordering Zhang Jingda and cohort to suppress his insurrection. Jingtang hence turned to the Khitan for assistance. In the ninth month, the Khitan ruler Yelü Deguang penetrated the empire via Yanmen to engage Tang armies in battle; Jingda was devastatingly defeated. Meanwhile, Jingtang departed through the city's northern gate under the cover of night to confer with Deguang, the two swearing allegiance as father and son.

On the twelfth day of the eleventh month [November 28], the Emperor [Jingtang] acceded to the throne and adopted the "Jin" as dynastic designation.[i] Relinquished to the Khitan were [sixteen] prefectures: You, Zhuo, Ji‡, Tan‡, Shun, Ying¶, Mo¶, Wei¶, Shuo, Yun‡, Ying‡, Xin, Gui¶, Ru‡, Wu, and Huan. The palace announced a general amnesty and change of calendar on the fourteenth, naming administrative secretary Sang Weihan as Hanlin academician, vice minister of rites, and commissioner of military affairs.

On the eleventh day of the intercalary month [December 27], the Hanlin recipient of edicts and vice minister of finance, Zhao Ying, was named deputy director at the Chancellery with ministerial powers; named deputy director at the Palace Secretariat was Sang Weihan, who shared ministerial powers while serving concurrently as military affairs commissioner. On the nineteenth, Zhao Dejun and his son, Yanshou, defected from the Tang to submit to the Jin; the Khitan took them back north in fetters. Imperial armies proceeded to Heyang on the twenty-fourth, where governor Chang Congjian defected from the Tang to submit to dynasty.[ii] The Emperor arrived from Taiyuan on the twenty-sixth, dismissing Lu Wenji and Yao Yi. After a general amnesty was announced on the twenty-ninth, Zhang Yanlang and Liu Yanlang were murdered, with only Fang Gao receiving a pardon.

On the first day of the twelfth month [C.E. January 16, 937], the Emperor departed for Heyang. Wang Congke was posthumously relegated to commoner status.[iii] On the third day, dignitary for public works Feng Dao received concurrent powers as deputy director of the Chancellery with ministerial powers. The military director at Caozhou, Shi Chongli, murdered his prefect, Zheng Wan [Ruan], on the fifth. The Emperor personally issued a plea for candid discourse, on the seventh. Two days later, the chief inspector at the Zhenzhou headquarters, Bi Qiong, purged deputy governor Li Yanqi. An assistant commander at Tongzhou, Men Duo, murdered his commander, Yang Hanbin. On the sixteenth, Tianping governor Wang Jianli murdered deputy governor Li Yanyun. There was drought.

In spring of the second year, tenth day of the inaugural month [February 22], Anyuan governor Lu Wenjin defected to surrender to the Wu kingdom. On the fourteenth day, Tianxiong governor Fan Yanguang murdered Bi Qiong, de-

i. The Basic Annals of Emperor Fei states that "the Khitan established the Jin," based on the Tang perspective. Here the words "he acceded to the imperial throne" imply that Jingtang installed himself and highlight his original intent. The defection and eventual installation of Jin founder Gaozu was certain even without Khitan assistance. Inasmuch as becoming emperor was his own ambition, Jingtang bears personal responsibility for his own vice.

ii. Emperor Fei was still alive at the time.

iii. "Wang Congke" [rather than Li Congke] represents the original wording of Jin times.

fense commissioner for Qizhou¶]. On the twenty-fifth, vice minister of war Li Song became vice director at the Palace Secretariat with powers as chief minister and commissioner of military affairs. The male descendants of the Tang imperial clan were invested as dukes; Duke Xi of the Sui dynasty was designated heir to the two royal princes, and Duke Jie of the Zhou dynasty was designated heir to the "three royal lines."[iv] Jieli, heir-apparent to the Khitan ruler, arrived in the capital as envoy on the fourteenth day of the second month. The Emperor departed for Bianzhou on the twenty-seventh day of the third month.

In summer, fifth day of the fourth month [May 17], pardons were issued for prisoners and land taxes remitted to the people. Zhao Ying served as envoy to the Khitan. On the ninth, the Xuanwu governor Yang Guangyuan made a monetary donation on behalf of the empire. Li Kexing, commissioner of imperial halls and parks for the Khitan, arrived as ambassador. On the eleventh day of the fifth month [June 21], the Emperor made a personal plea for candid discourse. On the twenty-sixth day, posthumous honors as "Emperor" were extended to paternal ancestors and "Empress" given to their wives: the imperial great-great grandfather, Jing, renamed Xiao'an, received the temple designation of Jingzu; the sobriquet Xiao'an Yuan went to his wife, née Qin. Great-grandfather Chen, renamed Xiaojian, received the temple designation of Suzu; the sobriquet Xiaojian Gong went to his wife, née An. Grandfather Yu, renamed Xiaoping, received the temple designation of Ruizu; the sobriquet Xiaoping Xian went to his wife, née, Lai. Imperial father Shaoyong, renamed Xiaoyuan, received the temple designation of Xianzu; the sobriquet Xiaoyuan Yi went to his wife, née He.

On the second day of the sixth month [July 12], a Khitan legal officer arrived in the capital as envoy. Tianxiong governor Fan Yanguang rebelled. On the eleventh day, arrows were conveyed [bearing military orders] to Fu Yanrao, the Yicheng governor. On the twenty-eighth, Yang Guangyuan was appointed chief officer for at-large forces on the four fronts of Weizhou. The inspector of military police for the eastern capital, Zhang Congbin, rebelled; Li Xia, administrative assistant to the interim custodian, died honorably resisting him. The suppression mission was entrusted to Hou Yi and Du Chongwei, chief directors of the Empire-Upholding and the Sage-Protecting guards, respectively. Congbin plundered Heyang, slaying imperial son Chongxin; he also sacked Henan Prefecture, where imperial son Chongyi was murdered.

During autumn, the seventh month, Zhang Congbin overran Sishui Pass, killing its inspector of military police, Song Tinghao. On the second day

....

iv. The personal names of imperial clansmen of the Tang have been lost to history. This citation serves to illustrate the continued existence of heirs to the two royal princes and the three royal lines; no need to cite the actual persons.

[August 10], the commandant of the Right Guard, Yin Hui, made an abortive attempt to defect and flee to the Wu kingdom, only to be executed. The commandant of the right guard for palace-gate security, Lou Jiying, mutinied to submit to Zhang Congbin. Turmoil erupted at the Yicheng command, resulting in the murder of Bai Fengjin, the chief director of cavalry and infantry in the Imperial Guard, then on regional assignment. On the fourth day, Ma Wan of the Empire-Upholding Guard on local assignment apprehended Fu Yanrao and returned him to the capital; the court ordered his murder at Chigang.[v] On the fifth, Yang Guangyuan became chief commissioner of the bandit-suppression forces at large at Weizhou. Du Chongwei conquered Sishui Pass on the eleventh.[vi] Yang Guangyuan conquered Bozhou on the twenty-second. On the twenty-sixth, Wang Hui, the director for defense reserves at Anzhou, assassinated his governor, Zhou Gui. The suppression was entrusted to Li Jinquan, commandant of the Right Guard.[vii]

On the sixteenth day of the eighth month [September 23], Jingnan governor An Shuqian donated horses to augment military forces. On the twenty-fifth, pardons were announced for noncapital offenses as well as partisans of Zhang Congbin, Fu Yanrao, and Wang Hui. Grains were donated by Yang Guangyuan during the ninth month. In winter, the second day of the tenth month, the production of military equipment was banned. In spring of the third year, twenty first day of the second month [C.E. March 24, 938], the various governors offered donations as subsidy to the government.[viii] Arriving on the fifteenth day of the third month was Zhai Quanfu, envoy of Renmei [Renyu], Khan of the Huihu Uighurs. The court banned private production of bronze objects.

In the autumn, sixteenth day of the seventh month [August 14], "monies for imperial enterprises" were used to produce coins celebrating the dynasty's new mandate.[ix] On the fourth day of the eighth month, Feng Dao and the left associate at the Imperial Secretariat Liu Xu received palace credentials as protocol ambassadors to the Khitan. On the eighth day, Chanzhou prefect Feng

....

v. Yanrao committed the crime of indulging his military, but was killed after being falsely accused of rebellion; thus, I do not say, "he was executed," but rather that "the court ordered his murder," to stress that Ma Wan killed him illicitly.

vi. Zhang Congbin killed himself by leaping into a river, so "execution" is not cited.

vii. Hui had fled before Jinquan arrived, subsequently to be killed. Thus, the citation here does not say that Hui "rebelled," nor does it mention the "conquest" of Anzhou or his "execution."

viii. Forcing the common people to provide for their superiors reflects a greed common to both ruler and official subjects. By now, practices of graft proved too numerous to count and are lumped together through simple reference to "[donations of] the various governors;" similar citations do not appear later.

ix. The production of coins need not be cited, but "monies for imperial enterprises" [*huangye qian*] represent the Son of Heaven's private reserve, our citation exposing the amassing of a private cache.

Hui surrendered. The court authorized the selection of palace-nominated officials on the twelfth, while remitting taxes for the victims of floods and droughts on the fifteenth. Court directors of actors and musicians were "reverted" to the Khitan on the twenty-seventh.[x] Fan Yanguang was pardoned on the fifth day of the ninth month [October 1].[xi] Reverted to the Khitan were Gentle Whip guardsman Liu Shouwei, document-verifying officer Wang Yin, and astronomy student Yin Hui, on the fifteenth.[1] Envoys Ma Jirong arrived from Yutian and Li Wanjin from the Huihu Uighurs. An amnesty was announced for Weizhou and the taxes of its people remitted on the twenty-fifth. The commissioner of the southern court for palace armies, Liu Churang, became commissioner of military affairs during this month.

In winter, the fifth day of the tenth month [October 30], the Khitan commissioned imperial secretary and envoy Han Jia [Jiong] to invest Gaozu as the "Heroically Martial and Eminently Righteous Emperor." On the seventh day, Bianzhou was designated as the "eastern capital," Luoyang designated the "western capital," and Yongzhou renamed Jinchang Commandery. On the fifteenth, chief of staff of the Imperial Insignia Right Bodyguard Ma Congbin was commissioned as ambassador to the Khitan. On the twenty-second, Khitan noblemen arrived as envoys. The court pronounced a general amnesty on the twenty-fifth and invested Li Shengtian as King of the Jewel Kingdom of Yutian on the twenty-seventh. On the eighth day of the eleventh month, Guangjin Commandery was renamed the Ye capital. The court abolished the director's position at the imperial mint on the nineteenth. On the third day of the twelfth month [December 27], it invested imperial son Chonggui as Prince of Zheng.

In the fourth year, spring, the inaugural month [C.E. 939], bandits plundered the tomb of Emperor Min of the Tang.[xii] On the ninth day, the defense commissioner for Chanzhou, Zhang Cong'en, was named deputy commis-

....

x. Gaozu treated the Khitan with the deference afforded fathers; thus, all things demanded by them were not said to have been "given" but rather "reverted," as if somehow presented to a superior.

xi. Yanguang had originally sought to surrender, but Gaozu rejected the offer. Yanguang subsequently delivered a staunch resistance such that he could not be overpowered even after prolonged siege. Gaozu ultimately regretted the matter and pardoned him. Thus, it is not said that Yanguang "surrendered."

xii. Emperor Min was interred within the burial compound of Mingzong: Huiling. Because his tomb lacked a formal name, there appears here only a general reference to "tomb." The posthumous title of Emperor Min was conferred retroactively by Gaozu of Jin upon his accession. Posthumous titles for emperors of the Five Dynasties, as they do not reflect normative practice, do not generally merit note. Citation is appropriate here, in the case of Emperor Min, in order to highlight his one-time demotion to the Prince of E. When empires collapse, rituals are slighted. The *Old History* and the *Veritable Records* for the period both lack dates for the request and conferral of posthumous titles. Events such as [the tomb desecration] remind us of the frustration of citing even matters that merit citation.

sioner of military affairs. The court authorized plaques and banners for the home of Shenzhou resident Li Zilun. Arriving on the third day of the third month [March 26] was the protector-general Yelidun, an envoy sent by the Huihu Uighurs. On the fourteenth, the *Modified Calendar* was promulgated. A garrison commander at Lingzhou‡, Wang Yanzhong, rebelled at Huaiyuan township; he surrendered on the seventeenth and was killed by Qi Yanzuo, manager of palace services.

In the summer, tenth day of the fourth month [May 1], the khan of the Huihu Uighurs, Renmei [Renyu], was invested Khan of Fenghua. The court abolished the military affairs commission on the thirteenth day. In autumn, the seventeenth day of the seventh month, the minting of coins was again proscribed. On the third day of the intercalary month [August 20], Sang Weihan was dismissed as minister. Dikes of the Yellow River ruptured at Boping [Bozhou] on the first day of the eighth month. The Xirong Tibetans pillaged Jingzhou‡, and the Zhangyi governor, Zhang Yanze, defeated them to apprehend ringleader Yeliluoxiadu. On the ninth day of the ninth month [October 24], Khitan envoy Nianmugu reached the capital. On the fifteenth, Li Congyi was invested Duke of Xun and ritual heir to the Tang royal line. The grand arbiter of Koryŏ, Heyong Soon [Xing Shun], arrived on the eighteenth day as envoy of the king, Wang Geon. In winter, the eighth day of the eleventh month, an ancestral temple was erected in the western capital for emperors of the Tang: Gaozu, Taizong, Zhuangzong, Mingzong, and Min. Khitan envoy Yaozhe arrived on the twenty-first. Bayanzu of Tubo offered his fealty.

In the fifth year, spring, first day of the inaugural month [C.E. February 11, 940], the public and private debts of the people were forgiven as part of a minor amnesty. The Huihu envoy Shihaijin arrived on the twenty-third. In summer, the twenty-ninth day of the fourth month, the Khitan Prince of Xinghua arrived. On the twenty-first day of the fifth month, Anyuan governor Li Jinquan defected to surrender to the Southern Tang. On the ninth day of the sixth month, [Tang ruler] Li Bian dispatched commander Li Chengyu to occupy Anzhou. In the aftermath of Jinquan's flight to the Tang, the new Anyuan governor, Ma Quanjie, engaged the army of Chengyu and prevailed. Anzhou was recaptured on the twenty-third, forcing Chengyu to flee to Yunmeng, where he was apprehended by Quanjie and killed.

In the autumn, fourth day of the eighth month [September 19], a royal inspection of farming occurred in the western suburbs. Yang Guangyuan, interim custodian of the western capital, murdered the grand preceptor to the heir-apparent, Fan Yanguang, on the twenty-sixth. In the ninth month, the fifth day, Hanlin recipient of edicts and vice minister of finance, He Ning, became deputy director of the Palace Secretariat with ministerial powers. A royal inspection of farming occurred on the nineteenth, at Shatai. During winter, the fifteenth day of the tenth month, Khitan noblemen reached the capital as envoys. On the fifteenth day of the eleventh month, the festival of the winter solstice was inaugurated with two ceremonial dances.

In the sixth year, spring, eighteenth day of the inaugural month [C.E. February 16, 941], Tang Shuyu was invested as King of Xing'an and Taitai as Duke of Changning. On the eighteenth day of the second month, the court ceased to charge officials for palace banquets. It abolished the collection of taxes two to four years in advance, during the third month.[xiii] In summer, the thirtieth day of the fourth month, Khitan envoy Shukuo reached the capital, as did the Tuhun chieftain Baichengfu in the fifth month and the Tujue envoy Xue Tonghai on the twenty-fourth day of the seventh month, the autumn.

On the fifth day of the eighth month [August 29], as the Monarch departed for the Ye capital, he entrusted the interim regency for the eastern capital to Chonggui, the Prince of Zheng and current metropolitan custodian of Kaifeng; the chief director of armed forces in and away from the capital became Zhang Cong'en, commissioner of the southern court for palace armies. A general amnesty was declared on the fifteenth. On the twenty-seventh, the court named Zhang Cheng, chamberlain of imperial recreations, as envoy to the Khitan, followed by former Anguo governor Yang Yanxun, on the eighteenth day of the ninth month. Envoy Baikejiu of the Tuhun arrived on the twentieth. Dikes on the Yellow River broke at the "central capital," its waters polluting the Ta River.

The Yellow River ruptured dikes at Hua, Pu, Yun, and Chan prefectures during the tenth month, wintertime. The governor of Shannan east circuit, An Congjin, rebelled. The suppression was entrusted to Gao Xingzhou, on the twenty-first of the eleventh month, the interim custodian of the western capital now empowered as chief officer for advance forces on the southern front. On the first day of the twelfth month [December 21], Chonggui, the Prince of Zheng, was named metropolitan custodian of Guangjin Commandery, his noble status changed to Prince of Qi. Guo Jinhai, the chief director of vanguard armies, engaged the men of An Congjin at Tangzhou and defeated them. An Chongrong, the Chengde governor, also rebelled. Entrusted with the suppression was Du Chongwei, the Tianping governor and now bandit-suppressing commissioner of at-large forces at Zhenzhou. Ambassadors for the Khitan arrived on the eleventh. Du Chongwei engaged An Chongrong in battle at Zongcheng [Beizhou] and prevailed, on the thirteenth.

....

xiii. This is an indication of the magnitude of current impositions and the people's inability to cope.

In the seventh year, spring, second day of the inaugural month [C.E. January 21, 942], Zhenzhou fell and rebel An Chongrong was executed. A pardon was announced for the Guangjin metropolis. Khitan envoy Dala arrived on the fifteenth. In the third month, Guide governor An Yanwei repaired ruptures in Yellow River dikes at Huazhou. In the intercalary month, locusts at Tianxing devoured the wheat crop. In the summer, twenty-second day of the fifth month, the Concubine Dowager Liu was honored as Empress Dowager.[xiv] On the fourth day of the sixth month, the ambassador for the Tuhun, Nianchouhan, reached the capital. On the thirteenth [July 28], the Emperor expired in the Baochang palace.[xv]

....

xiv. She was the biological mother of Gaozu.
xv. He was fifty-one *sui*.

CHAPTER 9

ANNALS IX: BASIC ANNALS OF JIN

Emperor Chu [Shi Chonggui, C.E. 914–947] was sired by Jingru, the elder brother of Gaozu and cavalry commander under Emperor Zhuangzong of the Tang. When he died young, Gaozu raised his orphan son, Chonggui, as son. Gaozu personally sired six boys, five of whom died prematurely while Chongrui was still a child, so Chonggui won installation.

As a youth, Chonggui was scrupulously principled and skilled as horseman and archer. Gaozu once arranged for doctoral degree holder Wang Zhen to instruct him in the *Book of Rites*. Unable to comprehend the work's general thrust even after much time, Chonggui asserted to Zhen, "This is not the calling of my family." Having been installed by the Khitan, Gaozu had planned to name a son as interim custodian of Taiyuan, but the Khitan ambassador personally lined up all of Gaozu's sons to make the selection himself. Pointing to Chonggui, the envoy pronounced, "The one with the large eyes will do!" Appointments ensued as grandmaster of imperial recreations with gold and purple insignia, acting metropolitan custodian of Taiyuan, and interim custodian of the northern capital, as well as governor of Hedong.

In the second year of Tianfu, the ninth month [C.E. 937], the capital summoned him to serve as generalissimo of the Imperial Insignia Left Guard. Appointed metropolitan custodian of Kaifeng in the third year, wintertime, he received investiture as Prince of Zheng and titular advancement to grand guardian with ministerial standing. In the sixth year, as Gaozu toured the Ye capital, Chonggui served as interim custodian of the eastern capital, and later, custodian of Guangjin metropolis with new vestments as Prince of Qi.

During the seventh year, thirteenth day of the sixth month [C.E. July 28, 942], Gaozu expired and the Prince acceded the imperial throne before his coffin. On the eighteenth, the palace dispatched commander Shi Dechao of the Valorous Right Guard to the western hills of Xiangzhou‡, where two of the Emperor's horses were sacrificed by pummeling.[i] Granaries officer Li Renkuo was commissioned as ambassador to the Khitan, just as Khitan noblemen arrived as envoys. On the twenty-fourth, the court named Feng Dao as dignitary for the grand procession to the imperial hillside mausoleum, Chancellery deputy director Dou Zhengu as deputy dignitary, chamberlain for imperial ceremonies Cui Zhuo as master of funeral ceremonies, vice minister of finance Lu Qi as escort for the royal carriage, and deputy censor Wang Yijian as master of funeral regalia.[ii] Named ambassadors to the Khitan on the twenty-seventh were Zhu Chongjie and Liang Yan, the master for diplomatic accommodations and the generalissimo of the Imperial Insignia Right Guard, respectively.

In the autumn, tenth day of the seventh month [August 24], Imperial Grandmother Liu expired and court audiences were suspended for three days.[iii] On the fifteenth, the court sent Shi Dechao to pummel horses to death in the western hills of Xiangzhou‡.[iv] A general amnesty was declared on the eighteenth. An interpreter for the Khitan arrived on the twenty-second.

On the seventh day of the eighth month [September 19], Gao Xingzhou seized Xiangzhou.[v] On the ninth, Tianping governor Jing Yanguang, Yicheng governor Li Shouzhen, and Zhangde governor Guo Jin each contributed cash and grain to defer construction costs for the hillside mausoleum. Khitan ambassador Langwu arrived on the thirteenth. On the nineteenth, the imperial grandmother was buried in Wei County. Director of accommodations Zhang Jiusi arrived as Khitan envoy on the twenty-second. In the ninth month, the twentieth day, Li Shouzhen became chief officer for the grand procession to the hillside mausoleum of the deceased Emperor.

....

i. This is a custom of the barbarians.
ii. The *Old History* and *Veritable Records* fail to mention the nomination of a deputy for accommodations and transportation: either the appointment never occurred or a citation was never made. The same holds for Gaozu of Han.
iii. The biological mother of Gaozu, she had been honored as Empress Dowager during his reign. Upon her death, however, the mourning and burial rites employed did not conform to the protocol for empresses—a sign of parsimony in the requisite protocol. She is not called "Empress Dowager," for she was simply [the adoptive] grandmother of Emperor Chu. The word "expired" [*beng*] is employed, a term appropriate to her status.
iv. A reference to the custom has been provided earlier, permitting economy on words here.
v. An Congjin died after setting himself afire, so no mention is made of "execution."

In winter, the ninth day of the tenth month [November 19], Khitan noblemen arrived as ambassadors, envoys for the Huihu Uighurs arriving on the twentieth. A Khitan minister came as envoy in the eleventh month. On the tenth day, the Sagaciously Literate, Martially [Enlightened, Virtuous,] and Filial Emperor was buried at the Xianling mausoleum.[vi] On the nineteenth, the steward for cattle and sheep, Dong Yin, was designated ambassador to the Khitan. The ancestral tablet for Gaozu was placed in the Imperial Ancestors' Temple on the twentieth. For residents along the cortege route for Gaozu, tax reductions by half were announced on the twenty-first. During the twelfth month, twenty-first day, interim custodian of the northern capital Liu Zhiyuan presented tents with white-coned roofs.[vii] A Khitan special envoy, Lingguzhi, reached the capital, as did their envoy Yelisi a day later. Arrivals were announced for Liu Zaisheng, protector-general from Yutian, on the twenty-seventh, accompanied by emissaries Cao Yuanshen of Sha Prefecture and Cao Yuanzhong of Gua. Droughts and locusts ravaged the empire.

In spring of the eighth year, the inaugural month, Wuduo'ao reached the capital on a mission for the Khitan court. On the fourth day of the second month [C.E. March 12, 943], Jing Yanguang was named commissioner of imperial encampments, the Monarch departing for the eastern capital on the eleventh. Prisoners at Guangjin metropolis received pardons. Proceeding to Chanzhou on the twelfth, a pardon for prisoners was issued once again. The Monarch arrived from the Ye capital on the seventeenth. On the twenty-second, the winter solstice, he conducted mountain sacrifices at the Southern Hamlet's Xianling mausoleum, the burning of imperial clothes and paper money attending the ceremony.[viii] With Zhao Ying dismissed on the first day of the third month, Jinchang governor Sang Weihan became director of the Chancellery. Meng Chenghui, the master of palace access and minister of supplemental revenues, was named ambassador to the Khitan. A locust blight occurred.

In summer, the twenty-third day of the fourth month [May 29], Dong Yin served as ambassador to the Khitan. Manager of palace services Zhang Fu led

....

vi. The mausoleum was located at Shou'an County, Henan. For times of such tumult as the Five Dynasties, five of the seven men to rule thus far did not die naturally. Mingzong may have died of natural causes, but Emperor Min did not succeed in burying him, the burial only undertaken upon Emperor Fei's accession. Such irregularities, therefore, are not cited. Emperor Chu represents the first son to manage to bury his father and even place his tablet in the Imperial Ancestors' Temple, so details are provided.

vii. "Tents with white-coned roofs" are used by the barbarians.

viii. Such practices as "burning imperial clothes" and "sacrificing in the wilderness" are practices of vulgar men whose adoption by the Son of Heaven reflects the severe degradation of rites and music.

the Inspired Submission Guard in trapping locusts at Chenzhou‡. In the fifth month, Taining governor An Shenxin trapped locusts in the "central capital." Imperial uncle Shi Jingru was posthumously invested Prince of Song on the tenth day. The court dismissed Feng Dao on the twenty-sixth, and a day later, announced a general amnesty in response to the ravages of drought and locusts. On the fourth day of the sixth month, sacrifices to ameliorate the locust blight were conducted at the palace's external gate. Seven managers of palace services led the Empire-Upholding Guard in trapping locusts within the capital, on the seventeenth. On the twenty-fifth day, grains of the people were collected in advance, death sentences imposed on those guilty of hoarding.

In autumn, the eighteenth day of the seventh month [August 21], the Empress Dowager received investiture. The Emperor practiced archery at the southern hamlet on the twenty-first. Khitan noblemen arrived as envoys. On the twenty-eighth, Li Hanchao of palace services directed Empire-Upholding guardsmen in trapping locusts within the capital. On the first day of the eighth month, the people were recruited to trap locusts, their services remunerated with grain. The court confiscated early harvests of the people on the fifth. On the third day of the ninth month, honors were extended to the Lady of Qin, née An, as the Consort Dowager. Imperial visits occurred at Danian hamlet, as well as Jing Yanguang's residence, on the twenty-first.

In winter, the third day of the tenth month [November 3], the Emperor installed Lady Feng as Empress.[ix] He hunted game in nearby suburbs, on the seventh, before departing for Shatai. Khitan interpreter Liu Yin arrived on the twenty-first. The advance collection of grains from the people occurred on the twenty-fifth. In the eleventh month, the fifth day, Dong Yin served as ambassador to the Khitan. The Emperor visited Bajiao to inspect grazing horses on the tenth. Khitan noblemen arrived as envoys on the twenty-first, and on the twenty-fourth, the Qizhou¶ prefect Yang Chengzuo fled to Qingzhou‡. On the twenty-seventh, the grand arbiter of Koryô, Kim In-bong [Jin Renfeng], arrived in the capital as its ambassador. In the twelfth month, the ninth day, the court named ambassadors to the Khitan: secretarial overseer Bian Guangfan and Dengzhou‡ prefect Guo Yanwei. The chief minister of Koryô arrived as ambassador. Pinglu governor Yang Guangyuan rebelled as prefect Zhai Jinzong of Zizhou died with honor.

In the inaugural year of Kaiyun, first day of the inaugural month [C.E. January 28, 944], spring, the Khitan invaded Cang Prefecture, overrunning Bei on the sixth. The court named Guide governor Gao Xingzhou, on the seventh day, chief officer of at-large forces on the northern front. Khitan

....

ix. Miss Feng was the aunt [*shumu*] of the Emperor.

armies infiltrated Yanmen to raid Daizhou. A day later, palace deputy Wang Ban departed as envoy to the Khitan, but could not advance beyond the Ye capital and returned.[x] A vast famine struck. On the ninth day, former Jingnan governor Li Zhou was named interim custodian of the "eastern capital" and Jing Yanguang named commissioner of imperial encampments. A northern expedition began on the twelfth. The Khitan raided Liyang a day later. On the eighteenth, military exercises took place at Chanzhou. The Khitan quartered men at Yuancheng, as Zhao Yanshou raided Nanle. On the twenty-first, the court named Liu Zhiyuan bandit-suppressing commissioner of at-large forces at Youzhou. Horses were appropriated. The Khitan raided Liyang on the twenty-third. Liu Zhiyuan, on the twenty-eighth, battled the Khitan Prince of Wei at Xiurong, defeating him. The prefect of Bozhou, Zhou Ru, defected to the Khitan to surrender the city.

On the fifth day of the second month, Li Shouzhen, the inspector-in-chief for advance contingents, battled Khitan forces at Majia Crossing and routed them. The inspector-in-chief of forces at large to the north, Ma Quanjie, engaged the Khitan at Beiping and prevailed, on the tenth. The Khitan met resistance at Qicheng as well, departing voluntarily.[xi] On the seventeenth, enemy armies met resistance at Hengshui from Bai Conghui, prefect of Jizhou¶, who vanquished them. Commoners were conscripted into the Martial-Resolve Militia on the twenty-first.

In summer, the fourth month, the Khitan overran Dezhou only to be defeated, the city recaptured by Liang Jin, the inspector of military patrols along the Yellow River. On the twelfth [May 7], the Emperor arrived from Chanzhou and announced an amnesty for the capital. Ma Quanjie engaged the Khitan at Dingfeng, on the seventeenth, to defeat them. Extensive confiscation of private property was ordered on the nineteenth. In the fifth month, the seventh day, Li Shouzhen led a punitive campaign against Yang Guangyuan. On the sixteenth, Zhang Cong'en, interim custodian of the Ye capital, was named inspector-in-chief for at-large forces at Beizhou. Li Shouzhen became inspector-in-chief for at-large forces at Qingzhou‡ on the twentieth. Zizhou was captured sometime during the sixth month. The post of military affairs commissioner was revived on the sixth day, and Chancellery director Sang Weihan was named palace secretary and concurrent military af-

x. Gaozu of Jin, since deferring to the Khitan ruler as father, was highly circumspect and sent envoys regularly, exchanges not cited in the *Old History* or the *Veritable Records*. With the installation of Emperor Chu, the endless traffic in envoys becomes too enormous to enumerate, so references here to lesser-ranked envoys are all deleted. Wang Ban is mentioned because he failed to progress beyond Ye.

xi. Both sides had sustained serious losses in battle and withdrew their men to regroup. Jin soldiers proved unable to pursue the Khitan; thus the phrase "they departed voluntarily."

fairs commissioner on the seventh. The Yellow River ruptured dikes at Huazhou on the seventeenth, encircling Mount Liang and infiltrating the Wen and Ji rivers.

In autumn, the first day of the seventh month [July 23], the court announced a general amnesty and change of calendar. On the nineteenth, it designated grand mentor to the heir-apparent Liu Xu provisional dignitary for public works and concurrent deputy director of the Chancellery with ministerial powers. On the first day of the eighth month, it designated Liu Zhiyuan as general commander of at-large forces on the northern front and Shunde governor Du [Chong]wei as chief commissioner of bandit suppression. On the twenty-eighth, it authorized banners and plaques for the gates of the home of Shi Renxu, a resident of Xiangcheng, Chenzhou‡. On the seventh day of the ninth month, the Khitan raided Suicheng and Leshou. The prefect of Daizhou, Bai Wenke repulsed them successfully at Qilifeng.

In winter, the eleventh day of the tenth month [October 30], the court appointed Wuning governor Zhao Zaili deputy commander of at-large forces to the north and interim custodian of the Ye capital, Ma Quanjie, deputy commissioner of bandit suppression. On the first day of the twelfth month, the Emperor hunted rabbits near the outer gates of the imperial compound. On the nineteenth, Yang Chengxun imprisoned his father, Guangyuan, in order to surrender and was murdered.[xii] On the seventeenth day of the intercalary month, prisoners at Qingzhou‡ received pardons under a minor amnesty. The Khitan raided Hengzhou.

In the second year, the Khitan overran Taizhou sometime during the inaugural month. On the fifteenth day [C.E. March 1, 945], Ma Quanjie engaged them at Yulin, both armies losing. On the twenty-first, as the Emperor departed for the southern hamlet, he named Zhang Cong'en as interim custodian of the eastern capital and Gao Xingzhou as commissioner of imperial encampments, on the twenty-fourth. A northern expedition, on the twenty-eighth, caused the Khitan to abscond. In the second month, the second day, the Emperor left for Liyang [Weizhou‡]. The Henghai governor Tian Wu, as a precaution against the Khitan, was appointed chief officer for at-large forces along the northeastern front.[xiii] A grand imperial inspection occurred at Qicheng on the ninth, and an inspection of horses at Tieqiu on the nineteenth. On the twenty-ninth, Feng Yu, the Hanlin academician and vice minister of finance became minister of finance and commissioner of military affairs.

....

xii. Emperor Chu had already agreed to spare Chengxun's life while at the same time ordering Li Shouzhen to kill him; thus the word "execution" is not used.

xiii. The phrasing "as a precaution" exposes the fact that commanders were commissioned only after the Khitan had departed.

On the second day of the third month [April 16], the Khitan felled Qizhou†, prefect Shen Bin perishing with honor. The Emperor hunted at Qicheng on the eleventh. Ma Quanjie overpowered Taizhou on the fourteenth. On the fifteenth, the garrison commander of Yizhou, Sun Fangjian, engaged Khitan commander Xieli at Langshan, defeating him. Du [Chong]wei overtook Mancheng on the eighteenth and Suicheng on the nineteenth. He also fought the Khitan at Yangcheng, defeating and pursuing them all the way to Weicun to prevail once again.

In summer, the thirteenth day of the fourth month [May 26], returning troops received rewards at Qicheng, as did troops along Wangmang River on the fourteenth. The Emperor arrived from Chanzhou on the nineteenth, pardoning prisoners of war in the immediate vicinity. He rendered a generous round of rewards for deserving troops, announcing a general amnesty in the fifth month, the first day. He departed for the southern hamlet on the eleventh day. He practiced archery at Fantai on the third day of the sixth month, visiting the residence of Du [Chong]wei afterward. Drought struck.

In autumn, the first day of the eighth month [September 9], the palace discontinued two forms of dances. It dismissed He Ning on the third day, naming Feng Yu as deputy director of the Palace Secretariat with ministerial powers. The Emperor inspected horses at Maoze Slope on the eighth and mandated an appropriation of horses on the fourteenth. After inspecting horses at Wanlong Ridge, the Emperor visited Li Shouzhen at home, on the sixth day of the ninth month.

In winter, the fourteenth day of the tenth month [November 21], grand arbiter Han Hyeon-gyu [Han Xuangui] and chamberlain for diplomacy Kim Ryeom [Jin Lian], among others, reached the capital as envoys of Koryô. The Emperor hunted rabbits at Yantai on the fifteenth. On the twenty-fifth, ambassadors Ryu Soong-gyu [Liu Chonggui], the vice minister of war, and Bak Ye-eon [Piao Yiyan], chamberlain for domestic armies, arrived from Koryô. On the fifth day of the eleventh month, the court invested Wang Moo [Wang Wu] as the King of Koryô. The Emperor hunted rabbits near the outer gates of the imperial compound, departing for Shatai on the twenty-sixth. On the fifteenth day of the twelfth month, on the full moon, the Emperor hunted in the suburbs. He dismissed Sang Weihan on the twenty-fifth, selected the Kaifeng custodian Zhao Ying to be palace secretary and Li Song to serve provisionally as director of the Chancellery and commissioner of military affairs.

In spring of the third year, fifteenth day of the second month [C.E. March 20, 946], an envoy arrived for the Huihu Uighurs: Tujuelu. Ducks were hunted at Banqiao on the twenty-first, the Emperor subsequently departing for the southern hamlet. In summer, the sixth month, defector Sun Fangjian surrendered Langshan to the Khitan. On the seventh day, the Khitan penetrated the border. On the thirtieth, the court named Li Shouzhen as chief officer for at-large forces and the Yicheng governor Huangfu Yu as deputy officer. The Yellow River burst its dikes at Yuchi. A vast famine ensued, and bandits rose in rebellion. In autumn, the seventh month, torrential rains and flooding occurred, the Yellow River overrunning Yangliu, Chaocheng, and Wude. Flood waters inundated Liting on the third day of the eighth month. During the ninth month, the Yellow River burst through dikes at Chan, Hua, and Huai‡ prefectures. Khitan forces were engaged at Xinxing by Zhang Yanze, the overseer of formations for at-large infantry and cavalry; their defeat occurred by the fourteenth. Hostilities with the Khitan erupted at Shuozhou on the sixteenth, Liu Zhiyuan defeating them. Heavy rains persisted, the Yellow River bursting through levies at Linhuang.

In winter, the Yellow River ruptured dikes at Weizhou‡, sometime during the tenth month. Dikes ruptured at Yuanwu on the ninth day [November 5]. On the fourteenth, Du [Chong]wei became chief commissioner of bandit-suppression forces at large to the north and Li Shouzhen director-in-chief of military forces. During the eleventh month, Yongqing governor Liang Hanzhang, resisting enemy armies at Yingzhou¶, was vanquished. The Khitan attacked Zhen and Ding prefectures.

On the third day of the twelfth month [December 28], Du [Chong]wei forted his men at Zhongdu. On the sixth, the chief director of the Empire-Upholding Guard, Wang Qing, engaged the Khitan at Hutuo and died honorably in defeat.[xiv] Du [Chong]wei, Li Shouzhen, and Zhang Yanze defected to surrender to the Khitan. The Emperor hunted rabbits at Shatai on the fourteenth. Zhang Yanze violated the capital on the sixteenth, slaying the metropolitan custodian of Kaifeng, Sang Weihan. The Khitan toppled the Jin dynasty.[xv]

WE LAMENT. I have written, "Imperial son Chonggui was invested Prince of Zheng," and elsewhere, "Imperial uncle Jingru was posthumously invested Prince of Song." To be sure, I do so with conscious intent! According to the *Book of Rites*, "The sons of a brother are like one's own sons." To refer to Chonggui as "royal son" makes sense, but Jingru was the father of Emperor

....

xiv. Even though commanders may have perished on the battlefield or died defending their cities, the dead are not cited for we cannot know their intent. Some may have sought to flee but simply failed, some may have sought to surrender but lacked the opportunity when suddenly stricken by death. Only those who refused to flee, refused to surrender, and clearly died out of ethical principle—as occurred with Wang Qing—are cited as "dying honorably."

xv. Although Emperor Chu survived, the Jin perished as a dynasty; thus the word "toppled" [*mie*].

Chu. By what reasoning do [contemporary documents] call him "imperial uncle?"

Emperor Chu, enthroned illicitly, renounced his own father by birth. Chu was adopted as Gaozu's son, but never named heir, for Gaozu had his own son. When a gravely ill Gaozu released that son, Chongrui, from his own embrace to entrust to Feng Dao's care, Chu hardly had a chance of succeeding. Yet the senior courtiers of Jin, violating both ritual propriety and the imperial will, enthroned him on the pretext of being Gaozu's son. They could not have done so if Chu were the son of Jingru. Hereafter, Emperor Chu imposed a strict taboo on discussion of his birth, renouncing his father to perpetrate a fraud on the world and present himself as Gaozu's true son.

The *Book of Rites* says, "Upon becoming heir to another line, the requiting of mother and father is still expected."[1] Were Gaozu childless and Emperor Chu installed properly, no need would have existed to deceive the world by renouncing the man to father him. I write, "imperial uncle Jingru was posthumously invested Prince of Song" intending to expose the illicitness of Chu's installation, but also his utter ravaging of human instinct by investing his father like an ordinary subject merely to swindle the world!

CHAPTER 10

ANNALS X: BASIC ANNALS OF HAN

Gaozu [Liu Zhiyuan, C.E. 895–948], the Profoundly Literate, Sagaciously Martial, Resplendently Majestic, and Filial Emperor, surnamed Liu, initially had the personal name Zhiyuan. His ancestors were Shatuo tribesmen, later generations living in Taiyuan. Zhiyuan tended to be weak to the point of impeding free movement. A man of few words and a sternly dignified deportment, he had a purplish face and eyes with whites so large as to seem frigid as ice.

He and the future Gaozu of Jin [Shi Jingtang] were both attending commanders under the future Mingzong of Tang when Mingzong engaged Liang armies at Desheng Commandery; the armor on Gaozu's horse broke, and Gaozu came perilously close to apprehension by the enemy when Zhiyuan gave his own horse to him, taking Gaozu's horse and returning behind him. Gaozu thereby came to value him, and during his tenure as interim custodian of the northern capital he selected Zhiyuan as military attaché.

The rebellion of Li Congke, the Prince of Lu, had forced Emperor Min of Tang into flight. Gaozu of Jin had left Zhenzhou for the capital, and en route to Weizhou‡, happened upon Emperor Min. They stopped at a relay station, where Zhiyuan arranged for the brave warrior Shi Gan, iron cudgel concealed up his sleeve, to assist Gaozu in anticipation of an incident. When Gaozu's differences with Emperor Min could not be resolved through negotiation, aides preferred a military solution. Zhiyuan escorted Gaozu into a side room, as Shi Gan and henchmen pummeled Min's aides to death. Zhiyuan subsequently led his men in assassinating the remaining escorts of Min, while confining the Emperor to a relay station, as he departed.

After the accession to the Tang throne of Emperor Fei, Gaozu of Jin regained the governorship of Hedong, but rifts between the two men had already surfaced. Gaozu was now on the verge of military action, Liu Zhiyuan and Sang Weihan assisting in setting strategy and encouraging action. Gaozu's succession to the Jin throne at Taiyuan resulted in Zhiyuan's promotion to inspector-in-chief of the Imperial Guard and Imperial Bodyguard, with concurrent powers as the Baoyi governor. The Khitan ruler Yelü Deguang, escorting Gaozu to Luzhou, pointed to Zhiyuan before parting to exclaim, "This inspector-in-chief is a man of rare bravado who should not be discharged except for some grave offense." [i]

In the second year of Tianfu [C.E. 937], Liu Zhiyuan became chief director of cavalry and infantry in the Imperial Guard and concurrently Zhongwu governor. Du Chongwei later replaced him at Zhongwu, Zhiyuan moving to the Guide command, but he was offended that Chongwei's name would appear on the same edict of appointment as rider, so he sequestered himself at home and refused to leave. A furious Gaozu considered stripping him of military powers, but chief minister Zhao Ying argued against it. Gaozu consequently dispatched He Ning, the Duanming academician, to the home of Zhiyuan to offer a public reading of imperial orders, Zhiyuan now accepting the appointment. In the fifth year [C.E. 940] he was reassigned interim custodian of the Ye capital. In the capital for an audience, in the ninth month, Gaozu paid a personal visit to his residence. During the sixth year [C.E. 941] he became governor of Hedong and interim custodian of the northern capital. Gaozu expired in the seventh year [C.E. 942].

Liu Zhiyuan had assisted Gaozu of Jin in raising armies at Taiyuan, proving his merit in establishing the dynasty's mandate. With the accession of Emperor Chu, the alliance with the Khitan was broken as armies were deployed northward. The Emperor often worried over Zhiyuan's loyalties in light of the high honors afforded him and possible alienation stemming from a string of incidents. The Emperor always strove to be indulging and deferential, in consequence. Honored as palace secretary and invested Prince of Taiyuan, Zhiyuan became commissioner of bandit-suppressing forces at large for Youzhou and, later, general commander of forces at large on the northern front.

During the second year of Kaiyuan [C.E. 945], the fourth month, Zhiyuan was invested Prince of Beiping, and in the fifth month of the third year, honored as ad hoc grand guardian. The Prince never deployed his troops, how-

....

i. In the idiom of the day, the word "bravado" [*caola*] implies ferocious valor; I have adopted the original terminology here.

ever: when the Khitan attacked Chanzhou, he sent detachments commander Wei Wang to attack Yanmen, resulting in a Khitan defeat at Xiurong. In the eighth month, the Prince murdered the Tuhun, Baichengfu, and his tribesmen while seizing tens of thousands of valuable objects and thousands of fine horses.

In the fourth year [C.E. 947], as the Khitan invaded the capital and retrieved Emperor Chu for exile in the north, the Prince [Zhiyuan] commissioned Wang Jun, military administrator to the governor, to present a petition to the Khitan. Their leader Yelü Deguang referred to Jun as "youth," then presented a wooden cane as gift. Among the barbarians, such canes are as precious as benches or handstaffs in the Middle Kingdom, going only to the highest and most favored of officials. Jun held the cane in hand for the trip home, its very sight causing barbarians along the route to yield to his entourage. Upon returning south, Jun reported that the Khitan had absolutely no potential for occupying the Middle Kingdom, encouraging the Prince to proceed in founding the dynasty.

On the twelfth day of the second month [March 7], a petition to the Prince urging his further elevation came from a cohort led by Zhang Yanwei, the manager-adjutant to the Hedong governor. On the fifteenth [March 10], the Emperor acceded to the throne and renamed this year "twelfth year of Tianfu."[ii] Bandits at Cizhou led by Liang Hui claimed Xiangzhou‡, reverting it to the dynasty.[iii] Shi Hongzhao, the chief director of the Martially Dedicated forces, seized Daizhou and killed prefect Wang Hui. A commander at Jinzhou, Yao Kechou, murdered defending commander Luo Conglang, along with Zhao Xi, the commissioner of revenues and admonitions master, reverting to the dynasty. Also submitting to the dynasty, on the twenty-fifth, were the interim regents of Shan and Lu prefectures, Zhao Hui and Wang Shou'en, respectively. On the first day of the third month, the court remitted miscellaneous taxes for Hedong. A mutiny erupted on the sixth within the Yanzhou‡ military, as governor Zhou Mi was purged, military director Gao

....

ii. Tianfu is the reign name for Gaozu of Jin, which ended during its eighth year, when Kaiyun became the reign name. Four years had lapsed by now. The Han established an empire but had no dynastic name, so it followed the Jin reign name. There was initially no symbolic message behind repudiating the recent Kaiyun and resuscitating the older Tianfu reign, so the citation is simply a statement of fact.

iii. The phrase "surrender to dynasty" [*laixiang*, in the *Old History*] has been rendered here as "revert to dynasty" [*laigui*] out of empathy with such men [as Liang Hui]. No ruler for the world existed at the time, so identifying a ruler and submitting to him differs vastly from cases where an official defects from X to follow Y. Gaozu of Han was a ruler of no great virtue, while these anxious men lacked better alternatives, so they identified with and submitted to him—thus, the wording "revert to dynasty."

Yanxun reverting the prefecture of Danzhou a day later. On the seventeenth, the Khitan retreated to safety,[iv] leaving behind their commander Xiao Han to defend Bianzhou as the Xuanwu governor.

In summer, fourth day of the fourth month [April 27], chief of the governor's guard, Yang Bin, became commissioner of military affairs, provisional powers as deputy military commissioner going to Guo Wei, the senior secretary for multiracial infantry and cavalry. The Khitan conquered Xiangzhou‡ and murdered Liang Hui. The Lady of Wei, née Li, was installed as empress on the eighth day. Named deputy directors at the Palace Secretariat with ministerial powers, on the ninth day, were Su Fengji, senior administrative aide to the Hedong governor, and Su Yugui, judicial officer of surveillance. Luzhou was captured on the tenth day by the chief director of infantry in the Imperial Guard and Imperial Bodyguard, Shi Hongzhao. Reverting to dynasty, on the thirteenth, was Wu Xingde, director of the Empire-Upholding Guard. Shi Hongzhao captured Zezhou. On the twenty-first day, the Khitan ruler Yelü Deguang died at Luancheng. The Khitan occupied Zhenzhou.

On the tenth day of the fifth month [June 1], the Taiyuan prefect Liu Chong became interim custodian of the northern capital. The Emperor departed for the eastern capital on the twelfth. Xiao Han retreated to Khitan domains for refuge, as Li Congyi, the Duke of Xun, was installed overseer of military affairs for the southern dynasty. On the twenty-fourth day, the Emperor proceeded to Jiangzhou, where prefect Li Conglang reverted to dynasty. He proceeded to Heyang [Luoyang], on the third day of the sixth month, ordering the deaths of Li Congyi and his mother in the capital. He arrived from Taiyuan on the eleventh day, the dynastic name changed to "Han" on the fifteenth.[v] He issued pardons for criminals and tax remissions for the people. Envoys from Yutian arrived. Liu Xu passed away during the summer.

In autumn, the thirteenth day of the intercalary seventh month [August 31], a ban was imposed on the production of Khitan-style costumes and paraphernalia. Tianxiong governor Du Chongwei rebelled.[vi] His suppression was

....

iv. Upon learning of the Han emergence at Taiyuan, the Khitan withdrew out of fear, thus the need for wording that distinguishes volition from involition. The word *dun*, "to retreat to safety," is thus employed.

v. Gaozu began with an empire but no dynastic name. The edict proclaiming empire, lacking clarity of language, does not merit citation here. Having employed the twelfth year of Tianfu for his reign, the dynasty was arguably still named Jin, although no definitive proof exists and caution is best for uncertainties of the sort. Here, it is said that "the dynastic name was changed to Han," so it is presumably acceptable to make use of the name for the period preceding its adoption.

vi. During the reign of Emperor Chu of Jin, Du Chongwei had dropped the character "Chong" from his personal name to avoid taboo use of a character in the Emperor's own name. Under the Han, he restored the character.

entrusted to Gao Xingzhou, the Tianping governor and now inspector-in-chief for at-large forces in the Ye capital. On the twenty-eighth day, posthumous honors as "Emperor" were extended to paternal ancestors and "Empress" given to their wives: the imperial great-great grandfather, Tuan, renamed Mingyuan, received the temple designation of Wenzu; the sobriquet Mingzhen went to his wife, née Li. Great-grandfather Ang, renamed Gongxi, received the temple designation of Dezu; the sobriquet Gonghui went to his wife, née Yang. Grandfather Zun, renamed Zhaoxian, received the temple designation of Yizu; the sobriquet Zhaomu went to his wife, née Li. Imperial father Dian, renamed Zhangsheng, received the temple designation of Xianzu; the sobriquet Zhangyi went to his wife, née An. Emperor Gao of the former Han dynasty was renamed Gaozu and Emperor Guangwu renamed Shizu; neither received ancestral temples.

In the eighth month, the director of the Sage-Protecting Guard, Bai Zairong, expelled the Khitan and relinquished Zhenzhou to the dynasty. On the fifteenth, upon killing Khitan commander Liu Duo, Anguo governor Xue Huairang entered Xingzhou. On the twenty-third of the ninth month [November 8], minister of personnel Dou Zhengu became ad hoc dignitary for public works and deputy director at the Chancellery, as Hanlin academician and secretariat drafter Li Tao became deputy director at the Palace Secretariat, both men conferred ministerial powers. The Emperor led a northern offensive on the twenty-ninth. In winter, the thirteenth day of the tenth month [November 28], the Emperor proceeded to Weicheng, announcing an amnesty for the northern Yellow River region. Du Chongwei surrendered on the twenty-second day of the eleventh month. The Emperor arrived from the Ye capital on the thirteenth day of the twelfth month.

In the inaugural year of Qianyou, spring, fifth day of the inaugural month [C.E. February 17, 948], the Emperor promulgated a general amnesty and a change of calendar. He changed his personal name to Gao, on the ninth day. On the twenty-seventh [March 10], he expired at the Wansui palace.[vii]

Emperor Yin [Liu Chengyou, C.E. 932–951] was the second son of Gaozu, named Chengyou. With the accession of Gaozu, he became generalissimo of the Right Guard and inspector-general of the imperial compound. Gaozu had especially loved the Prince of Wei, Chengxun, who was eldest son and of worthy character, preparing to name him successor when Chengxun died. An already unhealthy Gaozu deteriorated under the weight of the loss, prompting him to entrust Chengyou to the care of civil and military leaders. Chief min-

....

vii. He was fifty-four *sui*.

ister Su Fengji once warned, "Imperial son Chengyou, not yet invested as Prince, should be invested immediately." The Emperor expired, however, before making the investiture, so secrecy was imposed on the commencement of mourning. Du Chongwei was killed.

In the inaugural year of Qianyou, first day of the second month [March 14, 948], Chengyou was invested Prince of Zhou and, on the same day, acceded the throne before the imperial bier. On the twelfth day, an engagement with Shu armies occurred at Dasan Pass, led by Wang Jingchong, commandant of the Right Guard and commissioner of military police at Fengxiang; he defeated them. The palace announced a general amnesty on the thirteenth day. In the third month, the thirteenth day [April 24], Dou Zhengu was named dignitary for the grand procession to the imperial hillside mausoleum, with vice minister of personnel Duan Xiyao as deputy dignitary; chamberlain for imperial ceremonies Zhang Hao was named master of funeral ceremonies, vice minister of war Lu Jia named escort for the royal carriage, and deputy censor Bian Wei named master of funeral regalia. On the twenty-eighth, Li Tao was dismissed. Huguo governor Li Shouzhen rebelled, capturing Tongguan.

In summer, the second day of the fourth month [May 13], the military director-in-chief at Shanzhou, Wang Yu, conquered Tongguan. On the third day, commander Zhao Siwan of Yongxing defected, surrendering the commandery to Li Shouzhen. Master for diplomatic accommodations Wang Jun conducted armies to Guanxi, quartering them there.[viii] Yang Bin was named deputy director of the Palace Secretariat and concurrent minister of personnel with chief ministerial standing, Guo Wei becoming commissioner of military affairs. Named chief officer of the armed forces at Yongxing was Guo Congyi, the Zhenning governor. Baoyi governor Bai Wenke became chief officer for armed forces at Hezhong. Yellow River dikes were ruptured at Yuanwu. Envoys of the Huihu Uighurs arrived on the eleventh day of the fifth month. All-male triplets were born to Wu Jin, a resident of Neihuang, Weizhou. The Yellow River ruptured dikes at Yuchi, Huazhou. Drought and locust blight occurred.

In autumn, the first day of the seventh month [August 8], Zhangde governor Wang Jihong murdered administrative aide Zhang Yi. Having employed myna birds to feed on locusts, a ban on catching myna birds was imposed on the ninth day. Guo Wei received ministerial standing on the thirteenth. On the sixteenth, the prefect of Khitan-occupied Mozhou, Wang

....

viii. Jun was credentialed neither as commander nor bandit-suppressor, but had simply received orders to amass troops at Guanxi; his appointment as commander appears below.

Yanhui, came for sanctuary. On the twenty-third, Zhang Peng, deputy governor of the Chengde command, was murdered. Defector Wang Jingchong surrendered to Li Shouzhen on the twenty-eighth. In the eighth month, the eighth day, Guo Wei led the suppression of Li Shouzhen. The inspector-in-chief for at-large forces on the western front, Shang Hongqian, engaged the troops of Zhao Siwan and suffered defeat, during the ninth month.

In winter, the ninth day of the tenth month [November 12], a Tubo Tibetan envoy, Simandulinzhanyaosi, arrived. In the eleventh month, the ninth day, grand mentor to the heir-apparent Li Song was murdered along with his entire clan. On the twenty-seventh, the Profoundly Literate, Sagaciously Martial, Resplendently Majestic, and Filial Emperor was interred at the Ruiling mausoleum.[ix] On the fifth day of the twelfth month, Zhangwu governor Gao Yunquan murdered Liu Jingyan, the retired grand preceptor to the heir-apparent.

In spring of the second year,[x] first day of the inaugural month [C.E. February 1, 949], the government pardoned prisoners. Irregular taxes on the people were remitted on the second day of the second month. During the fifth month, summertime, a commander under Li Shouzhen, Zhou Guangxun, surrendered to the Khitan. Zhao Siwan surrendered on the twenty-second. The protector-general of the Huihu Uighurs, Yang Yanxun, reached the capital in the sixth month, the nineteenth day. Envoys from Xiliang Prefecture came also. Locusts struck.

In autumn, sixteenth day of the seventh month [August 12], Guo Wei murdered the interim regent for Huazhou‡, Zhao Siwan, at Jingzhao [Changan]. Hezhong was captured on the twenty-third.[xi] Guo Congyi killed the former chief of military police for Yongxing Commandery, Qiao Shouwen, during the eighth month. On the fifteenth day, a representative for Guo Wei presented prisoners of war to the court. In winter, the tenth month, the Khitan invaded Zhao and Wei prefectures, as the official rank and file donated horses to augment the metropolitan armed forces. The Khitan overran Neiqiu. A campaign against the Khitan was launched by Guo Wei and Wang

....

ix. Located in Gaocheng County, Henan.

x. Emperor Yin had already acceded to the throne and by now should have changed the reign name, but opted against it; details are provided in the note on "the second year of Xiande," in the Annals of Zhou. Moreover, the Emperor's personal name was Chengyou and his reign name Qianyou [containing the same final character], leading both officials and citizens of the empire to disregard the rules of avoidance in using the character. No misdeed of the day could be greater than this, yet the Basic Annals [in the *Old History*] merely cites the facts with no reproof, leaving later generations to discover the impropriety for themselves.

xi. Shouzhen died by setting himself afire, so no citation appears for "execution."

Jun, commissioner for the southern court of palace armies, on the twentieth day. The Khitan retreated to safety during the eleventh month.

In the third year, spring, the inaugural month [C.E. 950], the chief officer for at-large forces on the western front, Zhao Hui, conquered Fengxiang.[xii] On the eighth day [February 28], Guo Wei donated horses to augment the metropolitan armed forces. On the fourteenth, Zhao Hui presented to the court prisoners of war and the ears of war casualties. On the sixth day of the second month, the court ordered banners and plaques for the home of Qu Wen, [a moral exemplar] at Ruyin, Yingzhou¤. On the occasion of the winter solstice on the twelfth day of the third month were mountain sacrifices at the Nanyu gardens. In summer, the fifteenth day of the fourth month [May 4], Guo Wei, in his capacity as commissioner of military affairs, became the Tianxiong governor. The Yellow River ruptured dikes at Yuanwu, the seventh day of the sixth month. In autumn, the eighth month, the Tartars proffered fealty.

In winter, the eleventh month, thirteenth day [December 24], minister Yang Bin, chief director of the Imperial Guard and Imperial Bodyguard Shi Hongzhao, and fiscal commissioner Wang Zhang were all executed, their clans liquidated as well. Guo Wei rebelled. On the seventeenth, Yicheng governor Song Yanwo defected to relinquish his charge to Guo Wei. Fengqiu was invaded by Guo Wei on the nineteenth, with Taining governor Murong Yanchao deploying men at Qilidian in response. Troops received largess in the northern suburbs, on the twentieth, and again at Liuzipo a day later. Murong Yanchao engaged the armies of Guo Wei, his defeat causing Kaifeng custodian Hou Yi to defect and deliver the city to Wei. Guo Yunming rebelled. The Emperor expired on the twenty-second day [C.E. January 2, 951].[xiii] Su Fengji committed suicide. The Han dynasty collapsed.[xiv]

WE LAMENT. For the newly enthroned ruler of humanity to announce the inaugural year of his reign is only common, although the practice held no great symbolism in antiquity.[1] This was assuredly true for the period prior to Confu-

....

xii. Jingchong set himself afire, so, no citation appears for "execution."

xiii. He was twenty *sui* and interred, during the Zhou dynasty's inaugural year of Guangshun [C.E. 951], at Yangzhai County, Xuzhou‡. The mausoleum's name, Yingling, is not cited in the text, for he was buried by a renegade.

xiv. It was forty-two days after Emperor Yin's death before Taizu acceded to the Zhou throne. Upon the Emperor's death, however, I say that the Han "collapsed" [*wang*] to underscore the Emperor's death as the ruin of dynasty. The Empress Dowager may have presided at court and the Duke of Xiangyin may have been nominally installed, yet both were props of the Zhou upstart without genuine power. In order to expose his treachery, the citation here states, "the Han collapsed," thus stressing his deliberateness in delaying accession. The Zhou ruler moved slowly because of enduring obstacles to his installation, for he still had a sense of shame [as usurper].

cius' *Spring and Autumn Annals*. Despite arbitrary and banal rulers as well as inept and mediocre historians, events were always recorded in chronological progression from the remote to the recent: numbering years and months from one to two and so on provided a natural organization. Referring to "one" [*yi*] as the "inaugural" [*yuan*] never had underlying precepts either—it was simply an idiom of the ancients.[xv] Starting with the heterodox ideas of later thinkers, great symbolism came to be imposed upon Confucius' use of "inaugural month" in the *Annals*, causing changes in the inaugural year to acquire immense import.

After the Han dynasty, another practice evolved of prefixing citations for the new year with the words "initiating the inaugural" [*jianyuan*], whereby legitimate and illegitimate calendars came to be confused and reign names proliferated at innumerable levels. The Five Dynasties was an age of tumult, many of its affairs too devoid of method and reason to deserve mention. In the case of reign names, however, clarity is utterly imperative for their perversion facilitates the defrauding of posterity.

Taizu of the Liang succumbed to regicide [by son Yougui] in the second year of Qianhua. During the next year, Emperor Mo executed Yougui and rescinded his reign name, Fengli, reverting to Qianhua the third year. This is wholly justifiable. Once Gaozu founded the Later Han, he rescinded the Kaiyun reign of the Jin Emperor Chu, then in its fourth year, reverting back to [Chu's father's reign name], Tianfu the twelfth year. This derived purely from selfish impulse.

The future Gaozu of Han, posted at Taiyuan during Emperor Chu's reign, could be indignantly condescending toward the Jin ruler, who nonetheless persisted in public expressions of rare courtesy toward Gaozu and luckily avoided a rupture in relations. Once the Khitan uprooted the Jin court, the Han pretender evinced no interest in a rescue effort. A captive Emperor Chu was already headed northward before Han troops departed, ostensibly to stalk the entourage and liberate him, only to return upon reaching Tumen. We can well imagine, therefore, the self-consciousness of a newly enthroned emperor of Han when he abandoned the Kaiyun reign name [to invoke Tianfu]. His simple intent was to exploit the prevailing tumult to his own advantage, not reassert ruler-subject proprieties vis-à-vis Emperor Chu. For this, we can only sigh in lament! Herein lies the meaning of the phrase [from Mencius], "what appears within is invariably made manifest without."[2]

....

xv. The ancients called the first month of the year, not the "first month" [*yiyue*], but rather the "inaugural month" [*zhengyue*]. The *Narratives for the Kingdoms* [Guoyu] refers to the "sixth musical note" as the "great note in the initial group." The *Book of Changes* identifies the "six lines" [of a hexagram] with the "initial nine lines." When the ancients spoke numerically, they generally did not say "first," neither did they always use the word "initial" [*yuan*] for the year.

CHAPTER 11

ANNALS XI: BASIC ANNALS OF ZHOU

Taizu [Guo Wei, C.E. 904–954], the Sagacious and Spiritual, Reverent and August, Literate and Martial Emperor, surnamed Guo, was native to Yaoshan, Xingzhou. His father, Jian, had served the Prince of Jin as prefect of Shunzhou but was killed when Liu Rengong overran the city. His son, Wei, was orphaned young and relied upon the Chang family of Luzhou to survive.

The interim regent of Luzhou, Li Jitao, was recruiting men of daring valor for his army's lower ranks when the brave and muscular Wei, then eighteen, volunteered. The youth exuded a self-confident personality, while a propensity for assorted antics when drinking left Jitao thoroughly impressed. Sauntering about a marketplace, Wei once encountered a butcher given to intimidating marketgoers with his daring. An inebriated Wei called out to the butcher to slice some meat at his cutting board, then scolded him for his unconventional methods. The butcher, exposing his stomach, pronounced provokingly, "You're a brave man—brave enough to kill me?" Wei drew close and grabbed his knife to stab him to death. Shock reverberated throughout the market, although Wei kept his usually calm demeanor. Authorities apprehended him, but Jitao valued Wei's valor and provided cover for his disappearance, later recalling him to service under his command.

In time, Li Jitao rebelled against the Prince of Jin to submit to the Liang, only to be executed once Zhuangzong of Tang had overthrown the Liang dynasty. The troops formerly under Jitao's command were all reassigned to cavalry rotations, Guo Wei emerging as officer due to his skills at reading and arithmetic. He held an affinity for the [martial work] *Spring and Autumn Annals for a Wider World* and some facility in the art of war. He subsequently rose to senior administrative aide in the Imperial Guard. The future Gaozu of Han, then inspector-in-chief of the Imperial Guard and Imperial Bodyguard, acquired a special attachment to Wei and often brought him along during later tours as governor. Gaozu hence raised armies at Taiyuan after the Khitan purge of the Jin dynasty, naming Wei deputy commissioner of military affairs after his accession.

In the inaugural year of Qianyou, the inaugural month [C.E. 948], as Gaozu took gravely ill, he entrusted his son, Emperor Yin, to the care of Guo Wei, Shi Hongzhao, and cohort. Wei became military affairs commissioner upon Yin's accession. In the third month of the year, Li Shouzhen of Hezhong, Zhao Siwan of Yongxing, and Wang Jingchong of Fengxiang rebelled in rapid succession, causing Emperor Yin to entrust Bai Wenke, Guo Congyi, Chang Si, among others, with separate offensives, all of them failing despite prolonged effort. Emperor Yin now turned to Guo Wei, asking, "Might I impose upon your services?" "Your Subject dare not make such a request, but dare not spurn one either," Wei responded. "I will simply accept Your Majesty's orders." He now acquired ministerial standing and oversight over other commanders.

When entertaining guests in the military, Guo Wei liked to don official robes with broad sash, but when presiding over camps during campaigns, he insisted on wearing a scarf with short tail, not unlike his rank and file. As for gifts from the Emperor, he would allow commanders to take as they pleased after archery competitions, the remainder distributed to troops—to their uniform delight.

Upon reaching Hezhong Prefecture, Guo Wei erected palisades to the east of the city's walls, as did Chang Si to the south and Bai Wenke to the west. They also drafted twenty thousand adult men from the surrounding five counties to construct interconnected ramparts to protect the three sets of palisades. The various commanders all portrayed Li Shouzhen as a "destitute bandit" likely to capitulate in a matter of days, making superfluous such belaboring of the people. Wei ignored them. Shouzhen's men now emerged for several raids, hitting and damaging the connected ramparts, as Wei made quick repairs. They abruptly repeated their surprise strikes, every initiative ending in persistent loss. The city depleted supplies of troops and rations in due time, Wei now affirming that, "Victory is at hand!" He then gathered offensive weapons and launched a synchronized assault from all four directions, piercing the external wall of the city. Shouzhen and his wife set themselves afire, as Siwan and Jingchong surrendered in succession.

Emperor Yin rewarded Guo Wei with a jade sash and office as honorary grand preceptor and concurrent director of the Chancellery. Wei declined the sash, stating, "I observed many a subject of merit during service to the Former

Emperor, the jade sash never awarded to them." He further explained, "Your servant, privileged to lead our armies, succeeded in vanquishing the rebels through the august divinity of the Han dynasty and scarcely any special merit of my own. It is worthy military and civilian leaders who have restored order to the court, harmonized inner and outer realms, and guaranteed the timely provision of rations for our men. In this way, I could concentrate on military maneuvers." Wei's character now impressed Emperor Yin, who summoned Yang Bin, Shi Hongzhao, Su Fengji, Su Yugui, Dou Zhengu, Wang Zhang, and others to confer jade sashes on each. Wei now accepted his own.

Guo Wei further proposed increases in rank and rewards for meritorious senior officials, causing the elevation of Zhengu to dignitary for public works and Fengji to dignitary for education, while Yugui and Bin became left and right associates at the Imperial Secretariat. "This represents only a special cluster of trusted Han officials," he added, "and excludes the dynasty's imperial clan, regional governors across the northern realm and [southern tributaries] at Jinghu [Jingnan], Zhe [Wu/Yue], and Hunan [Chu]." Hereafter, extravagant awards prevailed across the world.

That winter, as the Khitan violated the border, Guo Wei directed a northern campaign against them as commissioner of military affairs. However, the Khitan had absconded as he reached Weizhou and his troops returned to the south by the second month of the third year [C.E. 950]. In the fourth month, Wei became interim custodian of the Ye capital and governor of Tianxiong, retaining powers as military commissioner from his district command. Yet Chief minister Su Fengji insisted that a standing commissioner of military affairs should not hold a concurrent governor's post, vigorously debating the issue with Shi Hongzhao. The concurrent assignment eventually did occur, the palace ordering all prefectural authorities in the northern Yellow River region to accept Wei's oversight.

Emperor Yin's schemes with Li Ye and others had already caused the murder of Shi Hongzhao, orders now going out to Li Hongyi, the Zhenning governor, to murder Wang Yin, the infantry director of the Imperial Guard, at Chanzhou. Imperial orders were also issued to Guo Chong, cavalry director of the guard, to slay Guo Wei and Wang Jun, the palace-armies commissioner then at Weizhou. The edict first reached Chanzhou, where Hongyi deemed the task impossible and instead showed the edict to Wang Yin, who now joined Hongyi in informing Guo Wei by messenger. Meanwhile, court mandates to murder Wei and Jun arrived by courier, but Wei concealed the edict and summoned Wei Renpu, an aide from the military commission, for consultations in the privacy of his own bedroom. Renpu encouraged Wei to rebel and taught him how to use the seal of the interim custodian, printed upside-down, to alter the imperial edict such that it instructs Wei to execute the commanders and their lieutenants. Renpu intended to incite their anger and he succeeded, making them more pliable to his will.

As Guo Wei raised troops to cross the Yellow River, on the fourteenth day of the eleventh month [December 25], Emperor Yin organized a resistance led by Kaifeng custodian Hou Yi, Baoda governor Zhang Yanchao, and master of diplomatic accommodations Yan Jinqing. To spy on Wei and assess his intentions, he also dispatched an attendant at the imperial kennel, Long Tuo. However, Tuo came under the sway of Wei instead, who prevailed upon him to petition the throne to arrest Li Ye and cohort for transfer to the military. Emperor Yin disclosed Tuo's memorial to Ye upon receiving it. Apprising this as incontrovertible evidence of Wei's treacherous intent, Ye and cohort executed all of Wei's dependents within the capital.

On the seventeenth day, Guo Wei reached Huazhou, where Yicheng governor Song Yanwo defected from the Han in surrender to him. Wei raided Fengqiu on the nineteenth. On the twenty-first, he engaged Taining governor Murong Yanchao at Liuzi Slope, a vanquished Yanchao fleeing to Yan Prefecture. Guo Yunming rebelled, committing regicide against Emperor Yin at Zhao village. Wei entered the capital on the twenty-third day, setting random fires and plundering widely. He led official multitudes, on the twenty-fifth, to meet with the Empress Dowager at the Mingde gate and request installation of a successor. The Empress Dowager directed civil and military officials, as well as commanders and their lieutenants in the Six Armies, to confer on nominating a man of noble character to succeed as sovereign. On the twenty-seventh day, Wei led the official multitudes to the Mingde gate to petition for Liu Yun, the Wuning governor, to succeed. The court dispatched grand preceptor Feng Dao to receive Yun at Xuzhou¶. On the twenty-eighth, officials asked the Empress Dowager to appear in court audience and govern. Wang Jun became commissioner for military affairs, the deputy commissioner now Fan Zhi, the Hanlin academician and minister of war.

On the first day of the twelfth month [C.E. January 11, 951], Guo Wei led a northern campaign against the Khitan and forted men at Hua Prefecture, only to return on the twentieth, upon reaching Chan. Meanwhile, Wang Jun arranged for Guo Chong, buttressed by seven hundred horsemen, to betray and murder Liu Yun at Songzhou, even as his commanders Gong Tingmei and Yang Wen defended Xuzhou¶ on Yun's behalf. Guo Wei proceeded to the external gate of Kaifeng, on the twenty-fifth day, where Dou Zhengu and Su Yugui, ministers of Han, appeared to encourage his accession. On the twenty-seventh, the Empress Dowager by rescript relinquished to Wei oversight over the empire's affairs.

In the inaugural year of Guangshun, springtime, fifth day of the inaugural month [February 13], the Emperor acceded to the throne, announced a general amnesty, change of reign name, and adoption of Zhou as dynastic designation. On the seventh day, the Empress Dowager of Han was elevated in title to the Luminous and Sagacious Empress Dowager. Liu Chong of the Han royal family enthroned himself at Taiyuan on the sixteenth.[i] Feng Dao became palace secretary on the seventeenth. On the ninth day of the second month [March 19], the protector-general for the Huihu Uighurs of Xizhou‡ reached the capital, as did Niaoguzhi, envoy of the Khitan ruler Wuyu [Yelü Ruan]. With the winter solstice on the twenty-first day, the Emperor conducted mountain sacrifices at Puchi Monastery.[ii] On the twenty-fifth, assistant director of the Imperial Secretariat, Tian Min, was named ambassador to the Khitan. An envoy for the Huihu Uighurs, Moni, arrived. On the ninth day of the third month, Wuning governor Wang Yanchao overtook Xuzhou¶.[iii]

In summer, the third day of the fourth month [May 11], the Emperor's wife, née Dong, was installed as the Virtuous Consort. On the tenth day of the fifth month, posthumous honors as "Emperor" were extended to paternal ancestors and "Empress" given their wives: the imperial great-great grandfather, Jing, renamed Ruihe, received the temple designation of Xinzu; the sobriquet Ruigong went to his wife, née Zhang. Great-grandfather Chen, renamed Mingxian, received the temple designation of Xizu; the sobriquet Mingxiao went to his wife, née Shen. Grandfather Yun, renamed Yishun, received the temple designation of Yizu; the sobriquet Yijing went to his wife, née Han. Imperial father [Jian], known posthumously as Zhangsu, received the temple designation of Qingzu; the sobriquet Zhangde went to his wife, née Wang.

On the twenty-first day, the sixth month [July 27], vice minister of revenues Fan Zhi and senior fiscal administrator Li Gu became deputy directors of the Palace Secretariat with ministerial standing, Dou Zhengu and Su Yugui dismissed. On the twenty-third, Fan Zhi became the associate commissioner of military affairs. On the twenty-seventh, the commissioner for the northern court of palace armies, Zhai Guangye, was named deputy commissioner of military affairs. In autumn, the eighteenth day of the seventh month [August 23], the Emperor visited the home of Wang Jun. In the eighth month, the thirteenth day, the Khitan returned the remains of Zhao Ying for burial rites. In winter, the eighteenth day of the tenth month, Han-dynasty royalists

....

i. Regimes such as Wu and Shu, having formed autonomous empires, are excluded from these [Annals of the north]. The citation occurs here because Liu Chong refused to submit to Zhou authority [as Han holdout]. See discussion in the "Chronological Charts of the Ten Kingdoms."

ii. Puchi is the name of a Buddhist monastery.

iii. No mention is made of Gong Tingmei and Yang Wen's "dying with honor," the reasoning for which appears in the biography of Liu Yun.

launched a punitive campaign,[iv] their assault emerging from the direction of Jinzhou.[v] In the eleventh month, Wang Jun and Wang Yanchao, the Jianxiong governor, were assigned to resist Han-dynasty warriors. Murong Yanchao rebelled during the twelfth month.

In the second year, spring, the seventh day of the inaugural month [C.E. February 5, 952], the chief director of infantry in the Imperial Guard, Cao Ying, was named chief officer for at-large forces at Yanzhou. On the thirteenth day, the grand arbiter Seo Bong [Xu Feng] arrived as ambassador of the King of Koryô, Wang So [Wang Zhao]. On the fourth day of the second month, the defense commissioner for Fuzhou†, Shedeyi, conquered Kelan Commandery. In the third month, the first day, winter solstice, mountain sacrifices were conducted in the suburbs. On the twelfth day, the palace master of diplomatic accommodations, Zheng Renhui, became deputy commissioner of military affairs, as Zhai Guangye was dismissed.

In summer, the fifth day of the fifth month [May 31], the Emperor departed for campaigns in the east, with Li Gu designated as interim custodian of the eastern capital and Zheng Renhui inspector-general for imperial precincts. The Emperor proceeded to Caozhou on the eighth, pardoning prisoners with sentences of lifelong exile and below. Yanzhou was conquered on the twentieth,[vi] a pardon issued for its residents on the twenty-seventh. On the first day of the sixth month, the Emperor visited Qufu to render sacrifices to Confucius. He arrived from Yanzhou on the seventeenth. In autumn, the twelfth day of the ninth month [October 3], Wang Yan, assistant equerry for the imperial stud, was appointed ambassador to Koryô. The Khitan violated the border.

In the third year, spring, fourth day of the inaugural month [C.E. January 21, 953], the prefect of Linzhou, Yang Zhongxun, defected from the Han to offer fealty. On the fifth day of the intercalary month, Duchengxiangwen arrived as emissary of the Huihu Uighurs. In the second month, the fourteenth day, the court demoted Wang Jun to manager-adjutant to the governor of Shangzhou. On the fifth day of the third month, it invested Rong as Prince of Jin,[vii] dismissing Zheng Renhui on the seventh. On the tenth, it named mili-

....

iv. The word for "punitive campaign" [*tao*] implies punishment for a crime. The Han used it with reference to the Zhou to suggest righteous reprisal as its goal.

v. Reference to an assault "from the direction of Jinzhou" simply underscores that Han troops had chosen an approach from Jinzhou when attempting to punish the renegades in their capital [of Kaifeng]. Raids on cities that do not produce a definitive win or loss are generally not cited. This citation is made to affirm the prerogative of the Han to conduct a punitive action.

vi. Yanzhao died by throwing himself into a well, so there is no citation for execution.

vii. The word "son" is not used because, by the rules of ritual propriety, Rong cannot be considered a son. Having not written the word "son," Rong's original surname [Chai] should be cited, but it is omitted here owing to the prevailing Zhou taboo about mentioning it.

tary training commissioner for Dizhou, Wang Rengao, commandant of the Right Guard and deputy commissioner of military affairs. During summer, the sixth month, heavy rains caused flooding.

In the seventh month of autumn, Zhang Cangying, governor of the Khitan-controlled Lutai Commandery, fled to the south. Envoys of the Tuhun led by Dangfuda reached the capital. In winter, thirteenth day of the tenth month, Feng Dao was named dignitary for greeting the "Spiritual Master" [for the four ancestral temples]. In the eleventh month, the seventh day, Tangut envoys Wutie'mowu and cohort reached the capital. On the second day of the twelfth month, the "Spiritual Master for the four ancestral temples" arrived from the western capital, the Emperor greeting the idol in the western suburbs and worshipping his ancestors at the Imperial Ancestors' Temple. On the twenty-sixth day, Tianxiong governor Wang Yin was slain. Ancestral sacrifices were conducted at the Imperial Ancestors' Temple on the twenty-ninth.

In the spring, first day of the inaugural month, the inaugural year of Xiande [C.E. February 6, 954], sacrifices were performed at the southern suburbs, a general amnesty declared, and a change in reign name announced. Ranking officials elevated the Monarch's title of honor to the "Sagacious and Enlightened, Literate and Martial, Benevolent and Virtuous Emperor." On the third day, Ye was stripped of its status as capital. Zhenning governor Zheng Renhui became commissioner of military affairs on the eleventh day. On the seventeenth, Duanming academician and vice minister of revenues Wang Pu was named deputy director of the Palace Secretariat with ministerial standing, and Wang Rengao was dismissed. On the same day,[1] the Emperor expired at the Zide palace.[viii]

....

viii. He was fifty-one *sui*. "[He expired] on the same day" is written to connect this passage to the preceding one; actually, the exact date of death is regrettably unknown.

CHAPTER 12

ANNALS XII: BASIC ANNALS OF ZHOU

Shizong [Chai Rong, C.E. 921–959], the Profound, Martial, Filial, and Literate Emperor, originally surnamed Chai, was native to Longgang, Xingzhou. A daughter of the Chai family married the future Taizu to become the Sagacious and Dignified Empress. Meanwhile, the elder brother of the Empress, Chai Shouli, had sired a son named Rong, who as a youth grew up with his aunt at the home of Taizu: the youth's earnest and genuine personality were so appealing that Taizu treated him as a son. As Taizu later acquired stature, Rong matured into a physically strong man, distinctly heroic in bearing with talents as horseman and archer. He also possessed a basic command of the classics, histories, and Daoist texts. In personality, he had a staid demeanor with few words. When Taizu became military commissioner under the Han, Rong served as left commandant for palace-gate security. Taizu was Tianxiong governor when Rong served under him as prefect of Guizhou‡ and chief director of military headquarters.

In the third year Qianyou, wintertime [C.E. 950], amid the uprising of Zhou armies at Weizhou and the raid on the capital, Rong stayed behind to defend Wei. He became prefect of Chanzhou, governor of the Zhenning command, and honorary grand mentor with ministerial standing upon Taizu's enthronement. The commissioner for military affairs, Wang Jun, had long been jealous of Rong, so after coming to the capital for audience, in the inaugural month of the third year of Guangshun [C.E. 953], Rong could not remain. Only after Jun had been executed for crimes did Rong, in the third month, receive appointment as prefect of Kaifeng and investiture as Prince of Jin. Sometime this winter, court oracles had picked New Year's Day of the coming year as the best time for ritual sacrifices in the southern suburbs, but Taizu fell ill and for long could not hold court.

During rites in the suburbs on the first day of the inaugural month, the inaugural year of Xiande [C.E. February 6, 954], Taizu could scarcely complete the ceremony.[1] He invested in the Prince oversight over armed forces in and away from the capital, then expired on the seventeenth day. Secrecy was initially imposed on public mourning, which began officially on the twenty-first, as the Emperor assumed power before the royal coffin.[i] The right commandant for palace-gate security, Wei Renpu, became deputy commissioner of military affairs.

On the fifth day of the second month [March 12], envoys of the Huihu Uighurs arrived. On the twenty-second, the court named Feng Dao as dignitary for the grand procession to the imperial hillside mausoleum, chamberlain for ceremonies Tian Min as master of funeral ceremonies, minister of war Zhang Zhao as escort for the royal carriage, deputy-censor Zhang Xu as master of funeral regalia, and the deputy custodian and concurrent administrator of Kaifeng, Wang Min, as master for accommodations and transportation. Han armies launched a punitive campaign from Luzhou.

On the seventh day of the third month [April 12], a general amnesty was declared. Zheng Renhui became interim custodian of the eastern capital on the ninth day. The Emperor departed for Luzhou, on the eleventh, to attack the [Northern] Han.[ii] On the eighteenth, he reached Zezhou, where troops were inspected in the northern suburbs. He engaged the troops of Liu Min on a plateau to vanquish them, on the nineteenth,[iii] then stalked them to Gaoping County for another victory. He reached Luzhou on the twenty-third day, then on the twenty-fifth executed the chief director of cavalry in the Imperial Guard, Fan Aineng, and chief director of infantry He Hui. On the twenty-eighth, Tianxiong governor Fu Yanqing became chief officer of at-large forces at Hedong.

In summer, the twelfth day of the fourth month [May 16], the Spiritual and Sagacious, Literate and Martial, Reverent, August and Filial Emperor[2]

....

i. The earlier mention of Rong's investiture as Prince of Jin has already clarified that he was not imperial son. In his appropriating of accession rituals for a new monarch, he certainly did not await critical input. Thus, no extraordinary elaboration appears here.

ii. Because fault lies with the Zhou [as usurper of the Later Han], the Emperor is not said to have led a "punitive drive" [*fa*]; the terminology for a superior power against an inferior is inappropriate here, so, the narrative employs "attack" [*gong*] for either side [as among peers].

iii. Liu Min refused to accept Zhou sovereignty, but he cannot be dignified with the title "Emperor," so his name is cited.

was buried at Songling.[iv] The defense commissioner of Fenzhou, Dong Xiyan, defected from the Han in surrender. On the thirteenth, the Liaozhou prefect Zhang Hanchao defected from the Han in surrender. The prefectures of Lan and Xian were captured on the eighteenth. The Lady of Wei, née Fu, was installed as empress on the nineteenth. The prefectures of Shi and Qin† were captured. Feng Dao passed away on the twenty-second. On the twenty-seventh, an amnesty was issued for criminals with sentences of lifetime exile and less. The Emperor departed for Taiyuan. The military overseer at Xinzhou‡, Li Jing, assassinated prefect Zhao Gao in mutiny against the Han, surrendering to Zhou.

On the third day of the fifth month [June 6], the defending commander at Daizhou, Zheng Chuqian, defected from the Han in surrender. The Khitan moved to rescue the Han. Yinnandilue arrived as ambassador of the Huihu Uighurs, on the twenty-fourth day. Fu Yanqing fought Khitan armies at Xikou and suffered defeat, the chief director of his vanguard, Shi Yanchao, dying with honor. In the sixth month, the third day, troops were withdrawn. On the thirteenth day, the Emperor reached Xinzheng where he worshipped at the Songling mausoleum. He arrived from Taiyuan on the twenty-eighth.

In autumn, the eighth day of the seventh month [August 9], the Emperor inspected farming at Nanyu hamlet. On the twenty-first, the auxiliary academician at the military bureau and vice minister of public works, Jing Fan, became deputy director at the Palace Secretariat with ministerial powers; Wei Renpu became commissioner of military affairs. In winter, third day of the tenth month [November 1], commandant of the Forest of Feathers Left Guard, Meng Hanqing, was murdered.

During spring of the second year,[v] the second month [C.E. 955], candid criticism was solicited by imperial directive. In summer, the fourth day of the fifth month [May 27], the punitive campaign against Shu was entrusted to Xiang Xun, commissioner for the southern court of palace armies, and the governor of Fengxiang, Wang Jing. On the seventh day, Buddhist temples were widely destroyed; the court also prohibited commoners with parents lacking caregivers from becoming Buddhist clerics and proscribed private

....

iv. Located in Xinzheng County, Zhengzhou.

v. The Five Dynasties being an age of turmoil, only five men to inherit the throne were actual heirs-apparent, while there are four cases of unconventional practices with reference to the adoption of calendars. Emperors Mo of the Liang and Chu of the Jin had acceded to power for a year without bothering to change the reign name, however necessary, and delayed doing so until the subsequent year; Emperors Yin of the Han and Shizong of the Zhou both employed the reign names of preceding monarchs and failed for the rest of their reigns to change them. The Basic Annals merely cites the facts without criticizing such practices, allowing the error to be self-evident.

conversions to the clergy. In autumn, the first day of the ninth month [September 19], a ban on bronze transfers was imposed. In the intercalary month, the eighteenth day, Xiang Xun seized Qinzhou. In winter, the seventh day of the tenth month [November 23], Chengzhou was captured. Reaching the capital on the fourteenth day was Yung [Rong], the ambassador of Koryô and grand advisor to its heir-apparent. Jiezhou was captured. On the first day of the eleventh month, the court charged Li Gu with the campaign against Southern Tang, as chief officer for at-large forces in the southern Huai. Wang Jing seized Fengzhou‡ on the fourteenth. Zheng Renhui passed away on the twenty-second day of the twelfth month.

In the third year, spring, the inaugural month [C.E. 956], fortifications were augmented in the capital. Xiang Xun became interim custodian of the eastern capital on the sixth day, the Emperor leading a campaign against the south on the eighth. On the seventeenth, the chief director of the Imperial Guard and Imperial Bodyguard, Li Chongjin, engaged Tang armies at Zhengyang, defeating them. He was named chief commissioner of bandit-suppressing forces at-large in Huainan circuit, on the twentieth. In the second month, the third day, the Emperor reached the suspension bridge at Xiacai, conquering Chuzhou‡ on the eighth day. On the tenth, an envoy for [Tang ruler] Li Jing arrived to plead for peace, but the court refused to respond. Jing sent a subject, Zhong Mo, with a letter of submission to the throne. Yangzhou was captured on the twenty-second, Taizhou on the twenty-seventh. In the third month, the seventh day, chief commander of cavalry and infantry in and away from the capital, Yuan Yan, became chief officer of the Bamboo-Dragon Guard. The prefectures of Guang, Shu, and Chang were captured during this month.[vi]

In summer, the fourth month, the prefectures of Chang and Tai were regained by the Tang. On the twenty-fourth day of the fifth month [July 4], the Emperor returned from the southern Huai and pardoned prisoners in the capital. Prisoners of war from Huainan were pardoned under a minor amnesty, on the eleventh day of the sixth month. In autumn, the seventh month, the Empress Fu expired. The prefectures of Yang, Guang, Shu, and Chu were regained by the Tang. In the eighth month, the sixth day, taxes were levied on the wood and leeks grown by the people. In the ninth month, the seventeenth day, the Duanming academician and left cavalier of palace remonstrance, Wang Pu, became minister of finance and deputy commissioner for military affairs. In winter, the second day of the tenth month [November

....

vi. "This month" is written to indicate that all three prefectures were not captured in a single day.

7], the Avowedly Moral Empress was buried at the Yiling mausoleum. In the eleventh month, the second day, the palace discontinued those ancestral sacrifices not sanctioned by assorted canons on sacrifices. Sun Cheng, a subject of [Tang ruler] Li Jing, was slain on the seventeenth.[vii]

In the fourth year, spring, the first day of the inaugural month [C.E. February 3, 957], the court announced an amnesty for all crimes below capital punishment. In the second month, the sixteenth day, it named Wang Pu interim custodian of the eastern capital, the Emperor directing a campaign against the south a day later. Shouzhou was conquered on the twentieth day of the third month.[viii] In summer, the twelfth day of the fourth month [May 14], the Emperor returned from Shouzhou. On the twenty-second day, the court released for repatriation to Shu some eight hundred surrendered troops. On the twenty-sixth, the Lady of Pengcheng, née Liu, posthumously became Empress. In the fifth month, the tenth day, the defense commissioner for Mizhou, Hou Xijin, was murdered.

In autumn, the twenty-first day of the eighth month [September 17], the palace dismissed Li Gu, naming Wang Pu as commissioner for military affairs. The Shu regime returned the prefect of Puzhou, Hu Li. In winter, the sixteenth day of the tenth month [November 10], the court appointed Wang Pu interim custodian of the eastern capital, as commissioner of the Three Fiscal Agencies Zhang Mei became inspector-general of imperial precincts. The Emperor launched a campaign against the south on the nineteenth. In the twelfth month, the third day, the defending commander of Sizhou, Fan Zaiyu, defected from the Tang to surrender his prefecture. On the eighth day, Guo Yanwei, the military training commissioner for Haozhou¶, surrendered his prefecture to the dynasty.[ix] Taizhou was claimed on the twenty-fifth.

....

vii. Writing "a subject of Jing was slain," rather than "Cheng died," serves to expose the serious crime committed by the Zhou in murdering a loyal subject while affirming the ethical death of Cheng [see chapter 33].

viii. On the reason for providing no citation for Liu Renshan's surrender, see "Biographies of Martyrs to Virtue" [chapter 32]. Renshan, in fact, did not surrender, so the Zhou itself "conquered" the prefecture. The word "conquer" [*ke*] implies a difficult conquest. The difficulty of claiming Shouzhou clearly reflects Renshan's loyal virtue. No mention is made of "dying with honor" [*sizhi*], inasmuch as Renshan actually died of illness. Still, he is included in the "Biographies of Martyrs to Virtue" for having preserved loyalist principle until death.

ix. The word "relinquishing land" [*fu*] is employed when the defector personally resides at the place being surrendered. Zaiyu and Tingwei, however, surrendered territory [in their official capacity] without actually residing in that territory. Therefore, the word "surrender" [*xiang*] is used instead of "relinquish land." On the reason for not mentioning Tingwei's "defection," see "Hereditary House of Southern Tang" [chapter 62].

In the fifth year, spring, fifth day of the inaugural month [C.E. January 27, 958], Haizhou was captured, and on the tenth, Jinghai Commandery. On the twenty-fifth, Chuzhou was conquered, commanders Zhang Yanqing and Zheng Zhaoye died with honor.[x] On the second day of the second month, Xiongzhou was captured. The Emperor departed for Yangzhou on the fifteenth, Gua peninsula on the twenty-first. On the first day of the third month, the Emperor left for Taizhou, departing once more for Yangzhou on the sixth. He visited Yingluan on the tenth. On the eighteenth day, fourteen prefectures were seized in Huainan, the southern border now drawn along the Yangzi River.[xi] Envoys of Li Jing came to offer a banquet and gifts. On the ninth day of the fourth month, the Emperor worshipped the "Spiritual Master for the Five Ancestral Halls" at the new Imperial Ancestors' Temple. On the twenty-first day, the Emperor returned from Huainan. Envoys arrived for the Huihu Uighurs and the Tartars. In the sixth month, the twenty-first day, some four thousand six hundred prisoners of war were repatriated to the Tang.

In autumn, the sixth day of the seventh month [July 24], the assistant director of waterways and irrigation, Han Yanqing, initiated trade in bronze with Koryô. On the eighth, the court reproduced the *Diagram of the Equitable Fields*. During the ninth month, Puhesan arrived as envoy of Shiliyindeman, the King of Zhancheng [southern Vietnam]. In winter, the twentieth day of the tenth month, a forage occurred for tax revenues. On the fourth day of the eleventh month, the court ordered reproduction of the *Comprehensive Rituals* and *Orthodox Music*. On the tenth day of the twelfth month, former distinctions were abolished in local administration between households providing taxes for imperial coffers and administrative coffers.

In the sixth year, spring, the inaugural month [C.E. 959], envoys arrived for the king of Koryô, So [Zhao]. Ambassador for the Jurchen, Abian, reached the capital on the fifteenth day [February 25]. In the third month, the fourth day, envoys for the Huihu Uighurs of Ganzhou came to offer jade presents, gifts rejected by the palace. Wang Pu passed away on the fifteenth day. On the twenty-first, commissioner of the southern court of palace armies, Wu Yanzuo, was named interim custodian of the eastern capital. The court dis-

....

x. The prefecture had been besieged since the ninth day of the twelfth month, the fourth year. Yanqing and cohort resisted defiantly for over forty days before succumbing, a clear indication that they neither fled not surrendered, so they are privileged to "die with honor." In the Basic Annals, the term "die with honor" is used for over ten persons. For lack in information, biographies were not written [in chapter 33] for Song Lingxun, Li Xia, Zhang Yanqing, and Zheng Zhaoye. As men whose value lies in their deaths, it is only appropriate for the Basic Annals here to highlight their great integrity.

xi. This includes the fourteen prefectures already cited; the citation here confirms that the Emperor had achieved his original objective.

continued the use of the bronze tally with fish motif [for imperial summons], on the twenty-eighth. The Emperor led a northern campaign on the twenty-ninth. Sometime this month, Wu Yanzuo became generalissimo of the Valorous Left Guard and commissioner of military affairs. Acquisition of the Qianning command occurred in the summer, seventeenth day of the fourth month [May 27], followed by Yijin Pass on the twenty-sixth, renamed Bazhou. On the twenty-eighth, Waqiao Pass was acquired and renamed Xiongzhou.[xii]

On the first day of the fifth month [June 9], Yingzhou¶ was acquired.[xiii] The Emperor returned from Xiongzhou on the thirtieth day. On the ninth day of the sixth month, Empress Fu was installed.[xiv] Imperial son Zongxun was invested Prince of Liang and Zongrang as Duke of Yan. The ambassador of Zhancheng, Puhesan, arrived on the fourteenth day. On the fifteenth, Fan Zhi and Wang Pu became associate commissioners of military affairs, as Wei Renpu assumed ministerial powers. The Emperor expired, on the nineteenth day [July 27], at the Zide palace.[xv]

Emperor *Gong* [Guo Zongxun, C.E. 953–973] was the fourth son of Shizong, Zongxun. Ever since Shizong's accession, leading officials had requested the investiture of his son as imperial prince, but the Emperor humbly deferred action for some time. In the midst of a northern campaign against the three passes, he took ill, and only after returning did he invest Zongxun as Prince of Liang. The youth was seven *sui*.

Shizong expired in the sixth year of Xiande, on the nineteenth day of the sixth month, the Emperor acceding to the throne before the royal coffin, on the twentieth. On the twenty-ninth, the palace designated Fan Zhi as dignitary for the grand procession to the imperial hillside mausoleum, Hanlin academician Dou Yan as master of funeral ceremonies, minister of war Zhang Zhao as escort for the royal carriage, deputy censor Bian Guidang as master of funeral regalia, and the commissioner of the southern court of palace armies

....

xii. District changes at the prefectural or county level are generally not cited. Yet the resuscitation of former lands of the Middle Kingdom is an event worth citing. It is clear that Shizong, after capturing the three passes, established prefectures at Waqiao and Yijin. Yukou Pass was simply made military outpost. The pertinent information is lacking in the *Old History* and *Veritable Records*, so the exact date of acquisition is uncertain. Yukou is now Xin'an Commandery.

xiii. Having reclaimed the former lands of the Middle Kingdom, the words "Khitan territory" are not employed.

xiv. Miss Fu did not hold noble rank. By refusing to use [the conventional phrase] "Miss Fu was installed as empress," there is an inference of impropriety. Inasmuch as her standing was fixed before the marriage itself, so "Empress Fu was installed" seems an appropriate narrative principle [*wenli*], without inference of praise or blame. [See chapter 20.]

xv. He was thirty-nine *sui*.

and administrator for Kaifeng, Zan Jurun, as deputy for accommodations and transportation. In autumn, the fourth day of the seventh month, minister of revenues Li Tao was named deputy dignitary for the funeral procession, and director of accounting Lu Yi was named his administrative aide.

On the seventeenth day of the eighth month [September 22], imperial younger brothers were invested princes: Xirang as the Prince of Cao, Xijin as the Prince of Ji, Xihui as the Prince of Qi. Ambassadors from Koryô arrived on the twenty-ninth. Commissioned as ambassador to Koryô, on the twenty-fourth day of the ninth month, was Dai Jiao, commandant of the Valorous Left Guard. In winter, the second day of the eleventh month, the Profound, Martial, Filial, and Literate Emperor was buried at the Qingling mausoleum.[xvi] Envoys from Koryô arrived.

On the fourth day of the inaugural month, the seventh year [C.E. February 3, 960], the Emperor relinquished the throne,[3] as the Song ascent begins.[xvii]

WE LAMENT. The Basic Annals for the Five Dynasties are, alas, complete.[xviii] Yet I could barely bring myself to describe ruler–subject relations! As evidenced by the rebellion of Yougui during the Liang [against his father], the lethal stabbing of Kening during the Tang [by a brother], and the murders of Cunyi and Congzan [by their father]—did not charity nearly vanish between father, son, and other blood kin? In simply "suspending court" when the Consort Dowager died while investing empresses in the manner of Liu and Feng—did not the perversity of husband–wife relations fall beneath beasts of

....

xvi. This is located in Guancheng County, Zhengzhou.

xvii. The collapse of the Five Dynasties has been depicted in varying ways, the language here simply following events. In earlier noting "the collapse of the Liang," I stressed the haste of the Later Tang ascent to power, while "the collapse of Han" stressed the delays in the Zhou accession. The Tang deceived the world by invoking the "suppression of renegades" as pretext, while the Zhou cheated the world in professing to install Liu Yun. The phrase "collapse of the Liang," stressing the speed of the Tang founding, makes it clear that the goal was never to "suppress renegades." The phrase "collapse of Han," by stressing the delays in founding the Zhou, makes it clear that the claim of installing Yun was bogus. No such words are used for the demise of Tang, for the Tang imperium effectively ended with the assassination of its ruler, Zhuangzong. Mingzong subsequently claimed to be successor to Tang, the Tang line ending for a second time following the flight of Emperor Min, before Fei came to reclaim it. To repeat citations in several separate places that the dynasty "collapsed" is unacceptable, so no citation is given at all. When the Jin fell, it is said that, "the Khitan toppled the Jin"—unambiguous words to convey a serious warning. For the Zhou, the Emperor "relinquished the throne," it is said, for "relinquishing" [*xun*] implies "obeying" [*shun*]—that is, the capacity to obey the Mandate of Heaven.

xviii. The word "complete" implies full inclusion herewith of all matters pertaining to the destruction and turmoil of the time.

the wild? By offering sacrifices in the wilderness during summer solstice and burning paper money, by engaging in merriment amid official mourning and calendar change, and by murdering Ma Yan and Ren Huan—do these not confirm the almost total desecration of rites and music, law and order? Raising effigies at Mt. Lei, passing arrows as military instructions, and pummeling horses to death—do these not confirm the almost total barbarizing of the Middle Kingdom? "Age of chaos" seems an apt characterization.

In the short span of five to six years, Shizong managed to reclaim the Qin and Long region [in the west], pacify the southern Huai region [to the south], and restore the three passes [in the north], his martial awe reverberating among barbarians and Chinese alike. Simultaneously, he invited to court the masters of Confucian crafts and literary composition to critique political institutions, revise the *Comprehensive Rituals*, systematize *Orthodox Music*, and deliberate on the *Uniform Penal Code*—creating methodologies for such studies, in the process, that became models for later generations. By character intelligent and intrepid, Shizong could be augustly decisive in deliberating affairs. Only a year after his accession, he eliminated 3,336 Buddhist temples across the empire. The Middle Kingdom faced a shortage of cash at the time, so the confiscation of all Buddhist statuary of bronze was mandated for recasting as coin. He once commented, "Tradition has it that the Buddha viewed his human existence as unreal, yet out of an urge to profit mankind [through his teachings], he chose to retain his true body. Having once chosen to forgo personal salvation to profit the world, how could he possibly begrudge us a bunch of bronze statues?" In this way, officialdom dared not criticize the action.

During his nighttime readings, the Emperor once came upon the *Charts on Equitable Fields* of the Tang courtier Yuan Zhen, then heaved a pensive sigh in remarking, "Here is the source of ultimate order—the policies of the true King must begin here!" He thus ordered instruction in the principles behind the charts to first expose administrators and commoners to them, hoping within a year to equalize fields across the world. The forethought behind his agendas was anything but trifling!

The Emperor consulted chief minister Li Gu on strategy during the campaign against the Southern Tang. Upon later conquering the southern Huai, he pulled out the letters from [a retired] Li Gu for comments from academician Tao Gu, the imperial brocade satchel replete with notes as the two men sat side by side in discussion. Shizong's capacity for martial valor deservingly dubbed "gallant heroism." His reception of opinions without prejudice and deployment of aides without second guessing truly merits his characterization as a "noble ruler!"

Shizong acquired the three passes to the north without bloodying the swords of troops, yet historians still censure him for "trivializing the security of the dynasty" in a rush for a chance victory. Astute in weighing the strategic strengths of the two sides and sensitive to the rare opportunity presented by opponent Shulü's overextension, who else could do so save for someone who appreciates the value of total victory? This is truly beyond the comprehension of official historians.[4]

CHAPTER 13

BIOGRAPHIES OF THE ROYAL FAMILIES: LIANG

We lament. The Liang was depraved to the extreme! Beginning with its rise through roguery and culminating in its purge of the Tang dynasty, its legacy poisoned an entire world. Throughout the realm, men of valor sallied forth at once, each harboring in his heart the wish to annihilate the Liang dynasty. Yet the failure to shake the dynasty's spirit even slightly would ultimately thwart those ambitions. Without peer in the world, the Liang had the might of tigers or wolves, so to speak. Yet eventual downfall occurred through fancy for a few women, culminating in men hacking at the chests or the bowels of fellow men to butcher one another like swine. In the calamity erupting between father and son, we can know the potential for the sensuous woman to ruin mankind.

Since antiquity, the calamity of women when severe could ruin the world, when less severe could ruin the family, when still less severe could ruin the individual. And even if the individual eludes extinction, his posterity can still be implicated—a matter of time only before calamity extends to everyone. Upon exploring the progression of it all, it invariably begins with ignoring subtle symptoms. The *Book of Changes*, "*Kun*, the Passive" says, "Six at the beginning: light frost underfoot suggests that solid ice is not far off." Another section, "*Jiaren*, the Family" adds, "Nine at the beginning: a king cloistered with family can forget all fears."[1] When words are so apt, we must surely be mindful! The affairs of the Liang royal family were akin to what the *Book of Odes* calls "unspeakable." But subsequently under the Later Tang and Jin, chaos persisted among people related by blood and marriage—inspiration for these "Biographies of the Royal Families."

The Refined and Charitable Empress, née Wang

The Refined and Charitable Empress, surnamed Wang [d. C.E. 891], was mother of Taizu of Liang and native to Shanfu, Shanzhou‡. She bore three sons: the eldest was named Zhu Quanyu, Prince of Guang; the next was named Zhu Cun, Prince of Lang; and then there was Taizu himself [Zhu Quanzhong].

Widowed young, the Empress carried her sons to the home of Liu Chong of Xiao County, where they worked for board. Locals especially suffered under the oppressive hand of Taizu, a wastrel with brawn and little else. Taizu seemed slothful and unwilling to work, as Chong saw it, so he repeatedly disciplined the youth with flogging. Chong's mother was alone in pitying the boy, often personally warning her family as she groomed him, "The third Zhu boy is no ordinary youth and should be treated kindly."

Taizu and Cun were both drawn to banditry in the wake of Huang Chao's rebellion, joining him in the offensive at Guangzhou‡, where Cun perished in battle. Taizu reversed course within a few years and defected to surrender to the Tang dynasty, eventually defeating Chao. Upon subsequently becoming the Xuanwu governor, he arranged for horses and carriages to greet the future Empress at Liu Chong's home in Xiao County. A nervous Empress ran off as the escort reached her door, exclaiming to Madame Liu, "The third Zhu boy lacked deportment and consorted with riffraff, only to die as a bandit. How could he have managed this?" The escort apprised the Empress of Taizu's current circumstances, and she wept in surprise and delight. The mother of Chong accompanied her on the return trip. The Empress was ennobled Grand Lady of Jin.

The Empress particularly relished an occasion when Taizu held a banquet for her and raised a goblet to toast her longevity. He began with the words, "Master of the Five Classics Zhu Cheng devoted his life to book learning, yet never passed a single examination. That his son could become governor is certainly no disgrace to that ancestor." The Empress reflected for some time before responding, "Your rise to such heights reflects rare valor, to be sure, but in practicing righteousness you are not necessarily a match for your ancestor." Taizu failed fully to appreciate her meaning, so the Empress continued, "You and Second Son both followed after Huang Chao, but he died in the mountains of the southern barbarians, and his children today are living as orphans at Wugou [the ancestral home]. How can their plight be ignored as you savor the rank and riches that are now yours?" Tearfully apologizing for his failings, Taizu summoned all sons of Cun to reunite with him. The temperamental and obstinate character of Taizu had caused many to be murdered, but whenever the Empress reproached him, most managed to survive.

In autumn, the second year of Dashun [891], the Empress grew ill, and prognosticators said that, "she should return to the old village." She did return to die at Wugou. Once Taizu acceded to the throne and constructed temples to the four ancestors, he honored his deceased father as the Majestic Emperor and her as the Refined and Charitable Empress, Wenhui.

The Maiden and Chaste Empress, née Zhang

The Maiden and Chaste Empress of Taizu, surnamed Zhang [d. C.E. 904], was the offspring of a prosperous clan at Juting village in Dangshan County, Shanzhou‡. Taizu had taken her as formal wife in youth, and their union yielded Emperor Mo. As his own stature grew, she was ennobled Lady of Wei.

Discerningly wise and deftly assertive, the Empress conducted herself with a strict sense of ritual decorum. For all of Taizu's bad temper and obstinacy, he nonetheless held her in awe. And whenever he sought her counsel on matters of the outer court, she was often on target. Taizu commonly murdered others in fits of rage, although many managed to survive when the Empress interceded on their behalf. Taizu once departed with his troops, when halfway into the journey, the Empress had second thoughts and promptly sent a servant to summon him back, and he arrived as promised.

Zhu Youyu, the Prince of Chen, once raided Xuzhou¶ and overpowered Zhu Jin at Mount Shifo, forcing his flight. Youyu's failure to pursue Jin left Taizu utterly livid, and he stripped him of command. A nervous Youyu and a handful of horsemen now absconded for the mountains, and sometime later hid at the Prince of Guang's residence. The Empress instructed Youyu by secret messenger to return of his own volition. He did indeed rush for an early morning meeting with Taizu, falling prostrate on the floor of his chambers and tearfully offering his life in contrition. Horrifically furious, Taizu ordered attendants to drag him away for beheading. As word reached the Empress, she spared not even a moment to slip into shoes, but rushed to chambers as she sobbingly propped up Youyu, telling him, "Having returned to throw yourself before the court in pleading mercy, why not prove yourself free of treachery?" Taizu's resolve abated and Youyu was spared.

After crushing Zhu Jin, Taizu returned to camp with Jin's wife and informed the Empress when she met him at Fengqiu County. The Empress hastened to meet Jin's wife, who bowed twice. The Empress reciprocated in kind, then said in tears of empathy, "The overseer of Yan and Yun [your husband] and the dignitary for public works [mine] share a common surname but different domains. For trivial reasons, my dear, wars waged among virtual brothers have wreaked such hardship for you. If Bianzhou had fallen, instead, I would be in your shoes today." Her words finished, she cried again. Taizu was so moved that he sent Jin's wife to a nunnery, the Empress providing clothing and food for her. "Dignitary for public works" refers to Taizu's honorary post at the time.

In the inaugural year of Tianyou [C.E. 904], the Empress died of illness. She was posthumously ennobled the Wise Consort after Taizu's accession to the throne. Originally buried in the Runse hamlet of Kaifeng County, her posthumous title changed to the Maiden and Chaste, Yuanzhen, Empress Dowager upon the accession of Empero Mo, her body interred at the Xuanling mausoleum [alongside Taizu]. Only after her death did Taizu turn to the debauchery that ultimately ruined him.

The Consort of Luminous Deportment, née Chen

The Consort of Luminous Deportment, Zhaoyi, surnamed Chen, was native to Songzhou. Her physical beauty in youth paved her path to the harem. Taizu would acquire several hundred female companions and concubines after achieving some stature, but Zhaoyi enjoyed his undivided favor. When Taizu took ill, she and several dozen nuns performed Buddhist ceremonies for his health, continuing day to night without a moment's rest. Taizu was moved by her love for him and especially favored her. In the third year of Kaiping [C.E. 909], initiated as a Buddhist novitiate, she assumed residence at a nunnery in Songzhou.

The Consort of Luminous Countenance, née Li

The Consort of Luminous Countenance, surnamed Li, also entered the palace through sensual appeal. A woman especially faithful, she never left the side of Taizu. When illness confined Taizu to bed during the daytime, the Consort was alone in his bedroom as a beam buckled: she quickly grabbed him by the clothes to permit a quick dodge, the broken beam landing on his bed. Taizu hence developed a special affinity for her, extending honors as the Consort of Luminous Countenance, Zhaorong. Nothing is known about her final whereabouts.

The Virtuous Concubine, née Zhang

The Virtuous Concubine of Emperor Mo, née Zhang [C.E. 892–915], was the daughter of Zhang Guiba, a meritorious subject under Taizu. The Emperor was still prince upon taking her as formal wife. After acceding the throne, he prepared to elevate her as Empress, but she preferred postponing the event until the Emperor had worshipped heaven at the southern suburbs. He never managed to conduct the rites when the Concubine succumbed to a serious illness, in the inaugural year of Zhenming [C.E. 915]. Investiture as the Virtuous Concubine, Defei, occurred on the very night of her death, at twenty-four *sui*.

The Secondary Concubine, née Guo

The Secondary Concubine was surnamed Guo and was a daughter of Guihou, a one-time prefect of Dengzhou‡ under the Liang. She entered the palace in youth based on physical appeal. When the Liang collapsed and Zhuangzong of Tang occupied its capital at Bianzhou, the former concubines and consorts of Liang all bowed in tearfully greeting the invader. The beautiful concubine of Zhu Youyong, the Prince of He, was summoned by Zhuangzong, only to revile him disparagingly. He murdered her, then summoned Concubine Guo, who obeyed his orders in fear. She was later initiated as a Buddhist nun and moved to Luoyang, the Emperor conferring the personal name Shizheng.

Earlier, as Zhuangzong occupied Bianzhou, Emperor Mo climbed the Jianguo Tower to address Huangfu Lin, his director of the Crane-Commanding Guard, saying, "Our feud with the Jin has spanned the generations, so I cannot afford to dally and succumb to its swords. You have permission to take my life—do not let me fall into enemy hands!" The two men held onto each other and wept bitterly. Lin subsequently raised his sword to fell the Emperor and hanged himself on the same night. Upon occupying Bianzhou, Zhuangzong ordered Zhang Quanyi of Henan to bury the corpses, storing their heads at the Grand Altar. In the third year of the Tianfu reign [C.E. 938], under Jin rule, authorities at the Grand Altar received directives to release the heads of former criminals to family survivors for burial. The head of Emperor Mo was released to the custody of An Chongruan, a commander of the Right Guard, and interred alongside the Concubine Guo, who had died in Luoyang.

Taizu [Zhu Quanzhong] had two elder brothers, Quanyu and Cun. He fathered eight boys: the eldest was Youyu, then Yougui, Youzhang, Youzhen,

Youyong, Youhui, and Youzi, respectively. His adopted son was Youwen. On the ninth day of the fifth month of the inaugural Kaiping year [C.E. June 22, 907], he ennobled Youwen as Prince of Bo, Yougui as Prince of Ying, Youzhang as Prince of Fu, Youzhen as Prince of Jun, Youyong as Prince of He, and Youhui as Prince of Jian. Youyu had died before the accession and posthumously became Prince of Chen. Only upon Emperor Mo's accession to the throne was Youzi invested Prince of Kang.

Zhu Youzhang originally served as military training commissioner for Shouzhou, group leader for the palace army's right and left wings, and overseer of the Fengde treasury. He served as interim regent for Yunzhou during the Yougui interlude, then governor of the Zhongwu and later Wuning commands under Emperor Mo. As for Youyong and Youhui, nothing is known of their fates.

Quanyu, Prince of Guang

Zhu Quanyu [d. C.E. 916] was ennobled Prince of Guang after the accession of Taizu. He alone remained with his mother as a boarder at Liu Chong's home when his younger brothers, Taizu and Cun, cast their lot with banditry. Once Taizu had achieved prominence, he and his mother rejoined the family at Xuanwu [Kaifeng], receiving temporary assignment as governor of Shannan west circuit. He eventually retired as grand preceptor.

As Taizu prepared to accept abdication of the Tang throne, Quanyu observed court authorities making ceremonial arrangements before the palace, asking as he turned to Taizu, "Third brother, are you capable of this?" Taizu had settled comfortably in the palace when the Prince joined him to imbibe and gamble. Intoxicated, Quanyu grabbed some dice to toss into a bowl, placing the bowl before Taizu to exclaim, "Third brother, you began as a common man from Dangshan with the good fortune to be favored by the Son of Heaven with four governorships. What disservice has he done you to justify annihilating the three-hundred year Tang imperium? I will surely witness your annihilation of its entire royal family as well. No need for gambling!" An irate Taizu abruptly terminated the gathering. Quanyu later grew dissatisfied with life in the capital and often stayed at the Dangshan ancestral home. His three sons all received investitures: Youliang as Prince of Heng, Youneng as Prince of Hui‡, and Youhui‡ as Prince of Shao.

In the inaugural year of Qianhua [C.E. 911], Songzhou was elevated to the Xuanwu command and Zhu Youliang assigned as governor. Youliang's offering of "auspicious wheat" with three buds on a stalk incited Taizu, who insisted, "This year, massive flooding afflicted Songzhou. Why bother with such things?" He dismissed Youliang, who now resided in the capital. When illness left Taizu bedridden and Quanyu came to visit him, the two embraced and wept uncontrollably. Taizu subsequently pardoned Youliang to permit his return eastward. Quanyu died of illness in the second year of Zhenming [C.E. 916], his noble rank as Prince of Guang inherited by Youliang, Prince of Heng.

As interim regent for Song and Hua prefectures and prefect for Chenzhou, Zhu Youneng acted improperly in every post, as many a malefactor presumed upon his patronage. Local customs at Chenzhou entailed a fascination with "temples to debauchery" and other heretical beliefs, where students of Buddhism celebrated one doctrine known as "ascending the vehicle"—worshippers assembling secretly from morning to night with the casual intermingling of men and women. Sorcerers Wu Yi and Dong Yi prodded their followers to call them "Sons of Heaven" and formed autonomous official organs. Initially tolerated by Youliang, once the two began plundering nearby cities and counties, Emperor Mo dispatched troops to liquidate them.

Ever since the rebellion and execution of Youzi, the Prince of Kang, Emperor Mo began distancing himself from the imperial clan, causing clansmen to squabble. In the fourth year of Zhenming [C.E. 918],[2] Zhu Youneng led a mutiny of Chenzhou armies and raided the capital. His men defeated at Chenliu, he retreated to Chenzhou, only to surrender a few months later. Emperor Mo issued a pardon while relegating his noble status to the marquis of Fangling. Zhu Youhui‡, governor of Shanzhou, had intended to mobilize prefectural armies in a mutiny as well, but Emperor Mo summoned him back to the capital, where he was incarcerated along with Youliang and Youneng. They were all killed once the dynasty fell and Zhuangzong occupied Bianzhou.

Cun the Prince of Lang, and Sons Youning and Youlun

Zhu Cun, the Prince of Lang, had formerly joined Taizu as Huang Chao [junior] lieutenants in the Guangzhou‡ assault, only to perish in battle. He was survived by sons Youning and Youlun.

Zhu Youning [d. C.E. 903] had the courtesy name Anren. Displaying a sharp mind in youth, he could suppress all outward expression of likes and dislikes. The future Taizu named him lieutenant because of his dexterity as archer and swordsman. Promotions ensued as director for Victorious brigades at headquarters and prefect of Gongzhou. As Taizu encircled Fengxiang, Youning was sent eastward to make military preparations at the Xuanwu command. The Liang came under a sudden storm from Wang Shifan, who surrounded Qizhou¶, so it deployed Youning and his men to retaliate. They carted off a thousand horses and severed several thousand human heads as spoils. The Tang court named Youning the Jianwu governor and conferred the title "Heroically Courageous Subject of Merit for the Royal Reception," coinciding with Taizu's reception of the Tang Emperor on his return to the capital. Taizu dispatched his men for another confrontation with Shifan. Surrounding Bochang County, they perpetrated a general massacre of sufficient magnitude to obstruct the flow of the Qing River. They battled at Shilou, and a vanquished Youning was slain after being thrown from his horse.

Zhu Youlun [d. C.E. 903] similarly possessed a sharp and lucid mind as a youth, acquiring a comprehensive knowledge of the Confucian *Analects* and *Lesser Learning*, as well as familiarity with musical notation. Cun had died when Taizu appointed Youlun director of the primary-cohort cavalry, petitioning for credentials as the Awesomely Martial right commander.

Once the armies of Yanzhou¤ attacked Neihuang County, Weizhou, Youlun headed an advance contingent to cross the Yellow River by night and commandeer a thousand of their horses. Luzhou governor Li Hanzhi's surrender to Liang prompted the Prince of Jin to storm Lu. Youlun's armies now occupied the city and retrieved Hanzhi for return to the capital. A series of promotions ensued, including honorary dignitary for public works and concurrent Tengzhou prefect. Jin forces rushed the Liang after Taizu's blockade of Fengxiang. Youlun responded by commanding a force of thirty thousand as far as Fanshan, forcing Jin regulars to retreat somewhat as Youlun headed westward to rendezvous with Taizu at Fengxiang. Emperor Zhaozong now returned to Changan and rewarded Youlun with the Ningyuan governorship.

Taizu returned to the east, but Youlun stayed behind in the capital with an Imperial Guard posting in order to monitor Zhaozong's actions. Youlun subsequently had an accidental fall from a horse during a polo match, his death inciting an utterly livid Taizu to direct seventy thousand men as far as Hezhong Prefecture. A confounded and crying Zhaozong considered flight to [the Prince of Jin] at Taiyuan, but never managed. Chief minister Cui Yin dispatched a messenger, meanwhile, to dissuade Taizu from advancing farther. Convinced that Cui Yin intentionally murdered Youlun, Taizu petitioned the palace to execute him and his supporters. Without authorization from Zhaozong, Taizu dispatched nephew Youliang to the capital. There he surrounded the Kaihua ward to murder Cui Yin, along with the metropolitan custodian Zheng Yuangui, commissioner for palace security Wang Jianxun, Flying Dragons commander Chen Ban, master of auxiliary palace gates Wang Jianxi, master of diplomatic accommodations Wang Jianyi, and a former left associate at the secretariat, Zhang Jun.

Once Taizu acceded to the throne and imperial clansmen received investitures, the Palace Secretariat further argued for noble titles for deceased imperial brother Cun, as well as imperial nephews Youning, the former Jianwu governor, and Youlun, the former Ningyuan governor. Thus, Cun was posthumously ennobled as Prince of Lang, Youning as Prince of An, and Youlun as Prince of Mi.

Youyu, Prince of Chen

Zhu Youyu [C.E. 904], the Prince of Chen, had the courtesy name Duanfu. A skilled horseman and archer since youth, he attended Taizu on campaign and won the hearts of troops through generous and genuine treatment. Taizu had once allied with the Prince of Jin to encircle Huang Ye at Xihua [Chenzhou], where an underling of Ye climbed the wall with spear in hand, defiantly cursing the enemy. The Prince of Jin deployed a foreign horseman to shoot him down, but a stream of arrows missed their mark. Taizu then witnessed Youyu hit the target at first shot, his soldiers all shouting in jubilation. Also amused was the Prince of Jin, who provided Youyu with fancy bows and a hundred arrows. Taizu was Xuanwu governor at the time, and he installed the youth as chief director of the governor's guard.

In the inaugural year of Jingfu [C.E. 892], Taizu opened hostilities against Yunzhou, while Youyu commanded a vanguard in proceeding next against Doumen. Hit by Yun belligerents in a nighttime strike, Youyu fled in defeat. As Taizu approached from his rear, he did not know of Youyu's defeat, so many troops on his own front lines perished at enemy hands. Only after retreating to a remote village did Taizu and Youyu manage to meet. Zhu Xuan was at Puzhou, then, so Taizu sent Youyu to lead an advance team of two hundred mounts; he arrived later but could not find Youyu. Ultimately, it was Taizu who engaged the enemy and absconded on the heels of defeat. With his opponents in hot pursuit, he initially reached a large water ditch, barely surviving them: his horses managed to pass only because of the dense accumulation of wooden logs in the ditch. The Liang side lost more than ten commanders, including Li Fan.

That winter, Zhu Youyu captured Puzhou and proceeded to blockade Shi Pu at Xuzhou¶. Zhu Jin now intervened on behalf of Pu, committing twenty thousand men, but Youyu defeated him all the same at Mount Shifo, as Jin fled. Inspector-in-chief Zhu Yougong addressed Taizu making the false charge that Youyu had failed to pursue Jin despite ample opportunity. A livid Taizu chose to reassign his army to Pang Shigu, while submitting Youyu to official authorities. The messenger delivered the wrong letter to Youyu, however, leaving him worried and confounded. Through guidance from Empress Zhang, he eluded the worst and later became interim prefect for Xuzhou‡.

The proximity of Xuzhou‡ to Caizhou had exposed the city to the ordeal of massive banditry, its residents ruined. Youyu managed to pacify such vagabonds and increase the city's population by thirty thousand households.

Promoted to chief director of the armed forces, Youyu was restored temporarily to Xuzhou‡, after pacifying Yan and Yun prefectures. He commanded armies in restoring order to Caizhou in the wake of Cui Hong's flight to Huainan, the markets continuing uninterrupted. Taizu was concurrent governor of the Huguo command upon selecting Youyu as his own interim regent. Reassignment as the Zhongwu governor followed. When Taizu attacked Fengxiang and failed to capture it, he departed to strike against Binzhou. Youyu overpowered Lingtai and Liangyuan, then subdued Long Prefecture, as Yang Chongben surrendered Bin. Later, Chongben defected once again and Taizu dispatched Youyu to raid him, his men quartered at Yongshou County. Youyu died of illness.

Youwen, Prince of Bo, and Yougui, Prince of Ying

Zhu Youwen [d. C.E. 911] the Prince of Bo had the courtesy name Deming. His original surname was Kang and personal name Qin. A handsome youth with refined features, he could be curious about learning, fond of debating affairs, and fairly competent at composing poetry. Taizu raised him as son.

As governor over four commands, Taizu named Youwen regional commissioner of salt and iron revenues: Taizu deployed armies across the four corners, but it was Youwen who amassed the tax revenues to satisfy military needs. After acceding to the throne, Taizu deposited revenues from the commands formerly governed by him—Xuanwu, Xuanyi, Tianping, and Huguo—into a newly established Jianchang Hall and named Youwen commissioner, investing him as Prince of Bo. During Taizu's visit to the western capital, Youwen stayed behind at the eastern capital as interim custodian.

A commoner later known as *Zhu Yougui* [d. C.E. 913] was the bastard son of Taizu: amid the pillaging of Song and Bo¶ prefectures during his early tenure as Xuanwu governor, Taizu had an illicit affair with a woman at an inn that produced the boy. Yougui matured into a discriminating man of many talents. The Prince of Bo, Youwen, was multifaceted in talents as well, and Taizu loved him dearly. He was the eldest son, no less, so despite having no designated heir at the time of formal accession, Taizu's heart was long set on Youwen as successor. Taizu did not take a second wife after Empress Zhang's death, so he appealed to sons in the districts to offer their own wives as harem candidates. He thereby developed a special attachment to Woman Wang, the attractive wife of Youwen. And throughout his lengthy illness, always in attendance at his bedside were either Woman Wang or Woman Zhang, the wife of Yougui. Once his illness abated somewhat, Taizu said to Woman Wang, "I will never rise from this bed again, I realize, so go to the eastern capital and summon back Youwen. I wish to see him for a final parting." His wish was clearly to entrust later affairs to Youwen as heir. He now addressed Jing Xiang, saying, "A district assignment may be given Yougui, arrangements for which should be made promptly." Yougui was named prefect of Laizhou.

Taizu was inherently obstinate and temperamental, but illness made his moods of pleasure and displeasure wholly unpredictable: at the time, those receiving orders of demotion faced the inevitable issue of a second order of still greater severity, which left Yougui utterly terrified. His wife, Woman Zhang, warned, "The Monarch has already transferred to Woman Wang the articles for imperial succession, arranging for her to go to the eastern capital to summon Youwen. Today you face certain calamity!" Husband and wife cried as they stood face to face. Aides to Yougui also prodded him, "In a matter of such life-or-death urgency, why did you not lay plans early on?"

Yougui changed clothes to proceed secretly to the Dragon and Tiger Left Guard to confer with its general commander, Han Jing. On the very same night, Jing provided five hundred troops from the governor's bodyguard to accompany Yougui, infiltrating the Crane-Commanding Guard to penetrate the palace. By the third drum that night, they smashed crossbars on the Wanchun gate to enter. Those attending to the sick Emperor had departed when intruders reached his bedroom, a startled Taizu rising as he shouted out, "I have long suspected your treachery and regret not killing you sooner. How can even an infidel manage to murder his own father?" A personal aide to Yougui, Feng Ting'e, leaped at Taizu with his sword, but the Emperor swung his body to the other side of a pillar, a pillar struck three times by the assassin's sword before an exhausted Taizu collapsed onto his bed: Ting'e now drove his sword into Taizu and ripped his belly open as stomach and intestines gushed out. Yougui employed underclothing and bedding to wrap the corpse in the bedroom, while conducting mourning in secret for four days. To lavish gifts on courtiers and soldiers, he tapped into the prefectural treasury. He also arranged for edict drafter Ding Zhaopu to hasten to the eastern capital with an edict authorizing the execution of Youwen. An edict [in Taizu's name] further declared:

> Through thirty years, I bore the weight of our dynastic enterprise, although rule over humanity was conferred only six brief years ago. Those near and far can now join hands in anticipation of a brief repose. How unthinkable that Youwen might secretly nurture seditious schemes and nearly commit a grave crime! Two nights ago, armored soldiers suddenly

> penetrated my palace and I escaped unscathed only through the intervention of a loyal and filial Yougui, who led guards in liquidating the intruders. But illness wracks my body and saps my spirits, as the end appears near. By suppressing the traitors, Yougui has evinced merit well beyond the ordinary, such that oversight over our armies and country should rightfully be entrusted to him.

Yougui only now assumed formal mourning.

In the second year of Qianhua, sixteenth day of the sixth month [C.E. August 1, 912], Yougui assumed the powers of Emperor before the coffin of Taizu. He rewarded Han Jing with the governorship for Zhongwu, while designating the future Emperor Mo as interim regent for Bianzhou and Zhu Youqian of Hezhong as palace secretary. Youqian refused the appointment. Meanwhile, a force of three thousand from the Dragon-Prancing Guard stationed at Huaizhou abducted commander Liu Chongba, occupied the city, and professed their wish to suppress the infidels. Yougui offered sacrifices to Heaven at the southern suburbs of Luoyang, in the inaugural month of the third year [C.E. 913], changing the reign to Fengli.

The maternal grandson of Taizu,[3] Yuan Xiangxian, laid plans with Zhao Yan, commander-in-chief for reserve mounts to assist Emperor Mo in suppressing the infidels. Palace guardsmen led by Xiangxian infiltrated the palace in the second month. Yougui slipped down the northern wall to ground level, joined by his wife, Woman Zhang. They were about to scale the city wall and flee, but failed to succeed. Yougui ordered Feng Ting'e to stab both himself and his wife to death. Ting'e committed suicide as well. Emperor Mo, after assuming the throne, restored titular honors to Youwen and relegated Yougui to commoner status.

Youzi, Prince of Kang

Zhu Youzi [d. C.E. 915], the Prince of Kang, had eyes with double pupils and once boasted privately of someday becoming the Son of Heaven. The Virtuous Consort of Emperor Mo died in the inaugural year of Zhenming [C.E. 915], and as her burial approached, Youzi arranged for an assassin to infiltrate Mo's bedroom under the cover of night. The Emperor was asleep at the time and dreaming that someone was about to harm him when he awakened to hear his sword on the reclining couch produce a clanging sound. Leaping to his feet and drawing his sword, he shouted, "Is this a mutiny?" He sealed off the room and apprehended the assassin, murdering him with his own hands and later executing Youzi. The next day, Mo turned to Zhao Yan and Zhang Hanjie, saying, "I came perilously close to never seeing you again." He hereafter kept the imperial clan weak and distanced, placing trust in Zhao and Zhang, even until his own demise.

WE LAMENT. It is an immense challenge to apply the rules of the *Spring and Autumn Annals* to assess right and wrong or pass judgment on sovereignty. Some have queried, "The crime of a subject who commits regicide against his monarch, as with Taizu of Liang, corresponds to a son's regicide against his father, as with Yougui. By the rules of the *Annals*, pretenders assuming the throne in the wake of regicide who change the reign name a year later are all treated as rulers. So why is Yougui denied a 'Basic Annal' in your history? Father and son being equally reprehensible, how is it consistent with the spirit of the *Annals* to exclude the son while including the father?" My response is this: affairs of the Liang are crystal clear, and exposing the father's vice does not rest upon whether we allow or disallow the son's imperium. Moreover, I cannot but consider Emperor Mo's just cause. By the rules of the *Annals*, when a ruler falls to regicide and the culprit eludes punishment, duty to exact justice falls on the subjects of that country. My treatment of Yougui derives from considering the just cause against him.[4]

CHAPTER 14

BIOGRAPHIES OF THE ROYAL FAMILIES: TAIZU OF TANG

The Formal Wife, née Liu, and the Secondary Consort, née Cao

The formal wife of Taizu [Li Keyong] was surnamed Liu [d. C.E. 925] and was native to Daibei. The Consort Cao [d. C.E. 925], a native of Taiyuan, was secondary consort.

After Taizu's investiture as Prince of Jin, Miss Liu was invested Lady of Qin. She commonly accompanied Taizu on military campaigns in the early days of his insurrection at Daibei. Possessed with a lucid intellect and multifaceted skills, she knew military tactics rather well and often helped Taizu by teaching archery and horseback riding to female attendants and concubines. Once, as Taizu pursued Huang Chao eastward, he passed through Liang territory on the return trip and billeted his men at Fengchan Monastery. The Prince of Liang invited him into the city [of Kaifeng] for a banquet at Shangyuan Post, his troops charging at Taizu halfway into the evening. Several of Taizu's aides managed to elude pursuers and return to the north beforehand, informing her of Taizu's uncertain fate. Without the faintest expression of emotion, the Lady Liu immediately decapitated the aides, then secretly summoned senior commanders to secure the armed forces for return. Taizu returned a day later, the two of them standing face to face and weeping uncontrollably. He now wanted to retaliate militarily against the Liang, but she counseled, "You began by suppressing rebels on behalf of the Tang empire. Were you now to send armies suddenly to retaliate against the Liang, even as its recent intrigues remain unknown to the outside, a world learning of the affair would find villain and victim indistinguishable. Better to withdraw your men and return to your assigned district, then personally lodge a complaint with the court over the incident." Taizu accepted her advice.

Sometime later, Taizu returned in defeat after storming Liu Rengong. The Liang now unleashed Shi Shucong, Kang Huaiying, and others for an offensive against the Prince of Jin, extending over several years. Their capital at Taiyuan surrounded, Jin forces suffered successive defeats, and a despondent Taizu seemed without recourse. Leading commanders such as Li Cunxin urged Taizu to take refuge in the northern border region, reorganizing himself for future insurgency. Taizu concurred and returned to the palace to tell Lady Liu, who promptly asked about the source of the recommendation. Taizu indicated Cunxin, and she responded indignantly, "Cunxin is the simple offspring of a Daibei shepherd. What makes him fit to counsel on life-or-death strategy? In the past, you scoffed at Wang Xingyu for abandoning Binzhou, only to be captured later on. Are your intended actions any different today? When formerly stranded in Tartar lands and barely managing an escape, the convergence of many factors across the land ultimately permitted your southward return. Our troops have mostly scattered after a succession of recent setbacks. Who will still follow, if you lose this city? And is there certainty that you could reach the northern border, in any case?" Fully persuaded, Taizu changed his plans as formerly dispersed troops gradually reverted to him.

The Lady had no sons, but her wise character kept her from becoming jealous. In fact, she once said to Taizu, "You should treat the Consort Cao kindly, for her physiognomy suggests that she will mother an esteemed son." Cao tended to shirk attention out of humility, causing the two women to share an extraordinary affinity.

Miss Cao, ennobled Lady of Jin, later gave birth to a son, namely Zhuangzong. Taizu's growing appreciation of the boy enabled Lady Cao to monopolize his affections. The fury of a temperamental Taizu often caused murders, a matter that close aides dared not address: only the Lady Cao proved frequently persuasive through her soberly worded admonitions. Once Zhuangzong succeeded as Prince, he treated his mother with utmost deference. However preoccupied with the rescue of Zhao, the raid against Yan¤, the conquest of Wei/Bo, plus a decade of skirmishes with the Liang along the Yellow River—Zhuangzong still insisted on hastening home to visit her up to three or four times a year, causing everyone to acknowledge his filial devotion. He invested Cao as Empress Dowager after assuming imperial powers, honoring stepmother Liu as Consort Dowager. When the Consort Dowager went to express gratitude to the Empress Dowager, the Empress blushed with embarrassment as the Consort said, "I hope our son enjoys an infinite reign. Because of him, I have been privileged to a future burial alongside the Former Monarch when I die. What more can I say!"

After purging the Liang and occupying Bianzhou, Zhuangzong arranged for the Empress Dowager to be escorted to Luoyang, where she resided in the Changshou palace. The Consort Dowager stayed behind in Jinyang County [Taiyuan]. In the third year of Tongguang [C.E. 925], the fifth month, the Consort Dowager Liu passed away. The Empress Dowager Cao passed away in the seventh month, receiving the posthumous title Chaste and Austere, Zhenjian; burial occurred at Kunling. Posthumous title was not afforded the Consort Dowager, interred at Wei County.

The two dowagers shared a profound love for one another, such that the Consort Dowager parted in tears when sending off the Empress Dowager for Luoyang. Upon returning to her own palace, her longing for the Empress left the Consort unable to rise from bed. The Empress wanted to hasten to Jinyang to care for the Consort, upon news of her illness, and also wanted to attend her funeral when her death was confirmed. A tearful Zhuangzong implored her against it, as did a succession of officials, so she stayed behind. The Consort Dowager's subsequent death left the Empress Dowager too bereaved to eat or drink—she died only a month later.

Empress Liu

The Divinely Dutiful and Deferential, Shenminjing, Empress of Zhuangzong, surnamed Liu, was native to Cheng'an, Weizhou. The Emperor's formal wife was Miss Han, the Lady of Wei‡, followed by Miss Yi, the Lady of Yan, and then the Empress herself, originally ennobled Lady of Wei.

The father of the Empress, a yellow-bearded Liu Sou who went by the name of "Mountain Man Liu," was gifted in medicine and prophecy. The future Empress was only five or six *sui* when the Prince of Jin, on campaign against Weizhou, pillaged Cheng'an. There, assistant commander Yuan Jianfeng captured the Empress and offered her to the Prince's palace. Thereafter, the Chaste and Austere Dowager trained her to play the flute, sing, and dance. By the time her hair was pinned [at fourteen *sui*], she had become exceptionally sensuous, and Zhuangzong relished her at first sight.

With Zhuangzong now Prince of Jin, the Empress Dowager Cao visited his palace for a banquet celebrating her longevity. He personally rose to sing and dance, causing the Dowager to savor the occasion profoundly, ordering Miss Liu to play the flute and pour wine. Once drinks were over, the young woman was left behind for Zhuangzong. Before this, Zhuangzong had obtained the Woman Hou, wife of Fu Daozhao, after a siege against Liang armies employing dual ramparts. She later emerged as the most favored woman in the palace, where her peers dubbed her, "Lady of the Dual Ramparts." Zhuangzong often brought along Woman Hou amid campaigns across the four corners. Later, Woman Liu gave birth to the son regarded by Zhuangzong as most like himself, Jiji, his love for the youth affording Liu a growing monopoly on imperial favor. Hence, Woman Liu singularly accompanied Zhuangzong on campaigns, beginning with the conquest of the Wei/Bo command and continuing through a decade or more of battles along the Yellow River. She possessed multifaceted knowledge and proved astute at satisfying the wishes of the throne, so other harem women had no way to win exposure.

Once her father learned of her new stature, he visited the Wei palace to pay respects. Zhuangzong summoned Yuan Jianfeng to inquire of the matter and Jianfeng reported, "Your Subject initially obtained Woman Liu from a village north of Cheng'an, where an old man with a yellow beard attempted to protect her." Liu Sou was now brought out to show Jianfeng, who affirmed that he was indeed the man. But Miss Liu was competing for imperial favor, at the time, against women from esteemed and pedigreed families, so she blurted out in rage, "Your Concubine largely recollects the circumstances of my departure from the countryside: my father's tragic death in a military mutiny and my weeping uncontrollably over his corpse, only to be dragged away. How dare this farm-patch peon appear here to suggest otherwise?" Liu Sou was thus ordered flogged with light rod at the gates of the palace.

Upon assuming the throne as emperor, Zhuangzong wished to install Miss Liu as empress. With the Lady Han already formal wife and the Lady Yi ranking above Liu, the Emperor was dissuaded by a recent history of insurmountable obstacles. Chief minister Doulu Ge and military bureau secretary Guo Chongtao, intuiting His Majesty's wishes, now petitioned on behalf of Liu's installation, Zhuangzong thoroughly pleased. In the second year of Tongguang, fifteenth day of the second month [C.E. March 22, 924], the Emperor appeared at Wenming Hall to arrange, by messenger, Liu's investiture as empress. The Empress, accepting the vestments, rode the feathered carriage with imperial insignia to the accompaniment of pipes and drums for an appearance at the Imperial ancestors' temple. Lady Han and others were disgruntled, so Han was ennobled as the Pure Consort and Yi as the Virtuous Consort.

Zhuangzong seemed to lose his sense of purpose after overturning the Liang, causing eunuchs and actors to wreak havoc upon governance, while the Empress came to command extraordinary clout from the palace. Emerging from obscure origins and leaping above others to become empress, the achievement reflected the powers of the Buddha, she reasoned. Given to hoarding things as well, she would dispatch cronies to the marketplaces acting as merchants under orders to sell items like firewood and mushrooms to her palace [and profiting as the merchants fled]. Meanwhile, tributary assessments from the four corners were always divided in half, one portion going to the Son of Heaven and the other to the Empress's palace, such that commodities were piled high as a hill within her palace precincts. She personally could transcribe Buddhist scripture, while lavishing feasts and presents on monks and nuns. Zhuangzong himself came to be deluded by Buddhism in consequence.

When a foreign monk arrived from Yutian, Zhuangzong led his Empress and sons in greeting him with bows. He even dispatched a palace commissioner to arrange food and lodging for the monk's travels about Wutai Mountain. Cities and counties along the path were wracked by the tumult. Another monk called Chenghui professed a capacity to induce dragons to descend from the heavens. Upon passing through Zhenzhou, governor Wang Rong's impolite reception caused an offended Chenghui to pronounce, "I possess five hundred poisonous dragons. One is enough to hoist a slab of a stone and reduce the entire Changshan populace to fodder for turtles." A year later, when massive flooding of the Hutuo River destroyed the suburban walls of Zhenzhou, the people all believed a spirit at work. The Emperor and Empress led royal sons and consorts in paying respects to Chenghui, who sat erect without rising. Literati of every station now followed suit in bowing to him, save for Guo Chongtao, who singularly refused.

At the time, when the Empress Dowager and the Empress communicated with the regional governors, the Dowager's communications were dubbed "palace orders" and the Empress's dubbed "directives," their frequency causing messengers for the two palaces to pass one another on the road. Xuzhou‡ governor Wen Tao knew of the Empress's partiality to Buddhism and proposed converting his private residence into a monastery, offering prayers to her prosperity there. During successive visits to the private homes of Guo Chongtao and Yuan Xingqin, Zhuangzong was commonly accompanied by the Empress. Later, they visited Zhang Quanyi at home, where they imbibed and an intoxicated Zhuangzong instructed the Empress to treat Quanyi as adopted father. Quanyi's attractive concubines thereby gained daily access to the Empress's palace, offering endless gifts and greetings.

Zhuangzong loved another concubine of extraordinary beauty, the mother of a son no less, causing the Empress to feel threatened. Amid relaxation one day in his palace, Zhuangzong asked of Yuan Xingqin, then sitting beside him, "You recently suffered the loss of your wife. Do you plan to remarry? Perhaps I can make arrangements?" The Empress interjected, pointing to the monarch's adored concubine, "If Your Majesty pities Xingqin, why not bestow her?" Without choice, Zhuangzong could only feign consent. The Empress rushed over to Xingqin to bow in gratitude, as he reciprocated with double bows before arising for a glance at the beauty, whom porters were already carrying from the palace. For days, a despondent Zhuangzong refused food on the pretext of illness.

Extreme floods, in the autumn of the third Tongguang year [C.E. 925], had forced residents of the Yellow River and Huai River valleys onto the highways and caused tax collections in the capital to fall short, soldiers in the Six Armies often dropping dead. The court still pressed for taxes for the next summer and fall, as an aggrieved populace took to the streets in embittered rancor. Zhuangzong and the Empress happened to be away for a hunting trip. On the day of the winter solstice, the twentieth day of the twelfth month [C.E. January 7, 926], their hunt continued at Baisha. There, the Empress and her entourage of royal sons and palace women passed through Yique and lodged at Kanjian, returning on the twenty-fourth day. Her return coincided with a heavy snowfall that left many soldiers with frostbite. The ten thousand mounts in the Golden Lance Guard, attending her, had commandeered from the people whatever they needed. They even destroyed the household utensils of commoners while razing their thatched huts and setting them afire. Local authorities, in fright, took cover in nearby hills and coves.

In the third month of the next year [C.E. 926], an unidentified star crossed paths with Tianku [near the North Star] and another strayed into the area of Tianpei [near Mars], prompting astrologers to say, "Military crises now plaguing the palace can only be countered by scattering your palace accumulations to assuage Heaven." The chief minister now requested withdrawals from the private treasury to pay the troops, which Zhuangzong approved when the Empress argued contrarily, "For you and I, husband and wife, to acquire the world stems from more than mere military feats—it also relates to the Mandate of Heaven. As the mandate rests with Heaven, how can ordinary humans affect us?" As the chief minister spoke at the Yanying palace, the Empress listened keenly through her screen, then ushered in the youngest royal son, Manxi. Displaying the contents of her cosmetics chest before the Emperor, she declared cynically, "The tribute from the governors has already been fully spent, leaving only such triflings in the palace. Maybe you can sell them to pay your armies!" The chief minister nervously withdrew. Only after the mutiny of Zhao Zaili and the issuing of suppression armies to Weizhou did the palace release items as incentive to the military. This caused soldiers to curse as they carried the gifts away, "Our wives have already starved to death. What can we do with these?"

Zhuangzong departed for Bianzhou with twenty-five thousand soldiers in tow. They could not proceed beyond Wansheng Garrison and returned, the bulk of his men having deserted or scattered. At Yingzi Canyon, where the road was narrow and riddled with obstacles, Zhuangzong noticed attending officials carrying weapons and assuaged them with kind words. "It has just been reported that the Prince of Wei, conquering Shu, has obtained a half million ounces of gold and silver. It is only fitting that it all be relinquished to you," he declared. But they insisted, "It is already too late for Your Majesty to offer such largess; recipients would feel no gratitude either." Zhuangzong shed tears; then, glancing at the palace treasury commissioner, Zhang Rongge, he ordered imperial gown sashes to be given them. "Nothing remains," Rongge exclaimed. But a soldier exclaimed, sneering at Rongge, "The likes of you are responsible for our ruler's coming to this!" The soldier drew his sword and lunged at Rongge, nearby attendants saving him from death. Rongge now exclaimed, in leaping to his death in a river, "The Empress values material things and failed to provide for our soldiers. Responsibility has nonetheless fallen on me: for failing to anticipate the problem, my body will be rendered into ten thousand pieces."

Guo Congqian then rebelled, and Zhuangzong was hit by a stray arrow and gravely injured. As he recuperated on the shaded verandah of Jiangxiao Hall and needed drink, the Empress directed eunuchs to provide food and milk without attending personally to him. And once Zhuangzong expired, she and Li Cunwo's cohort set fire to Jiaqing Hall. She then arrayed an escort of a hundred mounts to leave via the Shizi gate, her horse carrying a satchel stuffed with gold objects and precious sashes to erect a temple at Taiyuan for retirement as nun. She fornicated with Cunwo en route, only to shave her head to become a nun upon arriving at Taiyuan. Once Mingzong came to the throne, he sent an agent to oversee the Empress's suicide. In the fifth year of Tianfu, by the Jin calendar [C.E. 940], she was posthumously entitled Divinely Dutiful and Reverent Empress.

Since the turmoil of the late Tang, regulations were lacking for empresses and consorts. Thus, by the time of Zhuangzong, with the profusion of women in the inner palace, names and titles proliferated to indescribable heights: Luminous Countenance, Luminous Deportment, Luminous Beauty, Distinguished Servant, Principal Servant, Attendant to the Supreme One, Moral and Talented, Rare and Unique, Precious and Fragrant, Kind and Virtuous, Illustrious and Unique, and so forth. The women of his inner palace scattered after Zhuangzong's assassination, as Zhu Shouyin entered the palace to claim more than thirty women for himself, but he dared not keep the Lady of Guo, née Xia, a woman once favored by Zhuangzong. With the accession of Mingzong, the women of Zhuangzong's harem were all returned to their homes, except for Woman Xia, who had no home to return to and was reverted to the Heyang governor, Xia Luqi, owing to a common surname. She later married the Khitan chieftain Tuyu, known as Li Zanhua. A cruel and malicious man, he relished killing others: female servants and concubines making trivial mistakes were often tortured with stabbing or burning. A worried Woman Xia requesting divorce received permission to shave her head and live out her days as a nun. The Pure consort Han and the Virtuous consort Yi, however, both assumed residence at Taiyuan and fell captive to the Khitan after Gaozu of Jin rebelled.

After the Zhuye acquired the imperial Li surname, they ruled over a kingdom called Jin and a world called Tang. They initially ascended among the northern barbarians and ultimately perished amid turmoil, so few details can be found on their lineal descent. It can be verified that Taizu [Keyong] had four younger brothers, eight sons, and five grandsons—his line disrupted after the third generation. Taizu's four younger brothers were Kerang, Kexiu, Kegong, and Kening. Neither the personal names nor posthumous designations for their parents are known.

Li Kerang

An adept horseman and archer in youth, Li Kerang rose to lieutenant in the Zhenwu military. His merit in the campaign against Wang Xianzhi led to assignment as commander of the Imperial Insignia Guard, so he stayed in the capital. The Li clan had converted its tribesmen to the Tang dynasty since Emperor Xianzong's reign, the Tang reciprocating by accommodating them in Hexi circuit. Their potentate also sent a son to the capital for assignment in the Palace Guard, for whom an official residence was provided in the Qinren ward. Taizu subsequently raised armies at Yunzhong and killed the Tang defending commander, Duan Wenchu. The Tang unleashed armies against Taizu in retaliation. It further ordered Wang Chucun to surround the Qinren ward with troops and apprehend Kerang, the brother of Taizu, then in the guard. Yet more than ten horsemen led by stewards He Xiangwen and Shi Deli came to Kerang's assistance: astride galloping horses with bows taut, they broke the blockade and fled. Chucun commanded more than a thousand troops to pursue him up to Weiqiao, but the arrows of Kerang and his men killed more than a hundred pursuers, forcing them to desist as Kerang absconded for Yanmen. A year later, Taizu reasserted fealty to the Tang and Kerang returned to the capital as guardsman. He defended Tong Pass during the rebel Huang Chao's raid on Changan, only to be defeated by the renegade. Fleeing to the southern mountains, Kerang hid in a Buddhist monastery but was murdered by its monks.

Li Kexiu

His courtesy name Chongyuan, Li Kexiu [C.E. 860–890] had assisted in the suppression of rebel Pang Xun, becoming prefect of Shuozhou as reward for merit. He was named commander of the Sincere-in-Service Guard during Taizu's governorship at Yanmen and joined Taizu in penetrating the passes to suppress Huang Chao. Serving initially as vanguard, Kexiu rose to commander of the left encampment. Luzhou was acquired by the Jin after its governor, Meng Fangli, relocated to Xingzhou; Kexiu now became governor of its Zhaoyi command through Taizu's intervention at court. He repeatedly emerged from his base east of the [Taihang] mountains to storm Fangli, joining Li Hanzhi to pillage Huai‡ and Ming prefectures as well. Taizu later commanded a sortie against Fangli and passed through Luzhou on the return trip. There he was profoundly offended by the paltry rations provided his men by Kexiu, a man parsimonious by nature. A verbal thrashing attended flogging with light rod, an utterly mortified Kexiu dying of illness. He had two sons: Sibi and Sigong.

Li Sibi was prefect of Zhuozhou, in the nineteenth year of Tianyou [C.E. 922], when the Khitan attacked and toppled the city. He died at the hands of these barbarians.

Li Sigong [d. C.E. 923] combined martial bravado with strategic cunning at an early age. Having scored numerous military victories under Zhou Dewei, he became inspector-in-chief of cavalry and infantry. When Li Cunshen defeated Liang forces at Hubi, Sigong managed to capture alive one of its generals. Taizu of Liang then blockaded Xiu County, but Sigong assisted Cunshen in the county's rescue and Liang forces were compelled to dissolve their blockade. His merit notable, Sigong became prefect extraordinaire of Weizhou¶ and chief military commissioner for regiments north of Yanmen. Successive appointments ensued as prefect for Ze and Dai prefectures. The defection of Wang Yu of Xinzhou against Jin overlords and flight to the Khitan triggered defections of prefectural leaders across the Shanhou [northern Taihang] region, enabling Sigong to acquire the three prefectures of Gui, Ru, and Wu. He became the prefect of Xinzhou and chief commissioner for military training in Shanbei circuit, dying in office in spring, the inaugural year of Tongguang.

Li Kegong

Kegong was initially commander of Dedicated Victory forces, later becoming governor of the Zhaoyi command in the wake of Kexiu's death. Kexiu had been a frugal man, so Luzhou residents satisfied with his governance would mourn his flogging and death. An overbearing and intemperate Kegong, in contrast, abided by no rules at all, nor did he know much about military matters, such that Luzhou residents uniformly resented him. Kegong once offered to Taizu five hundred crack troops from his rear guard, but they had scarcely reached the county of Tongdi when commander Feng Ba led others in defecting. Taizu entrusted the suppression effort against them to Li Yuanshen, who was routed at Qinshui [Zezhou] and injured. Seeking sanctuary at Luzhou, the military attaché there, An Jushou, also defected and killed both Kegong and Yuanshen. Jushou then summoned Feng Ba by messenger, but his refusal to come induced a nervous Jushou to flee the city. He made it as far as Zhangzi County when a man of the wilderness murdered him and conveyed his head to Feng Ba, who now occupied Luzhou, pronounced himself interim regent, and defected to the Liang.

Li Kening

Kening was benevolent and filial by character, the noblest among the brothers, serving Taizu with unrelenting circumspection. From Taizu's battles at Yunzhou‡ and Weizhou¶ against Helian Duo and Li Keju, through his flight to Tartar lands and even his involvement in the Huang Chao suppression—Kening was never absent. As governor of Taiyuan, Taizu appointed him chief commissioner of multiracial infantry and cavalry empirewide, honorary grand guardian, and governor of the Zhenwu command. Military affairs now fell under Kening's purview, the serious and the trifling alike.

A bedridden Taizu, having invited the future Zhuangzong to care for him, turned to eunuch Zhang Chengye and brother Kening, saying, "I entrust Yazi [Zhuangzong] to your care." With the death of Taizu [C.E. 908], Zhuangzong approached Kening, "This nephew of yours, tender in years, remains deficient in governing skills. The Former Prince's mandate notwithstanding, I feel unready to assume the serious work of governing. Contrarily, my uncle's merits are exalted, such that the Former Prince once entrusted oversight of the kingdom to you. May I ask you, uncle, to preside over our affairs while deferring my own installation to the future?" "My elder brother expressly entrusted his young son to me," Kening insisted. "How dare I alter things?" He stepped down, then faced north in repeated bows of congratulations as Zhuangzong succeeded as Prince of Jin.

Among the warriors of martial bravado enlisted by Taizu during his insurgency at Yun‡ and Shuo prefectures, many were adopted as sons. Taizu could ultimately realize his ambitions as hegemon precisely because such daring men aided him in battle. And to the extent that the adopted sons tended to claim the most distinction in battle, Taizu especially favored and loved them, privileging them to costumes and courtesies like sons of a formal wife. These adopted sons had talented soldiers under their banners, men who presumed upon military attainments to act with reckless abandon, accustomed to being indulged under the Former Prince. After installation of a new prince tender in years, some sons declined appearances at court, feigning illness, and others appeared only to refuse to bow. Adopted sons Cunhao and Cunshi once warned Kening, "It is an old established practice for older brothers to be succeeded by younger brothers upon death. By what rationale, however, does an uncle defer to his nephew? In life, wealth and station are won only by the taking." But Kening responded, "Through three generations, our family has produced caring fathers and filial sons. So long as someone assumes sovereignty over the Former Prince's lands, I seek nothing else."

The Woman Meng, wife of Kening, was inherently stubborn and aggressive. Li Cunhao sent his wife, as did others, to enter and speak with Meng, who repeatedly intervened to pressure Kening. A man benevolent but indecisive, Kening could be swayed by the opinions of others, even to the point of causing calamity. Inspector-in-chief Li Cunzhi once incurred Kening's wrath and was killed. Meanwhile, Kening experienced tensions with [palace intimates] Zhang Chengye and Li Cunzhang, prompting his request for a temporary appointment as Datong governor. At this point, court favorite Shi Jingrong met with the Empress Dowager and charged Kening and Cunhao with conspiring to deliver the Prince and Dowager over to Liang rivals. Summoning Chengye and Cunzhang, Zhuangzong declared, "How can my uncle commit such an act? Flesh-and-blood kin cannot treat one another like fodder! To escape the perils of my own clan, perhaps I should defer to men more deserving." Chengye and cohort pleaded to execute Kening. Concealing troops in the prefectural offices with a large banquet as cover, Kening was seized and slain upon arrival.

Sons of Taizu: Cunmei, Cunba, Cunli, Cunwo, Cunyi, Cunque, Cunji

Among Taizu's eight sons, Zhuangzong [Cunxu] was eldest, then Cunmei, Cunba, Cunli, Cunwo, Cunyi, Cunque, and Cunji. In the third year of Tongguang, the fourteenth day of the intercalary twelfth month, Zhuangzong ordered investitures as Prince for Cunmei and his other brothers, seven in all. Cunba, Cunwo, and Cunji were born to the same mother as Zhuangzong; as for maternity of Cunmei, Cunyi, Cunque, and Cunli, neither the names nor titles of the women are known. Cunmei was ennobled as Prince of Yong‡, Cunba, as Prince of Yong, Cunli as Prince of Xue, Cunwo as Prince of Shen, Cunyi as Prince of Mu, Cunque as Prince of Tong, and Cunji as Prince of Ya.

Once governor of both the Jianxiong and Baoda commands, Cunyi married the daughter of minister Guo Chongtao. Influential at court, then, was a sorcerer from Weizhou, Yang Qianlang, who claimed to command the powers of the ancient Mozi to summon ghosts and spirits, even to transform cinnabar and mercury. Zhuangzong considered him divine and appointed him honorary gentleman at the Imperial Secretariat, conferring official robes purple in color. Qianlang's wife came to share his favor, gaining easy access to the forbidden precincts of the palace. Courtiers commonly sought office and title through them; royal sons like Cunyi and Cunwo often indecently fraternized at their home. In the wake of mass executions for Chongtao and his clan, Zhuangzong dispatched eunuchs to canvas discreetly opinion away from court concerning the incident. The eunuchs were intent on precluding some unforeseen peril by thoroughly eliminating the Chongtao faction, so they maliciously alleged that, "A drunken Cunyi once ran into Qianlang's home and curled his forearm, decrying in angry frustration the injustice against his own father-in-law, his words embittered to the extreme." A livid Zhuangzong directed guards to encircle Cunyi's residence and execute him, Qianlang as well.

Cunba was named governor of the Zhaoyi, Tianping, and Hezhong commands; Cunwo was named the Yicheng and Tianping governor, both men residing in the capital and enjoying salaries [without official duties]. Cunba was deployed at Hezhong in the wake of Zhao Zaili's mutiny. Once Li Siyuan rebelled and headed for the capital, Zhuangzong departed again for Sishui [Luoyang County], reassigning Cunba to interim custodian of the northern capital; replacing him as Hezhong governor was to be Cunwo. Reassignment orders were not even drafted when a mutinous Guo Congqian assailed the Xingjiao gate. Cunwo now assisted Zhuangzong in resisting the renegades. Hit by a stray arrow, Zhuangzong expired, and Cunwo joined Empress Liu in flight for Taiyuan, military subordinates at Fenggu County murdering Cunwo. News of tumult in the capital also caused Cunba to rush from Hezhong to Taiyuan. His troops had all scattered by the time of arrival, save for a page, Kang Congbian. Now assuming the tonsure and attire of Buddhist clerics, Cunba visited Fu Yanchao, imploring, "I wish to live reclusively as monk and seek your protection." Despite wanting to spare Cunba, Yanchao's rank and file murdered him.

Cunji and Cunque absconded for the southern mountains upon news of Guo Congqian's defection, hiding in the homes of commoners. Emperor Mingzong pronounced to Henan Prefecture [Luoyang] and the circuits elsewhere, "The royal princes having scattered, local authorities at such destinations should direct them to the capital. For the unfortunate ones now dead, burials should occur with the court informed." The family harboring Cunji and entourage informed minister An Chonghui, who addressed Huo Yanwei, in turn, saying, "His Majesty's search for the two missing princes may well be misguided. It is scarcely appropriate for a monarch new to power and immersed in mourning!" Yanwei responded, "The Emperor, a man of benevolence and compassion, cannot be burdened with petitions. We should act secretly on his behalf to calm the concerns of humanity." So, Yanwei proceeded to the commoner's home to kill them.

Cunmei suffered from some mental problems and lived in Taiyuan. Nothing is known of his final end, as is true for Cunli.

The Five Sons of Zhuangzong: Jiji, Jitong, Jisong, Jichan, and Jiyao

As for the five sons of Zhuangzong, the eldest was Jiji, then Jitong, Jisong, Jichan, and Jiyao. Jiji's mother was Empress Liu, but the mothers of the other four sons and their titles are unknown.

At the time of Zhuangzong's accession, son Li Jiji [d. C.E. 926] was interim custodian of the northern capital and administrator of the Six Armies. Promotions ensued as honorary grand guardian with ministerial standing. Minister Doulu Ge appraised the court of the Tang-dynasty precedent whereby imperial sons were named "commissioners at large." Jiji was thus designated commissioner at large for the Yezhou palace, renamed Xingsheng.

He was invested Prince of Wei in the third year of Tongguang [C.E. 925]. The campaign against Shu [Sichuan] began that year, Jiji named general commander of at-large forces in the southwest and Guo Chongtao chief commissioner for bandit suppression; minister of public works Ren Huan and Hanlin academician Li Yu‡ were assigned as adjutants. On the eighteenth day of the ninth month [October 8], Jiji led an army of sixty thousand through Dasan Pass from Fengxiang. He had less than ten days of rations for troops, but every city and town en route greeted them in surrender, his troops subsisting on the grains provided. At Xingzhou‡, the defecting Shu commander, Cheng Fenglian, with five hundred cavalry, deployed them to construct parallel roadways for the passage of Tang armies.

[Shu potentate] Wang Yan personally commanded ten thousand men to Lizhou, half of them diverted in the defense of Sanquan County. He met defeat at the hands of the Tang vanguard, Kang Yanxiao, and nervously severed the suspension bridge at Jibai River to return to Chengdu. Tang armies now advancing along alternate routes from Wenzhou, Jiji arrived at Mianzhou on the twentieth day of the eleventh month [December 8],[2] as Yan petitioned to surrender. Chengdu was occupied on the twenty-seventh day, Yan riding a bamboo carriage to the Shengxian bridge. Then he assumed plain clothes and a crown of weeds, with a lamb held on a leash and a coffin in tow, his lapel containing a band and his hand holding a jade disk. Aides joining him in surrender donned mourning garments and walked barefoot. Jiji alighted from his horse to accept the jade disk, as Chongtao loosened his girdle to set the coffin afire. From the dispatch of troops to the capitulation of Wang Yan, for a total of seventy-five days, soldiers had no need to bloody their knives: never in history have armies succeeded so handily. Jiji may have been general commander, but military policy and mandates emanated singularly from Chongtao.

Initially, Zhuangzong had dispatched officer of palace services, Li Congxi, to supervise the critical center armies, ranking eunuchs Li Ting'an and Lü Zhirou serving as communications escorts. Congxi and cohort had long begrudged Chongtao, his monopoly over military affairs further unsettling them. In the aftermath of the Shu conquest, esteemed courtiers and senior officers of the region, starting with Wang Zongbi [Yan's adopted son], scrambled to offer Chongtao and his sons the region's best in precious trinkets and carnal pleasures, the Prince of Wei receiving only some horses, hanks of silk, spittoons, and deer bridles. Chongtao exercised daily control over military decisions, so commanders, aides, and retainers flooded his reception room, while at the general commander's headquarters only ranking officers appeared in the morning, the office otherwise deserted. The indignation of Congxi and cohort was thus palpable. Zongbi later led Shu compatriots to meet with Jiji and request Chongtao's retention in Shu as governor. Congxi and the others now accused Chongtao of treacherous designs and urged Jiji to take countermeasures. "His Majesty relies on you, Mr. Minister, as he does the steadfast Heng and Hua mountains, honors you as he does the dynastic altars themselves," Jiji said to Chongtao. "Anticipating the day when the world is one and the four corners harnessed, he certainly does not intend to leave in the barbarian lands of the south a man of your stature, although I otherwise dare not address such matters."

Zhuangzong was distraught to learn that Chongtao wished to remain in Shu and rushed eunuch Xiang Yansi to aid Jiji in regrouping armies. Chongtao refused to go to greet Yansi upon arriving in Chengdu and proved ever rude when finally meeting him, inciting his ire. Congxi hence alerted Yansi to Chongtao's treachery and the possible threat posed to the Prince of Wei. Yansi fully apprised the court of conditions upon his return, and Empress Liu, in tears, pleaded for special protection for Jiji. Zhuangzong dispatched eunuch Ma Yangui personally to explore Chongtao's intent to stay or to leave.

In the wake of acquiring Shu yet prior to Meng Zhixiang's arrival, the hills and forests had attracted throngs of bandits. Guo Chongtao had recently sent Ren Huan and others along separate routes to enlist them; anticipating a possible mutiny, Chongtao's reinforcements remained at large. Meanwhile, Ma Yangui met with Empress Liu on the eve of his Shu journey, cautioning, "Your Subject has read Yansi's statements suggesting an already untenable position in Shu. The gap between opportunity and catastrophe being thin as hair's breadth, conveying commands back and forth across three thousand *li* is simply unfeasible." Empress Liu alerted Zhuangzong to Yangui's concerns, but he insisted, "In the absence of scrutinizing transmissions from the field, how can we casually change a course already set?" Her pleas unheeded, the Empress personally sent instructions to Jiji to assassinate Chongtao.

In the inaugural month of the next year [C.E. 926], Chongtao retained Ren Huan to defend Shu and awaited Meng Zhixiang's arrival, anticipating the court's designation of a date to withdraw troops. Yangui now reached Shu and pulled out the Empress's instructions to show Jiji, who exclaimed, "On the eve of issuing our great army, there exists no justification for action. How can I act so contrary to my heart?" Congxi pressed, tearfully, "Your Highness now possesses a secret command. In failing to implement it, we all are minced meat if Chongtao finds out!" "In the absence of an imperial edict, we have only the handwritten instructions of the Empress," Jiji countered. "Is it sufficient to slay the commissioner of bandit suppression?" Congxi continued his strenuous advocacy, leaving Jiji no choice but to concede. In the name of the general commander, Jiji, Congxi summoned Chongtao on the next morning. Jiji evaded him by ascending a tower. Chongtao entered and climbed the office steps when Jiji's confederate Li Huan struck him on the head and fractured it.

Jiji now withdrew his armies, which in the second month, reached Nixi County when vanguard Kang Yanxiao defected to occupy Hanzhou. Jiji charged Ren Huan with the suppression. He had only reached Xingping [Yuzhou], on the fifth day of the fourth month upon news of Mingzong's rebellion, his troops having taken the capital. Jiji wanted to withdraw his men to safety at Fengxiang, but Li Congxi urged him to rush the capital, upon reaching Wugong, to resolve the palace crisis. Approaching the Wei River, a suspension bridge was severed by Zhang Jian, interim custodian of the western capital. Unable to cross, Jiji followed the course of the river eastward to Weinan, his retinue having vanished. Congxi now conceded, "The critical events are already behind us and providence no longer ours. Your fate is up to you." An irresolute Jiji turned to Li Huan in tears, saying, "Having exhausted all conceivable paths, I wish for you to take my life." Irresolute for some time, Huan addressed Jiji's wet nurse, "I cannot bear to face the Prince. In the absence of a path to survival, the Prince should turn his back to me." Jiji faced his reclining couch to lay down, as Li Huan strangled him to death. Ren

Huan arrived afterwards to bury Jiji southwest of Huazhou‡. He had no sons, for a childhood illness had sterilized him. With Mingzong's accession, Ren Huan directed the Shu expeditionary force of twenty thousand back to the capital. The Emperor extended his visit to console him, then inquired of Jiji's whereabouts, with Huan giving a full account of his death.

By imperial rescript of the third year of Tongguang [C.E. 925], imperial sons Jisong, Jitong, Jichan, and Jiyao were named grandmasters of imperial recreations and honorary dignitaries for education. Because of their youth, none were ennobled. At the time that Zhuangzong fell to regicide, there were eleven surviving sons and grandsons of Taizu, four of whom were murdered after Mingzong's accession, the fates of the others unknown. The line of Taizu thereby came to an end.[i]

....

i. In these "Biographies of the Royal Families" of the Liang and Tang, brothers are placed first and sons given secondary placement, while the sons of royal brothers appear after their fathers; this reflects an established rule. In relating the lives of the seven brothers of Zhuangzong, rather than follow simple seniority, the narratives about them appear chronologically by the date of death. There is no other fixed rule for placement.

CHAPTER 15

BIOGRAPHIES OF THE ROYAL FAMILIES: MINGZONG OF TANG

Mingzong had three empresses and one consort: the Amiable, Martial, and Complacent Empress Cao gave birth to the Princess of Jin; the Luminous and Moral Empress Xia gave birth to the Prince of Qin (Congrong) and Emperor Min; the Illustrious and Complacent Empress Wei was the mother of the Prince of Lu (Congke); the Pure Consort Wang was the adopted mother of the Prince of Xu (Congyi).

No information exists on the ancestry of the Ladies Cao and Xia; Xia held no noble titles, having died before the accession of Mingzong. In the inaugural year of Tiancheng [C.E. 926], as Emperor Mingzong ennobled Cao as Lady of Chu with the title Pure Consort, he posthumously ennobled Xia as Lady of Jin. During the inaugural year of Changxing [C.E. 930], the Pure Consort was installed as empress. By then, two sons born to Woman Xia were now princes, so she was posthumously invested as empress and entitled Luminous and Moral.

Empress Wei

Woman Wei was a native of Pingshan, Zhenzhou. Originally married to a local man surnamed Wang, they had a son ten *sui* in age when Mingzong, as cavalry commander, plundered Pingshan and apprehended mother and son, returning them to the north. Dying some years later, she was buried at Taiyuan—her son none other than Congke, the Prince of Lu. By the reign of Mingzong, with Congke already prince, Woman Wei was posthumously elevated to the Lady of Lu, then further honored as Empress Dowager after Congke's accession as Emperor Fei. The erection of a mausoleum for her was proposed, although a temporary resting place had to be built east of the capital, at Henan Prefecture, because of the rebellion of Shi Jingtang at Taiyuan. In the third year of Qingtai, ninth day of the sixth month [C.E. June 30, 936], the court deputized minister of public works Cui Jian[1] to render vestments for the Empress Grand Dowager, her posthumous title changed to Illustrious and Complacent, Xuanxian.

The Pure Consort Wang and Empress Cao

The Pure Consort Wang [d. C.E. 947], from a family of pastry makers at Binzhou, possessed such beauty that others called her "the woman to shame flowers" [with her superior beauty]. While young, she was sold as servant to a one-time Liang commander, Liu Xun, only to be left homeless after his death. Mingzong's wife, née Xia, had died by then, and Mingzong was looking for another wife when someone mentioned the Woman Wang to An Chonghui, who spoke to Mingzong about her. He accepted. Having formerly acquired a sizable sum of gold from Liu Xun, Woman Wang donated it all to the Emperor's attendants and the mothers of his sons, winning praise from all. Mingzong came increasingly to love her. Meanwhile, the modest ways of Woman Cao, who preferred to avoid palace affairs, afforded Wang an opening to monopolize favor.

In the wake of Mingzong's accession, deliberations over the installation of an empress affirmed the superior claim of Miss Cao, but she turned to Wang, saying, "For long, I have suffered from numerous illnesses and I have a low tolerance for distractions. You, younger sister, should replace me." "An Empress is companion to the Emperor," Wang countered. "Who dares presume upon such an exalted position?" Woman Cao became empress, after all, and Wang was named the Pure Consort. The Consort ultimately served the Empress with scrupulous deference: when the Emperor arose at dawn, the Consort always personally organized attendants to prepare the royal toilet and wardrobe; and when he left court to dine with the Empress, the Consort sat in attendance without departing until the meal was over. Never lax in her duties, she commanded the growing affection of the Empress, as palace affairs fell under the Consort's sway.

Once illness afflicted Mingzong, the Consort and eunuch Meng Hanqiong mediated among aides to further their dominance of court affairs. They were implicated in the assassinations of both An Chonghui and the Prince of Qin, Congrong. Through Consort Wang, the various sons of Liu Xun all earned noble titles and official rank. Upon the accession of Emperor

Min, the Empress received investiture as Dowager and the Consort as Consort Dowager. Mingzong had heretofore instructed the Consort to raise a son of the inner palace as her own: this was *Li Congyi*, the future Prince of Xu [C.E. 931–947]. The wet nurse to Congyi, wardrobe stewardess Wang, observing the advanced age of Mingzong and the Prince of Qin's grip on the military, felt a need to plan strategically for her own future. "My son misses the Prince of Qin," she would say. Congyi was then four *sui* and was repeatedly prompted by wet nurse Wang to beg to visit the Prince of Qin. Mingzong arranged for the wet nurse to carry her son to the Prince of Qin's apartment, where she and Congrong had sexual relations. He hence exploited her to spy on palace activities. Congrong had already died, but wet nurse Wang believed that his armies had actually penetrated the palace to guard the Son of Heaven. After learning that he had already been executed for treason, she expressed words of umbrage. A furious Emperor Min, hearing the news, ordered Wang to commit suicide [C.E. 933]. Implicated in the affair was the Consort Dowager, a matter so troubling to the Emperor that he contemplated relocating her to the Zhide palace [Luoyang]. He decided otherwise for fear of hurting the Empress Dowager, whose close ties to the Consort were longstanding. Still, the Emperor treated the Consort most uncharitably.

With the accession of Emperor Fei, the Emperor once held a banquet at the Consort's courtyard, where she said with raised goblet, "I would like to take leave of Your Majesty to become a Buddhist nun." As a stunned Emperor inquired about the reasons, she added, "Younger Son [Congyi] retains this life only by a stroke of good fortune. Had you, Elder Son, not permitted his survival, how could I possibly stand face to face before the Former Monarch, upon my own death?" She now sobbed as an empathetic Emperor treated her with special kindness. Once Shi Jingtang invaded the capital and Emperor Fei gathered clansmen to set themselves afire, the Consort Dowager said to the Empress Dowager, "Under such serious deterioration of conditions, we should abscond and await assistance from brothers-in-law." The Empress insisted, however, "How could I countenance personal survival when family fortunes have come to this? My Sister may wish to flee alone." The Empress Dowager now perished with the Emperor in ritual fire, as the Consort Dowager hid in a polo arena, along with a younger sister and son Congyi, the Prince of Xu, thereby escaping.

Under the Jin dynasty reign of Gaozu, the Consort Dowager petitioned to become a nun, and once denied, relocated to the Zhide palace. The Consort Dowager and her son followed the Jin court when its capital shifted eastward to Bianzhou. Assuming residence in its palaces, she was treated by the Empress of Gaozu like a mother. In the fourth year of Tianfu, fifteenth day of the ninth month [C.E. October 30, 939], the Prince of Xu under Later Tang rule, Congyi, received investiture as Duke of Xun, with a feudatory of three thousand households called Xunguo. Investiture rituals were conducted in meticulous conformity to Tang protocol, as pertains to the color of costumes and the selection of banners. The ceremonies office proposed conversion of the Zhide palace to a temple to honor the three lines of Zhuangzong, Mingzong, and Emperor Min. The palace approved the building of a total of five temples, including those for [Former Tang] Emperors Gaozu and Taizong, authorizing Congyi to conduct annual rituals there.

The Consort Dowager and her son both returned to Luoyang once Emperor Chu came to power. After the Khitan invaded the capital, their ruler Yelü Deguang arranged the marriage of Zhao Yanshou to Congyi's younger sister, the Yong'an Princess; the widower Yanshou had formerly been married to a daughter of Mingzong. The Princess did not know her mother's identity, but she had been raised by the Consort Dowager, and it was the Consort who came to host the wedding ceremony in the capital. Deguang fixed his eyes on a portrait of Mingzong while burning incense and repeatedly bowing, then said to the Consort, "Mingzong and I were sworn brothers, so you are my sister-in-law." He continued with the insulting proposition, "And today, you can be my wife as well!" He offered Congyi the Zhangxin governorship, which he declined, returning with the Consort to Luoyang, disinterested in office.

Yelü Deguang departed for the north and left behind Xiao Han as prefect of Bianzhou. Once the Han-dynasty founder Gaozu raised armies at Taiyuan, Xiao Han summoned Congyi by messenger to the capital with promises of entrusting the Middle Kingdom to him, Han personally intending to depart for the north. To elude the messenger, Congyi and his mother attempted flight toward the Hui mausoleum, but were coerced eastward and Congyi installed as provisional military counselor for the southern dynasty. As he ascended the Chongyuan palace, Xiao Han escorted leading Khitan commanders in paying homage at the palace's upper dais, the multitude of Jin courtiers paying homage at its lower dais. Rank-and-file courtiers also entered the palace to confer with the Consort Dowager, who admitted, "This family of mother and son, isolated and defenseless, was coerced by Xiao Han. How can this possibly be providential? A catastrophic end is imminent!" The court nonetheless named Wang Song and Zhao Shangjiao counselors of the left and right, Li Shi and Zhai Guangye commissioners of military affairs, and the Yan¤ commander, Liu Zuo, chief director of the Imperial Guard and Imperial Bodyguard. Xiao Han also left behind a thousand Khitan soldiers before heading northward.

As Emperor Gaozu of Han commanded armies southward [C.E. 947], Congyi ordered Gao Xingzhou and Wu Xingde by special messenger to render resistance, but they refused to respond. Alternatively, Congyi collaborated with Wang Song to employ armies from Yanzhou¤ in securing the city. The Consort Dowager protested, "Our family represents the remnants of a vanquished dynasty. How dare we enter contest with others over the world?" A messenger was sent with a letter of invitation to Gaozu. By now, Gaozu had learned of their abortive attempt to summon Xingzhou and instructed Guo Congyi to enter the capital beforehand, murdering the Consort and her son. She queried in the face of death, "What crime has this mother and son committed? In the least, why not spare my son, permitting offerings of rice and wine at the tomb of Mingzong during winter solstice?" Those hearing her words were stirred with sadness. Congyi was seventeen *sui* at the time of death.

Empress Kong

The Aggrieved Empress of Emperor Min, surnamed Kong, was fathered by the Henghai governor, Kong Xun. The Empress exuded a noble deportment and produced four sons. She was to become empress upon Emperor Min's enthronement, but the dynasty never acted on the investiture when events distracted it. As Emperor Min fled the capital, the illness of his Empress and youth of sons prevented them from accompanying him. She was slain, along with all four sons, when Emperor Fei came to power [C.E. 933]. The posthumous title "Aggrieved," Ai, was conferred by Gaozu of Jin.

Congjing, Son of Mingzong

Mingzong had four sons: Congjing, Congrong, Conghou, and Congyi.

Originally named Congshen, Li Congjing [d. C.E. 926] evinced daring valor and a gift for combat, as well as humility and courtesy. He distinguished himself over and again in battle under Zhuangzong's banner, becoming director of the Golden Lance Guard. In the wake of Mingzong's mutiny at Weizhou, Zhuangzong instructed Congjing, "Your father's meritorious service to the country is distinguished, his loyal and filial devotion permitting my total trust in him. As he today faces coercion from mutinous armies, it is critical for you to go and convey my intentions in unequivocal terms." Departing in haste, Congjing reached Weizhou‡ when Yuan Xingqin apprehended him. On the verge of being killed, Congjing blurted out, "My father has been pressured by mutinous armies and You Gentlemen do not appreciate his true heart. If you will not permit my advance to Weizhou, I would be happy to return to the Son of Heaven." Xingqin decided to release him. Congjing's words stirred Zhuangzong's compassion, so he conferred the name Jijing and treated him as his own son.

Many to follow Zhuangzong to Bianzhou, commanders and combatants alike, vanished along the way, Congjing alone refusing to leave. He also refused to listen to aides encouraging his flight from imminent peril. Once Mingzong crossed the Yellow River at Liyang, Zhuangzong again wished to send Congjing to mediate, which Xingqin deemed a mistake, killing Congjing. He was posthumously entitled Grand Guardian upon Mingzong's accession.

We lament. There is no life without a father, no supports through life without a ruler. Yet for generations people say, "Loyal duty and filial piety are not equally perfectible." How can this possibly be true? Ruler and father provide the grand foundation for human ethics, loyalty and filial devotion constitute cardinal principles for official subjects. How inconceivable that the two, rather than complements to be practiced together, might actually prove mutually harmful! The problem lies, quite simply, with whether motivation is selfish or selflessly righteous: when acting selfishly, both virtues are diminished; when acting righteously, both virtues can be attained.

Should a son, if his father deploys armies against his ruler, follow his father or follow his ruler? I say, "It is enough that one's physical being honor its dwelling place, while one's ethical will abide by righteous principle." A person who physically dwells with the monarch should abide by the monarch; one who physically dwells with the father should abide by the father. The follower of a ruler must then decline his ruler's charge, indicating, "A son cannot injure his father, so I wish not to receive a command." He should protest to his father as well, "Can you not relinquish your army and revert to my ruler?" Then, if his ruler suffers defeat, the subject dies honorably for him; if his father falters, the son completes mourning duties for the father before resuming service to his monarch. The person who follows his father, on the other hand, must warn him, "As my ruler cannot be targeted for assault, can you not leave your army and revert to my ruler?" Then, if the ruler suffers defeat, he dies honorably for him; if his father fails, he submits to punishment and awaits the pardon of his ruler, resuming service after completing mourning for the father.

No person in ancient times understood filial devotion like Shun, none understood righteous principle like Confucius and Mencius—men meticulous about ruler/subject, father/son relations. Had they tragically confronted such dilemmas, they would have acted only in this manner. With reference to Congjing and Zhuangzong, the former accepted death as the cost of abiding by his ruler—an event to lament!

Congrong, Prince of Qin

In the inaugural year of Tiancheng [C.E. 926], the Prince of Qin, Li Congrong [d. C.E. 933], was named honorary dignitary for education, censor-in-chief, and governor of Tianxiong with ministerial standing. Reassigned as Hedong governor in the third year, he became metropolitan custodian of Henan Prefecture and concurrent administrator of the Six Armies during the inaugural year of Changxing [C.E. 930].

In the wake of Congjing's death, Congrong emerged as eldest of the royal sons to exert control over military power. As for character, he exuded carefree elegance in demeanor and the perspicacity of an eagle in appraising others. Possessing an affinity for Confucian teachings, he learned to compose songs and poems to the point of inviting literary scholars to gatherings for poetry writing and wine. In this way, frivolous youth flocked around him, feeding his arrogant impulses through flattering words. Everyone from commanders and ministers to senior courtiers saw potential peril in him. His defects were clearly visible to Mingzong, who nonetheless could not restrain him.

Congrong once attended to Mingzong, who asked of him, "What other activities do you enjoy, apart from military governance?" "During leisure, I like nothing more than reading books and exploring interpretations of the classics with Confucian scholars," Congrong said. Mingzong cautioned, in response, "Command of ruler and subject, father and son relations requires support from Confucians of erudition and scholars of rectitude, making proximity to them permissible. I recall the Former Emperor's propensity for composing songs and poems, however, something wholly uncommendable! Hailing from a family of military leaders, you have limited facility in the written word while literary finesse is simply unachievable. Should stories circulate among the people [of your writing deficiencies], they would surely cause ridicule. As an old man, the symbolic meaning of the classics eludes me, although I enjoy occasionally inquiring about them. Study beyond that is simply not worthwhile." In the autumn of the same year, Congrong was invested Prince of Qin.

By tradition, royal princes receiving formal investiture did not make ritual appearances at the Imperial Ancestors' Temple. The relevant officials, intuiting the Monarch's wishes to enhance the ritual's importance, now proposed, "The ancients formerly apportioned noble titles and emoluments during the *di* and *chang* sacrifices, demonstrating that they dared not apportion unilaterally [in disregard of the gods]. Today, no gathering occurs at the ancestral temples to announce major investitures, which is not the way to foster submission." Congrong thus presented himself at court riding a palace carriage replete with shield of the royal house. After receiving investiture at the audience hall of the palace, he departed by carriage with noble credentials to pay respects at the Imperial Ancestors' Temple. Residents of the capital all deemed the event glorious.

In the third year [C.E. 932], Congrong was elevated to palace secretary. The relevant officials again interjected, "By precedent, royal princes stand behind chief ministers during audience formation. Today, the Prince of Qin still appears to their rear despite his superior stature, an inadvisable practice." Hereafter, he and the ministers made separate formations, with Congrong at their right. Rising to imperial secretary in the fourth year, his fiefs of maintenance were increased to ten thousand households.

The deputy equerry for the imperial stud, He Ze, petitioned the throne to install Congrong as imperial heir. Already sickly, Mingzong was nonetheless displeased by the memorial and turned to those around him to pronounce, "The official multitudes seek to install an heir-apparent, so that I may live out my last years at Hedong [Taiyuan]." He now summoned leading courtiers to debate the designation of an heir, but they dared neither agree nor disagree. Congrong personally came to tell the Emperor, "Some sinister men, I hear, wish to install Your Subject as heir-apparent. This is not my wish, in fact." "But it is the wish of the official multitudes," Mingzong added. Congrong encountered Fan Yanguang and Zhao Yanshou in departing and blurted out to them, "In proposing my installation as heir, You Gentlemen obviously want my military commands stripped away and my movements confined to the eastern palace!" Yanguang and cohort, troubled by the comments, arranged for Congrong's elevation to supreme marshal for armed forces across the world. The pertinent officials again interjected: "Supreme marshals sometimes oversee armies across the circuits and sometimes dominate only a single theater. Because the title of 'supreme marshal for armed forces across the world' did not exist in the previous reign, we have no basis to examine the relevant protocol. We request that all persons commanding armies, beginning with governors and extending downward, appear in the uniforms and decorations appropriate to military protocol during appearances for consultations at the Prince's court—similar to initial treatment for those with concurrent ministerial standing, who are later afforded the protocol for temporary appointees. The documents and tallies of the supreme marshal's office, in order to have efficacy across the world, should employ the standard sealed forms. Meanwhile, the marshal should stand before chief ministers during court audiences."

Congrong held a grand feast in the supreme marshal's residence, where commanders all received special supplements: each director of the Crane-Commanding, Sage-Honoring, and Awesome Duty guards received a horse and ten bolts of raw silk; each commander in these guards received ten bolts of raw silk; the leaders of brigades and below received three to seven bolts. Congrong also petitioned for a thousand troops from the Awesome Duty and Sage-Sustaining guards to form a governor's bodyguard. Every time he entered court, the spectacle of several hundred cavalry to his front and rear, galloping swiftly with bows taut and arrows cocked, left roadside observers awestruck. Congrong also pressed subordinate officials and vagabond scholars at large to try to compose a "Call to Campaign against the Huai," celebrating his ambition to unify the world.

Policy critics once requested that distinguished tutors be selected for the royal princes to enhance their moral instruction. The chief ministers had difficulty acting on the proposal and invited Congrong to make the selection. He proposed nominating erudites such as Hanlin academician Cui Zhuo and Ren Zan, the vice minister of punishments, as administrative assistants to the supreme marshal. Mingzong demurred, insisting, "For an academician to speak on my behalf is unacceptable." Congrong left the palace in a rage, declaring, "It is beyond my comprehension that, as grand marshal, I still cannot choose my own subordinates." Commanders, ministers and senior courtiers, bearing witness to Congrong's expanding power and position, as well his improprieties, all recognized the peril presented by him, but none dared to speak out. Fan Yanguang and Zhao Yanshou were unique in quietly acknowledging the need to avoid the threat. In repeated meetings with Mingzong, they tearfully made plaintive pleas for release as military affairs commissioners. With the departure of these two men, Congrong's difficulties began.

On the sixteenth day of the eleventh month [C.E. December 5, 933], after a snowfall, Mingzong visited the Shihe pavilion, west of the imperial palaces, returning [to Kaifeng] with pneumonia. Congrong appeared at Guangshou Hall, flanked by military affairs commissioners Zhu Hongzhao and Feng Yun, on the seventeenth day to inquire after the Emperor's condition, only to learn that he could no longer recognize others. Pure Consort Wang [at his side] said to Mingzong, "Congrong is here" or "Hongzhao is there," without eliciting a response. The Emperor was removed to Yonghe Hall after the departure of Congrong and the others, palace residents weeping uncontrollably. Halfway into the night, as those attending him had all parted, the Emperor abruptly awakened on his reclining couch and turning to a female timekeeper for the palace, asked, "How late into night is it?" "It is the fourth watch," she said. He then coughed up many bits of flesh, apparently pieces of lung, and released enough urine and sputum to fill more than a pot. The timekeeper inquired, "Your Majesty, are you clear-headed?" "I do not know," was his response. Residents of the six palaces all arrived shortly afterward. "The Monarch has given up his ghost," they marveled, offering a bowl of rice gruel to the Emperor. His illness improved by the next morning, but Congrong did not come to pay his respects, professing illness.

Before this, Congrong had long been jealous of Conghou, Prince of Song, whom he considered a more worthy man capable of jeopardizing his own succession. Although usually someone confident and conceited, Congrong suddenly turned melancholy and insecure whenever others mentioned the Prince of Song's merits. He had earlier visited the palace to inquire of the Emperor's condition and witnessed his inability to recognize others. Once the wailing of attendants could be heard upon departure, Congrong believed the Emperor dead and conspired to infiltrate the palace with troops. His military attaché Ma Chujun was sent to inform Zhu Hongzhao that troops from Congrong's personal guard were to be accommodated at the Imperial Guard encampments. Chujun asked Hongzhao where to place them and he indicated, "Any place within the palace precincts is permissible. The Prince can personally decide." Hongzhao added privately, "Our Sage Monarch continues to be blessed [with life]. As for the Prince, he should exert his instincts as loyal subject and filial son, refraining from acting precipitately." Chujun made a full reporting to Congrong, who sent him back to Hongzhao and cohort, threatening, "Do your men have no regard for their own families?" At this point, Hongzhao entered the palace flanked by Feng Yun and Meng Hanqiong, the commissioner of palace armies, to apprise the Pure Consort Wang of circumstances and counsel, "This matter requires assistance from the Imperial Guard." They now ordered Kang Yicheng, director of the guard, to gather allies beneath the bamboo forest to lay plans. Yicheng dared not commit himself to leading the cabal, for his son was stationed at the Prince of Qin's residence. Deferring to Hongzhao, he insisted, "I am a mere lieutenant. For this matter, you must act." The response terrified Hongzhao.

On the next day, Congrong informed Feng Yun through Ma Chujun, "On this day, I intend to occupy the Xingsheng palace." Kang Yicheng was informed as well and gave his consent. As Yun rushed into the imperial compound, he noticed Yicheng, Hongzhao, Hanqiong, and cohort sitting in a side room of Zhongxing Hall in deliberation. Yun proceeded to upbraid Yicheng, "It was for precisely such times that Our Monarch has fed and clothed the likes of you! At a moment when the chasm separating security and peril is a hair's breadth thin, worries over your son have allowed the Prince of Qin to reach our very gates. What recourse will be afforded Our Monarch, and what will remain of our descendants?" Hanqiong now interjected, "I cannot take this humble life of mine too seriously: I will personally lead forces in resistance." He promptly entered the palace to report, "Congrong has rebelled and his armies are attacking Duan gate." The news left palace residents wailing as they stared at one another. Mingzong asked, "Is this true?" Hongzhao answered in the affirmative. Pointing his finger to the heavens, Mingzong cried at length. "Yicheng, you should handle the matter yourself. No need to alarm the capital," he indicated. Mingzong now said to Chongji, the Prince of Lu's son, then at his side, "Your father [Congke] and I emerged from an obscure and impoverished past. I can today claim the world because he provided repeated relief in assorted tight spots. The temerity of Congrong to commit a deed so sinister! You and your men must rush to guard all gates." Chongji deployed the Crane-Commanding Guard to secure the palace gates.

On the same day, Congrong departed from Henan Prefecture [Luoyang] with a thousand troops in tow. He once had a sizable staff of subordinates but often detested the more forthright among them: Liu Zan and Wang Jumin were especially held in contempt, as Congrong cultivated intimacy with Liu Zhi and Gao Nian. Departing in the company of Zhi and Nian, Congrong whispered along the way and pointed to a shadow at the southern approach to Tianjin bridge, remarking to Nian, "This time tomorrow, Wang Jumin will be executed!" He now encamped armies north of the bridge and sat down personally on a northern chair, sending a messenger to summon Kang Yicheng. With the southern formal gate already sealed shut, the messenger proceeded to knock at the Zuoye gate, also shut. A crevice between the doors, however, revealed a contingent of northern horsemen brought by Zhu Hongshi, director of the Sage-Sustaining Guard. The messenger hastened to inform Congrong, who, in shock, adjusted bow and arrow with weaponry tools. Some three hundred mounts rushed Congrong, led by the commissioner of security of the royal city, An Congyi, who pulled back after being hit by an arrow from Congrong's side. Five hundred horsemen commanded by Hongshi now departed from the Zuoyi gate, who were about to cross the river when rear-guard reinforcements arrived in vast numbers. Congrong could only flee back toward Henan Prefecture. Everyone from administrative assistant Ren Zan on down had absconded via the Dingding gate [of Kaifeng] by now, the governor's guard plundering Jiashan ward before being vanquished. Congrong and his wife, hiding under a bed, were killed by Congyi.

News of Congrong's death caused a grief-stricken Mingzong nearly to collapse on his couch, only to fall unconscious before regaining composure. Visited by Feng Dao and a full complement of courtiers, the Emperor remarked, "I am embarrassed to meet you, My Subjects, under such tragic family conditions." Ruler and subjects, eyes fixed on one another, sobbed as tears drenched their lapels. Congrong's two sons, still young, perished with him and Mingzong expired six days later.

Nephews of Mingzong

Li Congcan. The brothers of Mingzong did not produce hereditary houses. He did have four nephews: Congcan, Congzhang, Congwen, and Congmin.

Li Congcan [d. C.E. 929] originally served as commandant of the Right Guard. Once affairs of court were dominated by An Chonghui, everyone from royal princes to martial ministers submitted to him. Yet a relentlessly aggressive Congcan could not accommodate in the least, and his freewheeling spirit and propensity for ostentation left Chonghui resentful. Congcan was named commissioner of security of the royal city and the imperial precincts during Mingzong's stay at Bianzhou. In a drinking event at the Huijie gardens, an inebriated Congcan pretended to climb atop the imperial couch, an incident reported to the court by Chonghui. He was initially demoted to revenues adjutant for Fangzhou‡, and the court later mandated his suicide. Congcan's official rank was restored after the Chonghui execution and the posthumous title of grand guardian conferred.

Li Congzhang. His courtesy name Ziliang, Congzhang [C.E. 887–937] had been adept as horseman and archer since youth. In the era of Zhuangzong, his armies were garrisoned at Changshan when news arrived of the Mingzong mutiny at Weizhou, so he similarly rebelled to occupy Xingzhou. He became chief director of the Sage-Sustaining Guard's left wing, upon Mingzong's enthronement, then reassigned commissioner of security for the royal city and concurrent prefect of Raozhou. The Zhangguo and later Yicheng governorships were assigned as well. When Mingzong departed for Bianzhou, Congzhang wanted to coerce private citizens to offer gifts, an act deemed improper by an aide. His remonstrance incited Congzhang to draw his bow in an effort to shoot the aide, an incident punished with demotion to generalissimo of the Valorous Right Guard. He held that post for a considerable time before reassignment locally as the Baoyi and later Hezhong governor. Invested Prince of Yang in the fourth year of Changxing [C.E. 933], he was reassigned to the Weisheng governorship and relegated to Duke of Longxi, upon Gaozu's accession to the Jin throne. A man of greed and vulgarity, Congzhang began mending his ways while posted at the Baoyi command, such that an endearing legacy was actually left at Nanyang. He died in the second year of Tianfu [C.E. 937], at fifty-one *sui*.

Li Congwen had the courtesy name Deji. Originally interim deputy custodian of the northern capital, he proceeded to serve as governor of five commands: Anguo, Zhongwu, Yiwu, Chengde, and Wuning. He was invested Prince of Yan. After Gaozu assumed the Jin throne, reassignment as the Zhongwu governor occurred. An insatiably vile man, Congwen had reproduced numerous accessories and costumes of the Son of Heaven for his own illicit use. Many an imperial clansman and staff retainer expressed objections, all to no avail. His desperate wife, Woman Guan, now screamed aloud at the magistrate's office, "Wishing to rebel, Congwen has reproduced the paraphernalia of the Son of Heaven." A terrified Congwen destroyed them all.

Of the eight sons of Emperor Mingzong, six had died by the Jin reign of Emperor Chu. Congwen and Congmin alone survived, causing the Empress

Dowager often to insist, "I have only one elder brother. Why should laws encumber him?" Congwen thereby grew ever arrogant. He once maligned a trusted senior aide, Xue Rensi, charging theft to permit his own confiscation of the Xue family's properties, worth several tens of millions in cash. Rensi and kinsmen went to the capital to protest and the case was referred to the relevant officials, Congwen confessing to his crime. Emperor Chu opted to pardon him with no further punishment, for fear of offending the Empress Dowager. In the second year of Kaiyun [C.E. 945], Congwen was reassigned to the three cities of Heyang and died in office.

The son of Congzhang, Li Chongjun, was prefect of Guozhou when charged with graft. Administrative assistant Gao Xian received punishment instead, out of consideration for the Dowager. Chongjun was later resuscitated as prefect of Shangzhou. Later charges of fornicating with a younger sister and killing servant Sun Hanrong to steal his wife caused the court to order his suicide.

Li Congmin. His courtesy name Shuda, Congmin [d. C.E. 951] was extremely genuine in character and sparing in words, as well as skilled as an archer and horseman. Chief director of cavalry and infantry and concurrent manager-adjutant to the governor, initially under Zhuangzong, he rose to commissioner of security of the royal city and governor of the Baoyi command under Mingzong. He further participated in the suppression of Wang Du, holding in succession the governorships for Henghai, Yiwu, Chengde, Guide, Baoyi, Zhaoyi, and Heyang, while ennobled Prince of Jing. He became interim custodian of the western capital after Gaozu acceded to the Han throne, ennobled Duke of Qin. Dying under the Zhou, the inaugural year of Guangshun [C.E. 951], the posthumous post of palace secretary and the title Revered and Charitable, Gonghui, were conferred upon him.

CHAPTER 16

BIOGRAPHIES OF THE ROYAL FAMILIES: EMPEROR FEI OF TANG

Empress Liu

The Empress of Emperor Fei, surnamed Liu, was fathered by Liu Maowei, a native of Hunyuan, Yingzhou‡. The Empress had such an overbearing personality that she used to intimidate Emperor Fei. Ennobled as Lady of Pei, she was installed as empress upon Emperor Fei's accession.

The younger brother of the Empress, *Liu Yanhao,* had served in youth as military attaché to Emperor Fei, then governor. After the accession, he won appointments as master of imperial palaces and parks and commissioner for the southern court of palace armies. In the second year of Qingtai [C.E. 935], he became commissioner of military affairs and governor of the Tianxiong command. Yanhao began as serious and sincere, only to change as he rose in stature. Gaining access to power through the Empress, he began soliciting bribes and appropriating the gardens and manors of others. Failure to share spoils during tenure at the Ye capital left soldiers disaffected, as garrison troops led by Zhang Lingzhao, inspector-in-chief of the Sage-Sustaining Guard, expelled him. He fled to Xiangzhou‡. Shi Jingtang had rebelled at the time and deployed armies of conquest. Lingzhao also mutinied and sealed up the city, requesting a governorship through messenger Bian Rensi. The Emperor conceded to appointments as commander of the Thousand-Bull Right Guard and provisional prefect of the Tianxiong command. Later, the suppression effort against Lingzhao, led by Fan Yanguang, prompted flight to Xingzhou. Pursuers tracked Yanhao to Shahe County and beheaded him there. More than three thousand garrison troops perished during the mutinies. The relevant officials sought punishment for Yanhao by the strict rules of martial law, but Emperor Fei decided merely to strip him of office and title, in deference to the Empress.

Emperor Fei had two sons, Chongji and Chongmei. His sole daughter became a Buddhist nun nicknamed Youcheng. Nothing is known of the children's maternity.

Li Chongji [d. C.E. 934], director of the Crane-Commanding Guard when Emperor Fei was governor of Fengxiang, had been detained in the capital along with the nun [his sister]. The Crane-Commanding Guard is bodyguard to the emperor, and a newly ascended Emperor Min, reluctant to entrust his personal security to Chongji, assigned him away from the capital as commissioner of military training at Bozhou¶. Emperor Min detained Youcheng in the imperial city while forcibly relocating the future Emperor Fei to the northern capital. Fei's insecurities caused him to rebel, and Emperor Min retaliated by having Chongji murdered at Songzhou. Youcheng also perished.

Li Chongmei [d. C.E. 937], as a child, had the acuity of an adult. At the time of Emperor Fei's accession, he was generalissimo of the Left Guard, concurrent governor of the Chengde command, metropolitan custodian of Henan Prefecture, and administrator of the Six Armies. After the accession he was reassigned as concurrent Tianxiong governor with ministerial standing, invested Prince of Yong.

Emperor Fei favored personally leading a northern campaign after Shi Jingtang's rebellion, but Chongmei argued adamantly for restraint and composure. The Emperor had long found Jingtang intimidating, leaving him predisposed against proceeding. The words of Chongmei thus proved compelling. Yet relentless pressure from Liu Yanhao and Liu Yanlang forced Emperor Fei to proceed to Heyang, leaving Chongmei in the capital as interim custodian. The capital's residents in horror attempted a mass exodus from the city, only to be blocked by gatekeepers. Yet Chongmei insisted, "As the empire's hazards abound, rather than extend protection, we try to forbid the people's flight from calamity. How is this acceptable?" The people were now free to leave. As the Jin armies [of Jingtang] approached, Empress Liu piled firewood on the floor to set the palaces afire. Chongmei intervened, saying, "A new Son of Heaven having arrived, he will hardly sit in the open air. Days later, he will simply ply the people once more to rebuild—their wrath ultimately borne by us, even in death!" The Empress concurred, she and Chongmei perishing with the Emperor as he set himself afire.

WE LAMENT. The moral way for families cannot but exemplify rectitude. The notion of ritual propriety, after all, entails distinguishing the abhorrent and highlighting the subtle. Deplorable was the perversion of ethics among rulers, subjects, fathers, and sons of the Five Dynasties as order was lost at the ancestral temples, at the imperial courts, and among the living and the dead. It truly deserves the characterization "tumultuous age," without precedent since ancient times!

The Later Tang represents one dynasty ruled by three surnames, the Zhou a dynasty ruled by two surnames. Emperors Taizu and Zhuangzong of the Tang belonged to one family, Mingzong and Min belonged to another, and Fei to yet another. Emperor Taizu of Zhou represented one family and Shizong another. Why retain a single dynastic name for different family lines? Retention of the Tang dynastic name by later rulers exposes the illicitness of their successions, while retention of the Zhou name shows the volition involved in Shizong's ascent.

Distinguishing family lines serves to preclude posterity's confusion about kinsmen. Dynastic designations can be the same, but family relations require discriminations—precisely the meaning of distinguishing the abhorrent and highlighting the subtle. Zhu Youwen of Liang (Prince of Bo) reflects the lack of discriminations, and at what price? It was the basis for calamity: the peril to Taizu of Liang began with [adopted son] Youwen. His inclusion here should be a lesson for us all.

CHAPTER 17

BIOGRAPHIES OF THE ROYAL FAMILIES: JIN

Empress of Gaozu, née Li

Woman Li [d. C.E. 950], the Empress of Gaozu [Shi Jingtang], was a daughter of Emperor Mingzong of the Tang. Initially honored as the Princess of Yongning, her title changed to Senior Princess of Wei in the second year of Qingtai [C.E. 935].[1] Early in his reign, Emperor Fei felt certain of the future Gaozu's intent to rebel. The Empress visited the capital from Taiyuan in the third year, on the occasion of his birthday. Fei decided to detain her, saying at a time of inebriation, "Why return in such haste, if not to join in the treachery of Gentleman Shi?" When he sobered, aides reminded the Emperor of his words, which he greatly regretted, and he allowed the Princess to return. There she informed Gaozu of the comment, only to compound his anxieties.

The Princess deserved installation as Empress after Gaozu's accession. In the third month of the second year of Tianfu [C.E. 938], the relevant officials stated, "The Consort Dowager already possesses appropriate titles of honor, so the articles of investiture are requested." The Consort Dowager was Gaozu's birthmother, Woman Liu. Temples to the imperial ancestors had yet to be erected, however, and a diffident Gaozu seemed in no rush to act on the request. Stricken by illness in the seventh year, Gaozu ordered elevation of the Consort Dowager to Empress Dowager, in the fifth month of summer; he expired before formal investiture could occur. The Empress Li, likewise, went without formal investiture for the duration of Gaozu's reign. Only under Emperor Chu, in the seventh month of the eighth year of Tianfu [C.E. 943], were formal vestments as Empress Dowager conferred.

The Empress Dowager was naturally forceful and astute, her seriousness often intimidating Gaozu. Under Emperor Chu, the Empress Feng dominated court affairs, and Dowager Li repeatedly decried such conduct, her counsel ignored by Chu to his own eventual detriment.

[Khitan ruler] Yelü Deguang had won the surrender of Jin armies by the twelfth month of the third year of Kaiyun [C.E. 947]. He now dispatched Zhang Yanze to occupy the capital in advance and convey a letter to the Dowager Li, informing her of the surrender of Jin armies. The letter further queried, "The slave girl so-and-so, once my hairdresser, later stole a medicine bag and fled to the Jin. Is she still around? I previously lost an imported chariot in battle at Yangcheng. Does it still exist?" The letter also inquired after Khitan soldiers formerly captured by the Jin and the whereabouts of courtiers including Jing Yanguang and Sang Weihan. The Empress Dowager and the Emperor intended to set themselves afire upon hearing of Yanze's arrival but were dissuaded by the favorite, Xue Chao. Receiving Deguang's letter, they extinguished the fire and left to ascend a nature park. Auxiliary academician Fan Zhi was summoned by the Emperor, who asked, "Why did Gentleman Du [Chongwei] suddenly forsake us [for the Khitan]? When the Former Monarch [Jingtang] emerged from his Taiyuan base and wanted to select a son as interim prefectural custodian, he consulted the northern emperor, who selected me for the post. Thus, I have long been known to the Khitan monarch, so draft a memorial for me to explain matters, permitting my sons and mother to survive." Zhi now composed for the ruler the following "Petition of Surrender":

> Your Grandson and Subject, Chonggui, begs to speak. Recently, as the Tang mandate met its end and the central plains lost its bearings, the consequent misfortunes caused the depletion of Heaven and the dissipation of Earth. My ancestors could claim a mere strip of land and a squad of soldiers, endless wars and related calamities having exposed our military as imperiled and isolated. However, You, Venerable Emperor, once delivered us from calamity while crushing the infidels, advanced gain while expelling peril—the royal armor donned for incursions deep into the lair of thugs. You braved the hardships of rain and frost to overcome nature's hazards, You assumed the speed of wind and the sting of lightning to exact retribution at Zhongshan and Jizhou. The world extensively settled under the banner with yellow halberd, Your might reverberated across the universe, and Your righteousness stirred the gods. Electing not to preside over your own feat [of conquering the Middle Kingdom], You allowed the rule of Jin to emerge, the Venerable Emperor gloriously contributing to its rule.

Amid a succession of calamities from Heaven, the Former Monarch [Jingtang] departed this world, Your Subject inheriting his dying wish to build upon the dynastic foundation. The distractions of a recent mourning, plus endemic turmoil in the land, caused me to entrust all important military decisions to my martial ministers and senior courtiers. They unilaterally fixed the royal succession and acted without court mandates, issued directives at whim and dared to defy superiors. Since the onset of armed conflict and the horrific anger unleashed by it, the severity of our calamity convinced the spirits that our fortunes were spent and the world lost. A hundred thousand soldiers, watching the winds of fate, hopelessly folded their hands; a hundred million commoners, extending their necks, resigned their hearts.

In repudiating a righteous path, Your Subject is ashamed; in clinging to life, I am humiliated. Since my world turned topsy-turvy, generations of my deceased ancestors pass days and nights in precarious uncertainty. You, Venerable Emperor, evince compassion for those ancestors resembling the clearing after a thunderstorm: by neither prosecuting vengeance against the spirits nor disrupting rites to ancestors, hundreds of mouths celebrate Your charity in regenerating life, just as this particular family appreciates Your irredeemable grace. Although I gladly accept such grace, never did I dare expect it. Your Subject, joined by the Empress Dowager and my wife, Woman Feng, will go to the distant suburbs with faces masked and await due punishment.

Chonggui petitioned Deguang on behalf of the Empress Dowager as well, stating:

Recently betrothed to the Jin house, I, Woman Li, humbly beg to speak. With the arrival of Zhang Yanze and Fu Zhu'er came the letter of consolation from You, the Venerable Emperor. I humbly recall an incident where the Former Emperor [Jingtang], happened upon border troops at Bing and Fen prefectures: his peril had to be handled as delicately as stacking eggs, his crisis addressed with the urgency of a man hanging upside down. Our cunning and our courage exhausted, our fates from dusk to dawn were uncertain. You, Venerable Emperor, left the northern reaches of Jizhou¶ to appear in person at Hedong command [Taiyuan]—crossing mountains and rivers, conquering obstacles of nature. Your Majesty promptly subdued the mighty and the malevolent to restore order to the Central Plains, delivering the Shi family from imminent demise and inaugurating the Jin dynastic line.

To our misfortune, the Former Emperor left this world, bequeathing the imperium to a son unable to restore goodwill with you nor comfort his own people. Rather, he squandered goodwill and slighted righteous duty. Successive waves of warfare proved uncontainable once unleashed and quickly strengthened of their own force. Who can possibly contain such disaster? Today, the heavens above are angry while inner and outer realms are disaffected. Generalissimos now herd goats as imperial guardsmen doff their armor.

On behalf of the clan, I accept responsibility for mistakes made and initially looked to the prospect of survival with apprehension. Then, Your condolences arrived with a clear pronouncement of charity and subtle reassurances of forbearance. Privileged to such conciliatory gestures, we are lifted in body and spirit. To enjoy such a sudden act of grace when death loomed above can only give cause to reflect on our errors and accept blame. Even nine deaths are not enough to repay our debt. Today, I send grandsons Yanxu and Yanbao to forward this plea for mercy, offering my gratitude in the interim.

"No need for worry," Deguang reported back. "Take care to eat properly."

He entered the capital in the fourth year, first day of the inaugural month [C.E. January 25, 947], but the Emperor and Empress Dowager had left by sedan chair for the suburbs, Deguang unable to meet them. They were lodged at Fengchan Monastery, so Deguang sent commander Cui Yanxun [Tingxun] to place them under guard. It was a time of sleet and frigid cold, and everyone was intensely hungry. The Empress Dowager directed a messenger to ask of the monks, "On this very ground, I once feasted tens of thousands of clerics. Why have you no empathy today?" The monks expressed fear of feeding them owing to the unpredictable reaction of the barbarians. The Emperor discreetly begged a guard for food, obtaining a bit.

On the fifth day, Yelü Deguang ordered the Emperor's demotion to grandmaster of imperial recreations and honorary grand marshal, with the noble rank Fuyi, mandating relocation to Huanglong Prefecture.[2] Yet Deguang proposed to the Empress Dowager, through a messenger, "I hear that Chonggui came to the current end for failing to heed his mother's admonitions. You may request a more convenient accommodation, as you need not accompany him." "Chonggui has been scrupulous in deference to me," the Empress Dowager responded. "His failings lie in defying the will of the Former Monarch by severing the amicable bonds between our two empires. He was purged for this reason. Yet privileged to this magnificent act of beneficence, his life and those of his family will be spared. Where would a mother wish to go, if not with her son?" The Dowager hence accompanied the Emperor in the journey northward, along with Empress Feng, younger brother Chongrui, imperial sons Yanxu and Yanbao, and the imperial clan. The entourage also included fifty women from the palace, thirty eunuchs, fifty courtiers representing the eastern and western formations, one imperial doctor, four officers of the Crane-Commanding Guard, seven cooks from the imperial kitchens, three tea and wine officers, another three imperial regalia officers, and twenty soldiers from the Six Armies—all under the guard of three hundred [Khitan] horsemen. The prefectures and counties along the route, then administered by one-time Jin military officers and their aides, donated food that never reached them. Fathers and old men on the road bearing lamb and wine struggled to offer these, only to be pushed away by bodyguards intent on preventing a glimpse of the Emperor. They all dispersed in tears.

The entourage, ten days after leaving You Prefecture, passed through Ping before departing via Yu Pass. Crossing a terrain of pebbles and stones and denied food when hungry, palace women and official companions were forced to forage for food, mostly tree fruits and wild plants. After another seven to eight days of travel, upon reaching Jinzhou‡, the barbarians coerced the Emperor and Empress Dowager to bow before a picture of [Khitan patriarch] Abaoji. The Emperor could no longer bear the indignity and cried out, "By not allowing me to die, Xue Chao did me a profound disservice!" Another five or six days of passage saw the entourage pass through Haibei Prefecture, where captors had Yanxu bow at the tomb of the Prince of Dongdan.[3] They crossed the Liao River ten days or so later, reaching Tiezhou, Bohai, before traversing Nanhai Prefecture for an additional seven to eight days to reach Huanglong Prefecture.

In the sixth month of the year, the Khitan royal mother ordered the Emperor and Empress Dowager relocated to Huaimi Prefecture, fifteen hundred *li* northwest of Huanglong. They had traveled only two hundred *li* beyond Liaoyang when the Khitan royal mother was imprisoned by the current Prince of Yongkang [Yelü Ruan], who had the Emperor and Empress Dowager return to Liaoyang. They settled there and received modest subsidies. During the fourth month of the next year [C.E. 948], the Prince of Yongkang reached Liaoyang, as the Emperor appeared in plain white gown and gauze cap to visit his tent, flanked by the Empress Dowager and the Empress. The Emperor bowed in obeisance, but the Prince interrupted to greet him under informal protocol. The Emperor's tears fell like rain as he lay flat on the ground, confessing to past excesses and errors. The Prince had an aide raise him by the elbow, the two men sitting together to savor some wine and musical performances. Entertainers and attendants in the Prince of Yongkang's retinue could only weep in indescribable grief upon seeing the Former Monarch, as they vied to leave clothes, medicine, and cakes for him.

In the fifth month, the Prince of Yongkang proceeded northward for Xing† and took as companions certain members of the Emperor's entourage, including fifteen eunuchs, fifteen courtiers from the eastern and western formations, and imperial son Yanxu. The Prince's brother-in-law, Channu, enamored of a young daughter of the Emperor, asked to claim her. The Emperor noted her youth in declining, whereupon the Prince scampered off to seize her as a gift for Channu. Xing† is a barbarian land, elevated and cold, where the Khitan often ascend during the fifth month to escape the summer heat, then descend in the eighth month. As the Prince of Yongkang departed in the eighth month, the Empress Dowager personally rushed to meet him at Bazhou and plead for a parcel of land adjacent to Hanercheng to plant or graze for a livelihood.[4] The Prince allowed the Empress Dowager to travel with him for roughly ten days, she and son Yanxu later permitted to return to Liaoyang together.

A year hence, namely, second month of the second year of Qianyou, under Han rule [C.E. 949], the Emperor and Empress Dowager were relocated to Jianzhou. The location was twelve hundred *li* to the southwest of Liaoyang, governor Zhao Yanhui setting aside the master bedroom to accommodate them. Acquiring more than fifty *qing* of land located several dozen *li* beyond Jianzhou, the Emperor sent his companions to till the land for food.

In the third month of the next year, an ill Empress Dowager, confined to bed and lacking medicine, often looked to Heaven to weep, while pointing a finger to the south to curse Du Chongwei, Li Shouzhen, and cohort. "Had we died, the lack of awareness would have been manageable; but having sensation, I will never forgive you in the netherworld." As her condition deteriorated, by the eighth month, she enjoined the Emperor, "After my death, send my cremated bones to the Buddhist monastery at Fanyang [Youzhou]. Please do not leave me to roam the barbarian netherworld as a ghost." She soon died. The Emperor was accompanied by his Empress, palace women, eunuchs, and courtiers of the eastern and western formations in walking barefoot to carry her coffin to the cremation site, their hair hanging loose. After the cremation, her ashes were scattered across the landscape.

Under the Zhou reign of Xiande [C.E. 954–959], someone from the Middle Kingdom who had fled Khitan lands returned to report a sighting of the Emperor, Empress, and royal sons, who were still alive. Their subsequent fates are not known.

Consort Dowager An

Native to Daibei, the pedigree of Consort Dowager An [d. C.E. 948] is unknown. She married Shi Jingru and gave birth to Emperor Chu. Initially invested as Lady of Qin, she became Consort Dowager after Emperor Chu's accession. She accompanied the Emperor on his northern exile despite the loss of eyesight, ultimately dying on the road in the relocation from Liaoyang to Jianzhou. She pleaded with the Emperor in her last moments, "You should cremate my body and toss the ashes into a southerly wind, allowing my soul to approximate a return to the Middle Kingdom." When she died, in the absence of weeds or trees among the pebbles and rocks, an imported carriage was set afire for the cremation, her ashes carried to Jianzhou. There the Empress Dowager Li similarly perished, and the two women were buried together.

Empress of Emperor Chu, née Feng

Woman Feng, a native of Dingzhou, was Empress to Emperor Chu. Her father, Feng Meng, had lived in the capital as prefectural liaison at court, his proclivity for flattery appealing to An Chonghui, who named him deputy interim custodian of the Ye capital. With the future Gaozu then custodian of Ye, he developed a close affinity for Meng and arranged for Meng's daughter to marry younger brother Chongyin; she was invested Lady of Wu. Chongyin later died prematurely and the Empress lived for a while as a widow, but her beauty proved alluring to Emperor Chu.

Precisely as the recently deceased Gaozu lay coffined for his wake and the Emperor assumed mourning rites, he [violated taboos by] naming Feng his empress. On the same day, he summoned the Empress, accompanied by funeral guards for the Six Armies and Fife and Drum ceremonial contingents, to rendezvous with him at Xiyu hamlet, with its Buddhist altar to Gaozu. When the official multitudes offered felicitations, the Emperor cautioned [satirically] as he looked to Feng Dao and cohort, "On instructions from the Empress Dowager, the grand celebration with courtiers [usually attending a marriage] is not permitted." Once the official rank and file departed, the Emperor accompanied his Empress in the merriment of heavy drink, song, and dance. The Emperor poured libations while passing the royal bier, asserting [as he looked to the corpse], "On orders from the Empress Dowager, I cannot celebrate with you either!" His aides could not contain their laughter, and the Emperor nearly tripped over in glee. Now glancing at those nearby, he added, "I became a groom today. What do you think of that!"[5] Empress Feng and the aides laughed so loud that they were heard beyond the palace.

The Empress monopolized palace favor from the outset of her installation, arranging honors as "Lady" for the various female officials and ushers of her palace. She even employed an uncastrated man, Li Yanbi, as chief bodyguard for her palace. Elder brother Feng Yu held the reins of government as well, managing affairs in and away from the palace to the eventual ruin of Jin rule. Once the Khitan overran the capital, they exposed the evils of the Emperor to the world, stating, "By recruiting his aunt for the Empress's palace, he committed incest in violation of the most fundamental of ethics." The Empress later accompanied him northward. She repeatedly requested poisonous drugs out of concern for the Emperor's humiliation, planning to consume them and die together with him. She never managed to acquire the drugs, and her fate thereafter is unknown.

A vulnerable Jin dynasty originated among the barbarians and ultimately came to ruin at barbarian hands. For this reason, details on the long-term genealogical evolution of its ruling family cannot be found. The following can be verified: Gaozu had two uncles, one elder brother and six younger siblings, seven sons and two grandsons. Information is scant for some and replete for others: this reflects more than merely the random loss of information attendant to tumultuous times, but the lack of noteworthy personages. I have modestly gathered information to supplement deficiencies in formal documents.

Gaozu had two uncles, Shi Wanyou and Wanquan, and an elder brother, *Shi Jingru*. Younger brothers included Jingwei, Jingde, Jingyin, Jingyun, Jinghui, and Chongyin. His sons were Chonggui, Chongxin, Chongyi, Chongying, Chongjin, Chongrui, and Chonggao. Yanxu and Yanbao were grandsons. The Xiaoping Emperor [Jingtang's grandfather] gave birth to the Xiaoyuan Emperor [his father], as well as Wanyou and Wanquan. The Xiaoyuan Emperor gave birth to Gaozu, Wanyou fathered Jingwei and Jingyun, Wanquan sired Jinghui. As for Jingru, Jingde, Jingyin, and Chongyin, the precise nature of their blood connection to Gaozu is unclear.

Gaozu was the Xiaoyuan Emperor's second son and Jingru his elder brother. Xiaoyuan questioned whether Jingru was actually his own and grew attached to Gaozu, treating him as the eldest, instead. And when posthumous office was conferred, Jingru was unconventionally ranked last among the brothers and was the only one never ennobled posthumously under Gaozu—another highly suspect matter. Chongyin was Gaozu's younger brother, although we cannot confirm the nature of blood relations. Gaozu loved him dearly, raising him as a son and adding the character "Chong" to his name to imply his standing among the younger of his blood sons. The uncles of Gaozu both died before his accession, as had elder brother Jingru, younger brother Jingyin, and son Chongjin. Perishing at the time of Gaozu's rebellion were Jingwei, Jingde, Chongyin, and Chongying. A young son of Gaozu, nicknamed "Feng the Sixth," died before receiving a formal name. Longstanding assertions that Chongrui was youngest son are erroneous.

The Shi family had served in the military for generations, although the ranks of Wanyou and Wanquan were too modest to merit citation. In the second year of Tianfu, the inaugural month [C.E. 937], Wanyou held the posthumous rank of grandmaster of imperial recreations with gold and purple insignia and honorary dignitary for education, rank elevated to censor-in-chief and supreme pillar of state with grand preceptor standing. Wanquan also held the posthumous rank of grandmaster of imperial recreations with gold and purple insignia, honorary dignitary of public works, and concurrent censor-in-chief and supreme pillar of state with grand mentor status. In the reign of Emperor Chu, fifth month of the eighth year of Tianfu [C.E. 943], imperial granduncle Wanyou was posthumously invested Prince of Qin. Wanquan was posthumously advanced to grand preceptor and invested Prince of Zhao.

Shi Jingwei

Jingwei had the courtesy name Fengxin. During the reign of Emperor Fei, he served the Tang as chief director of the Sage-Exalting Guard's right third brigade and concurrently prefect of Changzhou. He once said to someone, after learning of Gaozu's mutiny at Taiyuan, "With life there is inevitable death. What human is above this? As my elder brother embarks upon a major enterprise, I cannot accept humiliation for the simple sake of survival. It would make me a mockery before my contemporaries!" He committed suicide. Jingde was director of cavalry and infantry at Yinzhou†, at the time, Gaozu's rebellion causing him to be executed.

In the second year of Tianfu, the inaugural month, Jingwei and Jingde were both posthumously ranked grand mentor, and Jingyin was ranked honorary advisor to the heir-apparent and grand mentor. Jingru was not included. In the inaugural month of the seventh year, the court posthumously ennobled Jingwei as Prince of Guang, Jingde as Prince of Fu, and Jingyin as Prince of Tong—all with rank of grand mentor. Jingru received his first rank as grandmaster of imperial recreations with gold and purple insignia, honorary associate at the Imperial Secretariat, concurrent censor-in-chief and supreme pillar of state with grand mentor standing; he alone received no title of nobility. In the fifth month of the eighth year of Tianfu, under Emperor Chu, the three junior uncles of the Emperor were honored as grand preceptor, senior uncle Jingru now receiving investiture as Prince of Song with grand preceptor standing.

Shi Jingyun

Jingyun [C.E. 899–947] had the courtesy name Dehe. For lack of someone to support him in youth, he consorted with commoners. Gaozu ordered a search that located him, an appointment ensuing as military attaché at Taiyuan. He became commissioner for Flying Dragon security forces in the capital, upon the accession of Gaozu, and eventually defense commissioner for Caozhou. In winter, the fifth year of Tianfu [C.E. 940], he became governor of the three cities of Heyang.

Jingyun was a man of avarice and caprice, so Gaozu recruited worthy men to assist him as aides. And he dared not violate the laws due to Gaozu's intimidating sternness of character. A year or so later, he was reassigned as Baoyi governor, ministerial standing conferred under Emperor Chu. Arrogance and debauchery now began to set in. Whenever the Emperor's messengers arrived, he invariably asked, "And how is my young nephew, [the Emperor]?" The people of Shanzhou suffered under his tyranny, and the capital summoned him back. An uncle to the emperor could hardly be reprimanded, so the court warned him by banishing Su Yancun and Zheng Wenyu, his military attachés of primary-cohort standing.

Once the Khitan violated the border, Jingyun departed with Emperor Chu for Chanyuan. He was supposed to make military preparations at Wenyang in defense of Majia Crossing, but he never confronted the enemy and proved thoroughly undistinguished. In the inaugural year of Kaiyun, the seventh month [C.E. 944], a local assignment came as Weisheng governor. A year or so later, Emperor Chu designated Caozhou as the Weixin command, with Jingyun as governor. His greed and caprice proved especially onerous at Caozhou, although recall occurred much later. During Zhang Yanze's invasion of the capital [C.E. 947], Jingyun absconded by night to leap over an eastern embankment of the city: falling into a moat, he died by drowning at forty-nine *sui*.

Shi Jinghui, Prince of Han

Jinghui, the Prince of Han, had the courtesy name Dezhao.[6] By character sincere and solemn, resolute and direct, he had multiple talents to complement his valor, causing Gaozu to love him dearly. He served as defense commissioner for Caozhou during Gaozu's reign and was praised for his honest and frugal ways. He died in office. Initially given posthumous rank as grand mentor, he was elevated to grand preceptor in the eighth year of Tianfu and invested Prince of Han. His son, Xi, succeeded him.

Gaozu's Empress Li gave birth to the Prince of Chu, Chongxin. The maternity of other sons is unknown. When Gaozu raised armies at Taiyuan, Chongying served as commandant of the Right Guard and Chongyin as deputy commissioner of security of the imperial city, residing in the capital.

News of Gaozu's insurrection forced Chongying and Chongyin to hide in a well at a commoner's home. Authorities apprehended and executed them and even liquidated the commoners who sheltered them. In the inaugural month of the second year of Tianfu [C.E. 937], Gaozu held a memorial service for his two sons, conferring the posthumous rank of grand guardian. Chongjin was also honored posthumously as commander of the Imperial Insignia Left Guard with the rank of grand guardian. All three were elevated to grand mentor in the inaugural month of the seventh year. Investiture occurred for Chongying as Prince of Guo, Chongyin as Prince of Tan, and Chongjin as Prince of Kui. Their posthumous rank was further elevated to grand preceptor under Emperor Chu, in the fifth month of the eighth year of Tianfu.

Shi Chongxin, Prince of Chu

Chongxin [C.E. 918–937], the Prince of Chu, had the courtesy name Shoufu. Possessing an alert and agile mind, plus multiple talents, he also celebrated ritual propriety. In the second month of the second year of Tianfu [C.E. 937], he was named governor of the three cities of Heyang, with the rank of generalissimo for the Valorous Left Guard. Owing to sound administration there, Gaozu issued a proclamation in praise. Fan Yanguang rebelled that year and the court ordered the former Lingwu governor, Zhang Congbin, to lead Heyang armies in suppressing the rebel. Congbin rebelled as well to murder Chongxin, a man of twenty *sui*. Gaozu intended to confer posthumous rank as grand marshal when senior courtiers noted the old Han-dynasty precedent barring imperial sons from "grand duke" ranking. "This youth encountered calamity in pursuit of good, which leaves me grieved beyond measure," Gaozu insisted. "As the action emanates from me, there is scarcely precedent!" Conferral of grand marshal rank occurred. In the inaugural month of the seventh year, he was elevated to grand preceptor and invested Prince of Yi, then reinvested Prince of Chu in the fifth month of the eighth year of Tianfu, under Emperor Chu.

Shi Chongyi, Prince of Shou

The Prince of Shou, Chongyi [C.E. 923–941], with courtesy name Hongli, possessed a curiosity for learning and some facility in the art of war. Upon the accession of Gaozu, he became commandant of the Valorous Left Guard. He also served as interim custodian of the eastern capital during Gaozu's tenure at Bianzhou. When Zhang Congbin rebelled and invaded Henan Prefecture [C.E. 941], Chongyi was murdered at nineteen *sui*. His posthumous rank as grand mentor was changed to grand marshal in the inaugural month of the seventh year of Tianfu, ennobled Prince of Shou. Elevation to grand preceptor came under Emperor Chu, in the fifth month of the eighth Tianfu year. Neither he nor Chongxin sired sons.

Shi Chongrui

In facial appearance, Chongrui looked strikingly like Gaozu. Once illness confined Gaozu to bed, chief minister Feng Dao visited the bedroom to confer. Chongrui was still young, then. Gaozu had an attendant summon Dao to his bedside, the child placed into Dao's embrace by a eunuch. Although nothing was said, everyone nearby could clearly see that Chongrui had been entrusted to Dao's care. Once the Emperor expired, leading Jin courtiers debated the installation of a mature man as ruler, in light of the country's numerous challenges. By then, Jing Yanguang had already secretly endorsed Emperor Chu's enthronement, so Chongrui never ruled. Emperor Chu named Chongrui honorary grand guardian and metropolitan custodian of Kaifeng, the concurrent interim prefect of Kaifeng [his deputy] being Bian Wei, heretofore attending left cavalier of palace remonstrance. In the fifth month of the second year of Kaiyun [C.E. 945], Chongrui became governor of the Xiongwu command, and Zhongwu a year later, both titles with no office. Once the Khitan overturned the Jin dynasty, he accompanied Emperor Chu in relocating north. Nothing is known of his final years.

Shi Chonggao

The Prince of Chen, Chonggao, was Gaozu's youngest son, with the nickname "Feng the Sixth."[7] He died before a formal name could be given, so the court posthumously conferred the name of Chonggao and the rank of grand mentor, investing him as Prince of Chen. Elevation to grand preceptor came under Emperor Chu, in the fifth month of the eighth Tianfu year.

Shi Yanxu and Yanbao

Yanxu and Yanbao, grandsons of Gaozu, were treated by Emperor Chu as sons. In the second year of Kaiyun [C.E. 945], the autumn, Yanxu was named prefect of Zhengzhou. Too young at the time to conduct affairs, the court sent a eunuch to accompany him to the post and assigned the secretariat's gentleman-designate, Lu Hang, as provisional prefect. The eunuchs later to monopolize prefectural affairs often vilified Hang, so Emperor Chu recalled him. Yanxu hence rose to defense commissioner of Qizhou¶.

Yanxu became the Zhenning governor in the third year. At the time, war ravaged the Hebei region while droughts and locusts despoiled the world, the attendant famine claiming a million lives or more. Yet the various governors competed to accumulate things, like Zhao Zaili, whose tens of thousands in cash strings exceeded other governors and royal princes. Emperor Chu sought to tap into such wealth by arranging Yanxu's marriage to Zaili's daughter. And indeed, Zaili produced a dowry of three thousand rolls of raw silk, not including the incalculable sums given before and after the marriage. In the fifth month of the third year, the court sent its chamberlain for the imperial clan, Shi Guangzan, to greet Zaili at his official residence with one hundred and fifty chests of cash as betrothal gift. Emperor Chu feasted Zaili at Wansui Hall and presented a staggering number of gifts. As ruler and subject indulged in such obscene ostentation, the event was celebrated at the time as glorious. Zaili once said to someone, "This single wedding will cost a hundred thousand in cash strings!" Yanxu moved on to the Baoyi governorship in the eleventh month.

Yanxu's assignment as defense commissioner for Qizhou¶ permitted Yanbao to replace him as Zhengzhou prefect. In the wake of the Jin dynasty's purge by the Khitan, Emperor Chu and the Empress Dowager chose Yanxu and Yanbao to present to the Khitan a "Petition to Surrender," the imperial seal of jade, and the imperial seal of gold. Yanbao was also governor of the Weixin command at the time. After obtaining the jade seal, the Khitan believed the workmanship inferior and the imprint different from the seal described in earlier histories. Yanxu and cohort were returned to demand the authentic seal. Emperor Chu drafted a plaint for his response, saying, "When Congke, the Prince of Lu, set himself afire at Luoyang, the location of the jade seal was unknown and believed destroyed by fire. Once the Former Monarch inherited the mandate, he ordered jade craftsmen to make this seal—a matter widely known among courtiers of the time." This settled the matter. Yanxu and cohort later accompanied Emperor Chu in his northern exile, their final fates unknown.

We lament. In antiquity, the unfortunate without sons adopted male heirs from the same line of descent. The practice was condoned by the Sage [Confucius] and expanded upon in the classic on *Rites* without taboos [on parent's identity]. Only the boorish provincials of later times chose to impose taboos, suppression invariably fostering either deception or hypocrisy. Thus, persons secretly acquiring an infant in swaddling clothes tend to suppress the parents' identity and guilefully present the boy as born to them, saying defensively, "We would otherwise not enjoy the child's full love and dedication, his heart certainly divided." The adopted son then similarly suppresses the identity of birth parents and repudiates his natural-born parents, treating father like an uncle. In the process, clansmen across the generations are deceived, rendering chaos to relations between the living and the dead, between relatives close and distant. All sentient beings have consciousness at birth and none will not love their parents. To make a given child suffer true denial of his own natural instincts is something seen not even among beasts. Or to make a youth outwardly deny his parents when his heart resists, this is an enormous hypocrisy.

When boorish provincials are involved in public affairs, the consequences can be grave. Their reckless manipulations, deception, and hypocrisy in defiance of normative rules are the handiwork of petty men. Only a sage can recognize, contrarily, that nothing in human mores is more vital than continuing a disrupted family line. Such practices are universal for all ages and all places in the world. Why resort to taboos? Never has a so-called son been born without father and mother. Thus, the youth designated as heir to another necessarily has a father by birth and a father by adoption, a principle altogether self-evident. Why resort to taboos? The rule of the sages is to be simple and transparent—not reckless and manipulative, deceptive and hypocritical—thereby embracing universal procedures and common practice.

Some further believe that an adopted son, as primary mourner for adoptive parents, should assume a rigorous regimen [of three years]. Human instinct, however, will not allow him to ignore birth parents either, so reducing the mourning for birth parents to a year makes compassionate sense. The five degrees of mourning are external to the self and can be reduced, yet the names of father and mother can never be altered. The classics thus insisted: "the person to become heir to another must still requite father and mother." This spirit has invariably guided rulers of empire and universe since the ancient Three Dynasties, save for the Jin period. With reference to Jingru, Emperor Chu repudiated the moral way for fathers by ennobling Jingru as subject: lacking legitimate claim to the throne, he not only had no alternative to severing family ties, but was mimicking boorish provincials as well.

Amid the tumult of battles and banditry under the Five Dynasties, rites and music were desecrated, the "three relationships" and the "five constants" cast off, and the institutions and literatures of the ancient kings swept away entirely. Practices like "sacrificing in the wilderness during winter solstice" and "burning paper money" reflect the Son of Heaven's common mimicking of boorish provincials. Moreover, the Jin house emerged from among the barbarians to win the world through usurpation. Gaozu served Yelü Deguang as father, while Emperor Chu served Deguang as grandfather, called himself grandson, and referred to his own birth father as "subject." How is this compatible with human principles?

CHAPTER 18

BIOGRAPHIES OF THE ROYAL FAMILIES: HAN

Empress Li

Gaozu's Empress Li [d. C.E. 960] was a native of Jinyang County, Taiyuan, her father involved in farming. Gaozu was a young foot soldier grazing horses at Jinyang when he infiltrated her home by night to abduct her. She was invested Lady of Wei after his rise in stature, giving birth to Emperor Yin.

In the fourth year of Kaiyun [C.E. 947], as Gaozu raised armies in rebellion at Taiyuan, reserves in the treasury proved insufficient to reward troops, so he planned a collection from the people. The Empress admonished against it, arguing, "Precisely as you now rise defiantly to claim a righteous cause, the people will see you seize their properties before witnessing any acts of charity. This is scarcely compatible with a new Son of Heaven's calling to succor the people. I would rather empty the consort's inner palaces: the proceeds may not yield enough, but we will thereby avoid the wrath of troops." Gaozu's face changed color as he thanked her. She was installed empress after his accession and honored as Empress Dowager by Emperor Yin, upon Gaozu's death.

During his youth, Emperor Yin often consorted with the petty likes of Guo Yunming, Hou Zan, and Li Ye, their frolicking in the palace inciting a succession of cutting rebukes from Dowager Li. Yet the Emperor countered, "Affairs of empire reside with the outer court, which the Dowager has no right to address!" Chamberlain for ceremonials Zhang Zhao overheard the exchange, admonishing the Emperor by memorial, "Your Majesty needs proximity to the erudite and receptiveness to the upright to enhance your knowledge." Yin grew increasingly disinterested, ultimately turning to Yunming and cohort for strategic and other planning until the fatal end.

Formerly, Emperor Yin intrigued with Yunming and cohort to execute such statesmen as Yang Bin and Shi Hongzhao, the cabal already formulated when he went to inform the Dowager. "Important matters of the sort deserve consultation with chief ministers," she insisted. Emerging from his side was Li Ye, who interjected, "For the life of the Former Emperor, men of letters were never consulted about major court decisions." The Empress Dowager expressed profound reservations, but the Emperor departed, ruffling his clothing to murmur, "Why should I confer with the women's quarters?" In the wake of Bin's death, the future Taizu of Zhou raised armies against the capital, inflicting defeat on Murong Yanchao at Liuzi Slope. Emperor Yin wished to leave to personally join his troops, the Empress Dowager trying to dissuade him. "Guo Wei is my own flesh and blood," she noted. "If not for dangers and discord, he hardly would have chosen the current course of action. If you hold troops in abeyance for now and issue instructions to Wei, he is certain to provide an explanation, possibly permitting a virtual retention of ruler/subject relations." The Emperor refused to heed her and departed as planned, foundering in the end.

After entering the capital, the future Emperor of Zhou, Taizu, scrupulously conducted court affairs with rescripts in the Empress Dowager's name. Subsequent debate yielded the decision to elevate the Duke of Xiangyin, Liu Yun, to Son of Heaven. Taizu invited the Empress Dowager to preside at court in advance of his arrival, then departed for campaigns against the Khitan; he returned after military leaders rallied to enthrone him. His proposition to treat the Dowager as mother was spurned by her, her letter enjoining him: "You, Chancellor Guo Wei, are distinguished in merit and highly esteemed, your repute for virtue heralded widely. Eradicating a perilous tumult and stabilizing relations with neighbors, the world celebrates your feats. Celestial fortunes now favor you, as military and civilian leaders and commoners by the millions rally in your support. The countless ordeals in these waning years of life leave me resigned to entrust this frail body to your eternal care. Reading your noble offer to treat me as mother moves me to tears, which flow in profusion." Hereafter removed to the Taiping palace, the Empress's titular honors were advanced to the Luminous and Sagacious Empress Dowager. She expired in spring of the inaugural year of Xiande [C.E. 960].[i]

....

i. According to the *Old History* and the *Veritable Records,* Emperor Yin had no empress; having expired within three years of acceding to power, at twenty *sui,* Yin never managed to install one.

Gaozu's Brothers, Chong and Xin, Sons Chengxun‡, Chengyou, and Chengxun, and the Prince of Xu, Liu Yun

Gaozu had two younger brothers and three sons: the brothers were named Chong and Xin, the sons named Chengxun‡, Chengyou, and Chengxun. The son of Chong, Yun, was so loved by Gaozu that he made him son; he became governor of Xuzhou¶ in the inaugural year of Qianyou [C.E. 948]. Chengxun‡ died young and was posthumously invested Prince of Wei. Chengyou came after him, the future Emperor Yin. Chengxun served as metropolitan custodian of Kaifeng.

Once the future Taizu of Zhou vanquished Han armies in the northern suburbs and Emperor Yin succumbed to regicide, Taizu reached the capital convinced that leading Han courtiers would support his enthronement. Chief minister Feng Dao and cohort, however, barely noticed him during the initial meeting. Taizu had little recourse but to kneel in a bow to Dao, who treated the gesture rather casually, then reciprocated with a few measured words of consolation: "You have been arduous in your endeavors, Sir." Stymied in ambition and confounded in demeanor, Taizu concluded that Han-dynasty courtiers had no inclination to install him, while unilateral action on his part might be problematic. He thus told the Han-dynasty Dowager to designate an heir to the Han throne.

Four members of the imperial clan then alive, led by Hedong governor Liu Chong, enjoined the Empress Dowager, "Hedong governor Liu Chong and Xuzhou‡ governor Liu Xin are younger brothers of Gaozu, while Xuzhou¶ governor *Liu Yun* [d. C.E. 951] and Kaifeng custodian Liu Chengxun are his sons. Civil and military officials should select one as heir to this imperium, endowed by Heaven." The future Taizu of Zhou and Wang Jun now entered the palace to confer with the Dowager, proposing, "It is preferable to enthrone the custodian of Kaifeng and son of Emperor Gaozu, Chengxun." The Dowager opposed the designation of Chengxun, citing longstanding physical illnesses. Taizu now led a cohort of officials seeking a meeting with Chengxun to observe his deportment. The Dowager arranged for Chengxun to be carried out on a stretcher for the meeting, officials now believing her after observing him. Courtiers then petitioned together, "The governor of Xuzhou¶, Liu Yun, loved by Gaozu and born his son, should be named heir." Grand preceptor Feng Dao was sent with a cadre of officials to receive Yun and escort him back. Intuiting that Taizu had no intention to support Yun, Dao asked him, "Does this endorsement, Sir, come from your heart?" Taizu pointed to Heaven to swear in the affirmative. "I usually do not lie to others, but must now lie," Dao confided in someone while departing. He then met Yun to convey the Empress Dowager's summons to court.

Liu Yun's entourage had reached Song Prefecture when Taizu abruptly returned to the capital from Chan, his troops rallying. Wang Jun suspected a mutiny underway among Yun's own attendants and sent Guo Chong, director of cavalry and infantry for the Imperial Guard, to safeguard Yun with seven hundred horsemen. Upon Chong's arrival at Songzhou, Yun climbed a tower to explore his intent. Chong said, "A mutiny has erupted at Chanzhou. Anxious in the absence of knowledge about it, I was sent as protective escort for you. I have no sinister agenda." Yun invited him in. Chong dared not advance until Feng Dao emerged to address Yun, whereupon he ascended the tower to meet Yun, whose guards were now removed.

By letter, Taizu called Feng Dao back to the capital in advance, leaving behind deputy escorts Zhao Shangjiao and Wang Du to accompany Liu Yun for audience with the Dowager. Dao thus returned first, as Yun intimated to him, "It is based on your repute, Sir, as a seasoned minister of thirty years that I reach this point—the right course, I have no doubt." Dao kept his silence. Yun's attending commander, Jia Zheng and cohort, repeatedly espied Dao for possible assassination. "No need for haste," Yun insisted, "I hardly see a threat emanating from Dao!" After Dao's departure, Guo Chong isolated Yun in an outer guesthouse, proceeding to murder Jia Zheng, administrative assistant Dong Yi, inspector-in-chief of the governor's guard Liu Fu, governor's senior secretary Xia Zhaodu, and others.

Taizu already wielded supervisory powers over the empire when the Empress Dowager issued the following rescript: "Recently, commissioner of military affairs Guo Wei, intent on placating the imperial clan and securing dynastic continuity, proposed the installation of an adult to the throne. Xuzhou¶ governor Liu Yun, on intimate terms with Gaozu, was named successor to the Han line and summoned to the capital from his district command. My directive was already issued, but military conditions have since deteriorated: the Heavenly way rests to the north [with Guo Wei] while the loyalties of subjects founder to the east [for Liu Yun]. At a time deemed appropriate by divinations, Yun should receive hereditary lands and titles before relegation to Supreme Commandant, Honorary Grand Preceptor, and Supreme Pillar of State, ennobled Duke of Xiangyin." Yun died in captivity.

Formerly, as Liu Yun departed Xu¶ Prefecture for the capital, the area's defenses were entrusted to Gong Tingmei, chief military attaché to the governor, and training commissioner Yang Wen. On word that Yun was bypassed for the succession, Tingmei and cohort sealed up the city in defiance of the dynastic mandate. Taizu named Wang Yanchao governor of Xu¶, his edict offering Tingmei an assignment as prefect while authorizing Yun to pardon Tingmei and cohort. In the third month of the inaugural year of Guangshun [C.E. 951], Yanchao conquered Xu¶ Prefecture, killing Tingmei and his group.

Chengxun died of illness in the inaugural year of Guangshun [C.E. 951] and was posthumously ennobled Prince of Chen.

We lament. Attending my woe for the Duke of Xiangyin, Liu Yun, is a celebration of the deeds of Tingmei and Yang Wen. Yun had no seniority in the Han succession and became a mere puppet of the Zhou founder, who, facing obstacles to a change of dynasty, was merely waiting for the right moment. At the time, the whole world appraised Yun as certain not to assume power, yet Tingmei and Wen stoutly defended an isolated city, in his name, even unto death. Is their conduct, from start to finish, any less than our "Martyrs to Virtue?" Having scrutinized the *Veritable Records*, however, I find uncertainties about the circumstances surrounding both deaths. These two men knew their mission was surely doomed and valued the simple act of death. But in the absence of clarification by historians, the circumstances of death cannot be known.

Amid the assault on Xuzhou¶ by Wang Yanchao, the Zhou once tried to sway Tingmei and cohort through messenger. I have encountered four imperial edicts professing that Tingmei had made peace overtures to the Zhou, only to defect again for fear of punishment. I have seen no petition from Tingmei soliciting an accommodation, leaving the veracity of such accounts indeterminate. We can afford nothing less than caution where omissions in the historical literature are involved: recording dubious points in the inherited record permits credible portions to receive a credible reception, after all. I genuinely celebrate the loyal commitment of these two men and mourn their thwarted mission. My inability to place their biographies among the "Martyrs to Virtue" is a matter of immense regret.

Liu Xin, Prince of Cai

The Prince of Cai, Xin, was Gaozu's first cousin and during his governorship at Taiyuan, Xin served as chief director of the Ascending-Victory Guard and concurrent Yicheng governor, later to be reassigned to Xuzhou‡. Emperor Yin was next in line to succeed once Gaozu became incapacitated, so orders went out to Yang Bin and cohort to place Xin under surveillance. Xin's presence in the capital now unwanted, he was relocated to a district command, departing in tears.

Wherever he went, Liu Xin obsessed with material objects and relished in the commission of murder. For a soldier guilty of some crime, for example, he would force their wives and sons to bear witness to the severing of his limbs and then eat the flesh. As blood drenched the ground before him, Xin would summon forth music, song, and wine.

The death of Yang Bin and cohort thoroughly delighted Liu Xin, who said to aides, "I initially thought Heaven had no eyes [to witness my hardship], allowing me to languish for three years at this site. The Monarch reigns in isolation, having virtually fallen into the hands of villains. I hope that You Gentlemen can hearten me with a toast." Later news of peril for the Emperor left him depressed and unable to eat. In the wake of the mutiny at Chan Prefecture by Taizu of Zhou, Wang Jun sent Ma Duo, the former prefect of Shen‡, to patrol Xu‡ Prefecture with armed forces, prompting Xin to commit suicide. He was posthumously ennobled as Prince of Cai upon the accession of Taizu.[ii]

....

ii. In the biographical chapters, the placement of Yun before Xin [his junior] is done simply out of convenience in narrating events.

CHAPTER 19

BIOGRAPHIES OF THE ROYAL FAMILIES: TAIZU OF ZHOU

Empress Chai

Taizu had one empress and three consorts. The Sagely and Majestic Empress, surnamed Chai, was a native of Yaoshan, Xingzhou. She and Taizu hailed from the same village, so he married her. During relative obscurity, Taizu used to drink, gamble, and indulge in heroic escapades without regard for nuanced behavior—conduct curtailed after repeated reproof from the Empress. The physical demeanor of Taizu being uniquely august, the Empress had every faith in his future greatness and served him with scrupulous deference. The Empress had died before his accession, so an edict announced, "The former Lady Chai, posthumously invested as Empress, receives the title Noble and Majestic, Shengmu."

Pure Consort Yang

The Pure Consort Yang was native to Zhending, Zhenzhou, her father Hongyu a one-time deputy custodian of Zhending. Based on her physical beauty, the Consort was recruited for the Prince of Zhao's palace, serving Wang Rong. Rong was later slain by Zhang Wenli as tumult overtook Zhenzhou, the Consort mixing among the common people before marrying a local man, Shi Guangfu, who died some years later. The Lady Chai was already dead when Taizu, learning of the Consort's physical beauty and worthy character, married her as principal wife. The Consort's own death in the Tianfu era had coincided with Taizu's tenure at

Taiyuan, under the reign of Han Gaozu, so she was interred in the nearby suburbs of Taiyuan.

Posthumous investiture as the Pure Consort attended the accession of Taizu in the ninth month of the inaugural year of Guangshun [C.E. 951]. Younger brother Yang Tingzhang was appointed director of the Flying Dragon Right Guard, but he declined, saying, "Your Subject, whose father is already old, would rather the post go to him." Taizu concurred, "The very same thought came to me. Hardly can your father be overlooked!" He summoned Hongyu to court, but old age prevented him from going, so authorities went to his home to bestow honors as grandmaster of imperial recreations with gold and purple insignia and deputy custodian of Zhending.

Taizu was buried at the Songling mausoleum [near Kaifeng]. One empress and three consorts should have been buried with him. With Taiyuan having eluded Zhou conquest, Shizong directed the relevant authorities to construct a vacant tomb adjacent to Songling, in anticipation of a future burial there for the Consort. During the inaugural year of Xiande [C.E. 954], Shizong defeated Liu Min at Gaoping before undertaking the assault on Taiyuan. The city, sealed up by defenders, came under a Zhou blockade, enabling the Consort's coffin to be escorted to Songling for reburial.

Precious Consort Zhang

Precious Consort Zhang was native to Zhending, Zhenzhou. Her grandfather, Ji, was administrative assistant to the Chengde governor and honorary minister of war. Her father, Tongzhi, had served as consultant under the Prince of Zhao, Wang Rong, eventually to become honorary minister of public works. Turmoil plagued Zhenzhou in the wake of Rong's death, so Zhuangzong directed Youzhou governor Fu Cunshen to lead suppression armies against Zhang Wenli. His assisting commander, Wu Congjian, had stayed at the home of the Consort and her vulnerability as a young child stirred his compassion. Congjian brought her back to his native Taiyuan to be wife to his son.

Sometime later, Taizu was serving Gaozu at Taiyuan when he recruited Lady Zhang as his wife: Consort Yang had died by then, the son of Wu Congjian having died also. She ultimately was elevated to the Lady of Wu after Taizu achieved stature. Occupation of the capital by Taizu's armies incited the Han court to dispatch Liu Zhu to liquidate his family, the Consort perishing along with all of his sons. She was posthumously invested Precious Consort upon Taizu's formal accession.

Virtuous Consort Miss Dong, Her Sons Tong, and Xin, and Her Nephews Shouyuan, Fengchao, and Xun

The Virtuous Consort Dong [C.E. 915–953] was a native of Lingshou, Zhenzhou. Her grandfather, Wenguang, once served the Tang as administrative adjutant for Shenzhou, and her father Guangsi was one-time sheriff of Zhaoqing, Zhaozhou. The Consort proved precociously intelligent: from the outset of learning to speak, she could identify the musical note by simply hearing a sound.

At seven *sui* she was lost during turmoil at Zhenzhou, a military attaché to the Luzhou governor finding her and taking her home, mixing her into his military convoy. The commander's wife once had a daughter who died at birth, so she felt instant compassion for the Consort and raised her like her own, treating the girl better than her blood mother. Over the course of five to six years, the Consort's original family missed her with such anguish that brother Dong Yu conducted searches among the people, her location impossible to determine. Once the Luzhou commander served in the capital and became acquainted with Yu, he gladly arranged her return. She was thirteen *sui*.

Dong Yu later married the Consort to Liu Jinchao, a fellow villager who served the Jin dynasty as courtier. The husband perished at the hands of Khitan barbarians during their invasion of the capital, the Consort hence living as widow in Luoyang. The future Taizu of Zhou was assisting Gaozu of Han in a sweep from Taiyuan to the capital upon passing through Luoyang, where Taizu learned of the Consort's noble comportment. He proposed to marry her. The central palace of the empress had no occupant when Taizu founded the empire, so she was invested as the Virtuous consort, only to die in the third year of Guangshun [C.E. 953] at thirty-nine *sui*. The Consort had three older brothers: Yu rose to grand right admonisher to the heir-apparent, Xuanzhi and Ziming both rose to prefect.

Formerly, the Emperor's mutiny at Weizhou had caused the Han to retaliate by surrounding his residence with troops: Precious Consort Zhang, sons Qingge and Yige, and nephews Shouyun, Fengchao, and Dingge were all executed. The maternity of Qingge and Yige is unknown. Upon accession, Taizu mandated posthumous rank for the deceased: second son, Qingge, as grand marshal with the formal name Tong; third son Yige as dignitary for public works with the name Xin; imperial nephews Shouyun as general of the Palace Left Guard ("Shouyun" was later changed to "Shouyuan," for "Yun" sounded like "Yong [Rong]," the taboo character in Emperor Shizong's name), Fengchao as general of the Palace-Gate Left Guard, and Dingge as general of the Thousand-Bull Left Guard with the name Xun.

During the fourth year of Xiande, under the Shizong reign, twenty-sixth day of the fourth month, the summer [C.E. May 28, 957], the palace issued a proclamation: "Ritual propriety demands the expression of human sentiment while beneficence demands the expression of grief. This being common between friends, the case for compassion is even more compelling here. My former younger brothers, Tong and Xin, honored posthumously as grand guardian and dignitary for public works, respectively, both perished at the outset of our illustrious enterprise without reaching adulthood, my love for them genuinely heartfelt. Tong will receive the posthumous rank of grand mentor and the title Prince of Tan, Xin receiving rank as dignitary for education and the title Prince of Qi." It was further proclaimed: "Shouyuan, general of the Palace Left Guard; Fengchao, general of the Palace-Gate Left Guard; and Xun, general of the Thousand-Bull Left Guard, among others—my deceased royal first cousins—never reached maturity owing to conditions of dynastic tumult. My reflections on these innocent victims stir unforgettable memories. Shouyuan is now honored as commandant of the Left Guard, Fengchao as commandant of the Right Guard, and Xun as commandant of the Martial Right Guard."

CHAPTER 20

BIOGRAPHIES OF THE ROYAL FAMILIES: SHIZONG OF ZHOU

Chai Shouli

The Woman Chai, the Sagacious and Majestic Empress of Taizu of Zhou, in the absence of sons, adopted the son of elder brother Shouli as her own. This was Shizong.

Shouli had the courtesy name Kerang. A member of the Empress's family, he received honors as grandmaster of imperial recreations with silver and blue insignia, honorary minister of personnel, and concurrent censor-in-chief. With the accession of Shizong, he was elevated to grandmaster of imperial recreations with gold and purple insignia, honorary dignitary for education, and chamberlain for imperial entertainments. Shouli's retirement was spent in Luoyang. For the entirety of Shizong's reign, he never visited the capital and court aides dared not mention the problem, employing the simple protocol for imperial uncles in treating him.

Shouli tended to be rather arbitrary and dissolute. After he murdered someone at the marketplace, the matter was exposed by the relevant authorities, but Shizong refused further inquiry. At the time, Wang Pu, Wang Yan, Wang Yanchao, Han Lingkun, and others, members of his cohort of commanders and ministers, all had fathers residing in Luoyang. They consorted with Shouli on a near daily basis and he indulged their whim, causing many a Luoyang resident to avoid this feared group, dubbed the "Powerful Ten Godfathers." Shouli died at seventy-two *sui*, achieving grand mentor standing.

WE LAMENT. The charity between father and son should be supreme. According to Mencius, when Gusou murdered another man during Shun's reign as Son of Heaven, Shun preferred to relinquish the world and covertly take flight, bearing his father on his own back. The world could do without Shun, he reasoned, but could not do without ultimate justice; he could relinquish his sovereignty over the world, but not punish his own father.[1] These words provide a foundational principle for the ages. Yet on many occasions, reality certainly falls short of ideals. What is best for a Son of Heaven who must bear the weight of the dynastic lifeline, preserve the institutions of government, and sustain the dignity of the court—someone without the luxury of quiet flight?

I have read the histories of Zhou to learn of Shouli's act of murder and Shizong's suppression of the incident without further inquiry, such that he embraced the weighty responsibilities of the world while also extending supreme devotion to his father. Shizong could thereby countenance the indiscretion of bending laws to invigorate the moral way of father and son, his actions in accord with righteous principle and reflecting his appreciation of relative worth. The superior man, in the conduct of affairs, must quite simply separate the important from the unimportant: the slighting of punishments may be minor, but failings in filial piety are grave. Punishments serve to inhibit people from wrongdoing, while filial piety instructs them in goodness. Their purposes being one, which should receive stress? Punishing a single person will not necessarily create a world where no one kills. Yet the murder of one's father involves negation of one's natural constitution and disavowal of human mores. So, which deserves greater stress?

In balancing the important against the unimportant, even when sovereignty over the world cannot be surrendered, a ruler's father cannot be punished either. Had Shun and Shizong found some way to prevent Gusou and Shouli from killing others, their filial duty would have been better served. But when circumstances prove less than ideal, the weighing of relative import should attend any action. Shizong's balancing of the relative proved stunningly enlightened.

Empress Liu

Shizong had three empresses. The Chaste and Charitable Empress Liu [d. 951] was of unknown ancestry, having married Shizong during his days of obscurity. Once Shizong became commander of the Palace-Gate Left Guard and earned the noble title Lord of Pengcheng, he left the Empress behind in the capital to join Taizu in the Weizhou campaign; so, after Taizu rebelled, the Han court liquidated Shizong's entire family in retribution. Posthumous investment as the Lady of Pengcheng occasioned Taizu's accession. In the fourth month of the fourth year of Xiande, in the reign of Shizong [C.E. 957], the court mandated a new investiture as "Empress" for the Lady of Pengcheng and conferral of the title Chaste and Charitable, Zhenhui. Her mausoleum was called Huiling.

The Empresses Fu

The Avowedly Moral Empress Fu [d. 956] was the granddaughter of Cunshen, the Prince of Qin, and daughter of Yanqing, the Prince of Wei. Having descended from generations of princes and an eminent line of commanders and ministers, she proved sharp, resolute, and highly ambitious.

Formerly, she had been married to the son of Li Shouzhen, Chongxun. Shouzhen, who rose to Hedong governor under the Han dynasty, had already acquired ambitions of treachery. Upon learning of a fortuneteller adept at determining an individual's good or bad fortunes based on the sound of their voice, Shouzhen arranged for him to test the voices of some family members. The fortuneteller, startled by the voice of the Empress, declared, "Here we have the mother of the world." An increasingly imperious Shouzhen affirmed, "My daughter-in-law being mother of the world, there is no question that I will claim it." By now, he had decided to rebel, causing the Han court to dispatch the future Taizu of Zhou to lead the suppression. He overtook the city a year later. Chongxun fully recognized the inevitability of death, so he personally killed his own family. As he prepared to kill the Empress, however, she took cover and concealed herself under the curtains of her bedroom. His hurried search for her having failed, Chongxun killed himself.

When Han warriors entered her home, the Empress sat in the reception hall with dignified demeanor. Looking at the troops, she declared, "The Gentleman, Guo Wei, is an old acquaintance of my father.[2] Your sort would be wise not to violate me!" Witnessing this, the troops dared not presume upon her. News of the incident impressed Taizu—the spectacle of a solitary girl making mutinous troops afraid to violate her—and he consoled and reassured her by returning her to Yanqing. Taizu's decision to refrain from killing her had moved the Empress, who subsequently treated him as father. Her mother believed the Empress to be blessed by Heaven, having single-handedly escaped the enemy's swords even as her husband's entire family was liquidated; she thus encouraged her to shave her head and become a nun. The Empress refused, stating, "Life and death represent the handiwork of Heaven. Why should I deform my own body and hair?"

Taizu had already been charitable toward the Empress, but Shizong with his sharp intellect developed an even greater affinity for her upon hearing the story. Thus, she was selected as principal wife following Empress Liu's death and invested Empress after his formal accession. A temperamental Shizong often had fits of anger, only to express remorse later: in moments of anger with his attendants, the Empress always calmly observed his facial expressions and then explained matters methodically, at which point Shizong tended to lose his stridency. He thereby came to hold her in growing esteem.

In the campaign of Shizong against the Huai region [C.E. 956], the Empress did not support his personal command of armies and admonished forcefully against it, her words only to go unheeded. Shizong and his men, beset with the oppressive heat and heavy rains of summer, for long accomplished nothing strategically, which caused a nervous Empress to take ill and expire. Some at court proposed simplified burial rites owing to the ongoing war. In consequence, the official rank and file was instructed to meet at the western palace for provisional audience and relinquish mourning costumes after three days, while the Emperor shed his own costumes after seven days. She was buried at Xinzheng, the Yiling mausoleum.

The *Lady Fu*, younger sister of the Avowedly Moral Empress, was later installed as empress [C.E. 959]. At the outset of our own dynasty, she was relocated to the western palace and dubbed the Empress Dowager of Zhou.

The Seven Sons of Shizong

Shizong had seven sons: the eldest was Yige‡, the next two initially had no formal names, then came Emperor Gong, then Xirang, Xijin, and Xihui. Maternity is known for none of them. Yige and the next two siblings were executed by the Han court, so after the accession of Taizu, the court conferred the personal name Yi for the imperial grandson [Yige‡] and the title commandant of the Valorous Left Guard. It also conferred upon grandsons Cheng and Xian the titles commandant of the Martial Left Guard and commandant of the Garrison Left Guard, respectively.

In the third year of Xiande, leading courtiers requested investitures for imperial clansmen. Shizong wanted to defer such considerations, however. Noting that the empire, still in its infancy, had yet to extend charity and instill faith in the people, he preferred first to make some grand strategic and moral feats as cause for celebration across the realm. During the next summer, twenty-sixth day of the fourth month [C.E. May 28, 957], investiture of the sons of Taizu received priority. The palace further mandated as follows: "It is the moral way for father and son that the wise and worthy not be forgotten. Reflecting on these premature deaths, my heart is burdened with sorrow and remorse. In the former travails of these one-time imperial sons—commandant of the Valorous Left Guard (Yi), commandant of the Martial Left Guard (Cheng), and commandant of the Garrison Left Guard (Xian)—there is much to be cherished and mourned. We should rightfully elevate their noble status by one character and their posthumous titles by three levels: Yi should receive the title of Grand Marshal and investiture as Prince of Yue, Cheng should receive the title of Grand Mentor and investiture as Prince of Wu, and Xian should receive the title of Grand Guardian and investiture as Prince of Han." Imperial sons then alive were not invested.

In the sixth year, after recovering the Three Passes to the north, the Emperor contracted some disease that forced him back to the capital. On the ninth day of the sixth month [C.E. July 17, 959], imperial son Zongxun received special promotion as generalissimo of the Left Guard and investiture as Prince of Liang, and Zongrang received honors as generalissimo of the Valorous Left Guard and investiture as Duke of Yan. Emperor Shizong expired ten days later, succeeded by the Prince of Liang, namely, Emperor Gong. During the eighth month of the same year, the personal name of Zongrang was changed to Xirang, his investiture confirmed as Prince of Cao. To the extent that Xijin and Xihui received no noble titles in the past, Xijin was named commandant of the Martial Right Guard and invested Prince of Ji, Xihui named commandant of the Metropolitan Guard and invested Prince of Qi. Xijin passed away in the tenth month of the second year of Qiande [C.E. 964], under our own dynasty. Information is lacking on the deaths of Xirang and Xihui.

WE LAMENT. Ultimate consensus reflects the shared opinion of the world. A father sometimes is not free to act on personal whim, however much he loves his son, when right or wrong, veracity or mendacity are involved. As Taizu of Zhou raised armies at Taiyuan, the Han court directed Liu Zhu to execute his extended family in the capital, an act of ultimate savagery and malice. Taizu later acceded to the throne and sent a messenger to reprimand Liu Zhu, whose words remained unrepentant. Although he despised him, Taizu ultimately opted against extended punishment for Zhu's family due to the veracity of his words. During posthumous investitures for his own dead wife and sons, Taizu limited himself to expressions of profound inner anguish without daring to denounce the Han [for killing them], clearly recognizing his own mendacity. The edict is briefly cited to expose the shame felt by this Zhou-dynasty ruler.

CHAPTERS 21–23

BIOGRAPHIES OF LIANG SUBJECTS

WE LAMENT. Mencius once said, "No righteous wars occurred in the Spring and Autumn period,"[1] to which I would add, "no wholly ethical subjects" lived in the Five Dynasties. The word "none" does not suggest the absence of a single person, merely that there were scarcely any. I have identified only three men under "Martyrs to Virtue." Officials whose service did not extend into a second dynasty are clustered under their respective empires—the inspiration for composing "Biographies of Subjects for the Liang, Tang, Jin, Han, and Zhou." For others whose service is not limited to one dynasty, whereby clustering under a single empire is impossible, I have composed "Miscellaneous Biographies." To appear among the "miscellaneous" should shame the superior man of sincerity, yet servitors of a single dynasty do not always deserve esteem, so the reader must scrutinize the particulars of their virtues and vices.

Jing Xiang

His courtesy name Zizhen, Jing Xiang [d. C.E. 923] was native to Pingyi, Tongzhou. He professed to be a scion of Hui, the Prince of Pingyang in Tang times. Owing to fondness for learning in youth, he came to draft proclamations rather deftly and even made a failed attempt at the official examination of the Qianfu era, subsequently becoming a retainer at Daliang [Bian]. Once fellow villager Wang Fa became deputy surveillance commissioner for Bianzhou, Xiang entered his service.

After some time, Wang Fa no longer advanced men of talent, leaving Jing Xiang ever desperate in his capacity as retainer, so he started drafting memoranda for others that circulated within the command. The future Taizu began with no knowledge of books and hence acquired an affinity for Xiang's writings and the vulgarisms contained therein. He thus said to Fa, "I hear that you have an old acquaintance. Perhaps he can join us?" Taizu also asked Xiang, upon their meeting, "You have studied the *Spring and Autumn Annals*, I hear. What sorts of events do the *Annals* record?" "Merely the rivalries and wars of feudal lords," Jing responded. Taizu continued, "Is there anything in techniques of war that I might utilize?" "A military strategist must adjust to change and exploit the unexpected to seize victory," Xiang added. "The *Spring and Autumn Annals* contains ancient techniques of no use today." The response immensely delighted Taizu, who wished to give him a military office, but Xiang had other preferences and accepted an assignment as inspector of postal relay stations.

As Taizu battled Caizhou armies in the Bianzhou suburbs, Jing Xiang frequently assisted in setting strategies, often with success. Taizu's joy was tempered by chagrin over the rather late recruitment of Xiang, so he tended to address him spontaneously about matters. Taizu received Emperor Zhaozong on his return to Changan from Qizhou‡, and the Emperor summoned Xiang and Li Zhen to the Yanxi villa to commend them, appointing Xiang as chamberlain for supplemental revenues.

Previously, Taizu was often posted at imperial halls, while Emperor Zhaozong sensed himself vulnerable to apprehension by some within his bodyguard. Thus, he pretended to be loosening a shoestring as he gazed at Taizu, who now knelt to tie the shoestring for him. No one in the vicinity dared to move, as perspiration saturated Taizu's back. Hereafter, he rarely stepped forward again before the Emperor. Zhaozong held a banquet at Chongxun Hall after relocation to Luoyang. Halfway into the feast, he arose and summoned Taizu to an inner hall with the intent of assigning some duty, but an ever anxious Taizu declined on the pretext of illness. "If you prefer not to come, you can send Jing Xiang instead," Emperor Zhaozong declared. Taizu abruptly motioned for Xiang to leave, which he did, feigning to be drunk.

Upon vanquishing Zhao Kuangning and claiming the prefectures of Jing and Xiang, Taizu proceeded with a southern Huai offensive. Jing Xiang was strident in opposing the move, arguing that armies newly victorious should rather instill awe through circumspect posture. Taizu refused his counsel. His troops encountered heavy rain upon leaving Guangzhou, barely managing to advance. Once they did advance against Shouzhou, the assault failed and the casualties were so heavy that Taizu now felt profoundly contrite and bitter. Returning in rage, he murdered leading Tang-dynasty courtiers to almost the last man. Increasingly, he found Xiang deserving of trust.

Many of the Liang intrigues culminating in regicide and usurpation originated with Jing Xiang. The Palace Secretariat of Tang times had formerly been staffed by eunuchs, so Taizu changed the office to the Bureau of Venerable Governance upon assuming the throne, and he appointed Xiang commissioner. Promotions ensued as minister of war and academician of Jinluan Hall. Xiang was a man of profound cunning and grandiose schemes, and through thirty years of military actions, Taizu invariably involved him in decisions of any consequence. A thoroughly dedicated and disciplined Xiang slept neither day nor night, professing that only astride a horse could he manage to rest. Taizu could be stubborn, impulsive, and inapproachable. When he disapproved of something, therefore, Xiang carefully avoided direct discussion. Instead, he gingerly approached the pros and cons in hopes of stirring Taizu's awareness, often changing his views in the process.

Upon conquering Xuzhou¶, Taizu apprehended the beloved consort of Shi Pu, surnamed Liu, and came to love and favor her. Liu was the one-time wife of Shang Rang, then wife to Jing Xiang. Even after Xiang achieved some stature, she attended to Taizu and regarded as unremarkable her movements in and out of his bedroom. The matter rather troubled Xiang, inciting Woman Liu to say derisively to him, "You apparently consider me to have lost my virtue to bandits! Contrarily, Shang Rang once held ministerial rank under Huang Chao and Shi Pu was a loyal subject of empire. Being with someone of your station is utter humiliation for me and I beg to part ways." Out of concern for Taizu's reaction, Xiang apologized to dissuade her. Woman Liu tended to clad her carriage horses ostentatiously and employed a receptions officer to conduct business with governors. The rich and powerful commonly fraternized with her, and the affairs addressed by confidantes were never conveyed to Xiang. The esteemed families of the day often did her bidding.

Yougui succeeded to power after Taizu expired, and he feared that Jing Xiang, a trusted aide to the deceased emperor, might conspire against him. So that he would be excluded from the court's inner circle, Xiang was replaced by Li Zhen at the Bureau of Venerable Governance, becoming director of the Palace Secretariat with ministerial standing. Xiang intuited Yougui's fear of him, so he repeatedly professed illness and never actually handled affairs.

With the accession of Emperor Mo, Zhao Yan and cohort came to dominate the court and created rifts with older statesmen, an unfulfilled Jing Xiang now feeling ever melancholy. The Liang later lost the northern Yellow River region entirely and confronted the Prince of Jin's forces at Yangliu township [Jizhou]. Xiang now commented, "Formerly, despite possessing half of the northern Yellow River region, and despite the martial valor of the Former Emperor and the ferociousness of commanders, we failed to prevail over the Jin. Its strength now swells with each day as Liang power correspondingly shrinks.

Your Majesty inhabits the palace's inner recesses and confers with either personal intimates or self-serving relatives. How can you expect to accomplish anything meaningful? Jin armies have attacked Yangliu, I hear, with Li Yazi [Cunxu] crossing the Yellow River ahead of troops carrying firewood on his back. Your Majesty complacently indulges in literary arts and evinces an affinity for Confucian refinement, leaving command of armies to He Gui. How can he possibly rival their residual vanguard? Despite my personal exhaustion, Your Subject has enjoyed the empire's profound charity and offer to exert myself, should the empire fall short of talent." Yan and cohort considered the comments incendiary, thwarting Xiang's deployment.

Later, Emperor Mo became anxious after Wang Yanzhang's defeat at Zhongdu and directed Duan Ning to the northern side of the Yellow River. Ning commanded the cream of the Liang army at the time, but his own seditious impulses left him awkward, so Ning refused to come. The Emperor now desperately cried out to Jing Xiang, "I ordinarily slighted your words such that conditions have reached the urgency of today. Please bear no grudge and instruct me on a possible recourse." Xiang countered, "Your Subject assisted the Former Emperor for over thirty years. I may be minister today, but I am actually a mere slave to the Zhu house, willing to serve Your Majesty as if a young man. This loyal heart of mine can scarcely withhold anything of potential value. I previously challenged Your Majesty's trust in Duan Ning, and now Ning refuses to come, while pressures from the enemy are acute. I desire to counsel Your Majesty, but the counsel will surely go unheeded once petty men start to plant rifts. Witnessing the demise of the ancestral temples is beyond my endurance, so I beg to die first!" Ruler and subject faced each other, weeping loudly.

Jing Xiang and Li Zhen had both enjoyed the confidences of Taizu. With the occupation of Bianzhou by Zhuangzong of Tang [Li Cunxu], an amnesty for all courtiers of Liang was issued. Li Zhen remarked gleefully to Xiang, "An edict having cleansed away all, I will soon serve at a new court." He invited Xiang to enter for the audience with him. Xiang stopped off at the Gaotou carriage house for the night, and, by the next morning, companions informed him, "Commissioner Li has entered for audience already." Xiang responded with a sigh, "I genuinely mistook Li Zhen for a gentleman. How can I stand once more before the Jianguo gates of our dynasty?" He then strangled himself to death.

Zhu Zhen and Li Tangbin

A native of Feng County, Xuzhou¶, a youthful Zhu Zhen [d. C.E. 889] and Pang Shigu had followed the future Taizu and others as bandits. Once commander, Zhen had a facility for managing armies and recruiting warriors, so Taizu deployed him to create military institutions at the Xuanwu command. Soon after he became governor. Zhen also proved exceedingly rigorous in selecting commanders and training troops. Taizu chose to subordinate to Zhen all soldiers recruited by his commanders as well as those to surrender, with Zhen personally selecting fifty commanders, all capable of deployment. He invariably appeared in battle—from the Liang defeat of Huang Chao, to its rout of Qin Zongquan, and ultimately its absorption of Yan and Yun prefectures—his valor peerless among the various commanders.

Taizu of Liang and the Prince of Jin had together pursued Huang Chao eastward when they passed by Bianzhou on the return trip. Lodged at Shangyuan Post, Taizu instructed Zhu Zhen to lead a contingent in a nighttime raid on the Prince of Jin. The Prince absconded, but Zhen murdered every subordinate left behind.

When mutineers at the Yicheng command expelled An Shiru, he fled to the Liang. Zhu Zhen was sent by Taizu to rush Huazhou. His men encountered a snowstorm en route, but Zhen pressed them to quicken the pace to reach the city walls within one night. The troops scaled them. The leaders at Yicheng had not anticipated the arrival of Liang forces owing to the snowfall, and, unprepared, the command succumbed.

Qin Zongquan opened an offensive against the Liang, deploying Lu Tang and Zhang Zhi. Liang might remained modest, then, and the regime was often menaced by Zongquan. To enlist troops from Zi and Qing† prefectures, Taizu named Zhu Zhen prefect of Zi. The detachments commander under Zhen, Zhang Renyu, then requested of him, "For military men who violate orders, might I propose beheading first and notification later?" Zhen retorted, "Presumably, you intend to be the sole murderer!" Zhen summarily decapitated Renyu, instead, in a symbolic act that gratified all of his troops. When he returned with more than ten thousand enlistees, an elated Taizu pronounced, "The renegades had reached our suburbs: even if they chose to trample our wheat fields, I would have been helpless! But alas, the simple arrival of Zhen has now saved the day. The renegades have rested their men to recoup spirits, believing our army modest in size; they are also unaware of Zhen's arrival and presume that we will cling to an entrenched defense. We should thus strike fast to catch them off guard." Troops were now unleashed to raid Zhi and cohort, defeating them to deliver a fatal blow to Zongquan. Liang warriors now witnessed a dramatic revelry in martial zeal—Zhen's delivery of reinforcements creating it all.

Zhu Zhen accompanied Taizu in attacks on Zhu Xuan, yielding the acquisition of Caozhou and apprehension of prefect Qiu Hongli. They claimed Puzhou as well, where prefect Zhu Yu fled to Yunzhou. Zhen stayed behind for the Yun offensive, once Taizu returned to Bianzhou. Within twenty *li* of the prefecture, Zhen unleashed an advance of crack troops to provoke the enemy. Yun defenders refused to leave the city. Yu composed in guile a letter of surrender while secretly instructing a messenger to invite Zhen inside with promises of opening the gates to receive him. Zhen believed him and led troops by night to the city wall, knocking at the gates. The gates were opened for Zhen's men to enter as Yu climbed embrasures atop the wall, then dropped the gates after Zhen's men had passed through the barbican wall.[2] Yun troops, perched atop the wall, proceeded to pellet them with stones from launchers, and Zhen's men all perished at the wall. Zhen barely managed his own escape, although Taizu refrained from reprimanding him.

When mutineers at the Wei/Bo command incarcerated Le Yanzhen, Taizu entrusted the Weizhou relief effort to Zhu Zhen. He felled nearby Liyang, Linhe, and Ligu counties while dispatching Nie Jin and Fan Jushi to plunder Chanzhou. Two thousand troops in the "Leopard Army" of Wei were murdered at Linhuang, as Zhen's martial ardor reverberated across the northern Yellow River region. He withdrew once Weizhou mutineers murdered Yanzhen. The Liang proceeded to raid Xuzhou¶ and unleash Zhen for an advance against Feng County, which succumbed as Shi Pu met defeat at Wukang County. Zhen now quartered men at Xiao County, assisted by Li Tangbin.

Li Tangbin [C.E. 889] came from Shanzhou. Initially a detachments commander under Shang Rang, he was vanquished by Taizu amid hostilities at the Weishi gate [of Kaifeng] and surrendered to the Liang. Tangbin often served alongside Zhu Zhen as Liang armies plundered the four corners, establishing a comparable reputation for martial awe, his valor even surpassing Zhen. Whenever beleaguered by minor setbacks in battle, Zhen would emerge victorious after Tangbin lent assistance. Zhen once provided private cover within his military unit for his own family, stirring suspicions of ulterior motives in Taizu, who thus planted Tangbin as a mole. Zhen did not cooperate with Tangbin, who found conditions sufficiently unbearable to abscond overnight for Xuanwu [Kaifeng]. Zhen followed on horseback, and the two men exchanged invectives before Taizu, who cherished the talents of both men and mediated matters.

While quartered at Xiao County, Zhu Zhen learned of Taizu's impending arrival and alerted his military to arrange lodging and stables. Tangbin's division commander, Yan Jiao, had proven tardy in arranging stables, and a military aide intervened to direct matters. When Jiao complained to Tangbin, he referred the matter to Zhen, who now angrily rose with sword drawn. Tangbin adjusted his clothes and approached Zhen, who beheaded him and then sent a messenger to court charging Tangbin with sedition. Jing Xiang sequestered the messenger upon arrival in the morning, worried about Taizu's raging temper. He met the messenger that evening, but proposed waiting until the next morning for Taizu's temper to subside. The messenger was brought to meet Taizu that night. Taizu was simply shocked at the news, yet the lateness of the hour prevented him from venting his anger. Xiang now calmly laid plans with Taizu, pretending a day later to have imprisoned Tangbin's wife and sons. Taizu subsequently left for Zhen's camps, which were only one league from Xiao County. Zhen appeared there to greet him when Taizu ordered him seized by bodyguards. Over ten commanders, including Huo Cun, kowtowed in pleading to spare Zhen. An utterly livid Taizu, hoisting a northern chair to hurl their way, queried, "Why did you men not make a similar effort to spare Tangbin when Zhen murdered him?" Cun and cohort pulled away as Zhen killed himself by strangling.

Pang Shigu

Native to Nanhua County, Caozhou, Pang Shigu [d. C.E. 897] began with the personal name Cong. Early in the tenure of the future Taizu as Xuanxu governor, he acquired five hundred horses and formed a cavalry unit. Shigu commanded the unit, which distinguished itself in vanquishing Huang Chao and Qin Zongquan.

Taizu later turned to Shigu after an unsuccessful raid on Shi Pu, leaving him to maintain the siege. Shigu took Suqian County, then advanced to Lüliang [Xuzhou¶] to fort his men. Shi Pu emerged with twenty thousand men, Shigu defeating him and beheading two thousand. Sun Ru now expelled Yang Xingmi from Yangzhou to claim the prefecture, as tumult engulfed Huainan circuit. Taizu hence directed Shigu to cross the Huai River for an assault on Ru, who vanquished Shigu. Zhu Zhen and Li Tangbin were dead by now, their residual troops divided between Shigu and Huo Cun. Taizu then unleashed the Prince of Chen, Zhu Youyu, to attack Xuzhou¶, but Zhu Jin intervened militarily to rescue Shi Pu. Youyu prevailed over Pu at Shifo Mountain, as Zhu Jin regrouped the remnants to withdraw. Taizu nonetheless held Youyu responsible for failing to pursue a vulnerable enemy and reassigned his armies to Shigu. Overrunning Xu¶ Prefecture, Shigu decapitated Pu and became interim regent for Xu¶, upon Taizu's petition to the Tang court. Once Liang armies approached the Ji River in their Yunzhou offensive, Shigu harvested trees to make a causeway, then ordered center contingents to cross the river by night.[3] Zhu Xuan fled to Zhongdu, only to be killed.

Having conquered Yan and Yun prefectures, Taizu unleashed Pang Shigu and Ge Congzhou against Yang Xingmi at Huainan [C.E. 897]. The former departed from Qingkou and the latter from Anfeng. Ever since the early days of obscurity, Shigu served Taizu with utmost deference and never left his side. He never departed on independent missions without advance instructions on strategy. And his army did not act wantonly without mandates from Taizu. Because of the inferior geographic conditions of Qingkou, where Shigu's men were quartered, someone petitioned to erect barricades on the highlands, which Shigu refused for lack of approval from Taizu. As Huai armies ruptured dams to flood the region, the petitioner exclaimed, "Alas, the tide unleashed by Huai armies is imminent!" Shigu summarily beheaded him, believing such words might incite the troops. His men could no longer fight once floodwaters arrived, and Shigu was killed.

WE LAMENT. To be sure, the fortunes of war can defy easy explanations! Liang armies were the mightiest in the world, while Wu warriors were trivialized as weak. Yet in successive sorties against Wu, Pang Shigu faced speedy routs that ultimately claimed his life. Taizu personally campaigned sometime later against Shouchun, departing from Guangshan, and defeat was the outcome as well. Ever since the death of Gao Pian, the Tang court had vested concurrent authority over Huainan to Liang governors, the ensuing contention with Sun Ru and Yang Xingmi over three decades ending in defeats for all three Liang campaigns. In effect, the supremely mighty in contest with the supremely weak produced outcomes that simply defy ordinary reason. The art of warfare contains methods for the few to vanquish the many or the weak to conquer the strong. Wu seems scarcely capable, however, of commanding the requisite skills. If not timing and opportunity, how else do we explain things? It is therefore said, "However lethal one's weapons, war remains a risky affair."[4] Should we not be mindful?

Ge Congzhou

His courtesy name Tongmei, Ge Congzhou [d. C.E. 913] was native to Zhencheng County, Puzhou. Accompanying Huang Chao in youth, he surrendered to the Liang after defeat in battle. He later assisted Taizu in the Caizhou offensive, where Taizu fell from his horse and Congzhou lifted him back, sustaining injuries to his face and multiple punctures to his body during ground skirmishes with the enemy. Detachments commander Zhang Yanshou now charged from their side to permit Congzhou and Taizu to leave. Taizu hence relieved the other commanders to employ Congzhou and Yanshou alone as senior commanders.

During the plunders of Ying¤ and Bo¶ prefectures, Qin Zongquan engaged Liang armies at Jiaoyi County. Ge Congzhou captured one of his commanders, Wang Juan. The ability of Zhu Zhen's armies to return intact—in the wake of retreating at Zi and Qing† prefectures and unexpected battles with belligerents to the east—reflects largely the merit of Congzhou. Zhang Quanyi later stormed Li Hanzhi at Heyang, Hanzhi fleeing to the Prince of Jin [Li Keyong] to rally for reinforcements against Quanyi, who in turn begged the Liang for relief. Taizu dispatched Congzhou and Ding Hui, who vanquished Jin forces at the Yun River. Feng Ba of Luzhou now murdered Jin commander Li Kegong to surrender to Liang. Taizu had Congzhou occupy the prefecture, although harassment by Jin regulars prevented him from securing the city and he fled to Heyang. Taizu followed with an offensive against Weizhou, Congzhou and Ding Hui first felling Liyang and Linhe counties before rendezvousing with Taizu at Neihuang to defeat Wei forces at Yongdingqiao. Congzhou and Ding Hui assisted in the assault on Suzhou, where they flooded the city with water and overpowered it. Taizu now faced a standoff with Zhu Jin at Yan Prefecture, so Congzhou stayed behind to encircle it. With the city sealed off and Zhu Jin refusing to emerge, Congzhou guilefully announced the arrival of reinforcements for Yan and gave the appearance of departing for Gaowu County to evade them. In fact, he had returned undetected deep into the night to positions at the city wall. Zhu Jin was convinced of his departure and released men to secure the outer moat, whereupon Congzhou's men sallied forth from an ambush to slay more than a thousand.

In the wake of aggression from the Prince of Jin, Weizhou authorities turned to the Liang for relief. Taizu dispatched Hou Yan for the effort, and he erected defense fortifications along the Huan River but refused to emerge for battle. An indignant Taizu replaced him with Ge Congzhou. Upon reaching the command, Congzhou further enhanced defense fortifications without leaving the city, then carved three concealed sally-ports through the wall to await the enemy. Jin troops did attack and Congzhou's crack troops stormed through the sally-ports to vanquish them. A furious Prince of Jin then personally commanded a sortie against Congzhou to deliver a rout. Yet the Prince's son, Luoluo, was apprehended by Liang armies and conveyed to Weizhou for beheading. Congzhou proceeded with an assault on Yunzhou. Apprehending Zhu Xuan at Zhongdu, he raided Yan Prefecture to expel Zhu Jin. Taizu petitioned the court to name Congzhou interim regent for Yan.

Armies from Yan and Yun prefectures were now deployed for an offensive against the Southern Huai. Departing from Anfeng, the force rendezvoused with Pang Shigu at Qingkou [C.E. 897]. Congzhou had reached Haozhou¶ upon learning of Shigu's death and abruptly returned. He was harassed by Huai pursuers while preparing to cross the Pi River and suffered another rout. At the time, Jin troops issuing from east of the mountain raided Xiang‡ and Wei‡ prefectures, Taizu retaliating by unleashing Congzhou to plunder the eastern mountain region. He overran Ming Prefecture and decapitated prefect Xing Shanyi, then overran Xingzhou to expel prefect Ma Shisu, then felled Ci to murder prefect Yuan Fengtao—vanquishing three prefectures in only five days! Taizu petitioned for his concurrent assignment as interim regent for Xingzhou.

Liu Rengong's offensive against Wei Prefecture had culminated in a massacre at Bei when Luo Shaowei sought relief from the Liang. Congzhou assisted Taizu in the Wei rescue, and they entered the prefectural seat. As armies from Yanzhou¤ assaulted the Guantao gate, Congzhou committed five hundred mounts to battle and affirmed, "A mighty enemy stands before us. We can't look back!" He ordered the gates shut behind him and destroyed eight of the enemy's palisades. As Yan¤ troops fled, he pursued them to Linqing County, where they were driven into the Yu River, with vast numbers drowning to death. Taizu rewarded him with the post of manager-adjutant of the Xuanyi command.

For the offensive against Liu Shouwen at Cang Prefecture [C.E. 900], Taizu entrusted command to Congzhou and oversight for his armies to Jiang Hui. Shouwen turned to his father, Rengong, for assistance and he committed Yan¤ forces. The various commanders of Congzhou were then told by supervisor Hui, "Our Prince entrusted me as your overseer. Yan¤ armies have now arrived, but we should not intercept them militarily: they should instead be allowed to enter the city, where they will accelerate the depletion of rations. Once the city is doubly burdened, we can handily claim it." The commanders seemed to concur, although Congzhou countered angrily, "I, as your generalissimo, control this army. How can a supervising officer speak for me? Hui's views are mere common knowledge. The key to victory or defeat is in my own head, knowledge that Hui hardly possesses!" He exhorted his men, instead, to resist Rengong at Qianning County. Rengong was routed at Laoyati, as Congzhou's men severed more than thirty thousand enemy heads, apprehended a hundred commanders including Ma Shenjiao, and retrieved three thousand horses.

At the time, Liu Shouwen sought additional relief from the Prince of Jin, who authorized raids on Xing and Ming prefectures, as diversion. Congzhou promptly returned to defeat Jin forces at Mount Qing. He now joined Taizu in the Zhenzhou offensive, overpowering Lincheng County, where Wang Rong pleaded for a truce. Congzhou became Ningtai governor at Taizu's request.

Congzhou assisted Shi Shucong in the offensive against the Jin base at Taiyuan, which proved inconclusive. When the Liang attacked Fengxiang to the west, Qingzhou† governor Wang Shifan retaliated by ordering commander Liu Xun to storm Yanzhou [in the northeast]. There, Xun apprehended relatives of Ge Congzhou but chose a beneficent dispensation, not the usual death. Once Taizu returned from Fengxiang, he dispatched Congzhou to attack Xun, Congzhou ultimately convincing him to surrender. Congzhou was named generalissimo of the Imperial Insignia Left Guard after Taizu's accession, but opted for retirement owing to illness; honored instead as generalissimo of the Right Guard, he assumed residence at Yanshi. Further honors as the Zhaoyi governor and investiture as Prince of Chenliu occasioned Emperor Mo's accession, with stipends continuing while at home. Posthumous investiture as grand marshal attended his death.

Kang Huaiying

Native to Yanzhou, Kang Huaiying had served Zhu Jin as military attaché. Jin left to plunder for food in Feng and Pei counties, once the Liang had opened hostilities. Huaiying remained to defend Yan only to surrender it to Liang, Jin absconding for the Wu region [C.E. 897]. The conversion of Huaiying greatly pleased Taizu.

Huaiying later assisted Shi Shucong in an attack on Zhao Kuangning, overpowering Dengzhou. He also served as vanguard for the Liang offensive against Li Maozhen at Qizhou‡ [C.E. 901], pummeling his opponents at Wugong County and slaying more than a thousand of its men. Taizu now exclaimed gleefully, "The town's name is Wugong [martial feat] and this is a genuinely martial accomplishment!" A prize horse was conferred as reward. At the time, Li Zhouyi had deployed troops from Fu‡ and Fang prefectures to relieve Qi‡. Quartered on the Sanyuan border, they were stormed and run off by Huaiying, who returned only after claiming Zhai Prefecture. Huaiying then constructed palisades to the northeast of the Qizhou‡ garrisons at Fengtian County, fortifications attacked by the enemy deep into the night. Wishing not to alarm his men, Huaiying personally led during the night some two thousand warriors in battle. By daybreak, Qi‡ armies disbanded, and he emerged with more than ten punctures to the body. Li Maozhen now mended relations with the Liang, and the Tang Emperor Zhaozong, returning to the capital, honored Huaiying as "Meritorious Subject of Daring Valor in the Imperial Reception."

Taizu rushed Kang Huaiying to Suzhou after an attack from Yang Xingmi, expelling him. Huaiying's appointment as prefect of Suzhou ensued, then governor of Baoyi. Defecting from the Liang, Ding Hui surrendered Luzhou to the Prince of Jin. Taizu responded by naming Huaiying bandit-suppressing commissioner. A strictly worded admonition from Taizu, prior to leaving, left Huaiying flustered and convinced him that Luzhou could certainly be claimed on schedule, so he encircled the city with dual ramparts.

The Jin prince dispatched Zhou Dewei, forting at Luanliu, to launch successive raids on the ramparts. Huaiying dared not engage him in battle, so Taizu assigned a replacement, Li Si'an, demoting Huaiying to inspector-in-chief. Si'an similarly achieved nothing after some time, an utterly livid Taizu now dismissing him to assign pacification duties to Liu Zhijun of Tongzhou.

In advance of Liu Zhijun's arrival at the Luzhou command, Taizu personally reached neighboring Zezhou, intending to assist and oversee the armies of Kang Huaiying and cohort. The Prince of Jin, Li Keyong, had now died, and successor Zhuangzong recalled Zhou Dewei [C.E. 908]. Taizu returned to Luoyang upon news of the Jin mourning and Dewei's withdrawal. His commanders relaxed their diligence as well, causing Zhuangzong to propose to Dewei, "It was the Former Prince who made the Jin a fitting foe to the Liang, leaving the enemy faint of heart. Aware of our current mourning for the Former Prince and my own recent accession, they will certainly be inattentive, regarding our dispatch of armies as improbable. We should thus exploit the element of surprise and rush them: apart from breaking their blockade, we will affirm our hegemonic standing." He and Dewei now scurried to Beihuangnian, where encountering a dense fog, they concealed their men at Sanchui Ridge before rushing straightway to form dual ramparts around the city. Their attack proved a success, while a rout awaited Huaiying, who lost three hundred senior commanders. With only a hundred mounts, he managed to flee back to the capital, submitting himself to the court's mercy. Taizu issued a pardon. "When mobilizing forces last year," he admitted, "oracles considered conditions unpropitious due to a lunar eclipse. I alone defied them, culminating in the current defeat. Fault lies not with you." He was named generalissimo of the Right Guard.

When Liu Zhijun defected and absconded for Qizhou‡, Kang Huaiying became Baoyi governor and deputy commissioner of bandit suppression for the western circuits. Zhijun now surrounded Lingwu County with Qi‡ armies, and as a diversionary tactic, Taizu ordered Huaiying to strike against the Bing/Ning command. He acquired Ning, Qing, and Yan¶ prefectures. Returning via Shengping County, Zhijun stormed Huaiying from an ambush and routed him. Reassignment as Ganhua governor ensued. Huaiying later led the suppression of Zhu Youqian upon his defection to the Jin [C.E. 912], his engagement of forces at Baijing Ridge ending in another rout. Reassigned as Yongping governor, he died at the command.

Liu Xun

A native of Anqiu County, Mizhou, Liu Xun [C.E. 858–921] served Wang Jingwu of Qingzhou† in youth. After the death of Jingwu and succession of son Shifan as governor, the Dizhou prefect Zhang Chan defected. For the suppression, Shifan commissioned military director Lu Hong, who also defected. Shifan hence summoned Hong with pretenses of goodwill, but charged Xun with greeting him in the suburbs only to behead him in his carriage seat. Shifan arranged for Xun to attack Zhang Shan as well, who was overpowered. He became prefect for Dengzhou‡ and manager-adjutant, at Shifan's request. With the future Taizu of Liang campaigning to the west at Fengxiang, Wang Shifan intended to exploit the Liang vacuum by secretly deploying agents to harass its counties and prefectures, a ploy that failed, as numerous schemes leaked out in advance.

Liu Xun was unique in his longstanding affinity for writings on warfare as well as strategizing sensibilities. By now, the Liang had vanquished Zhu Jin and cohort to acquire the entirety of the Yan/Yun region, designating Ge Congzhou as Yanzhou governor. Congzhou happened to be outside the city commanding troops when Xun arranged for oil and congee to be transported into the city to identify points of vulnerability and access. The oil vendor identified a water drain at the base of the outer city, so Xun had five hundred infantry follow the water drain to access and overpower the city [reclaiming it for the Tang dynasty]. He then relocated family dependents of Congzhou to another residence and paid personal respects to his mother, consoling her with the utmost charity and courtesy. Taizu had now removed the Tang Emperor Zhaozong from Fengxiang and retreated eastward, yet ordered offensives by Zhu Youning against Wang Shifan and Ge Congzhou against Liu Xun. Xun directed the mother of Congzhou to be conveyed by carriage and to holler out to her son from atop the city wall, "Commander Liu has afforded me exceptional charity, hardly different from your very own. Each subject must work for his own master, a matter that you may wish to reassess." Congzhou now relaxed his offensive.

Liu Xun gathered for evacuation from the city all those unfit to resist the enemy, including women, the old, and the infirm. He now prepared for a dogged defense, personally sharing hardships as well as food and clothing with stalwart youth. Once outside relief failed to materialize, men's loyalties began to shift: deputy prefect Wang Yanwen leaped over a city wall to flee, as numerous guards manning embrasures along the wall deserted. Xun now notified Yanwen, by messenger, "As deputy prefect, you cannot leave with many men—only those with permission can leave." He also issued orders within the city, insisting that, "Only those released by me can leave with the deputy prefect—all others will be liquidated with their families!" City residents believed the ploy, and the desertions ceased. Meanwhile, the story left Liang officers ultimately suspicious of whether Yanwen had genuinely defected and they beheaded him at the foot of the city wall. Defenders toughened their resolve in consequence.

With the armies of Wang Shifan already in surrender, Ge Congzhou lectured Liu Xun on the volatility of military fortunes. "I will revert the city to the Liang only when my master capitulates," Xun affirmed, and, indeed, he did surrender once a defeated Shifan submitted to Liang. Congzhou came to assist Xun to pack possessions before a sendoff. "A vanquished commander, I am fortunate enough to be spared death through the beneficence of Liang," Xun insisted. "I can scarcely leave astride a horse and draped in fur!" He reverted to Liang, instead, in plain clothes and riding an ass. Taizu conferred official cap and sash, hosting a banquet replete with wine. Xun professed a low capacity for alcohol in spurning the wine, Taizu responding, "Did not the Yanzhou conquest demand a great capacity?" An appointment ensued as chief of the governor's guard with primary-cohort standing. Taizu controlled four commands at the time, his commanders and senior staff all accomplished officers and old acquaintances. By defecting, Xun leaped above them virtually overnight. The various commanders all extended military courtesies in greeting him, but Xun kept a casual demeanor, as Taizu's appreciation for him grew.

Liu Xun received promotions, after Taizu's enthronement, culminating in commander of the Dragonly Martial Left Guard. In the wake of Liu Zhijun's defection and conquest of Changan, Taizu turned to Xun and Niu Cunjie for the suppression. Zhijun subsequently fled to Fengxiang. Changan was renamed the Yongping command with Xun as governor. The accession of Emperor Mo saw Xun receive concurrent powers as the Zhennan governor and metropolitan custodian of Kaifeng.

The prefectures of Xiang‡ and Wei became two separate commands once Yang Shihou died. Emperor Mo still feared a mutiny by the Weizhou military and directed Liu Xun to quarter troops at Wei County. A mutiny at Weizhou did occur, where He Delun was coerced to surrender to the Prince of Jin [C.E. 915], the Prince now occupying the prefecture. Taiyuan seemed ripe for a raid, so Xun reasoned, assuming that Jin troops had all entered Wei as well. He then patched together a straw dummy to be mounted atop a donkey, hoisting a banner and pacing back and forth atop the city wall. Meanwhile, his troops departed in stealth from Huangze Pass for a storm on Taiyuan. Jin warriors, focused on the moving banner on the Liang wall, did not notice the departure, so no one pursued them. Xun encountered heavy rains at Leping, however, and returned after further advancement proved futile. He then rushed on Linqing County to commandeer millet stored at Weizhou, but Zhou Dewei had already reached the site, and Xun had to fort his men at Shen County, provisioning them by digging a tunnel extending to the Yellow River.

After a long while, Emperor Mo reprimanded Liu Xun by letter: "Matters beyond the palace have been entirely entrusted to you, yet prefectures north of the Yellow River have all fallen virtually overnight. Reserves in our granaries are now depleted and rapid conveyors are insufficient. As commander sharing a common purpose with your country, you should devise some effective strategies." "Jin troops so exceptionally fit cannot be assaulted immediately," Xun responded. "We should wait things out instead." Emperor Mo dispatched additional messengers for details on schemes to assure victory, Xun insisting, "Your Subject possesses no miraculous skills. I would simply request that the people remit ten pecks of rice: the enemy will be vanquished when the rice is gone." An infuriated Mo rebounded derisively, "Does the Commander need rice to eliminate hunger or foil the enemy?" An overseer was thus commissioned to supervise his armies. Xun summoned the commanders to brainstorm, asking, "Confined to the deep recesses of his palaces, Our Monarch sets plans with pretty boys—a guarantee for ruin in governing! As the enemy's powers thrive, our actions cannot be rash. What is your assessment?" The commanders all preferred to fight, so Xun invited them to sit at the portal to his barracks, giving each a cup of murky water from the Yellow River. The commanders were baffled, some drinking and others declining, as Xun interjected, "If a single cup is so hard to drink, how can you possibly swallow a surging river?" The faces of the commanders all changed color.

Zhuangzong [Prince of Jin], then at Weizhou, used successive contingents of hardened warriors to pressure Liu Xun's forts, Xun not daring to leave his holdout. Emperor Mo exhorted him, over and again, to emerge for battle. Zhuangzong noted to commanders in a planning session, "Liu Xun, having studied the *Six Secret Teachings*, prefers to deploy armies in reaction to opportune changes.[5] His original objective was to expose his opponent's vulnerabilities before striking. If he now comes under pressure, he will surely want a speedy engagement." Professing his own return to Taiyuan, Zhuangzong ordered Fu Cunshen to hold positions at Wei Prefecture, while he and his men actually took cover at Bei, appearing to head westward. Xun could finally report to Emperor Mo, "The Prince of Jin having returned westward, Wei is ripe for a raid."

Liu Xun led ten thousand men in an assault on the eastern wall of Wei Prefecture, just as Zhuangzong rushed back from Bei for a sortie. The sudden sighting of Jin armies startled Xun, who cried out, "The Prince of Jin is actually here!" His retreating soldiers were pursued as far as the former Yuancheng, where Zhuangzong and Fu Cunshen sandwiched Xun's men from both sides. Xun employed the "circular formation" to resist Jin troops. A rout ensued after armies clashed again, Xun fleeing southward to cross the Yellow River at Liyang and hold position at Huazhou. Emperor Mo assigned him governor of the Yicheng command. Within a year, the entirety of lands north of the Yellow River were in Jin hands, Xun's demotion to military training commissioner for Bozhou¶ soon following.

Liu Xun became commissioner for pacification and local order after Zhang Wanjin's rebellion there. The defeat and subsequent death of Wanjin led to Xun's advancement as the Taining governor. Once Zhu Youqian defected and felled Tongzhou, Emperor Mo named Xun commissioner of bandit suppression for Hedong. Xun wrote a letter seeking to sway Youqian upon reaching Shanzhou, waiting over a month with no response. In the interim, Yin Hao, Duan Ning, and others with longstanding grudges against Xun maligned him, noting his ties to Youqian through marriage and attributing his procrastination to aiding and abetting the rebel. Xun's armies later met with successive defeats, resulting in banishment to Luoyang. There he was poisoned to death at sixty-four *sui*. The posthumous rank of palace secretary was conferred.

Xun's sons, Suining and Suiyong, were both prefects under the Later Tang. Xun's comely concubine, surnamed Wang, managed to enter the palace of Mingzong after Xun's death, becoming the Pure Consort Wang. Her involvement in the court affairs of Mingzong's waning years afforded favor for Xun's two sons.

Liu Suiyong was deputy interim-regent for the western capital when the Prince of Lu, Congke, rebelled at Fengxiang. Interim regent Wang Sitong had led combined armies from several commands in the Fengxiang suppression, returning eastward after defeat. Suiyong sealed his gates in denying him entrance, while securing the local treasury in anticipation of the Prince of Lu. Those in the Prince's armies to arrive first all received gold and silk. A tearful Prince at the sight of Suiyong grabbed his hand, hereafter consulting him about all affairs, the important and trivial alike. He became prefect of Zizhou upon Congke's accession as Emperor Fei. His replacement as deputy interim-regent for the western capital was Suiqing, the son of Xun's elder brother, Qi.

Liu Suiqing served as prefect for five areas, including Yi and Di prefectures, consistently administering with distinction. He later became defense commissioner for Fengzhou‡, then commissioner of the northern court of palace armies with oversight over the Three Fiscal Agencies. During the Kaiyun era of Jin [C.E. 944–946], he died as defense commissioner for Anzhou. Exceedingly filial by character, mourning for his father had emaciated Suiqing and earned him the praise of fellow villagers. As prefect for Zizhou, he once went to the suburbs to greet his mother and held her horse reins for a trip of several tens of *li*—a splendid sight for the local people to behold.

Zhang Guiba

Zhang Guiba [d. C.E. 908] was native to Qinghe County [Shandong]. Emperor Mo married his daughter, who became the Virtuous Consort. In youth, Guiba and younger brothers, Guihou and Guibian, were minions of Huang Chao, all of whom surrendered to the Liang after a vanquished Chao fled to the east.

Attacks on Bianzhou by Qin Zongquan permitted Guiba to distinguish himself in battle over and again. Once struck by an arrow as Zhang Zhi rallied his cavalry from forts at Chigang [Kaifeng], Guiba plucked out the arrow and hurled it back at the renegades, killing his target with a single shot before spurring his horse to return. Taizu observed him from high ground and, impressed by his ruggedness, presented him with gold and silk, as well as his own horse. Five hundred archers were subsequently concealed in mud bogs in ambush, and several hundred horsemen formed a roving detachment under Taizu's command. Zhi's barricades having been crossed, he emerged with men to pursue Taizu. Guiba now sallied forth from the ambush to murder a thousand of Zhi's soldiers and seize several dozen horses.

As Taizu undertook the offensive against Caizhou, prefectural commander Xiao Hao retaliated with an intense barrage against his campsite. With no time for orders, Guiba and Xu Huaiyu issued from the barrack portals for the east and south, respectively. They rejoined in combat and vanquished the enemy, plucking Taizu from the campsite.

Taizu claimed Caozhou amid offensives on Yan and Yun prefectures, arranging for Zhang Guiba to secure the prefecture with several thousand troops. Guiba proceeded to engage Zhu Jin in battle at Jinxiang, routing him and overrunning Puzhou. Once Weizhou came under assault from the Prince of Jin, Guiba assisted Ge Congzhou in the relief. In battles at Huanshui, Guiba captured the son of Li Keyong, Luoluo, to deliver him to Weizhou authorities. He defeated Liu Rengong at Neihuang as well, his merit unique among commanders then. Guiba served provisionally as Xingzhou prefect, during the second year of Guanghua [C.E. 899], later as prefect of Lai, generalissimo of the Left Guard, and prefect of Cao. Appointments followed, in the inaugural year of Kaiping [C.E. 907], as commander of the Dragon and Tiger Right Guard and generalissimo of the Valorous Left Guard. Named the Hedong governor in the second year, he died of illness.

His son, *Zhang Hanjie*, held prominent positions at the court of Emperor Mo, achieving dominance through the Virtuous Consort Zhang's influence. When the Liang collapsed and Zhuangzong of Tang occupied Bianzhou, his family was executed.

Younger brother *Zhang Guihou* had the courtesy name Dekun. Adept as archer and lancer, he also had the capacity as commander to deploy the few against the many. Zhang Zhi's men were quartered at Chigang when Guihou engaged him in a duel on the battlefield. An exhausted Zhi withdrew as Guihou's commanders exploited his vulnerability to inflict a grave defeat. The action greatly delighted Taizu, who named Guihou chief of cavalry.

During the Liang assault on Shi Pu, Guihou led warriors in an advance on the Jiuli Hills, where he encountered and engaged Xuzhou¶ armies. Guihou immediately recognized the one-time Liang commander Chen Fan, who had defected to Xu¶. Looking Fan furiously in the eye for a harsh rebuke, he swiftly rode his horse straightway in Fan's direction as if to seize him, lodging an arrow into his left eye.

In his offensive against Yunzhou, the Prince of Chen, Youyu, had forted men at Puzhou. Taizu approached from the rear, but Youyu had moved his barricades and failed in a reconnaissance with Taizu. Upon finally encountering Yunzhou armies and observing them from an elevated position, Taizu realized that they comprised a mere thousand men. He now joined Guihou and a contingent of personal militia in a direct charge. Once he was engaged in battle, however, Yunzhou forces arrived in vast numbers. Guihou reckoned that holding ground was impossible and opted to lead several dozen cavalry to secure Taizu's advance return. Yet Guihou's horse collapsed after an arrow struck, forcing him to grab his lance and spar on foot. Taizu returned to his army and rushed Zhang Yun back to the location to retrieve Guihou, certain that he must be dead. More than ten arrows pierced his body, yet Guihou managed to return on a horse provided by Yun. Taizu sobbed at the sight of him, saying, "You are alive. We need hardly make issue of vanquished armies!" Carried back to the Xuanwu command on a stretcher, he was reassigned as commander of the Divinely Martial Right Guard. He also served as prefect for Ming, Jin, and Jiang prefectures successively, where he engaged the Prince of Jin's armies on several occasions, never to succumb. Becoming the Zhenguo governor in the inaugural year of Qianhua [C.E. 911], he died of illness and left a son, Hanqing.

Zhang Guibian was also a commander skilled at combat. He served as director of long-sword regiments at Huazhou, in the early years of Kaiping. His son was Hanrong. After the collapse of the Liang dynasty, his entire family was executed.

Yang Shihou

A native of Jin'gou, Yingzhou¤, a youthful Yang Shihou [d. C.E. 915] served Li Hanzhi of Heyang. Upon surrendering to the Prince of Jin, Hanzhi selected a hundred of his stoutest warriors as a gift to the Prince, Shihou among them. Under the Jin banner, Shihou won no recognition and later fled to the Liang after committing some offense. He was posted by Taizu to the governor's guard at Xuanwu command and made prefect of Caozhou. During the Liang offensive against Wang Shifan [C.E. 903], Shihou captured more than eighty of the enemy commanders in battles at Linqu, then claimed Dizhou. He became prefect of Qizhou¶ as reward.

Yang Shihou was vanguard during Taizu's offensive against Zhao Kuangning of Xiangyang [C.E. 905]. He managed to cross the Han River by making a suspension bridge from wood retrieved from the Xitong Hills at Gucheng County, then proceeded to storm and indeed defeat Kuangning, who abandoned the prefecture and absconded. Shihou further advanced against Jingnan and repulsed Kuangning's younger brother, Kuangming. His feats numerous, he became governor of Shannan east circuit with ministerial powers [C.E. 909].

With the defection of Liu Zhijun and his conquest of Changan, Liu Xun and Niu Cunjie directed a prolonged yet fruitless siege. Yang Shihou left with a contingent of special forces and approached from alongside the Southern Mountains to enter the city's western gate and force guards there to surrender, claiming the city. Zhou Dewei of Jin then came to Zhijun's relief with an assault on Jinzhou, but was vanquished at Mengkeng County. For such merit, Shihou became the Baoyi governor, a posting later changed to Xuanyi.

At the time, Liang armies had undertaken a prolonged siege of Zhaozhou without prevailing. Taizu personally commanded a new sortie after recuperating from illness in Luoyang. Shihou and Taizu had reached Huanshui County upon losing their way during a nighttime maneuver. Reaching Wei County the next morning, they heard rumors that the enemy was at hand, which incited uncontainable tumult in their armies. When no enemy surfaced after some time, stability returned. Then Taizu's ailments recurred and he returned.

Jin armies attacked Yanzhou¤ in the next year and the Prince of Yan, Liu Shouguang, approached the Liang for relief. Meanwhile, Taizu enjoyed a modest recovery and launched a raid against Zhao to deflect Jin armies [C.E. 912]. Quartered at Longhua County, he directed Yang Shihou to attack Zaoqiang, an effort yielding few fruits even after three months.[i] An angry Taizu went personally to oversee the conduct of combat, subduing the town and massacring all. He proceeded with a siege of Xiu County. Shi Jiantang of Jin led light cavalry in a nighttime raid against Liang armies, triggering massive tumult. Taizu and Shihou now abandoned their wagons for flight south,

i. One version gives "three days."

Taizu returning to the eastern capital and leaving Shihou to man positions at Weizhou. In the next year,[6] Taizu succumbed to regicide and Yougui enthroned himself. Shihou exploited the vacuum to murder Pan Yan and Zang Yanfan, military attachés at Weizhou, among others, expelling its governor, Luo Zhouhan. [Liang usurper] Yougui subsequently named him Tianxiong governor.

Ever since Taizu began engaging the Prince of Jin's armies along the Yellow River, Yang Shihou often served as commissioner of bandit suppression, with the fittest of Liang warriors under his control. Shihou now expelled his subordinate commanders in the wake of Taizu's death and turned uncontainably haughty. By then the Weizhou governors had grown dependent on their military attachés, which fostered arrogance in subordinate commanders. The military attachés had all perished by the time of Luo Shaowei, causing the powers of Wei authorities to grow isolated and enabling the Liang to exert control. Shihou had now accomplished his objective and resuscitated his own Silver Lance and Dedicated regiments. Yougui secretly wished to scheme against Shihou and summoned him to the palace, ostensibly to deliberate matters. Aides to Shihou, such as Tian Wen, tried to dissuade him from going, but he declared, "For twenty years, I have not forsaken the Zhu house. To refuse to go now would rouse suspicions and trigger some incident. I also understand the character of Our Monarch and have confidence, should I appear, that nothing will happen to me." Shihou appeared at the capital with twenty thousand select warriors in tow, which were left outside the city wall. He entered with an escort of more than ten guards to meet Yougui, who seemed ever nervous and offered magnificent largess before his sendoff.

Later, as Emperor Mo [Prince of Jun] contemplated punitive action against Yougui, he spoke to Zhao Yan, who informed him, "The success or failure of this matter rests solely with the commissioner of bandit suppression, Yang Shihou: a single directive from him to the Palace Guard can render immediate success." Emperor Mo sent Ma Shenjiao to confer secretly with Shihou and convey his heartfelt feelings. A vacillating Shihou asked of a subordinate, "When the Prince of Ying [Yougui] committed regicide, I was unable to lead the suppression against him. Today, our relationship as ruler and subject is already fixed and I have no cause to consider alternatives. What do others suggest I do?" The subordinate hypothesized, "Yougui committed regicide against his own father and ruler, such that all persons under Heaven despise him. If the Prince of Jun invokes moral principle to execute the renegade, he will handily accomplish his feat. And should he break the renegade's back virtually overnight [without your assistance], what recourse will you have?" Greatly awakened, Shihou thus dispatched commander Wang Shunxian to Luoyang to confer with Yuan Xiangxian, arranging for Zhu Hanbin to assist with troops from Huazhou. Emperor Mo and Xiangxian ultimately did murder Yougui.

After attaining the throne, Emperor Mo invested Shihou as Prince of Ye, his edict avoiding use of the personal name [in rare deference]. He also conferred with Shihou about all affairs, however trivial. Yet jealousy and fear increasingly filled his heart, and Shihou later developed ulcers and died. Emperor Mo celebrated his memory in the palace. Hereafter, Xiang‡ and Wei prefectures were divided into separate governorships. After a mutiny at Weizhou, Wei and Bo surrendered to the Prince of Jin, the Liang hence losing the entire stretch north of the Yellow River.

CHAPTERS 24–28

BIOGRAPHIES OF TANG SUBJECTS

Guo Chongtao

A native of Yanmen, Daizhou, Guo Chongtao [d. C.E. 926] was once military training commissioner for Hedong. Possessing a discerning mind and gift for argumentation, his genius won wide acclaim.

When Zhuangzong was still Prince of Jin and Meng Zhixiang senior military advisor, Guo Chongtao served as deputy advisor. The post as senior advisor was a critical organ for court consultation. Heretofore, Wu Gong and Zhang Qianhou, among others, had in succession fallen from grace as senior advisors. An anxious Zhixiang thus sought a posting away from the capital. "If you wish to elude service, you should nominate someone to replace you," Zhuangzong insisted. Zhixiang recommended as senior advisor Chongtao, who came to enjoy exceptional intimacy and confidence.

Armies of the Prince of Jin had long besieged Zhang Wenli at Zhen Prefecture without success, whereupon Wang Du[1] of Ding lured the Khitan to invade the country [C.E. 921]. Jin authorities were terrified as the Khitan approached Xinle County, preferring to dissolve their blockade and retreat. Zhuangzong remained undecided when Guo Chongtao interjected, "The Khitan came not to rescue Wenli, but rather because Wang Du saw advantage in luring them. Moreover, in the wake of our recent victories over Liang armies, we should maximize our already thriving powers. The dastardly act of sudden retreat is unacceptable." Zhuangzong concurred and defeated the Khitan in the end. After his enthronement, Chongtao became minister of war and commissioner of military affairs.

Once the Liang commander Wang Yanzhang successfully stormed Desheng Commandery, Tang armies proceeded eastward to secure Yangliu township [Jizhou], which Yanzhang encircled. Zhuangzong then climbed a rampart to observe that Yanzhang intended to thwart his armies with multiple rings of moats—a sign that Yanzhang had underestimated him. "I now understand his thinking: he intends to tire us by protracted conflict," Zhuangzong observed with relish. He promptly emerged for battle with weapons drawn for close combat, only to be struck by archers of Yanzhang lying in ambush, who rendered a devastating defeat. Tang forces retreated and Zhuangzong, turning to Chongtao, queried, "What do we do now?"

The Tang had acquired Yun Prefecture by then, so Chongtao proposed, "Yanzhang's purpose in the siege here is to claim Yun. Your Subject, with several thousand men, proposes coursing the Yellow River downstream to erect ramparts at prospective combat sites. We will profess a rendezvous with Yun defenders, such that Yanzhang must come to challenge us: once his army is divided, it will be vulnerable to intrigue. But constructing ramparts of wedged earth will be difficult. If Your Majesty can conduct crack troops for daily rallies, preventing Yanzhang's men from advancing eastward, the ramparts can be completed in ten days." Zhuangzong agreed, ordering Chongtao and Mao Zhang to command several thousand men by night. They plundered from local residents along the entire route, damaging homes and felling trees. Crossing the Yellow River, they erected ramparts east of Bozhou, construction continuing from morning to night to permit completion in six days. Yanzhang did finally conduct armies in an intense barrage, but faced oppressive summer heat that killed some soldiers and impeded a successful assault on the ramparts. Losing more than half of his army, he rushed toward Yangliu, Zhuangzong intercepting with a broadside assault that defeated him.

After Kang Yanxiao deserted the Liang for the Tang, he was first met by Guo Chongtao, who delayed his bedroom visit to be thoroughly briefed on conditions in the Liang. Zhuangzong was forted at Chaocheng County at the time, Duan Ning at Linhe. Liang armies had daily raided Chan and Xiang‡ prefectures ever since the Tang loss of Desheng, seizing Liyang County and Wei‡ Prefecture, while Li Jitao defected to the Liang to surrender Zelu. Moreover, the Khitan repeatedly invaded You and Zhuo prefectures. News from Kang Yanxiao that the Liang would summon governors for a sweeping offensive left Tang commanders worried and confused, as the outcome seemed wholly unpredictable. Zhuangzong found the news sufficiently threatening to inquire of commanders, who concurred, "Our Tang has claimed Yun Prefecture, but separation by the Yellow River makes defense difficult. Better that we relinquish Yun to the Liang while claiming Weizhou‡ and Liyang to the west, the Yellow River serving as a border.[2] We could thereby enter a truce with the Liang to disband armies and forswear aggression, as we set alternative strategies later on."

The commanders' comments displeased Zhuangzong. Retiring to his tent for rest, he summoned Guo Chongtao to probe further, Chongtao asserting,

> Your Majesty, for over ten years, has invoked righteous principle in raising armies: commanders and warriors have borne fatigue in battle and ordinary persons toiled to transport rations to them. We have now gloriously assumed a dynastic name, as people north of the Yellow River all extend their heads in anticipating our victory, longing for a rest of arms. Today, we hold a single Yunzhou [to the southeast]. If we abandon it as indefensible and set the Yellow River as border, who will secure that border for Your Majesty? Moreover, before our loss of Desheng Commandery, commodities impressed from merchants across the four corners invariably converged at the same time, our fuelwood and military rations piled mountain-high. After losing the southern city to preserve Yangliu, more than half of our grain revenues are wasted or lost in transport. Moreover, for the five prefectures of Wei/Bo command, the autumn plantings are not ripe: even if we milk the people to collect, the food will not last a few months. Is this not the time to entrench troops for the long haul? The arrival of Kang Yanxiao has afforded Your Subject a full appraisal of actual conditions in the Liang domain, proving this moment as truly one of ruin wrought by Heaven itself. Let me propose that Your Majesty divide his armies to defend Weizhou, fortify Yangliu, and expel the enemy from their nests at Yunzhou. In less than half a month the world could be settled.

His words delighted Zhuangzong. "The deed of a true man," he pronounced.

Zhuangzong now consulted astrologers, who indicated, "The year is not propitious for military deployments." Chongtao interjected, "When the ancients issued mandates to commanders, they axed down the inauspicious northern door for their departure. At a time of resolve about our course, such chatter has no credibility!" On the very same day, Zhuangzong issued commands to the military, returned his own family dependents to Weizhou for safety, then crossed the river to Yangliu for a sudden strike on Bian via Yun Prefecture. He managed to annihilate the Liang in a mere eight days! In recognizing the meritorious, he bestowed an iron writ of immunity on Chongtao.[3] Named director of the Chancellery and the Chengde governor, Chongtao retained former powers as military commissioner.

Zhuangzong and his commanders claimed the world through military actions, yet Chongtao never saw combat: his recognition as supremely meritorious derived solely from strategies set and mandates executed. Having consolidated both civil and military power, he took affairs of the world as his personal duty, evading nothing that came his way. Eunuchs and actors thus faced a serious impediment to wielding influence at court.

Previously, both Guo Chongtao and eunuch Ma Shaohong had served as senior military advisors, with Shaohong enjoying senior rank. The two were also named commissioners of military affairs upon Zhuangzong's accession, yet Chongtao balked at Shaohong's superior rank; Zhang Juhan thereby became military commissioner and Shaohong transferred to commissioner of palace armies. The reassignment frustrated Shaohong, such that Chongtao formed a commission of tax accounting for him to head. All cash and grains either collected or dispersed by revenues officers across the realm were supervised by the tax accounting office. This involved a plethora of documents, which, compounded by malefaction at the local level, caused Shaohong's abrupt dismissal. The incident proved particularly embarrassing for him.

A rather intimidated Chongtao once commented to the son of an old friend, "Despite assisting the Son of Heaven to acquire the entire world and accomplishing the grandest of feats, petty partisans are banding against me. I prefer to elude them by returning to govern Zhenyang, escaping peril in the process. Is this feasible?" The friend's son responded, "There is an idiom, 'For he who rides the tiger, forces of circumstance preclude descent.' Your powers are already thriving, Sir, causing many subordinates to be resentful and jealous. Should a shift occur in court power, you will scarcely be secure!" Chongtao asked for clarification, as the youth continued, "The palace of the empress now lacks an occupant, even as Miss Liu commands imperial favor. You should plead to install her as empress on the one hand, and propose wide-ranging policies to profit the country and benefit the people on the other. Then, you can petition to leave office. The Son of Heaven will surely not accept your departure, in recognition of a record of noble feats and few faults. In this way, you are celebrated at court for eschewing power and esteemed in the palace for aiding the empress, leaving the world at large grateful. Regardless of the slander, none could undermine you." Chongtao concurred, petitioning the palace to install Miss Liu as empress.

Chongtao began as an honest man, but after relocating to Luoyang, bribes and gratuities from the four corners started to come his way, a matter occasionally addressed by an old friend's son. Chongtao insisted, however, "I enjoy standing as both civil and martial minister, whose salary and perquisites run into the tens of thousands. Why accept less of such things? Many of today's governors and overlords are former commanders of a defunct Liang, all men who once came close to peril at Your Majesty's hand. If I adamantly spurn their gifts today, would they not turn rebellious?

Moreover, I see little difference between storing such things at home or in an official repository." A year later, the Son of Heaven performed rituals at the southern suburbs and Chongtao lavished the entire cache on awards for persons of merit.

Zhuangzong installed Miss Liu as empress after completing the suburban rites. Guo Chongtao filed successive petitions proposing to revert military commissioners to the palace inner circle, in accord with Tang-dynasty precedent, while personally resigning as Zhenyang governor. The throne cordially refused permission. He further requested, "As Your Majesty and I forted armies at Chaocheng and adopted the blueprint for vanquishing the Liang, Your Majesty patted my back and swore, 'I promise you a governorship when we're done.' A single house now rules the world, as the eminent and wise are advanced at court. Your Subject is truly weary and wishes to withdraw, as agreed." Zhuangzong responded upon summoning Chongtao, "My promise at Chaocheng involved conferring a governorship, not allowing your departure. In deserting me, where would you go?" Chongtao now set forth twenty-five matters of benefit or detriment to the empire, which were acted upon.

When Li Siyuan was Chengde governor, Chongtao received assignment as Zhongwu governor. Chongtao's assertions to enjoy supreme rank and power afforded him a rare measure of freedom to speak forthrightly. Zhuangzong admitted [in gratitude], "Occupying the world's most exalted position, how have I overlooked your lack of any land!" The imperial order for enfeoffment was rescinded after endless declensions by Chongtao, whom the court named director of the Chancellery and commissioner for military affairs.

In summer, the third year of Tongguang [C.E. 925], ceaseless rains had caused vast floodwaters to despoil private farms, as many people fled or even died. Zhuangzong fretted that heat and humidity might leave palaces uninhabitable, so he considered acquiring a towered mansion for summertime retreat. A eunuch further noted, "Your Subject recalls Changan in its full glory, towered mansions such as Daming and Xingqing numbering in the hundreds. Our imperial precincts today fail to compare to even a minister's residence of old." Zhuangzong thus insisted, "For a world with our wealth, why shouldn't I construct a single tower?" He then ordered its erection by Wang Yunping, the master of imperial palaces and parks.

The eunuch reminded the Emperor, "Without even the shift of an eyebrow or turn of the head, Guo Chongtao commonly begrudges spending from our revenues office. Even if Your Majesty wishes, construction may not be possible!" Zhuangzong now addressed Chongtao, through a messenger, "During our military standoff with Liang along the Yellow River, I expected no praise, despite exposure to bitter cold and sweltering heat as I donned full armor on horseback. Now that I occupy palace precincts with their cavernous mansions, why do I find them insufferably hot?" Chongtao rebounded, "Your Majesty's heart formerly focused on the welfare of the world, while you now act on personal interest. Naturally, concerns do vary when conditions of idle comfort replace exacting hardship. Your Majesty, I hope, will not trivialize our toil in this dynastic enterprise. You need only increase visits north of the river to exchange our dreadful summer heat for the crisp temperatures there." Zhuangzong sat in silence, although he ultimately had Yunping start construction. Chongtao's admonition was incisive as well, causing the eunuch to add, "The official residence of Chongtao is of imperial sumptuousness. How can he appreciate the swelter of Your surroundings?" Slanders against Chongtao hereafter increased.

The custodian of Henan County [Luoyang], Luo Guan, a man assertive and direct, was known to Guo Chongtao. He personally upheld the law with no regard for propositions from the powerful. Whenever eunuchs and actors approached him with requests, the letters would pile on his desk without a single response. He showed them to Chongtao instead, who in turn, publicly exposed their schemes over and again. Eunuchs and actors acrimoniously gnashed their teeth in consequence. Since the former Tang dynasty, when Zhang Quanyi served as custodian of Henan County, the custodians often represented protégés of Quanyi, who cultivated a whole cohort. Luo Guan, as custodian, refused to defer to Quanyi's authority, so county residents who relied upon Quanyi to engage in illegal practices were all punished accordingly. An utterly livid Quanyi sent a messenger to apprise Empress Liu calmly of the Luo Guan matter, as the Empress's immediate aides excoriated Guan for his failings from morning to night. Zhuangzong had yet to act on indignation against Guan when the Empress Dowager expired, her burial arranged at the Kunling mausoleum, in Shou'an County. During a trip to the mausoleum's construction site, Zhuangzong encountered mud obstructions on the highway and a collapsed bridge. Stopping his carriage, he asked, "Who has authority here?" Eunuchs indicated the custodian of Henan, so Zhuangzong promptly summoned Luo Guan. Guan responded upon arriving, "Your Subject received no advance notification, so inquiry of the relevant custodian is in order." The Emperor now rejoined, "This is your jurisdiction. Why must I speak to someone else?" Guan was confined to jail and beaten by jailors such that his body had no skin intact. The palace authorized his murder a day later.

In admonishing Zhuangzong, Chongtao argued, "Luo Guan committed no crime besides neglecting to repair a bridge access, which the law does not punish with death." Zhuangzong was adamant, "The bridge access stood in disrepair as the Empress Dowager's funeral cortege was to depart and the Son of Heaven's carriage had to make multiple crossings. To see no crime here reflects your own partisanship!" "Guan's guilt notwithstanding, the proper penal authorities should have applied the law," Chongtao added. "Your Majesty has angrily brought down the force of the throne itself upon a single county administrator, causing people of the world to characterize Your Majesty as lacking fairness in enforcing the laws—fault for which must ultimately rest with me." "In light of your affections for Guan, you can pass judgment yourself," Zhuangzong pronounced. He arose to enter the palace, Chongtao on his heels, continuing the exchange. Zhuangzong then personally slammed the palace door behind him and denied Chongtao entry. Guan was murdered, in the end.

In the next year,[4] deliberations with senior commanders occurred on the eve of the Shu campaign [to the southwest]. The future Mingzong, as the current chief military coordinator, should have assumed command. Chongtao felt threatened by recent slanders and sought further security through some grand feat, so he addressed the Emperor: "The chief military coordinator [Mingzong] is uniquely suited to harnessing the Khitan menace to our north. However, the Prince of Wei, Jiji, has yet to establish notable merit despite priority in the line of succession, while the posting of royal princes as field marshal has ample precedent in the former Tang." "Jiji is a youth," Zhuangzong insisted. "How can he undertake a major action? I must insist on personally selecting his deputy marshal." He then affirmed, before Chongtao could respond, "My selection is made—there is no substitute for you!" He now named Jiji general commander of at-large forces in the southwest and Chongtao commissioner of bandit suppression with Chongtao rendering all military decisions.

Tang armies occupying Shu met with surrender at every turn. The younger brother of potentate Wang Yan, Zongbi, made secret overtures of surrender to Chongtao in exchange for assignment as interim regent for armed forces in western Chuan, Chongtao conceding to an assignment as governor. Zongbi removed Yan to the western palace once northern armies approached Chengdu, relinquishing his entire harem and treasure to Chongtao and his son, Tinghui. He further joined Shu residents in lining up to catch a glimpse of the Prince of Wei, while asking Chongtao to stay on as governor of Shu. Jiji had grown suspicious of Chongtao, and Chongtao, having no way to clarify his intentions, exploited an incident to behead Zongbi and his younger brothers, Zongwo and Zongxun, confiscating their family property. The action outraged Shu locals.

Guo Chongtao's contempt for eunuchs was longstanding. He once said to Jiji, "You, my Prince, have established merit in vanquishing Shu and will certainly become heir-apparent upon returning. Once the ruling Monarch has lived out a long life, you as ruler should expel such castrates and never so much as ride a gelding horse again." A military overseer for Jiji, eunuch Li Congxi, among others, had grown uncomfortable with Chongtao's monopoly on military affairs: reports of such statements only made them grit their teeth and consider a cabal against him.

Reports of success at the Shu conquest prompted Zhuangzong to send eunuch Xiang Yansi to reward troops. Chongtao's refusal to greet him at the suburbs of Chengdu utterly infuriated Yansi, inciting him to enlist Congxi and cohort in the conspiracy against Chongtao. Returning north, Yansi presented the court with a list of items obtained at Shu, including 300,000 troops; 9,500 horses; 7,000,000 weapons; 2,530,000 piculs in grain; 1,920,000 strings of cash; 220,000 ounces of gold and silver; 20,000 objects made of pearls, jade, rhinoceros horn, or elephant tusk; and 500,000 bolts of either decorated silk or silk gauze. "People say that Shu is the richest kingdom in the world," Zhuangzong queried. "Is our loot limited to this?" Yansi explained that the treasures of Shu had been claimed by Chongtao. He also slandered Chongtao with treasonous designs that imperiled the Prince of Wei. A raging Zhuangzong deputized the eunuch Ma Yangui to proceed to Shu and ascertain whether Chongtao intended to stay or leave. Yangui informed Empress Liu as well, who instructed Yangui to forge the imperial edict directing the Prince of Wei to murder Chongtao.

Guo Chongtao had five sons. Two died with him in Shu; the others were slain. The objects obtained during the Shu conquest were entirely confiscated. Upon the accession of Mingzong, the court permitted Chongtao's body to return for proper burial, his former home at Taiyuan bestowed upon his two grandsons.

During Chongtao's domination, ministers like Doulu Ge and Wei Yue liked to curry his favor. His father had the personal name Hong, and in deference to him, Ge and cohort used a related matter to request changing the Hongwen institute's name to Chongwen. They also held that Chongtao had descended from the famed Guo Ziyi, due to a common surname, which Chongtao himself came to believe. Passing by the grave of Ziyi during the Shu campaign, Chongtao dismounted his horse to weep bitterly before leaving—making him the laughingstock of all to hear of the affair. Still, he was thoroughgoing in devotion to empire, and a man with grandiose plans. After conquering Shu, he sent envoys westward to the Nanzhao tribes to disseminate the august virtues of Tang, aspiring to win their submission. Amazing ambition, to be sure!

An Chonghui

An Chonghui [d. C.E. 931] was native to Yingzhou‡, his father Fuqian a commander under the Prince of Jin whose valor and daring were legendary. When the Liang attacked Zhu Xuan at Yunzhou, Jin armies came to Xuan's relief, but a defeated Fuqian died in battle.

Serving in youth the future Mingzong, Chonghui proved sharp of mind and deferential in character. During Mingzong's tenure as the Anguo governor, he became senior military advisor. The massive blueprint behind the Weizhou mutiny [enthroning Mingzong] was the handiwork of Chonghui and Huo Yanwei. Upon assuming power, Mingzong made him commandant of the Left Guard, commissioner of military affairs, and concurrent governor of Shannan east. Chonghui adamantly declined the posts and a change to minister of war followed, his governorship continuing as before. After six years in office, appointments culminated in director of the Chancellery and imperial secretary.

Chonghui came to enjoy intimacy and trust since serving as senior military advisor. Later, his merit in assisting in the succession led to assignment to strategically sensitive posts and consultation on all matters, great and small alike—his powers shaking the world. He could be steadfastly loyal, dedicated in mind, and reasonably effective at times. Nonetheless, he liked to boast of the favor enjoyed and the awesome powers generating from him. Once imperial powers emanated from him without wise or moral men around to assist, his own personal views could trigger perilous feuds and ultimately harm ruler and subject alike, virtually annihilating both clans. We may consider it a true tragedy.

Chonghui once emerged [from his office] to pass by the gates of the Censorate, where a deputy for palace security, Ma Yan, mistakenly intruded upon the path reserved for Chonghui's escorts. An indignant Chonghui beheaded Yan at the Censorate's gates, informing the court after the fact. The incident had coincided with the beating and injury of an administrative advisor for Xiangzhou‡ by Sang Hongqian, a guard for the imperial militia. In another incident, a commander of the imperial escort, An Qian, had walked his horse across a path reserved for the chief minister's escort: Hongqian was sentenced to death, whereas Qian received a simple flogging with heavy rod. Having already beheaded Yan, Chonghui requested an edict sanctioning the punishment. Mingzong could not but agree, as censorial and admonition officers no longer dared to speak out.

The chief minister and administrator of the Three Fiscal Agencies, Ren Huan, had had a history of conflict with An Chonghui. Failing to prevail, he angrily resigned to retire at Cizhou, using illness as pretext. After the rebellion of Zhu Shouyin at Bianzhou [C.E. 927], Chonghui directed couriers with a forged imperial edict to murder Huan, a matter reported to court only after the fact. Huan was falsely charged as co-conspirator with Shouyin, and Mingzong was powerless to inquire further. Chonghui nonetheless feared criticism of him across the realm and requested the absolution of some two million strings of accumulated debts to the fiscal agencies, hoping to placate others and thwart critics. Mingzong could do little but order the debt forgiven. Many similar cases suggested that imperial powers emanated from Chonghui.

At the time, memorials from the four corners were revealed to Chonghui before referral to the throne. Authorities at Henan County once presented auspicious grains and one stalk with five buds. Chonghui needed only a glance to pronounce the items bogus, flogging the courier with light rod and sending him off. Li Renfu of Xiazhou forwarded a white falcon that Chonghui declined, explaining a day later, "Your Majesty issued a proscription to the world against offering falcons, Renfu's gift a violation of the mandate. I have already refused it, in fact." After he departed, Mingzong had someone secretly retrieve the falcon for his palace. He held it in hand at the western suburbs, a day later, as attendants cautioned, "Take care that Chonghui does not learn of this." Authorities at Suzhou presented a white rabbit as well. "A rabbit symbolizes something secretive and sneaky," Chonghui observed. "Although white, it has no other value!" He refused the gift without notifying the court.

Mingzong was munificent in character, even though his barbarian nature inclined him to murder others. The horses in the care of Tian Lingfang, master for the imperial pasturage, started losing weight, with many dying. He was tried and sentenced to death when Chonghui admonished the throne, stating, "A world learning that the death of horses provided cause to kill an officer will conclude that herds are valued more than humans." Lingfang's death sentence was thereby reduced.

Mingzong once sent Housan, a Huihu Uighur, to carry an express letter to his country. He had reached the secluded county of Liquan when he found the courier station without relief horses and county magistrate Liu Zhizhang away hunting, a relief horse not provided in due time. Housan promptly informed the court and a livid Mingzong ordered Zhizhang shackled and brought to the capital. The Emperor prepared to murder him when Chonghui spoke, with deliberative demeanor, enabling Zhizhang to escape death. Chonghui's steadfast loyalty and considerable efficacy are reflected in such acts.

Taking governance of the world as his personal duty, Chonghui wished within court to set a course for the dynasty and away from court to harness unruly overlords. Still, he carelessly gave credence to the slanders of Han Mei, severing bonds with the vassal Qian Liu; he drove Yang Yanwen to his death without eliminating the peril of the Prince of Lu; he dallied in allowing Meng Zhixiang to turn treacherous and Dong Zhang to defect before intervening with Li Yan and Li Renju; he permitted tumult to engulf the four corners and warriors to rally everywhere—much like trying to stop a fire by tossing oil on top, he only accelerated the entire process. This is the meaning of "personal views that trigger perilous feuds."

Since occupying the Liangzhe region and claiming the title Prince of Wu/Yue, Qian Liu had been afforded extraordinary diplomatic courtesies, beginning with the Liang and continuing through the Tang reign of

Zhuangzong. The singular purpose was to preserve him as vassal. Occasioning the accession of Mingzong, Liu commissioned an envoy, who appeared in the capital for audience with a letter for An Chonghui. The envoy proved discourteous and offensive to Chonghui, who without outward expression of anger, responded to Liu with his own emissaries: confidante Han Mei and Wu Zhaoyu, the deputy for palace services. The favor of Chonghui emboldened Mei to insult repeatedly fellow envoy Zhaoyu [while in the south], beating him with a horsewhip after getting drunk. Liu intended to inform the court of the incident, but Zhaoyu pleaded to the contrary for fear of indignity to his empire. Once Mei returned and met with Chonghui, he instead maligned Zhaoyu: "Zhaoyu had sauntered about like a vassal during meetings with Liu and illicitly divulged court affairs to him." Zhaoyu was sentenced to death in the censor's jail, while Qian Liu, stripped of office and title, was retired as grand preceptor. The Qian household thus severed ties with the Tang.

Congke the Prince of Lu was Hezhong governor, a man not born to the Li clan. Chonghui thus appraised him as an inevitable threat to empire and quietly conspired against him. Congke was inspecting horses at Huanglong village when his bodyguard's director, Yang Yanwen, sealed up Hezhong city in mutiny. Congke sent a messenger to plead with him, "I have treated you generously. What hardship has driven you to rebellion?" "I have not defected, but merely act on orders of the Military Bureau," Yanwen responded. "You must hasten to court." Upon reaching Yu County, Congke rushed a courier to explain the mutiny to Mingzong, whose skepticism about the facts as known provided cause for further details. He therefore dispatched the chief intendant for palace armies, Fan Yun, who gave as inducement to Yanwen a gold sash for official gowns and gold halter for horse saddle, naming him prefect of Jiangzhou. Mingzong could do little in the face of Chonghui's obstreperousness, so he authorized a pacification campaign against Yanwen entrusted to Yao Yanchou, director of the Imperial Guard, and Suo Zitong, interim custodian of the western capital [C.E. 930]. He also exhorted them, "Be sure, on my behalf, to apprehend Yanwen alive, because I want to investigate the facts personally." Yanchou and cohort chose to follow Chonghui's instructions instead, after overtaking Hezhong, by beheading and thereby silencing Yanwen. Chonghui subsequently led the official multitudes to congratulate the throne, but Mingzong interjected furiously, "I have failed to manage the affairs of my own family. You Gentlemen have no cause to assemble in celebration!" He dismissed Congke as governor and placed him under house arrest at Qinghua village.

Chonghui prodded the chief minister over and again, insisting that Congke's loss of Hezhong should rightfully be considered a crime. Minister Feng Dao further endorsed strict enforcement of the law against Congke. An embittered Mingzong countered, "My son was victim of a treacherous man. You Gentlemen make such statements even as the facts await clarification, obviously refusing to entertain survival for my son." "When the *Spring and Autumn Annals* reproved commanders, its purpose was to foster vassal-like submission," Zhao Feng asserted. "Well, submission clearly does not motivate You Gentlemen," Mingzong countered as Dao and associates nervously withdrew. A few days later, Feng Dao and others reiterated their request for punishment, Mingzong turning to attendants to address other matters. Chonghui personally expanded upon the sober facts a day later. "I am willing to defer to you, however you decide the case," Mingzong conceded, but Chonghui demurred. "A matter between father and son such as this should not be handled by Your Subject. Your Majesty alone can dispose of it." Mingzong now elaborated, "I was a petty lieutenant short on food and clothing when this youth carried lime bricks and collected horse dung for me, one helping the other to survive. With my current stature as Son of Heaven, how am I powerless to shield him? Were he confined to private residence, he could hardly affect court affairs." Chonghui dared not raise the matter again.

Governors Meng Zhixiang of western Chuan circuit and Dong Zhang of eastern Chuan were both inclined to treachery. Whenever Chonghui took measures to bridle their powers, he simultaneously strived to harness their treacherous hearts. Many of the defending commanders newly assigned to the two Chuan circuits were personal confidantes of Chonghui, and, invariably, the commanders were accompanied by elite troops to be spread slowly across the prefectures as a garrison presence, anticipating emergency deployments. The two men recognized the activity as directed at them and turned ever restless. Later, the court's commissioning of Li Yan as military overseer for western Chuan so thoroughly incensed Zhixiang that he beheaded Yan. The court also moved to harness Zhang and contain his lands by partitioning Langzhou‡ into a separate Baoning command, naming Li Renju governor. Zhang proceeded to attack and murder Renju. Zhixiang and Zhang hereafter rebelled [C.E. 930], as Tang troops garrisoned in Shu peaked at thirty thousand. Zhixiang eventually killed Zhang to wrest control over both Chuan circuits, Tang elite forces all capitulating to the Shu potentate.

Earlier, as Mingzong visited Bianzhou, An Chonghui wanted to proceed with a campaign against Wu, a proposal that Mingzong had difficulty accepting. Minister of revenues Li Lin later procured information from a spy from the Wu region that "[Wu overlord] Xu Zhigao wishes to transform the Wu kingdom into a frontier command under Tang sovereignty. To establish good faith, a simple confirmation from Gentleman An will suffice." Lin led the spy in meeting Chonghui, who in immense delight believed him. As tokens of goodwill to Zhigao, he gave to the spy a jade sash worth a thousand cash strings. The court was originally uninformed of the initiative. Only a year later, in the absence of a response from Zhigao, Chonghui petitioned to banish Lin to manager-adjutant.

Later, Li Xingde and Zhang Jian, the chief commissioner of the Sage-Sustaining Guard and his squad leader, respectively, informed the court of an impending mutiny, indicating, "The military bureau's recipient of edicts, Li Qianhui, has revealed to attendant Bian Yanwen that Chonghui has informally enlisted warriors and amassed armor and weapons while conferring secretly with a spy, his intent to personally campaign against Wu." Mingzong inquired of Chonghui, who became flustered and welcomed an investigation. Mingzong began as somewhat skeptical of Chonghui, but as high officers and close attendants all argued in his defense, he grew less so and began to make Yanwen's allegations known to Chonghui. The court investigated Yanwen for false allegations, a tragedy bringing tears to the eyes of ruler and subject alike. Yanwen, Xingde, and Jian were all executed along with their families. Chonghui now sought release from office, but Mingzong said consolingly, "Investigation of the matter is over. Please dispel reservations from your heart." Chonghui continued with such requests and an incensed Mingzong rebounded, "I will face no shortage of replacements upon dismissing you!" He now motioned to Meng Hanqiong, the Wude commissioner for palace doors, to proceed to the Palace Secretariat to press minister Feng Dao and cohort to explore replacements for Chonghui as military commissioner. "If You Gentlemen genuinely care for Gentleman An's welfare," Feng Dao counseled his peers, "allowing his dismissal may well deliver him from looming calamity." However, Zhao Feng argued against frivolous shifts among senior officials. Fan Yanguang later became military commissioner even as Chonghui continued in the post.

Once Dong Zhang rebelled, Shi Jingtang was entrusted with the suppression. The hazardous highways in the Chuan circuits made the transport of provisions particularly onerous: for every bushel of grain, only a peck actually arrived. From the passes extending westward, the people toiling under the weight of transport costs often fled to mountains and forests to band as bandits. "Conditions are so critical that I should direct the drive in person," Mingzong proposed, although Chonghui asserted personal responsibility and begged leave to campaign. Authorities at the western passes uniformly panicked upon news of Chonghui's impending arrival, those near and far aghast at his frenetic pace of several hundred *li* each day. The hurried conveyance of rations proceeded day and night without stop, the bodies to collapse on the roadways utterly incalculable.

As Chonghui passed through Fengxiang [north of Shu], he lingered in the bedroom of governor Zhu Hongzhao, who arranged for his wife and sons to serve guests with utmost respect. Chonghui intimated to Hongzhao, once intoxicated, "Of recent, I barely survived a cabal of slander, me and my family spared through the enlightened sagacity of Our Ruler." Tears flowed amid heavy sighs. Promptly after his departure, Hongzhao rushed a courier to court to warn, "A man of thwarted ambitions, Chonghui should not command at-large armies for fear of some incident." The commissioner of palace armies, Meng Hanqiong, recently returned to the capital from an at-large assignment, commented on the fright felt by people out west as well as Chonghui's personal excesses. Chonghui had reached Sanquan County when his recall was mandated and passed through Fengxiang once again. Hongzhao now refused to receive him. In fear, he hastened for the capital, his reassignment as Hezhong governor announced before he could arrive.

Men at court, intuiting changing palace sentiments attendant to Chonghui's dismissal, vied to expose his excesses. The eunuch An Xilun faced charges of a secret liaison with Chonghui to monitor palace activities for him. Xilun was executed at the marketplace after revelations of the matter. An ever-anxious Chonghui now invoked advanced age in petitioning to resign, which the court confirmed with standing as Grand preceptor to the heir-apparent. In the interim, the rising governor of Hezhong, Li Congzhang, rushed troops led by Yao Yanchou to Hezhong in anticipation of a mutiny. The sons of Chonghui, Chongxu and Chongzan, as Palace Guard officers in the capital, rushed to their father on the day that dismissal orders were issued. Startled to see them, Chonghui asked of someone, "What brought them here?" He added, "They clearly came not of their own will, but at another's behest. If my death can serve to requite empire, why bother to complain?" He shackled his two sons for return to the capital [in a plea for clemency]. They were jailed at Shanzhou.

Mingzong further ordered Zhai Guangye to Hezhong to appraise the intentions of Chonghui [C.E. 931], warning, "If he turns treacherous, you should assist Li Congzhang in disposing of him." A eunuch envoy was sent to contact Chonghui as well, the eunuch crying uncontrollably and at length, upon meeting him. When asked why, the messenger said, "People allege that you, Sir, have treacherous designs, the court-commissioned armies of Yao Yanchou already at hand!" "My death does not absolve me of mistakes," Chonghui insisted, "yet such a sudden taxing of court energies to mobilize armies only affirms the grave danger looming over our Enlightened Monarch." Congzhang surrounded Chonghui's residence with troops as Guangye arrived, entering the courtyard to bow. Chonghui fell to his knees, returning the bow when Congzhang struck him to the head with a cudgel. His wife ran over to embrace him, crying out, "There is still time, if the Gentleman must die. Why such haste?" Congzhang hit her on the head as well, husband and wife dying together as blood filled the courtyard. Congzhang later located and seized his family possessions, which did not even amount to several thousand in cash strings.

Mingzong issued a proclamation citing the crimes of Chonghui that included severing ties with Qian Liu and culminated in the rebellions of Meng Zhixiang and Dong Zhang, in addition to his advocacy of war against Wu. His two sons were also murdered, although other male descendants were spared. Upon falling from grace and facing the certainty of death, Chonghui lamented, "If I absolutely must die, my only regret is failing to eliminate the Prince of Lu on my empire's behalf."[5] He most resented this.

We lament. Civil service posts can long lose their powers. I have read official copies of imperial proclamations from the Liang dynasty, when Jing Xiang and Li Zhen were commissioners at the Bureau of Venerable Governance, and noticed that all orders from the throne were communicated to chief ministers prior to promulgation. When the monarch had to act because chief ministers were not in regular audience or when the edict's recipient wanted to petition again, "full records"[i] were made prior to submission. Commissioners for venerable governance were then notified and they rewrote draft edicts upon receipt before final orders could be issued.

Venerable governance commissioners in Liang times functioned like military affairs commissioners under the preceding Tang, vested with powers to give and receive orders. Whereas eunuchs commonly filled the post during the Tang, the Liang was mindful of the earlier eunuch peril and began involving civil officials as consultants or in deliberations on strategy in the palace; never did the commissioners fully control the implementation of orders away from the capital, however. By the time men like Chongtao and Chonghui assumed the post, the Military Affairs Bureau resumed the old Tang name, but its powers now paralleled chief ministers. Later generations followed this practice of sharing power, entrusting civil affairs to chief ministers and military matters to the Military Affairs Bureau. The weighty responsibility afforded the military bureau caused chief ministers hereafter to lose some powers.

Yuan Xingqin

A native of Youzhou, Yuan Xingqin [Li Shaorong, d. C.E. 926] was an assisting commander under Liu Shouguang. After Shouguang purged his own father, Rengong, he sent Xingqin to attack Rengong at Mount Da'an and imprison him [C.E. 897]. Shouguang also orchestrated Xingqin's murder of his various

....

i. It is common parlance to speak simply of "making a record" [*jishi*], even though today the Institute of Academicians provides formal "consultations" [*zibao*], while the back-and-forth exchanges among literati at large are formally known as "briefs" [*jiantie*].

brothers. Later, Xingqin was sent to recruit militia in the vicinity of Yun‡ and Shuo prefectures, following the Prince of Jin's raid on Youzhou. The future Mingzong had plundered lands north of the mountains, at the time, and faced off Xingqin at Guangbian Commandery: through eight battles, Mingzong injured him in seven places, but Xingqin plucked out the arrows and continued to battle, managing to hit Mingzong's middle thigh. Repeated setbacks forced Xingqin to surrender, Mingzong patting him on the back in raising a toast, "A rugged warrior, for sure!" Subsequently adopted as son, Xingqin often attended Mingzong in battle, proving his merit over and again. Zhuangzong was expanding the selection of courageous commanders for his personal bodyguard, after vanquishing Weizhou, and enlisted Xingqin as chief officer of detachments upon word of his valor. He conferred a new name as well, Li Shaorong.

In his zeal for war, Zhuangzong tended to slight his opponents. An engagement of Liang troops at Panzhang village ended in defeat for his army, Zhuangzong abruptly absconding with only three or four horsemen. Several hundred Liang troops pursued and encircled him with lances drawn. Xingqin recognized Zhuangzong by his flag and charged at an enemy horseman, challenging him to a swordfight and breaking two of his lances before beheading the man. Liang armies now lifted their blockade and withdrew. Zhuangzong hugged him after returning to camp, saying tearfully, "My wealth and station will be shared with you!" Xingqin's favor hereafter eclipsed the other commanders. An appointment ensued as prefect of Xinzhou‡ and later governor of the Wuning command.

Zhuangzong once entertained assorted courtiers in a hall of his private palace, imbibing with relish and amusing all by recounting a lifetime of battle stories. Baffled by Xingqin's absence, he turned to attendants to ask, "Where is Shaorong?" "Banquet invitations were received by ministers and commissioners," the coordinator reported. "Shaorong, a detachments official, received none." A displeased Zhuangzong abruptly terminated the gathering and, on the next day, conferred ministerial standing on Xingqin. Hereafter, the Emperor refused to invite the official rank and file to his private palace, entertaining only military officers there.

With the rebellion of Zhao Zaili at Weizhou [C.E. 926], Zhuangzong prepared to select some senior commander for a sortie when Empress Liu intervened. "This is a minor assignment that Shaorong might well assume," she said. Named commissioner of bandit suppression for at-large armies against the Ye capital, he commanded a force of two thousand to assault the southern gate of Ye. At the same time, he tried to sway Zaili with the Emperor's edict. Zaili presented Xingqin with lamb and wine to feed his troops, then climbed the city wall to shout out, "My commanders and troops, after separation from father and mother for a year, returned home without awaiting imperial orders. His Majesty now expresses his wise concerns, while we have our own regrets. If you, Sir, can explain things effectively to the court, perhaps we can atone for our faults and renew ourselves." "The Son of Heaven considers you and your cohort meritorious in the dynastic enterprise," Xingqin responded. "Minor failings will surely be pardoned." Zaili twice bowed before showing the imperial edict to his armies. Huangfu Hui approached from his side to grab the edict and destroy it, the soldiers rendering a loud roar in response. Xingqin made a detailed accounting to Zhuangzong, who instructed Xingqin in fury, "On the day that the city falls, I want no survivors." He also assigned troops from various districts to Xingqin's command. Garrisoned at Chanzhou, Xingqin divided troops from the districts into five columns, which destroyed the cartwheels, door leaves, and house rafters of the people to construct rafts to cross the Changqing River and attack the gates of the Guanshi county seat, but they failed to overpower it.

At the time, authorities at Xing and Ming prefectures had mutinied in succession, Xingqin's raid against Ye proving fruitless as well. Zhuangzong wished personally to command the effort, although opposition from the official rank and file led to the future Mingzong's deployment for the suppression. Mingzong stationed his men west of the city wall upon arriving at Weizhou, with Xingqin forted to its south. Once his army mutinied, Mingzong entered Weizhou to reach an accord with Zhao Zaili, news of which caused Xingqin to withdraw and fort at Weizhou‡, informing the court of the rebellion.

Zhuangzong had earlier dispatched Li Congjing, director of the Golden Lance Guard, to rush strategy instructions to Mingzong. Congjing was the son of Mingzong. He had reached only Weizhou‡ when his father rebelled, so Xingqin had him fettered and intended to kill him. Congjing pleaded to be returned to the capital, instead, and Xingqin consented. As Mingzong directed his men southward from Wei County [Weizhou], Xingqin rushed his armies back toward the capital [Luoyang]. He then departed with Zhuangzong for Bianzhou when word arrived, after reaching Yingze County, that Mingzong had already crossed the Yellow River at Liyang. Zhuangzong wished to recommission Congjing to negotiate with Mingzong, but Xingqin deemed it unwise and pummeled Congjing to death.

With Bianzhou occupied by Mingzong, Zhuangzong could not advance beyond Wansheng Garrison, he and Xingqin climbing a hill near the highway to share wine and stare tearfully at each other. Offered pheasant by a man of the wilderness, they inquired after the hill's name. "Melancholy Lookout," he indicated, causing Zhuangzong to grow even more sullen and terminate things as everyone left. Proceeding westward to Shiqiao, he again served wine in the wilderness, saying to Xingqin, "You Gentlemen have long followed me through good and bad times, always unperturbed. Yet you sit quietly without uttering a word in the face of our perils today, simply awaiting the outcome of defeat or victory. Back at Yingze, I expressed my desire to cross the river alone by horse and seek out my military coordinator [Mingzong], but you gentlemen each elaborated on the risks entailed. Now that I am reduced to the present circumstances, what do you propose?" Xingqin tearfully declared, "I began as a man of no note, Your Majesty's nurturing enabling me to rank today among senior commanders and ministers. Were I to fail to repay empire in moments of such peril, even death would be too poor a price to pay." He and more than a hundred commanders then loosened hair-knots to cut their hair, the locks tossed on the floor in a vow to him. Ruler and subject embraced one another in uncontainable grief.

Zhuangzong returned to Luoyang, departing again for Sishui a few days later, only to expire through the treachery of Guo Congqian. Xingqin absconded and reached Pinglu before apprehension by a man of the wilderness for conveyance to Guozhou, where prefect Shi Tan lopped off both feet for return to the capital in a cage. Mingzong excoriated him at their meeting, asking, "How did my son betray you?" A scornful Xingqin, eyes fixed on him, countered, "And why did you betray the Former Monarch?" His beheading at the Luoyang marketplace brought onlookers to tears.

WE LAMENT. Death is precious when a person places righteous principle before life itself. Thus, the saying goes, "A dynasty's true subject lives when his ruler lives, dies when his ruler dies." In the context of the Mingzong mutiny at Weizhou and uncertainty among commanders about whom to follow, Xingqin singularly chose to report the rebellion to the court of Zhuangzong, murder Mingzong's son Congjing, and even cut his own hair in a pledge. Such sincerity and integrity certainly merit celebration! Yet unable to commit suicide once Zhuangzong expired, Xingqin instead fled death and coveted life, only to be caught and killed, in the end. He never uttered words of submission, but neither was his death volitional—it fell short of precious!

Doulu Ge

The father of Doulu Ge [d. C.E. 927], Zan, was prefect of Shuzhou in the former Tang dynasty. His was an eminent clan of the age, although tumult in a waning Tang caused Ge to abscond for Zhongshan County. He became administrative secretary to Wang Chuzhi once the dynasty collapsed.

Zhuangzong was still a prince at Weizhou when proposing adoption of "Tang" as the dynastic designation. Scions of former courtiers under the earlier Tang had entirely vanished in the recent turmoil and Doulu Ge, hailing from a famous clan, was summoned to serve as left-auxiliary councilor and chief minister after Zhuangzong's accession to the throne. Despite association with an eminent Tang family, Ge never pursued learning. He often breached seniority rules in assigning officials, such that adjustments had to be made repeatedly by Xiao Xifu, a gentleman at the Imperial Secretariat whom he considered a menace. Zhuangzong had annihilated the Liang regime when Ge recommended Wei Yue [d. C.E. 927] as chief minister. An associate palace censor in the waning years of Tang, Yue had been banished to Nanhai after committing some impropriety, later to serve the Liang as vice minister of rites. Yue was selected to assist Ge due to knowledge of Tang affairs, but proved similarly devoid of erudition and simply reveled in his own pedigree.

At the time, Zhuangzong was vulnerable to the intimidation of Empress Liu within the palace and the guile of eunuchs and actors without. Guo Chongtao also lacked erudition, however unstinting in loyalty to empire. The malleable likes of Ge and Yue thus sat in silence and did nothing, merely complying with Chongtao's wishes. Courtiers had scattered during the tumultuous transition between the Tang and the Liang dynasties, such that the Ministry of Personnel's evaluation documents were incomplete. In this way, crafty and devious manipulations occurred, even the private selling of palace pronouncements. The ancestry of prospective officeholders was manipulated as well, with paternal uncles treated as brothers' offspring and maternal uncles treated as sisters' offspring. Chongtao sought to introduce legal penalties in such cases, while critics called for gradual reform, citing the recent Tang purge of Liang and the precariousness of court rules and standards. Chongtao's contempt for the practice so strong, he was absolutely adamant about imposing legal regulations. Yue and Ge appraised his actions as premature, but lacked the competence to articulate their views.

In the winter of that year, it was revealed that an incoming official, Wu Yanhao, had altered the letter of appointment for a deceased uncle. He was sentenced to death, along with the selection officer, Yin Mei, as banishment awaited others including Cui Yi, the left secretary for evaluation at the Ministry of Personnel. Wei Yue and Doulu Ge, proceeding to the anterior-palace gate, submitted themselves for punishment. With the new laws now implemented, banishment for document fraud and other abuses became common, the numbers of men left wailing or even dying on the roadways beyond all calculation. After the death of Chongtao, Yue prompted a protégé to petition the court on the matter, but critics there held him culpable as well.

That year, the ravages of a vast flood shook the four corners and claimed the lives of tens of thousands of refugees, as the wives and children of soldiers picked wild weeds for food. Almost daily, Zhuangzong reproved fiscal commissioner Kong Qian, who had no remedy. A minor aide at the military bureau, Duan Hui, reminded the Emperor, "Your Subject is familiar with practices under the former dynasty, where in the face of a major dynastic crisis, the Son of Heaven made formal inquiry of chief ministers, employing vermilion ink on imperial stationary. Floods and droughts effectively belonged to the purview of chief ministers." Zhuangzong hence ordered academicians to draft the text of an edict, personally transcribed by him, to make formal inquiry of Ge and Yue. The two men had no response and simply said, "Your Majesty's dauntless virtue reverberates to the four seas. Today, our troops to the west have vanquished Shu and obtained untold millions in precious objects, enough to subsidize our armies. Floods and droughts, the constant way of Heaven, do not merit much concern."

An array of problems plagued the world during Doulu Ge's tenure as chief minister. In an effort to prolong his life, he once consumed cinnabar pills in combination with breathing exercises that caused him to cough blood for several days and nearly die. Sons of both Ge and Yue had been appointed proofreaders at the secretariat, such that father and son worked under the same department. When observers noted the impropriety, sudden reassignment to other posts occurred: Ge appointed Yue's son as Hongwen academician, while Yue appointed Ge's son as Jixian academician.

Once Zhuangzong expired [C.E. 926], Doulu Ge was named master of the imperial mausoleum. After completing temple rites for Zhuangzong, precedent required that Ge leave the capital for a district assignment. He returned to his private residence, instead, and when orders failed to arrive after several days, he promptly proceeded to court at the suggestion of old friends and retainers. Military commissioner An Chonghui received him in audience with rebuke, "You are nominally still master of the imperial mausoleum. Nonetheless, you appear at the new court without waiting for a change of post, doubtless thinking that a military man like myself is gullible to your guile!" Admonitions officers, following his lead, leveled false charges against Ge, alleging the dispatch of tenants to murder others. They also charged Wei Yue with appropriating a neighbor's well. The two men were banished, Ge as prefect of Chen Prefecture and Yue as prefect of Xu†, although horses and rations were to be provided along the route. Three petitions to the throne, from chief ministers Zheng Jue and Ren Huan, argued against issuing the latter mandate for accommodations, receiving no response. Charges were again leveled against Ge for requesting salary and entering court without permission, Yue accused of selling office to examination candidates. As reprimand, Ge was reassigned revenues adjutant for Feizhou and Yue as adjutant for Yizhou¶, both supernumerary offices already held by others. Later, the court exiled Ge to Lingzhou and Yue to Hezhou, the pair permanently relegated to commoner status.

Previously, Wei Yue was exiled to Nanhai for some infraction, then happened upon a general amnesty and returned. Staying briefly at Jiangling, he came to know [Nanping governor] Gao Jixing. After Yue became chief minister, the two often expressed regards for one another through letters and presents. Tang armies later campaigned against Shu and Jixing sought authorization to deploy troops in the three gorges region. Zhuangzong approved, which permitted Jixing to assume administration over such prefectures as Kui, Zhong, Wan, Gui, and Xia‡. He contributed nothing to the conquest of Shu, however, the Tang acquiring the five prefectures through the efforts of other commanders. Jixing repeatedly requested return of the prefectures at the outset of Mingzong's reign, insisting that the Former Emperor had so agreed; the court conceded against its better instincts. After the second exile of Ge and Yue, blame for this misjudgment was heaped upon them. In the second year of Tiancheng, summertime [C.E. 927], the prefects of Lingzhou and Hezhou received imperial directives to oversee the suicides of Ge and Yue.

Doulu Ge's son, Sheng, and Wei Yue's son, Tao, both of whom had risen to "gentlemen" at the Imperial Secretariat, were purged as punishment for their fathers. Tao became assistant director of the Imperial Secretariat's catering office at the outset of the Jin dynasty's Tianfu reign, dying soon thereafter.

Wu Zhen

Wu Zhen [d. C.E. 927] was native to Xindu, Jizhou¶, a foot soldier in youth under the Prince of Zhao, Wang Rong. Through considerable military merit, he rose to deputy lieutenant under Fu Xi's command.

Fu Xi was accompanying Zhuangzong on campaigns in the northern Yellow River region when Rong fell to regicide by Zhang Wenli, Zhen now assisting Xi in the suppression effort [C.E. 921]. With the family of Zhen residing at Zhaozhou, Wenli sought to sway him by apprehending his mother, wife, and more than ten sons. Zhen chose to ignore him, such that Wenli personally broke and severed their hands and noses to maim without killing them, then released them at Xi's camp. Soldiers could not bear to set their eyes on the spectacle, while Zhen regained composure after an initial outburst, then rallied out of indignation, placing himself before menial soldiers on the battlefront. Once the Prince of Jin's armies had vanquished Zhenzhou, a meritorious Wu Zhen became prefect for Shen and later Zhao prefectures.

A genuinely straightforward Wu Zhen enjoyed learning in his youth, later acquiring a comprehensive command of the Zuo Narratives for the *Spring and Autumn Annals*, an affinity for writing poetry, and a knack for composition. During tenure as prefect, he was celebrated for honest and fair governance, winning reassignment as prefect of Jizhou¶ and concurrent commissioner of land and water transport on the northern front. Mingzong learned of his reputation and named him deputy commissioner of bandit suppression for Hebei circuit with concurrent powers as Ningguo governor. He later replaced Fang Zhiwen in overseeing Lutai Commandery, but garrison commander Long Zhi mutinied at the outset of Zhen's arrival, murdering him. The posthumous rank of grand preceptor was confirmed.

WE LAMENT. As I have already affirmed, loyal devotion and filial piety are both attainable, when guided by righteous principle. Do we deem someone like Wu Zhen genuinely loyal? Emphatically not!

When a man accepts compensation from humanity and assumes office on its behalf, when he assumes the office and duties are exclusively his, and when the fortunes of dynasty hinge upon whether or not he serves—even then, he can relinquish salary and office, should harm come to his family in the process of profiting the state. Still more so in this case, where any subordinate could have served in his place, where responsibility was not singularly his, and where the empire's fortunes did not hinge upon whether he served. Under such circumstances, Wu Zhen should be deemed unfilial for disregarding his own kinsmen, his professed lack of selfish intent notwithstanding. Only after a man serves his parents with filial piety can he serve the ruler with loyal devotion. The actions of Wu Zhen may be considered emphatically unfilial. How can they possibly be loyal?

Zhao Feng

Native to Youzhou, Zhao Feng [d. C.E. 935] was acclaimed in youth for his command of Confucian learning. In the era of Liu Shouguang as Prince of Yan, as men there were all being tattooed for induction in the army, an anxious Feng accepted tonsure as a Buddhist monk, seeking sanctuary with Liu Shouqi, the Prince's younger brother. Shouqi subsequently fled to the Liang, which appointed him prefect of Bozhou. Feng served as his administrative assistant, only to leave after Shouqi's death, becoming administrative assistant at Yun Prefecture. Once the Jin acquired Yun, the future Zhuangzong learned of Feng's reputation and relished in having obtained him, so an appointment ensued as Huluan academician. Assignments as drafter at the Palace Secretariat and Hanlin academician occasioned Zhuangzong's formal accession.

Accompanied by Empress Liu, Zhuangzong once visited the home of Zhang Quanyi, metropolitan custodian of Henan, where an inebriated Emperor directed the Empress to treat Quanyi as adoptive father. He dispatched a eunuch, a day later, to order academicians to draft a memorandum affirming Quanyi's standing as the Empress's father. Zhao Feng petitioned the throne in strenuous opposition. Meanwhile, the adopted son of Quanyi, Hao Jisun, died after violating the law. Eunuchs and actors coveting their property tenaciously pleaded for its confiscation by the court. But in a petition to the throne, Feng insisted, "Jisun being the adopted son of Quanyi, a separate seizure of his own property is impermissible. When the law falls short of demanding confiscation, the law enforcer's avarice for property is behavior that the world can ill afford to witness!" The Empress and a coterie of petty men dominated at the time, so the views of Feng could never win an audience.

Mingzong was a martial ruler without full command of the written language, so he commonly employed An Chonghui to read memorials for him from the four corners. Chonghui had no book learning, so frequently his readings proved inadequate to the monarch's needs. Kong Xun advised Chonghui to identify Confucians to serve at his left and right, but the two men knew nothing of Tang precedent. Academicians led by Feng Dao and Zhao Feng were thus recruited for Duanming Hall.

Zhao Feng spoke with candor and tended to be overbearing in character. His cordial relations with Ren Huan early on led to further advancement, once Huan became chief minister. In audience formations, Duanming academicians formerly appeared after Hanlin academicians, their titular rank below office rank as well. Upon promotion to vice minister of rites a year later, Feng pressured Huan to place academicians before regular officials. An imperial decree ultimately mandated the placement of Duanming academicians before Hanlin academicians in audience formation. Huan was later murdered by An Chonghui and falsely charged with conspiring to rebel, Chonghui's dominance of affairs leaving even Mingzong powerless to probe allegations further. A singular Zhao Feng loudly blurted out in tears, "Ren Huan was a righteous officer of our realm. How could he possibly conspire to rebel? You have murdered him, yet what proof can you offer the world?" A mortified Chonghui had no response.

The occultist Zhou Xuanbao's ability to read faces and often accurate prediction of human events had earned the special trust and veneration of Zhuangzong, who named him military inspector for the northern capital [Taiyuan]. The future Mingzong was director of special forces for the palace when An Chonghui sought to test Xuanbao's skills: he had Mingzong exchange clothes with an imposter, then seated him in the lower chair. Xuanbao was now summoned to read the faces. "The special forces director is a commander of precious promise, traits lacking in this man," Xuanbao observed. Pointing to Mingzong in the lower chair, he declared, "This is the right man!" Xuanbao insisted, however, that his predictions of Mingzong's future promise should not be divulged to others. Mingzong deemed Xuanbao divinely inspired after assuming the throne and prepared to summon him to the capital. Zhao Feng admonished against it: "A ruler must be wary of his likes and dislikes. Your Majesty today summons him because his craft seems divine. Invariably, the entire country will rush to embrace predictions of good or ill fortune, inducing deception and tumult whose calamitous consequences are anything but trivial." Mingzong did not summon him again.

Mingzong departed for Bianzhou when Zhu Shouyin rebelled [C.E. 927], then announced a departure for Yezhou in the wake of Shouyin's execution. The various armies in Mingzong's entourage, still in the process of relocating their households from Henan to Bian prefectures, did not wish to leave for the north, so rumblings pervaded the military ranks. Meanwhile, Wang Du of Dingzhou, having witnessed the Shouyin execution that occasioned the Son of Heaven's trip to Bian, interpreted the trip to Ye as part of a conspiracy against him, causing him to grow suspicious and insecure. The chief minister thus led the official multitudes to the auxiliary palace to request cancellation of the trip, their words unheeded by Mingzong. A pervasive fear gripped the hearts of men, yet officialdom dared not broach the matter again. Feng now personally drafted a memorandum chiding An Chonghui with words profoundly incisive and direct. Chonghui conveyed his sentiments to the throne and the trip was suspended.

A monk roaming the western regions and obtaining a tooth of the Buddha once offered it to the court. Mingzong exhibited it before senior officials, only for Zhao Feng to insist, "The tooth of the Buddha, according to longstanding legend, can be damaged neither by water nor fire. I beg to test the truth of the matter." He smashed it with a hatchet, revealing tiny bits as he pulled his hand away. Palace items given to the monk had exceeded several thousands, at the time, a practice that ended after Feng's smashing of the tooth.

In summer, the fourth year of Tiancheng [C.E. 929], Zhao Feng became deputy director at the Chancellery with ministerial powers. The deputy director of the palace library, Yu Qiao, had served alongside Feng as Hanlin academician since the reign of Zhuangzong. Like him, Qiao was invariably direct and daring in speech, the two men once on cordial terms. The continuing rise of Feng, even as Qiao long went without further advancement, convinced Qiao that his own superior talents and reputation had gone unrecognized. He thus joined Xiao Xifu in finding frequent fault with affairs of the day, inveighing against Feng in particular, who refrained from ever expressing the umbrage in his heart. Qiao's seizure of a neighbor's water drain riled An Chonghui as well, so Feng ordered Qiao's demotion to deputy director of the Imperial Library. An intoxicated Qiao went to meet Feng, who feared his obstreperousness and declined on the pretext of having his hair washed. Qiao cursed his nighttime aide, and, before leaving, urinated contemptuously on the cottage for officers on guard. An aide at one of the government departments informed Feng that Qiao had urinated at the hut and cursed him. Feng made the affair known to Mingzong, who stripped Qiao of office, reduced him to commoner status, and exiled him indefinitely to Wuzhou, then the Zhenwu command—punishment deemed by the world as ill suited to the offense.

An Chonghui later came to be charged by Bian Yanwen with sedition. Mingzong summoned Yanwen to court for interrogation, his own duplicity exposed in the process and a summary beheading followed. Several days later, as Zhao Feng addressed current affairs at Zhongxing Hall, he began by saying, "A sinister man has slandered Chonghui, I hear." "This trifling matter has been discharged by me, further inquiry unnecessary," Mingzong asserted. "Rumors heard by Your Subject suggest that the very well-being of empire was at stake," Feng argued, "a matter that Your Majesty can hardly characterize as 'trifling.' " Pointing to a room within the palace hall, he continued, "The most awesome and expansive portions of this hall are the supports for the ridge beams and pillar blocks. If a beam is broken or a pillar removed, the structure itself becomes gravely imperiled. High officials are the ridge beams and pillar blocks of empire. Moreover, Chonghui, rising from humble circumstances, has withstood precisely the tribulations that make Your Majesty today the monarch to rejuvenate our dynasty. How did we allow a sinister Yanwen to create such tumult?" The facial demeanor of Mingzong changed, as he gratefully acknowledged, "Your words are correct." He then authorized the executions of the extended families of Yanwen and two others [Li Xingde and Zhang Jian].

Once Chonghui fell from grace, ranking courtiers dared not speak in his defense, save for Zhao Feng, who repeatedly depicted him as unstintingly loyal. Mingzong now deemed Feng a partisan of Chonghui and banished him to Anguo governor. Feng later apportioned his entire salary as governor to commanders, lieutenants, and retainers, inspiring a newly acceded Emperor Fei to name him grand guardian to the heir-apparent. Feng was confined to home after acquiring a foot malady, where he personally divined with taro stalks once the illness worsened. He tossed the milfoils and sighed at the outcome, "Over the generations, none in my family have reached fifty. Moreover, they knew only poverty and obscurity. I now have exceeded them in age as well as wealth and station. What more could I wish for?" He died at home in the second year of Qingtai [C.E. 935].

Zhang Xian

With the courtesy name Yunzhong, Zhang Xian was native to Jinyang. A man of quiet solemnity and few desires, he was fond of learning in youth and gifted at playing the lute to accompany wine. Zhuangzong had long known of his literary finesse and appointed him administrative secretary to the Tianxiong governor, then deputy director of public works and commissioner of revenues after the accession. Promotions ensued as deputy director of punishments, administrator for evaluation at the Ministry of Personnel, and interim deputy regent for the eastern capital. His knack for managing personnel made Xian an exceedingly capable administrator.

When Zhuangzong departed for the eastern capital, Wang Du of Dingzhou came for an audience and Zhuangzong ordered Zhang Xian to prepare the polo field for a match with Du [C.E. 925]. Prior to this, Zhuangzong had employed the polo field as accession altar when inaugurating the dynasty in the eastern capital. "The accession altar is the venue for the inauguration of kings," Xian observed. "Indeed, altars south of Hao County for the Han dynasty and at Fanyang County for the Wei survive to this day. Such sites cannot be destroyed." He began clearing for a separate polo field to the west of the imperial palaces, work unfinished when an indignant Zhuangzong directed his two military inspectors to raze the accession altar forthwith, reverting it to a polo field. "This is not an auspicious omen," Xian said with a sigh in leaving court.

Previously, in order to campaign against the Khitan, the future Mingzong obtained arms and armor from Weizhou that he distributed among his own troops. These included some five hundred pieces of high-quality armor that Zhang Xian subsequently gave to troops without informing the court. Zhuangzong was thoroughly riled at reaching Weizhou and planned to reprimand Xian for hastily seizing the armor for himself, but was dissuaded after remonstrance from attendants. In addition, he asked Xian about the amount of cash in the treasury. Xian submitted a treasury register indicating thirty thousand strings of cash. Zhuangzong was even more indignant now, commenting to his favorite, actor Shi Yanqiong, "I need a hundred thousand cash strings merely to gamble with you fellows, but Xian gives me some old papers as substitute. Before I crossed the Yellow River, my treasury commonly contained millions of cash strings. Where is it today?" Yanqiong explained matters on Xian's behalf, concluding the matter.

Guo Chongtao, campaigning in Shu, had recommended Zhang Xian as prospective chief minister, but eunuchs and actors opposed Xian's presence at court. The recipient of edicts at the military bureau, Duan Hui, chimed in, "Chief ministers work in the presence of the Son of Heaven, so if they commit some misdeed, a change of course is still possible. If the wrong person is employed locally, however, the potential peril is far from trivial. A gifted and genuine Xian has such potential that a local appointment is all the more preferable." An appointment followed as metropolitan custodian of Taiyuan and interim custodian of the northern capital.

Zhang Xian's family was in residence at Weizhou during the mutiny of Zhao Zaili [C.E. 926]. Zaili treated the family well and sent a letter by special messenger trying to win over Xian [at Taiyuan]. The messenger was beheaded by Xian and the letter forwarded to the throne unopened. Zhuangzong later fell to regicide as Mingzong entered the capital, the news yet to reach Taiyuan, where [Zhuangzong's brother] Cunba, Prince of Yong, had fled. Xian's attendants now proposed, "Today, as Weizhou armies [of Mingzong] proceed southward, we cannot affirm that the Monarch is even alive. Cunba arrives without an imperial mandate and astride a horse with broken crupper. Is there any question of his defeat in battle? We should detain him and await orders from the court." Yet Xian insisted, "I began as a student of books without a scrap of military distinction, only to happen upon Our Monarch's profound generosity. How can I exploit changes and countenance a heart of divided loyalties? I would rather for us to die together!" An aide to Xian, Zhang Zhaoyuan, urged him to write Mingzong and endorse his elevation to the throne, which Xian sobbingly resisted. Cunba had shaved his head hoping to survive as monk when he encountered Fu Yanchao, the border inspector for the northern capital. A great clamor erupted among Yanchao subordinates, however, who murdered Cunba as Xian fled to Yizhou† to be slain as well.

WE LAMENT. Among the "Martyrs to Virtue," I included three persons, but had to exclude three others, the deaths of Gong Tingmei and Yang Wen already mourned. The case of Zhang Xian stirs particular anguish in me. After examining the facts about Xian in the *Old History*, it is impossible to verify the record, for the biographies of Cunba the Prince of Yong, Fu Yanchao, and Zhang Xian are inconsistent throughout. Mistakes by their biographers were doubtless due to the rapid succession of changes at the time. Yet the essentials of Xian's superior probity are readily apparent, his sincerity of purpose making him assuredly loyal.

His intent was abundantly clear: without considering family interests, he broke with Zaili, beheaded his messenger, and tearfully rejected the compromise of Zhaoyuan. He even wished to die along with Cunba, but later reversed himself to abandon Taiyuan in the wake of Cunba's death. Still, we cannot know his heartfelt feelings at the time. The *Old History* writes that Xian, convicted of abandoning the city, was ordered to commit suicide. This argument also seems incorrect to me. I wished to show Xian as adamant in wanting to perfect his noble mission, but, lacking clarity on his relinquishing of the city and the circumstances of his death, inclusion among the "Martyrs to Virtue" is not possible.

CHAPTER 29

....

BIOGRAPHIES OF JIN SUBJECTS

Sang Weihan

Sang Weihan [C.E. 899–947], whose courtesy name was Guoqiao, was a native of Henan Prefecture. He was grotesque in physical appearance, with a short body and long face. He often acknowledged his own strangeness when gazing into a mirror, saying, "I prefer my own foot-long face to the seven-foot body of others." Indomitable in spirit, he still aspired to the upper echelons of court officers.

As Sang Weihan was sitting for the doctoral examination, the official in charge detested Weihan's surname, meaning "mulberry" but pronounced like the word for "mourning." Someone else argued against necessarily pursuing the doctoral degree in favor of a different path to office holding. A pugnacious Sang demonstrated his determination by composing an "Ode to the Rising Sun Buttressed by the Mulberry." He also had a cast-iron ink slab that he showed to a friend, commenting, "Only when this ink slab corrodes will I change my ways!" Such resolve ultimately yielded success at the doctoral examination. When the future Gaozu of Jin was Heyang governor, Weihan served under him as administrative secretary and often accompanied him later on.

Upon deciding to relocate from Taiyuan to the Tianping command, Gaozu acted without court authorization and for treacherous purposes. He inquired of attending commanders, but none dared comment owing to faintness of heart. Sang Weihan and Liu Zhiyuan alone sanctioned it, so Gaozu instructed Weihan to write the Khitan to solicit military aid. Yelü Deguang had already consented when

Zhao Dejun [of Youzhou] amassed a massive bribe to lure Deguang's support, hoping himself to supplant the Tang. Gaozu's fear that his own solicitations might fail prompted the dispatch of Weihan for a meeting with Deguang, where his exceedingly reasoned argument on the benefits of alliance persuaded Deguang. The eventual demise of Tang and ascent of Jin came through Weihan's efforts. Gaozu's accession thus saw his rise to Hanlin academician, vice minister of rites, and commissioner of military affairs. Promotion ensued as deputy director at the Palace Secretariat with ministerial powers and concurrent commissioner of military affairs. In the fourth year of Tianfu [C.E. 939], he left the capital for the governorship of Xiangzhou‡, then for the Taining command [Yanzhou] a year later.

The Tuhun protector-general Bai Chengfu, under Khitan pressure, secured mediation of the Zhenzhou governor, An Chongrong, in hopes of reverting to the Jin dynasty. Chongrong now requested the Jin's repudiation of its alliance with the Khitan and deployed the Tuhun for an offensive. Strong reservations about Chongrong prevented Gaozu from reaching a decision, while Sang Weihan raised "seven reasons for not waging war with the Khitan." Gaozu summoned Weihan's messenger to his bedroom, affirming, "Concerns over the northern border had weighed heavy on my heart when this petition arrived, but my course is now set and Weihan should not despair." Weihan also urged Gaozu to visit the Ye capital, which he did in the seventh year [C.E. 942], Weihan meeting him in audience there. He was reassigned as Jinchang governor.

After ascending the throne, Emperor Chu summoned Weihan as director of the Chancellery. Court affairs were then dominated by Jing Yanguang, who had repudiated the Khitan alliance. The critical opinions of Weihan had difficulty penetrating the court, causing him discreetly to approach the Emperor through an intermediary, who insisted, "For harnessing the Khitan and stabilizing the world, none can succeed but Weihan." Once Yanguang was reassigned to Henan Prefecture, Weihan was named imperial secretary, restored powers as commissioner of military affairs, and invested Duke of Wei. All affairs, from the momentous to the trivial, were uniformly entrusted to him. And indeed, he managed to impose systematic order on a myriad of affairs in a matter of only months. Previously, Hanlin academician Li Han, a man fond of wine, often drank to such excess that Gaozu considered him reckless. In the ninth month of the fifth year of Tianfu [C.E. 940], the court moved to eliminate Hanlin academicians and reassign them as drafting officers at the Imperial Secretariat, in accord with the *Six Canons of Tang*. Academicians at Duanming Hall and the military bureau were eliminated as well. Weihan petitioned to reintroduce academicians to the Military Affairs Bureau upon assuming its commissionership, nominating only old friends and associates to the post.

As the influence of Sang Weihan flourished, bribes and gifts from the four corners swelled to many tens of thousands each year. He shared power at the time with Li Yantao and Feng Yu, the palace master of diplomatic accommodations and academician for Duanming Hall, suffering the slanders of both men. The Emperor wanted to banish Weihan posthaste, but senior officials such as Liu Xu and Li Song argued against it. Yu eventually became military commissioner and chief minister, and Weihan was relegated progressively to the sidelines. The Emperor later took ill after some heavy drinking, prompting Weihan to approach the Empress Dowager discreetly through a messenger to ask about naming tutors for the Emperor's younger brother, Chongrui. Learning of the effort after he recuperated, an offended Emperor demoted Weihan to prefect of Kaifeng. Hereafter, Weihan rarely resurfaced at court, citing a foot malady as a pretext for his absence.

Khitan armies quartered at Zhongdu Bridge overran Luancheng County and fractured the large armies of Du Chongwei and cohort. "Conditions are absolutely critical," exclaimed Sang Weihan, who met to consult Feng Yu and others on strategy. Cooperation between them proved impossible, and Weihan pleaded to confer with the Emperor, who was training falcons in the royal park and had no time for him. As he withdrew, Weihan said in lament, "Alas, [extinction awaits] the Jin dynasty, whose prerogative to sacrifice to the gods will be lost!"

The Jin alliance with the Khitan, forged under Sang Weihan, eventually collapsed under Jing Yanguang. Once hostilities erupted, each and every declaration of war by the Khitan invoked these two men as cause. Yelü Deguang, after invading the capital, conveyed a letter to the Empress Dowager through Zhang Yanze, asking whether the two men were available to emerge in advance of others. The Emperor had formerly spurned Weihan's council against breaking the truce and did not wish Weihan to meet with Deguang. Therefore, he slyly inveigled Yanze to scheme against Weihan, for Yanze coveted his properties.

Weihan's odd physical appearance caused him to buttress himself through a strident sternness, such that seasoned commanders and senior officials of the Jin dynasty uniformly deferred to him in his presence. Zhang Yanze liked to boast of his own bravado, yet whenever greeting Weihan, he could not avoid breaking into a sweat, even in the cold of winter. Previously, Zhang Yanze's coming to the capital caused attendants to urge Weihan to avert impending calamity. "I am a senior official," he insisted. "The country having come to this, how dare I elude death?" He sat calmly in his office and refused to budge. As Yanze took troops inside and asked of his whereabouts, Weihan declared in an obstreperous voice, "A senior official of Jin, I should rightfully die for my country. How can you be so discourteous!" Shuddering and not daring to look up, Yanze commented to others as he withdrew, "I was formerly unappreciative of this person, Sang Weihan, but bear personal witness today to his capacity to intimidate others. Scarcely do I dare to meet him again!" He hence summoned Weihan in the name of the Emperor.

Sang Weihan encountered Li Song on departing, the two exchanging conversation from halted horses. A military aide then approached to ask Weihan to present himself to the Imperial Guard prison. Recognizing the inevitable calamity, Weihan glanced at Song to ask, "Mr. Minister, will I be the only casualty of your tenure?" Mortified, Song could barely respond. Zhang Yanze engineered his murder that night, silk pressed against the throat to strangle him. Deguang was later told that Weihan "strangled himself to death." "I originally had no intent to kill him, and he had no need to kill himself," Deguang insisted. He ordered Weihan's corpse examined upon reaching the capital, only then believing that he did indeed die by strangulation. He reverted the body to family survivors, but Weihan's properties were all pilfered by Yanze.

Jing Yanguang

His courtesy name Hangchuan, Jing Yanguang [C.E. 892–947] was native to Shanzhou. His father Jian, a skilled archer, once instructed him, "If your arrow cannot penetrate the opponent's metal armor, do not even bother to shoot." Yanguang hereafter acquired fame for the powerful punch of his bow and arrow. He was serving Youhui, Prince of Shao, when the Prince was confined after plotting sedition. Yanguang absconded, later to assist Wang Yanzhang in battle at Zhongdu. He emerged from the Yanzhang defeat with multiple wounds to his body and barely able to elude peril.

In the wake of Zhu Shouyin's rebellion at Bianzhou, in the Mingzong reign, the future Gaozu of Jin had overseen the execution of Shouyin's followers, in his capacity as deputy director of the Six Armies [C.E. 927]. A lieutenant at Bian, Yanguang should have been executed, but Gaozu appreciated his talents and secretly facilitated his flight, only to enlist him later as attending commander. The accession of Gaozu witnessed his rise to chief director of infantry of the Imperial Guard with concurrent powers as military training commissioner for Guozhou‡. Reassignment ensued as the concurrent Ningjiang governor. In the fourth year of Tianfu [C.E. 939], Yanguang left the capital to become governor of the Yicheng and Baoyi commands, returning to serve as inspector-in-chief of the Imperial Guard's infantry and cavalry. He also held the governorship of the three cities of Heyang before assuming powers as chief director of armed forces and concurrent governor of Tianping.

In the wake of Gaozu's death, Jing Yanguang played a key role in Chu's succession, and liked to boast of it. Emperor Chu was still new to the throne when the leading Jin officials debated the possible adoption of "vassal" protocol in petitions to the Khitan. Yanguang singularly opposed this, conceding only to "grandson" protocol. Leading courtiers confronted with such opposition all knew him to be wrong but dared not force the matter, even though the decision ultimately infuriated the Khitan, who repeatedly reprimanded the Jin court. In addressing Khitan envoy Qiao Ying, Yanguang elaborated, "The Former Monarch was installed by the northern court, while our current Son of Heaven enthroned himself over the Middle Kingdom: protocol as grandson is acceptable [under these circumstances], but not vassal. Our Jin possesses a formidable arsenal of a hundred thousand giant swords. If the Venerable Gentleman [Yelü Deguang] wants a contest, let him come: he will reap the ridicule of the world, if he fails to prevail over his so-called 'grandson' [Emperor Chu]!" Ying fully appraised such words as cause for certain war between the two empires; at the same time, he feared later questions about his own accurate representation, so he asked that the response be committed to paper, ostensibly as a personal reminder. Yanguang ordered the aide to provide a detailed record for Ying, who returned with the letter concealed in the sleeve of his gown. Yanguang's entire exchange was further conveyed to the Khitan ruler, whose fury intensified.

In autumn, the eighth year of Tianfu [C.E. 943], Emperor Chu returned from a trip to Danian hamlet and hosted a banquet at Yanguang's official residence. There, Yanguang presented him with utensils, costumes, horse saddles, tea couches, and reclining sofas—all sheathed in gold or silver and bearing the dragon or phoenix design. He further provided five thousand bolts of raw silk, fourteen hundred ounces of flossy silk, and twenty-two horses, plus jade-studded saddles, suits of clothing, rhinoceros jade, and golden belts. These were all to be distributed among attending officials starting with royal brother Chongrui and extending down to nominal prefects and personal attendants to Chongrui based on rank. Meanwhile, the Emperor conferred substantial gifts on Yanguang, his mother and wife, and his personal attendants, administrative aides, and senior secretaries in varied manner. Ruler and subject reveled in such pompous displays of profligate ostentation, even as the ravages of drought and locusts claimed each year the lives of a hundred thousand people across the world.

In spring of the next year, as the Khitan launched an invasion, Jing Yanguang assisted Emperor Chu in the northern campaign as commissioner for imperial camps. They faced off in the area between Chan and Wei prefectures. Vanguard Shi Gongba engaged the barbarians at Qicheng. Short on men and unable to secure relief from commanders Gao Xingzhou and Fu

Yanqing, they rushed couriers to urge the augmenting of forces by Yanguang, whose own armies were never deployed. With the three commanders encircled several times around, the Emperor led his personal army to relieve them, the three managing to escape and tearfully articulate their grievances. Yanguang controlled the Imperial Guard, at the time, his military feats feeding his arrogant whim. The various commanders all came under his tight control, leaving even the Emperor unable to restrain him.

Khitan warriors now shouted to Jin defenders, "Jing Yanguang had called us over. Why does he refuse to fight forthwith?" At a time when the commanders all fought with vigor, Yanguang never once confronted the enemy. Even after the Khitan retreat, Yanguang secured city walls without daring to emerge. A single sentence from Yanguang had soured Jin relations with the Khitan, and hereafter, all military commands or calls to war issued by Yanguang did not involve consultation with senior Jin courtiers. The Khitan thus invariably alluded to Yanguang in any letters or pronouncements to the Jin. Emperor Chu returned to the capital after the Khitan withdrawal, reassigning Yanguang as metropolitan custodian of Henan and interim custodian of the western capital. He brought along Yanguang for the drive against Chanyuan [Chanzhou] a year later, accomplishing nothing militarily.

Residing in Luoyang, Yanguang turned melancholy over the failure to prevail. He fully recognized that the Jin dynasty was steadily declining and anticipated its inability to withstand the Khitan, so he imbibed deep into the night while erecting a grand residence with gardens containing singing girls for his personal amusement. Emperor Chu later came to regret his actions and begged the Khitan for peace, sending palace-services officer Zhang Hui to convey his acceptance of vassal protocol. Yelü Deguang insisted, however, "Peace is possible upon delivery of Sang Weihan and Jing Yanguang, plus cession of Zhen and Ding prefectures." The Jin court deemed such conditions unacceptable and suspended talks. Yanguang had quartered troops at Heyang when the Khitan reached Zhongdu, only to return after the Du Chongwei surrender.

In his invasion of the capital [C.E. 946], Deguang arranged for the integration of several thousand Khitan cavalry into Jin forces at Xiangzhou‡, then a crossing of the Yellow River to rush Luoyang and seize Jing Yanguang. "Yanguang may flee south to Wu or west to Shu," he cautioned, "but he must be pursued and captured." Yanguang had refrained from committing suicide out of concern for his family when barbarian mounts suddenly arrived. He and an aide, Yan Pi, were rushed to meet Deguang at Fengqiu County, Pi in shackles. Yanguang protested, "An aide of mine, Pi followed me for professional reasons. What crime has he committed to justify shackles?" He was subsequently taken away. Deguang proceeded to reprimand Yanguang, "The ruin of harmonious relations between north and south is entirely your fault." Qiao Ying was now summoned to bear witness to his previous words, which Yanguang initially denied until Ying withdrew the concealed letter from his sleeve. Deguang now reprimanded Yanguang on ten counts, giving him one counting stick for every admission of culpability. When Yanguang received the eighth stick, he fell prostrate facing the floor and refused eye contact with Deguang, who reviled and shackled him. Escorting him on the journey north, their entourage stopped at Chenqiao to lodge at a commoner's home. At midnight, observing the weariness of guards, Yanguang choked himself to death. He was fifty-six *sui*. Posthumous honors as director of the Chancellery came under Gaozu of Han.

WE LAMENT. Since antiquity, the patterns for peril or prosperity, victory or defeat were never more eminently manifest as with the Jin house. The Khitan facilitated its ascent at the outset and its overthrow at the end. When the Jin went down the path of challenging its own court, critical events did not converge while a center [at Taiyuan], isolated and under siege, could expect no relief from district commands. A single solicitation cast in the forceful tongue [of Weihan] gave the Khitan due cause to empty their own country in raising armies in relief, armies whose actions were coordinated like converging halves of a tally. It was Weihan who most enabled Jin rule to evolve amid impediments and perils. Yet under a recently enthroned and young monarch, it was Yanguang who wrought perpetual war on rival armies, as abrogated alliances created causes for armed conflict. The Jin house thereby matured under Weihan and came to ruin under Yanguang. The two men, however different in intent, met the same fatal end. And why? For those who collude with barbarians in conducting affairs without knowing the entire course of events, calamity is the common outcome, but never good fortune. We must be mindful, we must take heed!

CHAPTER 30

BIOGRAPHIES OF HAN SUBJECTS

Su Fengji

Su Fengji [d. C.E. 950] was native to Changan County, Jingzhao Prefecture. His father Yue had served on the staff of the future Gaozu while governor of Hedong. Fengji often composed memorials and memoranda on Yue's behalf, which Yue mentioned to Gaozu. Summoning him for a meeting, Gaozu was drawn to Fengji's vitality and spirited refinement, appointing him administrative aide.

Gaozu's personality could be stubborn as well as stern, and his retainers and aides rarely invited to draw near. The singular exception was Fengji, who attended to Gaozu in his library until late into the evening. Documents and registers from the governors and commissioners were piled high there, no one daring to discuss them.[1] Fengji would hastily place some next to his chest and pull out the documents, having scrutinized Gaozu's facial expressions for the appropriate time to disturb him. Gaozu approved many of the requests, creating in him an exceptional attachment to Fengji. Still, in greed and deceit, Fengji lacked any sense of decorum and even proved fond of killing others. As alms to Heaven on the occasion of his birthday, Gaozu sent Fengji to clear the capital's jail of prisoners, dubbing the action a "calming of the jail." Fengji entered the jail to inspect the prisoners, only to murder them all without regard for the severity of their crimes or the content of their character, reporting back that "the jail is indeed calm."

With the inauguration of dynasty by Gaozu, Fengji became deputy director of the Palace Secretariat with ministerial powers. The basic fashioning of institutions and major decision-making at court all emanated from Fengji, who at the time viewed these as his personal responsibility. Yet he began not as a man of learning and reached decisions, as events unfolded, based on personal opinions. For this reason, the Han era suffered from a critical lack of legal precepts and failed to effect virtuous governance, the people finding nothing praiseworthy in its rule.

With order restored to the capital by Gaozu, Su Fengji and Su Yugui served together at the Palace Secretariat, where their personnel assignments often violated established rules. Fengji was particularly given to taking bribes, bartering power, and selling offices, as detractors all clamored in indignation. No one dared to expose the two men, so long as Gaozu trusted them. Fengji once expected some rare trinket from Li Yongji of Fengxiang during his first audience in the capital. The son of Congyan, the former Prince of Qin, and scion of generations of noblemen, Yongji was approached by a Fengji crony demanding the deceased Prince's jade sash in exchange for a post as prefect. Yongji professed to have nothing to tender, so Fengji arranged for a jade sash worth several thousand cash strings to be procured, demanding reimbursement from Yongji. Then there was the one-time master for diplomatic accommodations, Wang Yun, recently returned from a mission to Chu, begun in the late Jin era. Fengji believed that the King of Chu had lavished hefty bribes on him and plied for these through a messenger, offering a prefectural assignment in exchange. A dispirited Yun relinquished half of the possessions in his sack. Neither man managed to win a post.

After Gaozu of Han occupied the capital and the chief minister of Jin, Li Song, departed northward under Khitan imposed exile, his official residence was given to Fengji by the emperor. Song also owned some rural estates near the western capital that Fengji claimed in their entirety. Once released to return from the north, Song presented the deeds to his homes to Fengji, annoying him in the process. Song's children and brothers repeatedly expressed their umbrage as well. Later, Fengji induced someone to impeach Song and his younger brothers, including Yu and Yi, who were jailed. [Seeking clemency], Song actually impugned himself by confessing, "With assistance from twenty servants from home, I schemed to induce tumult at the burial site of Gaozu [by setting fires]." His statement was sent from the prison to the Palace Secretariat, where Fengji changed the characters for "twenty" to read "fifty," causing Song's extended family to be liquidated.

At the time, bandits proliferated across the world, so Fengji drafted an edict by hand for the prefectures and counties, mandating capital punishment for all families that harbor bandits and extended death sentences for their immediate neighbors. Someone reminded him that, "Even for a bandit's own extended family, entire liquidation is contrary to the laws of kings. How can one justify the inclusion of neighboring communities?" Not the least contrite, Fengji considered the policy correct, but had to concede grudgingly to dropping one clause—the one demanding liquidation of entire clans. When authorities at Yunzhou apprehended Zhang Lingrou, an officer for apprehending bandits, they thereby perpetrated mass murder against several hundred persons across seventeen villages at Pingyin County. The prefect of Weizhou‡, Ye Renlu, upon learning of bandit activity within his own divisions, now personally led troops to apprehend them. A dozen or so villagers had simultaneously banded to drive out the renegades, infiltrating nearby hills and forcing them to disperse. Renlu arrived after the villagers to find them apprehending the culprits. Mistaking them for bandits, he arrested the entire lot and lopped off their feet, leaving them exposed to the elements at the foot of the hill. There, the villagers wept and wailed for days on end before dying. The injustice seemed insufferable for those to learn of it, but Fengji considered Renlu a capable man. Hereafter, banditry provided cause for wanton murder across the world.

As Fengji grew in political eminence, his material extravagance increased as well. He considered the food in the secretariat dining hall to be inedible and ordered chefs from his own home to prepare exceedingly rare delicacies for his daily consumption. Meanwhile, he refused to assume formal mourning upon the death of his stepmother; and when the Lady Wu died, his wife, court officials and local governors were all plied to provide silk gauze for mourning attire. The sons of Lady Wu were all allowed to assume official posts before completing a year's mourning for her. Once, a stepbrother came from afar to visit Fengji's sons without informing him in advance and an angry Fengji exploited another issue to impeach the cousin before Gaozu, causing him to be flogged to death.

Fengji once accompanied Gaozu in the campaign against Ye, repeatedly getting drunk and insulting the future Taizu of Zhou before troops, incurring his wrath. Upon the accession of Emperor Yin, Fengji importuned longtime friend Li Tao to petition for Taizu and Yang Bin to be removed as military commissioners. Empress Dowager Li was infuriated that Tao intended to plant rifts between senior officials and the court, dismissing him as minister. Yang Bin now received concurrent powers as minister, to be consulted on all decisions, as Fengji and Yugui were relegated to nominal posts. In the second year of Qianyou [C.E. 949], Fengji was honored as dignitary for public works.

The future Taizu of Zhou was never relieved of commissioner duties when serving as Yezhou governor. Yet it was inconvenient, Fengji argued, for governors assigned away from the capital to serve as military commissioner. He challenged Shi Hongzhao on the issue, but ultimately Hongzhao's opinion prevailed. Differences with Fengji had already alienated Hongzhao, but he was further incited at a gathering at Wang Zhang's residence, where an inebriated

Fengji wiggled rudely in his seat. Fengji initially considered a district assignment in hopes of avoiding him, but he dropped the idea. Others inquired of his reasoning and Fengji responded, "If I relinquish the post and leave, the punishment exacted by Shi Hongzhao would reduce me to pulp in an instant!"

Emperor Yin was young in years and surrounded by petty men, while Shi Hongzhao and colleagues manipulated him through intimidation; Hongzhao thus came to be perceived as a threat to the Emperor and his intimate aides like Li Ye and Guo Yunming. Whenever coming into contact with Ye and cohort, Fengji intentionally said things to provoke them further, their eventual murder of Hongzhao permitting Fengji's nomination as provisional commissioner of military affairs. His letter of appointment was being drafted as news arrived of Taizu's mutiny, the appointment now suspended.

Spending the night at the eastern auxiliary hall to the Jinxiang palace, Fengji confided to Wang Chu'ne, the chief astronomer for the summer, "Before shutting my eyes last night, I saw Li Song at my side: the living receiving the dead is hardly propitious!" Taizu of Zhou had reached the northern suburbs as government regulars were vanquished at Liuzi Slope. Fengji stayed at Qili inn [Kaifeng] at the time, where he drank heavily with fellow lodgers and demanded a sword to kill himself, only to be stopped by attendants. He fled with Emperor Yin to Zhao village and committed suicide at a commoner's hostel, a day later. With the restoration of calm to the capital, Taizu had his head severed for exposure at the same site where Li Song was executed. At the outset of the Guangshun era, the court conferred on Fengji's surviving sons an estate, replete with residence, in the western capital.

Shi Hongzhao

Shi Hongzhao [d. C.E. 950], whose courtesy name was Huayuan, was native to Xingze, Zhengzhou. He was courageously daring in character and could overtake a galloping horse on foot. The waning Liang dynasty was conscripting for its military one man in every seven households when it enlisted Hongzhao. Named director of exploratory advance forces, he was selected for the Palace Guard. When Gaozu of Han rose to manager of the guard, Hongzhao served as his lieutenant. Gaozu later left the capital to serve as Taiyuan governor, Hongzhao now becoming director of left and right regiments of the Martially Dedicated Guard with concurrent powers as Leizhou prefect. Gaozu had inaugurated the dynasty at Taiyuan, but faced opposition from Wang Hui of Daizhou and sent Hongzhao in a successful assault. The victory was rewarded with assignment as Zhongwu governor and chief director of Imperial Guard infantry.

The Khitan had returned north at the time, leaving Geng Chongmei to attack Wang Shou'en at Luzhou. Hongzhao led an advance raid at orders from Gaozu, defeating and running off Chongmei as Shou'en reverted the city to Han rule. Wu Xingde of Heyang and Zhai Lingqi of Zezhou now joined others in welcoming Hongzhao and reverting to dynasty. Hongzhao now occupied Heyang and Gaozu arrived at his heels, soon to occupy the capital.

As commander, Shi Hongzhao could be sternly imposing and sparing in words: a subordinate flaunting his authority was once summarily pummeled to death, as Hongzhao's army trembled in awe. In the midst of Gaozu's righteous insurrection, therefore, Hongzhao's troops refrained from even the slightest pillage along the entire path. Stability prevailed in the two capitals, in consequence. Promotion ensued as chief director of cavalry and infantry for the Imperial Guard and Imperial Bodyguard with concurrent powers as governor of Guide and chief minister. With the radical deterioration of Gaozu's health, Hongzhao, Yang Bin, and Su Fengji received orders to safeguard the succession.

Under Emperor Yin, rebellions erupted at Hezhong under Li Shouzhen, Fengxiang under Wang Jingchong, and Yongxing under Zhao Siwan [C.E. 948]. The deployment of troops to the western passes filled the hearts of men with fright, as rumors abounded among the capital's residents that utterly petrified all. Hongzhao responded by directing soldiers in patrols of deterrence and indiscriminately murdering troublemakers, irrespective of the severity of their crimes. At the time, the planet Venus was visible during daylight hours, yet those people who looked up and gazed at it were summarily disjoined at the waist at the marketplace. A drunkard at the marketplace who offended a foot soldier was falsely charged with prevarication and publicly executed. When a person faced criminal punishment, an aide would inform Hongzhao, who needed only to show his third finger for the aide to conduct a summary severing at the waist. Other punishments involved the severing of tongues, mouths, joints, and feet. When Li Song's entire clan was liquidated after a slave's accusation of treachery, Hongzhao claimed Song's young daughter as servant. Former commanders fallen from office tended, hereafter, to spoil the young slaves in their homes, as menial domestics often manipulated their fearful masters.

The wily and malicious Xie Hui, a senior civilian secretary in the Imperial Guard, tended to exploit connections to perpetrate sinister deeds, those suffering at his hand never daring to protest. There was a jade pillow-rest at Yanzhou¤ worth a hundred and forty thousand in cash strings, whose owner He Fujin sent a young servant to the southern Huai region to exchange it for tea. The servant concealed the cash proceeds, and Fujin flogged him with a light rod. The youth now falsely accused Fujin of taking the pillow-rest from Zhao Yanshou as a gift for the Wu regime. Hongzhao arrested and prosecuted Fujin, executing him at the marketplace, while Hongzhao's subordinates laid individual claim to his women and children and confiscated his family property.

Shi Hongzhao eschewed personal retainers or attendants. "I have a low tolerance for literary men, who address me as 'soldier,' " he declared. While serving concurrently at Guide, his deputy governor and others personally tendered a thousand strings of cash as monthly gratuity to Hongzhao. A brewery officer at Ying¤ Prefecture, Qu Wen, had fought with commander He Zheng [Chen Zheng] over purview for administrative revenues. The case was litigated at the Three Fiscal Agencies, which exonerated Wen, whereupon Zheng protested to Hongzhao. He found fault with Wen instead for failing to speak with him in advance, even though Ying¤ belonged to the purview of Hongzhao, then tracked and murdered Wen; several tens of persons were implicated in the affair.

The future Taizu of Zhou, commending meritorious subjects after the Li Shouzhen pacification, arranged Hongzhao's appointment as palace secretary. Military operations in the western passes now suspended, Emperor Yin drew petty men ever closer, taking excursions with individuals like Hou Zan and Li Ye without any sense of decorum. And as the Empress Dowager's kinsmen bartered their influence, Hongzhao and Yang Bin managed modestly to restrain them. When the son of an old acquaintance of the Dowager requested a military appointment, Hongzhao summarily beheaded him. The Emperor's enchantment with music having begun, he conferred a jade sash and embroidered gown on the court master of music. The official went to thank Hongzhao, who indignantly declared, "Our young warriors campaigning for empire lack remuneration for their military units. What deeds of yours might justify such things?" He restored everything to the government.

Shi Hongzhao offered to serve as acting commissioner of military affairs, as the future Taizu of Zhou prepared to leave the capital as Weizhou governor. Opposition came from Su Fengji and Yang Bin, who incurred Hongzhao's resentment. Gathering for drinks at the residence of Dou Zhengu a day later, Hongzhao looked to Taizu with raised goblet, saying in a stern voice to the others, "Why did we differ in court debate, yesterday, when we can come together over drinks, today?" Fengji and Bin now raised large goblets, adding, "For such matters of empire, why insist on taking personal offense?" They drained their goblets dry as Hongzhao continued, "Harmonizing the court and expelling tumult requires only long lances and large swords—the awl is hardly up to the task!" The commissioner of the Three Fiscal Agencies, Wang Zhang, retorted, "Without the awl, however, how could you amass the monies for arms?" The "awl" refers to a writing brush. Hongzhao sat in silence.

During another social gathering at Wang Zhang's residence, some days later, they engaged in heavy drink and played hand-motion games. Shi Hongzhao, unable to play, received repeated promptings from Yan Jinqing, the master for diplomatic accommodations seated beside him. Su Fengji now poked fun at him, saying, "Having someone named Yan seated with him, he need not worry about drinking penalties!" The wife of Hongzhao was also surnamed Yan and a one-time tavern prostitute, so he took the words as a personal insult and furiously cursed Fengji in the foulest of language. Fengji never bothered to correct his mistake, and Hongzhao was planning to thrash him when Fengji left the event early. Hongzhao rose to find his sword and pursue Fengji, as a tearful Yang Bin implored him, "Gentleman Su is chief minister of Han. If you murder him, what recourse do you leave the Son of Heaven?" Hongzhao dashed off on a horse, and Bin escorted him to his residence before returning. Hereafter, commanders and ministers contended like fire and water. Emperor Yin thus importuned Wang Jun to banquet them at Gongzi pavilion and mediate matters.

The court was then run by the likes of Li Ye, Guo Yunming, Hou Zan, and Nie Wenjin, men who disliked court observers. Moreover, as Emperor Yin matured in years and senior officials tried to harness him, he expressed constant indignation. Ye and cohort now exploited such sentiments to engage in slander campaigns, arguing that Hongzhao's propensity for intimidating the Monarch meant certain turmoil if it was not addressed. Emperor Yin similarly wished to eliminate him. One night, hearing the clamor of armor being forged in a workshop, the Emperor feared the arrival of enemy troops and could not sleep until daybreak. He thus met secretly to conspire with Ye and others in the palace. On the third year of Qianyou, winter, thirteenth day of the eleventh month [C.E. December 24, 950],[2] Hongzhao, Yang Bin, Wang Zhang, and cohort entered for audience. They sat on the eastern verandah of Guangzheng Hall when several dozen armored soldiers emerged from inside and beheaded all three men. The three families were annihilated as well.

In the wake of Hongzhao's death, the Emperor presided at Chongyuan Hall and summoned ranked officials to inform them of a conspiracy to rebel by Hongzhao and cohort. Officials had nothing to counter. Furthermore, lieutenants in the various armies were summoned to Wansui Hall and reminded, "The monopoly on power of Hongzhao's group had caused you constantly to fret about dying at their whim. Today, alas, I have finally disposed of the matter for you!" The lieutenants all bowed. Upon the accession of Taizu to the Zhou throne, Hongzhao received posthumous investiture as Prince of Zheng, his burial with appropriate honors approved.

Yang Bin

Native to Guanshi County, Weizhou, Yang Bin [d. C.E. 950] was secretarial aide at the prefectural offices as a youth. Commissioner of revenues Kong

Qian, after receiving authority over the Office of Accounts, named Bin clerical assistant. He later served as commissioner of military revenues at Meng, Hua‡, and Yun prefectures before serving under the future Gaozu of Han as the right chief military attaché to the governor. He became commissioner of military affairs upon Gaozu's enthronement.

Having emerged from the lower ranks, Yang Bin had no affinity for literati, and his relations with Su Fengji and cohort were marred by prejudice and jealousy. When Li Tao petitioned, at the prompting of Fengji, for Bin's dismissal as military commissioner, along with the future Taizu of Zhou, Bin appealed tearfully before the Dowager Li. She angrily relieved Tao of ministerial duties, instead elevating Bin to deputy director of the Palace Secretariat and concurrent minister of personnel with ministerial standing. Fengji and Su Yugui had appointed officials based on favoritism or bribery, at the time, causing an abundance of blunders. With his own ascent as chief minister, affairs regardless of import required Bin's review and approval before presentation to the palace. Moreover, he extensively reformed the practices of Fengji, conducting a thoroughgoing purge of appointees selected by patronage or promotion through government agencies.

However effective at handling matters, Yang Bin appreciated little of the larger enterprise: the governing of empire involved the simple adequacy of wealth and abundance of warriors, as he saw it, with rites, music, and cultural relics all empty vessels. For this reason, he commanded supreme powers, yet was obsessed with petty details. Men with official credentials from the former dynasty, he proposed, should not reside away from the capital, while those traveling the country should receive travel permits from local authorities. Within a week, the proposal wreaked such havoc with popular sentiment that Bin himself found implementation impossible and retreated.

Yang Bin and Wang Zhang often deliberated affairs before the Emperor, who once insisted, "After an action is taken, do not allow further discussion." Bin promptly responded, "Your Majesty can prohibit our speech, but Your Servants will stand here in any case." Listeners were terrified for him. Li Ye was the younger brother of Dowager Li, who sought an appointment as commissioner of palace armies. The Emperor and Dowager discreetly inquired of Bin, who objected and blocked the appointment. Bin also opposed the Emperor on installing as empress the favored Lady Geng. When the Lady died and the burial rites for empresses were to be employed, Bin voiced further objection. Emperor Yin was utterly livid by now, attendants exploiting such rifts to plot against Bin, whose murder occurred on the same day as Shi Hongzhao.

By character, frugal and demure, Bin did not necessarily spurn bribes from the four corners, but frequently presented these to the Emperor. He refused to accept visitors to his home, although in later years, he did interact more with officials while drawing retainers. He recognized the utility of stories from the historical past and urged courtiers to commit these to writing. Peril struck not long afterward. Posthumous investiture as Prince of Hongnong followed Taizu's accession to the Zhou throne.

Liu Zhu

Native to Shanzhou, a youthful Liu Zhu [d. C.E. 950] served as military attaché to the Liang dynasty's Prince of Shao. Through an old friendship with the future Gaozu of Han, he became left chief military attaché once Gaozu became governor of Taiyuan. Zhu was inclined to savagery and fond of murder, yet his courage and decisiveness were considered by Gaozu as akin to his own, so he deployed Zhu with every confidence. Named Yongxing governor after Gaozu's accession and later Pinglu governor, he enjoyed standing as honorary grand preceptor with ministerial powers. He was director of the Chancellery as well.

The Huai and Yangzi regions were not passable at the time, for Qian Liu's envoys from Wu/Yue often traveled by sea to reach the Middle Kingdom. Prefectural authorities along the coast all established trade offices for commerce with the people. Yet when people failed to trade as scheduled, administrators exceeding their own authority opted to organize trade and impose legal penalties, rather than report to the prefectures and counties. And former administrators who once accepted their hefty bribes preferred to release them with no questions asked. The people toiled bitterly under such practices, all banned by Zhu.

Liu Zhu also prided himself as harsh in enforcing the laws. Transgressors would be asked their age, and after giving some number in response, the flogging received by heavy rod would accord with the number—a practice dubbed "flogging based on age." For every flogging, two rods were applied simultaneously, in a practice dubbed "double-delight flogging." He requested an increase in land taxes as well: for every *mou* of land owned, thirty copper coins were claimed by the state. The people's suffering was immeasurable. Emperor Yin saw potential peril in Zhu's obstinacy and bad temper and summoned him, Zhu refusing to come out of fear. Guo Huai of Yi† Prefecture happened to be returning north after an offensive against Southern Tang, his armies stopping off at Qing†. Emperor Yin could then dispatch Fu Yanqing to replace Zhu. Noticing the presence of palace armies, Zhu dared not act insubordinately and accepted the replacement, returning to the capital.

Liu Zhu had known stormy relations with Shi Hongzhao and Yang Bin, so he remarked to Li Ye upon Hongzhao's death, "You men have a lot of gall!"

As provisional prefect of Kaifeng when Taizu of Zhou invaded the capital with his armies, Zhu responded to the rebellion by entirely liquidating the family dependents of Taizu and Wang Jun, among others. Taizu subsequently occupied the capital, and Zhu's wife, found naked, tried to cover herself with a rolled mat, only to be apprehended along with him. Zhu encouraged his wife, "I will surely die, but you should offer yourself as someone's slave." Taizu had someone reprimand Zhu, saying, "You and I both served the Former Monarch. How can you lack any sentiment for an old colleague? The massacre of my family may have been mandated by the ruler, but the savage method was singularly yours to decide. You similarly have a wife and sons, today. Are you not concerned for them?" "I was simply punishing a seditious subject and cognizant of nothing else," Zhu affirmed. Concerned about winning the hearts of others, Taizu proposed to officialdom, "Chancellor Liu has sustained grave injuries in falling from a horse, while humiliated by his own troops to the point of near death. I wish to memorialize the Empress Dowager about pardoning his family dependents. What do you think?" The officials all considered it noble. Murder was thus limited to Zhu, whose head was hung at the marketplace along with Li Ye and cohort. Their wives received pardons and conferral of estates at Shanzhou upon Taizu's formal accession.

Li Ye

Li Ye [d. C.E. 950] was the younger brother of Gaozu's empress. She had seven brothers in all, the youngest, Ye, especially beloved. Named the Wude commissioner in the reign of Gaozu, he was drawn increasingly into court affairs after Emperor Yin's accession, through the Empress Dowager, involvement he never spurned.

In a world plagued by drought and locusts, the Yellow River also overflowed its banks. Turbulent winds in the capital uprooted trees and destroyed gates along the city wall. A strange creature was repeatedly sighted in palace precincts, throwing tiles and shaking its doors. Emperor Yin summoned court astronomer Zhao Yanyi to explore ways to eradicate such menaces through prayers. "My expertise involves celestial omens and solar seasons," Yanyi responded. "I examine only the movements of heaven to identify regularities and irregularities, auspicious and inauspicious episodes. Your Subject has no knowledge of prayers to eradicate such things, although I have heard rumors of an evil elf who roams the mountains." The Dowager summoned nuns to conduct eradication prayers by chanting Buddhist scripture. One nun returned from the toilet weeping woefully, unable to recognize others for several days. She was asked about the incident after regaining consciousness and had no recollection. By then, the Emperor had grown intimate with Nie Wenjin, Hou Zan, Guo Yunming, and cohort. They often employed euphemisms to poke fun at one another, flying paper kites within palace precincts as well. The Dowager often pointed to the natural anomalies as a warning to the Emperor, but to no avail.

A vacancy existed for commissioner of palace armies at the time. Li Ye wished to assume it, and the Empress Dowager directed a messenger to prod senior officials about it. Ranking officials such as Yang Bin and Shi Hongzhao deemed the assignment unacceptable, giving Ye cause for grievance that culminated in an assassination conspiracy against Bin and others.

With Yang Bin and the others now dead, Li Ye dispatched Meng Ye, a palace-services officer, with an edict mandating the murder of Guo Wei at Weizhou, causing Wei to rebel with his armies. The throne entrusted the mission of repulsing him, at Chanyuan, to Yuan E and Yan Jinqing, the left commander of the Divinely Martial Guard and the chief director of cavalry for the Imperial Guard, respectively. Armies were awaiting deployment when Guo Wei reached Huazhou, leaving an utterly terrified Emperor to admit to leading officials, "Earlier, we acted too rashly." Li Ye requested dispersals from government treasuries as incentive for troops. When chief minister Su Yugui opposed, he bowed before Yugui in the Emperor's presence, insisting, "Please, Mr. Minister, do not cling to your treasuries in the name of His Majesty!" The palace now ordered the dispersal of ten thousand cash strings per soldier in the capital, as well as for soldiers from Weizhou accompanying Guo Wei southward. The court also supervised the writing of letters by the sons and brothers of Weizhou troops revealing the identities of soldiers to the north. With Han armies now vanquished in the capital's northern suburbs, Ye seized gold and gems from the palace treasury, placing these against his chest in fleeing to an elder brother, the Baoyi governor, Li Hongxin. The brother refused to accept him and he fled to Jiangzhou, where someone killed him.

Guo Yunming

In youth, Guo Yunming [d. C.E. 950] was a household servant of Gaozu of Han, whose affections led to appointment as beverage master at the Hanlin academy. Emperor Yin especially cherished Yunming, who faced no impediments to his pompous whimsicality. Leading courtiers could refuse him nothing.

While serving as envoy to the Jingnan overlord Gao Baorong, Yunming employed the chariot decorations and escort of a governor, so Baorong treated him with exceptional generosity. Yunming discreetly arranged for someone, on foot, to measure the height of city walls and depth of its moats, as if planning an offensive. He had intended to unnerve them, and indeed the people of Jingnan were uniformly worried. Baorong thus tendered hefty bribes to him. He became director of the Flying Dragon Guard.

Later, Li Ye and Guo Yunming entered a conspiracy to assassinate Yang Bin and others. The day was dark even in the absence of clouds, the moisture from fog seemingly like tears. By high noon, the bodies of more than ten men, including Bin, were carried to the marketplace to be exposed. Yunming personally murdered the sons of Bin and cohort on the western verandah of an audience chamber, the blood of Zhang Yisu, the son-in-law of Wang Zhang, flowing backward. Emperor Yin returned to the Fengqiu gates [of Kaifeng] after a setback in the northern suburbs. The gatekeepers refused him entry. He now fled to Zhao village, hotly pursued by Yunming, who committed regicide against his Emperor at a commoner's home before killing himself.

CHAPTER 31

BIOGRAPHIES OF ZHOU SUBJECTS

Wang Pu

Wang Pu [C.E. 906–959], whose courtesy name was Wenbo, was native to Dongping Commandery. He received the doctoral degree in youth to become editor at the palace library, where he bonded with Yang Bin, commissioner of military affairs. Tensions had surfaced between Bin and men like Wang Zhang and Shi Hongzhao. Pu further appraised Han rule as still in its infancy, its enfeebled Emperor Yin too prone to invest substantive powers in petty men. Tumult also seemed unavoidable owing to sour relations between Bin as senior statesman and commanders and ministers at court. Parting with Bin, Pu decided to return to the east. Li Ye and cohort later goaded Emperor Yin into executing his domineering courtiers, causing the deaths of Bin, Zhang, and Hongzhao—many a retainer of the three families included. Through absence, Pu singularly escaped.

Wang Pu served as administrative secretary under the future Shizong of Zhou, then governor of Chanzhou. He became right proofreader and judicial officer during Shizong's tenure as metropolitan custodian of Kaifeng and director of disciplinary review after Shizong's enthronement. Offering a "Plan to Expand the Border," Pu wrote:

> When the [Later] Tang strayed from the Way, it forfeited the regions of Wu and Shu; when the Jin strayed from the Way, it forfeited the prefectures of You and Bing. By observing the reasons for their errors, we can acquire the methods to neutralize the threats. Such mistakes coincide with governance un-

raveled by gullible rulers and people hard-pressed by arrogant armies, villainy perpetrated by confidantes at court and sedition committed by the disaffected in the districts. The failure to contain lesser threats culminated in usurpation while failure to contain major threats culminated in insurgency. The alienation of men's hearts across the world caused actions to occur without proper mandate: overlords at Wu and Shu exploited the tumult to proclaim bogus titles, those at You and Bing exploited vacuums to usurp power at their districts.

The method for neutralizing these threats rests simply with recognizing the need to reverse the mistakes of the Tang and Jin dynasties. We must first elevate the worthy and eliminate the unworthy to purify the age, utilize the capable and eliminate the inept to identify talent, issue commands both charitable and credible to secure the loyalty of armies, reward merit and punish malefaction to maximize our might, embrace economy and reduce consumption to concentrate the country's wealth, and confine labor service to necessary seasons so people may prosper. Only with filled storehouses and fully stockpiled arsenals can the people be deployed for military action. Then, the citizens of rival states will witness our imperium universally accepted, our populace united in purpose, our military mighty and resources plentiful, our people secure and commanders harmonious. The momentum for certain victory lies herein. Then, persons possessing military intelligence about our foes will gladly be our spies, while persons familiar with their geography will gladly lead the way. Once the hearts of their people and our people achieve harmony, a harmony with Heaven will be won as well—and harmony with Heaven will leave nothing beyond our reach.

The key to a conquest involves commencing with easy targets. At present, the Wu domain offers the only easy target: extending eastward to the sea and southward to the Yangzi River, it has two thousand *li* of border vulnerable to raid. We could begin by raiding the lesser-prepared sites: if fortifications lie to the east, we should raid the west; if fortifications lie to the west, we should raid the east. It will surely rush to relieve vulnerable areas, and based on its relief movements, we can know the state of its preparations and the strength of its armies. Then, by attacking locations vulnerable and armies weak, nothing will impede us, anywhere. We would need no major military movements, as raids by light cavalry will suffice. Its men being cowardly, Wu leaders will surely greet news of our army's infiltration by rallying a vast force in confrontation. Repeated rallies, however, will drain personnel and exhaust the country, permitting us to seize the strategic advantage without a mass mobilization. With them tired and us enjoying the advantage, we will absorb the

> northern Yangzi region into our empire. Securing the northern Yangzi and absorbing their men will enable our own armies to expand, making pacification of even the southern Yangzi far from difficult. Our attainments will thereby be many, despite only modest effort.
>
> After securing the Wu region, prefectures from Gui† to Guang‡ [in the far south] will all become our vassals, while Shu [to the west] can be summoned by a simple courier's letter. If it fails to submit, a simultaneous assault from the four directions will pacify Shu with the effortless ease of rolling a floor mat. The pacification of Wu and Shu will cause political winds to shift, delivering Youzhou to our door. Only Bingzhou is certain to die as renegade, unresponsive to our overtures of charity and trust. It will be necessary to attack with hardened warriors. When its vigor is sapped and morale spent, such that it no longer presents a border menace, then we can intrigue against it. At present, with our warriors well trained and our weaponry in full supply, our subordinates accepting rules and our commanders obeying orders, we could pacify the border in merely a year.
>
> Your Subject, a man of books, has no standing to address important affairs and may even lack appreciation of the broader objectives and timeliness of strategizing. Thus, I beg for Your Majesty's indulgence.

Promoted to left master of admonitions and prefect of Kaifeng, he became left cavalier of palace remonstrance with concurrent standing as Duanming academician within a year.

A newly enthroned Shizong, keen to launch a campaign, now circumvented objections from his senior staff. After personally vanquishing Liu Min at Gaoping, he returned to begin augmenting the armed forces in a thoroughgoing commitment to unify the world. Repeatedly, he probed senior officials on the proper ways to govern, while selecting Xu Taifu, among twenty men of literary background, to compose the "Discussion of the Challenges to Ruler and to Subject" and the "Plan to Pacify the Border." Wang Pu was among that twenty.

Civilian literati at the time counseled the Monarch against a rush to arms: cultivating literary virtues should receive priority, they argued, before tumult and treachery could be arrested. The only courtiers to advance offensive strategies were Hanlin academicians Tao Gu and Dou Yi, deputy censor Yang Zhaojian, and Pu himself, who advocated initial conquest of the Huai and Yangzi regions. Shizong had frequently heard of Pu, but came to cherish him as a rare talent upon witnessing his heroic stand on policy issues. His consultations with Pu on world affairs yielded such total agreement that

Shizong resolved to employ him. With the Emperor campaigning against the Huai region, in the third year of Xiande [C.E. 956], Pu was named interim deputy custodian of the eastern capital. He became vice minister of revenues and deputy commissioner of military affairs upon Shizong's return. Elevation to military commissioner ensued, Pu serving as the capital's interim custodian during the Huai campaigns of the fourth year.

Under Shizong, military campaigns occurred at large while laws and institutions were reformed at court. Wang Pu's sharp intellect and multiple proficiencies were not only relevant to the affairs of his times, but included a comprehensive command of geomancy and calendar making. In the second year of Xiande, he prepared a definitive calendar under court auspices known as the *Qintian Calendar*, purging the "heavenly complements" popular in recent times that lacked classical foundation. Instead, he applied the three astronomical measures to calculate the timing for new and full moons each year and divination numbers for related events, casting horoscopes based on the sun, moon, and five stars. The court further charged Pu, in the sixth year [C.E. 959], with a critical review of ritual music. When the twelve pitch pipes are played together, he found, producing the right tones proved difficult; he restored harmony by adopting the pitch standards of Jing Fang and employing thirteen chords that were each nine feet long, with posts placed one inch apart and the seven tones employed in equal portions.

Enjoying the confidences of Shizong, a stubbornly determined Wang Pu refused to be challenged in any endeavor nor consider the demands of others. During Shizong's campaigns against the Huai, he remained in the capital to extend city walls and connect its roadways, lending an imposing dignity and ample space. Many a configuration in our capital today was designed by him. Similarly, his musical arrangements can still be employed without modification. Even the strategies delineated by him for military movements are far from relevant to his day alone. In predicting the sequence by which rival states would succumb, he asserted, "The Southern Huai can be conquered first, but Bingzhou is certain to die as renegade holdout and perish last." Our own Song dynasty later emerged to pacify the four corners, and precisely as Pu predicted, Bingzhou [Northern Han] was the last holdout.

Shizong had Wang Pu inspect the mouth of the Bian River for the building of a sluice, in the spring of the sixth year [C.E. 959]. He stopped off at the home of former minister Li Gu, where he slumped into his chair on account of illness. Carried home on a stretcher, he died afterward at fifty-four *sui*. Shizong appeared at his funeral and struck his jade halberd against the floor in anguish, greatly moved to tears four times in succession. Posthumous rank as director of the Chancellery was conferred.

Zheng Renhui

His courtesy name Rixin, Zheng Renhui [d. C.E. 955] was native to Jinyang, Taiyuan. He initially served under the Tang commander Chen Shaoguang, a man martially daring and fond of heavy drink, who once vented anger against Renhui when inebriated and drew his sword, intending to kill him. As terrified attendants all scattered, Renhui stood erect with no movement and no expression of fear. Shaoguang now tossed his sword to the floor and patted Renhui on the back, declaring, "With your natural gifts, you will surely achieve an eminence exceeding my own." Renhui subsequently parted with Shaoguang to return to his village, where people say he served his mother with filial devotion.

When the future Gaozu of Han was governor of Hedong, the future Taizu of Zhou regularly visited with Renhui, their conversations leaving him extremely light of heart. He invariably solicited Renhui's counsel when uncertain about matters, his responses never entailing flattery such that Taizu valued him even more. Taizu became commissioner of military affairs under a newly inaugurated Han dynasty and summoned Renhui for office, his appointments culminating in palace master for diplomatic accommodations. Many of the military strategies adopted by Taizu to rout Li Shouzhen of Hezhong involved consultation with Renhui.

After acceding to the Zhou throne, Taizu named Renhui inspector-general of the imperial precincts, military training commissioner for Enzhou, deputy commissioner of military affairs, and later commissioner of the northern court of palace armies before a local assignment as governor of the Zhenning command. Named military commissioner in the inaugural year of Xiande [C.E. 954], he served as interim custodian of the eastern capital during Shizong's offensive against Hedong, only to die of illness a year later, in winter. Shizong prepared to attend his funeral when court authorities reported that attending a funeral that year would be inauspicious. He refused to be swayed, but chose to attend preceded by a broom made of peach-tree branches [as protection against demons].

Since his days of obscurity, Zheng Renhui often strategized with Taizu, but there is no indication of contribution after Renhui achieved eminence. Esteemed and trusted by both Taizu and Shizong, Renhui nonetheless had a capacity for circumspection and humility, while extending courtesies to others without self-adulation—behavior praised by scholar-officials. Posthumously ranked as Palace Secretary, he was ennobled Duke of Han and conferred the title of Loyal and Upright, Zhongzheng.

Hu Zai

Hu Zai was native to northern Yan¤, his courtesy name Zhongxi. With an affinity for learning and a knack for composition, he passed with high honors the doctoral examination of the early Guangshun reign, becoming editor at the palace library and auxiliary at the History Bureau before assignment as investigating censor. He relished in the flair of his own compositions, composing an "Ode on the Origins of Dynastic Fortunes" to enumerate in some detail the historic rise and fall, order and chaos of empires. Once strolling through the Xiangguo monastery [of Kaifeng] and inspired by some bamboo in a courtyard, he composed an "Ode to Virgin Green" for inscription on a monastery wall. Shizong learned of the ode and sent a eunuch attendant to the wall to copy it, praising the piece upon reading it. He now appointed Zai as assistant director of waterways and irrigation and drafter of proclamations. Promoted to Hanlin academician and conferred the silk sash in purple, illness prevented Zai's appearance at court for the protocol of acknowledgement. A hundred days later, he still had to exert himself to appear at the office for auxiliary academicians. Shizong directed him to return to his official residence out of concern, dispatching an imperial doctor to examine him.

Before this, Hu Zai was celebrated among contemporaries for literary skills, talents especially esteemed by military commissioner Wang Pu, who recommended him to chief minister Li Gu. After a long wait for appointment, Pu inquired of Gu, "Why has Hu Zai failed to become secretary?" Gu confided, "The problem lies not in failure to appreciate his talents, but rather, in the destiny of his days to be short—a fate not to be overcome, I fear." "Your responsibility, as minister," Pu insisted, "is to elevate the worthy and eliminate the inept. Why speak of destiny?" Zai was already serving as drafter of proclamations, and within a year of becoming academician, died of illness at thirty-six *sui*. Observers consequently noted that Gu's gift lay in knowing people and Pu's in advancing officials.

The Son of Heaven in those days, with his heroically martial character, relished in embracing the exceptionally gifted from across the world and treated literati with special courtesy. Those advanced by him included Hu Zai, Zhang Zhao, Dou Yan, Tao Gu, and Xu Taifu. Among these, Gu emerged as the most inferior in literary finesse and most deficient in deportment. Zhao and Yan repeatedly addressed policy issues employing exquisite prose, but Gu's allies could anticipate their ruler's inclinations and offer flattering words to suit his whim. In this way, events both momentous and trivial invariably inspired fawning praise such that accolades attended even such events as the expansion of the capital's walls, the commissioning of wooden manikins of farmers, and the sighting of purple stalk or white rabbits—their expressions generally akin to a comedy act. Zai had the misfortune to die prematurely. His policy positions, although no match for Zhao and Yan, were at least not of the obsequious sort produced by Gu.

WE LAMENT. A builder can have skilled artisans but lack quality raw materials, while an aspiring dynast may make an able ruler but lack able officials. Just as raw materials await the right artisans for construction, official subjects await the right ruler for utilization. There is a saying, "Governing a country is like playing *weiqi* checkers." Victory occurs when the player appreciates how to utilize the pieces and positions them correctly; loss occurs when the player does not know the function of the pieces and positions them incorrectly. The loser will approach the board with eyes fixed on the checkers and agonize to day's end, causing the skilled player to survey things and occupy the opponent's positions to win the game. The victor utilizes the pieces of the loser, just as an ascending empire uses the subjects of the vanquished.

In terms of raw talent, Wang Pu truly seems capable. If not for encountering Shizong, however, what could he have done? At large, military campaigns were claiming victory at every turn, while the court reformed institutions, deliberated penal codes, regularized laws and calendars, and probed extant texts on rites and music—all in the age of Shizong! For officials employed during the Five Dynasties period, we should scarcely assume that all were stupid and spineless under Jin and Han rule, whereas all were able and astute under the Zhou. The issue is simply facility in using them.

Rulers who preside over tumultuous empires will commonly place the stupid and the inept in high positions, imposing duties beyond their abilities only to expose their deficiencies and despicableness. Such rulers will place the wise and gifted beneath them and squander their talents, causing superior and inferior men to lose their proper places and imperil the ruler himself. Rulers of ordered empires will keep the wise and gifted in close proximity, while keeping the stupid and inept at a distance, consigning superior and inferior men to their appropriate places, as the ruler revels in peace and glory. The chasm between orderly rule and tumult can be vast, but few factors affect them like assigning men to the wrong places.

WE LAMENT. Since ancient times, rulers presiding over order are few, while those presiding over tumult are many. We can hardly expect better of the Five Dynasties! Whether officials do or do not happen upon the right ruler is a matter of amazement.

CHAPTER 32

BIOGRAPHIES OF MARTYRS TO VIRTUE

There is a saying, "It takes times of turmoil to reveal truly loyal subjects." Such honest words! It is wrong to assume the total absence of loyal men in the Five Dynasties. I have found three of complete integrity, inspiring these "Biographies of Martyrs to Virtue."

Wang Yanzhang

Native to Shouzhang, Yunzhou, Wang Yanzhang [C.E. 863–923] had the courtesy name Ziming. He was a foot soldier in youth under Taizu of Liang, rising to military attaché at Kaifeng, left director of the Royal Guard, and director of cavalry for the advance guard at large. Appointment as prefect of Puzhou, then Chan, followed Emperor Mo's enthronement. A man of audacious valor and physical strength, Yanzhang could walk barefoot across a bed of thorny brambles for a hundred feet. With iron lance in hand, he could dash on horseback with the swiftness of virtual flight—a feat impossible for others. The military consequently dubbed him "Iron Lance Wang."

Although the Liang and the Jin [Later Tang] were militarily peers in the contest over the world, Yanzhang uniquely perceived the Prince of Jin as inferior, commenting, "Yaci [Zhuangzong] is a mere kid who fancies rooster fights. How does he merit worry?" The Liang was dividing the six prefectures formerly centering on Wei and Xiang‡ into two commands, yet fear that Wei armies might not comply prompted the dispatch of Yanzhang, with five hundred horsemen, to occupy Weizhou [C.E. 915]. They forted at [nearby] Jinboting in anticipation of a mutiny, which did occur as Wei armies raided Yanzhang by night. He fled southward, and Wei authorities surrendered to the Prince of Jin, who in turn, overran Chanzhou. Yanzhang's wife and sons were apprehended there and taken back to Taiyuan, a residence provided and their needs amply met. Jin authorities further dispatched a messenger to sway Yanzhang, but he decapitated the messenger to preclude any apostasy. Jin authorities nonetheless feared Yanzhang's continued presence on the Liang side and felt compelled someday to win him over, so they treated his wife and sons even more generously.

Having lost Wei and Bo prefectures, the Liang confronted Jin troops from opposing sides of the Yellow River, and Yanzhang often served as advance guard. Subsequent posts included defense commissioner for Ru and Zheng prefectures, governor of the Kuangguo command, deputy commissioner of bandit suppression for at-large armies to the north, and later governor of Xuanyi. The Prince of Jin already controlled all lands north of the Yellow River at the time, employing iron locks to disrupt access to Desheng Commandery and erecting fortifications on both northern and southern shores of the river, dubbed "dual ramparts." The Liang dynasty's muddled Emperor Mo, meanwhile, had turned to petty sorts such as Zhao Yan and Zhang Hanjie to make decisions, as many senior officials and Palace Guard commanders suffered from slanders. Yanzhang's strategies were therefore never adopted, his powers as deputy commissioner of bandit suppression notwithstanding.

In summer, the third year of Longde [C.E. 923], the Prince of Jin's conquest of Yunzhou utterly terrified Liang troops. Chief minister Jing Xiang, realizing the urgency of matters, placed a rope in his boot before entering the palace to meet Emperor Mo, stating tearfully, "The Former Monarch, having not spurned Your Subject as unfit, invariably adopted my plans in the wake of conquering the world. But today, Your Majesty casually rejects my proposals, even as a dangerous foe looms above. My person no longer of any use to you, I prefer to die!" He drew the rope intending to kill himself when Emperor Mo directed someone to stop him, then invited Xiang to express himself. "Circumstances are extremely dire, and Yanzhang alone is up to the task," he said. Emperor Mo now summoned Yanzhang for assignment as commissioner of bandit suppression, with Duan Ning as deputy. The Emperor inquired of the timetable for breaking the enemy, and when Yanzhang said "three days," anyone within earshot burst into laughter.

Wang Yanzhang departed promptly upon receiving orders. His rush to Huazhou took two days, and he held a large banquet there. Meanwhile, troops were secretly dispatched to mobilize ships at Yang village, and six hundred armored men were instructed to follow the river downstream, each wielding giant axes and accompanied by workmen with charcoal strapped to horses. Halfway into the banquet, Yanzhang rose as if to change clothes, only to lead several thousand elite troops in coursing along the river for a rush on Desheng. Sailors raised the locks from the water and applied heat to break them, deploying their large axes to hack down the suspension bridge, as Yanzhang's men stormed the southern wall. Collapse of the bridge had permitted the wall to be breached—precisely on the third day!

The future Zhuangzong of Tang, then at Weizhou, had deployed Zhu Shouyin to defend the "dual ramparts." The naming of Yanzhang as bandit-suppressing commissioner now alarmed Zhuangzong, who commented, "Yanzhang is heroically daring. Having once dodged one of his sallies, I recognize that Shouyin is no match for him. With few troops, however, Yanzhang will find it expedient to engage forthwith, making a sudden charge on our southern wall a veritable certainty." Zhuangzong rushed cavalry for relief, but only twenty *li* into their trip, reports from the "dual ramparts" indicated, "Yanzhang's men have arrived!" And, indeed, the southern wall was pierced upon their arrival. Zhuangzong destroyed the northern ramparts to make rafts to go downstream toward Yangliu, where he and Yanzhang both rafted on the water, advancing along opposite sides of the river. Whenever the rafts of one side approached the other, a skirmish ensued, with several dozen exchanges of the sort erupting daily. Upon reaching Yangliu, Yanzhang attacked and nearly toppled the town. Jin troops had constructed barricades on the eastern shore of Bozhou, against which Yanzhang launched a sortie without success. He returned to storm Yangliu, only to be defeated.

Duan Ning, already inclined toward treachery at the time, had formed liaisons with Zhao Yan and Zhang Hanjie. Yet a thoroughly intractable Wang Yanzhang was indignant about the Liang's steady decline and resentful of Zhao Yan's actions, once saying to someone, "Just wait until I return from crushing the renegades: I intend to execute evil courtiers on behalf of the world." Such words conveyed to Yan and cohort left them sufficiently frightened to ally with Duan Ning to subvert him. When they breached the southern wall, both Yanzhang and Ning had sent separate letters by courier apprising the court of events. Ning sent another messenger, however, telling Yan to conceal Yanzhang's letter and forward only his own. Emperor Mo initially received such representations skeptically, but messengers later went to the military camps to reward Ning alone without rewarding Yanzhang, causing his men's faces to change color. The setback at Yangliu led Ning to petition the court and insist, "Yanzhang brought on the current defeat by slighting enemy strength under the influence of wine." Zhao Yan and cohort joined in maligning Yanzhang, continuing from midday to nighttime and ending in his dismissal. Replacing him as commissioner of bandit suppression was Ning himself. Yanzhang rushed to the capital for an audience, where he explained the circumstances of victory and defeat by employing an official's handstaff to draw illustrations on the ground. Prodded by Yan and cohort, court authorities censured Yanzhang for disrespectful conduct and tethered him for return to his residence.

As Tang armies attacked Yanzhou, Emperor Mo summoned Yanzhang to seal off the eastern highways. The Liang's most awesome fighters were all subordinate to Duan Ning. Only five hundred mounts were in the capital's imperial security units, all recent and useless conscripts; subordinate to Yanzhang, they were supervised by Zhang Hanjie. Upon reaching Difang Garrison, Yanzhang's armies lost a skirmish owing to troop shortages and took shelter at Zhongdu. After another defeat, he and more than a hundred mounts from his personal guard engaged in a win-or-lose battle. Tang commander Xia Luqi, once closely tied to Yanzhang, recognized his voice and pronounced, "This is Iron Lance Wang!" He proceeded to stab him with a spear to inflict serious injury. Yanzhang's horse now buckled, permitting his capture.

Upon meeting him, Zhuangzong asked, "You once scoffed me as a child. Do you intend to submit today?" He continued, "With your proficiency at warfare, why did you defend Zhongdu rather than Yanzhou? Zhongdu has neither walls nor ramparts. How is entrenchment there possible?" "The critical decisions already in the past, human effort can change nothing," Yanzhang responded. Zhuangzong pitied him and provided medicines for his wounds. Yanzhang was a military man without book learning, but he often recited an idiom to others, "Just as the dying leopard leaves his skin, so a dying man bequeaths a reputation." His loyalist fervor seemed instinctive. Zhuangzong admired such valor and wished to spare him, sending someone to offer consoling words. Yanzhang declined. "Your Majesty and I have fought bloody battles for over ten years. Today, with troops vanquished and energy spent, what should I expect but death? Your Subject, moreover, has enjoyed the beneficence of the Liang and cannot requite dynasty except through death. How can I possibly serve the Liang dynasty at dawn and the Prince of Jin at dusk? To continue living, I could scarcely face the people of the world." Zhuangzong also sent the future Mingzong to sway him. Lying on his bed, injuries preventing him from rising, Yanzhang looked up to Mingzong and acknowledged him by informal name. "Are you not Miaojilie? Now, for certain, you cannot permit this trivial life to continue!" Then sixty-one *sui,* he was murdered. Posthumous rank as grand preceptor was conferred after Gaozu's founding of the Jin dynasty.

Pei Yue

Pei Yue [d. C.E. 923], a contemporary of Wang Yanzhang, was once military attaché to the Luzhou governor. When Zhuangzong of Tang appointed Li Sizhao as the Zhaoyi governor, he entrusted the defense of Zezhou to Pei Yue as assistant commander. In the wake of Sizhao's death, his son Jitao defected to surrender Ze and Lu prefectures to the Liang. Yue summoned the local rank and file, tearfully trying to persuade them, "Through twenty years, I served the deceased governor and witnessed his sharing of spoils to sustain his troops, hoping to exact revenge against the Liang. He met the misfortune of an early death. Today, the Young Master [Jitao], the mourning for his father still incomplete, has repudiated ruler and father alike. I may well die here, but I cannot follow him in converting to the Liang." The rank and file was left teary-eyed.

The Liang court unleashed Dong Zhang to encircle Pei Yue, whom local men aided in the resistance while seeking relief from Zhuangzong. Still engaging Liang armies along the Yellow River, Zhuangzong had only recently adopted the dynastic designation of Tang and the Jitao defection to Liang gave him cause for considerable concern. Thus, Yue's singular refusal to defect came as happy news to Zhuangzong, who observed, "Scarcely was I miserly in treating Jitao, nor was I munificent in treating Yue—but alas, only Yue could distinguish sedition from submission!" Turning to Fu Cunshen,[1] he added, "I do not begrudge the loss of Zezhou to the Liang—a single prefecture can be easily acquired—but obtaining the likes of Yue is truly difficult. If circumstances permit, please retrieve him for me." Cunshen rushed to Liaozhou with five thousand horsemen, but Liang armies had already breached Zezhou and killed Yue.

Liu Renshan

In the Zhou-dynasty reign of Shizong lived *Liu Renshan* [C.E. 901–958], his courtesy name Shouhui. Native to Pengcheng, his father Liu Jin had served Yang Xingmi as prefect for Hao¶ and Chu‡ prefectures, a man heralded widely for his audacious valor.

Renshan was a commander who valued soldiers over wealth, a rigorous enforcer of laws and mandates as well. He had possessed a broad command of literature on warfare since youth. In service to the Southern Tang, he was left commander of palace-gate security and prefect of Huang and Yuan‡ prefectures—his repute for sound administration universal. Li Jing entrusted oversight over his personal bodyguard to Renshan, naming him governor of Wuchang Commandery.

The Zhou having launched its campaign against the Huai with Li Gu attacking from the direction of Shouchun, [Tang ruler] Li Jing responded by dispatching commander Liu Yanzhen to fend off Zhou armies and naming Liu Renshan as Qinghuai governor with command at Shouzhou. Once Li Gu retreated to defend the suspension bridge at Zhengyang, the retreat convinced Yanzhen of the cowardice of Zhou men, so he aggressively pursued them. Renshan considered the pursuit unwise, and when Yanzhen refused to listen, he unilaterally withheld his men, securing the city instead. Yanzhen was ultimately vanquished at Zhengyang.

In the Shouzhou offensive, Shizong had formed several rings around the city and deployed square ships conveying catapults down the Fei River to storm the city wall. He further roped together several hundreds of thousands of giant bamboo poles as platform, with cabins constructed on top that contained armored men for an attack on the wall; those structures were dubbed "dragon-size bamboo." He even blocked the enemy's water bars from flowing into the Fei River. A barrage of assaults on the city, from the inaugural month to the fourth, nonetheless did not lead to submission. The arrival of blazing summer heat now coincided with persistent rains that left Zhou warriors, after a week, in tents inundated by several feet of water. The Huai and Fei rivers suddenly swelled, causing the catapult-carrying ferries and the dragon-bamboo flatbeds all to drift to the river's southern bank, where they were set afire by Li Jing's armies. Zhou casualties were heavy. Once Shizong departed eastward for Haoliang, he left behind Li Chongjin as chief commissioner of bandit suppression at Lu‡ and Shou prefectures. Li Jing [of Southern Tang] similarly directed supreme marshal Li Jingda, the Prince of Qi, to implant barricades below the Zijin Hills, forming a causeway directed toward the city for access. Mutual suspicions impeded cooperation between the two Zhou commanders, Chongjin and Zhang Yongde, Renshan persistently pleading for Jingda's permission to emerge for battle, only to be denied. The attendant frustrations turned Renshan physically ill.

Shizong returned to the northern Huai border, in the inaugural month of the next year [C.E. 958], entirely demolishing palisades along the Zijin Hills and the causeway as well. A resounding defeat awaited Li Jing's men: unable to defend their charge, a succession of commanders either absconded or surrendered, including Feng Yanlu of Guangling, Zhang Shao of Guang Prefecture, Zhou Zuo of Shu, Fang Ne of Tai, and Fan Zaiyu of Si. Back at Jing's court, both ruler and subject trembled in shock, petitioning the Zhou to assume vassal status and promising to cede lands, its gestures of goodwill seemingly sincere. Renshan alone held to a dogged defense that precluded capitulation. Shizong now directed Li Jing's envoy to him, Sun Cheng, to the city wall as a gesture of accommodation to Renshan. Because of Renshan's illness, his son Chongjian schemed with commanders to surrender, which resulted in Renshan's ordering a summary beheading of the son. His military overseer, Zhou Tinggou, appeared before the central gate in pleading tearfully to spare Chongjian, with no success. Warriors were all stirred to tears and hence committed themselves to a life-or-death defense.

By the third month, Renshan had become severely ill, unable to identify others. Deputy governor Sun Yu could thereby forge a letter in his name to relinquish the city. Shizong had Renshan carried out on a stretcher to appear before his tent, heaving a deep and sustained sigh. Conferring a jade sash and royal horse, Shizong also permitted Renshan's return for recuperation. He died the very same day, the imperial rescript in his honor declaring, "Liu Renshan proved exhaustively loyal in every activity, his virtue lofty and flawless. Few among the celebrated subjects of former dynasties can compare! During these campaigns against the south, in acquiring you, I have gained much." Renshan was named honorary grand marshal, concurrent palace secretary, and Tianping governor, although he died before formal acceptance at fifty-eight *sui*.[2]

Shizong sent a personal representative to Renshan's funeral, paid for funeral expenses out of state funds, and posthumously invested him Prince of Pengcheng. Renshan's son, Chongzan, was appointed prefect of Huaizhou‡ and conferred a rural estate and residence. News of Renshan's death led Li Jing to award posthumous rank as well, as grand preceptor. Shouzhou was formerly administered from the town of Shouchun. Because of the challenge of conquering it, Shizong moved the town to Xiacai [north of the Huai River] and reverted the town's commandery status, calling it Zhongzheng, Loyal and Upright. "I do so to honor the integrity of Renshan," he said.

We Lament. To be sure, the world had long despised the Liang! For the literati hapless enough to live in such an age, simple refusal to serve was permissible. But men subsisting on the salaries of mankind must accept possible death in its service. Someone like Yanzhang can surely be said to have died willfully, and Renshan murdered his son to signal his dedication. How inconceivable that he would compromise integrity on the verge of death!

Today the *Veritable Records for Shizong of Zhou* cites Renshan's letter of surrender, likely written by deputy governor Sun Yu. During the reign of Shizong, Wang Huan had defended Qinzhou on behalf of the Shu kingdom, the city refusing to capitulate despite a long siege. Huan ultimately surrendered under considerable coercion and Shizong exalted him for loyal integrity, but limited honors to the title of "commandant." In reviewing the disparity in treatment for the two men, in addition to scrutinizing Shizong's rescript, I know that Renshan was no capitulator.

Since antiquity, loyal subjects and righteous warriors have been a rare find. But to uncover these three men in the tumult of the Five Dynasties—some emerging from the ranks of foot soldiers, others as subjects of a bogus empire—I am simply, quite simply, astounded!

CHAPTER 33

BIOGRAPHIES OF MARTYRS IN SERVICE

We woefully lament. From the Kaiping to the Xiande reigns [C.E. 907–960], for a total of fifty-three years in a world ruled by five houses, so few of the officials with the sad fortune to live then had insisted on total integrity and undivided loyalty. To demand that officials of such times necessarily choose either death or resignation would, alas, deprive the world of officials. But it was prevailing custom for men to cling to their lives, their refusal to surrender office seen as somehow natural. We cannot count the number of Confucian students of benevolence and righteousness, loyalty and trust who savored the salary of mankind and served its empire irrespective of the existence or extinction of that empire. Clinging to life seemed their only wish: not only devoid of shame, they actually reveled in survival. As for those subjects who died in the service of their country, they appear below.[1]

The superior man, in treating others, would rather emphasize the positive than insist on perfection. Still more so when death is involved, something dreaded by all men. For the Five Dynasties era, I can identify only three men of total integrity. There were another fifteen, excluding ordinary casualties of war, without notable integrity at the outset who ultimately died in the service of humanity. The inclusion of Wang Qing and Shi Yanchao contains symbolism, great symbolism—inspiring these "Biographies of Martyrs in Service."[i]

i. There are five men for whom no biography could be written: Ma Yanchao is appended to the biography of Zhu Shouyin. Song Lingxun, Li Xia, Zhang Yanqing, and Zheng Zhaoye appear only in the Basic Annals.

Zhang Yuande

Nothing is known of the family heritage of Zhang Yuande [d. C.E. 916], although reports place him originally with the Jin [Later Tang]. Serving the Prince of Jin in youth, he evinced no particular distinction before joining Li Hanzhi to repudiate Jin and surrender Luzhou to the Liang. Hanzhi subsequently sent Yuande to meet with Taizu, whose later accession to the Liang throne saw Yuande rise to prefect of Caizhou with standing as commander of the Imperial Insignia Guard.

In the third year of Zhenming, under the Liang [C.E. 917],[2] Wei/Bo governor Yang Shihou died, and Emperor Mo divided the six prefectures centering on Wei and Xiang‡ into two separate governorships. Anxious about whether the Wei military would acquiesce, he sent Liu Xun to fort ten thousand men at Weizhou as precaution against insurrection. Wei authorities did rebel and coerced He Delun to surrender both Wei and Bo prefectures to the Jin. At the time, Zhang Yuande was defending Beizhou. The Prince of Jin's various commanders, after the Wei occupation, wanted Beizhou selected first for a sortie. However, the Prince argued, "Bei is a small yet fortified town, one not to fall quickly. Yuande's reliance on Liu Xun notwithstanding, his interdependence with Cangzhou is like head to tail. Positioned between them is Dezhou, now without defenses. Claiming it beforehand seems preferable, and with the power of Cang and Bei fragmented, intriguing against either will be simpler." They first targeted Dezhou for a sortie and overpowered it before proceeding with a raid against Yuande involving five thousand troops. He staunchly resisted and the city refused to fall, so Jin troops dug trenches around the city.

A rout at the old Yuancheng County forced Liu Xun to flee southward to Liyang, as Jin armies overran Mingzhou. The Weizhou‡ prefect Lai [Mi] Zhao and Xingzhou governor Yan Bao then relinquished their towns to Jin, as prefects Jin Zhao of Ci, Zhang Yun of Xiang‡, and Dai Siyuan of Cang all fled. The entire Yan¤ region had already been conquered by the Prince of Jin, Zhen and Ding prefectures now coming under his sway. He controlled, in effect, six garrisons and dozens of prefectures extending over four thousand *li* north of the Yellow River and east of the mountains. The prefecture of Bei alone, encircled for over a year, singularly refused to succumb. Yuande's resolve for a staunch defense notwithstanding, the Beizhou leadership knew the Jin to hold the entire landmass north of the Yellow River, while food supplies locally were depleted. They pleaded to surrender, Yuande refused, and they murdered him.

The Beizhou leadership now intrigued in the wake of Yuande's death, "With the Jin siege having continued for long and our surrender a consequence of depleted resources, we worry that none will escape death." They thereby proposed to the Jin, "We prefer to surrender with our armor in place and troops in tow, relinquishing these after receiving a pardon. Is this acceptable?" The Jin military conceded, and three thousand Beizhou soldiers emerged from the city to surrender. After removing their armor, they were girded by Jin soldiers on all four sides and massacred.

Xia Luqi

A native of Qingzhou†, Xia Luqi [C.E. 883–931] had the courtesy name Bangjie. The name Li Shaoqi was conferred under Zhuangzong of Tang, but he and the others given names by Zhuangzong later chose to restore their old names. Luqi initially served the Liang as lieutenant of the Xuanwu Command, later fleeing to the Prince of Jin to become director of the Security Guard. He assisted Zhou Dewei in the raid on Liu Shouguang at Youzhou. Under Shouguang's command were Shan Tinggui and Yuan Xingqin, men who made much of their daring valor. Still, whenever Luqi had fistfights with the two commanders, they could not be easily broken up, their two armies pausing to observe them.

Wei and Bo prefectures had fallen to the Jin when Liang commander Liu Xun forted troops at Huanshui County. Zhuangzong [Prince of Jin] was deploying a hundred mounts for reconnaissance against the enemy upon falling into Xun's ambush: encircled several times around, flight seemed nearly impossible. Luqi fought with such vigor that over a hundred men died at his hand, even as punctures to his own body exceeded twenty. Breaking the blockade, he and Zhuangzong escaped together. Zhuangzong increasingly valued him and named Luqi prefect of Cizhou. He entered combat at Zhongdu as well, where the capture of Wang Yanzhang impressed Zhuangzong, who conferred a thousand bolts of sheer silk and appointed him defense commissioner for Zhengzhou. Reassigned governor of Heyang, Luqi governed with charitable compassion. When the government arranged his transfer as Zhongwu governor, the people of Heyang attempted to block the reassignment, as local elders visited the capital to plead for his retention. Mingzong had to deploy a palace commissioner to persuade them before Luqi managed to leave.

Xia Luqi became deputy commissioner of bandit suppression during the Tang campaign against Jingnan, returning without notable feats. He was the Wuxin governor when Dong Zhang of eastern Chuan rebelled. During Zhang's assault on Suizhou‡, Luqi sealed up the city in defiance. Reinforcements did not arrive after a full month, and the city's rations were exhausted. Luqi slit his throat and died.[3] He was forty-nine *sui*.[ii]

....

ii. The armies of Wu Luan could still fight but refused, while Luqi died when food and vigor had been exhausted. There is a clear distinction in the measure of righteous principle for the two.

Yao Hong

Beginning as a petty lieutenant under the Liang, Yao Hong [d. C.E. 930] served under Dong Zhang after his reversion to the Liang, later becoming military director during the Tang.

In the Changxing era, the court dispatched Hong to station a thousand garrison troops at Langzhou‡. Once Dong Zhang mutinied against Tang, he sent a messenger to win over Hong, but he promptly tossed the letter into a toilet upon receipt. Zhang's armies later conquered Langzhou‡ and apprehended Hong, whereupon Zhang inquired of Hong, "A one-time foot soldier, you once enjoyed my generous treatment. How could you forsake me?" Hong responded with a curse, "You old scoundrel! As a one-time slave of Gentleman Li the Seventh who scooped up horse dung, you were once eternally grateful to obtain a simple slice of leftover meat. Today, the Son of Heaven employs you as governor. What hardship could possibly cause you to rebel? I can accept death for the empire, but cannot countenance saving my life by following somebody's slave!" A furious Zhang ordered a cauldron of boiling water placed before him and commanded ten of his stoutest warriors to slice pieces of Hong's flesh to eat, Hong cursing vociferously to his last breath. Mingzong wept at the news, registering his sons as officials and extending generous treatment to his family.

Wang Sitong

Wang Sitong [d. C.E. 934] was native to Youzhou. His father, Jingrou, married the daughter of Liu Rengong, who gave birth to him. Sitong served Rengong as director of the Silver and Gold Guard. The incarceration of Rengong by his own son, Shouguang, led Sitong to seek sanctuary with the Prince of Jin, becoming director of the Nimble-Prancing Guard.[4] With the armies of Liang and Jin in a standoff at Shen County [Weizhou], Sitong was sent to construct ramparts at Yangliu. His merit led to promotion to chief director of the Divinely Martial Guard's Tenth Regiment, then defense commissioner for Zhengzhou. Sitong was a man of daring valor, his skills as horseman and archer complemented by an affinity for learning and writing poetry. Stressing righteous principle over material wealth, he treated many a literatus with due courtesy. He won not a single victory in battle, however.

In the era of Mingzong, after a prolonged term of office, he was named Kuangguo governor, then Xiongwu governor. Repeated pillaging from Tubo Tibetans occurred at the time, Qinzhou having no defense barriers. Sitong thus arrayed more than forty palisades to resist the intruders. He visited court some five years later, where Mingzong inquired of border affairs and Sitong, drawing the area's mountains and rivers by hand, enumerated strategic advantages and disadvantages. Once he withdrew, Mingzong turned to nearby attendants, commenting, "Some say that Sitong does not manage affairs, yet he managed here to perform exquisitely!" Starting to appreciate his talents, Mingzong named him generalissimo of the Right Martial Guard, metropolitan custodian of Jingzhao, and interim custodian of the western capital. During the punitive campaign led by Shi Jingtang against Dong Zhang [C.E. 930], Sitong served as director of the vanguard. Soldiers to the rear failed to keep up as his men entered Jianmen, leaving Sitong to engage Zhang alone in battle. He failed to prevail and retreated. Once Jingtang was relieved of command, Sitong became governor of Shannan west circuit, later to be restored as custodian of Jingzhao and interim custodian of the western capital.

In the second month of the inaugural year of Yingshun [C.E. 934], Congke, the Prince of Lu, rebelled at Fengxiang and urgently summoned to war the four neighboring commands. In enumerating the reasons for raising armies to suppress turmoil, he charged wicked officials with suspicious visits to the deathbed of the Former Monarch, the renegade murder of the Prince of Qin to install a young heir, and the undermining of imperial clansmen and district commanders. He further arranged for slave-musician An Shishi to visit Sitong, employing a five-stringed instrument to relax him while exploring his preferences. The hearts of commanders at the time were inclined as much toward submission to as defiance against the court: without spurning the Prince's messengers, the commanders nonetheless informed the court of his letter of grievance. Sitong alone chose to gather musician An Shishi and judicial officer Hao Xu, Congke's emissary, and convey them to the capital. Emperor Min commended his loyalty, naming Sitong chief officer of armed forces at large on the western front.

In the third month, Sitong aided armies from the various commands to surround Fengxiang, overrunning cities along the passes from east to west. Congke's soldiers, although weak, defended with dogged determination, inflicting serious injury and heavy casualties on the aggressors. A tearful Congke, climbing atop the city wall, shouted out to those outside soldiers, "I followed the Former Monarch for twenty years and witnessed several hundred battles great and small, our armor never unfastened despite wounds covering our bodies. You and your men even accompanied us then. Today the Former Monarch has recently left this world and the court trusts villains who plant rifts between flesh-and-blood clansmen. What crime have I committed to be targeted for assault?" He cried uncontrollably, his words stirring the compassion and commiseration of rival troops.

Zhang Qianzhao of Xingyuan moved to assault the city's western wall, directing an intensive barrage, but his own overwrought troops proceeded to attack him and force his flight. The director of the Forest of Feathers Guard, Yang Siquan, now pronounced thunderously, "The Prince of Lu is my ruler!" His men were then led through the western gate to surrender to Congke. The defection was still unknown to Sitong, who continued to direct soldiers. But the commander of the Austere Guard, Yin Hui, motioned to troops, declaring, "Armies at the western wall have indeed entered the city to receive awards. Why bother with further battle?" The troops now doffed their armor and abandoned their weapons, their cheering heard for a distance of several *li* as they all entered the city to surrender. The armies of the governors fully vanquished, Sitong departed in defiance. Upon reaching Changan, its deputy custodian Liu Suiyong shut the gates to refuse him entry, with Sitong then proceeding to Tong Pass. Congke thus led his armies eastward, his advance guard pursuing and apprehending Sitong at Zhaoying. Reprovingly, Congke queried, "Did you think you could flee punishment?" "It is not that I failed to realize, by assisting you, My Prince, that I could keep my life. Rather, I feared being unable to meet the Former Monarch in the netherworld, when death finally did come." Such words filled Congke with shame and he killed Sitong. Posthumous rank as director of the Chancellery was conferred once Gaozu assumed the Han throne.[iii]

Zhang Jingda

Native to Daizhou, Zhang Jingda [d. C.E. 936] had the courtesy name Zhitong and the nickname "Raw Iron." Deft as horseman and archer, he served in youth as auxiliary commander under Zhuangzong of Tang. In the reign of Mingzong, he rose to chief director of armed forces for Hedong and concurrent prefect of Qinzhou‡. Successive promotions left him governor of the Zhangguo and Datong commands, then Wuxin and Jinchang.

In the second year of Qingtai [C.E. 935], repeated Khitan raids on the border forced Emperor Fei to name Shi Jingtang, the Hedong governor, concurrent chief coordinator of multiracial armed forces for the commands of Datong, Zhangguo, Zhenwu, and Weisai, among others. Quartered at Xinzhou‡, his men once greeted Jingtang with roars [reserved for monarchs] of "Ten Thousand Years!" Jingtang had to behead more than thirty of them to stop the seditious act. Emperor Fei suspected Jingtang of treacherous intent and siphoned off his men by reassigning Zhang Jingda as deputy coordinator

....

iii. In going eastward, Sitong intended to return personally to the Son of Heaven, circumstances different from the flight of Yuan Xingqin. Therefore, a death of integrity is acknowledged.

of the northern front. By the summer of the next year [C.E. 936], with Jingtang now reassigned as Tianping governor, Jingda became chief officer of multiracial armed forces for the Datong, Zhangguo, Zhenwu, and Weisai commands. For this reason, Jingtang rebelled. The court designated Jingda as commissioner of bandit suppression for the four fronts at Taiyuan. Surrounding Taiyuan in the sixth month, Jingda's men erected a long wall of interconnected palisades, intending to assault the city with scaling ladders and catapults. As the wall of palisades neared completion, however, a heavy wind and rain suddenly struck, torrents of water destroying them.

Shi Jingtang turned to the Khitan for relief. In the ninth month, their ruler Yelü Deguang entered the country from Yanmen, his banners forming an uninterrupted line fifty *li* in length. Deguang had a messenger indicate to Jingtang beforehand, "This very day, I want to break our opponent. Is this acceptable?" Jingtang responded, "Your great army has traveled a long distance, while our adversary's strength thrives. The objective is success, not necessarily speed." The envoy had not even reported on the mission when armies were engaged.

Zhang Jingda battled near the western mountains, where the Khitan deployed against the Tang some three thousand lean horsemen with leather horsewhips and wooden stirrups—neither men nor horses of the highest quality. The Khitan were engaged forthwith and scattered. Tang armies pursued them to the Fen River [Jinyang], only to be split in half after an ambush. Regiments in the north perished entirely as overall casualties exceeded ten thousand. Jingda regrouped his men and arrayed barricades at Jin'an. The Khitan now surrounded him, Emperor Fei providing relief through Zhao Yanshou and Fan Yanguang. Yanshou quartered troops at Tuanbo ravine and Yanguang at Liaozhou, more than a hundred *li* from Jingda. Khitan soldiers currently besieging Jingda now descended southward from Jin'an County outposts, spanning an area more than a hundred *li* in length and fifty *li* in breadth. Jingda looked out from his barracks, able only to see an endless stream of barbarian tents that looked like knolls with nets on top, ropes tied across all four sides and bells suspended to alert soldiers and unleash man-hunting dogs. Some in Jingda's army who departed at nighttime were promptly apprehended by the Khitan; hereafter, he sealed the city tight and dared not allow any more departures.

Zhao Yanshou and cohort were all duplicitous in heart and disinterested in rescuing Jingda, who still possessed fifty thousand troops and over ten thousand horses. Once food supplies were depleted, Jingda's soldiers used wood shavings and recycled dung to feed their horses, then ate dead horses to the point of depleting horse supplies. Pleas came from Yang Guangyuan, deputy commissioner of bandit suppression, to surrender to the Jin dynasty, but

Jingda could not bear to repudiate the Tang, convinced that relief armies would arrive. As Guangyuan continued his relentless pressure, Jingda taunted him, "Why do you gentlemen keep trying to persuade me? Why not simply kill me and capitulate?" So, Guangyuan beheaded Jingda to surrender. Khitan ruler Yelü Deguang mourned him as a loyal man upon learning of the death, arranging his body's retrieval for proper burial.[iv]

Zhai Jinzong and Zhang Wandi

The places of origin for Zhai Jinzong [d. C.E. 944] and Zhang Wandi [d. C.E. 944] are unknown. They both originally served the Tang, then the Later Jin: Jinzong as prefect of Zi Prefecture and Wandi as prefect of Deng‡. When Yang Guangyuan rebelled, he deployed a hundred horsemen to seize the two prefects by force for transfer to Qingzhou‡. Wandi acquiesced in his mandate, but Jinzong singularly refused submission and Guangyuan murdered him. Emperor Chu conferred posthumous rank on Jinzong as generalissimo of the Left Martial Guard. A special amnesty was declared for Qingzhou‡ after Guangyuan's pacification, his sons and grandsons reprieved. Singularly exempted from the pardon was Wandi, beheaded after his crimes were exposed. The palace ordered the retrieval of Jinzong's body for burial rites of elevated status, subsidizing burial costs from official funds. His son, Renqin, received military rank as *Dongtou* services officer.

Shen Bin

His courtesy name Anshi, Shen Bin [d. C.E. 945] was native to Xiapi, Xuzhou. A foot soldier in youth, he rose to chief director of the Salute-to-Monarch Guard under the Liang before serving the Tang. He accompanied the Prince of Wei, Jiji, in the conquest of Shu and assisted in pacifying Kang Yanxiao. His merit led to an assignment as prefect for Guozhou and eventually eight other prefectures, including Sui and Zhao.

In the inaugural year of Kaiyun, under Jin rule [C.E. 944], Shen Bin became prefect of Qizhou†. Khitan violation of the border had extended to

....

iv. In the Basic Annals he is censured for failing to kill Guangyuan, enabling Guangyuan to murder him instead and surrender to the enemy. Therefore, it is not said that he "gave his life," but that events unfolded as he intended. Accounts of his death ultimately celebrate him for not surrendering, yet his death cannot be considered one of integrity: despite personally refusing to submit, he facilitated another's surrender to renegades.

Yulin County, so they passed through Qizhou† on the return. Having penetrated deep into Jin territory, returning Khitan troops, starving and exhausted, seemed vulnerable to attack, or so Bin reasoned. He deployed prefectural militia to engage them, but their elite cavalry tore down the city gate, and many of Bin's men perished. The city lacked military preparations and the mercenary commander for the barbarians, Zhao Yanshou, kept a force behind to unleash against the city an intense barrage. He also tried to persuade Bin to surrender, Bin reviling him from atop the city wall, "Father and son, the two of you have reckoned wrong: sinking into a lair of stench and consorting with packs of dogs and goats, you desecrate and violate your mother country. I gladly die for dynasty, but refuse to do as you have done." The city later succumbed and Bin killed himself, his entire family perishing at barbarian hands.

Wang Qing

Wang Qing [C.E. 895–947] had the courtesy name Quxia. Native to Quzhou, Ming Prefecture, he initially served the Tang as director of the Pacific Guard and the Later Jin as inspector-in-chief of the Empire-Upholding Guard. In the wake of An Congjin's mutiny at Xiangzhou, he aided Gao Xingzhou in an offensive. The city could not be taken even after a year, and Qing advised Xingzhou, "Congjin seals off his isolated city in hopes of preserving it. How can strategic advantage possibly be retained for long?" He requested to scale the wall in advance, permitting a successful assault.

In the second year of Kaiyun, wintertime [C.E. 945], Qing assisted Du Chongwei in battles at Yangcheng [Zhongshan]. A vigorous fighter, Qing emerged as the most meritorious in his entire infantry unit, rising to honorary dignitary for education. That winter, Chongwei forted troops south of Zhongdu Bridge, confronted by the barbarian Khitan armies directly north. The barbarians employed elite cavalry to emerge from the mountains to the west and assault the Jin army's rear flank. They simultaneously launched a sortie against Luancheng to the south, severing supply lines for the Jin. Qing now proposed to Chongwei, "Our Jin armies face imminent peril: only five *li* from Zhenzhou, yet we insist on a fatal defense here. With our camps isolated and rations gone, what are our prospects? Give me two thousand infantry as vanguard and I will rush the bridge to open a path. You should follow up with residual forces, at that point, to occupy Zhenzhou, which we could then hold." Chongwei consented and provided Song Yanyun for his vanguard. Qing defeated the barbarians in battle and seized the bridge. Chongwei's heart had turned seditious by now, and he refused to advance for lack of resolve. Yanyun withdrew as well, leaving Qing to exclaim, "I will surely die here on my own!" He perished in vigorous combat at fifty-three *sui*. Posthumous rank as grand mentor was conferred upon Gaozu's accession to the Han throne.

Shi Yanchao

Native to Yunzhou, Shi Yanchao [d. C.E. 954] was a man of dauntless daring and indomitable courage. During the ascent at Weizhou of Taizu, the future Zhou ruler, Yanchao was chief director of the Dragonly Victorious Guard of the Han dynasty and placed his army in Taizu's service. Attending Taizu's accession, Yanchao became chief director of the Lionly Victorious Guard, his men garrisoned at Jinzhou.

When [Northern Han] ruler Liu Min raided Jinzhou [C.E. 951], the prefecture lacked a leading commander, and prefect Wang Wan'gan could not offer resistance. Yanchao thus mobilized his garrison regiments for a tenacious defense of the city that exceeded a month. Min's troops dispersed, however, after Taizu's dispatch of Wang Jun as reinforcement. Yanchao's merit led to promotion as chief director for the Dragonly Victorious Guard's right wing, with concurrent authority as defense commissioner for Zhengzhou. He also led the vanguard as Zhou and Northern Han armies battled at Gaoping, the first to leap into the fray. Assignment as Gande governor came in consequence.[5]

As Zhou armies besieged Taiyuan, under Northern Han control, the Khitan intervened on behalf of the Han, departing from Xin‡ and Dai prefectures. Shizong dispatched Fu Yanqing to repulse them with Shi Yanchao as vanguard. Yanchao reached his full daring and fury during combat at Xinkou, as warriors nearby stormed forth, dispersing and regrouping a total of four times. He succumbed to battle.

Shizong, having recently vanquished the Northern Han at Gaoping, wanted to exploit the momentum to advance further. Yet his commanders could reach no consensus on the siege of the city, so final victory had long eluded them. Shizong now preferred to dissolve the blockade, but could reach no decision. News of Yanchao's death in battle induced him to recall troops for sudden withdrawal, his haste causing vast numbers to perish. Grief over Yanchao and indignation at failing to prevail left Shizong so depressed and enraged that he could not eat for several days. Yanchao won posthumous rank as grand preceptor, and his family was privileged to exceptional generosity.

Sun Cheng

Sun Cheng [d. C.E. 956], originally named Feng, also went by the personal name Ji, a native of Mizhou. He was fond of learning and literarily refined, with a special facility for poetry. As a Daoist adept in youth, he lived at the Jianji temple at Lushan. He often painted portraits of the Tang-dynasty poet Jia Dao on the wall of his room and offered prayers to them from morning to night. The other monks at Jianji temple despised Cheng and considered him a demon, so he was expelled after a flogging with light rod. He now donned Confucian attire in heading northward to Zhao and Wei prefectures for a meeting with Zhuangzong of Tang at Zhenzhou. Cheng thus became assistant director of editing at the Secretariat.

In the Tiancheng era [C.E. 926–929], Zhu Shouyin was governor of Bianzhou and arranged Cheng's assignment as administrative assistant. The rebellion and execution of Shouyin caused Cheng to leave his wife and sons, abandoning himself in the area of Chen and Song prefectures. Minister An Chonghui detested Cheng and believed that he prodded Shouyin to rebel, so pictures were painted of him and bounty offered. Cheng was never obtained; his entire family was liquidated instead.

Cheng now absconded for the Wu kingdom, where Li Bian was purging the Yang house and wooing many literati from across the four corners. Bian reveled in obtaining someone with the literary finesse of Cheng, naming him compositor for draft edicts. Cheng hence acquired fame. He spoke with a stammer: in encountering others, he could not chatter even casually on matters. When sitting down, however, precision suddenly surfaced as he discussed and debated affairs, listeners forgetting their own fatigue. Bian proved especially fond of Cheng and consulted him on policy, the two men in frequent agreement. He thus named him right associate at the Secretariat, Cheng joining Feng Yansi as ministers to Bian. Cheng felt contempt for the character of Yansi, often stating, "How can gold bowls and jade cups be used to hold dog shit?" Cheng served Bian and his son for more than twenty years, rising to dignitary for public works. His family grew in wealth and arrogance as well. For daily meals, they dispensed with the usual dinner table, insisting instead on arraying a throng of prostitutes, each carrying one utensil as they formed a circle to serve, the women dubbed "human servers." The practice was imitated by many others.

As Shizong of Zhou campaigned against the Huai region, a nervous Li Jing dispatched the military attaché for Sizhou, Wang Zhilang, to convey a letter to his Xuzhou¶ camps suing for peace. Shizong did not respond. Hanlin academician Zhong Mo and Wenlin academician Li Deming also carried letters for Jing conceding to vassal status, again without reaction. Another petition was delivered by the minister of rites Wang Chongzhi, deputy envoy to Sun Cheng for the mission. Mo and Cheng further indicated that, "Li Jing concedes to ceding the six prefectures of Shou, Hao¶, Si, Chu, Guang, and Hai, while subsidizing your military with an annual tribute of a million strings of cash." Chu‡, Yang, Hao¶, and Si prefectures were already under Shizong's control, however, and he insisted on the entire southern Huai region before withdrawing. Shizong, therefore, detained the envoys and intensified the assault on Shouzhou.

Zhong Mo and cohort recognized that Li Jing was no rival to Shizong in martial magnetism, while Shouchun faced imminent peril from Zhou armies, with their powers thriving. They thus appealed to Shizong, "We request that Your Majesty defer our own punishment for five days to permit Your Subjects to return Jing's earlier letter and secure cession of the entire [southern] Huai."[6] Shizong consented to the return south of deputies Deming and Chongzhi, in the custody of palace services officer An Hongdao, detaining chief envoys Mo and Cheng.

Upon the return of Deming and cohort, Li Jing regretted earlier concessions and deemed the surrender of land unacceptable. Meanwhile, Shizong needed to withdraw armies owing to the summer heat and heavy rains, leaving Li Chongjin and Zhang Yongde to maintain separate offensives against Lu‡ and Shou prefectures. The Zhou acquisition of Yang and Tai prefectures now proved untenable, and retreat rejuvenated the spirits of the southern armies. Mutual suspicions and eventual rifts even surfaced between the camps of Chongjin and Yongde, the latter writing the Zhou court to accuse Chongjin of impending rebellion. Shizong gave no credence to this, yet the rifts between the two commanders was known to Li Jing, who delivered a secret letter under wax seal encouraging Chongjin to rebel.

When earlier commissioned as envoy, Sun Cheng intimated to Wang Chongzhi, "I cannot possibly survive this mission, but to my last days, I refuse to betray our Yongling sovereign." "Yongling" refers to the tomb of [Southern Tang founder] Li Bian. Sun Cheng and Zhong Mo both reached the capital [Kaifeng] after Chongzhi's return south. Housed at Duting postal station, they received exceptional treatment. Whenever assembling for audience through the palace's side door, they stood immediately behind department executives for the right. Moreover, they were always privileged to exquisite wines when chosen to address the court.

Zhou armies subsequently faced successive defeats, only to lose all the prefectures formerly claimed. Worried, Shizong summoned Sun Cheng to inquire about affairs of the southern Yangzi. Cheng refused to respond and Shizong, although angry, did not vent it. Commander Li Chongjin happened, then, to bring to court Jing's letter under wax seal, which rebuked the Zhou for numerous mistakes and vices. The fury of Shizong now surfaced, as he pronounced, "When Cheng arrived as envoy to me, he spoke of Jing's awe for my martial genius and desire to face north in vassal-like submission, even guaranteeing the absence of duplicity in Jing. What can explain such words of rebuke in this letter?" He immediately ordered Han Tong, inspector of the Imperial Guard, to arrest Cheng and jail him, killing more than two hundred in his entourage. As Cheng neared death, Shizong again sent a confidante to reiterate his former inquiries, but he ultimately refused to respond, his demeanor calm and pious throughout. Adjusting his official robe and hat, Sun faced southward to bow, declaring, "Only through death can I repay my empire!" He now accepted punishment. Zhong Mo was then banished to manager adjutant for Yaozhou. Once his rage subsided, Shizong came to empathize with Cheng as a loyal subject and to regret slaying him. Zhong Mo, summoned back, was named vice minister for imperial regalia. Jing had ceded the northern Yangzi lands, by then, and Mo was permitted to return. Jing also conferred posthumous honors on Cheng as Duke of Lu after news of his death.

CHAPTER 35

BIOGRAPHIES OF SIX COURTIERS OF TANG

The calamity at Baima Post, a deplorable tragedy that truly brings tears to my eyes, symbolizes far more than the lives of the literati lost![1]

Earlier, in the third year of the Tang dynasty's Tianyou reign [C.E. 906], the Prince of Liang wanted a favored aide, Zhang Tingfan, posted as chamberlain for ceremonials. Chief minister Pei Shu demurred, pointing to dynastic practice where chamberlains are officials with pedigree, whereas Tingfan was a mere commander's attendant to the Prince of Liang. A thoroughly incensed Prince exclaimed, "I often cited Pei Shu as pure and genuine, not given to indulge frivolity. Still, he responds so callously!" In the fourth month of that year, a comet in the northwestern skies passed over the stellar spheres of Wenchang, Xuanyuan, and Tianshi. Chief minister Liu Can, at the Prince of Liang's prodding, held senior courtiers responsible. In this way, left associates at the Secretariat Pei Shu and Dugu Sun, right associate Cui Yuan, acting grand guardian emeritus Zhao Chong, vice minister of war Wang Zan, minister of public works Wang Pu, and minister of personnel Lu Yi—all innocent men—were banished and, on the same day, ordered to commit suicide at Baima Post. And civilian courtiers supporting the Tang over the Liang were uniformly branded factionalists: several hundred men were exiled or slain, the court purged in the process.

In the third month of the next year, Emperor Ai relinquished the Tang throne to the Liang. He named Zhang Wenwei, deputy director of the Palace Secretariat with ministerial powers, as dignitary for investiture protocol, and minister of rites Su Xun as his deputy; deputy director of the

Palace Secretariat with ministerial powers Yang She as dignitary for conveying the seal for dynastic succession, and Hanlin academician and Secretariat drafter Zhang Ce as his deputy; censor-in-chief Xue Yiju as dignitary for conveying the gold imperial seal; and left administrative aide at the Imperial Secretariat Zhao Guangfeng as his deputy. On the sixteenth day of the fourth month, arriving from Shangyuan Post, Wenwei and cohort presented the articles of investiture; riding sedan chairs, they led the Imperial Insignia Guard and chamberlain for attendance at the Liang court's Jinxiang Hall. The Prince donned the imperial robe and hat, then faced south as Subject Wenwei and Subject Xun ascended the hall to present investiture documents. After stepping forward for the citation, Subject She and Subject Ce presented the seal of dynastic succession; Subject Yiju and Subject Guangfeng presented the gold seal. In sequence, each ascended the stairs and stepped forward to read the citation. Upon their descent, the myriad of civil and military officials were ushered in for felicitations; facing north, they glided into multiple bows.

Which is more critical: the single post of ceremonies chamberlain or the ritual altars of dynasty? Based on earlier stands in the chamberlain controversy, if Pei Shu and cohort had not died, would they have willfully ceded empire to another? Had they tried, Shu and cohort may not necessarily have preserved Tang rule, yet they most certainly would have refused to help overturn the dynasty, then survive in its wake.

WE LAMENT. When the Tang perished, wise and moral men expired with it. Those to survive were all mediocre cowards of little worth, men of sinister cunning who exploited peril and rushed to profit as traitors to their country. How else can we explain such shamelessly demeaning deeds at the Liang court? Thus, I write these "Biographies of Six Courtiers of the Tang."

Zhang Wenwei

With the courtesy name Youhua, Zhang Wenwei [d. C.E. 908], was native to Hejian County. Early on, he won recognition for literary talents and personal deportment, passing the doctoral examination and becoming Hanlin recipient of edicts in the Tang reign of Zhaozong. The Son of Heaven was enfeebled at the time and institutions already shattered. From his post in the Hanlin academy, Wenwei issued edicts to the four corners and singularly held the élan of the empire together. Once Zhaozong relocated to Luoyang, he became deputy director of the Palace Secretariat with powers as chief minister. Liu Can later murdered seven courtiers, including Pei Shu, while others implicated met with summary executions. The literary officials stared at each other in disbelief, sensing that they were defenseless, but Wenwei spoke forcefully to win their release, and many a courtier survived unscathed through his intervention.

Taizu of Liang, upon formal enthronement, retained Wenwei as chief minister. Indeed, the institutions of early Liang were all constituted by Wenwei. At home he was known to be filial and fraternal. In the second year of Kaiping [C.E. 908], Taizu led a northern inspection and left behind Wenwei in the western capital, where he died of sudden illness. Posthumous rank as right associate at the Secretariat was conferred.

Yang She

Yang She's grandfather, Shou, had been chief minister in the Tang reign of Yizong.[2] His father, Yan, had risen in office to vice minister of war. He personally passed the doctoral examination and served as minister of personnel in Zhaozong's reign, then deputy director at the Palace secretariat with ministerial powers, once Emperor Ai was enthroned. Yang She hailed from an eminent Tang family, which for generations had adhered to rules of ritual propriety. He possessed a personality especially circumspect and magnanimous, but haplessly encountered the tumult of late Tang, and during his days as chief minister he tended to shed tears in the company of family members. Turning to his son Ningshi, he said, "I cannot escape this net of calamity soon to envelop us, a net certain to entangle you as well." After the Tang collapse, Yang She served the Liang as deputy director of the Chancellery with ministerial powers. He chose to bow his head and do nothing of substance over his three-year tenure, leading to demotion to left associate at the Secretariat and administrator of civil service examinations. He died several years later.

His son, *Yang Ningshi*, was a man of literary finesse with a talent for drafting documents. Holding office through the Liang, Tang, Jin, Han, and Zhou, he repeatedly retired for psychological reasons to reside at Luoyang. His highest rank was grand guardian to the heir-apparent.

Zhang Ce

A native of Dunhuang Prefecture, Hexi circuit, Zhang Ce [d. C.E. 914] had the courtesy name Shaoyi. His father, Tong, had served the Tang as regional military commissioner for Rongguan. A youth nimble of mind and fond of learning, Ce acquired a comprehensive command of commentaries on the classics. When his father, Tong, lived in the Dunhua ward of Luoyang, he once scooped up an ancient tripod from a well with the inscription, "crafted by Jiqian of the Wei dynasty, in the second month of the inaugural year of Huangchu." Tong marveled at the object. Thirteen *sui* at the time, Ce sat beside Tong and explained, "In the Han dynasty's twenty-fifth year of Jian'an [C.E. 220], Gentleman Cao Cao perished and the reign was changed to Yankang. In the tenth month of the same year, Emperor Wen assumed the Wei throne and further changed the reign to Huangchu. Thus, the inaugural year of Huangchu has no second month. How can a genuine inscription be in error?" Tong was flabbergasted and considered him a prodigy.

In youth, Zhang Ce was drawn to the teachings of Buddhism and even cropped his hair to become a monk, residing at the Ci'en temple of Changan. Once the rebel Huang Chao invaded Changan, Ce resumed wearing his original attire and assisted parents in evading the turmoil, residing on a farm for more than ten years. The court later named him erudite at the Guangwen academy, as Wang Xingyu of Binzhou arranged his posting as assistant to the surveillance commissioner. Once Xingyu came under attack from the Prince of Jin, Li Keyong, Ce and a female servant had to carry his aging mother by sedan chair to the east, along roads covered with snow. The spectacle elicited pity from passersby.

The future Taizu of Liang, then concurrent governor of four commands, arranged for Zhang Ce's posting as governor's deputy for Zheng and Hua prefectures. Relieved of duties to mourn his mother's death, he served the Tang court as assistant director of catering after the mourning period. An assignment as administrative aide was arranged by Han Jian of Hua‡ Prefecture. Jian's relocation to Xuzhou‡ caused Ce to be nominated administrative secretary to him. Jian once selected him as emissary to the future Taizu, who delighted upon meeting Ce, exclaiming, "Master Zhang has arrived, alas!" Taizu retained him as his own administrative secretary and even recommended him to the court, Ce eventually rising to drafter at the Palace Secretariat and Hanlin academician. Assignment as edict recipient for the vice minister of public works occasioned Taizu's formal accession to the Liang throne. In the second year of Kaiping [C.E. 908], Ce became vice minister for punishments with chief ministerial standing and later vice director of the Palace Secretariat. Owing to cold-related illness, he retired with rank of minister of punishments, dying in Luoyang.

Zhao Guangfeng

Zhao Guangfeng had the courtesy name Yanji, his father Yin a one-time left associate at the Secretariat in Tang times. Guangfeng had earned some personal renown under the Tang for literary skills and moral character. Contemporaries even celebrated his combination of direct honesty and amiable personality with the nickname "Jade Yardstick." In the reign of Zhaozong, he was named Hanlin recipient of edicts and deputy censor, only to forfeit office owing to tumultuous times: living in Luoyang, he shut his doors and spurned public affairs for five or six years. The rise of Liu Can to chief minister caused Guangfeng's resuscitation as vice minister of personnel and chamberlain for ceremonials, his friendship with Can of long standing.

Zhao Guangfeng proceeded to serve the Liang after the Tang collapse, as deputy director at the Palace secretariat with ministerial powers. Further promotions culminated in his being named left associate at the Secretariat. He retired with the rank of grand guardian to the heir-apparent; his resuscitation as dignitary for public works with ministerial standing attended Emperor Mo's accession. He retired again as dignitary of education, and in the Tiancheng reign of Tang he received honors at home as grand guardian, invested Duke of Qi. The rank of grand mentor followed his death.

Xue Yiju

Xue Yiju [d. C.E. 912] had the courtesy name Xiyong. Native to Wenxi, Hedong, he served the Tang as vice minister of war and Hanlin recipient of edicts. Emperor Zhaozong had returned to Changan from Qizhou‡ to conduct a mass execution of eunuchs precisely as Yiju was writing the caption for a portrait of Han Quanhui, a eunuch commandant, for which he received a demotion. Yiju hence allied with the future Taizu of Liang, whose favorable words to the court led to appointment as minister of personnel and later censor-in-chief.

In the third year of Tianyou [C.E. 906], when Taizu returned from Changlu to his command, Emperor Ai dispatched Yiju to confer awards on him. Yiju greeted Taizu with the protocol of subject, as Taizu cordially waived clenched hands in the air, inviting him to ascend the stairs. Yet Yiju insisted, "Your Highness's merit and virtue extend to humanity, while the spirits of Heaven and Earth now portend Your Majesty as undertaking the sacred mission of [ancient rulers] Shun and Yu. How dare Your Subject violate protocol?" He proclaimed himself royal subject and performed an elaborate bow of submission, Taizu shifting his own body to avoid him. After returning to the capital, Yiju prodded Emperor Ai to relinquish the throne. He became deputy director of the Palace Secretariat once Taizu assumed the throne, with ministerial powers. Honors as dignitary for public works eventually followed. He served as minister of Liang for five years, receiving rank as director of the Chancellery upon death.

Su Xun and Du Xiao

Nothing is known of the background of Su Xun. Crafty and obsequious, he flattered others with no sense of shame, assuming any posture of benefit to him. He served the Tang as minister of rites. The future Taizu of Liang had committed regicide against Zhaozong by now, installing Emperor Ai. The senior statesmen of Tang were uniformly outraged and indignantly critical: some bowed their heads for fear of calamity, while others left the capital to avoid service. Yet Xun's shameless patronizing of the Liang to win advancement was unparalleled. As Liang armies assaulted Yang Xingmi and suffered a rout at the Pi River, an indignant Taizu turned impatient about transferring imperial powers and sought the nine official privileges with vestments. The official rank and file dared not discuss so sensitive a matter, making Xun the sole advocate of conferral: "The Prince of Liang has evinced such merit and virtue that Heaven's mandate has reverted to him. The abdication should be executed promptly." Taizu formally assumed the throne a year later, Xun presiding as deputy master of investiture protocol.

Xun's son *Su Kai* had passed the doctoral examination in the Qianning era [C.E. 894–898], but Zhaozong directed academician Lu Yi to delete him from the list, causing Kai to feel frequent chagrin. Once Zhaozong fell to regicide and Tang administration reverted to the Liang, Kai became imperial diarist. This permitted him to cultivate ties to Liu Can and Zhang Tingfan, intimating to the latter, "In selecting a posthumous title to replace the personal name, credibility is critical. Earlier court authorities gave the Former Monarch the posthumous name 'Zhao' [Illustrious], but the titular and actual status were inconsistent. You, Sir, are chamberlain for ceremonials while I am court historian. We cannot but address the matter." Su Kai now argued the issue at court, point by point. Originally a commander's attendant under the Liang, Tingfan had once sought appointment as chamberlain of ceremonies; failing to obtain it, he similarly harbored resentment for the Tang dynasty. Kai's petition was thereby presented to Tingfan, who argued before the court, "For former monarchs who are unstintingly devoted to conducting affairs, it is said, the appropriate posthumous title is Dedicated [Gong]. For monarchs who face chaos but elude personal harm, the appropriate title is Astute [Ling]. For monarchs who are martial but fail in their goals, the appropriate title is Sober [Zhuang]. For monarchs who reign over a beleaguered empire, the appropriate title is Disconsolate [Min], and for monarchs who make strides during crises, the appropriate title is Facilitator [Xiang]. I petition that the posthumous title for Emperor Zhaozong be changed to the Dedicated, Astute, Sober, Disconsolate, and Facilitating Emperor with the temple name Xiangzong.[3]

After acceding the throne, Taizu held a banquet at Xuande Hall, where, glancing at courtiers, he professed himself too deficient in virtue to deserve the Mandate of Heaven, attributing his elevation to their efforts. Senior courtiers of Tang like Yang She and Zhang Wenwei stood in embarrassed shock, left speechless as they bowed. In fact, only Su Xun, Zhang Yi, and Xue Yiju proceeded to praise the merits of the Prince of Liang profusely, characterizing his accession as faithful to Heaven and responsive to the people. Xun and Kai, father and son, both acquired trust through submission to the Liang, yet rarely managed further advancement at court, despite protruding their heads from morning to night. Jing Xiang held them in particular contempt, saying to Taizu, "A newly ascendant Liang dynasty should recruit upright scholars to enrich current customs. The deficiencies in deportment of Xun and son make them unacceptable for the new dynasty." Father and son were thereby prodded to return to their village, where they enjoyed the patronage of Zhu Youqian of Hezhong.

Zhu Youqian later defected from the Liang to capitulate to the Prince of Jin [Li Cunxu]. As the Prince of Jin prepared for his accession, he solicited former officials of the Tang dynasty to fill vacancies in the civil service, Youqian sending Xun to his Weizhou camp. At the time, many a Jin commander preferred that the Prince not accede the imperial throne, for the purge of Liang had yet to occur. The Prince's commanders, ministers and senior courtiers remained unsupportive as well, even in the face of his own urgency. From the outset of Xun's arrival at Weizhou, however, he bowed during official visits to the prefectural offices, characterizing himself as "bowing before the imperial hall." When entering to meet with the Prince personally, he would glide into an elaborate bow, extend felicitations for "ten thousand years," and profess himself a "royal subject"—all to the Prince's immense delight. On the next day, Xun presented thirty "brushes for painting the sun" [to celebrate an ascendant monarch]. This pleased the Prince still more and resulted in appointment as deputy governor. Later dying of illness, Xun was posthumously entitled left associate at the Secretariat upon Zhuangzong's accession.

Su Kai became assistant director at the Imperial Secretariat during the Tongguang era [C.E. 923–926]. Upon the enthronement of Mingzong, however, senior courtiers wished to hold him culpable for the crime of reversing Zhaozong's posthumous title, the attendant anxieties causing his death.

When the Tang dynasty collapsed, there was also a man named *Du Xiao* [d. C.E. 913], whose courtesy name was Mingyuan. His grandfather Shenquan and father Rangneng both served as chief ministers of Tang. In the

Zhaozong reign, after assaults on the capital by Wang Xingyu and Li Maozhen, Zhaozong killed Rangneng at Lin'gao as a scapegoat for himself. Xiao considered his father's death unjust and physically wasted away while mourning for him. He donned the attire and headband of commoners, once mourning was over, to spend the next ten years in abandoned despair. With Cui Yin serving as senior administrator of the salt and iron monopolies, he nominated Xiao as patrol officer, and the court offered assignments as sheriff for a metropolitan county and auxiliary at the Zhaowen academy. Xiao spurned them all. Senior administrator for finance Cui Yuan similarly nominated him as patrol officer, whereupon someone reminded Xiao, "Upon the death of Ji Kang [centuries ago], his self-abnegating son, Shao, initially refused only later to accept office, once a reproachful Shantao pragmatically assessed things. My friend, can you imagine your own progeny, in seasonal rites to ancestors, being reduced to the protocol for commoners?" Xiao now agreed to be resuscitated. Successive appointments culminated in director of palace catering and Hanlin academician.

Taizu's accession to the Liang throne saw Xiao become edict recipient for the vice minister of public works. Promotion ensued, in the second year of Kaiping [C.E. 908], to deputy director of the Palace Secretariat with ministerial powers. Reassignment as minister of rites and academician for Jixian Hall attended the installation of Zhu Yougui. Later, in the suppression of renegade Yougui, the armies of Yuan Xiangxian pillaged widely, Xiao perishing at the hands of unruly troops. The posthumous title of right associate at the Secretariat was conferred.

WE LAMENT. Who will first raise the factionalist banner? I believe most emphatically that those most devoid of benevolence will cast the first mold [to stigmatize others].

During a visit to Fancheng, I once read the Wei-dynasty stele, "Commemorative for the Abdication," where courtiers of the preceding Han celebrated the merits and virtues of the new Wei dynasty. The large letters incised deep into the stone cited their names to celebrate contributions to their times. I have also read the *Veritable Records for the Liang*, where Wenwei and cohort comported themselves similarly. I can never read such passages without sobbing. To cede one's country to another and celebrate oneself as glorious, only later to minister to the new regime, who deigns to do so save for petty men?

At the end of the Han and Tang dynasties of old, the courts contained only petty men. Where were its superior men? As the Han faced imminent ruin, first came charges of factionalism to persecute the wise and morally superior, leaving the court with only petty men, and the Han collapse ensued. Similarly, as the Tang faced imminent ruin, initially factional slanders provided cause to liquidate the court's entire cohort of literati, residuals representing unfit mediocrities who induced the peril that brought the Tang to its knees.

Persons seeking to empty the people's empire and purge its superior men will surely accuse others of factionalism, those wanting to isolate the powers of the people's ruler and mask his eyes and ears will surely accuse others of factionalism, and those given to usurping empire for surrender to another will surely accuse others of factionalism. For moral men who commit some minor misdeed, petty men will try to elevate the misdeed to a crime, thereby providing something to malign. For others with nothing to malign, extending recrimination becomes impossible. Yet by simply raising the banner of "factionalism," petty men can purge moral men across the world for simply associating with their own kind. In this way, one's relatives and old associates can be branded as factional partisans, one's companions and friends can be branded factional partisans, fellow officeholders and classmates can be branded factional partisans, even student disciples and former secretaries can be branded factional partisans. And to the extent that these several groups share a common character, they all tend to be noble persons. Thus, it is said, persons intent on emptying the people's empire and eliminating its superior men need only allege factionalism, and no one will escape persecution.

It is naturally inherent for moral men to relish in associating with others of common character. Upon learning of other moral men, praise for one another will surely occur, and such simple praise leads to slurs of factionalism; in recruiting moral men for government, recommendation of one for another will surely occur, and such a simple recommendation leads to slurs of factionalism. If persons hear of moral men but dare not offer praise, then news of such men below never reaches our ruler's ears; and if people observe moral men but dare not recommend them, then the witnessing of such men never reaches our ruler's eyes. And with each day the moral become estranged as the petty become intimate. Who will then assist a dumbfounded ruler of humanity in laying plans for political order? As the saying goes, "Persons wanting to isolate the powers of the people's ruler and mask his eyes and ears will surely accuse others of factionalism."

In the presence of a single superior man, swarms of petty men, despite their vast numbers, will surely have some inhibitions, some moves that they dare not make. Upon purging the empire of all superior men, the petty are free to indulge their own fancy, leaving nothing beyond their reach. This was precisely the case for transitions from the Han to Wei dynasties as well as the Tang to Liang. Thus, the potential to usurp and even surrender empire to another emanates from the absence of superior men, and their total absence at court emanates from purges related to factionalism.

WE LAMENT. The ruler of humanity must cast a scrutinizing eye on charges of factionalism. This is precisely the meaning of the saying, "A single word can ruin a country,"[4] as conveyed [in the *Analects*]. To be reflective and vigilant, a ruler can afford nothing less!

CHAPTER 36

BIOGRAPHIES OF RIGHTEOUS SONS

We Lament. Once the Way of the times degenerates and the mores of humanity decline, the norms for regulating family relations can be subverted, culminating in strife among kinsmen as persons of different blood bond, like father and son. In the fifty years from the Kaiping to Xiande reigns, the Five Dynasties to rule the world represented eight surnames, in fact. The three extraneous surnames emanated from adoptions. The most eminent of adoptees claimed the world; the less prominent won renown for military achievements and ranked among the country's commanders and ministers. I can only assume that prevailing rivalries had made such liaisons somehow profitable.

Later Tang rulers, adopting the name Shatuo and emerging from Daibei, had assembled the most intrepid and fiercely martial warriors of the age, often raising them like sons to constitute the "Army of Righteous Sons." Many contributed to its success at winning the world, yet the Tang unraveled at their hands as well. The sons adopted by Taizu were truly numerous, nine of whom can be chronicled. One was Emperor Mingzong, and the others were Sizhao, Siben, Si'en, Cunxin, Cunxiao, Cunjin, Cunzhang, and Cunxian.[i]

Li Sizhao

Originally surnamed Han, Li Sizhao [d. C.E. 922] was born to a commoner family at Taigu County, Fenzhou. The fu-

i. With great conspicuousness, Li Cunshen later restored his original name, Fu, and therefore has received a separate biography.

ture Taizu [Li Keyong] once approached his home during a hunt, noticing a vapor of vast dimensions within the woods. He marveled and summoned the father to make inquiries. The father indicated that a son had recently been born to the family, so Taizu left behind gold and silk and took the boy, hence instructing younger brother Kerou to raise him as son. The youth, initially given the name Jintong, later received the new name of Sizhao. Although short in physical stature, he excelled others in daring. He was initially given to indulging in wine until Taizu admonished him subtly, and he refrained from drink for the rest of his life. Taizu cherished his scrupulous and substantial character. Often assisting Taizu in battle, Sizhao rose to director of the governor's guard.

As Wang Gong of Shanzhou challenged elder brother Wang Ke to inherit control over Hezhong, Taizu deployed Sizhao to assist Ke. They defeated Gong at Yishi County [Hezhong] and apprehended three of his commanders. Liang armies came to Gong's relief, but Sizhao defeated them at Hubi Fort and captured a Liang commander. In the inaugural year of Guanghua [C.E. 898], Li Hanzhi of Zezhou stormed Luzhou in surrendering to the Liang, the Liang responding by dispatching Ding Hui to rendezvous with Hanzhi. Sizhao engaged Hui in battle at Hanshan and apprehended one of his commanders, claiming the heads of three thousand soldiers. He then captured Zezhou. The Prince of Jin instructed Li Junqing, in the second year, to raid the Liang prefecture of Lu. Junqing suffered defeat at Liang hands, and Taizu of Jin poisoned him to death as punishment. Sizhao hence attacked and conquered Lu. Departing from east of the mountains in the third year, Sizhao seized the Liang prefecture of Ming. Taizu of Liang personally commanded the offensive against him and instructed Ge Congzhou to lay an ambush at Qingshankou. Word of Taizu's personal arrival caused Sizhao to abandon the city and abscond, his men falling into the ambush before them and routed.

In the inaugural year of Tianfu [C.E. 901], Liang armies overran Hezhong Prefecture to capture Wang Ke. Laying claim to the prefectures of Jin, Jiang, Ci‡, and Xi, it now began a sweeping offensive against the Jin, encircling Taiyuan. Li Sizhao emerged from the city with elite horsemen for daytime sorties against Liang forces. His efforts coincided with heavy rains that forced Liang men to dissolve their blockade and leave. The Fenzhou prefect Li Tang had defected from the Jin to surrender to Liang. Once Liang armies had left the area, Sizhao could regain Fenzhou and decapitate Tang. Sizhao now emerged from Yindi Pass to claim Cizhou‡, winning the surrender of its prefect, Tang Li. He further claimed Xizhou, as prefect Zhang Gui capitulated.

That year Liang armies invaded the capital to the west and besieged Fengxiang. Li Sizhao exploited the opportunity to attack the Liang prefectures of Jin and Jiang, joining battle at Pingyang and apprehending a Liang commander. He then advanced against Pu County. In response, Liang commanders Zhu Youning and Shi Shucong stormed him with a hundred thousand warriors. Sizhao's men fled after defeat, only to be pursued by Youning. The Prince of Jin directed Li Cunxin to lead a force to rendezvous with Sizhao, which met with defeat as well. Liang armies thereby surrounded Taiyuan, the prefectures of Ci‡, Xi, and Fen all having been restored to its control. Utterly terrified, Taizu considered flight to Yunzhou, but Li Cunxin and others encouraged him to take refuge with the Khitan. Sizhao argued strenuously against it and importuned Consort Dowager Liu to speak with Taizu as well, the plan now scrapped. From morning to night, Sizhao emerged from Taiyuan to storm Liang armies with his special forces, eventually reclaiming the prefectures of Fen, Ci‡, and Xi. At a time when the prefectures of Zhen and Ding had severed ties with the Jin in favor of Liang, a time when the Jin had lost assistance from a major ally abroad and relinquished most prefectures at home, a time when blockades of its isolated capital occurred twice in a single year—in such times, the merits of Sizhao as a dedicated warrior mattered for much.

In the third year of Tianyou [C.E. 906], Li Sizhao and Zhou Dewei attacked the Liang prefecture of Lu, forcing Ding Hui to surrender. Sizhao then became governor of the Zhaoyi command. The Liang sent Li Si'an, commanding a force of a hundred thousand, to attack Luzhou, where he encircled the prefecture by erecting dual ramparts. Taizu of Liang now dispatched a messenger to persuade Sizhao to capitulate, but Sizhao beheaded the envoy and sealed up the city in defiance. After a year, Zhuangzong began to bombard the dual ramparts and destroy them, as Sizhao completed the induction of commoners into the army, proving extremely charitable in caring for them.

Liang and Jin armies had engaged at Huliu, resulting in a Jin defeat and the loss of commander Zhou Dewei, who died in battle. A frightened Zhuangzong wanted to regroup his men and retreat to Linpu, but Sizhao countered, "Liang troops have already claimed victory and their hearts long, day and night, to return home. If we regroup our armies and allow them to recuperate, we will be no match for them in some future offensive. It is better to invest crack cavalry in harassing their men, winning victory by tiring them out." Zhuangzong concurred.

Liang armies had already ascended Wushi Mountain at the time, so Zhuangzong sent Li Sizhao back for a raid north of the mountain. Personally commanding the Silver Lance armies, Sizhao shouted as he sallied forth, "In today's battle, he who takes this mountain is the victor!" Jin warriors all vied among themselves to ascend the mountain just as Liang armies descended with a rush, the two battling on its western edge. Jin men vastly overpowered the Liang in their spirited storm up the mountain. The Jin now proceeded to erect walls around Desheng Commandery. In the wake of Zhou Dewei's death, Sizhao became acting prefect of Youzhou, to be replaced by Li Shaohong after several months. As he prepared to depart, the people of Youzhou all wept bitterly and sealed the locks on the city's gates, hoping to retain him. Only by wearing a disguise and departing by night did Sizhao manage to leave.

In the nineteenth year [C.E. 922], he assisted Zhuangzong in a sortie against the Khitan at Wangdu County. The Khitan had encircled Zhuangzong several times around, but with three hundred horsemen, Sizhao succeeded in breaking the blockade to permit Zhuangzong's escape. At the time, the Jin had unleashed Yan Bao against Zhang Wenli at Zhenzhou. Vanquished by Zhenzhou defenders, Bao was replaced by Sizhao. As forces at Zhen emerged from the city to raid Jiumen Commandery, Sizhao stormed with his elite troops. The Zhen armies had been virtually depleted, save for three men still hiding in the ruins of an earthen wall. Rushing at them on his horse, Sizhao drew his arrow, only to be struck on the head by a renegade arrow. Looking into his quiver to discover his spare arrows depleted, he wrenched the arrow from his head to fire at the renegade, killing him before returning to his own barracks to die.

Among the sons of Sizhao, the eldest, *Li Jichou*, proved rather timid, such that his younger brother *Li Jitao* imprisoned him to install himself. The future Zhuangzong was preoccupied with the face-off along the Yellow River with Liang armies, leaving no time to investigate the incident. Jitao consequently won confirmation as interim regent of the Zhaoyi command. Jitao tended to invest administrative duties to Wei Zhuo and Shen Meng, men who often prodded him to rebel, but Jitao remained undecided. Some other matter had caused Zhuangzong, then at Weizhou, to summon military overseer Zhang Juhan and Ren Huan, administrative assistant to the governor. Zhuo and others presumed Zhuangzong's summons of Juhan to pertain to the Jitao affair, and that an execution awaited him. Their words so incited Jitao that he sent his younger brother Jiyuan to the Liang court [in submission]. Its ruler, Emperor Mo, conferred ministerial powers on Jitao.

Zhuangzong overthrew the Liang only months later, and Jitao came close to fleeing to the Khitan when a pardon arrived. He desisted and instead prepared to accompany his mother for audience in the capital. Jiyuan admonished against it, warning, "My brother is a subject who once raised the banner of rebellion. What face is left to meet the Son of Heaven again? Moreover, the walls of Lu remain sturdy, its granaries replete with provisions. Better to seal off the city and subsist on grain reserves to lengthen your life than willfully walk to your own slaughter!" Jitao refused to listen.

Jitao's mother, surnamed Yang, had a proclivity for hoarding wealth, collecting objects eventually worth millions in cash over the course of her life. For a full year, the Woman Yang's wealth had assisted Li Sizhao during the dual-ramparts siege of the Liang, when his own military resources were direly deficient. Now she forwarded to the capital several hundred thousand ounces of silver to bribe eunuchs and actors, who observed for the Emperor, "Jitao began with no sinister intent and was merely deluded by evil men." Woman Yang bribes extended to Empress Liu as well, who added, "Sizhao having been a meritorious officer, leniency is rightfully due his son." Zhuangzong hence pardoned Jitao and even took him on hunting excursions, favoring him with no sign of friction. Still, Li Cunwo [Zhuangzong's brother] proved especially harsh and persistent in excoriating him, leaving Jitao sufficiently insecure to bribe eunuchs and actors once again, seeking restoration as regional governor. When Zhuangzong refused, Jitao secretly intrigued with Jiyuan to incite a military mutiny, expecting the Son of Heaven to send him to arrest the suspects. The ploy leaked out, and Jitao was beheaded at Tianjin Bridge.

The two sons of Li Jitao, once hostages in the Liang capital, were captured by Zhuangzong after the overthrow of the dynasty. Stroking their backs, he said, "You boys could aid and abet in your father's sedition, despite your youth. What might you do, should you grow up?" He executed them before dispatching an agent to behead Jiyuan. Replacing him as prefect of Luzhou was Jichou. The court summoned him to the capital, but Jichou did not depart on time, preoccupied with the harem and precious trinkets of Jitao, only recently claimed by him. This infuriated his younger brother Jida, who exclaimed, "My older brother [Jitao] and his sons have been executed, while Eldest Brother [Jichou] proves so morally bankrupt as to covet his properties and fornicate with his wife and concubines. I can no longer bear it!" Donning mourning clothes of hemp, he directed several hundred mounts to Jichou's front door with halberd emblem, where they entered to murder him. Jida now came under assault from deputy governor Li Jike, who had enlisted at the marketplace more than a thousand commoners. Jida hence fled beyond the city walls to strangle himself to death.

Li Sizhao had seven sons. In the Mingzong reign, son Jineng faced charges of flogging to death a servant responsible for his mother's valuables. The servant's family turned informants and implicated Jineng in a rebellion. He and brother Jixi were both killed. Only one son was spared, Jizhong, whose home at Jinyang [Taiyuan] was used by Woman Yang to store her residual wealth, still countless tens of thousands. Gaozu of Jin later raised armies at Taiyuan and sought assistance from the Khitan; they demanded bribes of

Gaozu, who borrowed enough from Jizhong to satisfy them. After assuming the throne, Gaozu found himself extremely indebted to Jizhong, who became prefect for Yi†, Di, and Shan‡ prefectures. He died in the Kaiyun era [C.E. 944–946]. The possessions amassed by Woman Yang over a lifetime ultimately proved critical for three in her family—Sizhao and his two sons.

Li Siben

Originally surnamed Zhang, Li Siben [d. C.E. 917] was native to Yanmen, his family for generations overseeing bronze production at their command. Having served Taizu in his youth, Siben was so cherished that Taizu conferred a new name and raised him as a son. He assisted Taizu in raids against Juyong Pass, becoming commissioner of the Army of Righteous Sons for merit won. He joined in the defeat of Wang Xingyu to become the Weiyuan governor, then the offensive against Luo Hongxin, leading the vanguard to vanquish Tang Yin. His assistance to Zhuangzong in breaching the dual ramparts at Luzhou led to further advancement to prefect of Daizhou, defense commissioner for Yunzhou, and Zhenwu governor. He was popularly dubbed the "Khan of Weixin." In the thirteenth year of Tianyou [C.E. 916], he attended Zhuangzong in the storm against Liu Xun at the former Yuancheng County [Daming], overpowering Ming and Ci prefectures, among others, before returning his armies to Zhenwu in the sixth month. The Khitan occupation of Daibei and raid on Weizhou¶ saw Siben die in battle [C.E. 917].

Li Si'en

Initially surnamed Luo, Si'en [d. C.E. 918] belonged to a tribe of the Tuyuhun. As a young man serving Taizu, he proved deft at mounted archery and rose to commander in the Forest of Iron armies. Before long, he became director of surprise-sally units through merit in battle. Taizu now conferred new names and treated him as son. Si'en participated in the rout of Kang Huaiying at Hexi, hence becoming chief director of cavalry for left-wing contingents.

Si'en attended Sizhao in the relief effort for Zhu Youqian at Hezhong Prefecture. He was engaging Liang armies in vigorous battle when a spear lodged in his mouth, although he fought on. Si'en became prefect of Liao Prefecture, then aided Zhuangzong to occupy Weizhou, becoming chief director of armed forces for the Tianxiong command.

As Liu Xun opened hostilities against Taiyuan and his men advanced against Leping, Si'en pursued him from the rear, then employed an alternate road to enter Taiyuan and defend it. Once the armies of Xun had withdrawn, Si'en led his own men in a rendezvous with Zhuangzong at Weizhou, joining battle at Shen County. Promotions ensued as prefect of Daizhou, commandant of armed forces north of Shiling Pass, and Zhenwu governor. He died at Taiyuan in the fifteenth year of Tianyou [C.E. 918], the posthumous rank of grand marshal conferred.

Li Cunxin

Li Cunxin [C.E. 862–902] had the original surname of Zhang. His father, Junzheng, came from the Huihu Uighur tribe of Li Sizhong. A youthful Cunxin, adept as horseman and archer, also knew four barbarian spoken languages and six barbarian writing systems. He joined Taizu in the insurgency at Daibei, crossing the border to break the back of Huang Chao. He eventually rose to chief director of armed forces through military merit. Conferred new names, he was treated as a son.

Cunxin had been adopted like Cunxiao, but was no match for him in talent and daring. Cunxin nonetheless refused to accept himself as inferior, causing a souring of relations as Cunxin persistently thwarted each and every deed of Cunxiao. Cunxiao eventually died after some infraction, but Cunxin assisted in repeated campaigns, his merits rewarded with a prefect's posting at Chenzhou¶.

As Taizu dispatched commanders to relieve Zhu Xuan, Cunxin's men were quartered at Shen County and met defeat in a sortie by Luo Hongxin. Taizu thereby lost his son, Luoluo. Later, assisting Taizu in a punitive action against Liu Rengong, Cunxin was routed at Ansai. An utterly incensed Taizu thus pronounced, staring him in the face, "Yesterday, when I was drunk, you could not fight in my stead. The ancients allowed for three defeats—you've already had two!" He prepared to murder him when Cunxin kowtowed in acknowledging his errors, managing to be spared. He thereby experienced such terror as to often excuse himself from battle, claiming illness. He died in the second year of Tianfu [C.E. 902] at forty-one *sui.*

Li Cunxiao

Native to Feihu, Daizhou, Li Cunxiao [d. C.E. 894] was originally surnamed An and called Jingsi. Obtained by Taizu during the pillage of the Daibei region, he assisted in his retinue before conferral of a new name, Cunxiao, and treatment as a son. He often served under Taizu as cavalry commander.

In the inaugural year of Wende [C.E. 888], Zhang Yan of Henan stormed and overran Heyang Prefecture, as Li Hanzhi reverted to the Prince of Jin [Li Keyong]. Hanzhi was temporarily relocated to Zezhou by the Prince, who also sent a force of seven thousand to assist him in returning fire against Heyang. The effort involved Xue Atan and Anxiuxiu, as well as Cunxiao. The Liang [Zhu Quanzhong] reciprocated by sending Ding Hui and Niu Cunjie to assist Zhang Yan. They battled at Wen County, Liang armies first seizing Taihang. Cunxiao was routed and Anxiuxiu apprehended. At the time, the Jin had seized Ze and Lu prefectures, emanating from the eastern mountains every year to challenge Meng Fangli over Xing, Ming, and Ci prefectures. Cunxiao was invariably in the thick of these battles. The Jin success at claiming the three prefectures, in the wake of Fangli's death, derived substantially from his merit.

The military at Luzhou mutinied in the next year, slaying Li Kegong to revert to the Tang dynasty. The Liang retaliated by sending Li Dang to raid Li Hanzhi at Zezhou; and to relieve him, Li Cunxiao came with five thousand cavalry. Liang soldiers taunted Hanzhi, saying, "You often act on instructions from [the Prince of Jin] at Taiyuan, but today Shangdang has reverted to the Tang court while Tang armies have massively assembled to encircle Taiyuan. You Shatuo hereafter will have no hole to hide in. Where else can you turn to avoid surrender?" With five hundred crack horsemen, Cunxiao surrounded the Liang palisades, then shouted back, "We Shatuo, in search of a hole, look forward to feeding your flesh to our troops: perhaps the fat ones should enter combat first!" The Liang generalissimo, Deng Jiyun, had emerged with warriors for battle, and Cunxiao managed to capture him by artful manipulation of his spear. Li Dang fled in defeat and Cunxiao pursued him aggressively to Malao Pass, raiding Luzhou on the return trip.

The Tang court had appointed Sun Kui as governor of Luzhou. A man of Confucian background, he pushed ahead, employing three thousand Liang foot soldiers as bodyguard and personally donning long robes with a capacious umbrella as shield and the tallies of office squeezed in his hand. Cunxiao had directed three hundred horsemen in laying an ambush near a canyon west of Zhangzi. After detecting the passing of Kui's troops, his men stormed in unison to cut them off, returning with Kui as hostage. The Liang had formerly ordered Ge Congzhou and Zhu Chongjie to defend Luzhou in advance of Kui's arrival. News of Kui's capture caused them to scatter, enabling the Jin to regain control of Luzhou.

At the time, Zhang Jun and Han Jian campaigned against the Prince of Jin and rushed Yindi pass. To thwart Jun, the Jin deployed Li Cunxin and Xue Atan, sending Cunxiao separately to fort his men at Zhaocheng. Tang armies lost the battle at Yindi Pass, and Jun withdrew to protect Jin Prefecture, Han

Jian fleeing to Jiangzhou. Cunxiao proceeded to attack Jinzhou, where Jun's men emerged to fight and quickly suffered their second defeat; he subsequently sealed off the city, no longer daring to leave. Cunxiao moved on to raid Jiangzhou, after which Jun and Jian both absconded.

His arms long like an ape, Cunxiao had a natural facility for archery. He tended to cover his body with multiple layers of armor, his bow and spear fixed in place as he whipped about his iron cudgel. Whenever he entered or left a battle site, two reserve horses invariably rode behind, enabling him to change fatigued horses in battle, mounting and dismounting with the speed of flying. Previously, the contributions of Cunxiao to acquiring Luzhou were considerable, yet the future Taizu [Li Keyong] decided to name senior commander Kang Junli as interim regent of the prefecture, Cunxiao becoming prefect of Fenzhou. For several days, Cunxiao refused to eat because of the slight. He became prefect of Binzhou after Zhang Jun's flight, reassigned interim regent of Xingzhou in the second year of Dashun [C.E. 891].

At the time Jin armies had for two years been attacking Changshan, lands subordinate to the Zhao, with Li Cunxiao frequently serving as vanguard. They eventually overran Lincheng and Yuanshi counties, Zhaozhou. The Prince of Zhao turned to Li Kuangwei of Youzhou for relief. When the troops of Kuangwei arrived, Jin armies abruptly withdrew. Owing to longstanding frictions between Cunxiao and Cunxin, the latter maligned the former, saying, "Cunxiao is seditious in mind and often avoids attacking Zhao." Cunxiao grew ill at ease, reverting to the Liang while holding discussions with the Zhao and personally professing loyalty to the Tang. He hence requested a joint campaign against the Jin. The Tang court ordered Wang Rong, the Prince of Zhao, to lend assistance. A year later tensions surfaced between the Prince of Zhao and authorities at Youzhou. A nervous Prince, now seeking cordial relations with the Jin, reversed himself and provided thirty thousand troops to assist the Jin in storming Cunxiao.

Li Cunxiao mounted the city wall for a staunch defense, as Taizu [Li Keyong] personally commanded troops in approaching it, digging trenches to encircle the city. Cunxiao emerged from the city for a rousing counterattack, thwarting completion of the trenches. An assistant commander, Yuan Fengtao, employed someone to advise Cunxiao, "You should fear the Prince of Jin, and him alone. As the Prince awaits completion of the trenches, he will leave behind some contingents and depart. None among his commanders can rival you. Even with their trenches, what can they do?" Cunxiao concurred and allowed the enemy to finish its trenches, which upon completion had a deep cavity and high ramparts, making them unapproachable. Cunxiao became distraught and, as the city's food supplies vanished, climbed the wall to shout across, "Your Son, owing to the beneficence of the Prince, is ranked among the domain's commanders and ministers. How could I forsake the bond of father and son in submitting to our erstwhile enemy? This is merely a trap set by Cunxin! My simple wish is to meet the Prince and make a statement while alive, after which I can die." Taizu felt compassion for him and arranged for the Lady Liu to enter the city to console him. She accompanied Cunxiao in appearing before Taizu, his head covered in mud as he submitted himself for punishment. "Your son, serving the Prince of Jin, has a record of contributions without excesses," Cunxiao said. "It is solely through the machinations of Cunxin that things have come to this." Derisively, Taizu responded, "By drafting your call to war, you wronged me in every way. Did Cunxin do this as well?" In fetters, Cunxiao rode in a rear carriage to Taiyuan, and there, upon his arrival, his limbs were drawn by horse-carts. Taizu came to miss his talents and, resenting his own commanders for refusing to consider leniency, was unable to conduct affairs for more than ten days.

Kang Junli shared cordial relations with Cunxin from early on. As relations between the two brothers soured, Junli always assisted Cunxin in undermining Cunxiao. Cunxiao had died when Taizu, gambling with commanders, cried uncontrollably at the very mention of him. Junli criticized such conduct, and a livid Taizu killed him with poison. Junli began as military attaché to the Yunzhou governor and helped purge Duan Wenchu in the Tang reign of Emperor Xizong. Participating in Taizu's uprising at Yunzhong was his earliest feat. He came to win a succession of military victories, Taizu petitioning for his nomination as Zhaoyi governor. His murder occurred because of Cunxiao.

Li Cunjin

Native to Zhenwu, Li Cunjin [d. C.E. 922] had the original surname Sun and personal name Chongjin. Taizu obtained him in the conquest of Shuozhou, only to confer a new name and raise him as a son. He joined Taizu in penetrating the passes to suppress the rebel Huang Chao, becoming commissioner for his Army of Righteous Sons.

Cunjin attended Taizu in battles at Baixiang, winning advancement to inspector-in-chief of forces at large, as well as prefect for Cizhou‡ and Qinzhou†. He became chief officer of the Tianxiong command once Zhuangzong had acquired Wei and Bo prefectures. There he ended turmoil in the old Liang military and applied the law in all matters: for those guilty of crimes, Cunjin moved promptly to expose their heads or dismember their bodies at the marketplace, causing the people of Wei to hold their breath in awe. He joined in battles along the Yellow River, his merit acknowledged by promotion as Zhenwu governor. At the time, Jin forces were lodged at Desheng Commandery, where they erected barricades to the north and south, seeking to sap the energies of sailors trying to pass through. Because of the absence of bamboo and stone north of the Yellow River, Cunjin used reed fasteners to tie together large boats [at the side] and form a pontoon bridge—his inventiveness relished by Zhuangzong, who removed his own shirt to give to Cunjin.

When the Jin campaigned against Zhang Wenli at Zhenzhou, the city did not capitulate even after a long siege [C.E. 921]. Moreover, the battlefield claimed the lives of Shi Jiantang, Yan Bao, and Li Sizhao, in succession, so the Jin replaced Sizhao with Cunjin as commissioner of bandit suppression. He quartered his men at Dongyuan Crossing. The poor soil at Dongyuan proved unfit for constructing ramparts, forcing Cunjin to harvest trees for making palisades instead. Jin troops emerged in the early morning to graze animal herds, whereupon more than a thousand troops led by Zhang Chuqiu, the son of Wenli, harassed the palisades of Cunjin. Cunjin appeared atop a bridge to do battle and decimated Chuqiu's entire army. He died in battle, the rank of grand marshal conferred on him posthumously.

The son of Cunjin, *Li Hanshao*, reverted to his original surname during the era of Mingzong, becoming governor of Yangzhou‡. Congke the Prince of Lu having rebelled at Fengxiang, Hanshao and Zhang Qianzhao allied with government regulars to suppress him. Tang armies all eventually surrendered to Congke. The armies of Hanshao and Qianzhao singularly refused capitulation, later fleeing to Shu, where Hanshao was governor of the Yongping, Xingyuan, and Wuxin commands. He was over seventy *sui* old when stricken by death in Shu.

Li Cunzhang

Cunzhang [d. C.E. 922] had the courtesy name Dehuang. He originally followed Taizu [Li Keyong] in entering the passes to suppress the rebel Huang Chao, as had Kang Junli and Xue Zhiqin. Successive assignments culminated in his being named commissioner of the Army of Righteous Sons. As the illness of Taizu turned grave, Cunzhang supported eunuch Zhang Chengye and others in respecting the affirmation by glance from his deathbed that the future Zhuangzong be installed Prince of Jin. The Prince named Cunzhang commissioner of armed forces in Hedong. The Jin had treated its soldiers quite liberally since the days of the deceased Prince, such that many tended to violate the laws and ignore prohibitions. Zhuangzong, however, considered the problem particularly worrisome from the outset of his installation. Cunzhang hereafter harnessed the military by imposing the law in all matters, purifying the realm. He participated in the raid on the dual ramparts and saw action at Baixiang, contributions acknowledged by assignment as Fenzhou prefect. With Zhuangzong in the thick of battle against Liu Xun at the Wei/Bo command, the Liang directed Wang Tan to exploit the vulnerability of Taiyuan to storm it. Cunzhang responded by drawing on Fenzhou troops to defend Taiyuan. He became defense commissioner and later governor of the Datong command through such merit, dying of illness in the nineteenth year of Tianyou [C.E. 922], his posthumous rank grand marshal.

Li Cunxian

Native to Xuzhou‡, Cunxian [C.E. 860–924] had the original surname Wang and personal name Xian. A foot soldier in youth with a knack for arm wrestling, he was obtained by Taizu during a raid against Huang Chao at Chenzhou‡, Taizu eventually changing his name and raising him as a son. Cunxian later served as deputy commissioner of the Army of Righteous Sons and prefect of Qinzhou†.

Before this, the prefecture of Qin†, under enemy barrage, was moved more than a hundred *li* to the south, where palisades were erected at strategic positions and the site occupied. Once Cunxin became prefect there, he reasoned, "Moving a city to avoid an enemy is scarcely the deed of brave men!" He hence restored walls to the old prefectural site. The Liang repeatedly assaulted it, but Cunxian's vigorous defense prevented the enemy from ever drawing near. He was advanced to prefect of Wuzhou and military training commissioner for Shanbei, later moving to Cizhou‡.

In the eighteenth year of Tianyou [C.E. 921], Liang armies attacked Zhu Youqian at Hezhong Prefecture, Zhuangzong designating Cunxian for the relief. Youqian had only recently defected from the Liang in submission to Jin, while Hezhong was short on food supplies and many of its troops were disloyal in heart. A spy consequently informed Cunxian, "The Hezhong rank and file wish to assassinate you to revert to the Liang. You should leave promptly." But Cunxian insisted, "I aim to die serving the Prince. What possible regrets might I have?" He ultimately ran off the Liang army in a spirited rally.

Once Zhuangzong acceded to the throne [C.E. 923], Cunxian became generalissimo of the Martial Right Guard. Zhuangzong was similarly fond of arm wrestling and once matched up with the royal princes, repeatedly winning and priding himself for this. Now, looking to Cunxian, he promised, "If you can beat me, I will give you a governorship." Cunxian won at the first lift of his fist. In spring, the second year of Tongguang [C.E. 924], Fu Cunshen of Youzhou took ill and Zhuangzong sighed during a palace banquet, "The old cohort to assist in founding the dynasty has thoroughly vanished, with Cunshen the sole survivor. Now that he is so severely ill, who can possibly replace him at the northern border?" He glanced at Cunxian and added, "You won the arm wrestle and I will not eat my words—no one will take your place." On the same day, Cunxian became governor of the Lulong command. He died that year at Youzhou, at sixty-five *sui*, posthumously ranked grand mentor.

CHAPTER 37

BIOGRAPHIES OF COURT MUSICIANS AND ACTORS

We Lament. The principle behind the splendor or ruin of dynasty is the Mandate of Heaven, some say. Yet how can we possibly deny human actions? In contrasting Zhuangzong's original winning of the world with his later loss of it, we can know for certain.

Legends of the day say that the Prince of Jin [Li Keyong], approaching death, presented three arrows to Zhuangzong. "The Liang is our hated enemy," he said. "The Prince of Yan, whom I once installed, and the Khitan, who once shared a fraternal alliance with us, have both repudiated our Jin to revert to Liang. These three arrows, representing a vengeance still unrequited for each foe, I bequeath to you, wishing that you do not forget such indignities." Zhuangzong took the arrows to store at the Imperial Ancestors' Altar. Later, when deploying armies, he would send an aide to offer one yearling as sacrifice at the temple, then request the arrows. With imposing ceremony, the arrows were placed in a brocade sack and carried on the aide's back as he charged forth to return triumphantly to Zhuangzong, giving them to him. After roping along the father and son renegades of Yanzhou¤ or boxing the heads of the Liang ruler and his courtiers for presentation at the ancestral altar, Zhuangzong would return the arrows to the deceased Prince and announce the victory, his valor so awesome that the word "imposing" seems apt!

In contrast, after annihilating his erstwhile adversary to settle the world, the destitution turned palpable: mutineers springing from every corner in response to a single sentry's summons in the night, flustered flights eastward as soldiers scatter even before rebels appear, ruler and subject with nowhere to go staring bewilderingly, as locks of hair are sheared and Heavenly vows sworn by tearful men with wet lapels.[1] How can an effort so hard won be squandered so callously? At the root of all such feats and defeats are human factors, to be sure!

According to the *Book of Documents*, "Arrogance invites adversity, modesty incurs gain."[2] The amply industrious can erect an empire, the overly idle can forfeit his life—this is a natural principle. A peerless Zhuangzong, at the peak of his powers, had attracted the most gallant warriors under heaven. Yet degradation of the regime came through the shenanigans of several dozen musicians and actors, a ruler dying as his empire crumbles and the world scoffs. To be sure, calamity commonly reflects the accumulated effect of slighting subtle signs, the intelligent and brave often harmed by persons they most adore. As this scarcely applies to musicians and actors alone, I write these "Biographies of Court Musicians and Actors."

With an affinity for actors and musicians, Zhuangzong could identify musical tones. He wrote songs and often perfomed them, which is the meaning of "imperial compositions," the ballads associated with Fen and Jin prefectures to this day. He had the nickname Yazi, but some contemporaries called him Yaci.[3] He also adopted a stage name for himself, Li Tianxia, or "Li's World." After installation as Prince, even after ascent to Son of Heaven, Zhuangzong often mixed with musicians and actors in courtyard performances, enabling them to be drawn into court affairs to his eventual ruin.

Empress Liu began as a woman of humble station. Her father, Liu Sou, a peddler of medicines with a facility for divination, went by the sobriquet "Mountain Man Liu." Woman Liu could be a forbidding person. With the various royal concubines vying for favor at the time, shame about her own family background commonly caused the imposition of strict taboos on the matter. [In jest,] Zhuangzong acquired clothing like that of Liu Sou and personally donned the attire, while carrying milfoil sacks and medicine boxes; he was joined by his own son, Jiji, who carried a tattered cap akin to Sou's very own. The two now went to her palace bedroom, as Jiji announced, "Mountain Man Liu comes to visit his daughter." Utterly livid, Woman Liu beat Jiji with a light rod before expelling him, peals of laughter erupting among the amused in the palace.

During the battle at Huliu, the actor *Zhou Za*, favored by Zhuangzong, was apprehended by Liang victors. Once the Liang was overturned and Kaifeng occupied, Za appeared formally before the horse of Zhuangzong, who reveled at finding Za and lavished him with gold and silk. He commended Za for the prolonged ordeal, as Za responded, "I fell into the enemy's lair and managed to survive only through the efforts of the master for court music, Chen Jun, and master for palace gardens Chu Deyuan. May I beg for prefectural assignments to repay the two men." Once Zhuangzong consented to postings as prefect, Guo Chongtao admonished, "The warriors to assist Your Majesty in claiming the world are all valorous and venturesome, dedicated and daring. Your great achievements now newly won, you have rewarded not a single one of them and first name a mere actor as prefect. This is unacceptable, and, I fear, may cause Your Majesty to forfeit the loyalties of the world." Zhuangzong thus suspended the order. He confided to Chongtao a year later, after persistent prodding from the actors, "Having already consented to Zhou Za, I feel awkward at the mere sight of the three men. However fair your views, you should indulge me by implementing instructions." Jun finally became prefect of Jingzhou and Deyuan prefect of Xianzhou.

Fond of the hunt, Zhuangzong was coursing through Zhongmou County [Zhengzhou] when the farmlands of commoners were trampled upon. The magistrate for Zhongmou, on behalf of the people, strenuously censured such conduct before Zhuangzong's horse. A cursing Zhuangzong had the magistrate removed with the intent of murdering him when actor *Jing Xinmo* interceded. The reaction seemed unfair to him, so he led other actors in pursuing the magistrate on foot, then planted him before Zhuangzong's horse for a [farcical] tongue-lashing, "You are county magistrate. How can you possibly be ignorant of our Son of Heaven's affinity for hunting? Moreover, why didn't you callously seize the people's harvests to meet the tax quotas? And to accommodate the galloping steeds of our Son of Heaven, why didn't you simply starve the people and despoil the lands in your district? Yours are crimes truly deserving of death!" Xinmo now pleaded for summary execution, as the actor-musicians chanted songs in support. Zhuangzong now roared with laughter, the magistrate spared and allowed to leave.

Performing with some actors in the palace, Zhuangzong once peered in every direction and cried out [invoking his own name], "Li Tianxia, Li Tianxia—where are you?" Xinmo scampered forth to slap his face. Zhuangzong changed color, as those nearby panicked. The actors, similarly shocked, grabbed Xinmo to restrain him, inquiring, "Slapping the Son of Heaven on the face—how could you!" "Li Tianxia is merely one person," he responded. "For whom does he make the second cry?"[4] Everyone thus burst into laughter, as a thoroughly humored Zhuangzong bestowed bounty on Xinmo.

Jing Xinmo once addressed affairs in an audience chamber containing many ferocious dogs. One dog leaped after him as he departed, causing Xinmo to cry out from behind a pillar, "Surely, Your Majesty would not unleash his own child to nip at me!" Zhuangzong hailed from barbarian stock, and barbarians enforce taboos about dogs.[5] Xinmo seemed to be mocking these, and Zhuangzong, utterly livid, drew bow and arrow to shoot him. Xinmo now shrieked nervously, "Your Majesty cannot kill me! You and Your Subject are inseparable, so killing me would be inauspicious." The words startled Zhuangzong, who invited him to elaborate. Xinmo continued, "Your Majesty, when founding the empire, changed the reign to Common Brilliance, so all under Heaven now call you the Tongguang Emperor. The word 'common' is a homonym for 'copper' [in reflecting mirrors]: if you kill Xinmo, the Mirror Brush, your commonwealth will lose its luster." Zhuangzong roared with laughter and forgave him.

Of the assorted actors at the time, only Jing Xinmo evinced a special gift for acting, his verbal articulations most expressive. Little evidence exists of excessive evil on his part, either. Yet the three men most prominent in thwarting governance and ruining dynasty were Jing Jin, Shi Yanqiong, and Guo Men'gao. Musicians and actors at the time, given privileged access to the palace's inner apartments, enjoyed ridiculing courtiers. Yet the courtiers, despite contempt for the entertainers, dared not vent their indignation. Some even resorted to fraternizing with them to win imperial favor, as governors across the four corners tendered gifts and bribes.

At the center of such illicit activity was *Jing Jin.* Sent by Zhuangzong to mingle among people in the locales, Jin's cohort came to be consulted on all matters, regardless of import. Whenever he memorialized the throne in audience chambers, men nearby uniformly stepped back in deference. Jin participated in matters of military strategy as well as domestic governance. The commissioner for the Three Fiscal Agencies, Kong Qian, treated him as elder brother and employed the appellation "Eighth Brother."

At the outset of occupying Luoyang, Zhuangzong resided in the former palaces of the defunct Tang dynasty, palaces not yet furnished with imperial consorts. Eunuchs intuiting their monarch's wishes often reported the nighttime sighting of ghosts in the palaces that frightened them. Zhuangzong inquired of ways to appease the ghosts, and the eunuchs replied, "During the former Tang, ten thousand persons resided in the inner palaces. Today, strange events are common because palaces are empty: they will cease as people fill the spaces." The observation pleased Zhuangzong, who during a subsequent visit to the Ye capital arranged for a thousand local beauties to be selected by Jing Jin and cohort for the inner palaces, a mission exploited by Jin to engage in vile acts. Apprehensive wives and daughters of soldiers thus fled by the thousands. And Zhuangzong's retinue for the return trip to Luoyang now included a thousand Ye women conveyed personally by Jin, the roadways packed with no segregation of men and women.

The Prince of Wei, Jiji, had recently conquered the Shu region when Empress Liu, swayed by the slanders of eunuchs, illicitly instructed Jiji to murder Guo Chongtao. To the extent that Chongtao had formerly resented musicians and actors and often reined them in, they uniformly reveled in his death. A younger brother of the Emperor, Li Cunyi, was also son-in-law to Chongtao, so Jin slandered him before Zhuangzong, "Cunyi is certain to rebel to exact revenge for his wife's father." Cunyi was thus incarcerated and killed. Formerly, Zhu Youqian defected from the Liang in surrendering Hezhong to the Prince of Jin, who proceeded to occupy Luoyang. Musicians and actors approached Youqian for bribes, demands that he could not satisfy. Jing Jin now moved to malign him, "With Chongtao executed, Youqian will be unsettled of heart and inclined to rebel. He should be similarly executed." Youqian perished along with five or six commanders, their clans included—an injustice that appalled the world. Jin reached the rank of grandmaster of imperial recreations, interim left cavalier of palace remonstrance, concurrent censor-in-chief, and supreme pillar of state.

Shi Yanqiong was the Wude governor, residing at the Ye capital. Holding full administrative sway over the Wei/Bo command's six prefectures, everyone from interim prefect Wang Zhengyan on down bowed their heads to serve him. Guo Chongtao had been killed without cause in the Shu region at the time. A world still uninformed of the death, yet witnessing metropolitan soldiers murder his sons at their residence, concocted the rumor that "Chongtao had murdered Jiji the Prince of Wei and proclaimed himself King of Shu, his family being liquidated as punishment." Authorities at Ye initially suspected something of a ruse upon hearing such reports. The additional slaying of Zhu Youqian followed. His son was Chanzhou prefect Zhu Tinghui [Jianhui], whom Yanqiong received a court mandate to murder. Concealing the directive, Yanqiong abruptly left the city late at night. Shocked Ye authorities witnessing his nighttime departure without cause would circulate a rumor that "the Empress Liu, enraged over Chongtao's murder of Jiji, committed regicide against the Emperor to install herself, Yanqiong being summoned for urgent consultations." Abject fear gripped the Ye capital, and a Beizhou native then visiting Ye carried the rumor back home. The rumor spread to the border guard Huangfu Hui, who prodded Zhao Zaili to mutiny. Zaili had already reached Guantao County when the military police commissioner at Ye, Sun Duo, met with Yanqiong to seek reinforcements against the renegades. Yanqiong was unwilling. "The renegades have yet to arrive," he insisted. "Awaiting their arrival to release reinforcements is time enough." Yanqiong led troops up the northern gate upon their arrival, the sound of renegade shouts so terrorizing him that he abandoned armies to return alone on horseback to the capital. Zaili's success at claiming Ye and prosecuting his agenda of treasonous tumult emanated from Yanqiong's actions.

Guo Men'gao had the personal name Congqian and the stage name Men'gao. Winning favor for acting abilities, he nonetheless accomplished some military feats to become director of the rotating cavalry: "rotating cavalry" belong to the Imperial Guard. Sharing the surname of Guo Chongtao, Congqian regarded him as an uncle, while imperial brother Cunyi treated Congqian as an adopted son. With Chongtao now dead and Cunyi incarcerated, Congqian wept and brooded about the injustice against the two men during a banquet in his barracks. At the time, a rotating cavalryman posted within imperial precincts, Wang Wen, having conspired to mutiny that night, was executed after exposure of the affair. Zhuangzong now asked Congqian, partly in jest, "Members of your faction, Cunyi and Chongtao, betrayed me and even drove Wang Wen to treachery. What else do you intend?" A frightened Congqian withdrew, only to address troops provokingly, "You should squander your possessions on meats and wines with no thought of the future." As troops inquired after his meaning, he added, "Because of the Wang Wen incident, the Monarch merely awaits victory at Ye to bury you all!" The troops all believed him and embraced treachery.

Li Siyuan's armies had now mutinied and headed for the capital. Zhuangzong departed eastward for Bianzhou, but Siyuan [Mingzong] reached it first to occupy the city. Zhuangzong failed to advance beyond Wansheng garrison [Bian's western suburbs] and returned to the western capital, desertions leaving a residual twenty thousand or so troops. Within a few days, he again departed eastward for Sishui, planning to thwart Siyuan by dominating the pass. On the first day of the fourth month [C.E. May 15, 926], he met officialdom in audience at the Zhongxing hall [of Luoyang], deliberations with chief ministers lasting only several tens of minutes. Zhuangzong's yellow-armor cavalry were positioned at the Xuanren gate, as infantry awaited him in formations at the Wufeng gate. He entered the palace's private chambers for a meal. Having drawn his sword and cocked an arrow, Congqian left the barracks beyond the wall to storm the Xingjiao gate, exchanging fire with the yellow-armor cavalry. Zhuangzong learned of the mutiny and rushed mutineers with a special guard for royal princes, hoping to exit the gate. Yet the rebels had set the gate afire and scaled the wall to enter. Zhuangzong personally killed dozens, perhaps even a hundred men, in the raid, although rebels shooting from a tower wounded him with an arrow to inflict serious injury. He fell motionless under the eaves of Jiangxiao Hall as everyone absconded, from the Empress to royal princes to close aides. The Emperor expired by noontime. An imperial caretaker for hunting dogs, Shanyou, piled up musical instruments to cremate him, his bones retrieved by Siyuan after occupying Luoyang for burial at the Yong mausoleum, Xin'an. Siyuan initially named Congqian prefect of Jingzhou, only to murder him later.

The Narratives of Zuo states, "The way a ruler begins reveals the way he will surely end."[6] Zhuangzong loved actors and musicians, only to be killed by actor Men'gao and burn with his own musical instruments. Is the statement not credible? Are we not admonished?

CHAPTER 38

BIOGRAPHIES OF EUNUCHS

WE LAMENT. Since antiquity, the havoc wrought by eunuchs and women has been grave! The enlightened ruler knows to shun them long before problems arise. The muddled ruler stays smug even as peril approaches and expresses no regrets as tumult and extinction overtake him. All the same, I cannot fail to forewarn—the inspiration for these "Biographies of Eunuchs."

Zhang Chengye

Zhang Chengye [C.E. 846–922] was a eunuch of the Xizong era of Tang times, his courtesy name Jiyuan and original surname Kang. Castrated as a child, he was adopted as son to Zhang Tai, attendant for palace eunuchs. When troops of the Prince of Jin stormed Wang Xingyu, Chengye repeatedly shuttled between battling armies, and the Prince of Jin came to appreciate his character. Later, Emperor Zhaozong considered flight to Taiyuan under pressure from Li Maozhen and commissioned Chengye as emissary to Jin, conveying his intentions beforehand. Chengye thereby became military overseer for Hedong. Minister Cui Yin later conducted a mass execution of eunuchs: all those away from the capital were to be murdered at their local postings. The Prince of Jin pitied Chengye and could not countenance killing him, so Chengye was hidden at the Hulü temple. His release followed Zhaozong's death, resuscitation to military overseer ensuing.

As the Prince of Jin [Li Keyong] turned fatally ill, he entrusted the future Zhuangzong to Zhang Chengye, saying "I must place Yazi in your care." Zhuangzong tended to treat Chengye as an older brother. Through regular visits to his own mother's home, he developed enormous love and esteem for the eunuch. For more than ten years, as he battled Liang armies along the Yellow River from his base at Weizhou, Zhuangzong delegated all military affairs to Chengye, who proved thoroughly dedicated and never remiss. All of the gold and grains accumulated by the regime, all of the soldiers enlisted and horses procured for its armies, all of the foodstuffs produced and silk taxed to further the dynastic agenda—much of the merit for these belongs to Chengye. He consistently applied the rule of law to rein in everyone at the Jinyang [Taiyuan] court, from the Chaste and Austere Dowager, to the Virtuous Consort Han, to the Pure Consort Yi, to the royal sons. The rich and powerful all held back their hands in response to an intimidating Chengye.

Often returning home from Weizhou to visit family, Zhuangzong needed cash to gamble with and patronize his retinue of actors. Chengye presided over the treasury, however, making it impossible to obtain cash. At a banquet on treasury grounds, an inebriated Zhuangzong prodded son Jiji to rise in a dance for Chengye. The dance finished, Chengye provided from the treasury some precious sashes, silks, and steeds. Zhuangzong pointed to a pile of cash and employed Jiji's nickname in yelling out to Chengye, "The 'Amicable Brother' is short on cash and a pile of cash strings is available. Why bother with sashes and steeds?" Chengye declined, saying, "The monies of the empire cannot be tapped by Your Subject for private purposes." The words of Zhuangzong turned aggressive, and a defiant Chengye retorted, "Your Subject, as eunuch commissioner of long standing, does not act out of concern for my own posterity. Rather, I treasure the money, quite simply, because it will advance the Prince's mission of world dominance. If you really wish to spend it, why inquire of me? Once our wealth vanishes and soldiers scatter, I will scarcely face calamity alone!" Zhuangzong looked to Yuan Xingqin. "Bring me my sword," he said. A weeping Chengye arose and gripped Zhuangzong's garment, adding, "Entrusted with the Former Prince's death wish to care for you, Your Subject swore to satisfy the vendetta of family and country. Should I die today because the Prince covets objects in the treasury, at least my death will bring no shame to the Former Prince!" Approaching from the side, Yan Bao tried to release the grip of Chengye and remove him, but an indignant Chengye clenched his fists to beat him to the floor, cursing him: "A hooligan under Zhu Wen of Liang, you, Yan Bao, have enjoyed the charity and beneficence of our Jin. Still, you present not a single word of loyal candor, only flatter to aggrandize yourself."

Once the Empress Dowager learned of the matter, she summoned Zhuangzong. Exceedingly filial by character, Zhuangzong was utterly petrified by news of the Dowager's summons. He thus poured two goblets of wine to apologize to Chengye, saying, "I have misbehaved under the influence of wine, even offended the Empress Dowager. I hope you will accept this drink and excuse my excesses." Chengye refused the drink, and Zhuangzong entered the palace. Dowager Cao hence had a messenger convey gratitude to Chengye, stating, "The youth, having been rude to you, was flogged with a light rod." On the next day, she accompanied Zhuangzong to Chengye's residence to console him further.

Lu Zhi was a man fond of drink and arrogantly dismissive, someone Zhuangzong loathed ever since Lu Zhi treated him and the other royal princes insolently. Chengye exploited the rift to request, "In his affinity for wine, Lu Zhi lacks decorum and Your Subject wishes to kill him, on the Prince's behalf." "I am in the throes of calling men of character and talent to the cause of dynasty," Zhuangzong responded. "How can your convictions be so extreme?" Chengye rose to congratulate him, adding, "If the Prince can abide by this principle, then not even pacification of the world will be enough!" Lu Zhi thereby escaped death.

By the eighteenth year of Tianyou [C.E. 921], Zhuangzong had secured his commanders' support to become emperor. Zhang Chengye lay bedridden with illness as the news arrived but insisted on traveling from Taiyuan to Weizhou by sedan chair to admonish him. "For thirty years, Your Eminence the Prince joined his father in fighting bloody battles against the Liang: our original intent was to satisfy the vendetta of family and country while restoring the ancestral altars of the Tang dynasty. If you hastily assume esteemed titles today, even as the primal monster [the Liang] remains unvanquished, you would contradict the original will of father and son and lose the world's respect—something wholly unacceptable!" An unpersuaded Zhuangzong insisted, "This represents the wish of the commanders." Chengye now enjoined, "They are wrong! The Liang is the erstwhile enemy of both Tang and Jin, loathed by the entire world as well. The Prince today should simply expel this horrific scourge on the world's behalf, reiterate its profound offense against your Sagacious Predecessor, then search for descendants of Tang royals to install. If heirs to the Tang are found alive, how can you presume to replace them? If no heirs are found, then who in the world would challenge the Prince's accession? Your Servant is merely an old slave of the Tang dynasty, who genuinely wishes to witness the success of our Eminent Prince. Then, I could retire to the countryside, with ranked officiary escorting me beyond Luoyang's eastern gates as sendoff, commoners along the road exclaiming as they pointed, 'He was the imperial commissioner for our dynasty and served as military overseer for the Former Prince.' This would be a common honor for ruler and subject alike." Zhuangzong failed to heed him, and Chengye reckoned further remonstrance to be futile, so, looking to the heavens, he wept aloud and declared, "My Prince will claim the title for himself and repudiate this old slave." Returning to Taiyuan by sedan chair, he starved himself to death at seventy-seven *sui*. In the inaugural year of Tongguang [C.E. 923], he received posthumous rank as generalissimo of the Left Martial Guard and the title "Forthright and Illustrious."

Zhang Juhan

With the courtesy name Deqing, Zhang Juhan [C.E. 858–928] was the adopted son of Zhang Congmei, the one-time director of women's services under the former Tang. Juhan served as military overseer at Fanyang Commandery during the reign of Zhaozong, developing amicable relations with governor Liu Rengong. During the liquidation of eunuchs in the Tianfu era, Rengong concealed Juhan in a gorge north of the Da'an Hills, enabling him to survive. Rengong later came under Liang attack and ordered Juhan to join the Prince of Jin in a diversionary action against Luzhou, Liang territory. Luzhou was subsequently seized by the Jin, Juhan becoming military overseer of the Zhaoyi command. Upon the imperial accession of Zhuangzong, Juhan and Guo Chongtao served together as commissioners of military affairs. Zhuangzong had grown imperious after supplanting the Liang and allowed eunuch intrusion into politics. But owing to Guo Chongtao's monopoly on court affairs, Juhan kept silent for survival's sake.

The Prince of Wei [Jiji] having overtaken Shu, [surrendered potentate] Wang Yan had reached Qinchuan Post en route to the capital for audience when Mingzong's armies mutinied at Weizhou [C.E. 926]. Zhuangzong had departed for the east on campaigns and feared a mutiny on the part of Yan, so an express courier was dispatched with a mandate that the Prince of Wei murder him. The edict with imperial seal and imprimatur was concealed by Zhang Juhan, who opened it and read the words, "execute Yan and all companions." Juhan considered it inauspicious, however, to kill men already in surrender, so he placed the edict against a pillar to blot out the characters for "all companions" and insert the character for "one family." The vanquished from Shu then accompanying Yan eastward numbered over a thousand, all of whom thereby eluded death.

After Zhuangzong perished in an act of regicide, Juhan met Mingzong at the Zhide palace to request retirement to the countryside. He died at Changan in the third year of Tiancheng [C.E. 928], at seventy-one *sui*.

The writings of the Five Dynasties were truly scarce, the office of court historian a casualty of the prevailing tumult. Many informal records and stories failed to be transmitted, thwarting any complete account of events for the full period, exaggeration and error abounding, instead. Chivalrous men in contention, wars won and lost, empires rising and falling—for such times, how do we explain the dearth of strategies by courtiers or oratory by polemicists? Perhaps the written word was too deficient to convey the ideas, causing such writings to vanish without transmission to later generations. Zhang Chengye singularly served with such dignity before the eyes and ears of men that elders still speak of him to this day. His oratory truly merits the characterization "intrepid," hardly typical of eunuch views.

Since antiquity, when eunuchs wreaked havoc on the empire of men, its roots ran deeper than the calamity of women. Women possess mere physical appeal, but eunuch ravages have no single source. Their proximity in serving the palace affords familiarity, even as their hearts brood endlessly on matters. They can target petty kindnesses to suit the impulses of their master and manipulate petty confidences to ensnare his heart, the ruler of men invariably trusting and cherishing them. Upon winning that trust, they deploy the monarch's awesome powers to manipulate him. Despite the presence of loyal subjects and erudite scholars at court, the ruler of men feels distanced from them, unlike his intimacy with those eating and sleeping and serving at his very side, men deemed deserving of his trust. In this way, those serving at his side are more cherished by the day, as the loyal and erudite become ever distant—the powers of the ruler of men increasingly isolated. After the monarch's powers are isolated, he will turn ever anxious about potential calamity; but the powers of his manipulators having grown secure, his own security now rests upon their whim as calamity festers in his very bedroom. Thus, persons formerly deemed by the monarch as trustworthy can now imperil him.

When the monarch finally awakens to the severity of things, he may want to enlist once estranged subjects to conspire against nearby confidantes. If he acts too slowly, the festering calamity will ultimately assume greater gravity. If he acts in haste, the ruler of men might be abducted as their hostage. By then, even someone of sagacious wisdom could not plot against them; if a plot emerged it could not be implemented, and if implemented it could not succeed. At its worst, in fact, rulers and eunuchs alike face potential harm and mutual demise. Serious cases can ruin a country, lesser cases can claim lives. And should men of villainy or valor seek to exploit conditions as cause to rebel, they will stop at nothing short of liquidating the entire eunuch cohort to appease men's hearts across the world. The calamity of eunuchs that conforms to this pattern in earlier histories is hardly confined to a single generation.

The ruler of men scarcely wants calamity to fester in his palace or loyal and erudite subjects consigned to the periphery. These emanate from the gradual accumulation of forces. In the case of delusion by beautiful women, the hapless ruler may prove unwary to the point of near peril, yet eradication is still possible upon awakening to the threat. For eunuch calamity, the force of circumstances may not permit eradication despite awareness and contrition by the ruler. Emperor Zhaozong of Tang is characteristic; thus my earlier statement that "its roots run deeper than the calamity of women." We must be mindful! Emperor Zhaozong found trust and intimacy with eunuchs, culminating in his confinement to the eastern palace. He later emerged from confinement to plot with Cui Yin against them. Although chief minister, Yin fully appraised his own powers as inadequate and summoned Liang armies. With the armies soon to arrive, eunuchs abducted the Son of Heaven to Qizhou‡, which the Liang blockaded for three full years before Zhaozong could emerge, the Tang dynasty now overturned.

Previously, coinciding with Zhaozong's emergence from Qizhou‡ [C.E. 903], the Prince of Liang executed all eunuchs of the Tang dynasty, over seven hundred men led by Diwu Kefan. For eunuchs in the locales, an imperial edict mandated a systematic arrest and murder, although many were concealed by local governors and not killed. Local governors then in the throes of usurping powers were employing eunuchs exclusively to manage affairs, a practice most prevalent at Wu/Yue. Once Zhuangzong acceded to Later Tang, he mandated to the world that all former eunuchs of the previous Tang be located for conveyance to the capital. Several hundred surfaced, only to be reinserted into court affairs, up to the dynasty's very demise. This hardly differs from seeking out a carriage already overturned only to return and drive down precisely the same path again. How tragic!

Zhuangzong had yet to purge the Liang dynasty when Chengye died. He later named Zhang Juhan military commissioner, but Juhan did not monopolize court business. One commissioner for palace armies, Ma Shaohong, conferred the imperial Li surname, did enjoy Zhuangzong's considerable trust. He went on to malign and murder senior courtiers, sully himself through graft, and monopolize monarchical powers to the outrage of the world—the typical product of the eunuch quarters privileged to improper intimacies with his monarch. The future Mingzong was approaching the capital from Zhenzhou at the time, responding to an imperial summons for audience. Zhuangzong now suspected him of some sinister agenda and secretly planted Shaohong to spy on his activities. Shaohong instead apprised Mingzong of circumstances. Once Mingzong rebelled at Weizhou, the world attributed the calamity to Weizhou upstarts. Who could ever guess that Mingzong's duplicity originated with Shaohong?

At the time of Guo Chongtao's victory in Shu [Sichuan], the insinuations of Zhuangzong's trusted eunuchs had left him suspicious of Chongtao. Zhuangzong never realized that Chongtao's death was the handiwork of eunuchs. The elite armies of Tang were all concentrated in Shu, then. If Chongtao had not died, how could Mingzong have occupied Luoyang, able to ignore perils to the west as he calmly claimed the Tang throne? After the accession, Mingzong again mandated the arrest and liquidation of eunuchs across the world, causing their flight to mountains and ravines for refuge, many accepting tonsure as Buddhist monks. More than seventy eunuchs reached as far as Taiyuan: rounded up for murder at Duting Post, their blood covered the courtyard.

Mingzong suffered from numerous ailments in his last years, permitting Pure Consort Wang to intrude into political affairs from her dominant position in the palace. The eunuch Meng Hanqiong hence came to manage affairs. The Prince of Qin had appeared at the palace to visit Mingzong, whose illness was already grave. The Prince heard the sound of sobbing as he left and believed the Emperor dead. Fearing his own installation in jeopardy, he thereby conspired to penetrate palace precincts with troops. Senior courtiers such as Zhu Hongzhao were in the throes of planning things, plans not yet finalized when Hanqiong abruptly entered Mingzong's chambers to expose the Prince of Qin's treachery. Troops went out to execute him, as Mingzong became consumed by outrage for his own vulnerability to the Prince of Qin's treachery, his death a consequence thereof. In the wake of Emperor Min's flight to Weizhou‡, Hanqiong went westward to receive Emperor Fei on the highway, but Fei despised Hanqiong and killed him.

We Lament. Humans are predisposed toward self-contentment: except for the sagaciously wise, arrogant indifference is unavoidable as time passes. The havoc of eunuchs and women occurs not in a single day, for these must await arrogant indifference to sink in gradually. Hardly a diffident ruler, Mingzong perhaps succumbed owing to a relatively long reign. Most other rulers of the period began as military men whose successors faced fleeting reigns and short lives. Eunuchs thus had little time to do their deeds, so the wreaking of serious havoc is scarcely visible. The statements of Chengye emerge as singularly venerable and splendid, while Juhan spared a thousand persons by altering one word. When a superior man appraises others, he will recognize any good deed. For these two persons, I have chosen to cite the good while exposing the bad in the spirit of "rendering respect but acknowledging evil, harboring contempt but acknowledging good."[1] This chapter further reveals how the calamities and defeats of others came about.

CHAPTER 39

MISCELLANEOUS BIOGRAPHIES

Wang Rong

The ancestor of Wang Rong [C.E. 873–921], Monuogan, was descended from Abusi, a man of Huihu Uighur extraction. Monuogan was cavalry commander under Wang Wujun of Zhenzhou, formally adopted by him as son and given the surname Wang. The son of Monuogan had the name Motanhuo, and his son had the name Sheng; Sheng's son was Tingcou, and his son was Yuankui; Yuankui's sons were Shaoding and Shaoyi, and Shaoding had a son named Jingchong. For the three generations up to Sheng, kinsmen often served as cavalry commanders for Zhenzhou; and for the four generations up to Jingchong, five men served as governors of the Chengde command. Jingchong rose in official rank to ad hoc grand marshal, invested as Prince of Changshan. He died in the Tang dynasty, second year of Zhonghe [C.E. 882], his son Rong inheriting his office at ten *sui*.

The Jin [under Li Keyong] had recently acquired Taiyuan at the time, as Li Kuangwei occupied Youzhou, Wang Chucun occupied Zhongshan, Helian Duo occupied Datong, and Meng Fangli took Xingtai—men of martial valor from the four corners of the world all contending for dominance. Positioned between these men, Rong inherited the century-old legacy of his ancestors: his warriors and horses were hardy, riches were stored away, and the family had served as vassals of the Tang for generations. Rong may have been young in years, but the hereditary standing of his family made him important: thus, action on all petitions to the Tang court to appoint or replace governors across the realm required Rong's involvement.

Jin armies, since departing from the eastern mountains [Shandong], had already broken the back of Meng Qian and acquired the three prefectures of Xing, Ming, and Ci. The launch of a major offensive occurred in the inaugural year of Jingfu [C.E. 892], storming Zhaozhou and felling its Lincheng County. Wang Rong turned to Li Kuangwei for relief, and Kuangwei's assistance forced Jin armies to disband and retreat. A year later, the Jin aligned with Wang Chucun for a raid on Jiangu and Xinshi counties, territory of Rong. The Prince of Jin and Chucun both personally commanded their men. Rong never even appeared before his armies, but instead sent training commissioners Duan Liang of the Zhuifeng brigade and Ma Ke of the Jiankou brigade, their armies simply placed under the command of Kuangwei. Upon engaging Jin armies at the Ci River, Kuangwei delivered a rout. In spring of the next year, the Jin raided Tianchang Commandery. Rong dispatched men for relief, but they were defeated at the Chiri Mountains. Jin armies later emerged from Jingxing [Hengzhou], and Rong again turned to Kuangwei for relief, after which Jin armies disbanded and withdrew.

Before this, Li Kuangwei had developed a physical attraction to the wife of his younger brother Kuangchou, his intimate relations with her offending his brother in the process. During Kuangwei's absence for the Rong relief effort, Kuangchou incited his military to mutiny and installed himself. Kuangwei was ashamed about returning, so he transferred to his younger brother the tallies and seals of office, preparing himself to seek refuge in the capital. His entourage had reached Shenzhou when a messenger from Rong arrived to extend an invitation, Rong feeling obliged for Kuangwei's former help for him. Housing them at Meizi [Haizi] gardens, Rong treated Kuangwei as father.

A retainer under Kuangwei, Li Zhengbao [Baozhen], who had traveled between Yan¤ and Zhao prefectures in youth, so loved his travels in Changshan [near Zhao] that he could not bring himself to leave. Having lost their kingdom, Zhengbao and Kuangwei had little else to do and climbed together a tall pavilion west of the city walls, surveying the mountains and rivers of Zhenzhou as tears fell in profusion. Zhengbao and Kuangwei thus conspired to replace Wang Rong by force.

Dropping by the hostel to console the two with an early morning visit, Wang Rong had relieved his bodyguard escorts, having been misinformed that the day was an inauspicious anniversary. Once he was seated comfortably, armored soldiers emerged from behind a curtain to grab Rong by his two sleeves, as he declared, "Our kingdom exists today by virtue of you, Kuangwei. I truly have nothing to offer as recompense for your profound charity, however. The incident today provides an opportunity to satisfy that debt." He now kowtowed in relinquishing to Kuangwei his own position. Kuangwei had long slighted Rong and considered him inept, so the two rode side by side on horseback to the prefectural seat in anticipation of replacing him. Once the entourage passed the barracks of the personal bodyguard, the soldiers shut the gates and created a huge clamor, while the heavens unleashed rain, thunder, and lightning, as wind gusts split trees and ripped tiles from homes. A butcher named Mo Junhe recognized Rong by sight and leaped out from behind a dilapidated wall, snatching him from his horse and carrying Rong off on his own back. Unruly troops rushed Kuangwei and Zhengbao to murder them, as Yan¤ soldiers all absconded. Kuangchou on principle now publicly censured Rong in the harshest of terms, despite hidden resentment toward his own elder brother. Rong thus lost support from allies at Yan¤, while Jin armies bombarding Pingshan forced Rong into an alliance with the Prince of Jin, which he accepted.

Taizu of Liang later overran the Jin prefectures of Xing, Ming, and Ci, then wrote Rong to demand a severing of ties with Jin and reversion to Liang. An irresolute Rong could reach no decision. Jin commander Li Sizhao recaptured Mingzhou but was defeated in a bombardment from Taizu of Liang, forcing Sizhao to abandon the prefecture. His equipment wagons were captured by Liang soldiers as well, along with Rong's letters to Sizhao containing many references to affairs of the Liang regime. An inflamed Taizu now advanced armies to Changshan, where he instructed Ge Congzhou, "I will entrust to you the conquest of Zhenzhou, you serving as my vanguard." Congzhou had only reached Lincheng when he was hit by a stray arrow and confined to a carriage, as Liang warriors faced a grave setback. Taizu personally commanded the charge on the city wall, setting afire its southern gates.

A frightened Wang Rong turned to subordinates, asking, "What can be done under circumstances so dire?" Administrative aide Zhou Shi, a deft polemicist, responded, "It will be difficult to challenge him with arms, but we can conquer with reason." An old acquaintance of Taizu, Shi requested to visit his barracks. Once there, Taizu cursed as he looked squarely at Shi, saying, "I sent many letters summoning Rong, who refused to come. Now, having reached this moment, your talents of persuasion come too late. Moreover, the Jin is my bitter rival and Rong allied with it. I believe Li Sizhao to be in the city, and he should emerge first." Rong's letter to Sizhao was then showed to Shi, who countered, "Does the Liang intend to stop after claiming the single prefecture of Zhen, or does it aspire to hegemonic powers over the world? The hegemon punishes others based on principle, not personal considerations. Today, as the Son of Heaven reigns on high, his lords hold fiefs as nonbelligerent neighbors in order to end wars and provide the people a respite. Long ago, Cao Cao defeated Yuan Shao and obtained letters to Shao from Wei commanders and their aides, deciding to burn them all. Is this not the deed of a hero? The Liang today, knowing that it lacks pretext to raise armies, merely exploits Sizhao to create cause. Moreover, the Wang family has pacified this land through five generations and six men of noble standing. It scarcely suffers a shortage of death-defying warriors such that dependence on Sizhao is even necessary." Taizu appeared jubilant, tugging at Shi's garment and saying consolingly, "My words were spoken in simple jest!" He then invited Shi to sit beside him in discussing a truce with Rong. Later, Rong gave a son, Zhaozuo, as bonded hostage to the Liang, Taizu giving his daughter in marriage to him. After the formal accession of Taizu, Rong was invested Prince of Zhao.

During mourning for Wang Rong's grandmother, the various governors all extended condolences. When representatives for the Liang saw emissaries for the Jin at their hostel, they returned to report that the Prince of Zhao had seditious intentions. Luo Shaowei of the Wei/Bo command had died by then, whetting the Liang appetite to seize the entire Hebei region. In the fourth year of Kaiping [C.E. 910], winter, it dispatched an officer for palace services, Du Tingyin, to oversee the Wei/Bo commander, Xia Yin. The Liang also stormed the two prefectures of Shen and Ji¶ with three thousand troops, naming Wang Jingren commissioner of bandit suppression for at-large forces on the northern front. A frightened Rong requested reinforcements from Jin, which responded by storming and defeating Jingren at Baixiang County. The Liang consequently lost Zhen and Ding prefectures, while the future Zhuangzong emerged as increasingly formidable. As he overpowered the prefectures of You and Yan¤ to the north and assimilated Wei and Bo to the south, Rong's men often accompanied Zhuangzong in expression of his profound indebtedness to the Jin. A year later, in a meeting with Zhuangzong at Chengtian Commandery, Rong raised a goblet in a toast to longevity. Zhuangzong similarly treated Rong with deference and courtesy, as a friend of his father. Starting to sing as the wine moved him, Zhuangzong drew the sword from his waist to sever part of his garment in an oath of allegiance, promising a daughter as wife to another of Rong's sons, Zhaohui.

A man of benevolence, not warfare, Wang Rong dared not appear before his troops. Whenever outside forces attacked Zhao, he commonly enlisted neighboring armies to save himself. The various governors of the day suffered under the weight of warfare, Zhao alone enjoying peace. Delighting in the stability of Wang rule, the gentlemen and ladies of its capital tended to don long official robes with broad sashes, engaging in lavish forms of entertainment. Rong especially reveled in wealth and status while favoring heterodox teachings, the search to prolong life prompting him to make medicines of cinnabar. He once retained the Daoist master, Wang Ruone, for travels to the western mountains, where they ascended a shrine to the spirit of the "Supreme Mother." There they had women pull them up using their wraparounds of fine brocade. Whenever he left on excursions, over a month might pass without contemplating return, as governance devolved on eunuchs.

The eunuch Shi Ximeng used to share the bed of Wang Rong from dusk to dawn. In winter, the eighteenth year of Tianyou [C.E. 921], Rong had left the western mountains to rest at Huying hamlet in preparation for return to the prefectural seat, but Ximeng tried to dissuade him. Another eunuch, Li Honggui, criticized the delay: "Today, as the Prince of Jin rallies archers and stone-throwers with a personal appearance, our Esteemed Prince squanders the kingdom's wealth on excursions. Over a month has passed since the Prince threw open the city gates and vacated its palaces, without once returning. If a soldier were to shut the gates and turn away your entourage, where would the Esteemed Prince return?" A nervous Rong hastened to ride back, although Ximeng adamantly tried to dissuade him. This infuriated Honggui, who sent Su Hanheng, a commander in the personal bodyguard, to array troops before his tent, their armor fastened and swords drawn in declaring, "We soldiers are genuinely fatigued and seek to return with the Prince." Honggui now stepped forward to press the issue, "Delusion of the Prince is the doing of Ximeng. To appease the troops, I want him killed!" Rong refused to respond, whereupon Honggui shouted out to one of Rong's armored men to decapitate Ximeng, his head tossed before Rong. A flabbergasted Rong returned immediately, then directed son Zhaozuo and senior commander Zhang Wenli to liquidate Honggui and Hanheng, their entire families included, while arresting and jailing their detachments' commanders. A thorough investigation of the circumstances surrounding the mutiny also occurred, leaving the personal bodyguard anxious and permitting Wenli to incite a mutiny: he led over a thousand guardsmen in leaping over a wall to infiltrate the palace. Rong happened to be burning incense with Daoist monks to receive divine inscriptions, as a soldier decapitated him and departed with the head under his sleeve. Soldiers now set fires that engulfed the palaces, later liquidating the entire Wang clan.

Rong's son, *Wang Zhaohui* [C.E. 912–?], only ten *sui* at the time, had been hidden in a cave by a soldier personally obliged to Rong. With the mutiny over, the youth's hair was shaved and a monk's shroud placed on his back. He encountered at the time a certain Li Zhen from Hunan, who concealed Zhaohui in a tea hamper and carried him to Hunan. Somewhere south of Mount Yue, he joined the Buddhist clergy and changed his name to Chongyin. Already an adult by the Mingzong era, Zhaohui wished to return, as Li Zhen reverted to Fu Xi, a one-time commander under Wang Rong now governor of the Xuanwu command [Kaifeng]. Xi petitioned Zhaohui's case to the court [on Zhen's behalf]. During court appearance, Zhaohui presented himself as the "former commander of center armies at Chengde." The court honored him as director of personnel evaluation and deputy director of the national granaries. He reputedly also served, in the Zhou dynasty's Xiande reign, as director of imperial factories.

Wang Rong was beguiled by love for *Zhang Wenli*, a cunning and mischievous man whom he treated as a son and liked to call Wang Deming. Wenli installed himself as interim regent upon Rong's death, an action initially condoned by Zhuangzong of Tang. He later learned of Wenli's communications with the Liang and ordered a raid against him, led by Fu Xi, the one-time Zhao commander, and Yan Bao. The ghosts in Wenli's home reportedly cried through the night, and the waters of the Ye River changed to blood as the fish inside all died, so terrifying Wenli that he died of an ulcer. His son Chujin assumed private mourning while continuing resistance against the enemy, ultimately defeating Xi and cohort in a storm. Xi's replacement was Li Sizhao, who died after a stray arrow hit him. His replacement, Li Cunjin, similarly died rather soon on the battlefield. Fu Cunshen then became commissioner of bandit suppression and eventually overpowered the regime. He apprehended Wenli's wife, as well as sons Chujin, Chuqiu, and Chuqi, among others, their feet lopped off for the trip to Jin. As demanded by the people of Zhao, they were reduced to minced meat, save for Wenli, who was dismembered at the marketplace.

Luo Shaowei

Luo Shaowei had the courtesy name Duanji. His ancestors were native to Changsha, but grandfather Luo Rang had migrated north to Weizhou, Guixiang County. His father, *Luo Hongxin*, at the time of death, was a minor officer for horse pastures. In the inaugural year of Wende [C.E. 888], a mutiny erupted in the governor's guard at Wei/Bo, claiming the life of supreme commander Le Yanzhen. Commander Zhao Wenjian was installed as interim regent, although mutineers later killed him as well. The guard could not decide whom to install, so the men roared in unison, "Who can lead us?" And Hongxin shouted back from within the crowd, "I would be willing to lead you, Gentlemen!" Hongxin was strange in physical appearance, his face a bluish-black. The military therefore considered him a prodigy and together elevated him to interim regent. Upon the accession of Emperor Zhaozong of Tang, Hongxin became governor.

As Taizu of Liang prepared to attack the Jin, he requested grains from Luo Hongxin, his refusal causing a rift between the two men. Liang armies thus attacked Weizhou and claimed the counties of Liyang, Qimen, and Wei‡. For the five battles at Neihuang [Xiangzhou‡], troops from Wei lost each and every one, compelling a nervous Hongxin to pursue an alliance to end hostilities. At the time, the Liang undertook offensives against Yan and Yun prefectures in the east and threatened the Jin to the north. The Jin offered assistance to Zhu Xuan in the person of Li Cunxin, who sought passage through Weizhou. News of the request prompted Taizu to dispatch a messenger to Hongxin, insisting that "Jin armies aspire to claim all lands north of the Yellow River. When their troops return, they will surely destroy Weizhou." Hongxin was persuaded and issued troops to storm Cunxin at Shen County, as Taizu deployed Ge Congzhou to render assistance at Shen. Liang armies managed to apprehend Luoluo, son of the Prince of Jin, and convey him to Weizhou, where Hongxin murdered him and permanently severed ties with Jin in the process. Taizu still suspected Hongxin of a duplicitous heart, so he extended courtesies of elder brother and commonly employed humble language in diplomatic communications with Wei, presenting hefty sums of cash. Whenever envoys from Weizhou reached his lands, Taizu faced north and bowed before accepting their tribute, saying to the envoys, "Sixth Brother is twice my age. How dare I treat him rudely?" A jubilant Hongxin hence thought himself highly valued by Taizu. Weizhou thus saw no threat in Taizu's military movements between Yan¤ and Zhao prefectures, nor even in his ultimate occupation of the northern Yellow River region. Shaowei was installed upon the death of Hongxin.

Fond of learning and skilled at calligraphy, Luo Shaowei also proved highly adept at composition. His personal library swelled to several tens of thousands in scrolls, access to which he afforded scholars from across the four corners. In Tang times, father Hongxin had been enfeoffed as Prince of Changsha, where his ancestors had originated. Shaowei similarly inherited the noble standing of his father as Prince of Changsha. Soon after Shaowei's installation, Liu Rengong of Youzhou attacked Weizhou with an army of a hundred thousand, committing a slaughter at Beizhou. Shaowei turned to the Liang for relief, helping him to win a rout of Yanzhou¤ troops at Neihuang. A year later, Taizu of Liang dispatched Ge Congzhou to rendezvous with Wei troops in a joint assault on Cangzhou; the two seized Dezhou and subsequently defeated troops from Yan¤ at Laoyati. In this way, Shaowei became obliged to the Liang for its assistance.

The governor's guard at Wei/Bo began under the governorship of Tian Chengsi, the guard growing progressively arrogant over the years. By the time of Luo Shaowei, they had entrenched themselves for two hundred years through father-to-son successions and marriage bonds. Supreme commanders of the past such as Shi Xiancheng, He Quanhao, Han Junxiong, and Le Yanzhen—each installed by the guard—had been abruptly slain by it in fits of rage. Shaowei, a man of sharp mind and heavy hand, held a broad appreciation of personnel matters and governed with imposing discipline, yet his ancestors had been installed by the guard for generations. In the second year of Tianyou [C.E. 905], the earth shifted within the walls of Weizhou, convincing Shaowei of a rebellion underway. And indeed, a mutiny did occur by Li Gongquan, a guard lieutenant. Shaowei executed him, then sent a messenger requesting reinforcements from the Liang in order to execute the entire governor's guard. Approving the request, the future Taizu of Liang instructed Li Si'an to raid Cangzhou, summoning troops from Wei. Wei forces were all dispatched by Shaowei in the effort, leaving behind only the governor's guard.

Luo Shaowei's son, Tinggui, had married a daughter of Taizu of Liang, who happened to die at the time. Under the bogus pretense of attending the burial, Taizu secretly arranged for commander's attendant Ma Sixun to recruit elite fighters to fill a carriage, while in the wagons entering Weizhou, a thousand men from his long-distance regiments were mixed in among the porters. Taizu directed his own armies to their rear. Shaowei now dispatched several hundred slave-soldiers, under the cover of darkness, to join Sixun in storming guardsmen, liquidating everyone including family dependents. Taizu personally rushed from Neihuang to Weizhou. Wei regulars assisting in the Cangzhou offensive realized the fraud upon reaching Liting County and rebelled en masse, occupying Chan and Bo prefectures. Bedlam prevailed in the Wei region for months before Taizu finally quelled it. With the governor's guard entirely dead and Wei regulars in mutiny, Shaowei's strategic isolation only intensified. Taizu now coveted his land, and Shaowei's regrets turned profound.

That year [C.E. 906], Taizu resumed his offensive against Cangzhou, forting men at Changlu as Luo Shaowei supplied his armies. Across a distance of five hundred *li* from Cang to Wei prefectures, guard stations were set up by Shaowei, who also met the miscellaneous needs of Liang armies, enough to satisfy many tens of thousands or even a hundred thousand Liang warriors. It became an enormous imposition for Shaowei. Later, Emperor Zhaozong of Tang moved the capital eastward to Luoyang and summoned assistance from the governors to rebuild the city. Shaowei covered construction costs for the temple to the Imperial Ancestors, completion of which resulted in advancement to acting director of the Chancellery and investiture as the Prince of Ye.

Taizu had besieged Cangzhou without success when Liu Shouguang assisted Jin armies in overrunning the Liang prefecture of Lu. Deciding to return via Changlu, Taizu took ill during passage through Weizhou and was confined to bed at the prefectural offices. Even the city's leading commanders were denied visits, so Shaowei feared that Taizu might have finally begun a raid against him. He used the opportunity to enter for a visit, where he said, "With the four corners now at war, it is lingering Tang rule that most imperils the Liang cause. Heaven's mandate for the Tang now expired, you would do better to claim it sooner than later." Such sentiments immensely pleased Taizu, who returned in haste. He prepared to make Luoyang his capital after formal accession to power, and Shaowei selected the best of Weizhou's building materials to construct the Wufeng tower and Zhaoyuan anterior palace, transporting the materials by river for construction in the capital. Taizu now commented with a sigh, "I have heard that Xiao He, in defending the Guanzhong area, once erected the Weiyang palace for the Han dynasty. Yet even his feat scarcely compares to Shaowei's conveyance of over a thousand *li*—the materials appearing as if by some divine act, exceeding Xiao He by far!" Taizu conferred a precious sash and prize horse.

A rift had developed between the Prince of Yan, Liu Shouguang, and elder brother Shouwen after Shouguang imprisoned their mutual father, Rengong [C.E. 907]. Through express communications, Luo Shaowei urged Shouguang to surrender to the Liang. Hearing of the effort, Taizu commented with a smile, "My repeated attacks on Yanzhou¤ could not cause its surrender: a mere missive from Shaowei prevailing over an army of a hundred thousand." Whenever faced with a major decision, Taizu often sent messengers to inquire of Shaowei. Shaowei commonly employed express letters to convey his response, messengers for the two men crossing one another on the roadways. And their views were generally compatible.

For long, Weizhou did not deploy troops. Luo Shaowei thus offered to harvest trees of Anyang and Qimen to build boats to transport annually a million piculs of grain by river to Luoyang as subsidy for the capital. Taizu thus increasingly deemed Shaowei steadfastly loyal. Liang commanders Cheng Hou and Lu Ning were sent to supervise the delivery of the boats, but Shaowei fell ill before finishing them and petitioned Taizu, "Wei was once a large district with many outside troops, so I would request the assignment of an experienced and respected subject of the Liang to preside over the prefecture, permitting this tired body of mine to rest at home." Taizu promptly authorized Shaowei's son, Zhouhan, to supervise prefectural affairs, while imparting the following words to the messenger: "You should hurry back, at my behest, to urge your master to tend to his health. If the unthinkable should occur, I will ennoble his sons and grandsons for generations to come. I hereby authorize Zhouhan to supervise prefectural affairs, but Shaowei's recovery is my true wish." Under the Liang, Shaowei eventually rose to grand preceptor and concurrent palace secretary, dying at thirty-four *sui*. Posthumous rank as imperial secretary and the title "Dedicated and Strong" were conferred.

Shaowei had three sons: *Luo Tinggui* reached the rank of minister for national granaries before his death. *Luo Zhouhan* [C.E. 902–915] succeeded to his father's position [as Weizhou governor], but was purged by Yang Shihou in the second year of Qianhua, the eighth month [C.E. 912]. Reassigned as the Xuanyi governor, Zhouhan died in office at fourteen *sui*. Replacing him as governor was brother *Luo Zhoujing* [C.E. 906–937], then ten *sui*. He subsequently became the Zhongwu governor and, a year later, director of the Palace Library, commandant of reserve cavalry, and chamberlain of imperial recreations. In the Tang reign of Zhuangzong, he was named commandant of the Imperial Insignia Guard, then governor of the Kuangguo command under Mingzong, who later demoted him to commandant. He died in the second year of Tianfu, under the Jin dynasty [C.E. 937], at thirty-two *sui*. Tinggui had married two daughters of the Liang ruler Taizu: the Anyang Princess, first, and the Jinhua Princess, second. Zhouhan married the daughter of Emperor Mo, the Shouchun Princess. Zhoujing also married a daughter of Emperor Mo, the Jin'an [Pu'an] Princess.

Wang Chuzhi

With the courtesy name Yunming, Wang Chuzhi [C.E. 863–922] was native to Wannian, Jingzhao. His father, Wang Zong, had a talent for turning profits on properties, creating wealth for the nobles. He served as administrative aide in the Divine-Strategy Guard under Tang rule, his rank rising to commandant of the Imperial Insignia Guard and concurrent Xingyuan governor. His sons were Chucun and Chuzhi.

Owing to his father's standing, *Wang Chucun* [d. C.E. 895] became a commander in the Valorous Bodyguard, regional commissioner of imperial stables for the converted lands of Dingzhou, and commissioner of palace gardens. He was already serving as the Yiwu governor, in the sixth year of Qianfu [C.E. 879], when the rebel Huang Chao overran Changan. The experience brought a furious Chucun to tears, and he commanded district regiments to enter the pass for the suppression effort. In terms of the contribution to defeating Chao, Li Keyong ranked first in claiming cities and repulsing renegades, although Chucun ranked first in rallying recruits around the righteous principle of succoring their monarch. Chucun died at his command during the second year of Qianning [C.E. 895], and based on precedent north of the Yellow River, the three armies elevated the son of Chucun, Wang Gao, to interim regent. The court confirmed him as governor and conferred office as honorary interim dignitary of education with ministerial powers. Chuzhi served under him as intendant for the [elite] "rear" and [strategic] "center" armies.

In the third year of Guanghua [C.E. 900], Liang armies raided Dingzhou, and Wang Gao dispatched nephew Chuzhi to resist them. He was defeated by

Liang men in the battle at Shahe, Chuzhi's returning armies subsequently entering the city to expel Gao, who fled to the Prince of Jin. The mutinous troops now elevated Chuzhi to interim regent. The city then came under the siege of Liang armies. Through a messenger, Chuzhi proposed severing ties with Jin to serve the Liang, relinquishing forthwith a hundred thousand bolts of silk as subsidy for its army. The alliance with Liang began in this way. Through petition to the Tang court, Taizu of Liang arranged for Chuzhi to become the Yiwu governor with eventual investiture as Prince of Taiyuan. Investiture as Prince of Beiping attended Taizu's formal accession.

Liang troops later attacked Wang Rong, who sought assistance from the Jin. Chuzhi also approached the Prince of Jin about severing ties with Liang to serve it, contributing five thousand men to the Jin relief for Rong. Liang armies were vanquished at Baixiang. The Jin proceeded to overrun Yanzhou¤ to the north, seize the Wei/Bo command to the south, and face off Liang armies along the Yellow River for more than ten years—and throughout it all, Chuzhi's men invariably participated.

Wang Chuzhi, fond of sorcery, had a perverse man as retainer, Li Yingzhi. Chuzhi once took ill and Yingzhi employed some heretical techniques to heal him, such that Chuzhi increasingly believed him a spirit: clothing Yingzhi in the attire of Daoist monks, Chuzhi appointed him adjutant for mobile brigades. He came thereby to decide all military affairs, great and small alike. Prior to this, Yingzhi took in a small boy at Xingyi, Liu Yunlang, and raised him as son. Chuzhi had no son, then, so the youth was presented to him, Yingzhi ingenuously claiming that, "Prodigies had attended the birth of this boy." Chuzhi adopted the youth and changed his name to Du, loving him immensely. Yingzhi turned ever more unruly after this, enlisting rough-and-ready men from his district to create a new army personally commanded by him. Housed at his official residence in Boling ward, he opened his four doors to every conceivable sort, and they indulged in heretical practices one and all. The commanders and aides of Chuzhi fully foresaw calamity as an inevitable outgrowth of such conduct, but none could admonish him.

At the time, Li Kuangchou of Youzhou was passing through Zhongshan en route to the capital, and Wang Chuzhi, as a precaution against the unexpected, led armored men beyond the city walls to lie in ambush. With the safe passage of Kuangchou, the armored men infiltrated the city to surround the home of Li Yingzhi, seizing and killing him. They now approached Chuzhi begging for Du's murder, but he refused. Chuzhi rewarded men for merit in battle a day later and retaliated by refraining from citing the names of armored men. He further concealed a separate list of names for everyone above company commander, later exploiting assorted incidents to execute them:

over some twenty years, no one escaped retribution. Chuzhi was himself slain by Du.

Wang Du [d. C.E. 929] was a wily man of endless intrigue, whom Chuzhi named deputy governor. Zhang Wenli had committed regicide against Wang Rong when Zhuangzong of Tang dispatched troops to punish him [C.E. 921]. Plotting with aides, Chuzhi observed, "Zhen Prefecture is the shield for Ding: if Zhen falls, Ding cannot survive alone, the crimes of Wenli notwithstanding." A request thus went out to Zhuangzong to refrain from issuing troops. Zhuangzong arranged for Chuzhi to view the wax-sealed letter, then in his possession, which Wenli had written to the Liang, adding, "It was Wenli who disavowed me. The troops cannot be stopped!"

Chuzhi had fathered a son with a concubine, *Wang Yu*, who in the wake of [cousin] Wang Gao's flight to Jin sought sanctuary there as well. The Prince of Jin had given his own daughter to Yu in marriage, providing office as defense commissioner for Xinzhou. The realization that Zhuangzong was certain to attack Wenli left Chuzhi feeling vulnerable, so he secretly contacted Yu with the intent of inviting the Khitan to the north to cross the border as a check on Jin armies. He also promised to announce Yu's selection as heir, an offer that displeased his adopted son, Du. The military at Dingzhou uniformly opposed Khitan involvement for fear of wreaking future calamity, but Chuzhi ignored them. Moreover, Yu relished in the opportunity to exploit the conflict to possibly replace Chuzhi, whom Yu believed never forgave him for fleeing to the Jin. He thus provided hefty bribes as an inducement to Khitan ruler Abaoji. With Abaoji mobilizing his country for an invasion even as Dingzhou warriors all opposed Khitan intervention, a minor aide named He Zhaoxun urged Du to intervene. Du subsequently seized Chuzhi, imprisoning him at a west-side residence to assume the post of interim regent personally. He also systematically massacred all sons and grandsons of the Wang family, even the commanders and lieutenants of Chuzhi. Du visited Chuzhi at the west-side residence on New Year's Day of the next year. In fury, Chuzhi arose and struck Du's chest as he shouted, "You treacherous renegade! How have I wronged you?" With no weapons at hand, Chuzhi wanted to bite his nose, but Du shook his sleeve free of the man to depart, then murdered Chuzhi.

A yellow snake was once sighted under a shelter for commemorative steles, and Wang Chuzhi, believing it a dragon, gathered it up to offer sacrifices. There were also several hundred wild magpies nesting in a wheat field, which Chuzhi considered a sign of his personal virtue. The people of Dingzhou nonetheless appraised them as inauspicious, saying, "The snake that inhabits mountains and marshes now dwells in a house for humans, while the magpie that nests among birds now descends to inhabit fields. When things above abandon their proper habitat, they symbolize the presumptions of a petty man to high position." And indeed purge and murder was the ultimate fate of Chuzhi.

Zhuangzong had already defeated the Khitan at Shahe when he passed through Dingzhou while pursuing them. There he found Wang Du extremely amiable and arranged for the marriage of his own son, Jiji, to the daughter of Du, elevating Du to governor of the Yiwu command. In the second year of Tongguang [C.E. 924], as Zhuangzong sojourned at the Ye capital, Du came for an audience and received countless tens of thousands in cash gifts. In consideration of son Jiji, Zhuangzong treated Du with extreme generosity, denying nothing requested by him. Mingzong later assumed power and found him reprehensible in character, as An Chonghui came to insist on imposing the law to harness him. Du thus began to develop a duplicitous heart.

At the time, Tang armies engaging the Khitan repeatedly passed through Dingzhou, but the supplies provided by Wang Du often proved deficient, giving Du more reason to be uneasy. Thinking of his interests, the aide He Zhaoxun said, "With the Son of Heaven newly enthroned and men across the four corners not yet deferring to him, his standing could easily deteriorate. The time to consider your own welfare is at hand!" Zhu Shouyin subsequently rebelled at Bianzhou and Du rebelled as well, sending messengers with wax-seal letters to the governors of the five commands at Qing†, Xu¶, Qi‡, Lu, and Zi‡, seeking a pledge to raise arms collectively. None of the five opted to join him. Mingzong now deployed Wang Yanqiu for the suppression against him. Du again joined Yu in soliciting intervention from the Khitan, who committed ten thousand cavalry to Du's relief, led by Tunei. Du arranged for two thousand men to greet the Khitan, led by military director Zheng Jilin and the commander of Longquan Garrison, Du Hongshou. Yanqiu defeated and apprehended Jilin and Hongshou, saying to them reprovingly, "Through a messenger, I once implored you to submit. What kept you from surrendering?" "Through two generations, we enjoyed the beneficence of the Zhongshan commander," Hongshou responded. "We dared not entertain duplicity." Both were slain at once, the demeanor of Hongshou retaining its natural calm even as execution began. With troops garrisoned at Wangdu, Yanqiu engaged Du and his Khitan confederates in battle, routing them at Quyang. Du and Tunei managed to abscond with a handful of cavalry, hereafter sealing up the city and refusing to leave again.

Previously, the army of Zhuangzong contained an abandoned boy whom he looked after. He came to love the youth and had him assume the surname Li and personal name Jitao, raising him in the palace as son. Once Mingzong came to power, An Chonghui purged him from the palace, asking Duan Hui to assume care, but Hui also despised the youth and expelled him. Wang Du now sent someone to find and retrieve Jitao, then deceived his rank and file:

"Here we have the heir-apparent to Zhuangzong!" Du placed the Son of Heaven's costumes upon Jitao, parading him atop the city wall to show Yanqiu's men. Someone among the troops recognized him and yelled out, "It is only Jitao!" as they all jeered at him.

The forces of Wang Du within the city were few and city defenses rested solely on two thousand Khitan soldiers, so Du acknowledged Tunei as "Prince of Nei," humbling himself in service to him. As for commanders wishing to surrender, Du conducted intensive spying, not a day passing without murder or massacre. In this way, a rigorous defense lasted a full year. The city finally succumbed in the fourth year of Tiancheng [C.E. 929], the second month, Du and his family dependents dying by setting themselves afire, as the Wang clan vanished from Zhongshan.

Wang Chucun had a son, Ye, whose son *Wang Tingyin* [d. C.E. 944] shared marriage bonds with Zhuangzong's maternal family. He was a man of valor and daring who insisted on sharing the hardship of his soldiers upon becoming lieutenant. In the reign of Mingzong, he served as prefect at Bei, Xin‡, Mi, Chan, and Xi. After the mutiny of Fan Yanguang at Yezhou, Emperor Gaozu of Jin named Tingyin commander of center armies at large, under Yang Guangyuan's direction. His merit in the victory over Yanguang led to assignment as Zhangde governor.

Before this, the incarceration of Wang Chuzhi by Wang Du forced youngest son *Wang Wei* to abscond for Khitan territories to the north. The Khitan ruler now proposed to Emperor Gaozu of Jin, "I wish to employ Wei in a raid on the lands formerly bestowed upon his ancestors. What are your sentiments?" "By the rules of the Middle Kingdom," Gaozu responded, "a person is promoted from lieutenant commander to prefect, then from military training commissioner or military defense commissioner to governor. Please return Wei to the Middle Kingdom for a gradual advancement." The indignant Khitan countered, "You personally rose from feudal lord to Son of Heaven. What's gradual about that?" The comments forced Gaozu to reassign Tingyin to the Yiwu command at once, saying, "He is descended of the Wang clan, after all." Later reassigned to the Zhenhai [Henghai] command, Tingyin died there.

Liu Shouguang

Liu Shouguang [d. C.E. 914] was native to Leshou, Shenzhou. His father, *Liu Rengong* [d. C.E. 914] once served under Li Keju of Youzhou. Rengong had a facility for digging tunnels through earth to attack city walls, his army dubbing him "Liu, the Champion Excavator." Eventual rise to lieutenant occasioned such merit. A man of daring, Rengong was fond of grandiose talk as well. Following the death of Keju, his son Li Kuangwei detested such a person and no longer cared to have him on staff, so he banished Rengong to magistrate for Jingcheng County, Yingzhou¶. The military at Yingzhou¶ subsequently murdered their prefect in a mutiny. Rengong responded by recruiting a thousand volunteers from Jingcheng County to suppress and eventually pacify the mutineers. A delighted Kuangwei now restored him as commander for the border garrison of Weizhou¶. The tenure for his garrison troops had expired and no replacements arrived, so subordinates wishing to return home began openly to express umbrage. Word of the purge of Kuangwei by younger brother Kuangchou incited Rengong to command border troops in a raid on Youzhou. He had reached Juyong Pass upon suffering defeat, then defected to Jin to become commander of Shouyang Garrison.

Liu Rengong, a man of considerable guile, evinced a capacity for manipulating others. He proved especially deferential in serving the Prince of Jin's beloved commander, Ge Yu. During talks with Yu, Rengong sobbed in professing over and again, "I committed no crime at Yanzhou¤, my expulsion due to simple slander." He thus revealed the strategic strengths and weaknesses of Yan¤, providing possible strategies for conquest. The Prince of Jin increasingly trusted and prized him. In the inaugural year of Qianning [C.E. 894], Jin armies vanquished Kuangchou in a sortie, after which Rengong became interim regent for Youzhou, the Prince of Jin leaving behind more than ten men to supervise his armies, including his close confidante Yan Liude. He petitioned the Tang court for a post, Rengong becoming interim dignitary for public works and governor of the Lulong command.

The Jin later attacked Luo Hongxin and sought reinforcements from Liu Rengong, who declined. The Prince of Jin sent a letter of slight reprimand, causing an utterly livid Rengong to seize the Jin messenger and slay him along with Yan Liude, rebelling in the process. The suppression against Rengong was launched personally by the Prince of Jin, the Prince routed in battles at Ansai. In the inaugural year of Guanghua [C.E. 898], Rengong arranged for his son, Liu Shouwen, to storm Cangzhou and expel governor Lu Yanwei, seizing Cang, Jing, and De prefectures. Rengong requested formal appointment by the Tang court for his son. Its Emperor Zhaozong had dallied when Rengong indignantly told the Tang messenger, "Inform the Son of Heaven for me: I already have military banners and tallies of office, and need only a bit of acknowledgment from Changan. Why have repeated requests yielded no titles?" Zhaozong finally named Shouwen the Henghai governor.

Liu Rengong and his sons commanded armies that spanned two districts and included a hundred thousand men. They boasted a force of three hundred thousand in their sortie on Wei Prefecture, a massacre at nearby Beizhou ensuing. Luo Shaowei turned to the Liang for relief, and they dispatched Li Si'an to Wei, who routed Shouwen at Neihuang, where fifty thousand soldiers were decapitated. As Rengong fled, Liang armies harassed him in pursuit. From Weizhou to Changhe [Dezhou], a stretch of several hundred *li*, corpses were strewn everywhere. Liang armies hereafter attacked him every year, their conquest of Ying¶ and Mo‡ prefectures so terrifying Rengong that he aligned with the Jin once again.

The Liang raided Cangzhou in the third year of Tianyou [C.E. 906]. Rengong now inducted into military service all males in the district above fifteen and below seventy *sui*, tattooing their faces with the words, "Brigade of the Anointed Hegemon." He obtained two hundred thousand men in this way, forcing them to furnish their own rations and weapons; they were forted at Waqiao. Liang armies fortified Changlu, digging deep trenches and high ramparts, so that Rengong could not draw near. The siege of Cangzhou lasted more than a hundred days, the city depleting food supplies as its residents ate one another, hacking human limbs to cook, while others rolled balls of clay to eat. Six or seven out of ten perished. Rengong turned to the Jin for aid and the Prince of Jin acted to divert Liang armies with a raid on Luzhou. Jin warriors overran Luzhou as the Liang army dissolved its siege.

Liu Rengong lived at a time rife with incidents, enabling him to revel in wealth and stature. He built a palace at Da'an Mountain of exquisite sumptuousness, where the most beautiful women of Yanzhou¤ were selected to fill its precincts. Moreover, he and Daoist adepts produced cinnabar medicines with hopes of conquering death. He had the people of Yan¤ make money of clay, copper cash now collected for storage in a cave carved into a mountain. The artisans constructing the cave were later killed, forever sealing their mouths to preclude location of the site by posterity.

Liu Rengong had a beloved concubine, Miss Luo, with whom his son Shouguang once had incestuous relations. An infuriated Rengong flogged him with a light rod before expelling him from home. In the inaugural year of Kaiping [C.E. 907], the Liang launched an attack on Rengong led by Li Si'an. Rengong was at Da'an Mountain at the time, permitting son Shouguang to infiltrate Yan¤ with armed forces and overpower Si'an in a sortie. He now proclaimed himself the Lulong governor. Shouguang further arranged for a strike against the Da'an retreat by Li Xiaoxi and Yuan Xingqin, apprehending Rengong to place him under house arrest. When elder brother Liu Shouwen learned of the incarceration of their father, he led a punitive drive against Shouguang. Defeated at Lutai County, Shouwen advanced to Yutian for another battle, and another defeat, before begging the Khitan for reinforcements. He commanded a force of forty thousand a year later, containing Khitan as well as Tuhun warriors. Battling at Jisu, it was Shouguang who faced defeat, as Shouwen appeared on the battlefield and shouted out to his troops, "Do not kill Younger Brother"—insinuating that he could not countenance murdering a brother. The Shouguang commander, Yuan Xingqin, recognized Shouwen and leaped from his horse to apprehend him. He was locked in a separate room before being killed.

Assistant commanders under Liu Shouwen, chiefly Sun He and Lü Yan, installed his son, Liu Yanzuo, in opposition to Shouguang. A siege by Shouguang ensued, lasting a hundred days and depleting the city entirely of food supplies. A peck of rice could now sell for thirty thousand in cash strings, as people killed one another for food and others ate clay; horses even gnawed at the napes and tails of one another. Lü Yan and cohort had the city's starving people eat yeast plants before sending them to a so-called slaughterhouse, where they were killed on a daily basis to feed troops. Yanzuo's power was gradually sapped to the point of surrendering.

Liu Shouguang, always a mediocrity, now turned ever imperious. Iron cages and iron brushes were manufactured to punish people guilty of certain infractions: once placed in the cage, fire would be set all around; or in the case of iron brushes, the victim's skin would be pared away until rendering him dead. Subjects of Yan¤ often evaded such peril by fleeing to other districts. Once, wearing clothing of reddish yellow, Shouguang declared to military aides, "In wearing clothes of this color as I face south—I might well rule as emperor of the world!" Sun He stridently admonished against such pretense.

The Liang had begun an offensive against Zhao, whose prince, Wang Rong, turned to Shouguang for assistance. Commander Sun He now advised Shouguang, "Zhao has committed no offense to warrant today's action by the Liang. The local lord whose relief armies reach Zhao before the others will acquire hegemonic powers, and I fear that the Jin may well vanquish Liang armies before Yan¤ soldiers even depart. A moment so opportune cannot be missed." "The Prince of Zhao once entered an alliance only to disavow me," Shouguang countered. "He now wants to revert in simple desperation. When two tigers are sparring, it is best to wait things out. I will conduct myself like [the tiger hunter] Zhuangzi of Bian." He, therefore, did not issue troops. The Prince of Jin did assist Zhao, in the end: routing Liang armies at Baixiang, he advanced to pillage Xing and Ming prefectures and reached as far as Liyang. Once Shouguang learned that the Jin had virtually emptied its own lands to penetrate deep into Liang territory, he mobilized armies and declared a high alert. An emissary was also dispatched to incite authorities at Zhen and Ding prefectures, asking, "Three hundred thousand crack troops are available at Yan¤, representing two districts to join the Jin against the Liang. Who might best preside over such an alliance?" The Prince of Jin found the notion worrisome as he reasoned, "Long ago, Fu Chai insisted on a joint action at Huangchi, his domain at Wu ultimately occupied by Yue. Xiang Yu saw advantage in war against Qi, his Chu domain ultimately defeated by the Han. I have now traversed a thousand *li* in campaigns against others, yet the presence of a powerful Yan¤ to my rear threatens my very existence." He decided to withdraw his men.

Liu Shouguang, appraising the other governors as awestruck before his might, prodded them to recommend honors for him. In consequence, the Prince of Jin joined Song Yao of the Tiande command, Zhou Dewei of the Zhenwu command, Li Sizhao of Zhaoyi, Wang Chuzhi of Yiwu, and Wang Rong of Chengde, among others, in investing Shouguang, through special imperial rescript in black ink, as imperial secretary and Esteemed Father. At the same time, Shouguang informed the Liang by courier, requesting its appointment as chief of armed forces in Hebei in order to pacify Zhen, Ding, and Hedong prefectures. The Liang authorized its master of palace gates, Wang Tong, to confer on Shouguang powers as investigation commissioner for Hebei.

The relevant advisers informed Shouguang that his initiation as Esteemed Father would employ the same Tang-dynasty ceremonies for initiating grand marshals, causing him to inquire, "Why does performance of the ceremony not entail sacrifices to Heaven and a change of reign name?" "The latter attends rituals by the Son of Heaven," advisors reminded him. "Despite the honor of Esteemed Father, your ritual involves merely a subject." Shouguang then rebounded indignantly, "If I am Esteemed Father, who will be Emperor? Today, the world is split and partitioned, the mighty claiming the title of 'Emperor' and the humble claiming the title of 'Prince.' Why should my Yan¤, with an area of two thousand *li*, singularly go without an Emperor of its own?" Shouguang fettered the envoys of Liang and Jin for confinement in prison. Then, placing an executioner's hatchet in the courtyard, he pronounced, "Anyone daring to admonish me will die!" Sun He nonetheless stepped forward, declaring, "It was by virtue of the Prince's beneficence that Your Subject, after the defeat at Cangzhou, was spared death. Thus, I cannot but admonish against the matter at hand, today." In fury, Shouguang tossed him beneath the hatchet, ordering him sliced into bits and eaten alive by soldiers. "Within a hundred days, the enemy's formidable armies will surely arrive," Sun He blurted out. He was gagged and reduced to minced meat.

In the eighth month of the inaugural year of Qianhua [C.E. 911], by the Liang calendar, Shouguang proclaimed himself Emperor of the Great Yan, changing the reign name to Yingtian. He named Wang Tong and Qi She as ministers of the left and right. The Jin had commissioned the deputy prefect for Taiyuan, Li Chengxun, to congratulate him on investiture as Esteemed Father. By the time the envoy reached Yan¤, Shouguang had already assumed his bogus titles and his courtiers tried to compel Chengxun to employ the word "subject" in identifying himself. He refused such submission, only to appear for audience using the diplomatic protocol for peer kingdoms, incurring the wrath of Shouguang, who murdered him.

The next year [C.E. 912], the Prince of Jin directed Zhou Dewei, commanding a force of thirty thousand, to rendezvous with troops from Zhen and Ding prefectures in an offensive against Yan¤. They approached via Qigou Pass, as the prefectures of Chan, Zhuo, Wu, and Shun all received them in surrender. Under siege for a full year and often losing this long series of battles, Shouguang ultimately arranged for commander's attendant Wang Zunhua to deliver a letter to Dewei, begging, "I have committed crimes against Jin and failed to change my ways. As pertains to the current maelstrom, please convey some kind words on my behalf." Dewei responded to Zunhua with the comment, "The Emperor of Yan has yet to conduct sacrifices to Heaven! What causes such a turnaround? My orders are to suppress a usurper's turmoil. I know of nothing else."

Increasingly desperate, Shouguang offered up a thousand bolts of silk gauze, a thousand ounces of silver, and a hundred lengths of brocade. He even dispatched commander Zhou Zunye to tell Dewei, "My Prince has apprised you, Sir, of his circumstances. Wealth and station, success and failure, are normal for us humans, while accepting victory and forgiving transgressions are ideals for the hegemon. Last year, Shouguang illicitly assumed titles of honor and originally could not be subdued by Zhu Wen. Scarcely did he anticipate the consequent face-off with the formidable armies of Your great kingdom that lasted a full year. A modest indulgence would be appreciated." Dewei refused consent, so Shouguang personally climbed the wall, shouting out to him, "As the Worthy of Jin, you hardly need to insist on herding others to their peril!" He sent someone to exchange his horse for the horse of Dewei, then departed, saying, "I will wait for the Prince of Jin's arrival before surrendering." The Prince subsequently appeared in person, Shouguang now climbing the city wall for a face-to-face meeting. The Prince asked about the future, and Shouguang asserted, "I am now like meat on a chopping board, the Prince using me as he wishes." Shouguang had a favorite, Li Xiaoxi, who counseled him against surrender. He requested a delay, but Xiaoxi had defected to Jin armies that very night. By the next morning, those armies overran the city and apprehended Rengong, along with three hundred members of his clan.

Liu Shouguang fled south to Cangzhou in the company of his wives, née Li and Zhu, and sons Jixun, Jifang, and Jizuo. Yet they lost their way and reached the outskirts of Yanle County, having passed several days without eating. Lady Zhu was sent to beg for food at a family farm. The family thought circumstances strange and pressed for further information, whereupon the Lady Zhu divulged her true story. They were seized and sent to Youzhou, where the Prince of Jin was feasting his armies. A commander's attendant fetched Shouguang, the Prince poking fun upon meeting him, saying, "How can a host shun such an unexpected guest?" Shouguang kowtowed as he pleaded to die, but the Prince had him and father Rengong fettered and brought along in the army's convoy. As the army passed through Zhao, Wang Rong, the Prince of Zhao, banqueted the Prince of Jin. Once intoxicated, he intimated a desire to meet Rengong and his son. The Prince of Jin had the fetters broken for them to emerge and assume seats below theirs, the Liu men nonchalantly eating and drinking with no sense of shame.

When the Prince of Jin reached Taiyuan, Rengong and son were dragged by rope for presentation before the Imperial Ancestors' Temple. Shouguang cried out in the face of imminent death, "Your Subject does not regret dying, but Li Xiaoxi had advised me against surrender. If the true culprit is not killed, I will have to seek retribution in the netherworld." The Prince summoned Xiaoxi, who fixed his eyes contemptuously on Shouguang, saying, "No doubt, Shouguang's incarceration of his own father, assassination of his elder brother, and incest with his own flesh-and-blood kin all occurred at my prompting as well?" The Prince, now fuming, ordered the initial beheading of Xiaoxi. Seeing his own fate before him, Shouguang blurted out, "The Prince will soon restore the Tang house and complete his mission as hegemon. Why not pardon Your Subject to assist you?" His two wives now approached from his side to declare reprovingly, "With matters so dire and survival hopeless, we prefer to die first!" The women perished together. The Prince instructed Li Cunba to carry Rengong to Yanmen, where, at the grave of the Former Prince, he was stabbed in the heart, his blood rendered as sacrifice to the ancestor before beheading.

CHAPTERS 40–41

MISCELLANEOUS BIOGRAPHIES

Li Maozhen

Native to Boye, Shenzhou, Li Maozhen [C.E. 856–924] had the original surname Song and personal name Wentong. He began as a foot soldier in the Boye army stationed at Fengxiang. The ravaging of the capital by Huang Chao caused Boye detachments to be deployed under Zheng Tian for a storm on the renegade. The merits of Maozhen led to promotion from company commander to lieutenant.

Zhu Mei rebelled in the inaugural year of Guangqi [C.E. 885], forcing Emperor Xizong to assume exile at Xingyuan. Zhu Mei arranged a raid on Dasan Pass by Wang Xingyu, but Xingyu met defeat at Datang Peak at the hands of Maozhen and Li Shan, the area commander of royal security forces. Mei died in battle a year later, but an accomplished Maozhen rose from area commander of the imperial escort to governor of Wuding. A new surname and personal name were conferred by the court. The imperial escort was returning eastward when a conflict over roadway access erupted at Fengxiang between governor Li Changfu and Yang Shouli, the area commander of Celestially Awesome forces. In the ensuing row between their men, governor Changfu lost to the escort and absconded for Longzhou. Emperor Xizong directed Maozhen to storm Changfu in retribution, killing him. Maozhen was rewarded with appointments to the Longyou and Fengxiang governorships. Investiture as Prince of Longxi came in the inaugural year of Dashun [C.E. 890].

In the second year, commissioner of military affairs Yang Fugong committed some offense at court and fled for

Xingyuan, where he was received by Xingyuan governor Yang Shouliang, Fugong's adopted son. Li Maozhen thus petitioned the court, arguing that Fugong and son should pay for their crimes with death while seeking his own nomination as bandit-suppressing commissioner for Shannan circuit to exact punishment. Opposition from eunuchs made action by Zhaozong difficult, so no authorization occurred. An insubordinate Maozhen issued troops to raid Xingyuan all the same, overrunning the prefecture and murdering both Fugong and his son.

Li Maozhen now petitioned for provisional powers as prefect at Xingyuan Commandery for his son, Li Jimi. The Emperor instead reassigned Maozhen to governor for Shannan west circuit, assigning chief minister Xu Yanruo to the Fengxiang governorship. Maozhen refused to accept imperial orders and petitioned in his own defense, "My sole concern centered on sudden changes in military conditions that might make our military immune to political restraints and bring suffering to residents of the capital. I do not know, when Your Majesty takes flight again, where he will possibly go." The Emperor found Maozhen's petition insufferably irreverent in wording and spoke with chief minister Du Rangneng. "Maozhen's district is large and armies formidable, while the military might of Tang is inadequate for punitive action," Rangneng argued. "Fengxiang also enjoys proximity to the capital. Hazards may prove easier to risk today than contrition later on. In the future, I fear, we may want to appease feudal lords by executing the Chao Cuo of our times, yet lack capacity."[1] An angry Zhaozong responded, "I cannot sit in impotence and suffer the abuse of a bully." He then commissioned Rangneng to mobilize troops and named Li Sizhou, the Prince of Tan, bandit-suppressing commissioner for Jingxi circuit.

When mandates for the campaign came down, residents of the capital all deemed it unacceptable and gathered at the Chengtian gate to block the path of the chief minister, pleading not to raise armies. They also vied to throw stone tiles at the minister, forcing him to alight from his carriage and run, losing his seals of office. Trepidation in men's hearts was profound, just as Zhaozong's resolve intensified. The Prince of Tan, commanding fifty-four brigades from the imperial escort, battled at Zhouzhi only to witness his Tang armies vanquished. Li Maozhen proceeded to raid the capital, his troops garrisoned at Sanqiao. Emperor Zhaozong appeared at the Anfu gate, where he murdered the two commissioners of military affairs to appease Maozhen, thereby facilitating his withdrawal of troops. Maozhen had previously known differences with Rangneng and thus insisted, "It was not the two military commissioners who schemed to raise armies, but Rangneng himself." He instructed troops to assume formation at Lin'gao Post and called for the murder of Rangneng. At this point, Rangneng himself said, "Your Subject was first to address the matter. You need only kill me to dispel the menace to our country." As tears soaked Zhaozong's lapel, Rangneng was banished to fiscal adjutant for Leizhou, his suicide prescribed. Maozhen now withdrew his armies.

Hezhong governor Wang Chongying died in the next year [C.E. 892], causing a rivalry between his sons Ke and Gong over the succession. The Prince of Jin, Li Keyong, sought the installation of Wang Ke, but the succession of Wang Gong was endorsed by Maozhen, Han Jian, and Wang Xingyu. Emperor Zhaozong withheld approval of Maozhen's petition, causing Maozhen and his cohort to lead armies from their three districts to raid the capital, intending to purge Zhaozong and install Bao, the Prince of Ji. Before they could succeed, the Prince of Jin also mobilized armies, inciting a nervous Maozhen to assassinate chief ministers Wei Zhaodu and Li Qi. Upon departing, he left behind adopted son Li Jipeng with two thousand troops, now merged into the Imperial Guard. As Jin troops approached Hezhong Prefecture, Jipeng wrangled with Xingyu's younger brother, Xingshi, to abduct Zhaozong and reduce the capital to chaos. Zhaozong departed for sanctuary at Shimen as Maozhen directed armies to Hu County, decapitating son Jipeng as a gesture of atonement to the court.

Jin armies had already defeated Wang Xingyu and returned to barracks at Weibei when the Prince of Jin sought authorization to storm Li Maozhen. The Jin was remote and Maozhen nearby, Zhaozong reasoned, so he wanted to woo Maozhen to cultivate a sense of obligation and thereby avail of him in future emergencies. And with Maozhen having slain his own son as atonement, Zhaozong decided to direct Jin armies to withdraw. Li Keyong [Prince of Jin] now reacted with the lament: "Having refused to execute Maozhen, the menace to Tang is far from over."

After Zhaozong returned from Shimen, recruits for his Sage-Securing and Imperial-Sustaining guards were expanded by more than ten thousand men, their commands entrusted to the various imperial princes. Li Maozhen saw that the Tang was preparing a campaign against him, so he mobilized his own armies and requested an audience. Residents of the capital were utterly mortified and lost themselves in the surrounding mountains and ravines. Maozhen then invaded the capital, as Zhaozong charged the Prince of Tan with the resistance. The Prince's army was vanquished upon reaching Sanqiao and the Emperor forced to assume temporary residence at Huazhou‡. Chief minister Sun Wo was now under mandate to punish Maozhen, an effort abandoned after Han Jian intervened on Maozhen's behalf. Much later, Maozhen received court honors as imperial secretary, invested Prince of Qi.

The subsequent purge of Emperor Zhaozong, once reversed, left chief minister Cui Yin favoring the deployment of Liang armies to execute eunuchs, and he was in secret collusion with the future Taizu of Liang. Likewise, associate commandant Han Quanhui and other eunuchs depended on a powerful Li Maozhen to render assistance from the outside. Maozhen had even arranged for a son, Li Jiyun, to take several thousand troops to the capital for assimilation into the Imperial Guard. Relying on the might of Qi‡ armies, eunuchs grew ever imperious and unruly.

In the inaugural year of Tianfu [C.E. 901], Cui Yin summoned Taizu of Liang to the west. As his armies reached Tongzhou, fear gripped Han Quanhui and Li Jiyun, who abducted Zhaozong to Fengxiang. Liang armies besieged the prefecture for over a year, with Li Maozhen losing on short order each and every battle, ultimately sealing up the city and daring not leave. The city exhausted its supplies of food and firewood, as rain and snow continued without stop from winter through spring and thousands of people either froze or starved to death each day. With a peck of rice costing seven thousand in cash, human excrement came to be cooked and human corpses boiled for food. Fathers ate their own sons, and when others vied for some of the meat, they would insist, "This is my son. How dare you eat him!" Human flesh commanded a hundred cash per catty, dog meat commanded five hundred, as fathers found palatable their own sons and human flesh proved cheaper than dog meat. The Son of Heaven's palace had small cutting boards, and palace workers were directed to crush beans and wheat to feed him. From the inner palaces to the sixteen houses of royal princes, three or four persons succumbed each day to starvation or exposure.

City residents conducted searches for Li Maozhen, seeking some way to survive. As circumstances turned desperate for Maozhen, he schemed to deliver the Son of Heaven to the Liang to resolve the crisis. Zhaozong also pressured him, saying, "Occupants of the six palaces and myself have a single meal of congee on one day and *butuo* noodles on the other. Why refuse a truce with Liang?" Maozhen entered a pact with Liang in the inaugural month of the third year [C.E. 903]. He decapitated Han Quanhui and more than twenty others and delivered their heads to Liang barracks when the Liang lifted its siege. Although released, the Son of Heaven was abducted by the Liang for relocation eastward, the Tang dynasty now destroyed. Not only did Maozhen manage to ruin the Tang but alas, he also wrought hardship upon himself.

After Taizu acceded to the Liang throne, the strongest of the local overlords in succession declared themselves "Emperor." Li Maozhen alone refused, referring to himself simply as "King of Qi." He did establish an administration based on civil service, call his wife "Empress," and array feathered fans overhead during processions to and from audience much like the Son of Heaven, but nothing more. While presiding at Qizhou‡, Maozhen could be magnanimously benevolent and loving of others, the people finding comfort in his rule. The narrowness of his lands and the paucity of its tax revenues once caused him to impose a monopoly on oil [needed for lanterns] and proscribe the transport of pine timber into the city, for fear of people using the timber to make torches. An actor once ridiculed the proscription, saying, "Your Subject begs for a ban on moonlight as well!" Maozhen laughed without getting angry.

Before this, when Li Maozhen vanquished Yang Shouliang to claim Xingyuan, a total of twenty prefectures belonged to his domain, including Bing, Ning, Fu‡, and Fang. After coming under the Liang siege, Xingyuan became Shu territory. And after the Kaiping reign, the Liang assumed control over Bin, Ning, Fu‡, and Fang; the Shu kingdom took over Liang, Qin, Feng‡, Jie, and Cheng. Only seven prefectures remained with him in the Liang dynasty's last years.[i]

Zhuangzong of Tang had already overturned the Liang when Li Maozhen assumed the title King of Qi, Maozhen referring to himself as "uncle" in correspondence to him. Once Zhuangzong occupied Luoyang, Maozhen petitioned for recognition as vassal, while sending to court his son, Li Congyan. Zhuangzong regarded him as senior statesman and extended utmost courtesy and deference. Maozhen's investiture was changed to King of Qin and edicts written to him refrained from using his personal name in deference. He died of illness in the second year of Tongguang [C.E. 924], at sixty-nine *sui*, the posthumous title of "Loyal and Revered" conferred.

Li Congyan, a man soft in character, had a talent for calligraphy and painting. Maozhen won court authorization for his appointment as governor of the Zhangyi command. Assignment as Fengxiang governor occasioned Maozhen's death.

During campaigns against Shu by Jiji, the Prince of Wei, Li Congyan served him as commissioner of transportation of military supplies. In the wake of the Shu pacification, Jiji directed divisions under Congyan to escort [deposed potentate] Wang Yan; they had reached Fengxiang when military overseer Chai Chonghou refused them entry. Congyan subsequently went eastward as far as Huazhou‡ upon learning about Zhuangzong's recent setbacks and decided to return to the west. After his accession, Mingzong was informed of Chonghou's earlier defiance to Congyan and sent someone to execute him. Congyan wrote the court seeking a pardon for Chonghou, noting that under his tenure, Fengxiang's soldiers and residents had been free of abuse. The Emperor rejected the pardon, but Congyan nonetheless won

....

i. The twenty prefectures were Qi‡, Long, Xing¶, Yuan, Wei†, Wu, Qin, Cheng, Jie, Feng‡, Bin, Ning, Qing, Yan¶, Fu‡, Fang, Dan, Yan‡, Liang, and Yang‡.

praise from local leaders, later serving as governor of the Xuanwu and Tianping commands.

At Fengxiang, Li Congyan owned lands covering an area of a thousand *qing* as well as bamboo gardens covering a thousand *mou*. Out of concern for undermining the profits of the people, he never inquired about the lands and the people of Fengxiang loved him for this. Emperor Fei rose against the court at Fengxiang and, as he departed, authorities there whipped their horses in begging for Congyan to replace him. Congyan became governor for Fengxiang upon Emperor Fei's accession, dying at forty-nine *sui*.

Yang Chongben

Yang Chongben [d. C.E. 914] served Li Maozhen during his youth. Adopted by Maozhen as son, he assumed the surname Li and personal name Jihui. Chongben became governor of the Jingnan command as a consequence of Maozhen's petition to the court. Taizu of Liang, unable to prevail in his offensive against Qizhou‡, redeployed his men in an offensive against Binzhou, where Chongben greeted him in surrender. Taizu authorized the restoration of his original surname and conferred the personal name Chongben while relocating Chongben's family to Hezhong as bonded hostages.

Chongben's wife was of substantial beauty. On trips back and forth through Hezhong during campaigns, Taizu once had relations with her. Chongben's wife, rather ashamed by this, had someone ridicule him, saying, "You, Honored Gentleman, proved unable to protect his spouse such that I am now the woman of Mr. Zhu [Taizu]. I have no face to see you, only a knife and cord [to kill myself]." Chongben wept in indignation. Once Liang armies dissolved their siege of Qizhou‡, Chongben's wife managed to return, and he repudiated the Liang once again, reverting to Maozhen.

Li Maozhen once allied with Shu troops to the west in a joint offensive against Yong and Hua‡ prefectures, unleashing shock waves throughout the Western passes. Taizu had commanded armies westward as far as Hezhong when he dispatched Youyu, the Prince of Chen, to storm Qizhou‡. Youyu died, however, after reaching Yongshou County [Binzhou], forcing Liang armies to return. Yang Chongben had military farm colonies at Meiyuan [eastern Jingzhao], so Taizu orchestrated another raid by Liu Zhijun and Kang Huaiying. They routed Chongben, who never again allowed his ambitions to lead him eastward.

In the fourth year of Qianhua [C.E. 914], Chongben was assassinated by his own son, Yang Yanlu. An adopted son, Li Baoheng, then murdered Yanlu to surrender to the Liang.

Zhao Kuangning

With courtesy name of Guangyi, Zhao Kuangning hailed from Caizhou. His father, *Zhao Deyin*, served under Qin Zongquan as prefect of Shenzhou‡. Zongquan later rebelled, and Deyin attacked and felled Xiangyang on his behalf. Zongquan met successive defeats during Taizu of Liang's offensive against Caizhou, causing Deyin to surrender to him seven prefectures in Shannan east circuit. Earlier in his tenure as governor of the Xuanwu command, Taizu had been beleaguered by Zongquan, so he greatly savored news of Deyin's surrender, petitioning the court to name him deputy chief commander of mobile brigades and military adjutant of the three commands of Heyang, Baoyi, and Yichang. Their two armies once rendezvoused in a raid on Caizhou, whose fall involved the considerable merit of Deyin. His son Kuangning was installed upon Deyin's death.

Cheng Rui had died at the time, and Lei Yangong now rushed to seize Jingnan. Zhao Kuangning then dispatched his younger brother Kuangming to expel Yangong. Taizu thereby petitioned the court to post Kuangning as Jingxiang governor and Kuangming as interim regent of Jingnan. With the Tang despoiled and its governors no longer serving the court, Kuangning and his brother proved exceptions in submitting taxes without stop. Kuangning could be extremely imposing in temperament and bearing, his character forthright and stern. He enjoyed designing his own apparel and possessed a curiosity for learning: his book collection contained several thousand volumes. In administering government, he proved formidable yet charitable.

When Taizu attacked Yanzhou, Zhu Jin requested assistance from the Prince of Jin, who commissioned Shi Yan to command the relief effort with a few thousand troops. Zhu Jin was vanquished and fled to Huainan, accompanied by Shi Yan and cohort. The Prince of Jin, Li Keyong, now dispatched a messenger to Zhao Kuangning bearing documents and gifts, while seeking passage through his lands for emissaries to Yang Xingmi [of Huainan]. He also requested the return of Shi Yan and the others. The Jin messenger was apprehended by the Liang, leaving Taizu livid. At the time, the Liang had already overrun Yan and Yun prefectures, so it unleashed Shi Shucong and Kang Huaiying for a raid on Kuangning. Shucong seized Bi and Sui prefectures, with Huaiying seizing Deng. A nervous Kuangning hence sued for an alliance, ending the hostilities.

Once Taizu committed regicide against Zhaozong and schemed to supplant the Tang dynasty, he feared that Zhao Kuangning and his brother might not acquiesce and informed them by envoy. Kuangning tearfully responded, "We have enjoyed the profound beneficence of the Tang dynasty and dare not recklessly entertain seditious agendas." Taizu dispatched Yang

Shihou to raid them, as he personally directed a rear action from north of the Han River. Defeated in battle, Kuangning used a light boat to flee to Yang Xingmi. With Shihou now advancing against the Jingnan region, Kuangming absconded for Shu.

Zhao Kuangning conferred with Yang Xingmi once at Guangling, where Xingmi remarked in jest, "As regional governor, you shipped tax payments to the Liang every year, sometimes by swift carriage and sometimes by stout horse. Only now, in defeat, do you try to revert to me!" Kuangning responded, "For generations we were subjects of the Tang dynasty, our tribute never intended for a renegade. Now, it is because I refuse to follow a renegade that I submit heart and soul to you, Sir, living or dying for you alone!" Xingmi hence treated him with exceptional munificence. After Xingmi died, successor Yang Wo proved rather discourteous. At a banquet, [the twenty year-old] Wo was eating a green plum when Kuangning looked at him and blurted out, "Try not to eat too much—you may catch baby's fever." The various commanders considered him insulting, so Wo relocated Kuangning to Hailing, where he was later killed by Xu Wen. Kuangming died in Shu.

CHAPTERS 42–43

MISCELLANEOUS BIOGRAPHIES

Zhu Xuan and Zhu Jin

Zhu Xuan [d. C.E. 897] was native to Xiayi, Songzhou. In youth, he and his father traded illegally in salt, his father dying as stipulated by the law. Xuan then left to serve as lieutenant under Wang Jingwu, the Qingzhou† governor, and was subordinate to commander Cao Quancheng. In the second year of Zhonghe [C.E. 882], Jingwu ordered Quancheng to penetrate the Guanzhong Pass and help suppress the rebel Huang Chao. He passed through Yunzhou on the return trip, where governor Xue Chong had recently died and commander Cui Junyu had proclaimed himself interim regent. Quancheng attacked and murdered Junyu, occupying Yunzhou. Zhu Xuan's merits in battle led to appointment as chief commander of infantry and cavalry. Occasioning the death of Quancheng, the military elevated Xuan to interim regent, the Tang court under Xizong confirming him as governor of the Tianping command.

The governor of Xuanwu [Bianzhou] and future Taizu of Liang treated Zhu Xuan as elder brother. He had only recently reached the command, and his military might was still modest. In the face of sustained pressures from Qin Zongquan, Taizu requested reinforcements from Xuan. Troops from Yan and Yun prefectures were deployed by Xuan and his "brother" Jin in the Bianzhou relief, routing armies from Caizhou and running off Zongquan. By now, Taizu had already claimed Huazhou in a sortie and increasingly wanted to devour the various governors. Xuan and Jin were already returning when Taizu rushed a declaration of war to Yan and Yun prefectures, alleging that Xuan and Jin had tricked many Xuanwu warriors into fleeing to the east—his own deployment of armies designed to retrieve those men at large. His attack thus made them belligerent neighbors destined to fight bitter battles in and around Cao and Pu prefectures. The Liang simultaneously conducted raids against Xuzhou¶ to its east, confronted renegades at Caizhou to its west, and challenged a powerful Jin to its north even as the brothers Xun and Jin stood in succession at its head and tail—ultimately vanquishing them all. Amid defeat in the fourth year of Qianning [C.E. 897], Zhu Xuan absconded for Zhongdu, where Ge Congzhou apprehended him. Beheading occurred at Bian Bridge.[i]

Zhu Jin [C.E. 867–918], son of Xuan's paternal uncle, resided with Xuan at Yunzhou, eventually becoming his lieutenant. He proved a vivacious man with grand ambitions. The Yanzhou governor Qi Kerang had a special affinity for him and gave his daughter to Jin in marriage. During the ceremony to receive his bride, Jin selected numerous hardy men as porters, having them conceal weapons in a carriage for military supplies. The carriage had reached Yanzhou by nighttime, the troops then rallying to imprison Kerang, as Jin assumed the title of interim regent. Emperor Xizong subsequently confirmed him as governor of the Taining command.

Zhu Jin and Zhu Xuan, having vanquished Qin Zongquan at Bianzhou, came under Taizu's censure for inducing his soldiers there to return with them. Sent to attack Zhu Jin was Zhu Zhen, who claimed Caozhou before proceeding with an assault on Puzhou, as Taizu personally approached from Yunzhou. For more than ten years, Jin and his brother went back and forth to assist one another, fighting several dozen battles against Taizu, great and small, and winning as much as losing.

Taizu later acquired Xuan commanders He Gui and He Huaibao, along with the elder brother of Jin, Zhu Qiong. Preparing to have Qiong and the others appear at the base of the Yan city wall, Taizu told Jin, "Your elder brother now vanquished and Qiong in surrender, you would do better to revert sooner than later." Jin ingenuously gave his consent, then sent military attaché Hu Gui to make a formal request for surrender at Taizu's barracks, bearing the appropriate documents and gifts. An immensely pleased Taizu went to the Yanshou gate to converse with Jin, who said, "I prefer to have Qiong deliver to you the tallies and seals of office." Taizu found him credible and sent commander's attendant Liu Han to escort Qiong to the city. Beneath a bridge, Jin had hidden in ambush his strongest men as he individually went to greet Qiong by horse, informing Han with the wave of a hand that "Qiong must

....

i. Today it is widely held that Xuan, elder brother of Jin, should have the radical *wang* [king] in his personal name; this is incorrect [as they are actually cousins].

come alone." As Qiong stepped forward, the warriors seized him and shut the gates. Jin reprimanded him for an early surrender, then decapitated Qiong and tossed his head outside the city wall. Taizu now reasoned that the city would not succumb, so troops stayed behind to continue the siege as he departed.

Zhu Jin personally secured the city for defense while engaging Ge Congzhou's armies at the city wall. He met with successive defeats, much like Xuan at Yunzhou, so he joined Xuan in soliciting the Prince of Jin for relief. Five thousand cavalry, led by Li Chengsi and Shi Yan, were deployed by the Prince as assistance. Taizu of Liang had already vanquished Zhu Xuan by now and scurried for Yanzhou. The city's food supplies depleted, Zhu Jin and Chengsi had to forage for food in the vicinity of Feng and Pei counties. Liang troops then arrived triumphantly at Yan, the city surrendered by Kang Huaiying, a commander under Zhu Jin.

Troops remaining under Zhu Jin's control now sought sanctuary at Yizhou†, only to be rejected by local prefect Yin Chubin. They subsequently fled for Haizhou, but the intense pursuit of Liang armies forced them to turn to Huainan for sanctuary. Yang Xingmi reveled in news of their arrival, removing his own jade sash as a present for Zhu Jin. He further petitioned the court to name him concurrent governor of Wuning, while personally employing Jin as deputy commander of armed forces. When the Liang later unleashed Pang Shigu and Ge Congzhou for its Huainan invasion, Yang Xingmi turned to Zhu Jin, who handily vanquished interventionist armies at Qingkou, decapitating Shigu. Successive petitions from Xingmi caused Jin's rise to deputy chief commander of at-large armies in the southeast and concurrent Pinglu governor with ministerial standing.

Yang Wo and Yang Longyan succeeded Xingmi upon death, each man so young in years that Xu Wen and son Xu Zhixun could monopolize affairs. Both feared Zhu Jin and wanted to eliminate him, while Jin conspired to assassinate Zhixun. On the first day of the new month, Jin sent a beloved concubine to the home of Zhixun to offer the usual holiday greetings, and Zhixun forced himself upon her. The concubine revealed the incident on returning home, leaving Jin ever restless. He repeatedly prodded Longyan to execute the Xu family to eliminate a peril to the kingdom, but Longyan lacked the capacity to act. Upon establishing Sizhou as a separate Jinghuai command, Xu Zhixun arranged for Zhu Jin's departure to serve as its governor and summoned him for drinks on the night before departure. He visited Jin's residence on the next day to say farewell when Jin delayed him in the guest hall and called out his wife, Lady Tao. Just as Zhixun bowed to her, Jin used his own official staff to knock Zhixun flat on the floor, as troops concealed in the house suddenly surfaced to slay him.

Heretofore, Zhu Jin kept in his courtyard two untamed horses in restraints. They had been unleashed after Xu Zhixun entered, their kicking and screeching preventing outsiders from hearing the mutiny underway inside. Jin now grabbed Zhixun's head to show Longyan, saying, "Today, I have eradicated this peril to our Wu domain." "I dare not be informed of such matters," Longyan responded, rising swiftly to go inside. Livid, Jin hit the head against a post as he drew his sword to leave. With the palace gate already secured, he leaped over a wall and broke his feet. He now deduced that no alternatives remained and yelled aloud, "To eradicate a blight on tens of thousands, I lay down this one life of mine." He then slit his own throat.

After learning of the mutiny, Xu Zhigao at Runzhou led troops in a rush on Guangling, liquidating the entire family of Zhu Jin. His wife, née Tao, sobbed when the moment of execution arrived, as a concubine reminded her, "Why should you sob? Today, in passing on, you will meet Gentleman Zhu." Lady Tao now forced back the tears and went calmly to her death—her story causing listeners to despair for her.

Widely known in the Huai and Yangzi region, Zhu Jin's name instilled fear in the people. His corpse had been abandoned at the northern gate of Guangling upon death and passersby voluntarily buried him. Numerous contagious diseases were rampant at the time, but people who gathered some earth from atop the grave and swallowed it with water were immediately healed, or so rumor has it. A tall tumulus eventually emerged in the process of adding new earth to the grave. Xu Wen and cohort resented the attention and exhumed his body, tossing it into the Leigong pond. Xu Wen later took ill and dreamed that Jin was stretching a bow to shoot him. In fright, he had the bones collected by net and properly buried beside the pond, a ritual altar placed on top. Zhu Jin had once acquired an ulcerous growth as ailment, the very sight of which caused the doctor examining him to change facial color. "I only want you to tend to the wound, for my death will not come from illness," Jin declared, and indeed, this proved true. He died at fifty-two *sui*.

Wang Ke

Wang Ke was native to Hezhong and paternal nephew of Wang Chongrong. Chongrong had deployed Hezhong armies to rout the rebel Huang Chao, and in reward for his merit, rose in Tang times to Hezhong governor. He had no sons and adopted Ke, the son of an older brother Chongjian, as heir. Occasioning the death of Chongrong, younger brother Chongying was installed as governor, and after Chongying's death, the military installed Chongrong's son, Ke.

Contesting the succession of Wang Ke were the sons of Chongying: Wang Gong, the governor of Shanzhou, and Wang Yao, the prefect of Jiangzhou. The brothers Gong and Yao, in letters to Taizu of Liang, noted that Ke was merely an underling in the Wang house, nicknamed "Loyal Youth," who did not deserve to be installed. Meanwhile, Ke asked for intervention from the Prince of Jin, who in turn spoke to the court. Emperor Zhaozong consented because of that intervention. Gong and Yao buttressed themselves by allying to their west with Wang Xingyu, Han Jian, and Li Maozhen, men who expressed their views in successive writings to the court. Zhaozong refused to alter his decision, however, because Chongrong and the Prince of Jin had both contributed prominently to the Tang cause and the succession was already accepted. The decision infuriated Xingyu and cohort, who raided the capital with their armies and assassinated chief minister Li Qi before leaving. Gong and Yao now joined forces in attacking Ke at Hezhong, compelling Ke to beg the Prince of Jin for relief. The Jin, in launching a punitive drive westward against the three commanders, descended upon Jiangzhou and decapitated Yao before moving on. Approaching north of the Wei River, it stormed and defeated Xingyu. Emperor Zhaozong could finally appoint Ke as governor of Hezhong, the Prince of Jin giving his daughter in marriage. The Prince also had Li Sizhao assist Ke by directing an offensive against Gong at Shanzhou. Gong was a sadistic man: he once executed someone and continued to laugh and talk even as the head was tossed before him. His subordinates suffered under him. After Gong had lost in battle, his attending commander, Li Fan, murdered him to install himself as interim regent.

At the time, the Liang had felled Zhen and Ding prefectures and prepared to move troops westward, while Liu Jishu's purge of Emperor Zhaozong and the tumult created in the capital were pervasive. Cui Yin had secretly summoned Liang troops westward, but Taizu of Liang saw potential danger in Wang Ke's presence east at Hezhong. Giving a large rope to Zhang Cunjing and Hou Yan as he glanced their way, Taizu exclaimed, "Go and fetch for me a tethered Wang Ke." Cunjing and the others departed from Hanshan to overrun the prefectures of Jin and Jiang; they also had He Yin secure the two cities to sever Jin relief lines. Wang Ke alerted the Jin to the emergency as Cunjing besieged Hezhong, but the presence of Yin prevented its armies from advancing. He even had his wife write a letter to the Prince of Jin, insisting, "The renegades enjoy such power that, day and night, we desperately consider capitulation. My father, how can you bear to withhold relief?" "Blocked by Liang armies, our ranks do not rival theirs and a rescue effort is to our own detriment," the Prince of Jin reported back. "You and Gentleman Wang would better revert to the Tang dynasty." Ke then sent a letter to Li Maozhen, warning, "When the Son of Heaven was initially restored to his rightful position, he stipulated that regional governors should stabilize the royal house by refraining from invading one another. Mr. Zhu's repudiation of that promise has brought the current action against me. And surely, his ambitions will not stop at my own humble district. If my humble district faces obliteration, then no command in the northwest will be safe for you. I am willing to join Huazhou‡ forces in an action emanating from Tongguan." Maozhen did not respond. His schemes exhausted, Ke arranged boats on the Yellow River with plans to convert to the capital.

Climbing the city wall at night, Wang Ke issued commands to guards manning embrasures atop the wall, the guards uniformly ignoring them. Military attaché Liu Xun visited his bedroom that night to apprise Ke of matters, but he rebuked Xun: "Does the military wish to mutiny?" Loosening his shirt as he approached, Xun tied himself with rope as he insisted, "If you, Sir, harbor doubts, I beg you to break my arms immediately!" "Affairs are pressing," Ke responded. "What might I pursue as sound strategy?" Xun continued, "If tonight you try to cross the river along with your family, people will certainly fight you over the boats: you need only one man to stir trouble and your efforts will be for naught. I prefer waiting until daybreak to assess your armies, roughly half of which might still follow you. Otherwise, you can write a cordial letter to delay Liang armies while methodically planning to repudiate its rule." Ke concurred.

Taizu of Liang, ever since the surrender of Tongzhou to the Tang dynasty, had relied on Wang Chongrong, treating him as maternal uncle because of a common surname with his own mother. Climbing the wall to shout out to Cunjing, Wang Ke thus insisted, "Owing to my close family ties over generations to the Prince of Liang, your armies should pull up their stakes and await the Prince's arrival. I intend to respect his command." Cunjing pulled up stakes and dispatched a courier to Taizu at Luoyang. Taizu arrived at Hezhong and proceeded first to the eastern wall, where he wept at Chongrong's grave before entering the city. Ke had intended to meet Taizu face to face, his hands bound with a lamb on a leash before him. However, Taizu insisted, "How can I ever forget the charity of the grand preceptor, my dear uncle? If the Gentleman is reduced to the protocol for the vanquished in meeting me, what would the grand preceptor say?" Meeting Taizu on the road, instead, Ke grabbed his hand to heave a mournful sigh before being exiled to Bianzhou. Taizu nonetheless suspected Ke of a duplicitous heart, due to relations with the Prince of Jin as son-in-law. He thus arranged for someone to slay Ke at a hostel as his entourage approached the capital from the west, reaching only Huazhou‡.

Wang Zan was a son of Chongying. Taizu of Liang had won concurrent powers as Hezhong governor upon apprehending Wang Ke, Zan recruited as administrative aide to him. Zan served the Liang as commandant of the Imperial Guard and governor of the Taining and Zhenguo commands. Service as metropolitan prefect of Kaifeng coincided with Emperor Mo's reign. In the fifth year of Zhenming [C.E. 919], he replaced He Gui as commissioner of bandit suppression for at-large forces on the northern front. Jin armies had erected ramparts around Desheng Commandery by then, so Zan crossed the Yellow River from Liyang to raid Chanzhou, only to fail to take the city. He retreated to camps at Yangcun. Controlling the upper current of the Yellow River, he had standoffs with Jin armies for much of a year, his men engaging in more than a hundred battles, great and small, without success. Emperor Mo thus replaced him with Dai Siyuan, restoring Zan as metropolitan prefect of Kaifeng.

With Zhuangzong approaching the capital from Yunzhou, word of his army's imminent arrival had reduced Emperor Mo to tears, from day to night, for lack of recourse. He personally held the imperial seals in hand and pointed to his palaces in saying to Wang Zan, "The preservation of these palaces rests solely upon your cunning!" Tang troops were passing Wanqu when Zan coerced city residents to climb the wall in defense of it. Once Tang armies attacked the Fengqiu gate, however, Zan opened the gate in surrender and offered his life, lying flat against the ground in submission. Zhuangzong lifted him and conveyed words of consolation: "For generations, we have been related by marriage, although subjects of different rulers. I can scarcely continue to hold umbrage against you." Zan thereby became metropolitan prefect of Kaifeng and later governor of the Xuanwu command. The execution of other one-time Liang subjects such as Zhao Yan and Zhang Hanjie left Zan himself ever nervous and brought on his own death. The posthumous title "grand preceptor to the heir-apparent" was conferred.

Zhao Chou

The ancestors of Zhao Chou came from Qing† prefecture, later generations serving as military attachés at Chen‡. During play with other boys in the street, military formations would be formed with Chou assuming direction like a commander, causing even the larger boys to submit to his lead. Startled at the sight of this, his father, Zhao Shuwen, insisted, "This boy will someday make our household important." He grew up to exhibit talents for archery and swordsmanship, in addition to exuding courageous dedication and righteous resolve. The local prefect, learning of his talents, recruited Chou for his regiments, and he eventually rose to chief inspector of infantry and cavalry at the Zhongwu command.

A mutinous Wang Xianzhi, in pillaging Henan and overrunning Ruzhou, had prepared to raid the eastern capital, but Zhao Chou led armies in a successful storm against him to force Xianzhi's flight to the south. Huang Chao subsequently rose in rebellion, many of the prefectures and counties targeted by his renegades often succumbing. Several hundred daring men from Chenzhou‡, wishing to preserve the prefecture, went together to the Zhongwu command to plead for Chou's assignment as prefect, as Zhongwu authorities petitioned the court to name him prefect of Chenzhou‡. Huang Chao later overran Changan, Zhao Chou now addressing military authorities to predict, "As I see it, if Huang Chao manages to evade execution by Changan authorities, he is certain to press his men eastward, in which case, our prefecture lies precisely in the path of his onslaught." Zhao Chou thus prepared the city's moats for defense. He also relocated commoners within a radius of sixty *li* of the city proper, selecting youth among these to be equipped with armor, their command entrusted to younger brothers Chang and Xu. Huang Chao did flee for the east after defeat at Changan, dispatching Meng Kai for an advance occupation of Xiangcheng. Zhao Chang vanquished Kai in a sortie and returned with him as hostage. Huang Chao arrived afterward, utterly riled to learn of Kai's apprehension.

Qin Zongquan hereafter surrendered Caizhou to Huang Chao, whose powers now thrived immensely, all of which were invested in the siege against Zhao Chou. Forced to feed his troops by grounding human flesh through a grinder, Chou's actions alarmed defenders at Chenzhou‡. "Through three generations, my family has served as Chenzhou‡ commanders," Chou said trying to assuage subordinates. "I must doggedly preserve it. As you struggle for life while surrounded by death, such times are truly opportune to win personal merit through your feats." Chenzhou‡ warriors all leaped in enthusiasm.

Roughly three *li* to the north of the city wall, Huang Chao's men had constructed ramparts for its "Barracks of the Eight Immortals" while erecting royal palaces and forming a civil service. Stores of rations were accumulated as well to facilitate long-term harassment of neighbors, the rebels boasting an army two hundred thousand strong. Warriors of Chenzhou‡ once possessed several hundred giant crossbows, now all broken and discarded, as younger artisans of crossbow manufacture knew nothing of the device. Zhao Xu reintroduced their manufacture, the arrows launched by these new crossbows capable of shooting as far as five hundred feet and piercing holes in humans and horses alike. Huang Chao dared not draw near in consequence. The siege persisted for three hundred days. As food supplies came close to depletion, Zhao Chou requested reinforcements from the Liang. Taizu of Liang and Li Keyong of Jin both personally commanded troops in a rendezvous at Chenzhou‡, where they stormed Huang Chao's lieutenant, Huang Ye, and vanquished him at Xihua. To the extent that Xihua contained stores of grain on which Huang Chao depended for rations, Ye's defeat forced Chao to dissolve the siege and abscond.

Once Taizu of Liang entered Chenzhou‡, Zhao Chou and his brothers greeted him with extreme deference, standing before his horse. Chou privately sensed that Taizu was certain to accomplish something monumental, so he condescended to go through the motions of submission merely as a ploy to make Taizu obliged to him. Having secured merit in assisting the Liang, he erected an altar to the living Taizu, sacrificing to it at dusk and dawn. He married his son, Zhao Yan, to Taizu's daughter, namely, the Princess Changle. Once the peril of Huang Chao abated, Qin Zongquan reintroduced turmoil to the Huaixi region, felling more than twenty prefectures in the vicinity. Chenzhou‡, although in closest proximity to Caizhou, could never be vanquished because of the strident resistance of Zhao Chou and his brothers. Later, defeat and death befell both Huang Chao and Qin Zongquan, Emperor Zhaozong elevating Chenzhou‡ to the Zhongwu command with Zhao Chou as governor. The post reverted to his younger brother Chang after Chou took ill, dying within a few months.

Zhao Chang exploited the recent suppression of the once formidable bandits to rest arms and cultivate agriculture, serving the Liang with scrupulous dedication. Once its armies began wars against the world's four corners, Chang gladly forwarded provisions without ever slackening. He was replaced upon death by Xu.

Zhao Xu possessed a considerable knowledge of books and once sought to follow in the footsteps of Deng Ai in channeling waters at Zhaiwangpo to irrigate farmlands of the people. The Zhao brothers presided over Chenzhou‡ for more than twenty years, and its people depended profoundly on them. After the surrender of Han Jian and acquisition of Tong and Hua‡ prefectures, Taizu relocated Zhao Xu as interim regent of Tongzhou. Xu became generalissimo of the Imperial Insignia Right Bodyguard under the Tang. Ailments a year or so later caused him to resign from office, and he returned home to die. In his honor, the people of Chenzhou‡ suspended business at local markets.

The next son of Chou, *Zhao Yan*, rose to minister of finance and revenues commissioner in the Liang reign of Emperor Mo, holding office alongside Zhang Hanjie and Han Lun. The Liang regime had evolved from the raging violence and murderous craze of Taizu to the remarkably amiable and deferential traits of Emperor Mo. A man mediocre in abilities, Mo developed an abiding trust in Hanjie, as a member of the Empress's family, and in Zhao Yan, his in-law. Even in the face of strident resistance from high officials and seasoned officers, Mo singularly and until his own demise refused to take heed.

Before this, Zhu Yougui had murdered Taizu to install himself, naming the future Emperor Mo interim custodian of the eastern capital. Zhao Yan visited the capital and imbibed with Mo, who revealed his honest feelings with composure. Yan decided to conspire on his behalf, sending a messenger to incite the troops of Yang Shihou to rise in rebellion. Yan now returned to the western capital and ultimately assisted Yuan Xiangxian in using the Palace Guard to execute Yougui, conveying the seal for dynastic succession to Emperor Mo.

After the installation of Emperor Mo, Zhao Yan was ashamed to learn that despite his merit under the Liang and marriage to a princess, his own perquisites were less than those of [imperial in-law] Du Cong, the Tang-dynasty martial minister and commissioner of reserve cavalry. He hence appropriated the fertile fields and grand houses across the realm while ruthlessly milking merchants, the doors to his home bustling like a marketplace. Half of the tax revenues were diverted to his private coffers, with Yan insisting on spending on food and drink some ten thousand strings of cash.

In former times, an unruly governor's guard at Weizhou had repeatedly mutinied, ultimately to be executed entirely by Luo Shaowei. Yang Shihou purged the Luo family to occupy Weizhou after Emperor Taizu's death, restoring two thousand troops to the governor's guard. Emperor Mo deemed them a potential danger, so occasioning Shihou's death, Zhao Yan joined Shao Zan, an administrative aide for revenues, in proposing to the throne, "Weizhou threatened the former Tang dynasty for more than a hundred years. Since the reign of the Former Monarch [Taizu], they gnashed their teeth in confrontation with Shaowei, acting obedient in his presence but disobedient in his absence. The Former Monarch departed this world only recently, yet Shihou today reemerges as a worry for Your Majesty, owing to Weizhou's large area and vast number of troops. Should Your Majesty fail to exploit this opportunity to restrain him, we have no certainty that a successor will not follow in Shihou's steps. It would be better to divide Xiang‡ and Wei prefectures into separate commands, precluding a menace to our north." Emperor Mo concurred and partitioned Xiang‡, Chan, and Wei‡ prefectures to constitute the Zhaode command. The governor's guard did rebel and surrender the Wei/Bo command to the Jin, the Liang dynasty losing the entire northern Yellow River region in the process.

At the time, Liang commanders Liu Xun and others engaged the future Zhuangzong of Tang in a standoff near Chan and Wei prefectures, with the

Liang defeated repeatedly. Zhao Yan proposed to the throne, "The kings of antiquity had to offer sacrifices to Heaven and Earth, yet Your Majesty has still not performed the sacrifices since the accession, so observers regard the imperial court as scarcely different from a governor's command. How can you possibly instill awe and respect in the world, under such circumstances? Despite the loss of Hebei, the world enjoys stability. Your Majesty should make every effort to perform the rituals." Jing Xiang differed, arguing, "With storehouses now exhausted, we overly tax to support our armies. If the sacrifices are to be done properly, they must coincide with conferral of rewards—tantamount to employing an ingenuous pretext to perpetrate a genuine abuse." Emperor Mo refused to heed him, preparing instead the prescribed carriage and departing for the western capital. Zhuangzong had captured Yangliu by then, inspiring one rumor that "Jin armies have occupied the eastern capital," another rumor that they "snatched Sishui," and yet another rumor that they "felled Yun and Pu prefectures." Meanwhile, gusts of wind had uprooted trees in the capital to the utter horror of Emperor Mo, he and his officials staring at one another in tears. The Emperor returned to the eastern capital without ever conducting the sacrifices.

Zhang Wenli of Zhenzhou now murdered Wang Rong, then sent a messenger to inform the Liang, "Your Subject, having already invited Khitan armies from the north, wishes for the Liang to commit ten thousand men from De and Di prefectures to sap the Prince of Jin's troops of their stamina." Jing Xiang found the idea credible, but Zhao Yan and Zhang Hanjie both argued against deployment, effectively shelving the matter. The subsequent cashiering of Wang Yanzhang and commissioning of Duan Ning reflected special intervention by Yan as well.

As armies of Zhuangzong approached Bianzhou, an overwrought Emperor Mo did not know what to do, so he climbed the Jianguo tower to inquire of officials there. Some proposed, "Jin armies, having come from afar and operating in isolation from their base, will face difficulty preserving their powers over the long haul. Even if they occupy Bianzhou, they could not defend it. You should proceed to Luoyang, finding protection in its rugged terrain, then summon troops from across the world to strategize methodically against them. Neither victory nor defeat is certain." Emperor Mo lacked resolve when Yan interjected, "In light of deteriorating conditions, no one can protect you even at walking down these very stairs!" Emperor Mo ultimately perished in the tower.

Wen Tao of Xuzhou‡ had been especially spineless in serving Zhao Yan when in power, so Yan commented to those around him, "I always treated Tao generously, so I can entrust my current emergency to him. He will certainly find a way to turn this misfortune to my personal benefit." Yan then walked in

Tao's direction, only to be decapitated by him, his head conveyed to the enemy. Once Zhuangzong had fully vanquished the Liang, Yan's one-time close associate, Duan Ning, memorialized for the execution of his family dependents, the liquidation approved.

We lament. There is hardly a single governing principle for peril or prosperity, as superior and inferior men experience them differently. [Philosopher] Laozi once stated, "It is peril upon which prosperity rests and prosperity in which peril hides."[1] Later writers on good and ill fortune all acknowledge the statement's truth. In doing good, one should meet with good fortune—but what if the outcome is ill fortune instead? In doing evil, one should meet with peril—but what if the outcome is good fortune instead? The moral man facing undeserved calamity will not necessarily fail to find good fortune therein, yet petty men seeking undeserved prosperity will reap nothing but peril—a natural principle. At the outset, Zhao Chou formed close bonds to Taizu of Liang through astute foresight. By the time that his sons and grandsons all enjoyed salary and privilege, they knew where to place their trust. Scarcely could they have imagined that their clan would ultimately perish along with the Liang dynasty! Chou's expectations of prosperity under the Liang is precisely the prosperity [with hidden peril] alluded to by Laozi, not what the superior man seeks. We cannot but be mindful!

Shi Shucong

Shi Shucong [d. C.E. 904] was native to Weishi, Kaifeng. A squad commander in the Liang cavalry, he distinguished himself repeatedly in battles during its storm against the rebel Huang Chao, centering on Chen‡ and Xu‡ prefectures. Taizu admired his fortitude and placed with Shucong command of the Rear Cavalry. He assisted in battles against Xu¶ and Yan prefectures and received promotion, on the future Taizu's nomination, to prefect of Suzhou. Shucong served in the offensive against Xiangyang, where successive setbacks led to demotion to district commissioner of controls at Yangzhai. After a long while, reassignment came as prefect of Caozhou.

Once Taizu had conquered Hezhong to claim the prefectures of Jin and Jiang, the Prince of Jin had a messenger deliver a peace petition to Taizu. The letter's wording seemed insulting, and Taizu retaliated with a raid led by Shucong and He Delun. Shucong approached from Taihang Mountain, seizing Ze and Lu prefectures, then departed via Shihui to garrison armies at Dongwo. Considerably later, he depleted provisions and had to return. Nomination by Taizu as prefect of Jinzhou ensued.

As Jin armies recaptured Jiangzhou and proceeded to raid Linfen, Shi Shucong chose two rugged warriors with deep eyes and whiskers to herd horses beside the highway to Xiangling. Assuming them to be fellow Jin soldiers [of Shatuo blood], the Jin army allowed them to join in the passage. The two infiltrators, waiting until the others were off guard, then apprehended two soldiers before returning. A petrified Jin army presumed some ambush to be awaiting them and retreated to camps at Pu County. Taizu arranged for his own son, Zhu Youning, to command ten thousand men in rendezvousing with Shucong to resist Jin armies. Youning preferred to rest his men and await further developments, but Shucong insisted, "The enemy will certainly flee upon hearing that reinforcements have arrived. What feat lies in simply winning their flight?" He then stormed by night to rout Jin armies, pursuing them all the way to Taiyuan. Taizu now commented with great relish, "In the overpowering of Taiyuan, the Venerable Shi is singularly qualified." Later, a major epidemic infecting his ranks forced Shucong to withdraw forces. "Those too ill to travel should be set afire," he mandated, a message instilling terror in the sick, who now all professed to be healthy. Shucong thereby returned to Shihui with crack troops as rear guard. Several horsemen stayed behind at Shihui, the banner of a senior commander planted on the ridge of a high hill. Jin armies suspected an ambush and dared not pursue them. Reassignment as the Baoda governor occurred sometime later.

Upon the relocation to Luoyang of the Emperor Zhaozong, Shi Shucong became commander-in-general of the Dragonly Martial Right Bodyguard. Taizu arranged for Shucong and Li Yanwei to commit regicide against Zhaozong, later to murder them.

Li Yanwei

Native to Shouzhou, Li Yanwei [d. C.E. 904] served the future Taizu of Liang in his youth. He was a man of astute prescience who could intuit the intentions of others. Out of compassion, Taizu adopted him as a son and had him assume the surname Zhu and personal name Yougong. He eventually served as prefect of Ru and later Ying¤ prefectures, becoming commander-in-chief of the Dragonly Martial Right Bodyguard after the Tang Emperor Zhaozong's arrival at Luoyang.

Liu Jishu had formerly purged Emperor Zhaozong to install the heir-apparent, Li Yu, as Son of Heaven. Once restored to legitimate power, Zhaozong pardoned the heir-apparent in light of his youth and the fact of installation by a renegade, even restoring his original title, Prince of De. When the Emperor returned to the capital from Qizhou‡ and Taizu of Liang met Yu for the first time, he instantly detested his wide eyebrows [an auspicious trait], insisting to chief minister Cui Yin, "The Prince of De was once enthroned by Jishu. Why is he still around? Tell the Son of Heaven to kill him." Yin petitioned Zhaozong, but he refused to acquiesce. The Emperor addressed Taizu on the matter on another day, Taizu informing him, "Your Subject dares not raise the issue. Cui Yin is trying to sell me out!" After relocating to Luoyang, the Emperor commented to Jiang Xuanhui, "The Prince of De is my beloved son. How can Quanzhong [Taizu] seek his murder?" He shed tears and bit his finger to the point of drawing blood. Xuanhui reported the entire exchange to Taizu, who came increasingly to loathe the Prince of De.

Emperor Zhaozong had changed the reign to Tianyou at the time, moving to the eastern capital. He did so under Liang duress, so the satrapies of Jin and Shu refused to acknowledge the Tianyou reign, for the Tang court had not freely adopted it, and recognized only the preceding Tianfu reign. Moreover, a summons to war was issued to the world by Wang Jian to raise armies to punish the Liang. A terrified Taizu feared that Zhaozong might take refuge at some other military district, so he sent a force of seventy thousand to Hezhong and secretly dispatched Jing Xiang[2] to Luoyang, instructing Li Yanwei and Shi Shucong to commit the treachery of regicide against their ruler.

On the second day of the eighth month [C.E. September 13, 904], Li Yanwei and Shi Shucong stationed contingents from their own Dragonly Martial Bodyguard in palace precincts. At the second drum of nighttime, they appeared at palace gates with a hundred troops, knocking to enter to petition the court. Opening the gate, imperial spouse Pei the Proper asked, "Why must troops enter to memorialize on affairs?" An officer of the Dragonly Martial Guard, Shi Tai, murdered her, then rushed toward the Jiaolan palace and asked of Zhaozong's whereabouts. Drunk at the time, Zhaozong arose to flee as Shi Tai pursued him with sword drawn, Zhaozong swinging his sheer gown around a pillar as he tried to escape, but was struck by Tai's sword and expired. When the death announcement reached Hezhong, Taizu gave the appearance of shock in falling to the floor, weeping aloud and scolding the assassins: "Those men have betrayed me and guaranteed the smearing of my good name in coming generations!" Upon reaching Luoyang, Taizu banished Yanwei and Shucong to Lingnan, employing Zhang Tingfan to kill them. Yanwei blurted out, as punishment approached, "You have betrayed me to shut my mouth. How does this square with heavenly principle?" Looking at Tingfan, he added, "Do your best. Your end will surely be as mine!" The murder then occurred, his original name subsequently restored.

In the Zhuangzong reign, a one-time palace servant of the former Tang dynasty, Jing Cha, reported that several hundred imperial princes and clansmen also perished when Yanwei assassinated Zhaozong, their bodies thrown into a single burial pit north of the Longxing temple. The construction of a large burial mound for purposes of reburial was requested and the court agreed to burial rituals of the first order, with the former Prince of Pu heading the group.

Kong Xun

The origins of his family are not known, for Kong Xun was orphaned as a child. He wandered about Kaifeng and its environs, where he was taken in by a wealthy man named Li Rang and raised as son. During Taizu's tenure as Xuanwu governor [of Kaifeng], he adopted Li Rang as son, so Xun similarly assumed the surname Zhu. He was nearly grown and serving in the tents of Taizu when a wet-nurse for some of Taizu's sons, having grown attached to him, adopted Xun as son: the wet-nurse's husband was surnamed Zhao, so Xun assumed a new surname, Zhao, and personal name Yinheng. Upon relocation of Emperor Zhaozong eastward to Luoyang, Taizu thoroughly purged the attendants of the Son of Heaven, replacing them all with Liang men. Wang Yin became commissioner of palace armies, Xun consequently becoming deputy commissioner.

Kong Xun had participated, along with Jiang Xuanhui and Zhang Tingfan, in the conspiracy to murder their monarch, Zhaozong. Rifts later emerged between Xun and Xuanhui. So, in the wake of Emperor Ai's accession to the throne and preparation to conduct sacrifices at the southern suburbs, Kong Xun joined Wang Yin in slandering Xuanhui in the presence of Taizu. "Xuanhui secretly serves the Empress Dowager He," they argued. "Moreover, he and Tingfan assist the Son of Heaven in the suburban rites hoping to prolong Tang rule." Taizu was utterly livid. At the time, Liang troops attacking Shouchun had been routed before returning. Emperor Ai nonetheless dispatched Pei Di to reward troops. His meeting with Di extremely infuriated Taizu, so after Di's return to the capital, Emperor Ai dared not conduct the suburban sacrifices. Instead, he offered to invest Taizu as Prince of Wei and confer the "nine official privileges with vestments," which Taizu refused to accept. Jiang Xuanhui and chief minister Liu Can, in succession, rushed to the Liang to offer personal explanations for his actions. "Since antiquity, ascending kings have invariably received a feudal domain," Liu Can explained. "The Tang Emperor has not relinquished the throne to you because of the prior necessity of investiture replete with the nine official privileges and vestments. After this, formal abdication can occur." But Taizu queried, "Can I not become Son of Heaven without the nine privileges?" A frightened Can abruptly departed. Taizu subsequently sent Kong Xun and

Wang Yin to commit regicide against the Dowager He. Also slain were Can, Xuanhui, and Tingfan. In reward, Xun was promoted to deputy secretary of palace armies.

With the collapse of Tang rule, Kong Xun served the Liang as defense commissioner for Ruzhou, commandant of the Left Bodyguard, and commissioner of revenues. He now reverted to the surname Kong and personal name Xun. Assignment as provisional prefect of Bianzhou [Kaifeng] occurred in the Zhuangzong reign. As the future Mingzong headed southward after the mutiny at Weizhou and Zhuangzong departed eastward for Sishui [in a rush to Kaifeng], Kong Xun played to both sides. He arranged for Mingzong to be met at the northern gate while personally greeting Zhuangzong at the western gate, preparing sacrificial animals and identical rituals for both. He further cautioned subordinates, "Whoever arrives first, enters first." Mingzong arrived first and Xun received him.

Kong Xun became commissioner of military affairs upon Mingzong's accession, and during his visit to Bianzhou, Xun served as interim custodian of the eastern capital. Some individuals once violated monopoly laws by making their own wine, and Xun murdered them and their families as punishment. Mingzong recognized the injustice and repealed the ban on private brewing, permitting the people to produce their own spirits.

Kong Xun was a man given to spineless sycophancy and treacherous tricks. He enjoyed a relationship of special intimacy and trust with An Chonghui, who accepted anything said by Xun. Mingzong once wished to marry an imperial son to Chonghui's daughter. Chonghui inquired of Xun, who said, "You, Sir, are a courtier of critical importance whose family should not intermarry with imperial sons." A persuaded Chonghui spurned the offer. At the same time, Xun secretly had someone tell Mingzong of his own desire to give a daughter as wife to an imperial son. Mingzong consequently arranged for the Prince of Song, Li Conghou, to marry Xun's daughter. Chonghui now began to detest Xun, banishing him to be governor of the Zhongwu command. Later he was reassigned as governor of Henghai, dying there at forty-eight *sui*, the posthumous title grand marshal conferred.

CHAPTERS 44–45

MISCELLANEOUS BIOGRAPHIES

Liu Zhijun

With courtesy name Xixian, Liu Zhijun was native to Pei County, Xuzhou¶. He served Shi Pu as a young man and assisted him in an offensive against the Liang, where Zhijun and two thousand men under his banner eventually surrendered to the Liang, Taizu naming him left commander of exploratory armies.

Zhijun was heroically virile in physical presence. He could mount his horse while fastening his armor, brandish his sword while charging the enemy, his courage unique among the commanders. At the time, the appellation "Reconnaissance Man Liu" commanded wide respect within military circles. He proceeded to serve successively as prefect of Hai, Huai‡, and Zheng prefectures. He also aided in the conquest of Qingzhou†, Taizu nominating him as governor of the Kuangguo command in reward.

When Yang Chongben of Binzhou deployed a force of sixty thousand to attack Yongzhou and garrisoned his men at Meiyuan, Taizu and the other commanders were engaged in an offensive at Cangzhou. Liu Zhijun and Kang Huaiying thus did not await orders from him, but instead stormed Chongben to sever twenty thousand enemy heads, capture three thousand enemy horses, and apprehend a hundred commanders and assistant commanders.

In the offensive of Li Si'an against Luzhou, the dual ramparts did not succeed in bringing down the prefecture, despite a long siege. Taizu thus dismissed Si'an and named Liu Zhijun bandit-suppressing commissioner for at-large forces. Zhijun had yet to reach Luzhou when the ramparts were breached by the enemy, so he was reassigned as bandit-suppressing commissioner for at-large forces in the western circuits. He defeated troops from Bin and Qi‡ prefectures at Mugu. At the time, Gao Wanxing of Yanzhou‡ had mutinied against Yang Chongben in surrendering to the Liang. Taizu sent Zhijun to rendezvous with Wanxing, attacking and eventually overrunning the four prefectures of Dan, Yan‡, Fu‡, and Fang. Honored as interim grand marshal and concurrent director of the Chancellery, he was invested Prince of Dapeng.

As his merits accumulated, Liu Zhijun grew uneasy, for Taizu had a proclivity for suspicions and jealousies and murdered a succession of commanders, the death of an innocent Wang Chongshi leaving Zhijun ever anxious. Once Taizu descended upon Fu‡ and Fang, he dispatched Zhijun to resume the offensive against Binzhou, but Zhijun could not provision his armies and did not advance. Taizu now departed for Hezhong and ordered the commissioner of palace armies, Wang Yin, to summon Zhijun. In the interval, Zhijun's younger brother, Liu Zhihuan, a military director in the Imperial Guard, had warned him by messenger against coming, so he mutinied to declare fealty to Li Maozhen. Zhijun also led an attack on Yong and Hua‡ prefectures, apprehending Liu Han and conveying him to Fengxiang. Taizu sent a messenger to inquire of Zhijun, "I have extended myself in treating you. How can you turn your back on me?" "Wang Chongshi did not turn on Your Majesty," Zhijun responded, "yet he and his family were liquidated. Your Subject did not turn against your virtue, but merely acted on fear of death." Taizu dispatched another messenger to explain, "I genuinely understand your position. It was bad counsel from Liu Han that caused me to execute Chongshi. I cannot but loathe him for forcing such circumstances upon you! Han is now dead, although this scarcely absolves me of responsibility." Zhijun did not respond, deploying troops instead to cut off Tongguan.

Taizu dispatched Liu Xun and Niu Cunjie to attack Liu Zhijun, forcing him to take sanctuary with Li Maozhen. The lands of Maozhen were slight, however. Having no place to assign Zhijun, Maozhen instructed him to raid Lingwu to the west. Han Xun consequently informed the Liang of his new emergency, and Taizu directed Kang Huaiying, Kou Yanqing, and others to raid Binning to contain Zhijun. Huaiying was routed at Shengping County by Zhijun, who also killed Liang commander Xu Congshi. An utterly delighted Maozhen appointed Zhijun governor of Jingzhou‡, unleashing him for an offensive against Xingyuan Prefecture. Zhijun proceeded to claim the prefectures of Xing‡ and Feng‡, then encircle Xi County.

Later, aides to Li Maozhen grew jealous of Liu Zhijun and his feats, the ensuing conflicts between them prompting Maozhen to strip Zhijun of his armies. Zhijun now sought sanctuary in the Shu region, where overlord Wang

Jian made him governor of the Wuxin command, entrusting a counteroffensive against Maozhen to him. The four prefectures of Qin, Feng‡, Jie, and Cheng were claimed in consequence. Wang Jian treated Zhijun with extreme bounty, even as he privately resented his talents, once saying to aides, "I am old, to be sure. When I die, Zhijun will be beyond the ability of any of you to control. It is better to lay your schemes against him sooner than later." Many a Shu warrior shared his jealousy. Zhijun had a face dark in color and was born in the year of *chou* [the bull], while the scions of Wang Jian all had personal names with the character *zong* or *cheng* [a homonym for "rope"]. They circulated a rumor among the villages: "A dark bull will charge to break the rope on the corral."[1] Jian's increased animosity for Zhijun led to his murder.

He Delun

Native to Hexi, He Delun had served as attaché for the governor's guard at Huazhou in his youth. Taizu then held concurrent powers over the Xuanyi command, so Delun assisted him on assorted campaigns, rising to the Pinglu governorship.

In the inaugural year of Zhenming [C.E. 915], Yang Shihou died at Weizhou, and Emperor Mo, in response to the arrogant and contrary character of Weizhou authorities, partitioned the prefectures of Xiang‡, Chan, and Wei‡ to form a separate Zhaode command, naming as its governor Zhang Yun. The three prefectures of Wei, Bo, and Bei now formed the Tianxiong command, with Delun serving as governor. Emperor Mo dispatched Liu Xun, with a force of sixty thousand, to cross the Yellow River on the pretext of attacking Zhending. Wang Yanzhang's five hundred cavalry were to occupy Weizhou, forting at Jinboting in anticipation of a mutiny. Half of the governor's guard at Weizhou was assigned to Zhaode, while the secretary to the commissioner of revenues was also dispatched to oversee the recruitment of Wei soldiers and manage its treasury. When Delun pressed his guardsmen to prepare for departure, the cries of the soldiers' relatives parting in grief filled the highways. Zhang Yan, commander of Dedicated forces, plotted with his rank and file, argued, "The court, due to the might and prosperity of our command, has imposed rules to ruin it. Long ago, our six prefectures formed a garrison command, yet never did we leave our canal gate for distant parts. On the day that we leave our own relatives and villages, life becomes worse than death." Banding together for a nighttime raid on Jinboting, they forced out Yanzhang. By the next morning, Wei armies attacked the inner wall to kill more than five hundred men and seize Delun, carrying him up a tower. Marauding troops pillaged extensively.

Emperor Mo rushed palace-services officer Hu Yi to Weizhou with instructions for Zhang Yan and the promise of a post as prefect. Yan addressed Yi, saying, "Report back to the Emperor, for me, that these three armies did not defy the court; rather, the court betrayed the three armies: the current turmoil emanates entirely from curtailing powers without proper cause. Your Majesty need only restore all six prefectures to Weizhou's purview and direct Liu Xun's armies to return—then you can sleep at ease." Upon returning, Hu Yi reported that an impetuous Yan was of minor concern, such that Xun's troops should storm him. Emperor Mo thus had a messenger inform Yan that the institutions, already in place, would not be altered. Messengers made three trips, infuriating Yan, who blurted out, "That houseboy has such audacity!" Summoning Sikong Ting, a one-time aide to Luo Shaowei, Yan warned, "Petition the throne for me indicating that if such dickering continues, I personally intend to cross the river to imprison him." The Emperor responded with an amicably worded edict, "In the wake of Wang Rong's death, the people of Zhenzhou sought to surrender and Xun was deployed at Zhenzhou with his armies to restore order. I had no other intent. If his presence is inconvenient for Weizhou, I will summon Xun to return." Yan was also cautioned against creating troubles for the court.

To the extent that Yang Shihou, as Weizhou governor, once held concurrent powers as commissioner of bandit suppression, Zhang Yan pressured He Delun to propose the nomination of a new commissioner. Emperor Mo withheld consent and informed Yan of the decision by imperial edict. Tearing the edict to pieces, Yan tossed it to the floor and insisted, "This idiot of a ruler lets others run a hole through his nose [like a mindless ox]—a man impossible to work with." He then compelled Delun to surrender to the Jin. Delun declared in horror, "I simply follow my commander's orders," sending military attaché Cao Tingyin to present a letter to Zhuangzong.

As the future Zhuangzong approached Weizhou, He Delun secretly dispatched a messenger to apprise him of the previous pressure exerted by Zhang Yan. Thus, before occupying Wei, Zhuangzong arranged for Yan's beheading at Linqing County. Delun was reassigned as governor of Datong, only to be detained upon reaching Taiyuan by its military overseer, [eunuch] Zhang Chengye. Taiyuan later came under attack by Wang Tan and many men under Delun's banner defected to him. Chengye worried that Delun might mutiny and killed him.

Kang Yanxiao

Native to Daibei, Kang Yanxiao had been a foot soldier at Taiyuan, then cast his fortunes with the Liang after committing some crime. When Emperor Mo dispatched Duan Ning to fort armies north of the Yellow River, he named Yanxiao commander of the Left and Right Vanguard. Yanxiao could observe the band of petty men employed by Emperor Mo, convincing him that the dynasty was destined to soon perish. He defected to Tang, along with a hundred horsemen. Zhuangzong met him at Chaocheng, removing his own royal robe and gold staff to give him. He also appointed Yanxiao as prefect of Bozhou and commissioner of Bracing-the-Sun forces and bandit suppression along the southern front.

Zhuangzong emptied the room to probe Kang Yanxiao about conditions at the Liang court. He spoke at length, stating, "Emperor Mo is ineffectual and entrusts affairs to Zhao Yan, his brother-in-law, and Zhang Hanjie of his wife's family. Duan Ning is the sinister type, who appoints senior commanders based on how much gold they remit. Influential commanders since the days of his father are all consigned to lesser positions today. Wang Yanzhang is a commander of valor, yet the throne attempts to control his armies by employing Hanjie as overseer. Petty men are advanced to office, as loyal subjects and courageous warriors all end up banished afar. Such conditions are certain cause for debacle." Zhuangzong also asked about the nature of Liang strategies. Yanxiao responded, "Your Subject, when serving the Liang court, furtively overheard a discussion of a major offensive planned for the second month of winter [the eleventh month]: Dong Zhang will depart from Shihui in an attack on Taiyuan, deploying the multitudes from Shan, Guo, Ze, and Lu prefectures; Huo Yanwei will rush against Zhen and Ding prefectures, deploying troops from the western passes, Ru and Luo, and pillage Xing and Ming prefectures; Wang Yanzhang will storm Yunzhou with troops from the Metropolitan Bodyguard; and Duan will contest you, Your Majesty, with armies along the Yellow River."

Zhuangzong was initially delighted to hear Yanxiao's prediction of certain demise for the Liang, yet news of a major offensive made him nervous, so he queried, "How are we to resist them?" "Liang troops are numerous," Yanxiao continued, "but far less formidable when divided. Your Subject proposes waiting until they have divided, then deploy five thousand cavalry in iron armor to rush Bian Prefecture from the direction of Yun. Your action being unexpected, you can hit him with a surprise strike and successfully settle the world in ten days." Zhuangzong was immensely impressed by his comments. Later, Dong Zhang's cohort was not deployed in the action as predicted. Nonetheless, the entire investment of Liang armies along the Yellow River, under Duan Ning's command, left the capital undefended. Zhuangzong ultimately adopted Yanxiao's strategy, approaching Bian from Yun Prefecture, to annihilate the Liang within eight days. For such merit, Yanxiao was named defense commissioner for Zhengzhou and conferred the name Li Shaochen. Reassignment as Baoyi governor came in the second year [C.E. 924].

In its campaign against Shu, during the third year, the court named Kang Yanxiao commissioner of military formations and fuel for vanguard units. Overrunning Fengzhou‡, his men also claimed Guzhen County before winning the surrender of Xingzhou‡. He battled [Shu potentate] Wang Yan at Sanquan County, a vanquished Yan severing a suspension bridge at the Jibai River as he fled. Yanxiao built boats to cross the river, then advanced to claim Mianzhou. Wang Yan tore out another suspension bridge across the Mian River. This time, addressing pacification commissioner Li Yan, Yanxiao proposed, "I have led armies across a distant one thousand *li* to enter enemy territory, so the greater benefit lies in rapid engagement. In exploiting this moment when Wang Yan's spirit is broken, a mere hundred mounts infiltrating Lutou Pass will suffice to induce the surrender of an endless stream of his commanders. Yet the repair of bridges will surely delay us by several days and enable Wang Yan to seal off the passes and make preparations, leaving the outcome wholly uncertain." Yanxiao and Li Yan thus climbed their horses and floated across the river. Just over a thousand soldiers to cross the river with them proceeded to penetrate Lutou Pass and fell Hanzhou. Rear contingents began to arrive within three days. Wang Yan's younger brother, Zongbi, surrendered Shu, in the end, as Yanxiao forted at Hanzhou to await the arrival of Jiji, Prince of Wei.

In the pacification of Shu, the feats of Kang Yanxiao were numerous. Dong Zhang was chief commander of infantry and cavalry for left-wing regiments, his rank lower than Yanxiao's, but he commanded the special respect of Guo Chongtao. Chongtao only summoned Zhang for consultations on military affairs, never inquiring of Yanxiao. This so infuriated Yanxiao as to prompt the following reprimand against Zhang: "I accomplished the pacification of Shu, you and your cohort merely trailing closely on my heels. Now, at the doors of the Gentleman Guo, you bow your head. As chief commander, I am confounded that I cannot decapitate the likes of you by the rules of martial law!" Zhang complained of the affair to Chongtao, who petitioned the court to appoint Zhang governor of eastern Chuan, relieving him of military commands. The compromise further infuriated Yanxiao, who commented, "To secure the two circuits of Chuan, I confronted naked swords and perilous obstacles of nature. As for Zhang, by what merit does he acquire the banner of governor?" Meeting with Chongtao, he argued against the appointment, but Chongtao roared back, "Shaochen, are you rebelling? How dare you violate my commands!" A cowered Yanxiao retreated. Chongtao died a year later, Yanxiao now asking of Zhang, "At whose door will you bow your head, now?" Zhang sought release from assignment with plaintive pleas.

As the Prince of Wei, Jiji, withdrew his men from Shu, he instructed Kang Yanxiao to form a rear guard with twelve thousand men. Yanxiao had reached Wulian when word of Zhu Youqian's murder without cause reached him. Youqian had a son at Suizhou‡, Zhu Lingde, and Jiji received orders from Zhuangzong via messenger to execute him posthaste. To carry out the mandate, Jiji did not employ Yanxiao, but rather Dong Zhang—a snub already stirring his suspicions. Moreover, Zhang passed by the camps of Yanxiao without entering to meet him, a livid Yanxiao commenting to a subordinate, "Pacification of Liang to the south and Shu to the west may well emanate from the strategies laid by Gentleman Guo, but the toil of sweating horses, the assaults on cities and the vanquishing of rivals—these are my own. Gentleman Guo is now dead. How am I to survive? Youqian and I both repudiated the Liang to convert to Tang, his own peril destined to be visited upon me, next time around." The men under Yanxiao's banner were all one-time commanders under Youqian, news of his liquidation causing them to wail loudly before his barracks in defiance. "Gentleman Zhu committed no crime, yet two hundred members of his family were executed," they said. "Many a former commander followed him in death, and we will die as well."

Kang Yanxiao rallied his rank and file, reentering Shu from the direction of Jianzhou‡ and pronouncing himself governor of western Chuan and regional commissioner for the three circuits of Chuan. A summons to war was immediately issued to the people of Shu, causing Yanxiao's armies to swell in a matter of days to fifty thousand. To pursue him, Jiji sent Ren Huan, with seven thousand cavalry. Huan rendezvoused with Meng Zhixiang at Hanzhou for a pincer action, a defeated Yanxiao apprehended and carted away on a cage-wagon.

Ren Huan held a banquet in his barracks, ordering the cage-wagon to be rolled in and placed before his seat. Pouring wine into a large goblet, Meng Zhixiang extended his hand into the cage to give a drink, then asked of Yanxiao, "The Gentleman had fled the Liang in converting to our mandate, hence acquiring the banner of a governor. There is also your recent merit in the pacification of Shu. Why should worries about wealth and status relegate you to a cage like this?" Yanxiao responded, "Guo Chongtao, a subject to assist in the dynastic mandate, ranked first in merit: without shedding the blood of troops, he captured the two circuits of Chuan. Suddenly, his entire family is slain without commission of a crime. How is it possible for someone like myself to save his own neck? I dared not return to court for this reason." Ren Huan departed for the east, again, while Zhuangzong dispatched a eunuch to murder Yanxiao as the cage-wagon reached Fengxiang.

Zhang Quanyi

His courtesy name Guowei, Zhang Quanyi [C.E. 852–926] was native to Linpu, Puzhou. As a young peasant, he worked as a conscript laborer at

Linpu County, but owing to repeated insults and harassment from the county magistrate, Quanyi cast his fortunes with Huang Chao's rebel bands. Once the capital of Changan fell into the rebel's hands, Quanyi was appointed minister of personnel and commissioner of water transport. And upon the defeat of Chao and his gang, Quanyi proceeded to Heyang to serve Zhuge Shuang, and later Shuang's son Zhongfang upon Shuang's death. Zhuge Zhongfang came to be purged from power by Sun Ru, Quanyi and Li Hanzhi now seizing independent control of Heyang and Luoyang for reversion to Liang sovereignty.

The two men reveled in their individual attainments, yet Li Hanzhi was given to avarice and caprice, preoccupied each day with plundering. In contrast, Zhang Quanyi proved rigorously frugal, imposed laws to regulate the army, and presided over the people's tilling of lands. For this reason, Hanzhi commonly faced shortages of food while Quanyi often enjoyed surpluses. Hanzhi looked to Quanyi for subsidy, which Quanyi could not provide, creating frictions between the two men. Hanzhi subsequently deployed armies to raid Jin and Jiang prefectures, Quanyi responding with an assault on Heyang, whose occupation forced Hanzhi to take refuge in Jin lands. The Jin assisted Hanzhi militarily by forming an extremely tight blockade around Quanyi, as he turned to the Liang for military relief. The Liang sent a force of ten thousand commanded by Niu Cunjie and Ding Hui: departing from Jiuding, they crossed the Yellow River and stormed Hanzhi's men at Yanshui. Defeated, Jin armies disbanded and withdrew. The Liang now appointed Ding Hui as custodian of Heyang and Quanyi as metropolitan prefect of Henan. Obliged to the Liang for rendering assistance, Quanyi devoted his heart to it.

In the wake of the ravages of war wrought upon Henan Prefecture by Huang Chao and Sun Ru, the city in ruins contained not even a hundred households. Zhang Quanyi uprooted weeds and brambles in fostering the cultivation of fields, he personally carried wine and food to comfort people toiling on farms and erected ramparts to the north and south to be manned. After some years, the people and the community at Luoyang were completely restored, as residents came to depend immensely upon him. By the time that Emperor Zhaozong of Tang had been forcibly relocated eastward by Liang Taizu, the sound state of Luoyang's palace quarters, prefectural offices, and grain storehouses all reflected the industry of Quanyi.

His personal name, initially "Yan," was changed to "Quanyi" by Emperor Zhaozong. He requested a change once the Tang had fallen and he entered service under the Liang, Taizu conferring the personal name "Zongshi." Despite the suspicions and jealousies of Taizu that grew worse in later years, Quanyi served him with heightened diligence and escaped personal peril even until his last days.

Liang armies faced successive defeats since engaging Jin troops north of the Yellow River. Quanyi's foraging for foot soldiers and armored cavalry yielded enough recruits each month to cover the shortfall. Taizu's armies were vanquished at Xiu County, and he took ill on the road, returning to Luoyang. Seeking to escape the summer heat, he visited Quanyi at his Huijie gardens and stayed for ten days, during which Taizu forced himself on Quanyi's wife and daughter. Zhang Jizuo, Quanyi's son, could not contain his indignation and shame, so he intended to stab Taizu with a sword. He was stopped by Quanyi, who said, "When Li Hanzhi's men surrounded us at Heyang and we had to eat shavings of wood to survive, the slaughter of a single horse in our possession was intended to feed an entire army. Death loomed day and night when Liang troops emerged on the scene. Even today I cannot forget this charitable deed." Jizuo therefore desisted.

Someone once spoke ill of Zhang Quanyi to Taizu, so Taizu summoned him to court to kill him. Quanyi's wife, née Chu, with her sharp mind and deft polemical skills, abruptly entered to meet Taizu and spoke in a firm voice, "Zongshi is but an old farmer. As custodian at Henan for the past thirty years, he initiated the cultivation of once barren lands, gathering the tax revenues to assist Your Majesty in the dynastic enterprise. Now left decrepit by old age, he is incapable of doing anything. Why does Your Majesty doubt him?" Taizu responded with a smile, "I have no sinister intent, Old Woman. You need say no more." Under the Liang, Quanyi eventually rose to palace secretary, his fiefs of maintenance swelling to thirteen thousand households. He held provisional authority as governor of the Zhongwu, Shanguo, Zhenghua, and Heyang commands. Named administrator of the Six Armies and deputy marshal for forces empirewide, he was invested Prince of Wei.

In the past, Zhang Quanyi's defeat by Li Hanzhi caused his younger brother Zhang Quanwu to be apprehended by Jin armies, along with family dependents. The Prince of Jin now provided a rural estate for Quanwu, privileging him to exceptional bounty. Quanyi often sent secret messengers to Taiyuan to inquire after the brother. Once Zhuangzong [Prince of Jin] occupied Bianzhou to purge the Liang, Quanyi left Luoyang to stand for punishment at court, his face covered in mud. Zhuangzong said to him reassuringly, "Today, virtual siblings of a family have the good fortune to meet again." Quanyi fell prostrate on the floor, moved to tears. He could not proceed forward because of advanced age, so someone lifted him from the floor and up the dais. The ensuing banquet generated such mirth that Zhuangzong instructed his son Jiji and younger brother Cunji to honor Quanyi as elder brother. Quanyi had already abandoned the name conferred by the Liang dynasty and requested to revert to his earlier name. He still felt ill at ease, so he left a sizable bribe with Empress Liu, placing himself in her trust.

Emperor Mo of Liang had once departed for Luoyang in preparation for sacrificing to Heaven at the southern suburbs; he never performed the sacrifice, but the imperial-insignia staff and other regulation paraphernalia were still present. Zhang Quanyi thus requested an imperial progress to Luoyang, characterizing the related ritual paraphernalia as complete. Zhuangzong reveled in the notion and bestowed honors on Quanyi as grand preceptor and imperial secretary, leaving for offerings at the southern suburbs of Luoyang in the eleventh month of the next year.[2] The ritual implements proved incomplete, in fact, so he changed the date for conducting the rites to the second month of the coming year. Still, he did not reprimand Quanyi for the previous misrepresentation, Quanyi instead enjoying ever-growing bounty through the Empress's influence. Zhuangzong paid repeated visits to his home, where now the Empress was told to treat Quanyi as father. His investiture was changed to Prince of Qi.

After initially annihilating the Liang, Zhuangzong wanted to plunder the tomb of the Liang founder Taizu, unearthing the coffin to desecrate his corpse. Yet Quanyi argued that its entire royal family had already been massacred—enough to atone for the old vendetta, however bitter. For a king seeking to display great dignity to the world, the desecration of a coffin was inappropriate, he insisted. Zhuangzong was persuaded and settled for simply seizing some tomb paraphernalia from the burial mound.

Zhang Quanyi had a military overseer who once acquired the Pingquan stone for recovering from a hangover, formerly owned by Li Deyu. The grandson of Deyu, Li Yangu, requested Quanyi's intervention to recover it. The military overseer insisted irately, "Since the turmoil of Huang Chao, even ownership of homes or gardens in Luoyang could not be guaranteed. How can one expect restitution of a simple Pingquan stone?" Quanyi had once consorted with the Huang Chao gang, so the comments seemed as satire against him. In raging anger, he petitioned the palace to have the military overseer flogged to death with light rod, an action deemed unjust by the world. When the case came before legal authorities, the rule existed of "passing favorable judgment for the party to sue first" [regardless of merit], a judgment regarded by the people as oppressive.

In the fourth year of Tongguang [C.E. 926], Zhao Zaili rebelled at Weizhou, and Yuan Xingqin, charged with suppressing him, had not succeeded. Zhuangzong wanted to lead the suppression effort in person, but senior courtiers all admonished against it, proposing instead the future Mingzong for the command. Guo Chongtao and Zhu Youqian had both fallen to murderous plots by then, Mingzong now coming to court from Zhenzhou and staying at his private residence. Zhuangzong's suspicions of Mingzong having been roused, he did not support the assignment and refused even after persistent pleas from the multitude of courtiers. In the end, it was Quanyi's forceful endorsement of the assignment that caused Zhuangzong finally to concede. Mingzong did mutiny upon reaching Weizhou, and Quanyi died of attendant anxieties at seventy-five *sui*. He received the posthumous title "Loyal and Solemn."

His son, *Zhang Jizuo* [d. C.E. 937], eventually held the title of generalissimo. In the reign of Gaozu of the Jin dynasty, he and Zhang Congbin rebelled at Heyang. This should have entailed extended executions, but chief minister Sang Weihan intervened to spare the lives of the entire family: the one-time service of Weihan's father, Sang Gong, under Quanyi had left him obliged to the Zhang family. The court refused, but agreed to limit its executions to Jizuo, his wife, and sons.

Zhu Youqian

Native to Xuzhou‡, Zhu Youqian [d. C.E. 926] had the courtesy name Deguang and the original personal name of Jian. Having committed some offense as a foot soldier at Mianchi Garrison, he cast himself into a life of banditry in the area of Shihao and Sanxiang counties, visiting hardship upon merchants traveling its roadways. He moved on to Shanzhou after some time and rose to lieutenant in the military.

Shanzhou governor Wang Gong, a man of savage cruelty, struggled with younger brother Wang Ke to control Hezhong. Upon failing in battle, military attaché for the governor's guard, Li Fan, assisted Zhu Youqian in a conspiracy that produced the murder of Gong and conversion of the prefecture to Liang sovereignty. The future Taizu petitioned the court for Fan to replace Gong as governor, and once Fan was formally installed, Youqian raised armies in an offensive. Fan managed to abscond and Taizu petitioned the court once again, now for Youqian's replacement of Fan.

Taizu of Liang often passed through Shanzhou in raids to the west against Li Maozhen, with Zhu Youqian scrupulously dedicated in serving him. He thus asked of Taizu, "It is through the efforts of you, Mr. Marshal that Your Servant, originally lacking in personal merit, can still enjoy such wealth and stature. In that we already share a common surname, I wish to change my personal name in the manner of your sons." Taizu increasingly empathized with him, changing his name to Youqian and registering him as son. After formally acceding to the throne, Taizu reassigned him as governor of Hezhong with honors as palace secretary and investiture as Prince Ji.

Taizu later succumbed to an act of regicide, as Yougui installed himself and honored Youqian as director of the Chancellery. Although accepting the mandate, Youqian felt ill at ease. Later, Yougui summoned him for a formal appearance at court, which Youqian never undertook, having already converted to the Prince of Jin. Yougui unleashed a sally against him: a force of fifty thousand led by Kang Huaiying, a commander under Han Jing, the commissioner of bandit suppression. The Prince of Jin intervened on Youqian's behalf. Departing from Ze and Lu prefectures, he engaged Huaiying at Xie County, routing him. The Prince's men pursued Huaiying to Baijing Ridge, where his men carried torches by night in a storm that defeated Huaiying once again. Liang armies then disbanded. The Prince of Jin, with Youqian asleep in his tent after an inebriating celebration, turned to aides to observe, "The Prince Ji [Youqian] is a valuable asset, although, sadly, his arms are too short!"

With the accession of Emperor Mo, Zhu Youqian resumed fealty to the Liang without rupturing ties with the Prince of Jin. A sally against Tongzhou in the sixth year of Zhenming [C.E. 920], which Youqian entrusted to son Lingde, resulted in the expulsion of governor Cheng Quanhui. Youqian now requested concurrent authority as governor of the new district. Emperor Mo initially declined only later to consent; the rescript of approval had not arrived when Youqian rebelled anew, beginning a formal severing of ties with the Liang and submission to Jin rule. Emperor Mo entrusted Liu Xun with the suppression effort, but Li Cunshen prevailed over him. Youqian was invested Prince of Xiping by the Jin authorities and honored as acting grand marshal. His son, Lingde, became governor of Tongzhou.

Zhu Youqian came to court once Zhuangzong occupied Luoyang and supplanted the Liang dynasty. The court conferred a new name, Li Jilin, as well as tens of thousands in cash gifts. In the next year [C.E. 924], further honors came as acting grand preceptor and imperial secretary, including conferral of an iron writ affirming immunity to capital punishment. His son Lingde was named governor of Suizhou‡ and son Lingxi named governor of the Zhongwu command. Among his sons, commanders, and lieutenants more than ten received posts as prefect. The lavishness of court charity and favor had no parallel in those days.

Eunuchs and actors wielded influence at the time, many of whom demanded bribes from Youqian. Unable to pay, he declined and thereby incurred their wrath. Once the Tang campaign against Shu got under way, Youqian was to inspect crack troops and arranged for his son, Lingde, to lead an accompanying force. Actor Jing Jin now alleged, in the aftermath of Guo Chongtao's murder: "At the outset of issuing our Tang armies, Youqian worried that the pacification might be directed against him, so his inspection of troops had served as self-preparation." The actor added, "He was in conspiracy with Chongtao to rebel. Behind Chongtao's rebellion in Shu was the presumption that Youqian would respond militarily in the capital. Now confronted with Chongtao's death, Youqian conspires with Li Cunyi to avenge the injustice against Mr. Guo." Zhuangzong was initially skeptical, but the accusations of actors and eunuchs continued day and night.

News of such allegations left Zhu Youqian dreadfully afraid, so he prepared to appear at court to explain matters. Commanders and aides uniformly counseled against the trip, but Youqian insisted, "Gentleman Guo contributed eminently to the empire, yet died through slander. If I do not personally explain matters, who will speak for me?" He entered the capital riding a single carriage. Jing Jin arranged for someone illicitly to alter a letter, accusing Youqian of rebellion. A deluded Zhuangzong banished Youqian to the Yicheng governorship, dispatching Zhu Shouyin that night to surround his hostel with military regiments. Shouyin forced Youqian beyond the Hui'an gate to murder him, as the court restored his original name.

The court mandated that the Prince of Wei, Jiji, murder Youqian's son Lingde at Suizhou‡, that Wang Sitong murder son Lingxi at Xuzhou‡, and that Xia Luqi liquidate family dependents at Hezhong. Luqi was met by Youqian's wife, Woman Zhang, upon arrival at their home, along with two hundred members of her extended family. "The Zhu family must die, but I hope you do not extend punishments needlessly to commoners," she pleaded. After separating a hundred slaves and servants, a hundred Zhu kinsmen went to their deaths. Woman Zhang had earlier entered the home to show the iron writ to Luqi, as she asked, "This was conferred by the Emperor. The meaning of the words eludes me!" Luqi felt ashamed. In the aftermath of Youqian's demise, seven of his commanders, including Shi Wu, were executed through association, along with their entire families. The world deemed it an injustice.

Yuan Xiangxian

Native to Xiayi, Songzhou, Yuan Xiangxian [C.E. 864–923] descended from the Tang-dynasty Prince of Nanyang, Yuan Shuji. His father, Yuan Jingchu, held office under the Liang dynasty as minister of supplemental revenues and commissioner of reserve cavalry, having married the younger sister of Emperor Taizu, the Senior Princess Wang'an. As an in-law of Liang royalty, Xiangxian rose to chief commander of infantry and cavalry at the Xuanwu command. He also served successively as prefect of Su, Ming, and Chen‡ prefectures. The formal accession of Taizu led to promotions as commander-in-general of the Dragonly Martial Left Guard and chief commander of infantry and cavalry in the metropolitan area.

With Taizu falling to regicide as Yougui installed himself in power, the future Emperor Mo continued to defend the eastern capital and consulted Zhao Yan on the strategic challenge. Yan argued, "This matter is as simple as turning the palm of a hand. All you need to succeed is a single directive to the Imperial Guard from the Honorable Mr. Yang." Emperor Mo thus sent a messenger to Weizhou to apprise Yang Shihou of his plans, Shihou responding by sending his deputy commander, Wang Shunxian, to Luoyang to meet and strategize with Yuan Xiangxian, who consented to join the conspirators.

At the time, Dragon-Prancing contingents commanded by Liu Chongyu, garrisoned at Huaizhou‡, had turned mutinous. Yougui thus dispatched Huo Yanwei to storm them at Yanling. He prevailed and their residuals scattered, an intensive round of arrests ensuing. The future Emperor Mo [Prince of Jun] then called in Dragon-Prancing armies for the eastern capital to inform them, "Because of the Chongyu incident, His Majesty [Yougui] intends to summon all Dragon-Prancing contingents to Luoyang for liquidation." He also fabricated an edict in Yougui's name to show them, instilling terror in these men, who could not decide on a course of action. Mo thus proposed, "Yougui has committed regicide against his own father and ruler, making him the world's premier renegade. If you can rush to Luoyang to apprehend him and offer his head in sacrifice to the Former Emperor, you may well 'turn peril into prosperity,' as the adage goes." The soldiers all leaped in excitement as they cheered, "The Prince's words are right." Mo promptly petitioned the court to indicate, "the Dragon-Prancing armies are in mutiny." The message gave Xiangxian cause to direct a thousand men from the Palace Guard into the palace for an assault on Yougui, who perished. Emperor Mo now acceded to the throne, and Xiangxian became governor of the Zhennan command with nominal powers as chief minister, metropolitan prefect of Kaifeng, and administrator of all metropolitan infantry and cavalry. In the fourth year of Zhenming [C.E. 918], he became the Pinglu governor before reassignment as Xuanwu governor.

Yuan Xiangxian, as Liang commander, had never proven merit in battle, his control of armies based on connections as imperial in-law. His role in executing Yougui now created merit with Emperor Mo. Through ten years or more of administration at Songzhou, he exacted heavily from the people, building a cache worth tens of millions. He attended court at Luoyang upon Zhuangzong's conquest of Liang, bringing along valuables worth hundreds of thousands to bribe martial ministers, actors, eunuchs, Empress Liu, and the like. In this way, he won uniform praise from those in and away from the capital. Zhuangzong treated him with exceptional bounty, conferring the name Li Shao'an and changing the name of the Xuanwu command to Guide. "I name Guide [Return to Virtue] in your honor," Zhuangzong once declared.

Sent back to his home district, Xiangxian died that year [C.E. 923] at sixty *sui*, the posthumous rank of grand preceptor conferred.

Xiangxian had two sons: *Yuan Zhengci* rose in office to prefect and *Yuan Yi* to Henghai governor during the Zhou-dynasty reign of Shizong. Over his lifetime, Xiangxian had amassed a fortune worth countless millions,[3] in addition to four thousand estates and houses. These were not divided among surviving sons upon his death, but given entirely to Zhengci. His father's standing had initially enabled Zhengci to become deputy commissioner of Flying Dragon forces. He donated to the government some fifty thousand strings of cash, during the Tang reign of Emperor Fei, for which concurrent powers as prefect of Quzhou were conferred. He donated another fifty thousand strings upon the accession of Gaozu of Jin, seeking an appointment as prefect with substantive powers. The court named him prefect of Xiongzhou, a prefecture situated west of Lingwu and east of the Tubo Tibetan border. Zhengci dallied, not wishing to proceed, then presented several tens of thousands in cash for release from the post. Still unable to overcome the sense of indignity, Zhengci tried to use a cloth sash to hang himself, only to be saved by his family's intervention. The donation of thirty thousand strings of cash and ten thousand ounces of silver won over Emperor Chu, once in power: a post for Zhengci in the interior was planned, but he died beforehand.

Yuan Zhengci's cash holdings could fill an entire room. Sounds approximating those of oxen were once heard in the room, which people reckoned an evil spirit that would be appeased only if the wealth was scattered. But Zhengci retorted, "When animals make sounds, I am told, they are merely seeking one of their own. By increasing my cash, therefore, the sound will surely cease!" Listeners later passed the story around as a joke.

Duan Ning

Duan Ning [d. C.E. 927], a native of Kaifeng, began with the personal name Mingyuan and later adopted Ning. He was once a magistrate's assistant at Mianchi County. His father had served under Taizu of Liang but had been demoted owing to some incident. Ning later abandoned his own civil office to serve similarly under Taizu's command, becoming inspecting officer of the armed forces. His attractive younger sister entered the harem of Taizu and later became the "Beautiful Consort."

Duan Ning was a man clever at flattery and adept at intuiting and accommodating the wishes of others. This, combined with his younger sister's favor, enabled him gradually to enjoy the intimacy and confidence of Taizu, who named him inspector for a succession of armies. As prefect of Huaizhou‡, Taizu passed through the prefecture during a northern campaign; Ning provided a stunning array of rations, leaving Taizu exhilarated. When he passed through Xiangzhou‡, prefect Li Si'an afforded Taizu's men rations commensurate with current protocol, but seemingly parsimonious in comparison. Si'an thereby incited Taizu and incurred his wrath, dying in consequence. Ning now became prefect of Zhengzhou, assigned to supervise troops along the Yellow River. Li Zhen petitioned stridently for his dismissal. "Ning has done no wrong," Taizu insisted. To this, Zhen retorted, "If we wait until some offense is committed, the dynasty and its ritual altars will have perished!" Dismissal never came.

Zhuangzong had already conquered Wei and Bo prefectures and faced off the Liang from opposite sides of the Yellow River. The Liang deployed Wang Yanzhang as commissioner of bandit suppression, Ning serving as his deputy. At the time, a muddled Emperor Mo entrusted affairs to Zhao Yan and Zhang Hanjie, so Ning allied with Yan and cohort to act on his sinister agenda. As commissioner, Yanzhang had employed spectacular strategies to overpower, in only three days, the southern city of Desheng, a commandery under Tang control. Ning nonetheless submitted a report to the court, separate from Yanzhang, where he ruminated on his own feats. Yan and cohort chose to conceal the achievement report of Yanzhang and attribute to Ning all merit in the effort. Ning then plied Yan and cohort with gold, requesting to replace Yanzhang. Emperor Mo was duped by Yan's words and authorized appointment as bandit-suppressing commissioner. Ning's armies were stationed at Wangcun.

At the time, Tang armies had overpowered Yunzhou. Duan Ning responded by breaking dikes on the Yellow River to permit its flow eastward from Suanzao County to Yunzhou, cutting off Tang armies in the process—dubbed "waters to protect the imperial progress." Zhuangzong then rushed from Yunzhou to Bianzhou, where troops were entirely subordinate to Ning. The capital lacked defense preparations, so the court employed Zhang Hanlun as express courier to summon back Ning from the upper Yellow River region. En route, Hanlun was thrown from his horse and sustained injuries that prevented him from advancing. The Liang subsequently collapsed and Ning led fifty thousand crack troops in surrendering to Tang, as Zhuangzong conferred a gown of brocade and an imperial horse. Ning memorialized the court, on the next day, arguing, "When the sinister band of ten led by Zhao Yan and Zhang Hanjie dominated the former Liang dynasty, their power games had cost the lives of many. I beg to have them and their families liquidated."

Duan Ning felt no awkwardness about his comings and goings at the Tang court, performing like an actor before the dynasty's commanders and ministers. He bribed Empress Liu through the actor Jing Jin to gain the court's favor. Zhuangzong loved him enormously and conferred the name Li Shaoqin, appointing him governor of Taining. In just over a month at the command, he spent cash from its treasury totaling several hundred thousand strings, for which the relevant officials at court sought to hold him personally liable for restitution. Zhuangzong forgave the debt, even as Guo Chongtao adamantly insisted on indemnity. An agitated Zhuangzong roared back, "I use you to issue directives—nothing derives from your own authority!" The debt was ultimately forgiven.

Li Shaohong had been sent by Zhuangzong to supervise the preparation of commanders against the Khitan. Duan Ning, garrisoned at Waqiao Pass, used the occasion to flatter Shaohong, who in turn, recommended Ning as a great talent over and again. Each time, Guo Chongtao insisted to the contrary. Ning was governor of the Wusheng command when Zhao Zaili rebelled, Shaohong proposing that Ning lead the suppression. Zhuangzong probed Ning on line advances and strategies, but the officer assignments sought by Ning were all old cronies of his. Zhuangzong came to question his competence, and the appointment never occurred. He was compelled to retire upon the accession of Mingzong. In the next year [C.E. 927], exiled to a remote Liaozhou, he committed suicide at court orders.

CHAPTERS 46–47

MISCELLANEOUS BIOGRAPHIES

Zhao Zaili

His courtesy name Ganchen, Zhao Zaili [C.E. 881–942] was native to Zhuozhou. In youth, he served as a lieutenant under Liu Rengong, who had sent Zaili to assist his son, Liu Shouwen, in a successful sortie on Cangzhou. Younger brother Shouguang slew Shouwen as Zaili sought sanctuary with the Jin. He became commander of Dedicated forces in the reign of Zhuangzong, garrisoning troops from Weizhou at Waqiao Pass. He had reached Beizhou on the return trip when a mutiny erupted there, led by local warrior Huangfu Hui. The mutineers had initially elevated commander Yang Rencheng [Renzheng] as their leader, and when he refused to cooperate, murdered him to elevate a minor lieutenant, whose similar refusal led to his murder as well. Carrying the two heads, Hui went to confront Zaili. News of the mutiny prompted Zaili to attempt leaping over the wall of his home, his clothes still unfastened, but Hui grabbed his feet to pull him down. Hui now dangled the two heads, brandishing naked swords in forming a circle around Zaili and threatening, "If you fail to join us, your head will end up like these." Zaili thereby assisted their mutiny.

From Beizhou, Zhao Zaili returned for an assault on Weizhou, permitting troops to pillage extensively. Upon news of Zaili's arrival, the metropolitan custodian of Xingtang at the time, Wang Zhengyan—a man left decrepit and muddled by old age—summoned aides to draft petitions for him. His aides had scattered, yet a still unaware Zhengyan raged with fury as he leaned forward against his desk. Remaining aides informed him, "The renegades are already killing city residents, while aides and commoners have all absconded. Whom are we to summon?" Profoundly shocked, Zhengyan admitted, "I had an inkling of this!" He gathered reins to leave, but a stable hand informed him, "Your wife and sons have been taken captive, Sir. Why bother to find a horse?" In dreaded fright, Zhengyan emerged from his office gates on foot to meet Zaili, kneeling to bow in his direction. Zaili cried out to him, "The Gentleman scarcely needs to humble himself in this way! My actions reflect the wishes of troops, not myself." Zaili hence installed himself as interim regent for military affairs.

Zhuangzong entrusted the suppression effort against Zaili to Yuan Xingqin, but assaults on Weizhou proved inconclusive and the future Mingzong was sent to replace him. A mutiny in his ranks erupted as Mingzong reached the Ye capital, so he entered the city to mend relations with Zaili. Mingzong's armies later headed back to the capital, Zaili remaining behind at Weizhou. Upon acceding to the throne, Mingzong named him governor of the Yicheng command. Zaili declined the assignment, later to become interim custodian of the Ye capital and metropolitan custodian of Xingtang. Huangfu Hui and cohort all departed in time, leaving Zaili alone at Weizhou. He continued to worry that the arrogance of Wei troops might bring calamity upon himself and requested reassignment as the Henghai governor. He also served successively at the Taining, Kuangguo, Tianping, Zhongwu, Wuning, Guide, and Jinchang commands—official residences at every post brimming with objects valued at many tens of thousands.

Under Emperor Chu of the Jin dynasty, Zhao Zaili became chief inspector of infantry and cavalry at large in the northern theater, conducting sallies against the Khitan, although never once prevailing in battle. Toiling acutely under his administration were the people of Songzhou, such that Zaili's later reassignment delighted its residents, who exclaimed to one another, "A nail is being plucked from our eye. Why should we not celebrate?" The court decided to continue him in that post, however, and he imposed an assessment of a thousand cash for every person registered in his domain—dubbing these "monies for plucking the nail."

With the Khitan occupation of Bianzhou that attended the Jin dynasty's demise, Zhao Zaili rushed to Luoyang from Songzhou. There he met the Khitan, Yela, and bowed before his horse's head. Yela's troops joined in demeaning him, badgering him for money and valuables. Zaili could scarcely contain his fury. Upon proceeding to Zhengzhou, he learned that most senior officials of Jin had been fettered by the Khitan. Amid nocturnal anxieties and apprehensions, he loosened the sash from his robe and went to a horse stable to hang himself. He died at sixty-two *sui*. The posthumous title of palace secretary was conferred under Gaozu of Han.

Huo Yanwei

He had the courtesy name Zichong and was native to Quzhou County, Mingzhou. Facing tumult in his youth, Huo Yanwei [d. C.E. 928] was abducted by the Liang commander Huo Cun, who found the gallantry of the youth endearing and raised him as son. Assisting Cun in battle, Yanwei was once struck by an arrow and lost an eye. He later served Taizu of Liang, who grew similarly fond of him, resulting in eventual promotions to commissioner of the Dragon-Prancing Left Guard and generalissimo of the Palace-Gate Right Guard. His merit in the cabal to execute Zhu Yougui [C.E. 913] led to posting as prefect of Mingzhou, then governor of the Bin/Ning command.

Li Maozhen had commissioned Liu Zhijun, the former Liang commander who had defected to him, with an offensive against Binzhou, yet Huo Yanwei defended the city doggedly for over a year. Whenever obtaining Zhijun's troops, Yanwei invariably returned them, so impressing Zhijun that he later refused new attacks. Yanwei was reassigned to the Yicheng governorship, then that of Tianping, with concurrent powers as commissioner of bandit suppression for at-large armies on the northern front. In the standoff with the Prince of Jin's armies along the Yellow River, Yanwei suffered a string of defeats, demotion ensuing as interim regent of Shanzhou.

After the Liang was overturned by Zhuangzong of Tang, Huo Yanwei came to court from Shanzhou and Zhuangzong held a banquet at the former Chongyuan palace of Liang times. Yanwei and other Liang commanders such as Duan Ning and Yuan Xiangxian were all present. An inebriated Zhuangzong raised his goblet to [perceived rival] Mingzong while pointing to Yanwei and cohort, saying, "My most intimidating foes of yesterday accompanying us in drink today—and you pulled it off!" Struck with horror, Yanwei and cohort fell prostrate on the floor, submitting themselves for capital punishment. "I am merely poking fun at my top commander [Mingzong]," Zhuangzong said consolingly. "There is nothing to fear." He conferred the name Li Shaozhen and reassigned Yanwei to the Wuning command a year later. Yanwei assisted Mingzong in a raid on the Khitan, Mingzong growing fond of his character and developing a deep intimacy and favor.

The rebellion of Zhao Zaili later erupted, and Huo Yanwei conducted a separate punitive operation against Zhao Tai at Xingzhou, overrunning the prefecture. He then returned to assist in the suppression of Zaili [at Weizhou], subordinating his troops to the future Mingzong. With the mutiny in Mingzong's ranks, his cavalry-escort commander, Zhang Pobai, led subordinates in murdering lieutenant commanders, setting fire to their barracks, and inciting rancor. Mingzong railed at them, stating, "Through over a decade of commanding armies, have I ever failed you? Now conquest of the renegade city lies only a morning or evening away, an occasion for all of you to establish your merit while securing wealth and status. For the bodyguard of the Son of Heaven no less, how can you possibly turn around and mimic renegades?" The warriors countered, "What crime did the men in this city commit? They were merely soldiers on border assignment who wished to return home, acting without authorization. The Son of Heaven refused to extend leniency, intent on an oppressive eradication. Once Weizhou falls, we hear, he even intends a thorough liquidation of Wei/Bo armies, men merely fearful of death with no initial desire to defect. We prefer to consolidate our forces with men in the city, storming armies of the various governors [loyal to the court] to effect their retreat. We further wish for the Son of Heaven to preside over the southern Yellow River region, while you, Sir, govern the northern regions." Mingzong sobbed in admonishing them, but the renegades formed a circle around him, clamoring, "If you, Sir, will not be emperor of the northern regions, someone else will. Much like jackals or lions, discerning the noble from the ignoble is simply beyond us."

Yanwei joined An Chonghui in encouraging Mingzong to relent, his troops hence directed into the city to merge with Zaili's men. Only Yanwei's army was held back. After entering the city, Mingzong feasted grandly with Zaili. Divisions outside the city absconded upon news of his rebellion, save for five thousand troops brought by Yanwei, now posted at the northwest corner of the city and holding that position. Mingzong reemerged within two days: with Yanwei's remnants, he proceeded to Wei County, intending to return to Zhenzhou. At the insistence of Yanwei and Chonghui, he led armies southward instead.

Once Zhuangzong had expired, Huo Yanwei helped Mingzong occupy Luoyang, as Yanwei personally led a multitude of courtiers in rallying for Mingzong's accession to the throne. Important affairs of every sort, within or without the palace, all came to be decided by Yanwei in consequence. Longstanding rifts with Duan Ning and Wen Tao ultimately caused Yanwei to arrest and jail them illicitly, intending an assassination when An Chonghui intervened. "The evils of Ning and Tao are already known to the world," Chonghui asserted. "Yet precisely as His Majesty attempts to pacify domestic challenges and needs to demonstrate charity and confidence to the people, it is scarcely the occasion, Sir, for you to exact revenge!" Yanwei thus desisted. Upon formal accession, Mingzong pardoned Ning and Tao for return to their villages, where they eventually received orders to commit suicide.

Huo Yanwei was reassigned as the Pinglu governor. In the wake of rebel Zhu Shouyin's execution, Yanwei sent an express courier to present two arrows to the Emperor in celebration. Mingzong reciprocated by giving two arrows to him. When barbarians wish to instruct issuing armies, the passing of arrows [with attached message] occurs as a form of command. Therefore, a subordinate cannot employ arrows for his superior. Mingzong originated with the barbarians and Yanwei was a man of the military, yet ruler and subject alike failed to appreciate the protocol. Many similar actions occurred.

Yanwei had a retainer, Chunyu Yan, a native of Dengzhou‡ who had passed the "classics" examination in his youth. Happening upon tumultuous times, he became Yanwei's dependent and served him as early as his days as assisting commander. Yanwei was once vanquished in battle and barely managed to abscond, not a single soldier under his banner able to follow. Yan alone escaped on foot, carrying a single sword and trailing him through a thicket of thorns and brambles. Yan's righteousness thus commanded Yanwei's esteem, such that Yanwei arranged staff appointments for Yan through a string of assignments as governor. All affairs of his household, great or small, were decided by Yan. For this reason, Yanwei was given to committing minor mistakes or excesses. The rule permitting governors to bring along their own civilian aides began with Yan.

Huo Yanwei died in his district in the third year of Tiancheng [C.E. 928]. Mingzong was hunting in nearby suburbs when a courier from Qingzhou† announced the death. He returned to his palace in tears, suspending court and forgoing all merriment for the remainder of the month. The posthumous rank of grand preceptor and title "Loyal and Martial" were conferred.

Wang Yanqiu

Native to Luoyang, Wang Yanqiu [C.E. 868–929] had the courtesy name Yingzhi. Owing to the chaos of his early years, he was abducted by brigands, then acquired by a well-to-do man at Bianzhou, surnamed Du, who raised him as a son and had him assume the Du surname. Taizu of Liang, as Xuanwu governor, would later recruit youths with martial talents from the homes of the wealthy, placing them under his personal command and calling them the "Chamber Brigade." An animated man of immense integrity, Yanqiu became the brigade's chief commander, then commander of the Thousand-Bull Right Guard upon Taizu's accession to the throne. Dragon-Prancing garrison troops mutinied in the wake of Yougui's accession, rushing the capital from Huaizhou‡. Sent to storm them, Yanqiu prevailed at Heyang and consequently won promotion to premier commander of Dragon-Prancing contingents.

Reassignment as commander of the fourth contingent of Dragon-Prancing forces attended the accession of Emperor Mo. The Liang court had dispatched Li Ba, commander of the Life-Sustaining Guard, to station a thousand men at Yangliu. He mutinied one night and entered the town along its canal gate, setting random fires and inducing widespread rancor. He even employed long bamboo poles tipped with rags drenched in enriched oil to propel flames against the Jianguo gates. Learning of the mutiny, Yanqiu refused to await court orders and led five hundred horsemen from Dragon-Prancing contingents in a rush on the renegades, causing their powers to wane. Emperor Mo climbed the tower, exclaiming as he observed the rebels, "Is that not my Dragon-Prancing Guard?" "The rebels represent the single brigade of Li Ba," Yanqiu informed him. "Your Majesty should rigorously defend the royal city, leaving defeat of the brigands to me." The renegades were all dead by daybreak, Yanqiu's merit leading to appointment as prefect of Chan.

During the Liang/Jin standoff along the Yellow River, Yanqiu was named chief commander of infantry and cavalry at large. With Zhuangzong approaching Bianzhou, Yanqiu pursued him as far as Fengqiu County upon word of Emperor Mo's death. He doffed his armor in surrender to Tang, as Zhuangzong conferred the name Li Shaoqian and assigned him defense commissioner for Qizhou¶, his troops stationed at Waqiao Pass.

Later, Mingzong's armies forced their mutinous agenda upon him. As he proceeded from Ye, he dispatched a messenger to sway Wang Yanqiu, who now accompanied Mingzong to Luoyang. Yanqiu subsequently became the Guide governor. In the wake of Wang Du's uprising at Dingzhou, the court entrusted the pacification effort to Yanqiu, as commissioner of bandit suppression, and Zhang Yanlang, commissioner of the southern court of palace armies. Du now invited Khitan intervention through a messenger and they assisted with ten thousand cavalry under the command of Tunei. After receiving news that Tunei's men had arrived, Yanqiu left behind Yanlang at encampments in Xinle County and personally coursed upstream to Wangdu County. Meanwhile, the Khitan entered Dingzhou from another direction and assisted Wang Du in a surprise strike against Yanlang's armies, delivering a resounding defeat. Yanlang now collected remnant forces and rendezvoused with Yanqiu in a rush toward Quyang County. Wang Du pursued them, wishing to exploit his momentum.

Wang Yanqiu reached the waterside first and was directing bannermen from his northern chair when Wang Du arrived without warning.[1] Yanqiu and more than ten companions unleashed on them a relentless barrage of arrows, forcing Du's men to retreat somewhat, as Yanqiu's rear contingents caught up. Standing upon a high mound, Yanqiu instructed all commanders to stow their bows and arrows: dispatching weapons for close combat, he threatened to decapitate anyone looking back. Fu Yanqing now attacked Wang Du's left flank with the Left Guard as Gao Xinggui [Xingzhou] struck his right flank with the Right Guard; cavalry in the Center Guard, clinging to the napes of their horses' necks, lunged into Du's armies. Du was routed, the landscape littered for more than sixty *li* from Quyang to Dingzhou with human remains and abandoned armor. Du and Tunei then entered the city, not daring to leave again. The Khitan sent another seven thousand cavalry, under the command of an administrator for royal affairs, as reinforcements for Du. Yanqiu confronted them at Tanghe County and directed an aggressive pursuit to Mancheng, claiming two thousand human heads and commandeering a thousand horses.

Through the many preoccupations of the Middle Kingdom, the Khitan emerged as a mighty force to its north such that assorted barbarian tribes there, regardless of size, all deferred to them in fear. And whenever armies of the Middle Kingdom engaged the Khitan, never did they succeed even slightly at obtaining their goals. After Yanqiu stormed and vanquished Tunei, then ran off their administrator for royal affairs, the residuals of the two Khitan commanders scattered for rural areas. Villagers wielding hoes, harrows, and white sticks wherever available now beat them to death, leaving no survivors. The administrator for royal affairs and several dozen horsemen fled to the west of Youzhou, where they were apprehended by Zhao Dejun and conveyed to the capital. An edict rebuking the Khitan was issued by Mingzong. The Khitan themselves sent a succession of envoys to the Middle Kingdom seeking the return of their royal affairs officer, their emissaries especially humble and submissive in speech. Mingzong summarily executed the envoys and severed relations with the Khitan. The omnipotence of the Middle Kingdom reverberated like a powerful jolt, at the time, as Khitan power slackened somewhat. It began with Yanqiu.

Yanqiu's offensive against Dingzhou for a long while proved inconclusive, and Mingzong repeatedly urged him via special messenger to suppress the enemy swiftly. Yanqiu argued against an intensive onslaught, yet assisting commanders Zhu Hongzhao and Zhang Qianzhao, characterizing Yanqiu as "utterly craven," pressed armies to advance. Their men were ultimately vanquished and sustained more than three thousand deaths or injuries. Hereafter, the commanders never again demanded an offensive. Yanqiu rested his troops, subsisting on tax revenues from the three prefectures. He even lavished his entire salary on beef and wine, accompanying commanders in festive banquets each day. Wang Du's city did deplete food supplies after some time. Initially releasing more than ten thousand residents, he and Tunei often plotted to break the blockade and flee, never managing to act. Surrender of the city came at the hands of Du's own commander, Ma Rangneng, as he set himself afire and died.

As commander, Wang Yanqiu was a cunning strategist, adept at cultivating the loyalty of his men as well. In sorties against Tunei, he managed to turn old losses into new wins. His commanders all preferred to exploit the momentum of victory to vanquish Wang Du. Contrarily, Yanqiu alone opposed action and ultimately undermined Du through protracted resistance. Du rebelled in the fourth month of the third year of Tiancheng [C.E. 928], the suppression against him beginning to succeed in the second month of the next year. Throughout, never once did Yanqiu have to kill men in his own armies [for disciplinary problems]. Merit in vanquishing Du led to promotion as governor of the Tianping command and subsequently Pinglu. Yanqiu's official rank rose to palace secretary. He died in the same year at sixty-two *sui*, given posthumous rank as grand marshal.

Wang Jianli

Native to Yushe, Liaozhou, Wang Jianli [C.E. 877–946] had served as inspecting commander under the future Mingzong, then prefect of Daizhou. Zhuangzong once sent a female slave to Daizhou to sacrifice at a tomb site, but the slave harassed and harangued local authorities, prompting Jianli to arrest and flog her with a light rod. Angered by the affront, Zhuangzong wanted to kill him, but Jianli evaded punishment under the protection of Mingzong. In the wake of Mingzong's mutiny at Weizhou and raid on the capital, his wives at Changshan, the future Empress Cao and Pure Consort Wang, were both vulnerable. Jianli murdered the military overseer at Changshan and his defending troops to spare Mingzong's dependents the usual calamity. Mingzong grew ever fond of him, in consequence. Jianli became deputy governor of the Chengde command upon Mingzong's accession to the throne, later governor there, ranked provisional grand marshal with standing as chief minister.

Owing to Jianli's strained relations with An Chonghui, the treachery-minded Wang Du of Dingzhou contacted Jianli repeatedly by letter to swear fraternal bonds. Chonghui learned of the matter and reported it, but Mingzong refused to harm Jianli and ordered his prompt return to the capital. Entering for audience, Jianli proceeded to enumerate Chonghui's many failings, information that thoroughly riled Mingzong, who contemplated summary dismissal. He desisted only under the admonition of official multitudes and close aides. Jianli finally rose to right associate at the Imperial Secretariat with ministerial powers and senior administrator at the Three Fiscal Agencies. Over a year later, he wanted to relinquish powers as fiscal administrator on admission of being unable to read, Mingzong refusing. Jianli employed the pretext of illness sometime later, Mingzong now remarking in jest, "Surely there are men with contrived illnesses who actually get sick!" Assigned away from the capital as the Pinglu governor, then reassigned as governor of Shangdang, Jianli was disgruntled for failing to achieve his aims and hence sought release from official duties. He retired with the rank of junior guardian to the heir-apparent.

Wang Jianli, after numerous requests for court audience, then denials, proceeded to the capital on his own initiative, unceremoniously going to the rear tower to meet Mingzong. There, weeping and professing his own innocence, he blamed Chonghui for his banishment. "You accomplished nothing notable as governor," Mingzong countered. "Chonghui's presumable slanders against you cannot be singularly responsible!" He lavished gifts of tea and medicine on Jianli before sending him off. The enthronement of Emperor Fei saw Jianli's resuscitation as Tianping governor.

Reassignment to the Pinglu command occurred in the Jin-dynasty reign of Gaozu. Appearing at court in the fifth year of Tianfu [C.E. 940], Jianli was consoled by Gaozu's words, "My esteemed Elder brother of thirty years—you hardly need to bow before me!" He allowed Jianli to enter court on a sedan chair, providing two eunuchs to brace him by the arm in ascending the steps of the audience chamber, their meeting festive and their eyes reddened. He reassigned Jianli to the Zhaoyi command, conferring a jade ax and prize horse from Shu. Investitures culminated in the Prince of Han. Jianli had been fond of murdering others but began in waning years to succumb to Buddhist heresy, which renounces the killing of sentient beings. The people at his posts could now enjoy modest relief. He died at seventy *sui*, receiving posthumous rank as imperial secretary.

His son, *Wang Shou'en*, received office through family privilege, eventually rising to commander of the Imperial Guard. Jianli's family was at Luzhou when he died and Shou'en received notice from the capital of the need to return. The Khitan had just overturned the Jin dynasty, and Shou'en was appointed provisional military inspector for Luzhou by the Zhaoyi governor, Zhang Cong'en, a man related to Shou'en by marriage. Cong'en went to the capital to meet Khitan occupiers, and in his absence Shou'en pilfered his family possessions and surrendered Luzhou to the Han dynasty. With the accession of Gaozu to the Han throne, Shou'en became the Zhaoyi governor and later the Jingnan governor, with powers as interim custodian of the western capital and honorary rank as chief minister.

Shou'en was by character vulgar and greedy, the people toiling bitterly under his administration. At the time, the future Taizu of Zhou, then military commissioner, commanded the armies of Bai Wenke and others in suppressing the three mutinies out west. They passed through Luoyang on the return, where Shou'en rode a sedan chair to greet them, deporting himself with the pretense of a governor or minister. An angry Taizu, by informal military directive, ordered on the very same day that Wenke replace Shou'en as interim custodian. Having departed for the hostel to await a meeting with Taizu, Shou'en sat boldly in the seat of honor. An aide hastily entered to announce the commencement of business at the prefectural offices by the new interim custodian, leaving him thoroughly startled and speechless. Now dismissed, Jianli received the honorary rank of *fengchaoqing* in the capital.

Emperor Yin later murdered Shi Hongzhao and cohort, then summoned courtiers to audience chambers ostensibly to console and instruct him. The multitude of officials, anxious and afraid, dared not speak, except for Shou'en, who stepped forward to ask, "Has Your Majesty just awakened from sleep?" Listeners all drew back their necks in horror. He died in the Xiande era [C.E. 954–960] as left generalissimo of the Imperial Insignia Guard.

WE LAMENT. Morality and virtue, benevolence and righteousness—these are the tools of good governance. Rules and regulations, principles and precepts—these are needed to buttress it. Since antiquity, empires facing turmoil and ruin have invariably allowed rules and regulations to be destroyed first, turmoil later flowing from this. When turmoil and destruction feed on one another to ravage principles and precepts beyond the point of revival, the extreme of all-pervading turmoil must occur before a reversal is possible. This is an outgrowth of natural forces, and the Five Dynasties era is illustrative.

Bai Wenke and Wang Shou'en, both ranked as commanders and ministers, were senior officials of the Han no less. But Taizu of Zhou employed an informal directive as military commissioner to replace one for the other, as if changing mere border guards. Taizu had not reached the point of breaking with the Han dynasty, treacherous insubordination still unknown to his heart. Why, then, did he act in this way? Inasmuch as his habits were common knowledge and Taizu expressed pleasure or displeasure with the move of his chin, Wenke dared not act contrarily and Shou'en never offered resistance. Taizu disposed of the matter without vacillating, while subjects at the Han court conformed without questioning. When superiors and inferiors calmly consider such practices unexceptional, it can only suggest that the ravaging of dynastic rules and regulations, principles and precepts had already reached an extreme, even though evolving over a long course. This should concern those given to pondering world affairs, who know not to slight minor symptoms, but intervene as matters are gradually unfolding. Should we not take heed?

Zhang Yun

Zhang Yun was native to Haizhou, his family involved in commerce for generations. He served under governor Shi Pu as prefect of Suzhou, falling into the hands of Liang soldiers during their assault on Pu and conquest of Suzhou. Taizu of Liang, with an affinity for Yun's debating skills and beneficence, named him attending commander of four districts, commander of long-distance armies, and eventually commissioner of palace armies. Once the three prefectures of Xiang‡, Chan, and Wei‡ were diverted [from Weizhou] to form the Zhaode command, Yun became the governor there; a mutiny at the Wei/Bo command ensued, authorities surrendering to the Prince of Jin. The Prince now raided Xiangzhou‡ and forced Yun to flee the city, later becoming governor of the Yongping command.

With the Liang demise, Zhang Yun served the Tang as metropolitan custodian of Jingzhao [Changan]. He assisted Guo Chongtao in the campaign against Shu, as pacification commissioner for the two circuits of Chuan. The pacification of Shu led to appointment as metropolitan prefect of Henan, then governor of Xingyuan. He once refused to meet commanders or senior aides owing to illness. When deputy governor Fu Yanlin entered to inquire of his health and Yun again spurned visits, he suspected that Yun had already died and requested the immediate removal of official tablets and seals. The action infuriated Yun, who instructed aides to arrest and confine Yanlin to jail, informing the court of his mutiny. Mingzong found no evidence of Yanlin's intent to rebel and summoned him to court for a pardon. Formally ordering Yun's reassignment as interim custodian of the western capital, he advised authorities there against accepting him, at the same time. Unable to enter Changan upon arrival there, Yun went to the capital for audience. He was named generalissimo of the Valorous Left Guard.

Yun's younger brother *Zhang Jian* served as director of the governor's guard during Yun's tenure as metropolitan custodian of Jingzhao, as well as regional commissioner of agriculture for Sanbai Channel. Jian stayed behind as custodian of Jingzhao after Yun's departure for the Shu campaign. After pacifying Shu, the withdrawal of troops was mandated by the Prince of Wei, Jiji, and Jian proceeded to Xingping. Mingzong's armies turned mutinous at Weizhou as pandemic turmoil swept the capital. Jian now severed the suspension bridge at Xianyang County to resist Jiji, who committed suicide.

Before this, Yun had replaced Kang Huaiying as the Yongping governor [of Changan] and pilfered Huaiying's family possessions after his death. Yun even burrowed beneath the old palaces of Tang to obtain many items of gold and jade. Two assistant commanders, Hou Mo and Chen Wei, had assisted Wen Tao in plundering the Tang imperial tombs, the two dividing the treasure trove between them. Yun eventually murdered Wei over some incident and seized the treasure. Jiji, the Prince of Wei, later died at Weinan, his travel bags all looted by Jian. [Surrendered potentate] Wang Yan had reached the Qinchuan

River [near Luoyang] in the trek from Shu when Zhuangzong dispatched the eunuch Xiang Yansi to kill him, so Yansi obtained all of the precious treasures of Shu then in Yan's possession. Yansi absconded, however, after the accession of Mingzong, who sent agents to arrest and execute eunuchs, the Shu treasures in his possession confiscated by Jian as well. In this way, the combined wealth of the two brothers grew to countless millions. Yun could be a charitable man, who, because of his wealth, did not exact heavily at the sites he served, the people finding security in his administration. However, Jian was given to heavy drinking, avarice, and rustic ways while governor of Yi† and later Mi prefectures. Under the Jin dynasty's Emperor Chu, he traded in horses with the Huihu Uighurs in his capacity as commander, but charges of importing horses below specifications were leveled against him. When judicial authorities demanded a full restitution of costs, a gauche Jian died of despondency.

The wealth carried by Zhang Yun to Luoyang, during his residence there, was enough to cover more than ten years of indulgence in wine, companions, and prostitutes—the people calling him the "Immortal on Earth." In the second year of Tianfu [C.E. 937], he relocated to Changan, but Zhang Congbin mutinied to occupy Luoyang the same year, Yun thereby escaping a violent end. He received posthumous rank as junior preceptor to the heir-apparent.

WE LAMENT. Rebels of the Five Dynasties are numerous, to be sure, but only for Mingzong do I have problems explaining things. He completed his usurpation only after the death of Jiji, the Prince of Wei.[2] The eldest son after Zhuangzong's death who controlled a vast army, Jiji died away from court and thereby lost the succession. Although a major incident, previous histories do not indicate how it came about. Whether Jiji lived or died had no impact, positive or negative, on Zhang Jian. Why did Jian offer the resistance that prevented Jiji from proceeding eastward? Did someone else facilitate Jian's interception? Mingzong felt profoundly obliged to Fu Yanchao, yet evinced no special generosity for Jian—another suspect issue. Subjects prone to exploit turmoil will simply look to the wind and follow its drift. Had the suspension bridge not been severed by Jian and Jiji managed to proceed eastward with his men, the installation of Mingzong might not have occurred. The death of Jiji stemming from Jian's resistance contains anything but trivial ramifications!

Zhang Xichong

With courtesy name Defeng, Zhang Xichong [d. C.E. 939] was native to Ji County, Youzhou. A youth fond of learning, he acquired a thoroughgoing command of the *Spring and Autumn Annals* and its Zuo Narratives. Liu

Shouguang disliked Confucian scholars, however, so Xichong served as assistant commander in his army, directing garrison forces at Pingzhou. The Khitan later attacked and felled Pingzhou, obtaining Xichong. They named him military adjutant of the Lulong command upon identifying him as a Confucian scholar.

Lu Wenjin abandoned Pingzhou to revert to the Tang dynasty during Mingzong's reign, the Khitan replacing him as Pingzhou governor with Xichong. The Khitan also stationed three hundred cavalry and a trusted commander to supervise him. After more than a year, the barbarian commander became attracted to his personality, causing some laxness in the oversight of armies that enabled Xichong and his bannermen to set plans to revert to the south. His subordinates argued that troops were too numerous to depart all at once, fearing that slipping away might be difficult, so they urged him to leave alone. Xichong insisted, "Barbarian forces contain a mere three hundred cavalry. We need only boil their commander alive and troops will surely scatter. Moreover, a thousand *li* separates Pingzhou from major barbarian camps. By the time they learn of the turmoil and rally troops, we all will have reached our own Han-Chinese border." His rank and file responded favorably and first dug pits to fill with lime. The barbarian commander visited him a day later, Xichong wining and dining him before slaying him in the lime pit. Khitan troops all absconded and Xichong managed to revert south with twenty thousand living souls under his banner. Mingzong applauded him with appointment as defense commissioner for Ruzhou.

Zhang Xichong later became the Lingwu governor. Ling Prefecture sits in close proximity to the northern and western barbarians, the supply lines for garrison troops often suffering under their plunder. Xichong later formed farm colonies, where soldiers were taught to till land. The armies came to have sufficient food, saving on the transportation of supplies. Mingzong issued an edict of praise, in fact. Xichong proved caring for his troops, while harmonizing relations with barbarian tribes: from Huihu-Uighur domains to prefectures such as Gua and Sha [Dunhuang], they all sent emissaries tendering tribute to the court. He held the post for four years upon petitioning to return to the interior, assuming the Bin/Ning command.

Reassignment to the Lingwu command attended Gaozu's accession to the Jin throne, prompting Xichong to comment, "It must be my destiny to die an old man on the frontier!" He served his mother with utmost filial devotion: at every morning and evening meal, he insisted on standing to her right or left side, waiting for the food to be taken away before leaving. He was a commander with no proclivity for indulgence in sensual pleasures. He liked reading books and knew a good deal about astronomy and calendars. In the third year of Tianfu [C.E. 938], the moon eclipsed the vast constellation of Hyades,

Xichong lamenting, "The vast Hyades symbolizes the commander at the border. [Its eclipse by the moon] can only pertain to my fate!" He died in the inaugural month of the next year, receiving posthumous rank as grand preceptor. He had a son named Renqian.

Huangfu Yu

Huangfu Yu was native to Zhending, Changshan. Brave and strong, he had curly whiskers and a gift for archery. In youth, he assisted Mingzong on campaign, rising under Tang rule to governor of the Wusheng command. He proved harsh and arbitrary wherever he served, concentrating on abusive exactions from the people: private secretaries and aides often abandoned offices or absconded to escape his peril.

In the reign of Gaozu of Jin, successive assignments came as governor of the Yiwu, Zhaoyi, Jianxiong, and Heyang commands, afterward becoming general commander of the Divinely Martial Guard. When the Khitan trespassed upon our lands to overrun Beizhou [C.E. 944], Emperor Chu designated Gao Xingzhou as chief officer for at-large forces on the northern front, Huangfu Yu serving as overseer of cavalry formations for right-wing contingents. At the time, Yang Guangyuan of Qingzhou† had occupied the city in rebellion, as Emperor Chu directed Li Shouzhen and Yu to launch independent efforts to defend Yunzhou. When Yu approached Majia Crossing, the Khitan prepared to ford the Yellow River to assist Guangyuan. Yu and his men stormed and defeated them, merit rewarded with assignment as the Yicheng governor and chief director of cavalry.

The Khitan having raided Xishan in the second year of Kaiyun [C.E. 945], the court instructed vanguard Zhao Yanshou to surround Zhenzhou. Du Chongwei dared not emerge for battle. Yanshou split his armies to plunder widely, raiding and overpowering nine counties, including Luancheng and Baixiang, extending southward as far as Xingzhou. All this coinciding with New Year's Eve, Emperor Chu and his intimates had been drinking so excessively that the sick Emperor could not leave on campaign. He entrusted the resistance instead to Zhang Cong'en, chief director of at-large forces in the northern theater, who rendezvoused with Ma Quanjie, An Shenqi, and Huangfu Yu. Upon arriving at Xiangzhou‡, Cong'en and the others stationed men south of the Anyang River, sending ahead several thousand cavalry under the command of Huangfu Yu and Murong Yanchao to observe barbarian movements. Ferrying across the Zhang River, Yu's men confronted several tens of thousands of barbarian soldiers and alternated in battles across an area exceeding ten *li*. Surrounded by the barbarians at Yulin, Yu's horse was hit by an arrow and fell to the ground. He now seized the horse of servant Du Zhimin and rode it into battle. Zhimin was captured by the barbarians. "Zhimin is a righteous soldier," Yu insisted to Yanchao. "How can we lose him?" The two men, leaping on their horses, lunged into the enemy to seize the youth and return.

Barbarian armies battled Huangfu Yu from early noon to late afternoon, dispersing and realigning as fresh troops increasingly emerged. Their powers thrived enormously. Turning to Yanchao, Yu asserted, "Strategic conditions today permit either combat or escape, nothing more. If exceptional at waging war, we may well survive; if we flee, we will surely die. Whether we die after waiting out the enemy or perish today in combat—both are sufficient to repay our empire!" In the absence of news from Yu, Zhang Cong'en and the other commanders suspected that he had fallen into enemy hands. A courier later reported the enemy's encirclement of Yu, An Shenqi now preparing to command a contingent to assist. Cong'en suspected some deception by the courier and opposed their departure. Yet Shenqi insisted, "Success or failure rests with Heaven. The barbarians might refrain from coming south, if you and I join forces. Still, how can we ever look the Son of Heaven in the face again, if we lose Yu?" Directing their own horsemen across the river, the other armies all followed them northward and repulsed the enemy over an area of ten *li* or more. Witnessing the arrival of reinforcements caused the barbarians to disband and withdraw. Yu and Cong'en could thereby recall soldiers for the return south, the Khitan likewise returning north. Khitan armies had intruded deep into the country at the time, tiring both men and horses. When they returned, the various commanders were unable to pursue them: Cong'en had directed Yu and cohort to retreat and preserve Liyang instead, allowing barbarian forces to slip away.

The court named Du Chongwei chief commissioner of bandit suppression in the winter of the third year [C.E. 946], and Huangfu Yu chief commander of right-wing cavalry, stationed at Zhongdu farm colonies. Having already made friendly overtures to the Khitan, Chongwei concealed troops under his own tent while summoning the various commanders to assume their positions, then announced his impending capitulation to the barbarians. Yu and other commanders, thoroughly startled, had no response. Chongwei revealed his petition of surrender, Yu and the others bowing their heads and following the others in signing their names to the document. Soldiers under their command now doffed their armor in surrender. The Khitan entrusted Yu and Zhang Yanze with the advance occupation of the capital, but after reaching Pingji, Yu slit his throat and died.

WE LAMENT. When the Liang dynasty collapsed and Jing Xiang died, he fell short of being a "Martyr to Virtue." When the Jin dynasty collapsed and Huangfu Yu died, he failed to make a "Martyr in Service." I have hardly written without conscious intent! Once the Liang had usurped the Tang dynasty, to the extent that many of its strategies derived personally from Xiang, he became the veritable son who assists his father in murdering his grandfather. This is hardly acceptable. He should consider himself lucky to have escaped a violent end under the executioner's hatchet!

When armies of the Jin dynasty surrendered to the barbarous Khitan, troops had no foreknowledge, so once compelled to doff their armor, their outbursts of grief virtually shook the heavens. Scarcely did they intend to surrender. If only Huangfu Yu had rolled up sleeves to bare his arms, rising defiantly to slay Chongwei in his very seat! He may not have eluded an untimely death, but he would have died honorably at least. His righteous fervor would have left men trembling in awe, to be sure. Instead, he bowed his head and obeyed orders, much like those actually toppling the empire, his eventual death unable to redeem him. How does he merit our esteem?

When superior men are among people, some employ forgiveness to commend others, some hold to the standard of perfection. Forgiveness permits goodness to expand along new paths, while perfection is immensely, immensely difficult to achieve—precisely the reason for valuing it. To understand what can be forgiven and what can be valued, this is more difficult still!

CHAPTERS 48–50

MISCELLANEOUS BIOGRAPHIES

Lu Wenjin

A native of Fanyang, Lu Wenjin had the courtesy name Dayong. He served as cavalry commander under Liu Shouguang. Once Zhuangzong attacked Fanyang, Wenjin surrendered early on to become prefect of Shouzhou. He came under the command of Zhuangzong's younger brother, Li Cunju. As military training commissioner for Xinzhou, Cunju oversaw the eight armies of the Shanhou region.[1] Zhuangzong had been in a standoff with Liu Xun at Shen County and summoned Cunju to assist him in a sortie against Xun. Cunju recruited from Shanhou several thousand crack troops while demanding horses of its people, the people trading ten oxen for a single horse and uniformly resenting the assessment. Moreover, troops displeased at having to campaign to the south, upon reaching Qigou Pass, coalesced to stage a mutiny. Then there was Wenjin, whose young and beautiful daughter had been requested by Cunju as concubine. Wenjin dared not resist because of Cunju's standing as senior commander, so he consented only to feel constantly contrite in his heart. This caused him to collude with unruly troops to assassinate Cunju and rebel. He raided Xin prefecture, which did not fall, then Wu, which did not fall either. He hence took refuge with the Khitan, who entrusted to him the defense of Pingzhou.

With the accession of Mingzong, Lu Wenjin commanded a force of several tens of thousands from Pingzhou to revert to Tang rule, a conversion immensely pleasing to the Emperor, who named him governor of the Yicheng command. Reassigned to the Weisheng command in just over a year's time, Wenjin also received nominal standing as minister and elevation to generalissimo. He later emerged as governor of the Zhaoyi and later Anyuan commands.

Once Gaozu came to the Jin throne and allied with the Khitan as "father to son," Lu Wenjin became apprehensive and insecure. In winter of the inaugural year of Tianfu [C.E. 936], Wenjin murdered military adjutant Feng Zhizhao and deputy governor Du Chonggui; gestures were also made to Li Bian [of Southern Tang], who arranged a military contingent as escort for him. As governor of a succession of districts, Wenjin was a considerably effective administrator, loved by both soldiers and civilians. So, as he prepared to leave, he followed several horsemen to tents to offer parting words to his commanders and acknowledge his intent to flee the Khitan, the commanders all bowing as they bid him farewell. After absconding for the south, Li Bian named him commander general of the Tianxiong command and governor of Xuanrun.

Seven feet in height, Lu Wenjin was imposing in physical presence. Beginning with his conversion to the Khitan, he repeatedly led them in raids and plunder against the region centering on You and Ji‡ prefectures, enslaving its people. He also taught the Khitan the art of textile weaving in the Middle Kingdom, sparing nothing. The Khitan grew ever more powerful in consequence. During the Tongguang era, the Khitan used cavalry of Xi tribesmen to cross the frontier over and again, pillaging Yan and Zhao prefectures as residents enjoyed not a year of peace. Tang armies stationed at Zhuozhou regularly transported rations via Waqiao Pass to Youzhou, only to be harassed by hardened troops serving as sentries along the way: Wenjin bears personal responsibility for a calamity to plague the Tang for over a decade. Yet he began devoting himself to a reclusive lifestyle after flight to the south, making efforts to be deferential and courteous to the learned, his actions humble and self-effacing. In discussing affairs, he confined himself to the ceremonies of recent dynasties or the precedent of government agencies without ever addressing military affairs. He held rank of generalissimo of the Left Guard upon his death at Jinling.

Li Jinquan

The ancestors of Li Jinquan emerged from Tuyuhun tribes. In his youth he served Mingzong of Tang as a menial servant, later proving a brave warrior skilled at mounted archery. He frequently assisted Mingzong in battle, rising to prefect through related merit. In the Tiancheng era, as the Zhangyi governor, he was given to greed and violence. Once dismissed from office, he presented a herd of several dozen horses to the court, presenting another herd several days later. Mingzong thus commented, "You must suffer from a plentitude of horses. Why else would you offer so many? Moreover, you serve at Jingzhou‡. How would you characterize conditions there? Surely, you do more than merely trade in horses?" An embarrassed Jinquan had no response. He was reassigned as Henghai governor, and after some time, named generalissimo of the Right Guard.

In the Jin-dynasty reign of Gaozu, the chief director of defense colonies at Anzhou, Wang Hui, assassinated governor Zhou Gui. Gaozu dispatched to the location Li Jinquan, with a thousand-man cavalry, while issuing a rescript hoping to win over Hui and promising, "If you surrender, I will name you prefect of Tangzhou." He further employed a "letter-on-arrow" to advise authorities at Anzhou against slaughtering a single person. He further admonished Jinquan, "Do not compromise my credibility!" Before Jinquan's arrival, An Congjin of Xiangzhou sensed Hui's inevitable flight to the southern Yangzi region and deployed crack troops to obstruct the principal roads. Hui did, indeed, head southward upon news of Jinquan's arrival, only to be slain by Congjin's men. Arriving later, Jinquan obtained several hundred of Hui's associates and sent them all to the capital.

During Wang Hui's mutiny, a vast plunder of the city continued for three days, Jinquan later making personal use of the valuables formerly pilfered by him. Jinquan apprehended more than ten of Hui's commanders as well, including Wu Kehe, to murder them. Kehe now cried out, "Even to the mutiny's ringleader, Wang Hui, you promised in writing an appointment as prefect. What crime have we committed to be killed instead? And what does this say about the credibility of court mandates? If commanders contravene imperial rescripts to kill surrendering soldiers, then you may not escape peril yourself!" Still, Gaozu could not vet further inquiry and later named Jinquan governor of Anyuan.

Hu [Ming] Hanrong, a chief military attaché under Jinquan, acted improperly in every undertaking. Gaozu found him worrisome and hesitated to cite Jinquan as a distinguished officer because of Hanrong's excesses, so he selected an honest administrator, Jia Renzhao, to replace Jinquan while recalling Hanrong. Hanrong persuaded Jinquan to retain him, thwarting recall to the capital. The retainer Pang Lingtu admonished Jinquan, stating, "Renzhao formerly served under Wang Yanqiu. During Yanqiu's offensive against Wang Du at Zhongshan, Du arranged for a skilled archer to climb the wall and shoot Yanqiu, hitting his helmet. Renzhao, approaching from the rear, then drew his bow and with a single shot killed the archer. Yanqiu later sought to identify the man, intending to lavish largess on him, but Renzhao retreated without uttering a word—here is a loyal subject for the whole world. After defeating Du, Yanqiu dispatched Renzhao to make formal announcement of victory to the capital, but the generous bounty given him was entirely divided among the poorest of his old associates and relatives—here is an honest subject for the whole world. Any undertaking attempted in consultation with such a man can produce nothing but good! It is only fitting to receive Renzhao and release Hanrong for recall." Upon hearing this, Hanrong arranged for someone to assassinate Lingtu that very night and poison Renzhao, whose tongue was mangled before death.

In summer, the fifth year of Tianfu [C.E. 940], Gaozu replaced Li Jinquan with Ma Quanjie. The two sons of Renzhao sought to visit the capital and file a complaint to redress the injustice against their father. The news utterly terrified Hanrong, who inveigled Jinquan, stating, "Formerly, the Son of Heaven summoned me, but you violated imperial orders by refusing to relieve me. The two sons of Renzhao will soon file a court complaint about his death. Today's appointment of Quanjie to replace you is tantamount to a call to jail." Jinquan believed him and rebelled, making gestures of goodwill to Li Bian. Gaozu then committed a force of thirty thousand to assist Quanjie in the suppression effort, while Bian had commander Li Chengyu enter Anzhou to facilitate Jinquan's flight to the south. Arriving at Chachuan, he extended his neck to face north and shed tears before departing. Li Bian now named him commander general of the Tianwei command.

In the Han reign of Emperor Yin, Li Shouzhen rebelled at Hezhong and requested reinforcements of Li Bian. As governor of Runzhou under Li Bian, Li Jinquan was to join Zha Wenhui and others in departing from Muyang. The various commanders of Bian all spoke eloquently on the prospects for claiming Hezhong, except for Jinquan, who considered it to lie too far to coordinate efforts, and the deployment was suspended because of his opposition. Jinquan never managed another major assignment, and we know nothing of his final years.

Gao Xingzhou and Gao Xinggui

Gao Xingzhou had the courtesy name Shangzhi. Native to Guizhou¶, he hailed from generations of frontier commanders at Huairong. His father Siji and Siji's brothers all employed their martial daring and valor along the northern border, serving as frontier commanders under Li Kuangwei, the governor of Youzhou. After the purge of Kuangwei by younger brother Kuangchou, the Prince of Jin [Li Keyong] prepared to suppress the mutiny, reasoning that, "Gao Siji and his brothers, with three thousand troops at Kongling Pass, pose a serious future threat. Sending someone to sway them is better. Should Siji agree to work for me, there is nothing beyond my reach!" Keyong thus dispatched someone to persuade the brothers.

At Yanzhou¤, local customs revere bravado and righteousness. When Siji and his brothers learned that Jin armies wished to exact revenge for Kuangwei, they gladly joined the effort as vanguard for the Jin. Once alerted to the brother's defection, Kuangchou abandoned the city and fled. Keyong thereby appointed Liu Rengong to preside over Youzhou, an elder brother of Rengong becoming chief director of the vanguard. Siji was named chief director of center armies and a younger brother named chief director of rear armies, while control over Yan¤ armies was divided among the Gao brothers. Keyong said to Rengong as parting words, "With Siji and his brothers dominating an entire region, the Gao family will surely bring calamity to Yan¤—an event that you must effectively guard against." Keyong left behind a thousand Jin warriors under Rengong's command. Yet frequent infractions of law by Jin troops prompted Siji and cohort to conduct multiple executions. Keyong blamed Rengong for the deaths, and he in turn placed blame on the Gao family. The Jin liquidated Siji and his brothers in consequence.

Rengong appointed a nephew of Siji, *Gao Xinggui* [d. C.E. 926], as military attaché. Siji's own son, Gao Xingzhou, just over ten *sui* at the time, similarly served in his army, receiving military rank upon reaching maturity. With the imprisonment of Rengong and installation of Liu Shouguang, Xinggui became prefect of Wuzhou. Shouguang later renounced the Jin, which retaliated militarily against him. Shouguang commander Yuan Xingqin was herding horses in the northern [Taihang] mountain region when he learned of the blockade against Shouguang, immediately leading his herd of horses to offer assistance. The men under his banner mutinied en route, however, elevating Xingqin to interim regent for Youzhou. "It is Xinggui who worries me," Xingqin exclaimed, whereupon a messenger was sent to Huairong to apprehend and rope-tie the son of Xinggui. Xingqin tried to sway Xinggui, as his troops passed through Wuzhou, asserting, "We can overpower Shouguang and replace him, assuming that you follow me. Otherwise, I will murder your son." Xinggui declined, adding, "You and I were both commanders of Mr. Liu. How can you consider defection? I must stand with the Liu house without consideration for my son." Xingqin swiftly surrounded Xinggui with troops.

Food supplies were depleted at Wuzhou after more than a month's siege. Gao Xinggui now gathered the men in the prefecture, admitting, "On behalf of community leaders, I cannot but defend the city. Reinforcements from Mr. Liu have yet to arrive. What choice do you have beyond killing me to surrender to the Jin?" The elders sobbed one and all, affirming their resolve to defend until death. Gao Xingzhou had followed Xinggui to Wuzhou at the time, then under the cover of night, hoisted himself over the city wall to rush to Jin barracks for a meeting with the future Zhuangzong. Zhuangzong subsequently sent the future Mingzong to relieve Wuzhou. Xingqin had disbanded and left as they arrived, Xinggui surrendering to Jin. Under the reign of Zhuangzong, Xinggui served as prefect of Shuo, Xin‡, and Lan prefectures, as well as governor of the Datong command. Reassignments to the Weisheng and Anyuan governorships came after the enthronement of Mingzong.

Gao Xinggui was predisposed to avarice and vulgarity, his actions often illegal. Deputy governor Fan Yance, a forthright man, admonished him over and again, Xinggui only ignoring and hating him. Later, Xinggui uncovered a plot in the making of frontier troops to mutiny, so he clandestinely moved armory weapons to another site. The frontier forces did rebel and rush the armory, finding no weapons to plunder. They scattered as Xinggui pursued and killed them. Xinggui falsely accused Yance of collaboration with rebels, and Yance was murdered, along with his sons—an injustice as the world saw it. Xinggui died in his district and received posthumous rank as grand marshal.

When Gao Xinggui surrendered to the Prince of Jin, Gao Xingzhou served under the future Mingzong's command. In his capacity as attending general, Xingzhou came to be known by Zhao Dejun, who said to Mingzong, "With his broad face and cautious heart, this youth is certain to rise someday to great eminence. Treat him well." Amid the Liang and Jin standoff along the Yellow River, Zhuangzong sent Mingzong eastward to storm Yunzhou. Xingzhou commanded forward contingents that encountered nighttime rains, his troops wishing to advance no farther. "This is a sign to me from Heaven," Xingzhou insisted. "The people of Yunzhou will not prepare for our arrival because of the rain, so we should exploit the element of surprise." They promptly crossed the Ji River that night to infiltrate the city, where Yunzhou soldiers happened to be asleep, and the city fell. After overturning the Liang dynasty, Zhuangzong rewarded his merit with appointment as concurrent prefect of Duanzhou, later moving him to Jiang prefecture. Xingzhou assisted in pacifying Zhu Shouyin and suppressing Wang Du during Mingzong's reign. Named military training commissioner of Yingzhou¤, he became governor of the Zhenwu command, then Zhangwu and Zhaoyi.

In the reign of Gaozu of Jin, Xingzhou became interim custodian of the western capital, then governor of Tianxiong. Named chief officer of at-large forces at Xiangzhou after the defection of An Congjin, his success at pacification led to reassignment as Guide governor. Xingzhou replaced Jing Yanguang, during the reign of Emperor Chu, as chief director of the Imperial Bodyguard. Conducting court affairs at the time were the likes of Li Yantao and Feng Yu, so Xingzhou requested restoration to a district post.

Once the Khitan had destroyed the Jin dynasty, they retained Xiao Han to defend the capital. Han was similarly purged by the Khitan, who now summoned the former Tang-dynasty Prince of Xu, Li Congyi, to occupy Bianzhou [C.E. 947]. Gaozu of Han hence rose in rebellion at Taiyuan, as [seventeen-*sui*] Congyi summoned Xingzhou by messenger to resist the Han. "An age in decline is hard enough to salvage, even without the games of children [on the throne]," he said with a sigh, refusing to come. Xingzhou received honors as palace secretary once Gaozu of Han took the capital. Later reassigned to the Tianping command, he was invested Prince of Linqing. Investiture as Prince of Qi attended the accession of Taizu to the Zhou throne, the posthumous rank of imperial secretary and title of Prince of Qin conferred upon death. He had a son, Huaide.

Wang Jun

Native to Anyang, Xiangzhou‡, Wang Jun had the courtesy name Xiufeng. His father, Feng, was once director of the army band. A youthful Jun proved a talented singer and served Zhang Yun, the one-time Liang governor. Zhuangzong of Tang had already overtaken the Wei/Bo command when Yun left Xiangzhou‡ to return to the capital [C.E. 915]. Revenues commissioner Zhao Yan passed by Yun's home, where Yun commanded Jun to complement the wine with a song, Yan stunned at the very sight of him. Yan enjoyed considerable standing at court, then, so Yun gave the youth to him. With the fall of the Liang, Yan's family was liquidated, and Jun drifted among the common people. After some time, he served under fiscal commissioner Zhang Yanlang, although Yanlang held no great affection for him. Yanlang was slain after Gaozu of Jin purged the Tang dynasty. The future Gaozu of Han joined ranks with the Jin in rebelling, so the former properties of Yanlang were all given to him. Jun managed to serve Gaozu of Han, in this way, serving as commander's attendant during Gaozu's governorship at Hedong. Named commissioner of diplomatic accommodations upon Gaozu's enthronement, Jun further rose to military overseer under Guo Congyi during the Han suppression of Zhao Siwan. Promotions culminated in commissioner of the northern court of palace armies.

Taizu of Zhou was still governor of Tianxiong when Wang Jun served as his military overseer. Emperor Yin had already killed senior Han courtiers such as Shi Hongzhao and unleashed agents to assassinate Taizu and Jun. The two thus turned their armies on the capital. Once Taizu came to supervise affairs of state, he had the Han-dynasty Dowager install Jun as commissioner of military affairs. Directing armies northward, Taizu had reached

Chanzhou only to redeploy his men toward the capital. He had already sent Feng Dao to Xuzhou¶ to receive Liu Yun, the Duke of Xiangyin; the Han-dynasty clansman Liu Xin, Prince of Cai, was in residence at Xuzhou‡. To thwart any untoward activities by the clansman, Jun conspired with Wang Yin, dispatching to Songzhou the chief cavalry director of the Imperial Guard, Guo Chong, as the one-time Shenzhou‡ prefect, Ma Duo, proceeded to Xuzhou‡. The commanders later murdered Yun and Xin.

The formal accession of Taizu [C.E. 951] saw Wang Jun become right associate at the Secretariat and deputy director of the Chancellery with ministerial powers. He supervised work on the national history as well. The assault on Jinzhou by Liu Min [of Northern Han] caused Jun to be designated chief officer of at-large forces, the court authorizing his conduct of civil affairs at personal convenience. Commissioned to join forces with him were Chen Sirang and Kang Yanzhao, departing from Jiangzhou via Wuling. Jun refused to advance beyond Shanzhou, however. Taizu dispatched to the prefecture an express messenger, Zhai Shousuo, to inform Jun of his wish to lead the campaign in person. Relieving his attendants, Jun confided in Shousuo, "The walls of Jin Prefecture are fortified beyond approach, whereas we are no match for Liu Min's formidable troops. This Subject persists at this site not for reasons of cowardice, but rather to await the right moment. His Majesty, newly acceded to the throne, has yet to instill awe in governors across the four corners. Is this the time for hasty action? Traces of treachery by Murong Yanchao of Yanzhou have also come to light. Should His Majesty depart from Sishui, Yanchao might occupy the capital. How could His Majesty possibly handle things, then?" Shousuo hurried back to the capital to provide a detailed accounting of Jun's words. By then, Taizu had issued commands for a progress westward, but Jun's sentiments left him suddenly pulling at his ears. "The matter nearly ruined me," he exclaimed, calling off the action.

Once the armies of Wang Jun issued from Jiangzhou, news that his vanguard had won passage through Mengkeng caused Jun to comment to a subordinate with relish, "Mengkeng is strategically vital to Jin and Jiang prefectures. Liu Min allowed us to pass without intercepting militarily, so we can surmise his inevitable defeat." Jun's armies were within a single league from Jinzhou when Min realized that a massive show of Zhou might had arrived; he disbanded and withdrew. The commanders all wanted to pursue him, but an initially indecisive Jun waited until the next day to dispatch horsemen, who failed to overtake Min and returned. As chief officer for imperial encampments, Jun later participated in the suppression of Murong Yanchao, leading troops to scale the walls ahead of others.

Ever since raising armies with Taizu at Weizhou, Wang Jun saw himself as instrumental to the dynasty's mandate and regarded world affairs as his personal duty. He expected to prevail in every debate or proposal, however salient or trifling. Whenever failing only slightly to have his way, his utterances and countenance would suddenly turn defiant, Taizu kindly indulging him on each occasion. Jun being two years older, Taizu often called him "elder brother" or sometimes employed his courtesy name, conduct fostering ever-whimsical behavior in Jun.

Zheng Renhui, Li Chongjin, Xiang Xun, and others, were all one-time assisting commanders under Taizu, men whom Taizu in the immediate wake of his accession initially refrained from advancing, Jun being jealous of them. After routing Murong Yanchao and returning to the capital, Jun asked to be relieved of powers as military commissioner, effectively to gauge the Monarch's instincts. Taizu consoled and commended him. Jun also wrote numerous letters to governors in the locales soliciting their recommendation of him. Within a matter of days, the governors all forwarded Jun's solicitous letter to the court by courier—utterly shocking Taizu. Jun repeatedly petitioned for release from duties and refused to conduct affairs in the interim. Taizu instructed a confidante to summon him. "If you do not emerge, I will have to go in person to inquire of you," he threatened. To this, Jun responded, "Should the royal carriage come, You will place Your Subject in a dangerous position." Still, he had absolutely no intent of leaving. Taizu now turned to an auxiliary academician at the military bureau with close ties to Jun, Chen Tong [Chen Guan], to summon him. Tong returned to report, "The resolve of Jun has abated somewhat. I beg Your Majesty to announce a solemn procession. Jun is certain to emerge once your departure is imminent." A reticent Taizu complied, news of Taizu's impending arrival forcing Jun to scurry off to court instead.

Wang Jun's erection of a new hall at the military bureau had been ostentatious in the extreme. Invited to visit the office was Taizu, who lavished gifts of rare bounty. When Taizu later erected a small hall in a garden within palace precincts, Jun abruptly petitioned, "Palace apartments are plentiful already. Why bother with this?" "The military bureau had quite a few rooms," Taizu countered. "Did you need to build yours?" Embarrassed, Jun had no response.

Although military commissioner with concurrent powers as chief minister, Wang Jun also sought concurrent authority as the Pinglu governor. And he held the post only briefly before seeking a loan of ten thousand bolts of gauze silk from the Left Treasury, which Taizu approved with reticence. Further requests to replace chief ministers Li Gu and Fan Zhi with Yan Kan and Chen Tong drew the following response from Taizu: "The installation or removal of chief ministers hardly involves such haste, but rather careful consideration." Failing to prevail on the issue, Jun's rhetoric turned progressively intractable, his wrangling continuing as the noon hour approached and Taizu had yet to dine. The occasion coincided with "cold foods" holiday,[2] and Taizu pronounced, "When the festival arrives, your bags should be packed!" Jun now withdrew, Taizu finding him insufferable. A day later, en route to an auxiliary palace where officials had been summoned, Taizu isolated Jun in a separate chamber, then met with Feng Dao. "Jun has insulted me beyond endurance," he acknowledged between sobs. Banished to military adjutant for Shangzhou, Jun died in exile.

After his banishment, Taizu worried that Wang Jun, as editorial overseer for the national histories, may have made inaccurate representations, so historians received instructions to review the calendar of daily events. Yet historians feared making the mistake of divulging matters unknown beyond the forbidden city. In that Li Gu directed the drafting of histories after Jun's exile, he petitioned to have palace confidantes provide a record of palace affairs for transfer to the History Bureau. This is the origin of the current practice where auxiliary academicians at the Military Affairs Bureau must provide copies of its internal records to the History Bureau.

CHAPTERS 51–53

MISCELLANEOUS BIOGRAPHIES

Zhu Shouyin

In youth, Zhu Shouyin [d. C.E. 927] was slave to the future Zhuangzong of Tang, nicknamed Nui'er. He often attended Zhuangzong as he read books, and after Zhuangzong's accession to the throne he rose from a menial services post in the long-distance armies to commander. Shouyin thus had no battlefield experience. He had a penchant for exposing the private lives or personal shortcomings of others to buttress his own standing such that Zhuangzong considered him loyal. Promoted to chief inspector of multiracial cavalry and infantry, Shouyin was commissioned to defend Desheng. During an offensive against the commandery by Wang Yanzhang, Shouyin's failure to prepare permitted Yanzhang to pierce the southern city. A cursing Zhuangzong exclaimed, "You thwarted the entire effort, you rotten scoundrel!" The future Mingzong sought Shouyin's punishment by the rules of martial law, Zhuangzong refusing to listen.

He received concurrent powers as the Zhenwu[‡] governor in the second year of Tongguang [C.E. 924]. Zhuangzong had only recently occupied Luoyang at the time, and Shouyin served as chief of military police for the capital. He grew arrogant through imperial beneficence, intentionally insulting men of accomplishment and seniority at court while colluding with actors such as Jing Jin. The Prince of Wei, Jiji, had already murdered Guo Chongtao when Jing Jin maligned Zhu Youqian as a Chongtao co-conspirator, so Zhuangzong had Shouyin encircle his official residence and kill him.

The future Mingzong had come to court from Zhenzhou, at the time, to stay at his private residence. Zhuangzong's current delusion by petty men left him suspicious of prominent officers, so he sent Zhu Shouyin to scrutinize Mingzong's movements. Clandestinely, Shouyin had someone inform Mingzong, "Peril looms over the life of an exalted subject: a man of accomplishment in the world will not receive just rewards. You are, alas, someone of exalted station and conspicuous attainment. To elude catastrophic fortunes, you must personally devise a way to return to your district." "I came to Luoyang a solitary man," Mingzong exclaimed. "What can I possibly do?" Mingzong later rebelled at Weizhou.

As Zhuangzong campaigned to the east, Zhu Shouyin organized cavalry formations outside the Xuanren gate [of Luoyang], anticipating the arrival of the imperial carriage. A mutinous Guo Congqian then raided the Xingjiao gate to enter. Zhuangzong issued an emergency summons to Shouyin, but he ordered armies to stay put, so only a hundred or so royal princes and eunuchs were available to fight the renegades. Shouyin's men never arrived, having been given repose at the foot of the Beimang Hills. There he learned of Zhuangzong's death and scurried back to Luoyang, infiltrating the palaces to cart off imperial concubines and precious objects, as unruly troops plundered. He then sent a messenger to invite Mingzong to occupy Luoyang.

Upon assuming the throne, Mingzong named Shouyin chief minister, metropolitan custodian of Henan Prefecture, and administrator of the Six Armies. A year later [C.E. 927], reassignment came as Xuanwu governor [of Bianzhou]. When Mingzong announced an imperial progress eastward to Bianzhou, in the ninth month, it stirred a rancor among observers: some presumed a campaign against the Wu region [to the southeast], while others inferred an action to harness certain overbearing overlords to the east. Feeling especially vulnerable, Shouyin assassinated military director Ma Yanchao, then sealed up the city in rebellion. Mingzong had reached Jingshui upon learning of Shouyin's mutiny and dispatched the swift mounts of Fan Yanguang to charge the city walls. Defenders at Bianzhou opened its gates to Yanguang, as Shouyin murdered his own family, then stretched out his neck and directed an aide to decapitate him. After reaching Bianzhou, Mingzong ordered the lashing of his corpse with a whip, his head hung at the marketplace for seven days before conveyance to Luoyang.

On the eve of rebelling, Shouyin approached Ma Yanchao, the chief military director, to join in his schemes. Yanchao refused, and Shouyin murdered him. Mingzong lamented the death of Yanchao and named his son, Ma Chengzuo, senior scribe for Ming Prefecture.

Fan Yanguang

Native to Linzhang, Xiangzhou‡, Fan Yanguang [d. C.E. 940] had the courtesy name Zigui. Mingzong of Tang, then governor, recruited Yanguang for his banner, although he did not yet prize him. Having conquered Yunzhou yet still facing stiff resistance from Liang troops at Yangliu, Mingzong received secret overtures from the vanguard commander for Liang, Kang Yanxiao. He needed someone to apprise Zhuangzong of the gesture, and Yanguang promptly pleaded to go. Bearing Yanxiao's letter with wax seal, he proceeded westward to deliver the letter in a meeting with Zhuangzong, commenting, "Yanxiao may wish to surrender, but Liang resistance at Yangliu is extremely resilient, the time to counter not at hand. Better to erect ramparts at Majia Crossing that extend to Wenyang." Zhuangzong concurred. With the new ramparts complete, the Liang unleashed a barrage against them by Wang Yanzhang. The future Mingzong had secretly sent Yanguang, along bypasses, to request military assistance when he was apprehended by Liang troops during a nighttime approach to the Yellow River. Sent to the capital and imprisoned, Yanguang endured several hundred floggings and the brandishing of swords, yet refused until the end to divulge information about the Jin. After confinement for several months, prison wardens gradually came to protect him. And once Bianzhou was occupied by Zhuangzong, the wardens, removing handcuffs and fetters, bowed as they released him. Zhuangzong, buoyed at the sight of Yanguang, appointed him honorary minister of public works.

Yanguang became commissioner of the southern court of palace armies during Mingzong's reign. Mingzong had departed for Bianzhou and reached Xingyang County when Zhu Shouyin rebelled. Yanguang now proposed, "The outlines of Shouyin's mutiny are becoming apparent. In delaying our response, we play into his own hand and the city will become entrenched and unapproachable. Nothing compares to a sudden sally to catch adversaries off guard. Your Subject requests five hundred horsemen to rush the city wall, our lightning speed certain to shock the enemy." Given five hundred cavalry, he traveled two hundred *li* in a frantic dash, from dusk to the wee hours of night, to reach city walls and enter combat. Mingzong arrived by daybreak after a hurried trip and Bianzhou warriors, upon sighting the Son of Heaven riding his carriage, opened the gates. Yanguang entered first and engaged in street combat, the injury and death of staggering dimensions. Shouyin was now dead and Bianzhou pacified.

Named commissioner of military affairs in the next year [C.E. 928], Yanguang left the capital as governor of the Chengde command. He was restored as military commissioner, alongside Zhao Yanshou, upon the death of An Chonghui. Once asked by Mingzong about the number of horses available, Yanguang responded that there were thirty-five thousand in the cavalry. Mingzong slapped his own thigh and sighed, "My involvement in the military spans forty years: since the days of Taizu at Taiyuan, when horses did not exceed seven thousand, to the time of Zhuangzong's occupation of the northern Yellow River region and standoff with the Liang along the river, when we had only ten thousand. We now possess thirty-five thousand horses and still cannot unify the world. Alas, I am old and a plentitude of horses hardly matters!" Yanguang added, "Your Subject once calculated that the cost of a single horse can support five men in infantry, so with thirty-five thousand horses, we can feed a hundred and fifty thousand soldiers." Mingzong retorted, "To fatten war horses, I have to emaciate my people—this would shame me."

Upon the death of Li Renfu of Xiazhou, his son Yichao installed himself and requested military banner and tassels of the court. Mingzong dispatched An Congjin to replace him, instead; and when Yichao rejected the replacement, Tang armies attacked him in a prolonged but fruitless effort. Xizhou prefect, Liu Suining, rode by courier path to Fan Yanguang to present an alternative strategy. Arguing that authorities at both Sui and Yin prefectures were sympathetic with the court, he proposed the assignment of prefects to the two places to win their surrender. Yanguang observed, "The misdeed now being punished by our troops originated with Yichao. Once Xiazhou is vanquished, what will we have to fear in Sui and Yin prefectures. If Xiazhou is not vanquished, then Sui and Yin cannot be retained, even if acquired." Suining further requested approval for an emergency meeting with Yichao to facilitate his surrender, but Yanguang countered, "If, by chance, we should lose a single Suining, its consequences do not merit worry. Rather, I worry over the grand polity of the royal court." The Pure Consort Wang dominated affairs of court, at the time, while Suining and his brothers were old acquaintances of the consort. The favor they enjoyed guaranteed a favorable audience for their words, many senior courtiers daring not challenge them for fear of the consort, save for Yanguang, who thwarted them with casual confidence.

When illness prevented Mingzong from holding audience, strange rumors were rife among residents of the capital, some of whom hid in mountains and ravines. Others hid themselves in military barracks, a practice that authorities could not prohibit. Recommendations came to Yanguang to stem the problem by strictly enforcing the law, but he insisted, "Maintaining calm is necessary to contain commotion. Indulge them a bit!" Later, Mingzong's illness improved modestly and calm returned to the capital.

At the time, the Prince of Qin was excessively insolent as military officer, the Prince of Song too weak and peripheral to court, and the Prince of Lu favored by many court insiders [to succeed Mingzong]. Fan Yanguang thus feared involvement in the inevitable calamity and requested release from duties. Zhao Yanshou hence abruptly sought reassignment as well, having subtly surmised Yanguang's intent to avoid peril. Mingzong attempted many times to retain them, their appeals to him only growing more earnest and adamant to the point of shedding tears. Without recourse, he dismissed both men. Yanguang was reappointed Chengde governor as Zhu Hongzhao and Feng Yun replaced him as military commissioners. Subsequently, the Prince of Qin faced execution for mutiny, Mingzong expired, the Prince of Lu rebelled, and murder befell Emperor Min. The pandemic tumult engulfing the Tang house brought calamity and death to Hongzhao and Yun, while Yanguang was restored as military commissioner under Emperor [Fei], with powers as Xuanwu governor. He also led the successful punitive campaign against the Tianxiong command, where a mutiny had caused governor Liu Yanhao to be expelled. Yanguang hence became Tianxiong governor.

He repeatedly dreamed of a large snake entering his abdomen through the navel, penetrating halfway when he pulled it out. Consulting a sorcerer in his entourage, Zhang Sheng, Yanguang was told, "The snake is related to the dragon: penetration of the abdomen is an auspicious mark for a future king." Sheng had predicted certain prominence for Yanguang ever since his days of obscurity, Yanguang for long deeming him a prophet and often including him in his entourage. The realization of many of Sheng's prophesies lent credibility to his utterances, and in turn nurtured Yanguang's treacherous impulses.

When Gaozu of Jin raised arms at Taiyuan, Emperor [Fei] ordered Yanguang to station at Liaozhou a force of twenty thousand, assisting Zhao Yanshou in a pincer envelopment against Gaozu. Yanguang singularly held out even as Yanshou surrendered. Once Gaozu acceded to the Jin throne, Yanguang's congratulatory letter arrived slightly later than did those from the other local lords. Moreover, his daughter was consort to Emperor [Fei's] son, Chongmei. Gaozu nonetheless chose to assuage him with investiture as Prince of Linqing.

There was a man from Pingshan named Bi Qiong, a commander in the metropolitan headquarters under Chengde governor Dong Wenqi. The governor was later enslaved by the Khitan, and Qiong liquidated his entire clan, tossed their bodies in a cave, and confiscated family valuables worth millions. Qiong became defense commissioner for Qizhou¶ once Gaozu of Jin assumed power, packing his belongings to depart from highways at Weizhou. Yanguang had a messenger quietly deliver a letter summoning him, which Qiong spurned. A now irate Yanguang selected a force to lie in ambush at the prefectural border to observe Qiong's passage, killing him at Xiajin County and commandeering his entire treasure. He then reported to court that border patrols had inadvertently killed him. This left Gaozu suspicious of a possible mutiny, so he personally visited Bianzhou.

In the sixth month of the second year of Tianfu [C.E. 937], Yanguang rebelled. He unleashed a force of twenty thousand, led by military attaché Sun Rui and Chanzhou prefect Feng Hui, to offer resistance at Liyang County, plundering Hua and Wei‡ prefectures. Gaozu named Yang Guangyuan bandit-suppressing commissioner: from Huazhou, he ferried across to Huliang for a raid. Sun Rui proved frivolous and devoid of any strategy, on the other hand, bringing along over ten female prostitutes as companions for the trip and raising tents and fans, only to frolic in wine, food, and song to his heart's content. His soldiers, toiling under oppressive heat, refused to be deployed. Guangyuan captured a spy and interrogated him about strategy, then induced Rui and cohort to cross the Yellow River, only to storm them midway. Many of Rui's soldiers drowned as Rui and Hui retreated to Weizhou, shutting its gates and refusing to reemerge.

Before deciding to rebel, Fan Yanguang came down with a sudden illness, unable to rise from bed. Rui secretly summoned Hui to enter the city to pressure him to rebel, a nervously deluded Yanguang following their wishes. News that Yanguang had rebelled with the assistance of Rui and cohort brought laughter to Gaozu, who commented, "Although not much of a warrior, I did assist Mingzong in seizing the world and, on many occasions, attacked fortified cities to overpower mighty enemies. Someone like Yanguang is no rival for me, let alone Rui and his gang with their infantile antics. Disposing of them is child's play!" Gaozu now grew committed to the pacification.

Yanguang initially had no compelling wish to rebel, so in the wake of Rui's defeat, he charged military attaché Wang Zhixin with delivering a petition to revert to the Jin dynasty. Gaozu refused to meet Zhixun, but assigned him to the Wude squads. Yanguang also petitioned for surrender to Yang Guangyuan, opting for a staunch defense only in the absence of a response. Meanwhile, Jin soldiers flooded the city with two hundred letter-bearing arrows promising amnesty for everyone at Weizhou and trying to woo some mercenary to behead Yanguang. But the walls of Weizhou were sturdy and difficult to pierce, remaining intact despite a yearlong siege. With troops weary and grains nearly depleted, assistant chamberlain for imperial affairs, Shi Ang, wrote a strident admonition against the action: requesting a pardon for Yanguang, he volunteered to ride a single cart into the city to negotiate surrender. Gaozu awakened to reality as well. In the ninth month of the third year [C.E. 938], after an emissary entered Weizhou to pardon Yanguang, he surrendered. Investiture ensued as Prince of Dongping and governor of Tianping. An iron writ of immunity was conferred as well. Yanguang came to court several months later, where in awkwardness, he asked to retire due to advanced age and received permission, the title grand preceptor to the heir-apparent conferred.

Previously, Gaozu pardoned Yanguang in exchange for surrender. The negotiator was ordered to deliver a promise, "The sparing of your life is assured. Should murder occur after your surrender, continuing to reign would be inconceivable to me!" Yanguang consulted deputy governor Li Shi, who interjected, "The Monarch is genuinely sincere and emphatically righteous. Having agreed to spare your life, you simply will not die!" Yanguang hence surrendered. Retired to the capital, he appeared at seasonal banquets, Gaozu treating him no different from other courtiers, but in his heart he preferred not to post Yanguang in the capital.

A year or so later, Gaozu arranged one night for Liu Churang, the commissioner of palace armies, to convey some wine to Yanguang. Churang informed him, "When His Majesty sent me, envoys for the Khitan had just arrived. The Northern Emperor had asked the Jin court about the whereabouts of once mutinous commanders of Wei/Bo, concerned that the court lacked the means to control them. Those mutineers should be presented in fetters [the envoy intimated] to preclude future calamity to the Middle Kingdom." The news brought tears to Yanguang, who could not decide on a recourse. "At Luoyang, you can perhaps avoid Khitan emissaries," Churang added. Yanguang interjected, however, "The interim custodian of Henan, Yang Guangyuan, is my bitter enemy. I do own a rural estate at Heyang, however. Is it feasible to go there?" Churang answered in the affirmative. Yanguang now gathered his cash to return to Heyang.

The profuse baggage for Yanguang's trip caused such a deluge on the roadway that Guangyuan came to covet the treasure and scheme against him. Memorializing the throne, Guangyuan insisted, "Yanguang is an untrustworthy and sinister subject. If not disposed of, he will certainly flee, if not north to the barbarians, then south to Wu/Yue. I seek his incarceration at Luoyang." Gaozu dallied in indecision, but Guangyuan was concurrent governor of Heyang and his son Yang Chengxun was civilian prefect. He thus instructed Chengxun to lead troops to compel Yanguang to commit suicide. "The Son of Heaven has provided an iron writ for me and agreed that I not die," Yanguang insisted. "How can you do this?" Pressed by burly troops to mount a horse, Yanguang had reached a suspension bridge when thrown into the water to die by drowning. The court was told that he willfully leaped into the water to his death. His entire treasure was seized. Gaozu vetted no inquiry, as the outcome suited his own wishes. He did suspend court and confer the posthumous title of grand mentor.

Yanguang's body was retrieved at the Miujia sandbank by Cao Qian, commissioner of water transport. The court authorized the return of the body to Xiangzhou‡ for burial at home. After the burial, the tomb abruptly ruptured as the inner and outer coffins broke to reveal a head and skull that had been crushed to pieces. Previously, Bi Qiong had murdered Dong Wenqi and claimed his property, Yanguang murdering Qiong to claim that same property. It was ultimately wealth that caused Yanguang's slaying by Guangyuan, yet Guangyuan could not elude the same fate.

At the time of Yanguang's rebellion, a man named *Li Yanxun* was military adjutant for Heyang. He allied with Zhang Congbin after his mutiny at Heyang, then fled to Weizhou in the wake of Congbin's defeat. Named chief director of infantry by Yanguang, Yanxun was entrusted with the city's defense. Yang Guangyuan, the commissioner of bandit suppression, knew Yanxun to be native to Xingzhou and his mother still there. A messenger was sent to Xingzhou to retrieve and bring her to the wall of Weizhou to show Yanxun, hoping to sway him. Yanxun shot and killed her upon sight with his arrow. Once Yanguang emerged to surrender, Gaozu of Jin named Yanxun prefect of Fangzhou[‡]. Senior officials insisted that he deserved execution for killing his mother, yet Gaozu argued that the amnesty order had been issued and his credibility could not be compromised. Yanxun was later executed for bribery.

We woefully lament. Human nature requires prudence with the familiar. Therefore, the Sage, a man steeped in benevolence and righteousness, exuded devotion without sloth, moderation without compulsion in the teaching of others. He aspired gradually to acquaint the people with virtues for purposes of assimilating them, familiarity over the long haul fostering good habits. The common people lack knowledge: accustomed to witnessing good, they accept goodness; accustomed to seeing vice, they accept vice.

The chaos of the Five Dynasties has remote origins. Since the decline of Tang and attendant wars and famine, fathers could not nurture sons and sons could not care for parents. At the onset, it was by mere misfortune that flesh-and-blood kin failed to protect each other, causing rites and righteousness to dissipate by the day, the charity of parents and the compassion of children to wane. After prolonged familiarity with these conditions, an all-pervading breakdown set in, as fathers and sons engaged in villainous acts of mutual destruction.

For the Five Dynasties era, the catastrophes and killings defy description. Human nature makes the love for parents a universal instinct and unfilial conduct a universal abomination. But when Yanxun stretched his bow to shoot an arrow into his mother and Gaozu acquiesced with a pardon, beyond symbolizing Yanxun's inability to appreciate his actions as abominable, it further shows Gaozu's condoning a deed not deemed perverse. This can scarcely happen except under the weight of bad habits over a long time. The *Analects* states, "In constitution we are close, in habit we are far apart."[1] When carried to an extreme, men's hearts do not differ from animals and beasts. Is it not harrowing? Based on the abominable conduct of Yanxun, who acted willfully with no sense of perversity, or an emperor such as Chu, who severed bonds with his own father, clearly the failure to recognize wrong characterized an entire age.

An Chongrong

Native to Shuozhou, An Chongrong [d. C.E. 942] had the nickname "Iron Barbarian." His grandfather, Congyi, was once prefect of Lizhou. His father, Quan, served as prefect of Shengzhou and chief director of infantry and cavalry of the Zhenwu command.

A man of physical strength, Chongrong was gifted as horseman and archer as well, becoming governor of the Zhenwu command. Once Gaozu of Jin raised armies at Taiyuan, he secretly charged Zhang Ying with recruiting Chongrong. His mother and elder brother both opposed his involvement, but Chongrong had already conveyed approval of the scheme to Ying. When mother and brother plotted to thwart him by assassinating Ying, Chongrong insisted, "Having not yet agreed, I should first consult the spirits out of consideration for mother." He then cocked his arrow and walked a hundred paces before shooting. "The Gentleman Shi [Gaozu] will become Son of Heaven if I hit this target," he declared. And indeed, he struck on the first shot. "I will become governor if I hit the target," he added. Again he struck on the first shot. His mother and brother now consented. Chongrong delivered a thousand border-patrol cavalry to the Taiyuan mutineers, becoming Chengde governor upon Gaozu's enthronement.

Although a military man, Chongrong understood administrative affairs such that subjects could not swindle him. A husband and wife once accused their son of unfilial conduct, so Chongrong drew his own sword to hand to the father, permitting him to kill the son. Yet the father insisted tearfully, "It is unbearable!" The mother approached from his side with verbal abuses, then grabbed the sword to pursue the son. Chongrong learned upon further inquiry that she was the youth's stepmother and chided her while chasing her off, later shooting her to death.

Emerging from the ranks of warriors, An Chongrong suddenly acquired riches and fame. He also witnessed men like Emperor Fei of Tang and Gaozu of Jin leap from governor-overlords to rulers of empire, exclaiming to someone, "Pedigree is scarcely necessary to become Son of Heaven. A man needs only strong armies and stout horses!" However predisposed to treachery, Chongrong had yet to act. Since Gaozu's assumption of a father-to-son covenant with the

Khitan, they had grown insufferably arrogant even as Gaozu served them with heightened circumspection. Chongrong thus commented in furor, "To demean the Middle Kingdom in order to venerate barbarians is already a hardship on our downtrodden people and feeds the insatiable desires of the Khitan. This blight on the Jin house will endure ten thousand generations!" He railed at Gaozu over and again on such matters. When Khitan emissaries passed through Zhenzhou en route to and from the capital, Chongrong insisted on sitting with legs crossed, rudely upbraiding them and refusing ordinary courtesies. He once even seized and murdered envoys.

At the time, Bai tribes of the Tuhun serving the Khitan as mercenaries had so toiled under their vicious oppression that Chongrong induced them to penetrate the frontier. The Khitan sent successive emissaries to reprove Gaozu and request the return of former envoys. Facing the envoy, Gaozu extended both head and torso in a bow of heightened deference while accepting the reproof, often employing plaintive language to explain himself. He indulged Chongrong out of impotence to scrutinize his conduct, but dispatched Zhang Cheng, officer of palace services, to direct a force of two thousand to round up Tuhun men concealed in the wilds of Bing, Zhen, Xin‡, and Dai prefectures, expelling them all beyond the frontier. The Tuhun departed, only later to return and ultimately receive sanctuary by Chongrong, who recruited local desperadoes and taxed every sort of grain from the people to feed ten thousand horses. He grew ever unruly, in consequence.

Chongrong killed military director Jia Zhang in a fit of anger, then falsely accused him of treachery. Zhang had a daughter still young, whom Chongrong wanted to exempt, but the girl insisted, "Thirty members of my family were slain by soldiers, only me and my father to survive. My father now dead, how can I bear to survive alone? I would rather die." Once killed, the people of Zhenzhou venerated the pious fervor of the Daughter Jia, while appraising Chongrong as destined to certain defeat. Chongrong now acquired pretenses to ostentation, no longer valuing the pouch with golden-fish ornament and preferring instead to adorn it with fish carved from jade. He married two women, both receiving additional investitures from Gaozu out of consideration for him.

In the sixth year of Tianfu, summer [C.E. 941], the Khitan envoy Yela passed through Zhenzhou and endured humiliation at Chongrong's hand. When the statements of Yela proved less than submissive, an indignant Chongrong seized him, then ordered light cavalry to force residents south of Youzhou to relocate to Boye. Petitioning the throne, he wrote:

> Your Subject recently witnessed the arrival for asylum of Bai Chengfu and Helian Gongde, assimilated Tuhun from Yingzhou‡, along with

> over thirty thousand tents [or households]. I have also witnessed the arrival for asylum of nonassimilated Tuhun, Hun, and Qibi tribesmen, plus three Tujue tribes from both northern and southern Turkish camps, who in turn command Shatuo, Anqing, and Jiufu tribes with their oxen and goats, wagons and tents, armor and horses, proceeding along seven or eight separate paths. They all speak of the callous depredations of the Khitan and the plunder involving human beings and livestock. Effective as of the second month of this year, orders went out to the border tribes to identify their stout and fit to enlist in the armed forces, providing military equipment in anticipation of an autumn invasion. Representing a combined force of perhaps a hundred thousand invincible warriors, the various border tribes genuinely want to revert to us early on, for fear that their clans face extinction, should Heaven's protection be lost.
>
> I have further witnessed, in the cases of the Tangut along the Yellow River plus the Yi and Yueli tribes to the south and north of the [Taihang] mountains, rulers who express goodwill through intermediaries and relinquish Khitan-conferred pronouncements of rank, proclamations from its court, as well as banners and pennants. Loudly, they all weep in enunciating hardships and conveying wishes for revenge by forming armies. I have even witnessed the deputy governor for Shuozhou, Zhao Chong, murder his governor, Liu Shan, and offer to convert the city. Observing the various border peoples coming voluntarily without summons and Shuozhou reverting willfully without attack—I can only attribute these to Heaven's designs, even though human sentiment is involved as well. I also realize that our commanders who converted to alien service, formerly distinguished for merit, had long enjoyed wealth and station before losing themselves along a barbarian frontier to suffer unspeakable oppression. They still stand on tipped toes in veneration of the court and earnestly aspire to revert to dynasty. If only they hear a summons to war, they will surely turn their weapons on their superiors.

His memorial contained several thousand words.

He further wrote letters to senior courtiers of the dynasty and governors across the four corners, insisting that the Khitan could be conquered. A threatened Gaozu visited Yezhou specifically for his sake and responded, "In generations past, a diplomacy of exchanging royal relatives with the barbarians emerged as the proper plan for the world. Today, I have placed our world in vassalage to them. For you as a single governor to try to resist them, disparities of power between you and them will reap nothing but humiliation for you." Chongrong no longer considered himself bound by Jin commands, fixed in his resolve to rebel. Despite using the Khitan as pretext, Chongrong turned around and secretly deployed a messenger to ally with Liu Xi, the governor of Youzhou. The Khitan, meanwhile, sought to exploit distractions at the Jin court and the turmoil induced by Chongrong, anticipating that the two would undermine one another and facilitate their own prying into the Middle Kingdom. For this reason, they no longer expressed indignation at Chongrong.

On the eve of his rebellion, the mother of Chongrong again expressed reluctance, so he "consulted the oracles on mother's behalf." Pointing to a post beyond their residence with flying streamer, he looked up to its dragon tip and declared in shooting at the aperture, "I will acquire the world if I hit the target." Having hit on the first shot, his mother approved. The county magistrate for Raoyang, Liu Yan, presented a waterfowl in five colors, Chongrong pronouncing it a phoenix and raising it on a lake to the rear of his home. He also arranged for someone to cast in iron a giant whip, perpetrating a fraud upon the people that, "A spirit occupies the whip: it need only be pointed at someone and the person will suddenly die." Dubbed the "Iron-whip Master," the object preceded Chongrong wherever he went. Atop the gates of Zhenzhou was an iron statue of a barbarian sentry [providing symbolic protection]. Without cause, its head fell to the ground and the incident left Chongrong bristling, inasmuch as his own nickname was "Iron Barbarian." Still, he never awakened to the event's symbolism.

That winter An Congjin mutinied at Xiangyang, the news prompting Chongrong to mobilize his troops to rebel as well. Zhengzhou had suffered that year from extensive drought and locust blight, as Chongrong impressed several tens of thousands of starving commoners in a movement toward Yezhou, purportedly to lend their services to the throne. Upon reaching the Pojia dikes of Zongcheng, Gaozu dispatched Du Chongwei to intercept. Hostilities had already commenced when commander Zhao Yanzhi, who had known differences with Chongrong, rolled down his banners on the verge of battle to flee to the Jin side. His armor and horse saddle were all plated in silver, so Jin troops unaware of his intent to surrender all vied to murder him and seize the loot. Chongrong was utterly terrified by word of Yanzhi's surrender to the Jin, forcing him to seek safety in a supply wagon, as twenty thousand of his troops scattered.

That winter proved bitterly cold, the vanquished soldiers all succumbing to starvation, cold, or murder with no survivors. Chongrong fled back with only a dozen or so cavalry. Making armor from the hides of oxen and horses, he compelled the people of Zhenzhou to defend the city while waiting out events. Once Chongwei's troops reached the city wall, an assisting commander under Chongrong personally led government regulars into the city from the west, via the Shuinian gate, slaying more than twenty thousand city defenders. Chongrong now employed several hundred Tuhun horsemen to defend the secondary wall of the inner city, but Chongwei had someone apprehend Chongrong and sever his head for presentation to the court. Gaozu ascended a tower to receive the head, then had it dipped in lacquer for conveyance to the Khitan. He also reportedly changed the name of Chengde command to Shunde, the prefecture of Zhen to Heng, and the mountain Changshan to Heng [words implying submission].

Yang Guangyuan

Yang Guangyuan [d. C.E. 944] had the courtesy name Deming. His father, Adengchuo, was a Shatuo tribesman. Guangyuan had the original name Atan and served as cavalry commander under Zhuangzong of Tang. While assisting Zhou Dewei in battle against the Khitan at Xinzhou, he broke an arm and suffered permanent loss of limb function. After a long time, he became chief director of infantry and cavalry for Youzhou, garrisoned at Waqiao Pass. Handicapped by baldness and a lame arm, Guangyuan did not command the written language either, but had a discriminating intellect and a facility for managing personnel. Over Mingzong's reign, he served successively as prefect of the four prefectures of Gui¶, Ying¶, Ji¶, and Yi, garnering a reputation for sound administration.

In the past, Tang armies had overrun Wang Du at Zhongshan and captured more than ten senior Khitan commanders, including Zela. The Khitan later entered amicable relations with the Middle Kingdom and their envoys demanded the return of Zela and cohort. Mingzong placed the matter before senior officials, who uniformly endorsed the return save for a singular Guangyuan, who insisted, "Zela and the others are the most gifted warriors of the northern barbarian, their loss akin to losing a hand or foot. Moreover, a long residence leaves them well versed in affairs of the Middle Kingdom, so their repatriation is scarcely in our interest!" "The barbarians attach great importance to sworn covenants," Mingzong reminded him. "They have already accepted a truce with us. How can we abrogate it unilaterally?" An emphatic Guangyuan concluded, "My greater fear is remorse that comes too late!" His words compelling, Mingzong ultimately refused the release of Zela and cohort. Guangyuan subsequently rose from Yizhou prefect to governor of the Zhenwu command. In the second year of Qingtai [C.E. 935], reassigned as Zhongshan governor, he received concurrent powers as chief inspector of at-large forces to the north, guarding against the Khitan at Yun‡ and Ying‡ prefectures.

When Gaozu of Jin raised armies at Taiyuan, Emperor [Fei] ordered Yang Guangyuan to assist Zhang Jingda in the suppression, as deputy commissioner of bandit suppression for Taiyuan. They retreated to defend Jin'ansai, the Khitan having defeated them. A blockade by the Khitan lasted several months and depleted food supplies for both humans and horses, as humans killed horses for food. Once without horses, Guangyuan slew Jingda to surrender. Yelü Deguang asserted in a stern voice upon meeting Guangyuan, "You and your men represent such thoroughly contemptible specimens of Han-Chinese!"[2] Guangyuan and the other commanders, initially failing to recognize the comments as reproof, continued with polite words until Deguang added, "Consuming ten thousand war horses without adding salt or butter, who else but a contemptible Han could do so?" Guangyuan and the others, now utterly mortified, fell prostrate on the floor as Deguang asked, "Are you scared?" "Extremely scared," they all responded. He asked their reason for fear. "We worry that Your Majesty will take us to the frontier," they said. "My country has neither the offices nor lands to accommodate you," Deguang informed them, "so you should exert yourselves on behalf of the Jin."

Gaozu of Jin subsequently named Yang Guangyuan governor of Xuanwu [Kaifeng] and chief director of infantry and cavalry of the Imperial Guard. Once entering the palace for meetings, Guangyuan appeared despondent, as if remorseful about something. Gaozu intuited some sort of dissatisfaction and arranged for someone to inquire, as Guangyuan confessed, "In riches or stature, Your Subject needs nothing. I am often contrite that I did not die on assignment, like Raw-Iron Zhang Jingda." Gaozu thus considered him loyal, placing considerable confidence in him.

In the wake of Fan Yanguang's rebellion, Yang Guangyuan became chief commissioner of bandit suppression for Wei Prefecture. Failure to take the city after a long siege convinced Gaozu ultimately to adopt another approach to win Yanguang's surrender. Guangyuan now started to turn self-aggrandizing and arbitrary: dominating a sizable army in the provinces, he presumed Gaozu to fear him. At every turn, Gaozu generously indulged him: he selected Guangyuan's son, Chengzuo, as husband for the Changan princess, while lavishing extraordinary official titles on younger sons such as Yang Chengxin—favor without parallel. Military commissioner Sang Weihan loathed and criticized him repeatedly. Upon visiting the court from Weizhou, Guangyuan proceeded to expose Weihan as power hungry and difficult to control. Gaozu had no choice but to reassign Weihan locally at Xiangzhou‡. He also relocated Guangyuan to the western capital [Luoyang] as interim custodian, conferring concurrent powers as Heyang governor and stripping him of military commands. The onset of such daunting frustrations prompted Guangyuan furtively to approach the Khitan with precious objects, complaining of rejection by the Jin court. His personal army of a thousand men was now violating the laws and vandalizing the Heyang and Luoyang region, its depredations worse than those of bandits. In the fifth year of Tianfu [C.E. 940], the Jin reassigned him as the Pinglu governor with investiture as Prince of Dongping. Guangyuan petitioned for his sons to accompany him, so Chengzuo was named prefect of Shanzhou‡ and Chengxun named defense commissioner for Laizhou. As father and sons departed for the east, their wagons and mounts stretched in a path several tens of *li* long. Guangyuan became grand preceptor and Prince of Shou upon the accession of Emperor Chu.

The Jin dynasty, facing a shortage of horses for military deployment, canvassed the entire country for them. Jing Yanguang thus sought the return of three hundred horses formerly borrowed from government stables by Guangyuan, causing him to retort angrily, "How can you reclaim these horses, gifts from the Former Monarch? You must suspect me of treachery!" He hereafter schemed to wreak havoc. His son Chengzuo then secretly fled Shanzhou‡ for home. Emperor Chu promptly appointed him prefect of Zizhou and conferred by messenger a jade sash and imperial horse, hoping to assuage him. Guangyuan turned even more arrogant by now and rebelled outright. He invited the Khitan to invade the country, overrunning Beizhou. The prefect of Bozhou, Zhou Ru, also defected to surrender his charge to the Khitan.

As Emperor Chu and Yelü Deguang faced off in the area of Chan and Wei prefectures, administrative assistant for surveillance at Yunzhou, Dou Yi, proposed as strategy to the military, "Today, if we fail to post overwhelming forces with seasoned commanders at Bozhou Crossing, we will permit Zhou Ru to direct Khitan armies eastward, where they will cross the Yellow River to converge with Guangyuan's men, imperiling the entire southern region." Emperor Chu thus dispatched Li Shouzhen and Huangfu Yu, commanding ten thousand troops, to course along the Yellow River downstream. Indeed, Zhou Ru did direct Khitan armies across the river at Majia Crossing: they were erecting ramparts when Shouzhen launched a surprise sortie, roundly defeating them and severing links to Guangyuan. Once Deguang learned of the rout of his men along the Yellow River, he entered a decisive battle with Jin armies at Qicheng, only to be defeated yet again.

The Khitan having returned to the north, Emperor Chu redeployed Li Shouzhen and Fu Yanqing eastward for the suppression effort. Guangyuan fortified defense parameters around the city for a staunch defense, which continued from summer to winter, as the people cannibalized one another to near extinction. Butting his head against the floor while looking northward to the Khitan, Guangyuan blurted out the name of Deguang, "Your Majesty, alas, has wronged me!" His sons, led by Chengxun, urged him to emerge for surrender, but Guangyuan declared, "While in Daibei, I once used ritual paper money to toss into the 'Heavenly Pond' in sacrifice, the paper promptly sinking to the bottom. Someone had then insisted that I would become Son of Heaven. I need only await the right moment, so do not bother me with frivolous proposals!" Chengxun now realized that Guangyuan would not consent and assassinated the governor's administrative aide, Qiu Tao, along with trusted commanders Du Yanshou, Yang Zhan, Bai Yanzuo, among others. He further placed Guangyuan under house arrest, dispatching a messenger with his confession of guilt [in a plea for mercy].

Brothers Chengxin and Chengzuo both went to the capital in an act of conversion, Guangyuan similarly making the gesture of offering his life. Emperor Chu appointed the two sons commanders in the Imperial Guard and forwarded a rescript to Guangyuan pardoning his death. Officials uniformly argued against the pardon, however, and Li Shouzhen received imperial instructions to dispose of him as conditions permitted. Shouzhen delegated to He Yanzuo, the deputy master for diplomatic accommodations, the task of killing Guangyuan at home. He was examining horses in a stable as Yanzuo reached his home, Yanzuo sending a brigade commander inside to inform Guangyuan, "The envoy of the Son of Heaven stands at your gate and wishes to report back to the Son of Heaven, but still lacks something to take along." Guangyuan inquired as to his meaning. "Simply put," the envoy declared, "he wants your head, Grand Prince!" A cursing Guangyuan continued, "What crime have I committed? I formerly surrendered Jin'ansai to the Khitan, enabling your family to continue as Sons of Heaven for generations to come. I similarly expect wealth and status for the rest of my life, rather than such betrayal of good faith!" He was murdered, although the court merely heard that he died of illness.

Yang Chengxun served the Jin dynasty as defense commissioner for Zhengzhou. After purging the Jin dynasty, Yelü Deguang summoned Chengxun to the capital, where he was reproved for abducting his own father and sliced to death before being cannibalized. Yet he appointed brother Chengxin as the Pinglu governor. Gaozu of Han conferred posthumous title on Guangyuan as imperial secretary, investing him as Prince of Qi. He also directed Secretariat drafter Zhang Zheng to compose a eulogy inscription for Guangyuan to be given to Chengxin and engraved on a stele at Qingzhou†. The stone tablet was hardly in place when thunder and lightning from the heavens cracked it.

Adengchuo began without a surname, later adopting the personal name Jian and surname Yang. The original name of Yang Guangyuan was Tan, but in the second year of Qingtai, court authorities ordered a change due to taboos involving characters in Mingzong's temple name, so he was conferred the name Guangyuan. Himself sickly and bald, his wife lame in the foot, others scoffed saying, "Since antiquity, has there ever been a bald and handicapped Son of Heaven with a lame-footed Empress?" Such stories passed around as jokes. Yet he summoned the northern barbarians to visit the first calamity on the world, one ultimately to ruin the Jin house and paralyze the Middle Kingdom for more than thirty years—these were the deeds of Guangyuan.

Du Chongwei

Du Chongwei [Du Wei, d. C.E. 948] was native to Shuozhou. His wife, née Shi, was younger sister of the Jin Emperor Gaozu. With the formal accession of Gaozu, the Lady Shi became Princess and Chongwei named prefect of Shuzhou and manager of the Imperial Guard. He attended Hou Yi in the successful assault on Zhang Congbin at Sishui, merit leading to appointment as Luzhou governor. After the mutiny of Fan Yanguang at Yezhou, Chongwei assisted Gaozu in the offensive that produced Yanguang's surrender. Chongwei received concurrent powers over the Zhongwu command and ministerial standing. Concurrent authority as Tianping governor ensued, later becoming chief director of the Imperial Bodyguard.

With the mutiny of An Chongrong, Chongwei engaged him in battle at Zongcheng. Chongrong organized his men in crescent formation, which Chongwei harassed without success. Chongwei preferred to pull back somewhat to observe their next move, but detachments commander Wang Zhongyin insisted, "When two forces are fully engaged, the one to retreat will be vanquished first." Splitting his army into three, Chongwei initially deployed his left and right companies to storm the opponent's two wings, and once hostilities turned intense, Zhongyin unleashed crack troops to storm the enemy's center armies. Chongrong commander Zhao Yanzhi then reverted to dynasty, causing Chongrong to be routed. He returned to Zhenzhou to secure the walls, refusing to leave. Chongwei attacked and overpowered him, receiving appointment as the Chengde governor in reward.

Du Chongwei emerged from the lower ranks of the military, his moral deportment deficient and facility in command strategies wholly lacking. In conquering Zhenzhou, he laid personal claim to the stores in the prefectural treasury as well as the personal wealth of Chongrong; Gaozu knew of the matter but refused to investigate. Once Emperor Chu abrogated the treaty with the Khitan and they began invading the country for successive years, Chongwei merely sealed off the city in self-defense. Many towns and villages subordinate to the prefecture faced massacre at Khitan hands. Sometimes barbarian mounts would forcibly parade untold thousands of his own people beneath city walls, Chongwei climbing the wall to peer out without ever trying to save them.

In the inaugural year of Kaiyun [C.E. 944], Chongwei received additional powers as commissioner of bandit-suppressing contingents at large on the northern front. He directed troops in an offensive against Taizhou a year later, overrunning Mancheng and Suicheng. Khitan armies had already withdrawn to Gubei, then returned for a sortie against Chongwei and cohort, who fled south. Under continued barbarian harassment at Yangcheng, Chongwei countered the sortie with the aid of turbulent winds and assistance from Fu Yanqing and Zhang Yanze, roundly routing the Khitan, who scattered. The various commanders wanted to pursue them, but Chongwei cited the popular idiom, "Persons lucky enough to elude the clutches of renegades can hardly expect to retrieve dependents as well!" He then proceeded to grab his horse and rush off.

While presiding at Zhenzhou, Du Chongwei milked the people mercilessly and wore its families ragged. He also worried over imminent Khitan incursions and made successive pleas to return to the capital. Even before the court could respond, he precipitately took to the highway. A court unable to stop him simply reassigned him as interim custodian of the Ye capital. The grains left behind at Zhenzhou as Chongwei's private cache amounted in excess of a hundred thousand pecks. Palace secretary Wang Qinzuo proposed that the court procure these for military needs based on rules for state procurement, compensating Chongwei with several tens of thousands in bolts of raw silk. The action utterly infuriated Chongwei, who insisted, "I am not a rebel. It is hardly acceptable to resort to stealing like this!"

In the autumn of the third year [C.E. 946], after Khitan commander Gao Mouhan swindled Yingzhou¶ into surrendering, Chongwei was restored as commissioner of at-large forces on the northern front. That autumn had witnessed vast flooding across the world, the rains continuing for more than sixty days as human corpses littered the highways. The people fed themselves on wood shavings, their horses and cattle subsisting on straw from sitting mats. As Chongwei's armies trudged through mud, they assessed villagers for rations along the way, leaving people near and far aggrieved by their toil. Mouhan had already relinquished Yingzhou¶ with the approach of Chongwei, who now retreated to Wuqiang. The Khitan proceeded to harass Zhen and Ding prefectures, forcing Chongwei to press westward to Zhongdu Bridge, where his men faced off barbarian armies from opposite sides of the Hutuo River. Detachments commanders Song Yanyun and Wang Qing crossed the river for an intense engagement. Chongwei intentionally held back his own men, causing Yanyun to be vanquished and Qing to die in battle. Commissioner of transport Li Gu taught Chongwei to use wooden triangles to form a pontoon bridge across the river, hoping to enlist death-defying warriors to cross over and storm the enemy. The commanders all supported the proposal, Chongwei alone rejecting it.

The Khitan unleashed cavalry from across the western mountains in a nighttime sortie against Luancheng, severing Chongwei from his rear guard. His inclination to treachery was already present, only to be reinforced by the disrupting of supply lines, so he clandestinely contacted the Khitan through a special messenger, offering to surrender. Immensely pleased, the Khitan promised the throne of the Middle Kingdom to Chongwei, a promise he believed. With armored soldiers concealed for protection, Chongwei summoned the various commanders to announce his impending capitulation to the barbarians. They all stood in shock, but obeyed orders owing to their senior commander's preemptive action. Chongwei pulled out the petition of surrender, making the commanders each sign their names to it, as troops were directed to assume formation beyond the barricades. Those troops were still reveling at the prospect of a decisive battle, only for Chongwei to pronounce rations exhausted and surrender necessary. The soldiers bawled while doffing armor, the sound reverberating from the plains to the wilderness. Chongwei received a robe of ocher-red from the Khitan, which he displayed before troops. The Khitan also honored him as grand mentor.

During the Khitan raids on the capital [of Kaifeng], Du Chongwei had forted Jin troops at Chenqiao, where soldiers suffered from exposure and hunger of indescribable dimensions. As he passed on the highways from one site to the next, marketgoers followed and cursed him, Chongwei lowering his head without daring to look up. After occupying the capital, the Khitan decided to appropriate a portion of the cash and silk gauze owned by city residents to reward troops, exempting not even commanders and ministers. Chongwei should have tendered ten thousand strings, yet he begged of the Khitan, "Your Subject must surely deserve special exemption. I led the way, after all, in relinquishing a hundred thousand Jin warriors to you!" The Khitan chuckled as they conceded to the exemption, then restored him to the Ye capital. The next year, as the Khitan headed back to the north, Chongwei visited their tents to offer parting words, accompanied by his wife, Lady Shi.

Once Gaozu of Han restored calm to the capital, he named Chongwei grand marshal and governor of the Guide command. A nervous Chongwei refused to accept the mandate, and Gaozu dispatched Gao Xingzhou to attack him, personally joining the offensive after the initial assault yielded no fruit. Secretarial overseer Chen Tong conveyed to Chongwei an imperial edict intended to sway him, but he still declined. Han soldiers suffered numerous setbacks in their blockade of over a hundred days' duration. The Khitan had previously left behind fifteen hundred Yanzhou¤ warriors in the capital. As the future Gaozu approached the capital from Taiyuan, informants reported that Yan¤ troops would soon rebel. Gaozu summarily liquidated their entire cohort at Fantai, as survivors fled to Ye. The Yan¤ commander Zhang Lian, with two thousand troops present at Ye, received news of the massacre by urging Chongwei to secure the city. Gaozu now regretted the killing and deployed a succession of messengers to woo Lian and cohort, but Lian climbed the wall to shout out, "What crime did we Yan¤ warriors commit to justify the Fantai executions? In the absence of a reason to expect survival, we beg to defend unto death."

With Du Chongwei's rations exhausted, the people of Ye survived on powdered distillery waste such that those to leap the wall to escape seemed wholly devoid of human coloring. Chongwei sent administrative aide Wang Min, and later his wife, to petition for surrender. Gaozu approved, and Chongwei emerged in plain clothes to meet him. A pardon followed, then honors for Chongwei as interim grand preceptor, acting grand mentor, and concurrent imperial secretary. Yet executions awaited Zhang Lian and the military aides to Chongwei, their personal wealth confiscated as well. Chongwei was returned to the capital.

His illness turning grave, Gaozu exclaimed as he looked to senior courtiers, "Be careful to guard against Chongwei." Once he expired, secrecy was imposed on official mourning, as senior officials allied to execute Chongwei, along with sons Hongzhang, Hongcan, and Hongsui. Their corpses exposed at the marketplace, passersby kicked and cursed them beyond any ability of authorities to control, frenziedly ripping limbs and trampling the remains to leave not a trace.

Zhang Yanze

The ancestors of Zhang Yanze hailed from Tujue tribesmen, who later relocated to Yinshan and subsequently Taiyuan. A man of galling ruthlessness and savagery, Yanze's yellow-colored pupils could glare in the dark of night—looking into his eyes much like staring at a ferocious animal. Through his gifts as an archer he became cavalry commander and frequently attended Zhuangzong and Mingzong in battle. Under the Jin dynasty, ties to Gaozu through marriage facilitated rise to chief director of the Sage-Protecting Guard's right-wing contingents and prefect of Caozhou. He assisted in the suppression of Fan Yanguang as well, becoming the Zhenguo‡ governor, and by mid-year, the Zhangyi governor.

He administered affairs with random violence, commonly venting anger against his own son and humiliating him with repeated floggings of the light rod. The son fled to Qizhou¶, where he was apprehended by local authorities and sent to the capital. Gaozu returned the youth to his father, who petitioned to kill him. The administrative secretary to Yanze, Zhang Shi, refused to write the petition. He also admonished repeatedly against such action, inciting an angry Yanze to draw his bow and arrow to shoot him. Shi managed to survive by absconding. He was formerly treated quite generously by Yanze, and many affairs were entrusted to him. Petty men surrounding Yanze envied Shi, however, and banded together to malign him, simultaneously applying pressure upon him by insisting, "If you fail to leave promptly, you face certain calamity!" Shi absconded and Yanze dispatched military director Li Xing and twenty horsemen to pursue him, with a warning as they departed, "Shi will not return of his own volition, so his head may be retrieved, instead!" Shi reached Yanzhou¶ when the local prefect assisted by military forces escorted him safely to Binzhou. Its governor Li Zhou, detaining Shi, informed the court by express courier. The court ordered Shi's exile to Shangzhou, but Yanze dispatched his manager-adjutant Zheng Yuanzhao to the capital to explain his position and demand Shi's return, adding, "If Yanze does not obtain Zhang Shi, the consequent calamity is unimaginable!" Gaozu could only relinquish Shi. Once in Yanze's custody, Shi's heart was ripped out, while tongue, hands, and feet were all severed before beheading.

Gaozu arranged for Wang Zhou to replace Zhang Yanze, naming him commandant of the Valorous Right Guard. Zhou then memorialized the court on the "twenty-six counts of illegal conduct" by Yanze, exposing his savage acts against residents of Jingzhou‡. And the father of Shi, Zhang Duo, filed a grievance in the capital of wrongful death. Also appealing the injustice of Yanze's murder of Shi were masters of remonstrance Zheng Shouyi and Cao Guozhen, directors of punishment Li Tao and Zhang Lin, and their assistant directors Ma Tao and Wang Xi—all of whom fell prostrate at the auxiliary palace. The court refused to investigate, so Tao met personally with Gaozu for a trenchant remonstrance. "Yanze is an accomplished subject whom I formerly granted immunity to capital punishment," Gaozu insisted. In a stern voice, Tao queried, "If we can tolerate the criminality of Yanze, what about the iron writ of immunity for Fan Yanguang?" An angry Gaozu rose to depart, Tao trailing him in ongoing admonition. Gaozu had no alternative: he summoned Shi's father, Duo, younger brother Shouzhen, and son Xifan, among others to confer official rank. He further waived taxes for Jingzhou‡ residents, along with labor services for a year. An edict even pronounced imperial culpability for the misdeeds, but punishment for Yanze involved simple reductions in official rank and titular standing. Guozhen again appeared at the palace's auxiliary doors, flanked by deputy censor Wang Yijian and heads of the three censorial agencies, a succession of appeals from them generating no response.

Under Emperor Chu, Zhang Yanze served successively as commandant of the Dragonly Martial Right Guard, commandant of the Martial Right

Guard, and general commander of the Divinely Martial Right Guard. Yanze emerged in many battles waged by the Jin against the Khitan in the Hebei region to distinguish himself in a string of battles, becoming governor of the Zhangguo [Zhangde] command. Surrounded by the Khitan in a contest at Yangcheng, Yanze's troops were without water as their well-water pump suddenly broke. Vast winds swept from the heavens as well, the Khitan launching a sally of rare intensity by riding the wind and creating commotion. The troops of Yanze were terrified. He solicited the counsel of commanders, who all insisted, "The barbarians today exploit an ascending wind, while we at the point of descent should await the wind's return to enter combat." Yanze concurred, but detachments commander Yao Yuanfu remained behind after commanders had departed to remind Yanze, "Hunger and dysentery in our ranks are already acute. Waiting for winds to shift will only deliver us to barbarian hands, to be sure. As the enemy certainly presumes that we are incapable of battling in unfavorable winds, we should, as they say, 'exploit the element of surprise.' " Yanze immediately dismantled the abatis [between him and the enemy] to lead a fierce scrimmage.[3] The Khitan fled more than twenty *li* to the north: pursued to Wei village, a rout forced them to abscond.

In the autumn of the third year of Kaiyun [C.E. 946], the court named Du Chongwei chief commissioner of bandit suppression, Li Shouzhen chief director of local forces, and Zhang Yanze chief overseer of cavalry formations. In maneuvers between Zhen and Ding prefectures, Yanze vanquished the Khitan at Taizhou and claimed two thousand heads. The offensive against Yingzhou¶] by Chongwei and Shouzhen had proven fruitless, so they retreated to Wuqiang. There they learned that the Khitan had virtually vacated their homelands to launch an invasion, which intimidated and confounded them. Yanze happened to arrive to present a scheme to break the barbarians, so he assisted Chongwei in a rush westward to Zhenzhou. As vanguard, Yanze met resistance from the barbarians at Zhongdu Bridge and fought fiercely over it, setting half of it afire. The barbarians suffered minor setbacks, after which the two sides erected ramparts on opposite banks of the river.

On the tenth day of the twelfth month [January 4, 947], Du Chongwei and Li Shouzhen defected to the Khitan and relinquished their charge. Yanze also surrendered. As [Khitan ruler] Yelü Deguang began his occupation of the capital, he provided Yanze and Fu Zhu'er with two thousand horsemen to enter in advance. Yanze proceeded frantically at twice the usual speed: upon reaching the Yellow River, he crossed by night with gags in the mouths of his men. On the night of the sixteenth, at the fifth drum [daybreak], he broke the crossbars of the Fengqiu gate to enter. A fire soon erupted within the palace, as Emperor Chu deployed swords to force more than ten palace women into the fire, only to be restrained by Xue Chao, a minor aide. Through the Kuanren gate, Yanze conveyed a letter from Deguang to the Empress Dowager, extinguishing the fire upon entering. On guard at the Kuanren gate was Kang Fuquan, chief inspector of the imperial precincts, who recognized the renegades after climbing the stairs. Yanze called out to him and he alighted to open all gates. Troops were posted before the Mingde mansion and Fu Zhu'er sent into the palace, conveying the proclamation of the Barbarian King. The Emperor changed from imperial robe of yellow into ordinary clothing, bowing twice in accepting the mandate. He had a messenger summon Yanze inside, who declined. "Your Subject is without face to stand before Your Majesty." The Emperor summoned him again by messenger, Yanze now laughing without a response.

A day later, the Emperor was relocated to Kaifeng, accompanied by the Empress and Empress Dowager, conveyed by sedan chair as more than ten palace consorts and eunuchs followed on foot. Zhang Yanze arranged for troops of Li Yun, director of the palace's Crane-Commanding Guard, to hold them in custody there, owing to disruptions in transportation between the capital and periphery. He reviewed all letters from the Emperor or Empress Dowager to Yelü Deguang, not daring to forward them otherwise. The Emperor attempted to take several lengths of silk gauze from official storehouses, but the manager insisted, "Your Majesty cannot have these!" He once asked for wine from Li Song, who said, "Your Subject has wine that I do not begrudge you but dare not offer for fear of provoking some mishap, should Your Majesty turn melancholy after consuming it and the unexpected occur." The Emperor's paternal aunt, the Wushi Princess, bribed a gatekeeper and managed to meet the Emperor, conveying parting words before returning to her room to hang herself. Once Deguang crossed the Yellow River, the Emperor proposed receiving him in the suburbs. Yanze withheld approval of the request and informed Deguang, who spurned the idea. "Two suns do not preside in the heavens," he argued. "How can two Sons of Heaven meet face to face on our roads?"

Upon Yanze's arrival in the capital, Li Tao commented to someone, "My calamity has arrived, a fate unavoidable even if I take cover in a waterhole!" At their meeting, Tao employed some idiomatic expression to convey his willingness to die, a statement met with laughter from Yanze, who treated him generously. Presuming upon his merit with the Khitan, Yanze drank from morning to night while indulging in sensual pleasures. The several hundred horsemen usually accompanying him carried banners still bearing the special designation "Red-Blooded Hearts Devoted to the Ruler." In the wake of forcibly relocating Emperor Chu, Yanze transferred items from the imperial treasury to his private residence, his soldiers plundering the capital widely. Soldiers once apprehended a criminal during patrols and Yanze proved too drunk to interrogate, so, looking scornfully at the suspect, he displayed three fingers and soldiers tossed the man outdoors for a summary severing at the waist. The mother of imperial son Yanxu, the Lady of Chu with the surname Ding, was a beauty whom Yanze approached the Empress Dowager about obtaining for himself. The dowager dallied without relinquishing her, so he abducted Lady Chu. Yanze also had a history of conflict with Gao Xun, master of palace gates: in a drunken stupor, he infiltrated Xun's home to slay several persons before leaving.

Yelü Deguang learned of Yanze's malevolence upon reaching the capital and angrily had him fettered. Gao Xun further raised his own grievances against Yanze with Deguang, who vetted the case with officials and civilians in the capital. "Should we not execute Yanze?" The officials uniformly opposed a pardon, as people in the capital vied to submit complaints concerning Yanze's evil. Deguang thus instructed Gao Xun to supervise the murder. Survivors of literati whom Yanze had killed trailed along in tears, donning the apparel and carrying the cane of mourners as they cursed and beat him with their canes. Yanze bowed his head without uttering a single word. Upon reaching the northern market, his wrists were broken to remove the shackles as the punishment commenced: Xun ripped out his heart in sacrifice to the dead, as marketgoers vied to crack his skull and remove the brains, his flesh sliced and eaten.

WE LAMENT. The events of the Jin dynasty were hideous, indeed, and its evil extreme as well! So, the reason for so quickly succumbing to calamitous turmoil was simple inevitability. Even if Du Chongwei and the others had not defected in surrender to barbarians, the dynasty would not necessarily have eluded overthrow. A single Jing Yanguang may have incited rifts with the barbarians, yet final calamity to the Jin house was wrought by three others [Du Chongwei, Li Shouzhen, and Zhang Yanze]. And through the deaths of Chongwei and Yanze and the deep-seated impulses of the Jin people for violence, we can see their intense hatred and wrath for these men—sentiments that did not surface overnight.

To reach the point of fighting over the corpse of a dead man, slicing flesh or dislodging brains to eat, trampling severed limbs to leave not a trace—since ancient times, such horrendous depravity has no precedent! With the entirety of Jin forces deployed to the north at the time, the empire's very survival hinged upon the victory or defeat of these three men—weighty duties, to be sure. For the world to hold them in such contempt precisely as the Jin emperor invested such powers without ever awakening to matters—surely, he typifies the ruler confronting imminent disaster who saw any subject as a worthy!

Murong Yanchao

Murong Yanchao [d. C.E. 952] came from a tribe of Tuyuhun and was brother of Gaozu of Han, born to the same mother. He once adopted the surname Yan, and, having black whiskers, Yanchao was dubbed "Yan the Dark Kunlun."[4] In his youth he served Mingzong of Tang as lieutenant and rose to prefect, similarly serving successively at Ci, Shan‡, Pu, and Di prefectures from the Tang to Jin dynasties. Once convicted of receiving bribes related to wine production, he should have died by rule of law, but the future Gaozu of Han petitioned from Taiyuan to spare him. The sentence was commuted to exile at Fangzhou‡.

After the Khitan had annihilated the Jin dynasty and Gaozu of Han raised armies at Taiyuan, Yanchao returned to the Han domain from his place of exile to become governor of the Zhenning command. In the wake of Du Chongwei's mutiny at Weizhou, Gaozu named the Tianxiong governor, Gao Xingzhou, chief officer for the suppression, Yanchao serving as deputy. The two men often could not cooperate on strategic matters. Xingzhou deployed armies with circumspection, so he did not advance even long after reaching the city walls. Yanchao preferred a speedy engagement, which Xingzhou refused. Inasmuch as Xingzhou's daughter was married to the son of Chongwei, Yanchao alleged that his disinclination to attack the renegade city grew out of consideration for the daughter. This left Xingzhou utterly livid. News of the two men's incompatibility worried Gaozu, who feared another mutiny in the making and abruptly directed the campaign in person. Yanchao tended to create occasions to demean Xingzhou in insufferable ways, such that in a meeting with chief ministers, a tearful Xingzhou stuffed his own mouth with excrement in protest. Gaozu believed the fault lay with Yanchao and sent a messenger to assuage Xingzhou, then summoned Yanchao for a reprimand and forced him to visit Xingzhou to apologize for improprieties. Xingzhou was somewhat mollified.

At the time, Han-dynasty troops had long been assigned to the walls of Weizhou in the face of Du Chongwei's heightened commitment to a staunch defense. The various commanders, all recognizing that the time had not come to act, preferred waiting for an opening of vulnerability. Murong Yanchao singularly argued for a speedy assault, convincing Gaozu, only to preside personally over a sally ending in more than ten thousand deaths and injuries. Never again did he dare propose another offensive. Chongwei later emerged in surrender and the post of Tianxiong governor went to Xingzhou, who did not hazard accepting it until Gaozu promised through Su Fengji, "to reassign Yanchao in consideration of you." Xingzhou accepted and Yanchao moved on to the Taining command.

Emperor Yin having murdered Shi Hongzhao and cohort, he dispatched others to Weizhou to assassinate the future Taizu of Zhou and Wang Jun. At the same time, he summoned commanders back to positions in the capital, for fear of failing. Yanchao was halfway into a meal when the Emperor's envoy reached Yan Prefecture: dropping spoon and chopsticks, he took directly to the highway. With Zhou armies invading the capital, the metropolitan custodian of Kaifeng, Hou Yi, advised Emperor Yin, "Northern armies have arrived, but the family dependents of leaders all reside in the capital. We should shut the city gates to resist their vanguard, while planting their wives and sons in embrasures atop the wall as an inducement to northern troops, perhaps succeeding in forcing them to relinquish armor in submission." Yanchao railed at him, arguing, "Hou Yi is an old fogy with the conniving of a coward!" Emperor Yin now assigned Yanchao as Yi's deputy in directing a force to the northern suburbs. Zhou armies arrived and Yi defected to the Zhou during the night. Yanchao continued to fight vigorously at Qili, as Emperor Yin emerged to reward troops. The Empress dowager had a messenger remind Yanchao "to guard the Emperor with care." He responded in a loud voice, "What can northern troops possibly do? Once on the battlefield, I will force them back to their barracks with a simple howl!" He then said to Emperor Yin, "Your Majesty's palaces face no threat, so you can emerge tomorrow to watch me wage war." Emperor Yin reappeared a day later to rally troops, as a vanquished Yanchao absconded for Yan Prefecture and the Emperor succumbed to regicide in the northern suburbs.

Murong Yanchao proved unsettled of heart upon Taizu's accession as Zhou ruler [C.E. 951] and often presented the court with gifts. Taizu reciprocated with a jade sash and even employed an imperial rescript to assuage him, politely calling him "younger brother" in lieu of personal name. Hanlin academician Lu [Yu] Chongliang was sent to assuage him as well, yet Yanchao grew ever suspicious and nervous. Liu Min [of Northern Han] subsequently installed himself at Taiyuan and launched raids against Jin and Jiang prefectures, prompting Taizu to deploy armies westward under Wang Jun. Yanchao also wanted to exploit the occasion to rebel and sent his own military attaché, Zheng Lin, to the capital to request a personal audience. Taizu approved his request in a handwritten rescript, fully appraising Yanchao as ingenuous. Repeatedly, Yanchao invoked serious bandit activity in his domain as pretext for declining an appearance. At the same time, he produced a letter attributed to Gao Xingzhou excoriating the Zhou for its failings and inferring that Xingzhou wished to recruit him for rebellion. Taizu examined the imprint on the letter to confirm it as forged, then showed it to Xingzhou. Meanwhile, Yanchao dispatched a messenger to the south to strike an alliance with Li Bian [of Southern Tang]. Bian accommodated him with a raid against

Muyang, but Zhou troops prevailed. Liu Min's offensive against Jin and Jiang prefectures had proven fruitless by now, forcing him to disband and retreat. Taizu now entrusted the suppression of Yanchao to the director of infantry in the Imperial Guard, Cao Ying, and master of diplomatic accommodations Xiang Xun. Yanchao sealed off the city in defense.

When Yanchao initially rebelled, administrative aide Cui Zhoudu had admonished, "The Lu domain [Yanzhou] appears in the *Odes* and *Documents* but has failed to produce a hegemon since the days of Boqin [of Western Zhou], its men often preferring to celebrate their times by embracing rites and righteousness. You are now resplendently martial, Sir, and a brave hero for your age. If you assess your strengths and act at favorable occasions, you may well secure riches and standing for life. Yet the examples of [renegades] Li Shouzhen of Hezhong, An Chongrong of Xiangyang, and Du Chongwei of Zhenyang provide a recent mirror for you to reflect upon." Yanchao, although utterly livid, had yet to harm him.

Having come under siege, Yanchao abusively appropriated the valuables of city residents to pay his troops, such that one manager-adjutant of Shanzhou, Yan Honglu, relinquished the entirety of his household wealth for fear of being horsewhipped. Yanchao suspected that everything had not been turned over and saw an opportunity to place blame on Cui Zhoudu, so he instructed Zhoudu to oversee the forage of Honglu's home for valuables. Zhoudu warned him, "Your destiny to live or die hinges on the measure of your wealth. I hope you have hidden nothing." Honglu directed a family servant to accompany Zhoudu in a search, digging holes in the ground only to obtain nothing. Yanchao further pressured Honglu by sending Zheng Lin to threaten him with daggers. A nervous Honglu pleaded with wife and concubines and they affirmed the absence of hidden objects. Zhoudu went to inform Yanchao, who did not believe them and confined both Honglu and Zhoudu to prison. The wet-nurse of Honglu, seeking to ransom him, uncovered a gold bracelet in the mud and presented it to Yanchao, whose anger was now uncontrollable. He instructed a lieutenant to flog Honglu and his wife, who died from the consequent flesh rot, then decapitated Zhoudu at the marketplace.

That year, the planet Saturn crossed paths with the star [cluster] Jue and Kang,[5] the astrologer saying, "Jue and Kang belong to the Zheng constellation and preside over Yan Prefecture." Yanchao thus led military and civilian officers through the western gate, walking on foot for thirty *li* to offer sacrifice. Greeted at Kaiyuan Monastery, where idols were produced for ritual purposes, they made return trips most days. The people were ordered to place yellow streamers in their homes and offer prayers.

Murong Yanchao was a man of guile with a propensity for accumulating possessions. He once built a storehouse in his district for pawning cash, where some sinister person pawned counterfeit silver and the storehouse custodian took a long time to detect the counterfeit. Yanchao secretly instructed the custodian, under cover of night, to dig a hole through the storehouse wall and remove to another site all gold and gauze-silk deposits, declaring these stolen. Yanchao then carried a register to the marketplace and instructed the people to identify their own pawned items and thereby qualify for restitution. The people all vied to profess ownership of pawned items, and in this way, Yanchao apprehended the person making the bogus silver. Placed into a deep underground cellar, the man was forced to teach more than ten persons working from dusk to dawn to make iron ingots coated in silver called "Silver with Iron Womb." Once the city came under siege, Yanchao tried to rally defenders along the wall, promising, "I have several thousand ingots of silver to give entirely to you." But the soldiers, declining deployment, privately said to one another, "With a core of iron, of what possible use is it?"

A year later, in the fifth month [C.E. 952], Taizu personally campaigned against him and overran the city. Yanchao and his wife both died after leaping into a well. His son Murong Jixun had led five hundred followers in flight, but they were apprehended and the entire family annihilated. The prefecture of Yan now pacified, Taizu conferred posthumous rank on Yan Honglu as commandant of the Valorous Left Guard and Cui Zhoudu as director of the Palace Library.

CHAPTERS 54–55

MISCELLANEOUS BIOGRAPHIES

It is said, "A sense of rites, righteousness, integrity, and shame constitute the 'four covenants' of the country. If these four covenants do not thrive, the country will perish."[1] Excellent indeed is Guan Zhong's way with words! Rites and righteousness are the premier methods for governing men, integrity and shame the premier maxims to anchor them. Without integrity everything is acceptable, without shame anything is done. When ordinary men are so disposed, every sort of catastrophic turmoil and devastating defeat can occur. Worse yet, when high officials will accept or do anything, chaos for the world and peril to empire can scarcely be eluded. I have read Feng Dao's "Jottings of the Old Man of Eternal Joy" and witnessed the glories that he personally professes: indeed, he emerges as a man utterly devoid of integrity or shame—a reality now clear to the whole world.

For the entire Five Dynasties era, I found three officials of complete virtue and fifteen to die honorably in service. It is perplexing that a great many literati presented themselves as Confucians and claimed to study antiquity, enjoyed the remuneration of mankind and served its empire. However, inasmuch as those to act on principles of righteous loyalty hailed solely from the ranks of military leaders and warriors, it only affirms the total absence of peers within Confucian ranks. Did literati of less lofty virtue so disdain the times that they dared not surface, their revulsion for the prevailing tumult notwithstanding? Or were monarchs then too undeserving to reach them? Confucius believed, "Even in a hamlet of ten families, the loyal and trustworthy are certain to exist"—no hollow words![2]

I once acquired a short story from the Five Dynasties concerning the Woman Li, wife of Wang Ning. If one woman can evince such moral girth, then surely the age produced others gone unnoticed by history. Wang Ning, his ancestral home located between Qing‡ and Qi¶ prefectures, was fiscal administrator of Guozhou upon dying of illness. His family being poor and his sole surviving son still young, his widow set out for home alone, escorting the child and Wang's corpse. Heading eastward, she passed through Kaifeng and stopped at an inn, where the keeper refused her lodging owing to the suspicious spectacle of [an unaccompanied] woman with child in hand. The sun had already set and Woman Li refused to leave, so the innkeeper grabbed her arm to evict her. The Woman now let out a long wail of protest in peering at the heavens, declaring, "How have I, the wife of another man, failed to protect my chastity by allowing this arm to be touched by another? And surely, I cannot permit a single arm to defile my entire body!" So, drawing an ax, she lopped off her own arm. Roadside observers then surrounded and comforted her, some pointing their fingers accusingly as others wept. Upon learning of the matter, the custodian of Kaifeng informed the court and tapped official funds to provide medicines to cover the wound. He extended generous relief to the Woman Li, the innkeeper flogged with light rod.

WE LAMENT. Literati lacking similar regard for their moral repute, men suffering shame for the simple sake of survival should be considerably ashamed to learn of this woman's integrity.

Feng Dao

Feng Dao [C.E. 882–954] had the courtesy name Kedao. Native to Jingcheng County, Yingzhou, he worked as consultant under Liu Shouguang, then for eunuch Zhang Chengye upon Shouguang's demise. With Chengye administering the Hedong command, Dao became his local inspector. He was recommended to the Prince of Jin, in recognition of literary talents, and named administrative secretary to the governor of Hedong. Appointments as vice minister of finance and concurrent Hanlin academician attended the accession of Zhuangzong.

Dao could be frugal to the point of severe self-deprivation. When the Princes of Jin and Liang faced off from opposite sides of the Yellow River, Dao lived in a thatched hut within the military compound and slept simply on bundles of straw, rather than on a sleeping mat. And whenever receiving salary, he found quiet contentment in lavishing it on servants, permitting them to enjoy the same food and wine as he. Commanders then given to abducting the beautiful girls of the vanquished often presented some to Dao, who could not well reject them, so he would furnish a separate room as accommodation while inquiring about their original father or husband, discreetly returning the women.

Taking leave as academician to mourn for his father, he found his native Jingcheng plagued for years with famine, so Dao relinquished all possessions to relieve the villagers, retreating to the wilderness to till the land and haul his own firewood. When others let their own lands grow wild or lacked the strength to till themselves, he would quietly proceed at nighttime to till for them. Such persons might later express an embarrassed gratitude, yet Dao saw nothing particularly noble in his deeds.

Reappointment as Hanlin academician followed his parental mourning. Dao had reached Bianzhou when Zhao Zaili rebelled and Emperor Mingzong directed armies southward from Weizhou to invade the capital. Kong Xun implored Dao to remain at Kaifeng to wait things out, but he insisted, "With an imperial summons to appear in the capital, how can I possibly dally?" He thus hastened to the capital of Luoyang. Mingzong ascended the throne after regicide against Zhuangzong, and having long heard of Dao's personal conduct, inquired of An Chonghui, "What was the standing of Feng Dao under the Former Monarch?" "He was an academician," reported Chonghui. "I have long known of his reputation and consider him the perfect minister for me," Mingzong affirmed, naming Dao academician of the Duanming pavilion and later vice minister of war. Only a year later, he became deputy director at the Secretariat with ministerial powers.

In the Tiancheng and Changxing reigns [C.E. 926–933], material bounty had persisted year after year, the Middle Kingdom spared major incidents. Dao often admonished Mingzong all the same, saying, "During my tenure as administrative secretary at Hedong, I served as envoy to Zhongshan and passed through the difficult terrain of Jingxing along the way. Fearing my horse might stumble, I dared not relax the reins and bit. It was on level land where conditions were seemingly harmless, however, that the horse suddenly stumbled and sustained injury. Thus, humans have a proclivity in the face of peril to save themselves by thoroughgoing vigilance, while tranquil times leave them careless about threats to their very life." Mingzong further inquired, "The world may be prosperous, but have the masses truly seen relief?" Dao responded, "Expensive grains leave farmers starving, but cheap grains will ruin their farms." Reciting the poem of literatus Nie Yizhong, "Farmer's Song," there was immediacy and clarity in his locution.[3] Glancing at scribes on the left and right, Mingzong had the poem recorded and often recited it personally.

A commander of water transport once obtained a jade dish from Linhe County inscribed with the characters, "Longevity Dish for the Seal of Dynastic Succession." Emperor Mingzong, terribly fond of the cup, indicated so to Dao, who surmised, "This treasure is simply a physical representation of a former age, while the moral King is a treasure who transcends form." Mingzong inquired further and Dao responded, "Benevolence and righteousness should be treasures for a monarch. It is said [in the *Book of Changes*], 'The greatest treasure is the throne, but the way to preserve the throne is through benevolence.' "[4] Mingzong was a martial ruler unable to appreciate his words, so after Dao's departure, he summoned aides to explain his meaning, embracing it with relish.

Dao served Mingzong as minister for more than ten years, and after Mingzong expired, he ministered to Emperor Min.[5] In the wake of the Prince of Lu's rebellion at Fengxiang and Emperor Min's flight to Weizhou‡, Dao led official multitudes in welcoming the Prince to the capital. The Prince became Emperor Fei, Dao ministering to him. Emperor Min was at Weizhou‡ at the time of Fei's accession, but perished in an act of regicide three days later. Emperor Fei subsequently transferred Dao locally as governor of Tongzhou, extending honors as duke a year later. Dao likewise served the Jin after its conquest of Tang, the Jin monarch, Gaozu, naming him dignitary for public works with ministerial powers, honorary dignitary of education, and concurrent director of the Secretariat, while elevating his noble status to Duke of Lu. He ministered to Emperor Chu once Gaozu expired, receiving honors as grand marshal and Duke of Yan as noble rank; reassignment to the Kuangguo and later Weisheng governorships ensued.

Feng Dao even served the Khitan after they annihilated the Jin, meeting Yelü Deguang for audience in the capital. Deguang reprimanded him for a record of little distinction under Jin rule, and Dao was unable to defend himself. Deguang further inquired, "Why have you come for audience?" "I have no city to administer and no troops to command," Dao told him. "Refusal is hardly an option!" Deguang now retorted in jest, "And what sort of Old Gentleman are you?" "An absent-minded Old Man bereft of talent or virtue" was his humble response. The words pleased Deguang, who named him Grand mentor. Dao followed Deguang upon his return north as far as Changshan, then reverted to the Han upon the accession of Gaozu, serving as grand preceptor with the prestige-rank of *fengchaoqing*. He further served the Zhou when it conquered Han, Taizu of Zhou honoring him as grand preceptor and concurrent palace secretary.

A youthful Feng Dao succeeded in making a name for himself by dint of contrived manners, and as high official, strove to impress others with his staid demeanor. Having served four royal houses and ten sovereigns, he increasingly presumed upon bygone merits to glorify himself. Yet courtiers of the age, the wise and witless alike, all celebrated Dao as senior statesman and heaped praises on him. Yelü Deguang once asked of him, "How are we to render assistance to commoners of the world?" Dao responded with a riddle, "Times like ours would be hard to salvage even for the Buddha, should he appear. Only a man like Your Majesty will do." The Khitan decision not to exterminate subjects of the Middle Kingdom is uniformly attributed to the goodwill fostered by Dao through such deeds [of flattery].

As Zhou armies rebelled and invaded the capital, and with Emperor Yin already dead, Taizu expected support for his own enthronement from senior courtiers of Han. Feng Dao, however, expressed not the slightest interest during their encounter. Taizu had heretofore bowed to Dao and could not do otherwise now [without appearing presumptuous], but Dao treated the gesture as unremarkable. Taizu could only modify his plans, therefore, recognizing that the time was not ripe for supplanting Han rule. He thus publicly endorsed the enthronement of Prince Xiangyin, Liu Yun, as heir to the Han line, dispatching Dao to escort Yun back from Xuzhou¶. Yun had yet to arrive, however, when supporters in Taizu's army rebelled during a journey northward to Chanzhou. He now supplanted Han rule. Having once thwarted Taizu in his ambitions, Dao tends by observers to be exonerated of complicity in the demise of the Jin and Han dynasties. Yet he never seemed especially upset at witnessing the death of rulers or the dissolution of empires.

In a world beleaguered by the universal chaos and alien invasion that gravely imperiled the fates of all living souls, Dao adopted "Old Man of Eternal Joy" as his style name. He even composed a letter of several hundred words celebrating service to four separate houses, plus the Khitan, only to find glory in the offices and titles acquired. "I have been filial to family and loyal to dynasty," he proclaims, "and experienced being a son, brother, official, teacher, husband, and father, as well as begetter of sons and grandsons. In occasionally opening a tome or drinking a draft, but also in consuming food, savoring songs, or enjoying human beauty, I have always found contentment with the times. And with age, I find contentment within. What joy could be greater?" And so goes the language of his autobiography!

In his service to nine previous rulers, Dao never admonished or challenged them. Upon Shizong's enthronement, however, as Liu Min [of Northern Han] campaigned against Shangdang, Shizong proposed, "Liu Min slights me for my youth, regarding my recent installation and formal mourning duties as virtual guarantee that I will not emerge for battle. Those adept at deploying armies must value the element of surprise: I should thus personally command a raid." With Dao admonishing stridently against the action, Shizong added, "I have heard that Taizong of Tang, in pacifying the world, personally campaigned against all foes, great and small alike." Dao now cautioned, "Your Majesty has not reached the point to invite comparisons with

Tang Taizong!" The Emperor continued, "Should the vultures of Liu Min engage my soldiers, they will be crushed like eggs under a mountain," to which Dao retorted, "And presumably Your Majesty will be the mountain that crushes them!" An angry Shizong arose to leave, eventually commanding the raid against Liu Min that vanquished him at Gaoping. Indeed, the martial awe of Shizong that culminated in acquiring the Southern Huai and Three Passes had its roots in the Gaoping victory. Out of contempt for Dao, Shizong thus refused to take him along once the offensive against Liu Min began; Dao was selected to represent the court at the mausoleum of Taizu instead. He died after completion of those burial rites, seventy-three years in age and given the posthumous title of "Literate and Worthy," later to be ennobled Prince of Ying.

After his death, contemporaries all marveled that Dao lived to the same age as Confucius—such was the prevailing proclivity for praising him. Dao's son was Ji.

Zheng Jue

Zheng Jue was a grandson of Zheng Qi, chief minister under the Tang. His father, Zheng Hui, once served as administrative assistant to the custodian of Henan, Zhang Quanyi. And a youthful Jue himself, through the favor of Quanyi, assumed residence in Henan. He failed successive doctoral examinations and secured the degree only after Quanyi impressed upon the relevant officials. An investigating censor during the reign of Zhaozong, Jue became left rectifier of palace documents after Taizu assumed the Liang throne. Further promotions ensued as drafter at the Palace Secretariat and Hanlin academician for communications, having been repeatedly recommended by senior Liang officials on intimate terms with Quanyi. Under Emperor Mo, he was named deputy director of the Imperial Secretariat with standing as chief minister.

Upon learning that Tang armies under Zhuangzong, approaching from Yunzhou, had already reached Bianzhou, a horrified Emperor Mo anguished over the appropriate response. He even wept aloud in the embrace of Li Zhen and Jing Xiang, then summoned Jue to weigh options. "I have only one plan, but do not know if Your Majesty is willing to implement it," Jue stated. Emperor Mo inquired of the plan's thrust, and he continued, "I would take the imperial seal for dynastic succession posthaste to the barracks of the Tang military, hoping to slow its advance while awaiting the arrival of relief troops." To this the Emperor responded, "With matters so urgent, we surely should not cling to a seal. But will your scheme succeed?" Jue lowered his head in contemplation before admitting, "It will not be easy, I fear." Those around him all burst into laughter.

As Zhuangzong entered Bianzhou, Jue led the throngs of officials in a reception on the left side of the road. He was exiled to revenues adjutant for Laizhou, then relocated closer as adjutant for Caozhou. And after Zhang Quanyi intervened with Guo Chongtao, Jue was summoned back to the capital as adviser to the heir-apparent. Mingzong, upon his accession, wanted Ren Huan as chief minister, but An Chonghui did not wish for the novice Huan to be sole minister, so he inquired of Kong Xun, the commissioner of military affairs. As former courtier of the Liang, Xun was on cordial terms with Jue, and spoke of his own ministry under the Liang and Jue's proclivity to be cautious and mature. An appointment came as chief minister.

When Mingzong departed for Bianzhou, the dependents of men in the Six Armies were removed from Luoyang to Bian as well; once Mingzong expressed a desire to leave for the Ye capital, his soldiers were embittered as high officials spoke out. The Emperor failed to reconsider and uproar erupted at every level, conditions reaching near tumult. Jue alone spoke favorably of the trip. Zhao Feng made a desperate plea to An Chonghui, and he, alarmed, presented a forceful remonstrance in meeting the Emperor, who now announced suspension of the trip. Even then, Jue persevered, now praising the Emperor for his new decision to suspend the trip.

As chief minister, Jue seemed perpetually busy without achieving anything. He was also losing his hearing and grew unsettled by Kong Xun's dismissal as commissioner of military affairs, promptly invoking illness as pretext for his own resignation. Mingzong persisted in trying to retain him, Jue submitting four petitions before the court authorized retirement as chief minister emeritus, conferring an estate at Zhengzhou. The posthumous title of dignitary for public works came with death.

Li Yu‡

Li Yu [d. C.E. 935] had the courtesy name Zihui and was native to Wudi County, Bohai. A man of staid dignity and few words, he loved learning and wrote in the classical style. The governor of Cangzhou, Lu Yanwei, named him magistrate's assistant for Anling County, an appointment disrupted to mourn his mother. He was traveling the area within the Guanzhong passes when Liu Jishu confined Emperor Zhaozong to his eastern palace, prompting Yu to write Han Jian and enlist him in plans to revive the throne. His words were stunningly imposing in fortitude. Jian proved of little use, and Yu left him for Luoyang. He later won doctoral degree and erudite literatus honors to become adjutant for the Henan yamen, then left for Shandong following the calamity at Baima Post. On close personal terms with Li Yanguang, who had served Emperor Mo of Liang as classical expositor-in-waiting, Yu was repeatedly recommended by him and thereby won recall to the capital. Eventually, he rose to senior proofreader of documents and auxiliary Chongzheng academician.

Youliang, the Prince of Heng and elder brother of Emperor Mo, was acknowledged by senior Liang courtiers such as Li Zhen with the standard bow, save for a singular Yu, who insisted on an extended bow in his presence. The Emperor thus reprimanded him, saying, "I acknowledge the Prince of Heng with the informal bow. How can you alone bow extendedly?" But Yu countered, "Your Majesty views matters from the etiquette of family, such that the standard bow is appropriate. Your Subject, lacking personal ties to the Prince, can scarcely countenance so thoughtless an offense." Coming under criticism for "indecent statements," reassignment occurred as administrative assistant to the Dingzhou surveillance commissioner.

Li Yu was serving at court when the Tang Emperor Zhuangzong purged the Liang. The respect of leading officials of Tang familiar with him as classical scholar facilitated postings as gentleman at the Bureau of Receptions and Hanlin academician. As Jiji, the Prince of Wei, campaigned in Shu, he invited Li Yu to be administrative assistant to the generalissimo. Owing to the natural obstacles on the road to Shu, many advisors preferred to delay troops and advance only after local circumstances had changed. Commissioner of bandit suppression Guo Chongtao turned to Li Yu to decide, and he said, "The regime of Wang Yan, wreaking havoc on his kingdom through indolence, is hated by his people. We should exploit the prevailing confusion to storm sites without defenses. The advantage rests with speed and dallying will not do." Chongtao embraced the idea, surrender occurring along his entire path as the Shu satrapy was annihilated. His armies had previously reached only Baoji [Qizhou‡] when an administrative assistant to Commissioner Guo, Chen Yi, pleaded illness as an excuse to stay behind. Li Yu asserted in a stern voice, "Chen Yi seeks to advance when seeing benefit and wishes to stop when sensing a challenge. Now, as our great army confronts serious impediments and men's minds can easily waver, a summary beheading is wholly fitting!" Hereafter, no warrior dared propose staying behind again.

Promotions culminated in assignment as deputy director of communications at the Ministry of War upon the accession of Mingzong. When the Emperor sacrificed to Heaven at the southern suburbs, Li Yu drafted the rescript of special beneficence for chief ministers Feng Dao and Zhao Feng. The rescript's wording seemed indecent to Dao, who reassigned Yu as director of the Court of Imperial Sacrifices. After Ren Huan's removal as minister,[6] Yu became deputy director of the Palace Secretariat with ministerial powers. For his entire tenure, Yu never arranged his own official residence and rented space in a guesthouse instead. When he took ill, eunuchs sent personally by Mingzong out of concern found him lying on tattered rugs and mat, his four walls bare. Mingzong heaved a heavy sigh at the news and provided proper bedding for him.

The Prince of Lu later rebelled to invade the capital, as Emperor Min fled under the cover of night. Li Yu and Feng Dao went to the formal gate a day later to learn of the Emperor's departure. Zhu Hongzhao and Feng Yun were already dead by now, so Yu wanted to proceed to the Palace Secretariat to await the Empress Dowager's instructions on whether to go ahead, but Dao declared, "The Prince of Lu has publicized his cause everywhere and won the hearts of man. Having already arrived, why await instructions from the Empress Dowager?" The two men emerged from the city to greet him. After the Prince was installed as Emperor Fei, he reassigned Feng Dao locally as governor of Tongzhou. Replacing him as minister was Liu Xu, a man impetuous by nature. Li Yu was always stubborn and direct, the two thus often at odds. Moreover, Liu Xu's marriage ties with Feng Dao's family gave Li Yu cause for repeated ridicule, their mutual recrimination ending in reassignment for both men. Yu retained honors as acting minister.

With wars erupting and assorted incidents preoccupying the world, Yu aspired as minister to organize governance along ancient models. He thus petitioned for the *Six Canons of Tang* to be recited before the official multitudes and its principles implemented in their jobs: the ritual banquets in the village of examination graduates at the prefectural or county level, for example, could be dropped when deemed unconventional. Emperor Min aspired to orderly governance upon assuming power, often summoning academicians to discuss current affairs, yet, intuiting Yu as the pedantic sort, never bothered to address him. Emperor Fei also concluded that Yu and his cohort were unaccomplished in office, turning repeatedly to chief ministers to say, "They are nothing but gluttonous monks—stuffing their bellies all day while applying their minds to nothing!" Yu died of illness in the second year of Qingtai [C.E. 935].

Liu Xu

Native to Guiyi County, Zhuozhou, Liu Xu [C.E. 885–944] was a man of elegant deportment, who along with older brother Xuan and younger brother Jiao, were renowned across Yan¤ and Ji‡ prefectures for their celebration of learning. He later served surveillance commissioner Wang Chuzhi of Dingzhou as legal administrator. Upon Chuzhi's imprisonment by own son

Wang Du and the assassination of Xu's elder brother Xuan in a family vendetta, Xu sought sanctuary at Cangzhou.

Zhuangzong acceded the Tang throne and named Liu Xu erudite of ceremonials and Hanlin academician. Xu rose eventually to vice minister of war under Mingzong, who had long respected him and admired his refined bearing. He rose to Duanming academician, and in the third year of Changxing [C.E. 932], deputy director of the Palace Secretariat and concurrent minister of punishments with ministerial powers.[7] Appearing at the doors of Zhongxing Hall to express gratitude, a major sacrifice happened to be underway that day, preempting audience, so Xu proceeded to Duanming Hall to do so. To rise from Duanming academician to chief minister was reckoned an honor in his day. The enthronement of Emperor Fei led to reassignment as minister of personnel and vice director at the Chancellery. Xu oversaw compilation of the national history as well.[8]

Soon after Emperor Fei's accession, he asked Wang Mei, commissioner of the Three Fiscal Agencies, "How much cash is in our treasury?" Mei indicated "Several million strings." But his insistence on allocating not even one-tenth of that sum to reward troops utterly infuriated the Emperor, who dismissed him and invested Xu with concurrent powers as fiscal administrator. A scrupulous man who detested the acute corruption and malpractices at the fiscal agencies, Xu made emendations to accounting registers based on actual conditions, while eliminating oppressive assessments and advance payments altogether. Administrative aides could once conceal without forwarding to superiors the sums acquired as tax advances, holding them back to solicit illegal bribes from prefectures and counties. Xu's total eradication of such practices delighted the people, who considered him virtuous, although aides at the fiscal agencies resented such subversion.

Heretofore, Feng Dao and Liu Xu were related by marriage and served simultaneously as ministers. Once Dao was dismissed, his replacement, Li Yu‡, had long held Dao's character in contempt. Upon detecting any mishandling of affairs, therefore, Yu‡ invariably exposed these to reprove Xu, "Your actions are taken on Dao's behalf, your in-law!" Xu was disinclined to accommodate and forgive others, while Yu‡ proved relentlessly stubborn, giving rise to mutual recrimination. Secretaries and aides at the chief minister's office resented the inflexibility of the two and all spoke openly of the conflict. Emperor Fei dismissed both men after realizing the problem, demoting Xu to right associate at the Secretariat. Administrators of the Three Fiscal Agencies, having assembled that day outside the Yuehua gate carrying seals of office, welcomed news of Xu's dismissal with outbursts of celebration, pronouncing, "We are at last without care!"

As chief minister, Liu Xu proved ignorant of ceremony and precedent. In the wake of Mingzong's death, chamberlain for ceremonials Cui Jujian should by convention have been appointed master of funeral ceremonies; he declined because his grandfather's personal name was Li. Feng Dao thus named him director of the Palace Secretariat, causing a dispirited Jujian to be negligent in office. The reassignment notice by Secretariat drafter Li Xiang employed the words, "His heart grew anxious after learning of the taboo name," words abruptly revised by Xu to read, "He had a sense of shame and rectitude." The change led Jujian to complain, "We have standard rules and regulations when a personal name contravenes some taboo. What offense have I committed?" Men of the day who learned of the incident circulated the story in jest.

On another occasion Liu Xu was associate at the Secretariat when rain fell as courtiers approached for audience, so the official formation moved to a shaded corridor. Administrative aides from the Censorate now guided Secretariat associates for placement after deputy censors. Xu asked the aides about the relevant precedent, but no one from chief ministers to officers of the three departments knew for sure. Dao had been dismissed as minister by then and held the rank of dignitary for public works. Since the Sui and Tang dynasties, the three dignitaries had had no official function and received no special accommodation in audience. Once Dao became dignitary, he asked the relevant authorities about his proper place in the official lineup, and again, no one knew. In consequence, he did not enter the audience chamber, but waited for Censorate and Department officers to enter, then followed chief ministers in leaving. Xu became associate at the Secretariat after removal as minister, like Feng Dao himself, so he followed Dao both in and out of audience. Court authorities by now could not correct things even through censure, and many a court observer secretly scoffed at them.

When Zhang Congbin rebelled in the reign of Gaozu of Jin, murdering imperial son Chongyi at Luoyang, he named Liu Xu interim custodian of the eastern capital and administrator of salt and iron. In the Kaiyun era, Xu received honors as dignitary for public works with ministerial powers, serving again at the Three Fiscal Agencies as administrator. Owing to problems with eyesight, he was dismissed from office once the Khitan invaded the capital, then honored as grand guardian. He died the same year at sixty *sui*.

Lu Wenji

Lu Wenji [C.E. 876–951] had the courtesy name Zichi. His grandfather, Lu Jianqiu, had served in the Tang dynasty as governor of Taiyuan. His father, Lu Siye, rose to right rectifier of omissions. Wenji earned the doctoral degree and served the Liang as vice minister of punishments, as well as academician for Jixian Hall. He became deputy censor during the Later Tang reign of Mingzong.

Assuming duties and meeting court officials before the Censorate, aides formally acknowledged communications representatives for the governors waiting to congratulate him. Wenji questioned the reasons for such a protocol and aides responded, "At the Tang court at Changan, communications representatives treated senior and junior censors like mere scribes. And after the decline of dynastic power and evisceration of the Tang throne, after the waxing of local overlords and waning of the civil service, the court indulged the governors by coddling their visiting representatives at court. As senior and junior censors addressed court affairs, communications officers of the governors were sent to guest rooms, their names announced while tea and wine were lavished on them, without ever meeting the censors. This has persisted to become precedent." Wenji interjected, "My modest virtues do not permit repeal of longstanding protocol!" He subsequently directed an aide to apprise the representatives, who clamored to leave, yet entered for a meeting grudgingly. Wenji leaned against his recliner to adjust his official staff, as Censorate personnel recited the names and announced bows to him. The anger and indignation of the communications officers were difficult to contain as they departed, complaining to An Chonghui, the commissioner of military affairs. "I know nothing of precedent, although you may take your complaint to the court," he said. They went in unison to the auxiliary palace hoping to air their grievance. Mingzong hence inquired of chief minister Zhao Feng, "What other groups of regional officials are comparable to communications representatives?" "Couriers or liaisons for prefectures and counties," was Feng's response. Mingzong then retorted, "Mere minor aides. How dare they insult my censors!" He ordered beatings with heavy rod before releasing them for home. Wenji also requested a systematic restoration of rules to evaluate officials in and away from court, with commanders and ministerial-level officials examined by the Son of Heaven personally. The reform won court endorsement, but officials were never examined, in the end. Wenji became minister of public works a year or so later.

Frictions between Lu Wenji and chief minister Cui Xie were longstanding, making him all the more livid when Xie appointed Yu Ye vice minister of public works, a man whose personal name sounded like his own father's name. When Ye went to bureau offices to confer with superiors, Wenji declined a meeting and requested successive absences for himself. Later, Ye's assignment orders were still pending when Wenji emerged to conduct business. An embittered Ye consequently got drunk and hanged himself, causing Wenji to be banished to manager-adjutant at Shizhou.

After some time, Wenji became director at the Palace Library and chamberlain for ceremonials. Serving as emissary to the Shu region, he passed through Fengxiang, where the future Emperor Fei was governor. Wenji's poised physical presence and lucid diction convinced Fei of his rare talent. Once installed as Emperor, Fei wished to name a chief minister and inquired of his aides, who universally agreed, "Wenji and Yao Yi are both held in high regard." Emperor Fei then wrote on strips of paper the names of all officials famed for their honesty and placed these inside a glass bowl, burning incense that night to invoke Heaven. Grabbing one strip with his chopsticks, the name of Wenji appeared on the first draw, so he confidently named him chief minister and deputy director of the Palace Secretariat.

In a world then beset with many problems, Emperor Fei often had to impose upon Wenji, who consequently requested elimination of the "rise and repose audiences" [*qiju*] every five days, returning instead to Tang traditions, while opening the Yanying hall to facilitate more informal discussion of the world's affairs. Emperor Fei noted that the "rise and repose audiences" every five days had enabled Mingzong to see his officials informally, so their suspension was unacceptable. Moreover, informality was also possible at adjacent chambers, such that convening at the Yanying hall was unnecessary. He instructed chief ministers wishing to discuss affairs beyond regular audience hours to appear at the auxiliary palace gate, when convenient.

Once Gaozu of Jin rebelled at Taiyuan, Emperor Fei led a northern expedition and stopped at the Hui mausoleum en route. Now resting at the barracks for his bodyguard, he looked to Wenji and asked, "I have known you since my days at Fengxiang and never treated you like ordinary men. Since your tenure as minister, my inquiries about current affairs have invariably met with your assertions of a great peace at hand. Having led me down this path today, how do you now explain yourself?" Nervous and afraid, Wenji sought clemency by confessing his crimes. Once Emperor Fei reached Heyang, Wenji urged him to hold firm in defending the bridge, but he did not listen. Gaozu's accession to the Jin throne resulted in Wenji's demotion to minister of personnel and eventually Grand preceptor to the heir-apparent prior to retirement. He received honors at home as dignitary for public works after the enthronement of Taizu of Zhou, dying in his home at seventy-six *sui*. The court conferred the posthumous title dignitary for education.

Liu Yue

With courtesy name of Zhaofu, Liu Yue was native to Luoyang and an eighth-generation descendant of Liu Zhenghui, the minister of revenues in Tang times. His uncles included Chonggui and Chongwang. As scion of a famous family, Yue was fond of learning and sensitive to the written word, in addition to his skills as interlocutor. Recipient of the doctoral degree, he served the

Liang as left-proof reader at the Chancellery and attending censor. He rose to Hanlin academician under Emperor Mo and eventually became vice minister of war.

Demoted to manager-adjutant to the Junzhou governor after the Liang demise, Liu Yue was later restored as supervisor over the heir-apparent's household, becoming vice minister of personnel under Mingzong of Tang. By precedent, the Ministry of Personnel's notification of office for civil and military appointees invariably involved tendering rolled paper money with vermilion imprint before delivering the document. Men of high rank and social station thereby received the proclamations, but the poor, unable to tender money, often got only the imperial letter of appointment, with no formal proclamation. In a tumultuous age like the Five Dynasties, such malpractices became normal such that officials of lesser station no longer received the proclamation of office: the Palace Secretariat merely recorded the words of the court's assignment orders for storage in edict albums. Yu proposed the following change, "The words of a court order sometimes mention the nominee's exceptional talent, sometimes cite his achievements, or even at times include instructions or admonitions. Those appointees who do not receive the proclamation will never know the basis for the assignment, for the mandate does not contain the words of their king. I request that everything be given them." Yue thus inaugurated the practice of giving proclamations to all officials.

Chief minister Feng Dao came from generations of farmers to till the land, his physical appearance plain and unkempt such that many courtiers reviled him as vulgar. He once approached the court, trailed closely by Liu Yue and Ren Zan, the vice minister of war. Dao looked back repeatedly as he walked, prompting Zan to ask of Yue, "Why does Dao look back?" "He simply misplaced his *Manual for a Rabbit Garden*," Yue responded. The manual is recited by rustic Confucians in rural schools to teach farmers and herders of animals. Yue's comment was intended as ridicule of Dao, who was utterly livid after learning of it and demoted him to Palace Library director. Later, with Li Yu‡ as chief minister, Yue received advancement to chamberlain for ceremonials.

Previously, Zheng Yuqing had gathered writings on techniques for interpreting auspicious and inauspicious omens for officials and commoners of the Tang, subsuming these under the family rituals for the age as part of a two-volume *Book on Ceremonies*. Mingzong noticed that the book included advice on "restoration to office" and "marrying dead persons," prompting him to say with alarm, "Confucians should exalt filial piety and fraternal devotion, rectifying customs of the day. Why must they be concerned with 'restoration to office' when not [indispensable] as men of war? Moreover, marriage is an auspicious ritual. It should scarcely be employed for the dead!" He ordered Yue to recruit literati with broad learning in ancient and modern times to produce a revised version. Yue assisted men like Duan Yong and Tian Min, erudites of ceremonials, in selecting source material to include. Their concerns related to rustic customs, however, and the customs of contemporary families toward sons and daughters, where the original essence was often missing; nonetheless, the work reflects a legacy of the rituals of the time. Once lost to posterity, it became all the more impossible to investigate the evolution of such practices. Especially without foundation in the classics were legends about receiving relatives during the wedding ceremony or sitting a bride on the groom's saddle with their hair joined. Families of officials tended to venerate such practices, and after a long time, perverted them so outrageously as to be utterly ludicrous. Such cases are countless.

Dying in office at fifty-six *sui*, Liu Yue was posthumously named minister of personnel. His son was Liu Wensou.

WE PROFOUNDLY LAMENT. Men are fond of practicing the rites. When the rites are not displayed on high, the people are left without an appreciation of their essence. But when unorthodox customs are passed down, the people will cling to their practice all the same. The Five Dynasties, an age of war-induced turmoil, had precious little time to lavish on the rites. Moreover, Mingzong was a man of war who hailed from barbarian stock: without possessing a full command of the written language, he nonetheless aspired to acquaint the people with the rites. Liu Yue and cohort, eminent Confucians of the day, ultimately discovered nothing new, making mere emendations to existing works. Yet in later generations, writers on auspicious or inauspicious omens for officials and commoners invariably took Yue's work as their model, even though he lost three or four out of ten relevant works. My sorrow is indescribable!

CHAPTERS 56–57

MISCELLANEOUS BIOGRAPHIES

He Ning

With the courtesy name Chengji, He Ning [C.E. 898–955] was native to Xuchang, Yunzhou. His ancestor nine generations removed, He Fengyao, was investigating censor in Tang times, although later generations did not pursue learning for purposes of holding office. Ning's father, He Ju, a man fond of drink, refused to be confined to trivial matters, preferring instead to extend courtesies to literati. His riches flowed liberally whenever fraternizing with them and Ning traveled along.

A child of nimble mind, Ning exuded refinement both physically and mentally. He passed the doctoral examination and received appointment as clerical aide to He Gui, governor of the Yicheng command. Gui once engaged Zhuangzong of Tang in battle at Huliu, only to be defeated, escaping with barely his own life. His only remaining follower was Ning, whom Gui noticed after looking back and motioned to leave. Ning insisted, however, "A gentleman should rightfully die for a true friend. My sole regret is failing to find the appropriate venue. How can I possibly leave?" An enemy horseman in pursuit of Gui was gaining ground as Ning cursed him incessantly, then extended his bow to shoot him dead. Gui thereby escaped, and upon returning, admonished his sons, "Disciple He, a warrior of righteous purpose, will surely enjoy wealth and station, someday. You should be circumspect in serving him." He consequently gave Ning a wife in the person of his daughter.

During the Tiancheng era, Ning rose to palace censor and, later, incoming minister of receptions, drafter of proclamations, Hanlin academician, and chief examiner for the civil service. At the time, doctoral candidates were often a bawdy lot who reveled in shocking the chief examiner with rancorous outbursts. Whenever the chief examiner prepared to post the list of new graduates, they commonly surrounded the office with thorn bushes to seal off the gates and prevent entry or exit. Ning tossed aside the thorns to open the gates, as students all stood solemnly without rancor. He eventually won praise for selecting the cream of the literati crop of his day.

At the outset of the Jin dynasty, He Ning became academician for Duanming Hall, concurrent administrator of fiscal accounts, and Hanlin recipient of edicts. Gaozu summoned him to court on many occasions to explore current affairs, and Ning's replies won universal praise. Appointment ensued, in the fifth year of Tianfu [C.E. 940], as deputy director of the Palace Secretariat with powers as chief minister. Gaozu was preparing to depart for Yezhou when it became apparent that An Congjin of Xiangzhou would rebel. Ning now queried, "Your Majesty's departure for Ye will give Congjin a chance to rebel, in which case, how will we manage?" Gaozu asked how he might handle Congjing. "By acting before others, we can outmaneuver them," Ning asserted. "I propose drafting more than ten imperial orders, entrusting these to the Prince of Zheng. If there is an emergency, then commanders can be directed to storm Ye." Gaozu concurred. The Prince of Zheng, as the current metropolitan custodian of Kaifeng, did not accompany Gaozu to the Ye capital, but stayed behind and received the imperial orders. Congjin did, indeed, mutiny at Xiang as Gaozu approached Ye, the Prince of Zheng employing imperial instructions to dispatch cavalry commanders Li Jianchong and Jiao Jixun for the suppression. Knowing Gaozu to be currently at Ye, Congjin did not anticipate the speed of Jin armies: upon encountering Jianchong's men at Mount Hua, he thought he had seen a mirage! He fled in defeat.

The accession of Emperor Chu saw Ning's advancement to right associate at the Secretariat. Divested of ministerial powers over a year later, he became left associate. Gaozu of Han bestowed honors as grand mentor to the heir-apparent, investing him as Duke of Lu. He died in the second year of Xiande [C.E. 955], at fifty-eight *sui*, honored posthumously as director of the Chancellery.

Ning was fond of adorning carriages and costumes. He also saw merit in the prolific profusion of writings. With personal writings in excess of a hundred chapters, he once personally had them cut into printing blocks to permit circulation in his day—an act ridiculed by many men of knowledge. In personality, he liked performing good deeds and celebrated himself as a scholar advancing the next generation of talent. By custom in Tang times, the chief civil service examiner, when releasing the new list of holders of doctoral degrees, paid special attention to the sequence of names relative to the examination that he had passed earlier. Ning had passed in fifth place on his own doctoral examination, and when administering the examination later, he selected Fan Zhi for fifth place. Zhi subsequently rose to chief minister, with investiture as Duke of Lu and ultimate rank as grand mentor to the heir-apparent—in each case, the same as Ning himself. Men of the age considered it glorious.

Lu Zhi

Native to Henan Prefecture, Lu Zhi [C.E. 876–942] had the courtesy name Zizheng [Ziwei]. His father, Lu Wang, served the Tang as director of personnel merits. Zhi proved intelligent and charitable as a youth, commanding a flair for literary composition. Serving the Tang as assistant palace librarian, he later left office to mourn for his mother. Subsequent sojourns to Taiyuan led to appointment from the Prince of Jin as administrative secretary to the governor of Hedong.

He joined Zhang Chengye and cohort in settling the princely succession in favor of Zhuangzong. Named commissioner of grand ceremonies and acting minister of rites prior to the Zhuangzong accession as emperor, Zhuangzong expressed a desire to make him chief minister after acceding the throne. Zhi's personality preferred aloof reclusion and eschewal of exceptional responsibility, so he was adamant in declining. He did become metropolitan custodian of Taiyuan and interim custodian of the northern capital, and later minister of revenues and Hanlin academician. Since pacification of the Liang dynasty, he served as provisional administrator of revenues, minister of war, and then edict recipient at an academy—the court conferring the honored title "Meritorious Subject, Reasoned in Thought and Devout in Service." In the inaugural year of Tiancheng [C.E. 926] he was named the Kuangguo governor, and by the third year, minister of war and senior administrator to the chamberlain of ceremonials. He was governor of the Heyang and Henghai commands as well.

Formerly, after the Liang dynasty had overturned the Tang, it invested the former Emperor Ai as Prince of Jiyin, only to assassinate him by poisoning and inter him unceremoniously at Caozhou. Zhuangzong was contemplating a change in burial in the third year of Tongguang, but postponed consideration because of Dowager Cao's death. Instead, he settled for slightly enlarging the mound above the tumulus and arranging for regular sacrifices. Lu Zhi now recommended the erection of a ritual temple for Jiyin and conferral of posthumous title, so a title was confirmed as the "Illustriously Enlightened and Radiantly Noble and Filial Emperor," his temple designation Jingzong. Mingzong paid a personal visit to Wenming Hall in the fourth year of

Tiancheng, twelfth day of the eighth month [C.E. September 17, 929], charging Zhi with officially inaugurating a ritual temple at Caozhou. Court observers argued against such changes, for Prince Hui [Jiyin] had been installed unpropitiously by renegades, while predecessor Zhaozong and Empress He had both succumbed to regicide by the Liang as their empire collapsed, such that the posthumous title "Illustriously Enlightened and Radiantly Noble" was wholly inappropriate; they also noted the impropriety of erecting a tomb for Jiyin's direct ancestors, rather than include him in the Temple to imperial ancestors of Tang. They all found fault with Zhi in consequence. Senior officials also deemed the proposal unacceptable and petitioned simply to abandon the temple designation of Jingzong.

In the wake of executing the Prince of Qin, Congrong, on charges of plotting to rebel, the court named Lu Zhi provisional prefect of Henan Prefecture, with standing as associate at the Secretariat. The future Emperor Fei then rebelled at Fengxiang and Emperor Min unleashed armies to punish him, depleting the imperial treasury in order remunerate troops generously. The armies nonetheless defected upon reaching Fengxiang. Fei took eastward the entire cache, lavishing spoils on troops after prevailing militarily, his soldiers excessive in their expectations. Once Fei was enthroned, court authorities could muster only a paltry sum from confiscated properties, inciting his sudden rage. Everyone from district governors to prefects now had to submit cash and silk gauze as subsidy for the state. These proved inadequate as well, so fiscal commissioner Wang Mei proposed augmenting resources by appropriating private property. The court directed him and Lu Zhi to explore rates of appropriation. Inequities between rich and poor triggered acrimony and legal action, as prisoners flooded the jails. Six or seven days later, the collection did not amount to even a hundred thousand strings of cash, which alarmed Emperor Fei and prompted orders for Zhi to collect urban taxes five months in advance. The people's revulsion was thereby immense.

Once Gaozu came to the Jin throne, Lu Zhi received an at-large assignment at the western capital due to illness and honors as grand guardian to the heir-apparent. He died at seventy-six *sui*, given the posthumous rank of grand preceptor to the heir-apparent and the title "Literate and Loyal."

Lü Qi

Lü Qi [d. C.E. 943], courtesy-named Huishan, came from Anci, Youzhou. His father, Lü Yan, was once the Henghai governor's administrative assistant. Governor Liu Shouwen and his younger brother Shouguang were at war when Shouwen died in defeat; Lü Yan played a leading role in the cabal of officers and subjects that installed as successor the son of Shouwen, Yanzuo. Yanzuo later met defeat at the hands of Shouguang, who murdered Yan and liquidated his family in angry retribution. Qi was fifteen *sui* when apprehended and brought before the executioner, who was misled by Zhao Yu, a one-time retainer of his father, to think that the youth was his own younger brother. The executioner believed him, and Qi was released to join Yu in departing. The boy's feet were too weak to walk, so Yu carried him piggyback across several hundred *li*, the youth eluding death by changing his name and begging for food on the roadways.

A man with exquisite deportment, Lü Qi had an indomitable sense of purpose as well. Owing to the loss of his family in youth, he roamed the region of Fen and Jin prefectures. Zhuangzong of Tang, then governor of Taiyuan, named him military judge for Daizhou. Qi later served as judge under the Henghai governor, Zhao Dejun, then came to the capital as palace censor. He rose to assistant director of imperial brigades and concurrent associate censor for miscellaneous affairs in the reign of Mingzong. The administrator of the prefectural treasury at Heyang, having pilfered properties under his control, had been confined to the military inspector's jail, only for warden Yin Xun to accept a bribe permitting his escape. The aggrieved families pleaded their case to the court, which entrusted investigation to the Censorate. Upon obtaining evidence of Xun's illicit wealth, the Censorate petitioned for his appearance. Yet Xun enjoyed the patronage of An Chonghui, who refused to surrender him. Lü Qi proved so unrelenting in petitioning for the Censorate that a frazzled Xun committed suicide. The criminal case was now clarified and the livelihoods of vast numbers of people saved. Over a year later, Qi became director at the Ministry of Rites and compiler at the History Bureau.

During the Changxing era, the future Emperor Fei had lost the defense of Hezhong. Placed under house arrest at the city's Qinghua ward, he lived on the same lane as Lü Qi, who often visited him there. Fei later assumed the throne and treated Qi with extreme bounty, appointing him drafter of imperial edicts, secretarial overseer, auxiliary academician at the Bureau of Military Affairs, and Duanming academician.

The future Gaozu of Jin, governor of Hedong at the time, was already inclined to sedition such that Emperor Fei saw a threat in him and installed Lü Qi and Li Song to provide strategic counsel, the two devising many valuable plans. Qi once advised, "The menace from Taiyuan lies in the certainty that it will invite Khitan intervention. We should preferably launch a preemptive strike to contain the problem." Since the rebellion of Wang Du at Dingzhou, in the Mingzong era, the Khitan had lent assistance to Du by dispatching Tunei and Zela. They were vanquished by Zhao Dejun and Wang Yanqiu,

Tunei slain and Zela and others sent to the capital. The Khitan later dispatched successive envoys seeking the return of Zela and cohort, their words exceptionally deferential, but Mingzong summarily beheaded the envoys and refused to respond.

Once the King of the Dongdan entered the Middle Kingdom for sanctuary, the Khitan pleaded often for peace. Qi said, in response, "In light of current strategic conditions, a truce with the Khitan is the better alternative: based on Han-dynasty precedent, we would provide annual payments of gold and silk, while offering our daughters as wives for them. In this way, powerful commanders on the border and influential governors within cannot look to the outside for intervention, their propensity to incite tumult thus thwarted." Li Song conveyed the views of Qi to Zhang Yanlang, commissioner of the Three Fiscal Agencies, who responded gleefully, "If we can thwart a grave threat to empire at roughly a hundred thousand cash strings a year—the mere cost of a county official—I can pay out of pocket!" So they banded together in pursuing an accommodation.

An uplifted Emperor Fei, a day later, discussed Lü Qi's ideas with Xu Wenyu, auxiliary academician at the Bureau of Military Affairs. He considered it gravely misguided and recited a poem by [Tang literatus] Rong Yu, "Survival of dynastic altars relies upon enlightened rulers, but security in peril rests with mere women." He was chiding Qi and cohort. Emperor Fei now became livid and summoned Song and Qi to inquire about specifics in the peace plan with the barbarians. Qi noticed the anger on the Emperor's face and impulsively responded, "Your Subjects weigh the interests of country in proposing policy, which does not mean helping the Khitan exact benefit from the Middle Kingdom." The Emperor's temper had now surfaced, as he retorted, "You counselors once aspired to help me attain universal peace. How have we come to this? My sole daughter remains a mere child, yet you want to forsake her to barbarian lands; gold and silk are needed to support troops and protect the empire, yet you want to relinquish these as barbarian subsidy. Is this acceptable?"

Afraid and nervous, Li Song and cohort bowed apologetically, but even before he could complete a few bows, Lü Qi stopped due to weak feet. The Emperor chided, "Lü Qi, you still have the stiff neck [of a stubborn man]. Are you willing to behold me as your ruler?" "Your Subject, beset by old afflictions, lacks energy after repeated bows," Qi countered. "Please indulge a slight rest." Once his panting had subsided, he continued, "Should Your Majesty find fault with Your Subject's proposals, punishment is always possible. What more does bowing accomplish?" The Emperor's anger subsided and he excused Qi from bowing, then ordered a goblet of wine for him to drink, the debate suspended. Qi was later named deputy censor and, within a few months, reappointed academician for Duanming Hall.

Later, when the future Gaozu of Jin rose in rebellion at Taiyuan, he did, indeed, lure the Khitan to intervene and bring the Tang to its knees. Lü Qi served the Jin as director of the Palace Library and ultimately vice minister of war. He died in the eighth year of Tianfu [C.E. 943].

Zhao Yu held official posts culminating in assistant director of the Bureau of Operations. Lü Qi treated him like a father, and when Yu took ill, he personally tended to him with medicines. Qi even assumed responsibility for the funeral and burial expenses after Yu's death. Yu's son, Zhao Wendu, orphaned at a young age, received instruction from Qi. Treated like a son, Wendu later passed the doctoral examination.

Lü Qi's offspring include sons Yuqing and Duan.

Li Song

Native to Raoyang, Shenzhou, Li Song [d. C.E. 948] was nimble of mind as a child and a deft composer of prose. He served as adjunct to the governor of Zhenzhou. When Jiji, the Prince of Wei during Later Tang times, was named Xingsheng commissioner at large, he held concurrent powers as governor of Zhenzhou and decided to name the judge Li Yao as his administrative secretary. Song commented to the current secretary, Lü Rou, "The Prince of Wei, imperial son, is of eminent standing in the world, Yao unqualified to draft his petitions." Rou privately arranged for Song to replace him, then informed ministers Lu Zhi and Feng Dao, who received the choice favorably. Song became inspector of the Xingsheng palace [at Ye] and chief musician.

During campaigns against Shu by Jiji and Guo Chongtao, Li Song became administrative secretary to Jiji. The vanquishing of Shu had been accomplished when Empress Liu, believing the slanders of others, secretly dispatched an agent to Shu directing Jiji to murder Chongtao. Her orders so unsettled the hearts of the leadership that Song entered for a meeting with Jiji to counsel, "Why should you, my Prince, assume so hazardous an undertaking? If Chongtao is genuinely problematic, deferring execution until his return to Luoyang is hardly too late! With armies now posted a remote five thousand *li* from the capital, to assassinate a senior official without tangible authorization from an imperial rescript only jeopardizes the people's support and invites turmoil." "I am also reticent," Jiji confided, "but what can I do?" Song called three or four scribes up a tower, removing the ladder as they composed overnight an imperial edict on yellow paper, the seal of the general commander affixed upside-down. He gave instructions to the armies on the next morning, the hearts of its leadership now assuaged.

Jiji died on the highway, but his armies returned. Ren Huan was supervisor of the Three Fiscal Agencies once Li Song reached the capital, appointing him administrative assistant for salt and iron revenues. Song left office to return to the countryside due to mourning obligations. After mourning, Fan Yanguang presided over Zhenzhou and arranged for Song's assignment as administrative secretary. Yanguang later became military commissioner, Song serving as proofreader and auxiliary at the bureau. He continued to rise as vice minister of revenues and academician of Duanming Hall.

Mingzong was advanced in years by the Changxing era and Congrong, the Prince of Qin, commonly conducted himself illegally. The future Gaozu of Jin [Shi Jingtang], then deputy commissioner of the Six Armies, worried about involvement in the unfolding calamity and requested leave from the capital for a frontier assignment. The Khitan by now had penetrated the empire at Yanmen and Mingzong began selecting a commander to secure Taiyuan, a post that Gaozu desired. Military commissioners Fan Yanguang and Zhao Yanshou long deliberated on the command problem without reaching a decision, and a furious Mingzong issued a reprimand. Yanshou and cohort, nervous and afraid, wanted to name Kang Yicheng to the command, but Song singularly disagreed, saying, "Taiyuan, the northern door to the country, rightfully deserves a respected leader: none will do but Shi Jingtang!" The court adopted Song's proposal.

The future Gaozu of Jin, profoundly obliged to Li Song, dispatched a secret messenger to express his appreciation, stating, "To be a Buddhist monk requires coming to terms with the razor!" It seemed a sign that he desired to employ Song from start to finish in realizing his dynastic ambitions. When Gaozu's armies later occupied the capital, Song concealed himself in a residence of commoners of the Yinque district, but was summoned to serve as vice minister of revenues, vice director of the Palace Secretariat with ministerial powers, and concurrent military commissioner. The court restored him to office as he was in mourning for his mother.

With the death of Gaozu and accession of Emperor Chu to the throne, Li Song served concurrently as supervisor of the Three Fiscal Agencies. He shared the military commissionership with Feng Yu. Jin armies had vanquished the Khitan at Yangcheng by now, while Zhao Yanshou of Youzhou attempted to mislead the Jin military with promises to revert, intimations that Li Song and cohort believed. Previously, the future Gaozu of Han controlled the Imperial Bodyguard as chief director of the Metropolitan Guard, although he shared powers as "honorary" minister with Du Chongwei. Considering the arrangement a humiliation, Gaozu in anger refused formally to accept the appointment, doing so only after the Jin ruler sent He Ning to assuage him. Gaozu later left the capital for residence at Taiyuan. Chongwei replaced him as director of the Metropolitan Guard and won repeated praise from Song as a man of talent. Gaozu concluded that Song was biased against him and came to hold him in profound contempt. Song also considered credible Yanshou's lies about conversion, causing Chongwei to command a vast army that was ultimately defeated at Zhongdu, bringing the Jin dynasty to its knees.

Khitan ruler Yelü Deguang, prior to invading the capital, had heard Zhao Yanshou and cohort praise the character of Li Song. After occupying the capital, therefore, he exclaimed to someone, "In vanquishing the southern dynasty, I obtained [nothing more valuable than] a single Li Song!" An appointment as grand preceptor to the heir-apparent followed. As they returned north, the Khitan ordered Song and his entire family to join their procession, leaving them behind at Zhenzhou. Once Ma Da abandoned Zhenzhou, return became possible for Song, Feng Dao, and others. Gaozu's displeasure with Song was longstanding, at the same time that those harboring grudges against Song slandered him for presumably enjoying substantial Khitan favor. In relations with powerful courtiers of the Han regime, Song often forced himself into humble deference, without daring to be too strident.

Once Gaozu of Han occupied the capital, he conferred the official residence of Li Song on Su Fengji. Song's family had buried lots of gold and other valuables owing to the turmoil around them, wealth Fengji claimed for himself. The younger brothers of Song, Yu and Yi, later stayed at the same hostel as the sons of Fengji, and under the influence of heavy drink, began venting grievances about the theft of their properties. Song's personal surrender to Fengji of the deeds to the home further displeased Fengji. The laws of Han were originally quite harsh, Yang Bin and Shi Hongzhao having fostered a proliferation in criminal punishments. Yu had a servant, Ge Yanyu, who once conducted trade on his behalf and embezzled virtually all of his property, so Yu punished him with a light flogging. Yanyu spent the night at the home of Li Cheng, a man in Fengji's private guard, where he made the circumstances known to him. Gaozu was soon to be buried at the Rui mausoleum, at the time, while the Hezhong governor Li Shouzhen rebelled. Cheng thus prodded Yanyu to charge Song and his sister's son, Wang Ning, with conspiring to rebel and setting the capital afire during the funeral activities; they further alleged contact with Shouzhen by secret letter with wax seal. Fengji summoned Song by messenger to his residence, casually relating the charges to him. Song recognized punishment as inescapable and entrusted his youngest daughter to Fengji's care. Fengji arranged for his incarceration in the jail of the Imperial Guard, and upon leaving the residence on horseback, Song's followers had scattered down to the last man, such that Song said defiantly, "Since antiquity, no man has ever eluded death and no empire escaped collapse!" He admitted to the false accusation, his entire family executed.

On close personal terms with Li Song was *Xu Taifu*, a Hanlin academician. On the occasion of Taizu's accession to the Zhou throne, he approached chief minister Feng Dao seeking the execution of Ge Yanyu. Dao found it difficult to act, for Yanyu had already happened upon successive amnesties. Military commissioner Wang Jun learned of the affair and considered Taifu's views righteous, so he petitioned for Yanyu's execution.

Li Lin

Li Lin [C.E. 860–947] descended from the imperial clan of Tang times. His uncle, Li Yang [Tang], had served as secretarial overseer during the Xiantong reign of Tang. Lin took the doctoral examination in his youth, but failed over and again, becoming a retainer in the Heshuo region. He professed to be administrative secretary for the Qinghai governor when visiting Wang Chuzhi of Dingzhou, who treated him discourteously. He subsequently changed from a green-colored costume to adornments in purple upon visiting Li Honggui of Changshan. Honggui recommended him to the Prince of Zhao, Wang Rong, who retained him as assistant. After Rong's subsequent assassination by Zhang Wenli, Wenli installed himself in power and designated Lin as his emissary to Zhuangzong, the future Tang ruler at Taiyuan. A man with a sharp tongue and the courage to speak out, Lin secretly provided Zhuangzong with a plan to conquer Wenli. He was named deputy to Zhuangzong upon the defeat of Wenli.

On the occasion of Zhuangzong's enthronement, Li Lin was named minister to the Court of the Imperial Clan and Li Qiong named deputy minister. The tombs of imperial grandfather Xianzu and great-grandfather Yizu were located at Zhaoqing County, Zhaozhou. Lin and Qiong petitioned the Later Tang court, after its inauguration, proposing, "We wish to appoint directors for the Jianchu tomb of Xianzu, the Manifest Emperor, and the Qiyun tomb of Yizu, the Glorious Emperor." Living in the countryside were more than a hundred abandoned youth who claimed descent from the imperial clan; in the absence of genealogical documents among clan authorities at court, their claims could not be proven. A commoner went to the Court of Ceremonials to profess that his family had served as directors over the Jing mausoleum at Danyang for generations, delivering hefty bribes to senior officials at the ceremonies office. Lin and Qiong did not bother with careful scrutiny of the claim before appointing him director. The commoner then organized military contingents under a crimson banner to appropriate more than a hundred *qing* of private land as the outer parameters for the graveyard. The people lodged complaints with local officials, who failed to reach a decision and informed the court. Zhuangzong referred the matter to senior courtiers and erudites, inquiring about the location of the imperial tombs for all rulers of the defunct Tang dynasty. They reported, "Danyang is currently Runzhou and the Jing mausoleum is not a Tang relic. Moreover, an unlearned Lin is ignorant and unfit to stand among the nine ministers." Demoted to vice director of the treasury, Lin then left the capital as deputy governor of Hezhong.

As an old acquaintance of Mingzong, Li Lin was summoned back to the capital after his accession, rising to minister of finance. He aspired to some important post such that he once said to Feng Dao and Zhao Feng, "By established practice under the Tang, members of the imperial clan commonly became chief ministers. Today, Heaven has ushered in a restoration of the Tang imperium and we should conform to established rules. However modest my talents, I did serve at Zhuangzong's princely command and knew the current Son of Heaven as regional governor. I am second to none in ability and experience. Yet I have long occupied my current place in official formation. How can you condone this?" Dao and cohort found his words repulsive. Later, Lin conferred with a spy for Yang Pu on assorted matters, then spoke to An Chonghui, claiming, "Yang Pu has wished to revert to dynasty for some time. The court need only dispatch an emissary of goodwill to win him back." Chonghui believed him and presented a jade sash to the spy as a token of trust. When no positive outcome occurred after a long wait, Lin was banished to manager-adjutant to the governor of Yanzhou.

Li Lin enjoyed relations of long standing with the future Emperor Fei as well. News arrived of Fei's accession to the throne while Lin served as Emperor Min's envoy to Hunan [Chu], in his capacity as minister of war. He relished in the presumed certainty of becoming chief minister. Passing through Jingnan on the return trip, he intimated to Gao Conghui, "We servitors have times of good and bad fortune, to be sure, and for long I had no opportunity to serve. With a new Emperor on the throne today, I will surely be employed." He thereby approached Conghui for valuable presents to take back for celebrations, Conghui providing two streamers of red horsehair and one skin from the long-tailed monkey. Conghui arranged a banquet for Lin and turned to his deputy envoy, Ma Chenghan, to ask, "Who among the statesmen at court today hold high prospects for leadership posts?" Chenghan indicated, "Secretariat director Cui Jujian, Secretariat associate Yao Yi, and after him, ceremonials chamberlain Lu Wenji." Conghui smiled in glancing at the men around him, then showed to Lin the reports of communications representatives [recently returned from the capital], where indeed, Yi and Wenji were pronounced chief ministers. Lin lost his color in shock, returning to the capital to present the skin and streamers to Emperor Fei, who did not employ him in the end.

In the past, Li Yu‡ had risen from chamberlain of ceremonials to chief minister, Lu Wenji replacing him as chamberlain. Once Wenji became minister, Lin requested the chamberlain post, and when the appointment occurred, Lin gratefully accepted at the palace, stating, "Your Subject now possesses the credentials to be chief minister!" The story circulated among courtiers as farce.

Under the Jin dynasty, Lin rose as high as grand guardian to the heir-apparent. Named dignitary of education upon Gaozu's accession to the Han throne, he died several months later, at eighty-eight *sui*, the posthumous title of grand mentor conferred.

Jia Wei

Jia Wei [d. C.E. 952] was native to Huolu, Zhenzhou. Having failed as a young man to pass the doctoral examination, prefectural authorities arranged his assignment as adjutant. Named senior military administrator for Zhaozhou during Fan Yanguang's governorship over Chengde, in the Tiancheng reign of Tang, promotion ensued as magistrate of Shiyi.

Jia Wei's strength lay in the writing of history. *Veritable Records* had never been written for the reigns of Wuzong and later, the post of court historian having gone unfilled. He thus sorted through informal accounts of events to compile a *Supplemental Chronology for the Tang*, in sixty-five chapters. During the waning years of Tang, the royal family had languished as local lords reveled in their powers, military actions occurred without authorization as the entire world succumbed to assorted incidents. For this reason, omissions and errors are replete in Wei's description. Nonetheless, for an era of devastating tumult where the preserved record of events is haphazard at best, it remains a useful supplement for historians.

Wei was appointed erudite of ceremonials during the Tianfu reign of Jin. But this was not Wei's passion, and he requested a historical assignment on numerous occasions. The court approved a change to assistant director of military farms, imperial diarist, and senior compiler at the History Bureau to assist in the compilation of the *History of the Tang*. Completion of mourning for his mother led to appointments as drafter at the Palace Secretariat, master of admonitions, secretarial overseer, and senior compiler of history once again.

In the Han reign of Emperor Yin, Jia Wei received court orders to assist Wang Shen, Dou Yan, and others in coauthoring *Veritable Records* for Emperors Gaozu and Chu of the Jin, as well as Gaozu of Han. Formerly, chief minister Sang Weihan despised much of Wei's personality and proved exceptionally uncharitable toward him. When writing the biography of Weihan, therefore, Wei wrote, "Upon death, Weihan owned eight thousand ingots of silver." Xu Taifu of the Hanlin academy saw this as incredulous, his repeated challenges of Wei leaving him no alternative to altering the text: he wrote, instead, "several thousand ingots."

The *Veritable Records* were complete by the inaugural year of Guangshun [C.E. 951]. Jia Wei now requested official reassignment and became frustrated when approval did not come. At the time, chief minister Wang Jun supervised compilation of the national history, and Wei composed the calendar of daily events, where he often discussed the shortcomings of senior officials of the day. Jun was incensed upon reading it, saying, "Secretary Jia and his children wish to create a partisan fraternity while serving in office. If not to promote the official careers of his sons and grandsons, why else would he defame scholars of our own dynasty?" He raised the matter with Taizu, who banished Wei to manager-adjutant to the Pinglu governor. He died a year later at Qingzhou†.

Zhang Yun‡

Native to Zhenzhou, Zhang Yun [C.E. 887–951] had served the prefectural government in youth, as adjutant to Zhang Wenli. During the campaign against Wenli by Zhuangzong of Tang, he split with ranks to surrender. Zhuangzong imprisoned Yun, but released him after the defeat of Wenli, permitting his appointment as personnel evaluator at Weizhou. Becoming judicial officer at the recommendation of governor Zhao Zaili, he later served successively as administrative secretary for Cang and Yan prefectures. Posted in the capital as investigating censor, his career culminated as assistant director of waterways and drafter of proclamations. The son of Emperor Fei, Li Chongmei, then metropolitan custodian of Henan with oversight over the Six Armies, respected Yun's dedicated resolve and named him secretarial overseer and administrator of the Six Armies. He became remonstrance cavalier after Chongmei's dismissal.

Coinciding with Gaozu's accession to the Jin throne, a succession of amnesties were promulgated for the world. Zhang Yun thus presented to the throne a "Critique of Amnesties," writing:

> There is a saying from Guanzi, "Amnesties generally involve little virtue and much vice, causing boundless calamity if practiced over a long period. The absence of amnesties will yield little vice but much virtue, making for boundless blessings if continued over the long term."[1] When the Emperor asked Wu Han of the Han dynasty, then fatally ill, to ex-

press freely his wishes, Han said, "I wish only that Your Majesty issue no amnesties." After all, to implement an amnesty may not be seen as charitable, while refusing to implement an amnesty may not be seen as uncharitable, for it merely reflects deserved punishment for crimes.

In antiquity, minor amnesties as acts of leniency only attended floods and droughts. To fling open jail cells and release prisoners in hopes of stirring Heaven to relieve victims of natural disaster is simply wrong. This is tantamount to two parties in a legal case, one guilty and the other innocent, where the guilty person wins release while the innocent cannot redress a grievance. Such a path will induce calamity, not save people from calamity. It will even cause petty men to take uniform delight in meeting natural disasters, as they goad one another to acts of evil, reasoning that, "The empire will surely issue an amnesty and certainly release me as part of its relief for natural disaster." In this manner, the people are taught to do evil. According to the Way of Heaven, goodness is repaid with prosperity and indulgence repaid with calamity. If we release evil persons ostensibly to replace natural disaster with prosperity, it suggests that Heaven also likes men to commit evil. Whenever Heaven unleashes calamity, it serves solely to warn the ruler of humanity to curtail sensual indulgence, commit to scrupulous frugality, empathize with dependent persons, and rectify the enforcement of legal punishments.

At the time, Gaozu of Jin still welcomed the outspoken views of subjects and relished in reading such words.

Zhang Yun was serving at the Han court as vice minister of personnel when Emperor Yin massacred senior officials to terrorize the capital. Often absent from court audience, he dared not return home and stayed at Xiangguo Monastery [at Kaifeng]. When the armies of Taizu of Zhou occupied the capital, Yun hid in a Buddhist hall and died when a piece of the ceiling fell on him. He was sixty-five *sui*.

CHAPTER 61

HEREDITARY HOUSE OF WU

WE LAMENT. After the decline of Tang rule, bandits across the world with tattooed faces and shaved heads exploited conditions to assume the costumes and trappings of royals. The domains of Wu and Southern Tang usurped power through a mixture of villainy and valor. Insularity for Shu created prosperity while isolation for Southern Han caused destitution, yet the poor became entrenched while the prosperous met an early end. Uncouth were overlords of Min and exploitive were those at Jinghu, while barbarian submission motivated men of Chu. The worst in insufferable plunder occurred at Wu/Yue, although Lingnan peoples seemed grist for sacrifice under Liu overlords.

Through a century of contests among men of valor, mountains and rivers were sealed so tight that neither wind nor air could pass. There is a saying: "When a fresh wind arises, perpetrators of darkness will submit; when the sun and moon come out, torches will be extinguished." As a great man does his deeds, harmony overtakes the world—my inspiration for writing "Hereditary Houses of the Ten Kingdoms."

Yang Xingmi and Sons Wo, Longyan, and Pu

Yang Xingmi [C.E. 842–905], with courtesy name Huayuan, was native to Hefei, Luzhou‡. A tall and muscular man, he could lift a hundred catties with his bare hands. In the Qianfu era of Tang, as bandit throngs sprung up across the Yangzi and Huai regions, Xingmi was apprehended on suspicion of banditry, although his stalwart physical presence impressed prefect Zheng Qi, who untied and released him. Xingmi later volunteered for the prefectural armed forces and received a border assignment at Shuofang, becoming company commander. He returned from border service after a year, but a military administrator's contempt for him led to reassignment on the frontier. He passed by the administrator's station before departing, a man who feigned kindness by asking Xingmi if he desired anything for the trip. Xingmi responded indignantly, "Only your head, Sir!" He proceeded to sever the man's head and carry it away, triggering a mutiny among his troops, as he claimed the title of chief commandant of the eight regiments. Prefect Lang Youfu fled the city, with Xingmi now occupying Luzhou‡.

The Tang court confirmed Xingmi as prefect of Luzhou‡ in the third year of Zhonghe [C.E. 883]. The governor of Huainan, Gao Pian, had come under attack from Bi Shiduo and petitioned the court to assign Xingmi as his manager-adjutant. Xingmi led a force of several thousand to lend assistance, reaching only Tianchang when Pian was imprisoned by Shiduo, who ordered Qin Yan of Xuanzhou to occupy Yangzhou, thereby preventing Xingmi from entering himself, so he quartered troops at Shugang. With an army several tens of thousands strong, Shiduo launched a surprise strike against Xingmi, who feigned defeat and abandoned tents to flee. Shiduo's starving men rushed victoriously to the tents to gather residual rations, Xingmi now counterattacking. Roundly defeated, Shiduo singularly rode into the city to slay Gao Pian. News of the death prompted Xingmi to assemble troops for three full days before the city wall, donning the white clothing of mourning and crying loudly, then raiding the western gate. Yan and Shiduo hence absconded for Dongtang as Xingmi occupied Yangzhou.

After depleting the city's stores of grain, starving residents murdered each other for food—husband and wife, father and son selling one another to the butcher to be trimmed like sheep or swine. Unable to defend Yangzhou, Xingmi wished to withdraw. However, Qin Zongquan of Caizhou had unleashed younger brother Zongheng to plunder the southern Huai region, as Qin Yan and Bi Shiduo returned from Dongtang to join forces with Zongheng. Xingmi responded by sealing up the city, not daring to emerge. Zongheng subsequently died at the hands of attending commander Sun Ru, whose raid on Gaoyou proved successful. This further intimidated Xingmi, whose attendant Yuan Xi observed, "We have defended an empty city with a band of fresh recruits, but most commanders are old associates of Gao Pian, not men humbled in heart by your profound charity, enduring trust, and vigorous controls. The armies of Ru, during the current rally, manage to vanquish every target they choose. This is a time for commanders to weigh the strengths and weaknesses of both sides, following one and abandoning the other. The Hailing governor, Gao Ba, a former lieutenant of Pian, will never act on our behalf." Xingmi then summoned Ba through special military order, inciting him to lead armies to occupy Guangling. Xingmi wished to use Ba to preserve Tianchang, but Yuan Xi interjected, "Having summoned Ba out of suspicion, how can we employ him anew? Moreover, if we prevail over Sun Ru, Ba will serve little purpose. If we happen not to be victorious, how will Tianchang be ours to hold, in any case? Killing him is a better option, then absorbing his troops." Xingmi thus offered a bounty to troops to liquidate Ba and his kinsmen, obtaining several thousand of his warriors.

Sun Ru later murdered Qin Yan and Bi Shiduo and absorbed their armies in a raid on Xingmi, causing him to consider flight to Hailing. Yuan Xi again counseled, "Hailing will be difficult to defend, but Luzhou‡ is a prefecture formerly administered by us, its storehouses replete with provisions. It will serve us better in the future." Xingmi went to Luzhou‡, instead. With the passage of some time, he remained undecided about the proper course to pursue and asked Xi, "I prefer to gather our armor for a breakneck sally against Hongzhou to the west. Is this feasible?" "Zhong Chuan having newly acquired the Jiangnan west region, it is not a vulnerable target," Xi responded. "At Xuanzhou, however, the Chizhou prefect Zhao Huang has had to preside at the behest of Qin Yan ever since claiming Guangling. With Yan now dead, Huang has lost a patron. The assignment at Xuanzhou was never originally to his liking, nor can he rival you in abilities. The city can be taken!" Xingmi led his men against Huang, routing him in a contest at Heshan. A blockade ensued at Xuanzhou, compelling Huang to abandon the city, as pursuers overtook and killed him. Xingmi hence occupied Xuan.

In the inaugural year of Longji [C.E. 889], the court named Xingmi surveillance commissioner for Xuanzhou. In an offensive against western Zhe circuit, Xingmi unleashed Tian Jun, An Renyi, and Li Shenfu: they acquired Su‡, Chang, and Run prefectures, seizing Chu‡ and He‡ in the second year. The acquisition of Chuzhou came in the inaugural year of Jingfu [C.E. 891]. Sun Ru, since expelling Xingmi to acquire Guangling, now found the city indefensible over the long haul and set it afire. Residents old and infirm were killed to feed his armies, which were hence pressed to cross the Yangzi in an assault on Xingmi, boasting five hundred thousand men. Commanders such as Tian Jun and Liu Wei were vanquished immediately upon engagement, as Xingmi considered flight to Tongguan. But attendant Dai Yougui cautioned, "Ru arrived with imposing morale and a multitude of men. At a time when his advance is invincible, we can still harass his men; at a time when his army is peerless, we can still corrode its power. To abscond in an effort to elude him is to walk willfully into his trap." Liu Wei added, "With our backs against city walls and fortifications reinforced, we can wear him out without joining battle." Xingmi concurred. In time, starvation ravaged Ru's armies, then massive pestilence. Xingmi now unleashed his entire army in a storm against Ru, defeating and capturing him. As his execution approached, Ru looked to Wei, stating, "I hear that you were behind this strategy to defeat me. If only I had a commander like you: how could I have been defeated?" Several thousands of Ru's remnants were absorbed by Xingmi, who provided coats of mail in black such that they were dubbed "Black-Cloud Regiment"; these men often functioned as his bodyguard.

That year Xingmi occupied Yangzhou once again, the Tang conferring standing as governor of Huainan. Further honors as honorary grand mentor with ministerial standing came in the second year of Qianning [C.E. 895]. Xingmi, in turn, appointed Tian Jun and An Renyi as prefects of Xuan and Run prefectures, respectively. Shengzhou prefect Feng Hongduo entered into submission to Xingmi. He sent Jun and the others to take multiple routes in raids and plunder, as every prefecture south of the Huai River and east of the Yangzi succumbed to them. Advancing against Suzhou‡, the prefect Cheng Ji was apprehended.

In the fourth year [C.E. 897], Zhu Jin of Yanzhou sought sanctuary with Xingmi. Heretofore, Zhu Jin had come under a Liang offensive and requested relief from the Prince of Jin, who sent several thousand stalwart horsemen under Li Chengsi's command. Zhu Jin was defeated all the same and subsequently joined Chengsi in taking refuge with Xingmi. Xingmi's troops were all natives to the Huai and Yangzi regions: Huai men tend to be slim and frail, so the acquisition of Zhu Jin's sturdy horsemen served to invigorate his own army. During this year, Taizu of Liang ordered an attack on Shouzhou, territory of Xingmi, led by Ge Congzhou and Pang Shigu. Xingmi stormed and overpowered them at Qingkou, killing Shigu as Congzhou gathered his men and fled; he pursued Congzhou to the Pi River, this time inflicting a rout.

In the fifth year [C.E. 898], Qian Liu raided Suzhou‡ and engaged Zhou Ben at Baifang Lake, defeating Ben and restoring Suzhou‡ to the authority of Yue. Xingmi dispatched Li Shenfu to attack the Yue region in the inaugural year of Tianfu [C.E. 901], where he scored a major upset in battles at Lin'an County [Hangzhou] and apprehended commander Gu Quanwu for return to Yangzhou. Feng Hongduo mutinied during the second year [C.E. 902], storming Xuanzhou and battling Tian Jun at Heshan. A defeated Hongduo prepared for flight on the high seas when Xingmi arrived from Dongtang and arranged for someone to approach him, saying, "Victory and defeat occur commonly in war. How can a single setback in battle cause such bitterness that you abandon yourself on some island in the sea? Our prefecture may be small, but adequate to accommodate you." Hongduo was moved to tears, as Xingmi trailed ten horsemen in rushing into his barracks, naming Hongduo deputy governor and Li Shenfu prefect of Shengzhou to replace Hongduo.

Emperor Zhaozong of Tang, in residence at Qizhou‡ that year, authorized the pacification commissioner for the Huai and Yangzi region, Li Yan, to confirm Xingmi's powers as general commander of at-large forces for the eastern circuits, honorary grand preceptor, and palace secretary, ennobled Prince of Wu. The new commissioner of bandit suppression for E/Yue‡, Li Shenfu, opened hostilities against Du Hong during the third year [C.E. 903]. Relief to Hong came from Cheng Rui of Jingnan, Shenfu defeating Cheng Rui at Junshan. Once Liang armies opened an offensive against Qingzhou‡ and Wang Shifan requested relief, Xingmi committed Wang Maozhang to the effort and he handily defeated the Liang, murdering Zhu Youning. Youning was the nephew of Taizu of Liang,[1] the death so incensing Taizu that he personally led a purported two hundred thousand men in a raid on Maozhang, only to suffer a second defeat at his hands.

Tian Jun now mutinied to launch a surprise strike against Shengzhou, apprehending the wife and son of Li Shenfu and returning them to Xuanzhou. Xingmi arranged for Shenfu to suppress Jun, but Jun directed commander Wang Tan to intercept Shenfu while leaving a letter trying to sway him through his wife and son. "From a lowly foot soldier in the Prince of Wu's service, I have reached today's stature as commanding officer," Shenfu affirmed. "How could I bear to disavow such virtue merely out of concern for family?" He promptly beheaded the messenger in expression of resolve, an action stirring the sentiment and fury of troops learning of it. With Shenfu advancing to Jiyang Ridge, Jun seized Chengding, Shenfu's son, to try to sway him. Shenfu screamed out to aides to shoot the youth, then proceeded to defeat Tan at Jiyang. Xingmi further dispatched Tai Meng to storm Jun, who perished in defeat.

Tian Jun, An Renyi, and Zhu Yanshou were formerly of humble origin and arose alongside Yang Xingmi. After restoring order to the Yangzi and Huai regions, Xingmi wanted a respite from war, but these three ferocious hooligans proved difficult to harness: he wished to eliminate them, yet had no occasion. In the second year of Tianfu, Qian Liu confronted a mutiny by his commander, Xu Zaisi, who isolated Liu in the city and invited Jun to raid Liu's seat at Hangzhou. Having accepted a bribe from Liu, however, Xingmi instructed Jun to disband on the very brink of victory, incurring Jun's wrath in the process. Jun had served in an accounting capacity at Guangling and often faced demands for bribes from Xingmi's commanders, even from wardens at the prisons. An angry Jun thus exclaimed, "These men must want me in jail!" The plans to rebel were laid upon his return.

News of Tian Jun's action prompted An Renyi to revolt as well, setting Dongtang afire in advance of a charge against Changzhou. As Changzhou prefect Li Yu emerged from the city to fight, he glanced at Renyi, roundly rebuking him. Renyi stopped his army, exclaiming, "Insulting me with such audacity, Li Yu must have troops lying in ambush." As he withdrew troops, men in ambush did indeed rally forth. They pursued him as far as Jiagang, where Renyi had planted banners and removed his armor to eat. The troops of Yu grew anxious about continued pursuit, enabling Renyi to occupy Runzhou again. Commissioned by Xingmi to encircle Renyi were Wang Maozhang, Li Decheng, and Mi Zhicheng. The military of Wu liked to celebrate Zhicheng as their premier archer, just as they regarded Zhu Jin as premier lancer. Renyi nonetheless took considerable pride in his own talents as archer, boasting, "Ten of Zhicheng's bows are no match for the single lance of Jin, but ten of Jin's lances are no match for a single bow of mine." Whenever engaging Maozhang and cohort in battle, Renyi insisted on predicting the point of impact before releasing his arrow. The armed forces of Wu thus feared him and dared not draw near. Xingmi also wished to convince him to surrender, but Renyi procrastinated in indecision. Maozhang exploited his delinquency to dig an underground pathway to enter the city, seizing Renyi for beheading at Guangling.

Yang Xingmi's wife, née Zhu, had a younger brother named Zhu Yanshou. Xingmi came to question his loyalties, however, in the wake of mutinies by commanders Tian Jun and An Renyi. He thereby feigned impairment of vision, bumping into objects around him whenever meeting Yanshou's messengers for them to see. He once intentionally hit a pillar during some activity, only to collapse onto the floor, the Woman Zhu having to brace him. He took considerable time to regain consciousness, then said tearfully to her, "The loss of eyesight coinciding with the achievement of my goals indicates that Heaven has forsaken me. None of my sons are fit to govern, so scarcely should I begrudge Yanshou the inheritance." This pleased his wife and an urgent summons went out to Yanshou. Xingmi met Yanshou in his bedroom upon arrival only to stab him to death, then expel Woman Zhu from the palace to marry another.

In the second year of Tianyou [C.E. 905], Xingmi dispatched Liu Cun to attack Ezhou, which he set afire. As defending troops suddenly broke the blockade to flee, Cun's commanders proposed a sally to stop them. Cun differed, arguing, "To attack and thereby force them back into the city would leave the city stronger still. Better to let them leave, making the city an easy conquest." Ezhou fell on the very same day and Du Hong was apprehended, his beheading occurring at Guangling. In the ninth month, after Liang forces conquered Xiangzhou, Zhao Kuangning turned to Xingmi for sanctuary. Xingmi died in the eleventh month, at fifty-four *sui*, and received the posthumous title of Martial and Loyal, his son Wo installed as heir. Retroactive elevation to the Martial Emperor Taizu attended the bogus accession of Yang Pu, his mausoleum named Xingling.

Yang Wo [C.E. 886–908], with courtesy name Chengtian, was Xingmi's eldest son. A bedridden Xingmi reassigned him away from the capital as surveillance commissioner for Xuanzhou. The director of the Right Guard, Xu Wen, once intimated to Wo, "An ailing Prince expelling his primary heir can only reflect the conniving of some evil courtiers. If you are summoned to court someday, I warn you not to comply unless the messenger is my own." Wo sobbed in thanking Wen, then departed.

As his illness worsened, Xingmi instructed administrative assistant Zhou Yin to employ "matching tallies" to summon Wo, yet Yin worried that a young and vulnerable Wo was unfit to govern. He thus urged Xingmi to select a seasoned commander of imposing stature to oversee military affairs and recommended the eminent commander Liu Wei. Xingmi had not yet consented when Xu Wen and Yan Keqiu visited his residence to inquire of his health, as Xingmi revealed Yin's proposal to them. The two men in utter horror left immediately for Yin's office to deliberate. Wen spotted the summons with matching tallies on Yin's desk before his arrival and seized it for transmission. Wo departed at the sight of Xu's messenger to win installation upon Xingmi's death. Zhou Yin was now summoned for a verbal thrashing. "How dare you, a sellout to our kingdom, behold again the countenance of a Yang clansman?" Wo said before slaying him.

Wang Maozhang hence became surveillance commissioner for Xuan Prefecture. After assuming powers as governor, Yang Wo wanted to revert to Guangling [Yangzhou] many objects in the Xuanzhou treasury and Maozhang's disinclination to release them incurred for him the wrath of Wo, who deputized Li Jian to surround the treasury with five thousand troops. Maozhang fled to Qiantang [Wu/Yue].

In the second month of the third year of Tianyou [C.E. 906], Liu Cun claimed Yuezhou‡ for Wu. Zhong Chuan of Jiangnan west died in the fourth month to be replaced by son Zhong Kuangshi. Chuan had an adopted son, Yangui, who resented being bypassed in the succession and attacked Kuangshi with his governor's guard. Yang Wo now intervened by sending Qin Pei's armies. Hongzhou was overtaken in the ninth month, while Kuangshi and manager-adjutant Chen Xiang were apprehended for return to Guangling. Xiang faced beheading at the marketplace there, with Kuangshi pardoned. Qin Pei became commissioner of regional order for Jiangnan west.

Taizu of Liang had supplanted Tang rule and changed the reign to Kaiping, but Yang Wo continued to acknowledge Tianyou. [Wu surrogates] Liu Cun of E Prefecture and Chen Zhixin of Yue‡ now led naval forces in a campaign against Chu, defeat awaiting them at Liuyang. Chu soldiers apprehended Cun and Zhixin for return westward. The Prince of Chu, Ma Yin, long knew of their reputations and sought to spare their lives, but Cun roundly reviled him: "Last year at Xuan, you barely eluded death at my hand. Heaven having wrought ruin upon me today, how can I serve you in hopes of surviving? Repudiating the house of Yang is simply beyond me!" Ma Yin deemed their submission impossible and killed them, Yuezhou‡ reverting to Chu.

Upon previously moving to Guangling, Yang Wo left behind at Xuanzhou a governor's guard contingent of three thousand men directed by trusted commanders Chen Fan and Fan Yu. After assuming power, he came to resent Xu Wen's dominance of the governor's guard and, for his personal security, chose Chen Fan and cohort to control cavalry for the eastern court. Fan's infringement upon their powers was resented by one-time senior commanders of Xingmi, Xu Wen and Zhang Hao, chief director of the Left Guard. Both men had even contributed to Wo's installation. During the inaugural month, the fourth year [C.E. 907], Yang Wo was conducting affairs with Chen Fan and others attending nearby as Wen and Hao ushered in contingents from the governor's guard, dragging away Fan and his men for summary beheading. Powerless to stop them, Wo consequently lost his governing powers. He could never vent the indignation within, while Xu Wen and cohort grew ever unsettled.

In the fifth month of the fifth year [C.E. 908], Xu Wen and Zhang Hao conspired to unleash hooligans to infiltrate Wo's bedroom to assassinate him. Wo promised the post of prefect to those same men if they killed Wen instead. The thugs all consented, save for a recalcitrant Ji Xiang, who seized Wo and strangled him to death. Twenty-three *sui* at the time, the posthumous title of Jing was conferred and younger brother Longyan succeeded. Elevation to Jing Emperor and Illustrious Ancestor attended Yang Pu's bogus accession, his mausoleum named Shaoling.

Yang Longyan [C.E. 897–920], with courtesy name Hongyuan, was Xingmi's second son. Earlier personal names included Ying and Wei. When formerly committing regicide against Yang Wo, Xu Wen and Zhang Hao had pledged to divide the lands of Wu among themselves and become vassals of the Liang. Hao experienced a change of heart after Wo's death, however, preferring to install himself. Wen deemed him a menace and inquired of attendant Yan Keqiu, the attendant noting, "Hao may be the obstinate sort, but he will easily acquiesce in a fait accompli."

On the next day, Zhang Hao arrayed swords and halberds in his office while summoning commanders for consultations. The senior commanders, from Zhu Jin and down, all left behind their personal guards prior to entering, as Hao pressed the question, "Who truly deserves installation?" The commanders dared not respond after three such inquiries, only Keqiu stepping forward to say confidentially, "As peril looms today in every corner, a man of your greatness is singularly able to master things. But your actions appear premature, I fear. Currently away from headquarters are men like Liu Wei, Tao Ya, Li Jian, and Li Yu, officers of primary standing under the Former Prince. You may manage to install yourself, Sir, but cannot know whether men of the sort will submit their hearts in serving you. Better to install a child leader and allow time gradually to pass, waiting for sentiment to change before taking action." Hao stood speechless as Keqiu scampered off to draft an order: placing it within his sleeve, he ushered commanders inside to offer felicitations, even though they knew nothing of his intentions, then pulled the orders from his sleeve to recite. Written on behalf of Wo's mother, née Shi, it alluded to the ordeals overcome by the Yang house to establish itself and the mishaps of successor Pu; it further affirmed Longyan as next in the line of succession and implored commanders to serve the Yang house, not forsake it. The statement's wording, emotionally evocative, stirred the feelings of listeners. Hao had lost both color and breath, by now, but had no recourse, Longyan consequently assuming power.

Tensions hence surfaced between Zhang Hao and Xu Wen, Hao intoning Longyan to reassign Wen locally at Runzhou. Yan Keqiu thus counseled Wen, "Today, as you forfeit bodyguard for assignment in the locales, calamity is already being perpetrated." The comments worried Wen. Keqiu consequently asked Hao, "Both you and Xu Wen were entrusted [by Xingmi] with care for Longyan. Rumors allege that you have stripped Wen of his bodyguard with the intent of slaying him in the provinces. Is the story credible?" "Action has already been taken," Hao insisted. "How can it be stopped?" "With considerable ease" was Keqiu's response.

On the next day, following Zhang Hao and other commanders in confronting Xu Wen, Yan Keqiu feigned reproof of Wen in stating, "The ancients never slighted the charity of a single meal. For a commander serving three generations of Yang overlords, the debt is hardly less! At a time when a young heir is new to power and affairs abound, how can you consider the security of a local post?" Wen expressed gratitude with similar histrionics, insisting, "If you Gentlemen wish to retain me, I hardly intend to leave." And he never left. A manager-adjutant to the governor on cordial terms with Zhang Hao, Li Chengsi, intuited Keqiu's collusion with Wen and prodded Hao to use a retainer to assassinate Keqiu by stabbing, his stabs in the dark of night only to miss their target. A day later, Keqiu met Wen to conspire to assassinate Hao instead. They secretly arranged for Zhong Zhang to select thirty stout warriors and proceed to the reception hall of the guard, where they decapitated Hao. Responsibility for regicide against Wo was heaped upon him as well. In this way, Xu Wen came to monopolize government, with Longyan a mere puppet.

In the sixth month, Wei Quanfeng mutinied at Fu¤ Prefecture and attacked Hongzhou, which triggered mutinies by Peng Yanzhang at Yuan‡ Prefecture, Peng Gan at Ji¤, and Wei Zichang at Xin†. Longyan summoned Yan Keqiu to ask about whom to deploy in the suppression. He recommended Zhou Ben, but having only recently returned defeated in the Suzhou† offensive, Ben was disinclined due to shame. Keqiu pressed for the resuscitation of Ben, who insisted, "The defeat at Suzhou‡ cannot be blamed on cowardice, but rather reflects the diminished powers of top commanders and often unilateral mandates from lesser commanders. If I must be assigned, I insist on no detachment commanders or attending commanders." Requesting seventy thousand troops, he opened hostilities at Xiangya Lake, apprehending Quanfeng and Yanzhang; Gan hence fled to Chu and Zichang to Qiantang [Wu/Yue]. After the arrival of Quanfeng at Guangling, the various commanders conferred, concluding, "In the past, when the Former Prince attacked Zhaohuang, Quanfeng repeatedly provisioned our Wu armies." They thus released him, forgoing murder.

Before this, as Quanfeng contemplated raising troops in rebellion, he encountered Wang Maozhang on the highway, under escort by Qian Liu to the north. "I hear that you, Sir, intend to launch a major uprising," Maozhang stated. "Permit me, if you will, to observe your armies and assess their viability." Quanfeng instructed troops to assume formation, then joined Maozhang in ascending the city wall for the review. Maozhang now confided, "I once served the Wu kingdom, whose armed forces were divided into three grades. A force like yours befits a commander of merely the lowest grade. Your mission is impossible without another hundred thousand soldiers." Quanfeng ultimately failed for this reason.

In the eighth year [C.E. 911], Xu Wen concurrently became prefect of Shengzhou to organize a naval force at Jinling [Nanjing]. Infuriated by Wen's dominance of affairs, Li Yu of Xuanzhou, a senior commander of considerable stature since Xingmi's days, once commented, "Who is this fellow, Xu Wen, suddenly so eminent without ever having met me!" His comments were passed on to Wen, so incensing him that he dispatched Chai Zaiyong to escort Wang Tan as Yu's replacement, recalling him to the capital. Suspicious, Yu ignored the order, so Zaiyong surrounded the city. In the interim, Yang Longyan arranged for attending commander He Yao to persuade Yu to return voluntarily. Yao told him, "If your intent is to rebel, you can murder me as a statement to the troops. If you lack such intent, why refuse to leave with me?" Knowing himself not to be a rebel, Yu departed with Yao, only for Xu Wen to prod Zaiyong to observe Yu's emergence and murder him. His family was annihilated as well.

In the ninth year [C.E. 912], Xu Wen joined senior civil and military officers in elevating Yang Longyan to grand preceptor, palace secretary, and

Prince of Wu. The court, in turn, confirmed Wen as manager-adjutant and Zhenhai governor with standing as chief minister. [Wu surrogate] Chen Zhang attacked Chu and seized Yue‡ Prefecture, apprehending prefect Yuan Mei. An attack on Changzhou by armies from Wu/Yue occurred in the tenth year [C.E. 913], Xu Wen personally vanquishing them at Wuxi. The Liang unleashed Wang Maozhang for a raid against Shouchun, but he was defeated by Wen at Huoqiu. During the twelfth year [C.E. 915], invested Duke of Qi, Wen won new assignments as commissioner of bandit suppression in the Liangzhe region. His term as Runzhou governor began now, and he left in the capital a son, Zhixun, as deputy commissioner of the armed forces. Zhixun came to handle regular administration, while Wen disposed of major matters from afar. That winter, during the dredging of the Yanglin River, fire emitted from the waters and burned.

During the thirteenth year [C.E. 916], Imperial Guard commanders Li Qiu and Ma Qian coerced Longyan to ascend a tower and position treasury guards at a bridge accessing city gates, attempting to execute Zhixun. They were repeatedly repulsed in confrontations with Zhixun. Zhu Jin happened to arrive from regional assignment, at the time, and after his horseman advanced to observe their formations up close, concluded, "The challengers are not up to the task." Looking back, he motioned to his men, who sallied forth, decapitating Qiu and Qian, as their mutinous armies all scattered.

Xu Wen moved his command to Jinling during the fourteenth year [C.E. 917]. The court launched an offensive against Qian and Shao prefectures, in the fifteenth year [C.E. 918], led by Wang Qi and the combined forces of Hong, Yuan†, and Xin† prefectures. They failed to prevail after some time, and Qi took ill, with Liu Xin replacing him. During the fourth month, deputy general commander Zhu Jin murdered Xu Zhixun, then committed suicide. Xu Zhigao learned of the mutiny at Runzhou and directed troops on the capital to execute Li Yan, the Tang commissioner of reconciliation, and end the turmoil. He now personally monopolized power.

With the Xu family dominating, a young and timid Yang Longyan could not keep a sense of dignity under Zhixun's exceptionally demeaning treatment. Once imbibing in a tower, Longyan summoned actor Gao Guiqing to accompany him in drinks. Zhixun was manager-adjutant, at the time, while Longyan assumed the simplest of clothing and coif, with green-falcon garb. An inebriated Zhixun began to curse with utterances abusive to Longyan, who shed tears in shame as Zhixun's insults increased. Attendants propped up Longyan by the arm to leave, as Zhixun murdered an aide and stopped them in their tracks. The people of Wu all looked askance in outrage.

Xu Zhixun also experienced frictions with Zhu Jin, who, upon slaying Zhixun, snatched the head to take to yamen offices to show Longyan. "Today,

I have eradicated a hazard to our Wu kingdom," he declared. "I dare know nothing of the incident," Longyan insisted as he abruptly stood to enter his quarters. Livid, Jin hung the head from a pillar before clutching his sword to leave. The doors of the yamen were shut by now, so Jin leaped over a wall of pounded earth and broke his feet, then slit his own throat to die.

News that Zhu Jin had killed Xu Zhixun incited Mi Zhicheng to don armor and lead his household guards to the Tianxing gate, where he inquired of Jin's whereabouts, only to return upon learning of his death. Xu Wen nonetheless suspected Zhicheng of abetting Jin and dispatched an assassin to kill him. Yan Keqiu worried that the plot might fail, however, so he arranged for a messenger purportedly from beyond the Hunan border to report some military victory: summoning the various commanders for celebrations, he seized Zhicheng for beheading. The prefecture of Qian was conquered by Liu Xin, and Tan Quanbo apprehended for repatriation.

In spring, the second month of the sixteenth year [C.E. 919], Xu Wen led civil and military officers in enjoining Yang Longyan to accede as Son of Heaven; he withheld consent. In summer, the fourth month, Wen presented Longyan with a jade register and seal suspended from a corded sash, his title of honor advanced to King of Wu. Temples to the royal ancestors and spirits were erected, a civil service modeled on institutions of the Son of Heaven inaugurated, the sixteenth year of Tianyou changed to first year of Wuyi, and a general amnesty for the kingdom announced. Yang Xingmi received posthumous honors as the Filial and Martial King with the temple name of Taizu and Yang Wo as the Glorious Prince with the temple name of Liezu.

Xu Wen became grand counselor and protector-general of armed forces kingdomwide, invested Prince of Donghai. Appointments ensued for Xu Zhigao as left associate at the Secretariat and assistant counselor, Yan Keqiu as deputy director of the Chancellery, Luo Zhixiang as deputy director of the Palace Secretariat, Yin Wengui and Shen Yan as Hanlin academicians, Lu Zhe as minister of personnel, Li Zong and Chen Zhang as left and right commanders of the Ferociously Martial Guard, Chai Zaiyong and Qian Biao as left and right commanders of the Dragonly Martial Guard, Wang Lingmou as military commissioner for the palace, Liu Xin of Jiangxi as commandant for southern campaigns, Li Jian of Ezhou as commandant for western pacification, Li Decheng of Fuzhou¤ as commandant for southern pacification, Zhang Chong of Luzhou‡ as commandant for western pacification, and Wang Wan of Haizhou as commandant for eastern pacification. Civil and military officials were advanced one rank and imperial clansmen all invested as dukes.

With the reassignment of Xu Wen as governor of Jinling, adopted son Xu Zhigao oversaw Runzhou. Yan Keqiu once commented to Wen, "Second Son is not of the Xu clan, yet by promoting the worthy and humbling officers, the loyalties of men will likely revert to him. If he is not eliminated, I fear calamity later on." Wen could not embrace such advice, but the comments leaked out after Zhigao consolidated power and he moved to reassign Keqiu to Chuzhou. A nervous Keqiu decided to visit Jinling, where he counseled Wen, "Twelve years have now lapsed since the fall of the former Tang dynasty, yet our Wu domain still dares not abandon its defunct reign name of Tianyou—symbolizing our refusal to forsake the Tang cause. When we conduct campaigns against the four corners or lay institutional foundations, we commonly use words such as 'regeneration' to justify them. I hear that Liang armies repeatedly fall short in recent conflagrations north of the Yellow River. If the house of Li [Prince of Jin] accomplishes the regeneration instead, will it respect the status quo? This is a timely occasion to assert autonomy and declare empire in advance of rivals." Concurring fully, Wen retained Keqiu and refused a Chuzhou posting, the two prodding Longyan to assume illicit titles.

Yang Longyan died in the fifth month of the second year of Shunyi [C.E. 922]. Because he had inherited position in youth, power rested with the Xu family. It was never his intent to found a kingdom or adopt royal institutions. Often dispirited, he tended to drink heavily and rarely eat, to the point of turning sick and dying at twenty-four *sui*. After brother Pu assumed the illicit titles of emperor, Longyan was posthumously entitled "Illustrious" and invested the Illustrious Emperor Gaozu, his mausoleum named Suling.

Yang Pu [C.E. 901–938], the fourth son of Xingmi, had been invested Duke of Danyang when Longyan proclaimed Wu as independent kingdom. Upon Longyan's death, the next in line for succession was younger brother Meng, the Duke of Lujiang, but Xu men dominating government were predisposed against a mature ruler, installing Pu instead. In the seventh month, the "superior protectorate of Shengzhou" was renamed "Jinling Metropolis" and Xu Wen appointed custodian there. The reign was changed to Shunyi in the second month of the next year [C.E. 921], Heaven worshipped at the southern suburbs during the eleventh month, wintertime. A general amnesty was promulgated after Pu climbed the "Heavenly Ascent" tower. Xu Wen became grand preceptor and Yan Keqiu right associate at the Secretariat.

In the third year [C.E. 923], with Zhuangzong of Tang annihilating the Liang, the Wu court commissioned as envoy to Tang, Lu Ping, the master of national granaries. Before his departure, Yan Keqiu provided a secret enumeration of outstanding issues. And once in Luoyang, Zhuangzong questioned Ping about concerns and he responded in sequence, just as instructed. Pu arrived at Baisha during the fourth year [C.E. 924], to inspect naval forces, Xu Wen coming to meet him there. Baisha was renamed "Garrison of the Imperial Reception."

During the fifth year [C.E. 925], the Tang dispatched master of admonitions Xue Zhaowen as envoy to Fuzhou¶ [Min] and sought passage through the Jiangnan west region. Liu Xin went to extend hospitality and asked, "Does Yaci [employing Zhuangzong's nickname] know of me?" Zhaowen replied, "The Son of Heaven, Sir, is unfamiliar with your reputation, having only recently acquired the southern stretches of the Yellow River." Xin continued, "Just as the ancient Han dynasty possessed [military strategist] Han Xin, Wu today has Liu Xin. Tell Yaci for me, upon returning, that he should come to some site along the Huai border for a contest of archery skills." Pouring wine into a large goblet, Xin glanced a hundred feet away at the crown atop his headquarters' flagpole, affirming to Zhaowen, "Please accept this draft in celebration of longevity, if I hit target on the first draw. Should I fail, I will even accept the penalty of a drink." His arrow had already hit the target as these words were uttered.

In the sixth year [C.E. 926], four generations of ancestors to Xu Wen, the grand counselor, received posthumous noble titles, ancestral temples erected in their honor at Jinling. The Secretariat's left associate Xu Zhigao became director of the Chancellery, while its right associate Yan Keqiu received ministerial powers. Zhuangzong expired during this year. On the twelfth day of the fifth month, court was suspended for seven days in honor of the Tongguang Emperor [Zhuangzong].

During the seventh year [C.E. 927], the grand counselor Xu Wen had formerly led civil and military officials of Wu in petitioning Yang Pu to accede as emperor, but Wen died of illness before Pu could consent. On the third day of the eleventh month [November 29], Pu proceeded to the Wenming palace to accede the throne as emperor, announcing a change of reign to Qianzhen and general amnesty for the domain. Xingmi received posthumous honors as the Martial Emperor, Wo as the Glorious Emperor, and Longyan as the Illustrious Emperor. Xu Zhigao received honors as grand marshal and director of the Chancellery. Another of Xu Wen's sons, Zhixun, became "bulwark commandant of the empire," and custodian of Jinling, Wen's former command. The sons of Wen were all invested as princes.

In the inaugural month of the second year of Qianzhen [C.E. 928], Donghai was redesignated as the princedom of Guangde, Jiangdu as the princedom of Guangyuan, Huaidu as the princedom of Changyuan, the upstream prefectures of Madang as the princedom of Ningjiang, the midstream prefectures of Caishi as the princedom of Dingjiang, and the downstream prefectures of Jinshan as the princedom of Zhenjiang. Gao Jixing of Jingnan [Nanping] offered fealty to Wu, in the sixth month, receiving investiture as Prince of Qin. In the ninth month, Jixing defeated Chu troops at Baitian, capturing thirty-four commanders and their lieutenants for conveyance to Wu.

In the eleventh month of the third year [C.E. 929], the prefect of Jinling, Xu Zhixun, came to court. Falsely accused by his brother Xu Zhigao of sedition, he was not permitted to leave, but received nominal powers as left commander; his attending commander Zhou Tingwang was decapitated. Replacing him as prefect of Jinling was Xu Zhi'e. Yang Pu advanced his own title of honor to the Profoundly Sagacious, Literarily Luminous, and Filial Emperor. He announced a general amnesty for the realm, a change of reign to Dahe, and honors for Xu Zhigao as palace secretary.

In the second year of Dahe [C.E. 930], royal son Yang Lian, the Prince of Jiangdu, was invested as heir-apparent. In the third year [C.E. 931] Xu Zhigao became custodian of Jinling, his son Jingtong honored as dignitary for education, sharing ministerial powers with Wang Lingmou and Song Qiqiu, left and right associates at the Secretariat, respectively. Zhigao was invested Prince of Donghai, in the fourth year, and Jinling designated the capital during the fifth year.

In the intercalary first month of the sixth year [C.E. 934], fires ravaged Jinling and its inauguration as capital was suspended. The Prince of Linchuan, Meng, was demoted to Duke of Liyang. Zhigao dispatched confidante Wang Hong to direct armies to contain him. Wang Lingmou received honors as dignitary for education and Song Qiqiu as dignitary for public works. Zhigao summoned son Jingtong back to Jinling to become deputy governor of the Zhenhai command. Zhigao's son, Xu Jingqian, became grand guardian with ministerial powers, governing alongside Lingmou and cohort.

In the ninth month of the seventh year [C.E. 935], Yang Pu further elevated his own title of honor to the Profoundly Sagacious, Literarily Luminous, Radiantly Filial, Celestially Ordained, Resplendently Moral, and Expansively Virtuous Emperor. He announced a general amnesty and change of reign name to Tianzuo. Zhigao was advanced to grand preceptor and supreme marshal of armed forces across the world, and further invested Prince of Qi. Jingqian took ill in the second year [of Tianzuo, C.E. 936], so the son next in line, Xu Jingsui, became deputy director of the Chancellery and assistant minister.

In the third year [C.E. 937], Xu Zhigao founded the kingdom of Qi, erecting temples to the ancestors and spirits of the royal house, inaugurating a civil service led by chief counselors of the left and right, and designating Jinling as the "western capital" and Guangling as the "eastern capital." In winter, the tenth month, Yang Pu commissioned the Prince of Jiangxia, Yang Lin, to confirm abdication of his throne to the Prince of Qi. Pu died at Danyang in the twelfth month,[2] at thirty-eight *sui*, with the posthumous title of Rui conferred.

In the sixth year of Shengyuan [C.E. 942], Li Bian [formerly Xu Zhigao] relocated the sons and grandsons of Yang Pu to Hailing. Dubbed the Yongning palace, the area was strictly guarded by troops and isolated from contact with the outside. The men and women confined there eventually intermarried, causing many Wu subjects to pity them. As Shizong campaigned against Huainan in the third year of Xiande [C.E. 956], he issued an edict consoling scions of the Yang house. Once [Bian's successor] Li Jing learned of the gesture, he liquidated the entire clan. The chief officer of the Zhou vanguard, Liu Chongjin, later obtained and forwarded to court the family's ink slabs of jade, bowls of agate, and vases with kingfisher design—the Yang royal house eradicated.

Xu Wen

Xu Wen [C.E. 862–927] had the courtesy name Dunmei. Native to Qushan, Haizhou, he smuggled salt as a youth and later served under Yang Xingmi's command after his insurrection at Hefei. The band to join Xingmi in rebellion, dubbed the "thirty-six braves," included men such as Liu Wei and Tao Ya, but among them, Wen was singularly lacking in battlefield feats. When Xingmi decided to murder Zhu Yanshou and cohort, Wen entrusted the conspiracy to his retainer Yan Keqiu, who taught Xingmi about feigning problems with eyesight. Once successful, Wen was promoted to director of the Right Guard in reward, hereafter securing the confidences of Xingmi.

As illness afflicted Xingmi, commanders with lifelong service were all deployed in regional hotspots, while Xu Wen presided over headquarters and was thereby privileged to consultation concerning Yang Wo's installation. Frictions emerged with Zhang Hao in the wake of regicide against Wo, Wen arranging Hao's murder by Zhong Zhang. After recruiting thirty stalwart soldiers for the action, Zhang cemented their alliance by butchering an ox in sacrificial fashion and draining its blood. Wen nonetheless worried that Zhang might fail, so deep into the night he sent someone to probe into his will by positing, "Wen has an old mother who worries that the cabal will fail. It might be better to suspend it." "Instructions have already left my lips," Zhang responded. "How can we quit?" The response served to calm Wen. Zhang killed Hao a day later, as Wen proceeded to liquidate Ji Xiang and cohort, then place culpability for regicide against Wo wholly upon Hao. Wen entered the palace to report the incident to Wo's mother, née Shi, who, grief-stricken, acknowledged tearfully, "My son so young and conditions of tumult so grave, it is only by the grace of you, Sir, that the lives of a hundred kinsmen can return safely to Hefei."

The installation of Yang Longyan enabled Wen to monopolize administration. Once reassigned as prefect of Shengzhou to train sailors at Jinling, senior commander Li Yu, who resented Wen's dominance, [exploited the absence] to say disparaging things of him. Wen now arranged for Chai Zaiyong to liquidate Yu and his family at Xuanzhou. Each and every seasoned commander from the days of Xingmi was suspicious of Wen, but he guilefully humbled himself to them and acted with scrupulous deference, as if in the presence of Xingmi himself, thereby assuaging commanders. During the eighth year [C.E. 911], Wen received reassignment as manager-adjutant, prefect of Runzhou, and governor of the Zhenhai command with standing as chief minister.

In the tenth year [C.E. 913], an offensive against Yue was entrusted to Li Tao, the commissioner of bandit suppression. He battled at Lin'an County [Hangzhou], but after assisting commander Cao Yun fled for Yue, a defeated Tao was apprehended by Wu. Wen arranged for a messenger to reassure the defector Yun, saying, "I employed you as commander, so any incapacity in meeting your army's needs can only reflect my own failings." He thus pardoned the wife and sons of Yun, forgoing execution and treating them generously. That autumn, the armies of Yue attacked Piling and Wen engaged them at Wuxi. The earlier statements of Wen had moved Yun, who fled to the other side as battle approached, Wu's defeat of Yue ensuing.

Xu Wen was invested Duke of Qi, in the twelfth year [C.E. 915]. Named commissioner of bandit suppression for the Liangzhe region, he assumed command at Runzhou. The six prefectures of Sheng, Run, Xuan, Chang, Chi, and Huang came to constitute the Qi feudatory. A wall was erected around Shengzhou, now established by Wen as the supreme protectorate-general. In the fourteenth year, he moved to administer Shenzhou: his son, Zhixun, thereby came to counsel Longyan at Guangling, although major decisions were still made by Wen from a distance. After the assassination of Zhixun by Zhu Jin, Wen's adopted son Zhigao preceded him to the capital to assume governance.

Xu Wen, a deceitful and dubious character, could nonetheless manage commanders and their staffs quite effectively. When Liu Xin of Jiangxi besieged Qianzhou without prevailing after considerable time, he sent someone to negotiate surrender with Tan Quanbo and a messenger to apprise Wen. Wen was furious, pronouncing, "With a force ten times greater [than his foe], he cannot conquer this single city, but instead tries to employ a demagogue to induce surrender. How can this possibly serve to overawe our enemies?" He flogged the messenger with light rod before sending him off, insisting, "I flog you in Xin's place!" He hence commissioned relief armies that broke the back of Quanbo.

Someone once falsely accused Liu Xin of dawdling on the assignment and clandestinely releasing Quanbo, even insinuating that he intended to rebel. Upon learning of the charges, Xin went to Jinling to meet Wen and personally present the spoils of war. The two men began to gamble, and Xin gathered the dice, saying in a piercingly jubilant voice, "If I aspire to forsake Wu, I will draw the face with ferocious colors. If sedition is absent from my heart, I should draw the face with mixed colors." Wen promptly tried to stop him, but on the first throw, he drew a face of six eyes in bright red. A mortified Wen held the goblet to allow Xin to drink from it, but proved suspicious of him until the end. As the armies of Tang campaigned against Wang Yan, Wen urgently summoned Xin to Guangling to serve as left general commander and entrusted defenses for the palace to him—divesting him of his local satrapy in the process.

The retainers of Xu Wen to command special confidences were Luo Zhixiang and Yan Keqiu. Keqiu was deft at strategizing, Zhixiang gifted at managing wealth. Wen turned to Keqiu on questions of military policy and to Zhixiang on concerns about government expenditures—the people of Wu dubbing them "the Yan/Luo duo." Wen liked to revel in his own cleverness, presuming himself to have won the hearts of Wu subjects. Before this, commanders accompanying Xingmi in the conquest of Zhaohuang tended to fight among themselves over gold and silk booty, yet Wen simply took leftover grains from a storehouse to make gruel to feed the hungry.

In the sixteenth year [C.E. 919], Xu Wen urged Longyan's accession as emperor; Longyan demurred, agreeing only to a second request to succeed as the King of Wu. Occasioning the founding of kingdom and change of reign, Wen was named grand counselor and protector-general of armed forces empirewide, his investiture advanced to Prince of Donghai. Upon the death of Longyan, Wen decided to suspend seniority and install younger brother Yang Pu. In the seventh year of Shunyi [C.E. 927], Wen now entreated Pu to become emperor, a request not yet approved when illness claimed Wen's life at sixty-six *sui*. Posthumously ennobled Prince of Qi, the title "Martial" was initially conferred, then "Righteous Ancestor" [Yizu] following Li Bian's usurpation.

WE LAMENT. How credible the saying that even brigands have morals! Writings about Xingmi reveal a character generously benevolent and fastidiously trustworthy, traits that won the hearts of troops. Commander Cai Chou once defected at Luzhou‡ and thoroughly plundered the family tombs of Xingmi. When defeat finally overtook him, military leaders unanimously sought revenge by plundering his own family tombs. Sighing, Xingmi said, "Chou committed one act of evil. How can I possibly repeat it?" An attendant assigned by Xingmi to carry his sword, Zhang Hong, once grabbed the sword to assault Xingmi, only to miss his target and be killed. Xingmi hence entrusted his sword to Chen Shao, a previous friend to Zhang Hong, without evincing the slightest suspicion. Another time he upbraided commander Liu Xin so severely that an indignant Xin fled to Sun Ru. Aides wanting to pursue him were dissuaded by Xingmi, who said, "How could Xin possibly desert me? Having left in an intoxicated stupor, he will surely return upon sobering." And, indeed, he did return a day later.

For such reasons, Xingmi may have arisen among brigands, his subordinates all inclined to martial antics and vicious rage, yet they reveled in his service. Four rulers over two generations could thereby rule for nearly fifty years. Beginning with Yang Wo's reign, Xu Wen dominated government precisely as pandemic turmoil pervaded the world and calamity overtook the Middle Kingdom, with perpetual purge and regicide a common occurrence. Xu Wen and sons, despite their own arrant duplicity and the twists and turns of three successions, never dared a precipitate play for the throne. And why? Enduring fear and favor among Xingmi's rank and file provide the only explanation.[i]

....

i. According to *Wu lu, Yunli tu,* and *Jiuguo zhi,* Yang Xingmi reentered Yangzhou in the inaugural year of Jingfu, under the Tang [C.E. 892], while the usurpation by Li Bian occurred in the second year of Tianfu, under the Jin dynasty [C.E. 937], representing actually forty-six years. But the old histories of Tang and the Five Dynasties both place the occupation of Yangzhou in the second year of Dashun [C.E. 891], whereby forty-seven years elapsed before Bian's usurpation. *Wu lu* was written by Xu Xuan and *Yunli tu* written by Gong Ying, both former subjects of Jiangnan [Wu], whose records should be factual. Many documents of the court were lost in the turmoil of a waning Tang, so the writings of Xuan and Ying are accepted as authoritative.

CHAPTER 62

HEREDITARY HOUSE OF SOUTHERN TANG

Li Bian, Son Jing, and the Son of Jing, Yu

Li Bian [Xu Zhigao, C.E. 888–943], had the courtesy name Zhenglun. Native to Xuzhou¶, he belonged to a family of humble obscurity for generations. His father, Li Rong, died of unknown circumstances in the turmoil of the late Tang. Orphaned young, Bian drifted in the area of Hao¶ and Si prefectures, Yang Xingmi apprehending him during a raid on Hao¶. The youth's physical appearance impressed Xingmi, who raised him as a son. The other Yang siblings, however, could not tolerate the youth, such that Xingmi approached Xu Wen about having the boy assume the surname Xu and personal name Zhigao. Bian eventually grew to seven feet in height, his forehead broad and nose prominent. In personality, he could be amiable and sincere, as well as clever in strategizing. He came to command the multiple-deck ships of the Wu navy, his sailors stationed at Jinling.

In the wake of Chai Zaiyong's raid on Xuanzhou and the murder of Li Yu by his men, Li Bian's merit led to appointment as prefect of Shengzhou. The Huai and Yangzi regions only recently pacified, most senior administrators at the prefectural and county level were military men given to diverting tax receipts to their war chests. Bian was exceptional in his yearning to learn and his courtesy toward Confucian literati. He also evinced a capacity for disciplined frugality to promote benevolence in government, winning the considerable praise of the people.

As governor of Runzhou, Xu Wen presided over six prefectures including Sheng and Chi, learning there of Bian's exemplary governance at Shengzhou. During a personal inspection, Wen witnessed prefectural storehouses in full stock and city walls in excellent repair, so he relocated personally to Shengzhou, reassigning Bian as Runzhou prefect. Bian was disinclined to accept the assignment and repeatedly requested a posting at Xuanzhou, but Wen refused to accommodate. Later, when Zhu Jin assassinated Xu Zhixun, the news reached Bian at his Runzhou post, with its greater proximity to Guangling, before reaching Wen at Jinling. In response, Bian directed prefectural armies across the Yangzi to suppress mutineers on the very same day, becoming administrator at Guangling.

Li Bian's rare filial piety and deference toward Xu Wen once caused Wen himself to revile his own sons as Bian's inferior, comments that his sons generally, and especially Zhixun, found unbearable. Zhixun thus invited Bian for wine while planting a swordsman to kill him. A wine server, Diao Yanneng, uncovered the plot and pinched Bian with his fingernails as he approached with wine, alerting him to rise and leave. He thereby eluded harm. Bian later came from Runzhou to the capital for audience, as Zhixun joined him in a round of drinks at Shanguang monastery, intent on harming him. Informed of the plot by Xu Zhijian, Bian managed to arise and abscond. Zhixun handed a sword to Diao Yanneng with orders to pursue and kill him, but Yanneng returned midway, professing an inability to catch up. Bian averted peril once again. After achieving prominence, Bian named Yanneng governor of Fuzhou¤.

The Yang house was emasculated under Zhixun's dominance and commanders treated with condescending ridicule, bringing on his own death. Once affairs came under Bian's control, he aspired to win people's hearts by relaxing laws and punishments while promoting compassion and trust. He erected the Yanbin pavilion to woo learned men of the four corners, recruiting Song Qiqiu, Luo Zhixiang, Wang Lingmou, and others as itinerant strategists. Literati at large in the Wu region thereby became valued advisors. Bian sometimes sent men undercover to identify those people too poor to afford marriage or funeral rites, often extending relief to them. At the peak of summer's heat, he had no umbrellas raised or fans prepared, and if aides tried to provide cover of the sort, he invariably spurned them, saying, "The bulk of our soldiers are largely exposed to the elements. How can I possibly use such things?" In this way, Bian was converting the people, even as Xu Wen retained the reins of power from a distant command.

Li Bian became left associate at the Secretariat and associate minister in the inaugural year of Wuyi [C.E. 919]. The manager-adjutant to Xu Wen, Xu Jie, had often urged him to select among his sons someone to replace Bian: Zhixun was sent by Wen to Guangling in an effort to supplant Bian's political control. In the wake of Wen's death by illness, Zhixun hastened back to Jinling, as Jie reversed course to conspire on Bian's behalf. He falsely accused Zhixun of criminal activity, then beheaded his own attending commander,

Zhou Tingwang, and demoted Zhixun to right commander. Once Yang Pu assumed his illicit titles, he honored Bian as grand marshal and palace secretary. Assignment away from the capital ensued as governor of Jinling, in the third year of Dahe [C.E. 931], and conforming to the precedent for Wen, son Jingtong [Li Jing] stayed behind, receiving honors as dignitary for education and ministerial standing. Wang Lingmou and Song Qiqiu became left and right associates at the Secretariat with ministerial powers. Bian's investiture as Prince of Donghai occurred in the fourth year.

Once, gazing into a mirror to find his whiskers now white, Bian sighed as he said to Zhou Zong, a senior aide, "My feats are accomplished, but old age overtakes me. What can a man do?" Zong understood the inference and rushed to Guangling to confer with Song Qiqiu on a change of dynasty. Qiqiu considered such action untimely, and even requested summary decapitation for Zong to satisfy the people of Wu. Bian banished Zong to prefect of Chizhou.

The Prince of Linjiang under Wu rule, Yang Meng, disaffected ever since the Xu family had dispossessed him to install Pu, was often agitated at heart. As Bian undertook schemes to usurp the kingdom's sovereignty, he moved first to demote Meng to Duke of Liyang, then place him under military custody. Meng managed to kill the guards and flee to Zhou Ben, the governor of Luzhou‡. A commander of long standing under Wu rule, Ben intended to offer sanctuary upon news of Meng's arrival, but his own son, Zuo, intervened to stop him. "The Young Master is from my former ruler's family," Ben exclaimed. "How can I consider spurning him?" Hastily preparing to emerge from the city to greet him, Ben was obstructed from leaving by Zuo, who slammed the city gates shut, then sent Meng in shackles to Jinling to be slain.

Li Bian was invested Prince of Qi during the fifth year [C.E. 933]. By now, kingdoms such as Min and Yue had sent envoys encouraging his further advancement, while Bian portrayed himself as embodying the aspirations of humanity. The founding of the Qi empire occurred in the third year of Tianzuo [C.E. 937], with temples erected to the ancestors and spirits of the royal house. Song Qiqiu and Xu Jie became chief counselors of the left and right, respectively. During the tenth month, Yang Pu conceded his throne to Bian through emissary Yang Lin, the temporary Grand marshal, affirming Qi as dynastic designation and Shengyuan as reign name. Bian invested Pu, in turn, stating that, "This Venerable Subject, Zhigao, who inherits your powers, respectfully elevates His Majesty to the 'Yielding Emperor: Exalted in Conduct, Profound in Thought, and Versed in the Ancients.' " Honors were extended retroactively to Xu Wen as the Loyal and Martial Emperor, his own son Jing ennobled Prince of Wu and other Xu sons, Zhizheng and Zhi'e, were ennobled Princes of Jiang and Rao, respectively. Zhou Ben led fellow commanders in appearing at Jinling to urge Bian's further elevation, only to lament upon his return, "I failed to execute the usurper of our kingdom to requite the Yang royal house. I am now too old to serve two surnames?" Ben died in grief and indignation. Yang Pu was relocated to Danyang Mansion [Runzhou] in the fourth month of the second year [C.E. 936]. Wang Yu became governor of the western Zhe region and Ma Sirang commissioner of Danyang Mansion, as hardened guards held Pu under house arrest.

Sons of the Xu family now petitioned Li Bian to restore his old surname. His humility prevented Bian from slighting the beneficence of the Xu family, so he referred deliberations to the official rank and file, who uniformly concurred: he hence reverted to the Li surname and adopted Bian as his personal name. Moreover, he personally alleged that Li Ke, the Prince of Jian and son of the Tang Emperor Xianzong, had fathered Chao who himself had fathered Zhi, an administrator of Xuzhou¶, who in turn fathered Rong [father to Bian]. This ostensibly made Bian a fourth-generation descendant of the Prince of Jian, so, he changed the dynastic designation to Tang. A temple was erected in honor of the Tang-dynasty rulers Gaozu and Taizong, while his own progenitor of four generations past, Ke, posthumously became the Filial and Serene Emperor with the temple name Dingzong. Imperial great-grandfather Chao became the Filial and Pacific Emperor with the temple name Chengzong. Imperial grandfather Zhi became the Filial and Reposed Emperor with the temple name Huizong. Imperial father Rong became the Filial and Virtuous Emperor with the temple name Qingzong. Having treated Xu Wen as a surrogate father, the sons and grandsons of the Xu family all received investitures as princes and dukes, the daughters becoming princesses. Ministerial powers were conferred upon Zhang Juyong, deputy director of the Chancellery, Li Jianxun, deputy director of the Palace Secretariat, and Zhang Yanhan, right associate at the Secretariat. During the eleventh month, military exercises occurred for eighty thousand infantry and cavalry at Tongqiao County [Jinling].

Yang Pu died at Danyang mansion. His son Lian, while heir-apparent to the Wu throne, had married the daughter of Bian. Once Bian usurped power, he invested the daughter as Princess Yongxing. The daughter, after hearing someone call her princess, sobbed tearfully in declining the honor, causing those in her mansion to pity her. Lian became the Kanghua governor in the wake of Pu's death, later dying of illness.

In the fourth month of the third year [C.E. 939], Li Bian rendered sacrifices to the God of the High Heavens at the circular mound. The rites complete, his subjects proposed elevation of his title of honor, a request he refused, insisting, "Titles of honor did not exist in antiquity." Local authorities petitioned the court about seven families of the filial and fraternal that cohabited for five generations, so the court honored their homes with recognition placards and waived their duties for community service. Among the more illustrious of these were the Chen of Jiangzhou, an extended family of seven hundred mouths. Whenever setting a full table for meals, young and old would dine together and sit by order of age. They also raised more than a hundred dogs that all ate in a common pen: if a single dog failed to arrive, the rest refused to eat.

In the sixth month of the fourth year [C.E. 940], the governor of Anzhou, Li Jinquan, defected from the Jin dynasty and made diplomatic overtures to Li Bian. In response, Bian dispatched Li Chengyu, the commissioner of encampments at Ezhou, to rendezvous with him. Jin commanders Ma Quanjie and An Shenhui consequently engaged Chengyu in battle, three contests to the south of Anlu all ending in his defeat; Chengyu perished along with assisting commander Duan Chugong. His military director-in-chief, Du Guangye, and five hundred men under his command were apprehended and conveyed to the Jin capital, where Gaozu extended rare munificence and tried to repatriate them. But Bian returned Guangye and cohort to Gaozu, forwarding a letter seeking strict enforcement of laws pertaining to vanquished commanders. Once more, Gaozu attempted repatriation, although Bian now stationed armored troops along the Huai River to intercept, forcing them back.

In the sixth year of Shengyuan [C.E. 942], fires ravaged the Wu/Yue kingdom, completely destroying its royal palaces, government treasury, and the cream of its armed forces. Many a Tang official wished to exploit such vulnerability to raid Wu/Yue. Li Bian refused and instead dispatched an emissary to convey condolences, extending substantial relief in its hour of need. Qian royals [at Wu/Yue] had known hostile relations with its western neighbor ever since the days of the Wu regime. Li Bian often proved reticent to deploy armies, however, having witnessed prolonged chaos in the world. On the eve of usurping the Wu throne, he thus promptly entered a truce with Qian royals, returning their commanders and soldiers then in custody as war prisoners. The Qian house reciprocated by releasing vanquished commanders of Wu. Cordial ties were established in this way, not to be severed.

Feng Yansi, a Li Bian attendant fond of discussing military affairs and grand schemes, once said of Bian in ridicule, "How can a rustic farmer like yourself succeed in accomplishing great feats?" His aspirations confined simply to securing the original lands of Wu, Bian lacked a formula for empire-building. The people of Wu also took comfort in the respite. Bian died in the seventh year [C.E. 943] at fifty-six *sui*. Posthumously entitled the Radiantly Literate, Augustly Martial, Filial, and Exalted Emperor, his temple name was Liezu and mausoleum known as Yongling. His son Jing succeeded him.

Li Jing [C.E. 916–961] was originally named Jingtong. Bian's eldest son, his name was further changed to Jing after the accession. As court affairs came under Bian's control in the wake of Xu Wen's death, Jing was named minister of war with ministerial standing. A year later, Bian became governor of Jinling and Jing remained behind in the capital as dignitary for education with ministerial standing. He resided, along with Song Qiqiu and Wang Lingmou, at Guangling to assist Yang Pu. Bian summoned Jing to Jinling on the eve of his usurpation, naming him deputy general commander. Ennobled Prince of Qi after the accession, he succeeded Bian upon death, changing the reign name to Baoda.

The royal mother, née Song, was honored as Empress Dowager and Consort Zhong as Empress. Younger brothers were invested: Jingsui (Prince of Shou) as Prince of Yan and Jingda (Prince of Xuancheng) as Prince of E. Having never held princely rank, Jingti won his first as Prince of Baoning. Jingsui received a new investiture as Prince of Qi, the next autumn, and titular posts as supreme marshal of armed forces empirewide, grand marshal, and palace secretary. Jingda was now Prince of Yan and deputy supreme marshal. Before the coffin of Bian, they swore to a succession from older to younger brother in perpetuity. Jing's son, Ji, invested Prince of Nanchang, was designated metropolitan custodian of Jiangdu.

In the tenth month, wintertime, the Qianzhou sorcerer and renegade Zhang Yuxian, once a minor aide in Luo [Boluo] County, Xunzhou‡, was vanquished. Before this, a spirit had descended on a commoner's home at Luo County and predicted the imminent arrival of peril for some and prosperity for others. Yuxian's prayers to the spirit prompted it to declare, "Yuxian is an Arhat who should stay to serve me." At the time, Liu Yan of Nanhai was initially succeeded upon death by his son, Liu Bin, but rogues and rebels rose up in Lingnan, some groups numbering over a thousand without any leadership. When the spirit was asked who should lead, it named Yuxian, so the rogues banded to elevate him as commander. Yuxian proclaimed himself King of the Middle Heavens and the Eight Kingdoms, adopted the reign name Yongle, and established bureaucratic rule. All clothed in crimson, the renegades had formerly attacked and plundered the outer reaches of Lingnan, then consulted the spirit where to proceed. "You should cross the mountains and capture Qianzhou [Tang territory]," it responded. They subsequently stormed Nankang, where governor Jia Hao failed to fend them off. Yuxian occupied Baiyun Caverns as well, building palaces there. His force now in excess of a hundred thousand, he felled a succession of neighboring counties. Li Jing thus authorized an offensive against him, led by Yan Si, the inspector of military encampments at Hongzhou, and the receptionist at the Secretariat, Bian Hao. Yuxian made further inquiries of the spirit, but it spoke no more. In fear, the rebel bands apprehended Yuxian and surrendered him.

Li Jing appointed Feng Yansi and Chang Mengxi as Hanlin academicians, Feng Yanlu as drafter at the Palace Secretariat, Chen Jue as commissioner of military affairs, and Wei Cen and Zha Wenhui as deputy commissioners. Mengxi's position as auxiliary at Xuanzheng Hall enabled him to monopolize affairs and issue secret orders, Yansi and cohort serving as mere sycophants—the "five monsters," as the people of Wu called them. Mengxi repeatedly challenged use of the five men, but Jing ignored him.

During the twelfth month, Li Jing mandated that the Prince of Qi, Jingsui, be consulted on all domestic and foreign affairs: memorials to Jing could only come from Chen Jue and Zha Wenhui, while access to court was to be restricted to those specifically summoned. An incisive memorial against the policy was lodged by secretarial overseer Xiao Yan, without eliciting a response. Imperial Guard inspector-in-chief Jia Chong now appeared at palace side-doors to meet Jing and declare, "Your Subject, having served the previous reign for thirty years, witnessed the way that the Former Monarch [Bian] laid a successful foundation: invariably, this involved adopting the strategies of a multitude of worthies. Thus, those at a distance were drawn near without ever being obstructed. Even then, the sentiments of the rank and file sometimes failed to be articulated. Your Majesty being new to the throne, whom will he trust? And why would Your Majesty suddenly sever yourself from your subjects? Being old and near death, my own fear is never seeing Your countenance again." His tears and sobs visibly moved Jing, who consoled Chong by inviting him to sit while offering food, then rescinded the order.

Before this, among those conspiring with Li Bian to usurp the Yang house, Song Qiqiu was the most powerful. With the act now a fait accompli, Qiqiu feigned withdrawal to the Jiuhua Mountains, which he left only after a succession of appeals from Bian. It was not long into Bian's usurpation that illness led to Qiqiu's dismissal as minister, leaving the capital to be governor of Hongzhou. Recalled as minister after Jing's accession, he orchestrated the advancement of Chen Jue, Wei Cen, and their lot. Once rifts emerged between Jue and Cen, Cen maligned Jue before Li Jing, who demoted him to left director of imperial factories. Qiqiu was also dismissed as minister and named governor of western Zhe. A disgruntled Qiqiu preferred to return to Jiuhua Mountain, so the court conferred the sobriquet "Master of Jiuhua," ennobled him Duke of Qingyang, and set aside revenues for Qingyang County as a stipend for him.

In the second month of the second year [C.E. 944], Lian Chongyu and Zhu Wenjin of the Min kingdom committed regicide against their ruler, Wang Yanxi, Wenjin hence placing himself in power. At the time, Yanxi's younger brother, Yanzheng, similarly installed himself at Jianzhou, adopting Yin as dynastic name. The Wang family had waged war over many years and wrought utter havoc on the Min region. In response to such tumult, Li Jing dispatched Zha Wenhui and Zang Xun, an officer-in-waiting, with armies to raid Jianzhou. Upon learning that the Tang was soon to attack him as well, Yanzheng sent a messenger to deceive Fuzhou¶, asserting, "Tang troops are now assisting me to suppress the renegades." Military authorities there believed him and banded together to murder Zhu Wenjin and cohort, surrendering to Yanzheng, who dispatched nephew Jichang to secure Fuzhou¶. Zha Wenhui's armies were quartered at Jianyang, so Fuzhou¶ commander Li Renda killed Wang Jichang and pronounced himself interim regent. The Quanzhou commander Liu Congxiao similarly killed prefect Huang Shaopo, both men now making overtures of submission to Wenhui.

In the fourth year [C.E. 946], the eighth month, [Tang commander] Zha Wenhui exploited this momentum to overrun the four prefectures of Jian, Ting, Quan, and Zhang. Li Jing then reconstituted the three counties of Yanping, Jianpu, and Fusha as the new Jian‡ Prefecture. The family of Wang Yanzheng was relocated to Jinling, and he was named governor of Raozhou. Li Renda became governor of Fuzhou¶ and Liu Congxiao governor of the Qingyuan command. Jing now wished to recall armies, but Zha Wenhui and Chen Jue both insisted, "The vile likes of Renda and cohort remain present. Exploiting victory's momentum to seize his entire army is far more preferable." Chen Jue personally argued that Renda and cohort could be controlled without using weapons.

Appointing Chen Jue as commissioner of reconciliation, Li Jing summoned Li Renda to Jinling for an audience, which he refused. Jue thus felt mortified and returned promptly to Jianzhou to fabricate orders for an offensive against Renda, troops issuing from the prefectures of Ting, Jian, Xin†, and Fu¤. The pacification commissioner for Zhangzhou and Quanzhou at the time, Wei Cen, greeted news of Jue's deployment by illicitly issuing his own armies in a rendezvous with Jue. This left Li Jing utterly livid, but Feng Yansi and cohort insisted, "Once a military action is under way, it cannot be stopped." Wang Chongwen thus became commissioner of bandit suppression and Wang Jianfeng deputy commissioner. An augmenting of troop strength for a rendezvous also occurred, the court confirming Feng Yanlu, Wei Cen, and Chen Jue as military commissioners.

Li Renda made overtures to Wu/Yue, and it dispatched a force of thirty thousand to assist him. Jue and cohort, competing against one another for distinction, failed to coordinate their military movements: Feng Yanlu first engaged Wu/Yue armies and absconded after a rout, the other armies likewise vanquished as they returned. An angry Li Jing ordered a messenger to confine Jue and Yanlu to shackles for the trip to Jinling. The chief minister then was Feng Yansi, while Song Qiqiu had been summoned from Jiuhua to serve as grand mentor. Both men favored leniency, so Jue was exiled to Qizhou¤ and Yanlu to Shuzhou. A searing remonstrance against leniency came from Han Xizai, whose memorial demanded the execution of Jue and cohort, but Qiqiu took umbrage with his words and banished Xizai as manager-adjutant of Hezhou‡.

Sometime that year, the Khitan overran the capital as the Middle Kingdom went without a ruler. The drain on the military in the southeast due to Chen Jue's actions, however, left Li Jing no energy to shift his attention northward. Deputy censor Jiang Wenwei, in a memorial profoundly incisive and direct, accused chief minister Feng Yansi and master of admonitions Wei Cen of wreaking havoc on governance, their crimes akin to Jue's own without suffering dismissal. An even more incited Li Jing, wrote a personal response to the memorial and banished Wenwei to manager of personnel at Jiangzhou, demoting Yansi to junior mentor and Wei Cen to front rider for the heir-apparent.

During the fifth year [C.E. 947], Jingsui was acknowledged as "fraternal heir," with Jingda named supreme marshal with investiture as Prince of Qi. The Prince of Nanchang, Ji, was named deputy marshal and invested Prince of Yan. Envoys of the Khitan arrived to extend diplomatic courtesies, the court appointing minister of war Jia Tan to reciprocate.

Li Shouzhen of Han mutinied at Hezhong, during the sixth year [C.E. 948], his interim commander's attendant, Zhu Yuan, sent to request assistance. Li Jing named Runzhou governor Li Jinquan pacification commissioner for at-large armies on the northern front. His men attacked Shuyang [Haizhou], but returned upon learning of Shouzhen's defeat. At the time, Emperor Yin of the Han was young and the Middle Kingdom highly vulnerable. Many a rebel band north of the Huai made peace overtures to Jing, prompting him to authorize Huangfu Hui to enlist and organize them from his bases at Hai and Si prefectures.

During the eighth year [C.E. 950], a ruse at Fuzhou¶ [Min] created the rumor that "Wu/Yue troops stationed at Fuzhou¶ have mutinied and killed Li Renda before absconding." The perpetrators sent a messenger inviting Zha Wenhui, the governor of Jianzhou. Wenhui took along Chen Hui, the Jianzhou‡ prefect, in navigating ships swiftly down the Min River for a confrontation at Fuzhou¶. Authorities in the city sent troops to greet them, as Chen Hui declared, "The people of Min, with their multitude of ruses, are difficult to trust. We should anchor our men on the riverbank to plan methodically." "If deferred for too long, tumult will occur," Wenhui countered. "Better to exploit the current instability to seize the city promptly." Hui stayed behind with his men at the river's mouth, Wenhui advancing as far as the city's western gates, where troops lying in ambush sallied forth to capture him. Hui engaged armies from Yue and routed them, apprehending their commander, Ma Xianjin. Li Jing decided to return Xianjin to Yue, which repatriated Wenhui to him.

Sometime this year, the king of Chu, Ma Xiguang, succumbed to regicide by [elder] brother Ma Xi'e, who installed himself. In the ninth year, autumn [C.E. 951], the people of Chu imprisoned Xi'e at Hengshan and enthroned younger brother Xichong, while paying homage to Li Jing. With extensive tumult pervading the Chu domain, Li Jing dispatched Xinzhou¤ prefect Bian Hao to attack. He overtook Tanzhou and subsequently relocated to Jinling the entire Ma clan. Li Jing now named Xi'e as governor of Hongzhou, Xichong governor of Shuzhou, and Bian Hao governor of Hunan.

In the tenth year [C.E. 952], the four counties of Gao'an, Qingjiang, Wanzai, and Shanggao were partitioned from Hongzhou to form the new prefecture of Yun¶. Feng Yansi and Sun Ji became left and right associates at the Secretariat, respectively, with ministerial powers. Liu Cheng of Guangzhou‡, exploiting the turmoil in Chu, seized Guiguan; Li Jing dispatched commander Zhang Luan with a large force to challenge the action, but he failed. Order returned to Chu anew, although its treasuries and storehouses were depleted. Chief minister Feng Yansi, basking in the glory of the Chu conquest, did not wish to impose military costs upon his own empire, so he exacted heavily from the Chu people to subsidize his armies, only to incur their wrath and incite rebellion. The Chu commander Liu Xin attacked Bian Hao, who failed to hold his position and absconded. Extensive fires ravaged Jinling for over a month during the eleventh year [C.E. 953], and during the twelfth a harsh famine caused many deaths by disease.

In the eleventh month of the thirteenth year [C.E. 955], the Zhou unleashed armies for a southern expedition. The imperial declaration of war read:

> Burrowing yourself into a lower Huai satrapy, you dared to resist this great country; seizing one corner of the world, you laid larcenous claim to bogus titles. From the Jin and Han dynasties, amidst the ceaseless unrest that engulfed the world from land to sea, you enlisted treacherous wastrels and comforted depraved defectors. From Jinquan's seizure of Anlu to Shouzhen's betrayal at Hezhong, you raised armies on a vast scale to assist them. You encroached upon lands of Min and Yue, despoiled Xiang¶ and Tan, abetted commander Murong, and importuned others against armies of Xu¶. It is easy to assess right and wrong courses from the battle at Shuyang: you induced the Khitan to penetrate the country and formed alliances with Bingzhou [Northern Han], abetting my erstwhile enemy. Your transgressions are difficult to enumerate, but outrage against them is shared by humans and ghosts alike.

The Zhou court named Li Gu chief officer of forces at large, his offensive issuing from Shouzhou.

To foil Zhou armies, Li Jing summoned Song Qiqiu, then governor of Hongzhou, back to Jinling, while deputizing Liu Yanzhen as general commander of the Divinely Martial Guard and Liu Renshan as the Qinghuai governor. Meanwhile, Li Gu warned Shizong, "We lack the equipment for naval warfare. If Huai armies decided to sever the suspension bridge at Zhengyang, we would face harassment at both front and rear." He then set afire the fuel and rations of the enemy before retreating to quarter troops at Zhengyang. Emperor Shizong, in the midst of personally commanding the campaign, reached Yuzhen upon learning of Gu's withdrawal of men and commented, "As our men retreat, Tang forces will certainly pursue them." He thus instructed Li Chongjin to rush to Zhengyang, professing, "Tang armies will arrive and should be met with a sudden storm." Liu Yanzhen and cohort had taken Li Gu's withdrawal as a sign of cowardice and pursued him aggressively. By the time he reached Zhengyang, Chongjin's men had already arrived and entered battle before even bothering to eat, vanquishing Yanzhen and cohort.

Yanzhen's armies deployed sharp knives atop their abatis poles with iron wires wrapped around, carved images of wild beasts out of pieces of wood with the inscription "emblem of the nimble horse," and tossed metal studs across the ground from their leather saddlebags. Through such actions, Zhou troops appraised them as cowards and defeated them immediately after the war drums had rolled. Forted to the northern side of the Fei River, Shizong crossed a suspension bridge at Xiacai. Li Jing had sent Lin Renzhao and others to challenge him, but the chance did not come when Zhou troops claimed Chuzhou‡. An anxious Jing subsequently dispatched Wang Zhilang, military attaché at Sizhou, to Xuzhou¶, where he submitted a letter in the Tang Emperor's name conceding to tribute payments and "elder brother" protocol in relations with the Zhou. Shizong did not respond.

Li Jing's deputy custodian of the eastern capital, Feng Yanlu, along with Guangzhou prefect Zhang Shao, Shuzhou prefect Zhou Zuo, and Taizhou prefect Fang Ne, chose to abandon their cities to abscond. Yanlu shaved his head to become a monk before being apprehended by the Zhou. After the Zhou won the surrender of Li Fu, an assistant commander at Qizhou¤ who had murdered prefect Wang Chengjuan, Li Jing became so nervous that he changed his personal name [from Jingtong] to "Jing" out of deference to a Zhou-dynasty taboo. He even deputized as emissaries the Hanlin academician Zhong Mo and Wenli academician Li Deming, proposing the adoption of "subject" in future protocol. To end hostilities, the envoys offered to provision Zhou armies with five hundred head of cattle, two thousand piculs of wine, and thousands in gold, silver, and sheer silk, while ceding the prefectures of Shou, Hao¶, Si, Chu, Guang, and Hai. Shizong refused to respond, conducting separate sorties against Yang and Tai instead, felling both prefectures. Li Jing now dispatched an emissary to the Khitan in search of assistance, the envoy's letter bearing the formal raised-wax seal; he was captured by a border commander. Guangzhou prefect Zhang Chenghan relinquished the city to the Zhou.

In the third month of the fourteenth year [C.E. 956], Li Jing further dispatched dignitary for education Sun Cheng and minister of rites Wang

Chongzhi to petition the Zhou, employing expressions of still greater humility. Shizong continued to ignore him, ordering retention in the interim capital of envoys Cheng and Chongzhi, who now joined earlier envoys Zhong Mo and cohort. Mo sought to return to secure Jing's approval to relinquish all lands north of the Yangzi River. Shizong finally allowed Chongzhi, Deming, and the others to return and deliver a letter to Jing, stating:

> Since the former Tang dynasty lost power, now some six decades ago, the natural course of Heaven has been obstructed. With the realm fractured into separate spheres, men made personal claim to royal nomenclature and imposed their dominance over a populace, they struck alliances with the four barbarians and importuned other powers against our empire. With our customs as Chinese deteriorating and ill fortunes prevailing, what heart among the many feels no indignation? I have claimed the wealth of a hundred prefectures and amassed armed forces some three hundred thousand strong. Promoting farming alongside preparations for war, our warriors are happy to serve. Were I to fail to recover our lands at home and extend our borders abroad, then negotiating withdrawal of our armies would be tantamount to political theater! As for divesting yourself of royal honors and accepting "subject" protocol, much like Sun Quan served the Wei dynasty and Xiao Cha served the Northern Zhou, such schemes are unacceptable today despite ancient protocol. If you insist on retaining imperial titles, you will scarcely survive until winter. But if you are steadfast in loyal service to this great country, I will certainly not force you into a perilous corner.

After returning south, Deming and the others praised Shizong for his martial courage, assessments displeasing to Jing.

Song Qiqiu, Chen Jue, and cohort argued against the additional ceding of land, concluding that Deming had sold out his empire for personal gain. Li Jing decapitated Deming, in fury, then authorized a military advance on Shouchun, with the Prince of Qi, Jingda, as supreme marshal. Chen Jue, Bian Hao, and Xu Wenzhen joined him. Recovery of the three prefectures of Shu, Qi¤, and Tai occurred under Zhu Yuan, a commander of Jingda's.

In the face of heavy rains over the summer, Zhou armies withdrew from the prefectures of Yang, Chu‡, and He‡. The various commanders had wanted to exploit this critical moment of danger to strike against the enemy. Song Qiqiu disagreed, insisting, "A strike will only deepen their animosity. It would be better to relax hostilities as an act of virtue." He then exhorted commanders to secure their cities and fight no major battles. Zhou armies all converged on Shouzhou. As he garrisoned his men at Wokou, Shizong had wished to proceed to Yangzhou again, but chief minister Fan Zhi, a teacher and trusted aide, tearfully remonstrated against it. Shizong instructed troops to withdraw instead, deploying Li Chongjin to attack Lu‡ and Shou prefectures, while Xiang Xun was to defend Yangzhou. Xun sought to abandon Yangzhou to concentrate strength on the Shouchun offensive, so he sealed the city's treasury and gave oversight to its custodian. He further entrusted local police patrols to seasoned commanders of Li Jing, such that not a single feather was pilfered. The people of Huainan, greatly pleased, gladly carried grains on their back to feed Zhou soldiers.

In the fifteenth year [C.E. 957], Li Jingda directed Zhu Yuan and cohort to quarter troops at Zijin Mountain and construct a tunnel to provision Shouzhou. Shizong resumed his southern expedition, in the second month, moving from the Xiacai suspension bridge to Wokou, a town renamed Zhenhuai Commandery, where he erected two walls to apply pressure to both banks of the Huai River. Zhou troops repeatedly ruptured assorted fortresses at Zijin as well. Military decisions for the Tang were all made by Chen Jue, despite Jingda's standing as supreme marshal. Yet for long, Jue had strained relations with Zhu Yuan, a one-time retainer to Li Shouzhen, making trust between the two men an enduring problem. Li Jing thus recalled Yuan and named senior commander Yang Shouzhong his replacement. An embittered Zhu Yuan now surrendered to the Zhou, as the various other Tang armies were foiled. Xu Wenzhen and Bian Hao were both apprehended, Jingda returning to Jinling with the aid of sailors. With Liu Renshan nearly dead of illness, his deputy Sun Yu and cohort surrendered Shouzhou to the Zhou. Once Shizong ordered troops to withdraw, Li Jing dispatched men to Yangzhou to set it afire and reassign its troops before departing.

Resuming his southern expedition in winter, the tenth month, Shizong blockaded Haozhou¶, where prefect Guo Tingwei informed him, "Your Subject cannot secure this solitary prefecture against imperial troops, but it is my preference to surrender with the Tang court's consent." Shizong therefore delayed his assault as Tingwei had a messenger solicit authorization from Jing, Tingwei capitulating once consent came. The Zhou took Sizhou as well. Investing several tens of thousands in infantry and cavalry, Zhou warriors advanced in concert by land and sea. Soldiers crafted a song, "Ode to Tan," which could be heard at a distance of several dozen *li* when sung. They encamped at the northern gate of Chuzhou, during the twelfth month.

In the inaugural month of the inaugural year of Jiaotai [C.E. 958], a general amnesty and change of reigns were announced. As Zhou troops assaulted Chuzhou, defending commanders Zhang Yanqing and Zheng Zhaoye proved unflappable in their defense: even a forty-day offensive could not topple the city. Shizong personally oversaw troops in digging hollows into the city wall and setting them afire. They thereby pierced the wall, as Yanqing and Zhaoye perished in battle. In enraged retribution, Zhou troops prosecuted a thoroughgoing slaughter. Reclaimed by the Zhou were the prefectures of Hai, Tai, and Yang. Shizong visited Yingluan in approaching the great river, Yangzi. Li Jing appraised his own position as untenable and accepted the humiliation of relinquishing royal titles as an act of submission, so he commissioned Chen Jue to petition for Zhou authorization to transfer the throne to his heir and submit to Zhou directives.

At the outset of their southern offensive, the Zhou military possessed no implements for war on water. After inflicting a succession of defeats on Li Jing's forces, it captured some of its sailors and commissioned several hundred warships, as surrendering sailors taught them naval warfare. Wang Huan received commands to steer them down the Huai River. Li Jing's navies lost repeated battles, such that the ships best suited to the Huai River all fell into Zhou hands. The Zhou also commissioned several hundred "layered cloud" [multiple deck] ships. As Shizong arrived at Chuzhou's Beishen dikes, the "layered cloud" ships proved too large to pass through, so they navigated the Laoquan River to reach the great river, Yangzi.

Li Jing originally enjoyed the advantage of a naval force and considered the Zhou no rival—certainly incapable of reaching the Yangzi River. Once Chen Jue, his envoy to the Zhou, witnessed the stunning profusion of sailors arrayed along the Yangzi, he could only conclude that they had fallen from heaven. He promptly requested, "To return home to secure approval from Jing to cede all prefectures north of the Yangzi, as tentatively agreed." Shizong consented and finally forwarded a letter to Jing stating, quite simply, "The Emperor extends courtesies to the ruler of the southern Yangzi," then offered condolences for the hardship he has known. By now, the Zhou already held the prefectures of Yang, Tai, Chu‡, He‡, Shou, Hao¶, Si, Chu, Guang, and Hai, while the further cession of Lu‡, Shu, Qi¤, and Huang by Li Jing served, effectively, to realign the border along the Yangzi River. By the fifth month, Jing formally relinquished the title of "emperor" to call himself "ruler of the kingdom" and conformed to the Zhou reign name, fifth year of Xiande.

Previously, the Southern Tang envoy Sun Cheng had been detained by the Zhou, permitting Shizong to question him on real conditions in the southern Yangzi. When he refused to respond, Shizong murdered him in angry retribution. Once Zhou armies had withdrawn from Tang regions, Li Jing honored Liu Renshan posthumously as grand preceptor and invested Sun Cheng as Duke of Lu. Meanwhile, Shizong allowed Zhong Mo and Feng Yanlu to return home. Mo and cohort went back to the northern capital on Jing's initiative, bearing a letter written at his own hand, where he alluded to the unrequitable beneficence of the sovereign as heaven and earth, mother and father. Jing further invited the court to employ, in his case, the protocol for subordinate governors in future communications, using "edicts" over "letters." In face-to-face meetings with Shizong, Mo reiterated Jing's wish to transfer power to the crowned prince. Shizong extended formal expressions of consolation and commendation before returning him and the other envoys. Once back, Mo became vice minister of rites and Yanlu vice minister of revenues.

Feng Yanlu and associates had enjoyed access to the eastern palace ever since Li Jing's days as heir-apparent, access frequently opposed by minister of rites Chang Mengxi during the reign of Li Bian. Yanlu's visibility after Jing came to power caused Mengxi to disparage him whenever possible. In the wake of ceding land and accepting vassal status, whenever someone alluded to the Zhou as the "great court," Mengxi roared back with laughter, "You gentlemen were once given to celebrating our ruler as a Yao or Shun, while today you personally acknowledge ours as the 'little court'!"

Zhong Mo formerly enjoyed cordial relations with Li Deming, so upon returning to the south, reports that Song Qiqiu and cohort were behind the murder of Deming incited Mo to avenge the injustice, although the opportunity never came. Chen Jue, a partisan of Qiqiu with a history of conflict with Yan Xu, called for Xu's execution. Having returned as emissary to Zhou, Jue indicated that Shizong considered Xu responsible for Southern Tang intransigence, so Jue urged Jing to execute him as atonement for the crime. Jing proved skeptical, and Mo offered to return as envoy to Zhou to ascertain the facts. Jing had relinquished territory and title by now, Mo appearing in audience up north to apologize for Jing's past errors and seek authorization to pardon Xu, on condition that he was not involved in the refusal to cede lands. An utterly shocked Shizong responded, "Xu is a capable negotiator who exemplifies loyalty to ruler. How can I kill a loyal subject?" Once back in the south, Mo charged Jue with treacherous schemes, an angry Jing banishing Jue to Raozhou before arranging his death. Song Qiqiu faced charges of factional ties to Jue and returned to Qingyang County, where the court mandated his suicide.

Jing appointed fraternal heir Jingsui the governor of Hongzhou; the Prince of Yan, Li Ji, became heir-apparent. Li Jing faced financial pressures due to warfare, so Mo proposed the minting of large coins, where one of the new equaled ten of the old and bearing the inscription "currency negotiable in perpetuity." The large coins were abandoned after Mo fell from grace. Han Xizai also minted coins of iron, one new equivalent to two old coins. The heir-apparent, Li Ji, died during the ninth month [C.E. 959]. The next son in the line of descent, Congjia, ennobled Prince of Wu, took up residence in the eastern palace. Zhong Mo considered Congjia too dissolute and requested installation of Congshan, the Duke of Ji. Li Jing resented Mo's comments and demoted him to director of education, installing Congjia as heir-apparent.

Through a messenger, Shizong informed Jing, "I have already set forth the outlines of relations with the southern Yangzi, but I fear that my successors will be less accommodating of you. For now, you are free to repair city moats and take critical steps on behalf of your sons and grandsons." Jing now began erecting and repairing the walls of cities while planning to relocate the capital to Hongzhou. The official leadership uniformly opposed relocation, the only favorable view coming from military commissioner Tang Hao. Hongzhou, renamed Nanchang, became the "southern capital." In the second year of Jianlong [C.E. 961], the heir-apparent, Prince Jia, was left behind to oversee affairs of empire, Jing personally moving to the southern capital. A highly congested Hongzhou, however, could not accommodate royal palaces and state offices, and leading officials from day to night could think only of returning. Jing never overcame his remorse for the decision. Tang Hao, ashamed and afraid, took ill and died.

Li Jing died during the sixth month, at [forty-six] *sui.*[1] Congjia inherited his position, then returned to Jinling to conduct mourning rites. He also sent an envoy to the court seeking authorization to restore imperial titles to Jing. Emperor Taizu of Song consented, so he received a posthumous title as the Enlightened Way and Exalted Virtue, the Literarily Illustrious and Filial Emperor. Given the temple name of Yuanzong, his mausoleum was called Shunling.

Li Yu [C.E. 937–978] had the courtesy name Chongguang. Originally named Congjia, he was Jing's sixth son. Humane and filial in character, Yu had a flair for composition, calligraphy, and painting. His forehead was broad and teeth perfectly chiseled, while one eye contained double pupils. All five older sons, including the heir-apparent, Ji, had died young, leaving Yu next in line. He was invested Prince of Wu. With the relocation of Li Jing to the southern capital, in the second year of Jianlong [C.E. 961], Yu became heir-apparent with oversight over affairs of state. He formally succeeded Jing, at Jinling, upon his death. His mother's surname was Zhong and her father's personal name Taizhang. Yu honored his mother as the Sagacious and Esteemed Empress, installing his consort, née Zhou, as Empress of the kingdom. He also invested younger brothers Congshan as Prince of Han, Congyi as Prince of Zheng, Congqian as Prince of Yichun, Congdu as Duke of Zhaoping, and Congxin as Duke of Wenyang. He announced a general amnesty for the domain and dispatched deputy director of the Palace Secretariat Feng Yanlu to renegotiate tribute to the northern court. He further instructed unassigned officials below the rank of four[2] to proceed, two per day, to the palace's internal hall and await orders for an assignment.

Liu Congxiao of Quanzhou died during the third year [C.E. 962]. In the wake of Li Jing's conversion as vassal to the Zhou, Congxiao similarly petitioned to submit tribute to the northern capital. Shizong declined the offer out of consideration for Jing. Jing's relocation to Hongzhou left Congxiao anxious that he might be targeted for assault, so he dispatched his son, Shaoji, to tender tribute at Jinling. The illness and death of Congxiao prompted the military at Quanzhou to relocate his entire family to Jinling, installing deputy governor Zhang Hansi. An elderly Hansi could not assume duties, however, local man Chen Hongjin purging him and pronouncing himself interim regent. Hongjin was subsequently confirmed as governor by Li Yu.

In the second year of Qiande [C.E. 964], once the government introduced iron coins, the people often hoarded the old currency. As the old coins grew scarce, merchants traveling beyond the border often had to exchange ten iron coins for a single copper coin of the past. Officials proved unable to ban the practice, so Li Yu ordered the exchange of one for ten. He appointed Han Xizai as deputy director of the Palace Secretariat and academician at Qinzheng Hall, investing eldest son Zhongyu as Duke of Qingyuan and second son Zhongyi as Duke of Xuancheng.

During the fifth year [C.E. 966], Li Yu called nighttime deliberative meetings at Guangzheng Hall with the deputy directors of the two secretariats, secretarial overseers, secretarial drafters, and academicians at Jixian and Qinzheng halls. Considering Xizai thoroughly loyal and candid in discourse, Yu once wanted to name him chief minister. He anguished over the appointment, however, for Xizai had several tens of concubines and prostitutes within his inner chambers, many of whom went to other homes to provide private services for guests. Alternatively, Xizai received the lesser appointment of right mentor to the heir-apparent for the southern capital's branch office. Xizai decided to release the prostitutes and take to the road in a solitary carriage, inspiring Li Yu to retain and even restore his original office. Once the prostitutes gradually began to return, Yu declared, "I am left with no possible way of acting!" Xizai died that year. "Now, I will never have Xizai as minister," Yu said in lament. He considered posthumously naming Xizai chief minister and asked whether a precedent existed in earlier reigns. "Posthumous honors as supreme commandant were once afforded Liu Muzhi," officials indicated, so Xizai received recognition as minister.

Han Xizai hailed from a family of commanders at Beihai, his relations with Li Gu originally quite cordial. He fled southward to Wu during the reign of Mingzong, Li Gu personally sending him off as far as Zhengyang. The two men became intoxicated there, and Xizai said as parting words to Gu, "If I become minister in the southern Yangzi, I will head straight for the Central Plains and establish order." And Gu retorted, "If the Middle Kingdom makes me minister, I will capture the southern Yangzi with the ease of pulling something from my own pocket." Li Gu eventually won commission to lead Zhou armies in campaigns that captured the Huai region, while Xizai was able to accomplish nothing.

In the fourth year of Kaibao [C.E. 971], Li Yu sent younger brother Congshan, the Prince of Han, for an audience in the capital, where he was detained and not allowed to return home. Yu wrote, by his own hand, a plea for Congshan's repatriation, but Emperor Taizu of Song refused. Often melancholy and worried about the hardships besetting his kingdom, Yu tended to feast daily with officials and muse endlessly on sad songs.

During the fifth year [C.E. 972], Li Yu issued directives to downgrade existing institutions. Out of deference to the northern court, imperial "documents" now became "instructions," the Palace Secretariat and Chancellery became the Left and Right Palace Secretaries Bureau, the Imperial Secretariat became the Audit Bureau, the Censorate became the Justice Bureau, the Hanlin Academy became the Literary Arts Institute, the Military Affairs Bureau became the Enlightened Governance Institute, and royal "princes" all became "dukes." The personality of Li Yu tended toward arrogant extravagance and addiction to sensual pleasures. He had an affinity for Buddhism as well, engaging in lofty discourse without due concern for affairs of government. Secretarial drafter Pan You once wrote him in caustic remonstrance during the sixth year, but Yu tossed him into prison, where You strangled himself to death.

In the seventh year [C.E. 974], Emperor Taizu summoned Li Yu by messenger to the capital, but he declined by pleading illness. As troops of the Emperor launched their southern expedition, Yu had Xu Xuan and Zhou Weijian plead with the court for a postponement. Taizu gave no response. Imperial troops conquered Jinling in the twelfth month of the eighth year. In the ninth year [C.E. 976], Yu reached the capital as hostage, Taizu pardoning him. Investiture followed as Marquis of Weiming with titular rank as left commander of the Thousand-Bull Guard. On later events, see the national histories.[3]

My family for generations having resided in the southern Yangzi region, elders speak of the Li family and its times. It is said that Li Yu, confronting the dispatch of Song armies against the south by Emperor Taizu, sent courtier Xu Xuan to the capital for audience. A resident of the southern Yangzi with the self-assurance of a celebrated statesman, Xuan had hoped to deploy his oratory skills in defending his kingdom's autonomy. Day and night, he reviewed exhaustively in his mind possible responses for the audience. As the meeting approached, court leaders asked to enter before Xuan; characterizing him as a man broad in learning and gifted at debate, they advised special caution. Breaking into laughter, Taizu responded, "You may disband, for you have no sense of things."

Xuan appeared for court audience a day later, where falling prostrate he declared, "Li Yu has committed no crime, leaving Your Majesty no cause to issue troops." A composed Taizu courteously instructed him to stand and finish his statement, as Xuan continued, "Ruler of a small kingdom, Li Yu has served this great one as a son serves a father, committing no offense against you. Why target him for assault?" His speech dragged on through several hundred words, Taizu now responding, "Would your so-called father and son maintain two separate households?" Xuan had nothing to offer in response and withdrew.

WE LAMENT. Such grandeur, yet his words so simple! When a King is on the ascent, the entire world must revert to unified rule. Those willing to submit should be welcomed, those unwilling should be invaded, and pretenders to illicit power should all be eliminated in a timely sweep. In reading the "Proclamation for the Huainan Campaign" by Emperor Shizong of Zhou, I marveled at his extensive elaboration on past events and crafting of words to discern right from wrong. It was no trifling feat! The martial genius of Shizong is enough to relish. How are his words excessive?[i]

i. According to the *Jiangnan lu* of Tang Yue, "In the fifteenth year of Baoda, the inaugural month [C.E. 957], Li Jing changed the reign to Jiaotai; he relinquished fourteen prefectures of Huainan and drew the border at the Yangzi River in the same year." The fifteenth year of Baoda is the fourth year of Xiande, by the Zhou calendar. According to the *Old History of the Five Dynasties* and the *Veritable Records for Shizong*, in the fourth year of Xiande, fourteenth day of the tenth month, Shizong had just resumed his campaign against the south and only succeeded in vanquishing Chu in the fifth year, twenty-fifth day of the inaugural month. Not until the eighteenth day of the second month did Jing actually relinquish the various prefectures of Huainan and set the border at the Yangzi, which should actually represent the sixteenth year of Baoda. Tang Yue and cohort were former subjects of the Southern Tang, so why does their record of an event so prominent contain such discrepancies? Relative to works like *Jiuguo zhi* and *Jinian tongpu*, Yue's book is most authoritative, yet this discrepancy of one year is due to a lack of consultation.

Li Jing's overturn of the Min kingdom occurred in the fourth year of Baoda, yet *Jiangnan lu* gives the third year—again, a discrepancy of one year—and it gives as reference the *Min shijia*. Some suspect that Jing waited a year to change the reign name, thereby placing the overthrow of Min in the third year. There is no discrepancy about the year when the Zhou acquired Huainan: the fifteenth year; only *Jiangnan lu* mistakenly places in the same year the installation of Jing and the change of reign name—discrepancies of a year being indeed commonplace. Today, we know otherwise. By consulting the various texts, the murder of Wang Yanxi by the Min people occurred in the inaugural year of Kaiyun, by the Jin calendar [C.E. 944], while Zhou armies began their conquest of Southern Tang in the second year of Xiande [C.E. 955]. Assuming that Jing changed the reign at the time of accession, then this would be the inaugural year of Kaiyun or the second year of Baoda, while the second year of Xiande would be the thirteenth year of Baoda. Today, the *Jiangnan lu* records that Yanxi was murdered in the second year, while Zhou troops began campaigning in the thirteenth year, suggesting no error in the belief that Jing assumed power and changed reign in the same year. However, Tang Yue and other authors each indicate a year's difference between the overturn of Wang royals and the ceding of Huainan. From the founding of the Southern Tang by Li Bian, in the second year of Tianfu [C.E. 937], until the purge of his kingdom in the eighth year of Kaibao under our own dynasty [C.E. 975], some thirty-nine years had elapsed.

CHAPTER 63

HEREDITARY HOUSE OF FORMER SHU

Wang Jian and Son Yan

Wang Jian [C.E. 847–918] had the courtesy name Guangtu. Native to Wuyang County, Xuzhou‡, he had lush eyebrows, a broad forehead, and majestic bearing. He was a wastrel in youth, who made a living butchering cows, stealing donkeys, and pirating illegal salt, such that fellow villagers dubbed him "Wang the Bastard."[1] He later served as foot soldier at the Zhongwu command [Xuzhou‡] and rose to company commander.

In the wake of Huang Chao's conquest of Changan and Emperor Xizong's sojourn in the Shu region, the Zhongwu commander Lu Yanhong committed to Yang Fuguang a force of eight thousand to suppress the renegades. Chao subsequently fled in defeat, as Fuguang divided his army into eight brigades, each brigade containing a thousand soldiers: Wang Jian and Yanhong together headed a brigade. After Fuguang's death, Yanhong directed the eight brigades westward for a rendezvous with Emperor Xizong in Shu, plundering along the entire way. Yanhong removed governor Niu Cong upon reaching Xingyuan, pronouncing himself interim regent. Xizong subsequently named him governor, and Yanhong, in turn, temporarily subordinated Jian and the other heads of the eight brigades to the local prefect. In time, Yanhong conducted his armies in returning to the east, overrunning Chen‡ and Xu‡ prefectures. Wang Jian absconded westward for Shu, however, joined by other brigade commanders, including Jinhui, Han Jian, Zhang Zao, and Li Shitai. Emperor Xizong proved thoroughly delighted to secure them and conferred the appellation "Five

Brigades Attending the Royal Entourage," their oversight entrusted to Tian Lingzhi, surveillance inspector of the Ten Armies. Lingzi treated Jian and cohort as adopted sons, and after Xizong returned to Changan, he confirmed Jian, Jinhui, and cohort as commanders in the Divine Strategy Guard.

In the inaugural year of Guangqi [C.E. 885], Wang Chongrong of Hezhong sparred with Lingzi over a salt pond, consequently inviting the armies of the Prince of Jin [Li Keyong] to raid the capital. Xizong proceeded to Fengxiang, then relocated to Xingyuan [Shannan west], in the third month of the second year. Serving as his master of sojourn security, Jian trailed with the imperial seals of jade. The entourage approached Dangtu Post when Li Changfu set fire to a footbridge and nearly severed it. Jian held the reins of Xizong's horse, the two men hazarding smoke and flames as they passed. Resting below a cliff, Xizong used Jian's lap as a pillow for sleep, only to be moved to tears as he awoke. A piece of his own apparel was removed to give to Jian.

Emperor Xizong had already reached Xingyuan, but Lingzi believed that the Son of Heaven's itinerancy had been caused by him and worried about bearing the blame. With Lingzi's maternal brother Chen Jingxuan serving as governor of the western Chuan command, Lingzi requested an appointment as military overseer there. His replacement as armed forces inspector for the Ten Armies was Yang Fugong, who elevated Jian to prefect of Bizhou‡. There Jian recruited soldiers of fortune and "River and Cave" tribesmen, amassing eight thousand men, for an assault on Langzhou‡, where prefect Yang Xingqian was apprehended. A raid on Lizhou ensued as prefect Wang Gong abandoned the city and fled. Jingxuan now considered him a potential menace and spoke to Lingzi, who asserted, "Wang the Bastard is my son. With a simple summons, he can be called to service under my banner." He arranged for someone to convince Jian.

Lingzi's summons of Wang Jian came as a great delight, for Jian was an old acquaintance of Gu Yanlang of the eastern Chuan command, so he stopped by Zi‡ Prefecture en route. There he said to Yanlang, "My father of the Ten Armies has summoned me, and I intend to meet Gentleman Chen at Chengdu to request a governorship." Entrusting family members to the care of Yanlang, Jian then selected two thousand skilled warriors for a dash toward Chengdu. He reached Lutou Pass when Chen Jingxuan came to regret summoning him, sending someone to intercept. An utterly livid Jian thus stormed and overran Lutou Pass, capturing Hanzhou. News of the incident prompted Yanlang to assist Jian by deploying a force that forted at Xueshe. Jian faced resistance from Gou Weili, a commander sent by Jingxuan, but he vanquished Weili in a sortie. An assault on Pengzhou ensued. Jingxuan now dispatched the prefect of Meizhou, Shan Xingzhang, to command fifty thousand men to Xinfan, where a sudden strike from Jian induced similar defeat: over ten thousand were taken hostage, as corpses lay strewn across an area of forty *li*. Jingxuan unleashed another seventy thousand men to bolster Xingzhang's position. They engaged Jian at Mengyang and Xindu in a standoff exceeding a hundred days in duration.

Emperor Zhaozong instructed Yanlang and cohort to disband their armies, naming the left master of admonition, Liu Xun, commissioner of cooperation and reconciliation for the two commands of Chuan. Yanlang petitioned for a senior officer as Shu governor while seeking a command on Jian's behalf. In the sixth month of the inaugural year of Wende [C.E. 888], the court named chief minister Wei Zhaodu governor of western Chuan. The prefectures of Qiong, Shu‡, Li‡, and Ya were reconstituted as the new Yongping command, with Jian as governor.

Chen Jingxuan refused to accept the replacement mandated by the court, causing Emperor Zhaozong to authorize a suppression effort by Gu Yanlang, a commander under Zhaodu. The Emperor further named Wang Jian chief director of bandit suppression for the yamen. Unable to prevail after some time, Jian intimated to Zhaodu, "You, Sir, with a legion of several tens of thousands, have long pressed warriors of the two Chuan commands with no success. And to what end? The Tang dynasty is beset with countless problems, as governors in the east extend military conflict westward to the capital. You should revert to the Son of Heaven to fortify the empire's foundation by restoring order to the Central Plains. This land of southern barbarians cannot justify your permanent presence." Zhaodu proved too tentative to reach a decision, so Jian dispatched troops to the entrance of Zhaodu's barracks, where an aide was seized and dismembered, his flesh even eaten. Entering again, Jian said to Zhaodu, "The troops needed to eat him—they were starving!" A frightened Zhaodu now relinquished to Jian his tallies of office and absconded for the east. Jian promptly seized Jianmen after Zhaodu's departure, isolating the two Chuan commands from the outside.

The armies of Shan Xingzhang quartered at Guangdu came under Wang Jian's sally and were defeated. He then fled to Meizhou and surrendered the prefecture to Jian, who directed his men in an offensive against Chengdu. Civilian prefects of Zi¶, Jian¶, Rong, Mao, Jia, and Qiong were all murdered, the prefectures surrendered to Jian.

Wang Jian's attack on Chengdu being extremely ferocious, Tian Lingzi climbed atop the city's wall to shout out, "This old man shares deep bonds with you. How can you act so objectionably?" Jian shouted back, "The kindness of Mr. Inspector is akin to father and son, something scarcely to disappear from my heart. At the behest of the Son of Heaven, however, I take military reprisal against a man who refuses to be replaced." Lingzi entered Jian's army under the cover of night, giving to Jian the shield and seals of both the governor and his surveillance officer. Jingxuan opened the city's gates to welcome Jian on the very next day. As he prepared to enter, Jian named Zhang Jing military inspector-in-chief, while admonishing troops, "Zhang Jing will be inspector-in-chief and no one should violate his orders. If you happen to be detained by Jing and later brought before me, I might allow you to live. If Jing kills you first before informing me, there is surely no recourse for me to pursue." Troops did engage in pillage once Jian occupied the city, and Jing killed a hundred men before ending the rampage. Jingxun was subsequently relocated to Yazhou, Jian deploying someone to kill him. Lingzi was restored as military overseer, but Jian arranged his assassination as well.

In the tenth month of the second year of Dashun [C.E. 891], the court appointed Jian honorary dignitary for education, metropolitan custodian of Chengdu, distinguished deputy governor of the two Chuan circuits, commissioner of metropolitan surveillance and oversight, and commissioner of bandit suppression for the eight kingdoms of Yunnan.

With the death of Gu Yanlang of eastern Chuan, younger brother Yanhui succeeded him. The Tang court had arranged for eunuch Zong Daobi to confer Yanhui's banner and tallies of office when Chang Hou, the prefect of Mianzhou, kidnapped Daobi and raided Zizhou‡. Wang Jian retaliated against Hou by dispatching Li Jian, Wang Zongdi, and others. Ever since Yanlang's death, Wang Jian harbored covetous designs on eastern Chuan without acting on them. Once Li Jian and cohort undertook the suppression against Hou, Wang Jian warned, "After our armies vanquish Hou, Yanhui is certain to emerge to feast troops. You should bring back him as well, sparing me the trouble of a second mission." Li Jian and cohort now stormed and defeated Hou at Zhongyang. Hou returned to Mianzhou, having restored the Tang banners and tallies to Daobi before departing. Yanhui thereby gained possession of the tallies, yet refused to emerge to dine with troops, professing illness.

In the second year of Qianning [C.E. 895], Wang Jian unleashed Wang Zongdi to attack Yanhui, and he was vanquished at Qiulin in the twelfth month. Yanhui commander Luo Zhang was beheaded, a blockade of Zizhou‡ ensuing. In the fifth month of the third year [C.E. 896], Emperor Zhaozong deputized eunuch Yuan Yijian to convey a imperial mandate stripping Jian of his armies. Jian regrouped his men, instead, returning to Chengdu. The Qiannan governor Wang Zhao surrendered his charge to Jian.

During the fourth year [C.E. 897], Wang Zongdi resumed an offensive in eastern Chuan: Wang Zongkan, Zong Ruan, and others were sent separately to approach from Xiazhou‡, claiming the prefectures of Yu‡ and Lu¶. Wang Jian personally led an assault on eastern Chuan during the fifth month, in response to which Emperor Zhaozong named commissioners of reconciliation for the two Chuan commands: master of admonition Li Xun and administrative assistant Wei Zhuang. The court further instructed Jian to relinquish his armies. When he rebuffed the court, it retaliated by demoting him to prefect of Nanzhou and arranging replacements: the Prince of Tan as governor of Fengxiang and Li Maozhen as governor of western Chuan. Once Maozhen resisted the assignment, the court restored former offices and noble titles to Jian.

In winter, the tenth month, Wang Jian overran Zizhou‡, where Yanhui committed suicide. Once Yanhui commander Gu Yanyao appraised the city as imperiled, he turned to assorted commanders and their aides, declaring, "Service under the Gentleman Gu should rightfully involve a life or death commitment!" He then added, pointing to the metal sword hanging from his waist, "Those considering treachery at this moment of crisis will surely get a taste of my sword!" The city was on the brink of collapse when Yanyao and Yanhui gathered commanders and their aides for a round of drinks, everyone perishing together. On Jian's recommendation, Wang Zongdi became interim regent of eastern Chuan, the Tang court confirming powers as governor of the area. The entirety of eastern and western Chuan then came under their control.

At the time, Li Maozhen of Fengxiang also exerted control over the prefectures of Liang, Yang‡, Qin, and Long, repeatedly intruding militarily upon Wang Jian as well. In the inaugural year of Tianfu [C.E. 901], with Liang armies under Taizu conducting a mass execution of eunuchs, a eunuch group led by Han Quanhui abducted the Son of Heaven to Fengxiang. Liang troops surrounded the city, but Maozhen sealed it tight in a resistance lasting a year, seeking a truce only after his energies were sapped. In this context, Jian sent a messenger of inquiry to Maozhen urging a staunch defense of the city and repudiation of peace with Liang, while promising to extend his own military assistance. He further unleashed Wang Zongdi, commanding a force of fifty thousand, purportedly to welcome the imperial entourage. They attacked Xingyuan Prefecture and apprehended its governor, Li Jiye. The neighboring Wuding governor, Tuoba Sijing, thereafter surrendered his lands to Jian, delivering the entire command of Shannan west to him. This coincided with the death of Cheng Rui of Jingnan, Zhao Kuangning of Xiangzhou now unleashing younger brother Kuangming for a surprise strike and occupation. Wang Jian exploited the vacuum to launch eventually successful raids on the prefectures of Kui, Shi‡, Zhong, and Wan [in eastern Chuan].

In the eighth month of the third year [C.E. 903], the Tang court invested Wang Jian as Prince of Shu. It moved its capital to Luoyang during the fourth year, changing the reign name to Tianyou. Jian was not informed of the change owing to disruption in relations with the Tang court, so he continued to recognize the Tianfu calendar. He claimed Guizhou in the sixth year, giving him control over the Three Gorges region. Once the Liang had supplanted the Tang dynasty, during the seventh year [C.E. 907], an envoy was sent to sway Jian, but he declined to accept its appeals, instead issuing an immediate call to the four corners for war. He had hoped to align the world against the Liang, but a world fully aware of his ingenuousness refused to respond.

In the inaugural month of the year, a giant man was sighted in the Qingcheng Hills. Sightings of a phoenix at Wansui County and a yellow dragon at the Jiayang River occurred in the sixth month. Across the prefectures came reports of other auspicious omens such as sweet dew, white deer, white sparrows, tortoises, and dragons. In the autumn, twenty-fifth day of the ninth month [November 3], Jian succeeded to the throne as emperor, investing each of his sons as prince. Wang Zongji became palace secretary, Wei Zhuang became left cavalier of remonstrance and administrator at the Palace Secretariat and Chancellery, Tang Xi became commissioner of military affairs, Zheng Qian became deputy censor, Zhang Ge and Wang Kai became Hanlin academicians, and Zhou Boya became the metropolitan custodian of Chengdu.

Through insularity, Shu could prosper. During the last years of Tang, many literati turned to Wang Jian to escape tumult. Despite his roguish origins, Jian's personality exuded cleverness and guile, and his treatment of literati quite kind. Upon assuming bogus titles of royalty, he employed the famous courtiers and pedigreed men of Tang times: Wei Zhuang was the grandson of Wei Jiansu and Zhang Ge the son of Zhang Jun. He once commented to attendants, "As commander of the Divine Strategy Guard with men billeted in the Tang imperial palace, I observed the Son of Heaven summoning academicians in an endless stream. He afforded them the beneficent courtesies and genuine intimacy of friends or associates—his relations with the martial ministers scarcely comparable." Thus, Jian treated Ge and cohort with extraordinary beneficence and courtesy, Song Pin and a hundred others enjoying his confidences.

In the inaugural years of Wucheng, the inaugural month [C.E. 908], Wang Jian conducted sacrifices to Heaven in the southern suburbs, announced a general amnesty and change of reign name, and honored Wang Zongji as grand preceptor. Originally surnamed Gan, Zongji had been abducted by Jian, then a foot soldier at the Zhongwu command, who raised him as a son. A succession of promotions attended military feats, culminating in Zongji's assignment as governor of the Wuxin command. Once sons personally fathered by Jian, such as [Zongyi], became adults, the insecurity of adopted son Zongji caused him to conspire with Zheng Qian and others. He requested honors as grand minister of war, director of the Six Armies, and decorated supreme marshal—effectively enabling him to make military decisions at discretion, informing the court after the fact. Jian chose a generous accommodation of Zongji, owing to his many merits in founding the kingdom.

A certain Tang Xi had won the favor of Wang Jian as a child dancer, causing Zongji to trivialize him. Even after Xi became commissioner of military affairs, Zongji continued to employ his personal name: the resentment within was never expressed without, and Xi served Zongji with heightened circumspection instead. Zongji's informality nonetheless annoyed Jian, who commented, "Zongji's use of personal name in addressing my military commissioner suggests impending rebellion." Jian received three separate petitions from Zongji to become grand minister of war, inquiring of Xi, who intentionally incited Jian by stating, "As a meritorious subject, Zongji's formidable stature can humble the hearts of men. Your Majesty should make a prompt appointment." Jian's apprehensions only increased. Zongji now appeared to address affairs and Jian did not allow him to finish, yelling out to bodyguards to pummel him to death. Zheng Qian received orders to commit suicide as well.

During the sixth month, the Prince of Sui, Zongyi, became heir-apparent. Wang Jian elevated his own title of honor to the Courageously Martial, Profound, and Sagacious Emperor. The *zouyu* white tiger was sighted at Wuding County in the seventh month. The court published the *Yongchang Calendar* in the second year. Reports of "auspicious grains" and "twin seedlings" came from Guangdu County. During the eighth month of the third year [C.E. 910], fifty dragons were sighted in the waters of Xunyang, then unicorns at Bizhou‡ in the tenth month. In the twelfth month, a general amnesty was pronounced and next year's reign name was changed to Yongping the first.

The Prince of Qi, Li Maozhen, facing a blockade by Liang armies, relinquished the Shannan region to Shu, for his lands were small and power too isolated. He hence sought amicable ties with Wang Jian and arranged the marriage of his son to Jian's daughter, while requesting retention of control over his Shannan satrapy. An angry Jian refused, unleashing instead a campaign against Qizhou‡ with Wang Zongkan as general commander of the northern circuits and sons Zongyou and Zonghe assisting Tang Xi as commissioners of bandit suppression for the three fronts. Defeats in battle at Qingni County forced Zongkan to retreat to Xi County, where Maozhen's armies encircled him. Jian now personally commanded a strike against Qi‡ troops, which scattered after a defeat; he proceeded to Xingyuan before returning to Chengdu. Jian's title of honor was advanced to the Resplendently Martial, Profoundly Sagacious, Radiant, and Filial Emperor.

In the second year [C.E. 912], Wang Jian was elevated to the Resplendently Martial, Profoundly Sagacious, Divinely Accomplished, Literary and Moral, Radiant and Filial Emperor. Previously, under Tian Lingzi's tenure as military overseer, the Tang imperial seal of dynastic succession was pilfered and brought to Shu to be buried. During repairs to Lingzi's former home by the master of domestic services, Ouyang Rou, the seal was retrieved from a hold in the floor and forwarded to court in the second month.

In the fifth month, the Liang dynasty envoy Lu Pin, chamberlain of imperial recreations, arrived to extend recognition of Wang Jian as elder brother. The envoy's travel documents contained the stamp, "Insignia of the Great Liang for Admission to Shu." Chief minister Zhang Ge protested, saying, "By Tang-dynasty custom, envoys to barbarian lands all carried documents stamped, 'Insignia of the Great Tang for Admission to a Certain Country.' The Liang now serving Your Majesty as elder brother, how can it disparage us like barbarians?" An aggrieved Jian would have murdered the envoy, but Ge countered, "This reflects the simple oversight of some Liang official, an incident that should not disrupt amicable bonds between our two empires." Taizu of Liang later died, and Jian offered condolences through envoy Li Hong, director of palace buildings. His credentials contained the words, "Insignia of the Great Shu for Admission to the Liang."

Trees with spectacular interconnected branches were reported at Jianzhou‡. Sightings occurred of a unicorn at Wenzhou, in the sixth month; a yellow dragon in the Fuyi River, in the twelfth month; unicorns at Yongtai, in the inaugural month of the third year; and the *zouyu* tiger with two deer in tow, at Bishan, during the fifth month.

In autumn, the seventh month [C.E. 913], heir-apparent Wang Yuanying killed Tang Xi, junior guardian to the heir. The second son of Wang Jian, Yuanying's original name, Zongyi, had been changed to Zongtan and again changed to Yuanying after Jian obtained a bronze tablet at Shifang: inscribed with over twenty words, the tablet was considered a prophetic amulet and Jian chose personal names for his sons based on its words. Yuanying had a piglike snout and rotten teeth, but possessed many a talent and craft. He could shoot an arrow through the hole of a coin. He once threw a cluster of painted balls from his horse to hit every one with a spray of arrows. At seventeen, he was designated heir-apparent, administrator of the Six Armies, founder of the Celestially Martial and Spiritually Anointed Encampments, and inaugurator of the Eternal-Peace Commandery, with a full complement of officials. Recognizing the gravity of responsibilities for someone so young, Jian often had affairs recorded to serve as instructions for him, insisting, "Only by systematically studying my actions is preservation of empire possible." Jian also ordered the Daoist priest known as Master Guangcheng, Du Guangting, to tutor Yuanying.

Tang Xi enjoyed the favor of Wang Jian, but Yuanying trivialized him, often mocking him at court. For fear of an ugly turn of events, Jian transferred Xi locally as governor of Xingyuan with standing as military commissioner.

Once Xi returned from assignment, Yuanying relentlessly excoriated him at court, further annoying Jian. Yuanying invited royal princes and senior officials for a banquet, on the "seventh night" festival that month.[2] Zonghan the Prince of Ji, military commissioner Pan Qiao, and Hanlin academician Mao Wenxi all failed to come, causing Yuanying to exclaim in rage, "The Prince of Ji refused to come at the prompting of Qiao and Wenxi." Speaking with Jian a day later, he accused the two men of inciting rifts. Jian, now riled, prepared to punish the two as Yuanying departed and Tang Xi entered, so Jian inquired of Xi. "The heir-apparent conspires to wreak havoc by summoning commanders and royal princes to incarcerate Qiao and Wenxi, then rise in rebellion," Xi alleged. Jian remained skeptical, so Xi requested the summoning of troops from barracks to palace stations. Yuanying was caught off guard, but assumed Xi's military summons as a ploy to kill him. He responded by arranging the actor An Xixiang and commander Yu Quanshu to lead contingents from the Heavenly Martial Guard to their palace positions. He further arranged for the abduction and flogging of Qiao and Wenxi, confining them to home, then ordered commandants Xu Yao and Chang Qian to resist Xi with their armies. They battled him at the Shenwu gate, where Xi, hit by a stray arrow, fell to his death from a horse. Wang Jian now dispatched Wang Zonghe to direct armies against Yuanying, whose troops scattered in defeat. Hiding in a sieve at Yao long Pond, Yuanying was recognized by a Shu native upon leaving to beg for food. Once informed, Jian sent Zonghan to try to sway him into submission, but Yuanying was murdered by a guardsman before Zonghan's arrival. Jian later installed youngest son Zongyan, the Prince of Zheng, as heir. A white dragon appeared at a river in Qiongzhou.

In the fourth year [C.E. 914], Gao Jichang of Jingnan [Nanping] invaded the Shu territory of Wushan. The Prince of Jia, Zongchou, vanquished him at Qutang County. The Qiannan governor Wang Zongxun was murdered in the eighth month. In the winter, southern barbarians attacked and pillaged the border region. They met defeat at Dadu River after Jian dispatched the Prince of Kui, Zongfan. A unicorn was sighted at Changzhou‡.

During the fifth year [C.E. 915], a "Longevity Hall" was erected in the Longxing palace, a portrait of Wang Jian painted on its walls. Also erected was the Heaven-Sustaining Pavilion, containing portraits of meritorious subjects. In the eleventh month, a vast fire destroyed palace apartments. Wang Zongshou‡ and cohort, sent to attack Qi‡, seized the four prefectures of Qin, Feng‡, Jie, and Cheng, extending as far as Dasan Pass. With the Liang defector Liu Zhijun at Qi‡, special arrangements were made to bring his extended family to the capital.

In the inaugural year of Tongzheng [C.E. 916], the court dispatched Wang Zongwan and others, commanding 120,000 men, in an offensive against

Qizhou‡. Departing from Dasan Pass, they acquired Longzhou. The "Hall of Refined Contemplation" was erected in the eighth month, piles of books to fill it procured by offering honorary office with rank of five. The military commissioner for the palace, Mao Wenxi, became academician for the new hall. A yellow dragon was sighted at Dachang Pond. A general amnesty was announced in the tenth month, the reign name Tianhan effective starting next year, and Han adopted as dynastic name. In the inaugural year of Tianhan [C.E. 917], Liu Zhijun was murdered. A general amnesty was promulgated in the twelfth month, the reign name Guangtian adopted for next year and Shu revived as dynastic name.

In the inaugural year of Guangtian [C.E. 918], the sixth month, Wang Jian died at seventy-two *sui*. Many palace favorites had been acquired in his waning years: the Wise Consort Xu and her sister the Pure Consort both won advancement based on sensual appeal, only to dominate the palace apartments and its affairs, allying with eunuchs such as Tang Wenyi to intrude into affairs of court. Growing senile in his old age, Jian named Wenyi as administrator of the Six Armies and permitted a range of affairs, great to small, to be singularly decided by him. As Jian took ill, Wenyi arranged for military contingents to infiltrate the palace stations of the bodyguard, planning to eliminate all of Jian's senior commanders. Once these commanders learned of Jian's illness, it proved impossible to enter for visits. It took some time before Zongbi and cohort thrust open the palace doors to enter, charging Wenyi with treacherous designs and killing him. Wang Jian had fully recognized that many of the old commanders and senior officials refused to serve the heir-apparent, being old associates of Xu Chang. He thus planned to select others, but his health deteriorated beforehand. The eunuch Song Guangsi was named commissioner of military affairs and administrator of the Six Armies on the eve of Jian's death. The heir-apparent inherited power, the character "Zong" deleted from his personal name, which now became "Yan."

Wang Yan [d. C.E. 926] had the courtesy name Huayuan. Jian sired eleven sons: Zongren the Prince of Wei, Yuanying the Prince of Jian, Zongji the Prince of Zhao, Zonglu the Prince of Bin, Zongzhi the Prince of Han, Zongte the Prince of Ju, Zongjie the Prince of Xing, Zongding the Prince of Lu, Zongze the Prince of Xin, and Zongping the Prince of Xue. Zongyan the Prince of Zheng was the youngest of these sons, but favor for his mother, the Wise Consort Xu, permitted his installation as heir-apparent. Presiding over the special district of Chongxian, he received a complement of officials, the district name later changed to Tiance.

He had square cheeks and large mouth, plus arms that extended beyond his knees. Looking through the side of his eye, he could see his own [auspiciously prominent] ears. He was a man of some learning with a penchant for frivolous embellishment in literary composition. Upon the death of Yuanying, Wang Jian considered selecting one of two other sons as successor: Zonglu the Prince of Bin, who resembled him in physical appearance, and Zongjie the Prince of Xin, who seemed the most able of his sons. However, Consort Xu monopolized his favor precisely as Jian grew muddled in old age. She and eunuch Tang Wenyi arranged for a face-reader to inform Jian of the superior physiognomy of Yan, while personally reiterating chief minister Zhang Ge's praise for Yan. In this way, he became heir-apparent.

Wang Yan succeeded Jian after his death. Jian received the posthumous title of Spiritual, Martial, Sagacious, Literate, Filial, Virtuous, Enlightened, and Charitable Emperor, his temple name Gaozu and mausoleum called Yongling. The formal wife of Jian, née Zhou, also known as the Luminously Sagacious Empress, died only a few days after him. Yan now moved to honor his own mother, née Xu, as Empress Dowager, the Empress Dowager's younger sister, the Pure Consort, becoming Consort Dowager. The Empress Dowager and Consort Dowager sold official posts on orders from her palace: for each vacancy of prefect and below, several persons were to compete, and the post was to be awarded to the highest bidder. From the capital to large towns, commercial shops were erected to snatch away the profits of the people.

Given to debauchery in youth, Wang Yan delegated affairs of government to eunuchs such as Song Guangsi, Guang Bao, Jing Runcheng, Wang Chengxiu, Ouyang Huang, and Tian Luchou. His illicitly intimate attendants included Han Zhao, Pan Zaiying, Gu Zaixun, and Yan Xu. He constructed a garden called Burgeoning Splendor, halls called Replenished Radiance, Supreme Purity, Prolonged Prosperity, and Authentic Assembly, palaces called Pristine Ambiance and Reception for Immortals, kiosks called Imminent Greatness, Idyllic Paradise, and Cinnabar Mist, a pavilion dubbed *Luan* Bird in Flight and a gate called Propitious Creatures. He also built the Convivial Spirits kiosk, where his intimate male attendants and wives drank to inebriation from morning to night. Feasting at the Burgeoning Splendor garden once continued for nine days, inciting the Prince of Jia, Zongshou, to invoke concern for the dynastic altars in reproof, tears falling as the words flowed. But Hanzhao and cohort said dismissively, "The Prince of Jia is simply left gloomy by the wine!" Those same intimates proceeded uniformly to insult and mock the Prince, creating around him a clamor as he sat, and preventing Yan from inquiring further.

Shu people are wealthy and given to merriment. In the later years of Wang rule, small caps had become a raging fashion. Barely covering the top of the head, the cap could fall off with a simple nod of the head, inspiring the name "precarious pate cap." Wang Yan considered it inauspicious and banned it. He personally preferred to wear large hats, donning these whenever mingling among the people incognito. The people thereby came to recognize Yan by the large hat, so he later directed all people of his kingdom to wear large hats.

Wang Yan also liked wrapping his head in a turban sharply creased and pointed like an awl. The women of his inner palace all wore head garlands of golden lotus flowers and the attire of Daoist nuns. Removing the head garlands at times of heavy drinking, they revealed hair twisted upward and accented with bright red powder. Called "drunkard's coif," the style drew reproof from his own subjects. Once, during travels to Qingcheng Mountain with the Empress Dowager and Consort Dowager, the palace women wore dresses painted with colorful clouds, the fluttering of which made the women look like immortals. Yan once composed the "Ode to Ganzhou" to describe this image of immortals, singing the song personally during travels through the ridges and ravines of the mountains, while instructing the ladies to accompany him in song. Within a year of taking power, he changed the reign year to "Power of the Primal Force," or Qiande [to celebrate immortals].

In the inaugural year of Qiande, the inaugural month [C.E. 919], sacrifices to Heaven were conducted at the southern suburbs, a general amnesty declared, and the monarch's title of honor advanced to the Sagacious, Virtuous, Enlightened, and Filial Emperor. Patrols along the northern border, as far as Xi County, occurred in winter of the second year [C.E. 920], the train of army banners and armored men stretching in a line over a hundred *li* long. On the return trip, Yan traveled up the [Jialing] river from Langzhou‡, his dragon boat and painted flotillas glistening in the water. Simply meeting their needs was more than people could bear. He returned to Chengdu in the inaugural month of the third year.

The Shangqing temple was erected in the fifth year [C.E. 923], where a clay statue of [Daoist progenitor] Wang Zijin was commissioned and honors conferred as Emperor of the Jade Palace and Sagacious Ancestor of Supreme Virtue. Statues of Wang Jian and Yan were also commissioned for placement at Zijin's left and right. For the anterior temple were statues of the Xuanyuan Emperor [Laozi] and all Emperors of the Tang dynasty. The monarch's chariot was prepared to render services.

In the sixth year [C.E. 924], Wang Chengxiu became the Tianxiong governor—that is, the Tianxiong command for Qinzhou.[3] He came to enjoy royal favor through eunuch influence and rose to commissioner of palace armies. He had a wife of stunning beauty, née Yan, with whom Wang Yan had illicit relations. At the time, annihilation of the Liang dynasty by Zhuangzong of Tang had alarmed the people of Shu. Zhuangzong deputized Li Yan as envoy to Shu and Wang Yan escorted the envoy to Shangqing, causing literati and commoners alike from the Shu capital to form an endless stream onto the roadways, appearing with screens, canopies, and jewel-studded headdress. The lavish wealth of Shu people was clearly visible to the envoy, as well as the arrogance and debauchery of Wang Yan, so he returned to propose war against Shu.

During the next year [C.E. 925], the Tang launched its campaign against Shu led by Jiji the Prince of Wei and Guo Chongtao. Wang Yan changed the reign name to Xiankang during the same year. Since his installation, Yan would go hunting at the Zilai Hills many times a year. This year, he also visited Yangpinghua at Pengzhou and the Sanxue Hills at Hanzhou. He further visited Qinzhou in the tenth month, out of consideration for Wang Chengxiu's wife, the Woman Yan. Courtiers had strenuously enjoined against the new trip, but Yan ignored them. His entourage reached Zitong [Jianzhou‡] when wind gusts uprooted the wooden posts for his tent, prompting his grand astrologer to comment, "This wind of the rapacious wolf symbolizes a vanquished army that murders its commander." Yan paid no heed. As his entourage reached Miangu, Tang troops had already penetrated the border and a nervous Yan returned in haste.

Tang armies met with surrender at every prefecture and county in their path. Wang Yan left behind [adopted brother] Wang Zongbi to defend Miangu, while mobilizing Wang Zongxun, Wang Zongyan, and Wang Zongyu to resist the invaders. Upon reaching Sanquan, Zongxun's men withdrew promptly as winds shifted. Yan ordered Zongbi to execute the deserters, but Zongbi on the contrary became coconspirator with Zongxun, making peace overtures to the Tang military. Yan now returned to Chengdu from Miangu, met at Qiliting by official multitudes and consorts of his inner palace. To enter Chengdu, Yan had to mix his palace personnel into contingents of Uighurs. Appearing at the Wenming palace a day later, he and his officials tearfully sobbed before each other. Zongbi similarly returned from Miangu in haste, climbing the Taixuan gate to apprehend Han Zhao, the custodian of Chengdu, and eunuchs Song Guangsi, Jing Runcheng, and Ouyang Huang, slaying them and severing their heads for conveyance to Jiji. Yan now petitioned the Tang for permission to surrender, Zongbi removing him to the Tianqi palace. Once Jiji the Prince of Wei reached Chengdu, Yan and his courtiers appeared with hands bound and coffins carried behind them, for the surrender at Qiliting.

Summoning Wang Yan to [the northern capital] at Luoyang, Zhuangzong declared by imperial edict, "Having already relinquished your territory to us, I promise no risk to human life. Swearing on the sun, moon, and stars above, I make no misrepresentations!" With edict in hand, Yan gladly took to the road. Escorting him eastward was an entourage of several thousands: members of the imperial clan, the bogus ministers Wang Kai, Zhang Ge, Yu Chuansu, and Xu Ji, Hanlin academician Li Min and assorted courtiers, commanders and their lieutenants, plus family dependents. As they reached Qinchuan post, in the fourth month of Tongguang the fourth year [C.E. 926], acting on the intrigues of actor-musician Jing Jin, Zhuangzong directed eunuch Xiang Yansi to execute Yan's entire family. The mother of Yan, née Xu, as her own punishment approached, cried out indignantly, "My son voluntarily relinquished his entire empire only to be slaughtered instead, contravening both honesty and integrity. There will be no retreat from calamity for you, I am sure." Yan's attractive Concubine Liu had hair so lush as to look like a cloud, such that the executioner considered exempting her. "My empire vanquished, righteous duty demands that I suffer no shame," she insisted before going willfully to her death.

Wang Zongbi [d. C.E. 925] originally had the surname Wei and personal name Hongfu before Wang Jian formally adopted him as son. When at war against Gu Yanhui, Jian's utterances to Zongbi were often divulged to Yanhui, but Jian treated Zongbi as usual in the wake of Yanhui's defeat. Upon the illness and death of Jian, Zongbi helped govern as acting grand preceptor, concurrent palace secretary, and administrator of the Six Armies. Zongbi presented the precious treasures of Shu to the Prince of Wei and Guo Chongtao, after Yan's surrender, requesting the governorship of western Chuan in exchange. The Prince insisted, "These possessions of my royal family hardly deserve to be called 'presents!' " Zongbi died at Chongtao's hands a few days later.

Wang Zongshou was born to commoners at Xuzhou‡ with the same surname as Wang Jian, who formally adopted him as son. He was fond of learning and could play the zither with grace. Composed and withdrawn by character, Zongshou was drawn to the Daoist occult. He served as governor of the Zhenjiang command under Wang Jian, then grand guardian to the heir-apparent with prestige-rank of *fengchaoqing* attending the accession of Yan. He tended to amuse himself, at the time, with pills of cinnabar to enhance his vital *qi* force. It was nonetheless Zongshou who singularly and repeatedly censured Yan for his debauched degeneracy, later becoming the Wuxin governor.

With Tang armies waging war against Shu and winning surrender at every turn, the Prince of Wei used personal letters to sway commanders into submission. Zongshou singularly refused to capitulate. After hearing that Yan had already left wearing pendants of royal power, Zongshou cried loudly and accompanied him in the journey eastward. Zongshou succeeded in bribing a guard, as they reached Qiyang, to meet with Yan, whose streaming tears drenched his lapel. "This day would scarcely have come, if only I had obeyed your counsel at the outset," Yan conceded. Zongshou proceeded to Mianchi following Yan's death, then absconded for the Xionger Mountains after word of regicide against Emperor Zhuangzong. He journeyed to the capital, in the second year of Tiancheng [C.E. 927], petitioning the throne to locate the bodies of Yan and his family for proper burial. Mingzong admired his sense of loyalty and named him manager-adjutant of the Baoyi command. Yan received posthumous investiture as Duke of Shunzheng and burial honors as ducal lord. Zongshou eventually obtained the remains of eighteen Wang royals for burial to the south of Changan, at Sanzhao village.

WE LAMENT. Since the Qin and Han dynasties, learned men have often addressed omens and auguries, but even for those astute at debating the issue, it was impossible to discredit such delusions. In reading the *History of Shu*, I found it perplexing that auspicious omens ostensibly associated with kingly rule such as the tortoise, dragon, unicorn, phoenix, and white *zouyu* tiger would ultimately surface in this domain, of all places. Yet the truth is eminently apparent based on the rise and fall, successes and failures of the Wang house. Some say that a single royal house like Wang was an unfitting candidate, which can be seen by observing general conditions of order and chaos across the world.

The dragon is a thing considered divine owing to rare sightings. It aspires simply to surge to the clouds and soar through the skies. Today there is nothing divine about a dragon's assuming a reclining position or revealing its likeness: to sight a dragon below in the water, not above in the heavens, is simply uncharacteristic. And for one dragon suddenly to become multiple dragons can only be deemed utter perversity!

The phoenix is a distant cousin to birds. Long ago, when Shun ruled over a world with effective governance and satisfied subjects, he commissioned Kui to compose music, the harmonious sounds causing birds and beasts to leap into dance upon hearing it. A phoenix happened to arrive at the time, and Shun's astrologer recorded its beauty, causing later generations to associate the phoenix's arrival with moral virtue. The phoenix appeared repeatedly in later times: sometimes coinciding with mediocre monarchs and inept rule, sometimes occasioning perilous catastrophe and chronic chaos. What is possibly propitious about this?

The unicorn is a distant cousin to beasts. Formerly, the Duke Ai of Lu went hunting and retrieved some unicorns without recognizing them. Having been obtained by hunt, furthermore, they emerged not of their own volition. In the *Spring and Autumn Annals*, Confucius states satirically that the duke "went westward for hunting and captured unicorns."[4] He deemed hunting excursions over such a distance wrong and the capture of unicorns down to the last one contemptible. References to hunting should always cite the location, but the Duke of Ai rode horseback across many a land, too many to be cited each time, so Confucius wrote "westward" to include many places. The statement also infers that the duke hunted in all kingdoms west of his own. The unicorn is a beast barely identifiable to humans. Intent on exposing the duke as plumbing the depths of mountains and marshes to seize the entire population—chasing, restraining, and retrieving beasts that no one can even recognize—the word "satire" seems fitting.

Spurious explanations flourished after the Sage's death, the unicorn becoming an omen for kingly rule and associated with perverse statements concerning "auguries of destiny" and "omens of fate." It seems reasonable that a phoenix emerging in the age of Shun is an auspicious omen. Its later appearance in times of chaos, however, surely reflects inauspiciousness. In earlier ages of orderly rule under Yao, Shun, Yu, Tang, Wen, Wu, and the Duke of Zhou, a beast like the unicorn never once appeared. What can possibly be propitious about sudden sightings in times of tumult?

The tortoise is a mysterious thing from turbid rivers and marsh waters, its numbers defying count. It acquires value after death simply because of its suitability for divination officials. According to the *Rites of Dai*, the tortoise exists in ponds of the royal palace, its auspiciousness related to the difficulty of attracting it. Then again, the *Rites of Dai* emerges from random writings of the Hundred Schools and contains numerous errors.[5]

I do not know what sort of thing the *zouyu* represents. The *Book of Odes* states, "We sigh before the *zouyu*."[6] Jia Yi [of Former Han] considered *zou* the walled garden of King Wen and *yu* his office of forestry. This being the standing assumption in Jia Yi's time, is it possible that depiction as a beast surfaced only in recent generations?

It is difficult to expose such delusions of the people when they enjoy credibility: awaiting an opening for doubt before proceeding with an attack is preferable. For omens of kingly rule such as the unicorn, phoenix, tortoise, and dragon to appear in the Five Dynasties era—sprouting up at Shu, no less—this is dubious even for someone otherwise receptive to theories of auguries and omens. To exploit such incredible episodes to revile them will likely cause second thoughts even for the most gullible.[i]

....

i. According to *Qian Shu shu*, *Yunli tu*, and *Jiuguo zhi*, Wang Jian entered Chengdu as governor for western Chuan in the second year of Dashun, by the Tang calendar [C.E. 891], establishing a royal house in the ninth month of the seventh year of Tianfu [C.E. 907], then changing the reign to Wucheng in the inaugural month of the next year—this is the accepted view today. Only the *Old History* mistakenly states that "he entered Chengdu in the inaugural year of Longji [C.E. 889], establishing a royal house and changing the reign in the fifth year of Tianyou [C.E. 908]." All works are consistent in placing the demise of Shu in the third year of Tongguang, under the Later Tang [C.E. 925]. The second year of Dashun until the third year of Tongguang represents a total of thirty-five years.

CHAPTER 64

HEREDITARY HOUSE OF LATER SHU

Meng Zhixiang and Son Chang

His courtesy name Baoyin, *Meng Zhixiang* [d. C.E. 934] was native to Longgang, Xingzhou. An uncle, Meng Qian, had occupied the three prefectures of Xing, Ming, and Ci during the final years of Tang, only to be taken captive by the Jin. Later, the Prince of Jin employed Qian to defend Zelu, but he surrendered the area to Liang after the Liang opened hostilities against Jin. The father of Zhixiang, Dao, singularly remained to serve the Jin, albeit without achieving prominence. Once Zhixiang gained maturity, the Prince of Jin gave the daughter of younger brother Kerang as his wife and named him left commissioner of military instructions.

Meng Zhixiang served as senior military advisor when the future Zhuangzong was Prince of Jin. As many senior military advisors of the past had been executed for assorted offenses, an anxious Zhixiang pleaded for reassignment. Zhuangzong instructed him to propose a potential replacement and he put forward Guo Chongtao, obliging Chongtao to him, in the process. Zhixiang advanced to inspector-in-chief of infantry and cavalry. In the wake of Zhuangzong's inauguration of dynasty and designation of Taiyuan as northern capital, Zhixiang became metropolitan custodian of Taiyuan and interim custodian of the northern capital.

With the campaign against Shu nominally led by Jiji, the Prince of Wei, Guo Chongtao as commissioner of bandit suppression said as parting words to Zhuangzong, "Your Subject embarks upon the pacification of Shu. Once Your

Majesty begins selecting commanders to defend the western Chuan region, no one can compare to Meng Zhixiang." After his armies had vanquished Shu, Zhuangzong made Zhixiang metropolitan custodian of Chengdu and deputy grand governor of the Jiannan/western Chuan theater. He first hastened to the capital, where Zhuangzong exhorted officials to lavish him with largess: many of the rare objects used as rewards came from the palace treasury itself. After heavy drinking, Zhuangzong turned jovial as he spoke of days past, saying with a sigh, "Jiji only recently had the stench of baby's milk and now can pacify the two Chuan circuits on my behalf. Growing older and witnessing the charm of this youth can leave a man like me ever melancholy. I recall the Former Monarch, upon leaving this world, beset by invasion from powerful neighbors that left in tact a mere corner of his domain. How unimaginable that the entire world would be ours today! The precious and rare treasures from the nine domains and four seas now fatten our bursary." Pointing to some of the objects, he said to Zhixiang, "I hear that Shu lands, however prosperous, have nothing as rare as these. As you are amiable and worthy, I offer them to you."

In the fourth year of Tongguang, twenty-first day of the inaugural month [C.E. March 7, 926], Chongtao had already died as Zhixiang reached Chengdu. The troops of Jiji the Prince of Wei now withdrawn and headed eastward, the vanguard Kang Yanxiao rebelled and raided Hanzhou, overpowering it. Zhixiang responded by dispatching commandant Li Renhan, rendezvousing with Ren Huan and Dong Zhang, in a successful storm on Yanxiao. Yanxiao lieutenants Li Zhao, Hou Hongshi, and several thousand infantry were captured by Zhixiang for the return trip. Mingzong came to power in the wake of Zhuangzong's passing and Jiji the Prince of Wei's death. Zhixiang now began training soldiers with the secret aim of ruling over Shu. The proliferation of armies occurred: units such as Righteous Victory, Settled Frontier, Intrepid Fortitude, Righteous Pacification, and Flying Oars represented a combined force of more than seventy thousand men. He split command over these among Li Renhan, Zhao Tingyin, and Zhang Ye.

Before this, as the Prince of Wei withdrew his men, Meng Zhixiang assessed the affluent of Chengdu and former subjects of Wang royals some six million strings of cash as bounty for his soldiers, with two million strings left unspent. Ren Huan left Shu to become chief minister and concurrent administrator of the Three Fiscal Agencies in the capital, keenly aware of the surplus in Shu. That winter the court named Zhixiang director of the Chancellery and deployed Zhao Jiliang, equerry for the imperial stud, to deliver the formal announcement of appointment. The court used the occasion to name Jiliang regional commissioner of the three commands of Chuan, responsible for forwarding to the capital all wealth beyond largess for onsite armies, while establishing oversight over the regular taxes for the two Chuan circuits. The intrusion infuriated Zhixiang, who refused to accept the edict. Jiliang stayed on in Shu, however, owing to relations with Zhixiang of long standing.

Commissioner of military affairs An Chonghui, having come to suspect Meng Zhixiang of seditious intent, aspired to contain him. At the outset of Zhixiang's governorship at Shu, Zhuangzong designated the eunuch Jiao Yanbin as military overseer. Mingzong systematically executed eunuchs after his accession, however, recalling all military overseers in the circuits. Chonghui decided to appoint another inspector following Yanbin's recall: the current master of diplomatic accommodations, Li Yan. A former envoy to Shu, Li Yan had returned north to orchestrate the campaign against it, so the Shu populace uniformly detested him. An equally irate Meng Zhixiang complained, "Jiao Yanbin's dismissal has been mandated and military overseers for the circuits abolished, an inspector named for my armies alone. Clearly, Yan intends to target Shu for some other adventure." Zhixiang's administrative secretary, Guan Zhaoyi, plus commanders and aides, all recommended cutting off Yan before entering the command, but Zhixiang insisted, "I will be prepared for his arrival!" As Yan approached the border, he had a messenger wait for Zhixiang with notice of his arrival. Zhixiang directed an imposing contingent of men to meet the messenger, hoping to frighten Yan against advancing. Yan kept his calm upon hearing the news, however.

In the second year of Tiancheng, the inaugural month [C.E. 927], Zhixiang banqueted Li Yan after arriving at Chengdu. Jiao Yanbin had stayed in Shu despite dismissal from office, so Yan pulled from his breast pocket an imperial edict mandating Yanbin's execution, showing it to Zhixiang. He refused to obey and upbraided Yan instead, asking, "Military overseers for the governors have recently been dismissed. What brings you here?" Then giving a glance at attending commander Wang Yanzhu, Yan was seized and decapitated. Mingzong proved powerless to pursue matters.

After initially assuming administration over Shu, Zhixiang sent someone to retrieve his family dependents from Taiyuan. Their entourage reached Fengxiang when the local governor, Li Congyan, detained them after word of Zhixiang's slaying of Li Yan, which he deemed an irrefutable act of sedition. Mingzong could not probe further into matters, so charity and trust were used to sway him. Master of diplomatic accommodations Li Renju then escorted back the Princess of Qionghua and Zhixiang's son, Chang, conveying consoling words.

Meng Zhixiang requested Zhao Jiliang's appointment as deputy governor, matters great and small all decided in consultation with him. During the third year [C.E. 928], the Later Tang court reassigned Jiliang as military training commissioner at Guozhou‡ and named He Zan as deputy governor. Zhixiang concealed the reassignment notice upon receipt and petitioned for retention of Jiliang. When the court refused, Zhixiang sent commander Lei Tinglu to the capital to clarify his position, leaving Mingzong no recourse but to accept. Zan's entourage had reached Miangu when fear kept him from advancing farther, so Zhixiang petitioned for Zan's assignment as manager-adjutant instead.

In the same year, with Tang armies campaigning against Jingnan, the court instructed Meng Zhixiang to deploy armies down the Yangzi against Xiazhou‡. He arranged for Mao Chongwei to post three thousand border troops at Kuizhou. Later, the governor of Jingnan [Nanping], Gao Jixing, died and his son Conghui sought court authorization to inherit the governorship, so Zhixiang asked to recall his own men. When the court refused, he provoked Mao Chongwei to scatter and return on the pretext of discontent in the ranks. The Tang court impeached Chongwei by imperial edict, but Zhixiang argued against impeachment in documents to the court. The entire affair only convinced leading courtiers of Zhixiang's resolve to rebel.

In the fourth year [C.E. 929], Mingzong prepared to conduct rites in the southern suburbs and sent Li Renju to ply Meng Zhixiang for a million strings of cash as subsidy for the rites. Zhixiang regarded the Tang request as a ploy to impoverish him. Not daring to decline outright, he procrastinated for some time before offering simply a half million strings. Previously, Jiji, the Prince of Wei, had left behind five thousand crack troops to secure the Shu frontier as he returned eastward. Subsequent suspicions about Zhixiang's loyalties on the part of An Chonghui prompted him, on the advice of policy advisors, to prepare a force for emergency purposes. He distributed authority among his own closest confidantes across prefectures in the two Chuan circuits: each defending commander received a company of crack troops as bodyguard, with an upper limit of two to three thousand and a minimum of five hundred.

That year the court named Xia Luqi governor of the Wuxin command. Langzhou‡ of eastern Chuan was reconstituted as the Baoning command and Li Renju named governor, Wu Qianyu becoming prefect of Mianzhou. Due to Renju's history of tensions with Dong Zhang of eastern Chuan and Qianyu's relations as maternal first cousin to military commissioner An Chonghui, Zhang and Zhixiang feared that the assignments signaled an impending campaign against them. Since assuming the governorship of eastern Chuan, Zhang had not bothered to contact Zhixiang, but now he began approaching him through intermediaries to augment personal bonds through marriage ties. Zhixiang despised Zhang and did not intend to consent. He inquired of Zhao Jiliang, who called for Zhixiang and Zhang to join ranks in resisting the court. Zhixiang consented, then petitioned the court, as did Zhang, to recall all governors and prefects assigned by the Tang to their domains. Mingzong employed an edict of extraordinary cordiality in hopes of assuaging them.

Mingzong conducted rites in the southern suburbs in the second month of the inaugural year of Changxing [C.E. 930], honoring Meng Zhixiang as palace secretary. Previously, Zhixiang and Zhang were equally inclined to sedition, but An Chonghui believed informers who appraised Zhang as unequivocally loyal to empire and Zhixiang as singularly suspect. Chonghui also hoped to enlist Zhang in a ruse against Zhixiang. Zhang was actually the first to rebel, in the ninth month, and overran Langzhou‡, where he captured and killed Li Renju. That month, on the Monarch's birthday,[1] Zhixiang held a banquet where he bowed repeatedly in looking to the northeast, then fell prostrate and sobbed, as tears soaked his lapel. His soldiers all whimpered empathetically for him, although he rebelled on the very next day.

That autumn, Mingzong decided to elevate the noble status of the Qionghua Princess to the Grand Princess of Fuqing. The relevant officials noted that investitures for princesses of generations past had not occurred under court orders to the locales, nor was there a ceremony for emissaries to invest them locally. Mingzong thus directed courtiers to create a new ceremony, deputizing as master of investiture Liu Yue, director of the Palace Library. Yue learned of Zhixiang's mutiny upon reaching Fengxiang and returned. Mingzong now mandated the stripping of Zhixiang's offices and titles, naming the Tianxiong governor, Shi Jingtang, chief commissioner of bandit suppression and Xia Luqi his deputy.

Meng Zhixiang dispatched Li Renhan, Zhang Ye, and Zhao Tingyin to direct a force of thirty thousand in rendezvousing with Dong Zhang to attack Suizhou‡. He also sent Hou Hongshi, with four thousand men, to assist Zhang in holding the eastern Chuan command and Zhang Wu down the gorge region to seize Yuzhou‡. Later Tang armies attacked Jianmen, killing three thousand of Zhang's defenders before occupying the city. Zhang visited Zhixiang to make his emergency known, a startled Zhixiang allocating ten thousand men to Tingyin for deployment eastward. Later, news arrived that Tang armies had stopped at Jianzhou‡ without advancing farther, as Zhixiang exclaimed gleefully, "If Tang armies had stormed eastern Chuan to break our blockade at Suizhou‡, I would have been strategically isolated and the two Chuan circuits shaken at their foundation. Their current failure to advance leaves me all the more confident of handily prevailing." Jingtang and Tingyin engaged in battle at Jianmen, in the twelfth month, where Tang armies were routed. Zhang Wu had claimed Yuzhou‡ before dying of illness. His successor as deputy commander, Yuan Yanchao, proceeded to claim Qianzhou‡.

In the inaugural month of the second year [C.E. 931], Li Renhan vanquished Suizhou‡, where Xia Luqi died with honor. Renhan was now named interim regent of the Wuxin command by Meng Zhixiang. Zhixiang directed a courier to rush Luqi's head for display to Jingtang's troops, who subsequently withdrew. Li Yanke of Lizhou abandoned the city and fled after learning of the Tang defeats and eastward retreat. Zhixiang hence named Zhao Tingyin interim regent of the Zhaowu command. Li Renhan advanced against Kuizhou; prefect An Chongruan absconded after relinquishing the city, Zhao Jiliang becoming its interim regent.

At the time, Tang armies confronting hazardous terrain had difficulty provisioning troops on the highway. Extending westward from the Tong Pass [Tongzhou], the transport of rations had taxed the people bitterly: for each picul of transport expense, scarcely a peck actually arrived. Cries of umbrage filled the roadways. As Jingtang's armies retreated, Tang commanders in the cities along the way all abandoned them. Troubled by such reversals, Mingzong blamed An Chonghui, who now nervously made a sudden request to lead a campaign. Chonghui faced malicious slanders at the time, precipitating his fall from grace and death. Mingzong had attributed the mutiny of Zhixiang and others to Chonghui's miscalculations, so after his death, tried to woo Zhixiang—returning the court liaison for western Chuan, Su Yuan, and commander of the Dutiful Service Guard, Du Shaoben. Once back, they both informed Zhixiang that his dependents in the capital had been spared harm.

In reaction to reports of Chonghui's execution and the Tang ruler's generous treatment of family dependents, Meng Zhixiang approached Dong Zhang about submitting simultaneous confessions for their crimes [as mercy plea]. Zhang countered, however, "Your dependents, Gentleman Meng, are still alive. Only my sons and grandsons were slain. What would my confession achieve?" Zhixiang dispatched three different messengers to meet him, none able to persuade Zhang. He also sent an administrative aide for surveillance, Li Hao, leaving Zhang suspicious that Zhixiang might sell him out. He used threatening language to address Hao, who subsequently urged Zhixiang to attack Zhang.

It was Dong Zhang who struck first, storming and overrunning Hanzhou, Zhixiang's domain. Zhixiang committed thirty thousand troops to Zhao Tingyin for retaliation, as he personally commanded a storm against Jijuqiao [Jizongqiao]. After apprehending one of Zhang's surrendering foot soldiers, Zhixiang provided him a brocade gown to wear and a letter entreating Zhang to capitulate. "Having reached this point, we will never waver," Zhang pronounced. "Better to fight immediately than to stand exposed in the daytime sun," his troops clamored back, whereupon they were promptly motioned into action.

Once their armies began to engage, an assistant commander to Dong Zhang, Zhang Shoujin, surrendered to Meng Zhixiang, who exploited the momentum to vanquish Zhang decisively. Upon crossing Jinyan Bridge on foot, Zhang tried to convince son Guangsi to coerce him into capitulating, thereby preserving the family line. The son said, in tears, "Since antiquity, when has a man ever killed his own father simply to stay alive? I would rather accept death with you." So, he departed with Zhang. Zhixiang unleashed Zhao Tingyin to pursue them, but he failed to catch up. Zhang now absconded for Zizhou‡, where he was slain, Guangsi hanging himself to death. Hence, Zhixiang absorbed the eastern Chuan region, and with Zhang dead, sent no more emissaries to the Tang court.

The military commissioner for the Tang, Fan Yanguang, now observed, "Zhixiang may have eliminated Zhang, but he will surely enhance the importance of the two Chuan commands by infringing upon the court's powers. We should not overextend ourselves to sway him nor expect his voluntary reversion to us." "Zhixiang and I are old acquaintances," Mingzong countered. "It was initially the manipulations of others that spawned the current hazards and suspicions. How can assuaging an old friend represent 'overextending ourselves'?" Li Kening had a wife, née Meng, who was Zhixiang's younger sister. She had been returned to Zhixiang after Kening's murder by Zhuangzong, but her son Gui remained in the Tang capital as palace services officer. Mingzong hence permitted Gui's return home to care for his mother, favoring Zhixiang with an edict to entreat and reassure him.

After consolidating control over the two circuits of Chuan, Meng Zhixiang installed Zhao Jiliang as interim regent of the Wutai command, Li Renhan as regent of Wuxin, Zhao Tingyin as regent of Baoning, Zhang Ye as regent of Ningjiang, and Li Zhao as regent of Zhaowu. Jiliang and cohort now beseeched Zhixiang to become king and conduct government business using handwritten communiqués in black ink. A final decision was still pending when Gui reached Shu, the very sight of which emboldened Zhixiang. Gui returned to the capital from Shu, in the ninth month, bearing Zhixiang's petition for confirmation of governorships for Zhao Jiliang and cohort, while requesting personal authority to appoint prefects and lesser local officials. He also requested investiture as King of Shu and informed the court of the Princess Fuqing's recent death. Personally conducting mourning rites for her, Mingzong also dispatched the master of palace gates, Liu Zheng'en, as commissioner of reconciliation. Zheng'en reported on the mission upon returning, as Zhixiang began sending a commander for audience in the capital, Zhu Huang.

In the fourth year, seventeenth day of the second month [C.E. March 15, 933], the court affirmed Zhixiang as honorary grand marshal and concurrent palace secretary, acting custodian of Chengdu, governor of the two circuits of Chuan, overseer for domestic surveillance, commander of southern barbarians at the immediate borders, and commissioners of pacification and regional order for Yunnan and the eight domains of the western mountains. The court further commissioned minister of works Lu Wenji to invest Zhixiang as King of Shu; the five governor appointments, led by Zhao Jiliang, were confirmed as well. Zhixiang had once subsidized the food and clothing costs for the tens of thousands of Tang troops stationed in Shu; he thus requested the return of dependents still in the north as consideration. Mingzong declined the request by formal edict.

Mingzong expired in the eleventh month. Zhixiang acceded to the throne as Emperor of Shu, in the intercalary first month of the next year [C.E. 934]. He named Zhao Jiliang as dignitary for public works with ministerial powers, senior military advisor Wang Chuhui as commissioner of military affairs, and Li Hao as Hanlin academician.

In the third month, the Later Tang Prince of Lu raised armies at Fengxiang against the court. Emperor Min entrusted the punitive campaign to Wang Sitong, whose men were vanquished. Subsequently capitulating to Shu were governors Zhang Qianzhao of Shannan west and Sun Hanshao of the Wuding command. Zhixiang changed the reign name to Mingde in the fourth month, Qianzhao and others arriving at Chengdu in the sixth month. He honored them with a banquet, but as Qianzhao rose to raise his goblet in a toast to longevity, Zhixiang's hands proved too paralyzed to lift his own goblet. He then took ill, his son Chang becoming heir-apparent and overseer of the empire. Upon death, he was called the Literarily Martial, Sagaciously Moral, Stridently Valorous, Enlightened, and Filial Emperor, his temple name Gaozu and mausoleum Heling.

Meng Chang [C.E. 919–965] was the third son of Zhixiang and one-time manager-adjutant during Zhixiang's governorship of the two Chuan circuits. He was named governor of eastern Chuan with ministerial standing, once Zhixiang assumed his bogus titles, and oversaw affairs of empire during his illness. Secrecy was imposed on Zhixiang's death and mourning deferred when Wang Chuhui happened upon Zhao Jiliang that night. The two faced each other and cried incessantly. Once Jiliang regained composure, he said, "Today, mighty overlords command armies and concentrate on exploiting opportune changes. By moving fast to install a successor, we can preclude the unexpected. Nothing is gained by crying!" Chuhui joined Jiliang in enthroning Chang, as formal mourning began. Chang did not change the reign name after accession and continued Mingde, waiting until the fifth year to adopt Guangzheng as reign.

In the third month, Mingde the third year [C.E. 936], the planet Mars crossed paths with Jishi [a cluster of five stars]. Chang worried that Jishi presided over Shu and considered prayers to it. He inquired of deputy astronomer Hu Yun, who reported, "According to the chart on twelve celestial positions, beginning with five degrees from Jing and extending to eight degrees from Liu, the so-called Quail's Head presides over the Qin region. Although Shu belongs to Qin, it lies to its extreme south. In earlier times, when Mars crossed paths with the constellation Gui, the attending resonance affected Qin. Therefore, during the Jin dynasty, third month of the ninth year of Xianhe [C.E. 334], Mars crossed paths with Jishi and, a month later, the Yongzhou prefect Guo Quan was killed. In the fourteenth year of Yixi [C.E. 418],[2] Mars crossed paths with Gui, and another Yongzhou prefect, Zhu Lingshi, was killed a year later. Nothing similar occurred in Shu, however." The prayers were suspended.

Meng Chang delighted in playing games from his horse. Moreover, to acquire the Daoist secrets of the bedchamber, he recruited numerous girls from upstanding families to fill his inner palaces. Such activities were stiffly rebuked by Han Baozhen, the deputy commissioner of military affairs, prompting a radical awakening in Chang himself: he purged those persons from the palace on the same day and conferred on Baozhen gold bullion weighing several catties. Someone at court petitioned him about the need to select men from upstanding families to administer the Three Departments and Censorate. Chang sighed before rebounding, "Why not simply speak of finding the right men for the job instead?" Aides now requested to use Chang's words to interrogate the petitioner, but he countered, "At the outset of the Tang reign of Taizong, I hear, prison official Sun Fujia memorialized on current affairs, and celebration attended his petition. How can you propose resisting remonstrance?"

Being young in years, Meng Chang did not personally preside over affairs: all commanders, ministers and senior statesmen were old Zhixiang associates, formerly treated by him with such leniency that it fostered excessively indulgent behavior in many. Their arrogance and pride only increased upon serving Chang, many violating the law to enlarge their estates, appropriating the finest of farmlands, and ransacking tombs of the dead. The most egregious cases were Li Renhan and Zhang Ye. Several months after assuming the throne, Chang seized and murdered Renhan, liquidating his entire family as well. Li Zhao had recently reached the capital from his district, at the time, and came to audience aided by a cane. He requested to forgo kneeling because of illness, but upon learning of Renhan's death, suddenly dropped the cane and knelt.

Zhao Jiliang died in the ninth year of Guangzheng [C.E. 946], causing Zhang Ye's involvement in decision making to expand. Nephew to Li Renhan, he happened to control the palace guard at the time of Renhan's execution. Meng Chang had reassigned him as chief minister for fear of possible rebellion. With concurrent oversight over the accounting office, Ye adjudicated criminal cases in his home and resorted to depraved devices to exact heavily from the Shu people, incurring their profound contempt. In the eleventh year [C.E. 948], Chang conspired with An Siqian, director of the Sage-Preserving Guard, leading to Ye's arrest and murder. Wang Chuhui and Zhao Tingyin retired in rapid succession, culminating in the total elimination of the seasoned commanders and trusted statesmen of the past. Chang now began to govern personally, setting up a small box at the court's reception hall to measure the sentiment of persons below.

The Khitan had overturned the Jin dynasty at the time, and Gaozu of Han raised arms at Taiyuan, the Middle Kingdom beset with a multitude of problems. The Xiongwu governor, He Jian, now relinquished to Shu the prefectures of Qin, Cheng, and Jie. Chang then unleashed a raid on Fengzhou‡ by Sun Hanshao, who overpowered the prefecture: Chang's regime could finally claim all Shu lands once held by Wang Yan [of Former Shu]. Also making diplomatic overtures to Chang were two mutinous commanders of Later Han, Zhao Siwan of Yongxing and Wang Jingchong of Fengxiang. To rendezvous with Siwan, Chang dispatched Zhang Qianzhao departing from Dasan Pass, He Jian departing from western Longzhou, and Li Tinggui from Ziwu Gorge. His minister then, Guan Zhaoyi, strenuously admonished against the decision, but Chang was keen in his ambition to appraise conditions within the northern passes and sent An Siqian eastward to augment forces. The Han later executed Siwan and Jingchong, causing Qianzhao and cohort to abort their mission and return. Siqian's sense of shame over accomplishing nothing militarily prompted him to kill numerous soldiers, intending to instill fear in his ranks. Chang now turned to the Hanlin academician Wang Zao to assassinate Siqian. A border officer happened to memorialize the court on a local emergency at the time; Zao failed to inform Chang in a timely fashion and further angered him by abruptly opening the sealed letter. Zao was at Chang's side during Siqian's murder, only to be seized on the spot and beheaded by Chang as well.

In the twelfth year [C.E. 949], the three promotion examinations of the Ministry of Personnel were instituted, as well as civil service examinations by the Ministry of Rites. In the thirteenth year, Meng Chang elevated his title of honor to the Profoundly Literate, Illustriously Martial, Benevolently Sagacious, and Luminously Filial Emperor. He invested son Xuanzhe as Prince of Qin and administrator of the Six Armies, second son Xuanjue as Prince of Bao, younger brothers Renyi as the Prince of Kui, Renzhi as Prince of Ya, and Renyu as Prince of Jia.[3]

In the eighteenth year [C.E. 955], Emperor Shizong of Zhou launched campaigns against Shu, raids starting at Qin Prefecture. Meng Chang had appointed Han Jixun as Xiongwu governor, but news of Zhou invaders en route caused him to lament, "How can Jixun withstand Zhou armies?" Master of diplomatic accommodations Zhao Jizha volunteered to advance and was named military overseer for Qin. He reached only Deyang upon learning that Zhou armies had actually arrived and returned in haste to petition the throne. Chang inquired of his mission, but Jizha proved paralyzed by nervousness and unable to utter a single word. Chang murdered him in fury. Gao Yanchou and Li Tinggui, departing from Tangcang, were now dispatched to thwart Zhou armies. Yanchou suffered a rout and fled to Qingni. The Zhou now managed to reclaim the prefectures of Qin, Cheng, Jie, and Feng‡. An anxious Chang hence dispatched envoys to both the Southern Tang and the Eastern [Northern] Han to enhance his strategic standing.

During the twentieth year [C.E. 957], Shizong repatriated prisoners of war formerly captured in Shu, as Meng Chang reciprocated by returning to the capital a Zhou commander in captivity, Hu Li. In correspondence to Shizong, however, Chang's failure to employ the protocol of "subject" so incited Shizong that he refused to respond. In the twenty-first year [C.E. 958], Zhou campaigns against the Southern Tang resulted in the capture of fourteen prefectures of the southern Huai region, alarming neighboring kingdoms one and all. Gao Baorong of Jingnan [Nanping], in a letter to Meng Chang, entreated him to revert to Zhou sovereignty, advice rejected owing to Shizong's lack of response to earlier correspondence.

When Chang's youngest son, Meng Xuanbao, died at a mere seven *sui*, the ceremonies officers argued against formal ceremonies for mourning and titular investiture. Chang subsequently inquired of Li Hao, who said, "Formerly, under the Tang, Emperor Dezong's son, Li Ping, died at four *sui* and still received posthumous honors as grand protector-general for Yangzhou and Prince of Su. This serves as precedent." The child received by Chang posthumous standing as grand protector-general for Qingzhou†, ennobled Prince of Sui. In the twenty-fifth year [C.E. 962], Chang installed Xuanzhe, the Prince of Qin, as heir-apparent.

Chang had the good fortune of living in the Jin/Han era, when a panoply of problems plagued the Middle Kingdom. Occupying an isolated corner of the world, ruler and subject could amuse themselves with extravagant living, decorating even urinals with the seven gems. After the rise of the Song dynasty and its conquest of Jing¶ and Tan prefectures, Chang grew ever uneasy. He sent by bypass his revenues officer, Sun Yu, bearing a letter with raised-wax seal, to the Eastern Han to propose a joint military harassment of the Middle Kingdom; Yu was apprehended by border guards. Emperor Taizu of Song later declared war against Shu: Wang Quanbin and Cui Yanjin departed from Fengzhou‡, Liu Guangyi and Cao Bin from Guizhou. He also had a residence for Chang built in anticipation of his relocation to the north; erected by the Office of the Eight Crafts along the Bian River and south of Kaifeng's Youye gate, it contained more than five hundred rooms replete with curtains and sundries.

Meng Chang deployed Wang Zhaoyuan and Zhao Yantao, among others, to resist the Song-dynasty mandate. A native of Chengdu, Zhaoyuan became a servant to Zhiyin, the Chan Buddhist master at Dongguo monastery, at thirteen *sui*. Meng Zhixiang invited the monk to his official residence, Zhaoyuan entering on his heels and carrying his cap and sandals. At first sight, Zhixiang loved the youth's kind and clever character. As his own son, Chang, was currently engaged in studies, Zhixiang arranged for Zhaoyuan to be his secretarial aide, the two developing intimacy. Zhaoyuan served as master of palace screens upon Chang's accession.

With the retirement of Wang Chuhui as commissioner of military affairs, Meng Chang worried over the excessive power and defiance of commissioners and named Zhaoyuan co-commissioner at the military bureau responsible for memorial reception. Affairs all falling under his purview regardless of import, Zhaoyuan was even permitted to take gold and silk from government treasuries with no questions asked. The mother of Chang, Dowager Li, often implored him against employing Zhaoyuan, only to be ignored. Zhaoyuan enjoyed military writings and celebrated a competence at military maneuvers. Chang once had Li Hao banquet armies departing from Chengdu, as Zhaoyuan smugly presided over the affair carrying in hand a metal amulet in the *ruyi* "as you wish" design. He even likened himself to [all-time strategist] Zhuge Liang. In a comment to Li Hao, an inebriated Zhaoyuan pronounced, "Why should our actions be limited to vanquishing the current foe? Twenty to thirty thousand of our youth with their ferociously tattooed faces can reclaim the entire Central Plains with the ease of turning the palm of a hand."

Meng Chang also dispatched son Xuanzhe, with several tens of thousands of crack soldiers, to defend Jianmen. Xuanzhe carried along a retinue of favorite concubines, musical instruments, and several dozen theatrical performers—a spectacle leaving onlookers in Shu chuckling in disbelief. [Song commander] Wang Quanbin confronted the forces of Zhaoyuan at Sanquan and vanquished them in a sally. Zhaoyuan burned a suspension bridge at the Jibai River to retreat, securing positions at Jianmen. A surrendering Shu foot soldier now informed Xiang Tao, a group commander for the Song, that, "A small road at Laisu emerges from the south of Jianmen, at Qingqiangdian, to merge into a major highway." Quanbin sent deputy commander Shi Yande with a separate force to depart from Laisu and rush northward against Jianmen, as Quanbin squeezed from the other direction in a pincer movement. Zhaoyuan and Yantao both fled in defeat and were captured, the defeat inducing Xuanzhe to flee for home.

Liu Guangyi attacked Kuizhou, where defending commander Gao Yanchou, after sustaining losses, sealed the gates of command headquarters in resistance. Administrative aide Luo Ji urged him to flee, but Yanchou insisted, "Having formerly failed to hold Qinchuan, I now flee northward. Although my ruler does not demand my life, how can I bear to face the people of Shu again?" New entreaties to surrender caused a defiant Yanchou to set himself afire and die. Shu armies hence scattered in defeat at every turn and many commanders became captives. Chang consulted aides on strategy and seasoned commander Shi Jun proposed amassing troops for a vigorous resistance to wear down the enemy, arguing that eastern troops deployed afar would not stay for long. Chang sighed as he rejoined, "For forty years, the Former Monarch and myself provided warm clothes and fine food for our troops. Yet once the enemy is at hand, they do not shoot a single arrow to the east on my behalf. My own wishes for a staunch defense of cities notwithstanding, who will do the defending?" Li Hao was directed to draft a petition of surrender in the inaugural month of the third year of Qiande [C.E. 965]. From the rallying of Song troops to the capitulation of Chang, a mere sixty-six days were involved. Previously, as Hanlin academician under [the Former Shu ruler] Wang Yan, Li Hao had personally drafted the petition of surrender attending the demise of Yan's regime. Now, he drafted a similar petition for Meng Chang. The people of Shu posted, one night, the following sign on his door, "The Li Household: Drafters of Surrender Petitions for Generations." The story made them the butt of jokes at the time.

Upon arriving in the capital, Meng Chang was named honorary grand preceptor and concurrent palace secretary, invested Duke of Qin. He died seven days later and received investiture as Prince of Chu. His mother, née Li, masterful at rhetoric, received extraordinary courtesies from the court, an imperial rescript referring to her as "Mother of the Empire." Emperor Taizu once summoned her to offer words of consolation, proposing, "Mother must take good care of herself and refrain from melancholy thoughts of Shu. Someday, Mother will be sent back." "Your Servant's home was originally Taiyuan," Woman Li interjected. "Perhaps I might return to the old ancestral home, such is my ultimate wish." At the time, Liu Chengjun was still in power at Taiyuan. Taizu took great relish in promising, "Once Liu Chengjun is pacified, I will accommodate Mother's wishes." Woman Li did not cry when Meng Chang died, but rather poured wine on the ground as libation, saying to him in prayers, "You could not die honorably for dynasty, but endured shame for the sake of survival. I initially decided to forgo death because you were alive. What purpose lies in continuing to live?" She subsequently refused food and died. For later events, see the "national histories."[i]

....

i. The years involved in the founding and overthrow of Meng Zhixiang's house are abundantly clear and all writings consistent: beginning with his arrival at Shu in the third year of Tongguang [C.E. 925] and ending in the third year of Qiande under our own dynasty [C.E. 965], when the kingdom expired, a total of forty-one years had elapsed. The *Old History* erroneously gives forty years, beginning with Tongguang the fourth year and ending in Qiande the third.

CHAPTER 65

HEREDITARY HOUSE OF SOUTHERN HAN

Liu Yin, Brother Yan, Yan's Son Bin, Bin's Brother Cheng, and Cheng's Son Chang

The grandfather of *Liu Yin* [C.E. 874–911], Liu Anren, hailed from Shangcai [Yuzhou] and later relocated to the Min region [Fujian]. Engaging in trade at Nanhai Commandery, Anren settled there. Yin's father, Liu Qian, was once military attaché to the Guangzhou‡ governor. During the Tang dynasty, fifth year of Qianfu [C.E. 878], Huang Chao overran Guang‡ before plundering the Hu and Xiang region [Hunan]. Authorities at Guang‡ petitioned the court for Liu Qian's assignment as prefect of Fengzhou¶ and overseer for bandit containment for the Hejiang region, defending lands to the west of Wu‡ and Gui† prefectures. After over a year, he commanded ten thousand troops and over a hundred warships. Qian had three sons: Yin, Tai, and Yan.

Upon the death of Liu Qian, Guangzhou‡ authorities petitioned the court for Yin to succeed him as prefect of Fengzhou¶. Governor Liu Chonggui died in the Qianning era and was replaced as commander by Li Zhirou, the prince-designate of Xue. His retinue had only reached Hunan, however, when Guangzhou‡ commanders Lu Ju and Tan Qi mutinied; Zhirou dared not advance farther. Yin employed his Fengzhou¶ armies to murder Ju and Qi, then received Zhirou, who subsequently recommended Yin as manager-adjutant. Later, Xu Yanruo replaced Zhirou as governor and sought Yin's appointment as deputy governor, military affairs now delegated to him. It was the military that installed Yin as interim regent once Yanruo died. His formal appointment as governor came in the second year of Tianyou [C.E. 905]. Under Liang rule, the inaugural year of Kaiping [C.E. 907], Yin became honorary grand marshal and concurrent director of the Chancellery. Concurrent assignments as Jinghai governor and protector-overseer of the Annan command [Hanoi] came in the second year, then in the third year, recognition as honorary grand preceptor, concurrent palace secretary, and Prince of Nanping.

Liu Yin and his sons rose up at Fengzhou¶ at a time when the world faced many problems, permitting a few military feats around the Lingnan command [Guangzhou‡] to win for them control over Nanhai Commandery. He also had an affinity for the wise and educated. In a world of tumult, many a courtier of the Middle Kingdom journeyed to the far reaches of Lingnan in search of sanctuary. There were famous courtiers banished for life to the far south during Tang times who often left behind survivors, or officials on recent assignment who encountered tumult that impeded their safe passage back north—these are the sorts of persons to become itinerants beyond the Lingnan Mountains. Liu Yin courteously wooed such men as Wang Dingbao, Ni Shu, Liu Jun, Li Heng, Zhou Jie, Yang Dongqian, and Zhao Guangyi [Guangyin]. Others came south to flee turmoil, such as Dingbao, patrol officer at the Rongguan command, Shu, erudite at the Imperial University of Tang, and Jun, the son of Chongwang. Li Heng, grandson of Deyu, had been right rectifier of omissions at the Tang court and came south as commissioner. Such men were recruited for military headquarters and were treated like honored guests. Zhou Jie was a skilled astrologer: serving the Tang as deputy master of national granaries, he came to flee chaos only to be frequently questioned by Yin about natural disasters. Jie was ashamed to serve Yin as mere astrologer, however, often avoiding court appearances by professing illness. Yin embraced him as retainer, all the same. Originally a patrol officer at the Yongguan command, Yang Dongqian became an immigrant to Nanhai after completing his term of office. Yin often treated him as teacher and later named him deputy governor. Once Liu Yan illicitly assumed royal titles, Dongqian provided justification by employing omens and ritual practices. Overall, the institutions for the kingdom and priorities for military strategy derived from consultations with these several men.

In the inaugural year of Qianhua [C.E. 911], Yin's noble rank was elevated to Prince of Nanhai. He died the same year at thirty-eight *sui*, younger brother Yan installed as successor.

Liu Yan [C.E. 889–942], originally named Yan‡, was born to Liu Qian's concubine, née Duan. His mother delivered him at an external residence, news of which incited the fury of Qian's jealous wife, Woman Wei. She grabbed a sword in leaving home, then ordered Yan brought over with the intent of killing him. One glance at the boy was enough to leave her trembling, the sword dropping to the ground. After an exceeding long pause, she exclaimed, "This is no ordinary boy!" Three days later, she murdered Woman Duan to raise Yan as her own son. He matured into a skilled archer and horseman, his body seven feet tall and his hands passing the knee when extended.

With Liu Yin as manager-adjutant, Yan was also named administrative advisor at the Prince of Xue's headquarters. Once Yin became governor of Nanhai, Yan served as deputy governor, replacing Yin upon his death. Appointments followed, in the second year of Qianhua [C.E. 912], as the Qinghai governor and honorary grand guardian with ministerial standing. Advancement to honorary grand mentor came in the third year. Occasioning the accession of Emperor Mo, all offices and titles formerly held by Yin were conferred upon Yan, including investiture as Prince of Nanhai.

In late Tang times, Nanhai was the last region to succumb to chaos, so senior courtiers after Xizong's reign serving locally as governors could find no place untouched by turmoil, save for Nanhai. Yet it also turned independent, beginning with Yin's rule. At the time, Qu Hao of Jiao prefecture, Liu Shizheng of Gui†, Ye Guanglue of Yong‡, and Pang Juzhao of Rong‡ had apportioned administrative authority among themselves. Lu Guangchou occupied Qian Prefecture for offensives north of the mountain range, as younger brother Guangmu occupied Chao and son Yanchang occupied Shao. Also beyond the court's control were Gaozhou prefect Liu Changlu, Xinzhou prefect Liu Qian, and over seventy military outposts east of the [Xun] river.

As Liu Yin attacked Shaozhou, Yan proposed, "Shao Prefecture is dependent on Guangchou at Qian, which will surely react in the event of a raid, causing both your head and your tail to be beleaguered by enemies. A direct attack is unnecessary when Shaozhou can be claimed through clever strategizing." Failing to heed him, Yin did indeed return in defeat. Hereafter, all military affairs were delegated to him. Yan completely pacified the various military outposts, subsequently murdering Changlu and cohort to install a new prefect. Ultimately, he unleashed armies in a successful strike against the Lu family, seizing Chao and Shao prefectures. He even managed to snatch Rong‡ and Gui† prefectures from Ma Yin [of Chu], to the west. Ma Yin claimed the Gui district and apprehended Liu Shizheng, but Liu Yan took the Rongguan command and expelled Juzhao, now capturing Yongguan as well. The Liu brothers, Yin and Yan, initially accepted noble titles from the Liang court, adopting its calendar and little else.

In the third year of Zhenming [C.E. 917], Liu Yan acceded to the throne as Emperor, adopted the dynastic name Great Yue, and changed the reign to Qianheng. Posthumous honors went to Anren as the Literary Emperor, Qian as the Sagaciously Martial Emperor, and Yin as the Facilitating Emperor. Three temples were erected for them. A civil service was established, naming

Yang Dongqian as vice minister of war, Li Heng as vice minister of rites, Ni Shu as vice minister of works, and Zhao Guangyin as minister of war, each with ministerial standing. Guangyin, hailing from one of the premier families of Tang times, felt shame about serving a bogus kingdom and had frequent bouts of depression as he contemplated returning. Yan learned to approximate Guangyin's handwriting to convey letters to Luoyang, his messengers escaping detection by taking side-roads, summoning to the south Guangyin's two sons, Sun and Yi, plus dependent kinsmen. Stunned and delighted by their arrival, Guangyin could now focus his heart on serving the Han.

Liu Yan was a man of sharp mind but savage impulses: whenever witnessing criminal punishments involving the slicing of bodies, severing of limbs, or tearing of flesh, he could not contain his pleasure in watching the victims die, unconsciously grating at the jaw and drooling from a sagging mouth. Some considered him a real-life [man-eating] serpent. He had a proclivity for material indulgence as well, amassing all of the precious gems of the Nanhai region to decorate his pavilions with jade and palaces with pearls.

During the second year [C.E. 918], sacrifices to Heaven were conducted at the southern suburbs, a general amnesty declared for the realm, and Han adopted as dynastic name. Resolved to assume his bogus royal titles, Yan nonetheless worried that Wang Dingbao might not cooperate, so Dingbao was sent off as emissary to Jingnan [Nanping]. Yan remained concerned, after Dingbao's return, that he might fault him and arranged for Ni Shu to visit and commend him on a successful mission, apprising Dingbao of the dynasty's recent inauguration as well. "The founding of dynasty should involve institutional adjustments," Dingbao exclaimed. "As I entered the southern gate, the placard for Qinghai Commandery remained in place. To people of the four corners, does this not seem sheer folly?" Chuckling, Yan commented, "I had long anticipated Dingbao's response, but never expected criticism so altogether fitting."

The Lady of Yue, Miss Ma, received investiture as Empress, in the third year [C.E. 919]. She was the daughter of the Prince of Chu, Ma Yin. During the spring of the fourth year, bureaus of recruitment and examination were established, which selected more than ten candidates for doctoral and *mingjing* degrees, in accordance with Tang practice. The exams were later held every year. In the seventh year [C.E. 923], the occupation of Bianzhou by Zhuangzong of Later Tang left Liu Yan rather nervous. Wanting to understand real conditions in the Middle Kingdom, he sent as envoy He Ci, master of imperial palaces and parks, bearing a letter from the "Ruler of the Great Han" to the "Emperor of the Great Tang." Ci returned to portray the Tang as facing certain tumult and not worth much worry, news pleasing to Yan. He had a proclivity for grand ostentation as well, luring many merchants from the Ling region to his north and the southern seas to his south, inviting them to visit his palaces and halls to show off their abundance of pearls and jade. His family allegedly originated at the Xianyang capital of the Qin dynasty and thus professed shame at ruling over the southern barbarians. He thus referred to the Later Tang dynasty's Son of Heaven [condescendingly] as "prefect of Luoyang."

That year, the Burmese chieftain of Yunnan, Zheng Min, sent an envoy presenting a white horse with red mane and requesting a marriage accommodation. The envoy professed to be blood brother of his monarch, with both *qingrong* and *buxie* rank, and appeared in a gown with gold brocade and tiger imprint, plus a decorative sword—clothes conferred by his ruler. Bearing credentials as the Marquis of Guirenqing with fiefs of maintenance for a thousand households, he carried tallies of office with the name Zheng Zhaochun. He appreciated learning and possessed literacy: while relaxing with Yan, Zhaochun composed poetry of a caliber that Yan and his courtiers could never match. Yan therefore sanctioned Zheng Min's marriage with the Zengcheng Princess, daughter of [Yan's predecessor] Yin.

During the eighth year [C.E. 924], after erecting the southern palace, Wang Dingbao celebrated its beauty with an "Ode to the Seven Wonders of the Southern Palace." Yan was originally named Yan‡ and later adopted Zhi as personal name. In the ninth year, after sighting a white dragon at the Sanqing Hall of the Southern Palace, Yan changed the reign name to Bailong [white dragon] and his personal name to Gong [with dragon radical]. A foreign monk predicted, however, "According to milfoils, it will be a 'Gong' who ruins the Liu house." He now selected the character "Yan" for personal name, employing allusions to "flying dragon in the heavens," in the *Book of Changes*—the character a homonym for his original name of Yan‡.

During the fourth year [C.E. 928], Chu warriors employed a naval force to attack Feng¶ Prefecture, resulting in defeat for Feng¶ defenders along the He River. An alarmed Liu Yan, conducting divination based on the *Book of Changes*, encountered a reference to the "Grand Possession" [*Dayou*[1]] and announced an amnesty for the domain and change of reign to Dayou. He also dispatched Su Zhang with three thousand men from Divine Bow regiments to relieve Fengzhou¶. Zhang submerged two metal locks into the He River while arranging large rotating wheels on the riverbanks, concealed by embankments. His small ships entered battle and gave the illusion of fleeing in defeat when Chu sailors pursued them. Zhang now employed the large wheels to extend the locks and freeze the Chu ships in place, as high-powered crossbows on both sides of the river pelted them. They totally annihilated the Chu armies.

During the third year [C.E. 930], commanders Li Shouyong and Liang Kezhen attacked Jiaozhi [northern Vietnam] and apprehended Qu Chengmei and cohort. As Chengmei and the other hostages reached Nanhai, Liu Yan climbed the Yifeng tower to receive them, saying to Chengmei, "You once dismissed my court as bogus. How did you end up as captive today?" Chengmei bowed his head to acknowledge his crimes and received a pardon. Chengmei was the son of Qu Hao. Kezhen also raided Zhancheng [southern Vietnam], pilfering its treasures before returning. Yang Tingyi of Aizhou defected during the fourth year, attacking Jiaozhou; prefect Li Jin absconded to return to Han. Yan dispatched Cheng Bao, his recipient for edicts, to retaliate against Yanyi, Bao dying in battle.

During the fifth year [C.E. 932], royal sons received investiture: Yaoshu as Prince of Yong, Guitu as Prince of Kang, Hongdu as Prince of Qin, Hongxi as Prince of Jin, Hongchang as Prince of Yue, Hongbi as Prince of Qi, Hongya as Prince of Shao, Hongze as Prince of Zhen, Hongcao as Prince of Wan, Honggao as Prince of Xun, Hongwei as Prince of Xi, Hongmiao as Prince of Gao, Hongjian as Prince of Tong, Hongjian‡ as Prince of Yi, Hongji as Prince of Bian, Hongdao as Prince of Gui, Hongzhao as Prince of Xuan, Hongzheng as Prince of Tong‡, and Hongyi as Prince of Ding.

General Sun Decheng, dispatched for a raid against Xiangzhou¶ in the ninth year [C.E. 936], did not prevail.[2] In the tenth year, a military attaché to the governor at Jiaozhou, Jiao Gongxian, killed Yang Tingyi to install himself. Retaliating against Jiaozhou was Wu Quan, a one-time commander under Tingyi. Gongxian now approached the Han for military assistance. Yan dispatched troops to the Baiteng River for a drive on Jiaozhou and invested his own son, Hongcao, as Prince of Jiao [and relief commander]. Yan personally lodged armies at Haimen. Quan had murdered Gongxian by now and engaged the enemy at the ocean port, planting iron rods in the water. Quan's troops advanced by riding a rising tide, Hongcao in pursuit. Yet the boats recoiled once tides receded, the iron rods now sticking into the wheel-ruts and overturning all of the affected ships. Hongcao died in battle and Yan regrouped his remaining men to return.

Liu Yan died in the fifteenth year [C.E. 942], at fifty-four *sui*. He received the posthumous title of the Grand Emperor of Heaven and temple name Gaozu, his mausoleum called Kangling. His son, Bin, succeeded him.

Liu Bin [C.E. 920–943] was originally named Hongdu and invested Prince of Qin. The older sons of Liu Yan, Yaoshu and Guitu, had both died young, leaving Bin next in line. As illness confined Yan to bed, he summoned right associate at the Secretariat, Wang Fan, and invoked the nicknames of Hongdu and Hongxi, saying, "Shou and Jun are older in age, but unfit for ruling in my place. I prefer installing Hongchang, who is most like me. How can my own sons and grandsons be so deficient? The empire's powers, by later generations, would otherwise be frittered away like rats descending the [funnel-shaped] horn of an ox!" Tears fell as he sobbed. Acting on his instructions, Fan removed Hongdu and Hongxi from the capital, the former to Yongzhou‡ and the latter to Rongzhou‡, Hongchang named heir-apparent. The succession matter had been settled when Xiao Yi, commissioner of the Chongwen Institute, entered the palace to inquire of Yan's health. Informed personally by Yan of the decision, Yi admonished, "Installation of a younger son and the attendant challenges of elder sons is a recipe for certain calamity!" In this way, Hongdu eventually inherited power, his personal name changed to Bin and the reign changed to Guangtian. His mother, the Illustriously Deported Consort Zhao, was honored as Consort Dowager and the Prince of Jin, Hongxi, designated regent.

Liu Bin proved utterly inept at governance after the accession. While the body of Yan lay in state, he summoned actor-musicians to make music, drinking wine in the palace and amusing himself with naked boys and girls. Occasionally donning a black hemp shirt, he consorted by night with prostitutes and casually roamed from one commoner's home to the next. In consequence, bandits from the mountains to the seas vied to rise up. The perverse Zhang Yuxian, declaring himself "King of the Middle Heavens and the Eight Kingdoms," overran Xunzhou‡, as Bin retaliated by dispatching Hongchang the Prince of Yue and Honggao the Prince of Xun. Yuxian managed to encircle Hongchang and the others at Qianbo hostel, yet assistant commanders Wan Jingxin and Chen Daoxiang fought ferociously, grabbing the two princes and piercing the blockade to flee. Bin failed to reflect sufficiently on such events, causing the eastern Ling region to slip into chaos.

Liu Hongxi accommodated Bin with progressively more singing girls to foster reckless abandon in him. Bin even suspected his younger brothers of conspiring against him, so eunuchs were directed to secure the palace gates and permit access only to those in constraints. Hongxi, Honggao, and Hongchang clandestinely enlisted the services of Chen Daoxiang's coterie of courageous men, including Liu Sichao, Tan Lingyin, Lin Shaoqiang, Lin Shaoliang, and He Changting—men skilled at wrestling who could perform before Bin. During a banquet at the Changchun palace, Bin arose in a drunken stupor after observing them perform. Daoxiang and Sichao trailed him to the bedroom door to assassinate him, along with an entire cohort of aides. In power for two years, Bin was twenty-four *sui* and posthumously entitled Shang. Younger brother Cheng succeeded.

Liu Cheng [C.E. 920–958] originally had the name Hongxi and standing as Prince of Jin. In the wake of regicide against Bin, he installed himself and changed the reign to Yingqian. He appointed Hongchang as supreme marshal and counselor of affairs and Honggao as deputy supreme marshal, with Sichao and cohort invested as "Subjects of Merit." Cheng came to power illicitly by murdering his brother, leaving him fearful of insubordination from the rank and file. To inspire awe, a heightened recourse to laws and punishments occurred. Subsequently, Honggao made repeated public pleas for punitive action against the renegade assassins of Bin, while privately urging Cheng's execution of Sichao and cohort to placate critics away from court. An utterly livid Cheng had a messenger summon Honggao by night, who now realized himself doomed. Detaining the messenger, Honggao drew a bath for himself, then prayed before a Buddhist statue, saying, "By some error of consciousness was I born as royal son, such that murder now awaits me. In the next life, I should be born to a commoner's household to elude such slaughter." Overcome with tears as he delivered parting words to family, he then went to the palace as ordered, only to be killed upon arrival. That winter, Cheng sacrificed to Heaven at the southern suburbs and announced a reign change to Qianhe. The multitude of courtiers elevated his title of honor to the Grandly Sagacious, Literarily Martial, Grandly Discerning, Preeminently Moral, Grandly Radiant, and Filial Emperor.

In summer of the second year [C.E. 944], Liu Hongchang was commissioned to conduct ancestral offerings at Emperor Xiang's tomb at Haiqu, but was intercepted by a renegade at the Changhua palace and stabbed to death, as prearranged by Cheng. Tensions with his other brothers had surfaced since Cheng's murder of Honggao. The wisest of the sons, Hongchang, was initially favored by their father for succession, so Cheng proved especially jealous of him, making him the first to fall to harm. Hongze the Prince of Zhen lived in Yongzhou‡ and enjoyed a reputation for exemplary governance. The sighting of a phoenix that year at Yongzhou‡, however, infuriated a jealous Cheng, who had him poisoned to death. In this way, his brothers would be murdered in succession.

In the third year [C.E. 945], Liu Cheng killed younger brother Hongya, followed by Liu Sichao and cohort, five in all. The deaths of Sichao and others frightened and unsettled Chen Daoxiang. A friend, Deng Shen, gave him a copy of Xun Yue's *Chronicles of Han*,[3] but Daoxiang initially failed to appreciate its import, prompting an upbraiding by Shen: "You savage idiot! The execution of Han Xin and the boiling alive of Peng Yue all appear in this book." A now alert Daoxiang grew ever nervous. News of the exchange profoundly upset Cheng, who imprisoned Daoxiang and Shen before decapitating both at the marketplace and liquidating their clans. He also banished the right associate at the Secretariat, Wang Fan, to prefect of Yingzhou†, then orchestrated his assassination on the highway. During the fifth year [C.E. 947], younger brothers Hongbi, Hongdao, Hongyi, Hongji, Hongjian, Hongjian‡, Hongwei, and Hongzhao were all slain on the same day.

Commissioned as envoy to Chu, in the sixth year [C.E. 948], was Zhong Yunzhang, director of public works and drafter at the Secretariat, the Han seeking a marriage accommodation that Chu declined. Cheng asked of Yunzhang upon his return, "Is the Gentleman Ma capable of another assault on the south?" Ma Xiguang had recently assumed power, then, as brother Xi'e rallied troops against him at Wuling. With pervasive tumult currently engulfing Hunan, Yunzhang interpreted conditions in Chu as favorable for invasion. Cheng thereby dispatched Wu Xun, director of the Giant Elephant regiments, and eunuch Wu Huai'en to attack Hezhou¶. Once they captured the prefecture, Chu sent reinforcements. Xun dug large pits at the base inside the city wall, covered the pits with screens, then lightly dusted the screens with dirt [as camouflage]. Chu troops scaling the wall all fell into the pits on the other side, as several thousands died and the rest fled. Xun proceeded to raid Guizhou‡ and the five prefectures of Lian, Yi‡, Yan·, Wu‡, and Meng‡, vanquishing all of them. He returned after pillaging Quanzhou‡.

In winter of the ninth year [C.E. 951], the eunuch Pan Chongche was sent for another offensive, now against Chenzhou¶. The armies of Li Jing [of Southern Tang] were already there and engaged Chongche, but suffered a rout at Yizhang, enabling the Han to win Chenzhou¶. Events seemed increasingly favorable to Liu Cheng, who deployed to the high seas a force led by Ji Yanyun, director of "sea-hulk" warships. They commandeered the gold and silk of merchants to erect palace retreats for Cheng. The royal house of Liu thus came to own hundreds of palaces too numerous to record: Nangong, Daming, Changhua, Ganquan, Wanhua, Xiuhua, Yuqing, Taiwei, and so on.

Liu Cheng raised no questions when eunuch Lin Yanyu and palace woman Lu Qiongxian arbitrarily killed enemies in and away from the palace. Often drinking by night to severe intoxication, Cheng once placed a melon on the back of actress Shang Yulou's neck, then grabbed his sword to test its sharpness by cutting the melon, only to sever Yulou's entire head. Upon sobering a day later, Cheng summoned Yulou to serve beverages when aides told him of her death: he heaved a sigh and nothing more.

During the tenth year [C.E. 952], Wang Jinkui of Hunan led a force of fifty thousand, composed mostly of "River and Cave" tribesmen, in a raid on Chenzhou¶. He met with defeat by Pan Chongche at Haoshi, where more than ten thousand vanquished soldiers were decapitated. Liu Cheng grew gravely ill during the eleventh year, prompting investitures for his sons: Jixing as Prince of Wei, Xuanxing as Prince of Gui, Qingxing as Prince of Jing, Baoxing as Prince of Xiang, and Chongxing as Prince of Mei.

In the twelfth year [C.E. 954], Liu Cheng personally tilled the royal fields. Wu Changjun of Jiaozhou sent an emissary to offer fealty in exchange for the tallies and halberds of subject. He was the son of Wu Quan, who had occupied Jiaozhou during the reign of Liu Yan. Yan had sent Hongcao to raid it, only to abandon the effort once he died, the prefecture not targeted again for attack. Succeeding Quan upon death was son Changji, and succeeding Changji was younger brother Changjun—the first to accept vassal status under Cheng. Secretarial overseer Li Yu was sent to deliver banner and tallies to accommodate Jun, but Yu was intercepted after approaching Baizhou, an agent of Jun insisting that the havoc wrought by pirates had left the road impassable, thwarting Yu's mission. Cheng murdered younger brother Hongmiao, then in the thirteenth year [C.E. 955], younger brother Hongzheng—the sons of Yan now entirely dead.

Emperor Shizong of Zhou was pacifying the northern Yangzi region, in the third year of Xiande [C.E. 956],[4] making Liu Cheng agitated and afraid. He dispatched an emissary to the capital to negotiate the terms of tribute, but obstruction by the Chu people prevented the envoy from advancing. The attendant anxiety visibly affected Cheng. He also professed knowledge of astrology, so when the moon eclipsed parts of Altair [*Qianniu*] and Vega [*Zhinü*], he produced a letter predicting the event, lamenting, "The eclipse pertains to my fate!" Afterward he had a long night of drinking.

In the sixteenth year [C.E. 958], a burial site was divined for Liu Cheng north of the city and glazed tiles transported there to decorate the burial vault, a site he personally inspected. He died that autumn at thirty-nine *sui*, receiving the posthumous title of the Literary and Martial, Brilliant and Sagacious, Enlightened and Filial Emperor. The temple name Zhongzong was conferred, his mausoleum Zhaoling. Son Chang succeeded him.

Liu Chang, originally named Jixing, had been invested Prince of Wei. As eldest son of Cheng, he was installed upon his death, the reign changed to Dabao. The stubborn and suspicious character of Cheng had precluded the proper utilization of courtiers, so he deployed only favored eunuchs such as Lin Yanyu and palace maidens like Lu Qiongxian. The stupendously stupid Chang considered officialdom incapable of complete loyalty because of family duties and concern for progeny, leaving only eunuchs as intimates capable of deployment. He entrusted governance, therefore, to such eunuchs as Gong Chengshu and Chen Yanshou. For courtiers that Chang wished to employ, he first insisted on their castration.

Because court affairs were monopolized by Gong Chengshu and cohort, Liu Chang in the inner palace could play his debauched games with female attendants, including a Persian. He never again emerged to inquire of state affairs. Meanwhile, Chen Yanshou brought to his attention the female sorcerer Fan Huzi, who claimed that the soul of the Jade Emperor had entered her own body. Chang raised a tent in a hall of the imperial compound to lay out precious objects. Huzi wore a hat for distant travel and a skirt of purple and pink, as she sat in the tent and portended future prosperity or peril. She addressed

Chang as the "emperor-designate." Affairs of empire all fell under her purview, the likes of Lu Qiongxian and Gong Chengshu vying to submit to her. Huzi once informed Chang that Chengshu and cohort were all "sent by the Supreme Heaven above to assist his heir-designate, so their misdeeds should be ignored." Left assistant director of the Imperial Secretariat Zhong Yunzhang, as assisting minister, held her in utter contempt. He also repeatedly proposed the execution of eunuchs, who all smugly squinted their eyes at him.

In the second year [C.E. 959], three days before Chang's conduct of sacrifices to Heaven at the southern suburbs, Yunzhang joined ritual experts in ascending the ritual mound and motioning in the four directions. The eunuch Xu Yanzhen observed them and concluded that, "this can only be a conspiracy to rebel." Drawing his sword, he climbed the mound to be met by curses from Yunzhang, as Yanzhen scurried off to accuse him of sedition. Chang ordered Yunzhang imprisoned, minister of rites Xue Yongpi charged with rendering a judgment. An old acquaintance of Yongpi, Yunzhen said to him, in tears, "I have committed no crime, yet may die through slander. For this, I feel no malice, although my two young sons do not appreciate their father's innocence. I hope you will tell them, once they are grown." His words triggered a swift rebuke from Yanzhen, "This treacherous thug obviously intends to facilitate retribution by his sons!" He returned to the palace to inform Chang, who ordered the two sons arrested and imprisoned as well, exterminating the entire family.

Chen Yanshou now reminded Chang, "The Former Monarch managed to transfer power to Your Majesty by exterminating all of his younger brothers." He pressed for the methodical execution or elimination of the royal princes. Chang agreed and murdered younger brother Xuanxing, the Prince of Gui. It was the inaugural year of Jianlong [C.E. 960]. A commander under Liu Chang, Shao Tingxuan, further counseled him, "Our Han dynasty exploited the tumult of the Tang to occupy this land for some fifty years. We were fortunate that the Middle Kingdom, with its assorted preoccupations, could not extend its armies this far. The Han grew ever arrogant in the face of such tranquility. Today, our armies know nothing of banner and drum, while our ruler knows nothing of dynastic fortunes. The world has long suffered from turmoil, and it is a natural tendency for order to replace prolonged turmoil. A genuine ruler has emerged [to the north], we now hear, who will certainly possess our entire continent, his powers permitting him to accept nothing short of complete unity of the world." He urged Chang to restore military readiness as precaution or, alternatively, offer the totality of the kingdom's treasures to the Middle Kingdom and establish cordial relations through diplomacy. In his ignorance, Chang saw nothing of concern and even resented Tingxuan's candor to the point of profoundly loathing him.

In the fourth year [C.E. 961], "purple mushrooms" sprouted on palace grounds, wild beasts knocked against the royal bedroom door, goats in the imperial gardens spewed pearls from their mouths, and stones along the side of a well levitated and moved over a hundred paces before falling to the ground. Fan Huzi regarded all as auspicious omens and prodded courtiers to enter the palace in celebration. Liu Chang named as Precious Consort, in the fifth year, a woman once adopted by the eunuch Li Tuo, favoring her exclusively. Tuo was grand preceptor for the inner palace, managing thereby to dominate governance from the palace. Having murdered Zhong Yunzhang, Xu Yanzhen resented Gong Chengshu and cohort for enjoying superior standing at court and schemed to assassinate them. Chengshu arranged for a crony to accuse Yanzhen of impending rebellion, and he was executed by Chang, along with his kinsmen.

In the seventh year [C.E. 964], imperial Song armies campaigned against the south, overtaking Chenzhou¶. The prefecture's leading commander Ji Yanyun and prefect Lu Guangtu, initially appointed by Liu Cheng, both perished in battle as residuals retreated to defend Shaozhou. Liu Chang only now recollected the counsel of Shao Tingxuan and sent him to resist imperial forces with a naval fleet emanating from Guangkou. At the time, imperial troops had retreated a full league, while Tingxuan instructed troops to enhance military preparedness—the people of Ling esteeming him as a superb commander. But anonymous letters to the court falsely accused Tingxuan of sedition, and Chang sent an agent to supervise his suicide. Tingxuan subordinates assembled before their camp entrance as the messenger arrived to assert the absence of sedition on Tingxuan's part, all to no avail. They later erected a shrine to him at Guangkou.

In the eighth year [C.E. 965], the death of Wu Changwen of Jiaozhou triggered a struggle for power between his assistant Lü Chuping and the prefect of Fengzhou†, Qiao Zhiyou. Utter bedlam beset the Jiaozhi region [northern Vietnam], prompting Ding Lian of Huanzhou‡ to raise troops in a successful storm against it. Lian was appointed by Chang as governor of Jiaozhou. A common woman at Nanhai, in the ninth year, gave birth to a son with two heads and four arms.

At the time, Emperor Taizu ordered Li Yu [of Southern Tang] to instruct Chang that he should accept vassal standing with the Song. An indignant Chang imprisoned Li Yu's envoy, Gong Shenyi. In the thirteenth year [C.E. 970], the Song court directed Pan Mei, its defense commissioner at Tanzhou, to issue troops. As they reached Baixia, Liu Chang took precautions by dispatching Gong Chengshu to defend He¶ Prefecture, Guo Chongyue to secure Gui†, and Li Tuo to secure Shao. Pan Mei pacified He¶ Prefecture sometime that autumn, then Zhao‡ and Gui† in the tenth month and Lian in the eleventh month. Chang seemed delighted, commenting, "Zhao‡, Gui†, Lian, and He¶ prefectures originally belonged to the Hunan [Chu] regime. Northern armies will surely be satisfied after claiming them, mitigating against further extension southward." Such was the measure of his stupidity! Shaozhou was pacified in the twelfth month.

Pacification of Ying¶ and Xiong prefectures occurred in the fourth year of Kaibao, the inaugural month [C.E. 971], Liu Chang's commander there, Pan Chongche, having capitulated in advance of hostilities. Northern troops proceeded to Longtou, as Chang sent an emissary suing for peace and a termination of hostilities. With northern troops approaching Majing, in the second month, Chang presented a petition of surrender through Xiao Cui, his right associate at the Secretariat. Chang grew anxious following Cui's departure and issued additional orders to regroup armies in resisting the northern mandate. As Pan Mei and cohort continued their advance, Chang offered to surrender through younger brother Baoxing, the Prince of Xiang, who led civil and military representatives to Mei's camp. Chang was spurned.

Gong Chengshu, Li Tuo, and others now presented another plan, stating, "Northern armies have come simply to take advantage of our kingdom's precious commodities. If we set the city afire, leaving nothing, their armies will have no place to lodge and need to return." They destroyed by fire all government treasuries, palaces, and halls. Anticipating his own flight to the high seas, Chang prepared more than ten oceanworthy vessels, brimming with precious gems and imperial concubines, but eunuch Le Fan commandeered the boats for flight to the Song side. Imperial troops now progressed to Baitian, where Chang emerged for surrender astride a white horse and wearing plain clothes. The captives were conveyed to the capital [Kaifeng], where Chang received a pardon and honors as left commandant of the Thousand-Bull Guard, in addition to investiture as the "Pardoned Marquis." For later events, see the "national histories."[i]

....

i. Various writings are consistent about the ascent and descent of Liu Yin's house: it began in the second year of Tianyou under the Tang [C.E. 905], when Yin became governor of Guangzhou, and ended in the fourth year of Kaibao [C.E. 971] under our own dynasty, when the kingdom was overturned—a total of sixty-seven years. The *Old History* traced the kingdom's founding to the assumption of illicit titles by Liu Yan, in the third year of Zhenming, by the Liang calendar [C.E. 917], thereby giving fifty-five years for its rule.

CHAPTER 66

HEREDITARY HOUSE OF CHU

Ma Yin and Sons Xisheng, Xifan, Xiguang, and Xi'e

Ma Yin [C.E. 852–930] had the courtesy name Batu, a native of Yanling, Xuzhou‡. During the Tang, third year of Zhonghe [C.E. 883], Qin Zongquan of Caizhou unleashed Sun Ru and Liu Jianfeng, with a force of ten thousand under younger brother Zongheng's direction, to plunder the southern Huai region. Yin initially served as assistant commander to Ru. The raid of Zongheng's cohort against Yang Xingmi at Yangzhou had yet to produce a definitive outcome when Zongquan, under the hammering of Liang armies, summoned Ru and cohort repeatedly. They were disinclined to return, and, after much prodding from Zongheng, a furious Ru killed him and personally commanded Zongheng's men against Gaoyou, expelling Xingmi. Xingmi now occupied Xuanzhou, as Ru's men surrounded the prefecture for a long yet indecisive siege. In the interim, Yin and Jianfeng were unleashed by Ru to plunder neighboring counties for food. Ru died in battle and Yin and confederates, without leadership, rallied behind Jianfeng as commander. Yin became his vanguard and was redeployed for an offensive at Yuzhang, during which he sacked Qian and Ji¤ prefectures, as his numbers swelled to several tens of thousands.

After entering Hunan in the inaugural year of Qianning [C.E. 894], Ma Yin had reached Liling when the Tanzhou prefect Deng Chune, departing with an army from Shaozhou‡, forted at Longhui Pass. Arrival at the pass of Jianfeng's contingent prompted Chune to force the surrender of his frontier commander, Jiang Xun. Jianfeng removed Xun's armor to place on the back of his own vanguard. Unfurling his banners and pennants, he rushed directly against Tanzhou. Once at the prefecture's eastern gate, the gatekeeper presumed the troops as their own returnees from the pass and opened the gates to admit them. Jianfeng subsequently murdered Chune and pronounced himself interim regent, Emperor Xizong [Zhaozong] confirming him as governor of Hunan and Ma Yin as chief director of infantry and cavalry. Jiang Xun sought appointment as prefect of Shaozhou‡, and, when Jianfeng refused, unleashed his men on Xiangxiang. Jianfeng turned to Yin for a sally against Xun at Shaozhou‡.

Liu Jianfeng, a mediocre man, had no facility for commanding armies and was given to carousing and creating a fracas with subordinates. After illicit relations with an attractive woman, the wife of infantryman Chen Shan, a furious Shan pummeled him to death with an iron wok. The military now raised as its leader Zhang Ji, the current manager-adjutant to the governor. As he approached headquarters, however, the horse carrying Ji began kicking its legs and gnawing at the bit, injuring his thigh. Ji had to admit to fellow commanders from his sickbed, "I am not the leader you need, but Gentleman Ma possesses eminent valor and should enjoy your combined support." The commanders first assassinated Shan and dismembered the corpse before sending Yao Yanzhang to retrieve Ma Yin from Shaozhou‡. Ji rode a sedan chair to headquarters upon Yin's arrival and Yin paid respects in the courtyard. Ji invited Yin to assume his platform and led commanders and their administrators in facing north in a double bow, relinquishing his position to Yin. It was the third year of Qianning [C.E. 896].

The Tang court formally appointed him prefect of Tanzhou, after which Ma Yin unleashed commanders Qin Yanhui and Li Qiong in raids on the six prefectures of Lian, Shao‡, Chen¶, Heng‡, Dao, and Yong¶, vanquishing them all. His actions alarmed Liu Shizheng of Guiguan, who directed commanders Chen Kefan and Wang Jianwu to retain control over the Quanyi Mountains. Yin dispatched an emissary to Shizheng, but Kefan's men turned him away upon approaching the border, inciting Yin to retaliate with a strike by seven thousand troops: he apprehended Kefan and more than two thousand of his men, burying them all alive. A blockade of the Guiguan command ensued, where Shizheng fell captive and its prefectures were seized, one and all. Yin now petitioned for court confirmation of Qiong as surveillance commissioner of the Guiguan command; he personally became the Wu'an governor in the fourth year [C.E. 897].

Previously, Yin's younger brother, Ma Bin, had been apprehended by Yang Xingmi in the wake of Sun Ru's defeat at Xuanzhou. Xingmi assimilated Ru's remnant soldiers into the Black Cloud Brigade, with Bin as director. Bin attended Xingmi into battle and distinguished himself on several occasions, but his earnest and serious character left him oblivious to vainglory. Xingmi grew to love him and inquired about his family. "I am the younger brother of Ma Yin," Bin indicated. His admission utterly astonished Xingmi, who exclaimed, "Your brother is distinguished indeed! With your permission, I will promptly return you to him." Bin did not respond, so Xingmi again raised the issue on another day and Bin declined, adding, "Your Subject, as the vanquished underling of Sun Ru, can never repay you for your compassion in sparing my life. Receiving regular news from the Hunan border about Yin's activities already suffices. I have no wish to leave." Xingmi said with a sigh, "In the past, I prized your demeanor, although now I finally can claim your heart! By motivating me to harmonize relations between our two kingdoms, facilitating trade, and assisting in the mutual exchange of commodities in short supply—in this way, you can repay me as well." Xingmi arranged a highly formal farewell for his return home. Bin's return exhilarated Yin, who petitioned for his assignment as deputy governor.

Once Yang Xingmi ordered a strike against Du Hong by commander Liu Cun, Ma Yin offered assistance as they encircled Ezhou, committing the naval forces of Qin Yanhui and Xu Dexun. Du Hong later died in defeat, after which Cun proceeded to attack Yin's men. Yin now deployed Yanhui to protect positions upstream while sending deputy commander Huang Fan, with three hundred boats, to lay in ambush at the mouth of the Liuyang River. Repeated battles had yielded no fruits for Cun, so he wrote to Yin seeking a truce, which Yin was inclined to accept. Yanhui countered, "The people of Huai are full of deceit and cannot be trusted, as they will await any vulnerability in our military to exploit." An intense sortie ensued, forcing Cun's men to withdraw. Huang Fan diverted to the Yangzi boats from the Liuyang River in a joint assault, winning resoundingly, as Liu Cun and Chen Zhixin both died in battle. Yanhui could thereby claim Yuezhou‡.

After Taizu acceded to the Liang throne, Ma Yin dispatched an envoy to tender tribute. Taizu named him director of the Chancellery and concurrent palace secretary, invested Prince of Chu. Gao Jichang of Jingnan [Nanping] led troops to cut off Hankou while intercepting the tribute emissaries of Yin, who responded with a military action against Shatou, led by Xu Dexun. Only after Jichang sued for peace did Yin desist.

Lü Shizhou, the Yuanzhou‡ prefect under Yang Xingmi, came to Chu for sanctuary. A brave and burly man of heroic stature, Shizhou possessed a substantial command of both classical exegeses and books on the art of warfare. He acknowledged a family with five generations of commanders and characterized his own professional choices as negligible. He often joined "drinking companions" in imbibing, rising to dance after intoxication as his melancholy songs induced a spontaneous flow of tears. Xingmi suspected some conflicted sentiments based on reports of such conduct and planted an informant to scrutinize his activities. A progressively nervous Shizhou asked of assistant commander Qiwu Zhang, "Standing opposite a hostile border with Chu peoples, I have often observed the extraordinary grandeur of the mists above its encampments, confirming its armies as not easily vanquished. Gentleman Ma is a benevolent man, I hear, who treats troops with decorum. Is it feasible for me to flee death in the land of Chu?" "You must set your own course," Zhang affirmed, "although I pledge not to divulge a word, even at risk of losing my tongue." Shizhou absconded for Chu during a hunt with his men along the border, Qiwu Zhang abandoning his own family dependents to join him. News of his arrival exhilarated Ma Yin, who declared, "To secure this single man while in the throes of strategizing against Lingnan [to the south] is enough for me to succeed!" Shizhou became chief director of infantry and cavalry, leading a drive on the Lingnan region that ended in the acquisition of Zhao‡, He¶, Wu‡, Meng‡, Gong, and Fu· prefectures, among others. Yin petitioned for Shizhou's nomination as prefect of Zhaozhou‡.

Lei Yangong of Langzhou¶ enlisted Wu troops to attack Pingjiang Prefecture, only to be defeated in a storm by Xu Dexun. Ma Yin dispatched Qin Yanhui to attack Langzhou¶. Once Lei Yangong fled to Wu, Ma Yin retaliated by apprehending his family of seven, including younger brother Yanxiong, for conveyance to the Liang.

Later, various "River and Cave" tribesmen reverted to Ma Yin through leaders Xiang Gui of Feng¤ Prefecture, Song Ye of Chen, and Chang Shiyi of Xu†. Yin petitioned to elevate Langzhou¶ as the Yongshun command with Zhang Ji as governor. He also requested the initiation of administrative offices with a full complement of officials, in accordance with the Tang precedent of Taizong. Taizu of Liang appointed Yin as generalissimo of the metropolitan government and Yin, in turn, named brother Ma Bin as councilor of the left, Cun as councilor of the right, and eighteen men as academicians, led by Liao Guangtu. In the reign of Emperor Mo,[1] Yin received additional powers as governor of commands including Wu'an [Wuping], Wuchang, Jingjiang, and Ningyuan, as well as general commander of at-large forces along the four fronts at Hong and E prefectures.

After the Liang dynasty was overturned by Zhuangzong of Tang, Ma Yin sent son Xifan to present tribute in the capital, surrendering the seal of "general commander" formerly conferred by the Liang. Zhuangzong asked about the length and breadth of [the expansive] Lake Dongting, Xifan responding, "If your carriage went southward for an inspection, you'd find its waters barely enough to water your horse." The Emperor was impressed [by his modesty]. Zhuangzong's pacification of the Shu region struck terror in Yin, who petitioned the court to retire. In a letter with the Emperor's personal seal,

Zhuangzong consoled and commended him. With the accession of Mingzong, Yin dispatched an envoy to tender tribute and convey congratulatory messages for the coming year. The envoy, Shi Guangxian, was apprehended by Gao Jichang of Jingnan. Yin retaliated militarily by unleashing the armies of Yuan Quan and Wang Huan. As they reached the city walls, however, Jichang sued for peace and they desisted.

The military might of Ma Yin began as modest, so he found particularly menacing such hostile neighbors as Yang Xingmi, Cheng Rui, and Liu Yan. He once inquired about strategy of commander Gao Yu, who counseled, "Cheng Rui's lands are trifling and troops too few to pose a serious menace while Liu Yan's ambitions are confined to the Wuguan [Lingnan] region. And the feud between Yang Xingmi and Sun Ru could not be ameliorated even with ten thousand ounces of gold. It is the mission of the 'hegemon' [Chu] to venerate the ruler and submit to him. As internal policy today, we should serve the imperial court to win noble titles, employing these externally to impress neighboring enemies [and inhibit aggression]. Then, we can rest our armies while rejuvenating agriculture, augment our might while awaiting an opportune moment." Hereafter, Yin began presenting tribute to the capital, although his annual tribute never exceeded even the tea production for his domain. Shops were set up to sell tea, extending from the capital all the way to Xiang, Tang, Ying, and Fu prefectures, which yielded a tenfold profit. Gao Yu further prodded Yin to mint coins of lead and iron, where ten iron strings were exchanged for one in copper cash. The people were also directed to produce tea for trade with itinerant merchants, the portion assessed by the government generating tens of thousands in cash every year. In this way, the domain expanded, its powers surged, and a succession of noble titles came its way.

In the second year of Tiancheng [C.E. 927], Ma Yin petitioned to establish locally an auxiliary Secretariat. Emperor Mingzong decided to invest him as "King" of Chu, when the relevant officials noted the absence of a ritual for investing the "king of a domain." Alternatively, they recommended sending the right associate at the Imperial Secretariat, Li Xu, to carry the tallies of office in "bamboo binders" for the investiture, consistent with the employment of bamboo binders for investing the three honorary dukes. Yin now gave Tanzhou the new name of Changsha Metropolis and inaugurated the trappings of kingdom, replete with full complement of self-appointed officials. He named younger brother Bin as the Jingjiang governor, son Xizhen as the Wushun governor, second son Xisheng as administrator of internal and external military affairs, Yao Yanzhang as minister of the left, Xu Dexun as minister of the right, Li Duo as dignitary for education, Cui Ying as dignitary for public works, Tuoba Chang as associate at the Secretariat, and Ma Gong as imperial secretary. Civil and military officials were all advanced in rank. He conferred the posthumous sobriquet Literate and August upon great grandfather Yun, Solemn and Majestic upon grandfather Zheng, and Glorious and Solemn upon father Yuanfeng. Ancestral temples for all three were erected at Changsha. Yin died in the inaugural year of Changxing [C.E. 930] at seventy-nine *sui*. By orders of the Tang court, "Ma Yin shall receive the posthumous title 'Martial and Majestic,' but no posthumous elevation in rank, his official and noble standing already high." His son Xisheng was installed.

Ma Xisheng [d. C.E. 932] had the courtesy name Ruone. The second son of Yin, he served as administrator of internal and external military affairs after the formal inauguration of kingdom. Gao Jichang of Jingnan came to regard Yin commander Gao Yu as threatening, for Chu's recent strength derived from Yu's strategic counsel. He even planted a spy to conduct subterfuge with Yin, but Yin ignored him. Once Xisheng managed affairs for his father, the spy informed him, "Chu's reliance on Yu has elated Jichang, convinced that ruin of the Ma house will occur at Yu's hand." A naive Xisheng believed him and summarily stripped Yu of military posts. "I have long served my Prince, but must now scurry to camps at Xishan," Yu exclaimed indignantly to others. "After all, I am getting old and the puppy [Xisheng], now grown up, is given to snipping at others!" The comments were conveyed to Xisheng, who forged orders in Yin's name to murder him. An aging Yin, no longer engaged in affairs, remained uninformed of Yu's death. A vast fog overtook the four passes on that very day, as a startled Yin reflected before attendants, "In my former service to Sun Ru, I always witnessed vast fogs filling the skies whenever Ru killed the innocent. What innocent life has ended in our own military prisons?" Aides divulged the affair a day later and Yin wept bitterly, pounding his own breast. "Am I so senile as to murder such a distinguished subject [without knowing it]?" Turning to attendants, he added, "Neither will I last long in this world!" He passed away in the next year.

With the installation of Ma Xisheng, the northern court confirmed him as the Wu'an and Jingjiang governor. Xisheng was impressed to learn of the Liang Emperor Taizu's affinity for chicken, so every day he had fifty chickens cooked for consumption in his own palaces. Xisheng did not cry during Yin's burial at Shanghuang, but in a single sitting consumed several bowls of chicken before departing. This prompted vice minister of rites Pan Qi to ask in satire, "Long ago, Ruan Ji prepared boiled pork while mourning.[2] Does our own age lack similar worthies?" Xisheng died in the third year of Changxing [C.E. 932], posthumously invested Prince of Hengyang. His successor was younger brother Xifan.

Ma Xifan [C.E. 899–947] had the courtesy name Baogui and was Yin's fourth son. Yin fathered more than ten boys: eldest son Xizhen, born to his formal wife, proved a worthy man. Next came Xisheng and Xifan, both born on the same day. The exceptional beauty and consequent favor of Xisheng's mother, the Lady Yuan, had facilitated his succession. Xizhen then relinquished official posts to become a Daoist adept residing at home, making Xifan next in line upon Xisheng's death. He inherited Yin's official posts and noble titles, invested King of Chu. The northern court conferred gifts of bow and arrow, cap and sword in the second year of Qingtai [C.E. 935]. It further elevated Xifan to generalissimo in the fourth year of Tianfu [C.E. 939], empowered to establish local administration consistent with precedent for Yin.

Fond of learning, Ma Xifan was a skilled poet. The eighteen literati at his court, including Liao Guangtu, Xu Zhongya, Li Gao, and Tuoba Chang, were already academicians in Yin's day, but they proved a frivolous lot who fed Xifan's own proclivities for extravagance and fostered drinking, gambling, and carousing. Tuoba Chang alone possessed maturity and gravitas, employing biting rebuke in remonstrance to Xifan, only to incur the resentment of Guangtu and cohort, in the process.

In the wake of mutinies by An Congjin of Xiangzhou and Li Jinquan of Anzhou, Emperor Gaozu of Jin ordered Xifan to dispatch troops. He rushed to Hanyang a naval force directed by Zhang Shaodi and transported fifty thousand pecks of rice to feed troops. Shaodi returned after defeating Jinquan and cohort. Once the Xizhou¶ prefect Peng Shichou organized assorted barbarians from Jin‡ and Jiang¶ prefectures to raid Fengzhou¤, Xifan dispatched Liu Qing and Liu Quanming, with five thousand infantry, to storm Shichou. He suffered a rout, Qing's men now proceeding to Xi¶ Prefecture, forcing Shichou to flee to Jiangzhou¶ while arranging for son Shigao to lead tribal chiefs in surrendering to Qing. To its west, Xizhou¶ borders Zangke and Lianglin, to the south it connects to Guilin and Xiangjun, so Ma Xifan commissioned a bronze ornamental column with an inscription by academician Li Gao [celebrating their submission]. The Nanning chieftain, Mo Yanshu, with tribes spread over eighteen prefectures; the Duyun chieftain, Yin Huaichang, with twelve tribes in the vicinity of Kunming; and Zangke chieftain Zhang Wanjun, with tribes spread over seven prefectures including Yi¶ and Bo‡, all were now subordinate to Xifan.

Xifan erected a "Garden for Greeting the Spring" and "Pavilion for Festive Repose," costing vast sums of cash and triggering supplemental taxes across the domain, a practice decried by Tuoba Chang as unacceptable. Xifan constructed a "Palace of the Nine Dragons" as well: with eight dragons encircling a pillar, Xifan fancied himself as the ninth dragon. By now, the Khitan had purged the Jin dynasty as bedlam overtook the Middle Kingdom. Military attaché Ding Sijin, admonishing Xifan at his office, observed, "The Former King [Ma Yin] climbed from foot soldier to claim these prefectures through hard-fought battles, relying on the northern court to restrain nearby enemies. Through three reigns power has passed, our lands now encompassing several thousand *li* and armies enrolling a hundred thousand men. Today, the Middle Kingdom goes without ruler, as its Son of Heaven suffers the indignity of imprisonment—an opportune moment for the genuine hegemon to do his deeds. If we can fully commit our armies in a storm on the northern capital via Jing and Xiang while proclaiming our cause to the world as righteous, our feat might be akin to ancient Kings Huan and Wen. We can scarcely afford to squander our kingdom's revenues and exhaust its natural resources on the pleasures of women and children!" Xifan politely spurned Sijin, who with an angry stare declared, "This youth will never learn!" He then choked to death.

Xifan perished in the fourth year of Kaiyun [C.E. 947] at forty-nine *sui* to receive posthumous title as the Literate and Illumined. Xiguang succeeded him.

Ma Xiguang [d. C.E. 950] had the courtesy name Depi and was Xifan's younger brother, his mother a commoner. Xifan always resented Tuoba Chang for being critical and contentious, so he once pointed to Chang as he entered the palace and shouted to doorkeepers, "I have no wish to see this man, and he should not receive access again." Chang was turned away. Only on his own deathbed did Xifan appreciate Chang's counsel as loyally inspired, summoning him and entrusting Xiguang to his care. Upon Xifan's death, Chang repeatedly urged Xiguang to offer the princedom to elder brother Xi'e, but he refused.

Ma Xi'e was governor of Langzhou¶ when Xifan died, whereupon he hastened to Changsha for mourning. One of Xiguang's commanders, Liu Yantao, counseled, "The Wuling governor does not come with honorable intentions. You should dispatch troops to greet him in anticipation of the unexpected, admitting him to the capital only after removing his armor and weapons." Zhang Shaodi and Zhou Tinghui even cautioned, "If the Prince wishes to relinquish the position to him, so be it; if not, you should dispose of him sooner than later." A tearful Xiguang admitted, "As my elder brother, I cannot bear to kill him! I would rather divide the kingdom under separate jurisdictions." He arranged an army to receive Xi'e at the Fushi district [of Changsha], then take him no farther than the Bixiang palace, lavishing largess before sending him off. Xi'e left bristling and sent an emissary to the northern capital to request noble standing and recognition of his autonomous satrapy. Emperor Yin of the Han declined permission, but forwarded a letter with his personal seal commending him and offering to mediate a resolution. This further incited Xi'e, who made diplomatic overtures to Li Jing [of Southern Tang]. He also unleashed armies against Changsha, Xiguang dispatching Liu Yantao and Xu Keqiong to resist him.

Liu Yantao defeated Xi'e at Puye Islet. After retreating, Xi'e incited assorted "River and Cave" tribes to plunder Yiyang. Xiguang directed Cui Gonglian to quarter seven thousand infantry at Yu Lake, Xiangxiang, to quell the barbarian menace. Meanwhile, Liu Yantao rushed a naval contingent to Wuling to attack Xi'e, but was vanquished at Meizhou‡. The defeat thoroughly alarmed Xiguang, who requested reinforcements of the northern capital, but Emperor Yin could not afford to deploy men. Xi'e unleashed a naval force up the Yangzi river, dubbing himself "Obeisance-to-Heaven commander." He proceeded with a strike against Yuezhou‡, where prefect Wang Yun remained in the fortified city refusing to fight. Xi'e screamed out to him, "You and I had formerly agreed to act in unison. Why has your heart now changed?" He shouted back, "The Prince and his brother cannot get along, yet he reproaches commanders and aides for 'changing their minds.' I hope Your Highness will enter Changsha without harming your own sibling. In the interim, Your Subject dares not devote himself absolutely to you." Xi'e withdrew and proceeded down to Xiangxiang [Xiangyin] before stopping at Changsha, quartering his men west of the [Xiang] river.[3] Liu Yantao and Xu Keqiong were forted east of the river.

Climbing the city wall, Peng Shigao surveyed armies west of the river and entered to inform Xiguang, "The armies of Wuling are arrogant, but also replete with barbarian boatmen, its powers easily broken. You should order Keqiong's men to rally at the foot of the hills, as I rush three thousand infantry to cross the river at Baxi for Yuelu, waiting until nighttime to storm him." Xiguang considered the proposal feasible, but Keqiong had already made secret gestures to Xi'e and obstructed the plan. Shigao visited Keqiong a day later for deliberations, where he gave an angry stare in scolding him, "I see the markings of a rebel on your very face. Is it your intent to surrender to that bandit [Xi'e]!" He dusted his clothes to depart, then rushed to request that Xiguang murder Keqiong, but he refused. Xi'e attacked the Changle gate, where military attachés Wu Hong and Yang Di offered resistance within the gate's vicinity and Xi'e suffered a slight setback. Hong and Di both scattered upon news of Keqiong's reversion to Xi'e.

Ma Xiguang, his wife, and sons, hiding at Ci Pavilion, were apprehended a day later. Xi'e seemed empathetic at first sight of Xiguang, saying, "How can so dimwitted a man commit so dastardly a deed? The delusion of aides offers the only explanation." Turning to his subordinates, he queried, "It is acceptable for me to spare him?" They did not respond, and Xiguang died by strangulation.

Ma Xi'e [r. C.E. 950–951] installed himself in the third year of Qianyou [C.E. 950]. Emperor Yin of the Han expired during the next year, his capital succumbing to bedlam. Xi'e now declared fealty to Li Jing [of Southern Tang], who invested him Prince of Chu. Xi'e decided to delegate all military and political affairs to younger brother Ma Xichong, but he entered a conspiracy to mutiny with senior commanders of Chu: Xu Wei, Lu Mengjun, and Lu Wan. Xichong once professed illness to forgo a banquet hosted by Xi'e at the Duanyang gate, where Xu Wei and cohort unleashed over ten wild horses trailed by stalwart soldiers wielding cudgels. They abruptly infiltrated his headquarters, commandeered storehouse guards, and tied up Xi'e. They further invited Xichong to assume power. Xichong instructed Peng Shigao and Liao Yan to incarcerate Xi'e at Hengshan, but Shigao instead acknowledged Xi'e as Prince of Hengshan and assumed vassal relations with Li Jing. A nervous Xichong also approached Jing about vassalage. At this point, Jing sent Bian Hao to Chu to relocate the entire Ma clan to Jinling [his own capital]. This was the inaugural year of Guangshun [C.E. 951], by the Zhou calendar. Xi'e was invested Prince of Chu and subsequently assumed residence at Hongzhou, while Xichong became concurrent governor of Shuzhou to reside at Yang Prefecture.

In the third year of Xiande [C.E. 956], Emperor Shizong felled Yangzhou in his campaign against the Huai region, then issued an edict consoling scions of the Ma clan. Once Yangzhou was regained by Li Jing [of Southern Tang], Xichong escorted to the northern capital an entourage including seventeen brothers. He received honors as right general commander of the Forest of Feathers Guard, Xineng as left commandant of the Garrison Guard, and Xiguan as right commandant of the Thousand-Bull Guard; Xiyin, Xijun, Xizhi, and Xilang were all named manager-adjutants to governors.

Liu Yan

Liu Yan [d. C.E. 953] was native of Luling County, Jizhou¤ and *Wang Jinkui* [d. C.E. 956] came from Wuling. Yan initially served under prefect Peng Gan, later following Gan in flight to Chu, there serving Ma Xifan as prefect of Chenzhou. A foot soldier in youth at the Jingjiang command, Jinkui rose to military director under Ma Xi'e.

Wang Jinkui was vanguard to Ma Xi'e during his offensive against Xiguang, resulting in the fall of Changsha. Owing to the turmoil and attendant destruction at Changsha, Xi'e deployed Jinkui with troops from Jingjiang to make repairs to the city. The soldiers all dejected and bitter, Jinkui spurred them on: wielding large axes with long handles, they smashed the crossbars on the city gates and fled back to Wuling. Xi'e happened to be drunk at the time and unable initially to pursue matters, but deployed commander Tang Zhu to track down Jinkui, a day later. A rout awaited Zhu at Wuling, forcing his return. Jinkui now expelled Ma Guanghui, the interim regent, inviting Liu Yan from Chenzhou to be commander; Jinkui became his deputy.

Utter chaos overtook Hunan after Xi'e commander Xu Wei and cohort mutinied, apprehending Xi'e and installing Xichong. Li Jing [of Southern Tang] sent Bian Hao into Chu to relocate Ma clansmen to Jinling and, at the same time, summoned Yan. Refusing the summons, Yan instead instructed Jinkui and manager-adjutant He Jingzhen to attack Hao at Changsha, Hao absconding after defeat.

In the third year of Guangshun [C.E. 953], by the Zhou calendar, Liu Yan petitioned the capital for noble titles. The ravaging of Changsha had made it uninhabitable, he also noted, and sought permission to move his administrative center to Wuling. Taizu of Zhou approved both requests, elevating Langzhou¶ to the Wuping command and ranking it above Wu'an, with Yan as governor. He later named Jinkui as Wu'an governor, but Jinkui refused to assume a post inferior to Yan, having installed Yan at the outset. Tensions began to surface between the two men, Yan viewing Jinkui as a menace and each plotting against the other. A scheming Jinkui reasoned, "Yan has only two commanders of any use, He Jingzhen and Zhu Quanxiu. If I summon and murder the two, Yan himself can be taken." At the time, Liu Cheng [of Southern Han] had seized the Chu prefectures of Wu‡, Gui†, Yi‡, and Meng‡. Jinkui thus asked Yan to order Jingzhen and others to rendezvous with him in a raid against Cheng. Yan believed Jinkui sincere, deploying Jingzhen and Quanxiu; both were killed upon arrival. Jinkui's men now stormed Wuling to apprehend and kill Yan. Upon petitioning the Zhou capital, Jinkui was confirmed by Emperor Taizu as Wuping governor.

Once Emperor Shizong launched his southern Huai campaign [C.E. 956], he named Wang Jinkui general commander of at-large forces on the southern front. Jinkui passed through Yue‡ Prefecture during the assault on E, and the prefect there, Pan Shusi, having shared military ranks with Jinkui in times past, treated him with extreme deference. The attendants to Jinkui approached Shusi for bribes, which he refused, so they maligned him for assorted failings. Jinkui now scolded him in person, leaving Shusi utterly mortified as he admitted to subordinates, "I have no chance of surviving once Jinkui returns victoriously from battle." As Jinkui occupied Ezhou and undertook the ultimately successful conquest of Changshan, Shusi stormed Wuling. Jinkui returned on light boats after hearing of the action, engaging Shusi outside the walls of Wuling, where his defeat led to his murder.

Zhou Xingfeng and Son Baoquan

A native of Wuling, Zhou Xingfeng [d. C.E. 962] had served alongside Wang Jinkui as a foot soldier at the Jingjiang command and later Xi'e as lieutenant.

As Jinkui attacked Bian Hao, Xingfeng led a separate force in vanquishing Yiyang, slaughtering over two thousand troops sent by Li Jing of Southern Tang and capturing his commander, Li Jianqi. Jinkui now became governor of the Wu'an command, with Xingfeng becoming prefect of Jizhou† and manager-adjutant to Jinkui. After rifts emerged between Jinkui and Liu Yan, Xingfeng plotted the surprise slaying of Yan. Jinkui hence controlled Wuling as Xingfeng controlled Tanzhou.

In the inaugural year of Xiande [C.E. 954], the court appointed Xingfeng as the Wuqing governor and provisional prefect of Tanzhou. Some had encouraged Pan Shusi, after slaying Jinkui, to occupy Wuling, but he admitted, "I killed Jinkui merely to escape death myself. Wuling offers no benefit to me." He returned to Yuezhou‡, sending attending commander Li Jian, with a force from Wuling, to retrieve Xingfeng from Tanzhou. Xingfeng had reached Wuling when someone recommended Shusi's assignment at Tanzhou, but Xingfeng insisted, "Shusi's murder of his chief commander is a crime deserving of death. But having arranged my reception, I could not bear to kill him. To entrust him with the Wu'an command [Tanzhou], however, might imply that I had orchestrated his murder of Gentleman Wang." Shusi was summoned to serve as manager-adjutant, a slight that embittered him; he declined, claiming illness. Xingfeng now angrily exclaimed, "He obviously intends to kill me as well!" Pretending to confer the Wu'an post, Xingfeng called Shusi to the Changsha offices to receive credentials, only to kill him on the spot.

A youthful Zhou Xingfeng was born to an impoverished family of Wuling farmers. Lacking proper deportment, he often spoke with uninhibited bombast. After presiding at Wuling, he could be materially frugal and self-restrained, but impetuous in personality and given to murdering others. Whenever commanders and aides presumed upon military feats to turn arrogantly unruly, he consistently disposed of them by the strict letter of the law. Once, ten or so senior commanders conspired to mutiny: Xingfeng invited the commanders to a banquet and arranged for the stoutest of warriors, halfway into an evening of drink, to seize and behead them—instilling fear across the domain.

As for misdeeds among the common people, regardless of severity, Xingfeng killed all transgressors. This prompted his wife, Woman Yan, to admonish: "Human nature consists of good and evil. How can you indiscriminately murder them all?" And he retorted, "What should a woman know of affairs beyond the home?" Displeased, Woman Yan now stated hypothetically, "Many tenant farmers currently enjoying privilege because of you no longer bother to farm and exploit influence to abuse the people. I beg to go and observe." Upon arriving, she assumed accommodations as in former times, and on the appropriate occasion, impressed upon tenant farmers to accompany her in delivering taxes to the city, wearing a dark-colored skirt like them.

Xingfeng went to visit her and said consolingly, "I am a man of stature, to be sure. Why must my wife personally taste such bitterness?" She continued, "Do you recall your days as head of local households? When people paid their taxes behind schedule, they often suffered a horsewhipping. With the stature now yours, you should lead the masses by reflecting on the past. How can you forget your days on the farm?" Xingfeng tried to force her return home, shoving his concubines onto sedan chairs. Woman Yan ultimately had no intention of remaining with him, saying, "Too severe in enforcing laws, you have lost your sense of human instinct. As for my reasons not to remain with you, I can more easily flee death in the countryside, if someday disaster strikes." Xingfeng now slightly modified his conduct.

In the third year of Jianlong [C.E. 962], as Xingfeng took ill, he summoned commanders and aides to entrust son Baoquan to their care. He further instructed them, "I emerged from the farms to join a company of ten men, all of whom have died by execution. The only survivor is the current prefect of Hengzhou‡, Zhang Wenbiao, and failure to become manager-adjutant often leaves him disaffected. He will surely defect upon my death, and Yang Shifan should lead the suppression. If he cannot, we should form a ring around the city without fighting and revert to the northern court."

Baoquan did succeed Zhou Xingfeng upon death, the news angering Wenbiao, "Xingfeng and I rose from impoverished obscurity to win repute for military merit. How can I now face north in service to a small child?" He led his men in a mutiny that succeeded in felling Tanzhou. Baoquan requested reinforcements from the capital, while also assigning Yang Shifan to direct the Wenbiao suppression. When told that these were his ancestor's very instructions, Baoquan was moved to tears, Shifan as well. Turning to his troops, Shifan declared, "Observe your young ruler: still shy of maturity, he possesses such character!" His troops in their excitement wanted to commit themselves fully. As Shifan reached Pingjinting, Wenbiao emerged to engage him in battle and was roundly defeated. Previously, in response to Baoquan's request for reinforcements against Wenbiao, Our Emperor Taizu [of Song] sent Murong Yanzhao; before he could arrive, Wenbiao had been apprehended by Shifan. The troops of Yanzhao subsequently occupied Langzhou¶, Baoquan leading his clan for audience in the northern capital. For later events, see the "national histories."[i]

....

i. From the third year of Qianning, by the Tang calendar [C.E. 896], when Ma Yin entered Hunan, until the inaugural year of Guangshun under the Zhou [C.E. 951], a total of fifty-seven years had elapsed. See the notes under "Genealogies" for further information.

CHAPTER 67

HEREDITARY HOUSE OF WU/YUE

Qian Liu, Son Yuanguan, Yuanguan's Son Zuo, and Zuo's Younger Brother Chu

Qian Liu [C.E. 852–932] had the courtesy name Jumei. Native to Lin'an County, Hangzhou, his village once had a large tree under which he played games as a child, accompanied by other boys. Liu liked to sit on a large rock to array banners as the boys assumed squad formation, keeping such disciplined demeanor in commanding others that the other boys were all intimidated. As an adult he had no affinity for ordinary professions and no one to support him, so he took to pirating in salt.

A secretary in his county, Zhong Qi, had several sons given to drinking and gambling with Qian Liu. He once prohibited such activity by his sons, but many still insisted on stealing away to carouse with Liu. In the interim, a man steeped in the occult from Yuzhang County once observed a "kingly force" in the area of Capricorn and Big Dipper, the two constellations that preside over the Qiantang area, so he roamed about Qiantang. He predicted the kingly force to reside at Lin'an county, so physiognomy experts scoured the county's marketplaces in search of the prodigy. Qi was on friendly terms with the occultist, who said to him confidentially, "I have divined that an important man inhabits your county and a scouring of the marketplace has yielded no trace of him. Reading your face reveals signs of greatness, but not enough for the prodigy." Qi now prepared wine and invited all worthy and brave men, secretly arranging for the prognosticator to examine each and every one, none of whom proved adequate. Qian Liu happened to approach Qi's house precisely as the prognosticator passed by, meeting Qi before returning. The visitor was astounded at the sight of him, declaring, "Our man of true greatness is here!" "He is simply the Youth Qian, my next door neighbor," said a humored Qi. The occultist summoned Liu for a studied look, then turned to Qi, adding, "Your own future eminence will come from this man." He further encouraged Liu, "Your facial patterns are beyond the ordinary. You must take special care." "It was not my desire to find this man—I simply bear witness to my craft," he said as parting words to Qi, leaving on the next day. Qi now freed his sons to join Liu in travels, often overextending his resources to support them.

Qian Liu was a deft archer and lance thrower, in addition to knowing books on fortune telling. A mutiny occurred in Tang times, the second year of Qianfu [C.E. 875], by an assistant commander in western Zhe circuit, Wang Ying. In response, the district commander of the Shijian Hills, Dong Chang, enlisted local men into militia to suppress the renegade. He petitioned the court to appoint Qian Liu as deputy commander, and they stormed and defeated Ying.

The followers of Huang Chao at the time, already numbering in the thousands, raided and pillaged across the eastern Zhe region. As they approached Lin'an County, Qian Liu proposed, "Local troops are scarce while renegade numbers abound, so prevailing today by arms alone will be difficult: better to send an elite force to confront them." He and twenty well-honed infantry then set an ambush in a mountain ravine, as Chao's vanguard in a single line crossed a narrow pass on horseback. From his ambush, Liu hit the enemy commander with a crossbow, slaying him and causing chaos in Chao's army. Liu now commanded his team of specialists in trampling underfoot residuals of the vanguard, severing several hundred heads. Liu added, however, "We can do this only once. The larger group will arrive and we are simply no match!" So, he redeployed warriors to Babaili [literally, "eight hundred villages"], which is a place name. He also informed an old woman on the roadside, "If anyone later asks, indicate that 'Lin'an troops are garrisoned at Babaili.' " Chao's men arrived and heard the old woman say that, "Lin'an armies are stationed at Babaili," not recognizing Babaili as place name. They thus concluded, "Earlier, we were no match when they had only ten infantry. How can we handle a force of eight hundred villages?" So, they hurriedly withdrew their men, bypassing the county.

Once general commander Gao Pian learned that Huang Chao's men dared not assault Lin'an, he was impressed by the fortitude of defenders and invited Dong Chang and Qian Liu to Guangling. Pian eventually lost interest in suppressing the renegade Chao, leaving Chang and cohort to feel underutilized. They requested to return home and Pian petitioned the court to appoint Chang prefect of Hangzhou. In a world of tumult, Chang organized men from the surrounding counties into eight brigades, installing Liu as chief director and Cheng Ji as chief commander of the Jingjiang‡ command.

In the second year of Zhonghe [C.E. 882], after rifts surfaced between Dong Chang and the surveillance commissioner for Yuezhou, Liu Hanhong, the latter directed younger brother Hanyou and inspector-in-chief Xin Yue to quarter troops at Xiling. Qian Liu led his eight brigades eastward to cross the Zhe River, seizing undetected the enemy's bugle and puncturing their tents with swords. Pandemonium ensued in enemy camps, now set afire. Hanyou fled along with his cohort. Brother Hanhong further dispatched commanders Huang Gui and He Su, who forted their men between Zhuji and Xiaoshan counties. Qian Liu broke both armies, then engaged Hanhong, whose stunning defeat led to the murders of He Su and Xin Yue. Hanhong changed clothes and grabbed a cleaver to take into hiding. As pursuers overtook him, he presented his cleaver in professing to be a butcher, eluding death.

In the fourth year [C.E. 884], Emperor Xizong sent palace commissioner Jiao Jufan as special peace emissary to Hang and Yue prefectures, directing Dong Chang and Liu Hanhong to disband their armies. They both declined, Hangong instead dispatching commanders Zhu Bao, Han Gongmei, and Shi Jianshi to position sailors at Wanghai County. Qian Liu departed from Pingshui and Cheng Ji led well-honed fighters by night, routing Bao's armies at the Cao'e dam. They then advanced to Fengshan and won the surrender of Shi Jianshi and cohort, the successful conquest of Yuezhou ensuing. Hanhong now absconded for Taizhou‡, where the prefect apprehended him for transfer to Liu. He was beheaded at Kuaiji and his family liquidated. Liu hence petitioned for Chang to replace Hanhong, while he personally assumed residence at Hangzhou.

In the third year of Guangqi [C.E. 887], the court named Qian Liu commandant of the Left Guard and prefect of Hangzhou, Dong Chang becoming surveillance commissioner for Yuezhou. The imprisonment of Gao Pian by rebel Bi Shiduo, during the same year, had reduced the southern Huai region to bedlam: the commander at Liuhe Garrison, Xu Yue, attacked and conquered Suzhou‡; the Runzhou military attaché, Liu Hao, expelled supreme commander Zhou Bao, who fled to Changzhou, installing accounting inspector Xue Lang as supreme commander. In response, Qian Liu raided Changzhou, sending brigade commanders Cheng Ji and Du Leng. They retrieved Zhou Bao for return to Qian Liu, who arranged a reception with full military honors and accommodated Bao at Zhangting. Bao died of illness. Du Leng and cohort advanced against Runzhou, expelling Liu Hao and apprehending Xue Lang, whose heart was ripped out in sacrifice to Bao. The younger brother of Qian Liu, Qiu, was later dispatched to attack Xu Yue, who absconded for the high seas in defeat as pursuers murdered him.

Emperor Zhaozong installed Qian Liu as defense commissioner for Hangzhou. Yang Xingmi and Sun Ru were vying for control over the Huainan command [Yangzhou], at the time, as Liu battled with them in the vicinity of Su‡ and Chang prefectures. Ru was eventually killed by Xingmi, who occupied Huainan and captured Runzhou. Liu captured neighboring Su‡ and Chang prefectures. Elevating Yuezhou to the Weisheng command, the Tang court named Dong Chang governor and invested him Prince of Longxi; it elevated Hangzhou to the Wusheng command, naming Qian Liu chief commissioner of military training and Cheng Ji deputy commissioner. Ji had the courtesy name Hongji and served alongside Liu through a range of military adventures, many a strategy emanating from him. Liu gave his daughter in marriage to Ji's son, Renxiu. Liu further selected a cohort of commanders, including Du Leng, Ruan Jie, and Gu Quanwu, plus attending officers Shen Song, Pi Guangye, Lin Ding, and Luo Yin.

The court affirmed Qian Liu as the Zhenhai governor and prefect of Runzhou, in the second year of Jingfu [C.E. 893], conferring ministerial standing in the inaugural year of Qianning [C.E. 894]. Dong Chang of Yuezhou rebelled in the second year [C.E. 895]. An inherently stupid Chang proved inept at making decisions: when adjudicating litigation among the people, he would throw dice and proclaim the winner innocent. He also came to be deluded by occultists Ying Zhi and Wang Wen, as well as the woman sorcerer, Han Yu, who represented certain birds and beasts as auspicious omens. Military attaché Ni Deru further informed Chang, "There is an old legend that a bird, *Luoping*, once presided over the peril or prosperity of Yuezhou, so many among the people crafted images in its likeness for prayers. I have observed that Your Highness writes his name in the form of that image." He now pulled out an image to show an exhilarated Chang, who proclaimed himself Emperor. He adopted the dynastic name of Luoping and the reign name Shuntian. He organized soldiers into two groups, the internal army wearing yellow uniforms and the external army wearing white, attaching to their uniforms the insignia "Converting to Righteousness." Deputy commissioner Huang Jie strenuously protested such actions but succeeded only in infuriating Chang, who had someone decapitate him and bring the head to him, as Chang cursed, "This renegade betrayed me. In this age of forbearance for men of wisdom, he refused to serve as honorary duke and brought on his own death." The head was then tossed into a toilet. Chang delivered a letter to Qian Liu apprising him of events, while Liu informed the court of his apostasy.

Emperor Zhaozong formally stripped Dong Chang of official and noble ranks, investing Qian Liu as Prince of Pengcheng and commissioner of bandit suppression for eastern Zhe circuit. "Obliged to Mr. Dong for his charity to me, I cannot suddenly wage war against him," Liu declared. So he garrisoned thirty thousand troops at Ying'enmen as his attending commander Shen Pang tried to persuade Chang to undo his misdeed. Chang distributed two million strings of cash to compensate troops, apprehended occultists like Ying Zhi for transfer to the military, and then threw himself at the mercy of the court. Liu's men subsequently returned. Yet Chang would defy the court once again, instructing commanders Chen Yu and Cui Wen to quarter men at Xiangyan and Shihou. He also turned for reinforcements to [Huainan potentate] Yang Xingmi, who committed An Renyi to the relief. Qian Liu now dispatched Gu Quanwu to attack Chang, and the henchman Cui Wen was beheaded. The commanders on whom Chang relied, such as Xu Xun, Tang Jiu, and Yuan Bin—a mediocre lot who knew nothing of military affairs—were swiftly vanquished upon confronting Quanwu. A nephew of Chang, Dong Zhen, emerged as exceptionally heroic in spirit and honed in war, such that Quanyu's offensive lasted over a year without overpowering him. A history of conflict between Zhen and Ci Yu, an assistant commander, culminated in defamation against Zhen by Yu and Zhen's eventual murder by Chang, whose armies hence succumbed. Chang personally ended up a hostage of Quanwu. Approaching the Xixiao River en route to Hangzhou, Chang turned to attendants and exclaimed, "Gentleman Qian and myself rose up from the same village, and I was once his superior officer. How can I countenance meeting him face to face today?" The attendants standing before him in tears, fury now filled his eyes as he bellowed, then leaped to his death in the river.

Emperor Zhaozong named chief minister Wang Pu governor of Yuezhou, but he requested that the assignment go to Qian Liu. The Weisheng command now renamed Zhendong, Liu was installed governor of both Zhenhai and Zhendong, his titular offices advanced to honorary grand marshal and palace secretary. He was also conferred an iron writ of immunity for up to nine capital offenses. After going to Yuezhou to receive credentials, Liu returned to administer the command from Qiantang County, Yuezhou becoming the Eastern Headquarters. He shifted the Zhenhai command to Hangzhou in the inaugural year of Guanghua [C.E. 898], his honors advanced to grand preceptor. The native village and hamlet of Liu were renamed "Village of the Extensively Righteous" and "Hamlet of the Accomplished and Venerable," his former barracks renamed the "Brocade Barracks."

After the prefect of Wuzhou¶, Wang Tan, defected to surrender the prefecture to Huainan, Yang Xingmi directed commander Kang Ru to join him in an attack on Muzhou. Qian Liu dispatched younger brother Qiu, who defeated Ru at Xuanzhu; Tan fled to Xuanzhou. Emperor Zhaozong ordered the likeness of Qian Liu for the Lingyan Pavilion [for meritorious subjects], while christening the Brocade Barracks as "Brocade City," Shijian Mountain as "Brocade Mountain," and Daguan Mountain as "Mountain of the

Meritorious Subject." Liu liked entertaining old acquaintances by strolling his Brocade City. Even trees on hills were covered with brocade. And the large tree that he played under as a child was dubbed "Brocade Commander."

He was invested Prince of Yue in the second year of Tianfu [C.E. 902]. A mutiny struck when Qian Liu was away touring the Brocade City. Led by Xu Wan and Xu Zaisi, the chief directors of the Martially Valorous Right Guard and Left Guard, respectively, they sacked the city's outer wall and set it afire, then stormed the inner wall. Sealing up the city in defiance were Liu's son, Qian Chuanying, and commanders Ma Chuo and Chen Wei. Liu returned to reach the northern gate of the outer wall, unable to enter. Replacing him in battle against Wan was Cheng Ji, who severed more than a hundred renegade heads as Wan took cover at Longxing Monastery.

Qian Liu now donned plain clothes in leaping over the outer wall to enter the city, then assigned Ma Chuo, Wang Rong, Du Jianhui, and others to man each of the city gates. He further arranged for Gu Quanwu to prepare the eastern headquarters for battle, but Quanwu argued, "The eastern headquarters is of no great concern, the greater worry being Huainan armies. A hard-pressed Xu Wan will surely summon Huainan troops, whose threat is hardly inconsequential! Yang Xingmi is a grand gentleman. Were we to report an emergency today, he will surely lend assistance." Liu concurred. "If I go alone, we will certainly not pull things off," Quanwu continued. "Please select one of your sons to come along." Liu admitted to formerly considering for his son, Yuanliao, a marriage accommodation with the Yang family, so he arranged for the youth, accompanied by Quanwu, to proceed to Guangling. Xu Wan did call Tian Jun's armies to Xuanzhou, but Xingmi recalled Jun after Quanwu arrived at Guangling and Xingmi consented to marry his daughter to Yuanliao. Jun returned with a million in cash from Liu and Liu's son, Yuanguan, as hostage.

In the inaugural year of Tianyou [C.E. 904], Qian Liu was invested Prince of Wu. He personally erected a hall for "meritorious subjects" and installed a stele commemorating his own achievements. The stele's reverse side contained the names of five hundred decorated commanders and lieutenants. Brocade City was now elevated to the "Brocade Command and Pacific Kingdom" during the fourth year [C.E. 907].

Qian Liu's investiture as Prince of Wu/Yue occasioned Taizu's accession to the Liang throne, concurrent powers as governor of Huainan [Yang Wo's satrapy] conferred as well. A retainer urged him to decline the Liang mandate, but Liu accepted it, saying, "I hardly intended to commit the error of Sun Quan!" Taizu once asked the prefectural liaison for Wu/Yue in the capital about "the sorts of things Qian Liu appreciates," the aide indicating a fondness for jade sashes and rare horses. This prompted a smiling

Taizu to comment, "The markings of a genuine hero!" He therefore conferred a jade sash and ten polo horses from the royal stables. Wei Zichang of Xinzhou† sought sanctuary with Qian Liu upon Yang Wo's defeat by Wei Quanfeng of Jiangnan west. Disliking his surname, meaning "danger," Liu changed it to Yuan. During the second year of Kaiping [C.E. 908], Liu was elevated to interim palace secretary, Lin'an County renamed Anguo County, and Guangyi Village renamed "Brocade Village." Honors as interim grand guardian came in the third year.

The blockade of Suzhou‡ by Zhou Ben and Chen Zhang, commanders under Yang Wo [of Huainan], caused Qian Liu to dispatch younger brothers Ju and Piao to render assistance. Huai armies had formed a ring around the [canalled] city with wooden rods planted in the water. Then, by submerging brass chains into the water to form a net, they could preclude access by interlopers. Wu/Yue sailor Sima Fu, a man of many talents and adept at maneuvering under water, initially employed a large bamboo pole to strike against the metal net: the clanging of the chains caused Huai armies to raise their nets as Fu slipped past their sentries to enter the city. He exited the very same way, then seized the enemy bugle to summon forces for a joint attack within and without the city. The responsive chanting of warriors so reverberated that Huai soldiers believed a spirit at hand and suffered a rout. Zhou Ben and cohort managed to flee, as commanders Lü Qiuzhi and He Ming were apprehended.

During a tour of his Brocade command, in the fourth year [C.E. 910], Qian Liu composed the following "Song for a Village Homecoming":

The governor of three districts returns to his village draped in brocade,
As local elders walk at a distance to greet and accompany him home.
No starbursts from Capricorn and Big Dipper, no guile among the people,
The Prince of Wu/Yue returns astride a single horse.

In the inaugural year of Qianhua [C.E. 911], the Liang court elevated Liu to interim imperial secretary with concurrent powers as general commander of at-large forces along the four fronts at Huainan, Xuan, and Run prefectures. While still alive, a temple for him was erected at the Brocade command. Qian Piao, Liu's younger brother in residence at Huzhou, illicitly murdered garrison commander Pan Zhang and fled to Huainan for fear of retribution. Zhu Yougui the Prince of Ying, acceding to the Liang throne during the second year, formally honored Liu as "Esteemed Father." Additional honors as supreme marshal without peer for military forces empirewide were conferred by Emperor Mo during the third year of Zhenming [C.E. 917], including authority to form a local administration with official complement. Yang

Longyan claimed Qianzhou, in the fourth year; [such expansion of Wu lands] caused Liu to start using the sea route to deliver tribute to the capital. In the inaugural year of Longde [C.E. 921], a store of blank imperial edicts was provided to Liu.

Once Emperor Zhuangzong of Tang occupied Luoyang [to supplant the Liang], Qian Liu sent an envoy to offer tribute and request his own jade registers for investitures. Zhuangzong referred the request for debate among the relevant officials. Ranked officiary uniformly believed that jade registers should only be employed by the Son of Heaven, Guo Chongtao especially emphatic in opposing the request, but ultimately Zhuangzong conceded to confer jade registers and a gold seal. Liu could now confer upon son Yuanguan the governorship of Zhenhai. Proclaiming himself "King of Wu/Yue," his homes were renamed royal palaces and halls, his administrative offices renamed a "court," and his officials all called themselves "subjects." Three buildings were erected at the Brocade command to store the jade register, gold writ, and imperial rescripts. He also sent envoys to invest the kings of Silla and Bohai, as rulers of coastal kingdoms all received his investiture.

An Chonghui managed political affairs after the accession of Mingzong and was infuriated by the insulting language of Qian Liu in a letter to him. At the time, palace managers Wu Zhaoyu and Han Mei had visited Wu/Yue as envoys; upon their return to the north, Mei falsely accused Zhaoyu of gesturing like a subject in Liu's presence. Chonghui thus petitioned the court to strip Liu of honors as king, marshal, and esteemed father while retiring him as grand preceptor. Yuanguan dispatched along bypass routes a messenger with silk petition to explain Liu's position. With An Chonghui now dead, Mingzong decided to restore offices to Liu. He died in the third year of Changxing [C.E. 932] at eighty-one *sui*. Given the posthumous title Martial and August, Wusu, he was succeeded by son Yuanguan.

Qian Yuanguan [C.E. 890–944] had the courtesy name Mingbao and was a hostage of Tian Jun in youth. Jun later defected from Wu and governor Yang Xingmi joined Wu/Yue armies in retaliation. Whenever suffering defeat, Jun would return with the intent of murdering Yuanguan, only for Jun's mother to intervene, shielding the youth. Jun finally departed for battle and promised aides upon leaving, "If we are not victorious on this day, we must decapitate the Youth Qian." Jun died in battle on that very day, enabling Yuanguan to return home.

An ill and bedridden Qian Liu summoned his leading officers, conceding, "My sons are all mediocre or inept, unfit for serving later on. I leave the selection of a successor after my death to you." Teary-eyed commanders responded in unison, "Among the sons to assist Your Highness on campaign,

Yuanguan is the most accomplished, your other sons no match for him. We propose his nomination." Liu pulled out several boxes of keys and summoned Yuanguan, saying in giving them to him, "The various commanders have consented to your installation." Yuanguan thus succeeded Liu upon death, inheriting his title as King of Wu/Yue, as well as jade registers and gold seal, in accord with precedent for his father.

The Min region had been reduced to utter bedlam after Wang Yanzheng installed himself at Jianzhou. Yuanguan thus intervened by sending Yang Quan and Xue Wanzhong. They returned a year later after sustaining a rout. Yuanguan proved masterful at assuaging his commanders, while at the same time, admiring Confucian learning and composing good poetry. He arranged for Shen Song, the kingdom's counselor, to form an "Academy for the Select and Gifted" that recruited men of learning from across the Wu region. He also had a propensity for extraordinary extravagance and an affinity for building mansions. During the sixth year of Tianfu [C.E. 941], raging fires at Hangzhou gutted each and every mansion, the flames seeming to leap in Yuanguan's direction as he fled. The terror so tormented Yuanguan that he turned delirious and died the same year at fifty-five *sui*. Receiving the posthumous title of Literate and Majestic, Wenmu, his son Zuo assumed power.

Qian Zuo [C.E. 928–947], with courtesy name You, was only thirteen *sui* at the time of installation. The various commanders all slighted him in consequence, but Zuo liberally indulged them at the outset. Once the commanders started to act illegally, he banished senior commanders Zhang De'an to Mingzhou‡ and Li Wenqing to Muzhou, then assassinated director-in-chief of the inner palace Du Zhaoda and military commissioner Kan Fan—striking an intimidating image across the kingdom.

The eruption of hostilities between the Wang brothers of Min, Yanxi and Yanzheng, triggered a cycle of murder and usurpation by the likes of Zhuo Yanming, Zhu Wenjin, and Li Renda, the warfare persisting without stop for several years. Renda was once allied to Li Jing [of Southern Tang] and now defected anew, prompting Jing to retaliate with a raid and Renda to approach Qian Zuo for relief. Summoning his commanders to strategize, Zuo intuited their predisposition against action and asked indignantly, "I am supreme marshal. Why can't I deploy armies? And why should you commanders, long nurtured by my family, singularly shrink from placing your lives before me? Anyone with a position contrary to mine faces summary beheading!" Military commanders Zhang Yun and Zhao Chengtai, among others, were subsequently unleashed for a land and sea offensive involving thirty thousand men. The commanders exacted pledges of restraint from their men while issuing orders both systematic and circumspect. Yun and cohort thereby routed Jing's men, claiming in excess of ten thousand enemy heads and capturing commanders such as Yang Ye and Cai Yu. Fuzhou¶ was also captured before returning. Hereafter, the commanders all submitted to Zuo.

In power for seven years, Zuo inherited the title of King of Wu/Yue, along with jade registers and gold seal, consistent with Yuanguan. He died in the fourth year of Kaiyun [C.E. 947], at twenty *sui*, receiving the posthumous title "Loyal and Accomplished," Zhongxian. Younger brother Chu was installed.

Qian Chu [C.E. 929–988] had the courtesy name of Wende. Upon the death of Zuo, younger brother Zong succeeded by virtue of seniority. Before this, when Yuanguan was a hostage at Xuanzhou, Hu Jinsi and Dai Yun had accompanied him. Jinsi and cohort thus became leading commanders upon Yuanguan's installation. The youthfulness of Zuo and the self-assurance of Jinsi as accomplished commander had privileged him to a rare measure of deference. Jinsi grew ill at ease, however, after the installation of Zong, who treated him rather dismissively. Once preparing to review troops at Biboting, Zong was drafting a schedule of rewards when Jinsi criticized beforehand the excessiveness of his largess. An angry Zong, tossing his brush into the water jar, pronounced, "How can I be selfish in material gifts to soldiers? And why should I accept censure?" The response thoroughly startled Jinsi. A year or so later, a painter presented a "Portrait of [the legendary] Zhong Kui Assailing Demons," Zong affixing a poem as lead for the painting. The spectacle stunningly alerted Jinsi to Zong's intent to murder him and he commanded imperial guardsmen, on the same night, to depose Zong and invite Chu to assume power. Initially detained at the Yihe bureau, Zong was later relocated to the eastern headquarters. Chu proceeded to inherit the title King of Wu/Yue through the Han and Zhou dynasties, receiving jade registers and gold seal.

As Shizong campaigned against the southern Huai, he ordered Qian Chu to attack the two prefectures of Chang and Xuan, thereby drawing Li Jing into the conflict. Chu mobilized his kingdom's armed forces in anticipation of action. Reports of a massive mobilization by the Zhou induced Jing to send northward an emissary of reconciliation and impose martial law on the border. The incoming administrator at Suzhou‡, Chen Man, did not know of Jing's mission and presumed northern armies to have already overtaken all of the region's prefectures, a representative being sent [as act of submission]. He thus urgently appealed to Qian Chu to raise troops in response. Sudden instructions to organize armies for deployment were issued by Chu's counselor, Wu Cheng, even as another counselor, Yuan Dezhao, challenged the directive in Chu's presence, convinced that royal troops should not cross the Huai River. He failed to change their minds, and Cheng and cohort proceeded with a raid on Changzhou. They were defeated by Chai Kehong, a Jing commander. Cheng's assisting commander, Shao Keqian, had fought with special vigor: even as his son fell dead before his own horse, Keqian fought on without looking back. Ultimately, Cheng and his men barely escaped with their very lives. By the time Zhou troops crossed the Huai River, Chu had already augmented armies by inducting all adult males in the kingdom. He now sent Shao Keqian, with four hundred warships and seventeen thousand sailors, to Tongzhou‡ for a prearranged rendezvous.

Wu/Yue had existed independently as a kingdom since the late Tang, precisely as Yang Xingmi and Li Bian occupied the Huai and Yangzi regions. To deliver tribute from the south and receive envoys from the northern court, it accessed the sea via ports at Deng‡ and Lai prefectures [Shandong], even as envoys died by maelstroms at sea each year. The envoys sent to Wu/Yue by the northern court, in the fourth year of Xiande [C.E. 957], were the left master of admonitions, Yin Rijiu, and director of personnel Cui Song. They received instructions from Emperor Shizong, who said, "I have now decided to pacify the northern Yangzi region. Upon your return, therefore, you should take the land route." Imperial troops campaigned in the Huai region in the fifth year and overtook the Jinghai command by the inaugural month, so Rijiu and cohort did ultimately return by land. With the lower Huai region pacified, Shizong sent envoys to honor Chu with gifts of military armor, banners, camels, goats, and horses.

The Qian house dominated the Liangzhe region for nearly a hundred years, and relative to other kingdoms, its leaders were reputedly more timid and weak. Having grown accustomed to decadent consumption, they devoted their lives to the clever and the crafty. Beginning with Qian Liu's generation, it became common to tax the people heavily to finance illicit extravagance, such that tax agents would appear at homes to claim the fledglings of chicken and fish on the very day of hatching. Whenever an individual was punished with flogging for tax arrears, the bookkeepers brought account books to the yamen for examination, then called out the amount of shortfall in their book and equated it with a prescribed number of beatings, their pronouncement followed by a succession of beatings. Even for lesser amounts, the penalty might still entail several dozen floggings with the light rod, while floggings could exceed a hundred for larger amounts—hardship the people found especially unbearable. Qian royals also pilfered the precious commodities of merchants from Lingnan and the Southern Seas.

Wu/Yue provided regular and uninterrupted tribute to the Middle Kingdom throughout the Five Dynasties era. As Shizong began to pacify the southern Huai and the Song dynasty entered its ascent, as the kingdoms of Jing and Chu in succession submitted to the new mandate, Qian Chu's powers grew ever isolated such that he nearly bankrupted his own kingdom to offer tribute to the north. Chu once visited the court in the Emperor Taizu's reign, where he received profound courtesy before returning home. In his delight, Chu presented as tribute still more precious and rare objects at levels beyond calculation. "These are mere objects from my treasury, to my mind," Taizu declared. "Why bother making tribute of them?" In the third year of Taiping-Xingguo [C.E. 978], having been summoned to the court, Chu and his family reverted permanently to the capital, his empire expired. For later events, see the "national histories."

WE LAMENT. The links between Heaven and humanity can defy explanation. Since antiquity, not only have occultists been favored for the novel, but ultimately valorous men turning to insurrection have anointed themselves through prodigies and omens. Such upstarts would scarcely have succeeded in deluding the gullible masses, if not for exploiting such superstitions. The gradual accumulation of proven merit did not cause their rise, but rather activities as tattooed bandits and baldheaded smugglers, making them noblemen almost overnight. Alas, people delight in perpetuating myths about them all the same.

In scrutinizing the full history of the Qian house, [we see that] it acquired a corner of the world through no great virtue, for it was gravely repressive through a century of rule. Instead, it exploited celestial phenomena in an utterly abominable fashion! An entire continent, fragmented at the time, faced unspeakable violence, yet everyone acquiesced in such fraud, as if no opening existed to apply reason. The predictions of occultists often miss the mark and are rarely on target. Why do men so relish in citing the few accurate hits?[i]

....

i. As for the rise and fall of the Qian house, all writings are consistent: beginning with the second year of Qianning, by the Tang calendar [C.E. 895], when conferred the Zhenhai and Zhendong governorships to control the Liangzhe region, and ending with the third year of Taiping-Xingguo, under our own dynasty [C.E. 978], a total of eighty-four years had elapsed.

CHAPTER 68

HEREDITARY HOUSE OF MIN

Wang Shenzhi, Sons Yanhan and Lin, and Lin's Sons Jipeng, Yanxi, and Yanzheng

Wang Shenzhi [C.E. 862–925] had the courtesy name Xintong and was native to Gushi County, Guangzhou [Huainan circuit]. His father, Wang Ren, came from generations of farmers and elder brother *Wang Chao* [d. C.E. 897] a county scribe.

As bandit bands emerged in the waning Tang dynasty, Wang Xu of Shouzhou overran Gushi, where he learned of the chivalry of Wang Chao and his younger brothers. Inviting them into his army, he named Chao lieutenant. Qin Zongquan of Caizhou was in the throes of enlisting men to expand his military, at the time, and installed Xu as prefect of Guangzhou, drawing upon his armies for a joint sortie against rebel Huang Chao. Xu dallied without advancing, and Zongquan retaliated militarily, forcing Xu to flee south with his men, plundering at every turn. He felled Zhangpu [Zhangzhou] in the approach from Nankang to Linting, amassing a following of several tens of thousands. Yet his suspicious character caused many talented commanders in his divisions to be slain in assorted incidents, actions that rather intimidated Wang Chao. As the military advanced to Nan'an, Chao turned to the commander of his vanguard, saying, "It was under coercion from Xu that we left our wives and sons and abandoned the ancestral tombs to become bandits—we hardly acted of our own volition! He has now turned tempestuous and suspicious such that any officer or aide of ability faces certain death. From morning to night, we go without any sense of security. How can we possibly manage to contribute meaningfully to his cause?" A sudden awakening overcame the vanguard as he tearfully embraced Chao. He now selected several dozen stalwart warriors to lay in ambush in a bamboo thicket to monitor Xu's approach, then scurry forth to seize him. Confined to a military compound, Xu later committed suicide.

Upon deposing Wang Xu, the vanguard supported the elevation of Wang Chao as leader, acknowledging, "I am alive through his virtue." The prefect of Quanzhou at the time, Liao Yanruo, had wrought hardship on its people through corrupt and abusive practices. As elders there learned of Chao's military operations in the area and the orderly discipline of his men, they intercepted him on the highway in hopes of retaining him. Chao now commanded men in surrounding Yanruo, overpowering him a year later.

In the second year of Guangqi [C.E. 886], Wang Chao was nominated prefect of Quanzhou by Chen Yan, the surveillance commissioner for Fujian. Yan died in the inaugural year of Jingfu [C.E. 892], whereupon son-in-law Fan Hui installed himself as interim regent. Chao sent brother Shenzhi to attack Hui. Unable to prevail after a long time and facing staggering injuries and deaths within his ranks, Shenzhi begged to retreat. Chao denied permission, so Shenzhi invited him personally to appear before soldiers while augmenting troop levels. "We have fully exhausted our soldiers and commanders, so I can only go myself," Chao responded. Shenzhi hence supervised armies in person and successfully overpowered Hui's army, killing him. The Tang court now named Chao surveillance commissioner for Fujian and selected Shenzhi as deputy.

Possessing an heroically imposing physical demeanor, Wang Shenzhi had a prominent nose and square mouth. He often rode a white horse, so the military dubbed him, "Third Gentleman on a White Horse." He replaced Wang Chao as commissioner upon his death in the fourth year of Qianning [C.E. 897]. The court renamed Fuzhou¶ the Weiwu command and appointed Shenzhi its governor, conferring honors culminating in ministerial standing and investiture as Prince of Langye. After overturning Tang rule, Emperor Taizu of Liang honored Shenzhi as palace secretary, invested him as Prince of Min, and elevated Fuzhou¶ to grand protectorate. With the Huai and Yangzi River regions currently controlled by Yang Xingmi, Shenzhi employed the sea route to exchange envoys and tender tribute each year to the Liang, approaching via the [Shandong] prefectures of Deng‡ and Lai. The conduct of such missions by sea, however, often claimed three or four lives out of ten by drowning.

Although he started as a brigand, Wang Shenzhi was a man of frugal ways and prone to treat underlings with courtesy. Entering public service under him, therefore, were men like Wang Dan, son of the Tang minister Wang Pu; Yang Yi, the younger brother of minister Yang She; and Xu Yin, the celebrated doctorate of the dynasty. Shenzhi also established schools of the "Four Gates" to educate the refined men indigenous to Min.[1] He even lured barbarians from coastal countries to conduct trade. The coastal site of Huangqi, formerly obstructed by billowing waves, was suddenly opened as a port after a night of blistering rains, thunder, and lightning. Considered as a sign of Shenzhi's virtuous governance, it came to be dubbed "Port of the Sweet Pear" by the people of Min. He died in the third year of Tongguang [C.E. 925], at sixty-four *sui,* and received the posthumous title "Loyal and Moral," Zhongyi, his son Yanhan securing the succession.

Wang Yanhan [d. C.E. 926], courtesy-named Ziyi, was Shenzhi's eldest son. The Later Tang court confirmed him as governor in the fourth year of Tongguang [C.E. 926], the same year that Zhuangzong fell to regicide and the Middle Kingdom faced innumerable problems. Yanhan showed his officers and their aides the biography of Wuzhu, the King of Min and Yue in Sima Qian's *Historical Records,* then queried, "Min has held kingdom status since ancient times, but I am not king. What is the justification for waiting?" Officers and aides at the command promptly urged his elevation through petitions. Yanhan inaugurated a kingdom with him as King, in the tenth month, still acknowledging the calendar of Later Tang.

A tall and rugged man, Yanhan possessed features as fine as jade, while his vulgar and lewd wife, Woman Cui, proved uncontrollable. Formal mourning for Shenzhi was yet incomplete when Yanhan cast aside the food table of mourners, taking numerous women from upstanding families as concubines. An instinctively jealous Woman Cui would isolate those pedigreed beauties in a back room, bind them in heavy chains, beat their cheeks with a wooden stick shaped like a human hand, then stab them to death with a metal awl. Eighty-four women died in a single year in that way. Woman Cui later took ill herself, and observers attributed her death to possession by an evil spirit.

The adopted son of Shenzhi, the Jianzhou prefect Yanbing, was originally surnamed Zhou. Yanbing had strained relations with Yanhan, since the days of Shenzhi, however. Yanhan inherited power and assigned younger brother Yanjun as prefect of Quanzhou, an assignment inciting Yanjun as well. He now joined Yanbing in infiltrating the palace with armed forces, during the twelfth month, to apprehend and slay Yanhan. Succeeding him was Yanjun, who changed his personal name to Lin.

Wang Lin [Yanjun, r. C.E. 927–936] was the next surviving son of Shenzhi. The Later Tang court confirmed him as governor, extending honors culminating in honorary grand preceptor and palace secretary, and investiture as King of Min.

Previously conspiring with Lin to assassinate Yanhan [C.E. 926], Yanbin came to seize and murder Yanhan a full day before Lin's men arrived. Yanbin nonetheless supported Lin's succession owing to his own lesser standing as adopted son. During a suburban banquet for Yanbin preceding his return to Jianzhou, he delivered as parting words to Lin, "You should ably preserve your ancestor's legacy and not trouble Elder Brother to come again!" The comments caused Lin to hold umbrage. In the second year of Changxing [C.E. 931], Yanbin led armies in a sally against Lin: he attacked the city's western gates and deployed son Wang Jixiong to raid the southern gate from the sea. Lin ordered Wang Renda to repulse them. Concealing armored men in a ship, Renda guilefully hoisted a white flag, as if to surrender. Jixiong considered him genuine and boarded the ship, as Renda's concealed men rallied to stab him to death. The spectacle of his head hanging from the western gate caused his men to scatter. With Yanbin also apprehended, Lin said scoffingly to him, "Alas, I ultimately could not preserve our ancestor's legacy and needed to trouble Elder Brother to come again!" Speechless, Yanbin was slain. His son Jisheng, then defending Jianzhou, fled to Qiantang [Wu/Yue] after learning of the upset.

In the third year of Changxing [C.E. 932], Wang Lin wrote to the court, "The now deceased Ma Yin (King of Chu) and Qian Liu (King of Wu/Yue) both formerly received honors as imperial secretary. Your Subject requests honors as secretary." The Tang court failed to respond, and Lin suspended tribute. He held a curiosity for ghosts and spirits as well as Daoist beliefs. The Daoist adept Chen Shouyuan exploited his heretical proclivities to win Lin's trust, Lin erecting a temple to the "Precious Emperor" for him to live in. Shouyuan once told him, "The Precious Emperor orders Your Highness to forfeit his position in youth. In this way, you can later rule as Son of Heaven for six full decades." Lin gladly relinquished power and instructed son Jipeng to assume temporary governance. Once restored to power, Lin enlisted Shouyuan to inquire of the Precious Emperor, "Where will I go after sixty years?" "You should become the Immortal of the Heavens," the Precious Emperor responded, according to Shouyuan.[2]

Lin now acceded the throne as Emperor, the ceremonies conducted at the temple to the Precious Emperor. He adopted the dynastic name of Min and the reign name of Longqi [Dragon's Inaugural], as a yellow dragon had appeared at his residence at Zhenfeng. The posthumous title of the Luminous, Martial, and Filial Emperor was conferred on Wang Shenzhi, who received the temple name Taizu. Five ancestral temples were erected, a civil service established, and Fuzhou¶ renamed Changle, "Forever Happy" district. Min lands being secluded and revenues perennially inadequate, Xue Wenjie, the commissioner of palace armies, was named fiscal commissioner. He often probed the secret dealings of the people, the misdeeds of the wealthy causing their properties to be confiscated as subsidy for the state. The people of Min all loathed him in consequence. Wenjie even recommended the sorcerer Xu Yan, insisting that, "Many of Your Majesty's closest aides are sinister men. Bedlam will come if you fail to consult the ghosts and spirits." Lin thereby enlisted Yan to identify ghosts within the palace.

Xue Wenjie had a history of conflict with Wu Ying [Wu Xu], the palace's military commissioner. Upon news of Ying's illness, Wenjie told him, "His Majesty entrusts to you positions involving special trust and intimacy. Excusing yourself repeatedly for illness will cause him to dismiss you." Ying asked for clarification and Wenjie advised, "The next time His Majesty's messengers inquire of your illness, simply say, 'I have merely a headache, no other malady.' " Ying agreed. On the next day, Wenjie prodded Lin to arrange for a sorcerer to evaluate Ying's illness. The sorcerer told Lin, "Entering the northern temple, I witnessed the Prince of Chongshun[3] strike Ying's head with a golden cudgel, asking, 'How dare you conspire to rebel?' " Lin conveyed the words to Wenjie, who added, "This is insufficient proof of sedition. You should rather ask Ying personally about his illness." Lin sent a messenger to inquire and Ying admitted to an "aching head." Lin now believed the sorcerer's premonition and imprisoned Ying, directing Wenjie to vet the investigation. Ying fell into a trap of slanders to end up murdered. News of his death riled the military, as Ying was once chief overseer of Min armies and commanded their loyalties.

In the same year, armies from Wu attacked Jianzhou and Wang Lin charged commander Wang Yanzong with the relief effort. Troops took to the highways but refused to advance, insisting, "We must obtain [Ying's murderer] Wenjie before proceeding." Lin was reticent to relinquish him, until son Jipeng intervened with pleas to overcome the current impasse by doing so. Wenjie was now delivered to the military on a flat cart for prisoners. Skilled at numerology, Wenjie had divined his own augury, "In three days, you will be safe from peril." His military escort learned of the prediction and scurried to arrive within two days, the troops deliriously leaping as they dismembered Wenjie at the marketplace. And the people of Min vied to toss ceramic tiles at his corpse, then devoured the entire body in short order. A pardon arrived a day later, delivered by messenger from Lin, but too late. Previously, the prisoner's cart had been constructed at Wenjie's behest, who insisted to Lin that the ancient style was archaic and should be altered: an opening now extended from top to bottom, and at the center were iron spikes that curled inward like hooks, digging into the victim at the slightest movement. Once the cart was complete, Wenjie was first to suffer from it.

In the third year of Longqi [C.E. 935], the reign was changed to Yonghe. Wang Renda had assisted Lin to assassinate Yanbin, his merit leading to posting as manager of the Imperial Bodyguard. Lin harbored suspicions toward him, all the same, and once inquired of Renda, "The legend that Zhao Gao 'pointed to a deer and called it a horse' to befuddle the Second Emperor—did it actually happen?" He responded, "Gao could represent a deer as a horse because the Second Emperor of Qin was himself muddled. It is not that he could make the Emperor muddleheaded. Today, Your Majesty is intelligent and his courtiers number fewer than a hundred. Their daily movements and activities are all known to Your Majesty, so anyone daring to presume upon your august powers can simply be liquidated." Embarrassed by his former suspicions, Lin reassured Renda with gifts of gold and silk. He told others once Renda withdrew, "The deft strategies of Renda should be exploited during my own reign to prevent peril from visiting later generations." In the end, slanders caused him to fall from grace and die.

The formal wife of Wang Lin died early on. Her successor, the Woman Jin, proved worthy yet received no recognition from Lin. Shenzhi had a female slave known as Jinfeng and surnamed Chen, a woman later favored by Lin and installed as empress. Originally, Lin was partial to aide Gui Shouming because of his physical appeal, dubbing him the "Youth Gui." During Lin's subsequent incapacity with pneumonia, Youth Gui and Woman Chen had illicit relations, and he even facilitated Woman Chen's fornication with Li Keyin, the master of imperial crafts. Thus, when Lin commissioned brocade craftsmen to produce a curtain with nine dragons, his subjects chanted a song, "To what does the 'nine-dragons curtain' refer—Youth Gui's hiding place!"

Wang Lin owned a female slave of considerable beauty, Chunyan. His son Jipeng had improper relations with her. Lin was ill when Jipeng sought permission to marry her, based on precedent for Empress Chen [Lin's one-time slave]. He consented, albeit with consternation. Younger son Jitao became angry at Jipeng and conspired to murder him. Jipeng now nervously conspired with Li Fang, commissioner of the imperial city. In the tenth month of the same year, as Lin banqueted troops at Dapu Hall, he sat in a stupor and reported seeing [the deceased] Yanbin approach him. Fang thereby realized the severity of his illness and deployed stalwart soldiers first to Li Keyin's home to kill him. Lin arrived at morning audience a day later, seemingly free of sickness, and asked Fang about the cause for Keyin's murder. Fang left in terror to meet Jipeng, then led imperial city guards into the palace. Lin ran to hide behind the curtain with nine dragons upon hearing the clamor. The guardsmen stabbed him short of death, leaving palace women to finish the deed, as they could not bear his anguish. Further perishing at Fang's hands were Jitao, Empress Chen, and Youth Gui. Lin was assassinated after ten years in power. He was posthumously entitled the Charitable Emperor, Hui, his temple name Taizong.

Wang Jipeng [Chang, r. C.E. 935–939] was Lin's eldest son. He changed his personal name to Chang and reign to Tongwen, upon accession. Li Fang became administrator over the Six imperial guards.

Having committed the crime of regicide against his ruler, Li Fang often felt precarious in the wake of Chang's installation and cultivated a cohort of diehard warriors in anticipation of the unforeseen. This presented a threat to Chang, who arranged for armored men to lie in ambush during a large banquet for troops and apprehend Fang, killing him and hanging his head at the marketplace. A thousand men in Fang's personal regiments later mutinied, setting the Qisheng gate afire and reclaiming his head before absconding for Qiantang [the Wu/Yue kingdom].

In the second year of Tianfu [C.E. 937], by the Jin calendar, Wang Chang sent envoys to present tribute in the northern capital. Gaozu reciprocated by deputizing Lu Sun, his cavalier for palace remonstrance, to invest Chang as Prince of Min and his [younger brother] Jigong, as Prince of Linhai. On the pretext of illness, Chang declined to meet Sun upon arrival in Min, ordering Jigong to preside over events. He also directed drafting official Liu Yi to pay respects to Sun at his guesthouse. Yi looked magnificent in his official garb, an abundance of child servants attending him. On another day on the highway, Sun saw Yi in simple commoner's clothes and straw sandals and had someone revile him, saying, "How has the drafting official of Phoenix Pavilion succumbed to such dire conditions?" Thoroughly embarrassed, Yi absconded with face covered by his hands. Chang learned of Sun's callous humiliation of Yi and, in anger, refused to address him upon his return to court.

An aide of Wang Chang's brother Jigong, Zheng Yuanbi, was sent to escort Lu Sun back to the northern capital to present local products as tribute. A letter conveyed to high officials of the Jin expressed Chang's wish, in future exchanges, to adopt the peer protocol accorded rival states. The request offended Gaozu as a sign of irreverence, so he issued an edict denouncing Chang's crimes and refusing his tribute items, which were to be returned. Assisting minister of war Li Zhisun memorialized the court seeking the confiscation of Min tribute and incarceration of its envoy. Once confined to prison and confronted with its contraptions of torture, Yuanbi fell prostrate on the ground and declared in desperation, "Chang is ruler of a barbarian land, a man ignorant of rites and propriety. Precisely as Your Majesty evinces profound trust before this man from afar, Your Subject carries instructions involving indecencies. I therefore willingly submit to the guillotine as atonement for Chang's crimes." Gaozu subsequently pardoned him to return home.

Like predecessors, Wang Chang favored the occult, honoring the Daoist adept Tan Zixiao as the "Orthodox Gentleman" and Chen Shouyuan as the "Celestial Teacher." The perverse Lin Xing acquired favor through command of the occult, needing only to invoke the name of the Precious Emperor to act upon all matters, great and small. On instructions from Shouyuan, Chang erected the Paradise of Immortals Pavilion, a three-story structure containing statues of [Daoist icons] the Precious Emperor, Primal Deity, and Supreme Sovereign.[4] The statues cost several thousand catties in gold. Burned daily were several catties of incense such as *longnao* and *xunlu*. And beneath the pavilion, Chang and his friends made music without stop from day to night, justifying this as part of their pursuit of an elixir for the "grand return" to immortality.

A rainbow appeared in the royal palace, during the summer of the third year [C.E. 938]. "This is an omen of impending mutiny by the imperial clan," so said the spirits as conveyed by Lin Xing. Chang now directed him to lead a band of stalwart soldiers in assassinating the sons of Shenzhi, Yanwu and Yanwang, along with their five sons. And when the scheme backfired, Xing himself was murdered. By now, Chang grew even more drawn down the path to turmoil, installing the slave of his father, Chunyan, as Pure Consort and later Empress. He also authorized a doctor, Chen Jiu, to sell official posts, providing a store of blank documents without names.

Wang Jiyan, Chang's younger brother, was administrator of the Six Armies before suspicions prompted Chang to replace him with youngest brother Jiyong. Chang entrusted his personal security to a special palace brigade composed of exceptionally courageous recruits, largess for which far exceeded the other armies. The practice provoked the ire of soldiers under Lian Chongyu, chief commander of the Crane-Commanding Guard, and Zhu Wenjin of the Palace-Saluting Guard. That summer, prognosticators warned Chang of a catastrophe striking the main palace, so he relocated to the southern palace to elude the menace. When fires did erupt within the palace, Chang suspected Chongyu's men of setting the fire. Eunuch academician Chen Tan, who held the confidences of Chang through sycophancy, was informed by him of suspicions about the fire, and he turned around to inform Chongyu. A nervous Chongyu led guardsmen by night in setting afire the southern palace, forcing Chang to join beloved concubines, children, and eunuch guardsmen in smashing the locks on the city gates to flee, camping in the wilds.

Lian Chongyu invited Yanxi to assume power, and he in turn directed his own son Jiye to lead a sortie against Chang.[5] After catching up with Chang's entourage, several were hit with arrows and killed. Chang now realized peril as inescapable and tossed his bow to the ground, Jiye seizing and slaying him. Wife and sons all perished as well, leaving no survivors. Chang received the posthumous title of Kangzong upon Yanxi's installation.

Wang Yanxi [Xi, r. C.E. 939–944], Shenzhi's youngest son, changed his personal name to Xi after installation. He sent envoys to offer tribute to the Jin, adopted the reign name Yonglong [C.E. 939], and minted large iron coins, exchanging one of the new for ten of the old.

An overbearing Wang Xi had been obstinate and uncontrollable since the days of Wang Chang, although the counselor under Chang, Wang Tan, made some progress such that Xi dared not act on impulse for fear of him. An emissary from Silla once presented a decorative sword to Chang; he showed it to Tan, asking, "What am I to do with this sword?" "Decapitate the disloyal and unfilial," Tan responded. Xi's face changed color as he stood nearby. Another sword from Silla envoys was presented to Xi after inheriting powers, reminding him of Tan's former words. Now already dead, Tan's body was exhumed from the grave: his face seemed lifelike and body covered in blood.

Quanzhou prefect Yu Tingying once forged directives in Wang Xi's name to abduct young women from upstanding families, causing an incensed Xi to vet a formal investigation at the Censorate. Tingying now presented ten million strings of cash to subsidize palace banquets, as Xi pressed further, "What about local tribute for the Empress?" After presenting another ten million strings to her, Tingying escaped prosecution. Upon the marriage of Wang Xi's daughter, courtiers who did not tender gifts of felicitation were to be flogged with light rod. Deputy censor Liu Zan now faced an imminent flogging for failing thoroughly to prosecute such cases, prompting a strident rebuke from Zheng Yuanbi, the master of admonitions. Xi fired back to him, "How dare you censure me with the stridency of the Gentleman Wei!" Yuanbi countered, "When Your Majesty assumes the traits of the Tang Emperor Taizong, I will gladly be your Wei Zheng!"[6] The response humored Xi, who released Zan without flogging.

From the outset of his installation, Wang Xi had strained relations with younger brother Yanzheng, the governor of Jianzhou with noble standing as Prince of Fusha. The two repeatedly raised armies against the other, as Xi developed contempt for the imperial clan and executed many clansmen for assorted reasons. Master of admonitions Huang Jun was vehement in remonstrance against Xi, going to audience chambers with a coffin carried behind him. A furious Xi banished him to fiscal adjutant for Zhangzhou. Imperial diarist Chen Guangyi wrote him a letter enumerating his more than fifty "excesses," and Xi directed an imperial guardsman to administer a hundred lashes of the horsewhip. Guangyi still did not die, so he was suspended from a wooden beam with rope around his neck: a long time still elapsed before death.

The commissioner of revenues collection, Chen Kuangfan, once presented new regulations to increase tax assessments on merchants. "Kuangfan is a gem among men," Xi said in his praise. Later, annual receipts failed to reach estimated levels, causing Kuangfan to meet the shortfall by borrowing from the people and creating such emotional stress as to kill him. After learning of such loans from the people, Xi had his corpse exhumed and dismembered before tossing it into the water.

Xi was debauched and sadistic by nature, while Woman Li proved a ruthless wife and raging alcoholic. The Worthy Consort Shang was favored for physical appeal, and nephew Li Renyu won favor similarly for his attractiveness, rising to counselor. Xi often drank like an ox. When entertaining officials with wine, those with a low tolerance might complain or furtively dispose of the wine, causing Xi to murder them on the spot. When son Jirou threw out his wine, Xi had him killed along with his herald.

Lian Chongyu had long feared reprisals from others in the empire for having slain Wang Chang. To secure himself, he arranged a marriage with the family of Zhu Wenjin. Xi nonetheless harbored suspicions toward him, often speaking derisively of Chongyu and cohort, as they in tearful desperation tried to defend themselves. Meanwhile, Woman Li remained jealous of Xi's favor for Consort Shang and wished to scheme against him to secure the succession of her own son, Yacheng. She thus conveyed a message to Chongyu and cohort: "His Majesty's heart is perturbed by the two of you. What can be done?" Her words haunted Chongyu and ally [Zhu Wenjin]. In the third month of the sixth year [C.E. 944], as Xi returned drunk after out-of-town travels, stalwart soldiers unleashed by Chongyu threw him from his horse to murder him. His posthumous title was Jingzong.

Wang Yanzheng [r. C.E. 943–946] was the son of Shenzhi. Wang Xi's debauched depravity after his own accession incited Yanzheng to write in repeated remonstrance. An embittered Xi dispatched Du Jianchong to assume oversight over his armies. Yanzheng expelled Jianchong and Xi retaliated by raising armies against him, only to lose. Yanzheng established a kingdom at Jian Prefecture called Yin and adopted the reign name Tiande [C.E. 943].

In the next year [C.E. 944], Lian Chongyu gathered the Min kingdom's official rank and file, in the wake of assassinating Wang Xi, informing them, "Formerly, the Martial Emperor Taizu [Wang Shenzhi] personally withstood the arrows and catapults of war to inaugurate Min rule, but his sons and grandsons are debauched and depraved beyond all description. Heaven now repudiates the Wang house, whose common people and capable men should join in elevating a man of virtue to calm their land." Courtiers in attendance dared not respond, whereupon Chongyu thrust Zhu Wenjin up the chamber platform as he led ranked officiary in facing north, affirming fealty as subjects of Wenjin. Chongyu was subsequently appointed administrator of the Six Armies, while all sons and brothers of Wang royals at Fuzhou¶ were liquidated, young and old alike. Huang Shaopo received the command at Quanzhou, Cheng Yun received the command at Zhangzhou, and Xu Wenzhen the command at Tingzhou. In recognition of the Jin calendar, the reign reverted to the inaugural year of Kaiyun.

A commander at Quanzhou, Liu Congxiao, created a ruse for the prefecture's soldiers, arguing, "Alas, armies of the Prince of Fusha have claimed Fuzhou¶. We were subjects of the Wang house for generations. How can we simply cross our arms in service to a renegade?" Local men now banded together to assassinate Huang Shaopo, inviting Wang Jixun to become prefect. Once news of the incident reached Zhangzhou, they similarly murdered Cheng Yun and invited Wang Jicheng to become prefect—both Wang men were scions of the royal house. Now nervous, Xu Wenzhen decided to surrender Tingzhou to Wang Yanzheng. With three prefectures now in Yanzheng's hands, Lian Chongyu murdered Zhu Wenjin and forwarded his head to Jianzhou, symbolizing his conversion to Yanzheng. He was killed, however, by Lin Renhan, an assistant commander at Fuzhou¶, who planned to invite Yanzheng to govern the prefecture.

Reports of such tumult in Min caused Li Jing of the Southern Tang to issue armies for an offensive. Wang Yanzheng responded by dispatching nephew Jichang to defend Fuzhou¶. In the midst of an intense pummeling of Yanzheng by Tang armies, Fuzhou¶ commander Li Renda warned underlings, "The Prince of Fusha cannot even preserve his position at Jianzhou, now under Tang assault. How can he possibly secure this site?" He promptly apprehended Jichang to slay him. Renda initially wished to install himself. Worried that his warriors might not coalesce, a monk from Xuefeng Monastery, Zhuo Yanming, was presented to them to pronounce, "This is no ordinary man!" Renda now thrust imperial robes upon Yanming, leading commanders and aides in facing north and declaring themselves his subjects. He later murdered Yanming and installed himself. Renda also made peace overtures to Li Jing, who in turn confirmed him as governor of the Weiwu command [Fuzhou¶] with the new personal name of Hongyi. The armies of Li Jing now felled Jianzhou. Yanzheng and his family were relocated to Jinling, and he was invested Prince of Poyang. This was the fourth year of Baoda, by Jing's calendar [C.E. 946].

Liu Congxiao responded to news of Yanzheng's surrender to Tang by seizing Wang Jixun for transfer to Jinling. He was rewarded by the Tang with the governorship of Quanzhou, now renamed the Qingyuan command. Li Jing sent a messenger to summon Li Renda to Jinling, in the wake of Yanzheng's rout, but he refused and subsequently surrendered to Wu/Yue. Meanwhile, Congxiao occupied the two prefectures of Quan and Zhang, having expelled Jing's defending armies; Jing now invested Congxiao as Prince of Jinjiang. During the reign of Shizong of Zhou, Congxiao sent military attaché Cai Zhongxing to the capital, along side-roads and in the guise of a merchant, to confirm a place of residence for him as subject of the Zhou dynasty. The border between the empires of Shizong and Jing had been only recently redrawn along the Yangzi River, so the envoy was turned away. Congxiao consequently assumed vassal relations with the Southern Tang. For later events, see the "national histories."[i]

i. The third year of Kaiyun, by the Jin calendar, is the fourth year of Baoda by the Southern Tang calendar [C.E. 946] as well as the *bingwu* year [in the cycle of sixty stems]. The armies of Li Jing overran Jianzhou during that year and overturned the Wang house. A misrepresentation in *Jiangnan lu* states, "In the third year of Baoda, the Wang clan was taken captive and relocated to Jinling." Wang Chao actually entered Fuzhou¶ in the inaugural year of Jingfu by the Tang calendar [C.E. 892], whereupon he became surveillance commissioner. Later chroniclers, however, based on a prophecy that he "rode in on the year of the horse and left on the year of the horse," implying a total of sixty-one years from the beginning of Jing's tenure as prefect of Quanzhou, in the second year of Guangqi [C.E. 886], until the fourth year of Baoda when the regime was overturned—both *bingwu* years [of the horse]. The inaugural year of Jingfu should actually be considered the beginning of Min rule over the area, in which case only fifty-five years elapsed. When writers today cite *bingwu* as the year that his empire was overturned, they are correct. The error with reference to the regime's inauguration has its origins in books on omens [which attach symbolism to matching years]. Moreover, the *Jiangnan lu* is short by one year.

CHAPTER 69

HEREDITARY HOUSE OF NANPING

Gao Jixing, Son Conghui, Conghui's Sons Baorong and Baoxu, and Baorong's Son Jichong

A native of Xiashi, Shanzhou, *Gao Jixing* [C.E. 858–928] had the courtesy name Yisun. He later changed his original name, Jichang, to Jixing to avoid the taboo name for the Xianzu Emperor [Li Guochang] of Later Tang. As a boy, Jixing was a servant at the home of Li Rang, a man of means at Bianzhou. Rang later offered largess to gain the goodwill of the future Taizu of Liang, early in his governorship of the Xuanwu command [Bianzhou]. Taizu eventually adopted Rang as son and changed his name to Zhu Yourang. Through Yourang, Jixing gained access to Taizu, who considered him a rare talent and directed Yourang to raise him as son. Jixing assumed the Zhu surname in this way, as well as direction of the Victory-Commanding Guard, and eventually direction of the Gallantly Valorous Guard.

The Prince of Liang's armies attacked Fengxiang in the second year of Tianfu [C.E. 902]. With Li Maozhen fortifying the walls and refusing to emerge from the city, Taizu of Liang now weighed the possibility of regrouping armies for return to the Hezhong command. Jixing singularly argued to the contrary, "For a full year, brave men across the world have anticipated this offensive. The soldiers of Qi‡ [Fengxiang] are now exhausted and within mere days of ruin. Our great Prince worries about fatigue to our men caused by this city's resilient resistance, but we can lure them out." Finding such words imposing, Taizu directed Jixing to recruit warriors of special valor. He identified the horseman Ma

Jing and set strategy with him before they went to meet Taizu. "This operation contains no design for return. I trust that office will be given to the heirs of participants," Jing told him. Out of compassion, Taizu initially suspended the plan, only to approve after Jing's adamant insistence. Jing led several horsemen in a rush toward the city walls, knocking at the gates and stating, "Liang armies will soon depart for the east, its vanguard having already departed." Qi‡ troops believed them and opened the gates for pursuit, as Liang warriors advanced from Jing's rear to murder more than nine thousand of the enemy. Jing perished with honor. Maozhen later struck a peace with the Prince of Liang as Emperor Zhaozong of Tang departed for Fengxiang. Jing received posthumous office and the title "Loyal and Determined." Jixing consequently acquired fame, becoming prefect of Songzhou a year later [C.E. 903]. After vanquishing Qing‡ Prefecture, he became defense commissioner for Ying¤ and reverted to the Gao surname.

In these, the waning year of the Tang dynasty, Zhao Kuangning of Xiangzhou rushed and routed Lei Yangong at Jingnan, installing as interim regent his own younger brother Kuangming. Xiangzhou came under the successful assault of Liang armies, forcing Kuangning to abscond for Wu and Kuangming to Shu. Jixing thereby won appointment as interim regent for surveillance under the Jingnan governor. Promotion to governor occurred in the inaugural year of Kaiping [C.E. 907], ministerial standing conferred in the second year [C.E. 908]. The ten prefectures constituting the Jingnan command, by the late Tang, had all been encroached upon by neighboring circuits, so only the city of Jiangling existed when Jixing first arrived, its communities desecrated under the fires of war. Jixing hence rallied to restore order to the region, giving soldiers and civilians reason to return. Men like Ni Kefu and Bao Tang served under him as commanders, while Liang Zhen, Sikong Xun, and Wang Baoyi became his military retainers.

Jixing observed the Liang daily wasting away after Taizu's passing and schemed to entrench himself through military intervention. Once dry ditches and observation towers along city walls were in place, he advanced against Gui and Xia‡ prefectures; the Shu commander Wang Zongshou defeated him. He now issued armies on the pretext of assisting the Liang against the Prince of Jin: his men raided Xiangzhou, but were vanquished by Kong Jing. Jixing hereafter suspended tributary taxes to the north for several years. Emperor Mo of Liang liberally indulged Jixing, investing him as Prince of Bohai and conferring royal attire and scabbard for his sword. Jixing revived tribute payments during the third year of Zhenming [C.E. 917].

With the Liang demise and the Tang occupation of Luoyang, Emperor Zhuangzong issued an edict of rapprochement to Gao Jixing. Sikong Xun and others urged him to enter the capital for audience, but Liang Zhen countered,

"The Liang and Tang have feuded for generations, conducting bloody battles from opposite sides of the Yellow River through two decades. Only recently did the monarch, Zhuangzong, annihilate the Liang, while the Great Prince is a former Liang subject with a powerful army and an important district. To enter the capital is to walk into jail." Jixing chose not to heed him, leaving behind two sons and personally appearing in Luoyang with a bodyguard of three hundred horsemen. Zhuangzong wished to detain him, although Guo Chongtao admonished, "Our recent conquest of the Liang and inheritance of the world came by demonstrating to others an abiding trust. Today overlords of the world's four corners offer tribute in succession, yet their representatives are merely sons, brothers, or commanders and their aides. The overlord Jixing, however, appears in person at court: he rightfully deserves a reception of exceptional charity and decorum as incentive for others to come forward. For you conversely to shackle him would only signal to the world a lack of munificence, thwarting the inclination of the four corners to submit." Zhuangzong now desisted, lavishing courtesies on Jixing before sending him off.

Zhuangzong had inquired of Jixing [during his visit], "Having already destroyed the Liang, I intend to campaign against Wu and Shu. Which deserves priority?" "Shu should come first," he indicated, "in which case, Your Subject requests the advance deployment of troops from my own circuit." An exhilarated Zhuangzong patted him on the back. Jixing subsequently had craftsmen embroider Zhuangzong's handprint on his clothes, which he considered a special honor after returning home.

Gao Jixing had already departed when Zhuangzong came to regret his release, sending secret directives for Liu Xun of Xiangzhou to eliminate him. Jixing's instincts were aroused upon reaching Xiangzhou, causing him to smash the gate locks and abscond by night, the instructions of Zhuangzong arriving as he left. He admitted to Liang Zhen upon returning, "I spurned your counsel and barely escaped calamity." He continued, "My trip entailed two mistakes: the first involved going to court and the second involved releasing me to return. Moreover, after hundreds of battles to capture the southern Yellow River region, His Majesty likes to boast before distinguished courtiers by copying passages from the *Spring and Autumn Annals*, commenting, 'I managed to obtain the world by the tips of these fingers!' He boasts and brags in this way, wasting time on hunting jaunts as affairs of state commonly get cast aside. I see little in him to cause worry."

Jixing was invested Prince of Nanping in the third year of Tongguang [C.E. 925]. Jiji, the Prince of Wei, had acquired more than four hundred thousand in ounces of gold and rolls of silk occasioning the conquest of Shu, wealth headed downstream from Xiazhou‡ when Zhuangzong succumbed to mutiny. Upon learning of insurrection in the Tang capital, Jixing intervened to divert to his satrapy the entire treasure trove from Shu, slaying its envoys, including Han Gong and more than ten others.

Previously, as the Tang campaigned against Shu, Jixing's offer to deploy armies from his own circuit enabled him to claim the prefectures of Kui, Zhong, Wan, Gui, and Xia‡, among others. He thereby became commissioner of bandit suppression in the southeastern Xiazhou‡ theater without ever actually issuing armies. In the aftermath of the Prince of Wei's conquest of Shu and Mingzong's accession to the throne, Jixing requested jurisdiction over the cluster of prefectures centering on Kui and Zhong, but leading officials of the Tang demurred, arguing that Jixing had formerly requested the prefectures without evincing any merit in the Shu offensive. Jixing persisted with petitions, leaving the Tang little option but to concede. He also rejected Tang attempts to control the appointment of local prefects. Mingzong now launched a strike against him, naming Liu Xun of Xiangzhou as commissioner of bandit suppression. When Xun's offensive stalled, the Tang dispatched detachments commander Xifang Ye, who overran the three prefectures of Kui, Zhong, and Wan. Jixing hence swore fealty to Wu and transferred to its sovereignty the prefectures of Jing, Gui, and Xia‡. Wu invested him Prince of Qin.

Gao Jixing died in winter, the third year of Tiancheng [C.E. 928], at seventy-one *sui* and received the posthumous title "Martial and Trustworthy," Wuxin. He had nine sons, the eldest of whom, Conghui, won installation.

Gao Conghui [C.E. 891–948] had the courtesy name Zunsheng. In the era of Jixing, he came to the Liang capital with appointments as manager of palace services and eventually rose to commissioner of the saddle storehouse. The court later granted a family leave to return home. Jixing now retained Conghui as chief director of infantry and cavalry and manager-adjutant to the governor. The Wu regime confirmed Conghui as governor of Jingnan upon Jixing's death. His father having severed relations with the Tang, Conghui worried about becoming a target for punitive action; he thus dispatched an emissary to the King of Chu, Ma Yin, seeking his intervention to secure Tang endorsement for his rule. He further sent Liu Zhiqian, the military attaché to Conghui, to offer fealty to the Tang court and forward three thousand ounces of silver as "atonement for crimes." Mingzong accepted the gesture. The Tang formally confirmed Conghui as governor in the inaugural month of the inaugural year of Changxing [C.E. 930], posthumously investing his father, Jixing, as Prince of Chu with the title Martial and Trustworthy. Invested as Prince of Bohai in the third year, Conghui became the Prince of Nanping in the inaugural year of Yingshun [C.E. 934].

Gao Conghui was a man with an astute mind and many an intrigue. The Hanlin academician Tao Gu once arrived as dignitary for official correspondence for Emperor Gaozu of Jin, on the occasion of Conghui's birthday. Entertaining Gu at Wangsha Tower, Conghui paraded a large armada of warships near the tower's base and commented, "Wu and Shu will not remain cordial for long. I intend to reconstitute weapons arsenals and conduct naval exercises in anticipation of deployment opportunities." Gu conveyed to Gaozu the entire conversation upon returning, as an elated Gaozu commissioned another envoy to give Conghui a hundred horses of superior stock. With the rebellion of An Congjin of Xiangzhou, Conghui was obliged to extend assistance, so he gave the outer appearance of resistance [to satisfy the Jin] while clandestinely cooperating with Congjin. Once Jin armies arrived for the suppression, Conghui deployed a naval force in a rendezvous with them, led by commander Li Duan. Conghui requested jurisdiction over Yingzhou, after Congjin's execution, but Gaozu refused.

The Khitan later overthrew the Jin dynasty, and Gaozu of Han raised armies at Taiyuan, so Gao Conghui dispatched a messenger via secondary roads to encourage his enthronement. He also sought jurisdiction over Yingzhou once the Han dynasty had consolidated power, a request that Gaozu seemed to approve. Conghui now sent an ambassador bearing tribute after Gaozu's occupation of Bianzhou, formally requesting Yingzhou. Gaozu refused, and an angry Conghui issued armies to raid the prefecture, where prefect Yin Shi defeated him. The Han later sent as envoy to Chu its director of education, Tian Min, and he sought passage through Jingnan. Conghui could thereby inquire about real conditions in the Middle Kingdom, and he characterized the north as depleted in both soldiers and food ever since the Khitan intervention, as if to belittle his guest. However, Min countered, "Once Du Chongwei surrendered the entire armed forces of Jin to the barbarians, those armies were positioned at Zhenzhou, not farther north: Jin armies thus all came under Han-dynasty control." The response annoyed Conghui. Min left behind a printed copy of the *Five Classics*, which Conghui declined, saying, "I am familiar with nothing beyond the eighteen chapters of the *Classic on Filial Piety*." "Indeed, that is sufficient as the principal path to ultimate virtue," Min responded. He then recited its *Regulations for Feudal Lords*, which reads, "To preside above without arrogance is to have status without intimidation; to restrain oneself with rigor is to have abundance without excess."[1] Conghui felt his words satirically directed at him and retaliated by employing large goblets to force drinking penalties upon him.

Jingnan was a small kingdom owing to its confined lands, weak military, and location between Wu and Chu. Rulers of Wu had assumed imperial trappings, yet the kingdoms of Southern Han, Min, and Chu continued to submit to Liang sovereignty, their envoys requiring passage through Jingnan to convey annual tribute. Those envoys were often intercepted by Jixing and Conghui for a layover, their possessions pilfered. Circuit authorities repeatedly filed complaints and occasionally unleashed armies to punish them, yet Gao overlords felt no shame even about having to return the loot. Later, as rulers of Southern Han, Min, and Shu all declared themselves emperors, Conghui pronounced himself vassal of whomever came along, so long as some benefit to him was involved. According to a popular saying, "He who illicitly purloins with no sense of shame is a 'parasite' or, said differently, 'someone with nothing to rely on.' " The other kingdoms dubbed them the "Gao Parasites."

Gao Conghui had severed relations after the Han refused his request to cede Yingzhou, a year later restoring communications and tribute. He died in the inaugural year of Qianyou, the tenth month [C.E. 948], at fifty-eight *sui*. Given the posthumous rank of imperial secretary and title of "Literate and Accomplished," Wenxian, he was succeeded by son Baorong. Conghui had fifteen sons: the eldest was Baoxun, then Baozheng and Baorong, who was third son. The reason for the latter's installation is unknown.

Gao Baorong [C.E. 920–960] had the courtesy name Dechang. He served as deputy governor and concurrent prefect of Xiazhou‡ during the Conghui era, named governor upon his death. Investiture as Prince of Bohai occurred in the inaugural year of Guangshun [C.E. 951] and elevation to Prince of Nanping during the inaugural year of Xiande [C.E. 954]. As Emperor Shizong campaigned in the Huai region, Baorong sent military director Wei Lin, with a force of three thousand, to depart from Xiakou and rendezvous with Zhou men. Through commander's attendant Liu Fu, he conveyed a memorandum to the Southern Tang urging its submission to Zhou sovereignty. Shizong obtained Baorong's memorandum once Li Jing assumed vassal relations and marveled, presenting Baorong with one hundred rolls of raw silk. Since the Later Tang, several years often elapsed before a single tribute mission to the capital came from Jingnan, relations disrupted twice in the interim. After the accession of Shizong, not a year passed without offering tribute. Baorong insisted that instruments of gold and silk, being native to the region, were a poor reflection of his sincere fidelity, so he sent younger brother Baoshen to court instead, causing Shizong to further cherish him.

Formerly, when Gao Jixing was governor and the Liang stationed a governor's guard of five thousand men at Nanping, both food and clothing were provided to Liang men. Annual subsidies had grown to thirteen thousand piculs of salt by the reign of Mingzong of Tang, payments later suspended by Nanping. Once Shizong of Zhou pacified the Huai region, he demanded similar protocol for authorities at Taizhou.[2]

Gao Baorong had an indecisive character and no particular talent, so he entrusted decisions of any import to younger brother Baoxu. When paternal cousin Congyi schemed to mutiny, his follower Gao Zhixun exposed the affair; Congyi was banished to Songzi and murdered as a result. The ascent of the Song dynasty worried Baorong, who in a single year tendered tribute three times. He died of illness in the inaugural year of Jianlong [C.E. 960], at forty-one *sui*, receiving the posthumous rank of grand marshal and title "Pure and Moral," Zhenyi. Younger brother Baoxu succeeded him.

Gao Baoxu [C.E. 924–962] had the courtesy name Xinggong. The tenth son of Conghui, he was named governor after Baorong's death. Once Baoxu himself took ill, in the third year [C.E. 962], he said to commander Liang Yansi, "I will not later recover from this illness. Among my brothers, who can be entrusted with the kingdom's future affairs?" Yanxi responded, "Are you not mindful of the Zhenyi Prince [Baorong]? The Former Prince, on his deathbed, entrusted this yamen to you. His son Jichong is now an adult." "Your words ring true," Baoxu conceded, hereafter entrusting to Jichong oversight over military forces across the domain. Baoxu died in the eleventh month at thirty-nine *sui*, posthumously ranked director of the Chancellery. The son of Baorong, Jichong, succeeded him.

Gao Jichong [r. C.E. 962–963], with the courtesy name Chenghe, became governor upon Baoxu's death. The death of Zhou Xingfeng of Hunan and succession of son Baoquan had caused commander Zhang Wenbiao to mutiny. It was the fourth year of Jianlong [C.E. 963], and Emperor Taizu of Song directed Murong Yanzhao to respond with a punitive action against Chu. Seeking passage through Jingnan, Yanzhao had promised to confine troops to the parameters of the walled city. "With a superior force and strategic cunning, he cannot be trusted to stay outside the wall, as promised," warned Li Jingwei, a leading commander under Jichong, who urged mobilization of a well-disciplined force as precaution. Administrative aide Sun Guangxian scoffed at Jingwei, saying, "What can a mere commoner from the Xia‡ River valley possibly know about fortunes of war? The commitment to unify the world has overtaken the Middle Kingdom ever since the days of Shizong, and even more so today, as a Sagacious Song ruler inherits Heaven's mandate. This reflects the emergence of a genuinely great line. How can we possibly rival its armies?" He therefore urged Jichong to abandon defenses and secure the treasury and storehouses as precaution. Jichong concurred. Jingwei now departed and said in lament, "A major decision has been made and my counsel rejected. Why continue to live?" He then choked to death. Jichong departed for the suburbs as Yanzhao's men arrived, Yanzhao's vanguard promptly occupying the city. Jichong hurried back to find, to his utter terror, armored horses and northern banners positioned along the alleys and thoroughfares. He proceeded to visit Yanzhao to surrender shield and seal, but the munificent edict of Taizu restored Jichong's powers as governor.

In the inaugural year of Qiande [C.E. 963], sacrifices were to be offered at the southern suburbs [of Kaifeng] and Jichong was petitioned to participate in conducting rites. In the ninth month, after impending sacrifices at the three ancestral temples were announced, Jichong led to the capital an entourage of five hundred, including commanders, their aides, and royal clansmen. Upon death, he held the title of Wuning governor. Sun Guangxian later served as Huangzhou prefect. For later events, see the "national histories."[i]

....

i. The dates for rise and fall of the house of Jixing are abundantly clear and all writings consistent: from inauguration of the Jingnan governorship under the Liang, in the inaugural year of Kaiping [C.E. 907], until the inaugural year of Qiande [C.E. 963] under this dynasty, when the kingdom was abolished, a total of fifty-seven years had elapsed.

CHAPTER 70

HEREDITARY HOUSE OF EASTERN HAN[1]

Liu Min, Son Chengjun, and Chengjun's Sons Ji'en and Jiyuan

Liu Min [C.E. 896–955] was the younger brother of Gaozu of the Later Han, born to the same mother. Originally named Chong, he had a handsome beard and double pupils in his eyes. A wastrel in youth, given to heavy drinking and frequent gambling, he was even tattooed upon induction as an ordinary foot soldier. He eventually rose to chief military director when the future Gaozu was Hedong governor. With the accession of Gaozu to the Han throne, Min was appointed metropolitan custodian of Taiyuan and interim custodian of the northern capital, with ministerial standing. Honors included palace secretary in the era of Emperor Yin.

The minority of Emperor Yin caused senior officials to govern on his behalf. The military commissioner at the time, the future Taizu of Zhou, had emerged as exceptionally distinguished in the wake of recent suppressions of three separate mutinies. Liu Min had a history of tensions with Taizu, however, leaving him uneasy. Turning to administrative aide Zheng Gong, he confided, "The monarch young and vulnerable, governance now rests with powerful officers. Moreover, my relations with Guo Wei have been strained. How do we cope with such times?" Gong confided, "The Han regime totters on chaos. As for Jinyang [your Taiyuan base], the valor of troops ranks first in the world, the terrain is securely defended, and its ten prefectures yield enough tax receipts to support autonomy. As a member of the imperial clan, should you fail to lay plans at this moment, Sir, your eventual domination by others is a certainty!" "Your words reflect precisely my own thoughts," Min responded, whereupon he ceased tax payments to the court and expanded his army by recruiting men of valor and enlisting commoners. Taizu's insurgency at Weizhou and the regicide perpetrated against Emperor Yin, in the third year [C.E. 950], convinced Min to consider military recourse.

Once Taizu of Zhou entered the capital from Weizhou, his intent to rebel was perfectly clear. However, leading Han courtiers had yet to support his further elevation, so he dared not claim the throne. Instead, he told the Empress Dowager of Han to install Liu Yun, the son of Min, as successor to the Han line and sent chief minister Feng Dao to escort Yun back from Xuzhou¶. Everyone at the time fully appraised Taizu as ingenuous, save for Min, who said joyfully, "My son will become Emperor. What peril need I fear?" He thus disbanded his army and dispatched a messenger to the capital.

Taizu of Zhou, humble in station as a youth, carried on his neck a flying-sparrow tattoo, so people commonly dubbed him the "Sparrow Guo." He spoke at length upon meeting Liu Min's messenger, reiterating his intent to install Yun. Pointing to the tattoo on his neck, he asserted, "Since antiquity, has a Son of Heaven ever carried such markings? I hope that you will find nothing suspect in me." His comments pleased Min, whose faith in their veracity only increased. The deputy custodian of Taiyuan, Li Xiang, had warned him, "The raising of troops by Mr. Guo is an act of insubordination. Political conditions will not permit him to remain loyal to Han and surely no scion of the Liu house will be installed by him." He thereby urged Min to lead an army down from Taihang to neutralize Meng Jin and hold vigil against a mutiny. If Yun managed to be enthroned, he could then disband his army. Min roundly reviled Li Xiang, however, stating, "A rotten Confucian, Xiang seeks to plant rifts between me and my son." Attendants were instructed to drag him away for beheading. As execution approached, Xiang said with remorse, "I conspired with an idiot and die out of sincerity, which I can wholly accept, but my infirm wife cannot live without me. Permit us to die together." The request incited Min to have the wife simultaneously stabbed to death at the marketplace. He also reported the incident to the Han court to affirm the absence of ulterior motives on his part.

Ultimately, Taizu of Zhou did overturn the Han and demote Liu Yun's noble status to Duke of Xiangying. Liu Min subsequently delivered a letter to Taizu through military attaché Li Bian requesting his son's return to Taiyuan, although he had died by now. Min wept bitterly. He also erected an ancestral temple to Li Xiang to conduct sacrifices every year.

In the inaugural year of Guangshun, by the Zhou calendar, sixteenth day of the inaugural month [C.E. February 24, 951], Liu Min acceded the imperial throne at Taiyuan. His son Chengjun was installed as metropolitan custodian of Taiyuan, administrative assistants Zheng Gong and Zhao Hua appointed chief ministers, military administrator Chen Guangyu named commissioner of palace armies, and diplomatic secretary Li Bian selected as special emissary to the Khitan. The Khitan Prince of Yongkang, Wuyu, proposed alliance with Liu Min's kingdom on a "father-to-son" basis. Min reciprocated with a letter delivered by chief minister Zheng Gong, where he referred to himself as the "Nephew Emperor," effectively conceding only to serve the Khitan ruler as "uncle." Wuyu now deputized the Prince of Yan, Shuya, and secretary of political affairs Gao Xun to invest Min as the Divinely Martial Emperor of the Great Han, investing his wife as Empress. Wuyu could be boorish in character: whenever envoys of Han arrived, he invariably ensnared them into binge eating and drinking. Gong was similarly plied to drink despite ongoing illnesses, and he died the next day of alcohol consumption. Wuyu saw opportunity in the Middle Kingdom's multitude of distractions attendant to Min's installation, so his return mission included the esteemed courtiers Shuya and Gao Xun. They brought as gifts a bay horse with yellow mane and the jade sash designed with nine dragons on twelve squares, so prized by Wuyu himself.

Once Wuyu succumbed to an act of regicide by Shuya, Shulü replaced him as ruler and Min commissioned Wang Dezhong, the auxiliary academician at the military bureau, as envoy to Shulü; he appealed for reinforcements to attack the Zhou. A force of fifty thousand led by Xiao Yujue was sent, as Min departed from Yindi Pass to launch a raid against Jinzhou. He was routed by Wang Jun, losing more than half of his men to starvation or exposure in the bitter cold of that winter. A raid on Fuzhou† occurred in the next year [C.E. 952], ending in Min's defeat by She Deyi, who now claimed the Kelan command for Zhou.

The Zhou ruler Taizu's passing came as good news to Liu Min, whose envoys conveyed a plea to the Khitan for troop support. They committed as relief some ten thousand "Iron Horse" cavalry and fifty to sixty thousand Xi tribesmen: commanded by Yang Gun, the force was allegedly a hundred thousand strong. Min designated as vanguard Zhang Yuanhui, while personally commanding thirty thousand horsemen in a raid on Luzhou. Li Yun of Luzhou responded by sending a mixed force of three thousand to intercept the intruders at Taiping station, led by Mu Lingjun. They were vanquished by Yuanhui in a sortie, the siege of Luzhou ensuing.

Newly acceded to power at the time, Shizong fully appreciated Liu Min's intention to exploit his disinclination to war owing to important mourning rituals and a recent accession to power. He thus preferred to storm Min unexpectedly. Many counseled against the action, including chief minister Feng Dao and cohort, although Shizong's resolve only intensified. Shizong personally led the campaign in the inaugural year of Xiande, opening hostilities at Gaoping County on the twentieth day of the third month [C.E. April 25, 954]. Commanding his left flank were Li Chongjin and Bai Chongzan, on his right were Fan Aineng and He Hui, presiding over regiments in the center were Xiang Xun and Shi Yanchao, while Zhang Yongde provided personal cover for Shizong with contingents of the Imperial Guard. Min similarly arrayed soldiers in three columns: Zhang Yuanhui served as eastern auxiliary, Yang Gun as western auxiliary, and Min presided over the center.

After a reconnaissance of Zhou armies, Gun said to Liu Min, "The enemy is exceptionally fit. We cannot act impetuously." Ruffling his beard, Min warned, "An opportunity of the sort cannot be squandered. Do not speak rashly!" Gun left embittered. Min ordered his eastern column to advance first, causing Wang Dezhong to complain as he struck furiously at his horse, "Extremely intense southern winds are unfavorable to this northern army—some delay is necessary." Min retorted angrily, "I warn you, crusty old fart, not to impede needlessly my armies." He promptly motioned to Yuanhui to storm the right flank of Zhou. Initial engagements forced Fan Aineng and He Hui to retreat as chaos overtook their cavalry. Several thousand of their infantry doffed armor to defect to Yuanhui, bellowing cheers for "Ten Thousand Years" with a sound that reverberated across the river canyon. A flabbergasted Shizong assumed personal direction of warriors, who were so invigorated as to vie for the chance to fight first. The winds had gathered such strength by now that Min motioned to Red Banner units to regroup, but his armies were out of control and met defeat. By sunset, Min withdrew remnants of roughly ten thousand to set up defenses in a ravine.

The Zhou army's rear regiments, commanded by Liu Ci, had yet to catch up when Shizong decided to avail himself of a speedy engagement. Ci's armies arrived on the heels of Shizong's victory and exploited this momentum to harass Min's men and deliver an even worse rout. Zhou armies now captured carts of heavy weapons and armor, plus the imperial carriage and other paraphernalia. Astride his bay horse with yellow mane from the Khitan, Min singularly absconded posthaste, taking side-roads through the Diaoke Mountains. There he lost his way in a ravine during nighttime travel and secured a villager as a guide, who mistakenly took him toward Pingyang before an alternate route back was found. Zhang Yuanhui died in the thick of battle. Yang Gun's indignation toward Min had incited him to immobilize the western column and refuse to fight, his army singularly managing to return completely intact. Once Min had returned, he built a special stable for the bay horse, which, outfitted in gold and silver, was provided meals of the superior third grade and dubbed the "Liberated General."

Resting armies at Luzhou, Shizong held a large banquet for commanders and troops and beheaded more than seventy of his own vanquished commanders such as Fan Aineng and He Hui—stirring imposing awe in his men. An offensive against Taiyuan ensued, Shizong sending to the north Fu Yanqing and Shi Yanchao to neutralize Xinkou and thereby sever Khitan relief routes. The walled city of Taiyuan was forty *li* in circumference, and Zhou troops, three hundred paces from the wall, formed a contiguous circle around it. From the fourth month through the sixth, their offensive yielded no concrete results. Meanwhile, Yanqing and his men were defeated by the Khitan and Yanchao died in battle. Shizong's armies quickly withdrew.

During the Zhou blockade of Taiyuan, Liu Min dispatched Wang Dezhong to escort Yang Gun back to the Khitan while requesting reinforcements. They followed through with several tens of thousands of cavalry as relief and allowed Dezhong to return in advance. Dezhong had reached Daizhou when local commander Sang Gui, having killed defense commander Zheng Chuqian, surrendered the city to the Zhou. He turned over Dezhong to the Zhou as well. Shizong summoned Dezhong to inquire about the number of troops in the barbarian relief and he indicated that Min had made no additional requests since Yang Gun's escort home. Shizong believed him. Later, the Khitan vanquished Fu Yanqing at Xinkou and Dezhong was slain [for misrepresentations].

In the wake of setbacks at Gaoping and the blockade at Taiyuan, Liu Min grew depressed and physically ill, dying in the eleventh month of the next year [C.E. 955] at sixty *sui*. His son Chengjun succeeded him.

Liu Chengjun [r. C.E. 955–967], second son of Min, had an affinity for learning and a proficiency at calligraphy in youth. Upon the death of Min, he petitioned the Khitan ruler for investiture, acknowledging himself as "baron." Shulü employed an imperial rescript in response, calling Chengjun "son" and approving his accession.

Before this, Liu Min often said to Zhang Yuanhui and cohort, "In preserving the legacy of Gaozu and redressing the injustice against Liu Yun, righteous principle precludes my submission to Guo Wei. I hope, along with you, to exert every effort in exacting revenge for family and country. As for declaring myself Emperor over one corner of the world, what could I possibly gain? What sort of Son of Heaven do you see in me, what sort of governors do you see in yourselves?" Although assuming bogus titles of royalty, he conformed to the Qianyou reign [of Later Han] with no changes. Nor did Min erect his own ancestral temple. In conducting the rituals of each season, he limited himself to the rites appropriate for a clansman. Only with the ascent of Chengjun was an amnesty announced for the domain, the tenth year of Qianyou changed to the inaugural year of Tianhui [C.E. 957], and seven ancestral altars erected in the Xiansheng temple.

The Khitan dispatched Gao Xun to support Chengjun, who in turn deployed Li Cungui to join Xun in a raid on Shangdang County [Luzhou]. They obtained nothing and retreated. In the next year [C.E. 958], Shizong launched a northern expedition against the Khitan, conquering the three passes. A Khitan envoy alerted Chengjun to emergency conditions, the incident ending after Shizong withdrew armies before Chengjun's reinforcements could depart.

After the Song-dynasty ascent, the Zhaoyi governor Li Yun betrayed the new mandate, directing commander Liu Jichong and administrative aide Sun Fu to seek "vassal" status under the Northern Han. He also delivered [Song-dynasty] military overseers Zhou Guangxun and Li Tingyu to Taiyuan, requesting military assistance. Chengjun had planned consultations with the Khitan, but Jichong conveyed Yun's opposition to Khitan involvement. Chengjun thus commanded only local troops in departing from Tuanbai Canyon. Leading officials held a farewell party at the Fen River, where Secretariat associate Zhao Hua cautioned, "Li Yun has endorsed a frivolous action and Your Majesty has depleted the empire's resources to wage war without due consideration for success or failure. Your Subject is genuinely distraught." Still, as Chengjun reached Taiping Post, he invested Yun as Prince of Longxi. Once Yun saw Chengjun without the escort of ceremonial guard and devoid of an imperial presence, he came to regret accepting vassalage under him. He now began affirming the Zhou dynasty's charity toward him, thereby making any disavowal of it unthinkable. Chengjun was especially displeased to learn of Yun's sentiments, in light of the historic feud between Han and Zhou, and sent Lu Zan, the commissioner of palace armies, to oversee his army. The appointment left Yun ill at ease, his conflicts with Zan so frequent that Chengjun had to dispatch chief minister Wei Rong to mediate matters.

Li Yun later perished in battle. Wei Rong was apprehended and taken to the Song capital, where Emperor Taizu asked about the level of Chengjun's involvement in Yun's rebellion. When his response seemed disrespectful, Taizu had Rong struck on the head with an iron cudgel. "Alas, I have found the right occasion to die," Rong shouted as blood covered his face. Taizu looked to attendants, admitting, "This is a truly loyal subject." Rong was released, provided the best of medicine for his wounds, and directed to write Chengjun a letter requesting the return of Zhou Guangxun and cohort in exchange for his own return to Taiyuan. Chengjun did not respond, and Rong remained in the capital. Turning to Zhao Hua, Chengjun admitted, "I was nearly ruined for not heeding your counsel, but my only regret is the loss of Wei Rong and Lu Zan."

Liu Chengjun came increasingly to value Confucians, and in consequence, appointed the recluse of Baofu Mountain, Guo Wuwei, as consultant on government affairs. This native to Dizhou had a square forehead and nose resembling a bird's beak. Fond of learning and well informed, Wuwei was a gifted rhetorician. He later donned coarse clothing to enter the Daoist priesthood, residing in the Wudang Mountains. The future Taizu of Zhou was in the throes of the Li Shouzhen suppression in Hezhong when Wuwei appeared at the portals to his barracks to visit. Taizu consulted him about affairs of the day and deemed him a rare talent. Someone remarked to Taizu, however, "For a senior officer of Han like yourself commanding vast armies away from court, such receptions of wandering scholars is not the most discreetly subtle and far-sighted approach." Taizu thus opted against recruiting Wuwei, and he departed for reclusion in the Baofu Mountains. A military commissioner for Chengjun's inner palace, Duan Chang, knew of Wuwei and praised his talents. Chengjun now summoned Wuwei to serve as master of admonitions and eventually chief minister. In the fifth year [C.E. 961], the palace uncovered a conspiracy to mutiny led by column leaders of the Palace Guard: Wang Yin, Liu Shao, and Zhao Luan. The conspirators were executed, and their confessions further implicated Duan Chang, who was demoted from military commissioner to prefect of Fenzhou, later to be murdered by hanging.

Since the times of Liu Min, affairs of the Han court invariably required written authorization from the Khitan, although Chengjun often slighted such procedures upon assuming power. The Khitan dispatched an emissary to censure him for ignoring consultations concerning the change in reign, relief for Li Yun, and Duan Chang's murder. The reproof left Chengjun flustered, and he issued a formal apology for his misdeeds. The Khitan inexplicably detained the envoy, causing Chengjun to serve them with heightened deference even as their contempt for him grew. In the wake of Li Yun's defeat and the loss of Khitan support, Chengjun grew uninterested in invading the south. Meanwhile, his kingdom's resources dwindled daily owing to his land's stunted size and meager manufactures, plus the flow of annual payments to the Khitan. The Buddhist monk Jiyong of Wutai Mountain was named master of state ceremonies.

The son of Liu Shouguang, the former Prince of Yan, Liu Jiyong was spared death along with him because his mother had been a mere concubine. He later accepted tonsure as a Buddhist cleric to reside in the Wutai Mountains. The Han had relied on Jiyong, a man of versatility who excelled at trade and finance, since the times of Liu Min. Jiyong could lecture so deftly on the *Huayan Sutra* that accumulated donations from the four corners often served to subsidize the state. With Wutai located inside the Khitan domain, Jiyong often obtained Khitan horses—several hundred a year—for transfer to the

Han as "cavalry supplement for the capital." He also established a silver refinery at Bai Canyon, conscripting commoners to harvest ore from nearby mountains to smelt silver for the government. The Liu ruling house depended on him to meet its needs and established the Baoxing command at the foundry site. Jiyong later held a succession of official posts culminating in grand preceptor and palace secretary. Dying of old age, he was posthumously invested Prince of Ding.

Emperor Taizu of Song once conveyed a message to Liu Chengjun through a spy in the north: "Your family feud with the Zhou dynasty having lasted generations, refusing to submit to its sovereignty seemed wholly fitting. Today, in the absence of rifts between you and me, why continue to impose such hardship on your own people? If you have designs on the Middle Kingdom, you should descend the Taihang Mountains to settle matters in a showdown!" Chengjun had the spy return with the response, "The territories and troops of the Hedong region do not even constitute one-tenth of those in the Middle Kingdom, while my royal house has never engaged in treachery. I defend this small land for fear that no one will offer rites to the Han gods." Sobered by his words, Taizu broke with a smile and said to the spy, "By speaking to Chengjun for me, you have opened a channel to life." He applied no further military pressure on the Han for the rest of his reign. In power for thirteen years, Chengjun died of illness, and adopted son Ji'en was installed.

Liu Ji'en [r. C.E. 967–974] was originally surnamed Xue, his father Xue Zhao a foot soldier to whom Liu Min married a daughter, the two giving birth to Ji'en. Zhao being a son-in-law, Gaozu of Later Han eliminated his armies to assume personal command of them. Zhao was devoid of talents, so Gaozu fed and clothed him without ever employing him. Because his wife was Min's daughter, she often stayed with him, and Zhao rarely saw her. This left him despondent, and, in a drunken stupor, he grabbed his hip-sword to stab her, injuring without killing her, and then killed himself. The daughter of Min later married into the He family and gave birth to Jiyuan. After Min's daughter and her husband had both died, Min instructed son Chengjun to adopt the two boys as sons, as he personally had none.

Upon the installation of Chengjun, Liu Ji'en became metropolitan custodian of Taiyuan. Chengjun once commented to Wuwei, "Ji'en is pure and filial in character, but lacks the skills to save the age and is unfit to assume family affairs, I fear." Wuwei did not respond. Later, as Chengjun lay bedridden in the Qinzheng chambers, he summoned Wuwei and clasped his hand in entrusting future decisions to him.

Ji'en deferred his own installation, following Chengjun's death, until the Khitan could be informed of the mourning underway. Presiding over affairs wearing the coarse skirt of mourning, he insisted on spending day and night in the Qinzheng chambers. But the former civil officials and bodyguard of Chengjun all remained at the Taiyuan prefectural offices. Summoning high officials and imperial clansmen for a banquet, in the ninth month, Ji'en returned to his Qinzheng chambers to rest after finishing drinks. That night, palace services officer Hou Barong led more than ten men with daggers into the chamber to slay him behind closed doors. Other men under Guo Wuwei's direction now infiltrated the room by ladder to murder Barong, his confederates perishing as well.

Earlier, during Chengjun's deathbed conversation with Guo Wuwei, Wuwei's lack of endorsement for Ji'en had incurred his resentment. Once in power, Ji'en wished to purge Wuwei but found no occasion. Everyone therefore considered Wuwei to have instigated the mutiny of Barong and killed him to seal his lips and protect the secret. Wuwei now invited Jiyuan to succeed him.

Liu Jiyuan [r. C.E. 974–979] was a vicious man. None of the over ten sons of Liu Min merit any note. During the times of Jiyuan, his uncles Hao, Kai, Qi, and Xi had all been slain by him, all but Xian, who feigned stupidity and survived. Since youth, Jiyuan and his brother had both treated Chengjun's wife, née Guo, as their mother. Woman Guo once scolded the wife of Jiyuan, Woman Duan, for some minor misdeed. Soon, Duan died of some illness and Jiyuan suspected Guo of murdering her. After formal installation, he arranged for favorite Fan Chao to assassinate Woman Guo: she was in mourning attire and weeping before Chengjun's coffin when Chao strangled her to death. The sons and grandsons of the Liu house hereafter had no survivors.

The reign was changed to Guangyun after Jiyuan's installation [C.E. 974]. As imperial troops of Song campaigned against the north, Jiyuan sealed off Taiyuan in defiance. Emperor Taizu, by formal edict, invited him to emerge and surrender, offering the Pinglu governorship to him and the Anguo command to Guo Wuwei. Wuwei's face changed color as he held the edict, but the military at Bing [Taiyuan] Prefecture and close aides to Jiyuan all insisted on defying the Song mandate with a staunch defense. Looking to the heavens, Wuwei wept bitterly as he drew a hip-sword, intending to kill himself, only to be restrained by attendants. Jiyuan lowered himself to clasp Wuwei's hand and invite him to sit down. "How can this isolated city," Wuwei queried, "resist a royal army of a million men?" His words were intended to jar the Bingzhou leadership, but served only to heighten their resolve. The eunuch Wei Degui managed to uncover evidence of treachery on the part of Wuwei and informed Jiyuan, who sent someone to strangle him to death.

Previously, Emperor Taizu of Song had waters from the Fen River diverted to flood the city. The waters seeped in through gates along the wall, but piles of hay within the city were thrown over the wall to obstruct the water. This coincided with summer rains, as imperial troops quartered in fields of tall weeds contracted assorted contagious diseases, inducing Taizu to withdraw his men. Once imperial armies had departed, Jiyuan could divert the water outside the city walls to Taitai Post, the subsiding waters revealing a city largely ravaged. A visitor currently at Taiyuan, Khitan envoy Han Zhifan, commented with a sigh, "When imperial troops diverted waters to flood the city, they demonstrated knowledge of the first step, but not the second. Had they flooded the city first and drained it later, they could have annihilated Bingzhou defenders."

Imperial troops resumed their campaign against the north in the fourth year of Taiping-Xingguo [C.E. 979]. Jiyuan's energy and morale were low, but the military leadership at Bingzhou preferred defiance. His deputy commissioner of military affairs, Ma Feng, who had been confined to home owing to illnesses of old age, proceeded on a stretcher to meet Jiyuan and make a tearful presentation on the rise and fall of dynasties, swaying him to surrender. Emperor Taizong accepted the surrender at an elevated pavilion to the north of the city, conferring honors on Jiyuan as generalissimo of the Right Guard and Duke of Pengcheng. For later events, see the "national histories."[i]

....

i. All writings are consistent about dates for the rise and fall of Liu Min's house: beginning with the inaugural year of Guangshun, by the Zhou calendar [C.E. 951], when dynastic titles were adopted, until the fourth year of Taiping/Xingguo in our own dynasty [C.E. 979], when it was overturned, a total of twenty-eight years had elapsed. For other details, see the notes under "Genealogical Charts."

NOTES

NOTES TO INTRODUCTION

1. The unusually high level of historical productivity in the Song period is quantified most emphatically in the *Siku quanshu zongmu tiyao*, the eighteenth-century encyclopedic catalog of most known writings up to that time, and the most comprehensive bibliography of its kind. Of the entries under history, 189 titles in a total of 564 (one-third) and 5,644 chapters in a total volume of 21,950 (one-fourth) represent works composed under the Song. See Gao, *Zhongguo shixueshi*, p. 243.

2. On Ouyang Xiu's political career and role as chief examiner, see Bol, *"This Culture of Ours,"* pp. 191–194; Egan, *Word, Image, and Deed*, pp. 3–8; Liu, *Ou-yang Hsiu*, pp. 69–70, 150–151; Mote, *Imperial China*, pp. 118–138.

3. Egan, *Literary Works*, pp. 12ff; Liu, *Ou-yang Hsiu*, pp. 131–154.

4. Tuo Tuo, *Song Shi*, chap. 319, p. 10381.

5. Egan, *Literary Works*, pp. 133ff.

6. Liu, *Ou-yang Hsiu*, pp. 85–99.

7. *Ouyang Xiu ziliao huibian*, vol. 1, pp. 120–121 and *Ouyang wenzhonggong wenji* (fulu), chap. 6, p. 44a.

8. Zhao, *Nianershi zhaji*, chap. 21, p. 455.

9. On the organization of Chinese official historiography and Sima Qian's contribution, see Yang, "Chinese Official Historiography," pp. 44–59.

10. Leslie, *Sources for Chinese History*, pp. 23–26. On the *Spring and Autumn Annals* and its commentary, see Nylan, *Five "Confucian" Classics*, pp. 253–306.

11. For some recent scholarship on Sima Qian's historical methodology as reflected in *Historical Records*, see Hardy, *Worlds of Bronze and Bamboo*, pp. 14 ff; Hulsewé, "Historiography of the Han Period," pp. 31–37; Nienhauser, *The Grand*

Scribe's Records, vol. 1, pp. v–xii; Watson, *Ssu-ma Ch'ien,* pp. 101–182; Zheng, "Sima Qian," pp. 134–166; Gao, *Shixueshi gaiyao,* pp. 64–93; Tao, *Shixueshi lue,* pp. 62–98; Cang, *Zhongguo shixue,* vol. 1, pp. 103–139; Zhang, *Zhongguo shixueshi,* pp. 116–144; Chen, *Zhongguo shixuejia,* vol. 1, pp. 18–52.

12. Sima Qian, *Shiji,* chap. 8, p. 393; chap. 28, p. 1356.

13. For an incisive discussion of Sima Qian's rather inconsistent views toward astrology and the supernatural, see Du, "Sima Qian," pp. 222–248.

14. Indeed, the original commentary on Qin is surprisingly free of moral pronouncements on the dynasty; see Dawson, *Historical Records,* p. 97; Watson, *Records of the Grand Historian: Qin Dynasty,* pp. ix–xvii, 1–87.

15. *Shiji,* chap. 9, pp. 395–411; Watson, *Records of the Grand Historian: Han Dynasty,* vol. 1, pp. 267–284.

16. For more on the *Old History* (Jiu wudai shi) and its defects, see Chai, "Lun Ouyang Xiu," p. 227; Chen, *Zhongguo shiliaoxue,* pp. 197–202; Gao, *Shixueshi gaiyao,* pp. 229–230; Lin, "Ouyang Xiu wudai shiji," pp. 305–306; *Nianwushi shuyao,* pp. 188–192; Qian, *Zhongguo shixue,* pp. 201–216; Tao, *Shixueshi lue,* pp. 281–288; *Siku quanshu congmu tiyao,* chap. 10, pp. 35–37; Zhang, *Shixueshi,* vol. 2, pp. 155–166; Zhao, *Nianershi zhaji,* chap. 21, pp. 445–452.

17. The exact length of the *Old History of the Five Dynasties* is problematic. Song dynasty sources indicate a total of 150 chapters, but the original was lost and current editions represent reconstructions by early Qing dynasty historians based on incomplete texts, the incomplete portions then supplemented with citations from other related sources. Thus, the current work, even with divisions based on 150 chapters, may actually be longer than the original text. See *Siku tiyao,* chap. 45, pp. 34–35.

18. On the format of the history, see Ishida, "Shin godai shi," pp. 31–45.

19. Ouyang Xiu's contempt for the institutions of this chaotic period is seen as the cause for omitting treatises; see Cang, *Zhongguo shixue,* vol. 1, p. 718; Zhang, *Zhongguo shixueshi,* vol. 2, pp. 160–161.

20. Hulsewé, "Notes on the historiography of the Han period," p. 35; Nienhauser, *The Grand Scribe's Records,* vol. 1, pp. xii–xiii. For a revisionist appraisal of Sima Qian's objectivity, see Hardy, *Worlds of Bronze and Bamboo,* Introduction.

21. Pulleyblank, "Chinese Historical Criticism," pp. 155–156; Cang, *Zhongguo shixue,* vol. 2, pp. 736–739.

22. In a 1037 letter, Ouyang Xiu had proposed that Yin Shu write Annals for the Tang and Jin, with Ouyang Xiu personally writing the remaining Annals for the north and the two sharing responsibility for the biographical chapters. Whether Shu actually accepted the arrangement and drafted portions prior to his death ten years later is unlikely, to my mind, although secondary scholars disagree. Curiously, Ouyang Xiu's tomb inscription for Yin Shu fails to mention any contribution to the *Historical Records,* noting only Yin's premature aging and the loss of four of six children before his death at forty-six years old, twenty-five years before Ouyang Xiu. See *Ouyang Xiu quanji,* "Jushi waiji," chap. 17, pp. 491–492; "Jushi ji," chap. 28,

pp. 199–200, respectively. For views both affirming and denying Yin Shu's consent to write, see Liu Deqing, *Ouyang Xiu zhuan*, p. 50; Cang, *Zhongguo shixue*, vol. 1, p. 710 and Preface to Taiwan reprint of *Xin wudai shi*, p. 6.

Interestingly, biographer James T. C. Liu seems to take two slightly different positions on the level of Yin Shu's contribution to the *Historical Records*. In the Chinese original, published in 1963, he asserts that Yin had never agreed to the offer and thus contributed nothing; but in the 1967 biography in English, Liu suggests that he made a partial contribution, stating, "Yin unfortunately died in the prime of life, having written only about four thousand words on the Five Dynasties." See Liu, *Ouyang Xiu de zhixue yu congzheng*, p. 50, and *Ou-yang Hsiu*, p. 106. Liu's wording can be misleading, inasmuch as Yin Shu's "four thousand words" should rightly refer not to his contribution to the *Historical Records* but to an independently authored work. A late contemporary of Ouyang Xiu, Wang Pizhi, makes the point more clearly, writing, "In the Tiansheng era [1023–32], the Esteemed gentleman Ouyang and Yin Shilu [Shu] once discussed joint authorship [of a New History], but later Shilu wrote a separate *Spring and Autumn Annals of the Five Dynasties*, a work of merely four thousand words, concise yet rich in historical method. In the end, the Esteemed gentleman Ouyang rewrote the [original] *History of the Five Dynasties*, a work brief in words yet detailed on events—ranking alongside Sima Qian's [*Historical Records*] and Ban Gu's [*History of the Han*] in integrating 'praise and blame' principles based on rules from the *Spring and Autumn Annals*" (*Ouyang Xiu ziliao huibian*, vol. 1, p. 76.

At first reading, Yin Shu seems to have contributed nothing to the *Historical Records*, the "discussion" of collaboration never progressing. But his *Spring and Autumn Annals for the Five Dynasties*, a chronological work, likely provided the inspiration for the Annals in Ouyang Xiu's own history, which are also celebrated for their rigorous historical method. This would imply that Yin Shu's contribution or influence was confined to the Annals and did not extend to the biographies, as initially proposed by Ouyang Xiu. Moreover, the extreme brevity of the extant *Spring and Autumn Annals for the Five Dynasties*, in two terse chapters, makes it a fraction of the length of similar chapters in the *Historical Records*, so it was hardly a foundation text. For the Yin Shu text, see *Wudai chunqiu* (Baibu congshu jicheng).

23. Liu, *Ou-yang Hsiu*, pp. 106–107; Cang, *Zhongguo shixue*, vol. 1, pp. 706–708.

24. Yan, *Ouyang Xiu nianpu*, p. 82.

25. *Ouyang Xiu quanji* (zouyi ji), chap. 16, p. 887; Cang, *Zhongguo shixue*, vol. 1, pp. 708–709.

26. Almost all authoritative sources refer to the work in "74 chapters," including the court-authorized tomb inscription *(shendaobei)* for Ouyang Xiu, whereas only one Song-dynasty contemporary, Chao Gongwu, cites "75 chapters." See *Ouyang Xiu ziliao huibian*, vol. 1, pp. 115 and 236, respectively. The eighteenth-century bibliography *Siku quanshu congmu tiyao*, an otherwise highly authoritative source, gives "75 chapters" as well (see *Siku tiyao*, chap. 46, p. 36 [1006]). Is it possible that the original 1077 edition contained another chapter, deleted from the extant 1199

edition? This is most unlikely, although some adjustment in organization may have occurred in the later edition, where two shorter chapters were conflated as one. With confidence, however, I am certain that nothing is missing.

27. *Ouyang Xiu quanji*, "shujian," chap. 6, pp. 1285–1286.

28. James T. C. Liu and countless others allude to personal objections to some historical interpretations in the work by Wang Anshi, the famous political reformer of the late 1060s and early 1070s. The origin of this allegation is apparently a twelfth-century chronological history of the Northern Song, *Xu zizhi tongjian changbian*, by Li Tao. See *Ouyang Xiu ziliao huibian*, vol. 1, p. 263. However, Ouyang Xiu's allusion to potential critics occurs in 1060, years before Wang Anshi's dominance at court.

29. *Jushi ji*, chap. 17, pp. 125–126.

30. Rao, *Zhengtong lun*, pp. 75–76.

31. Rao, *Zhengtong lun*, pp. 83–84.

32. De Bary, *Sources of Chinese Tradition*, vol. 1, pp. 391–392, with my own modifications. For the Chinese text, see Ouyang, *Ouyang Xiu quanji*, "jushi ji," chap. 17, pp. 124–125.

33. Liu, *Ou-yang Hsiu*, pp. 54–55.

34. See *Jin shi*, chap. 12, p. 282 and preface to the 1976 Taiwan reprint of *Xin wudai shi*, p. 10.

35. It was the late Song–early Yuan historian Ma Duanlin who seems to have coined the term "New Historical Records of the Five Dynasties," while referring to the Old History as simply "History of the Five Dynasties." See *Wenxian tongkao*, chap. 192, p. 1628.

36. Zhao, *Nianershi zhaji*, chap. 21, p. 445.

37. One school suggests that Ouyang Xiu personally wrote the notes but attributed them to another to avoid responsibility for sensitive statements; see Huang, *Song/Yuan xue'an*, chap. 4, p. 120; Liu, *Ou-yang Hsiu*, p. 110; Hervouet, *Sung Bibliography*, p. 63.

38. On Ouyang Xiu's contribution to official dogma on loyalty and its consequences at the end of dynasty, see Davis, *Wind against the Mountain*, pp. 14–15; Kobayashi, *Ōyō Shū*, pp. 120–146.

39. Xue Juzheng et al., *Jiu wudai shi*, chaps. 138–141.

40. *Jiu wudai shi*, chap. 1, p. 2; chap. 25, p. 332; chap. 75, p. 978; chap. 110, p. 1447.

41. For some examples of these attributions of historical events to Heaven or Fate, see *Jiu wudai shi*, chap. 10, p. 152; chap. 14, p. 200; chap. 15, p. 214; chap. 48, pp. 668–669; chap. 85, p. 1129; chap. 98, p. 1318; chap. 109, p. 1440; chap. 113, pp. 1505–1506; chap. 119, p. 1587; chap. 120, pp. 1597–1598.

42. Chapter 2, page 16, n. ix.

43. Intellectual historians have sometimes rendered the term *chang li* as "constant" or "moral" patterns. In the context of this particular historical text, however, the term is less abstract, thus my own preference for "common reasoning" or even "commonsense." See Bol, *"This Culture of Ours,"* p. 159; Smith, *Sung Dynasty I Ching*, p. 257.

44. Chapter 5, footnote xvii. Ouyang Xiu, incidentally, applied the same standard to the *New History of the Tang,* edited by him, where again he deleted speculative material and affirmed the importance of "recording the calamitous and strange while deleting commentary on political implications." See Davis, "Sung Historiography," pp. 113–114; Ouyang Xiu et al., *Xin Tang shu,* chap. 34, p. 873.

45. Ouyang Xiu, *Wudai shiji,* chap. 59, p. 711.

46. Liu, *Ou-yang Hsiu,* p. 157.

47. See *Wudai shiji,* preface by modern annotators, p. 8.

48. In combing through the *New History of the Tang,* I have found numerous references that seem to affirm the power of heaven: references to heaven's perfecting the virtue of loyalist martyrs while employing rebels to act on its will, references to heaven's alienation due to the inadequate virtue of later monarchs, references to heaven's intervening in the revival of Tang, references to the Tang demise as abandonment by heaven and to a "consensus" between heaven and man with regard to political change. Admittedly, nearly all of these references occur not in the early chapters attributed to the personal pen of Ouyang Xiu, but in later chapters authored by others, thus implying that Ouyang Xiu's own views were probably more radical than most contemporaries. See *Xin Tang shu,* chap. 85, p. 3703; chap. 184, p. 5399; chap. 192, p. 5544; chap. 80, pp. 3603–3604; chap. 135, p. 4582; chap. 179, p. 5326; chap. 185, p. 5414; chap. 105, p. 4036; chap. 124, p. 4395; chap. 82, p. 3640; chap. 181, p. 5355; chap. 215b, p. 6070; chap. 225c, p. 6369; chap. 9, p. 281, respectively.

49. *Wudai shiji,* chap. 37, p. 397, preface to "Musicians and Actors," pp. 309–310.

50. Zheng, "Ouyang Xiu tianrenguan," pp. 372–373.

51. For some of the more important secondary writings on these two historians and their attitude toward metaphysical speculations, see Henderson, *Chinese Cosmology,* pp. 104–105; McMullen, *State and Scholars,* pp. 177–178, 197; Pulleyblank, "Chinese Historical Criticism," pp. 136–151; Tao, *Shixueshi lue,* pp. 208–229; Yang, "Liu Zhiji," pp. 121–159; Yao, "Lun Tang/Song zhi ji," pp. 370–384.

52. Yao, "Lun Tang/Song zhi ji," pp. 378–379.

53. de Bary, *Sources of Chinese Tradition,* vol. 1, pp. 386–390; Liu, *Ou-yang Hsiu,* pp. 158–172.

54. Liu, *Ou-yang Hsiu,* p. 159.

55. Liu, *Ou-yang Hsiu,* pp. 159–162.

56. Davis, "The Heroism of Chou Shih-tsung."

57. *Wudai shiji,* chap. 49, pp. 558–559. The commentary does not appear in the translation below.

58. For more on Ouyang Xiu's attitude toward military men in general, see Davis, "Martial Men and Military Might," pp. 12–16.

59. On governors and their expanding role in Tang politics, see Wright, *Perspectives on the T'ang,* pp. 8–14; Twitchett, *Cambridge History of China,* vol. 3, pp. 586–601; Wang, *Structure of Power,* pp. 7–84. Chinese and Japanese secondary sources on the topic are too extensive to cite here.

60. On the relationship between military crisis and eunuch power, see Twitchett, *Cambridge History of China,* vol. 3, pp. 586–601.

61. Hebei Institute of Cultural Relics, *Wudai Wang Chuzhi mu.*

62. For more on Liang rule, see Eberhard, *Conquerors and Rulers,* pp. 97–99, 157; Wang, *Structure of Power,* pp. 26–29; Twitchett, *Cambridge History of China,* vol. 3, pp. 775–784; Zheng, *Wudai shiguo,* pp. 1–6.

63. Sima Guang et al., *Zizhi tongjian,* chap. 266, p. 8687.

64. For more on Zhu Quanzhong's lechery, see Li, *Zhu Wen,* pp. 145–150.

65. Li Keyong succeeded father Guochang in 883, but Guochang apparently died in 887; see *Zizhi tongjian,* chap. 256, p. 8345.

66. On the Later Tang, see Wang, *Structure of Power,* pp. 29–31; Franke, *Cambridge History of China,* vol. 6, pp. 6–7, 64–65, 161–163; Twitchett, *Cambridge History of China,* vol. 3, pp. 774–779, 784–787; Zheng, *Wudai shiguo,* pp. 6–8. For a valuable treatment of Shatuo culture, see Eberhard, *Conquerors and Rulers,* pp. 140–156.

67. Franke, *Cambridge History of China,* vol. 6, p. 8.

68. Twitchett, *Cambridge History of China,* vol. 3, pp. 777, 779.

69. Wang, *Structure of Power,* pp. 158, 170.

70. *Wudai shiji,* chap. 6, p. 63.

71. *Wudai huiyao,* chaps. 10–11, pp. 172–184.

72. Eberhard, *Conquerors and Rulers,* pp. 144–145. See also author's notes to chapters 4–7.

73. According to the famed Southern Song historian of institutions, Wang Yinglin, the burning of paper money on the occasion of "Cold foods festival" or "sacrifices in the wilderness" has its roots in the high Tang, starting in 728, not the Five Dynasties as suggested by Ouyang Xiu. See *Ouyang Xiu ziliao huibian,* vol. 1, p. 419.

74. For an insightful critique of Zhuangzong's reign from the perspective of Abaoji, ruler of the Khitan at the time, see Mote, *Imperial China,* pp. 45–47.

75. Wolfram Eberhard estimates that the Shatuo population peaked by the year 930 at roughly 100,000 and by 950 had plummeted due to a combination of war, natural disaster, and disease; see *Conquerors and Rulers,* pp. 142–143.

76. Wang, *Structure of Power,* pp. 188–191.

77. Franke, *Cambridge History of China,* vol. 6, p. 70.

78. Wang, *Structure of Power,* p. 164.

79. See Mote, *Imperial China,* p. 65. The author also notes that the so-called sixteen prefectures included eighteen, to be precise, but historical texts of the tenth century and later conventionally refer to sixteen.

80. Franke, *Cambridge History of China,* vol. 6, pp. 70–71.

81. Franke, *Cambridge History of China,* vol. 6, pp. 72–73.

82. *Wudai shiji,* chap. 9, pp. 92–93.

83. Franke, *Cambridge History of China,* vol. 6, pp. 72–74; Wang, *Structure of Power,* pp. 192–197.

84. *Wudai shiji,* chap. 10, p. 102.

85. *Wudai shiji,* chap. 18, p. 191.

86. *Wudai shiji,* chap. 18, pp. 191–192.

87. *Wudai shiji*, chap. 19, p. 197.

88. *Wudai shiji*, chap. 18, p. 192; Mote, *Imperial China*, pp. 93–95.

89. *Wudai shiji*, chap. 12, p. 117.

90. Franke, *Cambridge History of China*, vol. 6, p. 81.

91. *Wudai shiji*, chap. 12, pp. 117–126; Franke, *Cambridge History of China*, vol. 6, p. 81; Mote, *Imperial China*, pp. 92–93.

92. Fang, "Power Structures and Cultural Identities," chap. 5.

93. *Wudai shiji*, chap. 62, p. 776. I have written at greater length on Ouyang Xiu's portrayal of Shizong; see "The Heroism of Chou Shih-tsung." Also see Li, "Zhou Shizong lun," pp. 310–341.

94. *Wudai shiji*, chap. 67, p. 843.

95. *Wudai shiji*, chap. 54, p. 615; chap. 70, pp. 865–866.

96. *Song shi*, chap. 484, pp. 13,967–13,980. See pp. 13,969–13,970 for information on the Chenqiao mutiny and Han Tong's death. The late Song/early Yuan historian Ma Duanlin, writing before completion of the official history for the Song, acknowledges the omission of Han Tong as perhaps politically motivated. See *Wenxian tongkao*, chap. 192, p. 1628.

97. *Jiu wudai shi*, chap. 132–136. "Hereditary Regimes" included Chu, Eastern Han, Min, and Wu/Yue; "Illicit Usurpers" included Wu and Nanping, Former and Later Shu, Southern Han, and Southern Tang.

98. Ouyang Xiu is commonly identified as a native of Luling, modern Jiangxi, but he was born in Sichuan and raised in Hubei, spending little time in Luling even as an adult; see Liu, *Ou-yang Hsiu*, p. 25.

99. Davis, "Images of the South," pp. 147–150.

100. Elvin, *Pattern of the Chinese Past*, pp. 152–157.

101. Tsien, *Science and Civilisation in China*, pp. 154–159.

102. Mote, *Imperial China*, pp. 21–22. Reflecting the high level of local investment in some parts of the south during the tenth century, the Wu regime to precede Southern Tang had inherited a war-ravaged and bankrupt Yangzhou in the 890s, only to restore the city to its old glory by the early tenth century. See *Zizhi tongjian*, chap. 259, pp. 8430–8431, 8434–8435.

103. *Wudai shiji*, chap. 62, p. 775. On naval power in the south, see Zheng, *Wudai shiguoshi*, pp. 67–70.

104. Barfield, *Perilous Frontier*, pp. 131–150; Sinor, *Cambridge History of Early Inner Asia*, pp. 285–316; Zhang, *Sui/Tang/Wudai shi*, pp. 365–370.

105. On Uighur history for this period, see Barfield, *Perilous Frontier*, pp. 150–163; Mackerras, *Uighur Empire*, pp. 7–32; Sinor, *Cambridge History of Early Inner Asia*, pp. 317–342; Twitchett, *Cambridge History of China*, vol. 3, pp. 676–681; Zhang, *Sui/Tang/Wudai shi*, pp. 370–379.

106. Barfield, *Perilous Frontier*, p. 157.

107. For information on the Khitan and their expansion in the tenth century, see Barfield, *Perilous Frontier*, pp. 164–177; Franke, *Cambridge History of China*, vol. 6, pp. 43–153; Mote, *Imperial China*, pp. 31–48; Sinor, *Cambridge History of Inner Asia*, pp. 400–412; Wittfogel, *Chinese Society*, pp. 20–23.

108. Molé, *The Tu-yü-hun*, pp. xii–xxv.

109. On the conquest of Bohai see Franke, *Cambridge History of China*, vol. 6, p. 66.

110. On the symbolism of Abaoji's action see Mote, *Imperial China*, pp. 39–40.

111. Franke, *Cambridge History of China*, vol. 6, pp. 154–214; Zhang, *Sui/Tang/Wudai shi*, pp. 385–386; Mote, *Imperial China*, pp. 168–171.

112. On the history of military institutions for the period, see Wang, *The Structure of Power*; Hori, "Godai Sōsho ni okeru kingun no hatten," pp. 83–151; Sudō, "Godai setsudoshi no shihai taisei," pp. 521–539; Zhang, *Wudai jinjun chutan*.

113. Wang, *The Structure of Power*, pp. 47–148.

114. Zhang, *Wudai jinjun*, pp. 2 (preface), 5 (text).

115. On the origins and importance of this personal guard, see Hino, *Tōbatsu godaisho jiei gigunkō*, vol. 1, pp. 139–152; Zheng, *Wudai shiguoshi*, pp. 45–48.

116. In Song times, *li* refers to clerks in the subbureaucracy, that is, civilians. The status of *li*, based on a careful reading of the *Historical Records*, was much higher during the Five Dynasties, thus the translation "administrative aide." Usually, such aides are military advisors, not civilians, but not always.

117. Zhang, *Wudai jinjun*, p. 3; Zheng, *Wudai shiguoshi*, pp. 58–62.

118. The "Six Armies" for the early Liang were: Dragon and Tiger *(Longhu)*, Forest of Feathers *(Yulin)*, Divinely Martial *(Shenwei)*, Heavenly Martial *(Tianwu)*, Valorously Martial *(Yingwu)*, and Heavenly Awe *(Tianwei)*, each with a "left" and "right." The separate elite forces consisted of the Dragon-Prancing *(Longxiang)*, Divinely Victorious *(Shenjie)*, Crane-Commanding *(Konghe)*, and Divinely Awesome guards *(Shenwei)*. See Zhang, *Wudai jinjun*, pp. 7, 40. On the relationship of the Six Armies' commanders to the throne, see Wang, *The Structure of Power*, pp. 103–106.

119. *Wudai huiyao*, chap. 24, pp. 381–382.

120. For a detailed discussion of the evolution of the *Shumiyuan* in the Five Dynasties, see Su, "Wudai de shumiyuan," pp. 3–19. Also see Wang, *The Structure of Power*, pp. 89–93; *Wudai huiyao*, chap. 24, p. 377; *Cambridge History of China*, vol. 3, pp. 703–704, 780, Zhang, *Songchu zhengzhi*, pp. 21–32; Zheng, *Wudai shiguoshi*, pp. 23–27.

121. *Wudai huiyao*, chap. 24, p. 380; Wang, *The Structure of Power*, pp. 92–101.

122. *Wudai huiyao*, chap. 24, p. 381; Wang, *The Structure of Power*, p. 95.

123. Wang, *The Structure of Power*, pp. 127–131.

124. On these various changes in rules governing prefects, see Zheng, *Wudai shiguoshi*, pp. 49–54.

125. Zheng, *Wudai shiguoshi*, pp. 51–52; *Wudai huiyao*, chap. 19, pp. 312–313.

126. Wang, *The Structure of Power*, pp. 149–207, esp. 158; Zhang, *Wudai jinjun*, pp. 19, 87.

127. Zhang, *The Structure of Power*, pp. 31–38.

128. Zhang, *Wudai jinjun*, p. 87.

129. *Wudai shiji*, chap. 17, p. 185.

130. *Zizhi tongjian*, chap. 268, p. 8747.

131. Interestingly, parallels between the chastity of an upright woman and the loyalty of a Confucian male are further developed by the famed historian Sima Guang, a late contemporary of Ouyang Xiu and chief editor of the *Comprehensive Mirror for the Advancement of Governance*. For him, a courtier's relationship with the ruler is as inviolate as that between husband and wife, such that a courtier entering the service of a new ruler is tantamount to a wife's entering a new marriage after her husband's death. Sima Guang cites the preface from the *Historical Records* almost in its entirety, then proceeds with his own commentary, which merits substantial citation here:

> In my humble opinion, a proper woman should not submit to two husbands and a loyal subject should not serve two rulers. An improper woman, notwithstanding glamorous physical appeal or her craft as seamstress, does not deserve respect; the subject without loyalty, notwithstanding multiple talents and governing skills, does not deserve celebrity. Why? It is due to deficiencies in the basic rules of ethics. Dao served as minister to five dynasties and eight surnames [including the Khitan], like meeting passersby on a highway—his enemy in the morning becoming his overlord by night, altering facial expressions and utterances without ever feeling shame. Such was the case for his basic ethics, so regardless of minor good deeds, how can they possibly deserve celebration? Since the demise of Tang rule, some have argued, royal houses would come and go, the farsighted surviving barely beyond a decade while the shortsighted survived a mere three or four years. Even for a subject dedicated and bright, what possibly could be done? And at the time, Dao was hardly alone in compromising the integrity of a subject. Why isolate him for recrimination, they ask?
>
> The loyal subject, I humbly believe, anguishes over civic matters as he would his own family, exposing his very life in the face of peril. When a ruler is in error, he admonishes in strident opposition; and when his empire faces ruin, he exhausts integrity even unto death. The astute servitor surfaces when the Way prevails in the empire and hides away in its absence: some vanish into the hills and forests, while others join companions in roaming the world. Dao received deference as one of the Three preceptors, at the time, and enjoyed powers as the senior among ministers. Yet through the life of each dynasty, he passively folded hands and kept silent to secure posts and perquisites. When these empires collapsed, he schemed to escape harm and cling to life, while even welcoming upstarts and prodding successors. As rulers were enthroned and dethroned, Dao stayed content with wealth and station—an act of villainy too extraordinary for him to be compared to others.

Sima Guang reaffirms Ouyang Xiu's negative appraisal of Feng Dao as self-absorbed and self-interested, his political maneuverings making him a veritable "traitor" [*jianchen*], a word implying evil of the first order. The commentary also articulates cogently a point only implied in the *Historical Records*: Feng Dao's conduct did differ from others due to his unparalleled powers at court, powers that demanded a level of devotion and sacrifice exceeding men of lesser station. In effect, expectations of loyalty should mirror the political hierarchy, and for those at the pinnacle of power, the level of loyal commitment and personal sacrifice should be higher. See *Zizhi tongjian*, chap. 291, pp. 9510–13.

132. On rising Song standards for loyalist virtue, see Davis, *Wind against the Mountain*, pp. 14–16.

133. In the *New History of the Tang*, compiled by the court under the general editorship of Ouyang Xiu, there occurs a parallel process of narrowing the definition of "loyalist," where nearly one-fourth of the biographies in the *Old History of the Tang* were purged to make way for more credible entries. See Davis, *Wind against the Mountain*, p. 15

134. Mote, *Imperial China*, pp. 49–51.

135. On marriage age for the Song dynasty, see Chu Hsi, *Family Rituals*, pp. 48–49.

136. Such views are better articulated in his *New History of the Tang*. See Davis, "Chaste and Filial Women in the Historical Writings of Ouyang Xiu."

137. For further information, see Nienhauser, *The Grand Scribe's Records*, vol. 1, pp. xxxi–xxxiv.

138. Needham and Yates, *Science and Civilisation in China*, vol. 5, part VI, pp. 54–66, 101 passim.

NOTES TO CHAPTER 1

The Zhonghua shuju (Beijing) annotated reissue of the *Historical Records*, reproduced as *Xin wudai shi* in 1974 and slightly revised in 1992, is the foundation for the translation and annotation to follow. Consulting the various critical editions from traditional China, the editors also added their own comments and emendations. Reference below to "notes" within the *Wudai shiji* generally indicates that their annotation is the basis for my comments. But I have also consulted and included important notes from Zeng Sanyi of the mid-Southern Song, which appear as footnotes in the Zhonghua edition. Reference to his notes will be specifically indicated. Annotation on the annotation also exists for the first chapter, which I have once cited; see Yan Yiping, *Wudai shiji zhu jiaoding*. Many notes in the Zhonghua text are devoted to alternative readings of Chinese characters, particularly personal or place names. Rather than provide a full citation, I simply indicate the alternate spelling with brackets, as with "Lai Zhao" [Mi Zhao], where the *Historical Records* gives "Lai" as surname but other sources provide "Mi." The alternate reading appears after the original in brackets. See chapter 33.

1. The date given by Ouyang Xiu for the death of Xizong, April 17, is inconsistent with other authoritative sources, which give April 19; but I have chosen not to alter the entry; see *Wudai shiji*, chap. 1, p. 10, note 1.

2. This event occurred in 884, according to the Annals of Tang, p. 32.

3. Biyang was a county at the time, not prefecture, according to Zeng Sanyi commentary; see *Wudai shiji*, chap. 1, p. 6.

4. The text reads "an armored Son of Heaven," but modern annotators believe the "armor" *(jia)* to be a reference to the *jiazi* day. See *Wudai shiji*, chap. 1, p. 10, note 1; *Zizhi tongjian*, chap. 263, p. 8593.

5. Modern annotators point to some confusion about the identity of the assassin of Cui Yin: Ouyang Xiu gives Zhu Youqian, annotator Zeng Sanyi gives Zhu Youmou, the *Historical Records* elsewhere gives Zhu Youliang; and Qing-dynasty annotator Yan Yiping describes the confusion at length. See *Wudai shiji*, chap. 1, p. 11, note 2; chap. 13, p. 134; Yan, *Wudai shiji zhu jiaoding*, pp. 50–52. All three interpretations assume Ouyang Xiu to be in error, when he was likely simply following the *Spring and Autumn Annals* tradition of blaming the responsible person, irrespective of who actually carried out the murder. For example, in the "Basic Annals" of the *New History of the Tang*, written personally by Ouyang Xiu, Cui Yin's assassination is intentionally attributed to Zhu Quanzhong himself—the man behind the act, not the actual murderer. (Ouyang Xiu et al., *Xin Tang shu*, chap. 10, p. 301) When a discrepancy emerges in the *Historical Records* between the Annals and the biographical chapters, it likely reflects some conflict between reporting the facts and fixing responsibility for a crime. In such cases, the biographical chapter is more likely to reveal the actual perpetrator.

6. The text by Ouyang Xiu gives "*jiachen* day of the fourth month," but there is no *jiachen* day for the "fourth month" only the "intercalary" fourth month. The intercalary month is also cited in *Zizhi tongjian*, chap. 264, p. 8631.

7. On the eve of usurping the Han throne in C.E. 9, chief minister Wang Mang had accepted from the throne the "nine official privileges with vestments" *(jiuxi)*, providing precedent for this action. See *Zizhi tongjian*, chap. 265, p. 8651.

8. Chanzhou, also known as Puyang County (modern Qingfeng County, Henan) during the Five Dynasties, has been widely rendered in secondary English scholarship as "Shanzhou" or "Shanyuan." Yet the most authoritative Chinese dictionaries, including *Kangxi cidian* (p. 520) and *Hanyu da cidian* (vol. 6, p. 178) all give "Chan" as the appropriate spelling. Perhaps the "Shan" rendering is based on the *Zizhi tongjian*, where a Song-dynasty annotator gives "Shan," not "Chan," as the pronunciation; see *Zizhi tongjian*, chap. 225, p. 7250. Was the annotator simply mistaken or was "Shan" the Song-dynasty pronunciation for the character? A brief note by student-annotator Xu Wudang, in the *Historical Records*, alludes to the character Chan as derived in ancient times from another character, pronounced "Shan," which might explain the dual pronunciations; see chap. 46, p. 509. In any case, I have consistently followed modern pronunciation for names and terms in this text, even when a different contemporary pronunciation is known.

NOTES TO CHAPTER 2

1. A number of subtle changes are introduced in this chapter, coinciding with the formal accession of Taizu to the throne: the "Prince" now becomes the "Son of Heaven," and announcement of each of the four seasons now precedes the dates, in affirmation of the Liang dynasty's legitimate authority over the calendar. The announcement of "spring" is particularly rich with symbolism about political authority and continuity.

2. For details, see chapter 35.

3. On the post in question, *Shumiyuan,* and its growing importance, see Introduction.

4. The word *hong,* used for the death of a feudal lord or leading courtier, is translated as "passed away" to be distinguished from the death of more ordinary men of stature, *zu,* which I translate as simple "died" or "perished." Ouyang Xiu saw Zhang Wenwei as a traitor to his country, yet still conformed to protocol in citing his death (chapter 35).

5. The biography of Li Qi has not been translated. In discussing the palace protocol of Tang times that became simplified in its waning years and further debased in the Later Tang, he states: "Since the disruption of ritual propriety in the Qianfu era [C.E. 874–879], the Son of Heaven no longer met with the official rank and file on a daily basis and met only on the new moon. In consequence, the honor guards at the formal entrance were not on regular duty, although the guards were present for informal audiences on the new moon. The latter practice subsequently became commonplace, the extent to which greater symbolism was attached to 'procession to the auxiliary palace.' At one point, even processions via the anterior palace were dubbed 'processions to the auxiliary palace,' a practice abandoned for awhile and then revived at this time [Later Tang]." Li Qi, a strict ritualist, opposed such informality, but did not win the day. See *Wudai shiji,* chap. 54, pp. 617–618.

6. The author is alluding here to the early version of his essay on "Legitimate Rule" *(Zhengtong lun).* See Introduction.

NOTES TO CHAPTER 3

Note: Taizu's direct successor, Zhu Yougui, assassinated his father to rule for only eight months, so he is not afforded an annal. On the reign of Zhu Yougui, see chapter 13, biography of Zhu Youwen.

1. "Commandant of reserve cavalry" [*fuma duwei*] is an honorary rank provided imperial in-laws. Zhao Yan's involvement in the coup of Zhu Youzhen is significant due to his standing as imperial in-law, not command of armies.

2. Emperor Mo would reign for the next two years using the reign name of the dynasty's founder. On the symbolism of this act, see commentary in chapter 10, p. 99.

3. The princedom of "Jin" is acknowledged as Later "Tang" only after the fourth month of 923, when Li Cunxu formerly assumes the throne, a principle followed throughout the Annals where titles must conform to real powers.

4. On the pilfering of these important seals, see the biography of Zheng Jue (chapter 54) pp. 443, 511 and *Zizhi tongjian*, chap. 272, p. 8898.

NOTES TO CHAPTER 4

1. The subject of this chapter, Li Keyong, or Taizu, never ruled as emperor, so his narrative is subsumed under that of his successor Zhuangzong.

2. On the date of Guochang's death, given as 887 elsewhere, see Introduction, note 65.

3. For citation in the *Old History of the Five Dynasties*, see *Jiu wudai shi*, chap. 25, p. 331.

NOTES TO CHAPTER 5

1. By other accounts, Cunxu had just been born in the year 884.

2. I have based names of Chinese stars and constellations on Needham, *Science and Civilisation*, vol. 3.

3. As historian Zhao Yi notes, the practice of citing the multiple birth of sons began with the *Old History of the Tang*; there they served as auspicious omens, whereas Ouyang Xiu uses them to indicate "change." See *Nianershi zhaji*, chap. 21, pp. 459–460.

4. On the symbolism of leveling the accession altar, see chapter 28, biography of Zhang Xian.

NOTES TO CHAPTER 6

1. Later known as Li Zanhua, the Prince of Dongdan was deposed as heir to Abaoji. See Mote, *Imperial China*, pp. 51–52.

2. See chapter 24, biography of An Chonghui.

NOTE TO CHAPTER 8

1. These several men were probably sent as technical consultants, inasmuch as a later chapter not translated here indicates that the Khitan were avid borrowers of Chinese ways, material as well as political; see *Wudai shiji*, chap. 72, p. 894.

NOTE TO CHAPTER 9

1. See original citation in *Yili* (Sibu congkan ed.), chap. 11, "sangfu," p. 7b.

NOTES TO CHAPTER 10

1. Reign names *(nianhao)* were introduced during the Han dynasty, 178 B.C.E., to be precise, with a single emperor often employing multiple names to symbolize some ideal or aspiration for the period. Before this, calendars and histories were ordered by the title of the monarch himself, "first year in the reign of King X."

2. In the original phrase, Mencius writes, "When one has something within, it necessarily shows itself without." See D. C. Lau, trans., *Mencius*, Book 6, Part B, p. 175.

NOTE TO CHAPTER 11

1. Both this text and the *Zizhi tongjian* give the seventeenth as the day of Taizu's death and the twenty-first as the day of Shizong's accession. Yet the *Zizhi tongjian* also reveals discrepancies between the *Veritable Records* of Taizu and those for Shizong on the date of accession; those records, extant during the Song period, are no longer available. See *Zizhi tongjian*, chap. 291, pp. 9500–9501.

NOTES TO CHAPTER 12

1. Xiande is the reign name adopted by Taizu on the lunar New Year of 954, two weeks shy of his death. The reign was not changed after Shizong assumed power nor after his son Gongdi succeeded him in 959—an unthinkable event the reason for which is uncertain.

2. There are slight discrepancies in the posthumous title of Gaozu; see Basic Annals, chapter 11.

3. The wording here for "relinquishing the throne" [*xun yu wei*] closely parallels the phrasing of Yin Shu [*xun wei*] in *Spring and Autumn Annals for the Five Dynasties*, suggesting that he inspired Ouyang Xiu. See *Wudai chunqiu*, chap. 2, p. 7a.

4. The "official historians" being referred to are the writers of the original dynastic history, who present a more critical treatment of Shizong for overextending the military and economic capacities of his own empire; see *Jiu wudai shi*, chap. 119, p. 1587.

NOTES TO CHAPTER 13

1. Citations from *Zhou Yi* (Sibu congkan ed.), chap. 1, pp. 5b–6a, and chap. 4, pp. 7b–8a; Richard Wilhelm, trans., *I Ching*, pp. 15, 143–146.

2. Other sources for the period give the inaugural year of Longde [C.E. 921], not the fourth Zhenming year [C.E. 918], as the year of the Youneng's rebellion. See *Wudai shiji*, chap. 13, p. 139 n. 4.

3. Yuan Xiangxian is reported as "nephew" of Taizu, not "grandson," in the *Old History*. See *Wudai shiji*, chap. 13, p. 139 n. 5.

4. The argument about whether to sanction the rule of Zhu Yougui seems the weakest in the entire history. In reality, the future Emperor Mo controlled the eastern capital of Kaifeng during Yougui's rule, effectively denying him undisputed rule over north-central China. Ouyang Xiu did not employ this argument, however, making a moralistic argument instead.

NOTES TO CHAPTER 14

1. "Eleventh month" is based on the Basic Annals of Zhuangzong. The original citation of "tenth month" is probably in error, an error overlooked by modern annotators. See *Wudai shiji*, chap. 14, p. 155 n. 1.

NOTE TO CHAPTER 15

1. "Cui Jian" may be an erroneous rendering of "Cui Jujian," but modern annotators indicate some confusion about whether this represents a single person or two persons. See *Wudai shiji*, chap. 15, p. 169 n. 1.

NOTES TO CHAPTER 17

1. As indicated by modern punctuators, other sources indicate investiture as "Princess of Jin," not "Wei," in the year C.E. 935. See *Wudai shiji*, chap. 17, p. 189 n. 1.

2. Huanglong Prefecture, in modern Jilin Province slightly north of Changchun city, would have been roughly two thousand kilometers from the Jin capital.

3. The Bohai kingdom of southern Manchuria, which fell to the Khitan in 926, was renamed Dongdan, its king assuming vassal status. See Franke, *The Cambridge History of China*, vol. 6, pp. 66ff.

4. Hanercheng or Hancheng, literally "Town of Han," in the Khitan domain, was populated mostly by Han Chinese settlers. See *Wudai shiji*, chap. 72, p. 886.

5. The rendering of this last sentence is based on Sima Guang's *Zizhi tongjian* (chap. 283, pp. 9254–9255). The passage as it appears in the *Historical Records* de-

clares, "I am a groom today. *Is this not like living!* [*he si sheng*]." The passage makes no sense to scholars that I consulted recently in China; in the late eleventh century it must have similarly confounded Sima Guang, who adopted a rather different and more direct wording. I suspect a problem with the final character for "life" [*sheng*], which if simply changed to *ru* [likeness], would conform to the Sima Guang reading.

6. The *Old History* renders Jinghui's personal name as "Hui." See *Wudai shiji*, chap. 17, p. 189 n. 3.

7. Other sources refer to Shi Chongrui as youngest son, the seventh son of Gaozu, and Chonggao as the sixth, which makes sense in terms of his nickname. See *Wudai huiyao*, chap. 2, p. 16.

NOTES TO CHAPTER 20

1. See D. C. Lau, trans., *Mencius*, VII.A.35.

2. Other editions read, "Guo is an old acquaintance of *our King*." See *Wudai shiji*, chap. 20, p. 205 n. 3.

NOTES TO CHAPTERS 21–23

1. D. C. Lau, trans., *Mencius*, Book VII, Part 2, chap. 2.

2. According to Joseph Needham and Robin Yates, "embrasures" [*pi*] were stations atop the city wall, some 3–5 feet high in classical times, where marksmen could shoot down on intruders. The "barbican" or "jar" wall [*weng (yong?) cheng*], located inside the main wall, was designed to "protect the gate" as a secondary line of defense. See *Science and Civilisation*, vol. 5, Part VI, pp. 307 and 336–337.

3. Chinese armies tend to be divided into "left" and "right," then "center" [*zhongjun*], containing the chief commander; see *Wudai shiji*, chap. 70, p. 865. Also see chapter 70 of the present text.

4. The quote comes from Chao Cuo, a famed strategist of the ancient Han dynasty. See *Chengyu da cidian*, p. 52.

5. For an English translation of the ancient military text *Liu tao*, see Ralph D. Sawyer, *The Seven Military Classics of Ancient China*, pp. 19–105.

6. The death of Taizu and the massacre at Zaoqiang both occurred in the same year, that is, C.E. 912; the events are not separated by a year, as indicated here; see *Wudai shiji*, chap. 23, p. 244 n. 1.

NOTES TO CHAPTERS 24–28

1. Modern annotators note inconsistencies in the sources about this personal name, which in some other texts appears as Wang Yu. See *Wudai shiji*, chap. 24, p. 257 n. 1.

2. The Yellow River, the critical barrier between the Liang and Jin armies, runs in a northeasterly direction in the Shandong region, so "west of Yun" refers to regions on the "upper" or northern side of the river.

3. Iron writs *(tiequan)* represent a promise of immunity from future prosecution; see the biographies of Zhu Youqian and Guo Chongtao in the present volume. Interestingly, both Zhu and Guo were ultimately killed despite their immunities. For additional references to the practice, see *Wudai shiji*, pp. 247, 493, 580, 705, 734, 838; *Zizhi tongjian*, chap. 276, p. 9025.

4. Modern annotators believe this event to have occurred in C.E. 925, not as presented here in the "next year"—i.e., 926. See *Wudai shiji*, chap. 24, p. 257 n. 2.

5. The veracity of this quote is questioned by annotators of *Zizhi tongjian*, who note that the Prince of Lu had not given any indication of rebelling in 931, when Chongtao died. See *Zizhi tongjian*, chap. 277, p. 9060.

NOTES TO CHAPTER 30

1. The *liang shi* sometimes refers to surveillance commissioners *(guanchashi)* and governors *(jiedushi)*; see Xue Juzheng et al., *Jiu wudai shi*, chap. 85, p. 1122. In this context, however, the reference to the fiscal commissioner *(sansishi)* makes more sense.

2. The text originally gave "tenth month" for the death of Hongzhao, contradicting the Basic Annals earlier, which gives the "eleventh month." See *Wudai shiji*, chap. 10, p. 106.

NOTES TO CHAPTER 32

1. Other sources, including the *Old History*, give "Li Shaobin," not Fu Cunshen, as the person being addressed by Zhuangzong. See *Wudai shiji*, chap. 32, p. 353 n. 2.

2. Earlier Ouyang Xiu states that Renshan died on the same day that he met Shizong. Other sources, such as the *Comprehensive Mirror*, suggest the lapse of several days between the meeting and his death, enough time for the Emperor to confer office. The distinction is an important one for Ouyang Xiu, as is reflected in the commentary that follows. See *Wudai shiji*, chap. 32, p. 353 n. 3.

NOTES TO CHAPTER 33

1. Martyrs in Service represent an ethically less perfect group relative to the preceding Martyrs to Virtue. Many of them have histories of service to other dynasties, whereas Martyrs to Virtue served a single dynasty; thus Ouyang Xiu's characterization as "men of complete integrity" *(quan jie)* in the preface to chapter 32.

2. The biography of Yuande gives "third year of Zhenming" (C.E. 917) as the date for this event, but the Basic Annals earlier gives Yuande's date of death as "second year of Zhenming;" see *Wudai shiji*, chap. 3, p. 26. The "third year" is inconsistent with other sources as well, according to modern annotators; see *Wudai shiji*, chap. 33, p. 367 n. 1.

3. According to the Basic Annals, the Dong Zhang rebellion began in the ninth month of 930, while Luqi died in the fourth month of 931; see *Wudai shiji*, chap. 6, pp. 62–63. The narrative here suggests that the two events were much closer in time.

4. The text here originally read "Nimble-Victory Guard" [*Feisheng*]. The *Old History* gives "Nimble-Prancing" [*Feiteng*], and modern annotators consider this more likely; see *Wudai shiji*, chap. 33, p. 367 n. 3.

5. The *Old History* gives "Huazhou‡" as the place of assignment, at the time; see *Wudai shiji*, chap. 33, p. 367 n. 4.

6. The Zhou dynasty already controlled the "entire northern Huai region," as originally worded.

NOTES TO CHAPTER 35

1. Located at Huazhou, Baima Post is where more than thirty Tang courtiers were massacred in the sixth month of 905, under pressure from Zhu Quanzhong. See *Zizhi tongjian*, chap. 265, p. 8643.

2. Based on an array of primary sources consulted by modern annotators, Yang Shou is not the grandfather of Yang She, but his uncle. See *Wudai shiji*, chap. 35, p. 383 n. 1.

3. This represents a posthumous demotion for the deceased Tang monarch, the "Illustrious Emperor," Zhaozong. Under the Later Tang a reversal occurs and proponents of demotion are punished.

4. See Legge, *Confucian Analects*, Book 13, chap. 15, p. 268.

NOTES TO CHAPTER 37

1. For details, see the biography of Yuan Xingqin.

2. For original citation, see James Legge, *Shoo King*, Part II, Book II, chap. 3, verse 21, p. 65.

3. Li Keyong's nickname was "Li the Crow" (Li Ya'er; see chapter 4). Li Cunxu's own nickname, Yazi, sounds somewhat like "crow" but contains the character for "inferior," not crow. According to the *Old History of the Five Dynasties*, the Tang Emperor Zhaozong once commented, upon meeting an already impressive Cunxu, "He can potentially make even his father look inferior [*ke ya qi fu*]." The nickname Yazi thereby stuck. See *Jiu wudai shi*, chap. 27, p. 366.

4. According to *Zizhi tongjian*, the passage should read, "There is only one person who manages [*li*] the world. Who else is he referring to?" The surname Li and the verb for "manage" are homonyms. See *Zizhi tongjian*, chap. 272, p. 8904.

5. The term "taboo pertaining to dogs" (*huigou* or *huiquan*) usually relates to taboos against female dogs giving birth in the home of humans. Here, the term clearly relates to broader proscriptions against Chinese subjects alluding to dogs, owing to myths associating barbarians with dogs. In another section of the *Historical Records*, not translated here, there is mention of a "dog country" *(gouguo)* to the far north where legend has it that humans mixed with dogs, producing male offspring that looked like dogs and female offspring that looked like humans. See *Wudai shiji*, chap. 73, p. 907.

6. For the original citation, see Yang Bojun, *Chunqiu Zuozhuan zhu*, "Prince Xuan, 12th year," p. 741.

NOTE TO CHAPTER 38

1. This passage derives from the *Book of Rites*. See *Liji* (Sibu congkan ed.), chap. 1 ("qu," 1a), p. 1b.

NOTE TO CHAPTERS 40–41

1. Chao Cuo had wanted to reduce the powers of the feudal lords in the early Han and died when they turned against him. See Burton Watson, *Records of the Grand Historian: Han Dynasty*, vol. 1, pp. 462–466.

NOTES TO CHAPTERS 42–43

1. For the original citation, see Lao Zi, *Laozi: Daode jing* (Sibu congkan ed.), Part 2, p. 10b, and D. C. Lau, trans., *Tao Te Ching*, p. 119.

2. "Jing Xiang" is probably an error for "Li Zhen," according to modern annotators. See *Wudai shiji*, chap. 43, p. 478 n. 1.

NOTES TO CHAPTERS 44–45

1. The "rope" represents the sons and grandsons of Wang Jian, with the generational identifier of "Cheng" in their personal names, a close approximation of the word for rope *(sheng)*.

2. Modern annotators believe "next year" to be a mistake, as other primary sources give C.E. 923, not 924, as the date for Zhuangzong's visit to Luoyang. See *Wudai shiji*, p. 501 n. 1.

3. Versions of the story in other sources give "hundreds of thousands" in cash as representing Xiangxian's fortune, which seems an understatement in light of the assertion, later in the same passage, that his cash fortune "filled an entire room." See *Wudai shiji*, chap. 45, p. 501 n. 2.

NOTES TO CHAPTERS 46–47

1. According to *Zizhi tongjian,* the "northern chair" *(hu chuang)* originated with the Shatuo, although the term may refer to any northern or imported chair with a raised back; see *Zizhi tongjian,* chap. 278, p. 9093. In personal communications, an art dealer and furniture historian in Taiwan, Hong Guangming, has suggested that "northern chairs" tend to be folding and thus more portable than Chinese alternatives.

2. According to the Basic Annals for Mingzong, Mingzong acceded to the throne on the twentieth day of the fourth month, nearly three weeks after Zhuangzong's death but six days before Jiji, the Prince of Wei, perished. Thus, Ouyang Xiu's commentary contains a slight overstatement.

NOTES TO CHAPTERS 48–50

1. One "army" *(jun)* consists of roughly twelve thousand men, or four "divisions" *(shi).* Command of "eight armies" suggests an unreasonable number of men, so perhaps "Eighth Army" is a more accurate rendering of the passage. "Shanhou" refers to the region of modern Hebei Province centering on the Taihang and Dujun Mountains and extending as far north as Beijing. See *Zhongguo lishi diming da cidian,* p. 68.

2. On the eve of Qingming, the fourth day of the fourth lunar month, when ancestors' graves are swept, the Chinese refrain from eating hot foods as a form of fasting.

NOTES TO CHAPTERS 51–53

1. For another rendering, see D. C. Lau, trans., *Analects,* Book XVII, chap. 2, p. 142.

2. The word for "contemptible" can mean "wicked" in the sense of awesome, which was the initial reading by Guangyuan.

3. The abatis, translated by Needham and Yates as "chevaux-de-frise," is a wooden skeleton set at an angle and supporting spears fixed tightly in place. See *Science and Civilisation,* vol. 5, Part VI, pp. 334–335.

4. Kunlun refers to the remote west or south and its darker inhabitants.

5. Jue is the first and Kang the second star in the Chinese constellation of twenty-eight, the two actually constituting a total of six stars, as we know today. They are associated by modern scholars with Virginis. See Needham, *Science and Civilisation,* vol. 3, pp. 234–238.

NOTES TO CHAPTERS 54–55

1. Ouyang Xiu does not quote, but paraphrases Guan Zhong. See *Guanzi* (Sibu congkan ed.), chap. 1, "Mumin," pp. 2a–2b.

2. For the original citation, see James Legge, trans., *Confucian Analects*, Book V, chap. 27, p. 183.

3. The poem by Nie Yizhong (b. 837) is cited in full in the *Old History of the Five Dynasties*; see *Jiu wudai shi*, chap. 126, p. 1658. There, the title "Farmer's Song" *(tianjia shi)* is preceded by the word *shang*, meaning an ill or downtrodden farmer.

4. *Yi ching*, "Xici zhuan," Part B, chap. 8, p. 1b.

5. Dao served Mingzong as minister from 927 to 933. Ouyang Xiu is guilty of intentional overstatement here.

6. Ren Huan had been dismissed as chief minister for five years prior to the appointment of Li Yu‡, according to modern editors, so "reassignment" must refer to Zhao Feng, not Ren Huan. See *Wudai shiji*, chap. 54, p. 624 n. 2.

7. The "third year" (C.E. 932) is probably an error for the "fourth year" (C.E. 933). See *Wudai shiji*, chap. 55, p. 638 n. 3.

8. The *Old History of the Tang* bears his name as chief editor, although his personal contribution to the effort is disputed.

NOTE TO CHAPTERS 56–57

1. For the original citation, see *Guanzi*, "Fafa," chap. 16, p. 2b.

NOTES TO CHAPTER 61

1. The text originally reads "son of Taizu," which is inconsistent with information elsewhere in this history. See *Wudai shiji*, chap. 61, p. 763 n. 2.

2. Here the *Historical Records* implies that two months separated Pu's dethronement from his death, whereas chapter 62 suggests that he died in late 938. Other authoritative texts give the "tenth month" of 937 as the date of dethronement as well as Pu's death. See *Wudai shiji*, chap. 61, p. 763 n. 3.

NOTES TO CHAPTER 62

1. The *Historical Records* originally gave "sixty-four *sui*" as Jing's age at death, making his date of birth roughly C.E. 898, which would make him only ten years younger than his father, Li Bian. The *Old History* gives forty-six at the age of death, which other authoritative sources tend to accept. See *Wudai shiji*, chap. 62, p. 781 n. 4.

2. On a scale of 1 to 9, with 1 as the highest.

3. "National histories" *(guoshi)* probably refer to the contemporary histories written by the courts for most of the Ten Kingdoms. It could also refer, however, to the contemporary histories authored by the Song court that contain information on the later years of the coterminous Ten Kingdoms. The latter would not have been

circulated beyond the court's History Bureau, but Ouyang Xiu served in an official capacity at that bureau as chief editor of the *New History of the Tang*, giving him access.

NOTES TO CHAPTER 63

1. The term *Wang ba*, literally "king or master of eight," invokes Wang's surname while alluding to his multitude of professions; meanwhile, the two characters in combination have the additional meaning of someone vulgar or bastardlike.

2. Seventh day of the seventh lunar month is known as "Chinese Valentine's Day," a festival celebrating enduring love.

3. The Tianxiong command at Qinzhou should be distinguished from the Tianxiong command at Weizhou, in the north.

4. For citation, see Yang Bojun, ed., *Chunqiu zuozhuan zhu*, p. 1680 (Duke of Xiang, 14th year).

5. This is a reference to Dai Yong (378–441), annotator of the *Book of Rites* during the Liu–Song dynasty. See *Song shu*, chap. 93, pp. 2276–2278.

6. Citation from *Mao Shi* (Sibu congkan ed.), chap. 1, p. 21b; James Legge, trans., *She King*, Part I, Book 2, verse 14, p. 36.

NOTES TO CHAPTER 64

1. The emperor's birthday was literally called "Day of the Sage's Reception" *(yingshengjie)*; see *Jiu wudai shi*, chap. 36, p. 499. The birthday being celebrated is that of the northern emperor, Mingzong of Tang.

2. The original entry reads "fourth year of Yixi," but as modern annotators indicate, other sources for the period give the "fourteenth year." See *Wudai shiji*, chap. 64, p. 808 n. 2.

3. Other sources indicate that Renyu was Prince of Peng, not Prince of Jia. See *Wudai shiji*, chap. 64, p. 808 n. 3.

NOTES TO CHAPTER 65

1. "Grand Possession" *(Dayou)*, translated by Wilhelm as "Possession in Great Measure," relates to the Sage-King's possession of Heaven's mandate. See *I Ching*, pp. 456–460.

2. According to modern annotators, most other sources give Meng‡, not Xiang¶ prefecture for the raid of 936; see *Wudai shiji*, chap. 65, p. 820 n. 2.

3. The *Han Ji* by Xun Yue (148–209) is a history of the Former Han dynasty written in the waning years of Later Han, namesake for the two Han dynasties of the Five Dynasties era.

4. In the Basic Annals, Ouyang Xiu gives the "fifth year"—C.E. 958—as the year that the Zhou pacified the northern Yangzi/southern Huai region, so modern annotators consider "third year" as a technical error; see *Wudai shiji,* chap. 65, p. 820 n. 2. However, the initial campaign against the region did begin in 956. If the word "pacify" *(ping)* is interpreted as a process, not merely an event, then no error may exist at all.

NOTES TO CHAPTER 66

1. Modern annotators, drawing on other primary sources, give 912 as the year of this assignment, which would be the reign of Taizu, not Mo; see *Wudai shiji,* chap. 66, pp. 832–833 n. 2.

2. Ruan Ji (210–263), famed as one of the "Seven Worthies of the Bamboo Grove," was a Daoist known for highly relaxed attitudes toward Confucian decorum.

3. Xiangyang lies to the southwest of Changsha and is not along the path from Yuezhou‡, directly to the north. Thus modern annotators consider Xiangxiang an erroneous rendering of Xiangyin County, just south of Yuezhou‡. See *Wudai shiji,* chap. 66, p. 833 n. 4.

NOTES TO CHAPTER 68

1. Schools of the "four gates" *(simen xue)* represents higher level institutions of education, modeled on the capital in the north.

2. "Daluo" represents the highest of the thirty-six heavens in religious Daoism.

3. The Prince of Chongshun probably represents Wang Shenzhi, the deceased founder of Min.

4. "Precious Emperor" *(Baohuang)* and "Primal Diety" *(Yuanshi tianzun)* are religious icons in Daoism. "Supreme sovereign" *(Taishang laojun)* represents Laozi, the founder of Daoist philosophy.

5. Other primary sources suggest that Jiye is the nephew, not son, of Yanxi; see *Wudai shiji,* chap. 68, p. 854 n. 3.

6. Taizong was the heroic second emperor of Tang, so Yuanbi is flattering Wang Yanxi by associating him with Taizong, even as he presses for the right to remonstrance.

NOTES TO CHAPTER 69

1. From chapter 3 of the *Classic on Filial Piety.* See *Xiao jing* (Sibu congkan ed.), pp. 4a–4b.

2. Taizhou lies on the eastern coast just north of the Yangzi River, a city formerly ruled by the Southern Tang but newly acquired by the Zhou. The relevance

of this information to the Nanping kingdom is unclear. The connecting passage seems to be missing.

NOTES TO CHAPTER 70

1. Ouyang Xiu prefers "Eastern Han" to "Northern Han" for the house of Liu Min. "Eastern" refers to the circuit Hedong (literally, "east of the Yellow River"), the heart of his satrapy.

OFFICES OF THE FIVE DYNASTIES

Ambassador for the grand procession, *dalishi* 大禮使
Academician, *xueshi* 學士
Accounts officer, *duzhi* 度支
Ad hoc prefect, *zhizhou* 知州
Adjutant, *sima* 司馬 *canjunshi* 參軍事
Administrative aide, *panguan* 判官
Administrative secretary, *zhangshuji* 掌書記 *shuli* 書吏
Area commander, *dutou* 都頭
Assisting commander, *pijiang* 裨將
Associate at the Secretariat, *puye* 僕射
Associate minister, *canzhi zhengshi* 參知政事
Attending censor, *shiyushi* 侍御史
Auxiliary, *ting* 廳
Cavalry rotation, *congmazhi* 從馬直
Chamber brigade, *tingzidu* 廳子都
Chamberlain for imperial ceremonies, *taichangqing* 太常卿,
supplemental revenues, *taifuqing* 太府卿
Chief coordinator, *zongguan* 總管
Chief counselor, *chengxiang* 丞相
Chief director, *du zhihuishi* 都指揮使 *dujian* 都監
Chief director of armed forces, *bingma dujian* 兵馬都監
Chief intendant, *duzhi* 都知
Chief minister, *zaixiang* 宰相
Chief officer, *dubushu* 都部署
Commandant, *dajiangjun* 大將軍
Commander, *tungjun* 統軍 *bingmashi* 兵馬使
Commander's attendant, *kejiang* 客將
Commissioner of alien suppression, *zhuoshengshi* 捉生使
Commissioner of armed forces, *xingjunshi* 行軍使
Commissioner of bandit suppression, *zhaotaoshi* 招討使
Commissioner of military affairs, *shumishi* 樞密使
Commissioner of palace armies, *xuanhuishi* 宣徽使

Commissioner of palace security, *huangchengshi* 皇城使
Commissioner of reconciliation, *xuanyushi* 宣諭使
Commissioner of regional order, *zhizhishi* 制直使
Commissioner of venerable governance, *chongzhengshi* 崇政使
Consultant, *zichengguan* 諮呈官
Counselor of affairs, *zhizhengshi* 知政事
Defense commissioner, *fangyushi* 防禦使
Deputy censor, *yushi zhongcheng* 御史中丞
Deputy director, *shilang* 侍郎
Detachments commander, *biejiang* 別將 *pianjiang* 偏將
Dignitary for education, *situ* 司徒 for public works, *sikong* 司空
Diplomatic accommodations master, *keshengshi* 客省使 *neikeshi* 内客使
Diplomatic secretary, *qiantongshi sheren* 遣通事舍人
Director, *langzhong* 郎中 *shizhong* 侍中
Domestic accounting commissioner, *neigoushi* 内勾使
Drafter, *sheren* 舍人
Emissary for state correspondence, *guoxinshi* 國信使
Equerry for imperial stud, *taipuqing* 太僕卿
Eunuch attendant, *neishi* 内侍
Eunuch deputy for the palace, *dianzhi* 殿直
General commander, *dutong* 都統
Generalissimo, *shangjiangjun* 上將軍
Governor, *jiedushi* 節度使
Governor's deputy, *zhishi* 支使
Governor's military attache, *yaya* 押衙
Grand marshal (*taiwei*) 太尉, mentor (*taifu*) 太傅, preceptor (*taishi*) 太師
Grandmaster of imperial recreations, *guanglu dafu* 光祿大夫
Grand minister of war, *da sima* 大司馬
Group commander, *juntou* 軍頭
Imperial Bodyguard, *qinjun* 親軍
Imperial escort commissioner, *hubishi* 扈蹕使
Imperial Guard, *shiwei* 侍衛 *suwei* 宿衛 *jinjun* 禁軍
Imperial Insignia Guard, *jinwuwei* 金吾衛
Imperial secretary, *shangshuling* 尚書令
Inspector general, *dudianjian* 都點檢
Inspector-in-chief, *duyuhou* 都虞候
Inspector of armies, *guanjunrongshi* 關軍容使
Interim custodian, *liushou* 留守
Interim regent, *liuhou* 留後
Judicial officer, *tuiguan* 推官
Local military commissioner, *jinglueshi* 經略使
Magistrate's assistant, *zhubu* 主簿
Manager adjutant, *xingjun sima* 行軍司馬
Master of admonition, *jianyi dafu* 諫議大夫

Master of auxiliary palace gates, *gemenshi* 閤門使
Master of granaries, *sinongqing* 司農卿
Master of imperial palaces and parks, *gongyuanshi* 宮苑使
Master of imperial pasturage, *mumashi* 牧馬使
Master of palace access, *yinjinshi* 引進使
Master of state ceremonies, *hongluqing* 鴻臚卿
Metropolitan headquarters, *yanei* 衙內
Military administrator or attaché to governor, *yajiang* 牙將
Military directives courier, *touzi* 頭子
Military director, *zhihuishi* 指揮使
Military formations officer, *paizhenshi* 排陣使
Military overseer, *jianjun* 監軍
Military police, *xunjiansi* 巡檢司
Military revenues commissioner, *liangliaoshi* 糧料使
Military training commissioner, *tuanlianshi* 團練使
Minister for the imperial clan, *zongzhengqing* 宗正卿
Minister of justice, *xingbu shangshu* 刑部尚書 personnel (*li*) 吏 public works (*gong*) 工 revenues (*hu*) 户 rites (*li*) 禮 war (*bing*) 兵
Officer's attendant, *suijun* 隨軍
Officer-in-waiting, *daizhao* 待詔
Pacification commander, *anfushi* 安撫使 *xuanfushi* 宣撫使 *xunfushi* 巡撫使
Palace Armies Secretariat, *nei shumishi* 內樞密使
Palace censor, *dianzhong yushi* 殿中御史
Palace commandant, *zhongwei* 中尉
Palace commissioner, *zhongshi* 中使
Palace Guard, *dianqianjun* 殿前軍
Palace library assistant, *bishulang* 祕書郎, assistant director (*cheng*) 丞, director (*ling*) 令
Palace remonstrance master, *sanqichangshi* 散騎常侍
Palace secretary, *zhongshuling* 中書令
Palace services officer, *gongfengguan* 供奉官
Prefect, *cishi* 刺史
Prefectural liaison in the capital, *jinzouguan* 進奏官
Primary cohort, *yuancong* 元從
Princely administrator, *wangfu* 王府
Proofreader, *shiyi* 拾遺
Protector-general, *dudufu* 都督府
Protector-overseer, *duhu* 都護
Recipient of edicts, *chengzhi* 承旨
Reconnaissance regiments, *changzhi* 長直
Reserve cavalry command, *fuma duwei* 駙馬都尉 (honorific title for imperial in-laws)
Revenues commissioner, *zuyongshi* 租庸使 *guojishi* 國計使
Royal security commissioner, *baoluanshi* 保鑾使

Secretarial overseer, *jishizhong* 給事中
Senior military advisor, central armies commissioner, *zhongmenshi* 中門使
Senior secretary to the governor, *kongmuguan* 孔目官
Six Armies, *liujun* 六軍
Special emissary, *jianxingshi* 間行使
Supervisor-in-chief, *duzongguan* 都總管
Supreme marshal, *yuanshuai* 元帥
Supreme commandant, *kaifu yitong sansi* 開府儀同三司
Surveillance commissioner, *xunchashi* 巡察使 *guanchashi* 觀察使
Temple representative, *gongshi* 宮使
Ten Armies, *shijun* 十軍
Three Fiscal Agencies commissioner, *sansishi* 三司使
Vice director, *shaoqing* 少卿
Wardrobe stewardess, *siyi* 司衣

PREFECTURES CITED

Ai [zhou] 愛州
An 安
Ba 霸
Bai 白
Bei 貝
Bi 泌
Bi‡ 壁
Bian 汴
Bin 邠
Bing 并
Bo 博
Bo‡ 播
Bo¶ 亳
Cai 蔡
Cang 滄
Cao 曹
Chan 澶
Chang 常
Chang‡ 昌
Chao 潮
Chen 辰
Chen‡ 陳
Chen¶ 郴
Cheng 成
Chi 池
Chu 楚
Chu‡ 滁
Ci 磁
Ci‡ 慈
Dai 代
Dan 丹
Dao 道
De 德
Deng 鄧
Deng‡ 登
Di 棣
Ding 定
Duan 端
E 鄂
En 恩
Fang 坊
Fang‡ 房
Fei 費
Fen 汾
Feng 風
Feng‡ 鳳
Feng¶ 封/峯
Feng† 峰
Feng¤ 灃
Fu 復
Fu‡ 鄜
Fu¶ 福
Fu† 府
Fu¤ 撫
Fu• 富
Gan 甘
Gao 高
Gong 龔
Gua 瓜
Guang 光
Guang‡ 廣
Gui 歸
Gui‡ 貴
Gui¶ 嬀

Gui† 桂
Guo 虢
Guo‡ 果
Hai 海
Han 漢
Han‡ 韓
Hang 杭
Hao 亳
Hao‡ 豪
Hao¶ 濠
He 合
He‡ 和
He¶ 賀
Heng 恒
Heng‡ 衡
Hong 洪
Hu 湖
Hua 滑
Hua‡ 華
Huai 淮
Huai‡ 懷
Huan 寰
Huan‡ 驩
Huang 黃
Hui 惠
Hui‡ 徽
Ji 濟
Ji‡ 薊
Ji¶ 冀
Ji† 紀
Ji¤ 吉
Jia 嘉
Jian 建
Jian‡ 劍
Jian¶ 簡
Jiang 絳
Jiang‡ 降
Jiang¶ 獎
Jiao 交
Jie 階
Jin 晉
Jin‡ 錦
Jin† 金
Jing 景
Jing‡ 涇
Jing¶ 荊
Jun 均
Kui 夔
Lai 萊
Lan 嵐
Lang 郎
Lang‡ 閬
Lang¶ 朗
Lei 雷
Li 利
Li‡ 黎
Lian 連
Liang 梁
Liao 遼
Lin 鱗
Ling 陵
Ling‡ 靈
Long 隴
Lu 潞
Lu‡ 盧
Lu¶ 瀘
Luo 洛
Mao 茂
Mei 眉
Mei‡ 湄
Meng 孟
Meng‡ 蒙
Mi 密
Mian 綿/緜
Ming 洺
Ming‡ 明
Mo 鄚
Mo‡ 漠
Mo¶ 莫
Mu 睦
Nan 南
Ning 寧
Peng 彭
Ping 平
Pu 濮
Pu‡ 普
Qi 崎
Qi‡ 岐

Qi¶ 齊
Qi† 祁
Qi¤ 蘄
Qian 虔
Qian‡ 黔
Qin 秦
Qin‡ 欽
Qin† 沁
Qing 慶
Qing‡ 青
Qiong 邛
Quan 泉
Quan‡ 全
Qu 衢
Rao 饒
Rong 戎
Rong‡ 容
Ru 汝
Ru‡ 儒
Run 潤
Sha 沙
Shan 陝
Shan‡ 單
Shang 商
Shao 韶
Shao‡ 邵
Sheng 昇
Shi 石
Shi‡ 施
Shou 壽
Shu 舒
Shun 順
Shuo 朔
Si 泗
Song 宋
Su 宿
Su‡ 蘇
Sui 隨
Sui‡ 遂
Sui¶ 綏
Sui† 隨
Tai 泰
Tai‡ 台
Tan 潭
Tan‡ 檀
Tang 唐
Tie 鐵
Ting 汀
Tong 同
Tong‡ 通
Wan 萬
Wei 魏
Wei‡ 衛
Wei¶ 蔚
Wei† 渭
Wen 文
Wen‡ 溫
Wu 武
Wu‡ 梧
Wu¶ 婺
Xi 隰
Xi‡ 西
Xi¶ 溪
Xia 夏
Xia‡ 峽
Xian 憲
Xiang 襄
Xiang‡ 相
Xiang¶ 象
Xin 新
Xin‡ 忻
Xin† 信
Xing 邢
Xing‡ 興
Xing† 陘
Xiong 雄
Xu 敘
Xu‡ 許
Xu¶ 徐
Xu† 漵
Xuan 宣
Xun 鄩
Xun‡ 循
Ya 雅
Yan 兗
Yan‡ 延
Yan¶ 衍
Yan† 鹽

Yan¤ 燕
Yan• 嚴
Yang 揚
Yang‡ 洋
Yao 耀
Yi 易
Yi‡ 宜
Yi¶ 夷
Yi† 沂
Yi¤ 益
Yin 銀
Yin‡ 巠
Ying 郢
Ying‡ 應
Ying¶ 瀛
Ying† 英
Ying¤ 穎
Yong 雍
Yong‡ 邕
Yong¶ 永
You 幽
Yu 豫
Yu‡ 渝
Yuan 原
Yuan‡ 遠
Yuan† 袁
Yue 越
Yue‡ 岳
Yun 鄆
Yun‡ 雲
Yun¶ 筠
Ze 澤
Zhai 翟
Zhang 漳
Zhao 趙
Zhao‡ 昭
Zhen 鎮
Zheng 鄭
Zhong 忠
Zhuo 涿
Zi 淄
Zi‡ 梓
Zi¶ 資

Desheng 德勝軍
Guangjin 廣晉府
Henan 河南府
Heyang 河陽府
Hezhong 河中府
Jinchang 晉昌軍
Kaifeng 開封府
Taiyuan 太原府
Wanan 萬安軍
Xingtang 興唐府
Yedu 鄴都
Yulin 鬱林
Zhending 真定

BIOGRAPHICAL ENTRIES

An Chonghui 安重誨
An Chongrong 安重榮
An, consort dowager [Jin] 安太妃
Cao, Secondary Consort 次妃曹氏
Chai, Empress 皇后柴氏
Chai Rong 柴榮, see Emperor Shizong [Zhou]
Chai Shouli 柴守禮
Chu, Jin emperor 晉出帝
Concubine of Virtue Zhang 德妃張氏
Dong, Virtuous Consort 德妃董氏
Doulu Ge 豆盧革
Du Xiao 杜曉
Du Chongwei 杜重威
Duan Ning 段凝
Fan Yanguang 范延光
Fei, Tang emperor 唐廢帝
Feng Dao 馮道
Feng, Empress [Jin] 皇后馮氏
Fu, Empress [Zhou] 皇后符氏
Gao Barong 高保融
Gao Baoxu 高保勗
Gao Conghui 高從誨
Gao Jichang 高季昌, see Gao Jixing
Gao Jichong 高繼沖
Gao Jixing 高季興
Gao Xinggui 高行珪
Gao Xingzhou 高行周
Gaozu, Jin emperor 晉高祖
Ge Congzhou 葛從周
Gong, Zhou emperor 周恭帝
Guo Chongtao 郭崇韜
Guo Congqian 郭從謙, see Guo Men'gao

Guo Fengchao 郭奉超
Guo Men'gao 郭門高
Guo Shouyuan(yun) 郭守愿/筠
Guo Tong 郭侗
Guo Wei 郭威, see Emperor Taizu [Zhou]
Guo Xin 郭信
Guo Xun 郭遜
Guo Yunming 郭允明
Guo Zongxun 郭宗訓
He Delun 賀德倫
He Ning 和凝
Hu Zai 扈載
Huangfu Yu 皇甫遇
Huo Yanwei 霍彥威
Jia Wei 賈緯
Jing Jin 景進
Jing Xiang 敬翔
Jing Xinmo 敬新磨
Jing Yanguang 景延廣
Kang Huaiying 康懷英
Kang Junli 康君立
Kang Yanxiao 康延孝
Kong, Empress [Tang] 皇后孔氏
Kong Xun 孔循
Li Bian 李弁
Li Chongji 李重吉
Li Chongjun 李重俊
Li Chongmei 李重美
Li Congcan 李從璨
Li Conghou 李從厚, see Emperor Min [Tang]
Li Congjing 李從璟
Li Congke 李從珂
Li Congmin 李從敏
Li Congrong 李從榮
Li Congshen 李從審, see Li Congjing
Li Congwen 李從溫
Li Congyan 李從曮
Li Congyi 李從益
Li Congzhang 李從璋
Li Cunba 李存霸
Li Cunji 李存紀
Li Cunjin 李存進
Li Cunli 李存禮
Li Cunmei 李存美

Li Cunque 李存確
Li Cunwo 李存渥
Li Cunyi 李存乂
Li Cunxian 李存賢
Li Cunxiao 李存孝
Li Cunxin 李存信
Li Cunxu 李存勗, see Emperor Zhuangzong [Tang]
Li Cunzhang 李存璋
Li, Empress [Jin, Han] 皇后李氏
Li Jichan 李繼蟾
Li Jichou 李繼儔
Li Jiji 李繼岌
Li Jinquan 李金全
Li Jisong 李繼嵩
Li Jitao 李繼韜
Li Jitong 李繼潼
Li Jiyao 李繼嶢
Li Jing 李景
Li Kegong 李克恭
Li Kening 李克寧
Li Kerang 李克讓
Li Kexiu 李克脩
Li Keyong 李克用, see Emperor Wu [Tang]
Li Lin 李鏻
Li Maozhen 李茂貞
Li Siben 李嗣本
Li Sibi 李嗣弼
Li Si'en 李嗣恩
Li Sigong 李嗣肱
Li Siyuan 李嗣源, see Emperor Mingzong [Tang]
Li Sizhao 李嗣昭
Li Song 李菘
Li Tangbin 李唐賓
Li Yanwei 李彥威
Li Ye 李業
Li Yu 李煜
Li Yu‡ 李愚
Liu Bin 劉玢
Liu Chang 劉鋹
Liu Cheng 劉晟
Liu Chengjun 劉承鈞
Liu Chengxun 劉承勳
Liu Chengxun‡ 劉承訓
Liu Chengyou 劉承祐, see Emperor Yin [Han]

Liu Chong 劉崇
Liu, Empress [Tang, Zhou] 皇室 [后] 劉氏
Liu Ji'en 劉繼恩
Liu Jiyuan 劉繼元
Liu Min 劉旻
Liu Rengong 劉仁恭
Liu Renshan 劉仁贍
Liu Shouguang 劉守光
Liu Suiqing 劉遂清
Liu Suiyong 劉遂雍
Liu, Wife 正室劉氏
Liu Xin 劉信
Liu Xu 劉昫
Liu Xun 劉鄩
Liu Yan 劉龑
Liu Yan‡ 劉言
Liu Yanhao 劉延皓
Liu Yin 劉隱
Liu Yue 劉岳
Liu Yun 劉贇
Liu Zhijun 劉知俊
Liu Zhiyuan 劉知遠, see Emperor Gaozu [Han]
Liu Zhu 劉銖
Lu Wenji 盧文紀
Lu Wenjin 盧文進
Lu Zhi 盧質
Lü Qi 呂琦
Luo Hongxin 羅弘信
Luo Shaowei 羅紹威
Luo Tinggui 羅廷規
Luo Zhouhan 羅周翰
Luo Zhoujing 羅周敬
Ma Gao 馬縞
Ma Xi'e 馬希萼
Ma Xifan 馬希範
Ma Xiguang 馬希廣
Ma Xisheng 馬希聲
Ma Yin 馬隱
Ma Yinsun 馬胤孫
Meng Chang 孟昶
Meng Zhixiang 孟知祥
Mingzong, Tang Emperor 唐明宗
Mo, Liang Emperor 梁末帝
Murong Yanchao 慕容彥超

Pang Shigu 龐師古
Pei Yue 裴約
Qian Chu 錢俶
Qian Liu 錢鏐
Qian Yuanguan 錢元瓘
Qian Zuo 錢佐
Sang Weihan 桑維翰
Second Concubine Guo 次妃郭氏
Shen Bin 沈斌
Shi Chonggao 石重杲
Shi Chonggui 石重貴, see Emperor Chu [Jin]
Shi Chongrui 石重睿
Shi Chongxin 石重信
Shi Chongyi 石重乂
Shi Hongzhao 史弘肇
Shi Jinghui 石敬暉
Shi Jingru 石敬儒
Shi Jingtang 石敬瑭, see Emperor Gaozu [Jin]
Shi Jingwei 石敬威
Shi Jingyun 石敬贇
Shi Shucong 氏叔琮
Shi Wanquan 石萬詮
Shi Wanyou 石萬友
Shi Yanbao 石延寶
Shi Yanchao 史彥超
Shi Yanqiong 史彥瓊
Shi Yanxu 石延煦
Shizong, Zhou emperor 周世宗
Su Fengji 蘇逢吉
Su Kai 蘇楷
Su Xun 穌循
Sun Cheng 孫晟
Taizu, Emperor [Liang, Zhou] 太祖
Wang Chang 王昶
Wang Chao 王潮
Wang Chucun 王處存
Wang Chuzhi 王處直
Wang Du 王都
Wang Jian 王建
Wang Jianli 王建立
Wang Jinkui 王進逵
Wang Jipeng 王繼鵬, see Wang Chang
Wang Jun 王峻
Wang Ke 王珂

Wang Lin 王鏻
Wang Pu 王朴
Wang, Pure Consort [Tang] 淑妃王氏
Wang Qing 王清
Wang Rong 王鎔
Wang Shenzhi王審知
Wang Shou'en 王守恩
Wang Sitong 王思同
Wang Tingyin 王廷胤
Wang Wei 王威
Wang Xi 王曦, see Wang Yanxi
Wang Yan 王衍
Wang Yanhan 王延翰
Wang Yanjun 王延鈞, see Wang Lin
Wang Yanqiu 王晏球
Wang Yanxi 王延羲
Wang Yanzhang 王彥章
Wang Yanzheng 王延政
Wang Ye 王鄴
Wang Yu 王郁
Wang Zan 王瓚
Wang Zhaohui 王昭誨
Wang Zongbi 王宗弼
Wang Zongshou 王宗壽
Wei, Empress [Tang] 皇后魏氏
Wenhui Empress Wang 文惠后王氏
Wu Zhen 烏震
Xia Luqi 夏魯奇
Xu Taifu 徐台符
Xu Wen 徐溫
Xu Zhigao 徐知誥, see Li Bian
Xue Yiju 薛貽矩
Yang Bin 楊邠
Yang Chongben 楊崇本
Yang Guangyuan 楊光遠
Yang Longyan 楊隆演
Yang Ningshi 楊凝式
Yang Pu 楊溥
Yang, Pure Consort 淑妃楊氏
Yang She 楊涉
Yang Shihou 楊師厚
Yang Xingmi 楊行密
Yang Wo 楊渥
Yao Hong 姚洪

Yin, Han Emperor 漢隱帝
Yuan Xiangxian 袁象先
Yuan Xingqin 元行欽
Yuan Yi 袁義
Yuan Zhengci 袁正辭
Yuanzhen, Empress Zhang 元貞后張氏
Zhai Jinzong 翟進宗
Zhang Ce 張策
Zhang Chengye 張承業
Zhang Guiba 張歸霸
Zhang Guibian 張歸弁
Zhang Hanjie 張漢傑
Zhang Jingda 張敬達
Zhang Jizuo 張繼祚
Zhang Juhan 張居翰
Zhang, Precious Consort 貴妃張氏
Zhang Quanyi 張全義
Zhang Wandi 張萬迪
Zhang Wenli 張文禮
Zhang Wenwei 張文蔚
Zhang Xian 張憲
Zhang Xichong 張希崇
Zhang Yanze 張彥澤
Zhang Yun 張筠
Zhang Yun‡ 張允
Zhang Yuande 張源德
Zhao Chang 趙昶
Zhao Chou 趙犨
Zhao Feng 趙鳳
Zhao Guangfeng 趙光逢
Zhao Kuangning 趙匡凝
Zhaorong Consort Li 昭容妃李氏
Zhao Xu 趙巖
Zhaoyi, Consort Chen 昭儀妃陳氏
Zhao Yu 趙珝
Zhao Yu‡ 趙玉
Zhao Zaili 趙在禮
Zheng Jue 鄭珏
Zheng Renhui 鄭仁誨
Zhou Baoquan 周保權
Zhou Xingfeng 周行逢
Zhou Za 周匝
Zhu Cun 朱存
Zhu Jin 朱瑾

Zhu Quanyu 朱全昱
Zhu Quanzhong 朱全忠, see Emperor Taizu [Liang]
Zhu Shouyin 朱守殷
Zhu Wen 朱溫, see Emperor Taizu [Liang]
Zhu Xuan 朱宣
Zhu Yougui 朱友珪
Zhu Youhui 朱友誨
Zhu Youlun 朱友倫
Zhu Youneng 朱友能
Zhu Youning 朱友寧
Zhu Youqian 朱友謙
Zhu Youwen 朱友文
Zhu Youyu 朱友裕
Zhu Youzhen 朱友貞
Zhu Youzi 朱友孜
Zhu Zhen 朱珍
Zhuangzong, Tang emperor 唐莊宗

WORKS CITED

Barfield, Thomas J. *The Perilous Frontier: Nomadic Empires and China, 221 B.C. to A.D. 1757*. Cambridge: Blackwell, 1989.

Bol, Peter K. *"This Culture of Ours": Intellectual Transitions in T'ang and Sung China*. Stanford: Stanford University Press, 1992.

Cang Xiuliang et al. 倉修良 *Zhongguo shixue mingzhu pingjie* [A critical introduction to China's celebrated historical writings]. 中國史學名著評介 Jinan: Shandong jiaoyu chubanshe, 1988.

Chai Degeng. 柴德賡 "Lun Ouyang Xiu de Xin wudai shi" 論歐陽修的新五代史 [On Ouyang Xiu's *New History of the Five Dynasties*]. In Wu Ze, ed., 吳澤 *Zhongguo shixueshi lunji* 中國史學史論集, vol. 2, pp. 226–234. Shanghai: Renmin chubanshe, 1980.

Chen Gao 陳高 and Chen Zhichao, eds. 陳智超 *Zhongguo gudaishi shiliaoxue* 中國古代史史料學 [Study of historical documents in ancient Chinese history]. Beijing: Beijing chubanshe, 1983.

Chen Guangchong. 陳光崇 "Ouyang Xiu de shixue" 歐陽修的史學 [Ouyang Xiu's historical method]. In *Songshi yanjiu ji* 宋史研究集,pp. 521–548. Shanghai: Guji chubanshe, 1982.

Chen Qingquan et al. 陳清泉 *Zhongguo shixuejia pingzhuan* 中國史學家評傳 [Biographies of China's historians]. Henan: Zhongzhou guji chubanshe, 1985.

Chu Hsi [Zhu Xi]. *Chu Hsi's Family Rituals: A Twelfth-Century Chinese Manual for the Performance of Cappings, Weddings, Funerals, and Ancestral Rites. Trans.* Patricia B. Ebrey. Princeton: Princeton University Press, 1991.

Chunqiu Zuozhuan zhu 春秋左傳注 [An annotated *Spring and Autumn Annals* with *Zuo Commentary*]. Yang Bojun, ed. 楊伯峻 Beijing: Zhonghua shuju, 1981.

Davis, Richard L. "Chaste and Filial Women in the Historical Writings of Ouyang Xiu." *Journal of the American Oriental Society* 121, no. 2 (April–June 2001): 204–218.

——. "The Heroism of Chou Shih-tsung in the Eleventh Century: Perspectives from the *Historical Records of the Five Dynasties*." In *Song Xuxuan jiaoshou bashi rongshou lunwenji* 宋旭軒教授八秩嵩慶論文集, pp. 1134–1148. Taipei: Huatai gongsi, 2000.

——. "Historical Critic or Cultural Mediator—Ouyang Xiu on Legitimate Rule." In *Qingzhu Deng Guangming jiaoshou jiushi huadan lunwenji*慶祝鄧廣銘教授九十華誕論文集, pp. 426–448. Shijiazhuang: Henan jiaoyu chubanshe, 1997.

——. "Historiography as Politics in Yang Wei-chen's 'Polemic on Legitimate Succession.'" *T'oung Pao* (Leiden) 69, nos. 1–3 (1983): 33–72.

——. "Images of the South in Ouyang Xiu's *Historical Records of the Five Dynasties*." *Shixue yu wenxian* 史學與文獻, pp. 97–157. Taipei: Xuesheng shuju, 1998.

——. "Martial Men and Military Might in the Historical Writings of Ouyang Xiu." In *Kim Hua Paksa Cengnyen Kinyem Sahak Nonchong*. 金燁博士停年紀念, series 21, pp. 753–784. Chungbuk, Korea: Chungbuk Historical Society, 1998.

——. *Wind against the Mountain: The Crisis of Politics and Culture in Thirteenth-Century China*. Cambridge, Mass.: Harvard University Council on East Asian Studies, 1996.

Dawson, Raymond, trans. *Historical Records: A New Translation*. Oxford: Oxford University Press, 1994.

de Bary, Wm. Theodore, et al., eds. *Sources of Chinese Tradition, vol. 1*. 2d ed. New York: Columbia University Press, 1999.

Du Shengyun. 杜升云 "Sima Qian de tianwenxue chẹngjiu ji sixiang" 司馬遷的天文學成就及思想 [Sima Qian on astronomy: His achievements and philosophy]. In Liu Naihe, ed. 劉乃和 *Sima Qian he Shiji*. 司馬遷和史記, pp. 222–248. Beijing: Beijing chubanshe, 1987.

Eberhard, Wolfram. *Conquerors and Rulers: Social Forces in Medieval China*. 2d ed. Leiden: E. J. Brill, 1970.

Egan, Ronald C. *The Literary Works of Ou-yang Hsiu (1007–72)*. Cambridge: Cambridge University Press, 1984.

——. *Word, Image, and Deed in the Life of Su Shi*. Cambridge, Mass.: Harvard University Council on East Asian Studies, 1994.

Elvin, Mark. *The Pattern of the Chinese Past*. Stanford: Stanford University Press, 1973.

Fang, Cheng-Hua. Power Structures and Cultural identities in Imperial China: Civil and Military Power from Late Tang to Early Song Dynasties (A.D. 875–1063). Ph.D. diss., Brown University, 2001.

Franke, Herbert, and Denis Twitchett, eds. *The Cambridge History of China*, vol. 6, *Alien Regimes and Border States*, 907–1368. Cambridge: Cambridge University Press, 1994.

Gao Guokang. 高國抗 *Zhongguo gudai shixueshi gaiyao* 中國古代史學史概要 [An introduction to the historiography of ancient China]. Guangzhou: Guangdong gaodeng jiaoyu chubanshe, 1985.

Guanzi 管子 [Writings of Guanzi]. Sibu congkan edition 四部叢刊. Shanghai: Shangwu yinshuguan, 1929–1934.

He Zeheng. 何澤恆 Ouyang Xiu zhi jing/shi xue 歐陽修之經史學 [Ouyang Xiu's classical and historical writings]. M.A. thesis, National Taiwan University, 1976.

Hebeisheng wenwu guanlichu河北省文物管理處 [Hebei Institute for Cultural Relics]. *Wudai Wang Chuzhi mu* 五代王處直墓 [The tomb of Wang Chuzhi of the Five Dynasties]. Beijing: Wenwu chubanshe, 1998.

Henderson, John B. *The Development and Decline of Chinese Cosmology*. New York: Columbia University Press, 1984.

Hervouet, Yves, comp. A *Sung Bibliography/Bibliographie des Sung*. Hong Kong: The Chinese University Press, 1978.

Hino Kaisaburō. 日野開三郎 *Tōbatsu godaisho jiei gigunkō.* 唐末五代初自衛義軍考 [On the Imperial Guard and Righteous Armies of the Late Tang and Five Dynasties]. 2 vols. Fukuoka: Kyūko Shoin, 1984–1988.

Hori Toshikazu. 堀敏一 "Godai Sōsho ni okeru kingun no hatten." 五代宋初における禁軍の発展 [Development of the Palace Guard in the Five Dynasties and Early Song]. *Tōyō bunka kenkyūko kiyō* 東洋文化研 所紀要 4 (1953): 83–151.

Huang Zongxi et al. 黄宗羲 *Song/Yuan xue'an* [Intellectual biographies for the Song and Yuan dynasties]. 宋元學案 Taipei: Shijie shuju, 1973.

Hulsewé, A. F. P. "Notes on the Historiography of the Han Period." In W. G. Beasley and E. G. Pulleyblank, eds., *Historians of China and China*, pp. 31–43. London: Oxford University Press, 1961.

Ishida Hajime. 石田肇 "Shin godai shi no tairei ni tsuyite." 新五代史の体例について [On the format of the *New History of the Five Dynasties*] *Tōyōgaku* 東洋学 (Tokyo) 54 (July 1977): 31–45.

Kobayashi Yoshihiro. 小林義廣 *Ōyō Shū: sono shōgai to sōzoku* 欧陽修その生涯と宗族. Tokyo: Sōbunsha, 2000.

Lao Tzu. *Tao Te Ching*. Trans. D. C. Lau. New York: Penguin, 1962.

Lau, D. C., trans. *Mencius*. New York: Penguin, 1970.

Laozi. 老子 *Daode jing* 道德經 [The Way and Its Power]. Sibu congkan edition.

Legge, James, trans. *The Chinese Classics*, vol. 1, *Confucian Analects*; vol. 3, *The Shoo King*; vol. 4, *The She King*. Rev. ed. Hong Kong: Chinese University of Hong Kong Press, 1960.

Leslie, Donald D., Colin Mackerras, and Wang Gungwu, eds. *Essays on the Sources for Chinese History*. Columbia: University of South Carolina Press, 1975.

Li Bingquan. 李炳泉 *Zhu Wen* 朱溫 [Biography of Zhu Wen]. Taipei: Wenjin chubanshe, 1994.

Li Ji 禮記 [Book of Rites]. Sibu congkan edition.

Li Zefen. 李則芬 "Ouyang Xiu de xin shishi" 歐陽修的新史識 [The new historiography of Ouyang Xiu]. In *Sui/Tang/Wudai lishi lunwenji* 隋唐五代歷史論文集, pp. 342–356. Taipei: Taiwan shangwu yinshuguan, 1989.

———. "Zhou Shizong lun" 周世宗論 [On Emperor Shizong of the Zhou]. In *Sui/Tang/Wudai lishi lunwenji*, pp. 310–341. Taipei: Taiwan shangwu yinshuguan, 1989.

Liangqiannian zhongxi li duizhao biao. 兩千年中西曆對照表 [A Sino-Western Calendar for Two Thousand Years, A.D. 1–2000] Taipei: Yumin chubanshe, 1969.

Lin Ruihan. 林瑞翰 "Ouyang Xiu Wudai shiji zhi yanjiu" 歐陽修五代史記之研究 [Studies on Ouyang Xiu's *Historical Records of the Five Dynasties*]. In *Songshi yanjiu ji* 宋史研究集, vol. 10, pp. 303–354. Taipei: Taiwan shudian, 1978.

Liu Deqing. 劉德清 *Ouyang Xiu zhuan* 歐陽修傳 [Biography of Ouyang Xiu]. Harbin: Haerbin chubanshe, 1995.

Liu, James T. C. *Ou-yang Hsiu: An Eleventh-Century Neo-Confucianist.* Stanford: Stanford University Press, 1967.

Liu Zijian [James T. C. Liu]. 劉子健 *Ouyang Xiu de zhixue yu congzheng* 歐陽修的治學與從政 [The scholarship and political activism of Ouyang Xiu]. Hong Kong: Xinya yanjiusuo, 1963.

Ma Duanlin. 馬端臨 *Wenxian tongkao* 文獻通考 [Comprehensive critique of the sources]. Taipei: Xinxing shuju, 1963.

Mackerras, Colin. *The Uighur Empire (744–840) According to the T'ang Dynastic Histories*. Columbia: University of South Carolina Press, 1972.

Mao Hanguang. 毛漢光 "Wei/Bo erbainian shilun" 魏博二百年史論 [Historical notes on the Wei/Bo command, spanning two hundred years]. In *Zhongguo zhonggu zhengzhi shilun* 中國中古政治史論, pp. 323–390. Taipei: Lianjing chuban shiye gongsi, 1990.

———. "Wudai zhi zhengzhi yanxu yu zhengquan zhuanyi" 五代之政治延續與政權轉移 [On political continuity and change during the Five Dynasties]. In *Zhongguo zhonggu zhengzhi shilun*, pp. 391–445. Taipei: Lianjing chuban shiye gongsi, 1990.

Mao shi 毛詩 [The Odes]. Sibu congkan edition.

McMullen, David. *State and Scholars in T'ang China*. Cambridge: Cambridge University Press, 1988.

Molé, Gabriella. *The T'u-yü-hun from the Northern Wei to the Time of the Five Dynasties.* Roma: Instituto Italiano per il Medio ed Estremo Oriente, 1970.

Mote, F. W. *Imperial China, 900–1800*. Cambridge, Mass.: Harvard University Press, 1999.

Needham, Joseph, and Robin D. S. Yates. *Science and Civilisation in China*, vol. 5, part VI, *Military Technology: Missiles and Sieges*. Cambridge: Cambridge University Press, 1994.

Nianwushi shuyao 廿五史述要 [Essentials for the twenty-five dynastic histories]. Taipei: Shijie shuju, 1994.

Nienhauser, William H. Jr., et al. *The Grand Scribe's Records*, vol. 1, *The Memoirs of Pre-Han China*. Bloomington: Indiana University Press, 1994.

Nylan, Michael. *The Five "Confucian" Classics*. New Haven: Yale University Press, 2001.

Ouyang Xiu. 歐陽修 [脩] *Ouyang Xiu quanji* 歐陽修全集 [Collected writings of Ouyang Xiu]. 2 vols. Beijing: Zhongguo shudian, 1986.

——. *Wudai shiji* 五代史記 [Historical Records of the Five Dynasties]. Bonaben edition (1199) 百衲本. Taipei: Taiwan shangwu yinshuguan, 1988.

——. *Xin wudai shi* 新五代史 or *Wudai shiji* [New history of the Five Dynasties]. Rev. ed. Beijing: Zhonghua shuju, 1974 and 1992. Reprint, Taiwan: Dingwen shuju, 1976.

Ouyang Xiu et al. *Xin Tang shu*新唐書 [New history of the Tang]. Beijing: Zhonghua shuju, 1975.

Ouyang Xiu ziliao huibian 歐陽修資料彙編 [Collection of sources pertaining to Ouyang Xiu]. Hong Benjian, comp. 洪本健. 3 vols. Beijing: Zhonghua shuju, 1995.

Pulleyblank, E. G. "Chinese Historical Criticism: Liu Chih-chi and Ssu-ma Kuang." In E. G. Pulleyblank and W. G. Beasley, eds., *Historians of China and Japan*, pp. 135–166. London: Oxford University Press, 1961.

Qian Mu. 錢穆 *Zhongguo shixue mingzhu* 中國史學名著 [The celebrated historical writings of China]. Taipei: Sanmin shuju, 1973.

Rao Zongyi. 饒宗頤 *Zhongguo shixueshang zhi zhengtonglun* 中國史學上之正統論 [Essays on legitimate succession in Chinese historiography]. Hong Kong: Longmen shudian, 1977.

Sanaka Sakan. 佐中壮 Shin godai shi senjutsu no jijō. 新五代史選述の事情 [On the compilation of the *New History of the Five Dynasties*] *Shigaku zasshi* 史学雑誌 (Tokyo) 50, no. 11 (Nov. 1939): 1376–1394.

Sawyer, Ralph D., trans. *The Seven Military Classics of Ancient China*. Boulder, Colo.: Westview, 1993.

Shibaki Kunio. 芝木邦夫 "Ōyō Shū no shigaku shisō" 歐陽脩の史學思想 [Historical thought of Ouyang Xiu]. *Kaga Hakushi taikan kinen: Chūgoku bunshi tetsugaku ronshū*, pp. 637–650. Tokyo: Kodansha, 1979.

Shigezawa Toshio. 重澤俊郎 "Ōyō Shū no seitōron" 歐陽脩の正統論 [Ouyang Xiu's essay on legitimate succession]. *Tōhōgaku ronshū*, pp. 395–406. Tokyo: Tōhōgakkai, 1972.

Siku quanshu zongmu tiyao 四庫全書總目提要 [Abstracts for the general index to the Four Treasuries collection]. 5 vols. Taipei: Taiwan shangwu yinshuguan, 1971.

Sima Guang, et al. 司馬光 *Zizhi tongjian* 資治通鑑 [Comprehensive mirror for the advancement of governance]. Shanghai: Guji chubanshe, 1956.

Sima Qian. 司馬遷 *Shiji* 史記 [Records of the Grand Historian]. Rev. ed. Beijing: Zhonghua shuju, 1959.

Sinor, Denis, ed. *The Cambridge History of Early Inner Asia*. Cambridge: Cambridge University Press, 1990.

Song Yanshen 宋衍申, Zhao Yi 趙毅, comps. *Liang Wudaishi cidian* 兩五代史辭典 [Dictionary for the two dynastic histories for the Five Dynasties]. Jinan: Shandong jiaoyu chubanshe, 1998.

Su Jilang 蘇基朗. "Wudai de shumiyuan" 五代的樞密院 [The bureau of military affairs in the Five Dynasties]. *Shihuo fukan* 食貨復刊 (Taipei) 10, nos. 1–2: 3–19.

Sudō Yoshiyuki. 周藤吉之 "Godai setsudoshi no shihai taisei" 五代節度使の支配体制 [Support structures for military governors of the Five Dynasties]. *Shigaku zasshi* 史学雑誌 61, no. 4 (1952): 289–329; no. 6: 521–539.

Tao Maobing. 陶懋炳 *Wudai shilue* 五代史略 [A concise history of the Five Dynasties]. Beijing: Renmin chubanshe, 1985.

——. *Zhongguo gudai shixueshi lue* 中國古代史學史略 [A concise historiography for ancient China]. Changsha: Hunan renmin chubanshe, 1987.

Tsien, Tsuen-hsuin, and Joseph Needham. *Science and Civilisation in China*, vol. 5, *Chemistry and Chemical Technology, part I, Paper and Printing*. Cambridge: Cambridge University Press, 1985.

Trauzettel, Rolf. "Ou-yang Hsius Essays über die legitime Thronnachfolge." *Sinologica* 9, nos. 3–4 (1967): 226–249.

Tuo Tuo et al. 脱脱 *Song shi* 宋史 [Dynastic history for the Song]. Beijing: Zhonghua shuju, 1977.

Twitchett, Denis, ed. *The Cambridge History of China, vol. 3, Sui and T'ang China, 589–906*. Cambridge: Cambridge University Press, 1979.

Wang, Gungwu, "Feng Dao: An Essay on Confucian Loyalty." In Arthur F. Wright and Denis Twitchett, eds., *Confucian Personalities*, pp. 123–145. Stanford: Stanford University Press, 1962.

——. *The Structure of Power in North China during the Five Dynasties*. Stanford: Stanford University Press, 1963.

Watson, Burton, *Ssu-ma Ch'ien: Grand Historian of China*. New York: Columbia University Press, 1958.

——, trans. *Records of the Grand Historian: Han Dynasty, by Sima Qian*, vol. 1. Rev. ed. New York: Columbia University Press, 1993.

——, trans. *Records of the Grand Historian: Qin Dynasty, by Sima Qian*. Rev. ed. New York: Columbia University Press, 1993.

Wilhelm, Richard, trans. *The I Ching, or Book of Changes*. Princeton: Princeton University Press, 1977.

Wittfogel, Karl A., and Feng Chia-sheng. *History of Chinese Society: Liao (907–1125)*. Philadelphia: American Philosophical Society, 1949.

Wright, Arthur F., and Denis Twitchett, eds., *Perspectives on the T'ang*. New Haven: Yale University Press, 1973.

Wu Huaiqi. 吳懷祺 *Songdai shixue sixiangshi* 宋代史學思想史 [A history of historical thought for the Song dynasty]. Hefei: Huangshan shushe, 1992.

Wu Renchen. 吳任臣 *Shiguo chunqiu* 十國春秋 [A Spring and Autumn Annals for the Ten Kingdoms]. Xu Minxia 徐敏霞 and Zhou Ying 周瑩, eds. Beijing: Zhonghua shuju, 1983.

Wudai huiyao 五代會要 [Documentary abstracts for the Five Dynasties]. Wang Pu 王溥, comp. Shanghai: Shanghai guiji chubanshe, 1978.

Xiao jing 孝經 [Classic of Filial Piety]. Sibu congkan edition.

Xiao Yishan 蕭一山, Qi Zhaonan 齊召南, comp. *Lidai diwang nianbiao* 歷代帝王年表 [Chronological charts for emperors in history]. Taipei: Shijie shuju, 1976.

Xue Juzheng, et al. 薛居正 *Jiu wudai shi* 舊五代史 [Old history of the Five Dynasties]. Beijing: Zhonghua shuju, 1976.

Yan Jie. 嚴杰 *Ouyang Xiu nianpu* 歐陽修年譜 [A chronology for Ouyang Xiu]. Nanjing: Nanjing chubanshe, 1993.

Yan Shenxiu. 閻愼修 *Xinbian Wudaishi pinghua ciyu huishi*. 新編五代史平話詞語匯釋 [Terminological explanations for common phrases in the *History of the Five Dynasties*]. Taipei: Wenshizhe chubanshe, 1988.

Yan Yiping, comp. 嚴一萍 *Wudai shiji zhu jiaoding* 五代史記注校訂 [Annotation and emendations for the *Historical Records of the Five Dynasties*]. Taipei: Yiwen yinshuguan, 1976.

Yang Yixiang. 楊翼驤 "Liu Zhiji yu Shitong" 劉知幾與史通 [Liu Zhiji and his *Historical Generalities*]. In Wu Ze, ed., *Zhongguo shixueshi lunji*, vol. 2, pp. 121–159. Shanghai: Renmin chubanshe, 1980.

Yao Yingting. 姚瀛艇 "Lun Tang/Song zhiji de tianming yu fan tianming sixiang" 論唐宋之際的天命與反天命思想 [Ideas supportive or critical of Heaven's mandate for the Tang-Song period]. In Deng Guangming 鄧廣銘 and Li Jiaju, eds. 酈家駒 *Songshi yanjiu lunwen ji* 宋史研究論文集, pp. 370–384. Henan: Henan renmin chubanshe, 1984.

Yili 儀禮 [The Rites]. Sibu congkan edition.

Yin Shu [Zhu]. 尹洙 *Wudai chunqiu*. 五代春秋 Baibu congshu jicheng. Taipei: Yiwen yingshuguan, 1965.

Zhang Guogang. 張國剛 *Sui/Tang/Wudai shi yanjiu gaiyao* 隋唐五代史研究概要 [General studies on the Sui, Tang, and Five Dynasties]. Tianjin: Tianjin jiaoyu chubanshe, 1996.

Zhang Menglun. 張孟倫 *Zhongguo shixueshi* 中國史學史 [China's historiography]. Lanzhou: Gansu renmin chubanshe, 1983.

Zhang Qifan. 張其凡 *Wudai jinjun chutan* 五代禁軍初探 [Preliminary studies on the Palace Guard of the Five Dynasties]. Guangzhou: Jinan daxue chubanshe, 1993.

———. *Songchu zhengzhi tanyan* 宋初政治探研 [Preliminary studies on politics of the early Song]. Guangzhou: Jinan daxue chubanshe, 1995.

Zhao Lü Fu. 趙呂甫 "Ouyang Xiu shixue chutan" 歐陽修史學初探 [Preliminary studies on the historical methods of Ouyang Xiu]. In Wu Ze, ed., *Zhongguo shixueshi lunji*, vol. 2, pp. 201–225. Shanghai: Renmin chubanshe, 1980.

Zhao Yi. 趙翼 *Nianershi zhaji* 廿二史箚記 [Miscellaneous notes on the twenty-two dynastic histories]. 1795. Ed. Du Weiyun. Taipei: Huashi chubanshe, 1977.

Zheng Han. 鄭涵 "Ouyang Xiu tianrenguan shitan" 歐陽修天人觀試探 [Hypothesis on Ouyang Xiu's views on Heaven's relations with man]. In *Songshi lunji* 宋史論集, pp. 363–377. Henan: Zhongzhou shuhuashe, 1983.

Zheng Xuemeng. 鄭學檬 *Wudai shiguoshi yanjiu* 五代十國史研究 [Studies on the history of the Five Dynasties and Ten Kingdoms]. Shanghai: Shanghai renmin chubanshe, 1991.

Zhongguo yeshi jicheng 中國野史集成 [Collection of the unofficial histories of China]. Chengdu: Bashu shushe, 1993.

Zhou Yi 周易 [Book of Changes]. Sibu congkan edition.

Zhu Yulong, comp. 朱玉龍 *Wudai shiguo fangzhen nianbiao* 五代十國方鎮年表 [Chronological charts for local governors of the Five Dynasties and Ten Kingdoms]. Beijing: Zhonghua shuju, 1997.

INDEX

....

Index compiled by Shelley Hawks and the translator